MODERN

MANAGEMENT

EDITION 8

MODERN

MANAGEMENT

Diversity, Quality, Ethics,
& the Global Environment

SAMUEL C. CERTO

Professor of Management
Roy E. Crummer
Graduate School of Business—Rollins College

PRENTICE HALL

UPPER SADDLE RIVER, NEW JERSEY 07458

Senior Editor: David Shafer
Managing Editor (editorial): Jennifer Glennon
Editorial Assistant: Shannon Sims
Editor-in-Chief: Natalie Anderson
Marketing Manager: Michael D. Campbell
Production Editor: Cindy Spreder
Associate Managing Editor (production): Judy Leale
Permissions Coordinator: Monica Stipanov
Manufacturing Buyer: Diane Peirano
Manufacturing Supervisor: Arnold Vila
Manufacturing Manager: Vincent Scelta
Senior Designer: Cheryl Asherman
Design Manager: Patricia Smythe
Interior Design: Ox & Company
Photo Research Supervisor: Melinda Lee Reo
Image Permission Supervisor: Kay Dellosa
Photo Researcher: Melinda Alexander
Photo Permissions Coordinator: Zina Arabia
Cover Design: John Romer
Illustrator (Interior): Carlisle Communications
Cover Illustration/Photo: Tony Craddock/Tony Stone Worldwide
Composition: Carlisle Communications

Credits and acknowledgments for materials borrowed from other sources and reproduced, with permission, in this textbook appear on pages 579–583.

Library of Congress Cataloging-in-Publication Data

Certo, Samuel C.
    Modern management : diversity, quality, ethics, and the global
environment / Samuel C. Certo.   8th ed.
      p.   cm.
Includes bibliographical references and index.
   ISBN 0-13-013307-8
    1. Management.   2. Industrial management.   3. Social
responsibility of business.   I. Title.
HD31.C4125   2000
658—dc21   99-12570
                                       CIP

Prentice-Hall International (UK) Limited, London
Prentice-Hall of Australia Pty. Limited, Sydney
Prentice-Hall Canada, Inc., Toronto
Prentice-Hall Hispanoamericana, S.A., Mexico
Prentice-Hall of India Private Limited, New Delhi
Prentice-Hall of Japan, Inc., Tokyo
Prentice-Hall (Singapore) Pte. Ltd.
Editora Prentice-Hall do Brasil, Ltda., Rio de Janeiro

Printed in the United States of America

10 9 8 7 6 5 4 3 2 1

To Sarah,

A cherished daughter who pulls people to the Lord through genuine excitement about spiritual life . . . a true gift to all who know her!

BRIEF
CONTENTS

Part One   INTRODUCTION TO MANAGEMENT

1 Management and Management Careers   2
   Skills Video LIVE! Introduction to Modern Management   23
2 Managing: History and Current Thinking   24
3 Corporate Social Responsibility and Business Ethics   46
4 Managing in the Global Arena   101

Part Two   PLANNING

5 Organizational Objectives   102
6 Fundamentals of Planning   124
7 Making Decisions   142
8 Strategic Planning   164
9 Plans and Planning Tools   188
   Skills Video LIVE! Planning   209

Part Three   ORGANIZING

10 Fundamentals of Organizing   210
11 Responsibility, Authority, and Delegation   232
12 Managing Human Resources   254
13 Managing Change: From Stress to the Virtual Organization   276
    Skills Video LIVE! Organizing   301

Part Four   INFLUENCING

14 Fundamentals of Influencing and Communication   302
15 Leadership   324
16 Motivation   352
17 Groups, Teams, and Corporate Cultures   374
18 Understanding People: Attitudes, Perception, and Learning   400
    Skills Video LIVE! Influencing   419

Part Five   CONTROLLING

19 Principles of Controlling   420
20 Production Management and Control   442
21 Information and the Internet Technology   470
    Skills Video LIVE! Controlling   501

Part Six   TOPICS FOR SPECIAL EMPHASIS

22 Competitiveness: Quality and Innovation   502
23 Management and Diversity   526
    Skills Video LIVE! Topics for Special Emphasis   549

CONTENTS

Part One INTRODUCTION TO MANAGEMENT

chapter 1 **Management and Management Careers** **2**

Introductory Case: *Managing Disney's New
Animal Kingdom* 2
The Importance of Management 4
The Management Task 5
  The Role of Management 6
  Defining Management 6
  *The Management Process: Management
    Functions* 7
  Management Process and Goal Attainment 8
  *Management and Organizational
    Resources* 8
The Universality of Management 11
  The Theory of Characteristics 11
Management Careers 12
  A Definition of Career 12
  *Career Stages, Life Stages, and
    Performance* 12
  Promoting Your Own Career 13
  Special Career Issues 15
Special Features for the Remaining
  Chapters 17
  Spotlights 17
  Across Industries 18
  Management and the Internet 18

Case Study: *Chrysler's Top Gun* 21

Skills Video LIVE! *Introduction to Modern
Management* 23

chapter 2 **Managing: History and Current Thinking** **24**

Introductory Case: *A Problem at
McDonald's* 25
The Classical Approach 26
  Lower-Level Management Analysis 26
♦ **Across Industries: Mail Order Retailing** 28
  Comprehensive Analysis of Management 30
  Limitations of the Classical Approach 31
The Behavioral Approach 32
  The Hawthorne Studies 32
  Recognizing the Human Variable 33
  The Human Relations Movement 33

The Management Science Approach 34
  *The Beginning of the Management
    Science Approach* 34
  Management Science Today 35
♦ **Quality Spotlight:** *Baldridge Award
  Exemplifies Quality* **35**
  *Characteristics of Management
    Science Applications* 35
The Contingency Approach 36
♦ **Management and the Internet:** *"If-Then"
  Necessary for XS New York
  Cybercafe does not Materialize* 37
The System Approach 37
  Types of Systems 37
  Systems and "Wholeness" 37
  The Management System 38
  *Information for Management
    System Analysis* 39
  *Learning Organization:
    A New Approach?* 39
♦ **People Spotlight:** *People for a New
  Learning Organization at Signicast* **40**

Case Study: *"Chainsaw Al Dunlap":
A New Breed of Manager?* 44

Video Case: *History and Current Thinking
at Texas Name Plate* 45

chapter 3 **Corporate Social Responsibility
and Business Ethics** **46**

Introductory Case: *Larami Corporation
"Super Soaks" Society?* **47**
Fundamentals of Social Responsibility **48**
  *The Davis Model of Corporate Social
    Responsibility Exists* 48
  Areas of Corporate Social Responsibility 50
  *Varying Opinions on Social
    Responsibility* 50
  *Conclusions About the Performance
    of Social Responsibility Activities
    By Business* 51
♦ **Global Spotlight:** *DuPont Protects the
  Environment* **53**
Social Responsiveness **55**

Determining if a Social Responsibility
Exists   55
Social Responsiveness and Decision
Making   55
Approaches to Meeting Social
Responsibilities   57
◆ Diversity Spotlight: *Social Responsiveness
and the Equal Opportunity Act at
Opryland*   57
Social Responsibility Activities and
Management Functions   **58**
Planning Social Responsibility Activities   58
Organizing Social Responsibility
Activities   60
Influencing Individuals Performing
Social Responsibility Activities   61
Controlling Social Responsibility
Activities   61
◆ Across Industries: *Food Processing*   62
How Society Can Help Business Meet
Social Obligations   **64**
Business Ethics   **65**
A Definition of Ethics   65
◆ Management and the Internet: *Better
Business Bureaus Helps Management
Project Ethics Position on Internet*   **66**
Why Ethics is a Vital Part of
Management Practices   65
A Code of Ethics   66
Creating an Ethical Workplace   67

Case Study: *Dow Corning: A Question of
Legality of Ethics?*   72
Video Case: *Corporate Social
Responsibility and Business Ethics*   73

chapter 4   **Managing in the Global Arena**   **74**

Introductory Case: *Baskin-Robbins
Brings U.S. Ice Cream to Vietnam*   75
Managing Across the Globe: Why?   **76**
Fundamentals of International
Management   **76**
Categorizing Organizations by
International Involvement   **78**
Defining the Multinational Corporation   78
◆ Ethics Spotlight: *U.S. Companies Send
Hazardous Waste to Mexico*   **81**
Complexities of Managing the
Multinational Corporation   81
◆ Management and the Internet: *Virgin
Atlantic Airways Bows to U.S. Law*   **82**
Risk and the Multinational Corporation   84
The Workforce of Multinational
Corporations   84
Types of Organization Members Found
in Multinational Corporations   84

Management Functions and Multinational
Corporations   **86**
Planning in Multinational Corporations   86
◆ Across Industries: *Transportation Equipment*   **87**
Organizing Multinational Corporations   89
Influencing People in Multinational
Corporations   92
Controlling Multinational Corporations   93
Transnational Organizations   93
International Management: Special Issues   **94**
Maintaining Ethics in International
Management   94
Preparing Expatriates for Foreign
Assignments   95
◆ People Spotlight: *Helping Expatriates
to Adjust*   96

Case Study: *A Global Success Story*   99
Video Case: *Managing in the Global
Arena at Tile Connection*   101

Part Two   PLANNING

chapter 5   **Organizational Objectives**   **102**

Introductory Case: *Blockbuster Chief
Sets Organizational Objectives*   103
General Nature of Organizational
Objectives   **104**
Definition of Organizational Objectives   104
◆ Global Spotlight: *Asea Brown Boveri
Decides on Global Objectives*   **106**
Importance of Organizational Objectives   106
Types of Objectives in Organization   **107**
Organizational Objectives   107
Individual Objectives   107
Goal Integration   108
Areas for Organizational Objectives   **108**
◆ Management and the Internet: *Internet
Trend Causes to Alter Objectives*   **109**
Working with Organizational Objectives   **110**
Establishing Organizational Objectives   110
◆ Across Industries: *Automobile Tire
Manufacturing*   **110**
◆ Diversity Spotlight: *Diversity: Objective
for the Whole Organization at the
Department of Transportation*   **111**
Guidelines for Establishing Quality
Objectives   114
Guidelines for Making Objectives
Operational   115
Attainment of Objectives   116
How to Use Objectives   116
Management by Objectives (MBO)   **117**
Factors Necessary for a Successful
MBO Program   118
MBO Programs: Advantages and
Disadvantages   118

Case Study: *The Atlanta Committee for the Olympic Games (ACOG): Setting Objectives for an Event and a City*   121

Video Case: *Organizational Objectives at Cultural Toys*   123

chapter 6   **Fundamentals of Planning**   **124**

Introductory Case: *DuPont Plans to Make Women's Clothes*   **125**
General Characteristics of Planning   126
   Defining Planning   126
◆ **Across Industries:** *Government*   126
   Purpose of Planning   127
   Planning: Advantages and Potential Disadvantages   127
   Primacy of Planning   127
Steps in the Planning Process   128
The Planning Subsystem   129
   Elements of the Subsystem   130
   The Subsystem at Work   130
Planning and the Chief Executive   131
   Final Responsibility   132
◆ **Management and the Internet:** *Digital's New Plan Based Entirely on the Web*   132
   Planning Assistance   132
The Planner   133
   Qualifications of Planners   133
   Duties of Planners   134
   Evaluation of Planners   135
Maximizing the Effectiveness of the Planning Process   136
   Top-Management Support   136
◆ **Ethics Spotlight:** *Top Management Supports Environmental Protection Planning at Shell Oil Company*   136
   An Effective and Efficient Planning Organization   136
   Implementation Focused Planning   137
   Inclusion of the Right People   137
◆ **Quality Spotlight:** *Including the Right People on Panning Enhances Quality at Sun Microsystems*   138

Case Study: *Quaker Oats Focuses on a Planning Problem*   141

chapter 7   **Making Decisions**   **142**

Introductory Case: *Gateway Chief Makes Daring Decisions*   **143**
Fundamentals of Decisions   144
   Definition of a Decision   144
   Types of Decisions   144
◆ **Management and the Internet:** *Internet Company Makes Unprogrammed Decision Situation*   148
   The Responsibility for Making Organizational Decision   146

   Elements of the Decision Situation   148
◆ **Global Spotlight:** *Executives at United Technologies Detect a Weakness among Japanese Decision Makers*   149
The Decision-Making Process   **150**
   Identifying an Existing Problem   151
   Listing Alternative Solutions   151
   Selecting the Most Beneficial Alternative   152
   Implementing the Chosen Alternative   152
   Gathering Problem-Related Feedback   152
◆ **People Spotlight:** *Decision at John Deere: Eliminate Problems by Building Employee Involvement*   153
Decision-Making Conditions   153
   Complete Certainty Condition   154
   Complete Uncertainty Condition   154
   Risk Condition   154
◆ **Across Industries:** *Soft Drink Industry*   154
   Decision-Making Tools   155
   Probability Theory   155
   Decision Trees   156
Group Decision Making   158
   Advantages and Disadvantages of Using Groups to Make Decisions   158
   Processes for Making Group Decisions   158

Case Study: *The Decision to Change at General Motors Corporation*   162

chapter 8   **Strategic Planning**   **164**

Introductory Case: *Gillette's New Strategy: Women*   **165**
Strategic Planning   166
   Fundamentals of Strategic Planning   166
◆ **Across Industries:** *Toy Manufacturing*   167
   Strategy Management   167
◆ **Ethics Spotlight:** *Quaker Oats Cashes in on Fitness Fad*   171
◆ **Management and the Internet:** *800 Travel Systems, Inc. Establishes Internet Strategy*   172
◆ **Quality Spotlight:** *Lutheran General Health System's Mission Emphasizes Quality*   174
Tactical Planning   181
   Comparing and Coordinating Strategic and Tactical Planning   181
Planning and Levels of Management   182

Case Study: *How New Strategies Could Make a Difference at IBM*   186

Video Case: *Strategic Planning at Cloud 9 Shuttle*   187

chapter 9 **Plans and Planning Tools** **188**

Introductory Case: *Fiat Plans Car*
   Production 189
Plans: *A Definition* 190
♦ Ethics Spotlight: **Toyota Uses Philanthropy**
   Plan to Take Aim at General Motors 190
   Dimensions of Plans 190
   Types of Plans 192
♦ Management and the Internet: *Salomon*
   Smith Barney Establishes Rules to
   Deal with Internet 193
   Why Plans Fail 194
   Planning Area: Input Planning 194
♦ Global Spotlight: *Mexico as an Attractive*
   Manufacturing Site 195
Planning Tools 198
   Forecasting 198
♦ Across Industries: *Airplane Manufacturing* 199

Case Study: *Plans and Planning Tools* 207

Skills Video LIVE! *Planning* 209

Part Three **ORGANIZING**

chapter 10 **Fundamentals of Organizing** **210**

Introductory Case: *Lucent*
   Technologies Organizes for Success 211
A Definition of Organizing 212
   The Importance of Organizing 212
   The Organizing Process 213
♦ Management and the Internet: *Ad*
   Council to put Smokey the Bear
   on the Internet 214
   The Organizing Subsystem 215
Classical Organizing Theory 216
   Structure 216
♦ Global Spotlight: *Crown Cork & Seal*
   Company Organizes by Territory to
   Boost International Expansion 219
   Division of Labor 222
♦ Quality Spotlight: *Daimler Chrysler*
   Improves Coordination to Improve
   Product Quality 223
   Span of Management 224
♦ Across Industries: *Health Care* 226
   Scalar Relationships 226

Case Study: *Three's a Company*
   at AT&T 230

Video Case: *Fundamentals*
   of Organizing at Urocor 231

chapter 11 **Responsibility, Authority,**
and Delegation **232**

Introductory Case: *"Famous" Amos: The*
   Organizing Challenge 233
Responsibility 234

♦ Management and the Internet:
   Information Systems Job Descriptions
   Focus More on Internet 234
   Dividing Job Activities 235
   Clarifying Job Activities of Managers 237
Authority 239
   Types of Authority 240
♦ Ethics Spotlight: **General Electric Staff**
   Organizes Renovation 241
   Accountability 243
Delegation 244
   Steps in the Delegation Process 244
   Obstacles to the Delegation Process 245
   Eliminating Obstacles to the Delegation
     Process 246
   Centralization and Decentralization 247
♦ Across Industries: *Publishing* 247

Case Study: *Change Agents in Midstream* 252

chapter 12 **Managing Human Resources** **254**

Introductory Case: *Northwestern*
   Mutual Life Focuses on Recruitment 255
Defining Appropriate Human Resources 256
Steps in Providing Human Resources 256
   Recruitment 256
♦ Management and the Internet: *Texas*
   Instruments Uses the Web to Recruit
   Engineers 257
♦ People Spotlight: *NationsBank Helps*
   Women Employees with Child Care 263
   Selection 263
♦ Global Spotlight: *Compaq Computer*
   Company's International Selection
   Slip-Ups 264
   Training 266
♦ Across Industries: *Furniture Manufacturing* 270
   Performance Appraisal 271

Case Study: *Why CEO's Are Looking*
   at PEOs 275

chapter 13 **Managing Change: From Stress**
to the Virtual Organization **276**

Introductory Case: *AT&T Changes*
   Where and How People Work 277
Fundamental of Changing an
   Organization 278
   Defining Changing and
     Organization 278
   Change Versus Stability 278
Factors to Consider When
   Changing an Organization 279
   The Change Agent 280
♦ Across Industries: *Microcomputer*
   Manufacturing 281
   Determining What Should be Changed 281

♦ Ethics Spotlight: *Attitude Change is the Key to Establishing a Socially Responsible Position on Job Safety at Sonoco* 282
The Kind of Change to Make 283
♦ Diversity Spotlight: *McDonald's Corporation is Changing the Way Employees Think about Disabled Workers* 286
Individuals Affected by the Change 288
Evaluation of the Change 289
Change and Stress 290
Defining Stress 290
The Importance of Studying Stress 290
Managing Stress in Organizations 290
Virtuality 293
Defining a Virtual Organization 294
Degrees of Virtuality 294
♦ Management and the Internet: *Virtual Training at Cable and Wireless Communications* 294
The Virtual Office 295
Case Study: *Layoffs—The Cost of Doing Business* 299
Video Case: *Organizational Change and Stress at Image Communications* 300
Skills Video LIVE! *Organizing* 301

Part Four   INFLUENCING

chapter 14   **Fundamentals of Influencing and Communication** 302

Introductory Case: *Eaton Managers Concentrate on Influencing People* 302
Fundamentals of Influencing 304
Defining Influencing 304
The Influencing Subsystem 304
♦ People Spotlight: *The U.S. Army Teaches Leadership by Teaching Communication* 306
Communication 307
Interpersonal Communication 307
Interpersonal Communication in Organizations 314
♦ Management and the Internet: *Wimbledon Uses a We Site to Communicate with Stakeholders* 314
♦ Across Industries: *Local Government* 316
♦ Quality Spotlight: *Enhanced Formal Communication Contributes to Improving Quality at Holiday Inn* 317
Case Study: *Communication Services at Chick-fil-A Restaurants* 323

chapter 15   **Leadership** 324

Introduction Case Study: *The New President of H.J. Heinz Company Sends a Letter* 325
Defining Leadership 326
Leader Versus Manager 326

The Trait Approach to Leadership 327
The Situational Approach to Leadership:
A Focus on Leader Behavior 328
Leadership Situations and Decisions 328
♦ Management and the Internet: *K-B Uses Internet to Provide Information for Making Decisions* 329
Leadership Behaviors 334
♦ Across Industries: *Recruitment* 328
Leadership Today 342
♦ People Spotlight: *Robert Eaton Gets People Involved at DaimlerChrysler* 343
Transformational Leadership 343
Coaching 344
Superleadership 345
Entrepreneurial Leadership 345
Current Topics in Leadership 346
Substitutes for Leadership 346
Women as Leaders 346
Ways Women Lead 346
♦ Diversity Spotlight: *For James G. Kaiser of Corning, Being Employee-Centered Includes a Focus on Diversity* 347
Case Study: *Come Fly the Turbulent Skies* 350
Video Case: *Leadership at On Target Supply and Logistics* 351

chapter 16   **Motivation** 352

Introductory Case: *American Greeting Motivates Through Lateral Moves* 353
The Motivation 354
Defining Motivation 354
Process Theories of Motivation 354
Content Theories of Motivation: Human Needs 357
Motivating Organization Members 361
The Importance of Motivating Organization Members 361
Strategies for Motivating Organizational Members 361
♦ Across Industries: *Pharmaceuticals* 363
♦ Quality Spotlight: *Apple Computer's Job Enrichment Excels* 365
♦ Management and the Internet: *Managers Punish Pornographic-Related Behavior* 366
♦ People Spotlight: *Job Satisfaction is a More Powerful Motivator than Money at Microsoft* 370
Case Study: *Why Bart Simpson Flies Western Pacific Airlines* 373

chapter 17   **Groups, Teams, and Corporate Cultures** 374

Introductory Case: *Work Groups are Important to Progress at Rolls-Royce* 375
Groups 376

Kinds of Groups in Organizations 376
  Formal Groups 377
♦ Diversity Spotlight: *Managing a Diverse Salesforce Takes Special Insight at Equitable* 377
♦ Ethics Spotlight: *Calvary Hospital Forms Ethics Committees* 379
  Informal Groups 383
Managing Work Groups 384
  Determining Group Existence 384
  Understanding the Evolution of Informal Groups 385
Teams 387
  Groups Versus Teams 387
♦ Management and the Internet: *The Virtual Team* 387
  Types of Teams in Organizations 387
♦ Across Industries: *Motorcycles Manufacturing* 389
  Stages of Team Development 390
  Team Effectiveness 391
  Trust and Effective Teams 392
Corporate Culture 393
  The Significance of Corporate Culture 393
Case Study: *Whose Turn Is It To Polish the Apple?* 398
Video Case: *Groups, Teams, and Corporate Culture at Cactus and Tropicals* 399

chapter 18 **Understanding People: Attitudes, Perception, and Learning** 400

Introductory Case: *Reviving Workplace Attitudes* 401
What are Attitudes? 402
  How Beliefs and Values Create Attitudes 402
  Attitude Surveys 403
♦ Management and the Internet: *H.T.E. Uses the Internet to Study Employee Attitudes* 404
♦ Quality Spotlight: *Nucor Steel* 407
Perception 409
  Perception and the Perceptual Process 409
  Attribution Theory: Interpreting the Behavior of Others 409
  Perceptual Distortions 410
♦ Across Industries: *Banking* 411
♦ Global Spotlight: *The Wide, Wide World of Cultural Perceptions* 412
  Perceptions of Procedural Justice 412
Learning 414
  Learning Strategies 415
Case Study: *Sending the Wrong Signal* 418
Skills Video LIVE! *Influencing* 419

Part Five CONTROLLING

chapter 19 **Principles of Controlling** 420

Introductory Case: *Controlling at Polaroid* 421
The Fundamentals of Controlling 422
  Defining Control 422
  Defining Controlling 422
♦ Across Industries: *Hotels* 425
♦ Management and the Internet: *NBC Focused on Reaching Future Profitability Standards by Adding Internet Focus* 427
♦ People Spotlight: *Toyota Takes Corrective Action by Changing its President* 429
  Types of Control 429
♦ Diversity Spotlight: *Feedback Control Induces Cosmetics Industry to Develop New Products for Diverse Population Segments* 430
The Controller and Control 431
  The Job of the Controller 431
  How Much Control is Needed? 432
Power and Control 433
  A Definition of Power 433
  Total Power of a Manager 433
  Steps for Increasing Total Power 434
Performing the Control Function 435
  Potential Barriers to Successful Controlling 435
  Making Controlling Successful 436
Case Study: *Who Killed Barings Bank?* 440
Video Case: *Principles of Controlling at Medallion Funding* 441

chapter 20 **Production Management and Control** 442

Introductory Case: *The Quick Turn at USAir* 443
Production 444
  Defining Production 444
  Productivity 444
♦ Management and the Internet: *Sallie Mae Uses the Internet to Improve Productivity* 445
  Quality and Productivity 445
♦ Quality Spotlight: *Focusing on Quality at Adidas USA* 448
  Automation 449
♦ Across Industries: *Tools and Appliance Manufacturing* 449
  Strategies, Systems, and Process 450
Operation Management 450
  Defining Operations Management 450
  Operations Management Considerations 450
♦ Ethics Spotlight: *Firestone Exit LaVergne* 452
Operations Control 456

Just-in-Time Inventory Control 456
Maintenance Control 457
Cost Control 457
Budgetary Control 458
Ratio Analysis 459
Materials Control 459
Selected Operations Control Tools 461
Using Control Tools to Control
Organizations 461
Inspection 461
Management by Exception 461
Management by Objectives 462
Break even Analysis 462
Other Broad Operations Control Tools 465
Case Study: Sun Also Rises 468

chapter 21 **Information Technology and the
Internet** 470

Introductory Case: Making Changes
Without the Right Information at
Sunbeam? 471
Essentials of Information 472
Factors Influencing the Value of
Information 472
Information Appropriateness 473
Information Quality 474
Information Timelines 474
Information Quantity 474
Evaluating Information 475
The Management Information
System (MIS) 476
♦ Global Spotlight: Pohang Iron & Steel
Company Needs a Complex MIS 477
Describing the MIS 477
♦ Diversity Spotlight: Target's MIS Focuses
on Hispanic Workers 478
Established an MIS 480
Information Technology 484
Computer Assistance in Using
Information 484
The Management Decision Support
System (MDSS) 487
Computer Networks 489
The Local Area Network 489
The Internet 490
♦ Management and the Internet: Dell
Computer Company Surfs the Internet to
Service Customers and Build Its Image 491
♦ Across Industries: Accounting Technical
Glitch at Arthur Anderson Renders
E-Mails Useless 494
Case Study: The Internet Becomes a
Technological Battlefield 498
Video Case: Information and
Technology at the King Company 500
Skills Video LIVE! Controlling 501

Part Six   TOPICS FOR SPECIAL EMPHASIS

chapter 22 **Competitiveness: Quality
and Innovation** 502

Introductory Case: Lego's Mindstorms
Market Research Causes Problem 503
Fundamentals of Quality 504
Defining Total Quality Management 504
♦ Quality Spotlight: "Quality is Job 1"
at Ford 504
The Importance of Quality 505
Established Quality Awards 506
Achieving Quality 507
Environmental Analysis and Quality 511
Establishing Organizational
Direction and Quality 511
Strategy Formulation and Quality 512
Strategy Implementation and Quality 513
Strategic Control and Quality 514
The Quality Improvement Process 515
The Incremental Improvement Process 515
♦ People Spotlight: Keeping People Involved
in Incremental Improvement:
Bearings, Inc. 517
Reengineering Improvements 517
Innovation and Creativity 519
♦ Management and the Internet: Bill Gross
Uses Creativity to Launch Idealab 519
Creativity in Individuals 520
♦ Across Industries: Candy Manufacturing 521
Case Study: Total Quality Management:
Learning to Make it Work 524
Video Case: Quality: Building Competitive
Organizations 525

chapter 23 **Management and Diversity** 526

Introductory Case: Ortho
Pharmaceutical: "Showcase"
for Cultural Diversity 527
Defining Diversity 528
The Social Implications of Diversity 528
Advantages of Diversity in
Organizations 529
Gaining and Keeping Market Share 529
Cost Saving 529
Increased Productivity and Innovation 529
Better-Quality Management 530
♦ Diversity Spotlight: General Electric
Values Global Sensitivity 531
Challenges that Managers Face in
Working with Diverse Populations 531
Changing Demographics 531
♦ Global Spotlight: AT&T Connects
the World 532
Ethnocentrism and Other Negative
Dynamics 533

◆ Across Industries: *Family Dining*   533
   Negative Dynamics and Specific
    Groups   534
Strategies for Promoting Diversity in
  Organizations   535
   Workforce 2000   536
   Equal Employment and Affirmative
    Action   537
◆ Management and the Internet: *EEOC*
  Uses Web Site to Inform Managers
  about Sexual Harassment   537
   Organizational Commitment to
    Diversity   538
   Pluralism   540

The Role of the Manager   542
   Management Development and
    Diversity Training   543
Case Study: *Levi Strauss: Valuing*
  Diversity   548
Skills Video LIVE! *Topics for*
  Special Emphasis   549

Glossary   **550**
Endnotes   **561**
Credits   **579**
Name and Company Index   **585**
Subject Index   **589**

PREFACE

Never before have managers faced such exciting challenges! Never before have managers had the potential to earn such high compensation for meeting these challenges. Today, your career as a manager will be extremely interesting and your rewards for competence could be very significant.

As it was in the previous seven editions of *Modern Management,* the purpose of this text is to prepare students to be managers. Coverage includes a wealth of conventional wisdom related to traditional management tasks. Contemporary management challenges related to such issues as people, diversity, quality, ethics, and the global environment are featured. New to this edition is an emphasis on the Internet as a new, evolving, and valuable management tool. New coverage also highlights topics such as innovation, learning organizations, and the application of management concepts across industries.

Overall, this book is carefully crafted to present traditional management concepts, important contemporary management issues, and insights regarding ways that students should apply these in order to ensure organizational success.

The eighth edition of the **Modern Management Learning Package,** the text plus its ancillaries, continues a recognized and distinctive 20-year tradition in management education. This tradition emphasizes clear, concise, current, and thorough coverage of management concepts. In addition, the learning materials are based on an understanding of and a determination to enhance the student learning process. Only instructional support materials that contribute to the design and conduct of the highest-quality principles of management course are included in the package.

Revisions to the **Modern Management Learning Package** have been spirited by a single objective—improving student learning. All revisions reflect responsiveness to instructor and student feedback regarding ways to refashion the package in order to further enhance student learning. Starting with the text, the following sections describe and explain each major component of this revision.

TEXT: THEORY OVERVIEW

Decisions about which concepts to include in this revision were indeed difficult. Such decisions were heavily influenced by information from accrediting agencies such as the American Assembly of Collegiate Schools of Business (AACSB), organizations established by professional managers such as the American

Management Association (AMA), and organizations established by management scholars such as the Academy of Management. Overall, management theory in this text is divided into the following six main sections:

- ► Introduction to management
- ► Planning
- ► Organizing
- ► Influencing
- ► Controlling
- ► Topics for special emphasis

Extensive updates of theory and examples have been made in every section. Detailed discussion of content and other revisions to each section follow.

INTRODUCTION TO MANAGEMENT

This section lays the groundwork necessary for studying management.

- ► **Chapter 1, Management and Management Careers,** not only exposes students to what management is, but also gives them an understanding of special career issues, such as the progress of women in management, dual-career couples, and the multicultural workforce. Revision focus includes updated coverage of executive salaries and comparisons of male and female executive salaries.
- ► **Chapter 2, Managing: History and Current Thinking,** presents several fundamental but different ways in which managers can perceive their jobs. The work of management pioneers like Frederick W. Taylor, Frank and Lillian Gilbreth, and Henry L. Gantt is highlighted. New material in this chapter discusses the *learning organization* as a possible new, evolving approach to managing. A learning organization is defined and the five features of a learning organization (systems thinking, shared vision, mental models, team learning, and personal mastery) are discussed. A new People Perspectives feature illustrates how managers at Signicast Corporation took practical steps to build their learning organization.
- ► **Chapter 3, Corporate Social Responsibility and Business Ethics,** discusses the responsibilities that managers have to society and how business ethics applies to modern management. Valuable discussion focuses on determining if social responsibility exists in a particular situation.

► **Chapter 4, Meeting the Global Challenge,** focuses on domestic versus international, multinational, and transnational organizations; expatriates and repatriation; and international market agreements like the European Union (EU) and the North American Free Trade Agreement (NAFTA). Discussion also extends to the evolving international market agreement among countries in the Pacific Rim. This chapter appears early in the text to better enable students to reflect on global management issues throughout the course. New topics for this edition include better preparing expatriates for assignments, ethics in international management, and foreign investments in the United States.

► PLANNING

This section elaborates on planning as a primary management function.

► **Chapter 5, Organizational Objectives,** begins this section in order to emphasize the setting of organizational objectives as the beginning of the planning process. Topics include the importance of objectives and guidelines for establishing sound objectives.

► **Chapter 6, Fundamentals of Planning,** presents the basics of planning. The purpose of planning steps in the planning process and qualifications of a planner are stressed.

► **Chapter 7, Making Decisions,** discusses the decision process as a component of the planning process. Coverage focuses on group decision processes like brainstorming, the nominal group technique, and the Delphi technique. Coverage also focuses on advantages and disadvantages of having groups make decisions and problems in evaluating the group decision process.

► **Chapter 8, Strategic Planning,** highlights Porter's model for industry analysis, the BCG Growth-Share Matrix, the GE Portfolio Matrix, strategy implementation, and strategic control.

► **Chapter 9, Plans and Planning Tools,** discusses various planning tools, and such as forecasting and scheduling, that are available to help formulate plans.

► ORGANIZING

This section discusses organizing activities as a major management function.

► **Chapter 10, Fundamentals of Organizing,** presents the basic principles of organizing. Concepts featured are organization structure, division of labor, span of management, and scalar relationships.

► **Chapter 11, Responsibility, Authority, and Delegation,** focuses on ways to organize worker activities. Emphasis is on holding organization members accountable for carrying out their obligations.

► **Chapter 12, Managing Human Resources,** discusses hiring and developing people who will make desirable contributions to the attainment of organizational objectives.

► **Chapter 13, Managing Change: From Stress to the Virtual Organization,** emphasizes ways in which managers change

organizations and the stress-related issues that can accompany such action. New coverage highlights increasing virtuality in organizations by establishing virtual offices, building alternative work situations, and communicating successfully in virtual offices.

► INFLUENCING

This section discusses ways in which managers should deal with people. Reflecting the spirit of AACSB guidelines encouraging thorough coverage of human factors in the business curriculum, the influencing section is comprehensive.

► **Chapter 14, Fundamentals of Influencing and Communication,** introduces the topic of managing people, defines interpersonal communication, and presents organizational communication as the primary vehicle that managers use to interact with people.

► **Chapter 15, Leadership,** highlights more traditional concepts, such as the Vroom-Yetton-Jago leadership model, the path-goal theory of leadership, and the life cycle theory of leadership. Coverage also includes newer concepts, like transformational leadership, coaching, super-leadership, and entrepreneurial leadership.

► **Chapter 16, Motivation,** defines motivation, describes the motivation process, and provides useful strategies that managers can use in attempting to motivate organizational members.

► **Chapter 17, Groups, Teams, and Corporate Culture,** emphasizes managing clusters of people as a means of accomplishing organizational goals. This chapter covers the management of teams. Discussion focuses on groups versus teams; virtual teams; problem-solving, self-managed, and cross-functional teams; stages of team development; empowerment; and factors contributing to team effectiveness.

► **Chapter 18, Understanding People: Attitudes, Perception, and Learning,** focuses on important characteristics of people that managers must understand. First, the relationship among attitudes, values, and beliefs is described. Then, the role of attitudes in influencing behavior is discussed. The chapter then turns to perception and the perceptual process, including detailed analyses of attribution theory and perceptions of procedural justice. Finally, the concept of learning is studied.

► CONTROLLING

This section presents control as a major management function.

► **Chapter 19, Principles of Controlling,** discusses the basics of control. Power and control as well as types of control are important topics.

► **Chapter 20, Production Management and Control,** focuses on the creation of goods and services, paying special attention on automation and production strategies, systems, and processes available to managers.

► **Chapter 21, Information Technology and the Internet,** in keeping with the spirit of AACSB guidelines, has been significantly revised to add more coverage of current technology via Internet-related discussion. The chapter emphasizes recent technology developments ranging from e-mail, electronic data interchange, and videoconferencing to the Internet and the World Wide Web. Emphasis on Intranets and firewalls complete this section. Discussion focuses on becoming a better manager by using technological tools, *not* by understanding the intricacies of technology.

▶ TOPICS FOR SPECIAL EMPHASIS

The last section of *Modern Management* discusses additional issues important to managers operating in an organization in today's global environment.

- ▶ **Chapter 22, Competitiveness: Quality and Innovation**, emphasizes building competitiveness through quality and innovation. Discussion focuses on defining quality, achieving quality through strategic planning, and describing the management skills necessary to build quality throughout an organization. The ideas of such internationally known quality experts as Philip B. Crosby, W. Edwards Deming, and Joseph M. Juran are highlighted. Significant revision in this chapter discusses the role of innovation in being organizationally competitive. Topics discussed include innovation and creativity, creativity in individuals, and encouraging creativity in organizations.

- ▶ **Chapter 23, Management and Diversity**, defines *diversity*, explains the advantages of promoting diversity in organizations, and outlines ways in which managers can promote it. This chapter also discusses some key challenges and dilemmas that manager's face in attempting to build a diverse workforce.

◼ TEXT: STUDENT LEARNING AIDS

Several features of this text were designed to make the study of management more efficient, effective, and enjoyable. Many are new to this edition. The following is a list of these features and an explanation of each.

▶ LEARNING OBJECTIVES

The opening pages of each chapter contain a set of learning objectives that are intended as guidelines for focusing study within the chapter.

▶ CHAPTER OUTLINES

The opening pages of each chapter also contain a chapter outline that previews the textual material and helps the reader keep the information in perspective while it is being read.

▶ CHAPTER HIGHLIGHTS

Chapter highlights are another exciting feature of this text. In essence, highlights are extended examples or boxes emphasizing the wide range of contemporary issues in real companies that modern managers face. Each chapter has four highlights. The highlights have been significantly revised in this edition and include the following elements in each chapter:

- ▶ **Spotlights**—Spotlights focus on the following major management themes: diversity, quality, ethics, people, and the global environment. Two Spotlights appear in each chapter, with all topics receiving equivalent emphasis throughout the book. In chapter 21, for instance, a Global Spotlight focuses on the complex MIS needs of Pohang Iron & Steel, a South Korean metals manufacturer. In the same chapter, a Diversity Spotlight reports on how Target, a major U.S. retailer, uses its MIS to keep track of Hispanic worker demographics and needs.

- ▶ **Across Industries**—*New* to this edition, each chapter contains a section called Across Industries, a feature emphasizing how chapter content relates to a specific industry. The purpose of this feature is to ensure that students get a full, rich understanding of how management can be applied to many different situations. Situations presented in Across Industries emphasize companies and industries such as L.L. Bean in mail order retailing, Black & Decker in tool manufacturing, Shoney's in dining, Mattel in toy manufacturing, Arthur Andersen in accounting, and Goodyear in tire manufacturing.

- ▶ **Management and the Internet**—Also new to this edition, Management and the Internet, featured in every chapter, emphasizes the Internet as a new, evolving, and practical management tool. Given the unprecedented growth of the Internet, today's management students must acquire a useful, applied knowledge of the Internet. Companies and issues discussed in this feature include Dell Computer Corporation surfing the Internet to service customers and build company image, the Equal Employment Opportunity Commission (EEOC) using the Internet to inform managers about the specifics of sexual harassment, Texas Instruments using the Internet to recruit new employees, Sega considering the Internet in how it develops organizational objectives, and the All England Lawn Tennis and Croquet Club using the Internet to communicate with fans about Wimbledon.

▶ INTRODUCTORY CASES WITH BACK-TO-THE-CASE SECTIONS

The opening of each chapter contains a case study that introduces readers to management problems related to chapter content. Detailed Back-to-the-Case sections appear throughout each chapter, applying specific areas of management theory discussed in the chapter to the Introductory Case. All cases involve real companies ranging from AT&T and Gateway 2000 to Blockbuster, Heinz, and Rolls-Royce. Over half of the cases in this edition are new or updated. New cases in this edition include "Managing Disney's Animal Kingdom," "Gillette's New Strategy for Women," "Lucent Technology Organizes for Success," "Making Changes without the Right Information at Sunbeam," and "LEGO's MindStorms Market Research Causes Problems."

▶ END-OF-CHAPTER PEDAGOGY

As in the previous edition of *Modern Management,* several pedagogical features are integrated at the end of each chapter.

CHAPTER INTERNET ICON A new Internet icon has been designed for this edition. This icon appears at the end of each chapter to remind students that additional study materials related to the chapter are available at *www.prenhall.com/certo* and can be used independently to enhance their learning about management even if their course does not require such usage.

ACTION SUMMARIES Each chapter ends with an action-oriented chapter summary that allows students to respond to several objective questions that are clearly linked to the learning objectives stated at the beginning of the chapter. Students can check their answers against the answer key at the end of the chapter. This key also lists the pages in the chapter that the students can reference for a full explanation of the answers.

INTRODUCTORY CASE WRAP-UP Each chapter ends with an Introductory Case Wrap-Up that includes learning materials to further illustrate the application of chapter content to the Introductory Case. New to this edition, the wrap-up section has two distinct parts. Part one is a set of *case discussion questions* intended to extend discussion of the application of chapter content to the case. Part two, also new to this edition, is a *skills exercise* that focuses on building management abilities of students via the case. Sample exercises are "Designing an MBO Program," "Building Useful Organization Charts," "Using Reinforcement Strategies," "Determining Symptoms and Problems," "Applying Total Quality Management," and "Evaluating a Web Site."

ISSUES FOR REVIEW AND DISCUSSION The concluding pages of each chapter contain a set of discussion questions that test the understanding of chapter material and can serve as a vehicle for study and class discussion.

► **ADDITIONAL FEATURES**

► *Marginal Notes*—Each chapter contains marginal notes that can be helpful both in initial reading and for review. These notes highlight key terms in each chapter while providing brief definitions for student review.
► *Glossary*—Major terms and their definitions are gathered at the end of the text. Terms appear in boldface type and include references to the text pages on which the discussion of the term appears.
► *Illustrations*—Figures, tables, and photographs depicting various management situations are used throughout the text to help bridge the gap between management theory and real-world facts and figures.

► **ADDITIONAL TEACHING MATERIALS**

INSTRUCTOR'S MANUAL Designed to guide the educator through the text, each chapter in the instructor's manual contains a brief summary, brief chapter outline, detailed lecture outline, suggested answers and solutions to questions in the text, a comprehensive video guide with discussion questions based on the Skills Video LIVE! and the Small Business 2000 chapter-ending videos, and Internet support.

ELECTRONIC INSTRUCTOR'S MANUAL Conveniently provided on a 3.5" floppy disk, the Electronic Instructor's Man-

ual includes all of the previously mentioned material, plus an option for professors to annotate and add their own material.

TEST ITEM FILE Each chapter contains multiple choice, true/false, and essay questions. Together the questions cover the content of each chapter in a variety of ways providing flexibility in testing the students' knowledge of the text.

WINDOWS/PRENTICE HALL TEST MANAGER VERSION 4.0 Containing all of the questions in the printed Test Item File, Test Manager is a comprehensive suite of tools for testing and assessment. Test Manager allows educators to easily create and distribute tests for their courses, either by printing and distributing through traditional methods, or by on-line delivery via a Local Area Network (LAN) server.

POWERPOINT ELECTRONIC TRANSPARENCIES WITH TEACHING NOTES A comprehensive package allowing access to all of the figures from the text, these PowerPoint transparencies are designed to aid the educator and supplement in-class lectures. To further enhance the lecture, teaching notes for each slide are included both electronically, and as a printed, punched, and perforated booklet for insertion into a three-ring binder, allowing the educator to further customize the lecture.

COLOR TRANSPARENCIES Designed to aid the educator and enhance classroom lectures, 100 of the most critical PowerPoint electronic transparencies have been chosen for inclusion in this package as full-color acetates and are provided on high quality mylar.

STUDY GUIDE Designed to aid student comprehension of the concepts presented in the text, a Study Guide is available containing chapter objectives, detailed chapter outlines, review, discussion, and study questions.

PHLIP What is PHLIP? Prentice Hall Learning on the Internet Partnership (PHLIP) is a content-rich, multidisciplinary business education Web site created *by* professors *for* professors and their students. Developed by Professor Dan Cooper at Marist College, PHLIP provides academic support for faculty and students using this text.

FOR STUDENTS
► **Student Study Hall**
    Ask the Tutor offers Virtual Office Hours
    Writing Center provides links to on-line resources
    Study Skills Center provides study skills tips and resources
    Career Center offers tips, sample résumés, and on-line job applications
► **Research Center** provides resources for using the Internet as a research tool
► **Current Events** summarize and link to current news articles. Each article is fully supported by group activities, critical thinking exercises, discussion questions, reference resources, key topics, and more.

- ▶ **Interactive Study Guide** offers multiple-choice and true/false questions for every chapter. Students submit responses to the PHLIP server for scoring and receive immediate feedback, including page references linked to the text. Students can e-mail their scores to their instructor or teaching assistant.
- ▶ **Internet Resources** provide links to related Web sites, complete with an Info button that offers professors and students a helpful description of each site.

FOR INSTRUCTORS
- ▶ **Text-Specific Resources**
  - Downloadable supplements
  - On-line faculty support
- ▶ **Faculty Lounge**
  - **Talk to the Team** is a password-protected conference and chat room system
  - **Teaching Archive** includes **Sample Syllabi**
  - **Help with Computers** provides tips and links to on-line tutorials
  - **Internet Skills** offers advice, tips, and tutorials for using the Internet

◼ NEW TO THIS EDITION

CHAPTER ENDING VIDEOS Based on the popular PBS series, the Small Business 2000 videos highlight interesting small businesses and their growth. They are linked to various chapters in the book and emphasize key concepts in the chapters. Introductory Case material for the student is found at the end of the chapter.

PART ENDING SKILLS LIVE VIDEOS These exciting new videos are scenario-based and feature real actors demonstrating important management skills. They are based on a small video and television production company and include questions at the end of each segment that relate to the material in the previous part of the book. Dr. Certo appears on the video to comment on how text material relates to the case.

CD-ROM A CD-ROM is included that provides exciting links to the Web site (www.prenhall.com/certo) and the skills videos. By placing the skills videos on the CD-ROM, the instructor can use these as an out-of-class assignment.

ACKNOWLEDGMENTS

Much positive feedback regarding the **Modern Management Learning Package** has continued for nearly a quarter of a century. The steady stream of compliments over the years from friends, colleagues, and students has certainly been gratifying! Over the years, this package has created a standard for high-quality learning materials in colleges and universities, as well as in professional management-training programs throughout the world. These materials have been translated into foreign languages for distribution throughout the world and have been used by over half a million students.

I have received much professional recognition for the success of this text. Considerable recognition for the success of this project, however, rightly should be given to valuable contributions made by many of my respected colleagues. I am pleased to recognize the contributions of these individuals and extend to them my warmest personal gratitude for their professional insights, as well as for their personal support and encouragement throughout the life of this project.

Professor Lee A. Graf, Illinois State University, has been a special contributor. As a close personal friend, he has been especially vigilant in helping to keep this text a market leader since the first edition in 1980. During this time, Dr. Graf has made many significant contributions in many different text areas. His overall professional competence and instructional insights have been a constant encouragement.

Other colleagues have also made important contributions to this text and its ancillaries. I would like to thank these individuals for their dedication and professionalism in making this project all that it can be. The following professionals have helped to shape chapters in previous editions and the contribution that each has made is listed below:

Robert E. Kemper, Northern Arizona University, for assistance in the revision of chapter 20, "Production Management and Control"

Toni Carol King, Binghamton University, for assistance in writing chapter 23, "Management and Diversity"

Maurice Manner, Marymount College, for assistance in the revision of chapter 4, "Managing in the Global Arena"

Richard Ratliff, Shari Tarnutzer, and their colleagues, Utah State University, for assistance in the revision of chapter 22, "Quality: Building Competitive Organizations"

Larry Waldorf, Boise State University, for assistance in the revision of chapter 15, "Leadership"

Michael Carrell, Morehead State University, for assistance in the composition of chapter 18, "Understanding People: Attitudes, Perception, and Learning," which is new to this edition.

New to this edition, are the contributions of Rob Panco, a doctoral student at Baruch, who is responsible for selecting the Small Business 2000 segments and the excellent case notes that accompany them. He is also responsible for bringing together all six of the Skills Video LIVE! sections.

Every author appreciates the valuable contribution reviewers make to the development of a text project. Reviewers offer that "different viewpoint" that requires an author to constructively question his or her work. I again had an excellent team of reviewers. Thoughtful comments, concern for student learning, and insights regarding instructional implications of the written word characterized the high-quality feedback I received. I am pleased to be able to recognize members of the review team for this edition and their valuable contributions to the development of this text:

Laurence Aaronson, Catonsville Community College

Robert W. Amundson, Ulster County Community College

William B. Anhalt, Golden Gate University

James W. Bishop, Maryville College

Robert E. Callahan, Seattle University

Douglas G. Campbell, California State University, Chico

Paul A. Fadil, Valdosta State University

Richard F. Gordon, Detroit College of Business

Michael J. Hamburger, Northern Virginia Community College

Barbara C. Howard, Northern Virginia Community College

Felix Kamuche, Morehouse College

Marybeth Kardatzke, Montgomery College

Jehan G. Kavoosi, Clarion University of Pennsylvania

Robert Keating, University of North Carolina at Wilmington

Beverly Linnell, S.A.I.T. Calgary

Christine Miller, Tennessee Technological University

Alfred A. Noto, Berkeley College

Cyndy Ruszkowski, Illinois State University

I would like to personally and sincerely thank my many colleagues and friends at Prentice Hall for their outstanding support, vision, and encouragement throughout the development and publication of my text and its ancillaries. David Shafer, my editor, has been an unheralded source of innovative ideas and encouragement. His industry insights and vigilant focus on producing only high-quality materials was a driving force throughout the project. Jennifer Glennon, editorial managing editor, was new to this project and contributed an eye for sound text design and overall project leadership. Other Prentice Hall professionals who have assisted greatly in this book are the following: Natalie Anderson, editor-in-chief; Michael Campbell, executive marketing manager; Shane Gemza, assistant editor; Shannon Sims, editorial assistant; Judy Leale, associate managing editor; Cindy Spreder, production editor; Diane Peirano, manufacturing buyer; and Cheryl Asherman, senior designer. I thank them.

On a personal note, I want to thank my wife Mimi for helping me keep the importance of this project in perspective. Through her efforts I have maintained my professional dedication and, more importantly, become a better person. In addition, my children, Brian, Sarah, Matthew, and Trevis have no idea how much they inspire me. A special treat is that Trevis, a doctoral student at Indiana University, contributed thoughts, ideas, and two Introductory Cases to this edition. Melissa, the newest Certo on the scene, unknowingly prods me toward excellence through her high dedication to meeting life's important challenges. I thank them all for being themselves. The work ethic taught to me by my father and mother, Sam and Annette, has been instrumental in helping me complete long-run projects of this nature. They have given me many such survival tools for life.

MODERN

MANAGEMENT

Management and Management Careers

CHAPTER OUTLINE

Introductory Case: *Managing Disney's New Animal Kingdom*

THE IMPORTANCE OF MANAGEMENT

THE MANAGEMENT TASK
The Role of Management
Defining Management
The Management Process: Management Functions
Management Process and Goal Attainment
Management and Organizational Resources

THE UNIVERSALITY OF MANAGEMENT
The Theory of Characteristics

MANAGEMENT CAREERS
A Definition of Career
Career Stages, Life Stages, and Performance
Promoting Your Own Career
Special Career Issues

SPECIAL FEATURES FOR THE REMAINING CHAPTERS
Spotlights
Across Industries
Management and the Internet

STUDENT LEARNING OBJECTIVES

From studying this chapter, I will attempt to acquire

1. An understanding of the importance of management to society and individuals

2. An understanding of the role of management

3. An ability to define *management* in several different ways

4. An ability to list and define the basic functions of management

5. Working definitions of managerial effectiveness and managerial efficiency

6. An understanding of basic management skills and their relative importance to managers

7. An understanding of the universality of management

8. Insights concerning what management careers are and how they evolve

MANAGING DISNEY'S NEW ANIMAL KINGDOM

REMINDER: THE INTRODUCTORY CASE WRAP-UP (PP. 20–21) CONTAINS DISCUSSION QUESTIONS AND A SKILLS EXERCISE TO FURTHER ILLUSTRATE THE APPLICATION OF CHAPTER CONCEPTS TO THIS VIGNETTE.

Walt Disney Company has recently opened its newest theme park, Animal Kingdom, in Orlando, Florida. Company projections forecast that 7 to 8 million people will visit the new park annually.

Disney invested $1 billion to build Animal Kingdom, the most ambitious and expensive theme park ever built. The park stars 1,000 live animals that include giraffes, lions, tigers, rhinos, and gorillas. A Florida cow pasture was transformed into the closest thing to an African savannah this side of Nairobi in order to allow park visitors to take a life-like African safari. Animal Kingdom's expansiveness is reflected in its foundation of 4 million cubic yards of dirt, 40,000 mature trees, 60 miles of underground utilities, waterways, and structures built by 2,600 construction workers.

Employees, or cast members as they are called at Disney, will play a key role in the success of Animal Kingdom. Take, for example, the safari ride. Guests travel in 32-person vehicles driven by cast members who must excitedly react to the animals that they see. In essence, cast members are considered a critical part of the show. The drivers must dispatch at the right time while keeping their eye on and contributing to the positive experience of the guests. Cast members cannot be distracted by the animals but must complement them in providing an exciting time for park visitors. Effective cast members are rated highly by park visitors, provide those visitors the highest levels of guest satisfaction, and in turn, encourage park visitors to spend more time and money at Disney World.

It took Disney CEO Michael Eisner 5½ years to decide to build Animal Kingdom. This long deliberation period

Peter Hoke, an animal keeper at Disney's new Animal Kingdom Theme Park, presents an afternoon treat to a tamarin monkey. Successful management of skilled employees like Peter will be one of the most important elements in the new park's success in the years ahead.

reflects the facts that the new park is a huge investment and cannot be easily divested if it turns out to be a failure. Flop theme parks are not like flop movies that simply can be sold or discarded. Now that Animal Kingdom is built, the success or failure of the park rests squarely in the hands of management.

What's Ahead

As discussed in the introductory case, Walt Disney Company has recently opened it newest theme park, Animal Kingdom. Although building the park is a significant accomplishment, the future success or failure of the park rests in the hands of management. Assume that you are the manager in charge of Animal Kingdom. The information in this chapter is designed to help you understand the basics of your management job. In this chapter, management is defined through the following:

1. A discussion of its importance both to society and to individuals
2. A description of the management task
3. A discussion of its universality
4. Insights about management careers

THE IMPORTANCE OF MANAGEMENT

Managers influence all phases of modern organizations. Plant managers run manufacturing operations that produce the clothes we wear, the food we eat, and the automobiles we drive. Sales managers maintain a salesforce that markets goods. Personnel managers provide organizations with a competent and productive workforce. The "jobs available" section in the classified advertisements of any major newspaper describes many different types of management activities and confirms the importance of management (see Figure 1.1).

Our society could neither exist as we know it today nor improve without a steady stream of managers to guide its organizations. Peter Drucker emphasized this point when he stated that effective management is probably the main resource of developed countries and the most needed resource of developing ones.[1] In short, all societies desperately need good managers.

Besides its importance to society as a whole, management is vital to many individuals who earn their livings as managers. Government statistics show that management positions have increased approximately from 10 percent to 18 percent of all jobs since 1950. Managers come from varying backgrounds and have diverse educational specialties. Many people who originally trained to be accountants, teachers, financiers, or even writers eventually make their livelihoods as managers. Although in the short term, the demand for managers varies somewhat, in the long term, managerial positions can yield high salaries, status, interesting work, personal growth, and intense feelings of accomplishment.

In fact, there is some concern that certain managers are paid *too* much. Consider the results of a 1997 poll by *Forbes* magazine ranking the highest-paid chief executives over the five-year period, from 1992 to 1996.[2] As a group, the top 25 highest paid executives during this period earned over $2.5 billion. Topping the list is Stephen Hilbert, who earned a total of $277 million as Chief Executive Officer of Conseco. As another example, Michael Eisner, CEO at Walt Disney, made $236 million during the same period. Table 1.1 shows the 10 highest paid female executives for 1997.[3]

BACK TO THE CASE

The information just presented furnishes you, as the manager of Animal Kingdom, with insights concerning the significance of your role as manager. Your role is important not only to society as a whole but also to yourself as an individual. In general, as a manager you make some contribution to creating the standard of living that we all enjoy and thereby earn corresponding rewards. Walt Disney Company is making societal contributions aimed at relaxing and entertaining people throughout the world. As the manager of Animal Kingdom, you would be helping Walt Disney Company in this endeavor. If you are of significant help, the company's contribution to society as well as your personal returns will probably be magnified considerably.

FIGURE 1.1 ▶ The variety of management positions available

SR. MANAGEMENT DEVELOPMENT SPECIALIST

We are a major metropolitan service employer of over 5,000 employees seeking a person to join our management development staff. Prospective candidates will be degreed with 5 to 8 years experience in the design, implementation, and evaluation of developmental programs for first-line and mid-level management personnel. Additionally, candidates must demonstrate exceptional oral and written communications ability and be skilled in performance analysis, programmed instruction, and the design and implementation of reinforcement systems.

If you meet these qualifications, please send your résumé, including salary history and requirements to:

Box RS-653

An Equal Opportunity Employer

BRANCH MGR—$30,500. Perceptive pro with track record in administration and lending has high visibility with respected firm.

Box PH-165

AVIATION FBO MANAGER NEEDED

Southeast Florida operation catering to corporate aviation. No maintenance or aircraft sales—just fuel and the best service. Must be experienced. Salary plus benefits commensurate with qualifications. Submit complete résumé to:

Box LJO-688

DIVISION CREDIT MANAGER

Major mfg. corporation seeks an experienced credit manager to handle the credit and collection function of its Midwest division (Chicago area). Interpersonal skills are important, as is the ability to communicate effectively with senior management. Send résumé with current compensation to:

Box NM-43

ACCOUNTING MANAGER

Growth opportunity. Michigan Ave. location. Acctg. degree, capable of supervision. Responsibilities include G/L, financial statements, inventory control, knowledge of systems design for computer applications. Send résumé, incl. salary history to:

Box RJM-999
An Equal Opportunity Employer

FINANCIAL MANAGER

CPA/MBA (U of C) with record of success in management positions. Employed, now seeking greater opportunity. High degree of professionalism, exp. in dealing w/financial inst., strong communication & analytical skills, stability under stress, high energy level, results oriented. Age 34, 11 yrs. exper. incl. major public acctng., currently 5 years as Financial VP of field leader. Impressive references.

Box LML-666

MARKET MANAGER

Major lighting manufacturer seeks market manager for decorative outdoor lighting. Position entails establishing and implementing marketing, sales, and new product development programs including coordination of technical publications and related R & D projects. Must locate at Denver headquarters. Send résumé to

Box WM-214
No agencies please

GENERAL MANAGER

Small industrial service company, privately owned, located in Springfield, Missouri, needs aggressive, skilled person to make company grow in profits and sales. Minimum B.S. in Business, experienced in all facets of small business operations. Must understand profit. Excellent opportunity and rewards. Salary and fringes commensurate with experience and performance.

Box LEM-116

FOUNDRY SALES MANAGER

Aggressive gray iron foundry located in the Midwest, specializing in 13,000 tons of complex castings yearly with a weight range of 2 to 400 pounds, is seeking experienced dynamic sales manager with sound sales background in our industry. Salary commensurate with experience; excellent benefit package.

Box MO-948

PERSONNEL MANAGER

Publicly owned, national manufacturer with 12 plants, 700 employees, seeks first corporate personnel director. We want someone to administer programs in:

- Position and rate evaluation
- Employee safety engineering
- Employee training
- Employee communications
- Employee benefits
- Federal compliance

Qualifications: minimum of 3–5 years personnel experience in mfg. company, ability to tactfully deal with employees at all levels from all walks of life, free to travel. Position reports to Vice President, Operations. Full range of company benefits, salary $32,000–$40,000. Reply in complete confidence to:

Box JK-236

THE MANAGEMENT TASK

Besides understanding the significance of managerial work to themselves and society and its related benefits, prospective managers need to know what the management task entails. The sections that follow introduce the basics of the management task through discussions of the role and definition of management, the management process as it pertains to management functions and organizational goal attainment, and the need to manage organizational resources effectively and efficiently.

TABLE 1.1	The 10 Highest Paid Female Executives for 1997		
Name	Title and Firm	Salary	Total Compensation*
Linda Wachner	CEO and president, Warnaco Group;	$2,470,000	$10,190,000
	CEO and chair. Authentic Fitness	$ 975,000	$ 975,000
	Combined:	$5,445,000	$11,165,000
Jill Barad	CEO, Mattel	$ 786,546	$ 6,170,000
Carol Bartz	Chair, CEO, and president, Autodesk	$ 475,000	$ 5,510,000
Sally Crawford	COO, Healthsource	$ 324,235	$ 4,020,000
Estée Lauder	Former chair, Estée Lauder	$2,970,000	$ 3,820,000
Ngaire Cuneo	Executive VP, Conseco	$ 250,000	$ 3,680,000
Jane Hirsh	President, international business Copley Pharmaceutical	$ 580,000	$ 3,390,000
Nancy Pedot	CEO and president, Gymboree	$ 570,184	$ 5,190,000
Donna Karan	Chair, CEO, and chief designer, Donna Karan International	$2,730,000	$ 2,730,000
Sharon Mates	President, North American Vaccine	$ 275,000	$ 2,330,000

*Note that total compensation includes payments such as salary, bonus, and stock options.

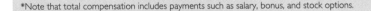

►THE ROLE OF MANAGEMENT

Essentially, the role of managers is to guide organizations toward goal accomplishment. All organizations exist for certain purposes or goals, and managers are responsible for combining and using organizational resources to ensure that their organizations achieve their purposes. Management moves an organization toward its purposes or goals by assigning activities that organization members perform. If the activities are designed effectively, the production of each individual worker will contribute to the attainment of organizational goals. Management strives to encourage individual activity that will lead to reaching organizational goals and to discourage individual activity that will hinder the accomplishment of those goals. "There is no idea more important to managing than goals. Management has no meaning apart from its goals."[4] Managers must, therefore, keep organizational goals in mind at all times.

►DEFINING MANAGEMENT

Students of management should be aware that the term *management* can be, and often is, used in different ways. For instance, it can refer simply to the process that managers follow in order to accomplish organizational goals. It can also refer to a body of knowledge; in this context, management is a cumulative body of information that furnishes insights on how to manage. The term *management* can also refer to the individuals who guide and direct organizations or to a career devoted to the task of guiding and directing organizations. An understanding of the various uses and related definitions of the term will help you avoid miscommunication during management-related discussions.

As used most commonly in this text, **management** is the process of reaching organizational goals by working with and through people and other organizational resources. A comparison of this definition with the definitions offered by several contemporary management thinkers shows that there is broad agreement that management has the following three main characteristics:

Scott McNealy, CEO of Sun Microsystems, speaking at a Harvard University conference on the future of electronic communications. McNealy's own vision became a reality with the enormous success of his firm, the marketer of Java applications software and powerful web servers that support the booming industry of electronic commerce. Sun's growth is a testament to McNealy's communicating, motivating, planning, and controlling skills.

Management is the process of reaching organizational goals by working with and through people and other organizational resources.

After taking over as CEO of Eastman Kodak Co. in 1993, George Fisher sought to focus the company's strategy on its core business—imaging. He realized, for example, that the company's efforts to develop and market new digital-imaging techniques were scattered among various divisions. He moved everyone involved into a single division, which is headed by a handpicked executive with experience in computer marketing.

1. It is a process or series of continuing and related activities
2. It involves and concentrates on reaching organizational goals
3. It reaches these goals by working with and through people and other organizational resources

A discussion of each of these characteristics follows.

▶ THE MANAGEMENT PROCESS: MANAGEMENT FUNCTIONS

The four basic **management functions**—activities that make up the management process—are described in the following sections.

PLANNING Planning involves choosing tasks that must be performed to attain organizational goals, outlining how the tasks must be performed, and indicating when they should be performed. Planning activity focuses on attaining goals. Through their plans, managers outline exactly what organizations must do to be successful. Planning is concerned with organizational success in the near future (short term) as well as in the more distant future (long term).[5]

Management functions are activities that make up the management process. The four basic management activities are planning, organizing, influencing, and controlling.

ORGANIZING Organizing can be thought of as assigning the tasks developed under the planning function to various individuals or groups within the organization. Organizing, then, creates a mechanism to put plans into action. People within the organization are given work assignments that contribute to the company's goals. Tasks are organized so that the output of individuals contributes to the success of departments, which, in turn, contributes to the success of divisions, which ultimately contributes to the success of the organization.

INFLUENCING Influencing is another of the basic functions within the management process. This function—also commonly referred to as *motivating, leading, directing,* or *actuating*—is concerned primarily with people within organizations.* Influencing can be defined as guiding the activities of organization members in appropriate directions. An appropriate direction is any direction that helps the organization move toward goal attainment. The ultimate purpose of influencing is to increase productivity. Human-oriented work situations usually generate higher levels of production over the long term than do task-oriented work situations, because people find the latter type of situations distasteful.

As CEO of Quantum Health Resources, a diversified health-care services organization providing therapies to individuals affected by chronic and other disorders, Douglas Stickney manages one of American's fastest-growing companies. Stickney sees influencing as one of his major jobs as a manager. Among other things, he likes to encourage employees to communicate more informally; the result, he believes, is a more creative environment for his workforce.

CONTROLLING Controlling is the management function for which managers:

1. Gather information that measures recent performance within the organization
2. Compare present performance to preestablished performance standards
3. From this comparison, determine if the organization should be modified to meet preestablished standards

*In early management literature, the term *motivating* was more commonly used to signify this people-oriented management function. The term *influencing* is used consistently throughout this text because it is broader and permits more flexibility in discussing people-oriented issues. Later in the text, motivating is discussed as a major part of influencing.

Controlling is an ongoing process. Managers continually gather information, make their comparisons, and then try to find new ways of improving production through organizational modification.

▶ MANAGEMENT PROCESS AND GOAL ATTAINMENT

Although we have discussed the four functions of management individually, planning, organizing, influencing, and controlling are integrally related and therefore cannot be separated in practice. Figure 1.2 illustrates this interrelationship and also indicates that managers use these activities solely for reaching organizational goals. Basically, these functions are interrelated because the performance of one depends on the performance of the others. For example, organizing is based on well-thought-out plans developed during the planning process, and influencing systems must be tailored to reflect both these plans and the organizational design used to implement them. The fourth function, controlling, involves possible modifications to existing plans, organizational structure, or the motivation system used to develop a more successful effort.

To be effective, a manager must understand how the four management functions must be practiced, not simply how they are defined and related. Thomas J. Peters and Robert H. Waterman, Jr., studied numerous organizations—including Frito-Lay and Maytag—for several years to determine what management characteristics best describe excellently run companies. In their book *In Search of Excellence*, Peters and Waterman suggest that planning, organizing, influencing, and controlling should be characterized by a bias for action; a closeness to the customer; autonomy and entrepreneurship; productivity through people; a hands-on, value-driven orientation; "sticking to the knitting"; a simple organizational form with a lean staff; and simultaneous loose-tight properties.

The information in this section has given you but a brief introduction to the four management functions. Later sections are devoted to developing these functions in much more detail.

▶ MANAGEMENT AND ORGANIZATIONAL RESOURCES

Organizational resources are all assets available for activation during normal operations; they include human resources, monetary resources, raw materials resources, and capital resources.

Management must always be aware of the status and use of **organizational resources.** These resources, composed of all assets available for activation during the production process, are of four basic types:

1. Human
2. Monetary
3. Raw materials
4. Capital

As Figure 1.3 shows, organizational resources are combined, used, and transformed into finished products during the production process.

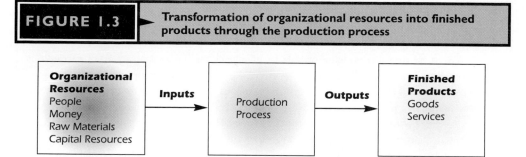

FIGURE 1.3 ▶ Transformation of organizational resources into finished products through the production process

Organizational Resources
People
Money
Raw Materials
Capital Resources

→ **Inputs** →

Production Process

→ **Outputs** →

Finished Products
Goods
Services

Human resources are the people who work for an organization. The skills they possess and their knowledge of the work system are invaluable to managers. Monetary resources are amounts of money that managers use to purchase goods and services for the organization. Raw materials are ingredients used directly in the manufacturing of products. For example, rubber is a raw material that Goodyear would purchase with its monetary resources and use directly in manufacturing tires. Capital resources are machines used during the manufacturing process. Modern machines, or equipment, can be a major factor in maintaining desired production levels. Worn-out or antiquated machinery can make it impossible for an organization to keep pace with competitors.

MANAGERIAL EFFECTIVENESS As managers use their resources, they must strive to be both effective and efficient. **Managerial effectiveness** refers to management's use of organizational resources in meeting organizational goals. If organizations are using their resources to attain their goals, the managers are said to be effective. In reality, however, there are degrees of managerial effectiveness. The closer an organization comes to achieving its goals, the more effective its managers are considered to be. Managerial effectiveness, then, exists on a continuum ranging from *ineffective* to *effective*.

> **Managerial effectiveness** refers to management's use of organizational resources in meeting organizational goals.

MANAGERIAL EFFICIENCY **Managerial efficiency** is the proportion of total organizational resources that contribute to productivity during the manufacturing process.[6] The higher this proportion, the more efficient the manager. The more resources wasted or unused during the production process, the more inefficient the manager. In this situation, *organizational resources* refers not only to raw materials that are used in manufacturing goods or services but also to related human effort.[7] Like management effectiveness, management efficiency is best described as being on a continuum ranging from inefficient to efficient. *Inefficient* means that a very small proportion of total resources contributes to productivity during the manufacturing process; *efficient* means that a very large proportion contributes.

> **Managerial efficiency** is the degree to which organizational resources contribute to productivity. It is measured by the proportion of total organizational resources used during the production process.

As Figure 1.4 shows, the concepts of managerial effectiveness and efficiency are obviously related. A manager could be relatively ineffective—with the consequence that the organization is making very little progress toward goal attainment—primarily because of major inefficiencies or poor utilization of resources during the production process. In contrast, a manager could be somewhat effective despite being inefficient if demand for the finished goods is so high that the manager can get an extremely high price per unit sold and thus absorb inefficiency costs.

For example, oil companies in Saudi Arabia can probably absorb many managerial inefficiencies when oil is selling at a high price. Management in this situation has a chance to be somewhat effective despite its inefficiency. Thus a manager can be effective without being efficient and vice versa. To maximize organizational success, however, both effectiveness and efficiency are essential.

BACK TO THE CASE

The above information contains more specific information on what management is and what managers do. According to this information, as the manager of Animal Kingdom, you must have a clear understanding of Walt Disney Company objectives and guide Animal Kingdom in a way that helps the company reach these objectives. This guidance, of course, will involve working directly

(continued)

with managers above you, the managers of other Disney theme parks in Orlando, and others who work at Animal Kingdom.

You must be sure that planning, organizing, influencing, and controlling are being carried out appropriately at Animal Kingdom. In other words, at Animal Kingdom you must outline how jobs are to be performed to reach objectives, assign these jobs to appropriate workers, encourage the workers to perform their jobs, and make any changes necessary to ensure reaching company objectives. As you perform these four functions at Animal Kingdom, remember that the activities themselves are interrelated and must blend together appropriately.

Your wise use of Animal Kingdom's organizational resources is critical. Strive to make sure that Animal Kingdom is both effective and efficient.

MANAGEMENT SKILLS No discussion of organizational resources would be complete without the mention of management skills, perhaps the primary determinant of how effective and efficient managers will be.

According to a classic article by Robert L. Katz, managerial success depends primarily on performance rather than personality traits.[8] Katz also states that managers' ability to perform is a result of their managerial skills. A manager with the necessary management skills will probably perform well and be relatively successful. One without the necessary skills will probably perform poorly and be relatively unsuccessful.

Katz indicates that three types of skills are important for successful management performance: technical, human, and conceptual skills.

> ► **Technical skills** involve using specialized knowledge and expertise in executing work-related techniques and procedures. Examples of these skills are engineering, computer programming, and accounting. Technical skills are mostly related to working with "things"—processes or physical objects.

> ► **Human skills** are skills that build cooperation within the team being led. They involve working with attitudes and communication, individual and group interests—in short, working with people.

Technical skills are skills involving the ability to apply specialized knowledge and expertise to work-related techniques and procedures.

Human skills are skills involving the ability to build cooperation within the team being led.

| FIGURE 1.4 | Various combinations of managerial effectiveness and managerial efficiency |

RESOURCE USE

Efficient
(most resources contribute to production)

| Not reaching goals and not wasting resources | Reaching goals and not wasting resources |

Inefficient
(few resources contribute to production)

| Not reaching goals and wasting resources | Reaching goals and wasting resources |

Ineffective
(little progress toward organizational goals)

Effective
(substantial progress toward organizational goals)

GOAL ACCOMPLISHMENT

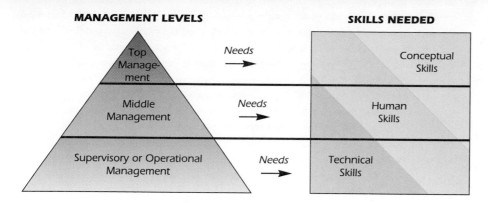

FIGURE 1.5 As a manager moves from the supervisory to the top-management level, conceptual skills become more important than technical skills, but human skills remain equally important

► **Conceptual skills** involve the ability to see the organization as a whole. A manager with conceptual skills is able to understand how various functions of the organization complement one another, how the organization relates to its environment, and how changes in one part of the organization affect the rest of the organization.

As one moves from lower-level management to upper-level management, conceptual skills become more important and technical skills less important (see Figure 1.5). The supportive rationale is that as managers advance in an organization, they become less involved with the actual production activity or technical areas and more involved with guiding the organization as a whole. Human skills, however, are extremely important to managers at top, middle, and lower (or supervisory) levels.[9] The common denominator of all management levels, after all, is people.

Conceptual skills are skills involving the ability to see the organization as a whole.

THE UNIVERSALITY OF MANAGEMENT

Management principles are **universal:** That is, they apply to all types of organizations (businesses, churches, sororities, athletic teams, hospitals, and so on) and organizational levels. Naturally, managers' jobs vary somewhat from one type of organization to another because each organizational type requires the use of specialized knowledge, exists in a unique working and political environment, and uses different technology. However, there are job similarities across organizations because the basic management activities—planning, organizing, influencing, and controlling—are common to all organizations.

Universality of management means that the principles of management are applicable to all types of organizations and organizational levels.

►THE THEORY OF CHARACTERISTICS

Henri Fayol, one of the earliest management writers, stated that all managers should possess certain characteristics, such as positive physical and mental qualities and special knowledge related to the specific operation.[10] B. C. Forbes has emphasized the importance of certain more personal qualities, inferring that enthusiasm, earnestness of purpose, confidence, and faith in their own worthwhileness are primary characteristics of successful managers. Forbes has described Henry Ford as follows:

> At the base and birth of every great business organization was an enthusiast, a man consumed with earnestness of purpose, with confidence in his powers, with faith in the worthwhileness of his endeavors. The original Henry Ford was the quintessence of enthusiasm. In the days of his difficulties, disappointments, and discouragements, when he was wrestling with his balky motor engine— and wrestling likewise with poverty—only his inexhaustible enthusiasm saved him from defeat.[11]

Fayol and Forbes can describe desirable characteristics of successful managers only because of the universality concept: The basic ingredients of successful management are applicable to all organizations.

MANAGEMENT CAREERS

Thus far, this chapter has focused on outlining the importance of management to society, presenting a definition of management and the management process, and explaining the universality of management. Individuals commonly study such topics because they are interested in pursuing a management career. This section presents information that will help you preview your own management career. It also describes some of the issues you may face in attempting to manage the careers of others within an organization. The specific focus is on career definition, career and life stages and performance, and career promotion.

▶ A DEFINITION OF CAREER

> A **career** is a sequence of work-related positions occupied by a person over the course of a lifetime.

A **career** is a sequence of work-related positions occupied by a person over the course of a lifetime.[12] As the definition implies, a career is cumulative in nature: As people accumulate successful experiences in one position, they generally develop abilities and attitudes that qualify them to hold more advanced positions. In general, management positions at one level tend to be stepping-stones to management positions at the next higher level.

▶ CAREER STAGES, LIFE STAGES, AND PERFORMANCE

Careers are generally viewed as evolving through a series of stages.[13] These evolutionary stages—exploration, establishment, maintenance, and decline—are shown in Figure 1.6, which highlights the performance levels and age ranges commonly associated with each stage. Note that the levels and ranges in the figure indicate what is *likely* at each stage, not what is inevitable.

> The **exploration stage** is the first stage in career evolution; it occurs at the beginning of a career, when the individual is typically 15 to 25 years of age, and it is characterized by self-analysis and the exploration of different types of available jobs.

EXPLORATION STAGE The first stage in career evolution is the **exploration stage,** which occurs at the beginning of a career and is characterized by self-analysis and the exploration of different types of available jobs. Individuals at this stage are generally about 15 to 25 years old and are involved in some type of formal training, such as college or vocational education. They often pursue part-time employment to gain a richer understanding of what a career in a particular organization or industry might be like. Typical jobs held during this stage include cooking at Burger King, stocking at a Federated Department Store, and working as an office assistant at a Nationwide Insurance office.

> The **establishment stage** is the second stage in career evolution; individuals of about 25 to 45 years of age typically start to become more productive, or higher performers.

ESTABLISHMENT STAGE The second stage in career evolution is the **establishment stage,** during which individuals about 25 to 45 years old start to become more productive, or higher performers (as Figure 1.6 indicates by the upturn in the dotted line and its continuance as a solid line). Employment sought during this stage is guided by what was learned during the exploration stage. In addition, the jobs sought are usually full-time. Individuals at this stage commonly move to different jobs within the same company, to different companies, or even to different industries.

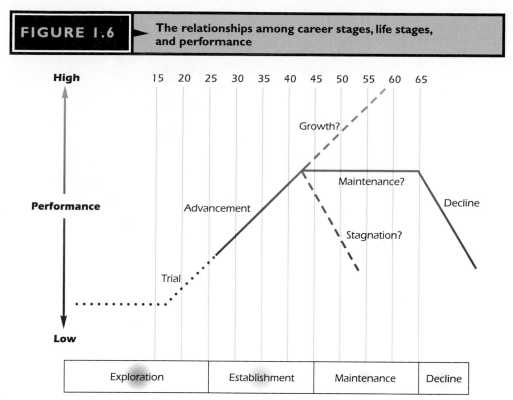

FIGURE 1.6 The relationships among career stages, life stages, and performance

MAINTENANCE STAGE The third stage in career evolution is the **maintenance stage.** In this stage, individuals who are about 45 to 65 years old show either increased performance (career growth), stabilized performance (career maintenance), or decreased performance (career stagnation).

From the organization's viewpoint, it is better for managers to experience career growth than maintenance or stagnation. That is why some companies, such as IBM, Monsanto, and Brooklyn Union Gas, have attempted to eliminate **career plateauing**—defined as a period of little or no apparent progress in the growth of a career.[14]

DECLINE STAGE The last stage in career evolution is the **decline stage**, which involves people about 65 years old whose productivity is declining. These individuals are either close to retirement, semiretired, or fully retired. People in the decline stage may find it difficult to maintain prior performance levels, perhaps because they have lost interest in their careers or have failed to keep their job skills up-to-date.

As Americans live longer and stay healthier into late middle age, many of them choose to become part-time workers in businesses such as Publix supermarkets and McDonald's or in volunteer groups such as the March of Dimes and the American Heart Association. Some retired executives put their career experience to good social use by working with the government-sponsored organization Service Corps of Retired Executives (SCORE) to offer management advice and consultation to small businesses trying to gain a foothold in their market.

▶ PROMOTING YOUR OWN CAREER

Both practicing managers and management scholars agree that careful formulation and implementation of appropriate tactics can enhance the success of a management career.[15] Planning your career path—the sequence of jobs that you will fill in the course of your working life—is the first step you need to take in promoting your career. For some people, a career path entails ascending the hierarchy of a particular organization. Others plan a career path within a particular profession or series of professions. Everyone, however, needs to recognize that career planning is an ongoing process, beginning with the career's early phases and continuing throughout the career.

In promoting your own career, you must be proactive and see yourself as a business that you are responsible for developing. You should not view your plan as limiting your options.

The **maintenance stage** is the third stage in career evolution; individuals of about 45 to 65 years of age either become more productive, stabilize, or become less productive.

Career plateauing is a period of little or no apparent progress in the growth of a career.

The **decline stage** is the fourth and last stage in career evolution; it occurs near retirement age, when individuals of about 65 years of age show declining productivity.

TABLE 1.2	Manager and Employee Roles in Enhancing Employee Career Development	
Dimension	**Professional Employee**	**Manager**
Responsibility	Assumes responsibility for individual career development	Assumes responsibility for employee development
Information	Obtains career information through self-evaluation and data collection: What do I enjoy doing? Where do I want to go?	Provides information by holding up a mirror of reality: How manager views the employee How others view the employee How "things work around here"
Planning	Develops an individual plan to reach objectives	Helps employee assess plan
Follow-through	Invites management support through high performance on the current job by understanding the scope of the job and taking appropriate initiative	Provides coaching and relevant information on opportunities

First consider both your strengths and your liabilities and assess what you need from a career. Then explore all the avenues of opportunity open to you, both inside and outside the organization. Set your career goals, continually revise and update these goals as your career progresses, and take the steps necessary to accomplish these goals.

Another important tactic in promoting your own career is to work for managers who carry out realistic and constructive roles in the career development of their employees.[16] (The cartoon on this page lightheartedly depicts a manager who is brutally uninterested in the careers of his employees.) Table 1.2 outlines what career development responsibility, information, planning, and follow-through generally include. It also outlines the complementary career development role for a professional employee.

To enhance your career success, you must learn to be *proactive* rather than *reactive*.[17] That is, you must take specific actions to demonstrate your abilities and accomplishments. You must also have a clear idea of the next several positions you should seek, the skills you need to acquire to function appropriately in those positions, and plans for acquiring those skills. Finally, you need to think about the ultimate position you want and the sequence of positions you must hold in order to gain the skills and attitudes necessary to qualify for that position.

Source: Warren Keith Schilit, "What's the Logic of Strategic Planning?" Management Review *(November 1988), 42. © Leo Cullum, 1991.*

"As this is your proposal, Cosgrove, its failure could mean the end of your career. I think, however, that is an acceptable risk."

Patricia F. Russo, executive vice president for strategy and administration, is Lucent Technology's highest-ranking woman. Although they now make up nearly half the workforce, women, and particularly minority women, still find it difficult to achieve positions such as Russo's. Savings institutions and financial firms tend to have the highest percentage of women officers, while trucking, semiconductor, and waste management industries have the lowest.

►SPECIAL CAREER ISSUES

In the business world of today, there are countless special issues that significantly affect how careers actually develop. Three issues that have had a significant impact on career development in recent years are:

1. Women managers
2. Dual-career couples
3. A multicultural workforce

The following sections discuss each of these factors.

WOMEN MANAGERS Women in their roles as managers must meet the same challenges in their work environments that men do. However, since they have only recently joined the ranks of management in large numbers, women often lack the social contacts that are so important in the development of a management career. Another problem for women is that, traditionally, they have been expected to manage families and households while simultaneously handling the pressures and competition of paid employment. Finally, women are more likely than men to encounter sexual harassment in the workplace.

Interestingly, Tom Peters, author of the aforementioned classic management book *In Search of Excellence,* believes that women may have an enormous advantage over men in future management situations.[18] He predicts that networks of relationships will replace rigid organizational structures and star workers will be replaced by teams made up of workers at all levels who are empowered to make decisions. Detailed rules and procedures will be replaced by a flexible system that calls for judgments based on key values and a constant search for new ways to get the job done. Strengths often attributed to women—emphasizing interrelationships, listening, and motivating others—will be the dominant virtues in the corporation of the future.

DUAL-CAREER COUPLES Because of the growing number of women at work, many organizations have been compelled to consider how dual-career couples affect the workforce.[19] The traditional scenario in which a woman takes a supporting role in the development of her spouse's career is being replaced by one of equal work and shared responsibilities for spouses. This requires a certain amount of flexibility on the part of the couple as well as the organizations for which they work. Today such burning issues as whose career takes precedence if a spouse is offered a transfer to another city and who takes the ultimate responsibility for family concerns point to the fact that dual-career relationships involve trade-offs and that it is very difficult to "have it all."

How Dual-Career Couples Cope Studies of dual-career couples reveal that many cope with their career difficulties in one of the following ways.[20] The couple might develop a commitment to both spouses' careers so that, when a decision is made, the right of each spouse to pursue a career is taken into consideration. Both husband and wife are flexible about handling home- and job-oriented issues. They work out coping mechanisms, such as negotiating child care or scheduling shared activities in advance, to better manage their work and their family responsibilities. Often dual-career couples find that they must limit their social lives and their volunteer responsibilities in order to slow their lives to a manageable pace. Finally, many couples find that they must take steps to consciously facilitate their mutual career advancement. Organizations that want to retain an employee may find that they need to assist that employee's spouse in his or her career development as well.

A MULTICULTURAL WORKFORCE The term *multicultural* refers to the mix of many different ethnic groups that are already working in business in the United States and will be increasingly in the twenty-first century. Various minority groups are included in the term, among them African Americans, Hispanics, Asians, Africans, Native Americans, and Caribbean Islanders. The U.S. Department of Labor estimates that almost one-third of new entrants into the labor force in the late 1990s and early 2000s will be members of various minority groups.

Minority groups are underrepresented in management today. The Rutgers University Graduate School of Management and the Program to Increase Minorities in Business found in an often-cited survey that of 400 Fortune 1,000 corporations, less than nine percent of all managers were members of a minority. One reason for this shortage is that minorities are often not educated in the fields most in demand by businesses: the hard sciences, business administration, and engineering. Many minority members therefore end up in staff rather than line positions and are consequently more likely to be laid off during a downturn. Finally, in some instances, discrimination is responsible for minority workers' being passed over for promotions.

Recruiting Minority Workers Since more and more new entrants into the labor market are members of minority groups, it is becoming essential for businesses to recruit talented minority workers. Building community visibility may be the first step companies can take to help minority applicants find them. Arranging internships and career fairs as well as providing financial support are other concrete steps a firm can take. Managers can look within the firm for minority employees who can be promoted. Finally, firms may need to conduct their own training and education programs to provide workers with the skills they need to join the ranks of management.

Valuing Diversity   Instead of looking for people who fit into the existing corporate culture, managers should consider talent in the context of diversity. Some managers are uncomfortable dealing with workers from different backgrounds and different cultures; corporations may need to provide support and reeducation for these managers so they will be sensitive to other cultures. To take one small example, much business jargon in the United States is sports-oriented. A manager who tells an employee from another culture to "play hardball" may not be understood.

Some U.S. businesses are making a concerted effort to attract and promote minorities. A *Black Enterprise* magazine survey listed 25 firms that were rated by African Americans as good places to work. Among them were Xerox, IBM, Hewlett-Packard, Avon, Philip Morris, AT&T, and Equitable. The multicultural workforce of the twenty-first century needs a new, more flexible, and open style of management to reflect the new mix of backgrounds and cultures.[21]

SPECIAL FEATURES FOR THE REMAINING CHAPTERS

The **law of the situation,** based upon the classic work of Mary Parker Follett, indicates that managers must continually analyze the unique circumstances within their organizations and apply management concepts to fit those circumstances.[22] Managers can understand planning, organizing, influencing, and controlling, but unless they are able to apply these concepts to deal with specific organizational circumstances, their knowledge will be of little value.

Spotlights, Across Industries, and *Management and the Internet* are special features in the remaining chapters that provide a wealth of examples on how chapter concepts can be applied to managing organizations. These features have been purposely designed to convey a practical understanding of chapter content by emphasizing the application of management principles by real managers in real organizations. Overall, they offer a rich assortment of applications in top-level to lower-level managerial positions in service, manufacturing, non-profit, for-profit, and other types of organizations. Additionally, smaller and midsize companies like Opryland, American Racing, RealNetworks, and 800 Travel Systems, are highlighted, as well as larger, better-known companies like L.L. Bean, DuPont, Virgin Atlantic Airways, and Sega.

The **law of the situation** indicates that managers must continually analyze the unique circumstances within their organizations and apply management concepts to fit those circumstances.

►SPOTLIGHTS

Spotlights appear throughout the text to focus attention on important contemporary management themes: global management, business or corporate ethics, diversity in organizations, quality in organizations, and people in organizations. Each chapter contains at least two *Spotlight* features, with all themes being equally developed throughout the book. Each type of *Spotlight* is discussed in the following paragraphs.

GLOBAL SPOTLIGHT   Modern managers are faced with many challenges involving global business. Some of these challenges involve building organizations in developing countries, fighting foreign competition, developing joint ventures with foreign companies, and building a productive workforce across several foreign countries. This feature illustrates the application of management concepts to meeting international challenges.

ETHICS SPOTLIGHT   Modern managers face the challenge of developing and maintaining social responsibility and ethical practices that are appropriate for their particular organizations. Some challenges involve such issues as settling on who within an organization should perform socially responsible activities, determining the role of ethics in an organization, encouraging ethical behavior throughout the organization, and determining internal funding for socially responsible activities.[23] This feature illustrates the application of management concepts to meeting a firm's social responsibility and ethical challenges.

DIVERSITY SPOTLIGHT Modern managers constantly face the challenge of handling situations involving diversity in organizations. *Diversity* is defined as differences in people in such areas as age, gender, ethnicity, nationality, and ability. In essence, today's managers must continually deal with significant variability in the people who interface with the organization. Thus organization members as well as customers may be a mix of African Americans, Hispanics, Asians, and Native Americans.[24] Or the mix may involve people who are older, women, and the handicapped. This management feature presents practical insights for appropriately building organizational diversity into a resource so that the organization can understand and respond to diversity in its broader environment (e.g., among customers) and thereby enhance its success. In addition, diversity is discussed in chapter 23, "Management and Diversity."

QUALITY SPOTLIGHT Contemporary managers, perhaps more than any other generation of managers, face the challenge of developing and maintaining high quality in the goods and services they offer.[25] High-quality products are defined as goods or services that customers rate as excellent. Most management theorists and practicing managers agree that if an organization is to be successful in today's national and international markets, it must offer high-quality goods and services to its customers.

Virtually every activity a manager performs can have some impact on the quality of goods or services that that manager's organization produces. Developing organizational objectives, training organization members, practicing strategic management, and designing organization structures—all affect the quality of a company's output. This management feature illustrates how various management activities affect product quality. In addition, quality is discussed in detail in chapter 22, "Competitiveness: Quality and Innovation."

You will find it valuable to study all of these management spotlights carefully, for they will help you build realistic expectations about your career as a manager. The cases detailed in the spotlights illustrate that as managers show the ability to solve various organizational problems, they become more valuable to organizations and are more likely to receive the organizational rewards of promotion and significant pay increases.

PEOPLE SPOTLIGHT This *Spotlight* concentrates on human issues in organizations. This feature emphasizes how crucial managing people is and illustrates that no management topic exists independent of people issues. In addition, the Influencing section of this text provides an in-depth theoretical look at many people-oriented topics, such as communication, managing teams, and motivation. The *People Spotlight* complements this theoretical focus by integrating human topics and their application into the entire book.

►ACROSS INDUSTRIES

Managers apply management principles daily in many different industries across the world. A rich understanding of management includes insights about how managers react to the varied situations that confront them. Studying how management principles are applied in different industries can provide managers with invaluable insights about facing the challenges of their industries. *Across Industries* is a new feature of this book that illustrates how management concepts are applied in different industries. An *Across Industries* highlight appears in each chapter. Industries highlighted in this text are varied and include mail-order retailing, food processing, automobile tire manufacturing, and government.

►MANAGEMENT AND THE INTERNET

Arguably, the Internet, including the World Wide Web (Web), its fastest growing part, is evolving into one of the most exciting new tools available to modern managers. Overall, the Internet is a vast, varied, and easily accessible source of management-related information.

More specifically, and perhaps more importantly, the Web is fast becoming an important influence on the way managers actually structure organizations and conduct business. *Management and the Internet* is a new feature of this text aimed at providing students with insights about how the Internet can be associated with the management process. *Management and the Internet* appears in each chapter and highlights how managers are using the Internet to help solve management problems. Examples of topics in this feature include plans based on the Web, changing objectives based on the growth of the Internet, managing within Internet-related laws, and the Better Business Bureau and the Internet. Also, new to this edition, chapter 21, "Information, Technology, and the Internet," discusses management and the Internet in detail.

BACK TO THE CASE

As with the managers of any company, managers at Walt Disney Company are at various stages of career development. As an example of how the stages of career development might relate to managers at Walt Disney Company, let us focus on one particular manager, Martin Plane. Assume that Martin Plane is a manager overseeing three different restaurants at Animal Kingdom. He is 45 years old and is considered a member of middle management.

Plane began his career (exploration stage) in college by considering various areas of study and by holding a number of primarily part-time positions. He delivered pizzas for Domino's Pizza and worked for Scott's, a lawn care company. He began college at age 18 and graduated when he was 22.

Plane then moved into the establishment stage of his career. For a few years immediately after graduation, he held full-time trial positions in the entertainment industry and the restaurant and retailing industries. What he learned during the career exploration stage helped him choose the types of full-time trial positions to pursue. At the age of 26, he accepted a trial position as an assistant manager of a restaurant at Walt Disney World in Orlando, Florida. Through this position, he discovered that he wanted to remain in the restaurant industry in general and more specifically with Walt Disney Company. From age 27 to age 45, he held a number of restaurant supervisory and management positions at Disney.

Now Plane is moving into an extremely critical part of his career, the maintenance stage. He could probably remain in his present position and maintain his productivity for several more years. However, he wants to advance his career. Therefore he must emphasize a proactive attitude by formulating and implementing tactics aimed at enhancing his career success, such as seeking training to develop critical skills or moving to a position that is a prerequisite for other, more advanced positions at Walt Disney World.

In the future, as Plane approaches age 65 (the decline stage), it is probable that his productivity at Disney will decline somewhat. From a career viewpoint, he may want to go from full-time employment to semiretirement. Perhaps he could work for Disney or another entertainment-based company on a part-time advisory basis or even pursue part-time work in another industry. For example, he might be able to teach a restaurant management course at a nearby community college.

For updated information on the topics in this chapter, Internet exercises, links to related Internet sites, an interactive study guide, and more, visit our companion Web site at

http://www.prenhall.com/certo

Additional information can be found on the inside front and back covers of this text.

Reread the learning objectives below. Each objective is followed by questions. Answering these questions accurately will help you retain the most important concepts discussed in this chapter. After answering each question, check your answer against the answer key at the end of this chapter. (*Hint:* If you have any doubts regarding the correct response, consult the page number that follows the answer.)

Circle:	From studying this chapter, I will attempt to acquire
	1. An understanding of the importance of management to society and individuals.
T F	**a.** Managers constitute less than one percent of the U.S. workforce.
T F	**b.** Management is important to society.
	2. An understanding of the role of management.
a b c d e	**a.** The role of a manager is to: (a) make workers happy (b) satisfy only the manager's needs (c) make the most profit (d) survive in a highly competitive society (e) achieve organizational goals.
T F	**b.** Apart from its goals, management has no meaning.
	3. An ability to define *management* in several different ways.
a b c d e	**a.** Management is: (a) a process (b) reaching organizational goals (c) utilizing people and other resources (d) all of the above (e) a and b.
T F	**b.** Management is the process of working with people and through people.
	4. An ability to list and define the basic functions of management.
a b c d e	**a.** Which of the following is not a function of management: (a) influencing (b) planning (c) organizing (d) directing (e) controlling.
a b c d e	**b.** The process of gathering information and comparing this information to preestablished standards is part of: (a) planning (b) influencing (c) motivating (d) controlling (e) commanding.
	5. Working definitions of managerial effectiveness and managerial efficiency.
T F	**a.** If an organization is using its resources to attain its goals, the organization's managers are efficient.
T F	**b.** A manager who is reaching goals but wasting resources is efficient but ineffective.
	6. An understanding of basic management skills and their relative importance to managers.
a b c d e	**a.** Conceptual skills require that management view the organization as: (a) a profit center (b) a decision-making unit (c) a problem-solving group (d) a whole (e) individual contributions.
T F	**b.** Managers require fewer and fewer human skills as they move from lower to higher management levels.
	7. An understanding of the universality of management.
T F	**a.** The statement that management principles are universal means that they apply to all types of organizations and organizational levels.
T F	**b.** The universality of management means that management principles are taught the same way in all schools.
	8. Insights concerning what management careers are and how they evolve.
T F	**a.** In general, as careers evolve, individuals tend to further develop job skills but show very little or no change in attitude about various job circumstances.
T F	**b.** Individuals tend to show the first significant increase in performance during the establishment career stage.

INTRODUCTORY CASE WRAP-UP

CASE DISCUSSSION QUESTIONS

"Managing Disney's New Animal Kingdom" (p. 3) and its related Back to the Case sections were written to help you better understand the management concepts contained in this chapter. Answer the following discussion questions about this introductory case to further enrich your understanding of the chapter content:

1. Do you think that it will be difficult for you to become a successful manager? Explain

2. What do you think you would like most about being a manager? What would you like least?

3. As part of this case, you were asked to assume that you are the manager in charge of Animal Kingdom. As such, list and describe five activities that you think you will have to perform as part of this job.

ISSUES FOR REVIEW AND DISCUSSION

1. What is the main point illustrated in the introductory case on Walt Disney Company?
2. How important is the management function to society?
3. How important is the management function to individuals?
4. What is the basic role of the manager?
5. How is *management* defined in this text? What main themes are contained in this definition?
6. List and define each of the four functions of management.
7. Outline the relationship among the four management functions.
8. List and describe five of Peters and Waterman's characteristics of excellent companies, and explain how each of these characteristics could affect planning, organizing, influencing, and controlling.
9. List and define the basic organizational resources managers have at their disposal.
10. What is the relationship between organizational resources and production?
11. Draw and explain the continuum of managerial effectiveness.
12. Draw and explain the continuum of managerial efficiency.
13. Are managerial effectiveness and managerial efficiency related concepts? If so, how are they related?
14. According to Katz, what are the three primary types of skills important to management success? Define each of these types of skills.
15. Describe the relative importance of each of these three types of skills to lower-level, middle-level, and upper-level managers.
16. What is meant by "the universality of management"?
17. What is a career?
18. Discuss the significance of the maintenance career stage.
19. What tips contained in this chapter for promoting the success of a career do you find most valuable? Explain.
20. What does the law of the situation tell you about the success of your management career?

ACTION SUMMARY ANSWER KEY

1. a. F, p. 4
   b. T, p. 4
2. a. e, p. 6
   b. T, p. 6
3. a. d, p. 7
   b. F, p. 7
4. a. d, p. 7
   b. d, pp. 7–8
5. a. F, p. 8
   b. F, p. 8
6. a. d, p. 11
   b. F, p. 11
7. a. T, p. 11
   b. F, p. 11
8. a. F, p. 12
   b. T, p. 12

CASE STUDY: Chrysler's Top Gun

More than any other of its current executives, President Robert Lutz personifies Chrysler's image as the brashest of the U.S. Big Three automakers. His flamboyant, often combative personality may have put off his former boss, Lee A. Iacocca, but it has endeared him to Chrysler's current low-key chairman, Robert Eaton. According to *Business Week*, their relationship is a textbook case of opposites attracting. Although it appears that Lutz will never achieve his dream of holding the top office at a U.S. automaker, he respects Eaton. In 1992, when Eaton left General Motors for Chrysler, hand-picked to succeed CEO and Chairman Iacocca, he called Lutz "integral to our success." Ever since then, the two leaders have bonded through their love of fast cars and their wish to see Iacocca retire. Once in control of Chrysler, Eaton approved a five-year product plan and gave his president free rein to execute it.

The son of a Swiss banker, Lutz became a citizen of the United States in 1943, along with his parents. He was captivated at an early age by motorcycles, cars, and planes, and became a fighter pilot in the Marine Corps in 1954. After five years in the service, he went on to earn a B.S. and an M.B.A. at the University of California. From there, he pursued his "need for speed" in the car industry, working first for General Motors as a planner, and later as a GM executive vice president in Europe. In 1971, he left GM to become vice president of sales and director at BMW. Eight years later, he was the head of Ford's European division. In

1982, Lutz returned to the United States as executive vice president for Ford's international operations.

Lutz's career at Ford soured, however, when Ford's European business fell through the floor. Held responsible for the collapse, he returned to Europe to correct it. Two years later, he was back in the United States again, heading Ford's sluggish truck operations. It was then that Lee Iacocca tapped Lutz for the position of executive vice president at Chrysler. Although his relationship with the charismatic Iacocca gradually decayed, Lutz moved up to the position of president in 1991.

By 1996, Lutz had convinced Chrysler's stockholders that he was almost exclusively responsible for boosting Chrysler's U.S. market share two points, to 14.3 percent, during his five-year tenure. Most shareholders tended to agree because of two key changes the tough-minded, dynamic new president had made:

1. He overhauled Chrysler's engineering ranks into skillful, cross-functional teams.
2. He supported daring styling in new performance models such as the Dodge Intrepid sedan and the Ram pickup.

According to Lutz, "I have an unusual ability to direct the product-creation process, sort of a gift," he says. "I'm much like the conductor of a symphony orchestra." Lutz conducted the "Chrysler automotive-symphony" in a 180-degree turnaround by helping to create Chrysler's vaunted "platform teams," in which engineers' work was organized around specific models. The team concept eventually came to include marketing, manufacturing, design, and financial personnel as well. Ultimately, product development became faster, cheaper, and more creative, as these cross-functional teams learned to build better-looking, better-performing models.

Widely regarded as the best product-development executive in the automotive industry, Lutz has also been blamed for the questionable quality of Chrysler's cars. Although he refuses to acknowledge that his company's cars are any lower in quality than other American autos, Lutz does admit that quality has to be Chrysler's major focus in the immediate future. Eaton agrees.

Quality complaints aside, Lutz is highly valued at Chrysler, and neither stockholders, board members, nor Eaton wants to lose him. The company has quietly overlooked its mandatory retirement age of 65 in his case and extended his contract through 1999. As Lutz puts it, "Reports of my pending retirement have turned out to be greatly exaggerated." Without question, Lutz's dynamic ideas—backed by solid experience, enthusiasm, and success with shareholders—have made him a valuable commodity at Chrysler now and in the years to come.

QUESTIONS

1. In what stage of the career cycle was Robert Lutz in each of the positions he held? What personal skills, interests, and abilities did he call upon in moving through his chosen career path? Explain.
2. What managerial characteristics described in the text are reflected in Robert Lutz? Cite examples from the case study to support your choices.
3. According to the text, "enthusiasm, earnestness of purpose, confidence, and faith in their worthwhileness are primary characteristics of successful managers." Use information about Robert Lutz contained in this case study to support or refute this statement.

A video has been created for each of the six parts of your textbook. It looks at specific areas which have been covered in detail in the individual chapters. The idea is not to isolate a point and focus on it exclusively. Instead, scenarios are developed that resemble situations you might experience in the real world. As a result, concepts are mixed together, experiences are not sequential (as they often are in a chapter in a textbook), and you may have to think about what you see to get the point. In fact, you will probably see things differently than some of your classmates. Each of you will see these scenes with the influence of what you have learned from the book, with influences from life's experiences, and from things that are important to you.

In the opening video, you are introduced to some of the main characters that appear throughout the series. John is a young guy who is trying to land a job as a production manager with a company that produces educational and news-type programs. He has experience in the field as a cameraman. This job, if he gets it, may begin to steer his career in a different direction. We get the feeling that he wants it to. You also meet Hal and Karen. They are partners who own the company, Quicktakes, with which John is trying to get a job.

A lot is gong on in this opening segment. There are a few things for which you may want to be on the lookout. First, pay attention to John as he prepares at home for the upcoming interview. He and his wife do not necessarily agree about the opportunity that exists at Quicktakes. Think about what the job really entails as you listen to the discussion John has with Hal and Karen, and pay attention to the way Hal and Karen interact. As partners, they both probably have a lot at stake in planning for the success and growth of this company. It is interesting to notice the way each sees the specific job John is applying for and also the way each views the overall objectives and plans for the company.

From a more general perspective, you may wish to consider how this company fits with some of the management concepts that you have learned about; how well this company is suited for doing business in other countries, under other social norms and standard business practices; and how well this company might do at adjusting to changes in its operating environment or to other changes in its internal environment as it grows.

QUESTIONS

1. John and his wife seem to have different ideas about the job description for the position John is applying for and different ideas about how qualified John is for the opening. What factors do you think influence an individual's perception, and why do you think they come up with different perspectives?

2. Hal and Karen are partners, but they seem to have their own ideas about the company and the way it runs. Do you think it is good for partners to have their own, and sometimes differing, opinions, or should they agree more? What do you think is good for the success of a company?

3. John was asked about how he would handle two particular issues in the company. One dealt with staffing multiple projects and one dealt with his use of company equipment to film a wedding for a friend. If you were Hal and Karen, what other hypothetical situations might you want to ask John about?

Managing: History and Current Thinking

STUDENT LEARNING OBJECTIVES

From studying this chapter, I will attempt to acquire

1. An understanding of the classical approach to management

2. An appreciation for the work of Frederick W. Taylor, Frank and Lillian Gilbreth, Henry L. Gantt, and Henri Fayol

3. An understanding of the behavioral approach to management

4. An understanding of the studies at the Hawthorne Works and the human relations movement

5. An understanding of the management science approach to management

6. An understanding of how the management science approach has evolved

7. An understanding of the system approach to management

8. Knowledge about the learning organization approach to management

9. An understanding of how triangular management and the contingency approach to management are related

CHAPTER OUTLINE

Introductory Case: *A Problem at McDonald's*

THE CLASSICAL APPROACH
Lower-Level Management Analysis

Across Industries: *Mail Order Retailing—"One Best Way" at L.L. Bean*
Comprehensive Analysis of Management Limitations of the Classical Approach

THE BEHAVIORAL APPROACH
The Hawthorne Studies
The Human Relations Movement

THE MANAGEMENT SCIENCE APPROACH
The Beginning of the Management Science Approach
Management Science Today

Quality Spotlight: *Baldrige Award Exemplifies Quality*
Characteristics of Management Science Applications

THE CONTINGENCY APPROACH

Management and the Internet: *"If-Then" Necessary for XS New York Cybercafe Does Not Materialize*

THE SYSTEM APPROACH
Types of Systems
Systems and "Wholeness"
The Management System
Information for Management System Analysis
Learning Organization: A New Approach?

People Spotlight: *People for a New Learning Organization at Signicast*

A PROBLEM AT McDONALD'S

REMINDER: THE INTRODUCTORY CASE WRAP-UP (P. 43) CONTAINS DISCUSSION QUESTIONS AND A SKILLS EXERCISE TO FURTHER ILLUSTRATE THE APPLICATION OF CHAPTER CONCEPTS TO THIS VIGNETTE.

McDonald's Corporation, perhaps the premier hamburger retailer in the world for decades, now faces significant problems. Within the last ten years, McDonald's share of fast food sales in the United States has slipped almost two percentage points. The drop has come despite the company's increasing its number of restaurants by 50 percent, thereby leading the industry.

How is the company trying to regain its lost sales? The primary solution involves re-engineering the company's system for making hamburgers. In the past, McDonald's used a *standard* way for making hamburgers. The customer could get a *custom* hamburger, but it would take much longer. In essence, the customer had to choose between a preferred hamburger and speed of service.

A new food preparation method requires McDonald's to prepare its food one order at a time as opposed to its traditional method of preparing its food in batches. Besides being more customer oriented, this "one order at a time" method should help McDonald's more effectively compete with the "one order at a time" methods used at Burger King and Wendy's, two of McDonald's primary competitors.

The new system has many advantages. First of all, the new system is very quick and accurate since its operation is computerized. Indeed, the system had to be designed to be quick because customers want food promptly and sandwiches are not made until customers actually order them. As another advantage, the new system will lower food costs. Company officials believe that the old system's batch-related cost of having to discard prepared food held

McDonald's is banking on its new "one order at a time" method of preparing its traditional burger and fries menu to help recover its dominant market share in the fast-food industry. Reduced waste, lower cost, and higher customer satisfaction are the goals.

too long in the warmer will be eliminated. Finally, the company believes that since food is no longer held in a warmer, the present high quality of food served should be raised even further.

Michael Quinlan, CEO at McDonald's, is very excited about the new system that is being introduced in his restaurants. He believes that the speedier system will enable restaurants to serve more customers at peak hours and offer more and different products. Quinlan, however, is an astute manager and knows that many problems will arise before the system contributes all that it can to the success of the organization.

There are several different ways to approach management situations and to solve related organizational problems. Managers like Michael Quinlan, the CEO of McDonald's mentioned in the Introductory Case, as well as all other managers at McDonald's must understand these approaches if they are to build successful organizations. This chapter explains six such approaches:

1. The classical approach
2. The behavioral approach
3. The management science approach
4. The contingency approach
5. The system approach
6. The learning organization approach

Chapter 1 focused primarily on defining *management*. This chapter presents various approaches to analyzing and reacting to the management situation, each characterized by a basically different method of analysis and a different type of recommended action.

There has been much disagreement on how many different approaches to management there are and what each approach entails. In an attempt to simplify the discussion of the field of management without sacrificing significant information, Donnelly, Gibson, and Ivancevich combined the ideas of Koontz, O'Donnell, and Weihrich with those of Haynes and Massie, and concluded that there were three basic approaches to management:[1]

1. Classical approach
2. Behavioral approach
3. Management science approach

The following sections build on the work of Donnelly, Gibson, and Ivancevich in presenting the classical, behavioral, and management science approaches to analyzing the management task. The contingency approach is discussed as a fourth primary approach, while the system approach is presented as a recent trend in management thinking. The learning organization is continually evolving and is discussed as the newest form for analyzing management.

THE CLASSICAL APPROACH

The **classical approach to management** is a management approach that emphasizes organizational efficiency to increase organizational success.

The **classical approach to management** was the product of the first concentrated effort to develop a body of management thought. In fact, the management writers who participated in this effort are considered the pioneers of management study. The classical approach recommends that managers continually strive to increase organizational efficiency in order to increase production. Although the fundamentals of this approach were developed some time ago, contemporary managers are just as concerned with finding the "one best way" to get the job done as their predecessors were. To illustrate this concern, notable management theorists see striking similarities between the concepts of scientific management developed many years ago and the more current management philosophy of building quality into all aspects of organizational operations.[2]

For discussion purposes, the classical approach to management can be broken down into two distinct areas. The first, lower-level management analysis, consists primarily of the work of Frederick W. Taylor, Frank and Lillian Gilbreth, and Henry L. Gantt. These individuals studied mainly the jobs of workers at lower levels of the organization. The second area, comprehensive analysis of management, concerns the management function as a whole. The primary contributor to this category was Henri Fayol. Figure 2.1 illustrates the two areas in the classical approach.

►LOWER-LEVEL MANAGEMENT ANALYSIS

Lower-level management analysis concentrates on the "one best way" to perform a task; that is, it investigates how a task situation can be structured to get the highest production from workers. The process of finding this "one best way" has become known as the *scientific method of management,* or simply, **scientific management.** Although the techniques of scientific managers could conceivably be applied to management at all levels, the research,

Scientific management emphasizes the "one best way" to perform a task.

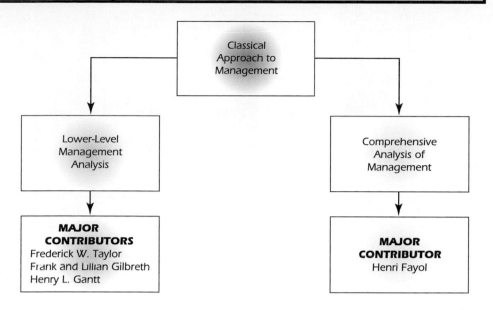

research applications, and illustrations relate mostly to lower-level managers. The work of Frederick W. Taylor, Frank and Lillian Gilbreth, and Henry L. Gantt is summarized in the sections that follow.

FREDERICK W. TAYLOR (1856–1915) Because of the significance of his contributions, Frederick W. Taylor is commonly called the "father of scientific management." His primary goal was to increase worker efficiency by scientifically designing jobs. His basic premise was that there was one best way to do a job and that that way should be discovered and put into operation.

Work at Bethlehem Steel Co. Perhaps the best way to illustrate Taylor's scientific method and his management philosophy is to describe how he modified the job of employees whose sole responsibility was shoveling materials at the Bethlehem Steel Company.[3] During the modification process, Taylor made the assumption that any worker's job could be reduced to a science. To construct the "science of shoveling," he obtained answers—through observation and experimentation—to the following questions:

1. Will a first-class worker do more work per day with a shovelful of 5, 10, 15, 20, 30, or 40 pounds?
2. What kinds of shovels work best with which materials?
3. How quickly can a shovel be pushed into a pile of materials and pulled out properly loaded?
4. How much time is required to swing a shovel backward and throw the load a given horizontal distance at a given height?

As Taylor formulated answers to these types of questions, he developed insights on how to increase the total amount of materials shoveled per day. He raised worker efficiency by matching shovel size with such factors as the size of the worker, the weight of the materials, and the height and distance the materials were to be thrown. By the end of the third year after Taylor's shoveling efficiency plan was implemented, records at Bethlehem Steel showed that the total number of shovelers needed had been reduced from about 600 to 140, the average number of tons shoveled per worker per day had risen from 16 to 59, the average earnings per worker per day had increased from $1.15 to $1.88, and the average cost of handling a long ton (2,240 pounds) had dropped from $0.072 to $0.033—all in all, an impressive demonstration of the applicability of scientific management to the task of shoveling.[4]

Unlike the women working in this World War I munitions factory, who had to contend with isolating and repetitive work in noisy surroundings, today's employee teams have the freedom to devise their own solutions to problems and put them into effect. Even factory workers in many firms are members of such teams. The members of this consulting team have just completed a project for Macy's, an elaborate computer model that will help the store determine how many salespeople are needed in each department based on how shoppers behave.

ACROSS INDUSTRIES — Mail Order Retailing

"ONE BEST WAY" AT L.L. BEAN

L.L. Bean, a mail-order outdoor sporting specialist, has built a legendary reputation for customer service on the ability to deliver to customers what they want when they want it. Not resting on past accomplishments, managers at L.L. Bean have recently been struggling with improving customer service by following the thrust of the classical approach to management—searching for the "one best way" to perform the task of filling customer orders.

Management determined that the "one best way" today to fill customer orders would be to upgrade its information system. This information system upgrade includes handling orders via bar codes.

Using bar codes will help employees to better identify and track the movement of inventory. The system upgrade also includes radio frequency communication between workers in the reserve storage warehouse and the order fulfillment center. Better information flow between these two organizational areas should help employees to more quickly find and mail ordered products. Lastly, the system upgrade includes electronic communication between L.L. Bean and its suppliers. This communication improvement should help L.L. Bean get products needed for shipping more quickly. Overall, the end result of the information system upgrade will be a significant cut in the amount of time necessary to fill customer orders.

FRANK GILBRETH (1868–1924) AND LILLIAN GILBRETH (1878–1972)

The Gilbreths were also significant contributors to the scientific method. As a point of interest, the Gilbreths focused on handicapped as well as normal workers.[5] Like other contributors to the scientific method, they subscribed to the idea of finding and using the one best way to perform a job. The primary investigative tool in the Gilbreths' research was **motion study,** which consists of reducing each job to the most basic movements possible. Motion analysis is used today primarily to establish job performance standards. Each movement, or motion, that is used to do a job is studied to determine how much time the movement takes and how necessary it is to performing the job. Inefficient or unnecessary motions are pinpointed and eliminated.[6]

Frank Gilbreth's experience as an apprentice bricklayer led him to do motion studies of bricklaying. He found that bricklayers could increase their output significantly by concentrat-

A **motion study** finds the best way to accomplish a task by analyzing the movements necessary to perform that task.

Operation No.	The Wrong Way	The Right Way	Pick and Dip Method: The Exterior 4 Inches (Laying to the Line)
TABLE 2.1 — Partial Results for One of Gilbreth's Bricklaying Motion Studies			
1	Step for mortar	Omit	On the scaffold, the inside edge of mortar box should be plumb with the inside edge of the stock platform. On the floor, the inside edge of mortar box should be 21 inches from wall. Mortar boxes should never be over 4 feet apart.
2	Reach for mortar	Reach for mortar	Do not bend any more than absolutely necessary to reach mortar with a straight arm.
3	Work up mortar	Omit	Provide mortar of right consistency. Examine sand screen and keep it in repair so that no pebbles can get through. Keep tender on scaffold to temper up and keep mortar worked up right.
4	Step for brick	Omit	If tubs are kept 4 feet apart, no stepping for brick will be necessary on scaffold. On floor, keep brick in a pile not nearer than 1 foot or more than 4 feet 6 inches from wall.
5	Reach for brick	Included in 2	Brick must be reached for at the same time that the mortar is reached for, and picked up at exactly the same time the mortar is picked up. If it is not picked up at the same time, allowance must be made for operation.

ing on performing some motions and eliminating others. Table 2.1 shows a simplified portion of the results of one of Gilbreth's bricklaying motion studies. For each bricklaying operation, Gilbreth indicated whether it should be omitted for the sake of efficiency and why. He reduced the five motions per brick listed under "The Wrong Way" to the one motion per brick listed under "The Right Way." Overall, Gilbreth's bricklaying motion studies resulted in reducing the number of motions necessary to lay a brick by approximately 70 percent and consequently tripling bricklaying production.

Lillian Gilbreth, who began as her husband's collaborator, continued to research and write on motion studies after his death. She is noted especially for her application of the scientific method to the role of the homemaker and to the handicapped.

HENRY L. GANTT (1861–1919) The third major contributor to the scientific management approach was Henry L. Gantt. He, too, was interested in increasing worker efficiency. Gantt attributed unsatisfactory or ineffective tasks and piece rates (incentive pay for each product piece an individual produces) primarily to the fact that these tasks and rates were set according to what had been done by workers in the past or on somebody's *opinion* of what workers could do. According to Gantt, *exact scientific knowledge* of what could be done by a worker should be substituted for opinion. He considered this the role of scientific management.

Gantt's management philosophy is encapsulated in his statement that "the essential differences between the best system of today and those of the past are the manner in which tasks are 'scheduled' and the manner in which their performance is rewarded."[7] Using this rationale, he sought to improve systems or organizations through task-scheduling innovation and the rewarding of innovation.

Scheduling Innovation The Gantt chart, the primary scheduling device that Gantt developed, is still the scheduling tool most commonly used by modern managers.[8] Basically, this chart provides managers with an easily understood summary of what work was scheduled for specific time periods, how much of this work has been completed, and by whom it was done.

Special computer software like MacSchedule has been developed to help managers more efficiently and effectively apply the concept of the Gantt chart today.[9] MacSchedule allows managers to easily monitor complicated and detailed scheduling issues like the number of units planned for production during a specified period, when work is to begin and to be completed, and the percentage of work that was actually completed during a period. (The Gantt chart is covered in much more detail in chapter 8.)

Wal-Mart gets help in scheduling orders and restocking operations from its satellite-based inventory system. Here in the satellite control room, technicians can upload and download sales information immediately and track which items need to be replenished in each store. Such state-of-the-art operations techniques build on the work of early management theorists like the Gilbreths and Henry Gantt.

Rewarding Innovation   Gantt was more aware of the human side of production than either Taylor or the Gilbreths were. He wrote that "the taskmaster (manager) of the past was practically a slave driver, whose principal function was to force workmen to do that which they had no desire to do, or interest in doing. The task setter of today under any reputable system of management is not a driver. When he asks the workmen to perform tasks, he makes it to their interest to accomplish them, and is careful not to ask what is impossible or unreasonable."[10]

In contrast to Taylor, who pioneered a piece-rate system under which workers were paid according to the amount they produced and who advocated the use of wage-incentive plans, Gantt developed a system wherein workers could earn a bonus in addition to the piece rate if they exceeded their daily production quota. Gantt, then, believed in worker compensation that corresponded not only to production (through the piece-rate system) but also to overproduction (through the bonus system).

BACK TO THE CASE

Michael Quinlan, the CEO of McDonald's mentioned in the Introductory Case, could attempt to use a classical approach to management to stress organizational efficiency—the "one best way" to perform jobs at McDonald's restaurants—and thereby increase productivity. To take a simplified example, McDonald's managers might want to check whether the dispenser used to apply mustard and catsup is of the appropriate size to require only one squirt or whether more than one squirt is necessary to adequately cover a hamburger.

To complement his new "made to order cooking system," Quinlan could use motion studies to eliminate unnecessary or wasted motions by his employees. For example, are Big Macs, french fries, and drinks located for easy insertion into customer bags, or must an employee walk unnecessary steps during the sales process? Also, would certain McDonald's employees be more efficient over an entire working day if they sat, rather than stood, while working?

The classical approach to management might also guide Quinlan to stress efficient scheduling. By ensuring that an appropriate number of people with the appropriate skills are scheduled to work during peak hours and that fewer such individuals are scheduled to work during slower hours, McDonald's would maximize the return on their labor costs.

Quinlan and other McDonald's managers also might want to consider offering their employees some sort of bonus if they reach certain work goals. Management should make sure, however, that the goals it sets are realistic because unreasonable or impossible goals tend to make workers resentful and unproductive. For example, management might ask that certain employees reduce errors in filling orders by 50 percent during the next month. If and when these employees reached the goal, McDonald's could give them a free lunch as a bonus.

Comprehensive analysis of management involves studying the management function as a whole.

►COMPREHENSIVE ANALYSIS OF MANAGEMENT

Whereas scientific managers emphasize job design approaching the study of management, managers who embrace the comprehensive view—the second area of the classical approach—are concerned with the entire range of managerial performance.

Among the well-known contributors to the comprehensive view are Chester Barnard,[11] Alvin Brown, Henry Dennison, Luther Gulick and Lyndall Urwick, J. D. Mooney and A. C. Reiley, and Oliver Sheldon.[12] Perhaps the most notable contributor, however, was Henri Fayol. His book *General and Industrial Management* presents a management philosophy that still guides many modern managers.[13]

HENRI FAYOL (1841–1925)   Because of his writings on the elements and general principles of management, Henri Fayol is usually regarded as the pioneer of administrative theory. The elements of management he outlined—planning, organizing, commanding, coordinating, and control—are still considered worthwhile divisions under which to study, analyze, and effect the management process.[14] (Note the close correspondence between Fayol's elements of management and the management functions outlined in chapter 1—planning, organizing, influencing, controlling.)

The general principles of management suggested by Fayol are still considered useful in contemporary management practice. Here are the principles in the order developed by Fayol, accompanied by corresponding definitional themes:[15]

1. *Division of work*—Work should be divided among individuals and groups to ensure that effort and attention are focused on special portions of the task. Fayol presented work specialization as the best way to use the human resources of the organization.

2. *Authority*—The concepts of authority and responsibility are closely related. *Authority* was defined by Fayol as the right to give orders and the power to exact obedience. *Responsibility* involves being accountable, and is therefore naturally associated with authority. Whoever assumes authority also assumes responsibility.

3. *Discipline*—A successful organization requires the common effort of workers. Penalties should be applied judiciously to encourage this common effort.

4. *Unity of command*—Workers should receive orders from only one manager.

5. *Unity of direction*—The entire organization should be moving toward a common objective, in a common direction.

6. *Subordination of individual interests to the general interests*—The interests of one person should not take priority over the interests of the organization as a whole.

7. *Remuneration*—Many variables, such as cost of living, supply of qualified personnel, general business conditions, and success of the business, should be considered in determining a worker's rate of pay.

8. *Centralization*—Fayol defined *centralization* as lowering the importance of the subordinate role. *Decentralization* is increasing the same importance. The degree to which centralization or decentralization should be adopted depends on the specific organization in which the manager is working.

9. *Scalar chain*—Managers in hierarchies are part of a chainlike authority scale. Each manager, from the first-line supervisor to the president, possesses certain amounts of authority. The president possesses the most authority; the first-line supervisor, the least. Lower-level managers should always keep upper-level managers informed of their work activities. The existence of a scalar chain and adherence to it are necessary if the organization is to be successful.

10. *Order*—For the sake of efficiency and coordination, all materials and people related to a specific kind of work should be assigned to the same general location in the organization.

11. *Equity*—All employees should be treated as equally as possible.

12. *Stability of tenure of personnel*—Retaining productive employees should always be a high priority of management. Recruitment and selection costs, as well as increased product-reject rates, are usually associated with hiring new workers.

13. *Initiative*—Management should take steps to encourage worker initiative, which is defined as new or additional work activity undertaken through self-direction.

14. *Esprit de corps*—Management should encourage harmony and general good feelings among employees.[16]

Fayol's general principles of management cover a broad range of topics, but organizational efficiency, the handling of people, and appropriate management action are the three general themes he stresses. With the writings of Fayol, the study of management as a broad comprehensive activity began to receive the attention it deserved.

►LIMITATIONS OF THE CLASSICAL APPROACH

Contributors to the classical approach felt encouraged to write about their managerial experiences largely because of the success they enjoyed. Structuring work to be more efficient and defining the manager's role more precisely yielded significant improvements in productivity, which individuals such as Taylor and Fayol were quick to document.

The classical approach, however, does not adequately emphasize human variables. People today do not seem to be as influenced by bonuses as they were in the nineteenth century. It is generally agreed that critical interpersonal areas, such as conflict, communication, leadership, and motivation, were shortchanged in the classical approach.

In the late 1980s, LSG/Sky Chefs, an airline caterer based in Arlington, Texas, reported 1,000 injuries—and 18,000 lost workdays—per year. The company has since instituted a safety-awareness program that also encourages employee initiative and what Henri Fayol called "esprit de corps." Here, for example, employees have taken over morning stretching exercises. Sky Chef also provides rewards to reinforce safe behavior.

The **behavioral approach to management** is a management approach that emphasizes increasing organizational success by focusing on human variables within the organization.

◢ THE BEHAVIORAL APPROACH

The **behavioral approach to management** emphasizes increasing production through an understanding of people. According to proponents of this approach, if managers understand their people and adapt their organizations to them, organizational success will usually follow.

▶ THE HAWTHORNE STUDIES

The behavioral approach is usually described as beginning with a series of studies conducted between 1924 and 1932 that investigated the behavior and attitudes of workers at the Hawthorne (Chicago) Works of the Western Electric Company.[17] Accounts of the Hawthorne Studies are usually divided into two phases: the relay assembly test room experiments and the bank wiring observation room experiment. The following sections discuss each of these phases.

THE RELAY ASSEMBLY TEST ROOM EXPERIMENTS The relay assembly test room experiments originally had a scientific management orientation. The experimenters believed that if they studied productivity long enough under different working conditions (including variations in weather conditions, temperature, rest periods, work hours, and humidity), they would discover the working conditions that maximized production. The immediate purpose of the relay assembly test room experiments was to determine the relationship between intensity of lighting and worker efficiency, as measured by worker output. Two groups of female employees were used as subjects. The light intensity for one group was varied, while the light intensity for the other group was held constant.

The results of the experiments surprised the researchers: No matter what conditions employees were exposed to, production increased. There seemed to be no consistent relationship between productivity and lighting intensity. An extensive interviewing campaign was undertaken to determine why the subjects continued to increase production under all lighting conditions. The following are the main reasons, as formulated from the interviews:

1. The subjects found working in the test room enjoyable
2. The new supervisory relationship during the experiment allowed the subjects to work freely, without fear
3. The subjects realized that they were taking part in an important and interesting study
4. The subjects seemed to become friendly as a group

The experimenters concluded that human factors within organizations could significantly influence production. More research was needed, however, to evaluate the potential impact of this human component in organizations.

THE BANK WIRING OBSERVATION ROOM EXPERIMENT The purpose of the bank wiring observation room experiment was to analyze the social relationships in a work group. Specifically, the study focused on the effect of group piecework incentives on a group of men who assembled terminal banks for use in telephone exchanges. The group piecework incentive system dictated that the harder a group worked as a whole, the more pay each member of that group would receive.

The experimenters believed that the study would show that members of the work group pressured one another to work harder so that each group member would receive more pay. To their surprise, they found the opposite: The work group pressured the faster workers to slow down their work rate. The men whose work rate would have increased individual salaries were being pressured by the group, rather than the men whose work rate would have decreased individual salaries. Evidently, the men were more interested in preserving work group solidarity than in making more money. The researchers concluded that social groups in organizations could effectively exert pressure to influence individuals to disregard monetary incentives.[18]

► **RECOGNIZING THE HUMAN VARIABLE**

Taken together, the series of studies conducted at the Hawthorne plant gave management thinkers a new direction for research. Obviously, the human variable in the organization needed much more analysis, since it could either increase or decrease production drastically. Managers began to realize that they needed to understand this influence so they could maximize its positive effects and minimize its negative effects. This attempt to understand people is still a major force in today's organizational research.[19] The cartoon below humorously illustrates how a manager's lack of understanding of an employee results in employee discontent and may eventually produce a less productive employee. More current behavioral findings and their implications for management are presented in greater detail later in this text.

► **THE HUMAN RELATIONS MOVEMENT**

The Hawthorne Studies sparked the **human relations movement,** a people-oriented approach to management in which the interaction of people in organizations is studied to judge its impact on organizational success. The ultimate objective of this approach is to enhance organizational success by building appropriate relationships with people. To put it simply, when management stimulates high productivity and worker commitment to the organization and its goals, human relations are said to be effective; and when management precipitates low productivity and uncommitted workers, human relations are said to be ineffective. **Human relations skill** is defined as the ability to work with people in a way that enhances organizational success.

The human relations movement has made some important contributions to the study and practice of management. Advocates of this approach to management have continually stressed the need to use humane methods in managing people. Abraham Maslow, perhaps the best-known contributor to the human relations movement, believed that managers must under-

The **human relations movement** is a people-oriented approach to management in which the interaction of people in organizations is studied to judge its impact on organizational success.

Human relations skill is the ability to work with people in a way that enhances organizational success.

cathy®   **by Cathy Guisewite**

Cathy Copyright © 1990, Cathy Guisewite. Reprinted with permission of Universal Press Syndicate.

stand the physiological, safety, social, esteem, and self-actualization needs of organization members. Douglas McGregor, another important contributor to the movement, emphasized a management philosophy built upon the views that people can be self-directed, accept responsibility, and consider work to be as natural as play. The ideas of both Maslow and McGregor are discussed thoroughly in chapter 16. As a result of the tireless efforts of theorists like Maslow and McGregor, modern managers better understand the human component in organizations and how to appropriately work with it to enhance organizational success.

BACK TO THE CASE

The comprehensive analysis of organizations implies that Michael Quinlan might be able to further improve success at McDonald's by evaluating the entire range of managerial performance—especially organizational efficiency, the handling of people, and appropriate management action. For example, Quinlan should make sure that McDonald's employees receive orders from only one source (be sure that one manager does not instruct an employee to serve french fries moments before another manager directs the same employee to prepare milk shakes). Along the same lines, Quinlan might want to make sure that all McDonald's employees are treated equally—that fry cooks, for example, do not get longer breaks than order takers.

The behavioral approach to management suggests that Quinlan strongly encourages McDonald's managers to consider the people working for them and evaluate the impact of their employees' feelings and relationships on restaurants' productivity. A McDonald's manager, for example, should try to make the work more enjoyable, perhaps by allowing employees to work at different stations (grill, beverage, or cash register) each day. A McDonald's manager might also consider creating opportunities for employees to become more friendly with one another, perhaps through a McDonald's employee picnic. In essence, the behavioral approach to management stresses that McDonald's managers should recognize the human variable in their restaurants and strive to maximize its positive effects.

THE MANAGEMENT SCIENCE APPROACH

The **management science approach** is a management approach that emphasizes the use of the scientific method and quantitative techniques to increase organizational success.

Churchman, Ackoff, and Arnoff define the management science, or operations research (OR), approach as (1) an application of the scientific method to problems arising in the operation of a system and (2) the solution of these problems by solving mathematical equations representing the system.[20] The **management science approach** suggests that managers can best improve their organizations by using the scientific method and mathematical techniques to solve operational problems.

▶ THE BEGINNING OF THE MANAGEMENT SCIENCE APPROACH

The management science, or operations research, approach can be traced to World War II, an era in which leading scientists were asked to help solve complex operational problems in the military.[21] The scientists were organized into teams that eventually became known as operations research (OR) groups. One OR group, for example, was asked to determine which gunsights would best stop German attacks on the British mainland.

These early OR groups typically included physicists and other "hard" scientists, who used the problem-solving method with which they had the most experience: the scientific method. The scientific method dictates that scientists:

1. Systematically *observe* the system whose behavior must be explained to solve the problem
2. Use these specific observations to *construct* a generalized framework (a model) that is consistent with the specific observations and from which consequences of changing the system can be predicted
3. Use the model to *deduce* how the system will behave under conditions that have not been observed but could be observed if the changes were made

4. Finally, *test* the model by performing an experiment on the actual system to see if the effects of changes predicted using the model actually occur when the changes are made[22]

The OR groups proved very successful at using the scientific method to solve the military's operational problems.

►MANAGEMENT SCIENCE TODAY

After World War II, America again became interested in manufacturing and selling products. The success of the OR groups in the military had been so obvious that managers were eager to try management science techniques in an industrial environment. After all, managers also had to deal with complicated operational problems.

By 1955, the management science approach to solving industrial problems had proved very effective. Many people saw great promise in refining its techniques and analytical tools. Managers and universities alike pursued these refinements.

By 1965, the management science approach was being used in many companies and being applied to many diverse management problems, such as production scheduling, plant location, and product packaging.

In the 1980s, surveys indicated that management science techniques were used extensively in very large, complex organizations. Smaller organizations, however, had not yet fully realized the benefits of using these techniques. Finding ways to apply management science techniques to smaller organizations is undoubtedly a worthwhile challenge for managers in the 1990s and beyond.[23]

QUALITY SPOTLIGHT ► Baldrige Award Exemplifies Quality

Since it was established in 1987, the Malcolm Baldrige National Quality Award has become the sought-after award for quality standards among U.S. businesses. In fact, it is to corporate America what the Oscars are to the motion-picture industry and the Grammys to the music industry.

The Baldrige Award's evaluation of a company's quality includes an examination of both efficiency and effectiveness. The guidelines for award application provide a detailed plan for improving quality in all areas of a company's business.

"The guidelines are outstanding," says James Houghton, chairman and chief executive officer of Corning Glass, which has competed for the award. "We have passed out the guidelines for our divisions and just said, 'If you want to know what quality is all about, take a look at this.'" Corning estimates that its staffers spent 14,000 hours competing for the award.

Six prizes are offered each year, two each for manufacturing and service companies and two for small businesses with fewer than 500 employees. Some past award winners are Motorola, Globe Metallurgical, IBM Rochester, Federal Express, Wallace Company, the Ritz-Carlton Hotel Company, AT&T Universal Card Services, Texas Instruments Defense Systems & Electronics Group, and Granite Rock Company.

The Baldrige Award is administered by the National Institute of Standards and Technology. To apply, a large company must pay a fee of about $4,000 and submit responses to a comprehensive 75-page questionnaire. A small company pays approximately $1,200 and answers a somewhat less comprehensive questionnaire.

Applications are scored by volunteer examiners, largely from industry. Companies that survive the initial screening enter the second phase of the competition, which includes an on-site visit by four to six examiners who verify information presented in the application.

Finally, application scores and examiners' reports are given to a panel of nine judges who submit their choices to the U.S. secretary of commerce.

Because the process is so detailed and exacting, merely applying for the Baldrige Award forces a company to review its entire operation with an eye to discovering quality weaknesses. Applicants also receive reports from the examiners highlighting strengths and weaknesses in their operations. Former Xerox Chairman David Kearns said that 90 percent of the value of applying for the award lies in that examiners' report. Adds David Luther, Corning Glass' vice president for quality, "It's the cheapest consulting you can ever get."

►CHARACTERISTICS OF MANAGEMENT SCIENCE APPLICATIONS

Four primary characteristics are usually present in situations in which management science techniques are applied.[24] First, the management problems studied are so complicated that managers need help in analyzing a large number of variables. Management science techniques increase the effectiveness of the managers' decision making in such a situation. Second, a management science application generally uses economic implications as guidelines for making a particular decision. Perhaps this is because management science techniques are best suited for analyzing quantifiable factors such as sales, expenses, and units of production.

Third, the use of mathematical models to investigate the decision situation is typical in management science applications. Models constructed to represent reality are used to determine how the real-world situation might be improved. The fourth characteristic of a management science application is the use of computers. The great complexity of managerial problems and the sophisticated mathematical analysis of problem-related information required are two factors that make computers very valuable to the management science analyst.

Today managers use such management science tools as inventory control models, network models, and probability models to aid them in the decision-making process. Later parts of this text will outline some of these models in more detail and illustrate their applications to management decision making. Because management science thought is still evolving, more and more sophisticated analytical techniques can be expected in the future.

◥ THE CONTINGENCY APPROACH

The contingency approach to management is a management approach emphasizing that what managers do in practice depends on a given set of circumstances—a situation.

In simple terms, the **contingency approach to management** emphasizes that what managers do in practice depends on, or is contingent upon, a given set of circumstances—a situation.[25] In essence, this approach emphasizes "if-then" relationships: "If" this situational variable exists, "then" this is the action a manager probably would take. For example, if a manager has a group of inexperienced subordinates, then the contingency approach would recommend that he or she lead in a different fashion than if the subordinates were experienced.

In general, the contingency approach attempts to outline the conditions or situations in which various management methods have the best chance of success.[26] This approach is based on the premise that, although there is probably no one best way to solve a management problem in all organizations, there probably is one best way to solve any given management problem in any one organization. Perhaps the main challenges of using the contingency approach are the following:

1. Perceiving organizational situations as they actually exist
2. Choosing the management tactics best suited to those situations
3. Competently implementing those tactics

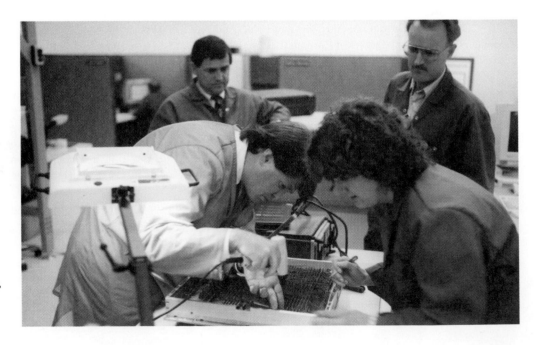

The organizational mission of Motorola University's Education Systems Alliance is to establish global alliances with school systems and not-for-profit educational institutions. New employees, like those shown here, are also trained at the company's schools. By fashioning itself as a learning corporation, Motorola helps its employees and managers make the best use of various approaches to management, like the contingency approach, and might even pave the way for new approaches to be developed for the future.

The notion of a contingency approach to management is not novel. The contingency approach has become a popular discussion topic for contemporary management thinkers. The general consensus of their writings is that if managers are to apply management concepts, principles, and techniques successfully, they must consider the realities of the specific organizational circumstances they face.[27]

MANAGEMENT AND THE INTERNET

"If-Then" Necessary for XS New York Cybercafe Does Not Materialize

Following the tenets of the contingency approach to management, *if* people surf the Internet in groups in social settings, *then,* at least based upon this one issue, it seems reasonable that management can take action to establish a Cybercafe. A cybercafe is a new type of restaurant that sells computer access along with light food and coffee. One cybercafe that was initiated based on this "if-then" relationship is the XS New York, a cybercafe and video game arcade in midtown Manhattan.

Mr. Rivera, who is 19 and recently interviewed at the XS New York, does not have a computer at home so he was trading messages with an unseen stranger. However, Rivera was the only person seated at the neat row of six shiny computers. Worse yet, Rivera, who works behind the pizza counter at XS, was not even a paying customer. Because someone left the computer, and the cafe was empty, he started playing with it.

In general, the popularity of cybercafes is declining. Many believe this is because of the increasing strength of people embracing the computer and the Internet. As people who sampled the World Wide Web in cafes liked it, they began buying their own computers and started surfing the Internet from their homes. As a result, the popularity of the cybercafe declined.

One new contingency puzzle that managers of cybercafes must now complete: *If* the declining popularity of the cybercafes continues, *then . . .*

THE SYSTEM APPROACH

The **system approach to management** is based on general system theory. Ludwig von Bertalanffy, a scientist who worked mainly in physics and biology, is recognized as the founder of general system theory.[28] The main premise of the theory is that to understand fully the operation of an entity, the entity must be viewed as a system. A **system** is a number of interdependent parts functioning as a whole for some purpose. For example, according to general system theory, to fully understand the operations of the human body, one must understand the workings of its interdependent parts (ears, eyes, and brain). General system theory integrates the knowledge of various specialized fields so that the system as a whole can be better understood.

> The **system approach to management** is a management approach based on general system theory—the theory that to understand fully the operation of an entity, the entity must be viewed as a system. This requires understanding the interdependence of its parts.
>
> A **system** is a number of interdependent parts functioning as a whole for some purpose.

▶ TYPES OF SYSTEMS

According to von Bertalanffy, there are two basic types of systems: closed and open. **Closed systems** are not influenced by, and do not interact with, their environments. They are mostly mechanical and have predetermined motions or activities that must be performed regardless of the environment. A clock is an example of a closed system. Regardless of its environment, a clock's wheels, gears, and so forth must function in a predetermined way if the clock as a whole is to exist and serve its purpose. The second type of system, the **open system,** is continually interacting with its environment. A plant is an example of an open system. Constant interaction with the environment influences the plant's state of existence and its future. In fact, the environment determines whether or not the plant will live.

> A **closed system** is one that is not influenced by, and does not interact with, its environment.
>
> An **open system** is one that is influenced by, and is continually interacting with, its environment.

▶ SYSTEMS AND "WHOLENESS"

The concept "wholeness" is very important in general system analysis. The system must be viewed as a whole and modified only through changes in its parts. Before modifications of the parts can be made for the overall benefit of the system, a thorough knowledge of how each part functions and the interrelationships among the parts must be present. L. Thomas Hopkins suggested the following six guidelines for anyone doing system analysis:[29]

1. The whole should be the main focus of analysis, with the parts receiving secondary attention
2. Integration is the key variable in wholeness analysis. It is defined as the interrelatedness of the many parts within the whole
3. Possible modifications in each part should be weighed in relation to possible effects on every other part
4. Each part has some role to perform so that the whole can accomplish its purpose
5. The nature of the part and its function is determined by its position in the whole
6. All analysis starts with the existence of the whole. The parts and their interrelationships should then evolve to best suit the purpose of the whole

Because the system approach to management is based on general system theory, analysis of the management situation as a system is stressed. The following sections present the parts of the management system and recommend information that can be used to analyze the system.

►THE MANAGEMENT SYSTEM

The **management system** is an open system whose major parts are organizational input, organizational process, and organizational output.

As with all systems, the **management system** is composed of a number of parts that function interdependently to achieve a purpose. The main parts of the management system are organizational input, organizational process, and organizational output. As discussed in chapter 1, these parts consist of organizational resources, the production process, and finished goods, respectively. The parts represent a combination that exists to achieve organizational objectives, whatever they may be.

The management system is an open system—that is, one that interacts with its environment (see Figure 2.2). Environmental factors with which the management system interacts include the government, suppliers, customers, and competitors. Each of these factors represents a potential environmental influence that could significantly change the future of the management system.

Environmental impact on management cannot be overemphasized. As an example, the federal government, through its Occupational Safety and Health Act (OSHA) of 1970, encourages management to take costly steps to safeguard workers. Many managers believe that these mandated safeguards are not only too expensive but also unnecessary.

The critical importance of managers knowing and understanding various components of their organizations' environments is perhaps best illustrated by the constant struggle of supermarket managers to know and understand their customers. Supermarket managers fight for the business of a national population that is growing by less than one percent per year. Survival requires that they know their customers better than the competition does. That is why many food retailers conduct market research to uncover customer attitudes about different kinds of foods and stores. Armed with a thorough understanding of their customers, gained from this kind of research, they hope to win business from competitors who are not benefiting from the insights made possible by such research.[30]

FIGURE 2.2 ► **The open management system**

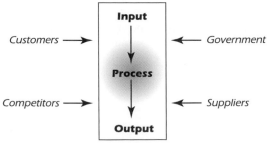

ENVIRONMENT

As noted earlier, general system theory supports the use of information from many specialized disciplines to better understand a system. This certainly holds true for the management system. Information from any discipline that can increase the understanding of management system operations enhances the success of the system. This is a sweeping statement. Where do managers go to get this broad information? The concise answer: To the first three approaches to management outlined in this chapter.

Thus the information used to discuss the management system in the remainder of this text comes from three primary sources:

1. Classical approach to management
2. Behavioral approach to management
3. Management science approach to management

The use of these three sources of information to analyze the management system is referred to as **triangular management.** Figure 2.3 presents the triangular management model. The three sources of information depicted in the model are not meant to represent all the information that can be used to analyze the management system. Rather, these are the three bodies of management-related information that probably would be most useful in analysis.

A synthesis of classically based information, behaviorally based information, and management science–based information is critical to effective use of the management system. This information is integrated and presented in the five remaining parts of this book. These parts discuss, respectively, management systems and planning (chapters 5–9), organizing (chapters 10–13), influencing (chapters 14–18), controlling (chapters 19–21), and topics for special emphasis (chapters 22–23). In addition, some information in these parts of the text is presented from a contingency viewpoint to emphasize the practical application of management principles.

Triangular management is a management approach that emphasizes using information from the classical, behavioral, and management science schools of thought to manage the open management system.

► LEARNING ORGANIZATION: A NEW APPROACH?

The preceding material in this chapter provides a history of management by discussing a number of different approaches to management that have evolved over time. Each approach developed over a number of years and focused on the particular needs of organizations at the time.

| FIGURE 2.3 | Triangular management model |

CLASSICALLY-BASED INFORMATION

MANAGEMENT SCIENCE-BASED INFORMATION

Customers → Input ← Government

Process

Competitors → Output ← Suppliers

ENVIRONMENT

BEHAVIORALLY-BASED INFORMATION

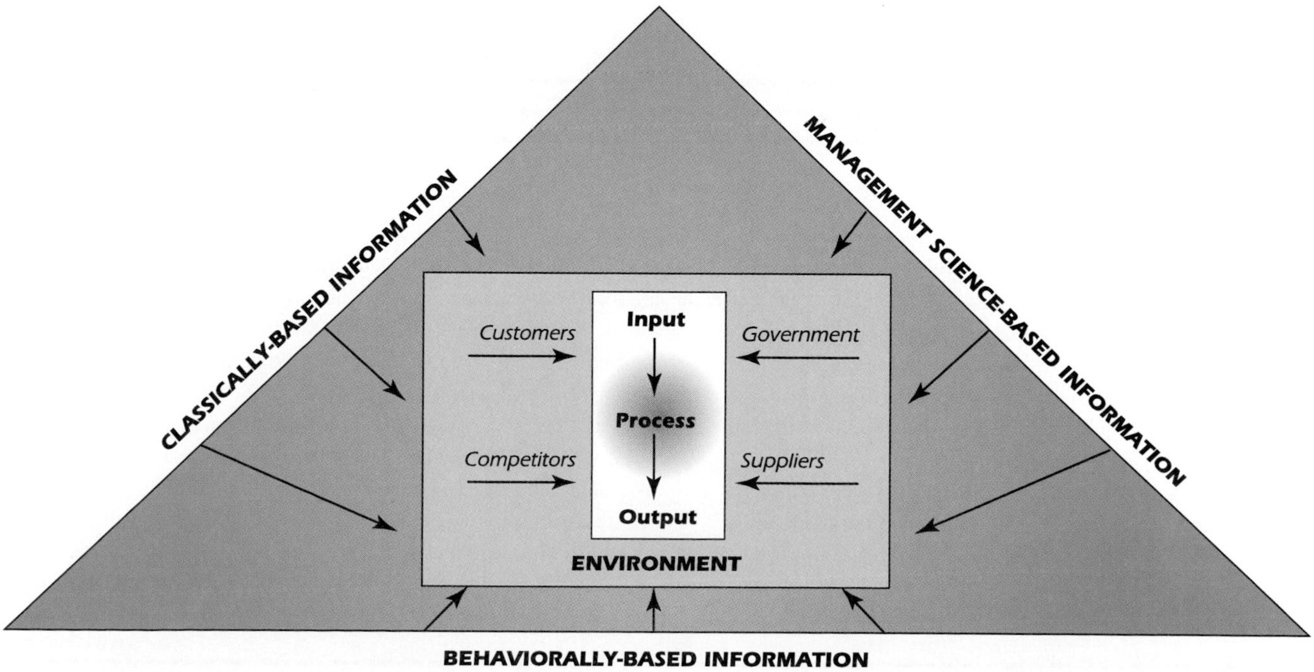

In more recent times, managers seem to be searching for new approaches to management.[31] Fueling this search is a range of new issues that modern managers face but that their historical counterparts did not. These issues include a concern about the competitive decline of Western firms, the accelerating pace of technological change, the sophistication of customers, and an increasing emphasis on globalization.

A new approach to management that is evolving to handle this new range of issues can be called the *learning organization approach*. A **learning organization** is an organization that does well in creating, acquiring, and transferring knowledge, and in modifying behavior to reflect new knowledge.[32] Learning organizations emphasize systematic problem solving, experimenting with new ideas, learning from experience and past history, learning from the experiences of others, and transferring knowledge rapidly throughout the organization. Managers attempting to build a learning organization must create an environment conducive to learning and encourage the exchange of information among all organization members. Honda, Corning, and General Electric are successful learning organizations.

The learning organization represents a specific, new *management paradigm,* or fundamental way of viewing and contemplating management. Peter Senge started serious discussion of learning organizations in 1990 with his book called *The Fifth Discipline: The Art & Practice of the Learning Organization.*[33] Since then, Senge, his colleagues at MIT, and many others have made significant progress in developing the learning organization concept. According to Senge, building a learning organization entails building five features within an organization:

1. *Systems Thinking*—Every organization member understands his or her own job and how the jobs fit together to provide final products to the customer.
2. *Shared Vision*—All organization members have a common view of the purpose of the organization and a sincere commitment to accomplish the purpose.
3. *Challenging of Mental Models*—Organization members routinely challenge the way business is done and the thought processes people use to solve organizational problems.
4. *Team Learning*—Organization members work together, develop solutions to new problems together, and apply the solutions together. Working as teams rather than individuals will help organizations gather collective force to achieve organizational goals.
5. *Personal Mastery*—All organization members are committed to gaining a deep and rich understanding of their work. Such an understanding will help organizations to reach important challenges that confront them.

The learning organization concept is being applied in many different sizes and types of organizations. The following People Spotlight discusses how Signicast Corporation took specific steps to help their employees become competent members of a learning organization.

A **learning organization** is an organization that does well in creating, acquiring, and transferring knowledge, and in modifying behavior to reflect new knowledge.

PEOPLE SPOTLIGHT · People for a New Learning Organization at Signicast

Signicast Corporation, a castings manufacturer based in Milwaukee, makes products like kickstands for Harley-Davidson motorcycles and various parts for John Deere tractors. When Signicast's executives decided to build a new $12 million automated plant, they knew they would need more than new technology—they would need new, learning-focused employees. Management decided to use the building of the new plant as a tool to transform employees into competent members of a learning organization.

In participating in the building of the new plant, employees were taught to become responsible and immersed in organizational issues, and to face and solve new and unique organizational problems. Every Signicast employee had an opportunity to contribute to how the new facility would finally appear. A core group of five executives would develop an idea, send it to employees, and ask for evaluation, soliciting both positive and negative reactions. Employees would meet with management to explain why plans would or would not work, how equipment would fit into the planned facility, and how expenses related to the new plant could be controlled. Employees even had the final word, through a formal vote, on whether the plant should be built. As by-products of the process, employees saw and understood that it was necessary to work 12-hour shifts, learn many different jobs, and be part of a team if the new plant was to be successful. Overall, management at Signicast initiated a learning culture by putting management and employees on the same team in planning for a new plant and by giving employees the power to function as real members of that team.

The above information suggests that Michael Quinlan could enhance the success of McDonald's by encouraging managers to use the management science approach to solve operational problems. According to the scientific method, a McDonald's manager would first spend some time observing. Next, the manager would use these observations to outline exactly how the restaurant operates as a whole. Third, the manager would apply this understanding of McDonald's operations by predicting how various changes might help or hinder the restaurant as a whole. Before implementing possible changes, the manager would test them on a small scale to see if they actually affected the restaurant as desired.

If McDonald's managers were to follow the contingency approach to management, their actions as managers would depend on the situation. For example, *if* some customers had not been served within a reasonable period because the equipment needed to make chocolate sundaes had broken down, *then* management probably would not hold employees responsible. But *if* management knew that the equipment had broken down because of employee mistreatment or neglect, *then* reaction to the situation would likely be very different.

A McDonald's manager could also apply the system approach and view a restaurant as a system, or a number of interdependent parts that function as a whole, to reach restaurant objectives. Naturally, a McDonald's restaurant would be viewed as an open system—one that exists in and is influenced by its environment. Major factors within the environment of a McDonald's restaurant would be its customers, suppliers, competitors, and the government. For example, if a McDonald's competitor lowered its price for hamburgers well below McDonald's price, McDonald's management might be forced to consider modifying different parts of its restaurant system in order to meet or beat that price.

Lastly, a McDonald's manager could apply the learning organization approach. Using this approach, a restaurant manager, for example, would see the restaurant as an organizational unit that needs to be good at creating, acquiring, and transferring knowledge, and at modifying behavior to reflect new knowledge. For example, all McDonald's employees at a restaurant would be involved in gathering new thoughts and ideas about running the restaurant and would be on a team with management, possessing a significant voice in establishing how the restaurant exists and operates.

For updated information on the topics in this chapter, Internet exercises, links to related Internet sites, an interactive study guide, and more, visit our companion Web site at

http://www.prenhall.com/certo

Additional information can be found on the inside front and back covers of this text.

ACTION SUMMARY

Reread the learning objectives below. Each objective is followed by questions. Answering these questions accurately will help you retain the most important concepts discussed in this chapter. After answering each question, check your answer against the answer key at the end of this chapter. (*Hint:* If you have any doubts regarding the correct response, consult the page number that follows the answer.)

Circle:

From studying this chapter, I will attempt to acquire

1. An understanding of the classical approach to management.

T F
    a. The classical management approach established what it considered the "one best way" to manage.

a b c d e
    b. The process of finding the "one best way" to perform a task is called: (a) comprehensive analysis of management (b) the concept of wholeness (c) the Hawthorne Studies (d) the management science approach (e) scientific management.

2. An appreciation for the work of Frederick W. Taylor, Frank and Lillian Gilbreth, Henry L. Gantt, and
   a b c d e   Henri Fayol.
      a. Fayol defines 14 principles of management. Which of the following is *not* one of those principles:
         (a) scalar chain of authority (b) esprit de corps (c) centralization (d) unity of command (e) di-
   a b c d e   rectedness of command.
      b. Which of the following theorists assumed that any worker's job could be reduced to a science:
   T F   (a) Gilbreth (b) Gantt (c) Mayo (d) Fayol (e) Taylor.
   T F   **c.** Gantt increased worker efficiency by setting standards according to top management's opinion of
         what maximum performance should be.

3. An understanding of the behavioral approach to management.
   a b c d e
      a. The behavioral approach to management emphasizes striving to increase production through an
         understanding of the organization itself.
   T F   **b.** The behavioral approach began with: (a) the Hawthorne Studies (b) the mental revolution (c) the
   T F   industrial revolution (d) motion studies (e) the Bethlehem Steel Studies.

4. An understanding of the studies at the Hawthorne Works and the human relations movement.
   T F   **a.** The Hawthorne Studies showed a direct relationship between lighting and efficiency.
      b. The Hawthorne experimenters found that people were more concerned with preserving the work
   a b c d e   group than with maximizing their pay.
      c. The human relations movement deemphasized the importance of people in organizations.

5. An understanding of the management science approach to management.
      a. Which of the following is *not* one of the philosophies of the management science approach:
   T F   (a) managers can improve the organization by using scientific methods (b) mathematical tech-
         niques can solve organizational problems (c) models should be used to represent the system (d) in-
         dividual work is better than teamwork (e) observation of the system must take place.
   a b c d e   **b.** In the management science theory, models are used to represent reality and then to determine how
         the real-world situation might be improved.

6. An understanding of how the management science approach has evolved.
   T F
      a. The management science approach emerged after: (a) World War I (b) the Civil War (c) the Korean
         War (d) World War II (e) the 1930s Depression.
   a b c d e   **b.** Although management science was first applied to military problems, it is now applied by compa-
         nies to diverse management problems.

7. An understanding of the system approach to management.
   a b c d e
      a. An organization that interacts with external forces is: (a) a closed system (b) a model (c) an inde-
         pendent entity (d) an open system (e) a contingency.
      b. Which of the following is *not* one of the guidelines proposed by Hopkins for doing system analysis
         according to the concept of wholeness: (a) the whole should be the main focus of analysis (b) all
         analysis starts with the existence of the whole (c) the nature of the part is determined by its posi-
   T F   tion in the whole (d) each part has some role to perform so that the whole can accomplish its pur-
   a b c d e   pose (e) modifications should be made as problems occur.

8. Knowledge about the learning organization approach to management.
      a. The learning organization approach to management reflects an old management paradigm.
      b. A learning organization is typically least characterized by: (a) systems thinking (b) shared vision
   a b c d e   (c) rigid job procedures (d) team learning (e) challenging mental models.

9. An understanding of how triangular management and the contingency approach to management are
      related.
   a b c d e   **a.** The contingency approach emphasizes the viewpoint that what managers do in practice depends
         overall on: (a) the worker (b) the situation (c) the task (d) the environment (e) the manager's
         personality.
      b. The three sources of information in triangular management are: (a) input, process, and output
         (b) management science, the classical approach to management, and the behavioral approach to
         management (c) mathematics, psychology, and sociology (d) managers, directors, and stockhold-
         ers (e) executives, administrators, and supervisors.

CASE DISCUSSION QUESTIONS

" **A** Problem at McDonald's" (p.25) and its related Back-to-the-Case sections were written to help you better understand the management concepts contained in this chapter. Answer the following discussion questions about this Introductory Case to further enrich your understanding of the chapter content:

1. Based on information in the introductory case, list three problems that you think future McDonald's managers will have to solve.

2. What action(s) do you think the managers will have to take to solve these problems?

3. From what you know about fast-food restaurants, how easy would it be to manage a McDonald's restaurant? Why?

SKILLS EXERCISE: APPLYING A COMPREHENSIVE VIEW OF MANAGEMENT

I n this chapter you studied a comprehensive view of management as outlined by 14 principles developed by Henri Fayol. Reflecting on the overall situation depicted in the introductory case about Mc-Donald's, discuss how you, as a manager of a McDonald's restaurant, would apply each of these principles to help ensure organizational success.

1. List the five approaches to managing.
2. Define the classical approach to management.
3. Compare and contrast the contributions to the classical approach made by Frederick W. Taylor, Frank and Lillian Gilbreth, and Henry L. Gantt.
4. How does Henri Fayol's contribution to the classical approach differ from the contributions of Taylor, the Gilbreths, and Gantt?
5. What is scientific management?
6. Describe motion study as used by the Gilbreths.
7. Describe Gantt's innovation in the area of worker bonuses.
8. List and define Fayol's general principles of management.
9. What is the primary limitation to the classical approach to management?
10. Define the behavioral approach to management.

11. What is the significance of the studies carried out at the Hawthorne Works of the Western Electric Company?
12. Describe the human relations movement.
13. What is the management science approach to management?
14. What are the steps in the scientific method of problem solving?
15. List and explain three characteristics of situations in which management science applications usually are made.
16. Define the contingency approach to management.
17. What is a system?
18. What is the difference between a closed system and an open system?
19. Explain the relationship between system analysis and "wholeness."
20. What are the parts of the management system?
21. Explain in your own words what is meant by a learning organization.

1. **a.** T, p. 26
   b. e, p. 26
2. **a.** e, p. 31
   b. e, p. 27
   c. F, p. 29
3. **a.** F, p. 32
   b. a, p. 32

4. **a.** F, p. 32
   b. T, p. 32
   c. F, p. 33
5. **a.** d, pp. 34–35
   b. T, pp. 34–36

6. **a.** d, p. 34
   b. T, p. 35
7. **a.** d, p. 37
   b. e, p. 38

8. **a.** F, pp. 39–40
   b. c, p. 40
9. **a.** b, p. 36
   b. b, p. 39

West Point graduate Albert J. Dunlap, former chairman and CEO of Scott Paper Company, claims that the U.S. Military Academy made him "tenacious and very organized." Others say his experience gave him an "in-your-face attitude rare among executives" and made him a valuable hired gun for straightening out troubled companies. Dunlap is known to attack and challenge nearly every premise and person that gets in his sight. Those who interfere with his efforts usually get chewed up by the experience.

Scott Paper is a familiar brand name to the American consumer. Founded by Clarence and Irvin Scott in 1879, the company eventually became the world's largest supplier of toilet tissue, paper napkins, and paper towels. As it matured, however, Scott's profitability suffered and growth stagnated when rival Procter & Gamble took an increasing market share. Between 1960 and 1971, Scott's market share of consumer paper products dropped from 45 to 33 percent. In the period 1990 to 1994, Scott continued to lose market share, and in 1993, the company lost $277 million and saw its credit rating deteriorate.

By 1994, Scott Paper was a moribund bureaucracy. In hiring Al Dunlap, Scott's board of directors signaled its determination to take decisive action. Dunlap initiated changes that would eliminate 11,000 employees (71 percent of headquarters staff, 50 percent of all managers, and 20 percent of hourly workers). He sold off unrelated business units—including publishing papermaker S.D. Warren Company, for $1.6 billion—and slashed spending—the research and development budget alone was cut in half, to $35 million.

Not surprisingly, Dunlap's cost cuts and increased prices achieved immediate bottom-line results. The company's profitability soared, as did the market value of its stock, which rose 225 percent under Dunlap's leadership. Dunlap claimed that by launching new products and selling unprofitable ventures, he had positioned Scott Paper for long-term positive returns for investors. Critics disagreed, seeing Dunlap's moves as constituting a short-term strategy to groom the company for a merger. In the words of one former marketing executive, Dunlap's strategy "became a volume-driven plan to pretty up the place for sale." In fact, on December 12, 1995, Scott shareholders approved a $9.4 billion merger with Kimberly-Clark Corporation.

As for Al Dunlap, he enjoys his "chainsaw" reputation and believes that his approach is helping to change the norms of corporate behavior. However, according to Peter D. Cappelli, chairman of the management department at the Wharton Business School, "He is persuading others that shareholder value is the be-all and end-all. But Dunlap did not create value. He redistributed income from the employees and the community to the shareholders."

Nevertheless, the cuts continued. Kimberly-Clark planned to remove 8,000 workers from the combined companies' 60,000 workforce by 1997 and to close Scott's headquarters in Boca Raton, Florida. One former high-level Scott executive believed that the company was now "just a hollow core."

Meanwhile Dunlap walked away with $100 million in salary, bonus, stock gains, and other perks. He offers no apologies for his approach: "I'm not going to apologize for success . . . for all this, for hard work. That's the free-market system." Dunlap does not believe that a business should be run for the stakeholders, such as employees or the communities in which they live, but for the shareholders—period. "Stakeholders are total rubbish," according to Dunlap. "It's the shareholders who own the company. Not enough American executives care about the shareholders."

The real question is whether short-term stockholder gains are good for business down the road. Says Sarah Teslik, executive director of the Council of Institutional Investors in Washington, a watchdog group for big shareholders: "Dunlap holds himself up as a role model, but any company is apt to have significant stock runup if current costs are reduced by a huge amount. That's no guarantee [Scott] will do well in the future."

On the other hand, some analysts contend that Dunlap has changed corporate America for the better. In a *Financial World* magazine poll, for example, CEOs voted Dunlap "most admired" chief executive officer. Certainly he is now a high-profile business leader who will be sought out by the boards of other troubled companies to enhance shareholder value. It remains to be seen, however, what impact the short-term and long-term consequences of Al Dunlap's management theory will have on corporate America and the American workforce.

QUESTIONS

1. Describe Al Dunlap's management approach. Does it fit any of the classical or modern approaches? Explain. How does it contradict some points in these approaches?

2. Delineate the good points and bad points of a massive downsizing effort such as that undertaken at Scott Paper—as if you were a stakeholder, and then, as if you were a shareholder. Are your two lists different? Explain.

3. What factors were the keys to increased productivity at Scott Paper? How was Dunlap responsible for the company's turnaround?

4. Describe the kind of company that might hire Dunlap next. What goals might its board of directors have? What problems might the company face? What companies in the news today fit your description?

SMALL BUSINESS 2000

Management has been considered a key ingredient to a company's success. Although management remains a key ingredient, the way in which companies view management continues to change and evolve.

Historically, three theories of management have been proposed: classical, behavioral, and management science. Today, management approaches are not considered in such clear-cut terms. Current thinking suggests that each approach may contribute to different parts of an organization and at different times to a venture's development. Most companies today display evidence of each approach, and the emphasis on each often changes as the company grows and as it responds to changes in its operating environment such as competition and changing customer requirements.

Texas Name Plate is such a company. Founded by three partners, it is a different company today than it was at its beginning. Texas Name Plate is experiencing significant growth and financial strength, but it has not always been so fortunate. It once was on the verge of bankruptcy. The company attributes its current strength to a major change taken by its founders to focus and redirect the company toward survival and profitability. The president of Texas Name Plate, Roy

Crownover, stepped down to appoint his son Dale, as president. Roy gave him complete control to lead the company as he saw fit. As you probably already know, changing leadership alone does not guarantee a change in the focus or performance of a company. If it is business as usual under new leadership, it is likely that very little has actually changed.

QUESTIONS

1. You have heard both a founder and current president of Texas Name Plate discuss the operations of this company. Identify and briefly discuss an example of each of the following management approaches: classical, behavioral, and scientific management.

2. How do you think the management of Texas Name Plate differs under Dale Crownover from the way the company was managed under Roy, his father?

3. Dale Crownover emphasizes the gathering and use of information in the decision-making process. He also emphasizes communication among individuals and organizations within the company. Do you think this is good or bad? When might information collection and emphasis on communication not be useful or necessary?

Corporate Social Responsibility and Business Ethics

STUDENT LEARNING OBJECTIVES

From studying this chapter, I will attempt to acquire

1. An understanding of the term *corporate social responsibility*

2. An appreciation of the arguments both for and against the assumption of social responsibilities by business

3. Useful strategies for increasing the social responsiveness of an organization

4. Insights on the planning, organizing, influencing, and controlling of social responsibility activities

5. A practical plan for how society can help business meet its social obligations

6. An understanding of the relationship between ethics and management

7. An understanding of how ethics can be incorporated into management practice

CHAPTER OUTLINE

Introductory Case: *Larami Corporation "Super Soaks" Society*

FUNDAMENTALS OF SOCIAL RESPONSIBILITY
The Davis Model of Corporate Social Responsibility
Areas of Corporate Social Responsibility
Varying Opinions on Social Responsibility
Conclusions About the Performance of Social Responsibility Activities by Business

Global Spotlight: *DuPont Protects the Environment*

SOCIAL RESPONSIVENESS
Determining If a Social Responsibility Exists
Social Responsiveness and Decision Making
Approaches to Meeting Social Responsibilities

Diversity Spotlight: *Social Responsiveness and the Equal Opportunity Act at Opryland*

SOCIAL RESPONSIBILITY ACTIVITIES AND MANAGEMENT FUNCTIONS
Planning Social Responsibility Activities
Organizing Social Responsibility Activities
Influencing Individuals Performing Social Responsibility Activities
Controlling Social Responsibility Activities

Across Industries: *Food Processing—Social Audits at Ben & Jerry's*

HOW SOCIETY CAN HELP BUSINESS MEET SOCIAL OBLIGATIONS

BUSINESS ETHICS
A Definition of Ethics
Why Ethics Is a Vital Part of Management Practices

Management and the Internet: *Better Business Bureau Helps Management Project Ethics Position on Internet*
A Code of Ethics
Creating an Ethical Workplace

LARAMI CORPORATION "SUPER SOAKS" SOCIETY

REMINDER: THE INTRODUCTORY CASE WRAP-UP (P. 71) CONTAINS DISCUSSION QUESTIONS AND A SKILLS EXERCISE TO FURTHER ILLUSTRATE THE APPLICATION OF CHAPTER CONCEPTS TO THIS VIGNETTE.

Larami Corporation produced a very hot toy in the summer of 1992. Super Soaker was a high-powered plastic toy gun that shot more water farther than any other toy gun on the market. It was a toy maker's dream—until it turned into a nightmare.

Soon after the toy's introduction, stories of Super Soaker-wielding youths squirting people with water, bleach, ammonia, and urine flooded the offices of lawmakers and police departments around the country. One youth in Boston died, and two others—one in New York, another in New Castle, Pennsylvania—were wounded in shootings triggered by dousings.

The controversy thrust closely-held Larami into a dilemma—particularly because the water gun was the company's biggest profit maker. Other companies made similar guns, such as Tyco Toys' Super Saturator, but Larami's Super Soaker was the top-selling water gun by far.

Larami took cover from the controversy by issuing a one-page statement expressing sympathy for the family of the 15-year-old Boston youth who was killed, but noting that violent misuse of the water gun is "something we cannot control." No one in the 50-employee company other than Al Davis, executive vice president, was authorized to speak to the media or public officials. But Mr. Davis, a spokesperson for the Philadelphia-based company said, was unavailable for comment.

The then-mayor of Boston, Raymond Flynn, urged retailers to stop selling the gun, and Michigan Senator Gilbert DiNello introduced a bill to outlaw the toy. In response, Woolworth's and Bradlees pulled the product off the shelves in some of their stores, and the Sharper Image said it would give to charity the money it made from the sale of the toy guns in its Boston stores. . . .

The Super Soaker came in three models that varied in price from $10 to $30 apiece. It was a best-selling toy, according to NPD Group, a Port Washington, New York, researcher that supplies industry sales figures to the Toys Manufacturers Association and to toy retailers. In fact, analysts estimated that Larami's water gun represented more than 70 percent of the water-gun market. The gun's air compression system, which propelled water as far as 50 feet away, was patented to keep competitors from copying the technology. But that did not stop others from riding

The Super Soaker water gun was a popular hit until a Boston teenager was killed in an incident involving the toy and the mayor of Boston urged retailers to stop selling it. Does the manufacturer have an ethical responsibility to consumers to stop distributing such a potentially dangerous item?

on the wave of this hot toy. For example, Tyco's Super Saturator, a battery-operated gun, was able to shoot water in spurts, lawnmower-style, as far as 35 feet. The Super Saturator, however, was not linked to any violent incidents.

Overall, the business attitude toward powerful water guns has been somewhat mixed. By including a miniversion of the Super Soaker water guns in its kids meals, Hardee's Food Systems seemed to be supporting Larami's right to sell this toy gun. On the other hand, by refusing to stock certain types of guns it believed could be dangerous, Toys "R" Us, the largest toy retailer in the United States, seemed to be saying that only clearly safe toy guns should be manufactured.

Needless to say, this kind of situation can put pressure on management and employees within any organization. Perhaps this pressure is one of the primary reasons that Larami is selling its water guns to Hasbro, another toy maker.

What's Ahead

The Introductory Case describes societal efforts to curb sales of a toy gun produced by Larami Corporation. Management at Larami faced the difficult challenge of making a profit from its Super Soaker while mollifying public criticism that this toy gun encouraged youth violence that resulted in serious injuries and even death. This chapter presents material that managers such as those at Larami can use to help analyze and handle the dilemma of reaching company objectives while protecting or improving the welfare of society. Specifically, the chapter discusses the following subjects:

1. Fundamentals of social responsibility
2. Social responsiveness
3. Social responsibility activities and management functions
4. How society can help business meet social obligations
5. Business ethics

FUNDAMENTALS OF SOCIAL RESPONSIBILITY

Corporate social responsibility is the managerial obligation to take action that protects and improves both the welfare of society as a whole and the interests of the organization.

The term *social responsibility* means different things to different people. For purposes of this chapter, however, **corporate social responsibility** is the managerial obligation to take action that protects and improves both the welfare of society as a whole and the interests of the organization. According to the concept of corporate social responsibility, a manager must strive to achieve societal as well as organizational goals.[1]

The amount of attention given to the area of social responsibility by both management and society has increased in recent years and probably will continue to increase.[2] The following sections present the fundamentals of social responsibility of businesses by discussing these topics:

1. The Davis model of corporate social responsibility
2. Areas of corporate social responsibility
3. Varying opinions on social responsibility
4. Conclusions about the performance of social responsibility actions by business

▶THE DAVIS MODEL OF CORPORATE SOCIAL RESPONSIBILITY

A generally accepted model of corporate social responsibility was developed by Keith Davis.[3] Stated simply, Davis' model is a list of five propositions that describe why and how business should adhere to the obligation to take action that protects and improves the welfare of society as well as of the organization:

Proposition 1: Social responsibility arises from social power—This proposition is derived from the premise that business has a significant amount of influence on, or power over, such critical social issues as minority employment and environmental pollution. In essence, the collective action of all businesses in the country primarily determines the proportion of minorities employed and the prevailing condition of the environment in which all citizens must live.

Davis reasons that since business has this power over society, society can and must hold business responsible for social conditions that result from the exercise of this power. Davis explains that society's legal system does not expect more of business than it does of each individual citizen exercising personal power.

Proposition 2: Business shall operate as a two-way open system, with open receipt of inputs from society and open disclosure of its operations to the public—According to this proposition, business must be willing to listen to what must be done to sustain or improve societal welfare. In turn, society must be willing to listen to business reports on what it is doing to meet its social responsibilities. Davis suggests that there must be ongoing honest and open communications between business and society's representatives if the overall welfare of society is to be maintained or improved.

Proposition 3: The social costs and benefits of an activity, product, or service shall be thoroughly calculated and considered in deciding whether to proceed with it—This proposi-

Faced with increasingly successful assaults by antismoking forces, the tobacco industry—a $47-billion concern—has retrenched. In the process, it has become a focal point in the debate about the interrelationship between business and society. In one 15-month period, for example, Philip Morris Co. and R.J. Reynolds Tobacco Co. spent $235 million on ads attacking antismoking laws, and in California alone, they have made $10 million in political donations in order to influence votes on pending legislation.

tion stresses that technical feasibility and economic profitability are not the only factors that should influence business decision making. Business should also consider both the long- and short-term societal consequences of all business activities before undertaking them.

Proposition 4: The social costs related to each activity, product, or service shall be passed on to the consumer—This proposition states that business cannot be expected to completely finance activities that may be socially advantageous but economically disadvantageous. The cost of maintaining socially desirable activities within business should be passed on to consumers through higher prices for the goods or services related to these activities.

Proposition 5: Business institutions, as citizens, have the responsibility to become involved in certain social problems that are outside their normal areas of operation—This last proposition makes the point that if a business possesses the expertise to solve a social problem with which it may not be directly associated, it should be held responsible for helping society solve that problem. Davis reasons that because business eventually will reap an increased profit from a generally improved society, business should share in the responsibility of all citizenry to generally improve society.

BACK TO THE CASE

Social responsibility obliges a business manager to take actions that protect and improve the welfare of society along with the interests of the organization. Larami's management, as discussed in the Introductory Case, faces the social responsibility issue of curbing youth violence. Following the logic of Davis' social responsibility model, if the sale of the Super Soaker actually does encourage youths to perform violent acts, Larami's management will probably have to address this violence issue by somehow modifying the design of the product and the way it is marketed. The real challenge in this situation is to determine whether the sale of the Super Soaker indeed causes these violent acts. Should Larami's management hold itself responsible for contributing to the delinquency of minors simply because some young customers use Super Soakers with violent intent? Larami's management must carefully weigh the social costs and benefits

(continued)

of providing society with such toys and then proceed with the course of action that will best benefit society as well as Larami.

The information presented thus far in this chapter also implies that Larami's management should seriously listen to society's concerns about the Super Soaker. Perhaps the best response to this situation is for Larami's management to gather as much information as possible concerning violent acts committed with the Super Soaker and take such steps as redesigning the product or refocusing its marketing to minimize future violent use of the toy gun.

As a consequence of handling this situation, Larami's management might acquire special expertise in developing products that not only discourage youth violence but also encourage young people to become a positive force in their communities. This expertise could certainly benefit society if Larami's management shared it with businesspeople in other fields. For example, Larami's management might be able to help the president of a publishing company publish books that discourage youth violence.

▶ AREAS OF CORPORATE SOCIAL RESPONSIBILITY

The areas in which business can act to protect and improve the welfare of society are numerous and diverse. Perhaps the most publicized of these areas are urban affairs, consumer affairs, environmental affairs, and employment practices affairs.

▶ VARYING OPINIONS ON SOCIAL RESPONSIBILITY

Although numerous businesses are already involved in social responsibility activities, there is much controversy about whether such involvement is necessary or even appropriate. The following two sections present some arguments for and against businesses performing social responsibility activities.[4]

ARGUMENTS FOR BUSINESS PERFORMING SOCIAL RESPONSIBILITY ACTIVITIES
The best-known argument for the performance of social responsibility activities by business was alluded to earlier in this chapter. This argument begins with the premise that business as a whole is a subset of society, one that exerts a significant impact on the way in which society exists. Since business is such an influential member of society, the argument continues, it has the responsibility to help maintain and improve the overall welfare of society. After all, since society puts this responsibility on its individual members, why should its corporate members be exempt?

In addition, some people argue that business should perform social responsibility activities because profitability and growth go hand in hand with responsible treatment of employees, customers, and the community. This argument says, essentially, that performing social responsibility activities is a means of earning greater organizational profit.[5]

Empirical studies, however, have not demonstrated any clear relationship between corporate social responsibility and profitability. In fact, several companies that were acknowledged leaders in social commitment during the 1960s and 1970s—including Control Data Corporation, Atlantic Richfield, Dayton-Hudson, Levi Strauss, and Polaroid—experienced serious financial difficulties during the 1980s.[6] (No relationship between corporate social responsibility activities and these financial difficulties was shown, however.)

ARGUMENTS AGAINST BUSINESS PERFORMING SOCIAL RESPONSIBILITY ACTIVITIES
The best-known argument against business performing social responsibility activities has been advanced by Milton Friedman, one of America's most distinguished economists. Friedman argues that making business managers simultaneously responsible to business owners for reaching profit objectives and to society for enhancing societal welfare sets up a conflict of interest that could potentially cause the demise of business

as it is known today. According to Friedman, this demise will almost certainly occur if business is continually forced to perform socially responsible actions that directly conflict with private organizational objectives.[7]

Friedman also argues that to require business managers to pursue socially responsible objectives may, in fact, be unethical, because it compels managers to spend money on some individuals that rightfully belongs to other individuals:[8]

> In a free enterprise, private property system, a corporate executive is an employee of the owners of the business. He has direct responsibility to his employers. That responsibility is to conduct the business in accordance with their desires, which generally will be to make as much money as possible while conforming to the basic rules of society, both those embodied in law and those embodied in ethical custom. . . . Insofar as his actions reduce returns to stockholders, he is spending their money. Insofar as his actions raise the price to customers, he is spending the customers' money.

An example that Friedman could use to illustrate his argument is the Control Data Corporation. Former chairman William Norris involved Control Data in many socially responsible programs that cost the company millions of dollars—from building plants in the inner city and employing a minority workforce to researching farming on the Alaskan tundra. When Control Data began to incur net losses of millions of dollars in the mid-1980s, critics blamed Norris's "do-gooder" mentality. Eventually, a new chairman was installed to restructure the company and return it to profitability.[9]

BACK TO THE CASE

There are many different areas of social responsibility in which Larami's management could become involved—for example, product line, marketing practices, employee education and support, corporate philanthropy, environmental control, and minority employment. The situation with the Super Soaker is best categorized under the heading of "product line," since society's criticisms focus on how misuse of the product can cause pain, injury, or even death to young people.

Whatever Larami's management might do to minimize the bad social effects associated with the Super Soaker would probably result in a short-run decrease in Super Soaker sales, and perhaps even cost the company additional money if management looked for and invested in better ways to manufacture the product. Although at first glance, such action might seem unbusinesslike, performing this type of social responsibility activities could significantly improve Larami's public image and be instrumental in maintaining the company's growth in the long run.

►CONCLUSIONS ABOUT THE PERFORMANCE OF SOCIAL RESPONSIBILITY ACTIVITIES BY BUSINESS

The preceding section presented several major arguments for and against businesses performing social responsibility activities. Regardless of which argument or combination of arguments particular managers embrace, they generally should make a concerted effort to do the following:

1. Perform all legally required social responsibility activities
2. Consider voluntarily performing social responsibility activities beyond those legally required
3. Inform all relevant individuals of the extent to which their organization will become involved in performing social responsibility activities

PERFORMING REQUIRED SOCIAL RESPONSIBILITY ACTIVITIES Federal legislation requires that businesses perform certain social responsibility activities. In fact, several government agencies have been established expressly to enforce such business-related

TABLE 3.1	Primary Functions of Several Federal Agencies That Enforce Social Responsibility Legislation
Federal Agency	**Primary Agency Functions**
Equal Employment Opportunity Commission	Investigates and conciliates employment discrimination complaints that are based on race, sex, or creed
Office of Federal Contract Compliance Programs	Ensures that employers holding federal contracts grant equal employment opportunity to people regardless of their race or sex
Environmental Protection Agency	Formulates and enforces environmental standards in such areas as water, air, and noise pollution
Consumer Product Safety Commission	Strives to reduce consumer misunderstanding of manufacturers' product design, labeling, etc., by promoting clarity of these messages
Occupational Safety and Health Administration	Regulates safety and health conditions in nongovernment workplaces
National Highway Traffic Safety Administration	Attempts to reduce traffic accidents through the regulation of transportation-related manufacturers and products
Mining Enforcement and Safety Administration	Attempts to improve safety conditions for mine workers by enforcing all mine safety and equipment standards

legislation (see Table 3.1). The Environmental Protection Agency, for instance, has the authority to require businesses to adhere to certain socially responsible environmental standards. Examples of specific legislation requiring the performance of corporate social responsibility activities are the Equal Pay Act of 1963, the Equal Employment Opportunity Act of 1972, the Highway Safety Act of 1978, and the Clean Air Act Amendments of 1990.[10] The Global Spotlight on page 53 discusses DuPont's handling of a clean air issue.

VOLUNTARILY PERFORMING SOCIAL RESPONSIBILITY ACTIVITIES Adherence to legislated social responsibilities is the minimum standard of social responsibility performance that business managers must achieve. Managers must ask themselves, however, how far beyond the minimum they should go.

Determining how far to go is a simple process to describe, yet it is difficult and complicated to implement. It entails assessing the positive and negative outcomes of performing social responsibility activities over both the short and the long term, and then performing only those activities that maximize management system success while making a desirable contribution to the welfare of society.

Events at Sara Lee Bakery's plant in New Hampton, Iowa, illustrate how company management can voluntarily take action to protect employees' health. Many employees at the plant began developing carpal tunnel syndrome, a debilitating wrist disorder caused by repeated hand motions. Instead of simply having their employees go through physical therapy—and, as the principal employer in the town, watching the morale of the town drop—Sara Lee thoroughly investigated the problem. Managers took suggestions from factory workers and had their engineers design tools to alleviate the problem. The result was a virtual elimination of carpal tunnel syndrome at the plant within a very short time.[11]

Sandra Holmes asked top executives in 560 major firms in such areas as commercial banking, life insurance, transportation, and utilities to state the possible negative and positive outcomes their firms could expect from performing social responsibility activities.[12] Table 3.2 lists these outcomes and indicates the percentage of executives questioned who expected them. Although this information furnishes managers with insights into how involved their organizations should become in social responsibility activities, it does not give them a clear-cut indication of what to do. Managers can determine the appropriate level of social responsibility involvement for a specific organization only by examining and reacting to specific factors related to that organization.

TABLE 3.2 ▸ Outcomes of Social Responsibility Involvement Expected by Executives and the Percent Who Expected Them

Expected Outcomes	Percent of Executives Expecting Them
Positive Outcomes	
Enhanced corporate reputation and goodwill	97.4
Strengthening of the social system in which the corporation functions	89.0
Strengthening of the economic system in which the corporation functions	74.3
Greater job satisfaction among all employees	72.3
Avoidance of government regulation	63.7
Greater job satisfaction among executives	62.8
Increased chances for survival of the firm	60.7
Ability to attract better managerial talent	55.5
Increased long-term profitability	52.9
Strengthening of the pluralistic nature of American society	40.3
Maintaining or gaining customers	38.2
Investor preference for socially responsible firms	36.6
Increased short-term profitability	15.2
Negative Outcomes	
Decreased short-term profitability	59.7
Conflict of economic or financial and social goals	53.9
Increased prices for consumers	41.4
Conflict in criteria for assessing managerial performance	27.2
Disaffection of stockholders	24.1
Decreased productivity	18.8
Decreased long-term profitability	13.1
Increased government regulation	11.0
Weakening of the economic system in which the corporation functions	7.9
Weakening of the social system in which the corporation functions	3.7

▸ GLOBAL SPOTLIGHT ◂ DuPont Protects the Environment

E. I. DuPont de Nemours and Company, a producer of chemical products, is certainly a company whose actions affect the environment at both the national and the international level. When scientists in the early 1970s theorized that certain types of gases—gases used in the production of some of DuPont's products—were contributing to the breakdown of the ozone layer, DuPont encouraged further research and began looking for alternative products. As the evidence that these gases caused ozone depletion became more conclusive, the company stepped up its research efforts so that management would be able to make informed decisions about its products and their impact on the environment. As a company that conducts business in many countries, DuPont wished to assure its customers and concerned citizens throughout the world that it was sensitive to the ozone issue and that it was acting in a socially responsible manner to ensure that its products would not contribute to further deterioration of the ozone layer.

Critics, however, could argue that DuPont was merely reacting to pressure from stakeholders and/or outside pressures from environmentalists instead of proactively seeking solutions to global environmental problems.

Volunteers for Habitat for Humanity put up low-income housing in Washington DC. Many firms encourage employee contributions to such socially responsible programs by allowing them time off to participate.

COMMUNICATING THE DEGREE OF SOCIAL RESPONSIBILITY INVOLVEMENT

Determining the extent to which a business should perform social responsibility activities beyond legal requirements is a subjective process. Despite this subjectivity, however, managers should have a well-defined position in this vital area and should inform all organization members of that position.[13] Taking these steps will ensure that managers and organization members behave consistently to support the position and that societal expectations of what a particular organization can achieve in this area are realistic.

Nike, the world famous athletic-gear manufacturer, recently felt so strongly that its corporate philosophy on social responsibility issues should be clearly formulated and communicated that the company created a new position, vice president of corporate and social responsibility. Maria Eitelto, a former public-relations executive at Microsoft, was hired to fill that position and is now responsible for clearly communicating Nike's thoughts on social responsibility both inside and outside the organization.[14]

BACK TO THE CASE

Some social responsibility activities are legislated and therefore must be performed by business. Most of this type of legislation, however, is aimed at larger companies. Even though Larami is a significant company in the toy industry, there probably is no existing legislation that would require its management to modify the Super Soaker.

Because Larami is not required by law to modify its Super Soaker for the benefit of society, whatever modifications management might decide to make would be strictly voluntary. In making a decision on modifications, Larami should assess the positive and negative outcomes of such action over both the long and the short term. Then it should make the modifications (if any) that would maximize the success of the company as well as offer some desirable contribution to society. Larami management should let all organization members, as well as the public, know how the company feels about the situation with the Super Soaker and why.

The previous section discussed social responsibility, a business' obligation to take action that protects and improves the welfare of society along with the business' own interests. This section defines and discusses **social responsiveness,** the degree of effectiveness and efficiency an organization displays in pursuing its social responsibilities.[15] The greater the degree of effectiveness and efficiency, the more socially responsive the organization is said to be. The next three sections take up the following issues:

1. Determining if a social responsibility exists
2. Social responsiveness and decision making
3. Approaches to meeting social responsibilities

Social responsiveness is the degree of effectiveness and efficiency an organization displays in pursuing its social responsibilities.

▶ DETERMINING IF A SOCIAL RESPONSIBILITY EXISTS

One challenge facing managers who are attempting to be socially responsive is to determine which specific social obligations are implied by their business situation. Managers in the tobacco industry, for example, are probably socially obligated to contribute to public health by pushing for the development of innovative tobacco products that do less harm to people's health than present products do, but they are not socially obligated to help reclaim shorelines contaminated by oil spills.

Clearly, management has an obligation to be socially responsible toward its stakeholders. **Stakeholders** are all those individuals and groups that are directly or indirectly affected by an organization's decisions.[16] Managers of successful organizations typically have many different stakeholders to consider: stockholders, or owners of the organization; suppliers; lenders; government agencies; employees and unions; consumers; competitors; and local communities as well as society at large. Table 3.3 lists these stakeholders and gives a corresponding example of how a manager is socially obligated to each of them.

Stakeholders are all individuals and groups that are directly or indirectly affected by an organization's decisions.

▶ SOCIAL RESPONSIVENESS AND DECISION MAKING

The socially responsive organization that is both effective and efficient meets its social responsibilities without wasting organizational resources in the process. Determining exactly which social responsibilities an organization should pursue and then deciding how to pursue them are the two most critical decisions for maintaining a high level of social responsiveness within an organization.

Figure 3.1 is a flowchart that managers can use as a general guideline for making social responsibility decisions that enhance the social responsiveness of their organization. This

TABLE 3.3	**Stakeholders of a Typical Modern Organization and Examples of Social Obligations Managers Owe to Them**
Stakeholder	**Social Obligations Owed**
Stockholders/owners of the organization	To increase the value of the organization
Suppliers of materials	To deal with them fairly
Banks and other lenders	To repay debts
Government agencies	To abide by laws
Employees and unions	To provide safe working environment and to negotiate fairly with union representatives
Consumers	To provide safe products
Competitors	To compete fairly and to refrain from restraints of trade
Local communities and society at large	To avoid business practices that harm the environment

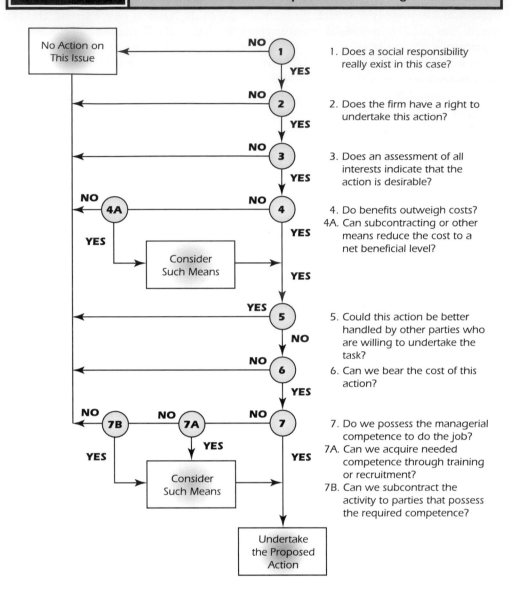

FIGURE 3.1 ▶ Flowchart of social responsibility decision making that generally will enhance the social responsiveness of an organization

No Action on This Issue

NO ① **YES**
1. Does a social responsibility really exist in this case?

NO ② **YES**
2. Does the firm have a right to undertake this action?

NO ③ **YES**
3. Does an assessment of all interests indicate that the action is desirable?

NO ④A **NO** ④ **YES**
4. Do benefits outweigh costs?
4A. Can subcontracting or other means reduce the cost to a net beneficial level?

YES

Consider Such Means **YES**

YES ⑤ **NO**
5. Could this action be better handled by other parties who are willing to undertake the task?

NO ⑥ **YES**
6. Can we bear the cost of this action?

NO 7B **NO** 7A **NO** ⑦ **YES**
7. Do we possess the managerial competence to do the job?
7A. Can we acquire needed competence through training or recruitment?
7B. Can we subcontract the activity to parties that possess the required competence?

YES **YES**

Consider Such Means

Undertake the Proposed Action

figure implies that for managers to achieve and maintain a high level of social responsiveness within an organization, they must pursue only those responsibilities their organization possesses and has a right to undertake. Furthermore, once managers decide to meet a specific social responsibility, they must determine the best way to undertake activities related to meeting this obligation. That is, managers must decide whether their organization should undertake the activities on its own or acquire the help of outsiders with more expertise in the area.

As an example of how the guidelines in Figure 3.1 can profitably be used, consider a recent decision made by Radisson Hotels International. Radisson's management determined that the company had an obligation to help preserve the environment. To proactively meet this obligation, management initiated a new concept called Green Suites. Along with the normally expected suite appointments, Green Suites feature recycled paper goods because Radisson managers believe that by offering its customers recycled paper products, the company can discourage the unnecessary cutting of trees. In order for this decision to be considered truly socially responsible, however, it must actually help to preserve the environment by saving trees and attract customer dollars that will help Radisson Hotels International reach such organizational objectives as making a profit.[17]

Various managerial approaches to meeting social obligations are another determinant of an organization's level of social responsiveness. According to Lipson, a desirable and socially responsive approach to meeting social obligations does the following:[18]

1. Incorporates social goals into the annual planning process
2. Seeks comparative industry norms for social programs
3. Presents reports to organization members, the board of directors, and stockholders on social responsibility progress
4. Experiments with different approaches for measuring social performance
5. Attempts to measure the cost of social programs as well as the return on social program investments

S. Prakash Sethi presents three management approaches to meeting social obligations:[19]

1. Social obligation approach
2. Social responsibility approach
3. Social responsiveness approach

Each of these approaches entails behavior that reflects a somewhat different attitude toward performance of social responsibility activities by business. The **social obligation approach,** for example, considers business as having primarily economic purposes and confines social responsibility activity mainly to existing legislation. The **social responsibility approach** sees business as having both economic and societal goals. The **social responsiveness approach** considers business as having both societal and economic goals as well as the obligation to anticipate potential social problems and work actively toward preventing their occurrence.

Organizations characterized by attitudes and behaviors consistent with the social responsiveness approach are generally more socially responsive than organizations characterized by attitudes and behaviors consistent with either the social responsibility or the social obligation approach. And organizations that take the social responsibility approach usually achieve higher levels of social responsiveness than organizations that take the social obligation approach. In other words, as one moves along the continuum from social obligation to social responsiveness, one generally finds management becoming more proactive. Proactive managers do what is prudent from a business viewpoint to reduce liabilities regardless of whether such action is required by law.

The **social obligation approach** is an approach to meeting social obligations that considers business to have primarily economic purposes and confines social responsibility activity largely to conformance to existing legislation.

The **social responsibility approach** is an approach to meeting social obligations that considers business as having both societal and economic goals.

The **social responsiveness approach** is an approach to meeting social obligations that considers business to have societal and economic goals as well as the obligation to anticipate potential social problems and to work actively toward preventing them from occurring.

►DIVERSITY SPOTLIGHT   Social Responsiveness and the Equal Opportunity Act at Opryland

The Equal Opportunity Act was passed in 1972 to eliminate employment discrimination based upon race, sex, or color. Management's attitude toward performing Equal Opportunity Act social responsibility activities at Opryland illustrates the social responsiveness approach.

The inevitability of having a future workforce characterized by cultural diversity is driving many hotels to aggressively recruit minorities for management-level positions. Such hotels see the careful building of a diverse workforce as a means not only of enhancing worker productivity but also of attracting a more diverse customer base since minorities are a growing segment of their market.

Because the pool of minority candidates for hotel manager positions is relatively small, many hotels and hotel chains are aggressively recruiting. At the Opryland Hotel, for example, the human resource department supports a wide range of special minority recruitment programs. One such program, called INROADS, gives minority college students the financial means to experience four years of hotel-management training. Upon completing such a college program, students are qualified for entry-level management positions in a hotel such as Opryland. Although participating in INROADS will not solve Opryland Hotel's minority recruitment problems in the short run, it will certainly increase the supply of minority candidates to fill the company's management positions in the longer run.

SOCIAL RESPONSIBILITY ACTIVITIES AND MANAGEMENT FUNCTIONS

This section considers social responsibility as a major organizational activity subject to the same management techniques used in other major organizational activities, such as production, personnel, finance, and marketing. Managers have known for some time that to achieve desirable results in these areas, they must be effective in planning, organizing, influencing, and controlling. Achieving social responsibility results is no different. The following sections discuss planning, organizing, influencing, and controlling social responsibility activities.

▶ PLANNING SOCIAL RESPONSIBILITY ACTIVITIES

Planning was defined in chapter 1 as the process of determining how the organization will achieve its objectives, or get where it wants to go. Planning social responsibility activities, then, involves determining how the organization will achieve its social responsibility objectives, or get where it wants to go in the area of social responsibility. The following sections discuss how the planning of social responsibility activities is related to the organization's overall planning process and how its social responsibility policy can be converted into action.

THE OVERALL PLANNING PROCESS The model presented in Figure 3.2 illustrates how social responsibility activities can be handled as part of the overall planning process of

| FIGURE 3.2 | Integration of social responsibility activities and planning activities |

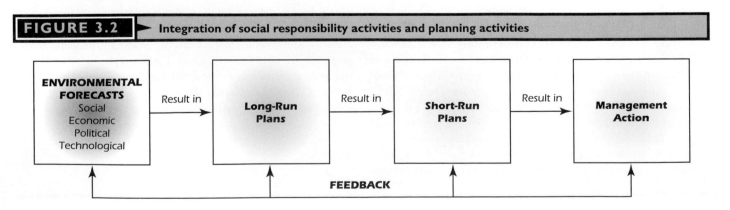

the organization. As shown in this figure, social trends forecasts should be performed within the organizational environment along with the more typically performed economic, political, and technological trends forecasts. Examples of social trends are prevailing and future societal attitudes toward water pollution, safe working conditions, and the national education system.[20] Each of the forecasts would influence the development of the organization's long-run plans, or plans for the more distant future, and short-run plans, or plans for the relatively near future.

CONVERTING ORGANIZATIONAL POLICIES ON SOCIAL RESPONSIBILITY INTO ACTION

A *policy* is a management tool that furnishes broad guidelines for channeling management thinking in specific directions. Managers should establish organizational policies in the social responsibility area just as they do in some of the more generally accepted areas, such as hiring, promotion, and absenteeism.

To be effective, social responsibility policies must be converted into appropriate action. As shown in Figure 3.3, this conversion involves three distinct and generally sequential phases.

► *Phase 1* consists of the recognition by top management that the organization has some social obligation. Top management then must formulate and communicate some policy about the acceptance of this obligation to all organization members.

► *Phase 2* involves staff personnel as well as top management. In this phase, top management gathers information related to meeting the social obligation accepted in phase 1. Staff personnel are generally involved at this point to give advice on technical matters related to meeting the accepted social obligation.

► *Phase 3* involves division management in addition to the organization personnel already involved from the first two phases. During this phase, top management strives to obtain the commitment of organization members to live up to the accepted social obligation and attempts to create realistic expectations about the effects of such a commitment on organizational productivity. Staff specialists encourage the responses within the organization necessary to meet the accepted social obligation properly. And division management commits resources and modifies existing procedures so that appropriate socially oriented activities can and will be performed within the organization.

BACK TO THE CASE

Larami's management should know that pursuing social responsibility objectives could be a major management activity within the company. Management must plan, organize, influence, and control Larami's social responsibility activities if the company is to be successful in reaching its objectives.

In terms of planning, management should determine how Larami can achieve its social responsibility objectives by incorporating social responsibility planning into the organization's overall planning process. That is, management should make social trends forecasts along with Larami's economic, political, and technological trends forecasts. In turn, these forecasts would influence the development of plans and, ultimately, the action taken by the company.

Management also must implement Larami's social responsibility policy. For example, management may decide to follow the policy of marketing the Super Soaker so that young people are better informed of the dangers of using this toy with undesirable chemicals like bleach or ammonia. To convert this policy into action, Larami's management should first communicate it to all organization members. Next, it should obtain additional knowledge of exactly how to market toys such as the Super Soaker in a way that encourages their safe use. Finally, management should make sure all organization members are committed to meeting this social responsibility objective and that lower-level managers are allocating funds and establishing appropriate opportunities for employees to help implement this policy.

FIGURE 3.3 ▶ Conversion of social responsibility policy into action

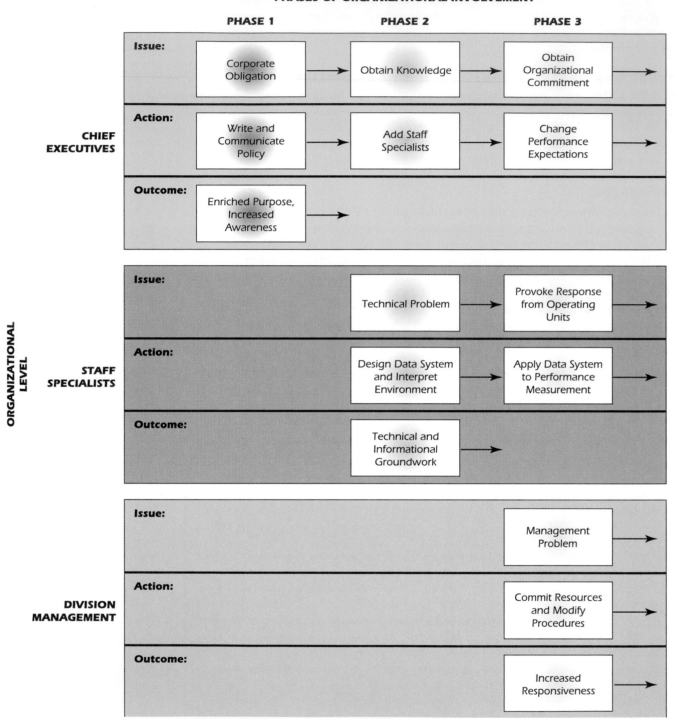

PHASES OF ORGANIZATIONAL INVOLVEMENT

ORGANIZING SOCIAL RESPONSIBILITY ACTIVITIES

Organizing was discussed in chapter 1 as the process of establishing orderly uses for all the organization's resources. These uses, of course, emphasize the attainment of management system objectives and flow naturally from management system plans. Correspondingly, organizing for social responsibility activities entails establishing for all organizational resources logical uses

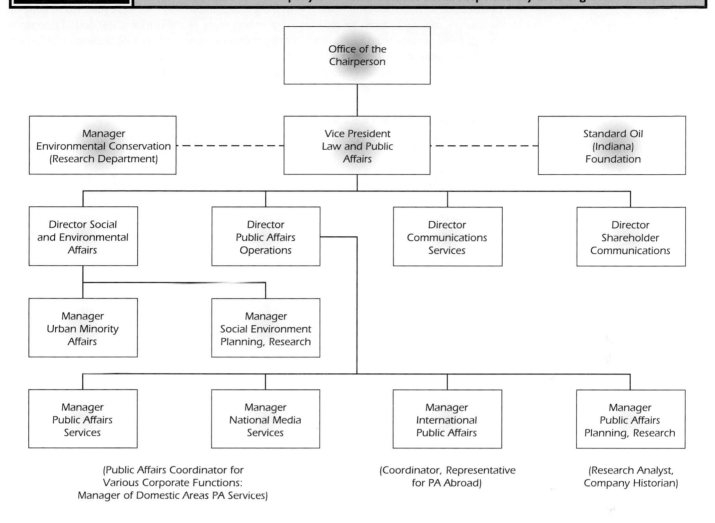

(Public Affairs Coordinator for
Various Corporate Functions:
Manager of Domestic Areas PA Services)

(Coordinator, Representative
for PA Abroad)

(Research Analyst,
Company Historian)

that emphasize the attainment of the organization's social objectives and that are consistent with its social responsibility plans.

Figure 3.4 shows how Standard Oil Company of Indiana decided to organize for the performance of its social responsibility activities. The vice president for law and public affairs has primary responsibility in the area of societal affairs and oversees the related activities of numerous individuals. This chart, of course, is intended only as an illustration of how a company might include its social responsibility area on its organization chart. Specific organizing in this area should always be tailored to the unique needs of a company.

► INFLUENCING INDIVIDUALS PERFORMING SOCIAL RESPONSIBILITY ACTIVITIES

Influencing was defined in chapter 1 as the management process of guiding the activities of organization members to help attain organizational objectives. As applied to the social responsibility area, then, influencing is the process of guiding the activities of organization members to help attain the organization's social responsibility objectives. More specifically, to influence appropriately in this area, managers must lead, communicate, motivate, and work with groups in ways that result in the attainment of the organization's social responsibility objectives.

Controlling, as discussed in chapter 1, is making things happen as they were planned to happen. To control, managers assess or measure what is occurring in the organization and, if necessary, change these occurrences in some way to make them conform to plans. Controlling in the area of social responsibility entails the same two major tasks. The following sections discuss various areas in which social responsibility measurement takes place and examine the social audit, a tool for determining and reporting progress in the attainment of social responsibility objectives.

AREAS OF MEASUREMENT Measurements to gauge organizational progress in reaching social responsibility objectives can be taken in any number of areas. The specific areas in which individual companies decide to take such measurements will vary according to the specific social responsibility objectives to be met. All companies, however, should probably take social responsibility measurements in at least the following four major areas:[21]

1. *The economic function area*—A measurement should be made of whether the organization is performing such activities as producing goods and services that people need, creating jobs for society, paying fair wages, and ensuring worker safety. This measurement gives some indication of the economic contribution the organization is making to society.

2. *The quality-of-life area*—The measurement of quality of life should focus on whether the organization is improving or degrading the general quality of life in society. Producing high-quality goods, dealing fairly with employees and customers, and making an effort to preserve the natural environment are all indicators that the organization is upholding or improving the general quality of life. As an example of degrading the quality of life, some people believe that cigarette companies, because they produce goods that can harm the health of society overall, are socially irresponsible.[22]

3. *The social investment area*—The measurement of social investment deals with the degree to which the organization is investing both money and human resources to solve community social problems. Here, the organization could be involved in assisting community organizations dedicated to education, charities, and the arts.

4. *The problem-solving area*—The measurement of problem solving should focus on the degree to which the organization deals with social problems, such as participating in long-range community planning and conducting studies to pinpoint social problems.

► ACROSS INDUSTRIES ◄ | Food Processing

SOCIAL AUDITS AT BEN & JERRY'S

Ben Cohen and Jerry Greenfield are chairman and vice-chairman, respectively, of Ben & Jerry's Homemade Inc., a business with $110 million in assets, 150 retail outlets, and about 700 employees. If you passed Ben and Jerry on the street, their sloppy T-shirts, portly figures, and worn jeans depict them as Grateful Dead roadies. Somewhat contrary to this image, Ben & Jerry's commands 39 percent of the U.S. marketplace for premium ice cream.

Ben & Jerry's has a great reputation for being a socially-responsible company. Management seems to include social responsibility issues in everything that it does. As an example, when recently looking for a site to build its new factory, the company was torn between building a new factory in its native Vermont to support strug-gling farmers or closer to the West Coast to avoid the pollution caused and energy expended by transporting the ice cream a couple of thousand miles. The Vermont site was eventually chosen.

Ben & Jerry's does not simply pay lip service to social and environmental concerns. The company invests in environmental concerns and then audits or follows up with environmental-impact reports on almost everything it does. Overall, management plans, organizes, influences, and controls for social responsibility activity. The company also donates a whopping 7.5 percent of its profits to charity. As you might suspect, following this emphasis on social responsibility creates a constant challenge for management to explain to stakeholders why making business decisions in such a fashion makes good business sense.

William D. Perez, president and CEO of S.C. Johnson & Son, competes in the CEO tricycle race during the 1998 United Way campaign kickoff in Racine, Wisconsin. Teams from various businesses competed in the corporate games to celebrate the start of the fund-raising season.

THE SOCIAL AUDIT: A PROGRESS REPORT A **social audit** is the process of measuring the present social responsibility activities of an organization to assess its performance in this area. The basic steps in conducting a social audit are monitoring, measuring, and appraising all aspects of an organization's social responsibility performance. Although some companies that pioneered concepts of social reporting, like General Electric, are still continuing their efforts, few companies, unfortunately, are joining their ranks.[23]

A **social audit** is the process of measuring the present social responsibility activities of an organization. It monitors, measures, and appraises all aspects of an organization's social responsibility performance.

BACK TO THE CASE

In addition to planning social responsibility activities at Larami, management must also organize, influence, and control them. To organize social responsibility activities, management must determine that all resources at Larami are used in an orderly fashion to carry out the company's social responsibility plans. It might be appropriate for management to develop an organization chart that shows the social responsibility area at Larami, along with corresponding job descriptions, responsibilities, and specifications for the positions on this chart.

To influence social responsibility activities, Larami's management must guide the activities of organization members in directions that will enhance the attainment of the company's social responsibility objectives. That is, management must lead, communicate, motivate, and work with groups in ways that encourage meeting those objectives.

To control, Larami's management must make sure that social responsibility activities within the company are happening as planned. If they are not, management should make changes to ensure that they will occur in the near future. One tool management can use to check Larami's progress in meeting social responsibilities is the social audit. With this audit, management can assess management system performance in such areas as economic functions, quality of life, social investment, and problem solving.

Although early in this chapter the point was made that there must be an open and honest involvement of both business and society for business to meet desirable social obligations, the bulk of the chapter has focused on what business should do in the area of social responsibility. This section emphasizes actions that society should take to help business accomplish its social responsibility objectives.

Jerry McAfee, chairman of the board and chief executive officer of Gulf Oil Corporation, says that although business has some responsibilities to society, society also has the following responsibilities to business:[24]

1. *Set rules that are clear and consistent*—This is one of the fundamental things that society, through government, ought to do. Although it may come as a surprise to some, I believe that industry actually needs an appropriate measure of regulation. By this I mean that the people of the nation, through their government, should set the bounds within which they want industry to operate.

    But the rules have got to be clear. Society must spell out clearly what it is it wants the corporations to do. The rules can't be vague and imprecise. Making the rules straight and understandable is what government is all about. One of my colleagues described his confusion when he read a section of a regulation that a federal regulatory representative had cited as the reason for a certain decision that had been made. "You're right," the official responded, "that's what the regulation says, but that's not what it means."

2. *Keep the rules technically feasible*—Business cannot be expected to do the impossible. Yet the plain truth is that many of today's regulations are unworkable. Environmental standards have on occasion exceeded those of Mother Nature. For example, the Rio Blanco shale-oil development in Colorado was delayed because air-quality standards, as originally proposed, required a higher quality of air than existed in the natural setting.

3. *Make sure the rules are economically feasible*—Society cannot impose a rule that society is not prepared to pay for because, ultimately, it is the people who must pay, either through higher prices or higher taxes, or both. Furthermore, the costs involved include not only those funds constructively spent to solve problems, but also the increasingly substantial expenditures needed to comply with red-tape requirements. Although the total cost of government regulation of business is difficult to compute, it is enormous. To cite an example, the Commission on Federal Paperwork estimated the energy industry's annual cost of complying with federal energy-reporting requirements at possibly $335 million per year.

4. *Make the rules prospective, not retroactive*—Nowadays, there is an alarming, distressing trend toward retroactivity, toward trying to force retribution for the past. Certain patterns of taxation and some of the regulations and applications of the law are indications of this trend.

    As a case in point, the U.S. government recently filed a multimillion-dollar lawsuit against Borden Chemicals & Plastics, a company operating in Louisiana and Illinois that produces various chemical products for construction, industrial, and agricultural markets.[25] The suit alleges that Borden released significant amounts of cancer-causing and other hazardous contaminants into the groundwater at its Louisiana complex. Borden maintains that recent changes to hazardous waste regulations are being applied retroactively to force the company to pay penalties for actions it took before the law existed. Borden charges that this type of action by the government violates the basic concepts of fairness and due process.

    It is counterproductive to make today's rules apply retroactively to yesterday's ball game.

5. *Make the rules goal-setting, not procedure-prescribing*—The proper way for the people of the nation, through their government, to tell their industries how to operate is to set the goals, set the fences, set the criteria, set the atmosphere, but don't tell us how to do it. Tell us what you want made, but don't tell us how to make it. Tell us the destination we're seeking, but don't tell us how to get there. Leave it to the ingenuity of American industry to devise the best, the most economical, the most efficient way to get there, for industry's track record in this regard has been good.

The study of ethics in management can be approached from many different directions. Perhaps the most practical approach is to view ethics as catalyzing managers to take socially responsible actions. The movement to include the study of ethics as a critical part of management education began in the 1970s, grew significantly in the 1980s, and is expected to continue growing into the next century. John Shad, chairman of the Securities and Exchange Commission during the 1980s when Wall Street was shaken by a number of insider trading scandals, recently pledged a $20 million trust fund to the Harvard Business School to create a curriculum in business ethics for MBA students. And television producer Norman Lear gave $1 million to underwrite the Business Enterprise Trust, which will give national awards to companies and "whistle blowers . . . who demonstrate courage, creativity, and social vision in the business world."[26]

The following sections define ethics, explain why ethical considerations are a vital part of management practices, discuss a workable code of business ethics, and present some suggestions for creating an ethical workplace.

►A DEFINITION OF ETHICS

The famous missionary physician and humanitarian Albert Schweitzer defined ethics as "our concern for good behavior. We feel an obligation to consider not only our own personal well-being, but also that of other human beings." This is similar to the precept of the Golden Rule: Do unto others as you would have them do unto you.[27]

In business, **ethics** can be defined as the capacity to reflect on values in the corporate decision-making process, to determine how these values and decisions affect various stakeholder groups, and to establish how managers can use these observations in day-to-day company management. Ethical managers strive for success within the confines of sound management practices that are characterized by fairness and justice.[28] Interestingly, using ethics as a major guide in making and evaluating business decisions is not only popular in the United States but also in the very different societies of India and Russia.[29]

►WHY ETHICS IS A VITAL PART OF MANAGEMENT PRACTICES

John F. Akers, former chairman of the board of IBM, recently said that it makes good business sense for managers to be ethical. Unless they are ethical, he believes, companies cannot be competitive in either national or international markets. According to Akers:[30]

> Ethics and competitiveness are inseparable. We compete as a society. No society anywhere will compete very long or successfully with people stabbing each other in the back; with people trying to steal from one another; with everything requiring notarized confirmation because you can't trust the other person; with every little squabble ending in litigation; and with government writing reams of regulatory legislation, trying business hand and foot to keep it honest.

Although ethical management practices may not be linked to specific indicators of financial profitability, there is no inevitable conflict between ethical practices and making a profit. As Akers' statement suggests, our system of competition presumes underlying values of truthfulness and fair dealing. The employment of ethical business practices can enhance overall corporate health in three important areas: productivity, stakeholder relations, and government regulation.

PRODUCTIVITY   The employees of a corporation constitute one major stakeholder group that is affected by management practices. When management is resolved to act ethically toward stakeholders, then employees will be positively affected. For example, a corporation may decide that business ethics requires it to make a special effort to ensure the health and welfare of its employees. To this end, many corporations have established Employee Advisory Programs (EAPs) to help employees with family, work, financial, or legal problems, or with mental illness or chemical dependency. These programs have even enhanced productivity in some corporations. For instance, Control Data Corporation found that its EAP reduced health costs and sick-leave usage significantly.[31]

Ethics is our concern for good behavior; our obligation to consider not only our own personal well-being but also that of other human beings.

Business ethics involves the capacity to reflect on values in the corporate decision-making process, to determine how these values and decisions affect various stakeholder groups, and to establish how managers can use these observations in day-to-day company management.

STAKEHOLDER RELATIONS The second area in which ethical management practices can enhance corporate health is by positively affecting "outside" stakeholders such as suppliers and customers. A positive public image can attract customers who view such an image desirable. For example, Johnson & Johnson, the world's largest maker of health-care products, is guided by a "Credo" addressed over 50 years ago by General Robert Wood Johnson to the company's employees and stockholders and members of its community (see Figure 3.5).

GOVERNMENT REGULATION The third area in which ethical management practices can enhance corporate health is in minimizing government regulation. Where companies are believed to be acting unethically, the public is more likely to put pressure on legislators and other government officials to regulate those businesses or to enforce existing regulations. For example, in 1995, Texas state legislators held public hearings on the operations of the psychiatric hospital industry. These hearings arose, at least partly, out of the perception that private psychiatric hospitals were not following ethical pricing practices.[32]

MANAGEMENT AND THE INTERNET — Better Business Bureaus Help Management Project Ethics Position on Internet

The Council of Better Business Bureaus, Inc. in Arlington, Virginia, is creating an "online ethical marketplace" by offering a digital seal of approval to online businesses. To earn the seal, a business must meet strict criteria for truthful advertising, quality service, and fair handling of customer complaints. Companies that have passed Better Business Bureau (BBB) checks may display a BBBOnLine seal at their World Wide Web sites. The online commerce of the companies will be monitored by the 150 Better Business Bureaus in the United States and Canada and sponsored by several companies including AT&T Corporation, Hewlett-Packard Company, and Netscape Communications Corporation.

To earn the BBBOnLine seal, companies must take a number of steps including submitting to a BBB site visit, participating in a self-regulated advertising review and changing any advertisements found to be wrong, agreeing to binding arbitration if customers request it, answering all complaints sent to the BBB, and possessing no significant ethical failures by management. After a company earns a seal, the challenge is not over. Any company that does not continue to meet BBBOnLine standards will lose its seal.

Because a sound ethical position makes good business sense in our modern society, many companies are interested in earning the BBBOnLine seal. Car rental giant Hertz Corporation said it will be among the first to earn a seal.

▶ A CODE OF ETHICS

A **code of ethics** is a formal statement that acts as a guide for making decisions and acting within an organization.

A **code of ethics** is a formal statement that acts as a guide for the ethics of how people within a particular organization should act and make decisions. Ninety percent of Fortune 500 firms, and almost half of all other firms, have ethical codes. Moreover, many organizations that do not already have an ethical code are giving serious consideration to developing one.[33]

Codes of ethics commonly address such issues as conflict of interest, competitors, privacy of information, gift giving, and giving and receiving political contributions or business. A code of ethics recently developed by Nissan of Japan, for example, barred all Nissan employees from accepting almost all gifts or entertainment from, or offering them to, business partners and government officials. The new code was drafted by Nissan President Yoshikazu Hanawa and sent to 300 major suppliers.[34]

According to a recent survey, the development and distribution of a code of ethics is perceived as an effective and efficient means of encouraging ethical practices within organizations.[35] The code of ethics that Johnson & Johnson drew up to guide company business practices (Figure 3.5) is distributed in its annual report, as well as to employees.

Managers cannot assume that merely because they have developed and distributed a code of ethics, organization members have all the guidelines they need to determine what is ethical and to act accordingly. It is impossible to cover all ethical and unethical conduct within an organization in one code. Managers should view codes of ethics as tools that must be evaluated

FIGURE 3.5 ▶ The Johnson & Johnson Credo

We believe our first responsibility is to the doctors, nurses, and patients, to mothers and all others who use our products and services.
In meeting their needs everything we do must be of high quality.
We must constantly strive to reduce our costs in order to maintain reasonable prices.
Customers' orders must be serviced promptly and accurately.
Our suppliers and distributors must have an opportunity to make a fair profit.

We are responsible to our employees, the men and women who work with us throughout the world.
Everyone must be considered as an individual.
We must respect their dignity and recognize their merit.
They must have a sense of security in their jobs.
Compensation must be fair and adequate, and working conditions clean, orderly and safe.
Employees must feel free to make suggestions and complaints.
There must be equal opportunity for employment, development, and advancement for those qualified.
We must provide competent management, and their actions must be just and ethical.

We are responsible to the communities in which we live and work and to the world community as well.
We must be good citizens — support good works and charities and bear our fair share of taxes.
We must encourage civic improvements and better health and education.
We must maintain in good order the property we are privileged to use, protecting the environment and natural resources.

Our final responsibility is to our stockholders.
Business must make a sound profit.
We must experiment with new ideas.
Research must be carried on, innovative programs developed and mistakes paid for.
New equipment must be purchased, new facilities provided, and new products launched.
Reserves must be created to provide for adverse times.
When we operate according to these principles, the stockholders should realize a fair return.

and refined periodically so that they will be comprehensive and usable guidelines for making ethical business decisions efficiently and effectively.

▶ CREATING AN ETHICAL WORKPLACE

Managers commonly strive to encourage ethical practices, not only to be morally correct, but also to gain whatever business advantage lies in projecting an ethical image to consumers and employees.[36] Creating, distributing, and continually improving a company's code of ethics is one common step managers can take to establish an ethical workplace.

Another step managers can take to create an ethical workplace is to set up a special office or department responsible for ensuring that the organization's practices are ethical. For example, management at Martin Marietta, a major supplier of missile systems and aircraft components, has established a corporate ethics office as a tangible sign to all employees that management is serious about encouraging ethical practices within the company (see Figure 3.6).

Another way to promote ethics in the workplace is to furnish organization members with appropriate training. General Dynamics, McDonnell Douglas, Chemical Bank, and American Can Company are examples of corporations that conduct training programs aimed at encouraging ethical practices within their organizations.[37] Such programs do not attempt to teach managers what is moral or ethical, but rather give them criteria they can use to help determine how ethical a certain action might be. Managers can feel confident that a potential action will

FIGURE 3.6 ▶ Martin Marietta's Corporate Ethics Statement

To ensure continuing attention to matters of ethics and standards on the part of all Martin Marietta employees, the Corporation has established the Corporate Ethics Office. The Director of Corporate Ethics is charged with responsibility for monitoring performance under this Code of Ethics and for resolving concerns presented to the Ethics Office.

Martin Marietta calls on every employee to report any violation or apparent violation of the Code. The Corporation strongly encourages employees to work with their supervisors in making such reports, and in addition, provides to employees the right to report violations directly to the Corporate Ethics Office. Prompt reporting of violations is considered to be in the best interest of all.

Employee reports will be handled in absolute confidence. No employee will suffer indignity or retaliation because of a report he or she makes to the Ethics Office. . . .

The Chairman of the Corporate Ethics Committee will be the President of the Corporation. The Committee will consist of five other employees of the Corporation, including representatives of the Corporation's operating elements, each of whom will be appointed by the Chairman of the Committee subject to the approval of the Audit and Ethics Committee of the Corporation's Board of Directors.

The Chairman of the Corporate Ethics Committee reports to the Audit and Ethics Committee of the Martin Marietta Corporation Board of Directors.

be considered ethical by the general public if it is consistent with one or more of the following standards:[38]

1. *The golden rule*—Act in a way you would expect others to act toward you.
2. *The utilitarian principle*—Act in a way that results in the greatest good for the greatest number of people.
3. *Kant's categorical imperative*—Act in such a way that the action taken under the circumstances could be a universal law, or rule, of behavior.

Although many consumer advocates believe all cigarette advertising is harmful, cigarette makers insist their messages have an appropriate audience. The furor over Joe Camel's apparent appeal to children resulted in the withdrawal of this advertising campaign.

4. *The professional ethic*—Take actions that would be viewed as proper by a disinterested panel of professional peers.
5. *The TV test*—Managers should always ask, "Would I feel comfortable explaining to a national TV audience why I took this action?"
6. *The legal test*—Is the proposed action or decision legal? Established laws are generally considered minimum standards for ethics.
7. *The four-way test*—Managers can feel confident that a decision is ethical if they can answer "yes" to the following questions: Is the decision truthful? Is it fair to all concerned? Will it build goodwill and better friendships? Will it be beneficial to all concerned?

Finally, managers can take responsibility for creating and sustaining conditions in which people are likely to behave ethically and for minimizing conditions in which people might be tempted to behave unethically. Two practices that commonly inspire unethical behavior in organizations are to give unusually high rewards for good performance and unusually severe punishments for poor performance. By eliminating such factors, managers can reduce any pressure on employees to perform unethically in organizations.[39]

BACK TO THE CASE

As indicated earlier, there is at present no legislation requiring Larami's management to modify its Super Soaker water gun to address the youth violence problem. Were such legislation to be considered, however, legislators could take certain reasonable steps to help Larami's management meet its social responsibilities in this area. For example, any laws enacted should be clear, consistent, and technically feasible to ensure both that Larami's management would know what actions were expected of the company and that the technology existed to help them take these actions.

Laws should also be economically feasible, and not be applied retroactively. That is, Larami's management should be able to obey the laws without going bankrupt and should not be penalized for what has happened in the past. Larami's management should also be given the flexibility to follow these laws to the company's best advantage. In other words, laws should not require management to follow specific procedures, but rather should set goals and allow the company to devise the most effective and efficient means for achieving those goals.

Ethical management is inclined to consider the well-being of other people. Assuming that Larami's management is ethical, then, it will seriously consider any reasonable action to aid society in its efforts to curb youth violence. If, however, Larami significantly reduces the overall appeal of its products to young customers because of management's desire to help curb violence among youths, employees, stockholders, and others who have a legitimate interest in the organization's success will probably consider management's actions to be unethical.

For updated information on the topics in this chapter, Internet exercises, links to related Internet sites, an interactive study guide, and more, visit our companion Web site at

http://www.prenhall.com/certo

Additional information can be found on the inside front and back covers of this text.

Reread the learning objectives below. Each objective is followed by questions. Answering these questions accurately will help you retain the most important concepts discussed in this chapter. After answering each question, check your answer against the answer key at the end of this chapter. (*Hint:* If you have any doubts regarding the correct response, consult the page number that follows the answer.)

Circle: From studying this chapter, I will attempt to acquire

1. An understanding of the term *corporate social responsibility.*

T F   **a.** According to Davis, since business has certain power over society, society can and must hold business responsible for social conditions that result from the exercise of this power.

a b c d e   **b.** Major social responsibility areas in which business can become involved include all of the following except: (a) urban affairs (b) consumer affairs (c) pollution control (d) natural resource conservation (e) all of the above are areas of potential involvement.

2. An appreciation of the arguments both for and against the assumption of social responsibilities by business.

T F   **a.** Some argue that since business is an influential component of society, it has the responsibility to help maintain and improve the overall welfare of society.

a b c d e   **b.** Milton Friedman argues that business cannot be held responsible for performing social responsibility activities. He does *not* argue that: (a) doing so has the potential to cause the demise of American business as we know it today (b) doing so is in direct conflict with the organizational objectives of business firms (c) doing so would cause the nation to creep toward socialism, which is inconsistent with American business philosophy (d) doing so is unethical because it requires business managers to spend money that rightfully belongs to the firm's investors (e) doing so ultimately would either reduce returns to the firm's investors or raise prices charged to consumers.

3. Useful strategies for increasing the social responsiveness of an organization.

a b c d e   **a.** When using the flowchart approach in social responsibility decision making, which one of the following questions is out of sequential order: (a) Can we afford this action? (b) Does a social responsibility actually exist? (c) Does the firm have a right to undertake this action? (d) Does an assessment of all interests indicate that the act is desirable? (e) Do benefits outweigh costs?

T F   **b.** The social obligation approach to performing social responsibility activities is concerned primarily with complying with existing legislation on the topic.

4. Insights on planning, organizing, influencing, and controlling social responsibility activities.

T F   **a.** Organizational policies should be established for social responsibility matters in the same manner as, for example, for personnel relations problems.

a b c d e   **b.** Companies should take social responsibility measurements in all of the following areas except: (a) economic utility area (b) economic function area (c) quality-of-life area (d) social investment area (e) problem-solving area.

5. A practical plan for how society can help business meet its social obligations.

T F   **a.** Ultimately, it is the citizens in a society who must finance the social responsibility activities of business by paying higher prices for goods and services or higher taxes or both.

a b c d e   **b.** The following is *not* one of the responsibilities that society has toward business, as listed by Jerry McAfee: (a) setting rules that are clear and concise (b) making rules prospective, not retroactive (c) making rules goal-setting, not procedure-prescribing (d) making rules subjective, not objective (e) making sure rules are economically feasible.

6. An understanding of the relationship between ethics and management.

T F   **a.** The utilitarian principle suggests that managers should act in such a way that an action taken under specific circumstances could be a universal law, or rule, of behavior.

a b c d e   **b.** Management might strive to encourage ethical behavior in organizations in order to: (a) be morally correct (b) gain a business advantage by having employees perceive their company as ethical (c) gain a business advantage by having customers perceive the company as ethical (d) avoid possible costly legal fees (e) all of the above.

T F   **c.** Once developed, a company's code of ethics generally does not have to be monitored or revised for at least two years.

T F   **d.** Some managers create a special "office of ethics" to show employees the critical importance of ethics.

CASE DISCUSSSION QUESTIONS

"Larami Corporation 'Super Soaks' Society?" (p. 47) and its related Back-to-the-Case sections were written to help you better understand the management concepts contained in this chapter. Answer the following discussion questions about this Introductory Case to enrich your understanding of the chapter content:

1. Do you think that Larami's managers have a responsibility to somehow modify the situation involving the Super Soaker so that this product does not encourage youth violence? Explain.

2. Assuming that Larami's managers have such a responsibility, under what conditions could they commit the company to assume that responsibility?

3. Assuming that Larami's managers have such a responsibility, when would it be relatively difficult for them to get the company to live up to it?

SKILLS EXERCISE: APPLYING ETHICAL STANDARDS TO A DECISION

In this chapter you studied seven standards that can be used to determine if management action is ethical. The Introductory Case in this chapter describes several issues that arose because Larami Corporation decided to make the Super Soaker. Use the seven standards to determine if the decision was ethical. Explain how you arrived at your determination.

◄ **ISSUES FOR REVIEW AND DISCUSSION** ►

1. Define *corporate social responsibility.*
2. Explain three of the major propositions in the Davis model of corporate social responsibility.
3. Summarize three arguments that support the pursuit of social responsibility objectives by business.
4. Summarize Milton Friedman's arguments against the pursuit of social responsibility objectives by business.
5. What is meant by the phrase *performing required social responsibility activities?*
6. What is meant by the phrase *voluntarily performing social responsibility activities?*
7. List five positive and five negative outcomes a business might experience as a result of performing social responsibility activities.
8. What is the difference between social responsibility and social responsiveness?
9. Discuss the decision-making process that can help managers increase the social responsiveness of their organizations.
10. In your own words, explain the main differences among Sethi's three approaches to meeting social responsibilities.
11. Which of Sethi's approaches has the most potential for increasing the social responsiveness of a management system? Explain.
12. What is the overall relationship between the four main management functions and the performance of social responsibility activities by business?
13. What suggestions does this chapter make concerning planning social responsibility activities?
14. Describe the process of turning social responsibility policy into action.
15. How do organizing and influencing social responsibility activities relate to planning social responsibility activities?
16. List and define four main areas in which any management system can take measurements to control social responsibility activities.
17. What is a social audit? How should the results of a social audit be used by management?
18. How can society help business meet its social responsibilities?
19. What is the relationship between ethics and social responsibility?
20. Explain how managers can try to judge if a particular action is ethical.
21. What steps can managers take to make their organizations more ethical workplaces?

◄ **ACTION SUMMARY ANSWER KEY** ►

1. **a.** T, p. 48
   b. e, p. 50
2. **a.** T, p. 50
   b. c, pp. 50–51

3. **a.** a, pp. 55–56
   b. T, p. 57
4. **a.** T, p. 60
   b. a, p. 62

5. **a.** T, p. 64
   b. d, p. 64

6. **a.** F, p. 65
   b. e, p. 65
   c. F, p. 66
   d. T, p. 67

Corporate social responsibility can be defined as the managerial obligation to take action to protect and improve both the welfare of society and the interests of the organization. In recent years, the public has placed more importance on corporate social responsibility, and businesses that violate this responsibility have suffered in both the courts and the marketplace.

The dilemma some companies confront in trying to meet their social responsibilities without sacrificing corporate objectives is exemplified by Dow Corning's legal problems over the safety of the company's silicone breast implants. Dow Corning introduced silicone breast-implant products in 1963, and by 1984, the company was enjoying $2.2 billion in annual sales of its line of silicone products. In 1984, however, the company was sued for fraudulently misrepresenting its product, and lost the case. This was only the first of many such suits Dow Corning lost. So far, the company's silicone implant business has cost it more than $1 billion in legal expenses, plunging it into bankruptcy and exposing its parent companies, Dow Chemical Company and Corning, Inc., to legal action as well.

John Swanson was 30 years old when he went to work for Dow Corning in 1966. He moved from the advertising to the industrial marketing department, and then went on to write speeches for CEOs William C. Goggin and Jack S. Luddington. In the mid-1970s, as corporations came under attack for unethical practices both at home and abroad, Swanson was given the task of creating an ethics committee to help Dow Corning measure its social responsibility.

Swanson and his new committee decided to promote the belief that the corporation should behave as if it were constantly in the public view. Meetings were held with managers who were part of Dow Corning's global operations in order to reinforce this decision and to determine ways to implement it. Implementation was considered so successful that by 1984 Swanson was a nationally recognized expert on the subject of corporate ethics. Unfortunately, Swanson's position was undermined when his superiors proved unwilling to allow the business ethics he preached to take precedence over the corporation's profit objectives in the matter of silicone implants.

Swanson was not a passive bystander during investigations into the ethics of Dow Corning's marketing of its silicone implants. In 1974, his own wife, Colleen, had had breast implants, and almost immediately afterward had developed illnesses for which no doctor could find a cause. It was 15 years after the surgery before Colleen Swanson learned of another woman who had also had the Dow implants and was suffering from similar maladies. Eventually, Colleen Swanson had the breast implants removed and filed suit against Dow Corning.

The next chapter in the story occurred in 1989, when the Food and Drug Administration was sued by a consumer group demanding to know the results of studies the FDA had done on the silicone gel used in breast implants. It became apparent that breast implants were not as strictly regulated by the FDA as other health-related products. After several reports concerning the effects of faulty implants appeared in the media, the adverse publicity prompted congressional hearings into the matter.

In December 1990, John Swanson received a memo alleging that some Dow Corning executives were attempting to destroy damaging internal reports on the complications of implant surgery. After an unsuccessful attempt to force the company to investigate these charges, Swanson resigned from Dow Corning to become an ethics consultant.

In 1991, a court awarded $7.3 million to a woman who had sued Dow Corning for damages resulting from her breast implants, and the verdict was upheld on appeal. In January 1992, Dow Corning announced that it was declaring a 45-day moratorium on the sale of breast implants, and in March of that year, the company formally ceased production of the implants. Three years later, a court determined that the corporation was unable to pay the estimated $4.23 billion needed to settle all the lawsuits that had been against it, and the company declared bankruptcy. Other health-product manufacturers have also had to contend with a barrage of lawsuits concerning silicone implants. Bristol-Myers Squibb, for example, has spent millions of dollars defending itself. Two other companies named in these lawsuits, Baxter Healthcare and 3M, have also expended large amounts on legal defense.

An interesting issue raised by this ethics struggle is whether so-called mass-tort lawsuits are valid. Such lawsuits are filed by hundreds—even thousands—of plaintiffs charging a company or product with the same violations. They often arise, as in the Dow Corning scenario, after a large settlement is awarded to one plaintiff—what was a trickle of lawsuits becomes an avalanche as the publicity about the defective product snowballs. It is then advantageous—and profitable to lawyers—to combine many suits into one mass-tort lawsuit.

Dow Corning—along with many other companies that fear being bankrupted by a mass-tort action—has pressed lawmakers to pass tort reform measures that will replace mass torts with "common issue" trials. These types of trials would set a limit on a company's liability.

Whatever the outcome of tort reform efforts, many people believe the legal issues in such cases as Dow Corning's are beside the point. For them, the issue is ethics.

QUESTIONS

1. What should a corporation learn from the experiences of Dow Corning? Why was setting up an ethics committee insufficient to monitor social responsibility?

2. How might Dow Corning argue its case using Milton Friedman's argument against corporations assuming social responsibility?

3. Had Dow Corning performed a social audit, what issues would have been raised by the audit and what outcome would have been likely?

4. What was the final outcome of Dow Corning's behavior? Role-play a conversation among Dow managers in 1963, when the company introduced silicone implants. Could you have convinced them to drop the project? Explain.

SMALL BUSINESS 2000

Corporate social responsibility and ethical business practices are characteristics of good business. To Judy Jacobsen, the founder and owner of Madison Park Greeting Card Company, it is not just good business—it pays off too, and the pay-off is not only in financial profits. Involvement in her community was one of the criteria that led to Judy being named Small Business Person of the Year for the State of Washington by the U.S. Small Business Administration.

Corporate social responsibility can be viewed at various levels ranging from simple legal compliance to making social contribution a key part of a company's philosophy and image. Madison Park Greeting believes in the value of being active in its community. Managers understand that when the company gets involved, the employees, the company, and the community stand to gain.

Judy Jacobsen sets the tone for the company's approach to working with people. She has a fundamental concern for meeting the financial obligations required to sustain and grow a viable company. Once that goal is met, the focus turns to the responsibility of the people who work in the company. Even in tackling its financial goals, a commitment to the well-being of the staff and employees of the company motivate them to get the job done.

As a potential customer of Madison Park Greeting Card Company, you might think that a company that shows such concern for its employees and its community might show the same concern for you. Madison Park Greeting may benefit from its role in the community and its value system. It is not uncommon for companies to seek out suppliers who share their interest in relation to a particular business practice or public issue. Consider the emphasis that is now placed on using recycled paper in packaging, or the emphasis that is placed on products that are less harmful to the environment. Madison Park Greeting, while helping its community, is also helping itself.

QUESTIONS

1. In this chapter, you have learned about various measures which can be used to evaluate a company's social responsibility activities. Evaluate the performance of Madison Park Greeting Card Company in the areas of *quality-of-life and social investment.*

2. Judy Jacobsen discussed the value of people many times and in many ways. She says that if she had to choose between profit or people, she would pick people first. Do you agree with this perspective? Why or why not?

3. Madison Park Greeting Card Company has a professional sales and distribution staff. It also has a special sales program for high school students. This special program takes time and money to run. Why do you think the company does it? What benefit does the company get from doing this?

Managing in the Global Arena

STUDENT LEARNING OBJECTIVES

From studying this chapter, I will attempt to acquire

1. An understanding of international management and its importance to modern managers

2. An understanding of what constitutes a multinational corporation

3. Insights concerning the risk involved in investing in international operations

4. Insights about those who work in multinational corporations

5. Knowledge about managing multinational corporations

6. Knowledge about managing multinational organizations versus transnational organizations

7. An understanding of how ethics and the preparation of expatriates relate to managing internationally

CHAPTER OUTLINE

Introductory Case: *Baskin-Robbins Brings U.S. Ice Cream to Vietnam*

MANAGING ACROSS THE GLOBE: WHY?

FUNDAMENTALS OF INTERNATIONAL MANAGEMENT

CATEGORIZING ORGANIZATIONS BY INTERNATIONAL INVOLVEMENT
Defining the Multinational Corporation

Ethics Spotlight: *U.S. Companies Send Hazardous Waste to Mexico*
Complexities of Managing the Multinational Corporation

Management and the Internet: *Virgin Atlantic Airways Bows to U.S. Law*
Risk and the Multinational Corporation
The Workforce of Multinational Corporations

MANAGEMENT FUNCTIONS AND MULTINATIONAL CORPORATIONS
Planning in Multinational Corporations

Across Industries: *Transportation Equipment— American Racing Exports to Build Business*
Organizing Multinational Corporations
Influencing People in Multinational Corporations
Controlling Multinational Corporations
Transnational Organizations

INTERNATIONAL MANAGEMENT: SPECIAL ISSUES
Maintaining Ethics in International Management
Preparing Expatriates for Foreign Assignments

People Spotlight: Helping Expatriates to Adjust

BASKIN-ROBBINS BRINGS U.S. ICE CREAM TO VIETNAM

REMINDER: THE INTRODUCTORY CASE WRAP-UP (P. 98) CONTAINS DISCUSSION QUESTIONS AND A SKILLS EXERCISE TO FURTHER ILLUSTRATE THE APPLICATION OF CHAPTER CONCEPTS TO THIS VIGNETTE.

Baskin-Robbins, an ice cream company based in Glendale, California, has a strong tradition of high-quality products. Rather than rest on its laurels, however, the company has taken several very aggressive steps to broaden its business in a very competitive marketplace.

One of these steps is the recent unveiling of the new Baskin-Robbins line of "Incredibles." These are ice cream cakes produced through a partnership with the Sara Lee Corporation. Baskin-Robbins has invested nearly $8 million in advertising for this new product.

In an effort to grow the company, Baskin-Robbins' management is also expanding sales at nontraditional store sites. For example, the company is exploring the sale of its new Yogurt Gone Crazy hardpack in coffee shops like Starbucks Coffee. It is also testing ice cream fountains in restaurants like Denny's and Miami Subs.

Baskin-Robbins' most aggressive attempt to grow its business, however, involves a business venture in Southeast Asia. By opening a Baskin-Robbins outlet in Ho Chi Minh City, the company brought American ice cream back to Vietnam. Baskin-Robbins was the first fast-food company to open a store in Vietnam after President Clinton lifted a 19-year economic embargo of that country.

According to the manager of the new Vietnamese outlet, Bui Vi Hoanh, the Baskin-Robbins store is attracting about 100 customers a day. This is a significant number of customers considering a single-scoop cone sells for 18,000 dong (about $1.60), which is more than a day's wage for the average Vietnamese factory worker. A double-scoop sundae costs about three days' wages.

Ho Chi Minh City was chosen for the store site because it is the most prosperous city in Vietnam and the country's chief tourist destination. Moreover, the older residents of the city remember American ice cream from

In order to grow its business in the international market, Baskin-Robbins built new stores like this one in Ho Chi Minh City—thus bringing American ice cream to Vietnam after an absence of 19 years.

the 1960s and 1970s, when thousands of U.S. soldiers were stationed there during the Vietnam War.

The Baskin-Robbins store in Vietnam is risky but potentially profitable. Only the future will tell if Baskin-Robbins has made a sound management decision.

What's Ahead

The Introductory Case illustrates several aggressive steps that Baskin-Robbins' management has taken to maintain the company's competitiveness. The boldest of these steps is opening a store in Vietnam. This move toward expanding the company's international presence is consistent with a worldwide trend in corporate management. This chapter provides insights about the challenge that firms like Baskin-Robbins face in expanding internationally and will give you an overview of the international management arena. The major topics covered are the following:

1. The need to manage internationally
2. The multinational corporation and its workforce
3. Management functions and multinational corporations
4. Transnational organizations
5. Special issues in international management

MANAGING ACROSS THE GLOBE: WHY?

Most U.S. companies see great opportunities in the international marketplace today.[1] Although the U.S. population is growing steadily but slowly, the population in many other countries is exploding. For example, it has been estimated that in 1990, China, India, and Indonesia together had more than 2 billion people, or 40 percent of the world's population.[2] Obviously, such countries offer a strong profit potential for aggressive businesspeople throughout the world.

This potential does not come without serious risk, however. Managers who attempt to manage in a global context face formidable challenges. Some of these challenges are the cultural differences among workers from different countries, different technology levels from country to country, and laws and political systems that can vary immensely from one nation to the next.

The remaining sections of this chapter deal with the intricacies of managing in a global context by emphasizing the following:

1. Fundamentals of international management
2. Categories of organizations by international involvement
3. Comparative management (with an emphasis on Japanese management)

FUNDAMENTALS OF INTERNATIONAL MANAGEMENT

International management is the performance of management activities across national borders.

International management is simply the performance of management activities across national borders. It entails reaching organizational objectives by extending management activities to include an emphasis on organizations in foreign countries. The trend toward increased international management, or *globalization,* is now widely recognized. The primary question for most firms is not *whether* to globalize, but *how* and *how fast* to do so and how to measure global progress over time.[3]

International management can take several different forms, from simply analyzing and fighting competition in foreign markets to establishing a formal partnership with a foreign company. AMP, Inc., for example, has been vigorously fighting competition in a foreign market. This company, a manufacturer of electrical parts, headquartered in Harrisburg, Pennsylvania, has achieved outstanding success by gaining significant control over a portion of its multinational market. The company built factories in 17 countries because experience showed management that competitors could best be beaten in foreign markets if AMP actually produced products within those markets. A message recently sent to AMP stockholders by company president William J. Hudson indicates that the company is continuing to make good progress in the international arena. Hudson has promised to persist in his efforts to develop AMP into a "globe-able" organization.[4]

An example of a formal international partnership involves Toshiba Corporation and Time Warner. Toshiba Corporation, a Japanese computer manufacturer, and Time Warner, a communications conglomerate that owns a major Hollywood film studio, recently formed a partnership to develop a new technology for presenting movies to consumers. This technology is

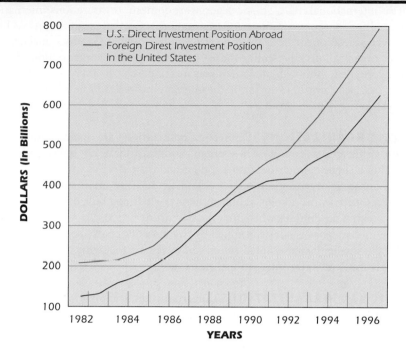

FIGURE 4.1 ▶ **U.S. investment in foreign countries versus foreign investment in the United States**

called digital video disc (DVD). In a natural division of labor, Toshiba will focus on making the hardware needed to deliver the new technology, and Time Warner will provide the movies to be presented on DVD. Both companies hope the partnership will give them an edge over formidable competitors like Sony.[5]

The notable trend that already exists in the United States and other countries toward developing business relationships in and with foreign countries is expected to accelerate even more in the future. As Figure 4.1 illustrates, U.S. investment in foreign countries and investment by foreign countries in the United States has grown since 1982 and is expected to continue growing, with only slight slowdowns or setbacks in recessionary periods. As an interesting side note, in the 1990s the growth rate of foreign investment in developing countries like India and China has increased, while the growth rate of foreign investment in the United States, Japan, and the European Community has slowed somewhat.[6] Information of this nature has spurred both management educators and practicing managers to insist that an understanding of international management is necessary for a thorough contemporary understanding of the fundamentals of management.[7]

BACK TO THE CASE

As you read in the Introductory Case, Baskin-Robbins is a U.S. organization that now operates in the global arena. In opening a store in Ho Chi Minh City, Baskin-Robbins, in essence, expanded management activities across the U.S. border into Vietnam. Given the international trend toward greater foreign investments, Baskin-Robbins is likely to continue to emphasize worldwide expansion, and foreign companies will attempt to compete in Baskin-Robbins' market in the United States. It is only a matter of time, for example, until companies like Delta Dairy, an ice cream maker based in Athens, Greece, start expanding to the United States.

A number of different categories have evolved to describe the extent to which organizations are involved in the international arena. These categories are domestic organizations, international organizations, multinational organizations, and transnational or global organizations. As Figure 4.2 suggests, this categorization format actually describes a continuum of international involvement, with domestic organizations representing the least and transnational organizations the most international involvement. Although the format may not be perfect, it is very useful for explaining primary ways in which companies operate in the international realm.[8] The following sections describe these categories in more detail.

A domestic organization is a company that essentially operates within a single country.

DOMESTIC ORGANIZATIONS **Domestic organizations** are organizations that essentially operate within a single country. These organizations normally not only acquire necessary resources within a single country but also sell their goods or services within that same country. Although domestic organizations may occasionally make an international sale or acquire some needed resource from a foreign supplier, the overwhelming bulk of their business activity takes place within the country where they are based.

Although this category is not determined by size, most domestic organizations today are quite small. Even smaller business organizations, however, are following the trend and becoming increasingly involved in the international arena.

An international organization is a company primarily based within a single country but having continuing, meaningful transactions in other countries.

INTERNATIONAL ORGANIZATIONS **International organizations** are organizations that are primarily based within a single country but have continuing, meaningful international transactions—such as making sales and/or purchases of materials—in other countries. Nu Horizons is an example of a small company that can be classified as an international organization. This distributor of electronic goods made mainly by some 40 U.S. manufacturers has about 5,000 customers and is the fastest-growing company in Melville, New York. Nu Horizons is an international organization because an important part of its business is to act as the primary North American distributor of electronic components made by Japan's NIC Components Corp.[9]

In summary, international organizations are more extensively involved in the international arena than are domestic organizations, but less so than either multinational or transnational organizations.

MULTINATIONAL ORGANIZATIONS: THE MULTINATIONAL CORPORATION

The *multinational organization,* commonly called the *multinational corporation (MNC),* represents the third level of international involvement. This section of the text defines the multinational corporation, discusses the complexities involved in managing such a corporation, describes the risks associated with its operations, explores the diversity of the multinational workforce, and explains how the major management functions relate to managing the multinational corporation.

▶ DEFINING THE MULTINATIONAL CORPORATION

The term *multinational corporation* first appeared in American dictionaries around 1970, and has since been defined in various ways in business publications and textbooks. For the pur-

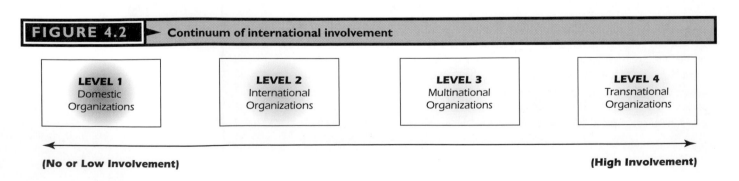

FIGURE 4.2 ▶ **Continuum of international involvement**

| **LEVEL 1** Domestic Organizations | **LEVEL 2** International Organizations | **LEVEL 3** Multinational Organizations | **LEVEL 4** Transnational Organizations |

(No or Low Involvement) — **(High Involvement)**

TABLE 4.1	▶ The 10 Largest U.S. Multinationals			
1995 Rank	Company	Foreign Revenue as Percent of Total	Foreign Profit as Percent of Total Profits	Foreign Assets as Percent of Total Assets
1	Exxon	77.8	76.5	59.0
2	General Motors	29.0	53.9	26.9
3	IBM	62.8	85.4	55.3
4	Mobil	66.4	69.2	61.7
5	Ford Motor	30.5	14.0	28.4
6	Texaco	56.1	69.2	46.5
7	Citicorp	59.3	57.9	57.6
8	Philip Morris Co.	34.2	24.3	36.2
9	Chevron	45.6	124.0	44.5
10	General Electric	25.5	13.4	26.0

poses of this text, a **multinational corporation** is a company that has significant operations in more than one country. Essentially, a multinational corporation is an organization that is involved in doing business at the international level. It carries out its activities on an international scale that disregards national boundaries, and it is guided by a common strategy from a corporation center.[10]

A **multinational corporation (MNC)** is a company that has significant operations in more than one country.

A list of the 10 largest multinationals in this country (see Table 4.1) includes 4 corporations whose major business is energy: Exxon, Mobil, Texaco, and Chevron. As the table implies, multinational organizations have significant foreign revenues, related profits, and foreign assets.

A list of the 12 largest foreign investments in the United States (see Table 4.2) includes an investment in Shell Oil by Royal Dutch/Shell Oil, an investment in BP America by British Petroleum, and an investment in MCI Communications by British Telecommunications. Other significant investments on the list include those in popular companies like Burger King, Pillsbury, Sony Electronics, Stop & Shop, Maybelline, and Citgo Petroleum. Foreign investment in the United States has reached a record high in recent years and will almost certainly continue to grow significantly in the future.

Neil H. Jacoby explains that companies go through six stages to reach the highest degree of multinationalization. As Table 4.3 indicates, multinational corporations can range from slightly multinationalized organizations that simply export products to a foreign country to

BFW, a small family-owned marketer of high-quality surgical and examination headlights and light sources in Kentucky, has expanded into Italy with the help of its distribution team of Levi Medica, pictured here with BFW president Lynn Cooper (standing, sixth from the left).

| TABLE 4.2 | ► The 12 Largest Foreign Investments in the United States |

1995 Rank	Foreign Investor	Country	US Investment	% Owned	Industry	Revenue ($mil)	Net Income ($mil)	Assets ($mil)
1	Royal Dutch/ Shell Group	Netherlands/ UK	Shell Oil	100	energy, chemicals	24,298	1,520.0	27,021
2	British Petroleum	UK	BP America	100	energy	16,206	−486.2	17,252
3	Grand Metropolitan	UK	Burger King	100	fast food	8,400	NA	NA
			Pillsbury	100	food processing	4,998	NA	NA
			Heublein	100	wines and spirits	1,265	NA	NA
			Pearle	100	eye care	354	NA	NA
			Other companies	100	wines and spirits	446	NA	NA
						15,463		
4	British Telecommunications	UK	MCI Communications	20	telecommunications	15,265	548.0	19,301
5	Sony	Japan	Sony Music Entertainment	100	music entertainment			
			Sony Pictures Entertainment	100	movies	14,141	NA	NA
			Sony Electronics	100	consumer electronics			
6	Toyota Motor	Japan	Toyota Motor Mfg	100	automotive	7,300E	NA	NA
			New United Motor Mfg	50	automotive	4,350E	NA	NA
	Nippondenso	Japan	Denso International America	100	auto parts	2,300	NA	NA
						13,950		
7	Matsushita Electric Industrial	Japan	MCA	20	entertainment	5,772	NA	9,997
			Matsushita Elec Corp America	100	electronics	7,300	NA	NA
						13,072		
8	Royal Ahold	Netherlands	Stop & Shop Companies	23	supermarkets	4,116	68.6	2,467
			BI-LO	100	supermarkets	2,511	NA	NA
			First National Supermarkets	100	supermarkets	2,462	NA	NA
			Tops Markets	100	supermarkets	1,719	NA	NA
			Other companies	100	supermarkets	1,726	NA	NA
						12,534		
9	Nestlé SA	Switzerland	Nestlé USA	100	food processing			
			Alcon Laboratories	100	pharmaceuticals	9,719	NA	NA
	L'Oréal	France	Cosmair	100	cosmetics	1,500	NA	NA
			Maybelline	100	cosmetics	368	17.1	215
						11,587		
10	Unilever NV	Netherlands						
	Unilever Plc	UK	Unilever United States	100	food processing, personal prod	9,600	NA	NA
			Helene Curtis Industries	100	personal products	1,255	8.0	612
						10,855		
11	Petróleos de Venezuela	Venezuela	Citgo Petroleum	100	refining, marketing	10,553	136.3	4,924
12	Tengelmann	Germany	Great A&P Tea	54	supermarkets	10,101	57.2	2,877

Note: Some foreign investors on the list own U. S. companies indirectly through companies in italics.
NA: Not available.

TABLE 4.3	► Six Stages of Multinationalization				
Stage 1	Stage 2	Stage 3	Stage 4	Stage 5	Stage 6
Exports its products to foreign countries	Establishes sales organizations abroad	Licenses use of its patterns and know-how to foreign firms that make and sell its products	Establishes foreign manufacturing facilities	Multinationalizes management from top to bottom	Multinationalizes ownership of corporate stock

highly multinationalized organizations that have some of their owners in other countries. According to Alfred M. Zeien, the chief executive officer of Gillette Company, it can take up to 25 years to build a management team with the requisite skills, experience, and abilities to mold an organization into a highly developed multinational company.[11]

In general, the larger the organization, the greater the likelihood it participates in international operations of some sort. Companies such as General Electric, Lockheed, and DuPont, which have annually accumulated over $1 billion from export sales, support this generalization. There are exceptions, however. BRK Electronics, for example, a small firm in Aurora, Illinois, has won a substantial share of world sales of smoke detectors. By setting up local distributors in Italy, France, and England, BRK caused its export sales to climb from $124,000 in one year to $4 million five years later.[12] As noted earlier, an increasing number of smaller organizations are undertaking international operations.

ETHICS SPOTLIGHT ◄ U.S. Companies Send Hazardous Waste to Mexico

The export of hazardous wastes by companies in more developed countries to companies in less developed countries is becoming commonplace. For example, U.S. companies commonly send large quantities of such waste to Mexico for disposal by Mexican companies. Although accidents related to this business could cause extensive environmental damage and even result in a loss of human life, useful international legislation governing the export of hazardous waste is virtually nonexistent.

Perhaps partly because of the absence of such legislation, there is much public controversy over the ethics of the international trade in the disposal of hazardous wastes. Citizens of underdeveloped countries have demonstrated against the disposal of hazardous wastes from developed countries in their areas, insisting that they have a right to a livable environment. They charge that dumping is a form of racism and should be halted immediately.

Managers involved in international hazardous waste disposal should ensure that the interests of domestic and foreign societies are protected along with the interests of their organizations. Although providing such protection is largely voluntary at this time, the evolution of legislation in this area will undoubtedly mandate protections in the future. To cope with the problem, the Japanese have drawn up a 100-year plan, called *New Earth 21*, that aims at developing ecologically efficient technology that will provide clean energy to the world.

►COMPLEXITIES OF MANAGING THE MULTINATIONAL CORPORATION

From the discussion so far, it should be clear that international management and domestic management are quite different. Classic management thought indicates that international management differs from domestic management because it involves operating:[13]

1. Within different national sovereignties
2. Under widely disparate economic conditions
3. Among people living within different value systems and institutions

Since 1987, Japan's Matsushita Electrical Industrial Co. has opened 13 new subsidiaries in the nation of Malaysia. The company has shown its sensitivity to the large Muslim segment of its workforce by providing special prayer rooms in each plant and permitting two prayer sessions during each shift.

4. In places experiencing the industrial revolution at different times
5. Often over greater geographical distance
6. In national markets varying greatly in population and area

Figure 4.3 shows some of the more important management implications of these six variables and some of the relationships among them. Consider, for example, the first variable. Different national sovereignties generate different legal systems. In turn, each legal system implies a unique set of rights and obligations involving property, taxation, antitrust (control of monopoly) law, corporate law, and contract law. In turn, these rights and obligations require the firm to acquire the skills necessary to assess the international legal considerations. Such skills are very different from those required in a purely domestic setting.

MANAGEMENT AND THE INTERNET | **Virgin Atlantic Airways Bows to U.S. Law**

By its nature, the World Wide Web allows management to cross national borders quickly, easily, and at a relatively low cost. Through the Web, management can readily provide information globally about issues like company operations, new products being developed, and even employment opportunities. As a result, many managers are opting to use the World Wide Web as one facet of conducting their international business.

There are, however, newly developing legal considerations to think about when conducting business on the Internet. Internet information received from a foreign company is subject to the laws of the recipient's country. If information received via the Internet violates the morals or laws of the recipient country, penalties, fines, damages, and conceivably a ban on the foreign company doing business are all possible. As an example, the British carrier Virgin Atlantic Airways recently announced over the Internet that a 21-day advance-purchase ticket fare between Newark and London was $499 on weekdays during certain travel periods. In a separate section of its site, Virgin Atlantic advised consumers to check with reservations or a local travel agent for the latest fare and availability, and any taxes, charges, or restrictions. The U.S. Department of Transportation fined the British company $14,000 for failing to disclose clearly that a tax of $38.91 applied to each ticket. Whether or not the announcement met legal standards in Great Britain, and regardless of where Virgin Atlantic's Internet server was located, the U.S. government successfully asserted jurisdiction over advertising that could be downloaded to a personal computer in the United States.

The World Wide Web undoubtedly presents new international opportunities for modern managers. Accompanying these opportunities, however, are risks and complexities related to established foreign laws.

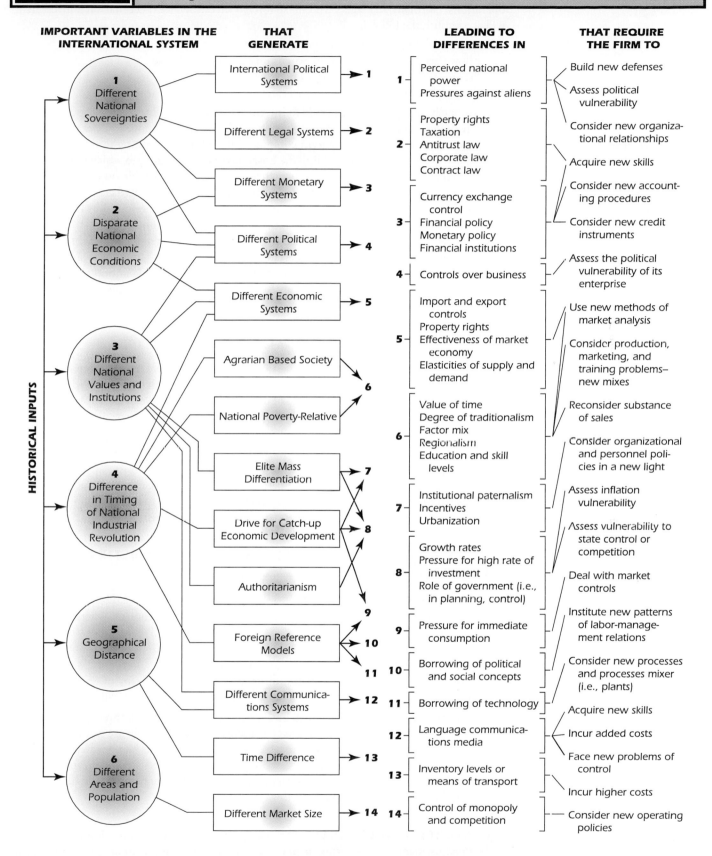

IMPORTANT VARIABLES IN THE INTERNATIONAL SYSTEM

HISTORICAL INPUTS

1 Different National Sovereignties

2 Disparate National Economic Conditions

3 Different National Values and Institutions

4 Difference in Timing of National Industrial Revolution

5 Geographical Distance

6 Different Areas and Population

THAT GENERATE

International Political Systems → 1

Different Legal Systems → 2

Different Monetary Systems → 3

Different Political Systems → 4

Different Economic Systems → 5

Agrarian Based Society

National Poverty-Relative

→ 6

Elite Mass Differentiation → 7

Drive for Catch-up Economic Development → 8

Authoritarianism

→ 9

Foreign Reference Models → 10 → 11

Different Communications Systems → 12

Time Difference → 13

Different Market Size → 14

LEADING TO DIFFERENCES IN

1 — Perceived national power
Pressures against aliens

2 — Property rights
Taxation
Antitrust law
Corporate law
Contract law

3 — Currency exchange control
Financial policy
Monetary policy
Financial institutions

4 — Controls over business

5 — Import and export controls
Property rights
Effectiveness of market economy
Elasticities of supply and demand

6 — Value of time
Degree of traditionalism
Factor mix
Regionalism
Education and skill levels

7 — Institutional paternalism
Incentives
Urbanization

8 — Growth rates
Pressure for high rate of investment
Role of government (i.e., in planning, control)

9 — Pressure for immediate consumption

10 — Borrowing of political and social concepts

11 — Borrowing of technology

12 — Language communications media

13 — Inventory levels or means of transport

14 — Control of monopoly and competition

THAT REQUIRE THE FIRM TO

Build new defenses

Assess political vulnerability

Consider new organizational relationships

Acquire new skills

Consider new accounting procedures

Consider new credit instruments

Assess the political vulnerability of its enterprise

Use new methods of market analysis

Consider production, marketing, and training problems– new mixes

Reconsider substance of sales

Consider organizational and personnel policies in a new light

Assess inflation vulnerability

Assess vulnerability to state control or competition

Deal with market controls

Institute new patterns of labor-management relations

Consider new processes and processes mixer (i.e., plants)

Acquire new skills

Incur added costs

Face new problems of control

Incur higher costs

Consider new operating policies

▶ RISK AND THE MULTINATIONAL CORPORATION

Developing a multinational corporation obviously requires a substantial investment in foreign operations. Normally, managers who make foreign investments expect that such investments will accomplish the following:[14]

1. Reduce or eliminate high transportation costs
2. Allow participation in the rapid expansion of a market abroad
3. Provide foreign technical, design, and marketing skills
4. Earn higher profits

The **parent company** is the company investing in international operations.

The **host country** is the country in which an investment is made by a foreign company.

Unfortunately, many managers decide to internationalize their companies without having an accurate understanding of the risks involved in making such a decision.[15] For example, political complications involving the **parent company** (the company investing in the international operations) and various factions within the **host country** (the country in which the investment is made) could prevent the parent company from realizing the desirable outcomes just listed. Some companies attempt to minimize this kind of risk by adding standard clauses to their contracts stipulating that in the event a business controversy cannot be resolved by the parties involved, they will agree to mediation by a mutually selected mediator.[16]

The likelihood of achieving desirable outcomes related to foreign investments will probably be somewhat uncertain and will certainly vary from country to country. Nevertheless, managers faced with making a foreign investment must assess this likelihood as accurately as possible. Obviously, a poor decision to invest in another country can cause serious financial problems for the organization.

▶ THE WORKFORCE OF MULTINATIONAL CORPORATIONS

As organizations become more global, their organization members tend to become more diverse. Managers of multinational corporations face the continual challenge of building a competitive business team made up of people of different races who speak different languages and come from different parts of the world. The following sections perform two functions that should help managers build such teams:

1. They furnish details and related insights about the various types of organization members generally found in multinational corporations
2. They describe the adjustments members of multinational organizations normally must make in order to become efficient and effective contributors to organization goal attainment, and they suggest how managers can facilitate these adjustments

▶ TYPES OF ORGANIZATION MEMBERS FOUND IN MULTINATIONAL CORPORATIONS

Workers in multinational organizations can be divided into three basic types:

▶ *Expatriates*—Organization members who live and work in a country where they do not have citizenship
▶ *Host-Country Nationals*—Organization members who are citizens of the country in which the facility of a foreign-based organization is located
▶ *Third-Country Nationals*—Organization members who are citizens of one country and who work in another country for an organization headquartered in still another country

Organizations that operate in the global businessplace often employ all three types of worker. The use of host-country nationals, however, is increasing because they are normally the least expensive to employ. Such employees, for example, do not need to be relocated or undergo training in the culture, language, or tax laws of the country where the organization is doing business. Both expatriates and third-country nationals, on the other hand, would have to be relocated and normally undergo such training.

WORKFORCE ADJUSTMENTS Working in a multinational corporation requires more difficult adjustments than working in an organization that focuses primarily on domestic activities. Probably the two most difficult challenges, which pertain to expatriates and third-country nationals rather than to host-country nationals, are adjusting to a new culture and repatriation.

Adjusting to a New Culture   Upon arrival in a foreign country, many people experience confusion, anxiety, and stress related to the need to make cultural adjustments in their organizational and personal lives. From a personal viewpoint, food, weather, and language may all be dramatically different, and driving may be done on the "wrong" side of the road. As an example of personal anxiety that can be caused by adjusting to a new culture, a U.S. expatriate recently working in Sao Paulo, Brazil, drove out of a parking lot by nudging his way into a terrible traffic jam. When a Brazilian woman allowed him to cut in front of her, the expatriate gave her the "ok" signal. To his personal dismay, he was told that in the Brazilian culture, forming a circle with one's first finger and thumb is considered vulgar.[17]

From an organizational viewpoint, there may be different attitudes toward work and different perceptions of time in the workplace. To illustrate, the Japanese are renowned for their hard-driving work ethic, but Americans take a slightly more relaxed attitude toward work. On the other hand, in many U.S. companies, working past quitting time is seen as exemplary, but in Germany, someone who works late is commonly criticized.

Members of multinational corporations normally have the formidable task of adjusting to a drastically new organizational situation. Managers must help these people adjust quickly and painlessly so they can begin contributing to organizational goal attainment as soon as possible.

Repatriation   Repatriation is the process of bringing individuals who have been working abroad back to their home country and reintegrating them into the organization's home-country operations. Repatriation has its own set of adjustment problems, especially with people who have lived abroad for a long time. Some individuals become so accustomed to the advantages of an overseas lifestyle that they greatly miss it when they return home. Others idealize their homeland so much while they are abroad that they become disappointed when it fails to live up to their expectations upon their return. Still others acquire foreign-based habits that are undesirable from the organization's viewpoint and that are hard to break.

Managers must be patient and understanding with repatriates. Some organizations provide repatriates with counseling so that they will be better prepared to handle readjustment problems. Others have found that providing employees, before they leave for foreign duty, with a written agreement specifying what their new duties and career path will be when they return home reduces friction and facilitates the repatriate's adjustment.

Repatriation is the process of bringing individuals who have been working abroad back to their home country and reintegrating them into the organization's home-country operations.

BACK TO THE CASE

As Baskin-Robbins expands internationally, it will become more of a multinational corporation—that is, an organization with significant operations in more than one country. In any company, international management is a complex undertaking. Baskin-Robbins' managers will have to learn how to operate successfully within different countries that are geographically separated and that are characterized by different economic conditions, cultures, technology levels, market sizes, and laws. Baskin-Robbins' experience with foreign expansion illustrates the potential rewards available to managers who can handle the complexity of doing business in other countries.

Naturally, management at Baskin-Robbins has tried to minimize the risk of investing in Vietnam. Other managements might see expansion into Vietnam as too risky to attempt at this time because Vietnam is still unstable economically and thus perilous for foreign investors. Moreover, many U.S. managers worry about an unfriendly reception to U.S. business because of the scars left by the Vietnam War.

The United States, however, is now attempting to establish a normal trading relationship with Vietnam, so Baskin-Robbins may have much to gain from being one of the first companies in its industry to establish a presence in Vietnam. Still, the company must be aware that the political situation between the United States and Vietnam can change quickly again. Therefore, Baskin-Robbins'

(continued)

management should monitor the political relationship between the two countries constantly so that it can quickly devise a response if the relationship changes.

Baskin-Robbins' management has obviously decided that its foreign investment entails a tolerable amount of risk when weighed against the prospect of increased return from operations in Vietnam. Only a significant period of operations in Vietnam will furnish the necessary feedback to determine whether this decision was sound.

Perhaps the most important variable for success in the Vietnam store is the employees working there. Baskin-Robbins must determine the best combination of expatriates, host-country nationals, and third-country nationals to run the store. Whatever blend of human resources the company ultimately decides on, management should be sensitive to helping individuals adjust both personally and organizationally to an international situation. In addition, if expatriates are involved in running the store, the company should plan on helping them adjust when they are repatriated.

MANAGEMENT FUNCTIONS AND MULTINATIONAL CORPORATIONS

The sections that follow discuss the four major management functions—planning, organizing, influencing, and controlling—as they occur at multinational corporations.

► PLANNING IN MULTINATIONAL CORPORATIONS

Planning was defined in chapter 1 as determining how an organization will achieve its objectives. This definition is applicable to the management of both domestic and multinational organizations, but with some differences.

The primary difference between planning in multinational versus planning in domestic organizations is in the plans' components. Plans for the multinational organization include components that focus on the international arena, whereas plans for the domestic organization do not. For example, plans for multinational organizations could include the following:

1. Establishing a new salesforce in a foreign country
2. Developing new manufacturing plants in other countries through purchase or construction
3. Financing international expansion
4. Determining which countries represent the most suitable candidates for international expansion

COMPONENTS OF INTERNATIONAL PLANS Although planning for multinational corporations varies from organization to organization, the following four components are commonly included in international plans:

- ► Imports/Exports
- ► License agreements
- ► Direct investing
- ► Joint ventures

This section discusses these four components as well as the responses of multinational corporations to international market agreements.

Imports/Exports Imports/Exports planning components emphasize reaching organizational objectives by **importing** (buying goods or services from another country) or **exporting** (selling goods or services to another country).

Organizations of all sizes import and export. On the one hand, there are companies like Auburn Farms, Inc., a relatively small producer of all-natural, fat-free snack foods that imports products to be resold. Auburn Farms is the exclusive U.S. importer of Beacon Sweets & Chocolates of South Africa. Auburn sees its importing activities as a way of expanding and diversifying.[18] On the other hand, there are extremely large and complex organizations, such as Eastman Kodak, which export photographic products to a number of foreign countries.[19]

Importing is buying goods or services from another country.

Exporting is selling goods or services to another country.

 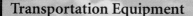

AMERICAN RACING EXPORTS TO BUILD BUSINESS

American Racing is a manufacturer of aluminum and steel wheels based in Rancho Dominguez, California. The company manufactures almost five million wheels per year in 80 different styles. Most of the wheels are used on small trucks, sport utility vehicles, and minivans. Half of the company's production goes to Chrysler and General Motors as original equipment parts, and the other half is sold to individual car owners through retail outlets and auto dealers. The company employs 2,200 people at 7 factories and 45 warehouse and distribution centers. In 1988, the company was purchased by a Canadian conglomerate.

With new ownership came the new strategy of exporting wheels to other countries. The new owners knew that selling abroad would be difficult and time consuming. To organize the new world-sized sales territory, countries were grouped into differ-ent regions then ranked according to potential sales. Different regions were given different attention and focus. Special strategies were developed to penetrate Japanese and German markets. In addition, agreements were made to allow foreign distributors to sell American Racing wheels.

American Racing has made significant progress in exporting its wheels. Since 1989, the company shipped $40 million worth of its product overseas, including more than $10 million in 1997. The export program has been so successful that about 100 new employees were hired to handle the new export business. American Racing wheels are now selling in more than 40 countries, and distribution agreements, presently being negotiated, will offer the wheels for sale in another 41 countries. The company expects that by the year 2000, American Racing will be selling an additional one million wheels per year through 100 dealers around the world.

License Agreements   A **license agreement** is a right granted by one company to another to use its brand name, technology, product specifications, and so on, in the manufacture or sale of goods and services. Naturally, the company to which the license is extended pays some fee for the privilege. International planning components in this area involve reaching organizational objectives through either the purchase or the sale of licenses at the international level.

> A **license agreement** is a right granted by one company to another to use its brand name, technology, product specifications, and so on in the manufacture or sale of goods and services.

For example, the Tosoh Corporation recently purchased a license agreement from Mobil Research and Development Corporation to commercialize Mobil's newly developed process for extracting mercury from natural gas. Tosoh, a Japanese firm, will use its subsidiaries in the United States, Japan, the Netherlands, Greece, Canada, and the United Kingdom as bases of operations from which to profit from Mobil's new process.[20]

Direct Investing   **Direct investing** is using the assets of one company to purchase the operating assets (for example, factories) of another company. International planning in this area emphasizes reaching organizational objectives through the purchase of the operating assets of another company in a foreign country.

> **Direct investing** is using the assets of one company to purchase the operating assets of another company.

A number of Japanese firms have recently been making direct investments in the United States. In fact, many people believe that a new wave of direct Japanese investment in the United States is building. Several large Japanese companies have announced plans to expand their U.S. production facilities. These planned direct investments are focused on building competitive clout for Japanese companies in such core industries as automobiles, semiconductors, electronics, and office products. Lower manufacturing wages and lower land costs in the United States are key attractions for the Japanese firms. For example, because the cost of building a factory was 30 percent cheaper in the United States than in Japan, Ricoh Company decided to spend $30 million to start making thermal paper products near Atlanta, Georgia. One of the largest Japanese direct investments in the United States was Toyota Motor Company's $900 million expansion of its Georgetown, Kentucky, plant. The lower costs associated with expanding and operating the Georgetown plant were the key reason Toyota decided to make this investment.[21]

Joint Ventures   An **international joint venture** is a partnership formed by a company in one country with a company in another country for the purpose of pursuing some mutually desirable business undertaking. International planning components that include joint ventures emphasize the attainment of organizational objectives through partnerships with foreign companies.

> An **international joint venture** is a partnership formed by a company in one country with a company in another country for the purpose of pursuing some mutually desirable business undertaking.

Daimler-Benz chairman Juergen Schrempp (left) and Chrysler chairman Robert Eaton prepare to sign the agreement that merged their two companies in May 1998. The deal, valued at over $40 billion, ranks as the biggest industrial merger to date and creates a new multinational corporation. The plans DaimlerChrysler will have to make affect its sales, manufacturing, and finance operations.

Joint ventures between car manufacturers are becoming more and more common as companies strive for greater economies of scale and higher standards in product quality and delivery.

General Motors and Suzuki Motor Company recently formed CAMI Automotive as a joint venture to manufacture the Geo Metro, touted as Chevrolet's most affordable car model. General Motors is based in the United States and is known throughout the world for its prowess as an automobile manufacturer. Suzuki is a leading minicar and motorcycle manufacturer based in Japan. General Motors' substantial size and marketing muscle make the joint venture desirable from Suzuki's viewpoint, and Suzuki's international presence through its subsidiaries in Spain, Canada, Australia, New Zealand, Germany, France, Italy, Belgium, the Philippines, Pakistan, and Colombia makes the partnership desirable from General Motors' viewpoint.[22]

PLANNING AND INTERNATIONAL MARKET AGREEMENTS In order to plan properly, managers of a multinational corporation, or any other organization participating in the international arena, must understand numerous complex and interrelated factors present within the organization's international environment. Managers should have a practical grasp of such international environmental factors as the economic and cultural conditions, the laws and political circumstances, of foreign countries within which their companies operate.

One international environmental factor impacting strategic planning that has lately received significant attention is the international market agreement. An **international market agreement** is an arrangement among a cluster of countries that facilitates a high level of trade among these countries. In planning, managers must consider existing international market agreements as they relate to countries in which their organizations operate. If an organization is from a country that is party to an international market agreement, the organization's plan should include steps for taking maximum advantage of that agreement. On the other hand, if an organization is from a country that is *not* party to an international market agreement, the organization's plan must include steps for competing with organizations from nations that are parties to such an agreement. The most notable international market agreements are discussed here.

The European Community (EC) The European Community (EC) is an international market agreement first formed in 1958 and dedicated to facilitating trade among member nations. To that end, the nations in the EC have agreed to eliminate tariffs among themselves and work

An **international market agreement** is an arrangement among a cluster of countries that facilitates a high level of trade among these countries.

toward meaningful deregulation in such areas as banking, insurance, telecommunications, and airlines. Longer-term members of the EC are Denmark, the United Kingdom, Portugal, the Netherlands, Belgium, Spain, Ireland, Luxembourg, France, Germany, Italy, and Greece. More recent members include Austria, Finland, and Sweden. Swedish businesses are particularly excited about their country's entrance into the EC because they are sure that membership will ultimately boost exports and encourage foreign investment from other member nations. The significance of the EC as an international environmental factor can only increase, since the number of member countries is expected to grow to over 25 by 2010.[23]

North American Free Trade Agreement (NAFTA)   The North American Free Trade Agreement is an international market agreement aimed at facilitating trade among member nations. Current NAFTA members are the United States, Canada, and Mexico. To facilitate trade among themselves, these countries have agreed to such actions as the phasing out of tariffs on U.S. farm exports to Mexico, the opening up of Mexico to American trucking, and the safeguarding of North American pharmaceutical patents in Mexico.

NAFTA has had significant impact since its implementation in January 1994. Recent figures show that since the agreement went into effect, there has been a 30 percent increase in U.S. exports to Mexico and a 15 percent increase in Mexican exports to the United States. Trade between the United States and Canada has exploded since NAFTA took effect. As with the EC, the significance of NAFTA as an international environmental factor can only grow in the future as other countries in the Caribbean and South America apply for membership.[24]

The Evolving Pacific Rim   Countries in the Pacific Rim area are commonly believed to be interested in developing an international market agreement among themselves that is as effective as the EC has proved to be in Europe. The countries categorized as belonging to the Pacific Rim are Japan, China, Malaysia, Singapore, Indonesia, South Korea, Thailand, Taiwan, Hong Kong, the Philippines, New Zealand, Pakistan, Sri Lanka, and Australia. One country on this list, Japan, is presently a world economic power, while others, like Taiwan and South Korea, are making good progress toward that status. The Pacific Rim countries as a group are anxious to develop an international trade agreement that can best serve their particular economic needs.[25]

To sum up, numerous countries throughout the world are already signatories to international market agreements. Moreover, the number of countries that are parties to such agreements should grow significantly in the future.

►ORGANIZING MULTINATIONAL CORPORATIONS

Organizing was generally defined in chapter 1 as the process of establishing orderly uses for all resources within the organization. This definition applies equally to the management of domestic and multinational organizations. Two organizing topics as they specifically relate to multinational corporations, however, bear further discussion. These topics are organization structure and the selection of managers.[26]

ORGANIZATION STRUCTURE   Basically, *organization structure* is the sum of all established relationships among resources within the organization, and the *organization chart* is the graphic illustration of organization structure.

Figure 4.4 illustrates several ways in which organization charts can be designed for multinational corporations. Briefly, multinational organization charts can be set up according to major business functions the organization performs, such as production or marketing; major products the organization sells, such as brakes or electrical parts; geographic areas within which the organization does business, such as North America or Europe; customers the organization serves, such as the Japanese or Swiss; or the way in which the organization manufactures and assembles its products. The topic of organization structure is discussed in much more detail in chapter 10.

As with domestic organizations, there is no one best way to organize a multinational corporation. Instead, managers must analyze the multinational circumstances that confront them and develop an organization structure that best suits those circumstances.

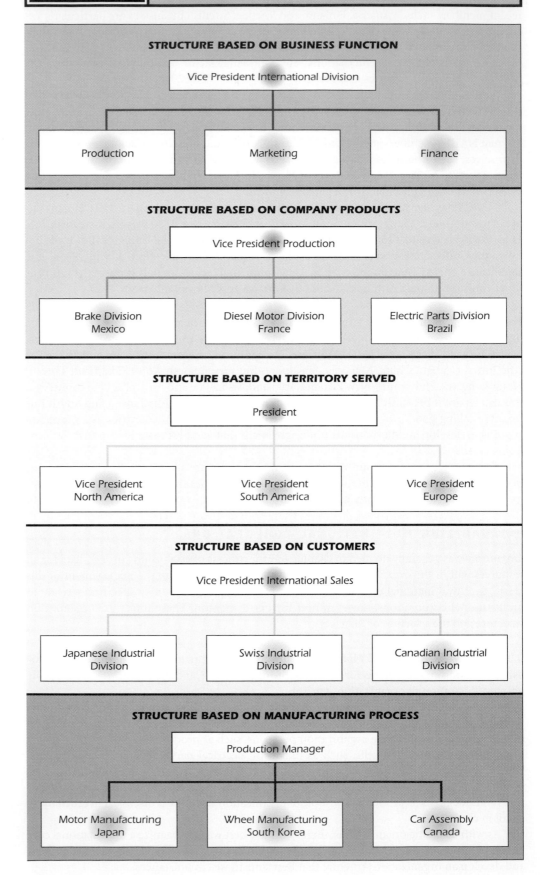

FIGURE 4.4 Partial multinational organization charts based on function, product, territory, customers, and manufacturing process

STRUCTURE BASED ON BUSINESS FUNCTION

Vice President International Division

- Production
- Marketing
- Finance

STRUCTURE BASED ON COMPANY PRODUCTS

Vice President Production

- Brake Division Mexico
- Diesel Motor Division France
- Electric Parts Division Brazil

STRUCTURE BASED ON TERRITORY SERVED

President

- Vice President North America
- Vice President South America
- Vice President Europe

STRUCTURE BASED ON CUSTOMERS

Vice President International Sales

- Japanese Industrial Division
- Swiss Industrial Division
- Canadian Industrial Division

STRUCTURE BASED ON MANUFACTURING PROCESS

Production Manager

- Motor Manufacturing Japan
- Wheel Manufacturing South Korea
- Car Assembly Canada

After the passage of the North American Free Trade Agreement (NAFTA), many economists and policy makers have pushed to extend the web of free-trade arrangements to more countries in Latin and South America. As the idea of hemisphere-wide free trade takes hold, more traffic will undoubtedly flow through such checkpoints as this U.S. Customs inspection station at the Mexican border in Del Rio, Texas.

SELECTION OF MANAGERS For multinational organizations to thrive, they must have competent managers. One characteristic believed to be a primary determinant of how competently managers can guide multinational organizations is their attitude toward how such organizations should operate.

Managerial Attitudes Toward Foreign Operations Over the years, management theorists have identified three basic managerial attitudes toward the operation of multinational corporations: ethnocentric, polycentric, and geocentric. The **ethnocentric attitude** reflects the belief that multinational corporations should regard home-country management practices as superior to foreign-country management practices. Managers with an ethnocentric attitude are prone to stereotype home-country management practices as sound and reasonable and foreign management practices as faulty and unreasonable. The **polycentric attitude** reflects the belief that because foreign managers are closer to foreign organizational units, they probably understand them better, and therefore foreign management practices should generally be viewed as more insightful than home-country management practices. Managers with a **geocentric attitude** believe that the overall quality of management recommendations, rather than the location of managers, should determine the acceptability of management practices used to guide multinational corporations.[27]

Advantages and Disadvantages of Each Management Attitude It is extremely important to understand the potential advantages and disadvantages of these three attitudes within multinational corporations. The ethnocentric attitude has the advantage of keeping the organization simple, but it generally causes organizational problems because it prevents the organization from receiving feedback from its foreign operations. In some cases, the ethnocentric attitude even causes resentment toward the home country within the foreign society. The polycentric attitude permits the tailoring of foreign organizational segments to their cultures, which can be an advantage. Unfortunately, this attitude can lead to the substantial disadvantage of creating numerous foreign organizational segments that are individually run and rather unique, which makes them difficult to control.

The geocentric attitude is generally thought to be the most appropriate for managers in multinational corporations. This attitude promotes collaboration between foreign and home-country management and encourages the development of managerial skills regardless of the organizational segment or country in which managers operate. An organization characterized by the geocentric attitude generally incurs high travel and training expenses, and many decisions are made by consensus. Although the risks from such a wide distribution of power are

The **ethnocentric attitude** reflects the belief that multinational corporations should regard home-country management practices as superior to foreign-country management practices.

The **polycentric attitude** reflects the belief that because foreign managers are closer to foreign organizational units, they probably understand them better, and therefore foreign management practices should generally be viewed as more insightful than home-country management practices.

The **geocentric attitude** reflects the belief that the overall quality of management recommendations, rather than the location of managers, should determine the acceptability of management practices used to guide multinational corporations. The geocentric attitude is considered most appropriate for long-term organizational success.

Japan's Mitsubishi Motors Corporation has been particularly successful in encouraging collaboration in its partnership with Malaysia's state-owned automaker, Proton. Mitsubishi, for example, gave expertise and technical assistance to Proton when it was in its infancy. Today, Proton is a $1.2 billion company whose biggest sellers are sedans and subcompacts developed jointly with Mitsubishi.

real, the potential payoffs—better-quality products, worldwide utilization of the best human resources, increased managerial commitment to worldwide organizational objectives, and increased profit—generally outweigh the potential harm. Overall, managers with a geocentric attitude contribute more to the long-term success of the multinational corporation than managers with an ethnocentric or polycentric attitude.

▶ INFLUENCING PEOPLE IN MULTINATIONAL CORPORATIONS

Influencing was generally defined in chapter 1 as guiding the activities of organization members in appropriate directions through communicating, leading, motivating, and managing groups. Influencing people in a multinational corporation, however, is more complex and challenging than in a domestic organization.

CULTURE The factor that probably contributes most to this increased complexity and challenge is culture. **Culture** is the total characteristics of a given group of people and their environment. The components of a culture that are generally designated as important are customs, beliefs, attitudes, habits, skills, state of technology, level of education, and religion. As a manager moves from a domestic corporation involving basically one culture to a multinational corporation involving several, the task of influencing usually becomes more difficult.

To successfully influence employees, managers in multinational corporations should:

1. *Acquire a working knowledge of the languages used in countries that house foreign operations*—Multinational managers attempting to operate without such knowledge are prone to making costly mistakes.
2. *Understand the attitudes of people in countries that house foreign operations*—An understanding of these attitudes can help managers design business practices that are suitable for unique foreign situations. For example, Americans generally accept competition as a tool to encourage people to work harder. As a result, U.S. business practices that include some competitive aspects seldom create significant disruption within organizations. Such practices could cause disruption, however, if introduced into either Japan or the typical European country.
3. *Understand the needs that motivate people in countries housing foreign operations*—For managers in multinational corporations to be successful at motivating employees in different countries, they must present these individuals with the opportunity to satisfy personal needs while being productive within the organization. In designing motivation

strategies, multinational managers must understand that employees in different countries often have quite different personal needs. For example, the Swiss, Austrians, Japanese, and Argentineans tend to have high security needs, whereas Danes, Swedes, and Norwegians tend to have high social needs. People in Great Britain, the United States, Canada, New Zealand, and Australia tend to have high self-actualization needs.[28] Thus, to be successful at influencing, multinational managers must understand their employees' needs and mold such organizational components as incentive systems, job design, and leadership style to correspond to these needs.

► CONTROLLING MULTINATIONAL CORPORATIONS

Controlling was generally defined in chapter 1 as making something happen the way it was planned to happen. As with domestic corporations, control in multinational corporations requires that standards be set, performance be measured and compared to standards, and corrective action be taken if necessary. In addition, control in such areas as labor costs, product quality, and inventory is important to organizational success regardless of whether the organization is domestic or international.

SPECIAL DIFFICULTIES Control of a multinational corporation involves certain complexities. First, there is the problem of different currencies. Management must decide how to compare profits generated by organizational units located in different countries and therefore expressed in terms of different currencies.

Another complication is that organizational units in multinational corporations are generally more geographically separated. This increased distance normally makes it difficult for multinational managers to keep a close watch on operations in foreign countries.

IMPROVING COMMUNICATION One action successful managers take to help overcome the difficulty of monitoring geographically separated foreign units is carefully designing the communication network or information system that links them. A significant part of this design requires all company units to acquire and install similar computer equipment in all offices, both foreign and domestic, to ensure the likelihood of network hookups when communication becomes necessary. Such standardization of computer equipment also facilitates communication among all foreign locations and makes equipment repair and maintenance easier and therefore less expensive.[29]

► TRANSNATIONAL ORGANIZATIONS

Transnational organizations, also called *global organizations,* take the entire world as their business arena. Doing business wherever it makes sense is primary; national borders are considered inconsequential. The transnational organization transcends any single home country, with ownership, control, and management being from many different countries. Transnational organizations represent the fourth, and maximum, level of international activity as depicted on the continuum of international involvement presented earlier in this chapter. Seeing great opportunities in the global marketplace, some MNCs have transformed themselves from home-based companies with worldwide interests into worldwide companies pursuing business activities across the globe and claiming no singular loyalty to any one country.

Perhaps the most commonly cited example of a transnational organization is Nestlé.[30] Although Nestlé is headquartered in Veney, Switzerland, its arena of daily business activity is truly the world. Nestlé has a very diversified list of products, including instant coffee, cereals, pharmaceuticals, coffee creamers, dietetic foods, ice cream, chocolates, and a wide array of snack foods. Its recent acquisition of the French company Perrier catapulted Nestlé into market leadership in the mineral water industry. Nestlé has over 210,000 employees and operates 494 factories in 71 countries worldwide, including the United States, Germany, Portugal, Brazil, France, New Zealand, Australia, Chile, and Venezuela. Of Nestlé's sales and profits, about 45 percent come from Europe, 35 percent from North and South America, and 25 percent from other countries.

Transnational organizations, also called *global organizations,* take the entire world as their business arena.

Planning is equally valuable to domestic and international companies. The primary difference in planning for Baskin-Robbins as an international rather than a domestic company is reflected in certain components of the company's plans. As an international corporation, Baskin-Robbins needs planning components that focus on the international sector, whereas a totally domestic organization obviously would not need such components. Examples of such components in Baskin-Robbins' case are establishing a partnership with a Vietnamese construction company to build ice cream stores throughout Vietnam, building an ice cream manufacturing facility in Vietnam that could furnish product to Baskin-Robbins' Vietnamese stores as well as prospective stores in nearby countries, choosing additional store locations in other countries, and selling the rights (license agreements) to a foreign company to use the name Baskin-Robbins in selling ice cream.

The organization structure of an international company such as Baskin-Robbins should generally be based on one or more of the important variables of function, product, territory, customers, and manufacturing process. In deciding on an organization structure, Baskin-Robbins' managers should consider all of these variables within the situations that confront them, and then design the structure that is most appropriate for those situations.

Over the long term, top management at Baskin-Robbins should try to select for international positions those managers who display geocentric rather than polycentric or ethnocentric attitudes. Such managers would be the most competent at building operating units in other countries and at using the best human resources available. They would also tend to be highly committed to the attainment of organizational objectives.

As Baskin-Robbins becomes more multinational, influencing employees will become increasingly complicated. The cultures of people in Vietnam and in whatever other countries the company expands into will have to be thoroughly understood by Baskin-Robbins' foreign operations managers. Those who are U.S. citizens will have to acquire a working knowledge of the languages spoken in the various host countries and an understanding of what attitudes and personal needs motivate individuals within the foreign workforce. For instance, the rewards used to motivate Vietnamese workers may need to be very different from the rewards the company uses to motivate U.S. workers.

The control process at Baskin-Robbins should involve standards, measurements, and corrective action where necessary, just as it would in a purely domestic company. But the currency used in Vietnam—and wherever else the company decides to set up foreign operations—will tend to make control more complicated for Baskin-Robbins than for a domestic organization. The geographic distance of its foreign operations from the United States will also complicate control at Baskin-Robbins.

INTERNATIONAL MANAGEMENT: SPECIAL ISSUES

The preceding section of this chapter discussed planning, organizing, influencing, and controlling multinational corporations. This section focuses on two special issues that can help to ensure management success in the international arena: maintaining ethics in international management, and preparing expatriates for foreign assignments.[31]

►MAINTAINING ETHICS IN INTERNATIONAL MANAGEMENT

As discussed in chapter 2, *ethics* is a concern for "good" behavior and reflects an obligation that forces managers to consider not only their own personal well-being, but that of other human beings as they lead organizations. Having a manager define what is ethical behavior can indeed be challenging. Defining what behavior is ethical becomes increasingly challenging as managers consider the international implications of management action. What seems ethical in a manager's home country can be unethical in a different country.

The following guidelines can help managers ensure that management action taken across national borders is indeed ethical. According to these guidelines, managers can ensure that such action is ethical by the following:

RESPECTING CORE HUMAN RIGHTS This guideline underscores the notion that all people deserve an opportunity to achieve economic advancement and an improved standard of living. In addition, all people have the right to be treated with respect. Much attention has been given recently by major sporting goods companies including Nike and Reebok to ensure that this guideline is followed in business operations they are conducting in other countries.[32] These companies have joined forces to crack down on child labor, establish minimum wages comparable to existing individual country standards, establish a maximum 60-hour workweek with at least one day off, and support the establishment of a mechanism for inspecting apparel factories worldwide. These companies have also committed themselves to the elimination of forced labor, harassment, abuse, and discrimination in the workplace.

RESPECTING LOCAL TRADITIONS This guideline suggests that managers hold the customs of foreign countries in which they conduct business in high regard. In Japan, for example, people have a long-standing tradition that those individuals who do business together exchange gifts. Sometimes, these gifts can be very expensive. When U.S. managers started doing business in Japan, accepting a gift felt like accepting a bribe. As a result, many of these managers thought that the practice of gift giving might be wrong. As U.S. managers have come to know and respect this Japanese tradition, most have come to tolerate, and even encourage, the practice as ethical behavior in Japan. Some managers even set different limits on gift giving in Japan than they do elsewhere.

DETERMINING RIGHT FROM WRONG BY EXAMINING CONTEXT This guideline suggests that managers should evaluate the specifics of the international situation confronting them in determining if a particular management activity is ethical. Although some activities are wrong no matter where they take place, some that are unethical in one setting may be acceptable in another. For instance, the chemical EDB, a soil fungicide, is banned for use in the United States. In hot climates, however, it quickly becomes harmless through exposure to intense solar radiation and high soil temperatures. As long as the chemical is monitored, companies may be able to use EDB ethically in certain parts of the world.

Most managers and management scholars agree that implementing ethical management practices across national borders enhances organizational success. Although following the above guidelines does not guarantee that management action taken across national borders will be ethical, it should increase the probability that such actions will be ethical.

► PREPARING EXPATRIATES FOR FOREIGN ASSIGNMENTS

The trend of U.S. companies forming joint ventures and other strategic alliances that emphasize foreign operations is increasing. As a result, the number of expatriates being sent from the United States to other countries is also rising.[33]

The somewhat casual approach of the past toward preparing expatriates for foreign duty is being replaced by the attitude that these managers need special tools to be able to succeed in difficult foreign assignments.[34] To help expatriates adjust, home companies are helping them find homes and high quality health care in host countries. Companies are also responding to expatriate feelings that they need more help from home companies on career planning related to foreign assignments, career planning for spouses forced to go to the foreign assignment country to look for work, and better counseling for the personal challenges they will face during their foreign assignment.

Many companies prepare their expatriates for foreign assignments by using special training programs. Specific features of these programs vary from company to company depending on the situation. Most of these programs, however, usually contain the following core elements:

Culture profiles—Here, expatriates learn about the new culture in which they will be working

Cultural adaptation—Here, expatriates learn how to survive the difficulties of adjusting to a new culture

Logistical information—Here, expatriates learn basic information, such as personal safety, who to call in an emergency, and how to write a check

Application—Here, expatriates learn about specific organizational roles they will perform

Expatriates generally play a critical role in determining the success of an organization's foreign operations. The tremendous personal and professional adjustments that expatriates must make, however, can delay their effectiveness and efficiency in foreign settings. Sound training programs can lower the amount of time expatriates need to adjust and can thereby help them become productive more quickly. The following People Spotlight discusses more detail on helping expatriates adjust.

PEOPLE SPOTLIGHT — Helping Expatriates to Adjust

As more companies initiate or expand overseas operations, the need to send employees on international assignments will increase. Because many companies use overseas assignments as a means of assessing which employees should be promoted to top-level positions, success in such positions is critical to both the individual and the organization.

Unfortunately, the success rate in foreign assignments is unimpressive. Up to 40 percent of expatriate employees leave their posts early. The reasons vary, but early termination is generally accompanied by negatives for both the organization and the employee. Each failure to complete a foreign assignment costs companies between $50,000 and $150,000 and usually derails the employee's career.

The primary reason for early termination is that the employee was not properly prepared for the foreign assignment. Poorly prepared expatriates find it very difficult to make the personal and organizational adjustments necessary for success in positions abroad.

Management can take certain steps to better prepare organization members for expatriate positions. For example, organization members who are eligible for expatriate positions should be involved in discussions concerning the challenges of working in another country before they are actually given an international assignment.

Employees chosen for an assignment should be given an early start on learning the language and etiquette of the host country where they will work, as well as the culture and value system of that country.

Finally, management should develop and refine the stress management skills of future expatriates. These employees will undoubtedly encounter high levels of stress related to their new foreign job, and they must know how to manage such stress if they are to be successful organization members.

BACK TO THE CASE

Based on the preceding information, managers at Baskin-Robbins should be concerned with promoting ethical behavior in its Vietnam operation. They can promote such behavior by only taking action that respects the core human rights of Vietnamese citizens, respects local Vietnamese traditions, and reflects what is "right" given Vietnamese culture. Examples of such behavior could be forbidding Vietnamese children from being hired as employees, paying a fair wage that reflects the national Vietnamese and Ho Chi Minh wage levels, and eliminating abuse and discrimination in Baskin-Robbins' stores.

In addition, Baskin-Robbins will have to properly prepare expatriates going to Vietnam in order for these individuals to be productive as quickly as possible. The company should take steps such as helping the expatriates find appropriate housing and health care, explaining how the Vietnamese assignment impacts the expatriates' long-term career at Baskin-Robbins, and providing counseling for personal problems that the expatriates could face by living in Vietnam. Formal training of expatriates going to Vietnam should include a description of the Vietnamese culture; steps that expatriates can take to adapt to that culture; basic information about logistics of life in Vietnam like who to call in case of emergency; and specifics about the job they will be performing in Vietnam.

For updated information on the topics in this chapter, Internet exercises, links to related Internet sites, an interactive study guide, and more, visit our companion Web site at

http://www.prenhall.com/certo

Additional information can be found on the inside front and back covers of this text.

◀ **ACTION SUMMARY** ▶

Reread the learning objectives below. Each objective is followed by questions. Answering these questions accurately will help you retain the most important concepts discussed in this chapter. After answering each question, check your answer against the answer key at the end of this chapter. (*Hint:* If you have any doubts regarding the correct response, consult the page number that follows the answer.)

Circle: From studying this chapter, I will attempt to acquire

1. An understanding of international management and its importance to modern managers.

T F
   a. To reach organizational objectives, management may extend its activities to include an emphasis on organizations in foreign countries.

a b c d e
   b. The U.S. multinational corporation with the highest foreign revenue as a percent of total revenue in 1993 was: (a) IBM (b) Citicorp (c) Exxon (d) General Motors (e) Mobil.

2. An understanding of what constitutes a multinational corporation.

a b c d e
   a. According to Jacoby, the first stage in a corporation's multinationalization is when the corporation: (a) multinationalizes ownership of corporate stock (b) multinationalizes management from top to bottom (c) establishes foreign manufacturing facilities (d) establishes sales organizations abroad (e) exports its products.

T F
   b. In general, the smaller the organization, the greater the likelihood that it participates in international operations of some sort.

3. Insights concerning the risk involved in investing in international operations.

a b c d e
   a. Managers who make foreign investments believe that such investments: (a) reduce or eliminate high transportation costs (b) allow participation in the rapid expansion of a market abroad (c) provide foreign technical, design, and marketing skills (d) earn higher profits (e) a, b, c, and d.

T F
   b. A manager's failure to understand different national sovereignties, national conditions, and national values and institutions can lead to poor investment decisions.

4. Insights about those who work in multinational corporations.

a b c d e   **a.** People who work in multinational corporations are generally categorized as: (a) expatriates (b) third-country nationals (c) host-country nationals (d) all of the above (e) a and b only.

T F   **b.** Personal adjustments that employees of multinational corporations must make can influence how productively they work.

T F   **c.** Repatriation is the process of sending an individual out of his or her home country to work for a multinational corporation.

5. Knowledge about managing multinational corporations.

T F   **a.** The primary difference between planning in multinational versus domestic organizations probably involves operational planning.

a b c d e   **b.** The attitude that regards home-country management practices as superior to foreign-country practices is known as a(n): (a) egocentric attitude (b) ethnocentric attitude (c) polycentric attitude (d) geocentric attitude (e) isocentric attitude.

6. Knowledge about managing multinational organizations versus transnational organizations.

T F   **a.** Generally speaking, a transnational organization transcends any home country, whereas a multinational organization does not.

T F   **b.** A multinational organization is basically the same as a transnational organization.

7. An understanding of how ethics and the preparation of expatriates relate to managing internationally.

T F   **a.** Examining context can help a manager determine if action taken in a foreign country or countries is ethical.

a b c d e   **b.** Which of the following is NOT commonly discussed in training programs aimed at preparing expatriates for foreign assignments: (a) culture profiles (b) cultural adaption (c) application (d) logistical information (e) all of the above are commonly discussed.

▶ INTRODUCTORY CASE WRAP-UP ◀

CASE DISCUSSSION QUESTIONS

"Baskin-Robbins Brings U.S. Ice Cream to Vietnam" (p. 75) and its related Back-to-the-Case sections were written to help you better understand the management concepts contained in this chapter. Answer the following discussion questions about this Introductory Case to enrich your understanding of the chapter content:

1. Do you think that at some point in your career you will become involved in international management? Explain.

2. Assume that you are about to become the manager of a Baskin-Robbins ice cream store in Japan. What challenges do you think will be most difficult for you? Why?

3. Evaluate the following statement: Baskin-Robbins can probably enhance its success in foreign countries by better preparing expatriates for foreign assignments.

SKILLS EXERCISE: PREPARING EXPATRIATES FOR FOREIGN ASSIGNMENTS

In this chapter you gained an appreciation for the importance of properly preparing expatriates for foreign assignments. In the Introductory Case you read how Baskin-Robbins opened an ice cream store in Vietnam. Assume that you are in charge of human resources at Baskin-Robbins and have just been notified that the company is sending an expatriate to Vietnam to oversee nine additional stores that will be run by locals. Do some research on Vietnam to uncover three issues that you would like the new expatriate to be aware of before taking the assignment. Be sure to discuss how each issue would impact the manner in which the expatriate would actually manage these stores and their employees in Vietnam.

1. More and more organizations are initiating business ventures in foreign countries. Explain why in detail.
2. Define *international management*.
3. How significant is the topic of international management to the modern manager? Explain fully.
4. What is meant by the term *multinational corporation?*
5. List and explain four factors that contribute to the complexity of managing multinational corporations.
6. Choose an organization and describe how it has become multinational by progressing through two or more stages of Jacoby's six stages of multinationalization.
7. List and define three types of organization members generally found in multinational corporations.
8. Describe personal and professional adjustments that members of multinational corporations generally must make. How should managers respond to employees making such adjustments? Why?
9. What is the difference between direct investing and joint ventures at the international level?

10. What is an international market agreement? Explain how these agreements can impact organization plans.
11. Draw segments of organization charts that organize a multinational corporation on the basis of product, function, and customers.
12. Is there one best way to organize all multinational corporations? Explain your answer fully.
13. What are the differences between ethnocentric, polycentric, and geocentric attitudes? Describe advantages and disadvantages of each.
14. How does culture affect the international management process?
15. Discuss three suggestions that would be helpful to a manager attempting to influence organization members in different countries.
16. What is a transnational organization? How does it differ from a multinational organization?
17. How can comparative management help managers of today?
18. Discuss three guidelines that managers can use to ensure that action taken across national borders is ethical.

1. a T, p. 76
  b. c, p. 79
2. a. e, pp. 79–80
  b. F, p. 81

3. a. e, p. 84
  b. T, p. 84
4. a. d, p. 84
  b. T, pp. 84–85
  c. F, p. 85

5. a. F, p. 86
  b. b, p. 91
6. a. T, p. 93
  b. F, p. 93

7. a. T, p. 95
  b. e, p. 96

► CASE STUDY: A Global Success Story ◄

Robert Goizueta, Coca-Cola's president and CEO since 1981, believed that "soft drinks are very much a local product. I'd love for the Chinese to arrive in New York" he explains, "and say, 'My goodness, they have Coca-Cola here, too,'" The hand-picked protégé of longtime Coca-Cola chairman Robert Woodruff, Goizueta recognized when he became CEO that changes had to be made in the company's way of doing business around the world to overcome the 1970s stagnation in Coca-Cola's growth. In the past, he says, "You'd plant your flag in a new country every time you needed to grow. We ran out of countries, so I had to do something different." In fact, Goizueta was recognized by *Fortune* magazine for his success in enhancing shareholder value—a crucial investment value that showed a significant loss in the 10-year period before he took over.

Atlanta-based Coca-Cola boasts one of the best-recognized logos in the world. Whether he or she speaks Japanese, Hebrew, or Russian, the world traveler knows the product inside the familiar tapered bottle or distinctively labeled can and trusts its consistently high quality. Even five years ago, however, Goizueta believed that Coca-Cola's marketing was flawed. Too much marketing money, he felt, was being devoted to advertising and too little to brand strategy and packaging. So Coca-Cola hired hundreds of new marketers to take a more "holistic" approach to the international market. At the same time, however, Goizueta cautioned a worldwide gathering of Coca-Cola's quality assurance staff about the dangers of change for its own sake. "It's extremely important," he reminded them, "that you show some sensitivity to your past in order to show the proper respect for the future."

Coca-Cola's push into the international market began during World War II, when company president Robert Woodruff announced, "We will see that every man in uniform gets a bottle of Coca-Cola for 5 cents wherever he is and whatever it costs." General Dwight D. Eisenhower, a

Coca-Cola fancier, agreed. Thus, as competing soft-drink companies watched helplessly, Coca-Cola established bottling plants near every battlefront. By the end of the war, the company had 64 international bottling plants, most of them built at the expense of U.S. taxpayers.

During the Cold War, however, the company faced severe criticism in certain countries as a symbol of American imperialism. For example, efforts were made to drive Coke from the shelves of French stores. "The moral landscape of France," declared the respected French newspaper *Le Monde,* "is at stake." In the end, of course, the company won this and other fights on foreign soil. Coca-Cola was once boycotted by Arabic countries because it had a franchised bottler in Israel, but over time, the company's persistence—and consumer demand—broke down this barrier.

Coca-Cola currently does business in 195 countries, deriving close to 70 percent of its total revenues and 80 percent of its operating profits from outside the United States. In 1994, Coke had revenues exceeding $15 billion and had more than doubled sales from the decade before. Today, the international market remains the key to Coca-Cola's future. With domestic per capita consumption leveling, the global market offers enormous potential.

Goizueta recognizes that Coca-Cola's present success comes from operating in different geographic locations. First, Coke pushed aggressively into foreign markets when the domestic market matured. Indeed, facing just 2 to 4 percent annual growth domestically, Coca-Cola *had* to concentrate on the world market. Coke managers reason that when sales drop in troubled economies like those of Mexico or Argentina, growth in new markets like India or China can create a hedge.

Today, Coca-Cola's International Business Sector is divided into four operating groups: the Greater Europe Group, the Latin America Group, the Middle and Far East Group, and the Africa Group. Moreover, Coca-Cola is putting major resources into continued international growth. The company has, for instance, targeted Eastern Europe and China for future expansion and has spent liberally to support business in these sizable markets. In addition, Coca-Cola plans a $250 million expansion in Russia. Bottlers in Venezuela anticipate a $200 million expansion, and in Brazil, $2 billion is slated to be spent in the next five years to add vending machines and coolers. Not forgetting the home market, Coca-Cola will also continue to add vending machines and coolers in U.S. gas stations, convenience stores, and grocery stores to help catch up with archrival Pepsi Cola in these areas.

Finally, since 1928, Coca-Cola has supported Olympic Games and athletes—this is the longest continuous support provided by a corporation. Through international and national sponsorship programs, Coca-Cola helps finance teams and aspiring athletes in 195 countries. The company has continued this worldwide marketing effort through the 1998 Winter Olympic Games in Nagano, Japan, and has agreed to be a sponsor for the 2000 Olympic Games in Sydney, Australia.

The key to Coca-Cola's future success is management's commitment to create value for shareholders. One of its major assets in this effort is the company's "strong global leadership in the beverage industry in particular and in the business world in general."

QUESTIONS

1. What does Goizueta mean when he says that "soft drinks are very much a local product"? Is Goizueta's vision of a "local" multinational company possible? Explain.
2. Cite evidence to illustrate ways in which Coca-Cola's management stresses the company's multinational status.
3. Consider past and current Coca-Cola advertising campaigns. Were these tailored for the international or the domestic market? Explain. How do these campaigns illustrate the concept of a "local" multinational?
4. Would a Coca-Cola bought in Atlanta taste the same as one bought in Moscow? Why or why not? What does this say about the company and its commitment to the international market?

SMALL BUSINESS 2000

When you think of international business, you might think of large corporations such as Volvo, Sony, or IBM. Many international companies are quite large, but smaller companies can be global too. Companies of any size may be attracted to an international perspective by either a need or an opportunity.

Jimmy Fand, the owner of Tile Connection, was motivated by both need and opportunity. Jimmy Fand discovered the need for importing high-quality tile, used in residential and commercial construction, when he was having a home built for his family. What Fand found was that the selection available to him was limited and that prices appeared to be much higher than he believed they needed to be. This simple personal event was the turning point which led to the establishment of Tile Connection, one of the largest tile importers in the United States. Mr. Fand quickly identified that he was not going to build the business he envisioned by simply relying on American manufacturers and suppliers. An interesting part of the Tile Connection story is that the opportunity that Mr. Fand developed and pursued guaranteed that his would be an international venture—it would be difficult to be a supplier of tile from all over the world without trading internationally.

Doing business internationally has its own set of interesting challenges. Tile Connection quickly became aware of them. One issue that required particular attention was the way in which relationships would be managed with international suppliers. Tile Connection had to establish supplier chains and build in safeguards to ensure that it received the products it wanted, when it wanted them, and in a condition that they could be sold. This may seem like basic business to you, but think about times that you went to purchase something and it was out of stock or you pulled something out of the box and parts were missing or broken. This is aggravating even when you live a walk or short drive away from the store, so imagine the hassles you would have if the store were thousands of miles away or the salesperson did not speak your language.

QUESTIONS

1. In this chapter you studied four levels of international business. Identify Tile Connection's level of international involvement and describe why you selected this level.

2. Mr. Fand has implemented various practices to ensure that Tile Connection benefits from its international trading relationships. Identify and describe examples of what has been done to safeguard and manage Tile Connection's interest.

3. Mr. Fand suggests that international trading is a two-way street. What has he done to make it desirable for his customers to do business with him?

4. Mr. Fand makes a comment that "the world is getting smaller." What do you think he means by that? Do you agree?

Organizational Objectives

STUDENT LEARNING OBJECTIVES

From studying this chapter, I will attempt to acquire

1. An understanding of organizational objectives

2. An appreciation for the importance of organizational objectives

3. An ability to tell the difference between organizational objectives and individual objectives

4. A knowledge of the areas in which managers should set organizational objectives

5. An understanding of the development of organizational objectives

6. Some facility in writing good objectives

7. An awareness of how managers use organizational objectives and help others to attain the objectives

8. An appreciation for the potential of a management-by-objectives (MBO) program

CHAPTER OUTLINE

Introductory Case: *Blockbuster Chief Sets Organizational Objectives*

GENERAL NATURE OF ORGANIZATIONAL OBJECTIVES
Definition of Organizational Objectives

Global Spotlight: *Asea Brown Boveri Decides on Global Objectives*
Importance of Organizational Objectives

TYPES OF OBJECTIVES IN ORGANIZATIONS
Organizational Objectives
Individual Objectives
Goal Integration

AREAS FOR ORGANIZATIONAL OBJECTIVES

Management and the Internet: *Internet Trend Causes Sega to Alter Objectives*

WORKING WITH ORGANIZATIONAL OBJECTIVES
Establishing Organizational Objectives

Across Industries: *Automobile Tire Manufacturing—Goodyear Uses Innovation to Support Profitability Objective*

Diversity Spotlight: *Diversity: Objective for the Whole Organization at the Department of Transportation*
Guidelines for Establishing Quality Objectives
Guidelines for Making Objectives Operational
Attainment of Objectives
How to Use Objectives

MANAGEMENT BY OBJECTIVES (MBO)
Factors Necessary for a Successful MBO Program
MBO Programs: Advantages and Disadvantages

BLOCKBUSTER CHIEF SETS ORGANIZATIONAL OBJECTIVES

REMINDER: THE INTRODUCTORY CASE WRAP-UP (P. 120) CONTAINS DISCUSSION QUESTIONS AND A SKILLS EXERCISE TO FURTHER ILLUSTRATE THE APPLICATION OF CHAPTER CONCEPTS TO THIS VIGNETTE.

Sumner Redstone, the chief executive officer (CEO) of Viacom Inc., made a tremendous gamble when his company purchased Blockbuster Entertainment in 1994 for $8.4 billion. At the time, Viacom already owned Paramount Pictures, MTV Networks, theme parks, and a dozen local television stations. Redstone hoped that the purchase of Blockbuster would result in tremendous synergies for the parent company; he thought that Blockbuster would be one of the final pieces of the Viacom entertainment puzzle.

In the two years following the acquisition, however, the Blockbuster unit struggled. Competition from local video stores diminished Blockbuster's market share, and new technology in the form of digital satellites and pay per view threatened Blockbuster's future. In addition to these external forces, internal problems plagued Blockbuster, as well. The company's marketing campaigns were ineffective, and customers often complained that stores did not carry enough copies of popular videos.

In 1997, however, Redstone hired John Antioco to take over the struggling Blockbuster unit. Before accepting his position at Blockbuster, Antioco served as the CEO of Taco Bell and Circle K Corporation. Redstone hoped that these experiences would help Antioco increase Blockbuster's profitability. Just 10 months after his arrival, Blockbuster's future already looked much brighter. Although Blockbuster had a 25 percent share of the rental market, Antioco wanted more.

In 1998, Antioco announced ambitious objectives to lead the once struggling unit into the new millennium; he believed that these objectives would enable the company to reach much higher levels of profitability. More specifically, Antioco announced that he expected the Blockbuster unit to sharply increase its share of the rental market to 40 percent in five years. To reach this objective, he

New long-term and short-term objectives as well as functional objectives are expected to help bring Blockbuster into the new century with a sharp increase in market share.

wanted Blockbuster to gain three market share points each year during the five-year period.

To gain the market share and support these long-term and short-term objectives, Antioco also issued functional objectives. For example, he planned to increase the number of copies of hit videos in the stores. In addition, he planned to aggressively match the price discounts given by local competitors. Last, Antioco felt that Blockbuster stores needed to match, if not exceed, the customer service provided by its smaller local competitors. By establishing and coordinating long-term, short-term, and functional objectives, Redstone and Antioco both hope that Blockbuster will return to its days of unprecedented profitability.

What's Ahead

Managers such as John Antioco, CEO of Blockbuster Entertainment, recognize that organizations without concrete objectives will encounter serious problems. This chapter can help other managers gain a broad appreciation for using objectives to appropriately guide organizations to success. This chapter discusses the following:

1. The general nature of organizational objectives
2. Different types of organizational objectives
3. Various areas in which organizational objectives should be set
4. How managers actually work with organizational objectives
5. Management by objectives (MBO)

GENERAL NATURE OF ORGANIZATIONAL OBJECTIVES

DEFINITION OF ORGANIZATIONAL OBJECTIVES

Organizational objectives are the targets toward which the open management system is directed. They flow from the organization's purpose or mission.

The **organizational purpose** is what the organization exists to do, given a particular group of customers and customer needs.

Organizational objectives are the targets toward which the open management system is directed. Organizational input, process, and output—topics discussed in chapter 2—all exist to reach organizational objectives (see Figure 5.1). Properly developed organizational objectives reflect the purpose of the organization—that is, they flow naturally from the organization's mission. The **organizational purpose** is what the organization exists to do, given a particular group of customers and customer needs. Table 5.1 contains several statements of organizational purpose, or mission, as developed by actual companies. If an organization is accomplishing its objectives, it is accomplishing its purpose and thereby justifying its reason for existence.

Organizations exist for various purposes and thus have various types of objectives. A hospital, for example, may have the primary purpose of providing high-quality medical services to the community. Therefore, its objectives are aimed at furnishing this assistance. The primary purpose of a business organization, in contrast, is usually to make a profit. The objectives of the business organization, therefore, concentrate on ensuring that a profit is made. Some companies, however, assume that if they focus on such organizational objectives as producing a quality product at a competitive price, profits will be inevitable. For example, although the Lincoln Electric Company is profit oriented, management has stated organizational objectives in these terms:[1]

> The goal of the organization must be this—to make a better and better product to be sold at a lower and lower price. Profit cannot be the goal. Profit must be a by-product. This is a state of mind and a philosophy. Actually, an organization doing this job as it can be done will make large

FIGURE 5.1	**How an open management system operates to reach organizational objectives**

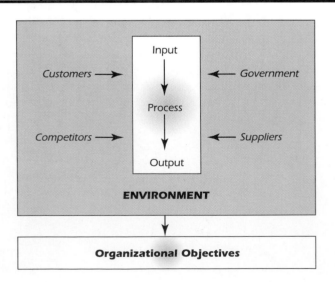

TABLE 5.1	Examples of Statements of Organizational Purpose
DuPont	DuPont is a multinational high-technology company that manufactures and markets chemically related products. It services a diversified group of markets in which proprietary technology provides the competing edge.
Polaroid	Polaroid manufactures and sells photographic products based on its inventions in the field of one-step instant photography and light-polarizing products. Utilizing its inventions in the field of polarized light, the company considers itself to be engaged in one line of business.
Central Soya	The basic mission of Central Soya is to be a leading producer and merchandiser of products for the worldwide agribusiness and food industry.
General Portland Cement	It has long been a business philosophy of Central Portland that "we manufacture and sell cement, but we market concrete." The company sees its job as manufacturing top-quality cement and working with customers to develop new applications for concrete while expanding current uses.

profits which must be properly divided between user, worker, and stockholder. This takes ability and character.

In a 1956 article that has become a classic, John F. Mee suggested that organizational objectives for businesses can be summarized in three points:[2]

1. Profit is the motivating force for managers
2. Service to customers by the provision of desired economic values (goods and services) justifies the existence of the business
3. Managers have social responsibilities in accordance with the ethical and moral codes of the society in which the business operates.

Deciding on the objectives for an organization, then, is one of the most important actions managers take. Unrealistically high objectives are frustrating for employees, while objectives that are set too low do not push employees to maximize their potential. Managers should establish performance objectives that they know from experience are within reach for employees, but not within *easy* reach.[3]

Outback Steakhouse, based in Tampa, Florida, set as its broad organizational goal to capture the middle range of the casual-dining steakhouse business. In order to maintain stable management and integrate employees into its organizational structure, Outback gives restaurant managers significant ownership stakes, maintains only one layer of management between the founders and the outlet managers, and permits in-store managers to handle all human resource decisions. Service quality is maintained because staff serve only three tables each, and product quality is high because everything is prepared on site.

An important part of being a manager is deciding on the objectives to formulate for an organization. Management at ASEA Brown Boveri (ABB) set the organizational objective of expanding its international business.

ABB, winner of R&D magazine's Corporation of the Year award, is a Swiss-Swedish corporation that was established in 1988. It is fast becoming a model for how to manage globally. Already, ABB is the world's largest manufacturer of railway vehicles, the world's leading equipment supplier to the electric power industry, and a major contender in robotics and worldwide pollution control equipment.

One of ABB's secrets in accomplishing its objectives to grow globally is that the company delegates large amounts of authority to managers around the world while maintaining influence over their important decisions regarding the business. Managers at ABB understand that reaching the organization's global objectives involves much more than generating international sales. A company like ABB must use management training sessions to inculcate global management skills in its managers. These skills include the ability to negotiate effectively with people from other cultures, the expertise to interpret market factors in different countries, and the competence to understand foreign politics. Such training will give a company like ABB a labor force that can compete effectively anywhere in the world.

▶ IMPORTANCE OF ORGANIZATIONAL OBJECTIVES

Managers use organizational objectives the way sailors use the North Star—they sight their compass by the objective, and then use it as the means of getting back on track whenever they go astray.[4] Organizational objectives give managers and all other organization members important guidelines for action in such areas as decision making, organizational efficiency, organizational consistency, and performance evaluation.

GUIDE FOR DECISION MAKING A significant part of managerial responsibility is making decisions that influence the everyday operation and existence of the organization and of organization members. Once managers grasp organizational objectives, they know the direction in which the organization must move. It then becomes their responsibility to make decisions that push the organization toward achieving its objectives.

GUIDE FOR ORGANIZATIONAL EFFICIENCY Because inefficiency results in a costly waste of human effort and resources, managers strive to increase organizational efficiency whenever possible. Efficiency is defined in terms of the total amount of human effort and resources that an organization uses to achieve organizational aims. Therefore, before organizational efficiency can improve, managers must have a clear understanding of organizational goals. Only then will they be able to use the limited resources at their disposal as efficiently as possible.

GUIDE FOR ORGANIZATIONAL CONSISTENCY Organization members often need work-related directives. If organizational objectives are used as the basis for these directives, the objectives will serve as a guide to consistent encouragement of productive activity, quality decision making, and effective planning.

GUIDE FOR PERFORMANCE EVALUATION Periodically, the performance of all organization members should be evaluated to assess individual productivity and to determine what might be done to increase it. Organizational goals are the guidelines or criteria that should be used as the basis for these evaluations. The individuals who contribute most to the attainment of organizational goals should be considered the most productive organization members. Specific recommendations for increasing productivity should include suggestions about what individuals can do to help the organization move toward goal attainment.[5]

Ben & Jerry set as an organizational objective the firm's entry into a new area—the market for rich, smooth ice cream, without chips, crunch, nuts, cherries, and other ingredients. Success in achieving this objective will bring positive results for Ben & Jerry's market share and profitability but will require targeted planning based on research about competitors' offerings and customers' tastes and preferences.

The above discussion of organizational objectives gives managers such as John Antioco, CEO of Blockbuster Entertainment, useful insights on how a company can be put and kept on the right track. The Introductory Case revealed that Blockbuster had few clear goals before Antioco's arrival. Soon after his arrival, however, Antioco established several organizational objectives. Perhaps the most important of these objectives involved drastically increasing Blockbuster's market share. In order to achieve his objective of market share growth, Antioco also established pricing, inventory, and customer service objectives. From a management viewpoint, these steps that Antioco took to pursue and reach his market share growth objective were logical. Antioco must be careful, though, to ensure that his market share objective does not conflict with Blockbuster's profit objectives. For example, decreasing the price of movie rentals might increase Blockbuster's market share, but it might actually decrease Blockbuster's profits.

TYPES OF OBJECTIVES IN ORGANIZATIONS

Objectives in organizations can be separated into two categories: organizational and individual. Recognizing the two categories and reacting appropriately to each are a challenge for all modern managers.

► ORGANIZATIONAL OBJECTIVES

Organizational objectives are the formal targets of the organization and are set to help the organization accomplish its purpose. They concern such areas as organizational efficiency, productivity, and profit maximization.

Y. K. Shetty conducted a study to determine the nature and pattern of corporate objectives as they actually exist in organizations. Shetty analyzed 193 companies in four basic industrial groups: (1) chemicals and drugs, (2) packaging materials, (3) electricity and electronics, and (4) food processing.[6] The results of his study indicate that the most common organizational objectives relate to profitability, growth, and market share. Social responsibility and employee welfare objectives are also common and probably reflect a change in approaches to management activities over a period of years. Still important, but less common, objectives relate to efficiency, research and development, and financial stability.

► INDIVIDUAL OBJECTIVES

Individual objectives, which also exist within organizations, are the personal goals each organization member would like to reach through activity within the organization. These objectives include high salary, personal growth and development, peer recognition, and societal recognition.

It is a problem for management when organizational objectives and individual objectives are incompatible. For example, a professor may have an individual goal of working at a university primarily to gain peer recognition. Perhaps she pursues this recognition by channeling most of her energies into research. This professor's individual objective could significantly contribute to the attainment of organizational objectives if she is at a university whose organizational objectives emphasized research. Her individual objective might contribute little or nothing to organizational goal attainment, however, if she is employed at a teaching-oriented university, because rather than improving her general teaching ability and the quality of her courses—which would be compatible with the teaching university's goals—she would be secluded in the library writing research articles.

One alternative managers have in situations of this type is to structure the organization so that individuals have the opportunity to accomplish their own objectives while contributing to the attainment of organizational goals. For instance, the teaching-oriented university could take steps to ensure that good teachers received peer recognition—by offering an "excellence in teaching" award, for example. In this way, professors could strive for their personal peer recognition goal while simultaneously contributing to the university's organizational objective of good teaching.

Individual objectives are personal goals that each organization member would like to reach as a result of personal activity in the organization.

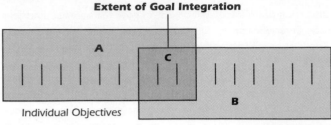

FIGURE 5.2 ► Goal integration model

►GOAL INTEGRATION

An objective, or goal, integration model can help managers understand and solve problems related to incompatibility between organizational and individual objectives. Jon Barrett's model, presented in Figure 5.2, depicts a situation in which the objectives in area C are the only individual ones (compare area A) compatible with organizational objectives (area B). Area C, then, represents the extent of **goal integration.**

> **Goal integration** is compatibility between individual and organizational objectives. It occurs when organizational and individual objectives are the same.

Managers should keep in mind two things about the situation depicted in this figure. First, the individual will tend to work for goals in area C without much managerial encouragement because the attainment of these goals will result in some type of reward the individual considers valuable. Second, the individual will usually not work for goals outside area A without some significant type of managerial encouragement because the attainment of these goals holds little promise of bringing any reward the individual considers valuable. Barrett suggests that "significant types of managerial encouragement" could take any one of the following forms:[7]

1. Modifications to existing pay schedules
2. Considerate treatment from superiors
3. Additional opportunities to engage in informal social relationships with peers

BACK TO THE CASE

Finding a common ground between organizational objectives and individual objectives is no easy task, and conflict between these two types of objectives can spell trouble for an organization. In the Blockbuster case, Blockbuster Entertainment is a franchise, and many of its stores are owned by individual franchisees. Perhaps part of Antioco's optimism is due to the compatibility between organizational and individual franchisee objectives. In Blockbuster's case, the goals of the corporation are similar to those of the individual franchisees. For example, both the organization and the franchisees know that improving customer service will bring more customers to the individual stores, and each store will rent more videos. By renting more videos, both the company and its individual franchisees will enjoy financial success. Consequently, individual franchisees will do all they can to help Antioco achieve the organizational goal of improved customer service. In this type of situation, a significant degree of goal integration should help Antioco achieve improved customer service and increased market share.

■ AREAS FOR ORGANIZATIONAL OBJECTIVES

Peter F. Drucker, one of the most influential management writers of modern times, believed that the very survival of a management system was endangered when managers emphasized only the profit objective because this single-objective emphasis encourages managers to take action that will make money today with little regard for how a profit will be made tomorrow.[8]

Managers should strive to develop and attain a variety of objectives in all areas where activity is critical to the operation and success of the management system. Following are the eight key areas in which Drucker advised managers to set management system objectives:

1. *Market standing*—Management should set objectives indicating where it would like to be in relation to its competitors
2. *Innovation*—Management should set objectives outlining its commitment to the development of new methods of operation
3. *Productivity*—Management should set objectives outlining the target levels of production
4. *Physical and financial resources*—Management should set objectives regarding the use, acquisition, and maintenance of capital and monetary resources
5. *Profitability*—Management should set objectives that specify the profit the company would like to generate
6. *Managerial performance and development*—Management should set objectives that specify rates and levels of managerial productivity and growth
7. *Worker performance and attitude*—Management should set objectives that specify rates of worker productivity as well as desirable attitudes for workers to possess
8. *Public responsibility*—Management should set objectives that indicate the company's responsibilities to its customers and society and the extent to which the company intends to live up to those responsibilities

According to Drucker, since the first five goal areas relate to tangible, impersonal characteristics of organizational operation, most managers would not dispute their designation as key areas. Designating the last three as key areas, however, could arouse some managerial opposition because these areas are more personal and subjective. Regardless of this potential opposition, an organization should have objectives in all eight areas to maximize its probability of success.

The information in this section pertains to all the different areas in which managers can establish organizational objectives. One relatively new area in which managers are setting objectives involves Internet usage. The following Management and the Internet discusses how one company recently altered its organizational objectives because of an increasing trend toward more Internet usage.

MANAGEMENT AND THE INTERNET — Internet Trend Causes Sega to Alter Objectives

Sega Enterprises, Inc., develops and markets video games and video game consoles. In 1997, the video game industry enjoyed record revenues of $5.5 billion, but Sega's once formidable grip on the industry virtually disappeared. In fact, Sega captured only four percent of the console market in 1997 while its main competitors, Sony and Nintendo, captured most of the remaining market. In the past, Sega's executives worried only about maintaining its huge market share, but two dynamics have forced the company to change its objectives: intense industry competition and the evolution of the Internet.

Due to intense industry competition, Sega changed its market share objective. More specifically, Sega's executives hope that sales of its new Dreamcast video game console, due to launch in the fall of 1999, match those of Sony's Playstation launch in 1995. In other words, Sega's objective changed from leading the market to simply keeping up with the market leader. Sega is concerned, however, that some consumers might skip its Dreamcast launch and wait until Sony introduces its new Playstation the following year.

Although intense competition obviously altered Sega's objectives, the company's executives might be even more concerned with the evolution of the Internet. Lower prices have made computers more affordable, and this increased computer ownership has provided more people with access to the Internet. This trend concerns Sega's executives because the Internet has spawned new games that enable users to play against thousands of strangers in real time on the Internet. As a result, Sega's new Dreamcast machine will include a first: a modem that allows users to connect to the Internet. With the modem, Sega executives hope to establish a presence in the Internet video game market. Obviously, these changes in the marketplace caused Sega to alter its objectives quite dramatically.

Appropriate objectives are fundamental to the success of any organization. Theodore Levitt noted that some leading U.S. industries could be facing the same financial disaster as the railroads faced years earlier because their objectives were inappropriate for their organizations.[9]

Managers should approach the development, use, and modification of organizational objectives with the utmost seriousness. In general, an organization should set three types of objectives:

Short-term objectives are targets to be achieved in one year or less.

Intermediate-term objectives are targets to be achieved within one to five years.

Long-term objectives are targets to be achieved within five to seven years.

The **principle of the objective** is a management guideline that recommends that before managers initiate any action, they should clearly determine, understand, and state organizational objectives.

1. *Short-term objectives*—targets to be achieved in one year or less
2. *Intermediate-term objectives*—targets to be achieved in one to five years
3. *Long-term objectives*—targets to be achieved in five to seven years

The necessity of predetermining appropriate organizational objectives has led to the development of a management guideline called the **principle of the objective.** This principle holds that before managers initiate any action, they should clearly determine, understand, and state organizational objectives.

ESTABLISHING ORGANIZATIONAL OBJECTIVES

Setting objectives is becoming an increasingly important part of a manager's job. Managers today are commonly asked to establish objectives for themselves, their departments, and their employees.[10] The three main steps a manager must take to develop a set of working organizational objectives follow:

1. Determine the existence of any environmental trends that could significantly influence the operation of the organization
2. Develop a set of objectives for the organization as a whole
3. Develop a hierarchy of organizational objectives

These three steps are interrelated and usually require input from several people at different levels and operational sections of the organization. Each step is further developed in the paragraphs that follow.

ANALYZING TRENDS The first step in setting organizational objectives is to list major trends in the organizational environment over the past five years and to determine if these trends have had a noticeable impact on organizational success. Conceivably, the trends could include changing customer needs,[11] marketing innovations of competitors, government controls, and social changes such as decreasing family size. Management should then decide which present and future trends are likely to affect organizational success over the next five years. This decision will determine what kinds of objectives are set at various levels of the organization. The following Across Industries feature shows how one company's innovation objectives and profitability objectives are interrelated.

ACROSS INDUSTRIES — Automobile Tire Manufacturing

GOODYEAR USES INNOVATION TO SUPPORT PROFITABILITY OBJECTIVE

Samir Gibara, the chairman and president of Goodyear Tire and Rubber Company, has an ambitious objective. Gibara wants Goodyear to be the low-cost manufacturer among the Big Three tire makers, and he believes that innovation will help the company reach that objective. Although Goodyear has always used innovation to develop new products, Gibara wants to use that same innovation to develop more efficient and less costly manufacturing processes. Gibara

hopes that innovation on both the product development side and the manufacturing side will help the company to outperform its main rivals, Michelin and Bridgestone.

To understand how innovation has helped Goodyear's product, one needs to look no further than the company's new run-flat tires. These new tires, considered to be an industry development comparable to the invention of radial tires, allow consumers to drive nearly fifty miles after getting a flat. As a result, the new tires enable consumers to drive without keeping spare tires in their cars.

Although the invention of these tires represents a major accomplishment, the high manufacturing cost results in a higher price for the consumer. Although the run-flat tires are only about 10 percent higher than the price of conventional tires, the sensor system required to alert drivers of flat tires costs an additional $250 per vehicle to install. Goodyear sees this high installation price as a major problem, and Gibara wants it to decrease to $50. For this dramatic price decrease to occur, he will have to further support innovation by maintaining the aggressive levels of research and development spending that Goodyear engineers have become accustomed to. If Goodyear can innovate successfully, it might just accomplish its objective of being the low-cost tire manufacturer.

DEVELOPING OBJECTIVES FOR THE ORGANIZATION AS A WHOLE After analyzing environmental trends, management should develop objectives that reflect this analysis for the organization as a whole. For example, the analysis may show that a major competitor has been continually improving its products over the past five years and, as a result, is gaining an increasingly large share of the market. In reaction to this trend, management should set a product improvement objective that will enable the organization to keep up with competitors. This objective would result directly from identification of a trend within the organizational environment and from the organizational purpose of profit. The paragraphs that follow illustrate how management might set financial objectives, product-market mix objectives, and functional objectives for the organization as a whole.

▸DIVERSITY SPOTLIGHT◂ Diversity: Objective for the Whole Organization at the Department of Transportation

Managers at the Department of Transportation (DOT), a major department within the U.S. government, appreciate the role that a properly managed diverse workforce can play in making an organization successful. In fact, management has set the objective of creating a work environment throughout DOT that fully values and uses the talents and capabilities of all employees, including employees of different cultures and colors.

DOT has taken several specific actions to try to accomplish this diversity objective. Management started out by holding sessions with DOT employees to hear their suggestions on how to create a diversity-sensitive environment. Building upon this employee input, DOT then held a diversity summit that was attended by over 650 department executives from across the country. The purpose of the summit was to pinpoint and explore diversity-related challenges and opportunities that confront DOT today. In addition, DOT assembled a team of human resources management professionals to work full-time on promoting diversity. This team works closely with managers throughout the department to create, plan, and implement diversity initiatives and to ensure that diversity issues are emphasized in all facets of DOT's operations. DOT also publishes a diversity newsletter to explain diversity issues to employees, provide them with information about department initiatives in this area, and suggest how diversity issues should be handled in the workplace.

Establishing Financial Objectives   **Financial objectives** are organizational targets relating to monetary issues. In some organizations, government regulations guide management's setting of these objectives. Managers of public utility organizations, for example, have definite guidelines for the types of financial objectives they are allowed to set. In organizations free from government constraints, setting financial objectives is influenced mainly by return on investment and financial comparisons with competitors.[12]

Return on investment (ROI) is the amount of money an organization earns in relation to the amount of money invested to keep the organization in operation. Figure 5.3 shows how to use earnings of $50,000 and an investment of $500,000 to calculate a return on investment. If the calculated return is too low, managers can set as an overall objective improving the organization's rate of return.

Information on organizational competition is available through published indexes, such as Dun & Bradstreet's *Ratios for Selected Industries*. These ratios reflect industry averages for

Financial objectives are organizational targets relating to monetary issues. They are influenced by return on investment and financial comparisons with competitors.

FIGURE 5.3 ▶ **Calculations for return on investment**

$$\text{Return on Investment} = \frac{\text{Total dollar amount earned}}{\text{Total dollar amount invested to keep organization operating}}$$

$$\text{Return on Investment} = \frac{\$50,000 \text{ (earnings)}}{\$500,000 \text{ (investment)}} = .10 = 10\% \text{ (return rate)}$$

key financial areas. Comparing company figures with the industrial averages should tell management about the areas in which new financial objectives should be set or the ways in which existing objectives should be modified.[13]

Product-market mix objectives are objectives that outline which products—and the relative number or mix of these products—the organization will attempt to sell.

Establishing Product-Market Mix Objectives **Product-market mix objectives** outline which products—and the relative number or mix of these products—the organization will attempt to sell. Granger suggests the following five steps in formulating product-market mix objectives:[14]

1. Examine key trends in the business environments of the product-market areas.
2. Examine growth trends (both market and volume) and profit trends (for the industry and for the company) in the individual product-mix areas.
3. Separate product-market areas into those that are going to pull ahead and those that are going to drag. For promising areas, the following questions need to be asked: How can these areas be made to flourish? Should additional capital, marketing effort, technology, management talent, or the like be injected into these areas? For the less promising areas, these questions are pertinent: Why is the product lagging? How can the lag be corrected? If it cannot be corrected, should the product be milked for whatever can be regained, or should it be withdrawn from the market?

His predecessor had insisted that each of the company's operating units remain independent so that they would be more responsive to changing consumer tastes. But when Philip B. Fletcher took over as CEO of ConAgra Inc., a consumer-foods giant based in Omaha, Nebraska, he instituted a program of cost controls that applied to the company as a whole. Thus while he still grants the virtues of independence, he has established executive councils on which division heads meet to discuss ways of sharing such costs as purchasing and warehousing.

4. Consider the need or desirability of adding new products or market areas to the mix. In this regard, management should ask these questions: Is there a profit gap to be filled? Based on the criteria of profit opportunity, compatibility, and feasibility of market entry, what are possible new areas of interest in order of priority? What sort of programs (acquisitions or internal development) does the company need to develop the desired level of business in these areas?
5. Derive an optimum yet realistic product-market mix profile based on the conclusions reached in steps 1 to 4. This profile embodies the product-market mix objectives, which should be consistent with the organization's financial objectives. Interaction while setting these two kinds of objectives is advisable.

Establishing Functional Objectives **Functional objectives** are targets relating to key organizational functions, including marketing, accounting, production, and personnel. Functional objectives that are consistent with the financial and product-market mix objectives should be developed for these areas. People in the organization should perform their functions in a way that helps the organization attain its other objectives.

> **Functional objectives** are targets relating to key organizational functions. They should be consistent with financial and product-market mix objectives.

BACK TO THE CASE

The information just presented implies that managers such as Antioco should set and strive to achieve objectives in addition to growth objectives. These other objectives should be set in such areas as profitability, market standing, innovation, productivity, physical and financial resources, managerial performance and development, worker performance and attitude, and public responsibility. Naturally, they should probably be set for the short, intermediate, and long term.

Before developing such objectives, however, a manager like Antioco should pinpoint any environmental trends, like the emergence of affordable satellite systems or the proliferation of pay-per-view systems, that could influence Blockbuster's operations. Objectives that reflect such environmental trends could then be set for the organization as a whole. They normally would include financial objectives like return on investment as well as product-market mix objectives like the number of days that a customer can rent a new release.

DEVELOPING A HIERARCHY OF OBJECTIVES In practice, an organizational objective must be broken down into subobjectives so that individuals at different levels and sections of the organization know what they must do to help reach the overall organizational objective.[15] An organizational objective is attained only after the subobjectives have been reached.

At 3M Corporation, Scotch-Brite, Never Rust soap pads are just one result of CEO L. D. DeSimone's focusing of short- and long-term objectives squarely on the new product pipeline. He has established, for example, a so-called 30-and-4 standard: 3M must generate 30 percent of its profits from products introduced within the previous four-year period. Within 18 months of their launch, the new Scotch-Brite soap pads captured 22 percent of the $100 million annual U.S. market.

FIGURE 5.4 ▶ Hierarchy of objectives for a medium-sized organization

TOP MANAGEMENT
1. Represent stockholders' interests—net profits of 10% or more
2. Provide service to consumers—provide reliable products
3. Maintain growth of assets and sales—double each decade
4. Provide continuity of employment for company, personnel—no involuntary layoffs
5. Develop favorable image with public

PRODUCTION DEPARTMENT
1. Keep cost of goods no more than 50% of sales
2. Increase productivity of labor by 3% per year
3. Maintain rejects at less than 2%
4. Maintain inventory at 6 months of sales
5. Keep production rate stable with no more than 20% variability from yearly average

SALES DEPARTMENT
1. Introduce new products so that over a 10-year period, 70% will be new
2. Maintain a market share of 15%
3. Seek new market areas so that sales will grow at a 15% annual rate
4. Maintain advertising costs at 4% of sales

FINANCE AND ACCOUNTING DEPARTMENT
1. Borrowing should not exceed 50% of assets
2. Maximize tax write-offs
3. Provide monthly statements to operating departments by 10th of following month
4. Pay dividends at rate of 50% of net earnings

SUPERVISORS
1. Handle employee grievances within 24 hours
2. Maintain production to standard or above
3. Keep scrappage to 2% of materials usage

DISTRICT SALES MANAGER
1. Meet weekly sales quotas
2. Visit each large customer once each month
3. Provide sales representatives with immediate follow-up support

OFFICE MANAGERS
1. Maintain cycle billing within 3 days of target date
2. Prepare special reports within 1 week of request

A **hierarchy of objectives** is the overall organizational objectives and the subobjectives assigned to the various people or units of the organization.

Suboptimization is a condition wherein organizational subobjectives are conflicting or not directly aimed at accomplishing the overall organizational objectives.

The overall organizational objective and the subobjectives assigned to the various people or units of the organization are referred to as a **hierarchy of objectives.** Figure 5.4 presents a sample hierarchy of objectives for a medium-sized company.

Suboptimization is a condition wherein subobjectives are conflicting or not directly aimed at accomplishing the overall organizational objective. Suboptimization is possible within the company whose hierarchy of objectives is depicted in Figure 5.4 if the first subobjective for the finance and accounting department clashes with the second subobjective for the supervisors. This conflict would occur if supervisors needed new equipment to maintain production and the finance and accounting department couldn't approve the loan without the company's borrowing surpassing 50 percent of company assets. In such a situation, in which established subobjectives are aimed in different directions, a manager would have to choose which subobjective would better contribute to obtaining overall objectives and should therefore take precedence.

Controlling suboptimization in organizations is part of a manager's job. Managers can minimize suboptimization by developing a thorough understanding of how various parts of the organization relate to one another and by ensuring that subobjectives properly reflect these relations.

▶ GUIDELINES FOR ESTABLISHING QUALITY OBJECTIVES

The quality of goal statements, like that of all humanly developed commodities, can vary drastically. Here are some general guidelines that managers can use to increase the quality of their objectives:[16]

1. *Let the people responsible for attaining the objectives have a voice in setting them*—Often the people responsible for attaining the objectives know their job situation better than the

managers do and can therefore help to make the objectives more realistic. They will also be better motivated to achieve objectives they have had a say in establishing. Work-related problems that these people face should be thoroughly considered when objectives are being developed.

2. *State objectives as specifically as possible*—Precise statements minimize confusion and ensure that employees have explicit directions for what they should do. Research shows that when objectives are not specific, the productivity of individuals attempting to reach those objectives tends to fluctuate significantly over time.

3. *Relate objectives to specific actions whenever necessary*—In this way, employees do not have to infer what they should do to accomplish their goals.

4. *Pinpoint expected results*—Employees should know exactly how managers will determine whether or not an objective has been reached.

5. *Set goals high enough that employees will have to strive to meet them, but not so high that employees give up trying to meet them*—Managers want employees to work hard but not to become frustrated.

6. *Specify when goals are expected to be achieved*—Employees must have a time frame for accomplishing their objectives. They then can pace themselves accordingly.

7. *Set objectives only in relation to other organizational objectives*—In this way, suboptimization can be kept to a minimum.

8. *State objectives clearly and simply*—The written or spoken word should not impede communicating a goal to organization members.

►GUIDELINES FOR MAKING OBJECTIVES OPERATIONAL

Objectives must be stated in operational terms. That is, if an organization has **operational objectives,** managers should be able to tell if these objectives are being attained by comparing the actual results with the goal statements.[17]

Assume, for example, that a physical education instructor has set the following objectives for his students:

1. Each student will strive to develop a sense of balance
2. Each student will attempt to become flexible
3. Each student will try to become agile
4. Each student will try to become strong
5. Each student will work on becoming powerful
6. Each student will strive to become durable

These objectives are not operational because the activities and operations a student must perform to attain them are not specified. Additional information, however, could easily make the objectives operational. For example, the fifth physical education objective could be replaced with: Each student will strive to develop the power to do standing broad jumps the distance of his or her height plus one foot. Table 5.2 lists four basically nonoperational objectives and then shows how each can be made operational.

Operational objectives are objectives that are stated in observable or measurable terms. They specify the activities or operations needed to attain them.

TABLE 5.2	**Nonoperational Objectives versus Operational Objectives**

Nonoperational Objectives	Operational Objectives
1. Improve product quality	1. Reduce quality rejects to 2%
2. Improve communications	2. Hold weekly staff meetings and initiate a newsletter to improve communications
3. Improve social responsibility	3. Hire 50 hard-core unemployed each year
4. Issue monthly accounting reports on a more timely basis	4. Issue monthly accounting reports so they are received 3 days after the close of the accounting period

Once managers like Antioco set overall objectives for their organizations, their next step is to develop a company hierarchy of objectives. The development of this hierarchy entails breaking down the organization's overall objectives into subobjectives so that all organization members know what they must do to help the company reach its overall objectives.

At Blockbuster, although a hierarchy of objectives probably exists, it should not include a wide array of objectives. Most franchisees would probably understand that the company places a serious emphasis on developing new business and their particular roles regarding this emphasis. In addition, a company like Blockbuster should be sure to address the setting and accomplishment of objectives in areas like social responsibility, employee welfare, and diversification.

In establishing a hierarchy of objectives, Antioco must be careful not to suboptimize, or establish objectives or subobjectives that conflict with one another. Suboptimization is probably somewhat of a problem at Blockbuster because market share growth objectives seem in conflict with objectives in areas like profitability. In most organizations, confusion about issues like not knowing what organizational objectives and subobjectives actually exist can make it difficult for managers to recognize when suboptimization is a problem.

Other guidelines for establishing useful objectives at a company like Blockbuster include making the objectives clear, consistent, challenging, and specific. Perhaps most important of all, organizational objectives should be operational. These are certainly good guidelines for Antioco to follow in formulating organizational objectives. In addition, if Antioco allows franchisees to participate in establishing organizational objectives, he can help to ensure that company objectives are realistic and that organization members are committed to reaching them.

ATTAINMENT OF OBJECTIVES

The attainment of organizational objectives is the obvious goal of all conscientious managers. Managers quickly discover, however, that moving the organization toward goal attainment requires taking appropriate actions within the organization to reach the desired ends. This process is called means-ends analysis.

Means-ends analysis is the process of outlining the means by which various organizational objectives, or ends, can be achieved.

Basically, **means-ends analysis** entails "(1) starting with the general goal to be achieved, (2) discovering a set of means, very generally specified, for accomplishing this goal, and (3) taking each of these means, in turn, as a new subgoal and discovering a more detailed means for achieving it."[18]

Table 5.3 illustrates a means-ends analysis for three sample goals for a hotel: increased market share, financial stability, and owner satisfaction. The goal of increased market share includes two means: good service and employee morale/loyalty. These two means are subgoals that the hotel manager must focus on attaining in order to reach the goal of increased market share. The last column of the table lists the measures that can be taken to operationalize the subgoals.

Effective managers are aware of the importance not only of setting organizational objectives but also of clearly outlining the means by which these objectives can be attained. They know that means-ends analysis is essential for guiding their own activities as well as those of their subordinates. The better everyone within the organization understands the means by which goals are to be attained, the greater the probability that the goals will be reached.

HOW TO USE OBJECTIVES

As stated earlier in the chapter, organizational objectives flow naturally from organizational purpose and reflect the organization's environment. Managers must have a firm understanding of the influences that mold organizational objectives for, as these influences change, so

TABLE 5.3	Sample Goals, Means, and Measures for a Hotel	
Increased market share	Good Service	Ratio of repeat business Occupancy Informal feedback
	Employee morale and loyalty	Turnover Absenteeism Informal feedback
Financial stability	Image in financial markets Profitability	Price-earnings ratio Share price Earnings per share Gross operating profit Cost trends Cash flow
	Strength of management team	Turnover Divisional profit Rate of proportion Informal feedback
Owner satisfaction	Adequate cash flow	Occupancy Sales Gross operating profit Departmental profit

must the objectives themselves. Managers should never look upon objectives as unchangeable directives. In fact, a significant managerial responsibility is to help the organization change objectives when necessary.

MANAGEMENT BY OBJECTIVES (MBO)

Some managers find organizational objectives such an important and fundamental part of management that they use a management approach based exclusively on them. This approach, called **management by objectives (MBO),** was popularized mainly through the writings of Peter Drucker. Although mostly discussed in the context of profit-oriented companies, MBO is also a valuable management tool for nonprofit organizations like libraries and community clubs.[19] The MBO strategy has three basic parts:[20]

Management by objectives (MBO) is a management approach that uses organizational objectives as the primary means of managing organizations.

1. All individuals within an organization are assigned a specialized set of objectives that they try to reach during a normal operating period. These objectives are mutually set and agreed upon by individuals and their managers
2. Performance reviews are conducted periodically to determine how close individuals are to attaining their objectives
3. Rewards are given to individuals on the basis of how close they come to reaching their goals

The MBO process consists of five steps (see Figure 5.5):

1. *Review organizational objectives*—The manager gains a clear understanding of the organization's overall objectives
2. *Set worker objectives*—The manager and worker meet to agree on worker objectives to be reached by the end of the normal operating period
3. *Monitor progress*—At intervals during the normal operating period, the manager and worker check to see if the objectives are being reached
4. *Evaluate performance*—At the end of the normal operating period, the worker's performance is judged by the extent to which the worker reached the objectives
5. *Give rewards*—Rewards given to the worker are based on the extent to which the objectives were reached

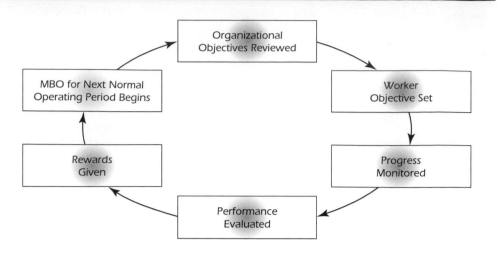

FIGURE 5.5 ► The MBO process

► FACTORS NECESSARY FOR A SUCCESSFUL MBO PROGRAM

Certain key factors are essential to the success of an MBO program. First, top management must be committed to the MBO process and set appropriate objectives for the organization. Since all individual MBO goals will be based on these overall objectives, if the overall objectives are inappropriate, individual MBO objectives will also be inappropriate and related individual work activity will be nonproductive. Second, managers and subordinates together must develop and agree on each individual's goals. Both managers and subordinates must feel that the individual objectives are just and appropriate if each party is to seriously regard them as a guide for action. Third, employee performance should be conscientiously evaluated against established objectives. This evaluation helps determine whether the objectives are fair and if appropriate means are being used to attain them. Fourth, management must follow through on employee performance evaluations by rewarding employees accordingly.

If employees are to continue striving to reach their MBO program objectives, managers must reward those who do reach, or surpass, their objectives more than those whose performance falls short of their objectives. It goes without saying that such rewards must be given out fairly and honestly. Managers must be careful, though, not to automatically conclude that employees have produced at an acceptable level simply because they have reached their objectives. The objectives may have been set too low in the first place, and managers may have failed to recognize it at the time.[21]

► MBO PROGRAMS: ADVANTAGES AND DISADVANTAGES

Experienced MBO managers say that there are two advantages to the MBO approach. First, MBO programs continually emphasize what should be done in an organization to achieve organizational goals. Second, the MBO process secures employee commitment to attaining organizational goals. Because managers and subordinates have developed objectives together, both parties are sincerely interested in reaching those goals.

MBO managers also admit that MBO has certain disadvantages. One is that the development of objectives can be time-consuming, leaving both managers and employees less time in which to do their actual work. Another is that the elaborate written goals, careful communication of goals, and detailed performance evaluations required in an MBO program increase the volume of paperwork in an organization.

On balance, however, most managers believe that MBO's advantages outweigh its disadvantages. Therefore, they find MBO programs beneficial.[22]

For updated information on the topics in this chapter, Internet exercises, links to related Internet sites, an interactive study guide, and more, visit our companion Web site at

http://www.prenhall.com/certo

Additional information can be found on the inside front and back covers of this text.

ACTION SUMMARY

Reread the learning objectives below. Each objective is followed by questions. Answering these questions accurately will help you retain the most important concepts discussed in this chapter. After answering each question, check your answer against the answer key at the end of this chapter. (*Hint:* If you have any doubts regarding the correct response, consult the page number that follows the answer.)

Circle:

From studying this chapter, I will attempt to acquire

1. An understanding of organizational objectives.

    T F   **a.** Organizational objectives should reflect the organization's purpose.

 a b c d e   **b.** The targets toward which an open management system is directed are referred to as: (a) functional objectives (b) organizational objectives (c) operational objectives (d) courses of action (e) individual objectives.

2. An appreciation for the importance of organizational objectives.

 a b c d e   **a.** Organizational objectives serve important functions in all of the following areas except: (a) making performance evaluations useful (b) establishing consistency (c) increasing efficiency (d) improving wages (e) decision making that influences everyday operations.

    T F   **b.** Implied within organizational objectives are hints on how to define the most productive workers in the organization.

3. An ability to tell the difference between organizational objectives and individual objectives.

 a b c d e   **a.** The following is considered to be an individual objective: (a) peer recognition (b) financial security (c) personal growth (d) b and c (e) all of the above.

 a b c d e   **b.** When goal integration exists: (a) there is a positive situation, desired by management (b) managers will not see conflict between organizational and personal objectives (c) the individual will work for goals without much managerial encouragement (d) additional opportunities to engage in informal social relationships with peers will not be necessary to encourage the individual (e) all of the above.

4. A knowledge of the areas in which managers should set organizational objectives.

a b c d e   **a.** The eight key areas in which Peter F. Drucker advises managers to set objectives include all of the following except: (a) market standing (b) productivity (c) public responsibility (d) inventory control (e) manager performance and development.

T F   **b.** Long-term objectives are defined as targets to be achieved in one to five years.

5. An understanding of the development of organizational objectives.

a b c d e   **a.** The following factor would *not* be considered in analyzing trends: (a) marketing innovations of competitors (b) projections for society (c) government controls (d) known existing and projected future events (e) product-market mix.

a b c d e   **b.** The following factor would *not* be considered in the "developing objectives for the organization as a whole" stage of setting organizational objectives: (a) establishing a hierarchy of objectives (b) establishing product-market mix objectives (c) establishing financial objectives (d) establishing return-on-investment objectives (e) establishing functional objectives.

6. Some facility in writing good objectives.

a b c d e   **a.** The following is an objective stated in nonoperational terms: (a) reduce customer complaints by 9 percent (b) make great progress in new product development (c) develop a new customer (d) increase profit before taxes by 10 percent (e) reduce quality rejects by 2 percent.

T F   **b.** An example of a good operational objective is: "Each student in this class will try to learn how to manage."

7. An awareness of how managers use organizational objectives and help others to attain the objectives.

T F   **a.** Means-ends analysis implies that the manager is results-oriented and discovers a set of means for accomplishing a goal.

a b c d e   **b.** Managers should use the following guidelines in changing objectives: (a) objectives should not be changed (b) adapt objectives when the organization's environmental influences change (c) change objectives to create suboptimization as needed (d) adapt objectives so that they are nonoperational (e) all of the above are valid guidelines.

8. An appreciation for the potential of a management-by-objectives (MBO) program.

T F   **a.** Both performance evaluations and employee rewards should be tied to objectives assigned to individuals when the firm is using MBO.

a b c d e   **b.** A method under which a manager is given specific objectives to achieve and is evaluated according to the accomplishment of these objectives is: (a) means-ends analysis (b) operational objectives (c) individual objectives (d) management by objectives (e) management by exception.

▶ INTRODUCTORY CASE WRAP-UP ◀

CASE DISCUSSSION QUESTIONS

"**B**lockbuster Chief Sets Organizational Objectives" (p. 103) and its related Back-to-the-Case sections were written to help you better understand the management concepts contained in this chapter. Answer the following discussion questions about this Introductory Case to further enrich your understanding of the chapter content:

1. If you were Antioco, what other objectives would you develop for Blockbuster? Discuss the importance of each objective to the success of the company.

2. Explain how Antioco's preoccupation with market share growth might cause problems in the company. List several of these problems, explain how they might be created, and discuss how they could be avoided.

3. As a manager, what strengths does Antioco have? What weaknesses does he have?

SKILLS EXERCISE: DESIGNING A MANAGEMENT-BY-OBJECTIVES (MBO) PROGRAM

In the Introductory Case, it is clear that one of Blockbuster's corporate objectives is to improve customer service. To reach this objective, design a management-by-objectives program that integrates the goals of the store employees with the goals of the store managers. First, identify the most important aspects of customer service and determine how to measure them. Second, establish what levels of performance result in employee awards. Lastly, determine appropriate employee awards that allow both the employees and the store managers to realize the successes of improved customer service.

1. What are organizational objectives and how do they relate to organizational purpose?
2. Explain why objectives are important to an organization.
3. List four areas in which organizational objectives can act as important guidelines for performance.
4. Explain the difference between organizational objectives and individual objectives.
5. What is meant by goal integration?
6. List and define eight key areas in which organizational objectives should be set.
7. How do environmental trends affect the process of establishing organizational objectives?
8. How does return on investment relate to setting financial objectives?
9. Define *product-market mix objectives*. What process should a manager go through to establish them?
10. What are functional objectives?
11. What is a hierarchy of objectives?
12. Explain the purpose of a hierarchy of objectives.
13. How does suboptimization relate to a hierarchy of objectives?
14. List eight guidelines a manager should follow to establish quality organizational objectives.
15. How does a manager make objectives operational?
16. Explain the concept of means-ends analysis.
17. Should a manager ever modify or change existing organizational objectives? If no, why? If yes, when?
18. Define *MBO* and describe its main characteristics.
19. List and describe the factors necessary for an MBO program to be successful.
20. Discuss the advantages and disadvantages of MBO.

1. **a.** T, p. 104
   b. b, p. 104
2. **a.** d, p. 105
   b. T, p. 105
3. **a.** e, p. 107
   b. e, p. 108
4. **a.** d, p. 109
   b. F, p. 110
5. **a.** e. p. 110
   b. a, pp. 111–113
6. **a.** b, p. 115
   b. F, p. 115
7. **a.** T, p. 116
   b. b, p. 117
8. **a.** T, p. 117
   b. d, p. 117

CASE STUDY: The Atlanta Committee for the Olympic Games (ACOG): Setting Objectives for an Event and a City

For Atlanta, Georgia, and the 1996 Olympic Committee, the Olympic motto, "Swifter, Higher, Stronger," was more than the objective for world-class competing athletes. It was their objective as well. Beginning in 1987, Billy Payne, a local real estate attorney, worked with city volunteers to convince the International Olympic Committee (IOC) that Atlanta was the best choice to host the centennial summer Olympic Games. In 1990, the IOC gave Atlanta the go-ahead, and the real work began. Considering the estimated $5.1 billion impact of the games on Georgia's economy, organizing was truly a task of Olympian proportions.

First, ACOG created advisory groups and task forces to help meet the city's objectives before, during, and after the games. Working with constituencies that included neighborhood groups affected by the construction of new Olympic venues; specialists in environmental, transportation, and security issues; and Olympic sponsors, artists, and artisans who would participate in the Olympics Arts Festival, ACOG eventually developed a process for planning and implementing a vast array of projects.

For example, ACOG worked with transportation officials from a wide range of public agencies to detail traffic circulation plans for movement of the Olympic Family, spectators, and the public in and around the "Olympic Ring"—an imaginary transportation circle encompassing Atlanta. The goal of the plan was to use lane restrictions and limited-hour street closings to keep major arteries and streets accessible to the Olympic Transportation System. In addition to the city's current transit buses and drivers, ACOG organized the delivery, prepa-

ration, maintenance, and return of a fleet of 2,000 new mass-transit buses borrowed from cities across the United States and hired 4,000 part-time drivers to supplement existing staff. Another 2,000 people— radio dispatchers, route supervisors, park-and-ride attendants, bus terminal managers, and baggage handlers—were engaged as support personnel. To further its mandate to protect the city's environment, ACOG tapped the American Gas Association to provide a fleet of 250 natural-gas vehicles, necessary infrastructure, and the natural-gas to fuel both the fleet and another 300 natural-gas-powered buses lent to the Olympic Games by municipalities around the nation. It was decided to include the cost of Olympic transportation for spectators in Atlanta in the price of an Olympic ticket.

To achieve the objective of safe and secure games, ACOG organizers brought together the State Olympic Public Safety Operations Task Force, the Georgia Emergency Management Agency, the Georgia National Guard, the CIA, the Bureau of Alcohol, Tobacco, and Firearms, the Immigration and Naturalization Service, the Secret Service, and U.S. Customs. An overall command and control center was established to divide tasks and coordinate the duties of these diverse groups.

From the beginning, construction around Atlanta was planned to have a major beneficial impact on neighborhoods. Olympic housing, the Olympic Stadium, and the Centennial Olympic Park (according to ACOG, the first urban park to be constructed in the nation in 52 years) are legacies of the games that will be part of the city landscape for years to come. At the same time, ACOG was committed to leaving no unwanted legacies—"white elephants" that the city could not maintain or support. Thus, the 1996 Olympics was planned to be the most transient in Olympics history.

To that end, 1 million square feet of tents, 24 miles of fencing, power backup, 4,000 tons of portable air-conditioning units, 1,800 portable toilets, and 186,000 temporary seats were all designed to disappear after the Olympics. Even some substantial construction was built to be torn down. For example, ACOG spent $6.5 million—much less than went into Barcelona's $25 million track—on a Velodrome track that could be disassembled after the games. A restaurant large enough to serve 3,000 athletes a day was built at the Olympic Village at a cost of less than one-tenth of the expense of a permanent building. According to John Hancock, ACOG's project manager for temporary structures, "We don't need to invest a lot of ACOG's money in owning things that are only going to be used for 16 days, then have a big fire sale later." ACOG's objective was to avoid the chastening experience of Montreal, whose taxpayers are still paying off the construction debt for the 1976 Summer Games.

Georgia Power, the Atlanta Chamber of Commerce, NationsBank, and other Georgia-based groups worked with ACOG to ensure that when the 1996 Olympic Summer Games were over, their legacy would be a powerful and positive one for Atlanta and the state. Almost two-thirds of the world's population watched the 1996 Olympics on television, and thousands of people coordinated their efforts to prove that through hard work and a shared vision, even the most complex goals could be reached.

QUESTIONS

1. List the areas in which ACOG had to set objectives. What factors inherent in the Olympic Games added to the difficulty of meeting those objectives?

2. Select one objectives area and list possible subobjectives. Consider transportation, traffic control, security, and marketing. What diverse groups of people were necessary to carry out these subobjectives? How were their efforts managed?

3. One of ACOG's major objectives was the international promotion of the city of Atlanta, the state of Georgia, and the southeastern United States. Based on your knowledge of these areas both prior to the Olympics and after the games, was ACOG successful in its promotion efforts? Search for news items showing whether or not there has been an ongoing positive impact from the 1996 Olympics. Why or why not has there been such an impact?

SMALL BUSINESS 2000

Hopefully, you are taking the courses you are enrolled in and studying toward the degree you have chosen because they will help you meet an objective you have established for yourself. This objective may have a near-term orientation, such as to earn an associate degree or bachelor's degree. Your objective may also have a more distant focus, such as becoming a lawyer. In order to get into law school you must have an undergraduate degree. Your current studies may be helping you meet both your near-term and longer-term objectives.

Once you enter the work world, you will probably face objectives at two levels, at least: those that are important to you personally and those that are important to the company for which you work. If you are happy in your job and enjoy working at your company, there will be a good chance that your objectives and those of your company have something in common.

Jake Miles has a set of personal objectives which are aimed at developing safe, nonviolent toys and published material for children. He is also concerned with providing toys for children with diverse cultural backgrounds, toys that reflect the cultural images with which they are familiar and comfortable. Jake spent over 20 years at two major U.S. toy manufacturers trying to get the company to adopt his ideas and add culturally sensitive toys to their product lines; his efforts never succeeded.

Jake's personal objectives and those of the companies that employed him were not fully aligned.

What could Jake do to close this gap? A change in his employer's organization provided him with the opportunity to start his own venture. Jake took a severance package and began to build a venture from the ground up. This was quite a switch from the work environment and resource availability that Jake was used to, but it did provide him with one thing he had not had in the past. The personality and culture of this new company, Cultural Toys, was his to mold and develop. Jake had his chance to create and work at a company whose corporate objectives were in line with his own personal objectives.

QUESTIONS

1. What do you think is the organizational primary objective of Cultural Toys?

2. Given what you have learned about Cultural Toys, what kind of people do you think are attracted to work at a company like this? Can you think of any other companies that may have focused objectives that attract a certain kind of person to work there?

3. Jake Miles got his customers involved in the development process of his Cultural Toys' products. Do you think this had an impact on the company's product market objectives? How?

Fundamentals of Planning

STUDENT LEARNING OBJECTIVES

From studying this chapter, I will attempt to acquire

1. A definition of planning and an understanding of the purposes of planning

2. A knowledge of the advantages and potential disadvantages of planning

3. Insights on how the major steps of the planning process are related

4. An understanding of the planning subsystem.

5. A knowledge of how the chief executive relates to the planning process

6. An understanding of the qualifications and duties of planners and how planners are evaluated

7. Guidelines on how to get the greatest return from the planning process

CHAPTER OUTLINE

Introductory Case: *DuPont Plans to Make Women's Clothes*

GENERAL CHARACTERISTICS OF PLANNING
Defining Planning

Across Industries: *Government—CIA Forms New Plan*
Purposes of Planning
Planning: Advantages and Potential Disadvantages
Primacy of Planning

STEPS IN THE PLANNING PROCESS

THE PLANNING SUBSYSTEM
Elements of the Subsystem
The Subsystem at Work

PLANNING AND THE CHIEF EXECUTIVE
Final Responsibility

Management and the Internet: *Digital's New Plan Based Entirely on the Web*
Planning Assistance

THE PLANNER
Qualifications of Planners
Duties of Planners
Evaluation of Planners

MAXIMIZING THE EFFECTIVENESS OF THE PLANNING PROCESS
Top-Management Support

Ethics Spotlight: *Top Management Supports Environmental Protection Planning at Shell Oil Company*
An Effective and Efficient Planning Organization
Implementation-Focused Planning
Inclusion of the Right People

Quality Spotlight: *Including the Right People in Planning Enhances Quality at Sun Microsystems*

DuPont Plans to Make Women's Clothes

REMINDER: THE INTRODUCTORY CASE WRAP-UP (P. 140) CONTAINS DISCUSSION QUESTIONS AND A SKILLS EXERCISE TO FURTHER ILLUSTRATE THE APPLICATION OF CHAPTER CONCEPTS TO THIS VIGNETTE.

DuPont is planning to make clothes as well as chemicals. Long known for its plastics and pesticides, the nation's biggest chemical producer now wants to make women's apparel. In less than a year, the company predicts, the first private-label sportswear designed and manufactured by DuPont Company will begin showing up in U.S. department stores and specialty retail chains.

Why would a $40 billion industrial giant decide to get into the rag trade? The new business, DuPont says, can yield a profit. At the same time, it can help boost DuPont's huge synthetic-fiber business.

Entering an arena ruled by the whims of fashion is a "nontraditional" move, DuPont concedes. In fact, its embryonic garment unit has yet to sign up a single customer. And even though the house-label apparel DuPont plans to make is the garment industry's fastest-growing segment, it remains a hotly competitive field.

The fashion game offers "no sure things," says Faye Landes, a Smith Barney footwear-and-apparel analyst. But "if DuPont can get the right designers and deliver the clothes at the right quality and price, they have a shot." She notes that it's relatively easy to enter the fragmented private-label industry and that it's "a business where you can definitely buy expertise."

DuPont's new unit, Initiatives Inc., is doing just that. Donald Linsenmann, former head of DuPont's Lycra spandex business in Europe and now Initiatives president, is interviewing designers and marketers for the unit's office in New York's garment district.

"I don't want people with a background in chemical engineering," says Mr. Linsenmann. "I want people who may have worked for a Liz Claiborne or DKNY."

DuPont notes that it has been a big provider of textile fibers for decades—in 1994, it sold apparel makers and textile companies more than $3 billion of nylon, Lycra spandex, and polyester fibers—and so already works with designers and retailers. "We've got a lot of experience" in apparel, says a spokesman. "Do we have enough experience? Probably not, yet."

Long a supplier of textile fibers for the fashion industry, DuPont is confident that if it can find the right combination of pricing and design, it can break into the world of private-label high fashions.

Most private-label concerns design clothing, then take orders from retailers and have the garments made in Asia. Initiatives will work with retailers to design house-brand clothing, then contract to have the apparel cut and sewn in Mexico.

What's Ahead

The Introductory Case discusses the initiation of a new product line, women's clothes, at DuPont. It leaves the impression that since DuPont has had little experience in manufacturing and selling women's clothing, the challenges of introducing and maintaining a new, successful line of women's clothing will be formidable. Material in this chapter will help managers like the ones at DuPont's Initiatives understand why planning is so important, not only for ensuring the success of a new-product introduction, but also for carrying out virtually every other organizational activity. The fundamentals of planning are described in this chapter. More specifically, this chapter does the following:

1. Outlines the general characteristics of planning
2. Discusses steps in the planning process
3. Describes the planning subsystem
4. Elaborates upon the relationship between planning and the chief executive
5. Summarizes the qualifications and duties of planners and explains how planners are evaluated
6. Explains how to maximize the effectiveness of the planning process

GENERAL CHARACTERISTICS OF PLANNING

This first part of the chapter is a general introduction to planning. The sections in this part discuss the following topics:

1. Definition of planning
2. Purposes of planning
3. Advantages and potential disadvantages of planning
4. Primacy of planning

▶ DEFINING PLANNING

Planning is the process of determining how the management system will achieve its objectives. In other words, it determines how the organization can get where it wants to go.

Planning is the process of determining how the organization can get where it wants to go. Chapter 5 emphasized the importance of organizational objectives and explained how to develop them. Planning is the process of determining exactly what the organization will do to accomplish its objectives. In more formal terms, planning is "the systematic development of action programs aimed at reaching agreed business objectives by the process of analyzing, evaluating, and selecting among the opportunities which are foreseen."[1]

Planning is a critical management activity regardless of the type of organization being managed. Modern managers face the challenge of sound planning in small and relatively simple organizations as well as in large, more complex ones, and in nonprofit organizations such as libraries as well as in for-profit organizations such as General Motors.[2]

ACROSS INDUSTRIES ◀ Government

CIA FORMS NEW PLAN

When the Soviet Union collapsed in the early 1990s, few doubted that the United States represented the only remaining true super power, and few Americans feared threats from any foreign country. One of the U.S. agencies hurt most by this sense of confidence was the Central Intelligence Agency (CIA). Because no single country represented a credible threat to the United States, many questioned the need for the large number of spies in the CIA, and Congress and the White House reduced the CIA's budget sharply. Consequently, the number of spies in the CIA diminished greatly in the mid-1990s.

When the CIA failed to accurately predict India's nuclear tests in 1998, however, many felt that it was time to return the organization back to its days of effectiveness. At the heart of the agency's weakness lay its dependence on advanced technologies. Relying on spy satellites, listening devices, and encryption techniques caused the CIA to lose its ability to place spies behind enemy lines effectively.

Due to these concerns, the CIA announced a new plan to re-establish itself as an espionage powerhouse. More specifically, the agency reported a plan to hire five times as many spies in 1998 as it did in fiscal year 1995. In addition, the agency reported that it would hire an even greater number of spies in 1999. To support these plans, the House of Representatives pushed through supplemental financing in 1998 and is again pushing for more financing in 1999. With this financing, the CIA hopes that this plan will help it to more accurately predict the unpredictable behind enemy lines.

► PURPOSES OF PLANNING

Over the years, management writers have presented several different purposes of planning. For example, a classic article by C. W. Roney indicates that organizational planning has two purposes: protective and affirmative. The protective purpose of planning is to minimize risk by reducing the uncertainties surrounding business conditions and clarifying the consequences of related management actions. The affirmative purpose is to increase the degree of organizational success.[3] For an example of this affirmative purpose, consider Whole Foods Market, a health-food chain in Texas. This company uses planning to ensure success as measured by the systematic opening of new stores. Company head John Mackey believes that increased company success is not an accident, but a direct result of careful planning.[4] Still another purpose of planning is to establish a coordinated effort within the organization. Where planning is absent, so, usually, are coordination and organizational efficiency.

The fundamental purpose of planning, however, is to help the organization reach its objectives. As Koontz and O'Donnell put it, the primary purpose of planning is "to facilitate the accomplishment of enterprise and objectives."[5] All other purposes of planning are spin-offs of this fundamental purpose.

► PLANNING: ADVANTAGES AND POTENTIAL DISADVANTAGES

A vigorous planning program produces many benefits. First, it helps managers to be future-oriented. They are forced to look beyond their normal everyday problems to project what situations may confront them in the future.[6] Second, a sound planning program enhances decision coordination. No decision should be made today without some idea of how it will affect a decision that might have to be made tomorrow. The planning function pushes managers to coordinate their decisions. Third, planning emphasizes organizational objectives. Because organizational objectives are the starting points for planning, managers are continually reminded of exactly what their organization is trying to accomplish.

Overall, planning is very advantageous to an organization. According to an often-cited survey, as many as 65 percent of all newly started businesses are not around to celebrate a fifth anniversary. This high failure rate seems primarily a consequence of inadequate planning. Successful businesses have an established plan, a formal statement that outlines the objectives the organization is attempting to achieve. Planning does not eliminate risk, of course, but it does help managers identify and deal with organizational problems before they cause havoc in a business.[7]

The downside is that if the planning function is not well executed, planning can have several disadvantages for the organization. For example, an overemphasized planning program can take up too much managerial time. Managers must strike an appropriate balance between time spent on planning and time spent on organizing, influencing, and controlling. If they don't, some activities that are extremely important to the success of the organization may be neglected.

Overall, the advantages of planning definitely outweigh the disadvantages. Usually, the disadvantages of planning result from the planning function's being used incorrectly.

► PRIMACY OF PLANNING

Planning is the primary management function—the one that precedes and is the basis for the organizing, influencing, and controlling functions of managers. Only after managers have developed their plans can they determine how they want to structure their organization, place

FIGURE 6.1

Planning as the foundation for organizing, influencing, and controlling

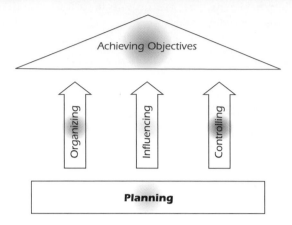

their people, and establish organizational controls. As discussed in chapter 1, planning, organizing, influencing, and controlling are interrelated. Planning is the foundation function and the first one to be performed. Organizing, influencing, and controlling are all based on the results of planning. Figure 6.1 shows this interrelationship.

BACK TO THE CASE

It is obvious from the information given in the Introductory Case that DuPont's managers must focus heavily on planning if the company's new line of women's clothing is to be successful. The planning process should help DuPont determine such issues as what and when equipment must be purchased to manufacture the new clothing, where the clothing will be manufactured, and how finished clothing will be delivered to customers.

Because of the many related benefits of planning, DuPont's managers should make certain that the planning process is thorough and comprehensive. One particularly notable benefit of planning is the probability of increased profits. To gain this and other benefits, however, DuPont's managers must see to it that the planning function is well executed, but not overemphasized.

DuPont's managers should also keep in mind that planning is the primary management function. Thus, when introducing new products like women's clothing, they should not begin to organize, influence, or control until they have completed their planning. Planning is the foundation management function upon which all other management functions at DuPont should be based.

STEPS IN THE PLANNING PROCESS

The planning process consists of the following six steps:

1. *State organizational objectives*—Since planning focuses on how the management system will reach organizational objectives, a clear statement of those objectives is necessary before planning can begin. In essence, objectives stipulate those areas in which organizational planning must occur.[8] Chapter 5 discusses how the objectives themselves are developed.
2. *List alternative ways of reaching objectives*—Once organizational objectives have been clearly stated, a manager should list as many available alternatives as possible for reaching those objectives.
3. *Develop premises on which to base each alternative*—To a large extent, the feasibility of using any one alternative to reach organizational objectives is determined by the **premises,** or assumptions, on which the alternative is based. For example, two alternatives a manager

Premises are the assumptions on which an alternative to reaching an organizational objective is based.

could generate to reach the organizational objective of increasing profit might be: (a) increase the sale of products presently being produced or (b) produce and sell a completely new product. Alternative (a) is based on the premise that the organization can gain a larger share of the existing market. Alternative (b) is based on the premise that a new product would capture a significant portion of a new market. A manager should list all of the premises for each alternative.

4. *Choose the best alternative for reaching objectives*—An evaluation of alternatives must include an evaluation of the premises on which the alternatives are based. A manager usually finds that some premises are unreasonable and can therefore be excluded from further consideration. This elimination process helps the manager determine which alternative would best accomplish organizational objectives. The decision making required for this step is discussed more fully in chapter 7.

5. *Develop plans to pursue the chosen alternative*—After an alternative has been chosen, a manager begins to develop strategic (long-range) and tactical (short-range) plans.[9] More information about strategic and tactical planning is presented in chapter 7 and 8.

6. *Put the plans into action*—Once plans that furnish the organization with both long-range and short-range direction have been developed, they must be implemented. Obviously, the organization cannot directly benefit from the planning process until this step is performed.

Figure 6.2 shows the sequencing of the six steps of the planning process.

THE PLANNING SUBSYSTEM

Once managers thoroughly understand the basics of planning, they can take steps to implement the planning process in their organization. Implementation is the key to a successful planning process. Even though managers might be experts on facts related to planning and the planning process, if they cannot transform this understanding into appropriate action, they will not be able to generate useful organizational plans.

| FIGURE 6.2 | ► Elements of the planning process |

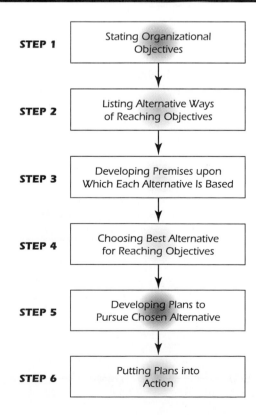

STEP 1 — Stating Organizational Objectives

STEP 2 — Listing Alternative Ways of Reaching Objectives

STEP 3 — Developing Premises upon Which Each Alternative Is Based

STEP 4 — Choosing Best Alternative for Reaching Objectives

STEP 5 — Developing Plans to Pursue Chosen Alternative

STEP 6 — Putting Plans into Action

CEO Gordon M. Bethune has stated quite clearly his objectives for Continental Airlines: He intends to reduce jobs, costs, and cut-rate fares while simultaneously improving service. The two prongs of the attack may seem contradictory, but Bethune is operating on a specific premise: Continental management, he maintains, can achieve both goals if it becomes more market-savvy and customer-oriented and less willing to let strictly financial considerations dictate marketing decisions.

A **subsystem** is a system created as part of the process of the overall management system. A planning subsystem increases the effectiveness of the overall management system.

One way to approach implementation is to view planning activities as an organizational subsystem. A **subsystem** is a system created as part of the overall management system. Figure 6.3 illustrates the relationship between the overall management system and a subsystem. Subsystems help managers organize the overall system and enhance its success.

►ELEMENTS OF THE SUBSYSTEM

Figure 6.4 presents the elements of the planning subsystem. The purpose of this subsystem is to increase the effectiveness of the overall management system by helping managers identify, guide, and direct planning activities within the overall system.

Obviously, only a portion of organizational resources can be used as input in the planning subsystem. This input is allocated to the planning subsystem and transformed into output through the steps of the planning process.

►THE SUBSYSTEM AT WORK

How planning subsystems are organized in the industrial world can be exemplified by the rather informal planning subsystem at the Quaker Oats Company and the more formal planning subsystem at the Sun Oil Company.[10]

QUAKER OATS COMPANY At Quaker Oats, speculations about the future are conducted, for the most part, on an informal basis. To help anticipate social changes, Quaker Oats management has opened communication lines with various groups believed to be harbingers

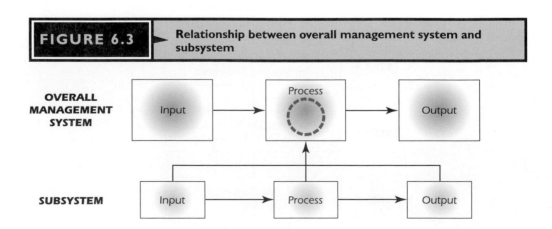

FIGURE 6.3 Relationship between overall management system and subsystem

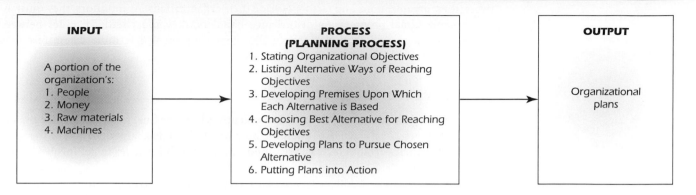

FIGURE 6.4 ▶ The planning subsystem

INPUT	PROCESS (PLANNING PROCESS)	OUTPUT
A portion of the organization's: 1. People 2. Money 3. Raw materials 4. Machines	1. Stating Organizational Objectives 2. Listing Alternative Ways of Reaching Objectives 3. Developing Premises Upon Which Each Alternative is Based 4. Choosing Best Alternative for Reaching Objectives 5. Developing Plans to Pursue Chosen Alternative 6. Putting Plans into Action	Organizational plans

of change. The company has organized a "noncommittee," whose members represent a diversity of orientations, to spearhead this activity. They monitor social changes—and thus augment the company's understanding of social change. Many companies throughout the world plan in an informal way, as Quaker Oats does.

SUN OIL COMPANY Several groups within Sun Oil Company are engaged in formal business planning and forecasting. Operational planning with a five-year horizon is done annually. The planning activity with the longest time horizon takes place within the Sun Oil Company of Pennsylvania, the corporation's refining, transportation, and marketing arm. A centralized planning group, reporting to the vice president of development and planning, is responsible for helping top management set the company's long-term objectives, develop plans to achieve those objectives, and identify future consumer needs and market developments that might indicate business areas for diversification. Current efforts focus on discussions on a series of long-range issues with the executive committee. This planning process is designed to generate a restatement of long-term objectives for the organization.

BACK TO THE CASE

The planning process at DuPont must result in a practical plan to manufacture and sell women's clothing. The process of developing this plan should consist of the six steps outlined in the text. That is, it should begin with a statement of the organizational objective to successfully introduce the new clothing and end with guidelines for putting the organizational plans into action.

To appropriately implement a planning process, managers should view planning as a subsystem of the overall management system and dedicate a portion of organizational resources to organizational planning. Using the new-product example detailed in the Introductory Case, we would say that the output of this subsystem would be the actual plans needed to introduce the private-label clothing. Areas such as refining a manufacturing process for the new clothing and ensuring that suppliers can furnish the materials necessary to produce it would be emphasized. Naturally, a comprehensive planning effort at DuPont would need to focus on many other organizational areas, such as obtaining funds for the venture and fighting established competitors for a share of the market for private-label women's sportswear.

PLANNING AND THE CHIEF EXECUTIVE

More than two decades ago, Henry Mintzberg pointed out that the top managers—the chief executives—of organizations have many different roles to perform.[11] As organizational figureheads, they must represent their organizations in a variety of social, legal, and ceremonial situations. As leaders, they must ensure that organization members are properly guided toward achieving organizational goals. As liaisons, they must establish themselves as links between their organizations and factors outside their organizations. As monitors, they must assess organizational progress. As disturbance handlers, they must settle disputes between organization members. And as resource allocators, they must determine where resources should be placed to benefit their organizations best.

►FINAL RESPONSIBILITY

In addition to these many varied roles, chief executives have the final responsibility for organizational planning. As the scope of planning broadens to include a larger portion of the management system, it becomes increasingly important for chief executives to get involved in the planning process.

As planners, chief executives seek answers to the following broad questions:[12]

1. In what direction should the organization be going?
2. In what direction is the organization going now?
3. Should something be done to change this direction?
4. Is the organization continuing in an appropriate direction?

Keeping informed about social, political, and scientific trends is of utmost importance in helping chief executives to answer these questions.

MANAGEMENT AND THE INTERNET — Digital's New Plan Based Entirely on the Web

Digital Equipment Corporation has long been known as a "cradle-to-grave" network designer. In other words, not only has the company been known for its ability to install networks, but it has also been known for its ability to design and manufacture the parts that it installs. With the proliferation of the Internet, however, that strategy changed. In fact, Digital CEO Robert Palmer announced a new plan that differs significantly from the cradle-to-grave strategy.

Instead of producing all of the parts that it assembles, Digital sold portions of its manufacturing facilities to companies such as Intel and Cabletron. Consequently, the company does not have to worry about the high costs associated with developing, manufacturing, and marketing commodity products. Now, the company will focus only on assembling the parts, and it has a new battle cry: "The Web Is the Platform." In other words, the company's new plan revolves solely around the Internet.

Digital once considered spinning off its popular AltaVista Internet service operation, but this new plan caused the company to abandon that idea. The company brought that operation back in-house and now considers it to be an essential element of the new plan. Although some think that Digital's plan is risky, others are applauding it. In fact, some say that this plan resembles that of companies such as IBM in the 1980s that changed from mainframe manufacturers to personal computer manufacturers. Palmer hopes that his plan will result in similar success.

►PLANNING ASSISTANCE

Given the necessity to participate in organizational planning while performing other time-consuming roles, more and more top managers have established the position of organization planner to obtain the planning assistance they require. Just as managers can ask others for help and advice in making decisions, so can they involve others in formulating organizational plans.[13]

The chief executive of a substantial organization almost certainly needs planning assistance.[14] The remainder of this chapter assumes that the organization planner is an individual who is not the chief executive of the organization, but rather a manager inside the organization who is responsible for assisting the chief executive on organizational planning issues.[15] Where the planner and the chief executive are the same person, however, the following discussion of the planner can, with slight modifications, be applied to the chief executive.

Richard Branson, CEO and founder of the innovative Virgin Atlantic Airways, has continued to strike out in new business directions with Virgin Records. While some planners have their hands full managing one type of business, Branson has managed to achieve success in two widely different business ventures due to his superb planning skills.

THE PLANNER

The planner is probably the most important input in the planning subsystem. This individual combines all other inputs and influences the subsystem process so that its output is effective organizational plans. The planner is responsible not only for developing plans but also for advising management on what actions should be taken to implement those plans. Regardless of who actually does the planning or what organization the planning is being done in, the qualifications, duties, and evaluations of the planner are all very important considerations for an effective planning subsystem.

QUALIFICATIONS OF PLANNERS

Planners should have four primary qualifications:

- First, they should have considerable practical experience within their organization. Preferably, they should have been executives in one or more of the organization's major departments. This experience will help them develop plans that are both practical and tailor-made for the organization.
- Second, planners should be capable of replacing any narrow view of the organization they may have acquired while holding other organizational positions with an understanding of the organization as a whole. They must know how all parts of the organization function and interrelate. In other words, they must possess an abundance of the conceptual skills mentioned in chapter 1.
- Third, planners should have some knowledge of and interest in the social, political, technical, and economic trends that could affect the future of the organization. They must be skillful in defining those trends and possess the expertise to determine how the organization should react to the trends to maximize its success. This qualification cannot be overemphasized.
- The fourth and last qualification for planners is that they be able to work well with others. Their position will inevitably require them to work closely with several key members of the organization, so it is essential that they possess the personal characteristics necessary to collaborate and advise effectively. The ability to communicate clearly, both orally and in writing, is one of the most important of these characteristics.[16]

Organizational planners have at least three general duties to perform:[17]

1. Overseeing the planning process
2. Evaluating developed plans
3. Solving planning problems

OVERSEEING THE PLANNING PROCESS   First and foremost, planners must see that planning gets done. To this end, they establish rules, guidelines, and planning objectives that apply to themselves and others involved in the planning process. In essence, planners must develop a plan for planning.

Simply described, a **plan for planning** is a listing of all of the steps that must be taken to plan for an organization. It generally includes such activities as evaluating an organization's present planning process with the intention of improving it, determining how much benefit an organization can gain from planning, and developing a planning timetable to ensure that all of the steps necessary to plan for the organization are performed by some specified date.

EVALUATING DEVELOPED PLANS   The second general duty of planners is to evaluate plans that have been developed. They must decide if these plans are sufficiently challenging for the organization, if they are complete, and if they are consistent with organizational objectives. Any developed plans that do not fulfill these three requirements should be modified appropriately.

SOLVING PLANNING PROBLEMS   Planners also have the duty to gather information that will help solve planning problems. Sometimes they find it necessary to conduct special studies within the organization to obtain this information. Effective planners continually evaluate the need for change and improvement. They then recommend what the organization should do to deal with planning problems and forecast how the organization might benefit from opportunities related to solving these problems.[18]

For example, a planner may observe that the organization's production objectives are not being met. This is a symptom of a planning problem. The problem might be that the objectives are unrealistically high, or it could be that the plans developed to achieve the production objectives are inappropriate. The planner must gather information pertinent to the problem and then suggest to management how the organization can solve it and become more successful.

Other symptoms that could signify planning problems are weakness in dealing with competition, declining sales volume, inventory levels that are either too high or too low, high operating expenses, and too much capital investment in equipment.[19] King and Cleland's presentation of the relationships among problems, symptoms, and opportunities is depicted in Figure 6.5.

The discussions of the three duties of the planner—overseeing the planning process, evaluating developed plans, and solving planning problems—were general comments on the planner's activities. The main focus of these activities is to advise management on what should be done in the future and to ensure that the timing of any managerial action is appropriate. A

A **plan for planning** is a listing of all the steps that must be taken to plan for an organization. It ensures that planning gets done.

When similar products compete against one another, as Snapple and Arizona brands of iced tea do, brand managers at both firms not only must make plans based on their head-to-head competition but also must consider the threat posed by other popular beverages such as soda and sports drinks, against which they both compete.

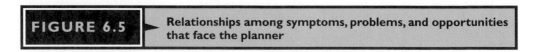

FIGURE 6.5 ▶ **Relationships among symptoms, problems, and opportunities that face the planner**

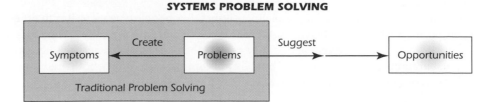

SYSTEMS PROBLEM SOLVING

Symptoms ← Create ― Problems ― Suggest → Opportunities

Traditional Problem Solving

planner, of course, can only recommend. Management may decide not to accept the planner's recommendations.

►EVALUATION OF PLANNERS

Planners, like all other organization members, should be evaluated according to the contribution they make toward helping the organization achieve its objectives.[20] The quality and appropriateness of the planning system and the plans that the planner develops for the organization are the primary considerations in this evaluation. Because the organizing, influencing, and controlling functions of managers all vitally depend on the fundamental planning function, an accurate evaluation of the planner is critically important to the organization.

OBJECTIVE INDICATORS Although the assessment of planners is necessarily somewhat subjective, there are several objective indicators. The use of appropriate techniques is one objective indicator. A planner who uses appropriate techniques is probably doing an acceptable job. The degree of objectivity displayed by the planner is another indicator. The planner's advice should be largely based on a rational analysis of appropriate information.[21] This is not to say that planners should abandon subjective judgment altogether, only that their opinions should be based chiefly on specific and appropriate information.

Malik suggests that a planner is doing a reputable job if the following objective criteria are met:[22]

1. Organizational plan is in writing
2. Plan is the result of all elements of the management team working together
3. Plan defines present and possible future business of the organization
4. Plan specifically mentions organizational objectives
5. Plan identifies future opportunities and suggests how to take advantage of them
6. Plan emphasizes both internal and external environments
7. Plan describes the attainment of objectives in operational terms whenever possible
8. Plan includes both long- and short-term recommendations

These eight criteria furnish objective guidelines for evaluating the performance of planners. Management's evaluation of planners should never be completely objective, however. Important subjective considerations include how well planners get along with key members of the organization, the amount of organizational loyalty they display, and their perceived potential.

BACK TO THE CASE

Technically, the chief executive officer (CEO) at DuPont is responsible for planning for the organization as a whole and for performing such related time-consuming functions as keeping abreast of internal and external trends that could affect the future of the company. Because planning requires so much time, and because the chief executive officer of DuPont has many other responsibilities within the company, the CEO might want to consider appointing a director of planning.

The director of planning at DuPont would need certain qualities. Ideally, this person would have considerable experience at DuPont, be able to see the company as an entire organization, have the ability to gauge and react to major trends that could affect the company's future, and be able to work well with others. The chief duties of the director of planning would be to oversee the planning process, evaluate developed plans, and solve planning problems. Naturally, the introduction of the company's new line of women's clothing would be an important area of focus for DuPont's director of planning. The evaluation of this person would be based on both objective and subjective appraisals of his or her performance.

Success in implementing a planning subsystem is not easily attainable. As the size of the organization increases, the planning task becomes more complicated, requiring more people, more information, and more complicated decisions.[23] Several safeguards, however, can ensure the success of an organizational planning effort:

1. Top-management support
2. An effective and efficient planning organization
3. An implementation-focused planning orientation
4. Inclusion of the right people

►TOP-MANAGEMENT SUPPORT

Unless top management supports the planning effort, other organization members may not take it seriously. This support is critical in planning for *any* type of organization—small or large, domestic or multinational.[24] Whenever possible, therefore, top management should actively guide and participate in planning activities. If the planner is furnished with the resources needed to structure the planning organization, if planning is a continuing process (not a once-a-year activity), and if people are adequately prepared for the changes that usually result from planning, it will be clear to organization members that top management is solidly behind the planning effort. Above all, the chief executive must give continual and obvious attention to the planning process if it is to be successful. The CEO must not allow concerns about other organizational matters to interfere with giving planning the emphasis it deserves.

ETHICS SPOTLIGHT — Top Management Supports Environmental Protection Planning at Shell Oil Company

The Shell Oil Company produces and sells various chemical and petroleum products such as gasoline and oil. To ensure that all organization members will take environmental planning seriously, top management at Shell solidly supports such planning within the company.

Shell's top managers began supporting environmental planning several years ago primarily because of the radical change in public attitudes toward the environment in recent decades. The credit for this change in attitude goes largely to the "green groups"—pressure groups that continually push business as well as society to strive to protect the environment. The pro-environment attitude of society has made companies like Shell look upon environmental protection not as a cost, but as an investment in the future that will impress present and potential customers. At Shell, environmental planning is a factor in every business venture, and such issues as health, safety, and environmental considerations are fundamental at every planning stage in the development of a project or product.

Shell continues to strive for improved response to accidents involving oil, gas, chemical, and any other business in which it is engaged. The company developed management guidelines for using environmental audits to determine whether a company activity complies with internal environmental standards.

►AN EFFECTIVE AND EFFICIENT PLANNING ORGANIZATION

A well-designed planning organization is the primary vehicle by which planning is accomplished and planning effectiveness is determined. Therefore the planner must take the time to design a planning organization as efficient and effective as possible.

The planning organization should have three built-in characteristics. First, it should be designed to use established management systems within the company. As expressed by Paul J. Stonich:[25]

> Many organizations separate formal planning systems from the rest of the management systems that include organization, communication, reporting, evaluating, and performance review. These systems must not be viewed as separate from formal planning systems. Complex

organizations need a comprehensive and coordinated set of management systems, including formal planning systems to help them toward their goals.

Second, the planning organization should be complex enough to ensure a coordinated effort of all planning participants, yet be simple as possible. Although the planning process may require a somewhat large planning organization, the planner should strive to make the complex facets of this planning organization as clear as possible to organization members.

Lastly, the planning organization should be flexible and adaptable. Planning conditions are constantly changing, and the planning organization must be able to respond to these changing conditions.

►IMPLEMENTATION-FOCUSED PLANNING

Because the end result of the planning process is some type of action that will help achieve stated organizational objectives, all planning should be aimed at implementation.[26] As Peter Drucker points out, a plan is effective only if its implementation helps attain organizational objectives. After a plan is developed, the planner should scrutinize it in light of how it is to be implemented.[27] Ease of implementation is a positive feature that should be built into the plan whenever possible.

THE BEST-LAID PLANS: THE EDSEL The marketing plan for the Edsel automobile introduced by Ford in the 1950s is an example of how a sound plan can fail simply because of ineffective implementation.[28] The rationale behind the Edsel was complete, logical, and defensible. Three consumer trends at that time solidly justified the automobile's introduction:

1. The trend toward the purchase of higher-priced cars
2. A general income increase in the society that resulted in all income groups purchasing higher-priced cars
3. The trend for owners of lower-priced Fords to trade them in for Buicks, Oldsmobiles, or Pontiacs after they became more affluent

Conceptually, these trends were so strong that Ford's plan to introduce the larger and more expensive model it called the Edsel appeared virtually risk-free.

Two factors in the implementation of this plan, however, turned the Edsel introduction into a financial disaster for Ford. First, the network of controllers, dealers, marketing managers, and industrial relations managers Ford created to get the Edsel to the consumer was overcomplicated and highly inefficient. Second, because Ford pushed as many Edsels as possible onto the road immediately after introducing the model, consumers found they were buying a poorly manufactured product. In summary, the plan to make and market the Edsel was defensible, but the manufacturing and marketing processes Ford used to implement the plan doomed it to failure.

►INCLUSION OF THE RIGHT PEOPLE

A plan is bound to fail unless the planning process includes the right people. Whenever possible, planners should obtain input from the managers of the functional areas for which they are planning. These managers are close to the everyday activity of their segments of the organization, therefore, they can provide planners with invaluable information. They also probably should be involved in implementing whatever plan is developed and should certainly be asked to furnish the planner with feedback on how implementation is working. As a general rule, managers who are to be involved in implementing plans should also be involved in developing the plans.[29]

Input from other individuals who will be directly affected by the plans also can be helpful to planners. Employees should be asked, for example, how various proposed plans will influence the work flow.

Not all organization members can or should be involved in the planning process. The kinds of decisions and types of data needed should dictate the choice of whom to involve.

Including the Right People in Planning Enhances Quality at Sun Microsystems

Sun Microsystems, Inc., is an integrated portfolio of businesses that supply computing technologies, products, and services. Its computing solutions include networked workstations and multiprocessing servers, operating system software, silicon designs, and other value-added technologies.

Management at Sun Microsystems has developed a team approach to planning. The planning team, known within the company as the business team, consists of representatives from design engineering, manufacturing, customer service, finance, and marketing. It is used primarily during the introduction of a new product.

The business team follows a very specific process. First, it creates a formal plan for the new-product introduction and submits it to an executive-level committee within the corporation. This plan, known as the Product Initiation Form (PIF), is essentially a business plan for a single new product. Once the executive committee approves a PIF, implementation proceeds by establishing an implementation team, which also consists of a number of individuals representing several different operational areas.

Through this cross-functional deployment of individuals in both business and implementation teams, Sun Microsystems has achieved more effective planning. This improved planning, in turn, has enhanced overall product quality by contributing to more on-time delivery of products, better product designs, and a higher proportion of manufactured products meeting established quality standards.

BACK TO THE CASE

A number of safeguards can be taken to ensure that the efforts of the person who has primary responsibility for planning at DuPont will be successful. First, top executives at the company should actively encourage planning activities and demonstrate their support of the planning process. Second, the planning organization designed to implement the planning process should use established systems at DuPont, be only as complex as necessary, and be flexible and adaptable. Third, the entire planning process should be oriented toward easing the implementation of generated plans. Finally, all key people at DuPont should be included in the planning process. With these safeguards, DuPont's management should be able to ensure sound planning for future new-product introductions as well as for all other organizational areas.

For updated information on the topics in this chapter, Internet exercises, links to related Internet sites, an interactive study guide, and more, visit our companion Web site at

http://www.prenhall.com/certo

Additional information can be found on the inside front and back covers of this text.

Reread the learning objectives below. Each objective is followed by questions. Answering these questions accurately will help you retain the most important concepts discussed in this chapter. After answering each question, check your answer against the answer key at the end of this chapter. (*Hint:* If you have any doubts regarding the correct response, consult the page number that follows the answer.)

Circle:

From studying this chapter, I will attempt to acquire

1. A definition of planning and an understanding of the purposes of planning.

    T F

  a b c d e

    a. The affirmative purpose of planning is to increase the degree of organizational success.

    b. The following is *not* one of the purposes of planning: (a) systematic (b) protective (c) affirmative (d) coordination (e) fundamental.

2. A knowledge of the advantages and potential disadvantages of planning.

  a b c d e

    a. The advantages of planning include all of the following except: (a) helping managers to be future-oriented (b) helping coordinate decisions (c) requiring proper time allocation (d) emphasizing organizational objectives (e) all of the above are advantages of planning.

  a b c d e

    b. The following is a potential disadvantage of planning: (a) too much time may be spent on planning (b) an inappropriate balance between planning and other managerial functions may occur (c) some important activities may be neglected (d) incorrect use of the planning function could work to the detriment of the organization (e) all of the above are disadvantages of planning.

3. Insights on how the major steps of the planning process are related.

  a b c d e

    a. The first major step in the planning process is: (a) developing premises (b) listing alternative ways of reaching organizational objectives (c) stating organizational objectives (d) developing plans to pursue chosen alternatives (e) putting plans into action.

  a b c d e

    b. The assumptions on which alternatives are based are usually referred to as: (a) objectives (b) premises (c) tactics (d) strategies (e) probabilities.

4. An understanding of the planning subsystem.

    T F

  a b c d e

    a. A subsystem is a system created as part of the process of the overall management system.

    b. The purpose of the planning subsystem is to increase the effectiveness of the overall management system through which of the following: (a) systematizing the planning function (b) more effective planning (c) formalizing the planning process (d) integrating the planning process (e) none of the above.

5. A knowledge of how the chief executive relates to the planning process.

    T F

  a b c d e

    a. The responsibility for organizational planning rests with middle management.

    b. The final responsibility for organizational planning rests with: (a) the planning department (b) the chief executive (c) departmental supervisors (d) the organizational planner (e) the entire organization.

6. An understanding of the qualifications and duties of planners and how planners are evaluated.

    T F

    a. The performance of planners should be evaluated with respect to the contribution they make toward helping the organization achieve its objectives.

  a b c d e

    b. The organizational planner's full responsibilities are: (a) developing plans only (b) advising about action that should be taken relative to the plans that the chief executive developed (c) advising about action that should be taken relative to the plans of the board of directors (d) selecting the person who will oversee the planning process (e) none of the above.

7. Guidelines on how to get the greatest return from the planning process.

    T F

  a b c d e

    a. Top management should encourage planning as an annual activity.

    b. The following is *not* a built-in characteristic of an effective and efficient planning organization: (a) it should be designed to use established systems within a company (b) it should be simple, yet complex enough to ensure coordinated effort (c) it should cover an operating cycle of not more than one year (d) it should be flexible and adaptive (e) all of the above are characteristics of an effective and efficient planning organization.

CASE DISCUSSSION QUESTIONS

"DuPont Plans to Make Women's Clothes" (p. 125) and its related Back-to-the-Case sections were written to help you better understand the management concepts contained in this chapter. Answer the following discussion questions about this Introductory Case to enrich your understanding of the chapter content:

1. What special challenges will DuPont face in planning for its new line of women's clothing? What steps would you take to meet these challenges?

2. Would you have the DuPont CEO or a DuPont planning executive do the planning for the new women's clothing? Why?

3. List three criteria that you would use to evaluate the planning done for DuPont's new women's clothing. Explain why you chose each criterion.

SKILLS EXERCISE: PLANNING TO OPERATE IN A FOREIGN COUNTRY

According to the Introductory Case, most private-label concerns design clothing in one country but have the clothing made in an Asian country. DuPont, however, plans to have its new clothing cut and sewn in Mexico. Assume that DuPont chose Mexico over another popular manufacturing country, Taiwan. Based on this information, answer the following questions:

1. Why would DuPont want to design its clothing in one country but manufacture it in another?

2. If you had to make the decision, on what factors would you compare Taiwan and Mexico?

3. What outside sources would you use to obtain the appropriate data so that you could compare the two countries accurately?

Now, use these sources to obtain the data and compare the two countries. Which country would you choose to manufacture DuPont's clothing? Why?

1. What is planning?
2. What is the main purpose of planning?
3. List and explain the advantages of planning.
4. Why are the disadvantages of planning called *potential* disadvantages?
5. Explain the phrase *primacy of planning*.
6. List the six steps in the planning process.
7. Outline the relationships among the six steps in the planning process.
8. What is an organizational subsystem?
9. List the elements of the planning subsystem.
10. How do the many roles of a chief executive relate to his or her role as organization planner?
11. Explain the basic qualifications of an organization planner.
12. Give a detailed description of the general duties an organization planner must perform.
13. How would you evaluate the performance of an organization planner?
14. How can top management show its support of the planning process?
15. Describe the characteristics of an effective and efficient planning organization.
16. Why should the planning process emphasize the implementation of organizational plans?
17. Explain why the Edsel automobile failed to generate consumer acceptance.
18. Which people in an organization typically should be included in the planning process? Why?

1. **a.** T, p. 126
   b. a, p. 127
2. **a.** c, p. 127
   b. e, p. 127
3. **a.** c, p. 128
   b. b, p. 128
4. **a.** T, p. 130
   b. b, p. 130
5. **a.** F, p. 132
   b. b, p. 132
6. **a.** T, p. 135
   b. e, p. 135
7. **a.** F, p. 136
   b. c, pp. 136–137

According to a 1996 fiscal report in the *Wall Street Journal*, venerable Chicago-based Quaker Oats Company was in the midst of a financial downturn indicating serious planning snafus. In particular, Quaker had lost $47.8 million in the second quarter of 1995, largely because of restructuring charges necessitated by its Snapple division's poor performance and the company's unsuccessful efforts to improve overseas sales. Quaker did not expect 1996 to begin any better.

Quaker Oats opened its doors to customers as the American Cereal Company of Chicago in 1891. Ten years later, the company changed its name to Quaker Oats Company and adopted the Quaker Man as its logo. Creative marketing practices and a powerful sales staff touted the healthful virtues of oatmeal and turned oatmeal cereal into a booming business. By 1911, Quaker had consolidated its mill operations and was ready to diversify, expanding into both animal feed and more grocery items. Acquisitions continued into the 1960s, as Quaker added Aunt Jemima pancake flour, Cap'n Crunch cereal, Fisher-Price toys, restaurants, and candies.

Until 1990, Quaker was still adding new products—everything from clothiers and opticians to Stokely-Van Camp, Gatorade, and Gaines dog food. A prime acquisition was Anderson Clayton & Company, a Houston food-products company that boasted such popular brands as Seven Seas salad dressings, Chiffon margarine, and Igloo ice chests. Then a downturn in 1990 convinced management to refocus the company on food.

Quaker implemented this new strategy by increasing its advertising budget, reformulating its dog foods, and launching new products. Determined to emphasize its core food categories, the company in 1993 sold Sutherland Foods, a British maker of sandwich-filling products, and purchased the Chico-San rice cake brand from Heinz. Then, in 1994, Quaker consolidated manufacturing, cut employment, and purchased Snapple.

Unfortunately, the Snapple deal did not fulfill Quaker's dreams of growth. Quaker had hoped to streamline distribution of its soft-drink products by combining the Snapple delivery system with Gatorade's. However, independent Snapple distributors, armed with ironclad contracts, refused to cooperate. They forced the company to abandon its plans for streamlining. And that was only the beginning of the brand's troubles. Huge inventories of obsolete products and packaging had to be dumped. And where Snapple had once created a cult following by running ads featuring offbeat celebrities, advertising of the brand under Quaker dried up. Competitors PepsiCo and Coca-Cola filled the marketing void with Lipton teas and Fruitopia juice drinks.

Another problem was that Quaker had counted on greater manufacturing synergies, or cooperative activities, but inherited contracts that locked it into unrealistic production levels with independent bottlers. To avoid paying penalties and to straighten out its supply-chain problems, Quaker eventually had to buy out some of these agreements.

Profits, predictably, disappeared for a while, but by the end of 1995, Snapple seemed to be rallying. Although some experts still question whether Snapple can help protect Quaker's market share in the soft-drink business, CEO William D. Smithburg rejects the suggestion that Quaker "bet the farm on a fad": "We certainly believe we bought a brand with legs." Smithburg has several plans to back up his belief:

1. Release a new ad campaign at the beginning of the soft-drink season to maintain Snapple's old quirky image despite its present association with a giant corporation
2. Promote an under-the-bottle-cap sweepstakes
3. Update flavors, improve taste, and jazz up the line with sporty new labels
4. Reduce customer confusion with a new shelf-stocking scheme that separates tea, juice, lemonade, and diet drinks

Besides solving its marketing problems, Quaker plans to improve Snapple's production systems. To cure production bottlenecks and overcome stocking problems, for instance, Quaker has eliminated one-third of its independent bottlers and introduced a centralized ordering system. Newly streamlined plants will produce a wider range of packaging, including a 32-ounce plastic bottle. Weak distributors will be bought out as Quaker takes additional territories in-house.

Some experts expect Snapple's growth to be slow—about $40 million in earnings in 1996. Others, however, contend that Quaker's global connections give the drink what beverage consultant Tom Pirko of Bevmark calls "colossal prospects." At the same time, of course, Snapple has lost its innovative edge as competitors have moved in with their own healthful teas and fruit juices. Only time will tell if the changes instituted by Quaker management are timely enough to make Snapple rise from the ashes of previous poor planning.

QUESTIONS

1. Classify the plans that Quaker made both before and after it purchased Snapple. Were they "protective"? "Affirmative"? Or were they established to coordinate efforts within the organization? Explain.
2. Use the example of the Quaker Oats Company's purchase of Snapple to illustrate the definition of *planning*.
3. What were Quaker's objectives when it bought Snapple? On what premises were these objectives based? Explain.
4. How would you say Quaker's decision to purchase and support Snapple illustrates planning activities as described in the text? Explain.

Making Decisions

**STUDENT LEARNING
OBJECTIVES**

**From studying this chapter, I
will attempt to acquire**

1. A fundamental understanding of
   the term *decision*

2. An understanding of each element
   of the decision situation

3. An ability to use the decision-
   making process

4. An appreciation for the various
   situations in which decisions are
   made

5. An understanding of probability
   theory and decision trees as
   decision-making tools

6. Insights about groups as decision
   makers

CHAPTER OUTLINE

Introductory Case: *Gateway Chief Makes Daring Decisions*

FUNDAMENTALS OF DECISIONS
Definition of a Decision
Types of Decisions

Management and the Internet: *Internet Company Makes Unprogrammed Decision*
The Responsibility for Making Organizational Decisions
Elements of the Decision Situation

**Global Spotlight: *Executives at United Technologies Detect a
Weakness among Japanese Decision Makers***

THE DECISION-MAKING PROCESS
Identifying an Existing Problem
Listing Alternative Solutions
Selecting the Most Beneficial Alternative
Implementing the Chosen Alternative
Gathering Problem-Related Feedback

**People Spotlight: *Decision at Deere & Company: Eliminate Problems
by Building Employee Involvement***

DECISION-MAKING CONDITIONS
Complete Certainty Condition
Complete Uncertainty Condition
Risk Condition

**Across Industries: *Soft Drink Industry—Coca-Cola CEO
Makes Key Decision in Midst of Uncertainty***

DECISION-MAKING TOOLS
Probability Theory
Decision Trees

GROUP DECISION MAKING
Advantages and Disadvantages of Using Groups to Make Decisions
Processes for Making Group Decisions

INTRODUCTORY CASE

GATEWAY CHIEF MAKES DARING DECISIONS

REMINDER: THE INTRODUCTORY CASE WRAP-UP (P. 161) CONTAINS DISCUSSION QUESTIONS AND A SKILLS EXERCISE TO FURTHER ILLUSTRATE THE APPLICATION OF CHAPTER CONCEPTS TO THIS VIGNETTE.

Although many are familiar with the histories of Bill Gates and Michael Dell, few know the story of Ted Waitt. Like Gates and Dell, Waitt left college to form Gateway, a multi-billion dollar company in the computer industry.

Gateway was started in an Iowa farmhouse by Waitt and Mike Hammond, who is now senior vice president of manufacturing for the company. Waitt's grandmother helped the two entrepreneurs secure a loan by offering a $10,000 CD from her nest egg as collateral. Waitt and Hammond started out by selling hardware peripherals and software to owners of Texas Instruments PCs. They then began designing and assembling their own fully configured PC-compatible systems for direct sale.

As the company grew, Waitt refused to abandon his Midwestern roots. In fact, he used these roots to differentiate the North Sioux City, South Dakota-based company from its competitors. More specifically, Gateway's use of cow spots helped it to establish a brand image, which is very difficult in the standardized computer industry. Waitt used Holstein cow-like themes in every way he could imagine. For example, Gateway shipped its computers to consumers in white boxes with cow-like black spots, and the company served cow-shaped cookies at its annual shareholder meetings. This brand image helped the company build a loyal customer base, and in 1998, Gateway reported revenues of $7.5 billion and a net income of $346 million.

To sustain the company's phenomenal growth, though, Waitt felt that he needed to make some changes. In April 1998, Gateway announced a major decision; Waitt, top executives, and assistants were relocating to an

Ted Waitt and partner Mike Hammond founded Gateway as a telephone sales operation using a $10,000 CD from Ted's grandmother as collateral for a loan. On the way to earning $7.5 billion in 1998, Waitt has learned to be comfortable making risky decisions.

administrative headquarters in San Diego. The expansion move was designed to help attract executive-level talent and place the company closer to partners and suppliers. Waitt also decided that the company needed to reduce its reliance on the cow motif to improve Gateway's position in the profitable business market. Some business executives may not clearly see the connection between high quality computers and cows.

Although Waitt views these decisions as necessary to increase the company's growth, some think the decisions are too risky. But Waitt believes that these decisions will benefit the company, and he is well aware of the risks.

This case contributed by: S. Trevis Certo, Doctoral Student, Indiana University.

What's Ahead

The Introductory Case discusses two decisions that Gateway's management recently made—to move the company's top management team to San Diego and to discontinue the use of its trademark cow logo in marketing campaigns. The information in this chapter discusses specifics surrounding a decision-making situation and provides insights about the steps that management at Gateway might have taken in making the decisions. This chapter discusses the following:

1. The fundamentals of decisions
2. The elements of the decision situation
3. The decision-making process
4. Various decision-making conditions
5. Decision-making tools

These topics are critical to managers and other individuals who make decisions.

FUNDAMENTALS OF DECISIONS

DEFINITION OF A DECISION

> A **decision** is a choice made between two or more available alternatives.

A **decision** is a choice made between two or more available alternatives. *Decision making* is the process of choosing the best alternative for reaching objectives. Decision making is covered in the planning section of this text, but since managers must also make decisions when performing the other three managerial functions—organizing, influencing, and controlling—the subject requires a separate chapter.

We all face decision situations every day. A decision situation may involve simply choosing whether to spend the day studying, swimming, or golfing. It does not matter which alternative is chosen, only that a choice is made.[1]

Managers make decisions affecting the organization daily and communicate those decisions to other organization members.[2] Not all managerial decisions are of equal significance to the organization. Some affect a large number of organization members, cost a great deal of money to carry out, or have a long-term effect on the organization. Such significant decisions can have a major impact, not only on the management system itself, but also on the career of the manager who makes them. Other decisions are fairly insignificant, affecting only a small number of organization members, costing little to carry out, and producing only a short-term effect on the organization.

TYPES OF DECISIONS

Decisions can be categorized according to how much time a manager must spend in making them, what proportion of the organization must be involved in making them, and the organizational functions on which they focus. Probably the most generally accepted method of categorizing decisions, however, is based on computer language; it divides all decisions into two basic types: programmed and nonprogrammed.[3]

> **Programmed decisions** are decisions that are routine and repetitive and that typically require specific handling methods.

Programmed decisions are routine and repetitive, and the organization typically develops specific ways to handle them. A programmed decision might involve determining how products will be arranged on the shelves of a supermarket. For this kind of routine, repetitive problem, standard-arrangement decisions are typically made according to established management guidelines.

> **Nonprogrammed decisions** are typically one-shot decisions that are usually less structured than programmed decisions.

Nonprogrammed decisions, in contrast, are typically one-shot decisions that are usually less structured than programmed decisions. An example of the type of nonprogrammed decision that more and more managers are having to make is whether to expand operations into the "forgotten continent" of Africa.[4] Another example is deciding whether a supermarket should carry an additional type of bread. The manager making this decision

Types of Decisions	Decision-Making Techniques	
	Traditional	Modern
Programmed:		
Routine, repetitive decisions	1. Habit	1. Operations research: Mathematical analysis models Computer simulation
Organization develops specific processes for handling them	2. Clerical routine: Standard operating procedures	2. Electronic data processing
	3. Organization structure: Common expectations A system of subgoals Well-defined information channels	
Nonprogrammed:		
One-shot, ill-structured, novel policy decisions	1. Judgment, intuition, and creativity	1. Heuristic problem-solving techniques applied to: Training human decision makers Constructing heuristic computer programs
Handled by general problem-solving processes	2. Rules of thumb	
	3. Selection and training of executives	

must consider whether the new bread will merely stabilize bread sales by competing with existing bread carried in the store or actually increase bread sales by offering a desired brand of bread to customers who have never before bought bread in the store. These types of issues must be dealt with before the manager can finally decide whether to offer the new bread. Table 7.1 shows traditional and modern ways of handling programmed and nonprogrammed decisions.

Programmed and nonprogrammed decisions should be thought of as being at opposite ends of the decision programming continuum, as illustrated in Figure 7.1. As the figure indicates, however, some decisions are neither programmed nor nonprogrammed, falling somewhere between the two.

MANAGEMENT AND THE INTERNET ▸ Internet Company Makes Unprogrammed Decision

Ron Glaser, a former executive at Microsoft, left that company to start RealNetworks, Inc., the software company that popularized the use of realtime audio and video on the Internet. Now the company has over 18 million registered users of its "streaming" software, and its success caught the attention of his former boss, Bill Gates. Like many successful software entrepreneurs, Glaser faced an unprogrammed decision: sell his company to Microsoft or compete directly with Microsoft and risk eradication.

When given the choice between competition and cooperation, Glaser chose "coopetition," a mix of the two strategies. In other words, Glaser sold 10 percent of his company to Microsoft for $30 million and licensed RealNetworks' technology to Microsoft for another $30 million. In addition, Microsoft agreed to bundle RealNetworks' streaming software with its popular Internet Explorer.

In the software industry, any company's success undoubtedly catches the eye of Microsoft. To survive battles with such enormous companies, managers must carefully make unprogrammed decisions. For the employees and shareholders of RealNetworks, Ron Glaser might have saved the company with his savvy decision making.

FIGURE 7.1 ▶ Decision programming continuum

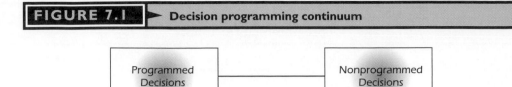

▶ THE RESPONSIBILITY FOR MAKING ORGANIZATIONAL DECISIONS

Many different kinds of decisions must be made within an organization—such as how to manufacture a product, how to maintain machines, how to ensure product quality, and how to establish advantageous relationships with customers. Since organizational decisions are so varied, some type of rationale must be developed to stipulate who within the organization has the responsibility for making which decisions.

One such rationale is based primarily on two factors: the scope of the decision to be made and the levels of management. The **scope of the decision** is the proportion of the total management system that the decision will affect. The greater this proportion, the broader the scope of the decision is said to be. *Levels of management* are simply lower-level management, middle-level management, and upper-level management. The rationale for designating who makes which decisions is this: the broader the scope of a decision, the higher the level of the manager responsible for making that decision. Figure 7.2 illustrates this rationale.

One example of this decision-making rationale is the manner in which E. I. DuPont de Nemours and Company handles decisions related to the research and development function.[5] As Figure 7.3 shows (see page 147), this organization makes both narrow-scope research and development decisions, such as "which markets to test" (decided by lower-level managers), and broad-scope research and development decisions, such as "authorize full-scale plant construction" (decided by upper-level managers).

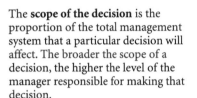

The **scope of the decision** is the proportion of the total management system that a particular decision will affect. The broader the scope of a decision, the higher the level of the manager responsible for making that decision.

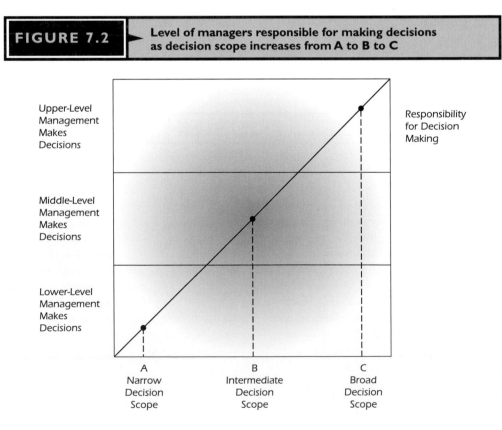

FIGURE 7.2 — Level of managers responsible for making decisions as decision scope increases from A to B to C

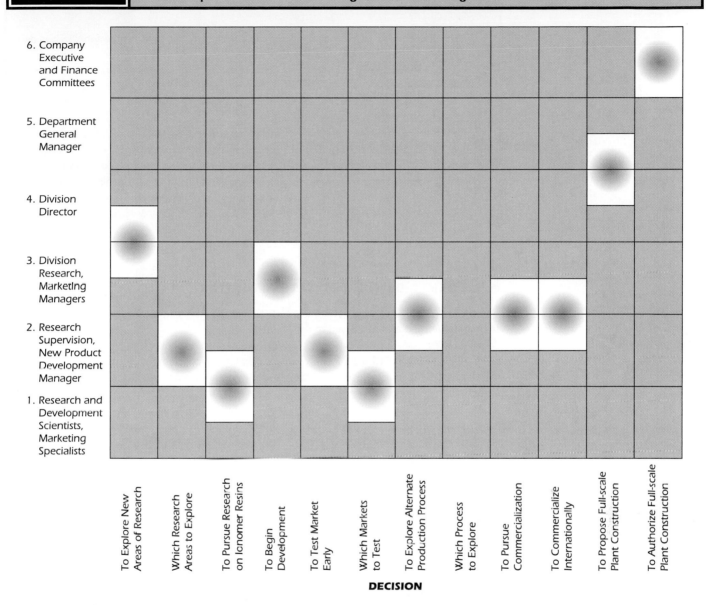

The manager who is responsible for making a particular decision, of course, can ask the advice of other managers or subordinates before settling on an alternative. In fact, some managers prefer to use groups to make certain decisions.

Consensus is one method a manager can use in getting a group to arrive at a particular decision. **Consensus** is agreement on a decision by all the individuals involved in making that decision. It usually occurs after lengthy deliberation and discussion by members of the decision group, who may be either all managers or a mixture of managers and subordinates.[6]

The manager who asks a group to produce a consensus decision must bear in mind that groups will sometimes be unable to arrive at a decision. Lack of technical skill or poor interpersonal relations may prove insurmountable barriers to arriving at a consensus. When a group is stalemated, a manager needs to offer assistance in making the decision or simply make it herself.

Decisions arrived at through consensus have both advantages and disadvantages. One advantage of this method is that it focuses "several heads" on the decision. Another is that employees are more likely to be committed to implementing a decision if they helped make it. The main disadvantage of this method is that it often involves time-consuming discussions relating to the decision, which can be costly to the organization.

Consensus is agreement on a decision by all individuals involved in making that decision.

Evaluating whether to move the location of its corporate headquarters to San Diego is definitely a formal decision situation; that is, one that requires management at Gateway to choose between a number of alternatives. Gateway's management must scrutinize this decision carefully because of the significance to the organization and to the careers of the managers themselves. Technically, this decision is nonprogrammed in nature and therefore is characterized more by judgment than by simple quantitative data.

Ted Waitt, the chief executive officer at Gateway, would probably have the ultimate responsibility, with the approval of the board of directors, for making such a broad-scope decision. This does not mean, however, that Waitt would have to make the decision by himself. He could ask for advice from other Gateway employees and perhaps even appoint a group of managers and employees to arrive at a consensus on which alternative the company should implement.

►ELEMENTS OF THE DECISION SITUATION

Wilson and Alexis isolate several basic elements in the decision situation.[7] Five of these elements are defined and discussed in this section.

THE DECISION MAKERS Decision makers, the first element of the decision situation, are the individuals or groups that actually make the choice among alternatives. According to Dale, weak decision makers usually have one of four orientations: receptive, exploitative, hoarding, and marketing.[8]

Decision makers who have a *receptive* orientation believe that the source of all good is outside themselves, and therefore they rely heavily on suggestions from other organization members. Basically, they want others to make their decisions for them.

Decision makers with an *exploitative* orientation also believe that the source of all good is outside themselves, and they are willing to steal ideas as necessary in order to make good decisions. They build their organizations on others' ideas and typically hog all the credit themselves, extending little or none to the originators of the ideas.

In retail stores like this Folsom, California Wal-Mart, lower-level managers oversee the stocking of inventory and numerous other functions on the selling floor. Sometimes called first-line managers, they also spend a good deal of their time working with and supervising the employees who report directly to them. They also interact with suppliers and middle-level managers at the home office.

The *hoarding* orientation is characterized by the desire to preserve the status quo as much as possible. Decision makers with this orientation accept little outside help, isolate themselves from others, and are extremely self-reliant. They are obsessed with maintaining their present position and status.

Marketing-oriented decision makers look upon themselves as commodities that are only as valuable as the decisions they make. Thus they try to make decisions that will enhance their value and are highly conscious of what others think of their decisions.

The ideal decision-making orientation emphasizes the realization of the organization's potential as well as that of the decision maker. Ideal decision makers try to use all of their talents when making a decision and are characterized by reason and sound judgment. They are largely free of the qualities of the four undesirable decision-making orientations just described.

GLOBAL SPOTLIGHT — Executives at United Technologies Detect a Weakness among Japanese Decision Makers

United Technologies is a company that designs, manufactures, and sells high-technology products, such as radar equipment and rocket motors. Executives at United Technologies think that they have identified a common weakness in Japanese multinational decision makers that Western firms can profitably exploit.

According to United Technologies' managers, in most Japanese companies, important corporate decisions regarding activities in foreign operations are made by top-management Japanese nationals who are quick to tell their foreign customers and managers that there is only one way to handle the design or delivery of a product or service—the way it is done in Japan. They seem to base decisions primarily on Japanese business custom at the home office rather than on the elements of the decision situation itself. This tendency makes Japanese operations in foreign countries particularly vulnerable to competition from Western manufacturers that can achieve Japanese standards of excellence in production *and* adjust to local customs and preferences. In the future, United Technologies intends to strive for those Japanese standards of excellence in production, while treating its foreign managers and partners with respect and deferring to their knowledge and ideas.

GOALS TO BE SERVED The goals that decision makers seek to attain are another element of the decision situation. In the case of managers, these goals should most often be organizational objectives. (Chapter 5 discusses the specifics of organizational objectives.)

RELEVANT ALTERNATIVES The decision situation is usually composed of at least two relevant alternatives. A **relevant alternative** is one that is considered feasible for solving an existing problem and for implementation. Alternatives that will not solve an existing problem *or* cannot be implemented are irrelevant and should be excluded from the decision-making situation.

> **Relevant alternatives** are alternatives that are considered feasible for solving an existing problem and for implementation.

ORDERING OF ALTERNATIVES The decision situation requires a process or mechanism for ranking alternatives from most desirable to least desirable. This process can be subjective, objective, or some combination of the two. Past experience of the decision maker is an example of a subjective process, and the rate of output per machine is an example of an objective process.

CHOICE OF ALTERNATIVES The last element of the decision situation is the actual choice between available alternatives. This choice establishes the decision. Typically, managers choose the alternative that maximizes long-term return for the organization.

As Gateway's management evaluates its decision about whether or not to abandon the company's popular cow-based marketing campaign, it must be aware of all the elements in the decision situation. Both the internal and external environments of Gateway would be one focus of the analysis. For example, internally, is there a sense of employee morale associated with the company's image? Externally, do customers in the highly profitable business market negatively perceive the company's products because of its cow-based marketing campaign? Management needs reason and sound judgment in making this decision. Also, management would have to keep Gateway's organizational objectives in mind and list relevant alternatives for additional marketing campaigns. For example, the company may decide to segment the market by keeping its current marketing campaign for consumers purchasing personal computers for home use while creating a new marketing campaign designed specifically for the business market. In addition, management would need to list such relevant alternatives in some order of desirability before choosing an alternative to implement.

THE DECISION-MAKING PROCESS

The **decision-making process** comprises the steps the decision maker takes to make a decision.

A decision is a choice of one alternative from a set of available alternatives. The **decision-making process** comprises the steps the decision maker takes to arrive at this choice. The process a manager uses to make decisions has a significant impact on the quality of those decisions. If managers use an organized and systematic process, the probability that their decisions will be sound is higher than if they use a disorganized and unsystematic process.[9]

A model of the decision-making process that is recommended for managerial use is presented in Figure 7.4. In order, the decision-making steps this model depicts are as follows:

1. Identify an existing problem
2. List possible alternatives for solving the problem
3. Select the most beneficial of these alternatives
4. Implement the selected alternative
5. Gather feedback to find out if the implemented alternative is solving the identified problem.

The paragraphs that follow elaborate upon each of these steps and explain their interrelationships.[10]

This model of the decision-making process is based on three primary assumptions.[11] First, the model assumes that humans are economic beings with the objective of maximizing satisfaction or return. Second, it assumes that within the decision-making situation all alternatives and their possible consequences are known. Its last assumption is that decision makers have some priority system to guide them in ranking the desirability of each alternative. If each of these assumptions is met, the decision made will probably be the best possible one for

FIGURE 7.4 ► Model of the decision-making process

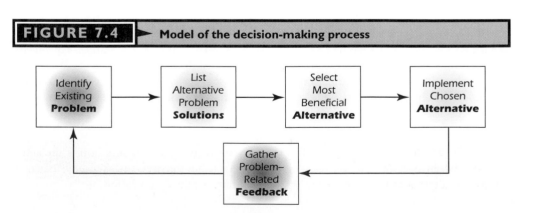

AMS Plastics in Mexicali, Mexico, is one state of the art firm that has benefited from the adoption of NAFTA's free trade provisions. The firm ships extruded and formed plastic parts to the United States. While some firms face stiffer competition with the lowered trade barriers NAFTA has achieved, others are finding they can thrive in their newly enlarged marketplace.

the organization. In real life, unfortunately, one or more of these assumptions is often not met, and therefore the decision made is less than optimal for the organization.

►IDENTIFYING AN EXISTING PROBLEM

Decision making is essentially a problem-solving process that involves eliminating barriers to organizational goal attainment. Naturally, the first step in this elimination process is identifying exactly what the problems or barriers are, for only after the barriers have been adequately identified can management take steps to eliminate them. Several years ago, Molson, a Canadian manufacturer of beer as well as of cleaning and sanitizing products, faced a barrier to success: a free-trade agreement that threatened to open Canadian borders to U.S. beer. Although the borders were not due to open for another five years, Molson decided to deal with the problem of increased beer competition from the United States immediately by increasing production and sales of its specialty chemical products. Within four years, Molson's chemical sales exceeded its beer sales. Essentially, the company identified its problem—the threat of increased U.S. competition for beer sales—and dealt with it by emphasizing sales in a different division.[12]

Chester Barnard has stated that organizational problems are brought to the attention of managers mainly by the following means:[13]

1. Orders issued by managers' supervisors
2. Situations relayed to managers by their subordinates
3. The normal activity of the managers themselves

►LISTING ALTERNATIVE SOLUTIONS

Once a problem has been identified, managers should list the various possible solutions. Very few organizational problems are solvable in only one way. Managers must search out the numerous available alternative solutions to most organizational problems.

Before searching for solutions, however, managers should be aware of five limitations on the number of problem-solving alternatives available:[14]

1. Authority factors (for example, a manager's superior may have told the manager that a certain alternative is not feasible)
2. Biological or human factors (for example, human factors within the organization may be inappropriate for implementing certain alternatives)

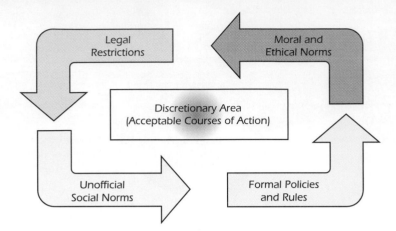

3. Physical factors (for example, the physical facilities of the organization may be inappropriate for certain alternatives)
4. Technological factors (for example, the level of organizational technology may be inadequate for certain alternatives)
5. Economic factors (for example, certain alternatives may be too costly for the organization)

Figure 7.5 presents additional factors that can limit a manager's decision alternatives. This diagram uses the term *discretionary area* to depict all the feasible alternatives available to managers. Factors that limit or rule out alternatives outside this area are legal restrictions, moral and ethical norms, formal policies and rules, and unofficial social norms.[15]

▶ SELECTING THE MOST BENEFICIAL ALTERNATIVE

Decision makers can select the most beneficial solution only after they have evaluated each alternative very carefully. This evaluation should consist of three steps. First, decision makers should list, as accurately as possible, the potential effects of each alternative as if the alternative had already been chosen and implemented. Second, they should assign a probability factor to each of the potential effects, that is, indicate how probable the occurrence of the effect would be if the alternative were implemented. Third, keeping organizational goals in mind, decision makers should compare each alternative's expected effects and the respective probabilities of those effects.[16] After these steps have been completed, managers will know which alternative seems most advantageous to the organization.

▶ IMPLEMENTING THE CHOSEN ALTERNATIVE

The next step is to put the chosen alternative into action. Decisions must be supported by appropriate action if they are to have a chance of success.

▶ GATHERING PROBLEM-RELATED FEEDBACK

After the chosen alternative has been implemented, decision makers must gather feedback to determine the effect of the implemented alternative on the identified problem. If the identified problem is not being solved, managers need to search out and implement some other alternative.

The text presents the decision-making process essentially as a problem-solving process. The following People Spotlight feature illustrates how top management at John Deere and Company decided to solve significant problems by getting employees more involved in the company.

To illustrate the above material, assume that Gateway's management is facing a decision to introduce a new line of computers. Management would first need to identify the problem. For example, management could find out that business customers are purchasing computers from other companies because they perceive Gateway's computers as inferior. Once the problem is identified, management would have to list all possible problem solutions—for example: Can the quality of computer parts be improved? Would a new line of computers capture more consumers? Would a new marketing campaign improve customer perception of Gateway's products?

After eliminating infeasible solutions, Gateway's management would have to evaluate all remaining solutions, select one, and implement it. If either improving the quality of parts or designing a brand new line of computers required too much capital, the best alternative might be to create a new marketing campaign for Gateway's products. Management would then have to initiate appropriate action to formulate and implement a new campaign. Problem-related feedback would be extremely important once the new campaign was formulated. For example, the marketing department could conduct a survey to evaluate the effectiveness of the new campaign. Management could then find out if the new campaign did, in fact, positively influence consumers' perceptions of product quality. If the campaign failed, management would need to decide what other actions should be taken to improve customer perception of Gateway's computers.

PEOPLE SPOTLIGHT — Decision at Deere & Company: Eliminate Problems by Building Employee Involvement

Hans W. Becherer, chief executive of Deere & Company, a firm that manufactures and sells farm equipment, recently faced two significant company problems: (1) the long-term demand for company products was weakening, and (2) competition from other companies was intensifying.

Becherer decided that the best way to deal with these problems was to get employees more involved in the company. For example, assembly-line workers were trained and then traveled across North America to explain Deere's new products to dealers and farmers. Becherer believed that this action would help the company fight its competition by impressing customers and dealers with the quality of Deere employees and hence its products. Becherer was also convinced that making production workers marketing emissaries for Deere's products would strengthen their commitment to manufacturing only the best products because they would feel more responsible for output once they had developed personal relationships with customers and dealers.

Another move Becherer has taken is to encourage employee involvement in maintaining customer relationships and monitoring product-quality feedback.

As Becherer expands the responsibilities of his employees, he has been careful to step up their training so they will be well prepared for their new roles. Preliminary reports indicate that Becherer's implementation of his decision to involve employees has indeed helped him solve Deere's problems of weakening product demand and increased product competition.

DECISION-MAKING CONDITIONS

In most instances, it is impossible for decision makers to know exactly what the future consequences of an implemented alternative will be. The word *future* is the key in discussing decision-making conditions. Because organizations and their environments are constantly changing, future consequences of implemented decisions are not perfectly predictable.

In general, there are three different conditions under which decisions are made. Each of these conditions is based on the degree to which the future outcome of a decision alternative is predictable. The conditions are as follows:[17]

1. Complete certainty
2. Complete uncertainty
3. Risk

►COMPLETE CERTAINTY CONDITION

The **complete certainty condition** is the decision-making situation in which the decision maker knows exactly what the results of an implemented alternative will be.

The **complete certainty condition** exists when decision makers know exactly what the results of an implemented alternative will be. Under this condition, managers have complete knowledge about a decision, so all they have to do is list outcomes for alternatives and then choose the outcome with the highest payoff for the organization. For example, the outcome of an investment in government bonds is, for all practical purposes, completely predictable because of established government interest rates. Deciding to implement this alternative, then, would be making a decision in a complete certainty situation. Unfortunately, most organizational decisions are made outside the complete certainty situation.

►COMPLETE UNCERTAINTY CONDITION

The **complete uncertainty condition** is the decision-making situation in which the decision maker has absolutely no idea what the results of an implemented alternative will be.

The **complete uncertainty condition** exists when decision makers have absolutely no idea what the results of an implemented alternative will be. The complete uncertainty condition would exist, for example, if there were no historical data on which to base a decision. Not knowing what happened in the past makes it difficult to predict what will happen in the future. In this situation, decision makers usually find that sound decisions are mostly a matter of chance. An example of a decision made in a complete uncertainty situation is choosing to pull the candy machine lever labeled "Surprise of the Day" rather than the lever that would deliver a familiar candy bar. Fortunately, few organizational decisions need to be made in the complete uncertainty condition.

►RISK CONDITION

The **risk condition** is the decision-making situation in which the decision maker has only enough information to estimate how probable the outcome of implemented alternatives will be.

The primary characteristic of the **risk condition** is that decision makers have only enough information about the outcome of each alternative to estimate how probable an outcome will be.[18] Obviously, the risk condition lies somewhere between complete certainty and complete uncertainty. The manager who hires two extra salespeople in order to increase annual organizational sales is deciding in a risk situation. He may believe that the probability is high that these two new salespeople will raise total sales, but it is impossible for him to know that for sure. Therefore, some risk is associated with this decision.

The risk condition is a broad one in which *degrees* of risk can be associated with decisions. The lower the quality of information about the outcome of an alternative, the closer the situation is to complete uncertainty and the higher is the risk of choosing that alternative. Most decisions made in organizations have some amount of risk associated with them.

As the previous discussion suggests, the risk condition lies somewhere in between the complete certainty condition and the complete uncertainty condition. The following Across Industries feature discusses a risky decision made by Coca-Cola's CEO, M. Douglas Ivester.

ACROSS INDUSTRIES | Soft Drink Industry

COCA-COLA CEO MAKES KEY DECISION IN MIDST OF UNCERTAINTY

On October 27, 1998, the stock market plunged, as investors feared the ramifications of the "Asian Crisis." Although most investors and companies developed strategies to exit Asian markets, M. Douglas Ivester, Coca-Cola's CEO, developed a strategy to increase the company's presence in Asian markets. When Ivester encountered the uncertainty of the crisis in Asia, he made an important decision that Coca-Cola's investors might applaud for years to come.

In South Korea and Thailand, Coca-Cola had partnerships with local bottlers to distribute the company's popular soft drinks. When the Asian Crisis occurred, the local bottlers had a difficult time obtaining credit lines from local banks; the uncertainty surrounding the crisis made investors and bankers nervous to lend out more money. While the bankers hesitated, Ivester stepped in and purchased full ownership of the South Korean bottler for $500 million, and he increased the company's stake in the Thai bottler for $50 million.

Although the uncertainty surrounding the crisis caused many investors to panic, Ivester saw the uncertainty as an opportunity. In fact, Ivester likens the crisis in Asia to the 1994 peso crisis in Mexico. During that crisis, Coca-Cola also took advantage of the uncertainty by increasing its investment in Mexico. Consequently, Coca-Cola's market share in Mexico increased from 51 percent to 68 percent. Today, Wall Street hopes that Ivester's decision in Asia's uncertain environment works as well as it did in Mexico.

BACK TO THE CASE

If Gateway's management decides to alter its marketing campaign, it must also face a decision regarding how to handle competition from other computer manufacturers like Dell and IBM. The decision-making condition for such a situation is somewhere between complete certainty and complete uncertainty about the outcome of the proposed alternatives. Gateway's management could decide, for example, to either lower prices or increase advertising to fight off the competition, but management has no guarantee that such measures would produce the desired results. Management *does* know, however, how its competitors have responded to price cuts in the past, and thus is not dealing with a complete unknown. Therefore, any decision that Gateway's management would make about handling increased competition would be made under the risk condition. In other words, management would have to determine the outcome probability for each proposed alternative and choose the alternative that looked most advantageous.

◣ DECISION-MAKING TOOLS

Most managers develop an intuition about what decisions to make—a largely subjective feeling, based on years of experience in a particular organization or industry, that gives them insights into decision making for that industry or organization.[19] Although intuition is often an important factor in making a decision, managers generally emphasize more objective decision-making tools. The two most widely used such tools are probability theory and decision trees.[20]

► PROBABILITY THEORY

Probability theory is a decision-making tool used in risk situations—situations in which decision makers are not completely sure of the outcome of an implemented alternative. *Probability* refers to the likelihood that an event or outcome will actually occur. It is estimated by calculating an expected value for each alternative considered. Specifically, the **expected value (EV)** for an alternative is the income (*I*) that alternative would produce multiplied by its probability of producing that income (*P*). In formula form, $EV = I \times P$. Decision makers generally choose and implement the alternative with the highest expected value.[21]

An example will clarify the relationship of probability, income, and expected value. A manager is trying to decide where to open a store that specializes in renting surfboards. She is considering three possible locations (A, B, and C), all of which seem feasible. For the first year of operation, the manager has projected that, under ideal conditions, her company would earn $90,000 in Location A, $75,000 in Location B, and $60,000 in Location C. After studying

Probability theory is a decision-making tool used in risk situations—situations in which the decision maker is not completely sure of the outcome of an implemented alternative.

Expected value (EV) is the measurement of the anticipated value of some event, determined by multiplying the income an event would produce by its probability of producing that income ($EV = I \times P$).

Alternative (Locations)	Potential Income	Probability of Income	Expected Value of Alternatives
A	$90,000	.2	$18,000
B	75,000	.4	30,000
C	60,000	.8	48,000

I	x	P	=	EV

historical weather patterns, however, she has determined that there is only a 20 percent chance—or a .2 probability—of ideal conditions occurring during the first year of operation in Location A. Locations B and C have a .4 and a .8 probability, respectively, for ideal conditions during the first year of operations. Expected values for each of these locations are as follows: Location A—$18,000; Location B—$30,000; Location C—$48,000. Figure 7.6 shows the situation this decision maker faces. According to her probability analysis, she should open a store in Location C, the alternative with the highest expected value.

▶ DECISION TREES

In the previous section, probability theory was applied to a relatively simple decision situation. Some decisions, however, are more complicated and involve a series of steps. These steps are interdependent; that is, each step is influenced by the step that precedes it. A **decision tree** is a graphic decision-making tool typically used to evaluate decisions involving a series of steps.[22]

> A **decision tree** is a graphic decision-making tool typically used to evaluate decisions involving a series of steps.

John F. Magee has developed a classic illustration that outlines how decision trees can be applied to a production decision.[23] In his illustration (see Figure 7.7), the Stygian Chemical Company must decide whether to build a small or a large plant to manufacture a new product with an expected life of 10 years (Decision Point 1 in Figure 7.7). If the choice is to build a large plant, the company could face high or low average product demand, or high initial and then low demand. If, however, the choice is to build a small plant, the company could face either initially high or initially low product demand. If the small plant is built and there is high product demand during an initial two-year period, management could then choose whether to expand the plant (Decision Point 2). Whether the decision is made to expand or not to expand, management could then face either high or low product demand.

Now that various possible alternatives related to this decision have been outlined, the financial consequence of each different course of action must be compared. To adequately compare these consequences, management must do the following:

1. Study estimates of investment amounts necessary for building a large plant, for building a small plant, and for expanding a small plant
2. Weigh the probabilities of facing different product demand levels for various decision alternatives
3. Consider projected income yields for each decision alternative

Analysis of the expected values and net expected gain for each decision alternative helps management to decide on an appropriate choice.[24] *Net expected gain* is defined in this situation as the expected value of an alternative minus the investment cost. For example, if building a large plant yields the highest net expected gain, Stygian management should decide to build the large plant.

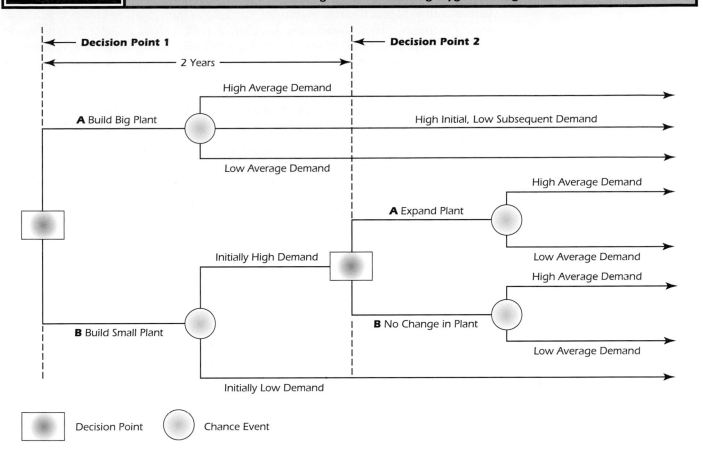

Decision Point 1 ←

← — 2 Years — →

Decision Point 2 ←

High Average Demand

A Build Big Plant

High Initial, Low Subsequent Demand

Low Average Demand

A Expand Plant

High Average Demand

Low Average Demand

Initially High Demand

High Average Demand

B No Change in Plant

B Build Small Plant

Low Average Demand

Initially Low Demand

☐ Decision Point   ◯ Chance Event

BACK TO THE CASE

According to the previous information, managers at Gateway have two tools that they can use to make better decisions. First, they can use probability theory to obtain an expected value for various decision alternatives and then implement the alternative with the highest expected value. For example, in determining a tactic for handling Dell and IBM competition, Gateway's management may need to decide either to devote more of the company's resources to making higher quality computers or to initiate more effective advertising for its existing products. This decision would depend on the projected value of each alternative once implemented.

Second, with decisions that involve a series of steps related to each of several alternatives, Gateway's management could use a decision tree to assist in picturing and evaluating each alternative. For example, to handle the competition, Gateway's management could choose to design an entirely new line of high-powered computers or to devote more resources to the improvement of its existing lines. Each of these alternatives would lead to different decision-making steps.

Gateway's management must remember, however, that business judgment is an essential adjunct to the effective use of any decision-making tool. The purpose of the tool is to improve the quality of the judgment, not to replace it. In other words, Gateway's management must not only choose alternatives based on probability theory and decision trees, but must also use good judgment in deciding what is best for the company.

Earlier in this chapter, decision makers were defined as individuals or groups that actually make a decision—that is, choose a decision alternative from those available. This section focuses on groups as decision makers. The two key topics discussed here are the advantages and disadvantages of using groups to make decisions, and the best processes for making group decisions.

► ADVANTAGES AND DISADVANTAGES OF USING GROUPS TO MAKE DECISIONS

Groups commonly make decisions in organizations.[25] For example, groups are often asked to decide what new product should be offered to customers, how policies for promotion should be improved, and how the organization should reach higher production goals. Groups are so often asked to make organizational decisions because there are certain advantages to having a group of people rather than an individual manager make a decision. One is that a group can generally come up with more and better decision alternatives than an individual can. The reason for this is that a group can draw on collective, diverse organizational experiences as the foundation for decision making, while the individual manager has only the limited experiences of one person to draw on.[26] Another advantage is that when a group makes a decision, the members of that group tend to support the implementation of the decision more fervently than they would if the decision had been made by an individual. This can be of significant help to a manager in successfully implementing a decision. A third advantage of using a group rather than an individual to make a decision is that group members tend to perceive the decision as their own, and this ownership perception makes it more likely that they will strive to implement the decision successfully rather than prematurely giving in to failure.

There are also several disadvantages to having groups rather than individual managers make organizational decisions. Perhaps the one most often discussed is that it takes longer to make a group decision because groups must take the time to present and discuss all the members' views. Another disadvantage is that group decisions cost the organization more than individual decisions do simply because they take up the time of more people in the organization. Finally, group decisions can be of lower quality than individual decisions if they become contaminated by the group members' efforts to maintain friendly relationships among themselves. This phenomenon of compromising the quality of a decision to maintain relationships within a group is referred to as *groupthink* and is discussed more fully in chapter 17, "Groups, Teams, and Corporate Culture."

Managers must weigh all these advantages and disadvantages of group decision making carefully, factoring in unique organizational situations, and give a group authority to make a decision only when the advantages of doing so clearly outweigh the disadvantages.

► PROCESSES FOR MAKING GROUP DECISIONS

Making a sound group decision regarding complex organizational circumstances is a formidable challenge. Fortunately, several useful processes have been developed to assist groups in meeting this challenge. The following sections discuss three such processes: brainstorming, nominal group technique, and Delphi technique.

Brainstorming is a group decision-making process in which negative feedback on any suggested alternative to any group member is forbidden until all group members have presented alternatives that they perceive as valuable.

BRAINSTORMING **Brainstorming** is a group decision-making process in which negative feedback on any suggested alternative by any group member is forbidden until all members have presented alternatives that they perceive as valuable.[27] Figure 7.8 shows this process. Brainstorming is carefully designed to encourage all group members to contribute as many viable decision alternatives as they can think of. Its premise is that if the evaluation of alternatives starts before all possible alternatives have been offered, valuable alternatives may be overlooked. During brainstorming, group members are encouraged to state their ideas, no matter how wild they may seem, while an appointed group member records all ideas for discussion.

Armstrong International's David Armstrong discovered an intriguing method for discouraging the premature evaluation of ideas during a brainstorming session. He allows only one negative comment per group member. Before discussion begins, he hands every member

FIGURE 7.8 ▶ **The brainstorming process**

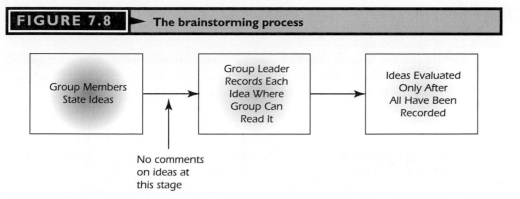

one piece of M&M's candy. Once a member makes a negative comment, he or she must eat the piece of candy. Because a group member is required to have an uneaten piece of candy in order to make a negative comment, members use their sole opportunity to be negative very carefully.[28] Once everyone's ideas have been presented, the group evaluates them and chooses the one that holds the most promise.

NOMINAL GROUP TECHNIQUE The **nominal group technique** is another useful process for helping groups make decisions. This process is designed to ensure that each group member has equal participation in making the group decision.[29] It involves the following steps:

▶ *Step 1*—Each group member writes down individual ideas on the decision or problem being discussed.

▶ *Step 2*—Each member presents individual ideas orally. The ideas are usually written on a board for all other members to see and refer to.

▶ *Step 3*—After all members present their ideas, the entire group discusses these ideas simultaneously. Discussion tends to be unstructured and spontaneous.

▶ *Step 4*—When discussion is completed, a secret ballot is taken to allow members to support their favorite ideas without fear. The idea receiving the most votes is adopted and implemented.

DELPHI TECHNIQUE The Delphi technique is a third useful process for helping groups make decisions. The **Delphi technique** involves circulating questionnaires on a specific problem among group members, sharing the questionnaire results with them, and then continuing to recirculate and refine individual responses until a consensus regarding the problem is reached.[30] In contrast to the nominal group technique or brainstorming, the Delphi technique does not have group members meet face to face. The formal steps followed in the Delphi technique are:

▶ *Step 1*—A problem is identified.

▶ *Step 2*—Group members are asked to offer solutions to the problem by providing anonymous responses to a carefully designed questionnaire.

▶ *Step 3*—Responses of all group members are compiled and sent out to all group members.

▶ *Step 4*—Individual group members are asked to generate a new individual solution to the problem after they have studied the individual responses of all other group members compiled in Step 3.

▶ *Step 5*—Steps 3 and 4 are repeated until a consensus problem solution is reached.

EVALUATING GROUP DECISION-MAKING PROCESSES All three of the processes presented here for assisting groups in reaching decisions have both advantages and disadvantages. Brainstorming offers the advantage of encouraging the expression of as many useful ideas as possible, but the disadvantage of wasting the group's time on ideas that are wildly impractical. The nominal group technique, with its secret ballot, offers a structure in which individuals can support or reject an idea without fear of recrimination. Its disadvantage is that there is no way of knowing why individuals voted the way they did. The advantage of the

Nominal group technique is a group decision-making process in which every group member is assured of equal participation in making the group decision. After each member writes down individual ideas and presents them orally to the group, the entire group discusses all the ideas and then votes for the best idea in a secret ballot.

Delphi technique is a group decision-making process that involves circulating questionnaires on a specific problem among group members, sharing the questionnaire results with them, and then continuing to recirculate and refine individual responses until a consensus regarding the problem is reached.

Delphi technique is that ideas can be gathered from group members who are too geographically separated or busy to meet face to face. Its disadvantage is that members are unable to ask questions of one another.

As with any other management tool, managers must carefully weigh the advantages and disadvantages of these three group decision tools and adopt the one—or some combination of the three—that best suits their unique organizational circumstances.

BACK TO THE CASE

The material in this section of the text offers insights about how a group at Gateway could be entrusted with the decision of whether to replace its marketing campaign. First, a decision of this magnitude and importance should probably be made by a group of top managers drawn from many different organizational areas. A group decision would almost certainly be better than an individual decision in this case because a group would have a broader view of Gateway and the market than any one person in the company would. Therefore, the group would be more likely to make an appropriate decision.

Perhaps the group decision-making process used in this case should be a combination of the three processes discussed in the text. Brainstorming sessions would ensure that all thoughts and ideas related to this crucial decision surface, while the nominal group technique would focus group members on the urgency of making the decision by requiring them to vote on whether or not to make the change. The Delphi technique could be used to obtain important input on the decision from experts around the country by asking them to present their written views through a specially designed questionnaire.

Unquestionably, using a group to make this decision would be time-consuming and expensive. Once the decision is made, however, group members will be committed to it, perceive it as their own, and do all in their power to ensure that they are successful—even if the decision is *not* to change the marketing campaign.

For updated information on the topics in this chapter, Internet exercises, links to related Internet sites, an interactive study guide, and more, visit our companion Web site at

http://www.prenhall.com/certo

Additional information can be found on the inside front and back covers of this text.

ACTION SUMMARY

Reread the learning objectives below. Each objective is followed by questions. Answering these questions accurately will help you retain the most important concepts discussed in this chapter. After answering each question, check your answer against the answer key at the end of this chapter. (*Hint:* If you have any doubt regarding the correct response, consult the page number that follows the answer.)

Circle: From studying this chapter, I will attempt to acquire

1. A fundamental understanding of the term *decision.*

   T F   **a.** A decision is a choice made between two or more alternatives.

   a b c d e   **b.** Decision making is involved in the following function: (a) planning (b) organizing (c) controlling (d) influencing (e) all of the above.

2. An understanding of each element of the decision situation.

a b c d e   **a.** The following type of decision-making orientation involves the belief that the source of all good is outside oneself and that, therefore, one must rely heavily on suggestions from other organizational members: (a) exploitation (b) hoarding (c) marketing (d) natural (e) receptive.

a b c d e   **b.** According to Wilson and Alexis, all of the following are elements of the decision situation except: (a) the ordering of alternatives (b) the decision makers (c) the goals to be served (d) the timeliness of the decision (e) the relevant alternatives.

3. An ability to use the decision-making process.

a b c d e   **a.** After identifying an existing problem, the next major step in the decision-making process is: (a) defining the terminology in the problem statement (b) listing possible alternatives to solve the problem (c) investigating possible alternatives to determine their effect on the problem (d) determining what parties will participate in the problem-solving process (e) identifying sources of alternatives to solve the problem.

a b c d e   **b.** After going through the decision-making process, if the identified problem is not being solved as a result of the implemented alternative, the manager should: (a) attempt to redefine the problem (b) turn attention to another problem (c) search out and implement some other alternative (d) attempt to implement the alternative until the problem is solved (e) accept the fact that the problem cannot be solved.

4. An appreciation for the various situations in which decisions are made.

T F   **a.** The risk condition exists when decision makers have absolutely no idea of what the results of an implemented alternative will be.

T F   **b.** When operating under the complete uncertainty condition, decision makers usually find that sound decisions are a matter of chance.

5. An understanding of probability theory and decision trees as decision-making tools.

a b c d e   **a.** Expected value is determined by using the formula: (a) $EV = I \times P$ (b) $EV = I/P$ (c) $EV = I + P$ (d) $EV = P - I$ (e) $EV = 2P \times I$.

a b c d e   **b.** In the case of the Stygian Chemical Company, the problem was solved through the use of: (a) executive experience (b) decision tree technique (c) queuing theory (d) linear programming (e) demand probability.

6. Insights about groups as decision makers.

T F   **a.** One disadvantage of using a group to make a decision is that members of the group will feel ownership of the decision.

a b c d e   **b.** The process for group decision making that involves the use of questionnaires is: (a) brainstorming (b) nominal group technique (c) Delphi technique (d) a and b (e) all of the above.

► INTRODUCTORY CASE WRAP-UP ◄

CASE DISCUSSSION QUESTIONS

"Gateway Chief Makes Daring Decisions" (p. 143) and its related Back-to-the-Case sections were written to help you better understand the management concepts contained in this chapter. Answer the following discussion questions about this Introductory Case to further enrich your understanding of the chapter content:

1. List three alternatives for handling competition that Gateway's management might consider *before* making a decision to abandon its popular marketing campaign.

2. What information would management need in order to evaluate these three alternatives?

3. Do you think that you would enjoy making this decision of whether to abandon the advertising campaign at Gateway? Explain.

SKILLS EXERCISE USING BRAINSTORMING TO MAKE A DECISION

Working in a group of four or five people, brainstorm as many alternatives as possible to Gateway's decision of how to improve market share in a highly profitable business market (use the brainstorming process as outlined in Figure 7.8). As a group, examine each suggested alternative and choose the one you think best. Now, list three disadvantages and three advantages of using brainstorming to solve such a problem. Will you use brainstorming when you become a manager? Explain.

1. What is a decision?
2. Describe the difference between a significant decision and an insignificant decision. Which would you rather make? Why?
3. List three programmed and three nonprogrammed decisions that the manager of a nightclub would probably have to make.
4. Explain the rationale for determining which managers in the organization are responsible for making which decisions.
5. What is the consensus method of making decisions? When would you use it?
6. List and define five basic elements of the decision-making situation.
7. How does the receptive orientation for decision making differ from the ideal orientation for decision making?
8. List as many undesirable traits of a decision maker as possible. (They are implied within the explanations of the receptive, exploitative, hoarding, and marketing orientations to decision making.)
9. What is a relevant alternative? An irrelevant alternative?
10. Draw and describe in words the decision-making process presented in this chapter.
11. What is meant by the term *discretionary area*?
12. List the three assumptions on which the decision-making process presented in this chapter is based.
13. Explain the difference between the complete certainty and complete uncertainty decision-making situations.
14. What is the risk decision-making situation?
15. Are there degrees of risk associated with various decisions? Why?
16. How do decision makers use probability theory? Be sure to discuss expected value in your answer.
17. What is a decision tree?
18. Under what conditions are decision trees usually used as decision-making tools?
19. Discuss the advantages and disadvantages of using a group to make an organizational decision.
20. In what ways are brainstorming, nominal group technique, and the Delphi technique similar? How do they differ?

1. **a.** T, p. 144
   b. e, p. 144
2. **a.** e, p. 148
   b. d, pp. 148–149
3. **a.** b, p. 150
   b. c, p. 152
4. **a.** F, p. 154
   b. T, p. 154
5. **a.** a, pp. 155–156
   b. b, p. 156
6. **a.** F, p. 158
   b. c, p. 159

CASE STUDY: The Decision to Change at General Motors Corporation

In 1992, unhappy with the company's direction and continuing operational losses, the executive board of General Motors Corporation made several major decisions to change GM. The positions of chairman and chief executive officer, then held by Robert Stempel, were separated. John G. Smale, former chairman of Procter & Gamble, became "nonexecutive chairman," and, under new guidelines that formalized stronger board oversight, John F. Smith, Jr., became CEO.

Smith, who proved a capable manager, in December 1994 hired Ronald Zarrella, formerly president of Bausch & Lomb, as head of marketing. Zarrella set out to dispel the long-held Detroit belief "that product is everything." Instead, he supported a strategy of emphasizing brand identification. As confirmation of the success of his strategy, Zarrella points to GM's popular Saturn, which has won more praise for its straightforward selling practices and unconventional ads than for its sedans and coupes. Says Lynn Upshaw, executive vice president of brand marketing for Ketchum Worldwide, "It's a nice little car, but what has really made [the Saturn] successful is its different marketing concept."

As part of this strategy of brand-name positioning, GM has adopted a concept known as "needs-based marketing," a brainchild of GM consumer research director Vincent Barabba. Barabba's concept required surveying car buyers on their preferences in order to make cars that fit what *customers* say they need rather than what *engineers* think they should have. According to Zarrella, "Part of this process is to get the decisions made on facts and data instead of emotion and history. Brand management will allow us to do that."

GM has targeted Cadillac, one of its most venerable divisions, to test the effectiveness of these branding decisions. Why Cadillac? According to one observer, "In the luxury-car business, where success hinges on luring affluent younger buyers, General Motors Corporation's Cadillac Motor Car Division is something of an industry joke." Since peaking at 351,000 cars in 1978, Cadillac sales have gone down steadily. In 1995, Cadillac's share of the roughly 1.2-million-unit luxury market stood at a mere 15 percent, down from 24 percent six years earlier.

The solution to this problem is to attract the segment of the luxury market that currently buys Cadillac's chief competitors—Lexus, BMW, and Infiniti. In 1994, this market of 40- to 50-year-old baby boomers accounted for one-third of all luxury car sales; by 2000, that figure will be 40 percent. The targeted market is younger and somewhat wealthier than present Cadillac buyers, and more likely to be college educated and female. In addition, it features very definite "psychographic" characteristics. For example, the average baby boomer was raised on imports and retains a youthful and busy lifestyle in middle age. Baby boomers are confident of their ability to shop and often have no brand loyalty. They expect high quality and reliability from their cars, and tend to avoid what they perceive as the common, the garish, and the excessive.

GM hopes that the new Catera model will solve the problem of Cadillac's sliding sales. True to their new commitment to design for the customer, Cadillac and GM's German subsidiary Opel created in the Catera a car to suit the American market. Confesses Opel engineer Willem Kohl, "We didn't realize you could know so much about your customer and what he wants in a car." Based on the data gathered from Saturn's foray into the market, Cadillac is requiring major changes in the methods that dealers use to sell the Catera. Catera brand manager Dave Nottoli believes the target market will demand "a hassle-free buying experience from a salesperson who is knowledgeable about the product and the competition."

Industry observers acknowledge that although the new Catera is a big improvement, it's only a start. According to David Bradley, an analyst at J. P. Morgan Securities, "If you need 10 steps to get [to targeted market share] this is half a step." Still, Cadillac hopes Catera will firmly establish the company as a viable producer in the minds of luxury-car buyers and thus prepare that market for more of the same from the company in the next century. If its expectations are off, Cadillac may fall completely out of the luxury-car market early in the twenty-first century.

The story of the Catera exemplifies one of the ways in which John Smith has positioned GM for long-term profitability. GM's board of directors has recognized his success. In 1995, it declared itself "free to [separate or recombine the positions of CEO and chairman] any way that seems best for the company." Thus the board voted in early 1996 to recombine the two positions, and Smith assumed both of them.

QUESTIONS

1. List all the decisions described in the story of Cadillac's Catera. How would you categorize each of these decisions? Explain. In your opinion, what decision-making techniques were used by GM's board and management?
2. What internal and external environmental factors influenced GM's decision to build the Catera? Which, do you think, had the greatest influence? Explain.
3. Illustrate the elements of the decision-making process with examples from the story of Catera's development.
4. Under which of the three decision-making conditions do you believe Cadillac's decision to build the Catera was made? Cite statements from the case to support your opinion.

Strategic Planning

STUDENT LEARNING OBJECTIVES

From studying this chapter, I will attempt to acquire

1. Definitions of both strategic planning and strategy

2. An understanding of the strategy management process

3. A knowledge of the impact of environmental analysis on strategy formulation

4. Insights about how to use critical question analysis and SWOT analysis to formulate strategy

5. An understanding of how to use business portfolio analysis and industry analysis to formulate strategy

6. Insights into what tactical planning is and how strategic and tactical planning should be coordinated

CHAPTER OUTLINE

Introductory Case: *Gillette's New Strategy: Women*

STRATEGIC PLANNING
Fundamentals of Strategic Planning

Across Industries: *Toy Manufacturing—New International Strategy at Mattel*

Strategy Management

Ethics Spotlight: *Quaker Oats Cashes in on Fitness Fad*

Management and the Internet: *800 Travel Systems, Inc. Establishes Internet Strategy*

Quality Spotlight: *Lutheran General Health System's Mission Emphasizes Quality*

TACTICAL PLANNING
Comparing and Coordinating Strategic and Tactical Planning

PLANNING AND LEVELS OF MANAGEMENT

GILLETTE'S NEW STRATEGY: WOMEN

REMINDER: THE INTRODUCTORY CASE WRAP-UP (P. 184) CONTAINS DISCUSSION QUESTIONS AND A SKILLS EXERCISE TO FURTHER ILLUSTRATE THE APPLICATION OF CHAPTER CONCEPTS TO THIS VIGNETTE.

Gillette has been producing technologically advanced safety razors since 1903. Although Gillette has long been concerned with men's faces, the company now has a new strategy: women's legs. Gillette executives hope that the market for women's razors will provide the company with growth well into the next century.

Gillette virtually ignored the women's market until 1975, when it unveiled the Daisy razor. In actuality, however, the Daisy represented little more than a pink version of the Good News disposable men's razor that it was already selling. Gillette's executives were afraid to invest too heavily in this market because they thought that it was too small, and their hesitation translated into poor unit sales. According to Mary Ann Pesce, vice president of female shaving for Gillette's North Atlantic group, women were not buying the new Daisy—literally.

In 1992, the introduction of the Sensor for Women, designed by a female industrial engineer, showed that management had taken a different view toward the women's market. Today, Gillette has turned its shaving line for women into a global business worth nearly $400 million. In the United States, women's blades represent 20 percent of Gillette's sales, compared to just 3 percent in 1991.

Gillette recognizes the opportunity that the women's market provides, and so do its competitors. For example, Warner Lambert, the producer of Schick razors, has introduced its Silk Effects line for women. For Warner Lambert, shaving products for women represent 35 percent of its total U.S. blade sales, compared with 20 percent for Gillette.

Although the women's line represents a larger portion of Warner Lambert's sales, Gillette is still the clear market leader. More specifically, Gillette's women's shaving products boast nearly a 13 percent share of the $1.3 billion U.S. market, which represents a substantial portion of Gillette's overall 67 percent share. At the same time, Warner Lambert has 16.5 percent share for both men's and women's products.

Strategic planning is what brings a business like Gillette's line of shaving products for women from zero in 1975 to nearly $400 million in 1998.

Gillette hopes to build on its women's market share by offering women their own version of the Mach3, Gillette's new three-bladed shaving system for men, and through its new "Gillette Women: Are You Ready?" advertising campaign. This campaign evolved from Gillette's market research showing that women regarded shaving as a chore separate from primping with makeup or clothing, and it attempts to establish a link between smooth-shaven legs and sex appeal.

Today, Gillette's management is much different from the cost conscious management of the 1970s that was hesitant to invest in the women's market. In fact, Gillette plans to spend $41 million in 1998 to promote its women's line in the United States and Western Europe. Gillette executives hope that this new strategic focus will provide it with higher revenues and profits well into the next century.

This case contributed by: S. Trevis Certo, Doctoral Student, Indiana University.

The Introductory Case highlights the new competitive course taken by Gillette. Developing a new course of this sort is actually part of Gillette's strategic planning process. The material in this chapter explains how developing a competitive strategy fits into strategic planning and discusses the strategic planning process as a whole. Major topics included in this chapter are as follows:

1. Strategic planning
2. Tactical planning
3. Comparing and coordinating strategic and tactical planning
4. Planning and levels of management

STRATEGIC PLANNING

If managers are to be successful strategic planners, they must understand the fundamentals of strategic planning and how to formulate strategic plans.

▶FUNDAMENTALS OF STRATEGIC PLANNING

This section presents the basic principles of strategic planning. In doing so, it discusses definitions of both *strategic planning* and *strategy* in detail.

Strategic planning is long-range planning that focuses on the organization as a whole.

DEFINING STRATEGIC PLANNING **Strategic planning** is long-range planning that focuses on the organization as a whole. In doing strategic planning, managers consider the organization as a total unit and ask themselves what must be done in the long term to attain organizational goals. *Long range* is usually defined as a period of time extending about three to five years into the future. Hence, in strategic planning, managers try to determine what their organization should do to be successful three to five years from now. The most successful managers tend to be those who are capable of encouraging innovative strategic thinking within their organization.[1]

The **commitment principle** is a management guideline that advises managers to commit funds for planning only if they can anticipate, in the foreseeable future, a return on planning expenses as a result of the long-range planning analysis.

Managers may have a problem trying to decide exactly how far into the future they should extend their strategic planning. As a general rule, they should follow the **commitment principle,** which states that managers should commit funds for planning only if they can anticipate, in the foreseeable future, a return on planning expenses as a result of long-range planning analysis. Realistically, planning costs are an investment and therefore should not be incurred unless a reasonable return on that investment is anticipated.

TABLE 8.1	Examples of Organizational Objectives and Related Strategies for Three Organizations in Different Business Areas		
Company	**Type of Business**	**Sample Organizational Objectives**	**Strategy to Accomplish Objectives**
Ford Motor Company	Automobile manufacturing	1. Regain market share recently lost to General Motors 2. Regain quality reputation that was damaged because of Pinto gas tank explosions	1. Resize and downsize present models 2. Continue to produce subintermediate, standard, and luxury cars 3. Emphasize use of programmed combustion engines instead of diesel engines
Burger King	Fast food	Increase productivity	1. Increase people efficiency 2. Increase machine efficiency
CP Railroad	Transportation	1. Continue company growth 2. Continue company profits	1. Modernize 2. Develop valuable real estate holdings 3. Complete an appropriate railroad merger

DEFINING STRATEGY Strategy is defined as a broad and general plan developed to reach long-term objectives. Organizational strategy can, and generally does, focus on many different organizational areas, such as marketing, finance, production, research and development, and public relations. It gives broad direction to the organization.[2]

Strategy is actually the end result of strategic planning. Although larger organizations tend to be more precise in developing organizational strategy than smaller organizations are, every organization should have a strategy of some sort.[3] For a strategy to be worthwhile, though, it must be consistent with organizational objectives, which, in turn, must be consistent with organizational purpose. Table 8.1 illustrates this relationship between organizational objectives and strategy by presenting sample organizational objectives and strategies for three well-known business organizations.

Strategy is a broad and general plan developed to reach long-term organizational objectives; it is the end result of strategic planning.

ACROSS INDUSTRIES — Toy Manufacturing

NEW INTERNATIONAL STRATEGY AT MATTEL

Mattel, Inc. has become a very popular toy manufacturer in the United States and a hot commodity on Wall Street. Although its main product lines such as Hot Wheels, Matchbox, and Barbie have shown recent strength, Mattel's management continues to look for new market opportunities. A recent study conducted by a group of consultants recommended that foreign markets represent an important opportunity that Mattel is neglecting. For example, Mattel sells nearly four dolls per child per year in the United States, but it sells only two in Europe and one in Japan.

In the past, Mattel simply modified U.S. manufactured toys for foreign markets, but its new strategy is based on manufacturing new products for the foreign markets. To better serve the needs of foreign consumers, each product category will have its own marketing and development managers in Europe, the United States, Latin America, and Asia. In addition to increasing revenues, these managers will also pay careful attention to decreasing costs. By focusing on both revenues and costs, Mattel's management hopes that this new strategy will capitalize on new opportunities and help it to capture $6 billion in revenues over the next five years.

►STRATEGY MANAGEMENT

Strategy management is the process of ensuring that an organization possesses and benefits from the use of an appropriate organizational strategy. In this definition, an appropriate strategy is one best suited to the needs of an organization at a particular time.

The strategy management process is generally thought to consist of five sequential and continuing steps:[4]

1. Environmental analysis
2. Establishment of an organizational direction
3. Strategy formulation
4. Strategy implementation
5. Strategic control

The relationships among these steps are illustrated in Figure 8.1.

Strategy management is the process of ensuring that an organization possesses and benefits from the use of an appropriate organizational strategy.

BACK TO THE CASE

In developing a plan to compete with its competitors, management at Gillette would normally begin by thinking strategically. That is, management should try to determine what can be done to ensure that Gillette will be successful with its women's shaving line three to five years in the future. Naturally, developing a women's shaving line that best suits the marketplace is part of this

(continued)

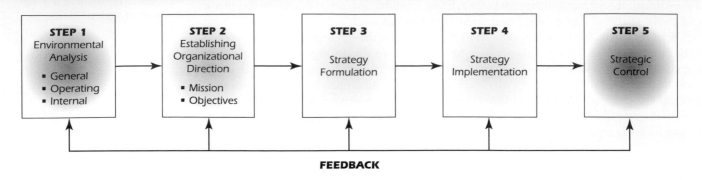

FIGURE 8.1 ▶ Steps of the strategy management process

STEP 1	STEP 2	STEP 3	STEP 4	STEP 5
Environmental Analysis	Establishing Organizational Direction	Strategy Formulation	Strategy Implementation	Strategic Control
• General • Operating • Internal	• Mission • Objectives			

FEEDBACK

thinking. Gillette's management must be careful, however, to spend funds on strategic planning only if they can anticipate a return on these expenses in the foreseeable future.

The end result of Gillette's overall strategic planning will be a strategy—a broad plan that outlines what must be done to reach long-range objectives and carry out the organizational purpose of the company. This strategy will focus on many organizational areas, one of which will be competing with other companies that develop similar shaving products. Once the strategy has been formulated using the results of an environmental analysis, Gillette's management must conscientiously carry out the remaining steps of the strategy management process: strategy implementation and strategic control.

ENVIRONMENTAL ANALYSIS The first step of the strategy management process is environmental analysis. Chapter 2 presented organizations as open management systems that are continually interacting with their environments. In essence, an organization can be successful only if it is appropriately matched to its environment. **Environmental analysis** is the study of the organizational environment to pinpoint environmental factors that can significantly influence organizational operations. Managers commonly perform environmental analyses to help them understand what is happening both inside and outside their organizations and to increase the probability that the organizational strategies they develop will appropriately reflect the organizational environment.

In order to perform an environmental analysis efficiently and effectively, a manager must thoroughly understand how organizational environments are structured. For purposes of environmental analysis, the environment of an organization is generally divided into three distinct levels: general environment, operating environment, and internal environment.[5] Figure 8.2 illustrates the positions of these levels relative to one another and to the organization; it also shows the important components of each level. Managers must be well aware of these three environmental levels, understand how each level affects organizational performance, and then formulate organizational strategies in response to this understanding.

The General Environment The level of an organization's external environment that contains components having broad long-term implications for managing the organization is the **general environment.** The components normally considered part of the general environment are economic, social, political, legal, and technological.

The Economic Component. The economic component is that part of the general environment that indicates how resources are being distributed and used within the environment. This component is based on **economics,** the science that focuses on understanding how people of a particular community or nation produce, distribute, and use various goods and services. Important issues to be considered in an economic analysis of an environment are generally the wages paid to labor, inflation, the taxes paid by labor and businesses, the cost of

Environmental analysis is the study of the organizational environment to pinpoint environmental factors that can significantly influence organizational operations.

The **general environment** is the level of an organization's external environment that contains components normally having broad long-term implications for managing the organization; its components are economic, social, political, legal, and technological.

Economics is the science that focuses on understanding how people of a particular community or nation produce, distribute, and use various goods and services.

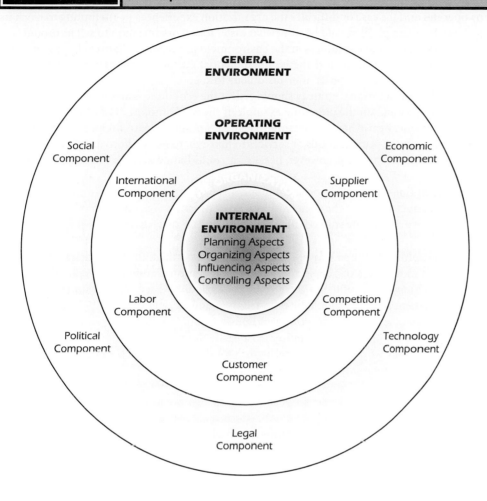

Factors that firms consider in formulating strategic plans to do business overseas, such as shipping these U.S.-grown apples to Yokohama, Japan, include aspects of the general environment such as possible legal considerations (tariffs, quotas, and so on); the operating environment, such as consumer tastes and preferences; and the internal environment, such as the firm's ability to transport perishable merchandise without loss.

materials used in the production process, and the prices at which produced goods and services are sold to customers.

Economic issues like these can significantly influence the environment in which a company operates and the ease or difficulty the organization experiences in attempting to reach its objectives. For example, it should be somewhat easier for an organization to sell its products at higher prices if potential consumers in the environment are earning relatively high wages and paying relatively low taxes than if these same potential customers are earning relatively low wages and have significantly fewer after-tax dollars to spend.

Naturally, organizational strategy should reflect the economic issues in the organization's environment. To build on the preceding example, if the total amount of after-tax income that potential customers earn has significantly declined, an appropriate organizational strategy might be to lower the price of goods or services to make them more affordable. Such a strategy should be evaluated carefully, however, because it could have a serious impact on organizational profits.

The Social Component. The social component is part of the general environment that describes the characteristics of the society in which the organization exists. Two important features of a society commonly studied during environmental analysis are demographics and social values.[6]

Demographics are the statistical characteristics of a population. These characteristics include changes in numbers of people and income distribution among various population segments. Such changes can influence the reception of goods and services within the organization's environment and thus should be reflected in organizational strategy.

For example, the demand for retirement housing would probably increase dramatically if both the number and the income of retirees in a particular market area doubled.[7] Effective organizational strategy would include a mechanism for dealing with such a probable increase in demand within the organization's environment.

An understanding of demographics is also helpful for developing a strategy aimed at recruiting new employees to fill certain positions within an organization. Knowing that only a small number of people have a certain type of educational background, for example, would tell an organization that it should compete more intensely to attract these people. To formulate a recruitment strategy, managers need a clear understanding of the demographics of the groups from which employees eventually will be hired.

Social values are the relative degrees of worth that society places on the ways in which it exists and functions. Over time, social values can change dramatically, causing significant changes in how people live. These changes alter the organizational environment and, as a result, have an impact on organizational strategy. It is important for managers to remember that

Demographics are the statistical characteristics of a population. Organizational strategy should reflect demographics.

Social values are the relative degrees of worth society places on the manner in which it exists and functions.

A Starbucks employee pours coffee beans into a grinder before the opening day ceremony at the Seattle-based company's first retail coffee shop in Beijing, China. The store, located in a 5-star hotel, is the first of 10 planned for the Chinese capital and marks the opening of Starbuck's ninth Asian market. Strategic planning for Starbuck's international operations would have begun with an environmental analysis and mostly likely focused on the question of whether Asian customers would be attracted to the idea of a retail specialty coffee shop.

although changes in the values of a particular society may come either slowly or quickly, they are inevitable. The following Ethics Spotlight shows how Quaker Oats responded to changing societal values.

ETHICS SPOTLIGHT — Quaker Oats Cashes in on Fitness Fad

As values of our society shifted toward exercising to achieve and maintain better physical health, Quaker Oats intensified its marketing of Gatorade, a drink used as an after-exercise refreshment that replaces body nutrients lost through exercise. Quaker Oats, however, has come under some attack for this marketing move because scientific analyses have shown that Gatorade is really no more effective than water in replenishing body fluids. Some might say that it is therefore unethical for Quaker Oats to present Gatorade as a worth-while product. The company could argue, however, that, as with other image products, merely consuming the drink gives a person an athletic self-image that makes him or her feel better.

Gatorade has the largest share of any product in the so-called sports drink market in the United States and is Quaker Oats' biggest brand. Competitors estimate that Gatorade spends about $100 million a year on marketing the drink. Many companies have tried to win market share from Gatorade, but none have been very successful.

The Political Component. The political component is that part of the general environment related to government affairs. Examples include the type of government in existence, government's attitude toward various industries, lobbying efforts by interest groups, progress on the passage of laws, and political party platforms and candidates. The reunification of Germany and the shift from a Marxist-Socialist government in the Soviet Union in the 1980s illustrate how the political component of an organization's general environment can change at the international level.

The Legal Component. The legal component is that part of the general environment that contains passed legislation. This component comprises the rules or laws that society's members must follow. Some examples of legislation specifically aimed at the operation of organizations are the Clean Air Act, which focuses on minimizing air pollution; the Occupational Safety and Health Act, which aims at ensuring a safe workplace; the Comprehensive Environmental Response, Compensation, and Liability Act, which emphasizes controlling hazardous waste sites; and the Consumer Products Safety Act, which upholds the notion that businesses

Since President Bill Clinton lifted the embargo against trade with Vietnam in February 1994, the communist country in Southeast Asia has ordered an annual average of 300,000 fiber-optic phone lines (plus advanced digital switches)—despite a per capita income of $220. Political factors, it seems, have been overridden by economic factors: Like most of their Third World counterparts, Vietnam's leaders realize that economic progress is dependent on a modern telecommunications infrastructure.

must provide safe products for consumers. Naturally, over time, new laws are passed and some old ones are amended or eliminated.

The Technology Component. The technology component is that part of the general environment that includes new approaches to producing goods and services. These approaches can be new procedures as well as new equipment. The trend toward exploiting robots to improve productivity is an example of the technology component. The increasing use of robots in the next decade should vastly improve the efficiency of U.S. industry.

MANAGEMENT AND THE INTERNET

800 Travel Systems, Inc. Establishes Internet Strategy

800 Travel Systems, Inc., a Tampa, Florida–based travel agent, uses toll-free telephone numbers to sell low-priced airline tickets. The company employs 145 reservation agents in Tampa and San Diego to generate revenue through commissions on airline tickets, service fees, and promotions with travel-service companies. Although the company advertises in 260 Yellow Page directories, it has been noticeably absent from the Internet.

Recently, however, the company announced a new strategy based primarily on the Internet. More specifically, the company announced plans to construct a new Web site by the end of the year. Although the company will finally have an Internet presence, this Web site will be far from ordinary. In fact, management is relying on the Web site's new chat feature. Because many consumers are afraid to give their credit card numbers to computers, this Web site will connect consumers directly to travel agents via chat boxes. The company hopes that this connection with real people will help hesitant consumers to conduct commerce on the Internet. Management is banking on the Web site and its new feature, and so is Wall Street. Reports of the new strategy have helped the stock price soar over 600 percent in the past month.

The **operating environment** is the level of the organization's external environment that contains components normally having relatively specific and immediate implications for managing the organization.

The Operating Environment   The level of an organization's external environment that contains components normally having relatively specific and immediate implications for managing the organization is the **operating environment.** As Figure 8.2 shows, major components of this environmental level are customers, competition, labor, suppliers, and international issues.

The Customer Component. The customer component is the operating environment segment that is composed of factors relating to those who buy goods and services provided by the organization. Businesses commonly create profiles, or detailed descriptions, of those who buy their products. Developing such profiles helps management generate ideas for improving customer acceptance of organizational goods and services.

The Competition Component. The competition component is the operating environment segment that is composed of those with whom an organization must battle in order to obtain resources. Organizational strategy requires searching for a plan of action that will give the organization an advantage over its competitors. Because understanding competitors is a key factor in developing effective strategy, understanding the competitive environment is a fundamental challenge to management. Basically, the purpose of competitive analysis is to help management comprehend the strengths, weaknesses, capabilities, and likely strategies of existing and potential competitors.[8]

The Labor Component. The labor component is the operating environment segment that is composed of factors influencing the supply of workers available to perform needed organizational tasks. Issues such as skill levels, trainability, desired wage rates, and average age of potential workers are important to the operation of the organization. Another important, but often overlooked, issue is potential employees' desire to work for particular organizations.

The Supplier Component. The supplier component is the operating environment segment that comprises all variables related to the individuals or agencies that provide organizations with the resources they need to produce goods or services. These individuals or agencies are called **suppliers.** Issues such as how many suppliers offer specified resources for sale, the relative quality of the materials offered by different suppliers, the reliability of supplier deliveries, and the credit terms provided by suppliers are all important to managing an organization effectively and efficiently.

Suppliers are individuals or agencies that provide organizations with the resources they need to produce goods and services.

TABLE 8.2	Important Aspects of the International Component of the Organization's Operating Environment

Legal Environment

Legal tradition
Effectiveness of legal system
Treaties with foreign nations
Patent and trademark laws
Laws affecting business firms

Economic Environment

Level of economic development
Population
Gross national product
Per capita income
Literacy level
Social infrastructure
Natural resources
Climate
Membership in regional economic blocs
(EEC, LAFTA, etc.)
Monetary and fiscal policies
Nature of competition
Currency convertibility
Inflation
Taxation system
Interest rates
Wage and salary levels

Cultural Environment

Customs, norms, values, beliefs
Language
Attitudes
Motivations
Social institutions
Status symbols
Religious beliefs

Political System

Form of government
Political ideology
Stability of government
Strength of opposition parties and groups
Social unrest
Political strife and insurgency
Government attitude toward foreign firms
Foreign policy

The International Component. The international component is the operating environment segment that is composed of all the factors relating to the international implications of organizational operations. Although not all organizations must deal with international issues, the number that have to do so is increasing dramatically and continually in the 1990s. Significant factors in the international component include other countries' laws, culture, economics, and politics.[9] Important variables within each of these four categories are presented in Table 8.2.

The Internal Environment The level of an organization's environment that exists inside the organization and normally has immediate and specific implications for managing the organization is the **internal environment.** In broad terms, the internal environment includes marketing, finance, and accounting. From a more specific management viewpoint, it includes planning, organizing, influencing, and controlling within the organization.

The **internal environment** is the level of an organization's environment that exists inside the organization and normally has immediate and specific implications for managing the organization.

BACK TO THE CASE

As part of the strategy development process, Gillette's management should spend time analyzing the organization's environment. Naturally, they should focus on Gillette's general, operating, and internal environments. Environmental factors that probably would be important for them to consider as they pursue strategic planning include the number of companies with which Gillette competes and knowing if this number will be increasing or decreasing, strengths and weakness of their products when compared to competitive companies, the reasons why people pay to use high-quality shaving products, and the methods competitors like Warner Lambert are using to promote their products to customers. Obtaining information about environmental issues such as these will increase the probability that any strategy developed for Gillette will be appropriate for its environment, and that the company will be successful in the long term.

ESTABLISHING ORGANIZATIONAL DIRECTION The second step of the strategy management process is establishing organizational direction. Through an interpretation of information gathered during environmental analysis, managers can determine the direction in which an organization should move. Two important ingredients of organizational direction are organizational mission and organizational objectives.

Determining Organizational Mission The most common initial act in establishing organizational direction is determining an organizational mission. **Organizational mission** is the purpose for which—the reason why—an organization exists. In general, the firm's organizational mission reflects such information as what types of products or services it produces, who its customers tend to be, and what important values it holds. Organizational mission is a very broad statement of organizational direction and is based upon a thorough analysis of information generated through environmental analysis.[10]

> The **organizational mission** is the purpose for which, or the reason why, an organization exists.

Developing a Mission Statement A **mission statement** is a written document developed by management, normally based on input by managers as well as nonmanagers, that describes and explains what the mission of an organization actually is. The mission is expressed in writing to ensure that all organization members will have easy access to it and thoroughly understand exactly what the organization is trying to accomplish. Here, for example, is the mission statement of Fedex:

> A **mission statement** is a written document developed by management, normally based on input by managers as well as nonmanagers, that describes and explains the organization's mission.

> Fedex is committed to our People-Service-Profit philosophy. We will produce outstanding financial returns by providing totally reliable, competitively superior, global air-ground transportation of high-priority goods and documents that require rapid, time-certain delivery. Equally important, positive control of each package will be maintained utilizing real time electronic tracking and tracing systems. A complete record of each shipment and delivery will be presented with our request for payment. We will be helpful, courteous, and professional to each other and the public. We will strive to have a completely satisfied customer at the end of each transaction.

The Importance of Organizational Mission An organizational mission is very important to an organization because it helps management increase the probability that the organization will be successful. There are several reasons why it does this. First, the existence of an organizational mission helps management focus human effort in a common direction. The mission makes explicit the major targets the organization is trying to reach and helps managers keep these targets in mind as they make decisions. Second, an organizational mission serves as a sound rationale for allocating resources. A properly developed mission statement gives managers general, but useful, guidelines about how resources should be used to best accomplish organizational purpose. Third, a mission statement helps management define broad but important job areas within an organization and therefore critical jobs that must be accomplished.[11]

> **QUALITY SPOTLIGHT** Lutheran General Health System's Mission Emphasizes Quality

A mission statement should emphasize the values that are important to a particular organization. The Lutheran General Health System, for instance, has a mission statement that emphasizes quality of services as an important value that managers should use to guide them in managing the organization.

Lutheran General Health System is a multiregional, multicorporate network of health and human service organizations, including the 742-bed Lutheran General Hospital. According to Dr.

Richard L. Phillips, chairperson of Lutheran General Health System's board of directors, the board's most important job is to review and define the mission and related core values of the organization as a whole. During the 1980s, each of the company's seven health-care facilities had a separate mission statement and a different strategic direction. As a result, there was very little coordination among the company's operating units in such areas as quality, long-term care, and substance-abuse treatment. Stephen L.

The Relationship between Mission and Objectives   Organizational objectives were defined in chapter 5 as the targets toward which the open management system is directed. Sound organizational objectives reflect and flow naturally from the purpose of the organization. The organization's purpose is expressed in its mission statement. As a result, useful organizational objectives must reflect and flow naturally from an organizational mission that, in turn, was designed to reflect and flow naturally from the results of an environmental analysis.

STRATEGY FORMULATION: TOOLS   After managers involved in the strategic management process have analyzed the environment and determined organizational direction through the development of a mission statement and organizational objectives, they are ready to formulate strategy. **Strategy formulation** is the process of determining appropriate courses of action for achieving organizational objectives and thereby accomplishing organizational purpose.

Managers formulate strategies that reflect environmental analysis, lead to fulfillment of organizational mission, and result in reaching organizational objectives. Special tools they can use to assist them in formulating strategies include the following:

1. Critical question analysis
2. SWOT analysis
3. Business portfolio analysis
4. Porter's Model for Industry Analysis

These four strategy development tools are related but distinct. Managers should use the tool or combination of tools that seems most appropriate for them and their organizations.

Critical Question Analysis   A synthesis of the ideas of several contemporary management writers suggests that formulating appropriate organizational strategy is a process of **critical question analysis**—answering the following four basic questions:[12]

➤ *What are the purposes and objectives of the organization?* The answer to this question will tell management where the organization should be going. As indicated earlier, appropriate strategy reflects both organizational purpose and objectives. By answering this question during the strategy formulation process, managers are likely to remember this important point and thereby minimize inconsistencies among the organization's purposes, objectives, and strategies.

➤ *Where is the organization presently going?* The answer to this question can tell managers if the organization is achieving its goals, and if it is, whether the level of progress is satisfactory. Whereas the first question focuses on where the organization should be going, this one focuses on where the organization is actually going.

➤ *In what kind of environment does the organization now exist?* Both internal and external environments—factors inside and outside the organization—are covered in this question. For example, assume that a poorly trained middle-management team and a sudden influx of competitors in a market are factors in, respectively, the internal and external environments of an organization. Any strategy formulated, if it is to be appropriate, must deal with these factors.

➤ *What can be done to better achieve organizational objectives in the future?* It is the answer to this question that results in the strategy of the organization. The question should be answered, however, only *after* managers have had an adequate opportunity to reflect on the answers to the previous three questions. Managers cannot develop an appropriate organizational strategy unless they have a clear understanding of where the organization wants to go, where it is going, and in what environment it exists.

Strategy formulation is the process of determining appropriate courses of action for achieving organizational objectives and thereby accomplishing organizational purpose. Strategy development tools include critical question analysis, SWOT analysis, business portfolio analysis, and Porter's Model for Industry Analysis.

Critical question analysis is a strategy development tool that consists of answering basic questions about the present purposes and objectives of the organization, its present direction and environment, and actions that can be taken to achieve organizational objectives in the future.

SWOT analysis is a strategy development tool that matches internal organizational strengths and weaknesses with external opportunities and threats.

Business portfolio analysis is the development of business-related strategy based primarily on the market share of businesses and the growth of markets in which businesses exist.

A **strategic business unit (SBU)** is, in business portfolio analysis, a significant organizational segment that is analyzed to develop organizational strategy aimed at generating future business or revenue. SBUs vary in form, but all are a single business (or collection of businesses), have their own competitors and a manager accountable for operations, and can be independently planned for.

SWOT Analysis **SWOT analysis** is a strategic development tool that matches internal organizational strengths and weaknesses with external opportunities and threats. (SWOT is an acronym for a firm's **S**trengths and **W**eaknesses and its environmental **O**pportunities and **T**hreats.) SWOT analysis is based on the assumption that if managers carefully review such strengths, weaknesses, opportunities, and threats, a useful strategy for ensuring organizational success will become evident to them.[13]

Business Portfolio Analysis Business portfolio analysis is another strategy development tool that has gained wide acceptance. **Business portfolio analysis** is an organizational strategy formulation technique that is based on the philosophy that organizations should develop strategy much as they handle investment portfolios. Just as sound financial investments should be supported and unsound ones discarded, sound organizational activities should be emphasized and unsound ones deemphasized. Two business portfolio tools are the BCG Growth-Share Matrix and the GE Multifactor Portfolio Matrix.

The BCG Growth-Share Matrix. The Boston Consulting Group (BCG), a leading manufacturing consulting firm, developed and popularized a portfolio analysis tool that helps managers develop organizational strategy based upon market share of businesses and the growth of markets in which businesses exist.

The first step in using the BCG Growth-Share Matrix is identifying the organization's strategic business units (SBUs). A **strategic business unit** is a significant organization segment that is analyzed to develop organizational strategy aimed at generating future business or revenue. Exactly what constitutes an SBU varies from organization to organization. In larger organizations, an SBU could be a company division, a single product, or a complete product line. In smaller organizations, it might be the entire company. Although SBUs vary drastically in form, each has the following four characteristics:[14]

1. It is a single business or collection of related businesses
2. It has its own competitors
3. It has a manager who is accountable for its operation
4. It is an area that can be independently planned for within the organization

After SBUs have been identified for a particular organization, the next step in using the BCG Matrix is to categorize each SBU within one of the following four matrix quadrants (see Figure 8.3):

▶ *Stars*—SBUs that are "stars" have a high share of a high-growth market and typically need large amounts of cash to support their rapid and significant growth. Stars also generate large amounts of cash for the organization and are usually segments in which management can make additional investments and earn attractive returns.

▶ *Cash Cows*—SBUs that are cash cows have a large share of a market that is growing only slightly. Naturally, these SBUs provide the organization with large amounts of cash, but since their market is not growing significantly, the cash is generally used to meet the financial demands of the organization in other areas, such as the expansion of a star SBU.

▶ *Question Marks*—SBUs that are question marks have a small share of a high-growth market. They are dubbed "question marks" because it is uncertain whether management should invest more cash in them to gain a larger share of the market or deemphasize or eliminate them. Management will choose the first option when it believes it can turn the question mark into a star, and the second when it thinks further investment would be fruitless.

▶ *Dogs*—SBUs that are dogs have a relatively small share of a low-growth market. They may barely support themselves; in some cases, they actually drain off cash resources generated by other SBUs. Examples of dogs are SBUs that produce typewriters or cash registers.

Companies such as Westinghouse and Shell Oil have successfully used the BCG Matrix in their strategy management processes. This technique, however, has some potential pitfalls. For one thing, the matrix does not consider such factors as (1) various types of risk associated with product development, (2) threats that inflation and other economic conditions can create in the future, and (3) social, political, and ecological pressures. These pitfalls may be the reason for recent research results indicating that the BCG Matrix does not always help managers make better strategic decisions.[15] Managers must remember to weigh such factors carefully when designing organizational strategy based on the BCG Matrix.

FIGURE 8.3 ► The BCG Growth-Share Matrix

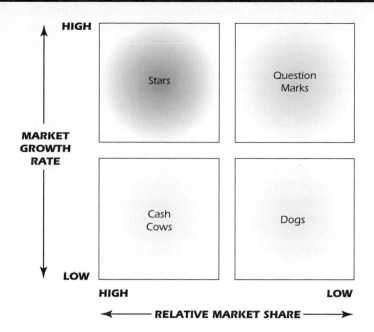

The GE Multifactor Portfolio Matrix. With the help of McKinsey and Company, a leading consulting firm, the General Electric Company (GE) has developed another popular portfolio analysis tool. Called the GE Multifactor Portfolio Matrix, this tool helps managers develop organizational strategy that is based primarily on market attractiveness and business strengths. The GE Multifactor Portfolio Matrix was deliberately designed to be more complete than the BCG Growth-Share Matrix.

Its basic use is illustrated in Figure 8.4. Each of the organization's businesses or SBUs is plotted on a matrix in two dimensions: industry attractiveness and business strength. Each of

FIGURE 8.4 ► GE's Multifactor Portfolio Matrix

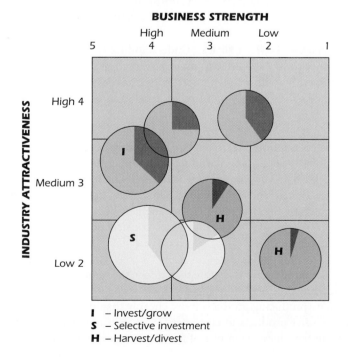

I – Invest/grow
S – Selective investment
H – Harvest/divest

these two dimensions is actually a composite of a variety of factors that each firm must determine for itself, given its own unique situation. As examples, industry attractiveness might be determined by such factors as the number of competitors in an industry, the rate of industry growth, and the weakness of competitors within an industry; while business strengths might be determined by such factors as a company's financially solid position, its good bargaining position over suppliers, and its high level of technology use.

Several circles appear on Figure 8.4, each representing a company line of business or SBU. Circle size indicates the relative market size for each line of business. The shaded portion of a circle represents the proportion of the total SBU market that a company has captured.

Specific strategies for a company are implied by where their businesses (represented by circles) fall on the matrix. Businesses falling in the cells that form a diagonal from lower left to upper right are medium-strength businesses that should be invested in only selectively. Businesses above and to the left of this diagonal are the strongest and the ones that the company should invest in and help to grow. Businesses in the cells below and to the right of the diagonal are low in overall strength and are serious candidates for divestiture.

Portfolio models are graphic frameworks for analyzing relationships among the businesses of an organization, and they can provide useful strategy recommendations. However, no such model yet devised gives managers a universally accepted approach for dealing with these issues. Portfolio models, then, should never be applied in a mechanistic fashion, and any conclusions they suggest must be carefully considered in light of sound managerial judgment and experience.

Porter's Model for Industry Analysis   Perhaps the best-known tool for formulating strategy is a model developed by Michael E. Porter, an internationally acclaimed strategic management expert.[16] Essentially, Porter's model outlines the primary forces that determine competitiveness within an industry and illustrates how those forces are related. The model suggests that in order to develop effective organizational strategies, managers must understand and react to those forces within an industry that determine an organization's level of competitiveness within that industry.

Porter's model is presented in Figure 8.5. According to the model, competitiveness within an industry is determined by the following: new entrants or new companies within the industry; products that might act as a substitute for goods or services that companies within the industry produce; the ability of suppliers to control issues like costs of materials that industry companies use to manufacture their products; the bargaining power that buyers possess within the industry; and the general level of rivalry or competition among firms within the industry. According to the model, then, buyers, product substitutes, suppliers, and potential new companies within an industry all contribute to the level of rivalry among industry firms.

STRATEGY FORMULATION: TYPES   Understanding the forces that determine competitiveness within an industry should help managers develop strategies that will make their companies more competitive within the industry. Porter has developed three generic strategies to illustrate the kind of strategies managers might develop to make their organizations more competitive.

Differentiation   **Differentiation,** the first of Porter's strategies, focuses on making an organization more competitive by developing a product or products that customers perceive as being different from products offered by competitors. Differentiation includes uniqueness in such areas as product quality, design, and level of after-sale service. Examples of products that customers commonly purchase because they perceive them as being different are Nike's Air Jordan shoes (because of their high-technology "air" construction) and Honda automobiles (because of their high reliability).

Cost Leadership   **Cost leadership** is a strategy that focuses on making an organization more competitive by producing products more cheaply than competitors can. According to the logic behind this strategy, by producing products more cheaply than its competitors do, an organization will be able to offer products to customers at lower prices than competitors can, and thereby increase its market share. Examples of tactics managers might use to gain cost leader-

Differentiation is a strategy that focuses on making an organization more competitive by developing a product or products that customers perceive as being different from products offered by competitors.

Cost leadership is a strategy that focuses on making an organization more competitive by producing products more cheaply than competitors can.

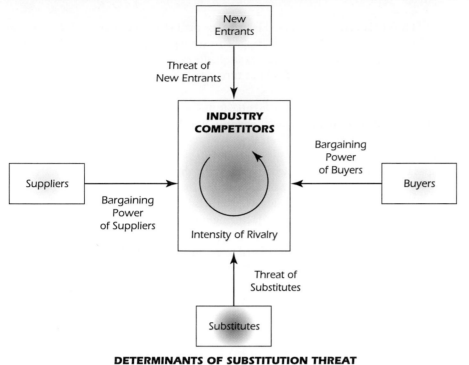

DETERMINANTS OF SUBSTITUTION THREAT
Relative Price Performance of Substitutes
Switching Costs
Buyer Propensity to Substitute

ship are obtaining lower prices for product parts purchased from suppliers and using technology like robots to increase organizational productivity.

Focus　**Focus** is a strategy that emphasizes making an organization more competitive by targeting a particular customer. Magazine publishers commonly use a focus strategy in offering their products to specific customers. *Working Woman* and *Ebony* are examples of magazines that are aimed, respectively, at the target markets of employed women and African-Americans.

Focus is a strategy that emphasizes making an organization more competitive by targeting a particular customer.

Sample Organizational Strategies　Analyzing the organizational environment and applying one or more of the strategy tools—critical question analysis, SWOT analysis, business portfolio analysis, and Porter's model—will give managers a foundation on which to formulate an organizational strategy. The four common organizational strategies that evolve this way are growth, stability, retrenchment, and divestiture. The following discussion of these organizational strategies features business portfolio analysis as the tool used to arrive at the strategy, although the same strategies could result from critical question analysis, SWOT analysis, or Porter's model.

Growth　**Growth** is a strategy adopted by management to increase the amount of business that an SBU is currently generating. The growth strategy is generally applied to star SBUs or question mark SBUs that have the potential to become stars. Management generally invests substantial amounts of money to implement this strategy and may even sacrifice short-term profit to build long-term gain.[17]

Managers can also pursue a growth strategy by purchasing an SBU from another organization. For example, Black & Decker, not satisfied with being an international power in power tools, purchased General Electric's small-appliance business. Through this purchase, Black & Decker hoped that the amount of business it did would grow significantly over the long term.

Growth is a strategy adopted by management to increase the amount of business that a strategic business unit is currently generating.

Similarly, President Enterprises, the largest food company in Taiwan, recently bought the American Famous Amos brand of chocolate chip cookies. Despite a downturn in the U.S. cookie market, management at President saw the purchase as important for company growth because it gave the company a nationally recognized product line in the United States.[18]

Stability is a strategy adopted by management to maintain or slightly improve the amount of business a strategic business unit is generating.

Stability Stability is a strategy adopted by management to maintain or slightly improve the amount of business that an SBU is generating. This strategy is generally applied to cash cows, since these SBUs are already in an advantageous position. Management must be careful, however, that in its pursuit of stability it does not turn cash cows into dogs.

Retrenchment is a strategy adopted by management to strengthen or protect the amount of business a strategic business unit is currently generating.

Retrenchment In this section, *retrench* is used in the military sense: to defend or fortify. Through **retrenchment** strategy, management attempts to strengthen or protect the amount of business an SBU is generating. This strategy is generally applied to cash cows or stars that are beginning to lose market share.

Douglas D. Danforth, the chief executive of Westinghouse, is convinced that retrenchment is an important strategy for his company. According to Danforth, bigger profits at Westinghouse depend not only on fast-growing new products but also on the revitalization of Westinghouse's traditional businesses of manufacturing motors and gears.[19]

Divestiture is a strategy adopted to eliminate a strategic business unit that is not generating a satisfactory amount of business and has little hope of doing so in the future.

Divestiture Divestiture is a strategy adopted to eliminate an SBU that is not generating a satisfactory amount of business and that has little hope of doing so in the near future. In essence, the organization sells or closes down the SBU in question. This strategy is usually applied to SBUs that are dogs or question marks that have failed to increase market share but still require significant amounts of cash.

Strategy implementation, the fourth step of the strategy management process, is putting formulated strategy into action.

STRATEGY IMPLEMENTATION Strategy implementation, the fourth step of the strategy management process, is putting formulated strategies into action. Without successive implementation, valuable strategies developed by managers are virtually worthless.[20]

The successful implementation of strategy requires four basic skills:[21]

1. *Interacting skill* is the ability to manage people during implementation. Managers who are able to understand the fears and frustrations others feel during the implementation of a new strategy tend to be the best implementers. These managers empathize with organization members and bargain for the best way to put a strategy into action.
2. *Allocating skill* is the ability to provide the organizational resources necessary to implement a strategy. Successful implementers are talented at scheduling jobs, budgeting time and money, and allocating other resources that are critical for implementation.
3. *Monitoring skill* is the ability to use information to determine whether a problem has arisen that is blocking implementation. Good strategy implementers set up feedback systems that continually tell them about the status of strategy implementation.
4. *Organizing skill* is the ability to create throughout the organization a network of people who can help solve implementation problems as they occur. Good implementers customize this network to include individuals who can handle the special types of problems anticipated in the implementation of a particular strategy.

Overall, then, the successful implementation of a strategy requires handling people appropriately, allocating resources necessary for implementation, monitoring implementation progress, and solving implementation problems as they occur. Perhaps the most important requirements are knowing which people can solve specific implementation problems and being able to involve them when those problems arise.

Strategic control, the last step of the strategy management process, consists of monitoring and evaluating the strategy management process as a whole to ensure that it is operating properly.

STRATEGIC CONTROL Strategic control, the last step of the strategy management process, consists of monitoring and evaluating the strategy management process as a whole to ensure that it is operating properly. Strategic control focuses on the activities involved in environmental analysis, organizational direction, strategy formulation, strategy implementation, and strategic control itself—checking that all steps of the strategy management process are appropriate, compatible, and functioning properly.[22] Strategic control is a special type of organizational control, a topic that is featured in chapters 19, 20, and 21.

Based on the previous information, after Gillette has performed its environmental analysis, it must determine the direction it will move regarding its competitive position. Issues like adding shaving products for women will naturally surface. Developing a mission statement with related objectives would be clear signals to all Gillette's employees about the role of new shaving products for women in the organization's future. Gillette's management has several tools available to assist them in formulating strategy. If they are to be effective in this area, however, they must use the tools in conjunction with environmental analysis. One of the tools, critical question analysis, would require management to analyze Gillette's purpose, direction, environment, and goals.

SWOT analysis, another strategy development tool, would require management to generate information regarding the internal strengths and weaknesses of Gillette as well as the opportunities and threats that exist within Gillette's environment. Management probably would classify the products of competitors like Warner Lambert's Schick division as threats and significant factors to be considered in their strategy development process.

One approach to business portfolio analysis would suggest that Gillette's management classify each major product line (SBU) within the company as a star, cash cow, question mark, or dog, depending on the growth rate of the market interested and the market share the Gillette product line possesses. Management could decide, for example, to consider the new Mach3 and each of its other major product lines as a unit for SBU analysis and categorize them according to the four classifications. As a result of this categorization process, they could develop, perhaps for each different product line that they offer, growth, stability, retrenchment, or divestiture strategies. Gillette's management should use whichever strategy development tools they think would be most useful. Their objective in this case, of course, is to develop an appropriate strategy for the development of Gillette's product lines.

To be successful at using the strategy that it develops, Gillette's management must apply its interacting, allocating, monitoring, and organizing skills. In addition, management must be able to improve the strategy management process when necessary.

TACTICAL PLANNING

Tactical planning is short-range planning that emphasizes the current operations of various parts of the organization. *Short range* is defined as a period of time extending about one year or less into the future. Managers use tactical planning to outline what the various parts of the organization must do for the organization to be successful at some point one year or less into the future.[23] Tactical plans are usually developed in the areas of production, marketing, personnel, finance, and plant facilities.

> **Tactical planning** is short-range planning that emphasizes the current operations of various parts of the organization.

▶COMPARING AND COORDINATING STRATEGIC AND TACTICAL PLANNING

In striving to implement successful planning systems within organizations, managers must remember several basic differences between strategic planning and tactical planning:

1. Because upper-level managers generally have a better understanding of the organization as a whole than lower-level managers do, and because lower-level managers generally have a better understanding of the day-to-day organizational operations than upper-level managers do, strategic plans are usually developed by upper-level management and tactical plans by lower-level management.

2. Because strategic planning emphasizes analyzing the future and tactical planning emphasizes analyzing the everyday functioning of the organization, facts on which to base strategic plans are usually more difficult to gather than are facts on which to base tactical plans.

3. Because strategic plans are based primarily on a prediction of the future and tactical plans on known circumstances that exist within the organization, strategic plans are generally less detailed than tactical plans.

TABLE 8.3	Major Differences between Strategic and Tactical Planning	
Area of Difference	**Strategic Planning**	**Tactical Planning**
Individuals involved	Developed mainly by upper-level management	Developed mainly by lower-level management
Facts on which to base planning	Facts are relatively difficult to gather	Facts are relatively easy to gather
Amount of detail in plans	Plans contain relatively little detail	Plans contain substantial amounts of detail
Length of time plans cover	Plans cover long periods of time	Plans cover short periods of time

4. Because strategic planning focuses on the long term and tactical planning on the short term, strategic plans cover a relatively long period of time whereas tactical plans cover a relatively short period of time.

All of these major differences between strategic and tactical planning are summarized in Table 8.3.

Despite their differences, tactical and strategic planning are integrally related. As Russell L. Ackoff states, "We can look at them separately, even discuss them separately, but we cannot separate them in fact."[24] In other words, managers need both tactical and strategic planning programs, and these programs must be closely related to be successful. Tactical planning should focus on what to do in the short term to help the organization achieve the long-term objectives determined by strategic planning.

PLANNING AND LEVELS OF MANAGEMENT

An organization's top management is primarily responsible for seeing that the planning function is carried out. Although all management levels are involved in the typical planning process, upper-level managers usually spend more time planning than lower-level managers do. Lower-level managers are highly involved in the everyday operations of the organization and therefore normally have less time to contribute to planning than top managers do. Middle-level managers usually spend more time planning than lower-level managers, but less time than upper-level managers. Figure 8.6 shows how planning time increases as a manager moves from lower-level to upper-level management. In small as well as large organizations, determining the amount and nature of the work that each manager should personally handle is extremely important.

FIGURE 8.6	Increase in planning time as manager moves from lower-level to upper-level management

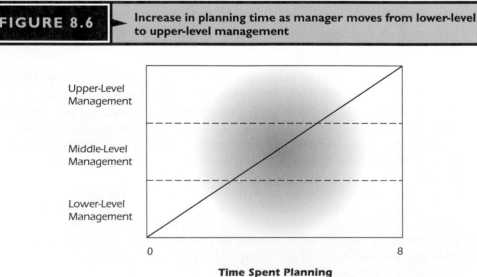

The type of planning done also changes as a manager moves up in the organization. Typically, lower-level managers plan for the short term, middle-level managers for the somewhat longer term, and upper-level managers for the even longer term. The expertise of lower-level managers in everyday operations makes them the best planners for what can be done in the short term to reach organizational objectives—in other words, they are best equipped to do tactical planning. Upper-level managers usually have the best understanding of the whole organizational situation and are therefore better equipped to plan for the long term—or to develop strategic plans.[25]

BACK TO THE CASE

In addition to developing strategic plans for its organization, Gillette's management should consider tactical, or short-range, plans that would complement its strategic plans. Tactical plans for Gillette should emphasize what can be done within approximately the next year to reach the organization's three- to five-year objectives and to steal competition from its competitors. For example, Gillette could devote more resources to aggressive, short-range advertising campaigns or increase sales by aggressively reducing the introductory prices of new products.

In addition, Gillette's management must closely coordinate strategic and tactical planning within the company. It must keep in mind that strategic planning and tactical planning are different types of activities that may involve different people within the organization and result in plans with different degrees of detail. Yet it must also remember that these two types of plans are interrelated. While lower-level managers would be mostly responsible for developing tactical plans, upper-level managers would mainly spend time on long-range planning and developing strategic plans that reflect company goals.

For updated information on the topics in this chapter, Internet exercises, links to related Internet sites, an interactive study guide, and more, visit our companion Web site at

http://www.prenhall.com/certo

Additional information can be found on the inside front and back covers of this text.

ACTION SUMMARY

Reread the learning objectives below. Each objective is followed by questions. Answering these questions accurately will help you retain the most important concepts discussed in this chapter. After answering each question, check your answer against the answer key at the end of this chapter. (*Hint:* If you have any doubts regarding the correct response, consult the page number that follows the answer.)

Circle:

From studying this chapter, I will attempt to acquire

1. Definitions of both strategic planning and strategy.

T F
    a. Strategic planning is long-range planning that focuses on the organization as a whole.

a b c d e
    b. Strategy: (a) is a specific, narrow plan designed to achieve tactical planning (b) is designed to be the end result of tactical planning (c) is a plan designed to reach long-range objectives (d) is timeless, so the same strategy can meet organizational needs anytime (e) is independent of organizational objectives and therefore need not be consistent with them.

2. An understanding of the strategy management process.

a b c d e
    a. Which of the following is *not* one of the steps in strategy management: (a) strategy formulation (b) strategy implementation (c) strategy control (d) environmental analysis (e) all of the above are steps.

T F
    b. The steps of the strategy management process are sequential but usually not continuing.

3. A knowledge of the impact of environmental analysis on strategy formulation.

T F   **a.** Environmental analysis is the strategy used to change an organization's environment to satisfy the needs of the organization.

a b c d e   **b.** All of the following are factors to be considered in environmental analysis except: (a) suppliers (b) economic issues (c) demographics (d) social values (e) none of the above.

4. Insights about how to use critical question analysis and SWOT analysis to formulate strategy.

a b c d e   **a.** The following is *not* one of the four basic questions used in critical question analysis: (a) Where has the organization been? (b) Where is the organization presently going? (c) What are the purposes and objectives of the organization? (d) In what kind of environment does the organization now exist? (e) What can be done to better achieve organizational objectives in the future?

T F   **b.** SWOT is an acronym for "Strengths and Weaknesses, Objectives and Tactics."

5. An understanding of how to use business portfolio analysis and industry analysis to formulate strategy.

a b c d e   **a.** Using the BCG Matrix requires considering the following factors: (a) types of risk associated with product development (b) threats that economic conditions can create in the future (c) social factors (d) market shares and growth of markets in which products are selling (e) political pressures.

a b c d e   **b.** To users of the BCG Matrix, products that capture a high share of a rapidly growing market are known as: (a) cash cows (b) milk products (c) sweepstakes products (d) stars (e) dog products.

T F   **c.** Use of the GE Multifactor Portfolio Matrix requires considering total market size for an SBU but usually not the amount of the market that the SBU has won.

6. Insights into what tactical planning is and on how strategic and tactical planning should be coordinated.

T F   **a.** Tactical plans generally are developed for one year or less and usually contain fewer details than strategic plans.

a b c d e   **b.** The following best describes strategic planning: (a) facts are difficult to gather, and plans cover short periods of time (b) facts are difficult to gather, and plans cover long periods of time (c) facts are difficult to gather, and plans are developed mainly by lower-level managers (d) facts are easy to gather, and plans are developed mainly by upper-level managers (e) facts are easy to gather, and plans are developed mainly by lower-level managers.

▶ INTRODUCTORY CASE WRAP-UP ◀

CASE DISCUSSSION QUESTIONS

"Gillette's New Strategy: Women" (p. 165) and its related Back-to-the-Case sections were written to help you better understand the management concepts contained in this chapter. Answer the following discussion questions about this Introductory Case to further enrich your understanding of chapter content:

1. For Gillette's management, is improving its women's line of shaving products a strategic management issue? Explain.

2. Give three factors in Gillette's internal environment that management should be assessing in determining the company's organizational direction. Why are these factors important?

3. Using the business portfolio matrix, categorize the new women's line of shaving products as a dog, question mark, star, or cash cow. From a strategic planning viewpoint, what do you recommend that Gillette management should do as a result of this categorization? Why?

SKILLS EXERCISE: PERFORMING AN ENVIRONMENTAL ANALYSIS

In this chapter you learned how managers study the environment to form a strategic plan. The Introductory Case details the new strategy at Gillette and how the company has increased its focus on women's shaving products. Describe two factors from each of Gillette's environments—general, operating, and internal—and discuss how each factor could increase the probability that the new women-oriented strategy will be successful. Discuss how each factor could decrease the probability that the new strategy will be unsuccessful.

1. What is strategic planning?
2. How does the commitment principle relate to strategic planning?
3. Define *strategy* and discuss its relationship to organizational objectives.
4. What are the major steps in the strategy management process? Discuss each step fully.
5. Why is environmental analysis an important part of strategy formulation?
6. List one major factor from each environmental level that could have a significant impact on specific strategies developed for an organization. How could the specific strategies be affected by each factor?
7. Discuss the significance of the questions answered during critical question analysis.
8. Explain in detail how SWOT analysis can be used to formulate strategy.
9. What is business portfolio analysis?
10. Discuss the philosophy on which business portfolio analysis is based.
11. What is an SBU?
12. Draw and explain the BCG Growth-Share Matrix.
13. What potential pitfalls must managers avoid in using this matrix?
14. Explain three major differences in using the GE Multifactor Portfolio Matrix to develop organizational strategy as opposed to the BCG Matrix.
15. Draw and explain Porter's model of factors that determines competitiveness within an industry. What is the significance of this model for developing an organizational strategy?
16. List and define four sample strategies that can be developed for organizations.
17. What is tactical planning?
18. How do strategic and tactical planning differ?
19. What is the relationship between strategic and tactical planning?
20. How do time spent planning and scope of planning vary according to management levels?

By the early 1990s, IBM Corporation was clearly in trouble. The company, whose past successes depended on mainframe personal computer (PC) sales, was in need of new direction. Lou Gerstner took command of IBM in April of 1993. His success outside the technology industry indicated the desire of IBM's board of directors to infuse new and productive approaches into the company's operations. From the beginning, Gerstner insisted he had no grand plan to turn IBM around. Instead, he concentrated on three major areas:

► Inefficient size of the company
► Loss of revenue that resulted when former customers took their business elsewhere
► Line of products that was lagging behind those of competitors

Gerstner has received high marks for the management team he assembled. Although most are IBM veterans, two are new to the IBM environment and culture. Jerry York was tapped to reduce IBM's size and to cut back on expenses. The number of employees on the IBM rolls has been slashed by more than 105,000, from a high of 407,080 in 1985 to 301,542 in 1995. High development costs have also hurt IBM. Thus far, York has reduced expenses by $5.6 billion. His eventual goal is to cut $8 billion in expenses. Richard Thoman was a member of Gerstner's team at other consumer-services companies and, like Gerstner, is a former McKinsey consultant. The sound decision to stop selling IBM PCs when a flaw was found in the Intel chip is attributed to him.

Gerstner and his new management team preach the concept of "network-centricity"—that is, basing company plans on computer networks and the products needed to complete this vision of the future. In a sense, this approach is a return to the computing concept of the single mainframe with multiple points of connectivity because a network-centric environment maintains the computing power of the mainframe while providing the connectivity and communication demanded by individual PC users. The advantage to customers is that they can reap the benefits of the network without making large outlays for mainframe computers and software. Gerstner is counting on IBM's ability to provide outsourcing and systems integration to its corporate customers. Current large corporate customers as well as the burgeoning—and as yet untapped—world of small businesses would benefit from the arrangement. IBM, which currently owns one-third of the world's data-processing centers, would retain ownership and maintenance of the mainframe that would be the center of each network.

A milestone in Gerstner's plan was the purchase of Lotus Development Corporation for $3.5 billion. IBM is betting big money on Lotus Notes, a "groupware" product that lets individuals communicate with others via E-mail and databases. This acquisition fits neatly with Gerstner's plan to free IBM from overdependence on the personal computer. Already, IBM has lost the lead in PC hardware sales to companies like Compaq and new mail-order companies like Dell and Gateway, and its OS/2 PC operating system is unable to compete successfully with Microsoft's Windows.

By and large, Gerstner's strategies have paid off. Most of IBM's product lines are showing not only higher sales but higher revenues as well. Even the mainframe sector has demonstrated growth, although many observers believe that this is not a long-term trend. In any case, customers now perceive IBM as more responsive to their needs, and the financial figures reflect this improvement in customer perception.

In addition to cutting costs and improving customer relations, Gerstner is forging new partnerships with other technology companies to reduce both the costs and time it takes to develop new products. IBM's new partnerships ensure that different perspectives will be incorporated into the product development process, which is especially important in the fast-paced world of technology. At the same time, Gerstner's plans capitalize on what made IBM successful in the past. He will use IBM's global presence, excellent consultant resources, and long-standing relationships with corporate customers to deliver solutions in the network-centric environment.

Of course, creating a network-centric plan for the future does not ensure its success. Gerstner must convince current and potential IBM customers that the plan offers important benefits to them. But even before he goes to the customer, he must sell his plan to those within the ranks of IBM who are not eager to abandon IBM's past model of success. The company's future depends on his success in both arenas.

QUESTIONS

1. What struggles does Lou Gerstner face in his plan to make IBM network-centric? Consider internal and external impediments.
2. Must IBM's basic corporate culture change in order to meet Gerstner's goal? Explain.
3. What strengths does IBM possess that make Gerstner's plan achievable? How do Gerstner's strategies incorporate those strengths?

SMALL BUSINESS 2000

In order to get the job done, employees need to know what the job is. A well defined and clearly communicated plan is a good way to ensure that people know what is expected of them. Cloud 9 Shuttle, a San Diego–based transportation company, was saved from the brink of failure by a management team that understood this and more.

The new owners of Cloud 9 understood that before they could communicate a plan, they needed to develop one. A plan is only as good as how well it helps accomplish the mission and objectives of the company. The new owners of Cloud 9 did a wise thing—they started over from the beginning. They started by defining a new mission for the company and developing a strategy for reaching their objectives. This of course was not enough because strategies are usually only broad-reaching and general descriptions of what is to be done.

Fortunately for Cloud 9, its leaders understood that. Cloud 9 did not turn into the company it is overnight. The company has grown gradually, but one thing has remained constant during its transition—the company has remained focused on the objectives put forth in its strategic plan. Cloud 9 has paid close attention to its market too. The strategy that the company follows is oriented toward changing the image that people have of the company and making it the service of choice for transportation to and from the San Diego airport. Cloud 9's management has been able to balance the internal demands of the firm with the needs of its market—the result has benefited the company, its customers, and the community in which it operates.

QUESTIONS

1. Some pretty big changes were implemented at Cloud 9 when it changed owners. Do you think such a big change in attitude and approach was necessary? What risks and advantages can you think of for taking this approach?

2. After the initial big change, it seems that Cloud 9's managers follow a more incremental approach to making changes at the company. Why do you think they have changed their tactics in this way? Is it a good idea? Why or why not?

3. You saw examples of investments the company made in maintenance and communication as well as an attempt to open the market to local customers. All of these things require the outlay of a lot of money. Do you think these are wise investments? Why or why not? What else do you think they might want to change or improve?

Plans and Planning Tools

STUDENT LEARNING OBJECTIVES

From studying this chapter, I will attempt to acquire

1. A complete definition of a plan
2. Insights regarding various dimensions of plans
3. An understanding of various types of plans
4. Insights on why plans fail
5. A knowledge of various planning areas within an organization
6. A definition of forecasting
7. An ability to see the advantages and disadvantages of various methods of sales forecasting
8. A definition of scheduling
9. An understanding of Gantt charts and PERT

CHAPTER OUTLINE

Introductory Case: *Fiat Plans Car Production*

PLANS: A DEFINITION

Ethics Spotlight: *Toyota Uses Philanthropy Plan to Take Aim at General Motors*
Dimensions of Plans
Types of Plans

Management and the Internet: *Salomon Smith Barney Establishes Rules to Deal with Internet*
Why Plans Fail
Planning Areas: Input Planning

Global Spotlight: *Mexico as an Attractive Manufacturing Site*

PLANNING TOOLS
Forecasting

Across Industries: *Airplane Manufacturing—Boeing Uses Forecasting to Alter Production*
Scheduling

FIAT PLANS CAR PRODUCTION

REMINDER: THE INTRODUCTORY CASE WRAP-UP (P. 206) CONTAINS DISCUSSION QUESTIONS AND A SKILLS EXERCISE TO FURTHER ILLUSTRATE THE APPLICATION OF CHAPTER CONCEPTS TO THIS VIGNETTE.

Automobile group Fiat, shrugging off the slowdown in European car demand, plans to build a major car plant in Basilicata, southern Italy, and expand and remodel an existing parts factory in Avelino, near Naples.

The decision involves investments totaling Lire 5 trillion ($4.5 billion) over a three-year period.

The Basilicata car plant will produce 1,800 cars a day and employ 7,000 workers, while the Avellino parts plant will be transformed into a factory producing 3,600 engines a day and employing 1,300 people.

The company is going ahead with the plan despite having cut back production because of slack European demand. [Recently,] Fiat doubled the number of workers temporarily laid off to 70,000 as part of a program of plant closures that cut planned output by about 90,000 cars. As a result, Fiat expects to produce about 2,150,000 cars a year worldwide, down from a level of about 2,250,000 sustained in previous years.

Susanne Oliver, European automotive analyst at London brokerage firm Hoare Govett, said the move was unexpected in the current depressed state of the market. "The move is a little bit surprising, given that they have announced production cutbacks. And that in the medium term there is no sign of an upswing in demand," she said.

"Obviously, it takes some years to bring the plants on stream . . . , nevertheless, capacity is being underutilized," she added. The Basilicata plant will have a theoretical capacity of almost 400,000 cars a year, working an average 220 days a year. Avellino could produce 790,000 engines a year.

"Fiat will be eligible for hefty state aid on both plants. The company declined to put a figure on the subsidies, but a [spokesperson] said, "We have asked the government for the maximum the law allows—nothing special, but the maximum."

Despite the slowdown in European car demand, Fiat has invested 5 trillion lire ($4.5 billion) in auto and parts factories.

An official of the ministry dealing with Italy's depressed south, the Mezzogiorno, said state grants of 15 percent were available on large productive investments of this type. On this calculation, Fiat could receive a subsidy of about 750 billion lire, though not all funds invested may be eligible.

In addition, soft loans, at 60 percent of prime rate, are available to cover 30 percent of the investment cost, and reductions will also be given on social security payments for workers. Extra subsidies may also be available because the plants are in zones that sustained earthquake damage in 1980.

Fiat, which already has ambitious production plans in Poland, is calculating that European car demand will sustain a further increase in capacity. "We think Europe will continue to absorb cars—maybe not at the record level of the past two to three years, but the market is healthy," a spokesperson said.

What's Ahead

The Introductory Case describes Fiat's plans to build one new plant and increase the capacity of another. This chapter emphasizes several fundamental issues about plans that should be useful to managers like those at Fiat. It describes what plans are and discusses several valuable tools that can be used in developing them.

The first half of the chapter covers the basic facts about plans. It does the following:

1. Defines what a plan is
2. Outlines the dimensions of a plan
3. Lists various types of plans
4. Discusses why plans fail
5. Explains two major organizational areas in which planning usually takes place

◤ PLANS: A DEFINITION

A **plan** is a specific action proposed to help the organization achieve its objectives.

A **plan** is a specific action proposed to help the organization achieve its objectives. A critical part of the management of any organization is developing logical plans and then taking the steps necessary to put the plans into action.[1] Regardless of how important experience-related intuition may be to managers, successful management actions and strategies typically are based on reason. Rational managers are crucial to the development of an organizational plan.

ETHICS SPOTLIGHT | Toyota Uses Philanthropy Plan to Take Aim at General Motors

The Toyota Motor Company, a Japanese firm, is one of the largest automobile manufacturers in the world. Toyota's top management has created a philanthropy plan to help the company better compete with General Motors.

Toyota has designed a comprehensive plan for the organization that has both domestic and overseas components. It outlines an enormous undertaking that calls for annual automobile production and sales equaling more than 6 million units within three to five years. Toyota's president, Shoichiro Toyoda, believing that the world automobile market has plenty of room to grow, is determined to overtake General Motors as the world's largest automaker by the end of this century.

Although GM's output and sales have declined in recent years while Toyota's output and sales have increased, some industry analysts doubt Toyota has the ability to develop a marketing effort that will enable the company to surpass GM. Toyota's management team, however, insists that the company's aspirations to overtake GM are realistic. One reason for Toyota's optimism is the company's philanthropy plan, which channels corporate profits into local communities, enhancing Toyota's public image and thus boosting sales. Over the last few years, Toyota has channeled about 1.5 percent of its profits into philanthropic programs. In the near future, the company's level of philanthropy will probably remain about the same or even increase.

▶ DIMENSIONS OF PLANS

Kast and Rosenzweig identify a plan's four major dimensions as follows:[2]

1. Repetitiveness
2. Time
3. Scope
4. Level

Each dimension is an independent characteristic of a plan and should be considered during plan development.

The **repetitiveness dimension** of a plan is the extent to which the plan is to be used over and over again.

REPETITIVENESS The **repetitiveness dimension** of a plan is the extent to which the plan is used over and over again. Some plans are specially designed for one situation that is relatively short-term in nature. Plans of this sort are essentially nonrepetitive. Other plans, however, are designed to be used time after time for long-term recurring situations. These plans are basically repetitive in nature.

Engineer Ron Shriver and his Japan-based counterpart Hiroyuki Itoh (second and third from the left, respectively) are celebrating the successful completion of a project to reduce the costs of building the Civic at Honda Motor Co.'s plant in East Liberty, Ohio. The project was a model of both team-based problem solving and creating plans across management levels. Originally, for instance, Shriver and Itoh had formed separate teams, but once they had begun pooling their resources, they were able to gather money-saving suggestions from suppliers and factory workers in both the United States and Japan.

TIME The **time dimension** of a plan is the length of time the plan covers. In chapter 8, strategic planning was defined as long term in nature, while tactical planning was defined as short-term. It follows, then, that strategic plans cover relatively long periods of time and tactical plans cover relatively short periods of time.

> The **time dimension** of a plan is the length of time the plan covers.

SCOPE The **scope dimension** of a plan is the portion of the total management system at which the plan is aimed. Some plans are designed to cover the entire open management system: the organizational environment, inputs, process, and outputs. Such a plan is often referred to as a *master plan*. Other plans are developed to cover only a portion of the management system. An example of the latter would be a plan that covers the recruitment of new workers—a portion of the organizational input segment of the management system. The greater the portion of the management system that a plan covers, the broader the plan's scope is said to be.

> The **scope dimension** of a plan is the portion of the total management system at which the plan is aimed.

LEVEL The **level dimension** of a plan is the level of the organization at which the plan is aimed. Top-level plans are those designed for the organization's top management, whereas middle- and lower-level plans are designed for middle and lower management, respectively. Because all parts of the management system are interdependent, however, plans designed for any level of the organization have some effect on all other levels.

> The **level dimension** of a plan is the level of the organization at which the plan is aimed.

Figure 9.1 illustrates the four dimensions of an organizational plan. This figure indicates that when managers develop a plan, they should consider the degree to which it will be used over and over again, the period of time it will cover, the parts of the management system on which it focuses, and the organizational level at which it is aimed.

FIGURE 9.1 ▶	Four major dimensions to consider when developing a plan

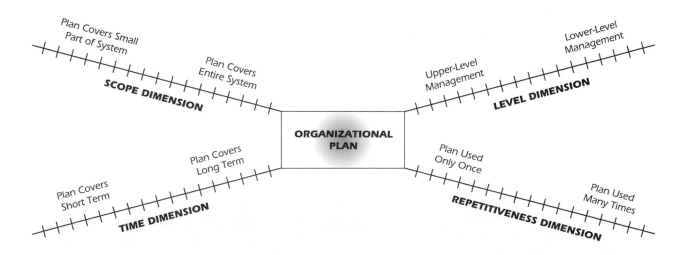

In developing plans for Fiat, management is devising recommendations for future actions. Therefore, plans should be action-oriented—that is, they should state precisely what Fiat is going to do to achieve its goals.

Fiat managers should consider how often the plans they are developing will be used and the length of time they will cover. Will a plan be implemented only once or will it be used over the long term to handle an ongoing issue such as maintaining product quality? A plan to build a new factory would probably not be used more than once and would be designed to cover a specific amount of time.

Fiat's managers should consider at which part of the organization to aim the plans they develop and on which organizational level the plans will focus. For example, a plan to cut costs might encompass all of Fiat's operations, whereas one to improve product quality might affect only one part of the production process. Similarly, a plan to cut costs might be aimed at top-level management, whereas a product quality plan might be aimed toward lower-level management and the auto assemblers themselves. Of course, managers must realize that, because management systems are interdependent, any plans they implement will affect the whole system.

►TYPES OF PLANS

Standing plans are plans that are used over and over because they focus on organizational situations that occur repeatedly.

Single-use plans are plans that are used only once—or, at most, several times—because they focus on unique or rare situations within the organization.

A **policy** is a standing plan that furnishes broad guidelines for channeling management toward taking action consistent with reaching organizational objectives.

With the repetitiveness dimension as a guide, organizational plans are usually divided into two types: standing and single-use. **Standing plans** are used over and over again because they focus on organizational situations that occur repeatedly. **Single-use plans** are used only once—or, at most, several times—because they focus on unique or rare situations within the organization. As Figure 9.2 illustrates, standing plans can be subdivided into policies, procedures, and rules and single-use plans into programs and budgets.

STANDING PLANS: POLICIES, PROCEDURES, AND RULES A **policy** is a standing plan that furnishes broad guidelines for taking action consistent with reaching organizational objectives. For example, an organizational policy relating to personnel might be worded as follows: "Our organization will strive to recruit only the most talented employees." This policy statement is very broad, giving managers only a general idea of what to do in the area of recruitment. The policy is intended to emphasize the extreme importance management attaches to hiring competent employees and to guide managers' actions accordingly.

As another example of an organizational policy, consider companies' responses to studies showing that one out of every four workers in the United States was attacked, threatened, or harassed on the job during a recent 12-month operating period. To deal with this problem, many managers are developing weapons policies. A sample policy could be: "Management

| FIGURE 9.2 | ► Standing plans and single-use plans |

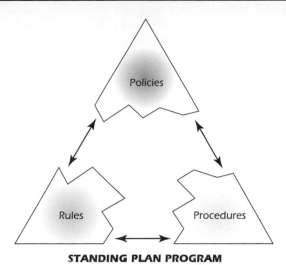

STANDING PLAN PROGRAM

strongly discourages any employee from bringing a weapon to work." This policy would encourage managers to deal forcefully and punitively with employees who bring weapons into the workplace.[3]

A **procedure** is a standing plan that outlines a series of related actions that must be taken to accomplish a particular task. In general, procedures outline more specific actions than policies do. Organizations usually have many different sets of procedures covering the various tasks to be accomplished. Managers must be careful to apply the appropriate organizational procedures for the situations they face and to apply them properly.[4]

A **rule** is a standing plan that designates specific required action. In essence, a rule indicates what an organization member should or should not do and allows no room for interpretation. An example of a rule that many companies are now establishing is No Smoking. The concept of rules may become clearer if one thinks about the purpose and nature of rules in such games as Scrabble and Monopoly.

Although policies, procedures, and rules are all standing plans, they are different from one another and have different purposes within the organization. As Figure 9.3 illustrates, however, for the standing plans of an organization to be effective, policies, procedures, and rules must be consistent and mutually supportive.

A **procedure** is a standing plan that outlines a series of related actions that must be taken to accomplish a particular task.

A **rule** is a standing plan that designates specific required action.

MANAGEMENT AND THE INTERNET

Salomon Smith Barney Establishes Rules to Deal with Internet

For many companies, the Internet has created opportunities that were once unimaginable. This technology has allowed some companies to reach markets that were once impossible, and it has helped other companies to literally start new businesses that did not exist previously. Although these benefits would seemingly result in a no-lose situation for all companies, some are struggling with the problems resulting from increased Internet use. Some of these problems include employees using company computers to access sports-related and pornographic Web sites and to send inappropriate e-mail messages.

To deal with these problems, some companies have created new rules, procedures, and policies. Surprisingly, however, there are many companies that still have not addressed these issues. According to a recent survey conducted by the Society for Human Resource Management, 70 percent of the organizations polled had no written Internet rules or policies. In addition, only half of the same organizations had written rules or procedures regarding the proper use of e-mail.

Salomon Smith Barney is one company that created new rules to protect it from the problems resulting from the Internet.

(continued)

A **program** is a single-use plan designed to carry out a special project in an organization that, if accomplished, will contribute to the organization's long-term success.

SINGLE-USE PLANS: PROGRAMS AND BUDGETS A **program** is a single-use plan designed to carry out a special project within an organization. The project itself is not intended to remain in existence over the entire life of the organization. Rather, it exists to achieve some purpose that, if accomplished, will contribute to the organization's long-term success.

A common example is the management development program found in many organizations. This program exists to raise the skill levels of managers in one or more of the areas mentioned in chapter 1: technical, conceptual, or human relations skills. Increasing managerial skills, however, is not an end in itself. The end or purpose of the program is to produce competent managers who are equipped to help the organization be successful over the long term. In fact, once managerial skills have been raised to a desired level, the management development program can be deemphasized. Activities on which modern management development programs commonly focus include understanding and using the computer as a management tool, handling international competition, and planning for a major labor shortage by the year 2000.[5]

A **budget** is a control tool that outlines how funds in a given period will be spent, as well as how they will be obtained.

A **budget** is a single-use financial plan that covers a specified length of time. It details how funds will be spent on labor, raw materials, capital goods, information systems, marketing, and so on, as well as how the funds will be obtained.[6] Although budgets are planning devices, they are also strategies for organizational control. They are discussed in more detail in chapter 20.

►WHY PLANS FAIL

If managers know why plans fail, they can take steps to eliminate the factors that cause failure and thereby increase the probability that their plans will be successful. A study by K. A. Ringbakk determined that plans fail when:[7]

1. Corporate planning is not integrated into the total management system
2. There is a lack of understanding of the different steps of the planning process
3. Management at different levels in the organization has not properly engaged in or contributed to planning activities
4. Responsibility for planning is wrongly vested solely in the planning department
5. Management expects that plans developed will be realized with little effort
6. In starting formal planning, too much is attempted at once
7. Management fails to operate by the plan
8. Financial projections are confused with planning
9. Inadequate inputs are used in planning
10. Management fails to grasp the overall planning process

►PLANNING AREAS: INPUT PLANNING

As discussed earlier, organizational inputs, process, outputs, and environment are major factors in determining how successful a management system will be. Naturally, a comprehensive organizational plan should focus on each of these factors. The following two sections cover planning in two areas normally associated with the input factor: plant facilities planning and human resource planning. Planning in areas such as these is called **input planning**—the development of proposed action that will furnish sufficient and appropriate organizational resources for reaching established organizational objectives.

Input planning is the development of proposed action that will furnish sufficient and appropriate organizational resources for reaching established organizational objectives.

TABLE 9.1	Major Areas of Consideration When Selecting a Plant Site and Sample Exploratory Questions To Be Asked

Major Areas of Consideration in Site Selection	Sample Questions To Be Asked
Profit	
Market Location	Where are our customers in relation to the site?
Competition	What competitive situation exists at the site?
Operating costs	
Suppliers	Are materials available near the site at reasonable cost?
Utilities	What are utility rates at the site? Are utilities available in sufficient amounts?
Wages	What wage rates are paid by comparable organizations near the site?
Taxes	What are tax rates on income, sales, property, and so on for the site?
Investment costs	
Land/development	How expensive are land and construction at the site?
Others	
Transportation	Are airlines, railroads, highways, and so on accessible from the site?
Laws	What laws related to zoning, pollution, and so on will influence operations if the site is chosen?
Labor	Does an adequate labor supply exist around the site?
Unionization	What is the degree of unionization in the site area?
Living conditions	Are housing, schools, and so on around the site appropriate?
Community relations	Does the community support the organization's moving into the area?

PLANT FACILITIES PLANNING **Plant facilities planning** involves determining the type of buildings and equipment an organization needs to reach its objectives. A major part of this determination is called **site selection**—deciding where a plant facility should be located. Table 9.1 lays out several major areas to be considered in plant site selection and gives sample questions that can be asked as these areas are being explored. Naturally, the specifics of site selection will vary from organization to organization.[8]

Plant facilities planning is input planning that involves developing the type of work facility an organization will need to reach its objectives.

Site selection involves determining where a plant facility should be located. It may use a weighting process to compare site differences.

GLOBAL SPOTLIGHT Mexico as an Attractive Manufacturing Site

For several years, U.S. companies have been building and running manufacturing plants just across the Mexican border. The mere existence of these plants—called *maquiladoras*—is evidence that Mexico has become an extremely attractive foreign manufacturing site for U.S. firms. The low cost of Mexican labor—significantly less than that in the United States—is the main reason for the success of the *maquiladoras*. Accompanying these lower labor costs, however, are several challenges that U.S. managers of *maquiladoras* must face: In general, the Mexican labor force employed at *maquiladoras* is young, inexperienced, and unskilled; because the labor force comes mainly from rural

Mexico, there are significant cultural differences between Mexican workers and U.S. owners or managers; Mexican labor laws are more protective of workers than are U.S. labor laws. As U.S. manufacturers find ways to improve the productivity of the Mexican labor force through special training for young, unskilled workers, they are gaining a real appreciation for Mexican culture and learning to manage effectively within the limits of Mexican labor laws. U.S. manufacturers are meeting the challenges of the *maquiladora* industry, improving the productivity of the Mexican labor force, and making Mexico an even more appealing site for foreign manufacturing plants.

Planning for plant facilities increasingly means planning to expand them overseas. At the Mexico factory of the South Korean electronics firm Daewoo, Lorena Lopez performs a quality control check on a computer monitor. Human resource planning is also needed to ensure that enough employees with the right skills are hired to run the plant, and quality planning must be done to provide guidelines for jobs such as Lopez's.

One factor that significantly influences site selection is foreign location. Management in a foreign country planning to select a site must deal with such issues as differences among foreign governments in time taken to approve site purchases and political pressures that may slow down or prevent the purchase of a site. For example, Japanese investors who locate businesses in the United States tend to select those states that have low unionization rates, low employment rates, relatively impoverished populations, and the highest possible educational levels under those conditions. Japanese managers believe that these factors enhance the chances of success of Japanese business in the United States.[9]

Many organizations use a weighting process to compare site differences among foreign countries. Basically, this process involves the following steps:

1. Deciding on a set of variables critical to obtaining an appropriate site
2. Assigning each of these variables a weight reflecting its relative importance
3. Ranking alternative sites according to how they reflect these different variables

Table 9.2 shows the results of such a weighting process for seven site variables in six countries. In this table, "living conditions" are worth 100 points and are the most important variable; "effect on company reputation" is worth 35 points and is the least important variable. The six countries are given a number of points for each variable, depending on the importance of the variable and how well it is reflected within the country. The table shows that, using this particular set of weighted criteria, Japan, Mexico, and France are more desirable sites than Chile, Jamaica, and Australia.

HUMAN RESOURCE PLANNING Human resources are another area of concern to input planners. Organizational objectives cannot be attained without appropriate personnel. Future needs for human resources are influenced mainly by employee turnover, the nature of the present workforce, and the rate of growth of the organization.[10]

The following are representative of the kinds of questions personnel planners should try to answer:

1. What types of people does the organization need to reach its objectives?
2. How many of each type are needed?
3. What steps should the organization take to recruit and select such people?
4. Can present employees be further trained to fill future needed positions?
5. At what rate are employees being lost to other organizations?

		Sites					
Criteria	**Maximum Value Assigned**	**Japan**	**Chile**	**Jamaica**	**Australia**	**Mexico**	**France**
Living conditions	100	70	40	45	50	60	60
Accessibility	75	55	35	20	60	70	70
Industrialization	60	40	50	55	35	35	30
Labor availability	35	30	10	10	30	35	35
Economics	35	15	15	15	15	25	25
Community capability and attitude	30	25	20	10	15	25	15
Effect on company reputation	35	25	20	10	15	25	15
Total	370	260	190	165	220	275	250

TABLE 9.2 ▶ **Results of Weighting Seven Site Variables for Six Countries**

Figure 9.4 shows the human resource planning process developed by Bruce Coleman. According to his model, **human resource planning** involves reflecting on organizational objectives to determine overall human resource needs, comparing these needs to the existing human resource inventory to determine net human resource needs, and, finally, seeking appropriate organization members to meet the net human resource needs.

Human resource planning is input planning that involves obtaining the human resources necessary for the organization to achieve its objectives.

FIGURE 9.4 ▶ **The human resource planning process**

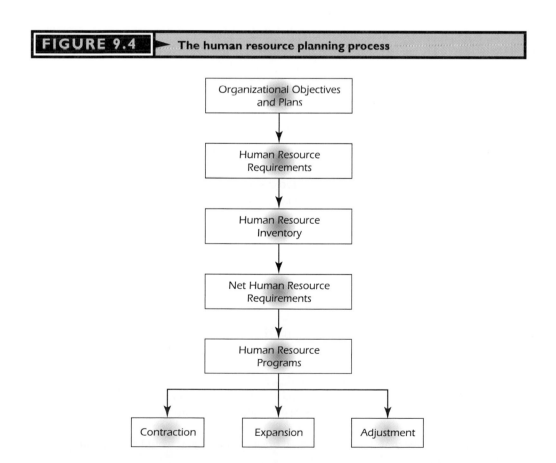

Managers at Fiat would use both standing plans and single-use plans. Standing plans include policies, procedures, and rules, and should be developed for situations that occur repeatedly. For example, Fiat might develop a standing plan that focuses on attaining and maintaining the degree of product quality management considers desirable.

Single-use plans include programs and budgets and should be created to help manage situations that occur once or only rarely. The Introductory Case implies that Fiat's management has worked on a budget for renovating an existing plant in Avellino, Italy. In developing such a single-use plan, Fiat's managers should make sure they thoroughly understand the reasons plans fail and take steps to avoid those pitfalls.

Planning plant facilities and human resource planning are two other types of planning that managers commonly perform. In Fiat's case, planning plant facilities entails designing the types of factories that the company needs to reach its objectives. The company has developed plans to build a new plant in Basilicata as well as to expand and remodel an existing parts factory near Avellino. Certainly, a strong influence on the decision to develop these plans was the financial support package offered to the company by the Italian government.

Human resource planning involves obtaining or developing the personnel an organization needs to reach its objectives. Fiat's management must have considered the numbers and kinds of employees required to run both the new and the renovated factories, and this discussion must inevitably have focused on such issues as when these employees would be needed, how they would be recruited, and how they would be trained appropriately after joining Fiat.

PLANNING TOOLS

Planning tools are techniques managers can use to help develop plans.

Planning tools are techniques managers can use to help develop plans. The remainder of this chapter discusses forecasting and scheduling, two of the most important of these tools.

FORECASTING

Forecasting is a planning tool used to predict future environmental happenings that will influence the operation of the organization.

Forecasting is the process of predicting future environmental happenings that will influence the operation of the organization. Although sophisticated forecasting techniques have been developed only rather recently, the concept of forecasting can be traced at least as far back in the management literature as Fayol. The importance of forecasting lies in its ability to help managers understand the future makeup of the organizational environment, which, in turn, helps them formulate more effective plans.[11]

HOW FORECASTING WORKS William C. House, in describing the Insect Control Services Company, has developed an excellent illustration of how forecasting works. In general, Insect Control Services forecasts by attempting to do the following:[12]

1. Establish relationships between industry sales and national economic and social indicators
2. Determine the impact government restrictions on the use of chemical pesticides will have on the growth of chemical, biological, and electromagnetic energy pest-control markets
3. Evaluate sales growth potential, profitability, resources required, and risks involved in each of its market areas (commercial, industrial, institutional, governmental, and residential)
4. Evaluate the potential for expansion of marketing efforts in geographical areas of the United States as well as in foreign countries
5. Determine the likelihood of technological breakthroughs that would make existing product lines obsolete

BOEING USES FORECASTING TO ALTER PRODUCTION

Boeing Company, the popular airplane manufacturer, has long used forecasting techniques to predict future sales. Although many companies use similar forecasting techniques, few attempt to match Boeing's long-term forecasting. Each year, Boeing revises its 20-year forecast of trends in the airline industry. Although some doubt the accuracy of such forecasts, many believe that these carefully determined forecasts lie at the heart of the company's success.

Boeing's most recent market forecast in 1998 provided a major surprise for the company's management and for its competitors. Now Boeing, long considered king of the jumbo jet, sees its future in smaller and less expensive planes. Boeing forecasters believe that more liberal airline regulations will result in airlines flying shorter and more frequent routes, and airlines will demand smaller and more efficient planes to fly these routes. Consequently, the company believes that the largest growth in the next 20 years will come from its intermediate-sized planes.

To capitalize on these forecasts, the company's management altered its production runs. Instead of producing more of the largest and smallest planes, management shifted its production so that the company produces more intermediate-sized planes. Boeing's management hopes that these forecasts will help the company produce more of the planes that the marketplace demands and less of the planes that are not in demand. If the forecasts are accurate, Boeing's management and shareholders might see even better times in the future.

TYPES OF FORECASTS In addition to the general type of organizational forecasting done by Insect Control Services, there are specialized types of forecasting, such as economic, technological, social trends, and sales forecasting. Although a complete organizational forecasting process should, and usually does, include all these types of forecasting, sales forecasting is considered the key organizational forecast. A *sales forecast* is a prediction of how high or low sales of the organization's products and/or services will be over the period of time under consideration. It is the key forecast for organizations because it serves as the fundamental guideline for planning. Only after the sales forecast has been completed can managers decide, for example, if more salespeople should be hired, if more money for plant expansion must be borrowed, or if layoffs and cutbacks in certain areas are necessary. Managers must continually monitor forecasting methods to improve them and to reformulate plans based upon inaccurate forecasts.[13]

METHODS OF SALES FORECASTING Modern managers have several different methods available for forecasting sales. Popular methods are the jury of executive opinion method, the salesforce estimation method, and the time series analysis method. Each of these methods is discussed in this section.

Jury of Executive Opinion Method The **jury of executive opinion method** of sales forecasting is straightforward. Appropriate managers within the organization assemble to discuss their opinions on what will happen to sales in the future. Since these discussion sessions usually revolve around hunches or experienced guesses, the resulting forecast is a blend of informed opinions.

A similar, more recently developed forecasting method, called the *delphi method,* also gathers, evaluates, and summarizes expert opinions as the basis for a forecast, but the procedure is more formal than that for the jury of executive opinion method.[14] The basic delphi method employs the following steps:

► *Step 1*—Various experts are asked to answer, independently and in writing, a series of questions about the future of sales or whatever other area is being forecasted.
► *Step 2*—A summary of all the answers is then prepared. No expert knows how any other expert answered the questions.
► *Step 3*—Copies of the summary are given to the individual experts with the request that they modify their original answers if they think it necessary.

The **jury of executive opinion method** is a method of predicting future sales levels primarily by asking appropriate managers to give their opinions on what will happen to sales in the future.

► *Step 4*—Another summary is made of these modifications, and copies again are distributed to the experts. This time, however, expert opinions that deviate significantly from the norm must be justified in writing.

► *Step 5*—A third summary is made of the opinions and justifications, and copies are once again distributed to the experts. Justification in writing for *all* answers is now required.

► *Step 6*—The forecast is generated from all of the opinions and justifications that arise from step 5.

The **salesforce estimation method** predicts future sales levels primarily by asking appropriate salespeople for their opinions of what will happen to sales in the future.

Salesforce Estimation Method   The **salesforce estimation method** is a sales forecasting technique that predicts future sales by analyzing the opinions of salespeople as a group. Salespeople continually interact with customers, and from this interaction they usually develop a knack for predicting future sales. As with the jury of executive opinion method, the resulting forecast normally is a blend of the informed views of the group.

The salesforce estimation method is considered to be a very valuable management tool and is commonly used in business and industry throughout the world. Although the accuracy of this method is generally good, managers have found that it can be improved by taking such simple steps as providing salespeople with sufficient time to forecast and offering incentives for accurate forecasts. Some companies help their salespeople to become better forecasters by training them to better interpret their interactions with customers.[15]

The **time series analysis method** is a method of predicting future sales levels by analyzing the historical relationship in an organization between sales and time.

Time Series Analysis Method   The **time series analysis method** predicts future sales by analyzing the historical relationship between sales and time. Information showing the relationship between sales and time typically is presented on a graph, as in Figure 9.5. This presentation clearly displays past trends, which can be used to predict future sales.

Although the actual number of years included in a time series analysis will vary from company to company, as a general rule, managers should include as many years as necessary to ensure that important sales trends do not go undetected. At the Coca-Cola Company, for example, management believes that in order to validly predict the annual sales of any one year, it must chart annual sales in each of the 10 previous years.[16]

FIGURE 9.5   ► **Time series analysis method**

The time series analysis in Figure 9.5 indicates steadily increasing sales for B.J.'s Men's Clothing over time. However, since in the long term products generally go through what is called a product life cycle, the predicted increase based on the last decade of sales should probably be considered overly optimistic. A **product life cycle** is the five stages through which most products and services pass. These stages are introduction, growth, maturity, saturation, and decline.

Product Stages. Figure 9.6 shows how the five stages of the product life cycle are related to sales volume for seven products over a period of time. In the introduction stage, when a product is brand new, sales are just beginning to build (WebTV and DVD videos). In the growth stage, the product has been in the marketplace for some time and is becoming more accepted, so product sales continue to climb (e.g., cellular phones and compact disc players). During the maturity stage, competitors enter the market, and although sales are still climbing, they are climbing at a slower rate than they did in the growth stage (e.g., personal computers). After the maturity stage comes the saturation stage, when nearly everyone who wanted the product has it (e.g., refrigerators and freezers). Sales during the saturation stage typically are due to the need to replace a worn-out product or to population growth. The last product life cycle stage—decline—finds the product being replaced by a competing product (e.g., black-and-white televisions).

Managers may be able to prevent some products from entering the decline stage by improving product quality or by adding innovations. Other products, such as scissors, may never reach this last stage of the product life cycle because there are no competing products to replace them.

EVALUATING SALES FORECASTING METHODS The sales forecasting methods just described are not the only ones available to managers. Other, more complex methods include the statistical correlation method and the computer simulation method.[17] The methods just discussed, however, do provide a basic foundation for understanding sales forecasting.

In practice, managers find that each sales forecasting method has distinct advantages and disadvantages. Before deciding to use a particular sales forecasting method, a manager must carefully weigh these advantages and disadvantages as they relate to the manager's organization. The best decision may be to use a combination of methods to forecast sales rather than just one. Whatever method or methods are finally adopted, the manager should be certain the framework is logical, fits the needs of the organization, and can be adapted to changes in the environment.

A **product life cycle** is the five stages through which most products and services pass: introduction, growth, maturity, saturation, and decline.

FIGURE 9.6 ▶ **Stages of the product life cycle**

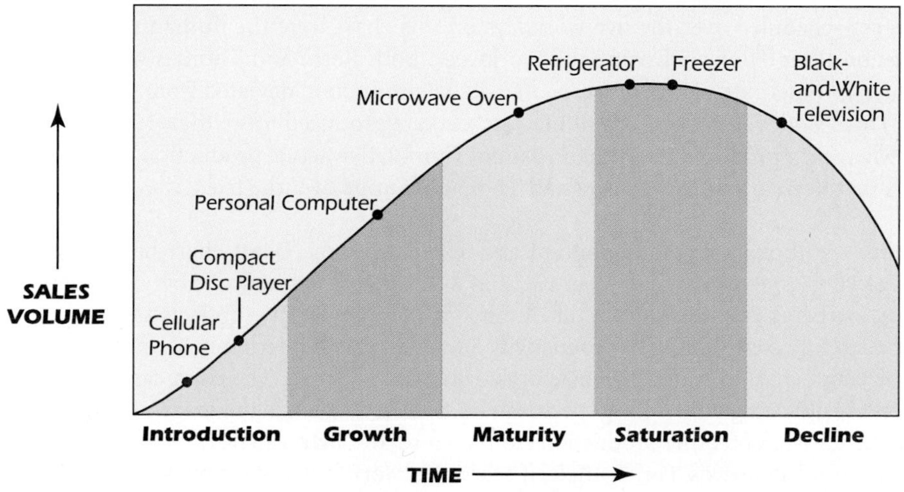

SCHEDULING

Scheduling is the process of formulating a detailed listing of activities that must be accomplished to attain an objective, allocating the resources necessary to attain the objective, and setting up and following timetables for completing the objective. Scheduling is an integral part of every organizational plan. Two popular scheduling techniques are Gantt charts and the program evaluation and review technique (PERT).

GANTT CHARTS The **Gantt chart,** a scheduling device developed by Henry L. Gantt, is essentially a bar graph with time on the horizontal axis and the resource to be scheduled on the vertical axis. It is used for scheduling resources, including management system inputs such as human resources and machines.

Figure 9.7 shows a completed Gantt chart for a work period entitled, "Workweek 28." The resources scheduled over the five workdays on this chart were the human resources Wendy Reese and Peter Thomas. During this workweek, both Reese and Thomas were supposed to produce 10 units a day. Note, however, that actual production deviated from planned production. There were days when each of the two workers produced more than 10 units, as well as days when each produced fewer than 10 units. Cumulative actual production for workweek 28 shows that Reese produced 40 units and Thomas 45 units over the five days.

Features Although simple in concept and appearance, the Gantt chart has many valuable managerial uses. First, managers can use it as a summary overview of how organizational resources are being employed. From this summary, they can detect such facts as which resources are consistently contributing to productivity and which are hindering it. Second, managers can use the Gantt chart to help coordinate organizational resources. The chart can show which resources are not being used during specific periods, thereby allowing managers to schedule those resources for work on other production efforts. Third, the chart can be used to establish realistic worker output standards. For example, if scheduled work is being completed too quickly, output standards should be raised so that workers are scheduled for more work per time period.

Scheduling is the process of formulating a detailed listing of activities that must be accomplished to attain an objective, allocating the resources necessary to attain the objective, and setting up and following timetables for completing the objective.

The **Gantt chart** is a scheduling tool composed of a bar chart with time on the horizontal axis and the resource to be scheduled on the vertical axis. It is used for scheduling resources.

FIGURE 9.7 ▶ **Completed Gantt chart**

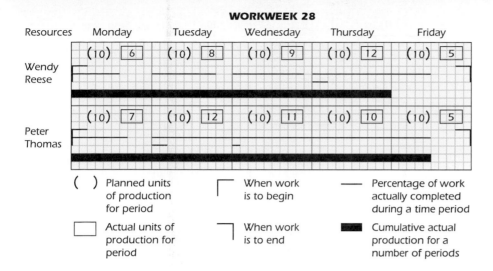

WORKWEEK 28

Resources	Monday	Tuesday	Wednesday	Thursday	Friday
Wendy Reese	(10) [6]	(10) [8]	(10) [9]	(10) [12]	(10) [5]
Peter Thomas	(10) [7]	(10) [12]	(10) [11]	(10) [10]	(10) [5]

( ) Planned units of production for period

☐ Actual units of production for period

⌐ When work is to begin

⌐ When work is to end

— Percentage of work actually completed during a time period

▬ Cumulative actual production for a number of periods

PROGRAM EVALUATION AND REVIEW TECHNIQUE (PERT) The main weakness of the Gantt chart is that it does not contain any information about the interrelationship of tasks to be performed. Although all tasks to be performed are listed on the chart, there is no way of telling if one task must be performed before another can be started. The program evaluation and review technique (PERT), a technique that evolved partly from the Gantt chart, is a scheduling tool that does emphasize the interrelationship of tasks.

Defining PERT PERT is a network of project activities showing both the estimates of time necessary to complete each activity and the sequence of activities that must be followed to complete the project. This scheduling tool was developed in 1958 for designing and building the Polaris submarine weapon system. The people who were managing this project found Gantt charts and other existing scheduling tools of little use because of the complicated nature of the Polaris project and the interdependence of the tasks to be performed.[18]

The PERT network contains two primary elements: activities and events. **Activities** are specified sets of behavior within a project, and **events** are the completions of major project tasks. Within the PERT network, each event is assigned corresponding activities that must be performed before the event can materialize.[19]

Features A sample PERT network designed for building a house is presented in Figure 9.8. Events are symbolized by circles and activities by arrows. To illustrate, the figure indicates that after the event "Foundation Complete" (represented by a circle) has materialized, certain activities (represented by an arrow) must be performed before the event "Frame Complete" (represented by another circle) can materialize.

Two other features of the network shown in Figure 9.8 should be emphasized. First, the left-to-right presentation of events shows how the events interrelate or the sequence in which they should be performed. Second, the numbers in parentheses above each arrow indicate the units of time necessary to complete each activity. These two features help managers ensure that only necessary work is being done on a project and that no project activities are taking too long.

Critical Path Managers need to pay close attention to the **critical path** of a PERT network—the sequence of events and activities requiring the longest period of time to complete. This path is called *critical* because a delay in completing this sequence results in a delay in completing the entire project. The critical path in Figure 9.8 is indicated by thick arrows; all other paths are indicated by thin arrows. Managers try to control a project by keeping it within the time designated by the critical path. The critical path helps them predict which features of a schedule are becoming unrealistic and provides insights into how those features might be eliminated or modified.[20]

The **program evaluation and review technique (PERT)** is a scheduling tool that is essentially a network of project activities showing estimates of time necessary to complete each activity and the sequence of activities that must be followed to complete the project.

Activities and events are the primary elements of a PERT network. **Activities** are specified sets of behavior within a project. **Events** are the completions of major project tasks.

A **critical path** is the sequence of events and activities within a program evaluation and review technique (PERT) network that requires the longest period of time to complete.

FIGURE 9.8 ► **PERT network designed for building a house**

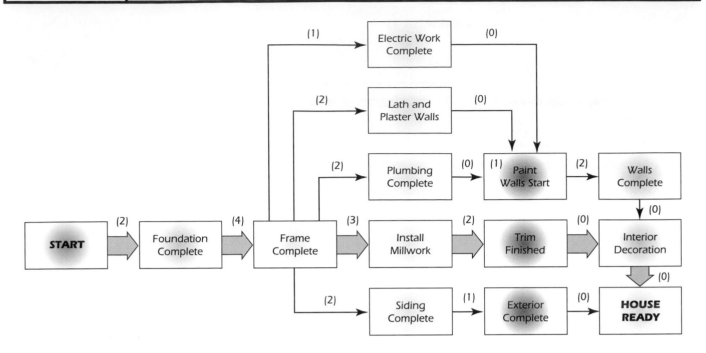

Steps in Designing a PERT Network When designing a PERT network, managers should follow four primary steps:[21]

► *Step 1*—List all the activities/events that must be accomplished for the project and the sequence in which these activities/events should be performed
► *Step 2*—Determine how much time will be needed to complete each activity/event
► *Step 3*—Design a PERT network that reflects all of the information contained in steps 1 and 2
► *Step 4*—Identify the critical path

BACK TO THE CASE

Scheduling is another planning tool available to Fiat's management. It involves the detailed listing of activities that must be accomplished to reach an objective. For example, if Fiat's goal is to have all its employees working proficiently on updated equipment in its planned renovated factory within two years, management needs to schedule activities such as installing the equipment, training the employees, and establishing new output standards.

Two scheduling techniques available to Fiat's management are Gantt charts and PERT. To schedule employee production output, Fiat's managers might want to use Gantt charts—bar graphs with time on the horizontal axis and the resources to be scheduled on the vertical axis. They might also find these charts helpful for evaluating workers' performance and for setting new production standards.

When Fiat's managers feel they need to see the relationships among tasks, they should use PERT to develop a flowchart showing activities, events, and the amount of time necessary to complete each task. For example, a PERT network would be helpful in scheduling the installation of new machines because this type of schedule would indicate which equipment needed to be installed first, the amount of time each installation would require, and how other activities in renovating an existing factory would be affected before the installation was completed. In addition, PERT would demonstrate to Fiat the critical path managers must follow for successful installation. This path represents the sequence of activities and events requiring the longest amount of time to complete, and it determines the total time required to finish the project. If, for example, new welding machinery takes longer to install than other types of equipment, Fiat's management should use this component's installation time as a basis for targeting the completion date for the entire equipment installation.

For updated information on the topics in this chapter, Internet exercises, links to related Internet sites, an interactive study guide, and more, visit our companion Web site at

http://www.prenhall.com/certo

Additional information can be found on the inside front and back covers of this text.

ACTION SUMMARY

Reread the learning objectives below. Each objective is followed by questions. Answering these questions accurately will help you retain the most important concepts discussed in this chapter. After answering each question, check your answer against the answer key at the end of this chapter. (*Hint:* If you have any doubts regarding the correct response, consult the page number that follows the answer.)

Circle:

From studying this chapter, I will attempt to acquire

1. A complete definition of a plan.

  a b c d e   **a.** A plan is: (a) the company's buildings and fixtures (b) a specific action proposed to help the company achieve its objectives (c) a policy meeting (d) a projection of future sales (e) an experiment to determine the optimal distribution system.

  a b c d e   **b.** The following is generally *not* an important component of a plan: (a) the evaluation of relevant information (b) the assessment of probable future developments (c) a statement of a recommended course of action (d) a statement of manager intuition (e) strategy based on reason or rationality.

2. Insights regarding various dimensions of plans.

  T F   **a.** Most plans affect top management only.

  a b c d e   **b.** The following is one of the four major dimensions of a plan: (a) repetitiveness (b) organization (c) time (d) a and c (e) b and c.

3. An understanding of various types of plans.

  a b c d e   **a.** Standing plans that furnish broad guidelines for channeling management thinking in specified directions are called: (a) procedures (b) programs (c) single-use plans (d) policies (e) rules.

  a b c d e   **b.** Programs and budgets are examples of: (a) single-use plans (b) standing rules (c) procedures (d) Gantt chart components (e) critical paths.

4. Insights on why plans fail.

  a b c d e   **a.** The following is a reason that plans fail: (a) adequate inputs are used in planning (b) corporate planning is integrated into the total management system (c) management expects that plans developed will be realized with little effort (d) management operates by the plan (e) responsibility for planning is vested in more than just the planning department.

  T F   **b.** The confusion of planning with financial projections will have no effect on the success of plans.

5. A knowledge of various planning areas within an organization.

  T F   **a.** Input planning includes only site selection planning.

  a b c d e   **b.** Personnel planners who reflect on organizational objectives to determine overall human resource needs and compare needs to existing human resource inventory are engaging in a type of planning called: (a) process layout (b) plant facilities (c) input (d) life cycle (e) delphi.

6. A definition of forecasting.

T F   **a.** Forecasting is the process of setting objectives and scheduling activities.

a b c d e   **b.** According to the text, the following product is in the growth stage of the product life cycle: (a) microwave oven (b) cellular phone (c) black-and-white television (d) personal computer (e) refrigerator.

7. An ability to see the advantages and disadvantages of various methods of sales forecasting.

a b c d e   **a.** The sales forecasting technique that utilizes specialized knowledge based on interaction with customers is: (a) jury of executive opinion (b) sales force estimation (c) time series analysis (d) a and b (e) b and c.

T F   **b.** One of the advantages of the jury of executive opinion method is that it may be the only feasible means of forecasting sales, especially in the absence of adequate data.

8. A definition of scheduling.

a b c d e   **a.** Scheduling can best be described as: (a) the evaluation of alternative courses of action (b) the process of formulating goals and objectives (c) the process of formulating a detailed listing of activities (d) the calculation of the break-even point (e) the process of defining policies.

T F   **b.** Scheduling is the process of predicting future environmental happenings that will influence the operations of the organization.

9. An understanding of Gantt charts and PERT.

a b c d e   **a.** The following is *not* an acceptable use of a Gantt chart: (a) as a summary overview of how organizational resources are being used (b) to help coordinate organizational resources (c) to establish realistic worker output standards (d) to determine which resources are consistently contributing to productivity (e) none of the above (all are acceptable uses of Gantt charts).

a b c d e   **b.** In a PERT network, the sequence of events and activities requiring the longest period of time to complete is: (a) called the network (b) indicated by thin arrows (c) the path that managers avoid (d) the critical path (e) eliminated from the rest of the project so the project will not take too long.

► INTRODUCTORY CASE WRAP-UP ◄

CASE DISCUSSSION QUESTIONS

"Fiat Plans Car Production" (p. 189) and its related Back-to-the-Case sections were written to help you better understand the management concepts contained in this chapter. Answer the following discussion questions about this Introductory Case to enrich your understanding of chapter content:

1. Should Fiat's plant facilities planning be related to its human resource planning? Explain.

2. Explain this statement: "The quality of Fiat's decision to build one factory and to expand and renovate another is largely determined by the validity of the company's sales forecast."

3. What sales forecasting method(s) do you think Fiat's management should have used as the basis for making its plant facilities decision? Explain.

SKILLS EXERCISE: PREPARING A SALES FORECAST

In the Introductory Case, Fiat's management decided to increase production capacity to satisfy future market demand in Europe. Do a time series analysis that enables you to forecast Fiat's sales in Italy for the next three years. Go to the library or the Internet to gather data. What are the strengths of your forecast? The weaknesses? What management action would you take at Fiat based upon this forecast? Why?

1. What is a plan?
2. List and describe the basic dimensions of a plan.
3. What is the difference between standing plans and single-use plans?
4. Compare and contrast policies, procedures, and rules.
5. What are the two main types of single-use plans?
6. Why do organizations have programs?
7. Of what use is a budget to managers?
8. Summarize the 10 factors that cause plans to fail.
9. What is input planning?
10. Evaluate the importance of plant facilities planning to the organization.
11. What major factors should be involved in site selection?
12. Describe the human resource planning process.
13. What is a planning tool?

14. Describe the measurements usually employed in forecasting. Why are they taken?
15. Draw and explain the product life cycle.
16. Discuss the advantages and disadvantages of three methods of sales forecasting.
17. Elaborate on the statement that all managers should spend some time scheduling.
18. What is a Gantt chart? Draw a simple chart to assist you in your explanation.
19. How can information related to the Gantt chart be used by managers?
20. How is PERT a scheduling tool?
21. How is the critical path related to PERT?
22. List the steps necessary to design a PERT network.

► ACTION SUMMARY ANSWER KEY ◄

1. **a.** b, p. 190
   b. d, p. 190
2. **a.** F, p. 190
   b. d, p. 190
3. **a.** d, p. 192
   b. a, p. 194

4. **a.** c, p. 194
   b. F, p. 194
5. **a.** F, p. 194
   b. c, p. 194

6. **a.** F, p. 198
   b. d, p. 201
7. **a.** b, p. 199
   b. T, p. 199

8. **a.** c, p. 202
   b. F, p. 202
9. **a.** e, p. 202
   b. d, p. 203

► CASE STUDY: Plans and Planning Tools ◄

On February 2, 1996, Congress passed a landmark bill deregulating every aspect of the communications business. Under this bill, cable-TV providers, local phone companies, and long-distance carriers will all be allowed to forage in one another's markets for profits. On the basis of past performance, MCI looks like the heir apparent in this competitive free-for all. But first the company must learn to sell a lot more than long-distance calls. According to UBS Securities analyst Linda B. Meltzer, "It's no longer a question of how large a share of the $75 billion long-distance market you can get. It's a question of how big a share of the $500 billion converged or integrated market [MCI] will get."

MCI responded to the new telecom opportunities with a series of contradictory starts and stops. For example, the company started and stopped two different wireless strategies and one on-line service effort. CEO Bert C. Roberts, however, contends that his company's erratic activities are evidence of its ultimate strength—the ability to be flexible: "We're quick to move forward and quick to pull back when we have to," says Roberts. Such flexibility, he argues, will enable MCI to conceive and implement a cohesive strategy for the new communications market.

Present MCI strategy concentrates company resources on current industry logic—namely, what *Business Week* magazine describes as: "Offer a single source for long-distance and local calling, video, data, and wireless services, bundle them onto one bill, and customers will come." Through joint ventures, partnerships, resale agreements, and its own initiatives, MCI expects to be able to offer almost every service that can be delivered over both wired and wireless communications systems—satellite TV, Internet connections, and electronic commerce transactions, as well as local, long-distance, and international phone service. "We want to get as many hooks into each of our customers as possible," says CEO Roberts, pointing to revealing MCI studies showing that customers who buy more than one service from a carrier switch carriers 40 percent less often than customers who buy only one service.

In fact, in support of MCI's new "diversify-or-die-mantra," Roberts says that he wants the company to earn 50 percent of its revenues from new ventures by the year 2000. To meet this objective, MCI spent more than $6 billion during the calendar year of 1995, buying everything from a cellular-phone reseller to SHL Systemhouse, a Canadian-based computer systems integrator. MCI has also built fiber links in 25 cities to provide local phone service to business customers.

Above all, the company shocked industry experts when it paid $2 billion for a 13.5 percent stake in News Corporation because the experts could not reconcile this investment decision with known MCI goals and objectives. Early in 1996, however, MCI and News Corporation announced a joint venture that entailed spending $1.3 billion to build a DBS (digital broadcast system) network. Soon afterward, MCI announced another broad alliance, this time with Microsoft Corporation, in which MCI would become the primary distributor of Microsoft's online network.

MCI claims to base its "scattershot" strategy on a consistent set of principles. "We buy when there are finite resources and [sell] when there is a glut," says Timothy F. Price, president of MCI's long-distance business. As an example of the first principle, MCI paid $628.5 million for the last available slot for its DBS satellite, despite analysts' protests that the price was twice the value. The second principle influenced MCI to resell wireless services purchased from other suppliers. MCI planners figured that once PCS (Personal Communications Service) networks were built—at high setup costs—there would be a glut of capacity. In support of its plans, MCI paid $190 million in September of 1995 for Nationwide Cellular Services, Inc., a large reseller.

Another strategic MCI tenet is to share the cost of its many ventures in order to spread the risk. To that end, Roberts hopes to take on partners as often as possible—whether Rupert Murdoch (News Corporation), Bill Gates (Microsoft), or British Telecommunications PLC (20 percent owner of MCI since 1994). "I'm not so visionary that I know where all the bucks are going to flow five years from now," says Roberts. Finally, MCI president Price points to the company's ultimate trump card—and one of the main tenets of its successful planning: killer marketing instincts. "We don't want to dive in ahead of where the customer is," he says. "We just want to move as fast as possible to where they are." According to British Telecom's new president, Peter Bonfield, that won't be a problem: "They are bloody fast. They can turn an idea into a product in a month."

QUESTIONS

1. Characterize the policy by which CEO Bert Roberts runs his company. Do you consider this a strong policy on which to base MCI's future? Explain.

2. Is the plan devised by MCI to take advantage of the new communications environment a *standing plan* or a *single-use plan?* Explain, using definitions and diagrams from the text section entitled, "Types of Plans."

3. Describe the forecasting process used by MCI to develop diversification plans. Review the text description of the five actions Insect Control Services took to forecast the future environment of its industry. What forecasting steps do you believe MCI followed in its planning procedures?

4. Consider all the products that MCI now offers from long-distance service to entertainment packages, and place each product on the *product life cycle.* What can MCI do to extend the life of the products on the far end of the curve and bring to maturity those at the beginning of the curve?

Remember John from the first part-ending video case? In this episode, we find out that John got the production manager job at Quicktakes. We meet up with John on his first day on the job; we join him at his first meeting at Quicktakes and are reintroduced to Hal and Karen, the owners of the company. We also meet Alexandra, the company's general manager. It seems that the purpose of this meeting is to give John an idea of how the company is organized, what its goals are, and how things run.

What can you learn from this meeting that relates to what you have learned about planning? Before considering this question, we might want to make some assumptions about the management of the company. Given that this meeting is set up to introduce John to the company, we assume that the people invited are those that the owners believe are important in setting the direction and focus of the company, or are those who are most responsible for keeping it running. This may not be a correct assumption, but it is logical that John might get this idea. He will only know for sure after he's been at Quicktakes for a while.

This meeting is John's first real chance to learn about who is really running Quicktakes and about how the people interact. In this meeting he gets some idea about how Hal and Karen operate and interact on the job. It is likely that someday, maybe soon, you will be in a meeting like this and you will be in John's shoes. Think about the kinds of information you would hope to get, the expectations you might have of new employers, and the kinds of things you would hope your new employer thinks are important. With these things in mind, you might now consider how you think John feels after this meeting.

There are a couple of important areas covered in this orientation meeting. First, we get some idea about the culture at Quicktakes. This comes across in the comments Hal makes to John about a dress code and the degree of formality that you observe in the meeting. You also get some hints about what Hal and Karen, and to some degree Alexandra, think Quicktakes' main product focus is. They tell John about things they think make them different from their competitors and things that they seem to think are important.

It is interesting that John asks about plans and goals, more than once. This gives us an idea about what is important to John. He does not necessarily get the answer he is looking for and seems to think that there might be more to planning than what is currently considered at Quicktakes.

QUESTIONS

1. Hal and Karen talk about their ideas for the company. Do you think they are both moving in the same direction and aiming for the same target? If not, how do you think this affects the ongoing operation of the company?

2. It was explained to John that it is difficult to plan because of changes in economic conditions and areas of public interest. What areas of Quicktakes' operation might economic and market factors affect the most? Do you think that these issues make it impossible to develop a general plan and goal for the company? What areas might be important to consider anyway?

3. There was some discussion of things that Quicktakes does other than video production. Why do you think they do these other things? To what degree should a small company like Quicktakes spread itself across multiple products?

10

Fundamentals of Organizing

STUDENT LEARNING OBJECTIVES

From studying this chapter, I will attempt to acquire

1. An understanding of the organizing function

2. An appreciation for the complexities of determining appropriate organizational structure

3. Insights on the advantages and disadvantages of division of labor

4. A working knowledge of the relationship between division of labor and coordination

5. An understanding of span of management and the factors that influence its appropriateness

6. An understanding of scalar relationships

CHAPTER OUTLINE

Introductory Case: *Lucent Technologies Organizes for Success*

A DEFINITION OF ORGANIZING
The Importance of Organizing
The Organizing Process

Management and the Internet: *Ad Council Organizes to Put Smokey the Bear on the Internet*
The Organizing Subsystem

CLASSICAL ORGANIZING THEORY
Structure

Global Spotlight: *Crown Cork & Seal Company Organizes by Territory to Boost International Expansion*
Division of Labor

Quality Spotlight: *DaimlerChrysler Improves Coordination to Improve Product Quality*
Span of Management

Across Industries: *Health Care—Circular Organization Chart at Our Lady of the Way Hospital*
Scalar Relationships

LUCENT TECHNOLOGIES ORGANIZES FOR SUCCESS

REMINDER: THE INTRODUCTORY CASE WRAP-UP (P. 229) CONTAINS DISCUSSION QUESTIONS AND A SKILLS EXERCISE TO FURTHER ILLUSTRATE THE APPLICATION OF CHAPTER CONCEPTS TO THIS VIGNETTE.

Lucent Technologies, headquartered in Murray Hill, New Jersey, designs, builds, and delivers a wide range of public and private networks, communications systems and software, wired and wireless business telephone systems, and microelectronics components. For businesses it produces and sells call center systems, Internet systems, and mobile phone systems.

Two years ago Lucent was spun off from AT&T and established as a stand-alone company. Major competitors of the newly formed company are Motorola, Tellabs, Harris Corporation, and Applied Signal. Even given such formidable competition, Lucent shows amazing success. The company reached annual revenues of more than $26 billion with a 20 percent annual growth rate. Lucent's outstanding performance has gained both national and international attention and respect.

A large part of the credit for this success goes to Lucent's organization structure. The company built a structure that facilitates internal autonomy to speed up the product development process and get products to market sooner. Managers can make decisions about what must be done and when it can be done without getting constant approval from managers higher up.

Lucent's organization structure also gives groups within the company the ability to respond quickly to an ever-changing marketplace. The company was divided into 11 groups with each group focusing on a major product or service being offered. According to Karyn Mashima, a vice president of the area entitled Enterprise Networks and Data Networks Systems, such groupings will help Lucent to get focused and be efficient in some very competitive business areas.

The new group-oriented structure allows groups autonomy but also encourages them to work together. As an

Lucent Technology's organizational structure speeds up the product development process by giving individual groups greater autonomy and the ability to respond quickly to the marketplace.

example, the Global Service Provider group was formed to support sales and service of several other groups. Groups are accountable for their individual missions, which at times include independence from other groups and at other times, cooperation with other groups.

Some question if Lucent can continue its rate of growth and success. According to Richard A. McGinn, Lucent CEO, the company's organization structure is one factor that assures this continuance.

What's Ahead

The Introductory Case describes, in general, how Lucent is being organized in order to be more competitive. Information in this chapter would be useful to a manager like Richard A. McGinn, Lucent's CEO, in contemplating organizing issues. This chapter emphasizes both a definition of organizing and principles of classical organizing theory that can be useful in organizing a company.

A DEFINITION OF ORGANIZING

Organizing is the process of establishing orderly uses for all the organization's resources.

Organizing is the process of establishing orderly uses for all resources within the management system. Orderly uses emphasize the attainment of management system objectives and assist managers not only in making objectives apparent but also in clarifying which resources will be used to attain them. A primary focus of organizing is determining both what individual employees will do in an organization and how their individual efforts should best be combined to advance the attainment of organizational objectives.[1] *Organization* refers to the result of the organizing process.

FAYOL'S GUIDELINES In essence, each organizational resource represents an investment from which the management system must get a return. Appropriate organization of these resources increases the efficiency and effectiveness of their use. Henri Fayol developed 16 general guidelines for organizing resources:[2]

1. Judiciously prepare and execute the operating plan
2. Organize the human and material facets so that they are consistent with objectives, resources, and requirements of the concern
3. Establish a single competent, energetic guiding authority (formal management structure)
4. Coordinate all activities and efforts
5. Formulate clear, distinct, and precise decisions
6. Arrange for efficient selection so that each department is headed by a competent, energetic manager and all employees are placed where they can render the greatest service
7. Define duties
8. Encourage initiative and responsibility
9. Offer fair and suitable rewards for services rendered
10. Make use of sanctions against faults and errors
11. Maintain discipline
12. Ensure that individual interests are consistent with the general interests of the organization
13. Recognize the unity of command
14. Promote both material and human coordination
15. Institute and effect controls
16. Avoid regulations, red tape, and paperwork

If a bumper crop is the objective, the organizing process can be divided into major tasks, like tilling, planting, fertilization, watering, and so on; then allocating resources like equipment and labor to accomplish subtasks like sorting the harvest, and finally evaluating the result for quality and quantity produced.

► THE IMPORTANCE OF ORGANIZING

The organizing function is extremely important to the management system because it is the primary mechanism managers use to activate plans. Organizing creates and maintains relationships between all organizational resources by indicating which resources are to be used for specified activities and when, where, and how they are to be used. A thorough organizing effort helps managers minimize costly weaknesses, such as duplication of effort and idle organizational resources.

Some management theorists consider the organizing function so important that they advocate the creation of an organizing department within the management system. Typical responsibilities of this department would include developing the following:[3]

1. Reorganization plans that make the management system more effective and efficient
2. Plans to improve managerial skills to fit current management system needs
3. An advantageous organizational climate within the management system

The steps in the organizing process are crucial to the success of operations like maintaining a fleet of cargo planes. Managers at Korean Air Cargo know how important it is to get their planes on the ground, unload them, service them, reload them, and get them back in the air. Not only must each individual job be done well, but the tasks must be coordinated so that, for example, they occur in the right sequence and the right equipment is at hand for each task when it is needed.

▶THE ORGANIZING PROCESS

The five main steps of the organizing process are presented in Figure 10.1:[4]

1. Reflect on plans and objectives
2. Establish major tasks
3. Divide major tasks into subtasks
4. Allocate resources and directives for subtasks
5. Evaluate the results of implemented organizing strategy

As the figure implies, managers should continually repeat these steps. Through repetition, they obtain feedback that will help them improve the existing organization.

The management of a restaurant can serve as an illustration of how the organizing process works. The first step the restaurant manager would take to initiate the organizing process would be to reflect on the restaurant's plans and objectives. Because planning involves determining how the restaurant will attain its objectives, and organizing involves determining how the restaurant's resources will be used to activate plans, the restaurant manager must start to organize by understanding planning.

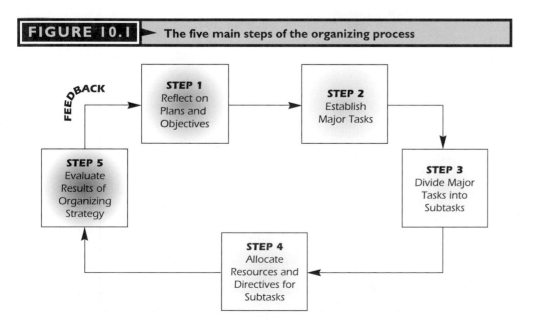

FIGURE 10.1 ▶ **The five main steps of the organizing process**

FEEDBACK

STEP 1 Reflect on Plans and Objectives

STEP 2 Establish Major Tasks

STEP 3 Divide Major Tasks into Subtasks

STEP 4 Allocate Resources and Directives for Subtasks

STEP 5 Evaluate Results of Organizing Strategy

The second and third steps of the organizing process focus on tasks to be performed within the management system. The manager must designate major tasks or jobs to be done within the restaurant. Two such tasks are serving customers and cooking food. Then the tasks must be divided into subtasks. For example, the manager might decide that serving customers includes the subtasks of taking orders and clearing tables.

The fourth organizing step is determining who will take orders, who will clear the tables, and what the details of the relationship between these individuals will be. The size of tables and how they are to be set are other factors to be considered at this point.

In the fifth step, evaluating the results of the implemented organizing strategy, the manager gathers feedback on how well the strategy is working. This feedback should furnish information that can be used to improve the existing organization. For example, the manager may find that a particular type of table is not large enough and that larger ones must be purchased if the restaurant is to attain its goals.

MANAGEMENT AND THE INTERNET

Ad Council Organizes to Put Smokey the Bear on the Internet

The Advertising Council is a nonprofit, public service advertising agency. For years, the Council's advertising campaigns such as Smokey the Bear, McGruff the Crime Dog, and test dummies have urged people to prevent forest fires, fight crime, and drive safely.

Following the steps of the organizing process, the Advertising Council recently reflected on its plans and objectives and discovered some new, contemporary, Internet-related tasks that must be performed to better reach various audiences. The process already started within the organization to allocate resources that will have the organization's public service messages appear as banners on many Web sites across the World Wide Web. Eventually, the Council could buy its own server and build a Web site presence that touts all of its causes. In this case, the Council might have to hire a totally different kind of employee than it presently has to build and maintain its Internet presence.

This new organizing strategy of the Advertising Council will almost certainly help the organization to become more successful. To maximize this success, however, management must remember to continually evaluate and improve its new organizing strategy.

FIGURE 10.2 ▶ Relationships between overall management system and organizing subsystem

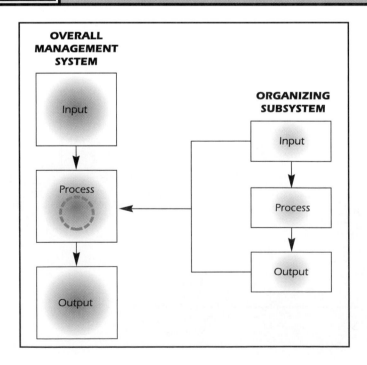

FIGURE 10.3 ► Organizing subsystem

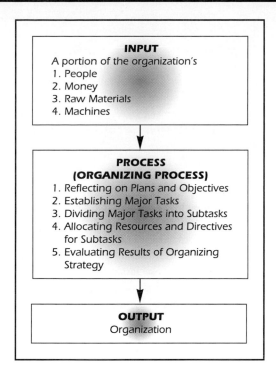

INPUT
A portion of the organization's
1. People
2. Money
3. Raw Materials
4. Machines

**PROCESS
(ORGANIZING PROCESS)**
1. Reflecting on Plans and Objectives
2. Establishing Major Tasks
3. Dividing Major Tasks into Subtasks
4. Allocating Resources and Directives
   for Subtasks
5. Evaluating Results of Organizing
   Strategy

OUTPUT
Organization

►THE ORGANIZING SUBSYSTEM

The organizing function, like the planning function, can be visualized as a subsystem of the overall management system (see Figure 10.2). The primary purpose of the organizing subsystem is to enhance the goal attainment of the general management system by providing a rational approach for using organizational resources. Figure 10.3 presents the specific ingredients of the organizing subsystem. The input is a portion of the total resources of the organization, the process is the steps involved in the organizing function, and the output is organization.

BACK TO THE CASE

In contemplating how Lucent should be organized, a manager like Richard A. McGinn can focus on answering several important questions. These questions should be aimed at establishing an orderly use of Lucent's organizational resources. Because these resources represent an investment on which he must get a return, McGinn's questions should be geared toward gaining information that will be used to maximize this return. Overall, such questions should focus on determining what use of Lucent's resources will best accomplish its goals.

Some preliminary questions could be as follows:

1. What organizational objectives exist at Lucent? For example, does Lucent want to focus on international markets as well as domestic markets? Does Lucent want to grow or maintain its present size?

2. What plans does Lucent have to accomplish these objectives? Is Lucent going to open more offices abroad? Are additional training programs being added to enable employees to effectively work abroad?

3. What are the major tasks Lucent must accomplish to offer message and voice products? For example, how many steps are involved in developing a new wireless telephone and making it available to appropriate customers?

(continued)

CLASSICAL ORGANIZING THEORY

Classical organizing theory comprises the cumulative insights of early management writers
> Classical organizing theory comprises the cumulative insights of early management writers on how organizational resources can best be used to enhance goal attainment.

Classical organizing theory comprises the cumulative insights of early management writers on how organizational resources can best be used to enhance goal attainment. The writer who probably had the most profound influence on classical organizing theory was Max Weber.[5] According to Weber, the main components of an organizing effort are detailed procedures and rules, a clearly outlined organizational hierarchy, and impersonal relationships among organization members.

> **Bureaucracy** is the term Max Weber used to describe a management system characterized by detailed procedures and rules, a clearly outlined organizational hierarchy, and impersonal relationships among organization members.

WEBER'S BUREAUCRATIC MODEL Weber used the term **bureaucracy** to label the management system that contains these components. Although he firmly believed in the bureaucratic approach to organizing, he was concerned that managers were inclined to overemphasize the merits of a bureaucracy. He cautioned that a bureaucracy is not an end in itself, but rather a means to the end of management system goal attainment. The main criticism of Weber's bureaucracy model, as well as the concepts of other classical organizing theorists, is that they give short shrift to the human variable within organizations. In fact, it is recognized today that the bureaucratic approach without an appropriate emphasis on the human variable is almost certainly a formula for organizational failure.[6] Considerable discussion on this variable is presented in chapters 13 through 18.

The rest of this chapter summarizes four main considerations of classical organizing theory that all modern managers should incorporate into their organizing efforts:

1. Structure
2. Division of labor
3. Span of management
4. Scalar relationships

▶ STRUCTURE

> **Structure** refers to the designated relationships among resources of the management system.

In any organizing effort, managers must choose an appropriate structure. **Structure** refers to the designated relationships among resources of the management system. Its purpose is to facilitate the use of each resource, individually and collectively, as the management system attempts to attain its objectives.[7]

> An **organization chart** is a graphic representation of organizational structure.

Organization structure is represented primarily by means of a graphic illustration called an **organization chart.** Traditionally, an organization chart is constructed in pyramid form, with individuals toward the top of the pyramid having more authority and responsibility than those toward the bottom.[8] The relative positioning of individuals within boxes on the chart indicates broad working relationships, and lines between boxes designate formal lines of communication between individuals.

Authority and Responsibility   Figure 10.4 is an example of an organization chart. The dotted line is not part of the organization chart but has been added to emphasize the chart's pyramid shape. The position of restaurant manager is at the point of the pyramid, and those positions close to the restaurant manager's involve more authority and responsibility, while

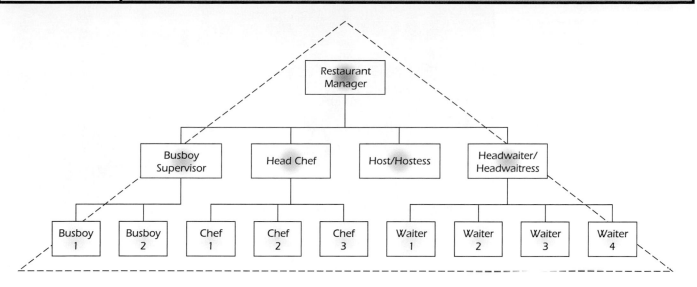

FIGURE 10.4 ► **Sample organization chart for a small restaurant**

those positions farther away involve less authority and responsibility. The locations of positions also indicate broad working relationships. For example, the positioning of the head chef over the three other chefs indicates that the head chef has authority over them and is responsible for their productivity. The lines between the individual chefs and the restaurant manager indicate that formal communication from chef 1 to the restaurant manager must go through the head chef.

Structure and Gender   Pyramidal organization structures are probably modeled on the hierarchical structure of military command. In the Western world, the structure of organized religion has also been hierarchical, with authority derived from the top. Some researchers have found that women are not comfortable with this type of structure. As more and more women enter the management field, therefore, a new type of structural model may be needed. In *The Female Advantage: Women's Ways of Leadership*, Sally Helgesen postulates that women create networks or "webs" of authority and that women's leadership styles are relational rather than hierarchical and authoritarian. Management writer Tom Peters suggests that these styles are inherently better suited to the new kinds of organizational structures, featuring teamwork and participative management, required for the competitive global environment of the 1990s.[9]

FORMAL AND INFORMAL STRUCTURE   There are two basic types of structure within management systems: formal and informal. **Formal structure** is defined as the relationships among organizational resources as outlined by management. It is represented primarily by the organization chart.

Informal structure is defined as the patterns of relationships that develop because of the informal activities of organization members. It evolves naturally and tends to be molded by individual norms and values and social relationships. Essentially, an organization's informal structure is the system or network of interpersonal relationships that exists within, but is not usually identical to, the organization's formal structure.[10] This chapter focuses on formal structure. Details on informal structure are presented in chapter 17.

DEPARTMENTALIZATION AND FORMAL STRUCTURE: A CONTINGENCY VIEWPOINT   The most common method of instituting formal relationships among resources is to establish departments. Basically, a **department** is a unique group of resources established by management to perform some organizational task. The process of establishing departments within the management system is called **departmentalization.** Typically, these departments are based on, or contingent upon, such situational factors as the work functions

Formal structure is defined as the relationships among organizational resources as outlined by management.

Informal structure is defined as the patterns of relationships that develop because of the informal activities of organization members.

A **department** is a unique group of resources established by management to perform some organizational task.

Departmentalization is the process of establishing departments within the management system.

Top management at GE Appliances headquarters in Louisville, Kentucky, uses such technologies as worldwide teleconferencing as more than communications tools: They are in fact one means of recognizing fundamental changes in the organization of today's big businesses. According to many experts, such factors as global markets and advances in communication are forcing businesses to reorganize more radically than at any time since the 1950s, when the multidivision corporation became commonplace.

being performed, the product being assembled, the territory being covered, the customer being targeted, and the process designed for manufacturing the product. (For a quick review of the contingency approach to management, see chapter 2.)

FUNCTIONAL DEPARTMENTALIZATION Perhaps the most widely used basis for establishing departments within the formal structure is the type of *work functions* (activities) being performed within the management system.[11] Functions are typically divided into the major categories of marketing, production, and finance. Figure 10.5 is an organization chart showing structure based primarily on function for a hypothetical organization, Greene Furniture Company.

PRODUCT DEPARTMENTALIZATION Organization structure based primarily on *product* departmentalizes resources according to the products being manufactured. As more and more products are manufactured by a company, it becomes increasingly difficult for management to coordinate activities across the organization. Organizing according to product permits the logical grouping of resources necessary to produce each product. Figure 10.6 is an organization chart for Greene Furniture Company showing structure based primarily on product.

GEOGRAPHIC DEPARTMENTALIZATION Structure based primarily on *territory* departmentalizes according to the places where the work is being done or the geographic mar-

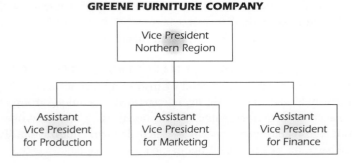

FIGURE 10.5 ▶ Organization structure based primarily on function

GREENE FURNITURE COMPANY

Vice President
Northern Region

Assistant Vice President for Production

Assistant Vice President for Marketing

Assistant Vice President for Finance

FIGURE 10.6 ▶ **Organization structure based primarily on product**

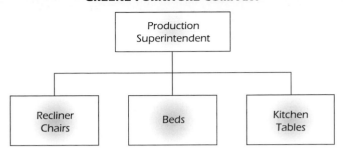

GREENE FURNITURE COMPANY

FIGURE 10.7 ▶ **Organization structure based primarily on territory**

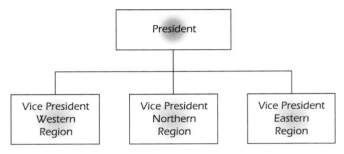

GREENE FURNITURE COMPANY

kets on which the management system is focusing. The physical distances can range from quite short (between two points in the same city) to quite long (between two points in the same state, in different states, or even in different countries).[12] As market areas and work locations expand, the physical distances between places can make the management task extremely cumbersome. To minimize this problem, resources can be departmentalized according to territory. Figure 10.7 is an organization chart for Greene Furniture Company based primarily on territory.

GLOBAL SPOTLIGHT ◀ **Crown Cork & Seal Company Organizes by Territory to Boost International Expansion**

The Crown Cork & Seal Company, headquartered in Philadelphia, Pennsylvania, manufactures and sells a variety of food and beverage packaging containers as well as packaging machinery. The company has designed its structure to ensure its continued international growth.

Crown Cork & Seal has experienced substantial international growth in recent years, virtually doubling its global sales to an estimated $3.8 billion. Today the company has 141 plants in 32 countries. When John F. Connelly took it over in 1956, it had worldwide sales of $100 million and a heavy debt load that brought it close to collapse. By 1962, Crown was relatively debt-free and positioned for growth, with the beverage industry as its main target. To focus organizational resources and efforts on continued organizational growth in the global arena, Connelly restructured the company into two basic divisions: North America and International. Present international efforts focus on Hong Kong, the People's Republic of China, Korea, Venezuela, and Saudi Arabia.

FIGURE 10.8 ▶ Organization structure based primarily on customers

CUSTOMER DEPARTMENTALIZATION

Structure based primarily on the *customer* establishes departments in response to the organization's major customers. This structure, of course, assumes that major customers can be identified and divided into logical categories. Figure 10.8 is an organization chart for Greene Furniture Company based primarily on customers. Greene Furniture obviously can clearly identify its customers and divide them into logical categories.

MANUFACTURING PROCESS DEPARTMENTALIZATION

Structure based primarily on *manufacturing process* departmentalizes according to the major phases of the process used to manufacture products. In the case of Greene Furniture Company, the major phases are woodcutting, sanding, gluing, and painting. Figure 10.9 is the organization chart that reflects these phases.

If the situation warrants it, individual organization charts can be combined to show all five of these factors. Figure 10.10 shows how all the factors are included on the same organization chart for Greene Furniture Company.

FORCES INFLUENCING FORMAL STRUCTURE

According to Shetty and Carlisle, the formal structure of a management system is continually evolving. Four primary forces influence this evolution:[13]

1. Forces in the manager
2. Forces in the task
3. Forces in the environment
4. Forces in the subordinates

The evolution of a particular organization is actually the result of a complex and dynamic interaction among these forces.

Forces in the manager are the unique way in which a manager perceives organizational problems.[14] Naturally, background, knowledge, experience, and values influence the manager's perception of what the organization's formal structure should be or how it should be changed.

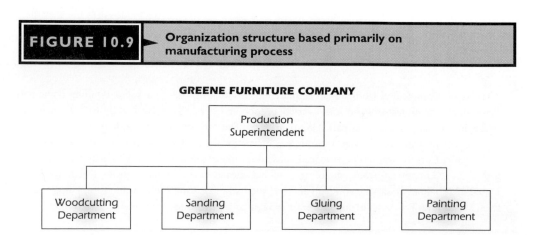

FIGURE 10.10 ► Combined organization chart for Greene Furniture Company

GREENE FURNITURE COMPANY

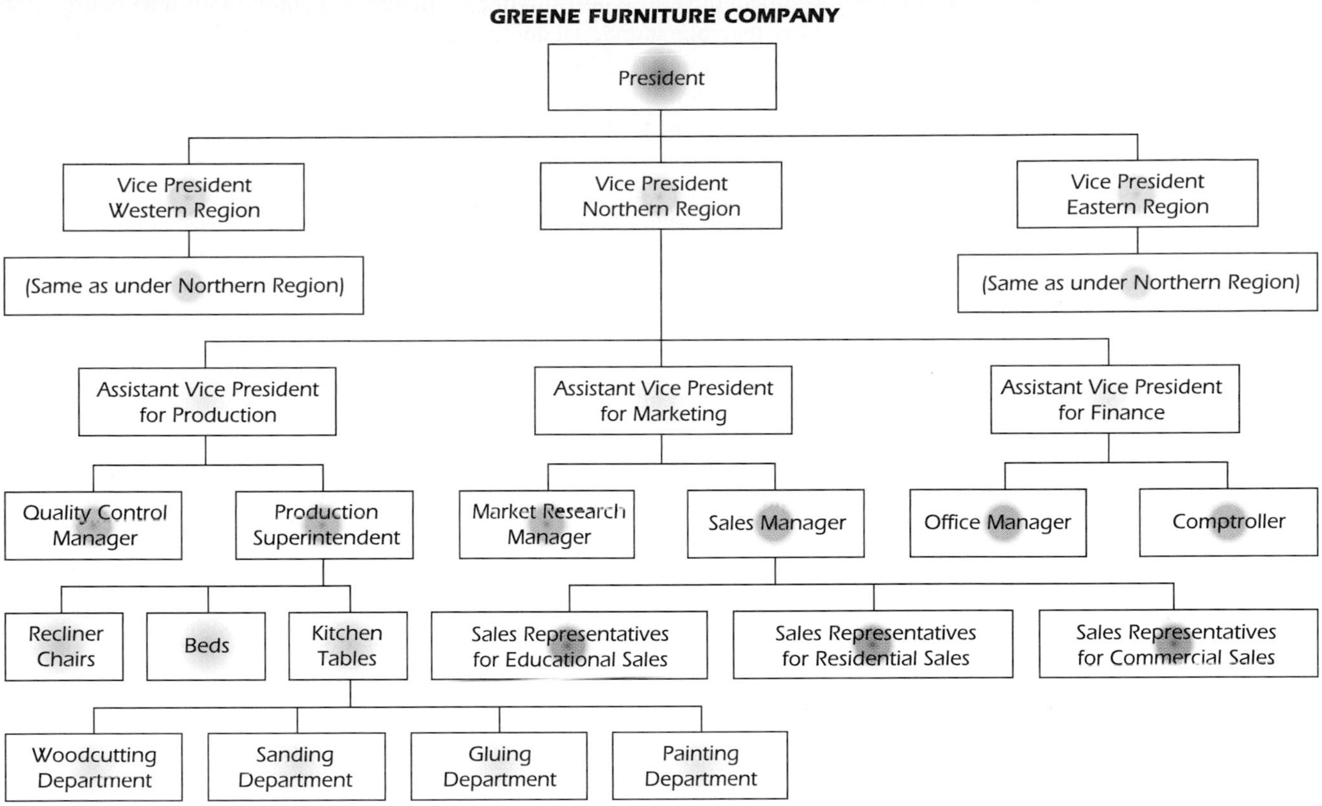

Forces in the task include the degree of technology involved in performing the task and the task's complexity. As task activities change, a force is created to change the existing organization. Forces in the environment include the customers and suppliers of the management system, along with existing political and social structures. Forces in the subordinates include the needs and skill levels of subordinates. Obviously, as the environment and subordinates change, forces are created simultaneously to change the organization.

BACK TO THE CASE

In order to develop a sound organizing effort, a manager like McGinn should take classical organizing theory into consideration. Of the four major elements of classical organizing theory, the first to be considered here is structure. McGinn's considerations regarding the structure of Lucent would be aimed at creating working relationships among all Lucent employees. In order to develop an effective organizational structure, McGinn must analyze situational factors in the company, such as functions, products, geographic locations, customers, and processes involved in offering its products to customers.

Within the case there is information indicating that McGinn's organization structure for Lucent is based primarily upon products or services offered. For example, 2 of the 11 main areas at Lucent are Global Service Provider and Enterprise Networks and Data Networks Systems. In essence, Lucent is arranging its resources to focus on its 11 main product/service areas.

A manager like McGinn typically uses an organization chart to represent organization structure. Such a chart would allow McGinn not only to see the lines of authority and responsibility at Lucent, but also to understand the broad working relationships among his employees.

Division of labor is the assignment of various portions of a particular task among a number of organization members. Division of labor calls for specialization.

The second main consideration of any organizing effort is how to divide labor. **Division of labor** is the assignment of various portions of a particular task among a number of organization members. Rather than one individual doing the entire job, several individuals perform different parts of it. Production is divided into a number of steps, with the responsibility for completing various steps assigned to specific individuals. The essence of division of labor is that individuals specialize in doing part of a task rather than the entire task.

A commonly used illustration of division of labor is the automobile production line. Rather than one person assembling an entire car, specific portions of the car are assembled by various workers. The following sections discuss the advantages and disadvantages of division of labor and the relationship between division of labor and coordination.

ADVANTAGES AND DISADVANTAGES OF DIVISION OF LABOR Even the peerless physicist Albert Einstein, famous for his independent theorizing, believed that division of labor could be very advantageous in many undertakings.[15] Several explanations have been offered for the usefulness of division of labor. First, when workers specialize in a particular task, their skill at performing that task tends to increase. Second, workers who have one job and one place in which to do it do not lose valuable time changing tools or locations. Third, when workers concentrate on performing only one job, they naturally try to make the job easier and more efficient. Lastly, division of labor creates a situation in which workers need only to know how to perform their part of the work task rather than the entire process for producing the end product. The task of understanding their work, therefore, does not become too burdensome.

Arguments have also been presented against the use of an extreme division of labor.[16] Essentially, these arguments contend that division of labor focuses solely on efficiency and economic benefit and overlooks the human variable in organizations. Work that is extremely specialized tends to be boring and therefore will eventually cause production rates to go down as workers become resentful of being treated like machines. Clearly, managers need to find a reasonable balance between specialization and human motivation. How to arrive at this balance is discussed in chapter 16.

Coordination is the orderly arrangement of group effort to provide unity of action in the pursuit of a common purpose. It involves encouraging the completion of individual portions of a task in an appropriate, synchronized order.

DIVISION OF LABOR AND COORDINATION In a division-of-labor situation, the importance of effective coordination of the different individuals doing portions of the task is obvious. Mooney has defined **coordination** as "the orderly arrangement of group effort to provide unity of action in the pursuit of a common purpose." In essence, coordination is a means for achieving any and all organizational objectives.[17] It involves encouraging the completion of individual portions of a task in a synchronized order that is appropriate for the overall task. Groups cannot maintain their productivity without coordination.[18] Part of the synchronized order of assembling an automobile, for example, is that seats are installed only after the floor has been installed; adhering to this order of installation is an example of coordination.

Establishing and maintaining coordination may require close supervision of employees, though managers should try to break away from the idea that coordination can only be achieved this way.[19] They can, instead, establish and maintain coordination through bargaining, formulating a common purpose for the group, or improving on specific problem solutions so the group will know what to do when it encounters those problems. Each of these efforts is considered a specific management tool.

Follett's Guidelines on Coordination Mary Parker Follett provided valuable advice on how managers can establish and maintain coordination within the organization. First, Follett said that coordination can be attained with the least difficulty through direct horizontal relationships and personal communications. In other words, when a coordination problem arises, peer discussion may be the best way to resolve it. Second, Follett suggested that coordination be a discussion topic throughout the planning process. In essence, managers should plan for coordination. Third, maintaining coordination is a continuing process and should be treated as such. Managers cannot assume that because their management system shows coordination today it will show coordination tomorrow.

Follett also noted that coordination can be achieved only through purposeful management action—it cannot be left to chance. Finally, she stressed the importance of the human element and advised that the communication process is an essential consideration in any attempt to encourage coordination. Employee skill levels and motivation levels are also primary considerations, as is the effectiveness of the human communication process used during coordination activities.[20]

QUALITY SPOTLIGHT — DaimlerChrysler Improves Coordination to Improve Product Quality

Improving coordination can improve the effectiveness and efficiency of the workforce in virtually any organization. DaimlerChrysler executives focus on improving coordination to improve product quality.

Although they acknowledge that new competitors such as Lexus and Infinity have made an impact in the upscale automobile market, DaimlerChrysler executives are neither discouraged nor digressing from decades-old organizational objectives. The company remains dedicated to the needs and wants of the upscale-but-unpretentious buyer who is looking for a vehicle that balances style and performance with form and function.

As in the past, the company will compete by remaining firmly committed to improving the overall quality of its products. Klaus-Dieter Vohringer, a member of the DaimlerChrysler top-management team, says the company will demonstrate this commitment to product quality through a plan that focuses on improving coordination among three different manufacturing and assembly plants. This major restructuring of the manufacturing process at DaimlerChrysler is expected to result not only in better product quality but also in more productive uses of existing facilities, quicker responses to changing customers' needs and competitive products, and lowered product costs. According to Vohringer, DaimlerChrysler has developed a sophisticated understanding of its customers over the years. In order to maintain a high level of customer satisfaction, management knows that it must constantly be on the alert for new methods of improving product quality, and is convinced that better coordination in the manufacturing process will help DaimlerChrysler achieve its quality goals.

BACK TO THE CASE

In developing the most appropriate way to organize Lucent employees, a manager like McGinn can reflect upon the second major element in classical organizing theory, division of labor. He could decide, for example, that instead of having one person do all the work involved in servicing a business customer, the labor could be divided so that for each business customer one person would make the initial contact, another would assess the communication needs of the organization, and a third would explore the alternative ways that Lucent could offer to meet those needs. In this way, employees could work more quickly and specialize in one area of business customer relations, such as business needs assessment or meeting business customer needs.

In considering the appropriateness of division of labor at Lucent, a manager like McGinn could also consider creating a mechanism for enhancing coordination. In order to develop such a mechanism, McGinn must have a thorough understanding of how various Lucent business processes occur so he can divide various tasks and maintain coordination within the various Lucent divisions. In addition, a manager like McGinn must stress communication as a prerequisite for coordination. Without Lucent employees continually communicating with one another, coordination will be virtually impossible. In taking action aimed at enhancing organizational coordination, McGinn must also continually plan for and take action toward maintaining such coordination.

The **span of management** is the number of individuals a manager supervises.

The third main consideration of any organizing effort is **span of management**—the number of individuals a manager supervises. The more individuals a manager supervises, the greater the span of management. Conversely, the fewer individuals a manager supervises, the smaller the span of management. The span of management has a significant effect on how well managers carry out their responsibilities. Span of management is also called *span of control, span of authority, span of supervision,* and *span of responsibility.*[21]

The central concern of span of management is to determine how many individuals a manager can supervise effectively. To use the organization's human resources effectively, managers should supervise as many individuals as they can best guide toward production quotas. If they are supervising too few people, they are wasting a portion of their productive capacity. If they are supervising too many, they are losing part of their effectiveness.

DESIGNING SPAN OF MANAGEMENT: A CONTINGENCY VIEWPOINT As reported by Harold Koontz, several important situational factors influence the appropriateness of the size of an individual's span of management:[22]

▶ *Similarity of functions*—the degree to which activities performed by supervised individuals are similar or dissimilar. As the similarity of subordinates' activities increases, the span of management appropriate for the situation widens. The converse is also generally true.

▶ *Geographic continuity*—the degree to which subordinates are physically separated. In general, the closer subordinates are physically, the more of them managers can supervise effectively.

▶ *Complexity of functions*—the degree to which workers' activities are difficult and involved. The more difficult and involved the activities are, the more difficult it is to manage a large number of individuals effectively.

▶ *Coordination*—the amount of time managers must spend synchronizing the activities of their subordinates with the activities of other workers. The greater the amount of time that must be spent on such coordination, the smaller the span of management should be.

▶ *Planning*—the amount of time managers must spend developing management system objectives and plans and integrating them with the activities of their subordinates. The more time managers must spend on planning activities, the fewer individuals they can manage effectively.

Table 10.1 summarizes the factors that tend to increase and decrease the span of management.

GRAICUNAS AND SPAN OF MANAGEMENT Perhaps the best-known contribution to span-of-management literature was made by the management consultant V. A. Graicunas.[23] He developed a formula for determining the number of *possible* relationships between a manager and subordinates when the number of subordinates is known. **Graicunas' formula** is as follows:

Graicunas' formula is a formula that makes the span-of-management point that as the number of a manager's subordinates increases arithmetically, the number of possible relationships between the manager and the subordinates increases geometrically.

$$C = n\left(\frac{2^n}{2} + n - 1\right)$$

C is the total number of possible relationships between manager and subordinates, and *n* is the known number of subordinates. As the number of subordinates increases arithmetically, the number of possible relationships between the manager and those subordinates increases geometrically.

A number of criticisms have been leveled at Graicunas' work. Some have argued that he failed to take into account a manager's relationships outside the organization and that he considered only *potential* relationships rather than *actual* relationships. These criticisms have some validity, but the real significance of Graicunas' work lies outside them. His main contribution,

TABLE 10.1 ▶ Major Factors That Influence the Span of Management

Factor	Factor Has Tendency To Increase Span of Management When—	Factor Has Tendency To Decrease Span of Management When—
1. Similarity of functions	1. Subordinates have similar functions	1. Subordinates have different functions
2. Geographic contiguity	2. Subordinates are physically close	2. Subordinates are physically distant
3. Complexity of functions	3. Subordinates have simple tasks	3. Subordinates have complex tasks
4. Coordination	4. Work of subordinates needs little coordination	4. Work of subordinates needs much coordination
5. Planning	5. Manager spends little time planning	5. Manager spends much time planning

in fact, was to point out that span of management is an important consideration that can have a far-reaching impact on the organization.[24]

HEIGHT OF ORGANIZATION CHART There is a definite relationship between span of management and the height of an organization chart. Normally, the greater the height of the organization chart, the smaller the span of management, and the lower the height of the chart, the greater the span of management.[25] Organization charts with little height are usually referred to as **flat,** while those with much height are usually referred to as **tall.**

Figure 10.11 is a simple example of the relationship between organization chart height and span of management. Organization chart A has a span of management of six, and organization chart B has a span of management of two. As a result, chart A is flatter than chart B. Note that both charts have the same number of individuals at the lowest level. The larger span of management in A is reduced in B merely by adding a level to B's organization chart.

An organization's structure should be built from top to bottom to ensure that appropriate spans of management are achieved at all levels. Increasing spans of management merely to eliminate certain management positions and thereby reduce salary expenses may prove to be a very shortsighted move. Increasing spans of management to achieve such objectives as speeding up organizational decision making and building a more flexible organization is more likely to help the organization achieve success in the long run.[26] A survey of organization charts of the 1990s reveals that top managers are creating flatter organizational structures than top managers used in the 1980s.

A **flat organization chart** is an organization chart characterized by few levels and a relatively broad span of management.

A **tall organization chart** is an organization chart characterized by many levels and a relatively narrow span of management.

FIGURE 10.11 ▶ Relationship between organization chart height and span of management

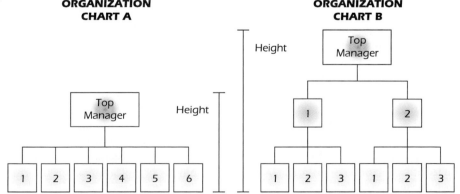

CIRCULAR ORGANIZATION CHART AT OUR LADY OF THE WAY HOSPITAL

Reflecting traditional organization theory, this chapter is filled with examples and discussions of organization charts built linearly and vertically. Given such organization chart construction, issues like height are relevant and important. However, in more recent times, some managers use circular organization charts.

Our Lady of the Way Hospital is a small, 39-bed hospital located in Martin, Kentucky. Like most hospitals, Our Lady of the Way historically had an organization chart built on straight lines and boxes that reflected a typical bureaucratic organization. The CEO of Our Lady of the Way Hospital had direct management responsibility for several functional departments.

Recently, however, management replaced the traditional, hierarchical organization chart with a circular structure. According to management, the new structure was built to emphasize an increased need for reliance on team processes throughout the hospital. The circular organization chart is represented by a series of diagrams in which the circle, a geometric form with no beginning or end points, symbolizes the ongoing nature of the team process. The circle also implies that decisions are reached by consensus, that no expertise within the organization is more important than any other, and that each person on the team is equally responsible for advancing its work.

► SCALAR RELATIONSHIPS

Scalar relationships refer to the chain-of-command positioning of individuals on an organization chart.

The fourth main consideration of any organizing effort is **scalar relationships**—the chain of command. Every organization is built on the premise that the individual at the top possesses the most authority and that other individuals' authority is scaled downward according to their relative position on the organization chart. The lower a person's position on the organization chart, then, the less authority that person possesses.[27]

Unity of command is the management principle that recommends that an individual have only one boss.

The scalar relationship, or chain of command, is related to the unity of command. **Unity of command** is the management principle that recommends that an individual have only one boss. If too many bosses give orders, the result will probably be confusion, contradiction, and frustration—a sure recipe for ineffectiveness and inefficiency in an organization. Although the unity-of-command principle made its first appearance in management literature well over 75 years ago, it is still discussed today as a critical ingredient of successful organizations.[28]

Fayol's Guidelines on Chain of Command   Fayol has indicated that strict adherence to the chain of command is not always advisable.[29] Figure 10.12 explains his rationale. If individual F needs information from individual G and follows the concept of chain of command, F has to go through individuals D, B, A, C, and E before reaching G. The information would get back to F only by going from G through E, C, A, B, and D. Obviously, this long, involved process can be very time-consuming and therefore expensive for the organization.

A **gangplank** is a communication channel extending from one organizational division to another but not shown in the lines of communication outlined on an organization chart. Use of Fayol's gangplank may be quicker, but could prove costly in the long run.

To avoid this long, involved, expensive process, Fayol has recommended that in some situations a bridge, or **gangplank,** be used to allow F to go directly to G for information. This bridge is represented in Figure 10.12 by the dotted line connecting F and G. Managers should be very careful in allowing the use of these organizational bridges, however, because although F might get the information from G more quickly and cheaply that way, individuals D, B, A, C, and E would be excluded from the communication channel, and their ignorance might prove more costly to the organization in the long run than would following the established chain of command. When managers allow the use of an organizational bridge, they must be extremely careful to inform all other appropriate individuals within the organization of any information received that way.

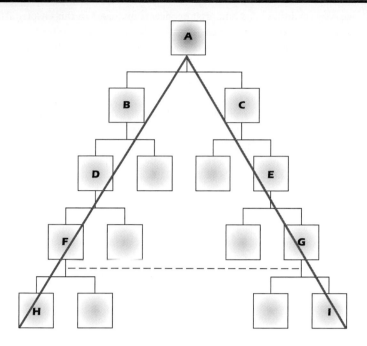

BACK TO THE CASE

The last two major elements in classical organizing theory that a manager like McGinn could reflect upon are span of management and scalar relationships. Span of management focuses on the number of subordinates that managers in various roles at Lucent can successfully supervise. In thinking about span of management McGinn might explore several important situational factors, such as similarities among various Lucent activities, the extent to which Lucent workers being managed are physically separated, and the complexity of various Lucent work activities.

For example, McGinn should consider that selling cordless phones to consumer outlets can be fairly simple and that installing a special equipment network within a company can be much more involved and complicated. Therefore, the span of management for workers doing the former job should generally be larger than the span of management for workers doing the latter job. Other important factors McGinn should consider in determining spans of management for various Lucent managers are the amount of time managers must spend coordinating workers' activities and the amount of time managers spend planning. With all of this information, a manager like McGinn should be quite capable of determining appropriate spans of management for their managers.

For updated information on the topics in this chapter, Internet exercises, links to related Internet sites, an interactive study guide, and more, visit our companion Web site at

http://www.prenhall.com/certo

Additional information can be found on the inside front and back covers of this text.

Reread the learning objectives below. Each objective is followed by questions. Answering these questions accurately will help you retain the most important concepts discussed in this chapter. After answering each question, check your answer against the answer key at the end of this chapter. (*Hint:* If you have any doubts regarding the correct response, consult the page number that follows the answer.)

Circle:	From studying this chapter, I will attempt to acquire
	1. An understanding of the organizing function.
a b c d e	**a.** Of the five steps in the organizing process, the following is grossly out of order: (a) reflect on plans and objectives (b) establish major tasks (c) allocate resources and directives for subtasks (d) divide major tasks into subtasks (e) evaluate results of the implemented organizational strategy.
T F	**b.** Proper execution of the organizing function normally results in minimal duplication of effort.
	2. An appreciation for the complexities of determining appropriate organizational structure.
a b c d e	**a.** The XYZ Corporation is organized as follows: it has (1) a president, (2) a vice president in charge of finance, (3) a vice president in charge of marketing, and (4) a vice president in charge of human resources management. This firm is organized on the: (a) functional basis (b) manufacturing process basis (c) customer basis (d) territorial basis (e) production basis.
a b c d e	**b.** All of the following forces are influences on the evolution of formal structure except: (a) forces in the manager (b) forces in subordinates (c) forces in the environment (d) forces in the division of labor (e) forces in the task.
	3. Insights on the advantages and disadvantages of division of labor.
a b c d e	**a.** Extreme division of labor tends to result in: (a) human motivation (b) boring jobs (c) nonspecialized work (d) decreased work skill (e) all of the above.
a b c d e	**b.** The following is *not* a generally accepted advantage of division of labor within an organization: (a) workers' skills in performing their jobs tend to increase (b) workers need to know only how to perform their specific work tasks (c) workers do not waste time in moving from one task to another (d) workers naturally tend to try to make their individual tasks easier and more efficient (e) none of the above (all are advantages of the division of labor).
	4. A working knowledge of the relationship between division of labor and coordination.
T F	**a.** Effective coordination is best achieved through close employee supervision.
T F	**b.** Mary Parker Follett contended that managers should plan for coordination.
	5. An understanding of span of management and the factors that influence its appropriateness.
a b c d e	**a.** Of the factors listed, the following would have a tendency to increase (expand) the span of management: (a) subordinates are physically distant (b) subordinates have similar functions (c) subordinates have complex tasks (d) subordinates' work needs close coordination (e) manager spends much time in planning.
a b c d e	**b.** The concept of span of management concerns: (a) seeing that managers at the same level have equal numbers of subordinates (b) employee skill and motivation levels (c) supervision of one less than the known number of subordinates (d) a determination of the number of individuals a manager can effectively supervise (e) a and d.
	6. An understanding of scalar relationships.
a b c d e	**a.** The management concept that recommends that employees should have one and only one boss is termed: (a) departmentalization (b) function (c) unity of command (d) scalar relationship (e) none of the above.
T F	**b.** According to Fayol, under no circumstances should a gangplank be used in organizations.

CASE DISCUSSSION QUESTIONS

"Lucent Technologies Organizes for Success" (p. 211) and its related Back-to-the-Case sections were written to help you better understand the management concepts contained in this chapter. Answer the following discussion questions about this Introductory Case to further enrich your understanding of the chapter content:

1. Does it seem reasonable that McGinn is attempting to better organize Lucent in order to remain more competitive? Explain.

2. List five questions that McGinn should ask himself in exploring how to best organize Lucent.

3. Explain why it would be important for McGinn to ask each of the questions you listed.

SKILLS EXERCISE: BUILDING A USEFUL ORGANIZATION CHART

In this chapter you studied several topics that apply to building organization charts. The Introductory Case discusses organizational structure at Lucent Technologies and how its CEO, Richard A. McGinn, has divided the organization into 11 operational units. Draw a partial organization chart for Lucent showing 11 vice presidents reporting to him (you do not need to name each area). Now, draw another chart showing 2 executive vice presidents between McGinn and the 11 vice presidents. Construct an argument for using this second chart at Lucent as opposed to the first chart.

1. What is organizing?
2. Explain the significance of organizing to the management system.
3. List the steps in the organizing process. Why should managers continually repeat these steps?
4. Can the organizing function be thought of as a subsystem? Explain.
5. Fully describe what Max Weber meant by the term *bureaucracy*.
6. Compare and contrast formal structure with informal structure.
7. List and explain three factors that management structure is based on, or contingent upon. Draw three sample portions of organization charts that illustrate the factors you listed.
8. Describe the forces that influence formal structure. How do these forces collectively influence structure?
9. What is division of labor?
10. What are the advantages and disadvantages of employing division of labor within a management system?
11. Define *coordination*.
12. Does division of labor increase the need for coordination? Explain.
13. Summarize Mary Parker Follett's thoughts on how to establish and maintain coordination.
14. Is span of management an important management concept? Explain.
15. Do you think that similarity of functions, geographic contiguity, complexity of functions, coordination, and planning influence appropriate span of control in all management systems? Explain.
16. Summarize and evaluate Graicunas' contribution to span-of-management literature.
17. What is the relationship between span of management and *flat* and *tall* organizations?
18. What are scalar relationships?
19. Explain the rationale behind Fayol's position that always adhering to the chain of command is not necessarily advisable.
20. What caution should managers exercise when they use the gang-plank Fayol described?

1. **a.** c, p. 213
   b. T, p. 212
2. **a.** a, p. 218
   b. d, p. 220

3. **a.** b, p. 222
   b. e, p. 222
4. **a.** F, p. 222
   b. T, pp. 222–223

5. **a.** b, p. 224
   b. d, p. 224

6. **a.** c, p. 226
   b. F, p. 226

In the fall of 1995, AT&T chairman Robert Allen announced that AT&T was separating into three publicly traded global companies. It is the fourth strategic restructuring in AT&T's history, and the biggest corporate reorganization ever in terms of stock market value. Under the terms of the split, AT&T shareowners will receive shares in each of the new companies.

In justifying the decision to reorganize, Allen pointed to transformations in the communications industry resulting from changes in customer needs, technology, and public policy. With AT&T at the intersection of all those changes, the restructuring had a single purpose—to give AT&T's businesses the agility to seize the best of new market opportunities. In Allen's view, restructuring was the only logical action for AT&T.

Three problems faced the old corporate giant: size, agility, and stock price. AT&T management realized that only companies would be positioned to take full advantage of the many new opportunities. Before the restructuring, AT&T was one company competing in four segments of information technology: (1) computing, (2) premises equipment, (3) network systems, and (4) communications services. The company had swollen to the point where advantages of size and scope were offset by the time and cost of coordinating and integrating sometimes conflicting business strategies.

At least two of the new companies have one important advantage: Although they are smaller and more focused than the parent company, they are by no means underfinanced. For example, the new AT&T communications group, holding almost 60 percent of the long-distance market, ranks no. 12 on the Fortune 500 list; moreover, its Universal card is the second-largest credit card in the country. In addition, the acquisition of McCaw Cellular Communications in 1994 made AT&T a powerhouse in wireless services, with 80 percent of the wireless market. Finally, with changes brought about by the 1996 telecommunications bill, the company is set to take a bite of the local phone market as well, as it bundles its services into one-stop consumer shopping handled on a single bill.

In Allen's view, restructuring offers shareholders several advantages. For example, each of the main AT&T businesses can follow its individual path, striving to create greater value without worrying about bumping into another AT&T unit along the way. Each can now transfer energy previously expended on coordinating complex strategies across businesses into new offers for customers. Finally, each company can be more responsive to customers and offer shareowners a more focused investment in a high-growth industry, allowing investors to evaluate each company on its own merits.

AT&T's voluntary restructuring is regarded by Wall Street as nothing less than miraculous. Shortly after the stunning announcement was made, stocks climbed by a little over 6 points. According to investment experts, the company that had long been synonymous with "Big Business" and the model for vertical integration had divested itself for its

own good. Because AT&T is now poised to jump into the newly opened local-phone-service business and to offer integrated services that rival cable companies' services, downsizing may make the company bigger and better than ever.

Of course, such radical restructuring does not come without pain. In early 1996, for instance, Allen announced 40,000 layoffs touching every area of the business: AT&T itself, the communications group; Lucent, the new equipment and research group; and NCR, the computer group. NCR was the company most in trouble at the time of the restructuring. Many observers thought that AT&T's hostile $7.4 billion takeover of NCR in 1991 was too costly. Others have argued that although communications and computers seemed a perfect marriage, integration of the two companies proved too complicated—that AT&T bet too much on synergies that did not materialize.

Many of AT&T's problems in the mid-1990s originated in the breakup of the early 1980s, when AT&T spun off seven regional telephone companies, known as the "Baby Bells." Problems arose when AT&T began to supply competitors and compete with its own customers. For example, loath to enrich a telephone service competitor after deregulation opened new markets, the Baby Bells started to buy new equipment from other suppliers—a major blow to the equipment side of AT&T.

Allen believes the new restructuring will eliminate the problems of internal competition and put all three companies on a clearer path. This CEO, who entered the telephone business in 1957 as a management trainee for Indiana Bell, could never have foreseen as a young manager that telephone companies would someday have to compete with software companies, data providers, cable groups, and broadcasters. But as the definition of communications expanded, he came to believe that restructuring was the only answer and that the three new parts of AT&T will be even greater than the old whole.

QUESTIONS

1. Discuss the problems that Robert Allen and his reorganizing team have identified. Which problems suggested restructuring? What alternatives might the team have considered? Explain.

2. Create a new AT&T organizational chart based on information given in the case study. Conduct research to find updated information so you can add further areas to the chart. On what principle(s) is this organizational strategy based? Explain.

3. Using information from the text, explain the statement made by one AT&T competitor and customer, Pacific Telesis' Robert I. Barada: "There has always been a cloud in dealing with AT&T. It makes you stop and think when you buy one of their [fiber-optic cable rings], because you know they're installing the same fiber ring in our territory to compete with us. This will take part of that cloud away."

SMALL BUSINESS 2000

Why is it that the structure of all companies is not the same? All companies are not alike. The attitudes of leaders about the span of control that should be assigned to any one manager differs. Additionally, the degree to which a firm's leaders are hands-on versus the degree to which they delegate differs. These, and any number of other variables, influence a company's structure.

Two other factors that may influence a firm's structure are its size and its age. At Urocor, a medical diagnostic company with annual sales of approximately $25 million, size is definitely a variable in determining the organization's structure. Roles and responsibility, delegation, expecting employees at many levels of the company to make decisions, and the characteristics that the company looks for in recruiting employees to the Urocor team, are all affected by the company's size and all affect the way the company is organized. The company currently has about 200 employees, a size that makes a formalized structure and process for managing the company necessary and important.

Urocor has not always been this large. When its current president joined the firm seven years ago, the company only had 12 employees. An early task for the new president was to determine and secure what he thought was an appropriate set of resources needed for the firm to grow. It also appears that he had some idea of how these resources (both equipment and staff) would be organized. Although the firm was not yet very large, its leader was already concerned about how the company would be organized and how it would function. Perhaps that is a large part of why Urocor has grown as fast as it has, and why it is a major player in the medical diagnostics industry.

QUESTIONS

1. Identify some key players at Urocor and describe how you think their roles fit into the overall structure of Urocor.

2. Bill Hagstrom, Urocor's president, discussed his philosophy of individual responsibility and how he expects people to work within the Urocor structure. What do you think of his attitude toward action and decision making? Would you like to work in a company like this? Why or why not?

3. Bill Hagstrom appears to have had a structure in mind before the company realized the sales and growth needed to justify a staff the size it has today. What do you think are some advantages and disadvantages of his doing this?

4. You heard Urocor's president say that he believed that the right management team and right management attitude was more important than a perfect technical base or product. What do you think he means by this? Do you agree?

11

Responsibility, Authority, and Delegation

STUDENT LEARNING OBJECTIVES

From studying this chapter, I will attempt to acquire

1. An understanding of the relationship of responsibility, authority, and delegation

2. Information on how to divide and clarify the job objectives of individuals working within an organization

3. Knowledge of the differences among line authority, staff authority, and functional authority

4. An appreciation for the issues that can cause conflict in line and staff relationships

5. Insights on the value of accountability to the organization

6. An understanding of how to delegate

7. A strategy for eliminating various barriers to delegation

8. A working knowledge of when and how an organization should be decentralized

CHAPTER OUTLINE

Introductory Case: *"Famous" Amos: The Organizing Challenge*

RESPONSIBILITY

Management and the Internet: *Information Systems Job Descriptions Focus More on Internet*
Dividing Job Activities
Clarifying Job Activities of Managers

AUTHORITY
Types of Authority

Ethics Spotlight: *General Electric Staff Organizes Renovation*
Accountability

Diversity Spotlight: *Procter & Gamble's Managers Held Accountable for Advancement of Minorities*

DELEGATION
Steps in the Delegation Process
Obstacles to the Delegation Process
Eliminating Obstacles to the Delegation Process
Centralization and Decentralization

Across Industries: *Publishing—Knight-Ridder Plans to Centralize Foreign Bureaus*

INTRODUCTORY CASE

"Famous" Amos: The Organizing Challenge

REMINDER: THE INTRODUCTORY CASE WRAP-UP (P. 251) CONTAINS DISCUSSION QUESTIONS AND A SKILLS EXERCISE TO FURTHER ILLUSTRATE THE APPLICATION OF CHAPTER CONCEPTS TO THIS VIGNETTE.

Wally "Famous" Amos, a pioneer of the now burgeoning $450-million-a-year gourmet cookie industry, is an entrepreneur who is famous not only for his delicious chocolate chip cookies but for his upbeat take on life as well. This former William Morris Talent Agency employee, the first African American ever hired by the agency to be a talent agent, founded his company in 1975 with $24,000 (in exchange for 25 percent of stock) lent by celebrity friends Helen Reddy, her husband Jeff Wald, and singer Marvin Gaye. Amos had been baking cookies since he was a teenager (his Aunt Della got him started), and he regularly used them as a "hook" to charm the producers and other Hollywood executives he met during his 14 years as an agent. People kept telling Amos he should sell his cookies, but it wasn't until his career as an agent took a downturn that he decided he wanted a more stable business of his own to run.

Amos opened his first store, which an artist friend designed, on Sunset Boulevard. He traded in his tailored suits for Hawaiian-style shirts, baggy pants, and a panama hat. Then he had himself photographed and the image put on each package of Famous Amos cookies. For the opening, he sent out 2,500 invitations to the press, and, as a band played, poured champagne and dispensed cookies to his willing publicity pawns. By the next morning, lines were forming outside his door as people tried to become part of L.A.'s latest media event.

The Famous Amos Chocolate Chip Cookie Company quickly grew to include stores in Santa Monica and Hawaii. The company grossed $300,000 in its first year, $4 million in 1979, and $10 million in 1987. Today "fresh-baked" retail outlets are located across the country, and Famous Amos cookies line the shelves of thousands of grocery stores and supermarkets worldwide. Recently, Amos sold his company to Denver real estate investors and entrepreneurs Jeffrey and Ronald Baer.

The outstanding initial success of Famous Amos Cookies was based primarily on the ability of Wally Amos

The challenge facing the Famous Amos Chocolate Chip Cookie Company is to organize the efforts of employees throughout the company.

to see a market and sell his vision. One of the most pressing challenges management must now meet is professionally managing the company that has evolved. Successfully organizing the efforts of employees throughout the company is a prerequisite to maintaining and expanding the company Wally Amos founded.

While the Baers are busy running his old company, Wally "Famous" Amos is deeply involved in establishing his new venture—Uncle Noname Cookie Company.

What's Ahead

The Introductory Case describes how Wally Amos initiated and built the Famous Amos Cookie Company into a thriving enterprise, which he later sold to Jeffrey and Ronald Baer. The case ends with the implication that the company has gone beyond the fledgling phase and management must now focus on meeting the normal challenges of an established company if it is to continue to prosper. The case indicates that one such challenge is how best to organize the efforts of employees throughout the company. The information in this chapter on organizing the job activities of individuals within an organization should be of great value to managers like the Baers. Three major elements of organizing are presented:

1. Responsibility
2. Authority
3. Delegation

Chapter 10 dealt with applying the principles of organizational structure, division of labor, span of management, and scalar relationships to establish an orderly use of resources within the management system. Productivity in any management system, however, results from specific activities performed by individuals within that organization. An effective organizing effort, therefore, includes not only a rationale for the orderly use of management system resources but also three other elements of organizing that specifically channel the activities of organizational members: responsibility, authority, and delegation.

RESPONSIBILITY

Responsibility is the obligation to perform assigned activities.

Perhaps the most fundamental method of channeling the activity of individuals within an organization, **responsibility** is the obligation to perform assigned activities. It is the self-assumed commitment to handle a job to the best of one's ability. The source of responsibility lies within the individual. A person who accepts a job agrees to carry out a series of duties or activities or to see that someone else carries them out.[1] The act of accepting the job means that the person is obligated to a superior to see that job activities are successfully completed. Because responsibility is an obligation that a person *accepts*, there is no way it can be delegated or passed on to a subordinate.

A **job description** is a list of specific activities that must be performed to accomplish some task or job.

THE JOB DESCRIPTION An individual's job activities within an organization are usually summarized in a formal statement called a **job description**—a list of specific activities that must be performed by whoever holds the position. Unclear job descriptions can confuse employees and may cause them to lose interest in their jobs. On the other hand, a clear job description can help employees to become successful by focusing their efforts on the issues that are important for their position. When properly designed, job descriptions communicate job content to employees, establish performance levels that employees must maintain, and act as a guide that employees should follow to help the organization reach its objectives.[2]

MANAGEMENT AND THE INTERNET

Information Systems Job Descriptions Focus More on Internet

The growth and popularity of the Internet have undeniably changed the way many managers are creating job descriptions for people working in Information Systems (IS) departments. In the past, IS job descriptions have focused mainly on programming. Programs were mostly written to facilitate handling and analyzing data related to various organizational functions. IS personnel were mainly attentive to designing their programs to best help "end users," people inside the organization who normally used the programs and data created by them.

With the growth of the Internet, management is seeing many new and exciting ways for IS personnel to assist in reaching organizational goals. As a result, many new job descriptions are being written to emphasize Internet usage, or existing ones are being changed, reducing the programming focus and emphasizing an Internet focus. This new Internet focus emphasizes not only communicating more closely with customers, but also having employees communicate more efficiently and effectively via Internet e-mail.

Managers are realizing more and more that a high-quality Internet presence is a prerequisite for organizational success. Success is encouraged as IS personnel make organizational information directly available to customers. Products are explained, press releases are posted, and management's views and philosophy are communicated. Success is also encouraged as management reaps the potential rewards of Internet commerce. Conducting business via Internet payments is becoming more commonplace everyday. Organizations that fail to capitalize on Internet opportunities are not only missing an opportunity today, but may be risking their future success if Internet business transactions become a dominant method of transacting business.

Job activities are delegated by management to enhance the accomplishment of management system objectives. Management analyzes its objectives and assigns specific duties that will lead to reaching those objectives. A sound organizing strategy delineates specific job activities for every individual in the organization. Note, however, that as objectives and other conditions within the management system change, so will individual job activities.

The following three areas are related to responsibility:

1. Dividing job activities
2. Clarifying job activities of managers
3. Being responsible

Each of these topics is discussed in the sections that follow.

►DIVIDING JOB ACTIVITIES

Obviously, one person cannot be responsible for performing all of the activities that take place within an organization. Because so many people work within a given management system, organizing necessarily involves dividing job activities among a number of individuals. Some method of distributing these job activities is essential.

THE FUNCTIONAL SIMILARITY METHOD The **functional similarity method** is, according to many management theorists, the most basic method of dividing job activities. Simply stated, the method suggests that management should take four basic interrelated steps to divide job activities in the following sequence:

1. Examine management system objectives
2. Designate appropriate activities that must be performed to reach those objectives
3. Design specific jobs by grouping similar activities
4. Make specific individuals responsible for performing those jobs

Figure 11.1 illustrates this sequence of activities.

> The **functional similarity method** is a method for dividing job activities in the organization.

FUNCTIONAL SIMILARITY AND RESPONSIBILITY At least three additional guides can be used to supplement the functional similarity method.[3] The first of these supplemental guides suggests that overlapping responsibility should be avoided when making

---

FIGURE 11.1   **Sequence of activities for the functional similarity method of dividing job activities**

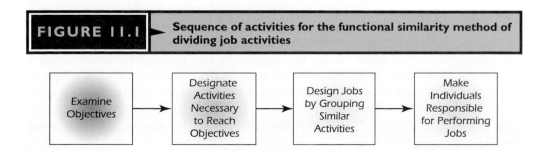

In addition to adopting such practices as just-in-time parts delivery and continuous improvement, General Motors' Adam Opel plant in Eisenach, Germany, has increased productivity by experimenting with new forms of job responsibility. Job applicants, for example, are tested for teamwork abilities and trained specifically in the demands of just-in-time operations. Two-thirds of all employees work in teams, and any individual can stop the assembly line to check or correct a defect in quality.

Overlapping responsibility refers to a situation in which more than one individual is responsible for the same activity.

A responsibility gap exists when certain organizational tasks are not included in the responsibility area of any individual organization member.

job activity divisions. **Overlapping responsibility** refers to a situation in which more than one individual is responsible for the same activity. Generally speaking, only one person should be responsible for completing any one activity. When two or more employees are unclear about who should do a job because of overlapping responsibility, it usually leads to conflict and poor working relationships.[4] Often the job does not get done because each employee assumes the other will do it.

The second supplemental guide suggests that responsibility gaps should be avoided. A **responsibility gap** exists when certain tasks are not included in the responsibility area of any individual organization member. This results in a situation in which nobody within the organization is obligated to perform certain necessary activities.

The third supplemental guide suggests that management should avoid creating job activities for accomplishing tasks that do not enhance goal attainment. Organization members should be obligated to perform *only* those activities that lead to goal attainment.

The absence of clear, goal-related, nonoverlapping responsibilities undermines organizational efficiency and effectiveness.[5]

When job responsibilities are distributed inappropriately, the organization will have both responsibility gaps and overlapping responsibilities.

The effects of responsibility gaps on product quality are obvious, but overlapping responsibilities also impair product quality. When two (or more) employees are uncertain as to who is responsible for a task, four outcomes are possible:

1. One of the two may perform the job. The other may either forget to or choose not to do the job—and neither of these is a desirable outcome for product quality control.
2. Both employees may perform the job. At the least, this results in duplicated effort, which dampens employee morale. At worst, one employee may diminish the value of the other employee's work, resulting in a decrement in product quality.
3. Neither employee may perform the job because each assumed the other would do it.
4. The employees may spend valuable time negotiating each aspect and phase of the job to carefully mesh their job responsibilities, thus minimizing both duplication of effort and responsibility gaps. Though time-consuming, this is actually the most desirable option in terms of product quality.

Note that each of these outcomes negatively affects both product quality and overall productivity.

The Baers face the challenge of organizing the activities of all the people working for the Famous Amos Cookie Company. If the company is to continue to be successful, the managers must derive these activities directly from company objectives. The Baers' specific organizing steps should include analyzing company objectives, outlining specific company activities that must be performed to reach those objectives, designing company jobs by grouping similar activities, and assigning these jobs to company personnel. In taking these steps, the Baers must be careful not to create, or allow, overlapping responsibilities, responsibility gaps, or responsibilities for activities that do not lead directly to goal attainment.

►CLARIFYING JOB ACTIVITIES OF MANAGERS

Clarifying the job activities of managers is even more important than dividing the job activities of nonmanagers because managers affect greater portions of resources within the management system. Responsibility gaps, for instance, usually have a more significant impact on the management system when they relate to managers than when they relate to nonmanagers.

One process used to clarify management job activities "enables each manager to actively participate with his or her superiors, peers, and subordinates in systematically describing the managerial job to be done and then clarifying the role each manager plays in relationship to his or her work group and to the organization."[6] The purpose of this interaction is to ensure that there are no overlaps or gaps in perceived management responsibilities and that managers are performing only those activities that lead to the attainment of management system objectives. Although this process is typically used to clarify the responsibilities of managers, it can also be effective in clarifying the responsibilities of nonmanagers.

MANAGEMENT RESPONSIBILITY GUIDE A specific tool developed to implement this interaction process is the **management responsibility guide,** some version of which is used in most organizations. This guide helps management to describe the various responsibility relationships that exist in the organization and to summarize how the responsibilities of various managers relate to one another.

The seven main organizational responsibility relationships covered by the management responsibility guide are listed in Table 11.1. Once it is decided which of these relationships exist within the organization, the relationships between these responsibilities can be defined.

A **management responsibility guide** is a tool that is used to clarify the responsibilities of various managers in the organization.

TABLE 11.1	► Seven Responsibility Relationships Among Managers, as Used in the Management Responsibility Guide

1. *General Responsibility*—The individual who guides and directs the execution of the function through the person accepting operating responsibility.

2. *Operating Responsibility*—The individual who is directly responsible for the execution of the function.

3. *Specific Responsibility*—The individual who is responsible for executing a specific or limited portion of the function.

4. *Must Be Consulted*—The individual whose area is affected by a decision who must be called on to render advice or relate information before any decision is made or approval is granted. This individual does not, however, make the decision or grant approval.

5. *May Be Consulted*—The individual who may be called on to relate information, render advice, or make recommendations before the action is taken.

6. *Must Be Notified*—The individual who must be notified of any action that has been taken.

7. *Must Approve*—The individual (other than persons holding general and operating responsibility) who must approve or disapprove the decision.

RESPONSIBLE MANAGERS Managers can be described as responsible if they perform the activities they are obligated to perform.[7] Because managers have more impact on an organization than nonmanagers, responsible managers are a prerequisite for management system success. Several studies have shown that responsible management behavior is highly valued by top executives because the responsible manager guides many other individuals within the organization in performing their duties appropriately.

The degree of responsibility that a manager possesses can be determined by appraising the manager on the following four dimensions:

1. Attitude toward and conduct with subordinates
2. Behavior with upper management
3. Behavior with other groups
4. Personal attitudes and values

Table 11.2 summarizes what each of these dimensions entails.

TABLE 11.2 ▶ Four Key Dimensions of Responsible Management Behavior			
Behavior with Subordinates	**Behavior with Upper Management**	**Behavior with Other Groups**	**Personal Attitudes and Values**
Responsible managers—	Responsible managers—	Responsible managers make sure that any gaps between their areas and those of other managers are securely filled.	Responsible managers—
1. Take complete charge of their work groups	1. Accept criticism for mistakes and buffer their groups from excessive criticism		1. Identify with the group
2. Pass praise and credit along to subordinates	2. Ensure that their groups meet management expectations and objectives		2. Put organizational goals ahead of personal desires or activities
3. Stay close to problems and activities			3. Perform tasks for which there is no immediate reward but that help subordinates, the company, or both
4. Take action to maintain productivity and are willing to terminate poor performers if necessary			4. Conserve corporate resources as if the resources were their own

BACK TO THE CASE

In organizing employees' activities, the Baers must recognize, for example, that a department manager's job activities, as well as those of his or her subordinates, are a major factor in the company's success. Because the activities of department managers have an impact on all personnel within the department, these activities must be well defined. In addition, within each company division, all department managers' job activities should be coordinated so that departments do not work at cross-purposes. The Baers might choose to use the management responsibility guide process to achieve this coordination of responsibilities across departments.

Overall, for managers within the Famous Amos Cookie Company to be responsible managers, they must perform the activities they are obligated to perform and respond appropriately to their subordinates, their superiors in the company, and their peers in other departments in the division.

Individuals are assigned job activities to channel their behavior within the organization appropriately. Once they have been given specific assignments, they must be given a commensurate amount of authority to perform those assignments satisfactorily.

Authority is the right to perform or command. It allows its holder to act in certain designated ways and to directly influence the actions of others through orders. It also allows its holder to allocate the organization's resources to achieve organizational objectives.[8]

Authority is the right to perform or command.

AUTHORITY ON THE JOB The following example illustrates the relationship between job activities and authority. Two primary tasks for which a particular service station manager is responsible are pumping gasoline and repairing automobiles. The manager has the authority necessary to perform both of these tasks, or he or she may choose to delegate automobile repair to the assistant manager. Along with the activity of repairing, the assistant should also be delegated the authority to order parts, to command certain attendants to help, and to do anything else necessary to perform repair jobs. Without this authority, the assistant manager may find it impossible to complete the delegated job activities.

Practically speaking, authority merely increases the probability that a specific command will be obeyed.[9] The following excerpt emphasizes that authority does not always exact obedience:[10]

> People who have never exercised power have all kinds of curious ideas about it. The popular notion of top leadership is a fantasy of capricious power: the top man [*or woman*] presses a button and something remarkable happens; he [*or she*] gives an order as the whim strikes him [*or her*], and it is obeyed. Actually, the capricious use of power is relatively rare except in some large dictatorships and some small family firms. Most leaders are hedged around by constraints—tradition, constitutional limitations, the realities of the external situation, rights and privileges of followers, the requirements of teamwork, and most of all, the inexorable demands of large-scale organization, which does not operate on capriciousness. In short, most power is wielded circumspectively.

ACCEPTANCE OF AUTHORITY As chapter 10 showed, the positioning of individuals on an organization chart indicates their relative amount of authority. Those positioned toward the top of the chart possess more authority than those positioned toward the bottom. Chester Barnard writes, however, that the exercise of authority is determined less by formal organizational decree than by acceptance among those under the authority. According to Barnard, authority exacts obedience only when it is accepted.

In line with this rationale, Barnard defines *authority* as the character of communication by which an order is accepted by an individual as governing the actions that individual takes within the system. Barnard maintains that authority will be accepted only under the following conditions:

1. The individual can understand the order being communicated
2. The individual believes the order is consistent with the purpose of the organization
3. The individual sees the order as compatible with his or her personal interests
4. The individual is mentally and physically able to comply with the order

The fewer of these four conditions that are present, the lower the probability that authority will be accepted and obedience be exacted.

Barnard offers some guidance on what managers can do to raise the odds that their commands will be accepted and obeyed. He maintains that more and more of a manager's commands will be accepted over the long term if:[11]

1. The manager uses formal channels of communication and these are familiar to all organization members
2. Each organization member has an assigned formal communication channel through which orders are received
3. The line of communication between manager and subordinate is as direct as possible
4. The complete chain of command is used to issue orders
5. The manager possesses adequate communication skills
6. The manager uses formal communication lines only for organizational business
7. A command is authenticated as coming from a manager

► TYPES OF AUTHORITY

Three main types of authority can exist within an organization:

1. Line authority
2. Staff authority
3. Functional authority

Each type exists only to enable individuals to carry out the different types of responsibilities with which they have been charged.

Line authority consists of the right to make decisions and to give orders concerning the production-, sales-, or finance-related behavior of subordinates.

Staff authority consists of the right to advise or assist those who possess line authority.

LINE AND STAFF AUTHORITY **Line authority,** the most fundamental authority within an organization, reflects existing superior-subordinate relationships. It consists of the right to make decisions and to give orders concerning the production-, sales-, or finance-related behavior of subordinates. In general, line authority pertains to matters directly involving management system production, sales, and finance and, as a result, the attainment of objectives. People directly responsible for these areas within the organization are delegated line authority to assist them in performing their obligated activities.[12]

Whereas line authority involves giving orders concerning production activities, **staff authority** consists of the right to advise or assist those who possess line authority as well as other staff personnel. Staff authority enables those responsible for improving the effectiveness of line personnel to perform their required tasks. Examples of organization members with staff authority are people working in the accounting and human resource departments. Obviously, line and staff personnel must work together closely to maintain the efficiency and effectiveness of the organization. To ensure that line and staff personnel do work together productively, management must make sure both groups understand the organizational mission, have specific objectives, and realize that they are partners in helping the organization reach its objectives.[13]

Size is perhaps the most significant factor in determining whether or not an organization will have staff personnel. Generally speaking, the larger the organization, the greater the need and ability to employ staff personnel. As an organization expands, it usually needs employees with expertise in diversified areas. Although small organizations may also require this kind of diverse expertise, they often find it more practical to hire part-time consultants to provide it as needed than to hire full-time staff personnel, who may not always be kept busy.

LINE-STAFF RELATIONSHIPS Figure 11.2 shows how line-staff relationships can be presented on an organization chart. The plant manager on this chart has line authority over each immediate subordinate—the human resource manager, the production manager, and the sales manager. But the human resource manager has staff authority in relation to the plant manager, meaning the human resource manager possesses the right to advise the plant manager on human resource matters. Still, final decisions concerning human resource matters are in the hands of the plant manager, the person holding line authority. Similar relationships exist between the sales manager and the sales research specialist, as well as between the production manager and the quality control manager.

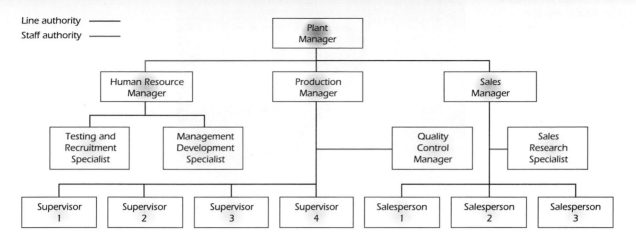

Roles of Staff Personnel   Harold Stieglitz has pinpointed three roles that staff personnel typically perform to assist line personnel:[14]

1. *The advisory or counseling role*—In this role, staff personnel use their professional expertise to solve organizational problems. The staff personnel are, in effect, internal consultants whose relationship with line personnel is similar to that of a professional and a client. For example, the staff quality control manager might advise the line production manager on possible technical modifications to the production process that will enhance the quality of the organization's products.

2. *The service role*—Staff personnel in this role provide services that can more efficiently and effectively be provided by a single centralized staff group than by many individuals scattered throughout the organization. This role can probably best be understood if staff personnel are viewed as suppliers and line personnel as customers. For example, members of a human resource department recruit, employ, and train workers for all organizational departments. In essence, they are the suppliers of workers, and the various organizational departments needing workers are their customers.

3. *The control role*—In this role, staff personnel help establish a mechanism for evaluating the effectiveness of organizational plans. Staff personnel exercising this role are representatives, or agents, of top management.

These three are not the only roles performed by staff personnel, of course, but they are the major ones. In the final analysis, the roles of staff personnel in any organization should be specially designed to best meet the needs of that organization. In some organizations, the same staff people must perform all three major roles.

ETHICS SPOTLIGHT ◄   **General Electric Staff Organizes Renovation**

At General Electric, a social responsibility project was organized and managed by one of GE's staff personnel, Bob Hess, a marketing specialist. As part of a sales meeting, GE salespeople renovated San Diego's Vincent de Paul–Joan Kroc urban center for the homeless. This project was part of a company program in which tired buildings used by worthy nonprofit organizations are selected to be renovated by GE employees. At the beginning of the renovation day at San Diego, GE workers formed teams, each with a captain, a safety expert, and a task expert. In about eight hours, the work teams completed 95 percent of the job, renovating space for 400 beds and preparing space for 200 additional beds.

The renovation program at General Electric reflects a very progressive management attitude. Through staff activities, the company has been able to demonstrate its desire and ability to make a worthwhile contribution to society.

Sheldon Laube became chief technologist—a staff position that ranks among the 20 most senior management jobs—at the accounting firm of Price Waterhouse in 1989. His first assignment: Make the firm's technology state-of-the-art. The screen in the background—on which each icon corresponds to a database that can be shared with 18,000 other people—is what Laube sees when he boots his computer.

Conflict in Line-Staff Relationships Most management practitioners readily admit that a noticeable amount of organizational conflict centers around line-staff relationships.[15] From the viewpoint of line personnel, conflict is created because staff personnel tend to assume line authority, do not give sound advice, steal credit for success, fail to keep line personnel informed of their activities, and do not see the whole picture. From the viewpoint of staff personnel, conflict is created because line personnel do not make proper use of staff personnel, resist new ideas, and refuse to give staff personnel enough authority to do their jobs.

Staff personnel can often avert line-staff conflicts if they strive to emphasize the objectives of the organization as a whole, encourage and educate line personnel in the appropriate use of staff personnel, obtain any necessary skills they do not already possess, and deal intelligently with resistance to change rather than view it as an immovable barrier. Line personnel can do their part to minimize line-staff conflict by using staff personnel wherever possible, making proper use of the staff abilities, and keeping staff personnel appropriately informed.[16]

BACK TO THE CASE

Assuming that a main objective of the Famous Amos Cookie Company is to produce the highest quality cookie possible, Famous Amos' personnel who are directly responsible for achieving this objective should possess line authority to perform their responsibilities. For example, individuals responsible for purchasing ingredients for the cookies must be given the right to do everything necessary to obtain ingredients that will result in the best possible cookies.

Famous Amos may need to hire one or more individuals to assist line personnel. Perhaps these staff personnel could be responsible for advising Famous Amos' management on such issues as how consumers rate Famous Amos Cookies relative to a competitor's product (Mrs. Fields' Cookies, for example) and on how employees should be trained to become more productive. Staff responsible for advising line personnel should be delegated the authority to do so.

As in all organizations, the potential for conflict between line personnel and staff personnel would be significant. Famous Amos Cookie Company's management should be aware of this potential and encourage both line and staff personnel to strive to minimize it.

Functional authority consists of the right to give orders within a segment of the management system in which the right is normally nonexistent.

FUNCTIONAL AUTHORITY **Functional authority** consists of the right to give orders within a segment of the organization in which this right is normally nonexistent. This authority is usually assigned to individuals to complement the line or staff authority they already possess. Functional authority generally covers only specific task areas and is operational only for

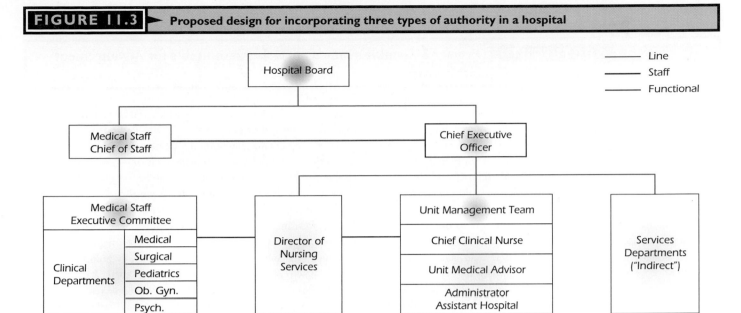

PROPOSED LARGE HOSPITAL ORGANIZATION
AUTHORITY AND RELATIONSHIPS

designated amounts of time. Typically, it is possessed by individuals who, in order to meet responsibilities in their own areas, must be able to exercise some control over organization members in other areas.

The vice president for finance in an organization is an example of someone with functional authority. Among his or her basic responsibilities is the obligation to monitor the financial situation of the whole management system. To do so requires having appropriate financial information continually flowing in from various segments of the organization. The vice president for finance, therefore, is usually delegated the functional authority to order various departments to furnish the kinds and amounts of information he or she needs to perform an analysis. In effect, this functional authority allows the vice president for finance to give orders to personnel within departments in which he or she normally cannot give orders.

From this discussion of line authority, staff authority, and functional authority, it is logical to conclude that although authority can exist within an organization in various forms, these forms should be used in a combination that will best enable individuals to carry out their assigned responsibilities and thereby best help the management system accomplish its objectives. When trying to decide on an optimal authority combination for a particular organization, managers should be aware that each type of authority has both advantages and disadvantages. The organization chart illustrated in Figure 11.3 shows how the three types of authority could be combined for the overall benefit of a hospital management system.

▶ ACCOUNTABILITY

Accountability refers to the management philosophy whereby individuals are held liable, or accountable, for how well they use their authority and live up to their responsibility of performing predetermined activities.[17] The concept of accountability implies that if an individual does not perform predetermined activities, some type of penalty, or punishment, is justifiable. The punishment theme of accountability has been summed up by one company executive: "Individuals who do not perform well simply will not be around too long."[18] The accountability concept also implies that some kind of reward will follow if predetermined activities are performed well.

Accountability refers to the management philosophy whereby individuals are held liable, or accountable, for how well they use their authority or live up to their responsibility of performing predetermined activities.

Organizations commonly hold their managers accountable for performance issues such as earning higher profits, developing new products, and keeping work environments safe. At Procter & Gamble (P&G), managers are also held accountable for a more rarely used performance variable: the advancement of minority workers.

Edwin L. Artzt, P&G's chairman, aims to build a tougher, faster, more global organization, and believes that the company must be able to harness the energies of a diverse workforce if this objective is to be accomplished. Hence Artzt has instituted a system to track minority employees' advancement and to hold managers accountable for their progress. P&G's participative approach to decision making, use of teams to accomplish company projects, and formulation and assignment of company goals will be useful only if the company is successful in building its workforce—which will inevitably become progressively more diverse—into a productive, dedicated work unit.

Diversity is not the only accountability issue at P&G. Artzt is taking other steps to build a faster, tougher company—demanding, for example, that his managers consistently beat the competition to market with the latest products. Many inside the company think that Artzt is pushing this first-to-market agenda too hard. He is also being criticized for focusing too much on short-term financial results, which some contend works against building a truly faster, tougher company. Artzt can easily counter this criticism, however, by pointing to his record on new-product development. In gearing Procter & Gamble to the longer term, Artzt spent $400 million in one recent year on developing new products—up 50 percent from previous yearly averages.

BACK TO THE CASE

Functional authority and accountability are two additional factors that the Baers must consider when organizing employee activities within the Famous Amos Cookie Company. Some employees may have to be given functional authority to supplement the line or staff authority they already possess. For example, the accountant, a staff person who advises management on financial affairs, may need to gather financial results of various company retail outlets throughout the country. Functional authority would enable individuals on the accountant's staff to command that this information be channeled to them.

In organizing employee activity, the Baers should also stress the concept of accountability—that living up to assigned responsibilities will bring rewards, while not living up to them will bring negative consequences.

DELEGATION

Delegation is the process of assigning job activities and related authority to specific individuals in the organization.

So far in this chapter we have discussed responsibility and authority as complementary factors that channel activity within the organization. **Delegation** is the actual process of assigning job activities and corresponding authority to specific individuals within the organization. This section focuses on the following topics:

1. Steps in the delegation process
2. Obstacles to the delegation process
3. Elimination of obstacles to the delegation process
4. Centralization and decentralization

STEPS IN THE DELEGATION PROCESS

According to Newman and Warren, the delegation process consists of three steps, all of which may be either observable or implied.[19] The first step is assigning specific duties to the individual. In all cases, the manager must be sure that the subordinate assigned to specific duties has a clear understanding of what these duties entail. Whenever possible, the activities should be stated in operational terms so the subordinate knows exactly what action must be taken to perform the as-

TABLE 11.3	► Guidelines for Making Delegation Effective

► Give employees freedom to pursue tasks in their own way

► Establish mutually agreed upon results and performance standards for delegated tasks

► Encourage employees to take an active role in defining, implementing, and communicating progress on tasks

► Entrust employees with completion of whole projects or tasks whenever possible

► Explain the relevance of delegated tasks to larger projects or to department or organization goals

► Give employees the authority necessary to accomplish tasks

► Allow employees access to all information, people, and departments necessary to perform delegated task

► Provide training and guidance necessary for employees to complete delegated tasks satisfactorily

► When possible, delegate tasks on the basis of employee interests

signed duties. The second step of the delegation process involves granting appropriate authority to the subordinate—that is, the subordinate must be given the right and power within the organization to accomplish the duties assigned. The last step involves creating the obligation for the subordinate to perform the duties assigned. The subordinate must be aware of the responsibility to complete the duties assigned and must accept that responsibility. Table 11.3 offers several guidelines that managers can follow to ensure the success of the delegation process.

►OBSTACLES TO THE DELEGATION PROCESS

Obstacles that can make delegation within an organization difficult or even impossible can be classified into three general categories:.

1. Obstacles related to the supervisor
2. Obstacles related to subordinates
3. Obstacles related to organizations

An example of the first category is the supervisor who resists delegating his authority to subordinates because he cannot bear to part with any authority. The cartoon below depicts a different sort of manager—one who delegates simply because he enjoys exercising the power to do so. Two other supervisor-related obstacles are the fear that subordinates will not do a job well and the suspicion that surrendering some authority may be seen as a sign of weakness.

Wall Street Journal, *March 9, 1990, A13.*

Moreover, if supervisors are insecure in their jobs or believe certain activities are extremely important to their personal success, they may find it hard to put the performance of these activities into the hands of others.

Supervisors who do wish to delegate to subordinates may encounter several subordinate-related roadblocks. First, subordinates may be reluctant to accept delegated authority because they are afraid of failing, lack self-confidence, or feel the supervisor doesn't have confidence in them.[20] These obstacles will be especially apparent in subordinates who have never before used delegated authority. Other subordinate-related obstacles are the fear that the supervisor will be unavailable for guidance when needed and the reluctance to exercise authority that may complicate comfortable working relationships.

Characteristics of the organization itself may also make delegation difficult. For example, a very small organization may present the supervisor with only a minimal number of activities to be delegated. In organizations where few job activities and little authority have been delegated in the past, an attempt to initiate the delegation process may make employees reluctant and apprehensive, for the supervisor would be introducing a significant change in procedure and change is often strongly resisted.

►ELIMINATING OBSTACLES TO THE DELEGATION PROCESS

Since delegation has significant advantages for the organization, eliminating obstacles to the delegation process is important to managers. Among the advantages of delegation are enhanced employee confidence, improved subordinate involvement and interest, more free time for the supervisor to accomplish tasks, and, as the organization gets larger, assistance from subordinates in completing tasks the manager simply wouldn't have time for otherwise. True, there are potential disadvantages to delegation—such as the possibility that the manager will lose track of the progress of a delegated task—but the potential advantages of some degree of delegation generally outweigh the potential disadvantages.[21]

What can managers do to eliminate obstacles to the delegation process? First of all, they must continually strive to uncover any obstacles to delegation that exist in their organization. Then they should approach taking action to eliminate these obstacles with the understanding that the obstacles may be deeply ingrained and therefore require much time and effort to overcome. Among the most effective managerial actions that can be taken to eliminate obstacles to delegation are building subordinate confidence in the use of delegated authority, minimizing the impact of delegated authority on established working relationships, and helping delegatees cope with problems whenever necessary.[22]

Koontz, O'Donnell, and Weihrich believe that overcoming the obstacles to delegation requires certain critical characteristics in managers. These characteristics include the willingness to consider the ideas of others seriously, the insight to allow subordinates the free rein necessary to carry out their responsibilities, trust in the abilities of subordinates, and the wisdom to allow people to learn from their mistakes without suffering unreasonable penalties for making them.[23]

BACK TO THE CASE

To delegate effectively within the Famous Amos Cookie Company, managers must assign specific duties to individuals, grant them corresponding authority, and create in them the awareness that they are obligated to perform these activities.

In encouraging the use of delegation within their company, the Baers must be aware that managers, subordinates, and departments may all present obstacles to the delegation process. They must strongly encourage managers to meet the delegation challenge—that is, to discover which delegation obstacles exist within their work environments and then take steps to eliminate them. If Famous Amos' managers are to be successful delegators, they must be willing to consider the ideas of their subordinates, allow them the free rein necessary to perform their assigned tasks, trust them, and help them learn from their mistakes without suffering unreasonable penalties.

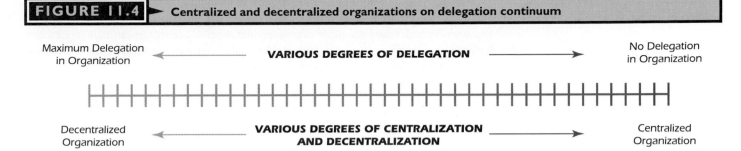

Maximum Delegation in Organization ◀——— **VARIOUS DEGREES OF DELEGATION** ———▶ No Delegation in Organization

Decentralized Organization ◀——— **VARIOUS DEGREES OF CENTRALIZATION AND DECENTRALIZATION** ———▶ Centralized Organization

▶ CENTRALIZATION AND DECENTRALIZATION

There are noticeable differences from organization to organization in the relative number of job activities and the relative amount of authority delegated to subordinates. This difference is seldom a case of delegation existing in one organization and not existing in another. Rather, the difference is degree of delegation.

The terms **centralization** and **decentralization** describe the general degree to which delegation exists within an organization. They can be visualized as opposite ends of the delegation continuum depicted in Figure 11.4. It is apparent from this figure that centralization implies that a minimal number of job activities and a minimal amount of authority have been delegated to subordinates by management, whereas decentralization implies the opposite.

The issues practicing managers usually face are determining whether to further decentralize an organization and, if that course of action is advisable, deciding how to decentralize.[24] The section that follows presents practical suggestions on both issues.

Centralization refers to the situation in which a minimal number of job activities and a minimal amount of authority are delegated to subordinates.

Decentralization refers to the situation in which a significant number of job activities and a maximum amount of authority are delegated to subordinates.

ACROSS INDUSTRIES ◀ Publishing

KNIGHT-RIDDER PLANS TO CENTRALIZE FOREIGN BUREAUS

Knight-Ridder is a publishing company that engages in newspaper publishing with products in print and on-line around the world. The company publishes 31 daily newspapers in 28 U.S. markets, maintains 34 associated Web sites, and operates news bureaus in locations like Brazil, Colombia, Nicaragua, and Mexico.

The purpose of the bureaus is to provide news from their regions, that can be published in all Knight-Ridder papers. The bureau system was created within the company about 20 years ago and has been run as a decentralized operating unit in an attempt to make operations more efficient. The largest newspapers in the Knight-Ridder group were established as "host" newspapers to loosely oversee one or more bureaus. As examples, the *San Jose Mercury News* runs bureaus in Tokyo and Mexico City while the *Detroit Free Press* runs bureaus in Warsaw and Zimbabwe.

Recently, a problem has arisen with this decentralized structure. Bureaus have become extensions of their host newspapers, writing stories with a slant for host newspaper communities rather than for all Knight-Ridder newspapers. As a result, less bureau material is being published by multiple newspapers than in the past. To eliminate this problem, management plans to establish a more centralized bureau system wherein procedures for choosing, writing, and evaluating articles are more uniform across all company bureaus.

DECENTRALIZING AN ORGANIZATION: A CONTINGENCY VIEWPOINT

The appropriate degree of decentralization for an organization depends on the unique situation of that organization. Some specific questions managers can use to determine the amount of decentralization appropriate for a situation are as follows:

1. *What is the present size of the organization?* As noted earlier, the larger the organization, the greater the likelihood that decentralization will be advantageous. As an organization increases in size, managers have to assume more and more responsibility and different types of tasks. Delegation is typically an effective means of helping them manage this increased workload.

In some cases, however, top management will conclude that the organization is actually too large and decentralized. One signal that an organization is too large is labor costs that are very high relative to other organizational expenses. In this instance, increased centralization of certain organizational activities could reduce the need for some workers and thereby lower labor costs to a more acceptable level.[25]

2. *Where are the organization's customers located?* As a general rule, the more physically separated the organization's customers are, the more viable a significant amount of decentralization is. Decentralization places appropriate management resources close to customers and thereby makes quick customer service possible. J.C. Penney, for example, decentralized its purchasing activities to give its managers the ability to buy merchandise best suited to the customers of their individual stores.[26]

3. *How homogeneous is the organization's product line?* Generally, as the product line becomes more heterogeneous, or diversified, the appropriateness of decentralization increases. Different kinds of decisions, talents, and resources are needed to manufacture different products. Decentralization usually minimizes the confusion that can result from diversification by separating organizational resources by product and keeping pertinent decision making close to the manufacturing process.

4. *Where are organizational suppliers?* The location of raw materials needed to manufacture the organization's products is another important consideration. Time loss and high transportation costs associated with shipping raw materials over great distances from supplier to manufacturer could signal the need to decentralize certain functions.

    For example, the wood necessary to manufacture a certain type of bedroom set may be available only from tree growers in certain northern states. If the bedroom set in question is an important product line for a furniture company and if the costs of transporting the lumber are substantial, a decision to decentralize may be a sound one. The effect of this decision would probably be building a plant that produces only bedroom sets in a northern state close to where the necessary wood is readily available. The advantages of such a costly decision, of course, would accrue to the organization only over the long term.

5. *Is there a need for quick decisions in the organization?* If speedy decision making is essential, a considerable amount of decentralization is probably in order. Decentralization cuts red tape and allows the subordinate to whom authority has been delegated to make on-the-

Some management functions can be delegated, others cannot. This supervisor retains the overall responsibility to ensure continued high quality of the uniforms produced in his department, although he may delegate the responsibility to monitor, for instance, the correct placement of buttons or the neatness of the finishing.

spot decisions when necessary. It goes without saying that this delegation is advisable only if the potential delegatees have the ability to make sound decisions. If they don't, faster decision making results in no advantage for the organization. Quite the contrary, the organization may find itself saddled with the effects of unsound decisions.

6. *Is creativity a desirable feature of the organization?* If creativity is desirable, then some decentralization is advisable, for decentralization allows delegatees the freedom to find better ways of doing things. The mere existence of this freedom encourages the incorporation of new and more creative techniques within the task process.[27]

DECENTRALIZATION AT MASSEY-FERGUSON: A CLASSIC EXAMPLE Positive decentralization is decentralization that is advantageous for the organization in which it is being implemented; negative decentralization is disadvantageous for the organization. To see how an organization should be decentralized, it is worthwhile to study a classic example of an organization that achieved positive decentralization: Massey-Ferguson.[28]

Guidelines for Decentralization Massey-Ferguson is a worldwide farm equipment manufacturer that has enjoyed noticeable success with decentralization over the past several years. The company has three guidelines for determining the degree of decentralization of decision making that is appropriate for a situation:

1. The competence to make decisions must be possessed by the person to whom authority is delegated. A derivative of this principle is that the superior must have confidence in the subordinate to whom authority is delegated.
2. Adequate and reliable information pertinent to the decision is required by the person making the decision. Decision-making authority therefore cannot be pushed below the point at which all information bearing on the decision is available.
3. If a decision affects more than one unit of the enterprise, the authority to make the decision must rest with the manager accountable for the most units affected by the decision.

Delegation as a Frame of Mind Massey-Ferguson also encourages a definite attitude toward decentralization in its managers. The company's organization manual indicates that delegation is not delegation in name only but a frame of mind that includes both what a supervisor says to subordinates and the way the supervisor acts toward them. Managers at Massey-Ferguson are prodded to allow subordinates to make a reasonable number of mistakes and to help them learn from these mistakes.

Complementing Centralization Another feature of the positive decentralization at Massey-Ferguson is that decentralization is complemented by centralization:

> The organization plan that best serves our total requirements is a blend of centralized and decentralized elements. Marketing and manufacturing responsibilities, together with supporting service functions, are located as close as possible to local markets. Activities that determine the long-range character of the company, such as the planning and control of the product line, the planning and control of facilities and money, and the planning of the strategy to react to changes in the patterns of international trade, are highly centralized.

Thus, Massey-Ferguson management recognizes that decentralization is not necessarily an either/or decision and uses the strengths of both centralization and decentralization to its advantage.

Management Responsibilities Not all activities at Massey-Ferguson are eligible for decentralization. Only management is allowed to follow through on the following responsibilities:

1. Responsibility for determining the overall objectives of the enterprise
2. Responsibility for formulating the policies that guide the enterprise
3. Final responsibility for control of the business within the total range of the objectives and policies, including control over any changes in the nature of the business
4. Responsibility for product design where a product decision affects more than one area of accountability

5. Responsibility for planning for achievement of overall objectives and for measuring actual performance against those plans
6. Final approval of corporate plans or budgets
7. Decisions pertaining to availability and application of general company funds
8. Responsibility for capital investment plans

BACK TO THE CASE

Centralization implies that few job activities and little authority have been delegated to subordinates; decentralization implies that many job activities and much authority have been delegated. Managers within the Famous Amos Cookie Company will have to determine the best degree of delegation for their individual situations. For guidelines, they can use the rules of thumb that greater degrees of delegation become appropriate as departments become larger, as retail outlets become more dispersed and diversified, and as the need for quick decision making and creativity increases.

Massey-Ferguson's experience with decentralization provides many valuable insights on what characteristics the decentralization process within the Famous Amos Cookie Company should assume. First, Famous Amos' managers should use definite guidelines in deciding whether their situation warrants more decentralization. In general, additional delegation would be warranted within the company as the competence of subordinates increases, as Famous Amos managers' confidence in their subordinates increases, and as more adequate and reliable decision-making information becomes available to subordinates. For delegation to be advantageous for the Famous Amos Cookie Company, managers must help subordinates learn from their mistakes. Depending on their situations, individual Famous Amos' managers may want to consider supplementing decentralization with centralization.

For updated information on the topics in this chapter, Internet exercises, links to related Internet sites, an interactive study guide, and more, visit our companion Web site at

http://www.prenhall.com/certo

Additional information can be found on the inside front and back covers of this text.

ACTION SUMMARY

Reread the learning objectives below. Each objective is followed by questions. Answering these questions accurately will help you retain the most important concepts discussed in this chapter. After answering each question, check your answer against the answer key at the end of this chapter. (*Hint:* If you have any doubts regarding the correct response, consult the page number that follows the answer.)

Circle: From studying this chapter, I will attempt to acquire

1. An understanding of the relationship of responsibility, authority, and delegation.

T F   a. Responsibility is a person's self-assumed commitment to handle a job to the best of his or her ability.

a b c d e   b. The following element is *not* an integral part of an effective organizing effort: (a) rationale for the orderly use of management system resources (b) responsibility (c) authority (d) delegation (e) none of the above (they are all important).

2. Information on how to divide and clarify the job activities of individuals working within an organization.

a b c d e
    a. The following is *not* one of the four basic steps for dividing responsibility by the functional similarity method: (a) designing specific jobs by grouping similar activities (b) examining management system objectives (c) formulating management system objectives (d) designating appropriate activities that must be performed to reach objectives (e) making specific individuals responsible for performing activities.

a b c d e
    b. A management responsibility guide can assist organization members in the following way: (a) by describing the various responsibility relationships that exist in their organization (b) by summarizing how the responsibilities of various managers within the organization relate to one another (c) by identifying manager work experience (d) a and b (e) none of the above.

3. Knowledge of the differences among line authority, staff authority, and functional authority.

a b c d e
    a. The production manager has mainly: (a) functional authority (b) staff authority (c) line authority (d) a and c (e) all of the above.

T F
    b. An example of functional authority is the vice president of finance being delegated the authority to order various departments to furnish him or her with the kinds and amounts of information needed to perform an analysis.

4. An appreciation for the issues that can cause conflict in line and staff relationships.

a b c d e
    a. From the viewpoint of staff personnel, a major reason for line-staff conflict is that line personnel: (a) do not make proper use of staff personnel (b) resist new ideas (c) do not give staff personnel enough authority (d) a and c (e) all of the above.

a b c d e
    b. From the viewpoint of line personnel, a major reason for line-staff conflict is that staff personnel: (a) assume line authority (b) do not offer sound advice (c) steal credit for success (d) fail to keep line personnel informed (e) all of the above.

5. Insights on the value of accountability to the organization.

T F
    a. Accountability refers to how well individuals live up to their responsibility for performing predetermined activities.

a b c d e
    b. Rewarding employees for good performance is most closely related to: (a) simplicity (b) a clear division of authority (c) centralization (d) decentralization (e) accountability.

6. An understanding of how to delegate.

T F
    a. The correct ordering of steps in the delegation process is: assignment of duties, creation of responsibility, and granting of authority.

a b c d e
    b. The following are obstacles to the delegation process: (a) obstacles related to supervisors (b) obstacles related to subordinates (c) obstacles related to the organization (d) all of the above (e) none of the above.

> **INTRODUCTORY CASE WRAP-UP** ◄

CASE DISCUSSSION QUESTIONS

❝❝❝**F**amous' Amos: The Organizing Challenge" (p. 233) and its related Back-to-the-Case sections were written to help you better understand the management concepts contained in this chapter. Answer the following discussion questions about this Introductory Case to enrich your understanding of the chapter content:

1. What first step would you recommend that the Baers take in organizing the activities of individuals within their company? Why?
2. Discuss the roles of responsibility, authority, and accountability in organizing the activities of individuals within Famous Amos.
3. At this time, do you think that the company should be more centralized or more decentralized? Why?

SKILLS EXERCISE: MANAGING LINE AND STAFF PERSONNEL

The Introductory Case ends with Wally Amos establishing his new Uncle Noname Cookie company. List two *line* positions and two *staff* positions that you think should exist in the new company. Describe the responsibility(ies) and authority that you think would characterize each position. What steps would you take to minimize conflict between the line and staff personnel?

1. What is responsibility, and why is it so important in organizations?
2. Explain the process a manager would go through to divide responsibility within an organization.
3. What is a management responsibility guide, and how is it used?
4. List and summarize the four main dimensions of responsible management behavior.
5. What is authority, and why is it so important in organizations?
6. Describe the relationship between responsibility and authority.
7. Explain Barnard's notion of authority and acceptance.
8. What steps can managers take to increase the probability that subordinates will accept their authority? Be sure to explain how each of these steps increases that probability.
9. Summarize the relationship that exists between line and staff personnel in most organizations.

10. Explain three roles that staff personnel can perform in organizations.
11. List five possible causes of conflict in line-staff relationships and suggest appropriate action to minimize the effect of these causes.
12. What is functional authority?
13. Give an example of how functional authority actually works in an organization.
14. Compare the relative advantages and disadvantages of line, staff, and functional authority.
15. What is accountability?
16. Define *delegation* and list the steps of the delegation process.
17. List three obstacles to the delegation process and suggest actions for eliminating them.
18. What is the relationship between delegation and decentralization?
19. What is the difference between decentralization and centralization?

1. **a.** T, p. 234
   b. e, p. 234
2. **a.** c, p. 235
   b. d, p. 237

3. **a.** c, p. 240
   b. T, pp. 242–243
4. **a.** e, p. 242
   b. e, p. 242

5. **a.** F, p. 243
   b. e, p. 243

6. **a.** F, pp. 244–245
   b. d, p. 245

CASE STUDY: Change Agents in Midstream

In today's fast-paced business world, companies need managers who can channel the activities of organization members through efforts that include responsibility, authority, and delegation. Companies that handle these tasks well will very likely see dramatic increases in speed, productivity, and profits.

Unfortunately, middle managers who have the skills to navigate the rapids of change associated with technology shifts, more sophisticated customers, and ever-growing competitors are often unrecognized by top executives, who often prefer more traditional managers. This fact seems to be true even though the consequence of "business as usual" may be failure to accomplish important company objectives.

Top managers must learn to recognize effective change leaders in their company. In a study of middle-manager change agents at organizations from Compaq Computer to the New York City Transit Authority, McKinsey & Company director Jon R. Katzenbach concluded that the most sought-after person in today's workplace is a new breed of middle manager—a focused, determined "maverick" who is willing to break rules if necessary to carry out responsibilities delegated by upper management.

According to Katzenbach, change agents tend to be between 25 and 40 years old and may be either men or women. (In the McKinsey study, about a third of the change agents identified were women.) As a rule, they are more flexible than ordinary general managers and much more people-oriented. In addition, they balance several abilities:

1. They are technically skilled and have the ability to develop and employ personal relationships very successfully

2. They are tough decision makers who are highly disciplined about performance results

3. They are capable of energizing people and getting them to focus on one agenda, often finding ways to get more out of people than might be expected

Typically, however, change leaders are rarely viewed by top management as high-potential company leaders. Katzenbach quoted one CEO as saying, "These are the funny little fat guys with thick glasses who always get the job done." Why does this perception prevail? For one thing, change agents usually do not come out of company training programs or standard business schools. Rather, they are often engineers, accountants, or production-line workers. Generally, they are not found in more traditional organizations dominated by strong role models. They are people who have figured out how to get jobs done by themselves, often by fighting their way out of tough situations. The best of them have developed skills that many more conventional managers simply do not have.

One of the outstanding traits of change agents is the ability to deploy more than one leadership style. They will use whatever works in an existing situation, especially if it helps them get more out of their people. Generally speaking, managers want more than rising financial numbers. Often their greatest satisfaction comes from getting people to do more than they thought they could. Therefore, change leaders like to use custom measurements that determine both customer and employee reactions. In addition, they instinctively look to people in front-line jobs for help and are generous in sharing the rewards of accomplishment.

Change leaders are also hungry for information from the marketplace. Because they want the facts badly, they will not wait for the system to deliver them. Instead, they go out and get direct feedback from customers and competitors. In turn, they use their findings to motivate their employees, firing up their desire to beat the competition and increase their own bottom lines—namely, higher salaries and greater job security.

Finally, change leaders tend to be problem solvers by nature. And they are more motivated by the results of their solutions than by the recognition those solutions may bring them. They really like delivering results, getting people to stretch. Once they have accomplished one assignment, they want to plunge into another. Over time, they become so confident of their own skills that they are free to focus on results rather than job security.

Katzenbach is quick to point out that a company needs a good mix of managers—from change leaders, who shake things up, to traditional managers who keep things under control. Both, he emphasizes, are needed in today's global business environment.

QUESTIONS

1. Explain how change leaders, as described by Jon Katzenbach, might handle the problems of responsibility gaps and overlapping responsibility.

2. Create job descriptions to suit the talents of a change leader. How would these differ from job descriptions for a more traditional manager? Use this comparison to explain Katzenbach's finding that the people identified as potential change leaders in a company were definitely not the same as the people identified as "high-potential" leaders.

3. Describe the different sources of authority that change agents use to motivate their people. For example, change agents derive authority from their positions of command and from the relationships that they have with their people. On what other sources do they depend for authority?

4. How do change agents measure accountability? Explain. Is this practice realistic? How does it differ from the norm? Why is it important to a company?

12

Managing Human Resources

STUDENT LEARNING OBJECTIVES

From studying this chapter, I will attempt to acquire

1. An overall understanding of how appropriate human resources can be provided for the organization

2. An appreciation for the relationship among recruitment efforts, an open position, sources of human resources, and the law

3. Insights on the use of tests and assessment centers in employee selection

4. An understanding of how the training process operates

5. A concept of what performance appraisals are and how they can best be conducted

CHAPTER OUTLINE

Introductory Case: *Northwestern Mutual Life Focuses on Recruitment*

DEFINING APPROPRIATE HUMAN RESOURCES

STEPS IN PROVIDING HUMAN RESOURCES
Recruitment

Management and the Internet: *Texas Instruments Uses the Web to Recruit Engineers*

People Spotlight: *NationsBank Helps Women Employees with Child Care*
Selection

Global Spotlight: *Compaq Computer Company's International Selection Slip-Ups*
Training

Across Industries: *Furniture Manufacturing—Training Is Critical at Keller Manufacturing*
Performance Appraisal

REMINDER: THE INTRODUCTORY CASE WRAP-UP (P. 274) CONTAINS DISCUSSION QUESTIONS AND A SKILLS EXERCISE TO FURTHER ILLUSTRATE THE APPLICATION OF CHAPTER CONCEPTS TO THIS VIGNETTE.

Northwestern Mutual Life is a Milwaukee-based insurance company. The company specializes in life and disability insurance and is the nation's sixth largest insurer with over $63 billion in assets. The company's major competitors include John Hancock Mutual Life, Aetna, and Prudential Insurance of America.

Since 1983, *Fortune* magazine has annually surveyed senior executives, outside directors, and securities analysts of the nation's largest companies to determine the most admired company in their industry based on eight key attributes of reputation. They are innovativeness, quality of management, employee talent, quality of products/services, long-term investment value, financial soundness, social responsibility, and use of corporate assets. Each year, Northwestern Mutual has been rated first in the life insurance industry.

Despite Northwestern Mutual's outstanding reputation, recruiting good employees is a major challenge and concern. The company is finding it very difficult to attract new, good people. This difficulty, however, is being experienced throughout the insurance industry. John Sheaffer, assistant director of career recruitment at Northwestern Mutual believes that it takes as many as 20 to 40 referrals to lead to one new prospect.

Sheaffer recently decided to concentrate on solving this recruitment problem at Northwestern Mutual. He established a committee for recruitment improvement and included Michael Van Grinsven, a commercial life underwriter and assistant director of campus recruitment; Blaise Beaulier, manager of systems development; and Laura Schmidt, project manager. The initial focus of the group was to automate the recruitment process. To start, the company's recruitment data was stored on a mainframe computer and was retrievable. Each area of the company, however, maintained its own manual recruitment tracking system, and people were reluctant to use the centralized mainframe system. Overall, the results of the mainframe-based recruiting were somewhat disappointing.

Next, the company began developing an Internet-based recruiting process. Following this process, prospec-

Northwestern Mutual recently focused on tackling the challenge of recruiting outstanding employees and agents. One of its initiatives revolves around an Internet-based qualifying exam. Those who pass are interviewed by the Northwestern recruiter closest to their home and the results are e-mailed to the home office.

tive recruits who enter Northwestern Mutual's recruitment Web site register and take a qualifying exam. Registrant demographic information and test scores are then automatically and electronically forwarded to the Northwestern Mutual home office. Information on the acceptable registrants is then e-mailed from the home office to company recruiters located in areas closest to the candidates. Recruiters interview candidates and then communicate interview results back to the home office via e-mail from their laptop computers. Depending upon the results of the field interview, the recruitment process of a candidate is either continued or terminated.

Northwestern Mutual's management is certainly excited about the potential of the company's new Internet-based recruitment process. As the process is used, improvements will undoubtedly be made to increase efficiency and effectiveness.

The Introductory Case discusses an intense effort by John Sheaffer and others at Northwestern Mutual to recruit good new people. The task of recruiting and hiring not just any people, but the *right* people is part of managing human resources in an organization. This chapter outlines that process of managing human resources within an organization and illustrates how recruiting and ultimately hiring the right people fit within this process.

The emphasis in chapter 11 was on organizing the activity of individuals within the management system. To this end, responsibility, authority, and delegation were discussed in detail. This chapter continues to explore the relationship between individuals and organizing by discussing how appropriate human resources can be provided for the organization.[1]

DEFINING APPROPRIATE HUMAN RESOURCES

Appropriate human resources are the individuals in the organization who make a valuable contribution to management system goal attainment.

The phrase **appropriate human resources** refers to the individuals within the organization who make a valuable contribution to management system goal attainment. This contribution results from their productivity in the positions they hold. The phrase *inappropriate human resources* refers to organization members who do not make a valuable contribution to the attainment of management system objectives. For one reason or another, these individuals are ineffective in their jobs.

Productivity in all organizations is determined by how human resources interact and combine to use all other management system resources. Such factors as background, age, job-related experience, and level of formal education all play a role in determining how appropriate the individual is for the organization. Although the process of providing appropriate human resources for the organization is involved and somewhat subjective, the following section offers insights on how to increase the success of this process.

STEPS IN PROVIDING HUMAN RESOURCES

To provide appropriate human resources to fill both managerial and nonmanagerial openings, managers follow four sequential steps:[2]

1. Recruitment
2. Selection
3. Training
4. Performance appraisal

Figure 12.1 illustrates these steps.

▶ RECRUITMENT

Recruitment is the initial attraction and screening of the supply of prospective human resources available to fill a position.

Recruitment is the initial attraction and screening of the supply of prospective human resources available to fill a position. Its purpose is to narrow a large field of prospective employees to a relatively small group of individuals from which someone eventually will be hired. To be effective, recruiters must know the following:

1. The job they are trying to fill
2. Where potential human resources can be located
3. How the law influences recruiting efforts

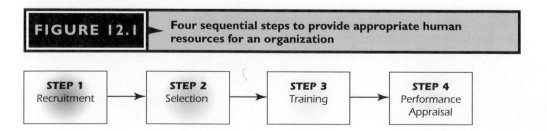

FIGURE 12.1 ▶ Four sequential steps to provide appropriate human resources for an organization

| STEP 1 Recruitment | → | STEP 2 Selection | → | STEP 3 Training | → | STEP 4 Performance Appraisal |

Texas Instruments is a global semiconductor company and is probably best known for its calculators and personal organizers. As with most companies of this size, recruiting appropriate people is a constant endeavor and challenge at Texas Instruments.

Management at Texas Instruments has recently taken a progressive and novel step to help meet this recruiting challenge. The company decided to initiate an Internet recruiting effort to complement its more traditional recruiting practice. John Nelson has been appointed as the company's full-time "cyber recruiter." As such, Nelson spends his day visiting Web sites to discover highly talented engineers who have posted their resumes and are looking for a new job. Nelson

can then use e-mail as a quick and efficient way to contact desirable candidates. In addition, the company is evaluating the use of a "robot service" to help keep track of engineering résumés on the Web. This service would automatically search for the type of résumé a company like Texas Instruments needs and would forward any to corporate recruiters.

Nelson is getting results. Last year about 10 percent of the company's newly hired engineers were first discovered through Internet contacts. That is about 8 percent more than previous years and is expected to grow even further in the future. According to Nelson, Internet recruiting not only has merit, it is the wave of the future.

KNOWING THE JOB Recruitment activities must begin with a thorough understanding of the position to be filled so the broad range of potential employees can be narrowed down intelligently. The technique commonly used to gain that understanding is known as **job analysis.** Basically, job analysis is aimed at determining a **job description** (the activities a job entails) and a **job specification** (the characteristics of the individual who should be hired for the job). Figure 12.2 shows the relationship of job analysis to job description and job specification.[3]

The U.S. Civil Service Commission has developed a procedure for performing a job analysis. As with all job analysis procedures, the Civil Service procedure uses information gathering as the primary means of determining what workers do and how and why they do it. Naturally, the quality of the job analysis depends on the accuracy of information gathered. This information is used to develop both a job description and a job specification.[4]

Job analysis is a technique commonly used to gain an understanding of what a task entails and the type of individual who should be hired to perform that task.

A **job description** is a list of specific activities that must be performed to accomplish some task or job.

A **job specification** is a list of the characteristics of the individual who should be hired to perform a specific task or job.

FIGURE 12.2 ▶ **Relationship of job analysis, job description, and job specification**

JOB ANALYSIS
A process for obtaining all pertinent job facts

JOB DESCRIPTION
A statement containing items such as:
- Job title
- Location
- Job summary
- Duties
- Machines, tools, equipment
- Materials and forms used
- Supervision given or received
- Working conditions
- Hazards

JOB SPECIFICATION
A statement of the human qualifications necessary to do the job. Usually contains such items as:
- Education
- Experience
- Training
- Judgment
- Initiative
- Physical effort
- Physical skills
- Responsibilities
- Communication skills
- Emotional characteristics
- Unusual sensory demands, such as sight, smell, hearing

KNOWING SOURCES OF HUMAN RESOURCES Besides a thorough knowledge of the position the organization is trying to fill, recruiters must be able to pinpoint sources of human resources. Since the supply of individuals from which to recruit is continually changing, there will be times when finding appropriate human resources will be much harder than at other times. Human resources specialists in organizations continually monitor the labor market so they will know where to recruit appropriate human resources and what kind of strategies and tactics to use to attract job applicants in a competitive marketplace.[5]

Sources of human resources available to fill a position can be generally categorized in two ways:

1. Sources inside the organization
2. Sources outside the organization

Sources Inside the Organization The pool of employees within the organization is one source of human resources. Some individuals who already work for the organization may be well qualified for an open position. Although existing personnel are sometimes moved laterally within an organization, most internal movements are promotions. Promotion from within has the advantages of building employee morale, encouraging employees to work harder in hopes of being promoted, and enticing employees to stay with the organization because of the possibility of future promotions. Companies such as Exxon and General Electric find it very rewarding to train their managers for advancement within the organization.[6]

Human Resources Inventory. A **human resource inventory** consists of information about the characteristics of organization members. The focus is on past performance and future potential, and the objective is to keep management up-to-date about the possibilities for filling a position from within. This inventory should indicate which individuals in the organization would be appropriate for filling a position if it became available. In a classic article, Walter S. Wikstrom proposed that organizations keep three types of records that can be combined to maintain a useful human resource inventory.[7] Although Wikstrom focused on filling managerial positions, slight modifications to his inventory forms would make his records equally useful for filling nonmanagerial positions. Many organizations computerize records like the ones Wikstrom suggests to make their human resource inventory system more efficient and effective.

► The first of Wikstrom's three record-keeping forms for a human resource inventory is the **management inventory card.** The management inventory card in Figure 12.3 has been completed for a fictional manager named Mel Murray. It indicates Murray's age, year of employment, present position and the length of time he has held it, performance ratings,

A **human resource inventory** is an accumulation of information about the characteristics of organization members; this information focuses on members' past performance as well as on how they might be trained and best used in the future.

The **management inventory card** is a form used in compiling a human resource inventory. It contains the organizational history of an individual and indicates how that individual might be used in the organization in the future.

FIGURE 12.3 ► Management inventory card

NAME Murray, Mel		AGE 47	EMPLOYED 1985
PRESENT POSITION Manager, Sales (House Fans Division)			On Job 6 years
PRESENT PERFORMANCE Outstanding—exceeded sales goal in spite of stiffer competition.			
STRENGTHS Good planner—motivates subordinates very well—excellent communication.			
WEAKNESSES Still does not always delegate as much as situation requires. Sometimes does not understand production problems.			
EFFORTS TO IMPROVE Has greatly improved in delegating in last two years; also has organized more effectively after taking a management course on own time and initiative.			
COULD MOVE TO Vice President, Marketing		**WHEN** 2000	
TRAINING NEEDED More exposure to problems of other divisions (attend top staff conference?). Perhaps university program stressing staff role of corporate marketing versus line sales.			
COULD MOVE TO Manager, House or Industrial Fans Division		**WHEN** 2001 2002	
TRAINING NEEDED Course in production management; some project working with production people; perhaps a good business game somewhere.			

strengths and weaknesses, the positions to which he might move, when he would be ready to assume these positions, and additional training he would need to fill the positions. In short, this card contains both an organizational history of Murray and an indication of how he might be used in the future.

► Figure 12.4 shows Wikstrom's second human resource inventory form—the **position replacement form.** This form focuses on position-centered information rather than the people-centered information maintained on the management inventory card. Note that the form in Figure 12.4 indicates little about Murray, but much about two individuals who could replace him. The position replacement form is helpful in determining what would happen to Murray's present position if Murray were selected to be moved within the organization or if he decided to leave the organization.

► Wikstrom's third human resource inventory form is the **management manpower replacement chart** (see Figure 12.5). This chart presents a composite view of the individuals management considers significant for human resource planning. Note on Figure 12.5 how Murray's performance rating and promotion potential can easily be compared with those of other employees when the company is trying to determine which individual would most appropriately fill a particular position.

The **position replacement form** is used in compiling a human resource inventory. It summarizes information about organization members who could fill a position should it open up.

The **management manpower replacement chart** is a form used in compiling a human resource inventory. It is people-oriented and presents a composite view of individuals management considers significant to human resource planning.

The management inventory card, the position replacement form, and the management manpower replacement chart are three separate record-keeping devices for a human resource inventory. Each form furnishes different data on which to base a hiring-from-within decision. These forms help management to answer the following questions:

1. What is the organizational history of an individual, and what potential does that person possess (management inventory card)?

FIGURE 12.4 ▶ Position replacement form

POSITION	Manager, Sales (House Fans Division)			
PERFORMANCE Outstanding	**INCUMBENT** Mel Murray		**SALARY** $44,500	**MAY MOVE** 1 Year
REPLACEMENT 1 Earl Renfrew			**SALARY** $39,500	**AGE** 39
PRESENT POSITION Field Sales Manager, House Fans			**EMPLOYED:** Present Job 3 years	Company 10 years
TRAINING NEEDED Special assignment to study market potential for air conditioners to provide forecasting experience.				**WHEN READY** Now
REPLACEMENT 2 Bernard Storey			**SALARY** $38,500	**AGE** 36
PRESENT POSITION Promotion Manager, House Fans			**EMPLOYED:** Present Job 4 years	Company 7 years
TRAINING NEEDED Rotation to field sales. Marketing conference in fall.				**WHEN READY** 2 years

2. If a position becomes vacant, who might be eligible to fill it (position replacement form)?
3. What are the merits of one individual being considered for a position compared to those of another individual under consideration (management manpower replacement chart)?

Considering the answers to these three questions collectively should help management make successful hiring-from-within decisions. Computer software is available to aid managers in keeping track of the organization's complex human resource inventories and in making better decisions about how employees can be best deployed and developed.[8]

Sources Outside the Organization   If a position cannot be filled by someone presently employed by the organization, management has available numerous sources of human resources outside the organization. These sources include the following:

1. *Competitors*—One often-tapped external source of human resources is competing organizations. Since there are several advantages to luring human resources away from competitors, this type of piracy has become a common practice. Among the advantages are the following:

   ▶ The individual knows the business
   ▶ The competitor will have paid for the individual's training up to the time of hire
   ▶ The competing organization will probably be weakened somewhat by the loss of the individual
   ▶ Once hired, the individual will be a valuable source of information about how to best compete with the other organization

2. *Employment agencies*—Employment agencies help people find jobs and help organizations find job applicants. Such agencies can be either public or private. Public employment agencies do not charge fees, whereas private ones collect a fee from either the person hired or the organization doing the hiring, once the hire has been finalized.

3. *Readers of certain publications*—Perhaps the most widely used external source of human resources is the readership of certain publications. To tap this source, recruiters simply place an advertisement in a suitable publication. The advertisement describes the open position in detail and announces that the organization is accepting applications from quali-

FIGURE 12.5 ► Management manpower replacement chart

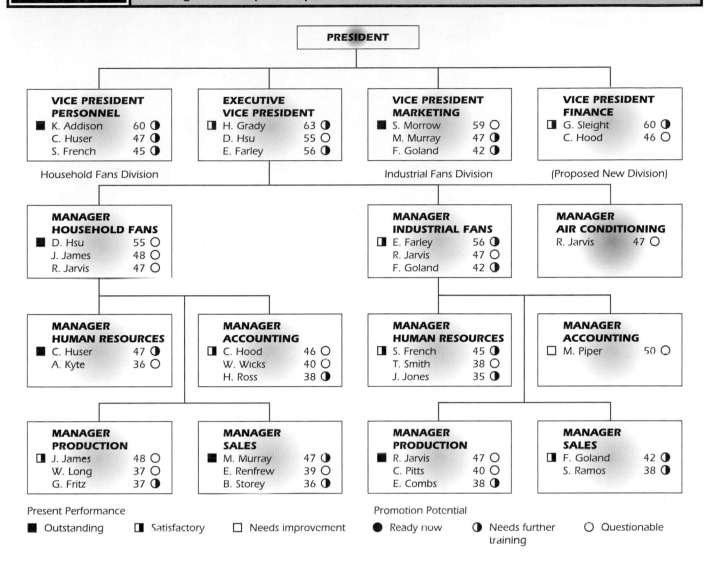

PRESIDENT

VICE PRESIDENT PERSONNEL
■ K. Addison   60 ◑
  C. Huser   47 ◑
  S. French   45 ◑

EXECUTIVE VICE PRESIDENT
◧ H. Grady   63 ◑
  D. Hsu   55 ○
  E. Farley   56 ◑

VICE PRESIDENT MARKETING
■ S. Morrow   59 ○
  M. Murray   47 ◑
  F. Goland   42 ◑

VICE PRESIDENT FINANCE
◧ G. Sleight   60 ◑
  C. Hood   46 ○

Household Fans Division   Industrial Fans Division   (Proposed New Division)

MANAGER HOUSEHOLD FANS
■ D. Hsu   55 ○
  J. James   48 ○
  R. Jarvis   47 ○

MANAGER INDUSTRIAL FANS
◧ E. Farley   56 ◑
  R. Jarvis   47 ○
  F. Goland   42 ◑

MANAGER AIR CONDITIONING
  R. Jarvis   47 ○

MANAGER HUMAN RESOURCES
■ C. Huser   47 ◑
  A. Kyte   36 ○

MANAGER ACCOUNTING
◧ C. Hood   46 ○
  W. Wicks   40 ○
  H. Ross   38 ◑

MANAGER HUMAN RESOURCES
◧ S. French   45 ◑
  T. Smith   38 ○
  J. Jones   35 ◑

MANAGER ACCOUNTING
☐ M. Piper   50 ○

MANAGER PRODUCTION
◧ J. James   48 ○
  W. Long   37 ○
  G. Fritz   37 ◑

MANAGER SALES
■ M. Murray   47 ◑
  E. Renfrew   39 ○
  B. Storey   36 ◑

MANAGER PRODUCTION
■ R. Jarvis   47 ○
  C. Pitts   40 ○
  E. Combs   38 ◑

MANAGER SALES
◧ F. Goland   42 ◑
  S. Ramos   38 ◑

Present Performance
■ Outstanding   ◧ Satisfactory   ☐ Needs improvement

Promotion Potential
● Ready now   ◑ Needs further training   ○ Questionable

fied individuals. The type of position to be filled determines the type of publication in which the advertisement is placed. The objective is to advertise in a publication whose readers are likely to be interested in filling the position. An opening for a top-level executive might be advertised in *The Wall Street Journal,* a training director opening might be advertised in the *Journal of Training and Development,* and an educational opening might be advertised in the *Chronicle of Higher Education.*

4. *Educational institutions*—Many recruiters go directly to schools to interview students close to graduation time. Liberal arts schools, business schools, engineering schools, junior colleges, and community colleges all have somewhat different human resources to offer. Recruiting efforts should focus on the schools with the highest probability of providing human resources appropriate for the open position.

KNOWING THE LAW Legislation has had a major impact on modern organizational recruitment practices. Managers need to be aware of the laws that govern recruitment efforts. The Civil Rights Act passed in 1964 and amended in 1972 created the **Equal Employment Opportunity Commission (EEOC)** to enforce federal laws prohibiting discrimination on the basis of

The **Equal Employment Opportunity Commission (EEOC)** is an agency established to enforce federal laws regulating recruiting and other employment practices.

In Louisville, Kentucky, a program called Job Link has been established by the nonprofit Louisville Private Industry Council. Job Link is a one-stop career center that helps job seekers prepare materials and devise strategies. Applicants with good skills are referred to current employment leads; in other cases, training is provided—for example, an unemployed data-processing clerk may be trained as a systems analyst. Most people find jobs within six weeks.

race, color, religion, sex, and national origin in recruitment, hiring, firing, layoffs, and all other employment practices. The EEOC report was amended in 1978 to include the Pregnancy Discrimination Act, which requires employers to treat pregnancy, insofar as leave and insurance are concerned, like any other form of medical disability.

Equal opportunity legislation protects the right of a citizen to work and obtain a fair wage based primarily on merit and performance. The EEOC seeks to uphold this right by overseeing the employment practices of labor unions, private employers, educational institutions, and government bodies.

AFFIRMATIVE ACTION In response to equal opportunity legislation, many organizations have established **affirmative action programs.** Translated literally, *affirmative action* means positive movement: "In the area of equal employment opportunity, the basic purpose of positive movement or affirmative action is to eliminate barriers and increase opportunities for the purpose of increasing the utilization of underutilized and/or disadvantaged individuals."[9] An organization can judge how much progress it is making toward eliminating such barriers by taking the following steps:

Affirmative action programs are organizational programs whose basic purpose is to eliminate barriers against and increase employment opportunities for underutilized or disadvantaged individuals.

1. Determining how many minority and disadvantaged individuals it presently employs
2. Determining how many minority and disadvantaged individuals it should be employing according to EEOC guidelines
3. Comparing the numbers obtained in steps 1 and 2

If the two numbers obtained in step 3 are nearly the same, the organization's employment practices probably should be maintained; if they are not nearly the same, the organization should modify its employment practices accordingly.

Modern management writers recommend that managers follow the guidelines of affirmative action, not merely because they are mandated by law, but also because of the characteristics of today's labor supply.[10] According to these writers, more than half of the U.S. workforce now consists of minorities, immigrants, and women. Since the overall workforce is so diverse, it follows that employees in today's organizations will also be more diverse than in the past. Thus today's managers face the challenge of forging a productive workforce out of an increasingly diverse labor pool, and this task is more formidable than simply complying with affirmative action laws.

Many managers confront special issues related to minority employees after they are hired. The following People Spotlight feature describes one issue pertaining to women employees and explains how NationsBank is responding to it.

Many managers are discovering that their women employees need child-care services during working hours. This is an important issue in today's workplace since many managers are finding that the quality of child care that employees can obtain for their children has a direct and measurable impact on those employees' productivity.

Companies are responding to the need for high-quality child care for the dependents of their employees out of sheer self-interest. NationsBank Corporation, for example, recently set aside $10 million for a five-year investment in such programs as developing a child-care center within the company and training outside caregivers to be made available for hire by NationsBank employees. This allocation of company funds is not viewed as a charitable donation by NationsBank management. Rather, management sees the $10 million as an investment in productivity, on the theory that by eliminating working parents' concerns about the care their dependents are receiving, the bank will gain more productive employees.

NationsBank decided to focus on child care because of the deplorable conditions in so many child-care facilities today. Many working parents are leaving their children in facilities that are unhealthy and unsafe, and studies show that such poor-quality care threatens children's cognitive and emotional development. A recent study of 400 day-care centers across the United States found that 73.7 percent of them were providing only average care that may compromise children's readiness to learn when they enter school. Another 12.3 percent of the centers studied were rated unacceptable.

BACK TO THE CASE

A successful recruitment effort at Northwestern Mutual would require recruiters to know where to locate the available human resources to fill open positions. These sources may be both within Northwestern and outside of it. In this case, employees at Aetna, John Hancock Mutual Life, and Prudential Insurance of America would probably be good candidates.

In supporting plans for the future, Northwestern Mutual's management must devise ways to obtain needed appropriate human resources along with other resources like equipment and buildings. To do this, management can keep current on the possibilities of filling positions from within by maintaining some type of human resource inventory. This inventory can help management organize information about (1) the organizational histories and potentials of various Northwestern employees, (2) the employees in other Northwestern positions who might be eligible to fill various roles in the future, and (3) the relative abilities of various Northwestern employees to fill openings. Some of the sources of potential human resources outside of Northwestern that a manager like John Sheaffer could be aware of are competitors, public and private employment agencies, the readers of industry-related publications, users of the Internet, and various types of educational institutions.

Northwestern's management must also be aware of how the law influences its recruitment efforts. Basically, the law says that Northwestern's recruitment practices cannot discriminate on the basis of race, color, religion, sex, or national origin. If recruitment practices at Northwestern are found to be discriminatory, the company is subject to prosecution by the Equal Employment Opportunity Commission.

⟩ SELECTION

The second major step involved in providing human resources for the organization is **selection**—choosing an individual to hire from all those who have been recruited.[11] Selection, obviously, is dependent on the first step, recruitment. The following cartoon lightheartedly points out the importance of selecting the right people for an organization.

Selection is choosing an individual to hire from all those who have been recruited.

MIKE SHAPIRO

"How many times do I have to tell Personnel we want a hip young crowd buying our products, not working for us?"

Selection is represented as a series of stages through which job applicants must pass in order to be hired.[12] Each stage reduces the total group of prospective employees until, finally, one individual is hired. Figure 12.6 lists the specific stages of the selection process, indicates reasons for eliminating applicants at each stage, and illustrates how the group of potential employees is narrowed down to the individual who ultimately is hired. Two tools often used in the selection process are testing and assessment centers.

GLOBAL SPOTLIGHT ▶ | Compaq Computer Company's International Selection Slip-Ups

At times, managers must handle selection mistakes—people who shortly after being hired leave the company voluntarily or are fired. In these cases, recruitment and selection expenses are lost.

Growth at Compaq Computer Company, a computer manufacturer based in Houston, Texas, has been phenomenal in recent years. In 1994, the firm had annual sales of $10.9 billion—up from $7.2 billion in 1993—with $887 million in net profit—up from $462 million in 1993. The company's expansion into international markets has played a major role in its success.

Selection mistakes in the international arena are likely to be more expensive for a company like Compaq than selection mistakes in the domestic arena because foreign assignments are usually more expensive to set up and maintain. Expenses incurred for employees posted to a foreign country include salary based on the value of the U.S. dollar in that country, housing allowance, cost-of-living adjustments, transportation allowances, and private-school tuition for employees' children.

Testing is examining human resources for qualities relevant to performing available jobs.

TESTING **Testing** is examining human resources for qualities relevant to performing available jobs. Although many different kinds of tests are available for organizational use, they generally can be divided into the following four categories:[13]

1. *Aptitude tests*—Tests of aptitude measure the potential of an individual to perform a task. Some aptitude tests measure general intelligence, while others measure special abilities, such as mechanical, clerical, or visual skills.[14]
2. *Achievement tests*—Tests that measure the level of skill or knowledge an individual possesses in a certain area are called achievement tests. This skill or knowledge may have been acquired through various training activities or through experience in the area. Examples of skill tests are typing and keyboarding tests.
3. *Vocational interest tests*—Tests of vocational interest attempt to measure an individual's interest in performing various kinds of jobs. They are administered on the assumption that

FIGURE 12.6 ► **Summary of major factors in the selection process**

STAGES OF THE SELECTION PROCESS	REASONS FOR ELIMINATION	
Preliminary screening from records, data sheets, etc.	Lack of adequate educational and performance record	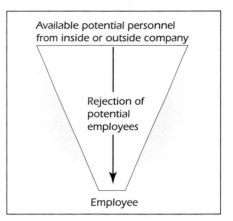
Preliminary interview	Obvious misfit from outward appearance and conduct	
Intelligence tests	Failure to meet minimum standards	
Aptitude tests	Failure to have minimum necessary aptitude	
Personality tests	Negative aspects of personality	
Performance references	Unfavorable or negative reports on past performance	
Diagnostic interview	Lack of necessary innate ability, ambition, or other qualities	
Physical examination	Physically unfit for job	
Personal judgment	Remaining candidate placed in available position	

certain people perform jobs well because they find the job activities stimulating. The basic purpose of this type of test is to select for an open position the individual who finds most aspects of that position interesting.

4. *Personality tests*—Personality tests attempt to describe an individual's personality dimensions in such areas as emotional maturity, subjectivity, honesty, and objectivity. These tests can be used advantageously if the personality characteristics needed to do well in a particular job are well defined and if individuals possessing those characteristics can be identified and selected. Managers must be careful, however, not to expose themselves to legal prosecution by basing employment decisions on personality tests that are invalid and unreliable. Test validity and reliability are discussed under "Testing Guidelines."[15]

Testing Guidelines   Several guidelines should be observed when tests are used as part of the selection process. First, care must be taken to ensure that the test being used is both valid and reliable. A test is *valid* if it measures what it is designed to measure and *reliable* if it measures similarly time after time.[16] Second, test results should not be used as the sole determinant of a hiring decision. People change over time, and someone who doesn't score well on a particular test might still develop into a productive employee. Such factors as potential and desire to obtain a position should be assessed subjectively and used along with test scores in the final selection decision. Third, care should be taken to ensure that tests are nondiscriminatory; many tests contain language or cultural biases that may discriminate against minorities, and the EEOC has the authority to prosecute organizations that use discriminatory testing practices.

ASSESSMENT CENTERS   Another tool often used in employee selection is the **assessment center.** Although the assessment center concept is discussed in this chapter primarily as an aid to selection, it is also used in such areas as human resource training and organization development. The first industrial use of the assessment center is usually credited to AT&T. Since AT&T's initial efforts, the assessment center concept has expanded greatly, and today it is used not only as a means for identifying individuals to be hired from outside an organization but also for identifying individuals from inside the organization who should be promoted. Corporations that have used assessment centers extensively include J.C. Penney, Standard Oil of Ohio, and IBM.[17]

An assessment center is a program (not a place) in which participants engage in a number of individual and group exercises constructed to simulate important activities at the organizational levels to which they aspire.[18] These exercises can include such activities as participating in leaderless discussions, giving oral presentations, and leading a group in solving some assigned problem. The individuals performing the activities are observed by managers or trained

An **assessment center** is a program in which participants engage in, and are evaluated on, a number of individual and group exercises constructed to simulate important activities at the organizational levels to which they aspire.

observers who evaluate both their ability and their potential. In general, participants are assessed according to the following criteria:[19]

1. Leadership
2. Organizing and planning ability
3. Decision making
4. Oral and written communication skills
5. Initiative
6. Energy
7. Analytical ability
8. Resistance to stress
9. Use of delegation
10. Behavior flexibility
11. Human relations competence
12. Originality
13. Controlling
14. Self-Direction
15. Overall potential

BACK TO THE CASE

After the initial screening of potential human resources, Northwestern Mutual will be faced with the task of selecting the individuals to be hired from those who have been screened. Two tools that Northwestern could suggest to help in this selection process are testing and assessment centers.

For example, after screening potential employees for positions at Northwestern, management could use aptitude tests, achievement tests, vocational interest tests, or personality tests to see if any of the individuals screened had the qualities necessary to work a specific job. In using these tests, however, management must make sure that the tests are both valid and reliable, that they were not the sole basis for its selection decision, and that they are nondiscriminatory.

Northwestern can also use assessment centers to simulate the tasks necessary to perform jobs that workers will be performing. Individuals who performed well on these tasks would probably be more appropriate for the positions than would those who did poorly. The use of assessment centers might be particularly appropriate in evaluating applicants for the position of sales agent. Simulating this job would probably give management an excellent idea of how prospective sales agents would actually interact with customers during sales presentations.

▶ TRAINING

Training is the process of developing qualities in human resources that will enable them to be more productive.

After recruitment and selection, the next step in providing appropriate human resources for the organization is training. **Training** is the process of developing qualities in human resources that will enable them to be more productive and thus to contribute more to organizational goal attainment. The purpose of training is to increase the productivity of employees by influencing their behavior. Table 12.1 provides an overview of the types and popularity of training being offered by organizations today.

The training of individuals is essentially a four-step process:

1. Determining training needs
2. Designing the training program
3. Administering the training program
4. Evaluating the training program

These steps are presented in Figure 12.7 and are described in the sections that follow.

TABLE 12.1	Types and Popularity of Training Offered by Organizations	
Types of Training		Percentage of Surveyed Companies That Offer the Training
1. Management skills and development		74.3
2. Supervisory skills		73.4
3. Technical skills and knowledge updating		72.7
4. Communication skills		66.8
5. Customer relations and services		63.8
6. Executive development		56.8
7. New methods and procedures		56.5
8. Sales skills		54.1
9. Clerical and secretarial skills		52.9
10. Personal growth		51.9
11. Computer literacy and basic computer skills		48.2
12. Employee and labor relations		44.9
13. Disease prevention and health promotion		38.9
14. Customer education		35.7
15. Remedial basic education		18.0

DETERMINING TRAINING NEEDS The first step of the training process is determining the organization's training needs.[20] **Training needs** are the information or skill areas of an individual or group that require further development to increase the productivity of that individual or group. Only if training focuses on these needs can it be productive for the organization.

The training of organization members is typically a continuing activity. Even employees who have been with the organization for some time and who have undergone initial orientation and skills training need continued training to improve their skills.

Determining Needed Skills There are several methods of determining which skills to focus on with established human resources. One method calls for evaluating the production process within the organization. Such factors as excessive rejected products, unmet deadlines, and high labor costs are clues to deficiencies in production-related expertise. Another method for determining training needs calls for getting direct feedback from employees on what they believe

Training needs are the information or skill areas of an individual or group that require further development to increase the productivity of that individual or group.

FIGURE 12.7 ▶ Steps of the training process

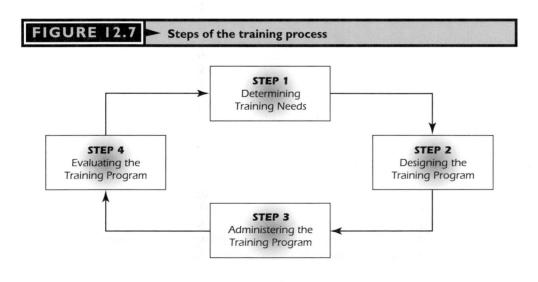

STEP 1
Determining
Training Needs

STEP 2
Designing the
Training Program

STEP 3
Administering the
Training Program

STEP 4
Evaluating the
Training Program

are the organization's training needs. Organization members are often able to verbalize clearly and accurately exactly what types of training they require to do a better job. A third way of determining training needs involves looking into the future. If the manufacture of new products or the use of newly purchased equipment is foreseen, some type of corresponding training almost certainly will be needed.

DESIGNING THE TRAINING PROGRAM   Once training needs have been determined, a training program aimed at meeting those needs must be designed. Basically, designing a program entails assembling various types of facts and activities that will meet the established training needs. Obviously, as training needs vary, so will the facts and activities designed to meet those needs.

BACK TO THE CASE

After hiring, Northwestern Mutual must train new employees to be productive organization members. To train effectively, Northwestern must determine training needs, design a corresponding training program, and administer and evaluate the program.

Designing a training program requires that Northwestern assembles facts and activities that address specific company training needs. These needs are simply information or skill areas that must be further developed in Northwestern's employees in order to make them more productive. Over the long term, training at Northwestern should focus on more established employees as well as newly hired employees.

For a company like Northwestern, future plans probably include continued expansion. In this situation, management should probably try to learn as much as possible from training programs that the company operated to support past expansion. Knowing strengths and weakness of training programs aimed at past expansion would undoubtedly help management at Northwestern in designing efficient and effective training programs for its newest expansion plans.

ADMINISTERING THE TRAINING PROGRAM   The next step in the training process is administering the training program—that is, actually training the individuals selected to participate in the program. Various techniques exist for both transmitting necessary information and developing needed skills in training programs, and several of these techniques are discussed in the sections that follow.

Techniques for Transmitting Information   Two techniques for transmitting information in training programs are lectures and programmed learning. Although it could be argued that these techniques develop some skills in individuals as well as transmit information to them, they are primarily devices for the dissemination of information.

> 1. *Lectures*—Perhaps the most widely used technique for transmitting information in training programs is the lecture. The **lecture** is a primarily one-way communication situation in which an instructor orally presents information to a group of listeners. The instructor typically does most of the talking, and trainees participate primarily through listening and note taking.
>
>   An advantage of the lecture is that it allows the instructor to expose trainees to a maximum amount of information within a given time period. The lecture, however, has some serious disadvantages:[21]
>
>> The lecture generally consists of a one-way communication: the instructor presents information to the group of passive listeners. Thus, little or no opportunity exists to clarify meanings, to check on whether trainees really understand the lecture material, or to handle the wide diversity of ability, attitude, and interest that may prevail among the trainees. Also, there is little or no opportunity for practice, reinforcement, knowledge of results, or

A **lecture** is primarily a one-way communication situation in which an instructor trains an individual or group by orally presenting information.

overlearning. . . . Ideally, the competent lecturer should make the material meaningful and intrinsically motivating to his or her listeners. However, whether most lectures achieve this goal is a moot question. . . . These limitations, in turn, impose further limitations on the lecture's actual content. A skillful lecturer may be fairly successful in transmitting conceptual knowledge to a group of trainees who are ready to receive it; however, all the evidence available indicates that the nature of the lecture situation makes it of minimal value in promoting attitudinal or behavioral change.

2. *Programmed Learning*—Another commonly used technique for transmitting information in training programs is called programmed learning. **Programmed learning** is a technique for instructing without the presence or intervention of a human instructor.[22] Small parts of information that require related responses are presented to individual trainees. The trainees can determine from checking their responses against provided answers whether their understanding of the information is accurate. The types of responses required of trainees vary from situation to situation, but usually are multiple-choice, true-false, or fill-in-the-blank.

> **Programmed learning** is a technique for instructing without the presence or intervention of a human instructor. Small pieces of information requiring responses are presented to individual trainees, and the trainees determine from checking their responses against provided answers whether their understanding of the information is accurate.

Like the lecture method, programmed learning has both advantages and disadvantages. Among the advantages are that it can be computerized and students can learn at their own pace, know immediately if they are right or wrong, and participate actively in the learning process. The primary disadvantage of this method is that no one is present to answer a confused learner's questions.

Techniques for Developing Skills Techniques for developing skills in training programs can be divided into two broad categories: on-the-job and classroom. Techniques for developing skills on the job, referred to as **on-the-job training,** reflect a blend of job-related knowledge and experience. They include coaching, position rotation, and special project committees. *Coaching* is direct critiquing of how well an individual is performing a job.[23] *Position rotation* involves moving an individual from job to job to enable the person to gain an understanding of the organization as a whole. *Special project committees* are vehicles for assigning a particular task to an individual to furnish him or her with experience in a designated area.[24]

> **On-the-job training** is a training technique that blends job-related knowledge with experience in using that knowledge on the job.

Classroom techniques for developing skills also reflect a blend of job-related knowledge and experience. The skills addressed through these techniques can range from technical, such as computer programming skills, to interpersonal, such as leadership skills. Specific

Solid employee skills training is what makes quick response times possible. Here workers package Microsoft Windows 98 in a Washington plant just before the new software went on sale in June 1998. The ability to deliver new products quickly is critical in the highly competitive software industry.

classroom techniques aimed at developing skills include various types of management games and role-playing activities. The most common format for *management games* requires small groups of trainees to make and then evaluate various management decisions. The *role-playing format* typically involves acting out and then reflecting on some people-oriented problem that must be solved in the organization.

In contrast to the typical one-way communication of the lecturer, the skills instructor in the classroom encourages high levels of discussion and interaction among trainees, develops a climate in which trainees learn new behavior from carrying out various activities, clarifies related information, and facilitates learning by eliciting trainees' job-related knowledge and experience in applying that knowledge. The difference between the instructional role in information dissemination and the instructional role in skill development is dramatic.[25]

EVALUATING THE TRAINING PROGRAM

After the training program has been completed, management should evaluate its effectiveness.[26] Because training programs represent an investment—costs include materials, trainer time, and production loss while employees are being trained rather than doing their jobs—a reasonable return is essential.

Basically, management should evaluate the training program to determine if it meets the needs for which it was designed. Answers to questions like the following help determine training program effectiveness:

1. Has the excessive reject rate of products declined?
2. Are deadlines being met more regularly?
3. Are labor costs per unit produced decreasing?

If the answer to such questions is yes, the training program can be judged as at least somewhat successful, though perhaps its effectiveness could be enhanced through certain selective changes. If the answer is no, significant modification to the training program is warranted.

In a noteworthy survey of businesspeople, 50 percent of respondents thought that their sales per year would be unaffected if training programs for experienced salespeople were halted.[27] This is the kind of feedback management should seek and scrutinize to see if present training programs should be discontinued, slightly modified, or drastically altered to make them more valuable to the organization. The results of the survey just mentioned indicate a need to make significant changes in sales training programs at the companies covered by the survey.

ACROSS INDUSTRIES — Furniture Manufacturing

TRAINING IS CRITICAL AT KELLER MANUFACTURING

The Keller Manufacturing Company, located in Corydon, Indiana, manufactures high-quality solid wood furniture for both dining rooms and bedrooms. Recently, management introduced a new, very complex, computer-assisted manufacturing system for better serving the customer through quicker and more reliable delivery of finished products. The process involved using more than 6,000 different components and more than 100 different procedures.

Training employees in how to use the new system was key to implementing the system successfully according to Marvin Miller, vice president of information services and the manager in charge of implementing the new process. The training program first focused on employees on the shop floor. A training room was set up to introduce 10 people at a time to the new system. Training began with 18 hours of keyboard work, learning how to operate the new system via the computer. Extensive on-the-job training in which employees actually operated the new system and gained insights followed keyboard training.

Miller evaluates the worth of this training by seeing how many employees opt to take voluntary, more advanced training. Results from one plant indicated that 93 percent of the employees volunteered for the extra training. Miller sees such feedback as indicating that employees value the training and feel that it is instrumental in doing good work.

► PERFORMANCE APPRAISAL

Even after individuals have been recruited, selected, and trained, the task of making them maximally productive within the organization is not finished. The fourth step in the process of providing appropriate human resources for the organization is **performance appraisal**—the process of reviewing individuals' past productive activity to evaluate the contribution they have made toward attaining management system objectives. Like training, performance appraisal—which is also called *performance review* and *performance evaluation*—is a continuing activity that focuses on both established human resources within the organization and newcomers. Its main purpose is to furnish feedback to organization members about how they can become more productive and useful to the organization in its quest for quality.[28] Table 12.2 describes several methods of performance appraisal.

Performance appraisal is the process of reviewing past productive activity to evaluate the contribution individuals have made toward attaining management system objectives.

WHY USE PERFORMANCE APPRAISALS? Most U.S. firms engage in some type of performance appraisal. Douglas McGregor has suggested the following three reasons for using performance appraisals:[29]

1. They provide systematic judgments to support salary increases, promotions, transfers, and sometimes demotions or terminations
2. They are a means of telling subordinates how they are doing and of suggesting needed changes in behavior, attitudes, skills, or job knowledge; they let subordinates know where they stand with the boss
3. They furnish a useful basis for the coaching and counseling of individuals by superiors

HANDLING PERFORMANCE APPRAISALS If performance appraisals are not handled well, their benefits to the organization will be minimal. Several guidelines can assist management in increasing the appropriateness with which appraisals are conducted. The first guideline is that performance appraisals should stress both performance in the position the individual holds and the success with which the individual is attaining organizational objectives. Although conceptually separate, performance and objectives should be inseparable topics of discussion during performance appraisals. The second guideline is that appraisals should emphasize how well the individual is doing the job, not the evaluator's impression of the individual's work habits. In other words, the goal is an objective analysis of performance rather than a subjective evaluation of habits.

The third guideline is that the appraisal should be acceptable to both the evaluator and the subject—that is, both should agree that it has benefit for the organization and the worker. The fourth, and last, guideline is that performance appraisals should provide a base for improving individuals' productivity within the organization by making them better equipped to produce.[30]

TABLE 12.2	Descriptions of Several Methods of Performance Appraisal

Appraisal Method	Description
Rating scale	Individuals appraising performance use a form containing several employee qualities and characteristics to be evaluated (e.g., dependability, initiative, leadership). Each evaluated factor is rated on a continuum or scale ranging, for example, from 1 to 7.
Employee comparisons	Appraisers rank employees according to such factors as job performance and value to the organization. Only one employee can occupy a particular ranking.
Free-form essay	Appraisers simply write down their impressions of employees in paragraph form.
Critical-form essay	Appraisers write down particularly good or bad events involving employees as these events occur. Records of all documented events for any one employee are used to evaluate that person's performance.

POTENTIAL WEAKNESSES OF PERFORMANCE APPRAISALS To maximize the payoff of performance appraisals to the organization, managers must avoid several potential weaknesses of the appraisal process, including the following pitfalls:[31]

1. Performance appraisals focus employees on short-term rewards rather than on issues that are important to the long-run success of the organization
2. Individuals involved in performance appraisals view them as a reward-punishment situation
3. The emphasis of performance appraisal is on completing paperwork rather than on critiquing individual performance
4. Individuals being evaluated view the process as unfair or biased
5. Subordinates react negatively when evaluators offer unfavorable comments

To avoid these potential weaknesses, supervisors and employees should look on the performance appraisal process as an opportunity to increase the worth of the employee through constructive feedback, not as a means of rewarding or punishing the employee through positive or negative comments. Paperwork should be viewed only as an aid in providing this feedback, not as an end in itself. Also, care should be taken to make appraisal feedback as tactful and objective as possible to minimize negative reactions.

BACK TO THE CASE

The last step in providing appropriate human resources at Northwestern Mutual is performance appraisal. This means that the contributions that Northwestern's employees make toward attaining management system objectives must be evaluated. Naturally, the performance appraisal process should focus on more recently hired employees as well as more established Northwestern employees.

It would be difficult to visualize a Northwestern employee who could not benefit from a properly conducted performance appraisal. Such an appraisal would stress activities on the job and effectiveness in accomplishing job objectives. An objective appraisal would provide Northwestern's employees with tactful, constructive criticism that should help to increase their productivity. Handled properly, Northwestern's appraisals would not be a reward or a punishment in themselves, but rather an opportunity to increase their value to the company. Such objective, productive analysis of performance should help Northwestern's employees to become more productive over time rather than to be without guidance and perhaps moving toward the inevitable outcome of being fired.

ACTION SUMMARY

Reread the learning objectives below. Each objective is followed by questions. Answering these questions accurately will help you retain the most important concepts discussed in this chapter. After answering each question, check your answer against the answer key at the end of this chapter. (*Hint:* If you have any doubts regarding the correct response, consult the page number that follows the answer.)

Circle:

From studying this chapter, I will attempt to acquire

1. An overall understanding of how appropriate human resources can be provided for the organization.

  T F   **a.** An appropriate human resource is an individual whose qualifications are matched to job specifications.

  a b c d e   **b.** The term *appropriate human resources* refers to: (a) finding the right number of people to fill positions (b) individuals being satisfied with their jobs (c) individuals who help the organization achieve management system objectives (d) individuals who are ineffective (e) none of the above.

2. An appreciation for the relationship among recruitment efforts, an open position, sources of human resources, and the law.

  a b c d e   **a.** The process of narrowing a large number of candidates to a smaller field is called: (a) rushing (b) recruitment (c) selection (d) enlistment (e) enrollment.

  a b c d e   **b.** The characteristics of the individual who should be hired for the job are indicated by the: (a) job analysis (b) job specification (c) job description (d) job review (e) job identification.

3. Insights on the use of tests and assessment centers in employee selection.

  a b c d e   **a.** The level of skill or knowledge an individual possesses in a particular area is measured by: (a) aptitude tests (b) achievement tests (c) acuity tests (d) assessment tests (e) vocational interest tests.

  a b c d e   **b.** The following guideline does *not* apply when tests are used in selecting potential employees: (a) the tests should be both valid and reliable (b) the tests should be nondiscriminatory in nature (c) the tests should not be the sole source of information for determining whether someone is to be hired (d) such factors as potential and desire to obtain a position should not be assessed subjectively (e) none of the above—all are important guidelines.

4. An understanding of how the training process operates.

  a b c d e   **a.** Four steps involved in training individuals are: (1) designing the training program (2) evaluating the training program (3) determining training needs (4) administering the training program. The correct sequence for these steps is:
    (a) 1, 3, 2, 4
    (b) 3, 4, 1, 2
    (c) 2, 1, 3, 4
    (d) 3, 1, 4, 2
    (e) none of the above

  T F   **b.** The lecture offers learners an excellent opportunity to clarify meanings and ask questions, since communication is two-way.

5. A concept of what performance appraisals are and how they can best be conducted.

  a b c d e   **a.** Performance appraisals are important in an organization because they: (a) provide systematic judgments to support promotions (b) provide a basis for coaching (c) provide a basis for counseling (d) let subordinates know where they stand with the boss (e) all of the above.

  a b c d e   **b.** To achieve the maximum benefit from performance evaluations, a manager should: (a) focus only on the negative aspects of performance (b) punish the worker with negative feedback (c) be as subjective as possible (d) focus only on the positive aspects of performance (e) use only constructive feedback.

CASE DISCUSSSION QUESTIONS

"Northwestern Mutual Life Focuses on Recruitment" (p. 255) and its related Back-to-the-Case sections were written to help you better understand the management concepts contained in this chapter. Answer the following discussion questions about this Introductory Case to further enrich your understanding of the chapter content:

1. How important is the training of employees to an organization such as Northwestern? Explain.

2. What actions besides training must an organization such as Northwestern take to make employees as productive as possible?

3. Based upon information in the case, what do you think will be the biggest challenge for Northwestern's management in successfully providing appropriate human resources for the future? Explain.

SKILLS EXERCISE: PERFORMING A JOB ANALYSIS

In this chapter you learned that performing a job analysis entails determining a job description and a job specification. Assume that you are John Sheaffer (as discussed in the Introductory Case) and are doing a job analysis of the "Insurance Sales Agent" position at Northwestern Mutual. Recognizing that you are not an insurance expert, write a job description and a job specification for this position.

1. What is the difference between appropriate and inappropriate human resources?
2. List and define the four major steps in providing appropriate human resources for the organization.
3. What is the purpose of recruitment?
4. How are job analysis, job description, and job specification related?
5. List the advantages of promotion from within.
6. Compare and contrast the management inventory card, the position replacement form, and the management manpower replacement chart.
7. List three sources of human resources outside the organization. How can these sources be tapped?
8. Does the law influence organizational recruitment practices? If so, how?
9. Describe the role of the Equal Employment Opportunity Commission.
10. Can affirmative action programs be useful in recruitment? Explain.
11. Define *selection*.
12. What is the difference between aptitude tests and achievement tests?
13. Discuss three guidelines for using tests in the selection process.
14. What are assessment centers?
15. List and define the four main steps of the training process.
16. Explain two possible ways of determining organizational training needs.
17. What are the differences between the lecture and programmed learning as alternative methods of transmitting information in the training program?
18. On-the-job training methods include coaching, position rotation, and special project committees. Explain how each of these methods works.
19. What are performance appraisals, and why should they be used?
20. If someone asked your advice on how to conduct performance appraisals, describe in detail what you would say.

1. **a.** F, p. 256
   b. c, p. 256
2. **a.** b, p. 256
   b. b, p. 257
3. **a.** b, p. 264
   b. d, p. 265
4. **a.** d, p. 266
   b. F, p. 268
5. **a.** e, p. 271
   b. e, p. 272

A new industry, sometimes called *employee leasing*, has emerged to help businesses cope with human resource management. Known as *professional employer organizations,* or *PEOs,* these firms have grown from a handful in 1984 to some 2,200 companies, leasing almost 2 million employees and generating $10 billion in revenues, in 1995. PEOs are valuable to all kinds and sizes of businesses. For example, with human capital an increasing cost of doing business, American companies are instituting downsizing programs, typically by eliminating or reorganizing their workforces. PEOs were developed to help companies outsource nonessential tasks related to their human resource needs. PEOs offer businesses two distinct options.

One option provides professional employees for specific projects. For example, a business can tap a pool of experienced executives or skilled workers to replace those lost in downsizing or to staff a special project. This option is particularly attractive to a company that needs engineers for a project that may last only a year or two.

The second option meets the needs of companies that do not want to bear the expense of full-time employees. The PEO can place *all* of the company's current employees on its own payroll, thereby becoming the employer of record and taking legal responsibility for them. The PEO takes care of paychecks, W-2 forms, workers' compensation claims, health insurance matters, personnel placement and safety, and even personnel training. It may even handle EEOC and other government agency matters, maintain a credit union, and manage the company's facilities.

Outsourcing the human resource function is a particularly valuable option for small businesses. A human resource department is often not economically cost-effective at a company with fewer than 100 employees, yet every company has personnel matters that must be attended to, even if it employs only one person. The business owner, for instance, can easily be overwhelmed by government-mandated policies and practices, often discovering costly regulatory changes after the fact. As much as 25 percent of an employer's time may be taken up by these matters.

PEOs were spawned both by increasing governmental pressures on businesses to remain in compliance with human resource laws and by the need to focus sharply on their core competencies in the face of severe competition. As a specialist, the PEO can administer payrolls in a more cost-effective manner. In the purchase of insurance and related matters, it can pool the employees into larger groups that have more economic clout. Generally, the business owner who uses a PEO saves money and has satisfied personnel whose needs are professionally met in accordance with governmental regulations.

It must be noted, however, that PEOs are neither management consulting firms nor payroll companies. A professional employer organization differs from the first in that it is a continuing on-site presence rather than a periodic advisor. A PEO differs from a payroll company in that it takes care of all other employee needs as well as paychecks. Thus the business owner is freed to concentrate on getting the product out the door. PEOs help businesses lower human resources costs in two ways:

1. Competitive pressures force smaller businesses to provide benefit packages in line with those offered by larger employers. The unique services of PEOs allow these businesses with limited resources to concentrate on developing their strategic strengths with minimum human resources expenditures.

2. Workers' compensation insurance can be an incredibly expensive benefit for certain companies or industries that have unsatisfactory claim histories. With workers' compensation mandated by law, a leasing company is ensured a steady source of motivated prospects.

For these reasons, the growth in PEOs in the next decade should be similar to the growth experienced by the payroll-processing industry in its infancy. From large companies such as AT&T and Delta Airlines to a plethora of smaller companies, PEOs are expanding their client portfolios around the nation. And there's still room for growth. Surveys indicate that PEOs are now used by only 1 percent of the 6.2 million small businesses in the United States. Since 42 percent of all U.S. workers are employed by small businesses, this field is obviously a fertile one for PEOs. Thus the industry should continue to grow well into the next century.

QUESTIONS

1. Does employee leasing diminish workers' loyalty toward a company? Is this a positive or a negative factor for workers? For the company?

2. Would employee leasing be an attractive alternative for Boeing? For Procter & Gamble? Which company would derive the greater benefit from employee leasing? Why?

3. Should employee leasing replace the human resource function in a company? Explain your answer.

4. During a business slowdown, would an employee of a leasing company have a better chance of staying employed than someone working for a large corporation? Explain your answer.

Managing Change: From Stress to the Virtual Organization

STUDENT LEARNING OBJECTIVES

From studying this chapter, I will attempt to acquire

1. A working definition of *changing an organization*

2. An understanding of the relative importance of change and stability to an organization

3. Some ability to recognize what kind of changes should be made within an organization

4. An appreciation for why the people affected by a change should be considered when the change is being made

5. Some facility at evaluating change

6. An understanding of how organizational change and stress are related

7. Knowledge about virtuality as a vehicle for organizational change

CHAPTER OUTLINE

Introductory Case: *AT&T Changes Where and How People Work*

FUNDAMENTALS OF CHANGING AN ORGANIZATION
Defining Changing an Organization
Change versus Stability

FACTORS TO CONSIDER WHEN CHANGING AN ORGANIZATION
The Change Agent

Across Industries: *Microcomputer Manufacturing—Steven Jobs: Apple's Remarkable Change Agent*
Determining What Should Be Changed

Ethics Spotlight: *Attitude Change Is the Key to Establishing a Socially Responsible Position on Job Safety at Sonoco*
The Kind of Change to Make

Diversity Spotlight: *McDonald's Corporation Is Changing the Way Employees Think about Disabled Workers*
Individuals Affected by the Change
Evaluation of the Change

CHANGE AND STRESS
Defining Stress
The Importance of Studying Stress
Managing Stress in Organizations

VIRTUALITY
Defining a Virtual Organization
Degrees of Virtuality

Management and the Internet: *Virtual Training at Cable and Wireless Communications*
The Virtual Office

AT&T CHANGES WHERE AND HOW PEOPLE WORK

REMINDER: THE INTRODUCTORY CASE WRAP-UP (P. 298) CONTAINS DISCUSSION QUESTIONS AND A SKILLS EXERCISE TO FURTHER ILLUSTRATE THE APPLICATION OF CHAPTER CONCEPTS TO THIS VIGNETTE.

AT&T is one of the world's premier communications and information services companies, serving more than 90 million consumer, business, and government customers. The company has annual revenues of more than $52 billion and employs more than 130,000 workers. It runs the world's largest, most sophisticated communications network and is the leading provider of long-distance and wireless services. AT&T operates in more than 200 countries and territories around the world. The company also offers online services and access to home entertainment, and has begun to deliver local telephone service. AT&T's mission statement is as follows:

> We aspire to be the most admired and valuable company in the world. Our goal is to enrich our customers' personal lives and to make their businesses more successful by bringing to market exciting and useful communications services, building shareowner value in the process.

In late 1994, AT&T formed an eight-member Alternative Work Arrangements (AWA) team. The purpose of this team was to assess and propose various new company options for alternative work arrangements—new and different work situations that could be instituted within the company. In essence, AWA was to develop a comprehensive plan for implementing new, desirable work situations. The plan was to include conclusions that were based on surveying employee ideas and assessing company work needs. In addition, the plan was to include proposed guidelines for implementing recommended new work situations along with new training packages necessary to acclimate people to these new situations. Lastly, the plan was to include recommended purchases of equipment, if any, necessary to make the new work situations functional.

Although AWA studied several options like continuously changing work schedules and a compressed workweek, the team finally settled on endorsing only the initiation of telecommuting, employees essentially working from home via e-mail, videoconferencing, and other information technology advances. One area of concern about instituting a new telecommuting work situation came from supervisors at AT&T. They were concerned about how to measure the productivity of telecommuting

About 12 percent of AT&T's workforce has a formal telecommuting arrangement with management, works from a virtual office, or works from a remote location. Michelle Swiatek works from her home in Illinois as billing coordinator for the Computer Technology Center, part of the Quality, Engineering, Software and Technologies (QUEST) group. Property of At&T Archives, reprinted with permission of AT&T.

employees. In order to address this concern, AWA actually devised a new feedback form focusing on telecommuter productivity. In essence, this form gave supervisors a new, useful tool for evaluating the performance of telecommuting workers.

Based on the recommendation of AWA, AT&T instituted a new telecommuting program. By the beginning of 1995, almost 28 percent of AT&T managers had become telecommuters. Although not without its problems, the general consensus today at AT&T is that the telecommuting program continues to be successful. The company benefits in areas like reducing office expenses because employees work from home and increasing productivity because workers are generally not interrupted as much at home as in traditional offices. Perhaps most importantly to employees, the new program gives them a better balance between their work and family lives.

In essence, the Alternative Work Arrangements (AWA) team discussed in the Introductory Case is faced with making a recommendation about what changes to make within AT&T and how to make them. The changes AWA must recommend focus on implementing new and better ways to do work. Members of teams like AWA as well as individual managers who face making similar organizational changes would find the major topics in this chapter very useful and practical. These topics are the following: fundamentals of changing an organization, factors to consider when changing the organization, organizational change and stress, and virtuality.

FUNDAMENTALS OF CHANGING AN ORGANIZATION

Thus far, discussion in this "Organizing" section of the text has centered on the fundamentals of organizing, furnishing appropriate human resources for the organization, authority, delegation, and responsibility. This chapter focuses on changing the organization.

DEFINING CHANGING AN ORGANIZATION

Changing an organization is the process of modifying an existing organization to increase organizational effectiveness—that is, the extent to which an organization accomplishes its objectives. These modifications can involve virtually any organizational segment, but typically affect the lines of organizational authority, the levels of responsibility held by various organization members, and the established lines of organizational communication. Driven by new technology, expanding global opportunities, and the trend toward organizational streamlining, almost all modern organizations are changing in some way.[1]

THE IMPORTANCE OF CHANGE Most managers agree that if an organization is to thrive, it must change continually in response to significant developments in the environment, such as changing customer needs, technological breakthroughs, and new government regulations. The study of organizational change is extremely important because all managers at all organizational levels are faced throughout their careers with the task of changing their organization. Managers who determine appropriate changes to make in their organizations and then implement such changes successfully enable their organizations to be more flexible and innovative. Because change is such a fundamental part of organizational existence, such managers are very valuable to organizations of all kinds.[2]

Many managers consider change to be so critical to organizational success that they encourage employees to continually search for areas in which beneficial changes can be made. To take a classic example, General Motors provides employees with a "think list" to encourage them to develop ideas for organizational change and to remind them that change is vital to the continued success of GM. The think list contains the following questions:[3]

1. Can a machine be used to do a better or faster job?
2. Can the fixture now in use be improved?
3. Can handling of materials for the machine be improved?
4. Can a special tool be used to combine the operations?
5. Can the quality of the part being produced be improved by changing the sequence of the operation?
6. Can the material used be cut or trimmed differently for greater economy or efficiency?
7. Can the operation be made safer?
8. Can paperwork regarding this job be eliminated?
9. Can established procedures be simplified?

CHANGE VERSUS STABILITY

In addition to organizational change, some degree of stability is a prerequisite for long-term organizational success. Figure 13.1 presents a model developed by Hellriegel and Slocum that shows the relative importance of change and stability to organizational survival. Although these authors use the word *adaptation* in their model rather than *change,* the two terms are essentially synonymous.

> **Changing an organization** is the process of modifying an existing organization to increase organizational effectiveness.

FIGURE 13.1 ▸ Adaptation, stability, and organizational survival

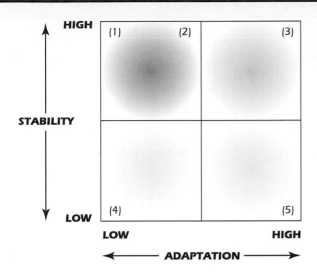

(1) High death probability (slow)
(2) High survival probability
(3) High survival and growth probability
(4) Certainty of death (quick)
(5) Certainty of death (quick)

The model stresses that organizational survival and growth are most probable when both stability and adaptation are high within the organization (number 3 on the model depicted in Figure 13.1). The organization without enough stability to complement change is at a definite disadvantage. When stability is low, the probability of organizational survival and growth declines. Change after change without regard for the essential role of stability typically results in confusion and employee stress.[4]

BACK TO THE CASE

The above information furnishes several insights about how AWA should make decisions, such as whether or not to recommend a particular type of change in AT&T's work arrangements. AWA should evaluate if a change would better enable AT&T to accomplish its objectives. It should also understand that making such change is extremely important. If AT&T is to have continued success over the long run, change will probably have to be made a number of times. In fact, appropriate change is so important to a company like AT&T that AWA might want to consider initiating some type of program that would encourage employees to submit their ideas continually on new alternative work ideas that could increase company effectiveness. When considering possible changes, however, AWA will have to keep in mind that some level of work arrangements stability is also necessary to survival and growth.

FACTORS TO CONSIDER WHEN CHANGING AN ORGANIZATION

How managers deal with the major factors that need to be considered when an organizational change is being made will largely determine how successful that change will be. The following factors should be considered whenever change is being contemplated:

1. The change agent
2. Determining what should be changed
3. The kind of change to make
4. Individuals affected by the change
5. Evaluation of the change

Although the following sections discuss each of these factors individually, Figure 13.2 makes the point that it is a collective influence that ultimately determines the success of a change.

FIGURE 13.2

The collective influence of five major factors on the success of changing an organization

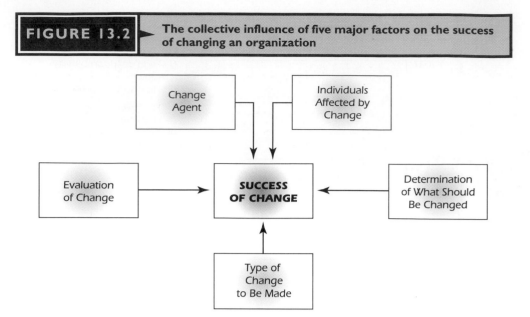

Change Agent

Individuals Affected by Change

Evaluation of Change

SUCCESS OF CHANGE

Determination of What Should Be Changed

Type of Change to Be Made

▶ THE CHANGE AGENT

A **change agent** is an individual inside or outside the organization who tries to modify an existing organizational situation.

Perhaps the most important factor managers need to consider when changing an organization is who will be the **change agent**—the individual inside or outside the organization who tries to modify the existing organizational situation. The change agent might be a self-designated manager within the organization or an outside consultant hired because of a special expertise in a particular area. This individual might be responsible for making very broad changes, like altering the culture of the whole organization, or more narrow ones, like designing and implementing a new safety program or a new quality program.[5] Although in some circumstances the change agent will not be a manager, the term *manager* and *change agent* are used synonymously throughout this chapter.

Special skills are necessary for success as a change agent. Among them are the ability to determine how a change should be made, the skill to solve change-related problems, and facility in using behavioral science tools to influence people appropriately during the change process. Perhaps the most overlooked skill of successful change agents, however, is the ability to determine how much change employees can withstand.[6]

Overall, managers should choose change agents who have the most expertise in all these areas. A potentially beneficial change might not result in any advantages for the organization if a person without expertise in these areas is designated to make the change.

VF Services is a division of the $5.5 billion holding company, VF Corp., whose subsidiaries design, manufacture, and market brand-name jeans, intimate apparel, knitwear, children's playwear, and other apparel. Some of VF's brands are Lee, Wrangler, Jantzen, and Healthtex. To function as a change agent at VF Services, someone like president Tom Payne would need the skill to evaluate situations, make decisions about the level of change needed, and communicate that change throughout the organization, ensuring that it is accepted and implemented.

STEVEN JOBS: APPLE'S REMARKABLE CHANGE AGENT

This section discussed change agents as a component of organizational change. Steven Jobs, the top manager at Apple Computer, Inc., is perhaps the most talked about change agent in the modern management world.

Apple Computer, Inc. ignited the personal computer revolution in the 1970s by introducing the Apple II, and then reinvented the personal computer in the 1980s with the Macintosh computer. Apple is now committed to its original mission—to bring the best personal computing products and support to students, educators, designers, scientists, engineers, businesspersons, and consumers in over 140 countries around the world. Apple owns manufacturing facilities in the United States, Ireland, and Singapore. Distribution facilities are located in the United States.

In December 1996, Steve Jobs returned to Apple Computer after having left the company he cofounded 20 years earlier, as special advisor to CEO Gil Amelio. As employees admitted, Apple was in a death spiral. Sales and market share were falling sharply. Expenses were ballooning out of control. Departments battled one another.

Some of Amelio's top managers were in denial while others were leaving. After spiraling downward for months, Amelio was ousted and the board of directors turned to Jobs, who quickly assembled a sympathetic core group of lieutenants. He then persuaded most of Amelio's board of directors to quit. Once they resigned, he appointed a new board. In September, the new board invited Jobs to serve as the interim CEO, and he agreed. Free to act, Jobs moved with great speed to make changes in Apple's products, structure, personnel, manufacturing, distribution, and marketing.

In its first fiscal year since Jobs took over as interim CEO in September 1997, the company made a profit of $309 million on revenues of $5.9 billion. The year before Jobs arrived, Apple had lost $1 billion on revenues of $7.1 billion. The crowd of press, analysts, and employees at the Flint Center gasped when Jobs revealed a $109 million profit for the fiscal fourth quarter ended September 25. That beat Wall Street's consensus estimate by 38 percent. When you consider all the changes that Jobs has made at Apple and the financial impact of these changes, one thing is clear: Jobs is a savvy change agent.

BACK TO THE CASE

Some appointed manager at AT&T would undoubtedly have the main role in deciding on what structural changes to make or upon which new alternative work arrangements to implement as well as actually implementing such changes. For these particular changes, therefore, this manager would be the change agent. The change agent should be carefully selected giving special consideration to individuals with abilities to determine if and how particular changes recommended by AWA should be made. The individual best suited for this change agent role is probably the individual best suited in the company to evaluate the advantages and disadvantages of having one type of structure or work situation as opposed to another.

The change agent must have the ability to use behavioral science tools to influence organization members during the implementation of planned change. As examples, the change agent must determine how much structural or new work situation change AT&T employees can withstand, influence employees so that they learn to work together in their new roles, and implement this change, perhaps gradually, so employees will not be overwhelmed. Overall, the ability to use behavioral science tools will help the change agent to be successful in implementing needed work situation changes at AT&T.

►DETERMINING WHAT SHOULD BE CHANGED

Another major factor managers need to consider is exactly what should be changed within the organization. In general, managers should make only those changes that will increase organizational effectiveness.

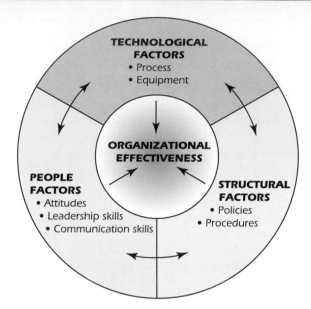

It has been generally accepted for many years that organizational effectiveness depends primarily on activities centering around three classes of factors:

1. People
2. Structure
3. Technology

People factors are attitudes, leadership skills, communication skills, and all other characteristics of the human resources within the organization. **Structural factors** are organizational controls, such as policies and procedures. And **technological factors** are any types of equipment or processes that assist organization members in the performance of their jobs.

For an organization to maximize its effectiveness, appropriate people must be matched with appropriate technology and appropriate structure. Thus people factors, technological factors, and structural factors are not independent determinants of organizational effectiveness. Instead, as Figure 13.3 shows, organizational effectiveness is determined by the relationship of these three factors.

People factors are attitudes, leadership skills, communication skills, and all other characteristics of the organization's employees.

Structural factors are organizational controls, such as policies and procedures.

Technological factors are any types of equipment or processes that assist organization members in the performance of their jobs.

ETHICS SPOTLIGHT

Attitude Change Is the Key to Establishing a Socially Responsible Position on Job Safety at Sonoco

Progressive companies take seriously the challenge to establish a safe working environment for their employees. They are determined to meet this challenge, not only because fewer accidents means a more productive workforce, but also because they recognize their social responsibility to provide a workplace in which employees are reasonably free from harm. The Sonoco Products Company, an organization that produces primarily paperboard packaging, had to change employee attitudes in order to reshape the company into one that is appropriately responsible for job safety.

The Corrugating Department of Sonoco Products Company's Paper Division in Hartsville, South Carolina, celebrated a milestone recently when its employees completed their first year of injury-free work. As a result, the Paper Division received the annual Best Safety Record award from the Southern Pulp & Paper Safety Association. To achieve this record, management had to instill in employees the attitude that job safety is important and worthy of serious attention from everyone at Sonoco. To that end, the company designed and implemented a program called STOP—Safety Training Observation

Program—to impress upon employees the importance of job safety and to help them develop safe work habits. STOP was successful because Sonoco management was solidly behind it and spared no effort in pushing the idea that employees and management share responsi-

bility for creating a safe work environment. Once Sonoco employees developed the attitude that a safe workplace is indeed important, actually establishing such an environment became a realistic objective for management.

►THE KIND OF CHANGE TO MAKE

The kind of change to make is the third major factor that managers need to consider when they set out to change an organization. Most changes can be categorized as one of three kinds:

1. Technological
2. Structural
3. People

Note that these three kinds of change correspond to the three main determinants of organizational effectiveness—each change is named for the determinant it emphasizes.

For example, **technological change** emphasizes modifying the level of technology in the management system. Because this kind of change so often involves outside experts and highly technical language, it is more profitable to discuss structural change and people change in detail in this text.

Technological change is a type of organizational change that emphasizes modifying the level of technology in the management system.

STRUCTURAL CHANGE Structural change emphasizes increasing organizational effectiveness by changing controls that influence organization members during the performance of their jobs. The following sections further describe this approach and discuss matrix organizations (organizations modified to complete a special project) as an example of structural change.

Describing Structural Change   **Structural change** is change aimed at increasing organizational effectiveness through modifications to the existing organizational structure. These modifications can take several forms:

Structural change is a type of organizational change that emphasizes modifying an existing organizational structure.

1. Clarifying and defining jobs
2. Modifying organizational structure to fit the communication needs of the organization
3. Decentralizing the organization to reduce the cost of coordination, increase the controllability of subunits, increase motivation, and gain greater flexibility

Although structural change must take account of people and technology to be successful, its primary focus is obviously on changing organizational structure. In general, managers choose to make structural changes within an organization if information they have gathered indicates that the present structure is the main cause of organizational ineffectiveness. The precise structural changes they choose to make will vary from situation to situation, of course. After changes to organizational structure have been made, management should conduct periodic reviews to make sure the changes are accomplishing their intended purposes.[7]

Matrix Organizations   Matrix organizations provide a good illustration of structural change. According to C. J. Middleton, a **matrix organization** is a traditional organization that is modified primarily for the purpose of completing some kind of special project. Essentially, a matrix organization is one in which individuals from various functional departments are assigned to a project manager responsible for accomplishing some specific task.[8] For this reason, matrix organizations are also called *project organizations*. The project itself may be either long term or short term, and the employees needed to complete it are borrowed from various organizational segments.

A **matrix organization** is a traditional organizational structure that is modified primarily for the purpose of completing some kind of special project.

John F. Mee has developed a classic example showing how a traditional organization can be changed into a matrix organization.[9] Figure 13.4 presents a portion of a traditional organizational structure based primarily on product line. Although this design is generally useful, management might learn for example, that it makes it impossible for organization members to give adequate attention to three government projects of extreme importance to long-term organizational success.

FIGURE 13.4 **Portion of a traditional organizational structure based primarily on product line**

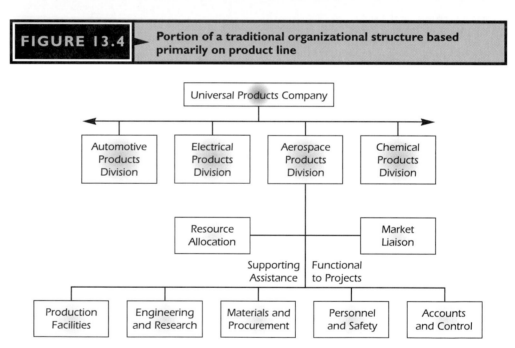

Making the Change to Matrix: An Example. Figure 13.5 illustrates one way management could change this traditional organizational structure into a matrix organization to facilitate completion of the three government projects. A manager would be appointed for each of the three projects and allocated personnel with appropriate skills to complete the project. The three project managers would have authority over the employees assigned to them and be accountable for the performance of those people. Each of the three project managers would be placed on the chart in Figure 13.5 in one of the three boxes labeled Venus Project, Mars Project, and Saturn Project, and the work flow related to each project would go from right to left on the chart. After the projects were completed, the organization chart would revert to its original design—assuming that design is more advantageous under most circumstances.

There are several advantages and disadvantages to making structural changes such as those reflected by the matrix organization. The major advantages are that such structural changes

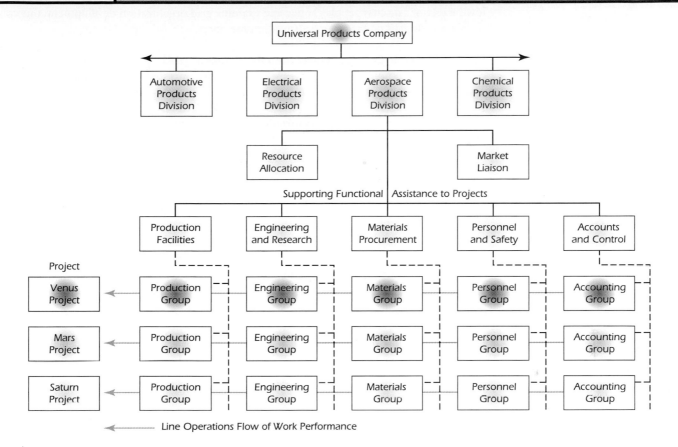

Line Operations Flow of Work Performance

generally result in better control of a project, better customer relations, shorter project development time, and lower project costs. In addition, matrix organizations are flexible enough to allow managers to shift resources to special projects as needed. The downside is that such structural changes generally create more complex internal operations, which commonly cause conflict, encourage inconsistency in the application of company policy, and result in a more difficult situation to manage.

The advantages and disadvantages of changing a traditional organization into a matrix organization will have different weights according to the situation. One point is clear, however. For a matrix organization to be effective and efficient, organization members must be willing to learn and execute somewhat different organizational roles than they are used to.[10]

BACK TO THE CASE

The AT&T change agent chosen to put AWA recommendations into action must make different types of changes. The preceding information discussed how a change agent can change technological factors, people factors, and structural factors in order to increase organizational effectiveness. AWA's recommendation will likely include change in all these factors. New work arrangements would be categorized as changing structural factors. In addition, however, such new work arrangements would include technological change centering on features like using new computers and the Internet. Lastly the new work situation changes must focus on people—changing the way people actually do their work at AT&T will be facilitated through actions such as the change agent communicating with off-site workers, molding off-site workers into a team with a distinctive culture, and motivating off-site workers.

PEOPLE CHANGE Although successfully changing people factors necessarily involves some consideration of structure and technology, the primary emphasis is on people. The following sections discuss people change and examine grid organization development, one commonly used means of changing organization members.

People change is a type of organizational change that emphasizes modifying certain aspects of organization members to increase organizational effectiveness.

Describing People Change: Organization Development (OD) People change emphasizes increasing organizational effectiveness by changing certain aspects of organization members. The focus of this kind of change is on such factors as employees' attitudes and leadership skills. In general, managers should attempt to make this kind of change when human resources are shown to be the main cause of organizational ineffectiveness.

DIVERSITY SPOTLIGHT | **McDonald's Corporation Is Changing the Way Employees Think about Disabled Workers**

In 1990, President George Bush signed into law the Americans with Disabilities Act (ADA), which bans discrimination against disabled workers. Although some employers may be concerned about hiring the disabled, companies like DuPont and Target Stores have found that employing the disabled is a sound business practice. Their history in this area shows that many disabled workers are loyal, enthusiastic employees and make valuable contributions toward attaining organizational goals.

To effectively integrate disabled workers into the organization, however, some managers have discovered that they must change the way other employees think of their disabled coworkers. These managers have developed specific programs to prepare employees for appropriate interaction with disabled workers. For example, McDonald's

Corporation sponsors awareness training in which employees role-play disabled workers to experience how these workers feel and how they may react to other employees' statements or attitudes concerning them. The experience of companies with a successful history of employing and integrating the disabled into the workforce indicates that awareness training should avoid prejudging disabled people's limitations. Employees who have not had direct experience with disabled workers often overestimate their limitations and consequently buffer them from challenges they can actually handle quite well.

Hiring the disabled can provide significant benefits to an organization. One is that the disabled usually are loyal and productive workers and managers. Another is that consumers commonly develop a deep sense of respect for companies that hire the disabled.

Organization development (OD) is the process that emphasizes changing an organization by changing organization members and bases these changes on an overview of structure, technology, and all other organizational ingredients.

Grid organization development (grid OD) is a commonly used organization development technique based on a theoretical model called the *managerial grid.*

A **managerial grid** is a theoretical model based on the premise that concern for people and concern for production are the two primary attitudes that influence management style.

The process of people change can be referred to as **organization development (OD)**. Although OD focuses mainly on changing certain aspects of people, these changes are based on an overview of structure, technology, and all other organizational ingredients.

Grid OD One commonly used OD technique for changing people in organizations is called **grid organization development,** or **grid OD.**[11] The **managerial grid,** a basic model describing various managerial styles, is used as the foundation for grid OD. The managerial grid is based on the premise that various managerial styles can be described by means of two primary attitudes of the manager: concern for people and concern for production. Within this model, each attitude is placed on an axis, which is scaled 1 through 9 and is used to generate five managerial styles. Figure 13.6 shows the managerial grid, its five managerial styles, and the factors that characterize each of these styles.

The Ideal Style. The central theme of this managerial grid is that 9,9 management (as shown on the grid in Figure 13.6) is the ideal managerial style. Managers using this style have a high concern for both people and production. Managers using any other style have lesser degrees of concern for people or production, and are thought to reduce organizational success accordingly. The purpose of grid OD is to change organization managers so they will use the 9,9 management style.

Main Training Phases. How is a grid OD program conducted? The program has six main training phases that are used with all managers within the organization. The first two phases focus on acquainting managers with the managerial grid concept and assisting them in determining which managerial style they most commonly use. The last four phases of the grid OD

FIGURE 13.6 ► The managerial grid

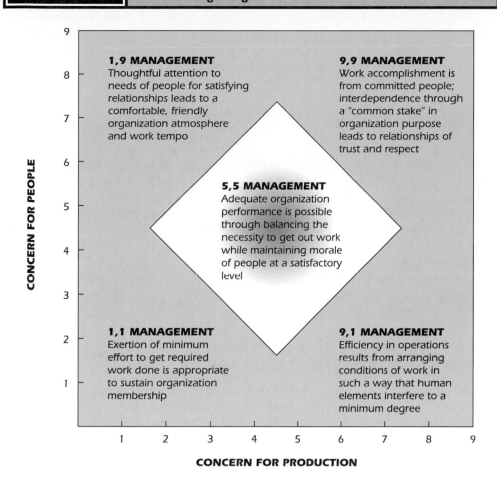

CONCERN FOR PEOPLE

1,9 MANAGEMENT
Thoughtful attention to needs of people for satisfying relationships leads to a comfortable, friendly organization atmosphere and work tempo

9,9 MANAGEMENT
Work accomplishment is from committed people; interdependence through a "common stake" in organization purpose leads to relationships of trust and respect

5,5 MANAGEMENT
Adequate organization performance is possible through balancing the necessity to get out work while maintaining morale of people at a satisfactory level

1,1 MANAGEMENT
Exertion of minimum effort to get required work done is appropriate to sustain organization membership

9,1 MANAGEMENT
Efficiency in operations results from arranging conditions of work in such a way that human elements interfere to a minimum degree

CONCERN FOR PRODUCTION

program concentrate on encouraging managers to adopt the 9,9 management style and showing them how to use this style within their specific job situation. Emphasis throughout the program is on developing teamwork within the organization.

Some evidence suggests that grid OD is effective in enhancing profit, positively changing managerial behavior, and positively influencing managerial attitudes and values.[12] Grid OD will have to undergo more rigorous testing for an extended period of time, however, before conclusive statements about it can be made.

The Status of Organization Development   If the entire OD area is taken into consideration, changes that emphasize both people and the organization as a whole seem to have inherent strength. There are, however, several commonly voiced weaknesses in OD efforts. These weaknesses are as follows:[13]

1. The effectiveness of an OD program is difficult to evaluate
2. OD programs are generally too time-consuming
3. OD objectives are commonly too vague
4. The total costs of an OD program are difficult to gauge at the time the program starts
5. OD programs are generally too expensive

These weaknesses, however, should not eliminate OD from consideration, but rather should indicate areas to perfect within it. Managers can improve the quality of OD efforts by doing the following:[14]

1. Systematically tailoring OD programs to meet the specific needs of the organization
2. Continually demonstrating exactly how people should change their behavior
3. Conscientiously changing organizational reward systems so organization members who change their behavior in ways suggested by the OD program are rewarded

The software manufacturer PeopleSoft employs a diverse workforce whose members function in a casual environment. Competitors and customers know, however, that PeopleSoft's concern for its employees' welfare should not be mistaken for a low priority on business matters such as quality and market responsiveness.

Managers have been employing OD techniques for several decades, and broad and useful applications of these techniques continue to be documented in the more recent management literature. OD techniques are currently being applied not only to business organizations but also to many other types of organizations, such as religious organizations. Moreover, OD applications are being documented throughout the world, with increasing use being reported in countries like Hungary, Poland, and the United Kingdom.[15]

BACK TO THE CASE

Technically, changing work situations at AT&T would not be classified as people change. Although the people involved in the change must be considered to some extent, the main emphasis of this change is on structural factors.

If, however, a change agent at AT&T would believe that problems with human resources are the main cause of organizational ineffectiveness and *not* the work situation, he or she would probably plan and initiate an organization development program rather than a work situation improvement focus. On the other hand, the change agent may find it necessary to use grid OD in order to modify management styles and produce more cooperative team effort once established work changes are in place and a "new" kind of worker is operating.

▶ INDIVIDUALS AFFECTED BY THE CHANGE

A fourth major factor to be considered by managers when changing an organization is the people who will be affected by the change. A good assessment of what to change and how to make the change will be wasted if organization members do not support the change. To increase the chances of employee support, managers should be aware of the following factors:

1. The usual employee resistance to change
2. How this resistance can be reduced

RESISTANCE TO CHANGE Resistance to change within an organization is as common as the need for change. After managers decide to make some organizational change, they typically meet with employee resistance aimed at preventing that change from occurring.[16] Behind this resistance by organization members lies the fear of some personal loss, such as a reduction in personal prestige, a disturbance of established social and working relationships, and personal failure because of inability to carry out new job responsibilities.

REDUCING RESISTANCE TO CHANGE To ensure the success of needed modifications, managers must be able to reduce the effects of the resistance that typically accompanies proposed change. Resistance can usually be lowered by following these guidelines:[17]

1. *Avoid surprises*—People need time to evaluate a proposed change before management implements it. Unless they are given time to evaluate and absorb how the change will affect them, employees are likely to be automatically opposed to it. Whenever possible, therefore, individuals who will be affected by a change should be informed of the kind of change being considered and the probability that it will be adopted.
2. *Promote real understanding*—When fear of personal loss related to a proposed change is reduced, opposition to the change is also reduced. Most managers find that ensuring that organization members thoroughly understand a proposed change is a major step in reducing this fear. Understanding may even generate enthusiastic support for the change if it focuses employees on individual gains that could materialize as a result of it. People should be given information that will help them answer the following change-related questions they invariably will have:

   ▶ Will I lose my job?
   ▶ Will my old skills become obsolete?

- Am I capable of producing effectively under the new system?
- Will my power and prestige decline?
- Will I be given more responsibility than I care to assume?
- Will I have to work longer hours?
- Will it force me to betray or desert my good friends?

3. *Set the stage for change*—Perhaps the most powerful tool for reducing resistance to change is management's positive attitude toward the change. This attitude should be displayed openly by top and middle management as well as by lower management. In essence, management should convey that change is one of the basic prerequisites for a successful organization. Management should also strive to encourage change for increasing organizational effectiveness, rather than for the sake of trying something new. To reinforce this positive attitude toward change, some portion of organizational rewards should be earmarked for those organization members who are most instrumental in implementing constructive change.

4. *Make tentative change*—Resistance to change can also be reduced if the changes are made on a tentative basis. This approach establishes a trial period during which organization members spend some time working under a proposed change before voicing support or nonsupport of it. Tentative change is based on the assumption that a trial period during which organization members live under a change is the best way of reducing feared personal loss. Judson has summarized the benefits of using the tentative approach:

- Employees affected by the change are able to test their reactions to the new situation before committing themselves irrevocably to it
- Those who will live under the change are able to acquire more facts on which to base their attitudes and behavior toward the change
- Those who had strong preconceptions about the change are in a better position to assess it with objectivity. Consequently, they may review and modify some of their preconceptions
- Those involved are less likely to regard the change as a threat
- Management is better able to evaluate the method of change and make any necessary modifications before carrying it out more fully

► EVALUATION OF THE CHANGE

As with all other managerial actions, managers should spend some time evaluating the changes they make. The purpose of this evaluation is not only to gain insights into how the change itself might be modified to further increase its organizational effectiveness but also to determine whether the steps taken to make the change should be modified to increase organizational effectiveness the next time they are used.

According to Margulies and Wallace, making this evaluation may be difficult because the data from individual change programs may be unreliable.[18] Nevertheless, managers must do their best to evaluate change in order to increase the organizational benefits from the change.

Evaluation of change often involves watching for symptoms that indicate that further change is necessary. For example, if organization members continue to be oriented more to the past than the future, if they recognize the obligations of rituals more readily than they do the challenges of current problems, or if they pay greater allegiance to departmental goals than to overall company objectives, the probability is high that further change is necessary.

A word of caution is needed at this point. Although symptoms such as those listed in the preceding paragraph generally indicate that further change is warranted, this is not always the case. The decision to make additional changes should not be made solely on the basis of symptoms. More objective information should be considered. In general, additional change is justified if it will accomplish any of the following goals:[19]

1. Further improve the means for satisfying someone's economic wants
2. Increase profitability
3. Promote human work for human beings
4. Contribute to individual satisfaction and social well-being

The change agent at AT&T must realize that even though he or she may formulate a structural change that would be beneficial to the company, any attempt to implement this change could prove unsuccessful if it does not appropriately consider the people affected by the change. For example, if a new work arrangement is implemented requiring certain employees to work from home, employees may fear that this change will diminish their opportunities for promotion within the company. As a result, they may subtly resist the change.

To overcome such resistance, the change agent could use strategies like giving employees enough time to fully evaluate and understand the change, presenting a positive attitude about the change, and, if resistance is very strong, making the proposed change tentative until it is fully evaluated.

All work situation changes at AT&T need to be evaluated after implementation to discover if further organizational change is necessary and if the change process used might be improved for future use. For example, concerning the change of establishing a new work situation requiring certain workers to work only from home, the evaluation process could indicate that managers needed more personal contact with workers and that workers should work only half-time at home and half-time in the office.

CHANGE AND STRESS

Whenever managers implement changes, they should be concerned about the stress they may be creating. If the stress is significant enough, it may well cancel out the improvement that was anticipated from the change. In fact, stress could result in the organization being *less* effective than it was before the change was attempted. This section defines stress and discusses the importance of studying and managing it.

DEFINING STRESS

Stress is the bodily strain that an individual experiences as a result of coping with some environmental factor.

The bodily strain that an individual experiences as a result of coping with some environmental factor is **stress.** Hans Selye, an early authority on this subject, said that stress constitutes the factors affecting wear and tear on the body. In organizations, this wear and tear is caused primarily by the body's unconscious mobilization of energy when an individual is confronted with organizational or work demands.[20]

THE IMPORTANCE OF STUDYING STRESS

There are several sound reasons for studying stress:[21]

- ▶ Stress can have damaging psychological and physiological effects on employees' health and on their contributions to organizational effectiveness. It can cause heart disease, and it can prevent employees from concentrating or making decisions.
- ▶ Stress is a major cause of employee absenteeism and turnover. Certainly, such factors severely limit the potential success of an organization.
- ▶ A stressed employee can affect the safety of other workers or even the public.
- ▶ Stress represents a very significant cost to organizations. Some estimates put the cost of stress-related problems in the U.S. economy at $150 billion a year. As examples of these costs, many modern organizations spend a great deal of money treating stress-related employee problems through medical programs, and they must absorb expensive legal fees when handling stress-related lawsuits.

MANAGING STRESS IN ORGANIZATIONS

Because stress is felt by virtually all employees in all organizations, insights about managing stress are valuable to all managers. This section is built on the assumption that in order to appropriately manage stress in organizations, managers must do the following:

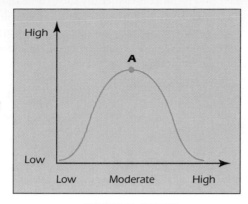

1. Understand how stress influences worker performance
2. Identify where unhealthy stress exists in organizations
3. Help employees handle stress

UNDERSTANDING HOW STRESS INFLUENCES WORKER PERFORMANCE

To deal with stress among employees, managers must understand the relationship between the amount of stress felt by a worker and the worker's performance. This relationship is shown in Figure 13.7. Note that extremely high and extremely low levels of stress tend to have negative effects on production. Additionally, while increasing stress tends to bolster performance up to some point (Point A in the figure), when the level of stress increases beyond this point, performance will begin to deteriorate.

In sum, a certain amount of stress among employees is generally considered to be advantageous for the organization because it tends to increase production. However, when employees experience too much or too little stress, it is generally disadvantageous for the organization because it tends to decrease production. The cartoon below lightheartedly illustrates the profoundly negative effect that too much stress can have on job performance.

IDENTIFYING UNHEALTHY STRESS IN ORGANIZATIONS
Once managers understand the impact of stress on performance, they must identify where stress exists within the organization.[22] After areas of stress have been pinpointed, managers must then determine

Keller is a good man but totally lacking in stress-management skills.

Harvard Business Review (July/August 1987), 64. © Lee Lorenz 1989.

whether the stress is at an appropriate level or is too high or too low. Because most stress-related organizational problems involve too much stress rather than too little, the remainder of this section focuses on how to relieve undesirably high levels of stress.

Managers often find it difficult to identify the people in the organization who are experiencing detrimentally high levels of stress. Part of this difficulty is that people respond to high stress in different ways, and part is that physiological reactions to stress are hard, if not impossible, for managers to observe and monitor. Such reactions include high blood pressure, pounding heart, and gastrointestinal disorders.

Nevertheless, there are several observable symptoms of undesirably high stress levels that managers can learn to recognize. These symptoms are as follows:[23]

- ► Constant fatigue
- ► Low energy
- ► Moodiness
- ► Increased aggression
- ► Excessive use of alcohol
- ► Temper outbursts
- ► Compulsive eating
- ► High levels of anxiety
- ► Chronic worrying

A manager who observes one or more of these symptoms in employees should investigate to determine if those exhibiting the symptoms are indeed under too much stress. If so, the manager should try to help those employees handle their stress and/or should attempt to reduce stressors in the organization.

A **stressor** is an environmental demand that causes people to feel stress.

HELPING EMPLOYEES HANDLE STRESS A **stressor** is an environmental demand that causes people to feel stress. Stressors are common in situations where individuals are confronted by circumstances for which their usual behaviors are inappropriate or insufficient and where negative consequences are associated with failure to deal properly with the situation. Organizational change characterized by continual layoffs or firings is an obvious stressor, but many other factors related to organizational policies, structure, physical conditions, and processes can also act as stressors.[24]

REDUCING STRESSORS IN THE ORGANIZATION Stress is seldom significantly reduced until the stressors causing it have been coped with satisfactorily or withdrawn from the environment. For example, if too much organizational change is causing undesirably high levels of stress, management may be able to reduce that stress by improving organizational training that is aimed at preparing workers to deal with job demands resulting from the change. Or management might choose to reduce such stress by refraining from making further organizational changes for a while.[25]

Management can also adopt several strategies to help prevent the initial development of unwanted stressors in organizations. Three such strategies follow:[26]

1. *Create an organizational climate that is supportive of individuals*—Organizations commonly evolve into large bureaucracies with formal, inflexible, impersonal climates. This setup leads to considerable job stress. Making the organizational environment less formal and more supportive of employee needs will help prevent the development of unwanted organizational stressors.
2. *Make jobs interesting*—Routine jobs that do not allow employees some degree of freedom often result in undesirable employee stress. If management focuses on making jobs as interesting as possible, this should help prevent the development of stressors related to routine, boring jobs.
3. *Design and operate career counseling programs*—Employees often experience considerable stress when they do not know what their next career step might be or when they might take it. If management can show employees that next step and when it can realistically be achieved, it will discourage unwanted organizational stressors in this area.

Gateway Computers recently supplemented its former mail-order operation with more traditional retail outlets like the one shown here. A major change like this can sometimes be accompanied by employee resistance and accompanying stress. It is management's role to reduce resistance and manage stress to accomplish the needed change.

IBM is an example of a company that for many years has focused on career planning for its employees as a vehicle for reducing employee stress.[27] IBM has a corporationwide program to encourage supervisors to annually conduct voluntary career planning sessions with employees that result in one-page career action plans. Thus IBM employees have a clear idea of where their careers are headed.

BACK TO THE CASE

The change agent should be careful not to create too much stress on other organization members as a result of planned change. Such stress could be significant enough to eliminate any planned improvement at AT&T and could eventually result in such stress-related effects on employees as physical symptoms and the inability to make sound decisions.

Although some additional stress on organization members as a result of a change agent's newly implemented work situations could enhance productivity, too much stress could have a negative impact on production. The change agent could look for such signs as constant fatigue, increased aggression, temper outbursts, and chronic worrying.

If the change agent determines that undesirably high levels of stress have resulted from new work situation changes, he or she should try to reduce the stress. The change agent may be able to do so through training programs aimed at better equipping organization members to execute new job demands resulting from the change. Or he or she may want to simply slow the rate of planned change.

It would probably be wise for the change agent to take action that would prevent unwanted stressors from developing as a result of planned, work situation change. In this regard, the change agent could ensure that the organizational climate at AT&T is supportive of individual needs and that jobs resulting from the planned change are as interesting as possible.

◤ VIRTUALITY

One specific, commonplace type of organizational change being made in modern organizations throughout the world is the trend toward "virtuality."[11] Since this trend is indeed significant and expected to grow even more in the future, this section emphasizes it by defining a virtual organization, discussing degrees of virtuality in organizations, and describing the virtual office.[28]

►DEFINING A VIRTUAL ORGANIZATION

Virtual organization is an organization having the essence of a traditional organization, but without some aspect(s) of traditional boundaries and structure.

Overall, a **virtual organization** has the essence of a traditional organization but without some aspect of traditional boundaries and structure.[29] Virtual organizations are also referred to as *network organizations* or *modular corporations*.[30] In essence, managers go beyond traditional boundaries and structure for the good of the organization by using recent developments in information technology. Perhaps the most prominent of these developments are the Internet, the World Wide Web, and hardware and software tools enabling managers to use these two more easily.[31] Both large and small organizations can have virtual aspects.[32]

►DEGREES OF VIRTUALITY

Virtual corporation is an organization that goes significantly beyond the boundaries and structure of a traditional organization.

Organizations can vary drastically in terms of their degree of virtuality. Perhaps the company exhibiting the most extensive degree is known as the **virtual corporation,** an organization that goes significantly beyond the boundaries and structure of a traditional organization by comprehensively "tying together" a company's stakeholders like employees, suppliers, and customers via an elaborate system of e-mail, the World Wide Web, and other Internet-related vehicles like videoconferencing. This tying together allows all stakeholders to communicate and participate in helping the organization to become more successful.

Virtual teams are groups of employees formed by managers that go beyond the boundaries and structure of traditional teams.

Virtual training is a training process that goes beyond the boundaries and structure of traditional training.

On the other hand, some organizations have much lesser degrees of virtuality. As an example, some organizations limit their virtuality to **virtual teams,** groups of employees formed by managers that go beyond the boundaries and structure of traditional teams by, for example, having members in geographically dispersed locations meeting via real-time messaging on an intranet or the Internet to discuss special or unanticipated organizational problems.[33] As another example, organizations may limit their virtuality to **virtual training,** a training process that goes beyond the boundaries and structure of traditional training. Such training can go beyond traditional training limits by, for example, instructing employees via Internet-assisted learning materials.[34] The following sections discuss virtual offices, a popular type of virtuality being introduced into many organizations.

MANAGEMENT AND THE INTERNET

Virtual Training at Cable and Wireless Communications

Cable and Wireless Communications is a global telecommunications company operating in over 50 countries across the world. The conglomerate is highly diversified, focusing in areas like telephone switching, cable television, and Internet communications.

Naturally, helping organization members learn how to solve job-related problems in an organization of this size is a significant challenge. To help meet this challenge, the company instituted and operates its own training organization called The Cable and Wireless College. The purpose of this college is to provide training, development, and education that will enable the company to lead the world in integrated communications.

One of the college's recent learning experiments that has received widespread acclaim involves virtual training. The experiment was based on the hypothesis that managers, with the assistance of a facilitator, could train one another in how to solve mutual problems. To actually run the experiment, small groups were established with members who had similar challenges and who could share their experiences, practices, and problems. Next, small-group members were given the opportunity to communicate about their challenges via the Internet with the help of a facilitator. Essentially, the

rationale of the experiment featured managers training or giving advice to one another.

One established learning group was made up solely of marketing directors from six different islands in the Caribbean. Although they knew each other, face-to-face meetings were difficult to organize, time-consuming, and usually involved commuting to Miami. This group was asked to discuss via the Internet how to solve problems preventing their short-run success. The group used a dedicated chat room for its conversations. Also, the group discussion was led and supported by a facilitator, a line manager within the company.

The results obtained within the marketing directors group were remarkable. In some cases, directors brought up problems that others already had struggled with and solved, everyone's commuting time was eliminated, and their commitment was raised through the virtual training process to solving problems discussed. Based upon these results, The Cable and Wireless College will undoubtedly organize more virtual training sessions in the future. As the company gains more experience with the virtual training process, such learning will undoubtedly increase in value.

This section discusses an exciting component of organization virtuality, the virtual office.[35] The following sections discuss the definition of the term, various reasons for establishing a virtual office, and challenges to managing a virtual office.

DEFINING A VIRTUAL OFFICE A **virtual office** is a work arrangement that extends beyond the structure and boundaries of the traditional office arrangement. Specifics of the arrangements vary from organization to organization, but can be conceptualized using the alternative work arrangements continuum shown in Figure 13.8. This continuum is based upon the degree of worker mobility reflected within a particular virtual office, moving from "occasional telecommuting" to "fully mobile." The definitions of the alternative work arrangements shown on the continuum follow:

> A **virtual office** is a work arrangement that extends beyond the structure and boundaries of the traditional office arrangement.

Occasional Telecommuting Workers have fixed, traditional offices and work schedules, but occasionally work at home. In this situation, most are traditional workers in traditional office situations.

Hoteling Workers come into the traditional office frequently, but because they are not always physically present they are not allocated permanent office space. Instead workers can reserve a room or cubicle in advance of their arrival, sometimes called a "hotel room," where they can receive and return telephone calls and link into a computer network.

Tethered in Office "Tethered" workers have some mobility, but are expected to report to the office on a regular basis. As an example, some tethered workers are expected to appear at the office in the morning to receive a cellular phone and portable computer. The equipment is returned to the office in the afternoon, sometimes accompanied by meeting or progress reports for the workday.

Home-Based, Some Mobility A home-based worker has no traditional office. The workspace of this type of worker could be a kitchen table or a bedroom desk. A home-based worker may visit customers or go outside the home occasionally, but his or her work is mainly done via the telephone or computer inside the home. Some companies support home-based workers through activities like leasing office furniture, providing computers, and procuring high-speed phone lines.

Fully Mobile A worker who is fully mobile works out of a car. In essence, the car is an office containing equipment like a cellular phone, portable computer, and fax machine. This type of worker is expected to be on the road or at work areas like customer locations during the entire workday, and they are typically field sales representatives or customer service specialists.

REASONS FOR ESTABLISHING A VIRTUAL OFFICE Managers design and implement virtual offices for many different reasons. Cost reduction is the most commonly cited reason and real estate or rental costs are the most commonly cited costs to be reduced. Traditional office space needed for an organization can be reduced by over 50 percent by using virtual offices. Managers also use virtual offices to increase productivity. History in some organizations shows that people work faster and are interrupted less when working at home. Thirdly,

FIGURE 13.8 ► **Continuum of alternative work arrangements**

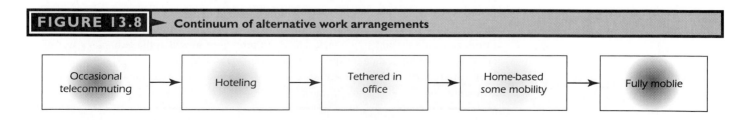

firms also establish virtual offices as part of redesigning jobs to make employees more effective and efficient. For example, some organizations need to decrease the amount of time necessary for eliminating customer problems. Some managers meet this need by establishing fully mobile customer service employees. According to the rationale, fully mobile customer service employees have a better chance of arriving at customer locations quickly than customer service employees in traditional offices, and thereby have a better chance of solving customer problems quickly.

CHALLENGES TO MANAGING A VIRTUAL OFFICE Undoubtedly, managers face many new and different challenges when using the virtual office concept. For example, virtual offices make it more difficult to build desired corporate culture. For employees, traditional offices represent a place to become familiar with fellow workers and socialize into a purposefully designed corporate culture. Due simply to their proximity, employees working in virtual offices are more physically distant from other employees and more difficult for managers to build into the fabric of organizational culture. Another management challenge to using virtual offices is that such offices make it more difficult for managers to control workers. An individual's presence in a traditional office can give a manager constant feedback throughout the day concerning worker commitment and performance, whereas in a virtual office situation, it is not as easy. Lastly, virtual offices make communication more difficult. Planned or unplanned face-to-face communication that takes place in a traditional office is essentially nonexistent in a virtual office. As a result, management has a difficult time gathering information relevant to employee attitudes and work concerns. Table 13.1 contains several steps managers can take to ensure good communication in virtual offices.

TABLE 13.1	► **Tips to Ensure Good Communication in a Virtual Office**

► Establish regular, mutually agreed-upon communication times. Telephone calls, e-mail messages, teleconferences, videoconferences and chat areas can all be entered at an agreed-upon time. Team meetings and group think-sessions can be carried out efficiently and effectively this way.

► Make certain that offsite workers understand their worth to the organization. Devise methods to make these workers feel included in the team spirit. For example: If there are good-natured team contests, ensure that workers in the virtual workplace are included; or, you might create a virtual coffee break wherein spontaneous humor and light chat are exchanged.

► Have social events periodically where all workers can meet in person.

► Circulate an online newsletter to keep everyone abreast of projects, discoveries, innovations and even errors. Communicating errors—and fixes—prevents others from making similar mistakes. Solicit contributions from all team members.

► If in-person meetings are out of the question at a particular time, do your best to hold a videoconference. Visual communication enhances verbal communication.

► If your workers are regionalized, appoint one of the workers to be orchestrator of communication and social activities. Groups that meet informally to share values or special interests can be effective.

► If team members are within convenient driving (or flying) distance, it is still a great idea to have weekly meetings at most or monthly meetings at least. There is no replacement for "in person" sessions.

► If it is convenient for you to visit telecommuters occasionally, it would be helpful to visit them in their work environments. Team meetings might be held in various homes/work environments to legitimize the workplace of the telecommuter.

► Contact each team member regularly to offer support and to facilitate the work process. Probe for training needs to enhance productivity. Provide these training opportunities.

► If workers are job sharing, have a formal hand-off procedure, as well as the technology available for informal communication for special situations and questions.

► Constantly research and implement state-of-the-art technology for [maintaining] productive communication.

This last chapter section contains material that illustrates the type of content the AWA team's report could feature. First, the AWA report could recommend establishing a virtual organization at AT&T. This type of recommendation would focus on keeping the essence of traditional organization, but without some aspects of traditional boundaries and structure. The team's recommendation probably would not recommend drastic measures like establishing AT&T as a virtual corporation, but rather some degree of virtuality like establishing virtual teams.

As the Introductory Case indicates, the AWA team's actual recommendation focused on establishing a type of virtual office that had workers telecommute. Other options available for establishing a virtual office at AT&T could have included workers hoteling, tethered in the office, home-based with some mobility, or fully mobile. The AWA team's rationale for establishing this type of virtual office at AT&T probably included cost savings due to rent savings and enhanced worker productivity.

The AWA team's report probably also included challenges that must be met in order for a newly established virtual office at AT&T to be successful. Perhaps the most significant of these challenges is appropriately integrating virtual workers into the AT&T corporate culture. The report probably reasoned that building good communication among AT&T's managers and virtual workers is an important step for integrating these workers into the culture and maintaining their continued presence. To build this communication, AT&T's managers could take steps like establishing regular communication times with virtual workers, publishing an online newsletter aimed at helping virtual workers deal with their unique problems, and having regular social events where virtual workers can meet and interact with other virtual workers as well as with AT&T's employees in traditional work settings.

For updated information on the topics in this chapter, Internet exercises, links to related Internet sites, an interactive study guide, and more, visit our companion Web site at

http://www.prenhall.com/certo

Additional information can be found on the inside front and back covers of this text.

ACTION SUMMARY

Reread the learning objectives below. Each objective is followed by questions. Answering these questions accurately will help you retain the most important concepts discussed in this chapter. After answering each question, check your answer against the answer key at the end of this chapter. (*Hint:* If you have any doubts regarding the correct response, consult the page number that follows the answer.)

Circle: From studying this chapter, I will attempt to acquire

1. A working definition of *changing an organization.*

T F   **a.** The purpose of organizational modifications is to increase the extent to which an organization accomplishes its objectives.

a b c d e   **b.** Organizational modifications typically include changing: (a) overall goals and objectives (b) established lines of organizational authority (c) levels of responsibility held by various organization members (d) b and c (e) all of the above.

2. An understanding of the relative importance of change and stability to an organization.

a b c d e   **a.** According to the Hellriegel and Slocum model, the following is the most likely outcome when both adaptation and stability are high: (a) high probability of slow death (b) high probability of survival (c) high probability of survival and growth (d) certainty of quick death (e) possibility of slow death.

T F   **b.** According to Hellriegel and Slocum, repeated changes in an organization without concern for stability typically result in employees with a high degree of adaptability.

3. Some ability to recognize what kind of changes should be made within an organization.

T F   **a.** Although managers can choose to change an organization in many ways, most changes can be categorized as one of three kinds: (1) people change (2) goal or objective change and (3) technological change.

a b c d e   **b.** Decentralizing an organization is a structural change aimed at: (a) reducing the cost of coordination (b) increasing the controllability of subunits (c) increasing motivation (d) all of the above (e) a and b.

4. An appreciation for why the people affected by a change should be considered when the change is being made.

a b c d e   **a.** The following is *not* an example of personal loss that organization members fear as a result of change: (a) possibility of a reduction in personal prestige (b) disturbance of established social relationships (c) reduction in overall organizational productivity (d) personal failure because of an inability to carry out new job responsibilities (e) disturbance of established working relationships.

T F   **b.** Support for a proposed change may be altered by focusing attention on possible individual gains that could materialize as a result of the change.

5. Some facility at evaluating change.

a b c d e   **a.** Symptoms indicating that further change is necessary are that organization members: (a) are oriented more to the future than to the past (b) recognize the challenge of current problems more than the obligations of rituals (c) pay more allegiance to overall company goals than to departmental goals (d) none of the above (e) a and b.

T F   **b.** Change is an inevitable part of management and considered so important to organizational success that some managers encourage employees to suggest needed changes.

6. An understanding of how organizational change and stress are related.

T F   **a.** Stress is simply the rate of wear and tear on the body.

T F   **b.** From a managerial viewpoint, stress on employees can be either too high or too low.

T F   **c.** Stressors are the factors within an organization that reduce employee stress.

7. Knowledge about virtuality as a vehicle for organizational change.

a b c d e   **a.** The continuum of alternative work arrangements contains a work circumstance called: (a) work surfing (b) fully tethered (c) fully mobile (d) occasional hoteling (e) none of the above.

T F   **b.** Lowering expenses is the reason managers least cite for establishing a virtual office.

T F   **c.** Workers in virtual office work situations are harder for managers to control.

▶ INTRODUCTORY CASE WRAP-UP ◀

CASE DISCUSSSION QUESTIONS

"AT&T Changes Where and How People Work" (p. 277) and its related Back-to-the-Case sections were written to help you better understand the management concepts contained in this chapter. Answer the following discussion questions about this Introductory Case to further enrich your understanding of chapter content:

1. How complicated would it be for a change agent at AT&T to implement the change of establishing new work situations in the company? Explain.

2. Do you think that certain AT&T employees would subtly resist this change? Why or why not?

3. What elements of this change could cause organization members to experience stress, and what might the change agent do to help alleviate this stress? Be specific.

SKILLS EXERCISE: BUILDING A MATRIX ORGANIZATION

The Introductory Case discusses AT&T's efforts to change where and how people work. Assume that you have been appointed a project manager at AT&T who is responsible for implementing needed changes in these areas. Draw a matrix organization chart that you would use to implement these needed changes. Explain in as much detail as possible how your matrix organization would function. The name your project has been given is "Alternative Work Project."

1. What is meant in this chapter by the phrase *changing an organization?*
2. Why do organizations typically undergo various changes?
3. Does an organization need both change and stability? Explain.
4. What major factors should a manager consider when changing an organization?
5. Define *change agent* and list the skills necessary to be a successful change agent.
6. Explain the term *organizational effectiveness* and describe the major factors that determine how effective an organization will be.
7. Describe the relationship between "determining what should be changed within an organization" and "choosing a kind of change for the organization."
8. What is the difference between structural change and people change?
9. Is matrix organization an example of a structural change? Explain.
10. Draw and explain the managerial grid.
11. Is grid OD an example of a technique used to make structural change? Explain.
12. What causes resistance to change?
13. List and explain the steps managers can take to minimize employee resistance to change.
14. How and why should managers evaluate the changes they make?
15. Define *stress* and explain how it influences performance.
16. List three stressors that could exist within an organization. For each stressor, discuss a specific management action that could be taken to reduce or eliminate it.
17. What effect can career counseling have on employee stress? Explain.
18. Define *virtual organization* and explain how different organizations can have different degrees of virtuality.
19. Discuss three challenges that you might face in managing a virtual organization. Be sure to explain why the issues you raise are indeed challenges.
20. Discuss three suggestions that you would make for maintaining good communication between a manager and workers in a virtual office situation.

► ACTION SUMMARY ANSWER KEY ◄

1. **a.** T, p. 278
   b. d, p. 278
2. **a.** c, pp. 278–279
   b. F, pp. 278–279
3. **a.** F, p. 282
   b. d, p. 283

4. **a.** c, p. 288
   b. T, p. 288
5. **a.** d, p. 289
   b. T, p. 289

6. **a.** T, p. 290
   b. T, p. 290
   c. F, p. 292

7. **a.** c, p. 295
   b. F, p. 295
   c. T, p. 296

► CASE STUDY: Layoffs—The Cost of Doing Business ◄

In 1995, 385,000 American jobs were cut across a broad base of industries—manufacturing, telecommunications, finance and securities, and retailing. From 1990 to 1995, U.S. corporations slashed 2.9 million jobs. The largest of these cuts came in 1993, when IBM cut 60,000 and Sears Roebuck 50,000 workers from their payrolls. On January 2, 1996, AT&T rang in the new year with the announcement that 40,000 workers would be asked to leave as part of its mass restructuring into three separate companies.

According to the American Management Association, however, this trend in corporate downsizing has been slowing. Each year in the period from 1990 to 1992, almost 8 percent of the U.S. workforce was laid off; 1993 saw the highest number of layoffs, with over 8 percent of U.S. workers dismissed. The percentage decreased in 1993–1994, to less than 6 percent; in 1994–1995, just 1 percent of workers lost their jobs because of corporate downsizing.

National statistics, however, do not tell the whole story, especially the human side. AT&T's announced breakup stunned its 300,000 employees. In his announcement speech, AT&T Chairman Robert E. Allen, who has presided over five large workforce reductions in the past eight years, declared that "to the extent we can get in trim, we'll produce better margins, more flexibility and more cash flow to invest in other opportunities." Officials admitted it was impossible to predict when layoffs would end because no one knew how many employees would be required to run the new AT&T. Throughout the company, employees felt the stress of job insecurity.

Two months after the layoffs announcement, the stress hit home as 72,000 managers—about half of AT&T's total administrative staff—were offered buyout packages. Managers were given until the end of December 1996 to decide. The offer was not that "sweet"; in fact, managers who waited to see if they would be among those laid off stood to receive quite similar severance packages. Analysts believe AT&T management decided not to make the buyout too attractive for fear of losing talent that they hoped to capitalize on in their new companies. Only 6,500 managers accepted the buyout prior to the deadline.

On January 2, 1996, Allen announced that "the reduction in our workforce will be the most difficult and painful step we've had to take in this restructuring process. Compassion will be an essential ingredient in the handling of the job cuts. . . ." In an e-mail message to employees, he explained that job reductions "are being driven by changes in our marketplace—changes in customer needs, technology and public policy—not through any fault of the people who will leave."

Whether or not they were included in the first round of layoffs, virtually all AT&T employees felt the stress of downsizing. Morale was low. In New Jersey, a state where the company is the largest private employer and 6,000 to 7,000 workers were laid off in the beginning of January, entire communities stood to suffer at least a temporary downturn in their economies. According to Don Jay Smith, an AT&T worker in Parsippany, "I think there were a lot of people who were very nervous about this and about their prospects for getting a replacement job. I think most people felt this was pretty much the end of it."

One top AT&T executive, a 36-year veteran and key architect of the 1984 breakup, decided to leave the company before the new restructuring took place. In an Associated Press interview, Victor A. Pelson, who ended his AT&T career as chairman of global operations, said, "It's absolutely necessary, but when you go through changes of this sort, there's a tremendous amount of work that has to be done—separation of all kinds of assets, most importantly human assets . . . and I've been through that."

According to *The Wall Street Journal,* insiders feared that years of downsizing have devastated morale at AT&T just when the company needed "an esprit de corps among its workers to attack new markets." Says John Challenger, an employment consultant at Challenger, Gray & Christmas, Inc., a Chicago outplacement firm, "Cutbacks such as these throw the organization into chaos, making it harder for the company that remains to get back on its feet."

Nevertheless, according to Richard Klugman of Paine Webber, corporate moves that hurt employees but benefit stockholders are on the rise: "You [will see] more and more companies . . . take a realistic approach that the shareholders come first and employees are there to serve the shareholders." It seems, therefore, that Americans entering the workforce will have to develop a mind set about their careers that is very different from the mind set their parents had when they were young. White- and blue-collar workers can expect to change jobs six or seven times throughout their careers.

Job insecurity is a stress that afflicts corporate workers at all levels. "Managers used to be impervious to changes in the economy," says Paul Osterman, a human resources professor at Sloan School of Management. "Now, they feel like their world is falling apart, even though they are still better off than most folks."

QUESTIONS

1. Should all American workers feel insecure about their jobs, or are specific areas and types of workers targeted in downsizing? Cite examples to support your opinion.
2. How does AT&T's restructuring plan effect change in the three main classes of organizational factors—people, structure, and technology? Describe how effectiveness might be maximized in each area.
3. Massive layoffs like those at AT&T obviously have a strong effect on the people who lose their jobs, but they also affect employees who remain at the company. List the negative effects of layoffs on remaining human resources. Brainstorm a list of ways in which companies might reduce this negative impact.

►VIDEO CASE STUDY: Organizational Change and Stress at Image Communications◄

SMALL BUSINESS 2000

In today's business environment nothing stands still. Changes in the competitive mix, influence from the expanding world market, changes in buyers' preferences, and innovations such as e-commerce all affect the way businesses organize and run. The opportunity to find the best way to do things and to simply maintain them does not exist any longer.

Companies today continually face new challenges and new opportunities. An encouraging and motivating element of this demand for change is the opportunity it creates for individuals and businesses. On the other hand, not every individual or business may be interested in or prepared for this endless cycle of evolution and reinvention. Change is not without its downside. Sometimes companies miss the mark and use up significant resources with little or negative results; sometimes people lose jobs.

Image Communications is a company that thrives on change. In fact, the company's founder is quite sure that change is the only thing that is certain for his company. He believes that change is not only necessary, but that savvy change is the difference between companies that grow and those that remain flat or eventually go away. This does not

mean that he believes a firm should jump on every opportunity that it encounters. In his discussion of Image Communications' evolution, you will begin to see a process that supports the trade-off between stability and change within the company. You may also observe the existence of a corporate culture which supports top management's interest in transitioning this company from its current focus and product mix toward what it will be next.

QUESTIONS

1. Identify and describe the change agent(s) at Image Communications. How do you think they go about determining what needs to be changed and when they should change?
2. How do you think the pace at which the company evolves and the energy of the firm's leaders affect others' reaction to change? What do you think the company does to ensure that it has the right team to meet the challenges it faces?
3. Jeff Gordon is quoted as saying, "I think we are always on the brink of failure; success is a moving target." Do you think such a statement might be stressful to employees watching this video? Explain your answer.

In this segment, our new production manager is being tested by a Quicktakes producer. We are not given an organizational chart to look at, but it comes across as if Susan does not report directly to John, but that she is at a lower level in the organization's overall scheme. Given John's broader role and responsibility, it seems appropriate that the decisions that need to be made in this video segment are John's shots to call. As a result, we get our first idea of how John handles conflict and whether or not he accepts the responsibility that comes along with the job he has taken. In segment one, we heard John tell his wife that he wanted to be a manager; in this segment, he gets his chance to be just that.

It is not uncommon for new employees to be tested by people who have been working at a company for a long time. This is especially true when someone inside the company thinks that they were more qualified for the job than the newcomer. Pressure like John is getting from Susan is pretty common. We learn a lot about John, Susan, and Hal from watching how all three of them deal with the task of getting a couple shoots set up. We also learn about how this company is organized by watching who takes, or gets stuck with, certain parts of the task.

A final thought might be to consider why Susan got upset about the way the shoots were planned. It could have been her basic frustration with John. On the other hand, maybe something else is going on. Hal talks about Susan as if she has been with Quicktakes for a long time. Perhaps Susan is showing some of her feelings toward the way the company is changing. Very few successful companies stand still. Sometimes people who work at a company roll with the changes and progress with the company, and sometimes people are overwhelmed and wish it was the "same old company" it used to be. We do not know exactly what Susan's concerns are but there are certainly many ideas to think about.

QUESTIONS

1. John and Susan get into a debate about resource allocation. John seems to be understanding but stern in his approach. He addressed Susan's concerns by stating that he knows the crew she is worried about, but he does not back down. Do you think he handles this situation properly? How else might he have handled it?

2. After he deals with staffing assignments and Susan's disagreement, John talks with Hal. Why do you think he does this? What might John be hoping to get from Hal? Do you think he gets it?

3. In the end, Susan runs into trouble and John's plan seems to have paid off. He and Susan have a phone discussion and come up with a solution to their dilemma. What do you think about the way Susan and John dealt with the issue? Think about other ways each might have dealt with the problem. What do you think would be some of the advantages and disadvantages to your solution?

14

Fundamentals of Influencing and Communication

STUDENT LEARNING OBJECTIVES

From studying this chapter, I will attempt to acquire

1. An understanding of influencing

2. An understanding of interpersonal communication

3. A knowledge of how to use feedback

4. An appreciation for the importance of nonverbal communication

5. Insights on formal organizational communication

6. An appreciation for the importance of the grapevine

7. Some hints on how to encourage organizational communication

CHAPTER OUTLINE

Introductory Case: *Eaton Managers Concentrate on Influencing People*

FUNDAMENTALS OF INFLUENCING
Defining Influencing
The Influencing Subsystem

People Spotlight: *The U.S. Army Teaches Leadership by Teaching Communication*

COMMUNICATION
Interpersonal Communication
Interpersonal Communication in Organizations

Management and the Internet: *Wimbledon Uses a Web Site to Communicate with Stakeholders*

Across Industries: *Local Government—How David Bell Communicates with City Employees*

Quality Spotlight: *Enhanced Formal Communication Contributes to Improving Quality at Holiday Inn*

EATON MANAGERS CONCENTRATE ON INFLUENCING PEOPLE

REMINDER: THE INTRODUCTORY CASE WRAP-UP (P. 322) CONTAINS DISCUSSION QUESTIONS AND A SKILLS EXERCISE TO FURTHER ILLUSTRATE THE APPLICATION OF CHAPTER CONCEPTS TO THIS VIGNETTE.

It is 7:30 A.M., time for the morning quiz at Eaton Corporation's factory. Ten union workers, each representing work teams, sit around a boardroom table. "What were our sales yesterday?" asks a supervisor at the head of the table. A worker, glancing at a computer printout, replies that they were $625,275. "And in the month?" From another worker comes the response: $6,172,666.

Eaton may not be a household name, and its products—including gears, engine valves, truck axles and, at Lincoln, Nebraska, circuit breakers—aren't glamorous. But its success in raising productivity and cutting costs throws plenty of doubt on recent hand-wringing about unmotivated American workers and flaccid American corporations.

Getting people to think for themselves—and work in teams—is important to Eaton. The company starts by hiring managers who are not autocratic and training them to accept encroachments on their authority. Not everyone can hack it: When engineers at Lincoln were evicted from their office enclave and the department was moved out onto the shop floor, the department chief and a colleague quit in protest.

Managers who adjust, however, tend to stay at one plant a long time. The same person has been plant manager at Lincoln since 1980. The Kearney manager, Nebraskan Robert Dyer, is an area native who was hired as a machine operator in 1969, when the plant opened. That, too, is not unusual: 23 of Lincoln's salaried staff of 57 came up from the rank and file.

Management shares extensive financial data with employees at the two plants to underscore the link between their performance and the factory's. At Kearney, a TV monitor in the cafeteria indicates how specific shifts and departments did the previous day against their cost and performance goals. Lincoln gets the message out via computer printouts. "It gives you a sense of direction," says Ricky Rigg, a metal fabricator, " and makes you appreciate what you do more."

At Kearney, where workers labor amid the noise and heat of hot forged metal, bonuses are based on the entire

These team workers at Eaton Corporation are planning and evaluating their own work. The company provides them with the financial information and other data they need to make their own decisions.

plant's performance compared with the prior year. In the first quarter, for instance, Kearney topped the year-earlier profit and cost criteria by 7 percent—and workers got a quarterly bonus of 7 percent, or about $500 each. Kearney employees have earned a bonus every quarter since the system was introduced six years ago.

There's noncash recognition as well. On a recent Wednesday, the Kearney plant held a lunchtime barbecue to mark the first shift's 365th consecutive day without any injuries. Plant Manager Dyer and his staff prepared the meal—hamburgers, hot dogs, potato salad, and baked beans—while the first shift chowed down.

"Bob personifies what I look for in a plant manager," says George Dettloff, general manager of Eaton's engine-components division and Robert Dyer's boss. "He manages, but he gives people freedom."

That style was evident a year ago, when Kearney was looking for a human resources manager to replace one who had resigned. A joint labor-management committee of 18 people whittled the field down to 3 candidates. And when it came time for a final decision, Dyer asked the committee to decide on its own.

What's Ahead

In the Introductory Case, Eaton Corporation's success in enhancing company productivity and efficiency is credited largely to how its managers manage people. According to the case, Eaton managers manage by encouraging employees to think for themselves, to make decisions about who is hired at Eaton, and to make changes in the organization that will result in improvements. The information in this chapter emphasizes the value of such managers and offers insights into what additional steps managers might take to guide organization members' activities in directions that lead to the attainment of management system objectives. The chapter is divided into two main parts:

1. Fundamentals of influencing

2. Communication

FUNDAMENTALS OF INFLUENCING

The four basic managerial functions—planning, organizing, influencing, and controlling—were introduced in chapter 1. *Planning* and *organizing* have already been discussed; *influencing* is the third of these basic functions covered in this text. A definition of *influencing* and a discussion of the influencing subsystem follow.

▶ DEFINING INFLUENCING

Influencing is the process of guiding the activities of organization members in appropriate directions. *Appropriate directions,* of course, are those that lead to the attainment of management system objectives. Influencing involves focusing on organization members as people and dealing with such issues as morale, arbitration of conflicts, and the development of good working relationships. It is a critical part of a manager's job. In fact, the ability to influence others is a primary determinant of how successful a manager will be.[1]

▶ THE INFLUENCING SUBSYSTEM

Like the planning and organizing functions, the influencing function can be viewed as a subsystem within the overall management system (see Figure 14.1). The primary purpose of the

Influencing is the process of guiding the activities of organization members in appropriate directions. It involves the performance of four management activities: (1) leading, (2) motivating, (3) considering groups, and (4) communicating.

FIGURE 14.1	Relationship between overall management system and influencing subsystem

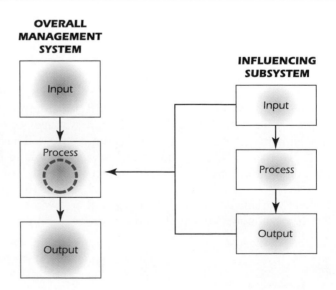

influencing subsystem, as stated above, is to enhance the attainment of management system objectives by guiding the activities of organization members in appropriate directions.

Figure 14.2 shows the constituents of the influencing subsystem. The input of this subsystem is composed of a portion of the total resources of the overall management system, and its output is appropriate organization member behavior. The process of the influencing subsystem involves the performance of four primary management activities:

1. Leading
2. Motivating
3. Considering groups
4. Communicating

Managers transform a portion of organizational resources into appropriate organization member behavior mainly by performing these four activities.

As Figure 14.2 shows, leading, motivating, and considering groups are interrelated. Managers accomplish each of these influencing activities, to some extent, by communicating with organization members. For example, managers can only decide what kind of leader they need to be after they analyze the characteristics of the various groups with which they will interact and determine how those groups can best be motivated. Then, regardless of the leadership strategy they adopt, their leading, motivating, and working with groups will be accomplished—at least partly—through communication with other organization members.

In fact, all management activities are accomplished at least partly through communication or communication-related endeavors. Because communication is used repeatedly by managers, ability to communicate is often referred to as the fundamental management skill.

Communication is critical at all levels of an organization, even between colleagues like Microsoft's founder, Bill Gates, and its new president, Steve Ballmer, who have worked together for many years.

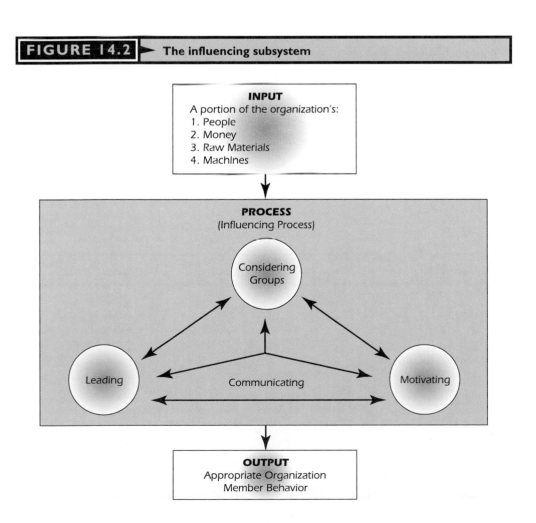

FIGURE 14.2 ▶ **The influencing subsystem**

INPUT
A portion of the organization's:
1. People
2. Money
3. Raw Materials
4. Machines

PROCESS
(Influencing Process)

Considering
Groups

Leading   Communicating   Motivating

OUTPUT
Appropriate Organization
Member Behavior

Rank*	Key Learning Area	Frequency Indicated
1	Oral and written communication skills	25
1	Interpersonal skills	25
3	Financial/managerial account skills	22
4	Ability to think, be analytical, and make decisions	20
5	Strategic planning and goal setting—concern for long-term performance	13
6	Motivation and commitment to the firm—giving 110%	12
7	Understanding of economics	11
8	Management information systems and computer applications	9
8	Thorough knowledge of your business, culture, and overall environment	9
8	Marketing concept (the customer is king) and skills	9
11	Integrity	7
11	Knowledge of yourself: Setting long- and short-term career objectives	7
13	Leadership skills	6
13	Understanding of the functional areas of the business	6
13	Time management: Setting priorities—how to work smart, not long or hard	1

*1 is most important.

A recent survey of chief executives supports this notion that communication is the fundamental management skill. The results, which appear in Table 14.1, show that CEOs ranked oral and written communication skills first (along with interpersonal skills) among the skills that should be taught to management students.

The information in the text indicates that managers lead, at least partly, by communicating with organization members. The following People Spotlight feature explains why the U.S. Army has made teaching communication skills an important part of its leadership training program.

PEOPLE SPOTLIGHT ◂ **The U.S. Army Teaches Leadership by Teaching Communication**

The U.S. Army claims that it can teach people how to lead. Cadets get their leadership training in Advance Camp, a six-week summer program for officer candidates held at Fort Bragg, North Carolina, and at Fort Lewis, Washington.

One of the issues the Army emphasizes in its leadership training program is communication. Future leaders are taught how to communicate, both orally and in writing. Making presentations to groups is especially stressed.

Other areas emphasized in the Army leadership training program are planning and organizing, technical competence, judgment,

sensitivity, and delegation. Physical exercises aimed at building leadership skills include crawling out on a rope to drop 40 feet into water, directing a squad to build a bridge over fast-running water, and leading a squad through obstacles.

In sum, the Army wants officers who can lead intellectually and physically. Thus it emphasizes teaching cadets both intellectual and physical skills to prepare them for their future as officers.

Communication is discussed further in the rest of this chapter. Leading, motivating, and considering groups are discussed in chapters 15, 16, and 17, respectively.

COMMUNICATION

Communication is the process of sharing information with other individuals. Information, as used here, is any thought or idea that managers desire to share with other individuals. In general, communication involves one person projecting a message to one or more other people that results in everyone's arriving at a common understanding of the message. Because communication is a commonly used management skill and ability and is often cited as the skill most responsible for a manager's success, prospective managers must learn how to communicate. To help managers become better interpersonal communicators, new communication training techniques are constantly being developed and evaluated.[2]

The communication activities of managers generally involve interpersonal communication—sharing information with other organization members. The following sections feature both the general topic of interpersonal communication and the more specific topic of interpersonal communication in organizations.

> **Communication** is the process of sharing information with other individuals.

▶ INTERPERSONAL COMMUNICATION

To be a successful interpersonal communicator, a manager must understand the following:

1. How interpersonal communication works
2. The relationship between feedback and interpersonal communication
3. The importance of verbal versus nonverbal interpersonal communication

HOW INTERPERSONAL COMMUNICATION WORKS Interpersonal communication is the process of transmitting information to others.[3] To be complete, the process must have the following three basic elements:

1. *The source/encoder*—The **source/encoder** is the person in the interpersonal communication situation who originates and encodes information to be shared with others. Encoding is putting information into a form that can be received and understood by another individual. Putting one's thoughts into a letter is an example of encoding. Until information is encoded, it cannot be shared with others. (From here on, the *source/encoder* will be referred to simply as the *source*.)

> The **source/encoder** is the person in the interpersonal communication situation who originates and encodes information to be shared with another person or persons.

A **message** is encoded information that the source intends to share with others.

The **signal** is a message that has been transmitted from one person to another.

The **decoder/destination** is the person or persons in the interpersonal communication situation with whom the source is attempting to share information.

2. *The signal*—Encoded information that the source intends to share constitutes a **message.** A message that has been transmitted from one person to another is called a **signal.**

3. *The decoder/destination*—The **decoder/destination** is the person or persons with whom the source is attempting to share information. This person receives the signal and decodes, or interprets, the message to determine its meaning. Decoding is the process of converting messages back into information. In all interpersonal communication situations, message meaning is a result of decoding. (From here on, the *decoder/destination* will be referred to simply as the *destination.*)

The classic work of Wilbur Schramm clarifies the role played by each of the three elements of the interpersonal communication process. As implied in Figure 14.3, the source determines what information to share, encodes this information in the form of a message, and then transmits the message as a signal to the destination. The destination decodes the transmitted message to determine its meaning and then responds accordingly.

A manager who desires to assign the performance of a certain task to a subordinate would use the communication process in the following way: First, the manager would determine exactly what task he or she wanted the subordinate to perform. Then the manager would encode and transmit a message to the subordinate that would accurately reflect this assignment. The message transmission itself could be as simple as the manager's telling the subordinate what the new responsibilities include. Next, the subordinate would decode the message transmitted by the manager to ascertain its meaning and then respond to it appropriately.

Successful communication refers to an interpersonal communication situation in which the information the source intends to share with the destination and the meaning the destination derives from the transmitted message are the same.

Successful and Unsuccessful Interpersonal Communication **Successful communication** refers to an interpersonal communication situation in which the information the source intends to share with the destination and the meaning the destination derives from

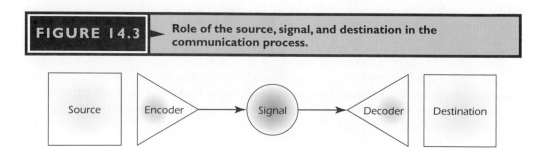

| **FIGURE 14.3** | Role of the source, signal, and destination in the communication process. |

Source → Encoder → Signal → Decoder → Destination

the transmitted message are the same. Conversely, **unsuccessful communication** is an interpersonal communication situation in which the information the source intends to share with the destination and the meaning the destination derives from the transmitted message are different.

To increase the probability that communication will be successful, the message must be encoded so that the source's experience of the way a signal should be decoded is equivalent to the destination's experience of the way it should be decoded. If this is done, the probability is high that the destination will interpret the signal as intended by the source. Figure 14.4 illustrates these overlapping fields of experience that ensure successful communication.

Barriers to Successful Interpersonal Communication Factors that decrease the probability that communication will be successful are called *communication barriers*. A clear understanding of these barriers will help managers maximize their communication success. The following sections discuss both communication macrobarriers and communication microbarriers.

Macrobarriers. **Communication macrobarriers** are factors that hinder successful communication in a general communication situation.[4] These factors relate primarily to the communication environment and the larger world in which communication takes place. Some common macrobarriers are the following:[5]

1. *The increasing need for information*—Because society is changing constantly and rapidly, individuals have a greater and greater need for information. This growing need tends to overload communication networks, thereby distorting communication. To minimize the effects of this barrier, managers should take steps to ensure that organization members are not overloaded with information. Only information critical to the performance of their jobs should be transmitted to them.

2. *The need for increasingly complex information*—Because of today's rapid technological advances, most people are confronted with complex communication situations in their everyday lives. If managers take steps to emphasize simplicity in communication, the effects of this barrier can be lessened. Furnishing organization members with adequate training to deal with more technical areas is another strategy for overcoming this barrier.

3. *The reality that people in the United States are increasingly coming into contact with people who use languages other than English*—As U.S. business becomes more international in scope and as organization members travel more frequently, the need to know languages other than English increases. The potential communication barrier of this multilanguage situation is obvious. Moreover, people who deal with foreigners need to be familiar not only with their languages but also with their cultures. Formal knowledge of a foreign language is of little value unless the individual knows which words, phrases, and actions are culturally acceptable.

4. *The constant need to learn new concepts cuts down on the time available for communication*—Many managers feel pressured to learn new and important concepts that they

Unsuccessful communication refers to an interpersonal communication situation in which the information the source intends to share with the destination and the meaning the destination derives from the transmitted message are different.

Communication macrobarriers are factors hindering successful communication that relate primarily to the communication environment and the larger world in which communication takes place.

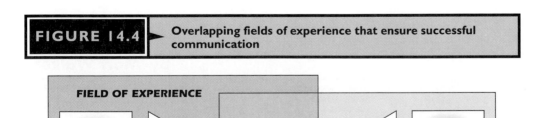

FIGURE 14.4 Overlapping fields of experience that ensure successful communication

FIELD OF EXPERIENCE

Source → Encoder ▷ Signal ◁ Decoder Destination

FIELD OF EXPERIENCE

did not have to know in the past. Learning about the intricacies of international business or computer usage, for example, takes up significant amounts of managerial time. Many managers also find that the increased demands that training employees makes on their time leaves them with less time for communicating with other organization members.

Communication microbarriers are factors hindering successful communication that relate primarily to such variables as the communication message, the source, and the destination.

Microbarriers. **Communication microbarriers** are factors that hinder successful communication in a specific communication situation.[6] These factors relate directly to such variables as the communication message, the source, and the destination. Among the microbarriers are the following:[7]

1. *The source's view of the destination*—The source in any communication situation has a tendency to view the destination in a specific way, and this view influences the messages sent. For example, individuals usually speak differently to people they think are informed about a subject than to those they believe are uninformed. The destination can sense the source's attitudes, which often block successful communication. Managers should keep an open mind about the people with whom they communicate and be careful not to imply any negative attitudes through their communication behaviors.

Message interference refers to stimuli that compete with the communication message for the attention of the destination.

2. *Message interference*—Stimuli that compete with the communication message for the attention of the destination are called **message interference,** or noise. An instance of message interference is a manager talking to an office worker while the worker is trying to input data into a word processor. The inputting of data is message interference here because it is competing with the manager's communication message. Managers should attempt to communicate only when they have the total attention of the individuals with whom they wish to share information. An amusing example of message interference is depicted in the cartoon below.

3. *The destination's view of the source*—Certain attitudes of the destination toward the source can also hinder successful communication. If, for example, a destination believes that the source has little credibility in the area about which the source is communicating, the destination may filter out much of the source's message and pay only slight attention to that part of the message actually received. Managers should attempt to consider the worth of messages transmitted to them independently of their personal attitudes toward the source. Many valuable ideas will escape them if they allow their personal feelings toward others to influence which messages they attend to.

Perception is the interpretation of a message by an individual.

4. *Perception*—**Perception** is an individual's interpretation of a message. Different individuals may perceive the same message in very different ways. The two primary factors that influence how a stimulus is perceived are the destination's education level and the destination's amount of experience. To minimize the negative effects of this perceptual factor on interpersonal communication, managers should try to send messages with precise meanings. Ambiguous words generally tend to magnify negative perceptions.

5. *Multimeaning words*—Because many words in the English language have several meanings, a destination may have difficulty deciding which meaning should be attached to the words of a message. A manager should not assume that a word means the same thing to all the people who use it.

BEETLE BAILEY ®   **By Mort Walker**

A classic study by Lydia Strong substantiates this point. Strong concluded that for the 500 most common words in our language, there are 4,070 different dictionary definitions. On the average, each of these words has over 18 usages. The word *run* is an example:[8]

Babe Ruth scored a *run.*
Did you ever see Jesse Owens *run?*
I have a *run* in my stocking.
There is a fine *run* of salmon this year.
Are you going to *run* this company or am I?
You have the *run* of the place.
What headline do you want to *run?*
There was a *run* on the bank today.
Did he *run* the ship aground?
I have to *run* (drive the car) downtown.
Who will *run* for president this year?
Joe flies the New York–Chicago *run* twice a week.
You know the kind of people they *run* around with.
The apples *run* large this year.
Please *run* my bathwater.

When encoding information, managers should be careful to define the terms they are using whenever possible, never use obscure meanings for words when designing messages, and strive to use words in the same way their destination uses them.

BACK TO THE CASE

In discussing Robert Dyer's ability to communicate, we are really discussing his ability to share ideas with other Eaton employees. For Dyer to be a successful communicator, he must concentrate on the three essential elements of the communication process. The first element is the source—the individual who wishes to share information with another. In this case, the source is Dyer. The second element is the signal—the message transmitted by Dyer. The third element is the destination—the Eaton employee with whom Dyer wishes to share information. Dyer should communicate with Eaton's employees by first determining exactly what information he wants to share, encoding the information, and only then transmitting the message. Communication is complete when his subordinates interpret the message and respond accordingly. Dyer's communication would be termed successful if his subordinates interpreted his messages as he intended.

If Dyer is to be a successful communicator, he must also learn to minimize the impact of numerous communication barriers. These barriers include the following:

1. Eaton's employees need to have more information and more complex information to do their jobs
2. Message interference
3. Dyer's view of the destination as well as the destination's view of Dyer
4. The perceptual processes of the people involved in the communication attempt
5. Multimeaning words

FEEDBACK AND INTERPERSONAL COMMUNICATION Feedback is the destination's reaction to a message. Feedback can be used by the source to ensure successful communication. For example, if the destination's message reaction is inappropriate, the source can conclude that communication was unsuccessful and that another message should be transmitted. If the destination's message reaction is appropriate, the source can conclude that communication was successful (assuming, of course, that the appropriate reaction did not happen merely by chance). Because of its potentially high value, managers should encourage feedback whenever possible and evaluate it carefully.[9]

Feedback is, in the interpersonal communication situation, the destination's reaction to a message.

Gathering and Using Feedback   Feedback can be either verbal or nonverbal.[10] To gather verbal feedback, the source can simply ask the destination pertinent message-related questions; the destination's answers should indicate whether the message was perceived as intended. To gather nonverbal feedback, the source can observe the destination's nonverbal response to a message. Say a manager has transmitted a message to a subordinate specifying new steps that must be taken in the normal performance of the subordinate's job. Assuming there are no other problems, if the subordinate does not follow the steps accurately, this constitutes nonverbal feedback telling the manager that the initial message needs to be clarified.

If managers discover that their communication effectiveness is relatively low over an extended period of time, they should assess the situation to determine how to improve their communication skills. It may be that their vocabulary is confusing to their destinations. For example, a study conducted by Group Attitudes Corporation found that when managers used certain words repeatedly in communicating with steelworkers, the steelworkers usually became confused.[11] Among the words causing confusion were *accrue, contemplate, designate, detriment, magnitude,* and *subsequently.*

Achieving Communication Effectiveness   In general, managers can sharpen their communication skills by adhering to the following "ten commandments of good communication" as closely as possible:[12]

1. *Seek to clarify your ideas before communicating*—The more systematically you analyze the problem or idea to be communicated, the clearer it becomes. This is the first step toward effective communication. Many communications fail because of inadequate planning. Good planning must consider the goals and attitudes of those who will receive the communication and those who will be affected by it.

2. *Examine the true purpose of each communication*—Before you communicate, ask yourself what you really want to accomplish with your message—obtain information, initiate action, change another person's attitude? Identify your most important goal and then adapt your language, tone, and total approach to serve that specific objective. Don't try to accomplish too much with each communication. The sharper the focus of your message, the greater its chances of success.

3. *Consider the total physical and human setting whenever you communicate*—Meaning and intent are conveyed by more than words alone. Many other factors influence the overall impact of a communication, and managers must be sensitive to the total setting in which they communicate. Consider, for example, your sense of timing—that is, the circumstances under which you make an announcement or render a decision; the physical setting—whether you communicate in private or otherwise, for example; the social climate that pervades work relationships within your company or department and sets the tone of its communications; custom and practice—the degree to which your communication conforms to, or departs from, the expectations of your audience. Be constantly aware of the total setting in which you communicate. Like all living things, communication must be capable of adapting to its environment.

4. *Consult with others, when appropriate, in planning communications*—Frequently, it is desirable or necessary to seek the participation of others in planning a communication or in developing the facts on which to base the communication. Such consultation often lends additional insight and objectivity to your message. Moreover, those who have helped you plan your communication will give it their active support.

5. *Be mindful while you communicate of the overtones rather than merely the basic content of your message*—Your tone of voice, your expression, your apparent receptiveness to the responses of others—all have a significant effect on those you wish to reach. Frequently overlooked, these subtleties of communication often affect a listener's reaction to a message even more than its basic content. Similarly, your choice of language—particularly your awareness of the fine shades of meaning and emotion in the words you use—predetermines in large part the reactions of your listeners.

6. *Take the opportunity, when it arises, to convey something of help or value to the receiver*—Consideration of the other person's interests and needs—trying to look at things from the other person's point of view—frequently points up opportunities to convey something of

immediate benefit or long-range value to the other person. Subordinates are most responsive to managers whose messages take the subordinates' interests into account.

7. *Follow up your communication*—Your best efforts at communication may be wasted, and you may never know whether you have succeeded in expressing your true meaning and intent, if you do not follow up to see how well you have put your message across. You can do this by asking questions, by encouraging the receiver to express his or her reactions, by following up on contacts, and by subsequent reviewing performance. Make certain that you get feedback for every important communication so that complete understanding and appropriate action result.

8. *Communicate for tomorrow as well as today*—Even though communications may be aimed primarily at meeting the demands of an immediate situation, they must be planned with the past in mind if they are to be viewed as consistent by the receiver. Most important, however, communications must be consistent with long-range interests and goals. For example, it is not easy to communicate frankly on such matters as poor performance or the shortcomings of a loyal subordinate, but postponing disagreeable communications makes these matters more difficult in the long run and is actually unfair to your subordinates and your company.

9. *Be sure your actions support your communications*—In the final analysis, the most persuasive kind of communication is not what you say, but what you do. When your actions or attitudes contradict your words, others tend to discount what you have said. For every manager, this means that good supervisory practices—such as clear assignment of responsibility and authority, fair rewards for effort, and sound policy enforcement—communicate more than all the gifts of oratory.

10. *Last, but by no means least: Seek not only to be understood but also to understand—be a good listener*—When you start talking, you often cease to listen, or at least to be attuned to the other person's unspoken reactions and attitudes. Even more serious is the occasional inattentiveness you may be guilty of when others are attempting to communicate with you. Listening is one of the most important, most difficult, and most neglected skills in communication. It demands that you concentrate, not only on the explicit meanings another person is expressing, but also on the implicit meanings, unspoken words, and undertones that may be far more significant.

VERBAL AND NONVERBAL INTERPERSONAL COMMUNICATION Interpersonal communication is generally divided into two types: verbal and nonverbal. Up to this point, the chapter has emphasized **verbal communication**—communication that uses either spoken or written words to share information with others.

Nonverbal communication is the sharing of information without using words to encode thoughts. Factors commonly used to encode thoughts in nonverbal communication are gestures, vocal tones, and facial expressions.[13] In most interpersonal communication, verbal and nonverbal communications are not mutually exclusive. Instead, the destination's interpretation of a message is generally based both on the words contained in the message and on such nonverbal factors as the source's gestures and facial expressions.

Verbal communication is the sharing of information through words, either written or spoken.

Nonverbal communication is the sharing of information without using words.

The Importance of Nonverbal Communication In an interpersonal communication situation in which both verbal and nonverbal factors are present, nonverbal factors may have more influence on the total effect of the message. Over two decades ago, Albert Mehrabian developed the following formula to show the relative contributions of verbal and nonverbal factors to the total effect of a message: Total message impact = .07 words + .38 vocal tones + .55 facial expressions. Other nonverbal factors besides vocal tones that can influence the effect of a verbal message are facial expressions, gestures, gender, and dress. Managers who are aware of this great potential influence of nonverbal factors on the effect of their communications will use nonverbal message ingredients to complement their verbal message ingredients whenever possible.[14]

Nonverbal messages can also be used to add content to verbal messages. For instance, a head might be nodded or a voice toned to show either agreement or disagreement.

Managers must be especially careful when they are communicating that verbal and nonverbal factors do not present contradictory messages. For example, if the words of a message express approval while the nonverbal factors express disapproval, the result will be message ambiguity that leaves the destination frustrated.

Managers who are able to communicate successfully through a blend of verbal and nonverbal communication are critical to the success of virtually every organization. In fact, a recent survey of corporate recruiters across the United States commissioned by the Darden Graduate School of Business at the University of Virginia revealed that the skill organizations most seek in prospective employees is facility at verbal and nonverbal communication.

BACK TO THE CASE

Employees' reactions to Dyer's messages can provide him with perhaps his most useful tool for honing his communication skills—feedback. He must be alert to both verbal and nonverbal feedback. When feedback seems inappropriate, Dyer should transmit another message to clarify the meaning of his first one. Over time, if feedback indicates that he is a relatively unsuccessful communicator, he should analyze his situation carefully to improve his communication effectiveness. He might find, for instance, that he is using a vocabulary that is generally inappropriate for certain employees or that he is not following one or more of the ten commandments of good communication.

In addition, Dyer must remember that he communicates to others without using words. His facial expressions, gestures, even the tone of his voice, say things to his employees. In most communication situations, in fact, Dyer is sending both verbal and nonverbal messages to Eaton's employees. Because a message's impact is often most dependent on its nonverbal components, Dyer must make certain that his nonverbal messages complement his verbal messages.

►INTERPERSONAL COMMUNICATION IN ORGANIZATIONS

Organizational communication is interpersonal communication within organizations.

To be effective communicators, managers must understand not only general interpersonal communication concepts but also the characteristics of interpersonal communication within organizations, or **organizational communication.** Organizational communication directly relates to the goals, functions, and structure of human organizations.[15] To a major extent, organizational success is determined by the effectiveness of organizational communication.

Although organizational communication was frequently referred to by early management writers, the topic did not receive systematic study and attention until after World War II. From World War II through the 1950s, the discipline of organizational communication made significant advances in such areas as mathematical communication theory and behavioral communication theory, and the emphasis on organizational communication has grown stronger in colleges of business throughout the nation since the 1970s.[16] The following sections focus on three fundamental organizational communication topics:

1. Formal organizational communication
2. Informal organizational communication
3. The encouragement of formal organizational communication

MANAGEMENT AND THE INTERNET — Wimbledon Uses a Web Site to Communicate with Stakeholders

The All England Lawn, Tennis & Croquet Club hosts Wimbledon, a 121-year-old tennis championship. For the 1998 championship, the club decided to take a giant step forward by communicating to its stakeholders about Wimbledon via a Web site. To build the site, the club teamed up with IBM, one of the sponsors of Wimbledon. To enhance ease of use and overall effectiveness, the site was based upon Notes, an IBM software package. The club increased its usual five-person information systems staff to 150 in order to handle operations of the new Web site.

The site was very flexible and was used by different groups in different ways. Wimbledon players registered for the tournament via e-mail. Club reporters and sports writers entered their news or human interest stories and simply pressed a "Publish" button to have their stories appear live on the Internet. Fans entered the site to get player profiles, up-to-date scores, and match summaries. In addition, broadcasters of the event searched the site for interesting information to tell listeners.

Looking back, the use of the Web site at Wimbledon was quite successful. The site averaged 9,000 hits per day. The highest number of hits for a single day was 25,000. A major factor contributing to this success is the fact that the Web site was structured so that it was easy to bring in nontechnical help for the two weeks of competition without having to provide lots of training. Naturally, IBM's experience in building such sites contributed to this success. IBM has built similar sites for the 1996 Summer Olympic Games in Atlanta, the 1998 Winter Olympics in Nagano, Japan, and the 1998 World Cup soccer championships.

FORMAL ORGANIZATIONAL COMMUNICATION In general, organizational communication that follows the lines of the organization chart is called **formal organizational communication**.[17] As discussed in chapter 10, the organization chart depicts relationships of people and jobs and shows the formal channels of communication among them.

Types of Formal Organizational Communication There are three basic types of formal organizational communication:

1. Downward
2. Upward
3. Lateral

Downward organizational communication is communication that flows from any point on an organization chart downward to another point on the organization chart. This type of formal organizational communication relates primarily to the direction and control of employees. Job-related information that focuses on what activities are required, when they should be performed, and how they should be coordinated with other activities within the organization must be transmitted to employees. This downward communication typically includes a statement of organizational philosophy, management system objectives, position descriptions, and other written information relating to the importance, rationale, and interrelationships of various departments.

> **Formal organizational communication** is organizational communication that follows the lines of the organization chart.

> **Downward organizational communication** is communication that flows from any point on an organization chart downward to another point on the organization chart.

Open, inviting office spaces in bright and cheerful colors are a trend in organizational decor in some industries. Some people feel they encourage formal organizational communication in all directions, although employees may need to adjust to the relative lack of privacy that comes with extremely open spaces. Jay Chiat, of the advertising agency TBWA Chiat/Day, is shown here enjoying his own "virtual office."

Upward organizational communication is communication that flows from any point on an organization chart upward to another point on the organization chart.

Lateral organizational communication is communication that flows from any point on an organization chart horizontally to another point on the organization chart.

Upward organizational communication is communication that flows from any point on an organization chart upward to another point on the organization chart.[18] This type of organizational communication contains primarily the information managers need to evaluate the organizational area for which they are responsible and to determine if something is going wrong within it. Techniques that managers commonly use to encourage upward organizational communication are informal discussions with employees, attitude surveys, the development and use of grievance procedures, suggestion systems, and an "open door" policy that invites employees to come in whenever they would like to talk to management.[19] Organizational modifications based on the feedback provided by upward organizational communication will enable a company to be more successful in the future.

Lateral organizational communication is communication that flows from any point on an organization chart horizontally to another point on the organization chart. Communication that flows across the organization usually focuses on coordinating the activities of various departments and developing new plans for future operating periods. Within the organization, all departments are related to all other departments. Only through lateral communication can these departmental relationships be coordinated well enough to enhance the attainment of management system objectives.

ACROSS INDUSTRIES   Local Government

HOW DAVID BELL COMMUNICATES WITH CITY EMPLOYEES

The previous information discusses organizational communication and describes various directions in which it can occur. David Bell, a city administrator in Columbus, Nebraska, understands that sound organizational communication is important in building successful city government. Bell believes that public administrators should encourage employee participation and feedback on such issues as working conditions, employee benefits, and personnel policies. To encourage this feedback, Bell constantly strives to maintain good relationships with diverse employee groups like police officers, firefighters, and street maintenance workers.

According to Bell, public administrators must make a serious effort to improve the quality of communication in their organizations. Local government employees want to know more about their organizations, and a lack of information flowing from administrators to employees forces employees to rely on the local newspaper and the rumor mill as their two primary sources of information. Unless employees are kept informed of a local government's activities, they seek out information elsewhere—and that information may be drastically incorrect. Also, administrators should strive to improve organizational communication because such improvement generally leads to improved employee relations and, resultantly, better city government.

Bell has his own style in staff meetings. These meetings with department heads occur directly after the city council meets. Bell presents issues and official actions of the council in a written summary. Department heads then post the meeting summary on all employee bulletin boards on the same day to ensure that employees have quick access to the information.

According to Bell's philosophy, communicating with employees is also the key to updating and improving personnel policies. City government personnel policies should be updated annually to reflect both changes in employment law and organizational and employee needs. Bell encourages all departments to review and suggest changes in personnel policies. City employees are aware of problems in the day-to-day administration of these policies and generally have excellent ideas for improvement. In addition, employee participation in improving such policies leads to greater employee acceptance of the policies and greater ease for Bell in implementing the policies.

Modern managers in city governments face the serious and formidable challenge of building successful organizations. Building sound organizational communication within city government seems to be an important key to meeting this challenge.

Patterns of Formal Organizational Communication   By its very nature, organizational communication creates patterns of communication among organization members. These patterns evolve from the repeated occurrence of various serial transmissions of information. According to Haney, a **serial transmission** involves passing information from one individual to another in a series. It occurs under the following circumstances:[20]

A **serial transmission** involves the passing of information from one individual to another in a series.

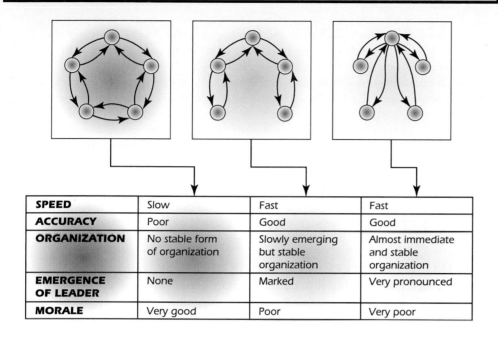

FIGURE 14.5

Comparison of three patterns of organizational communication on the variables of speed, accuracy, organization, emergence of leader, and morale

SPEED	Slow	Fast	Fast
ACCURACY	Poor	Good	Good
ORGANIZATION	No stable form of organization	Slowly emerging but stable organization	Almost immediate and stable organization
EMERGENCE OF LEADER	None	Marked	Very pronounced
MORALE	Very good	Poor	Very poor

A communicates a message to *B; B* then communicates *A*'s message (or rather his or her interpretation of *A*'s message) to *C; C* then communicates his or her interpretation of *B*'s interpretation of *A*'s message to *D;* and so on. The originator and the ultimate recipient of the message are separated by middle people.

One obvious weakness of a serial transmission, of course, is that messages tend to become distorted as the length of the series increases. Research has shown that message details may be omitted, altered, or added in a serial transmission.

The potential inaccuracy of transmitted messages is not the only weakness of serial transmissions. A classic article by Alex Bavelas and Dermot Barrett[21] makes the case that serial transmissions can also influence morale, the emergence of a leader, the degree to which individuals involved in the transmissions are organized, and their efficiency. Three basic organizational communication patterns and the corresponding effects on the variables just mentioned are shown in Figure 14.5.

▶ QUALITY SPOTLIGHT ◀   Enhanced Formal Communication Contributes to Improving Quality at Holiday Inn

Improving the flow of communication dictated by the organization chart can be of immense benefit to an organization. Holiday Inn discovered that improving the flow of such communication enhanced the quality of customer service throughout the organization.

Marketing and product quality were the themes at a recent Holiday Inn Worldwide Franchise Conference. Individual Holiday Inn operators expressed more confidence in the company after it announced it had a new plan to improve customer service as well as customer attitudes toward Holiday Inn by improving Holiday Inn's

formal communication system. The company stated it would extend its satellite communication system into Europe to allow for more efficient communication of hotel room rate information between North American and European operations.

Mike Leven, president of the Holiday Inn franchise division, said that franchisees have always depended on Holiday Inn's commitment to maintaining quality service. Company Chairman Bryan Langton believes that this focus on quality has helped Holiday Inn outperform the industry in occupancy rates in recent years.

Informal organizational communication is organizational communication that does not follow the lines of the organization chart.

INFORMAL ORGANIZATIONAL COMMUNICATION Informal organizational **communication** is organizational communication that does not follow the lines of the organization chart.[22] Instead, this type of communication typically follows the pattern of personal relationships among organization members: One friend communicates with another friend, regardless of their relative positions on the organization chart. Informal organizational communication networks generally exist because organization members have a desire for information that is not furnished through formal organizational communication.

The **grapevine** is the network of informal organizational communication.

Patterns of Informal Organizational Communication   The informal organizational communication network, or **grapevine,** has three main characteristics:

1. It springs up and is used irregularly within the organization
2. It is not controlled by top executives, who may not even be able to influence it
3. It exists largely to serve the self-interests of the people within it

Understanding the grapevine is a prerequisite for a complete understanding of organizational communication. It has been estimated that 70 percent of all communication in organizations flows along the organizational grapevine. Not only do grapevines carry great amounts of communication, but they carry it at very rapid speeds. Employees commonly cite the company grapevine as the most reliable and credible source of information about company events.[23]

Like formal organizational communication, informal organizational communication uses serial transmissions. The difference is that it is more difficult for managers to identify organization members involved in these transmissions than members of the formal communication network. A classic article by Keith Davis that appeared in the *Harvard Business Review* has been a significant help to managers in understanding how organizational grapevines spring up and operate. Figure 14.6 sketches the four most common grapevine patterns as outlined by Davis. They are as follows:[24]

1. *The single-strand grapevine—A* tells *B,* who tells *C,* who tells *D,* and so on. This type of grapevine tends to distort messages more than any other.
2. *The gossip grapevine—A* informs everyone else on the grapevine.
3. *The probability grapevine—A* communicates randomly—for example, to *F* and *D. F* and *D* then continue to inform other grapevine members in the same way.
4. *The cluster grapevine—A* selects and tells *C, D,* and *F. F* selects and tells *I* and *B,* and *B* selects and tells *J.* Information in this grapevine travels only to selected individuals.

Dealing with Grapevines. Clearly, grapevines are a factor managers must deal with because they can, and often do, generate rumors that are detrimental to organizational success. Exactly how individual managers should deal with the grapevine, of course, depends on the specific organizational situation in which they find themselves. Managers can use grapevines advanta-

FIGURE 14.6 ▸ Four types of organizational grapevines

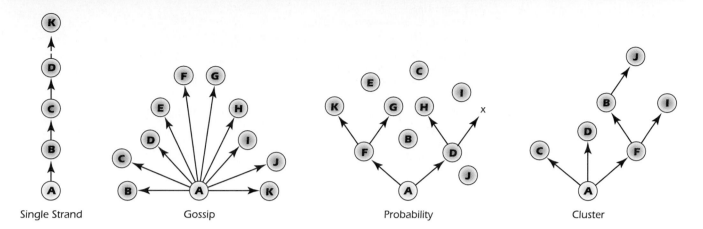

Single Strand   Gossip   Probability   Cluster

geously to maximize information flow to employees. When employees have what they view as sufficient organizational information, it seems to build their sense of belonging to the organization and their level of productivity. Some writers even argue that managers should encourage the development of grapevines and strive to become grapevine members in order to gain feedback that could be very valuable in improving the organization.[25]

ENCOURAGING FORMAL ORGANIZATIONAL COMMUNICATION Since the organization acts only in the way that its organizational communication directs it to act, organizational communication is often called the nervous system of the organization. Formal organizational communication is generally the more important type of communication within an organization, so managers should encourage its free flow.

One strategy for doing this is to listen attentively to messages that come through formal channels. Listening shows organization members that the manager is interested in what subordinates have to say and encourages them to use formal communication channels in subsequent situations. Table 14.2 presents some general guidelines for listening well.

Some other strategies to encourage the flow of formal organizational communication are as follows:

▸ Support the flow of clear and concise statements through formal communication channels. Receiving an ambiguous message through a formal organizational communication channel can discourage employees from using that channel again.

At Disneyland one means of bolstering formal communication is substituting camaraderie and enthusiasm for an overabundance of procedures and policies. Newcomers are immediately exposed to the company culture, and although there are fairly strict rules about dress, hairstyle, and makeup, managers encourage imagination and independence when it comes to dealing directly with guests like Minnie Pepito, who is being celebrated here for becoming the 400 millionth guest at the park.

TABLE 14.2	► Ten Commandments for Good Listening

1. *Stop talking!*
   You cannot listen if you are talking.
   Polonius *(Hamlet):* "Give every man thine ear, but few thy voice."

2. *Put the talker at ease*
   Help the talker feel free to talk.
   This is often called establishing a permissive environment.

3. *Show the talker that you want to listen.*
   Look and act interested. Do not read your mail while he or she talks.
   Listen to understand rather than to oppose.

4. *Remove distractions*
   Do not doodle, top, or shuffle papers.
   Will it be quieter if you shut the door?

5. *Empathize with the talker*
   Try to put yourself in the talker's place so that you can see his or her point of view.

6. *Be patient*
   Allow plenty of time. Do not interrupt the talker.
   Do not start for the door to walk away.

7. *Hold your temper*
   An angry person gets the wrong meaning from words.

8. *Go easy on argument and criticism*
   This puts the talker on the defensive. He or she may "clam up" or get angry.
   Do not argue: even if you win, you *lose.*

9. *Ask questions*
   This encourages the talker and shows you are listening.
   It helps to develop points further.

10. *Stop talking!*
    This is the first and last commandment, because all other commandments depend on it. You just can't do a good listening job while you are talking. Nature gave us two ears but only one tongue, which is a gentle hint that we should listen more than we talk.

► Take care to ensure that all organization members have free access to formal communication channels. Obviously, organization members cannot communicate formally within the organization if they don't have access to the formal communication network.

► Assign specific communication responsibilities to staff personnel who could be of enormous help to line personnel in spreading important information throughout the organization.

BACK TO THE CASE

It is virtually certain that there is an extensive grapevine in Dyer's plant—there is one in nearly every organization. Although Dyer must deal with this grapevine, he may not be able to influence it significantly. Eaton employees at his plant, like employees everywhere else, will latch onto a grapevine out of self-interest or because the formal organization has not furnished them with the information they believe they need.

By developing certain social relationships, Dyer could conceivably become part of the grapevine and obtain valuable feedback from it. Also, because grapevines generate rumors that could have a detrimental effect on the success of Dyer's plant, he should make sure that all personnel at his plant receive all the information they need to do their jobs well through formal organizational communication channels, thereby reducing their reliance on the grapevine.

Because formal organizational communication is vitally important to Dyer's plant, he should strive to encourage it by listening intently to messages that come to him over formal channels, supporting the flow of clear messages through formal channels, and making sure that all employees at his plant have access to these formal channels.

For updated information on the topics in this chapter, Internet exercises, links to related Internet sites, an interactive study guide, and more, visit our companion Web site at

http://www.prenhall.com/certo

Additional information can be found on the inside front and back covers of this text.

ACTION SUMMARY

Reread the learning objectives below. Each objective is followed by questions. Answering these questions accurately will help you retain the most important concepts discussed in this chapter. After answering each question, check your answer against the answer key at the end of this chapter. (*Hint:* If you have any doubts regarding the correct response, consult the page number that follows the answer.)

Circle:

From studying this chapter, I will attempt to acquire

1. An understanding of influencing.

T F   **a.** The influencing function can be viewed as forcing the activities of organization members in appropriate directions.

a b c d e   **b.** The following activity is *not* a major component of the influencing process: (a) motivating (b) leading (c) communicating (d) correcting (e) considering groups.

2. An understanding of interpersonal communication.

a b c d e   **a.** Communication is best described as the process of: (a) sharing emotion (b) sharing information (c) sending messages (d) feedback formulation (e) forwarding information.

a b c d e   **b.** The basic elements of interpersonal communication are: (a) source/encoder, signal, decoder/destination (b) sender/message, encoder, receiver/decoder (c) signal, source/sender, decoder/destination (d) signal, source/decoder, encoder/destination (e) source/sender, signal, receiver/destination.

3. A knowledge of how to use feedback.

T F   **a.** Feedback is solely verbal.

a b c d e   **b.** Robert S. Goyer suggested using feedback: (a) as a microbarrier (b) as a way for sources to evaluate their communication effectiveness (c) to ensure that instructions will be carried out (d) to evaluate the decoder (e) all of the above.

4. An appreciation for the importance of nonverbal communication.

T F   **a.** In interpersonal communication, nonverbal factors often play a more influential role than verbal factors.

T F   **b.** Nonverbal messages can contradict verbal messages, creating frustration in the destination.

5. Insights on formal organizational communication.

a b c d e   **a.** The following is *not* upward communication: (a) cost accounting reports (b) purchase order summary (c) production reports (d) corporate policy statement (e) sales reports.

a b c d e   **b.** The primary purpose served by lateral organizational communication is: (a) coordinating (b) organizing (c) direction (d) evaluation (e) control.

6. An appreciation for the importance of the grapevine.

a b c d e   **a.** The following statement concerning the grapevine is *not* correct: (a) grapevines are irregularly used in organizations (b) a grapevine can and often does generate harmful rumors (c) the grapevine is used largely to serve the self-interests of the people within it (d) some managers use grapevines to their advantage (e) in time, and with proper pressure, the grapevine can be eliminated.

T F   **b.** The grapevine is much slower than formal communication channels.

7. Some hints on how to encourage organizational communication.

a b c d e   **a.** To encourage formal organizational communication, managers should: (a) support the flow of clear and concise statements through formal channels (b) ensure free access to formal channels for all organization members (c) assign specific communication responsibilities to staff personnel (d) a and b (e) all of the above.

T F   **b.** Since formal organizational communication is the most important type of communication within an organization, managers must restrict its flow if the organization is to be successful.

CASE DISCUSSSION QUESTIONS

"Eaton Managers Concentrate on Influencing People" (p. 303) and its related Back-to-the-Case sections were written to help you better understand the management concepts contained in this chapter. Answer the following discussion questions about this Introductory Case to enrich your understanding of the chapter content.

1. List three problems that could be caused at Eaton's Kearney plant if Robert Dyer were a poor communicator.

2. Explain *how* the problems you listed in number 1 could be caused by Dyer's inability to communicate.

3. Assuming that Dyer is a good communicator, discuss three ways that he is having a positive impact on Eaton's Kearney plant as a result of his communication expertise.

SKILLS EXERCISE: ENCOURAGING FORMAL ORGANIZATIONAL COMMUNICATION

In this chapter you studied about encouraging formal interpersonal communication in organizations. The Introductory Case explains how Eaton Corporation focuses on building work teams. Assume that you supervise a work team at Eaton. List five actions you would take to encourage upward formal organizational communication from the team to you. Be sure to explain why you would take each action.

1. What is influencing?
2. Describe the relationship between the overall management system and the influencing subsystem.
3. What factors make up the input, process, and output of the influencing subsystem?
4. Explain the relationship between the factors that compose the process section of the influencing subsystem.
5. What is communication?
6. How important is communication to managers?
7. Draw the communication model presented in this chapter and explain how it works.
8. How does successful communication differ from unsuccessful communication?
9. Summarize the significance of field of experience to communication.
10. List and describe three communication macrobarriers and three communication microbarriers.
11. What is feedback, and how should managers use it when communicating?
12. How is the communication effectiveness index calculated, and what is its significance?
13. Name the ten commandments of good communication.
14. What is nonverbal communication? Explain its significance.
15. How should managers use nonverbal communication?
16. What is organizational communication?
17. How do formal and informal organizational communication differ?
18. Describe three types of formal organizational communication, and explain the general purpose of each type.
19. Can serial transmissions and other formal communication patterns influence communication effectiveness and the individuals using the patterns? If so, how?
20. Draw and describe the four main types of grapevines that exist in organizations.
21. How can managers encourage the flow of formal organizational communication?

1. **a.** F, p. 304
   b. d, pp. 304–305
2. **a.** b, p. 307
   b. a, pp. 307–308
3. **a.** F, p. 312
   b. b, p. 312
4. **a.** T, p. 313
   b. T, pp. 313–314
5. **a.** d, p. 316
   b. a, p. 316
6. **a.** e, p. 318
   b. F, p. 318
7. **a.** e, pp. 319–320
   b. F, p. 319

Chick-fil-A, the Atlanta-based chicken restaurant chain, went through some major growing pains in the past 13 years as it changed from an operation predominantly located in shopping malls to one that expanded into at least eight different restaurant concepts. Along the way, this close-knit family-owned company doubled its number of locations to over 600.

For the past 30 years, Truett Cathy, the charismatic founder, has held the company together. Corporate communication for most of the company's history was through traditional methods—personal contact, telephone calls, and written memos. Cathy went to considerable effort to ensure that he communicated successfully with his operators, whether through personal appearances at operator get-togethers or through routine visits at company locations.

Chick-fil-A restaurants are not franchises. Owner/operators, who are considered employees by the company, split restaurant profits with corporate headquarters. They are rewarded financially for profitable performance and have the opportunity to add units or move into more profitable markets. This entrepreneurial arrangement serves to motivate direct communication between owner/operators and corporate headquarters.

As the corporation grew, field management consultants became part of the organizational structure. These consultants helped resolve problems and assisted owner/operators in running profitable restaurants according to corporate guidelines. Whenever owner/operators needed assistance, they would simply leave messages at Atlanta corporate headquarters for the field consultants. As operations exploded, however, responses were delayed or even lost because of consultants' heavy travel schedules.

According to Mark Ashworth, Chick-fil-A's manager of communication services, the need for better communication was initially a result of the rapid increase in the number of restaurant units that the corporation owned. Personal contact by headquarters, except at regional workshops and annual meetings, became almost logistically prohibitive. Thus the field consultants' role in effective corporate communication became more imperative. Later, the introduction of new food items and expansion into new markets heightened the need for fresh ideas in communicating quality guidelines.

Chick-fil-A headquarters consequently began expanding its communication procedures to include different kinds of media; soon newsletters, audiotapes, and videotapes were spreading the corporate message. At first, corporate communications were highly decentralized.

Not only were employees getting different messages from different people, but messages sometimes lacked relevance and timeliness or were duplicated or poorly implemented. In short, few communications were used to the fullest potential. In addition, production quality was inconsistent, and managers often chose the wrong communication tools to reach intended audiences.

Under Mark Ashworth's direction, corporate communications have not yet become totally centralized, but department managers at Chick-fil-A headquarters have begun to deliver their messages more effectively. Because the communication needs of the owner/operators are sometimes different from those of front-line employees, managers are encouraged to choose from an arsenal of communication programs. Being able to pick the right medium for their message has not only helped people at Chick-fil-A headquarters become better communicators, but has also saved the company money. Managers who once requested only expensive videos are now using other media, such as newsletters or audiotapes, to communicate.

According to Ashworth, even after they switched to more effective media, corporate managers were still doing a lot of one-way communicating with owner/operators. To rectify this situation, voice mail and e-mail were recently added to Chick-fil-A's arsenal of communication tools. Now, says Ashworth, owner/operators are trained to use personal computers to expedite the flow of two-way communications. Field consultants, who are still the front-line communicators, receive messages in a more timely manner as owner/operators communicate with absent colleagues or leave e-mail messages for people at corporate headquarters. Important voice and electronic mail messages are now broadcast immediately, without any of the delays associated with traditional communications methods. The Internet is the next communication tool to be exploited by Ashworth and his colleagues.

QUESTIONS

1. How has communication changed over the corporate life of Chick-fil-A? What precipitated the changes?
2. Define successful communication. Why is the choice of medium so important to successful communication?
3. According to Ashworth, communication at Chick-fil-A is still one-way in many circumstances. Do you consider this a problem? Explain. How is the company attempting to encourage two-way communication and make it more effective. What other ways would you suggest?

15

Leadership

STUDENT LEARNING OBJECTIVES

From studying this chapter, I will attempt to acquire

1. A working definition of leadership

2. An understanding of the relationship between leading and managing

3. An appreciation for the trait and situational approaches to leadership

4. Insights about using leadership theories that emphasize decision-making situations

5. Insights about using leadership theories that emphasize more general organizational situations

6. An understanding of alternatives to leader flexibility

7. An appreciation of emerging leader styles and leadership issues of today

CHAPTER OUTLINE

Introductory Case: *The New President of H.J. Heinz Company Sends a Letter*

DEFINING *LEADERSHIP*
Leader versus Manager

THE TRAIT APPROACH TO LEADERSHIP

THE SITUATIONAL APPROACH TO LEADERSHIP:
A FOCUS ON LEADER BEHAVIOR
Leadership Situations and Decisions

Management and the Internet: *K•B Uses Internet to Provide Information for Making Decisions*
Leadership Behaviors

Across Industries: *Recruitment—Dan Caulfield Changes His "High Task" Leadership Style*

LEADERSHIP TODAY

People Spotlight: *Robert Eaton Gets People Involved at DaimlerChrysler*
Transformational Leadership
Coaching
Superleadership
Entrepreneurial Leadership

CURRENT TOPICS IN LEADERSHIP
Substitutes for Leadership
Women as Leaders
Ways Women Lead

Diversity Spotlight: *For James G. Kaiser of Corning, Being Employee-Centered Includes a Focus on Diversity*

The New President of H.J. Heinz Company Sends a Letter

REMINDER: THE INTRODUCTORY CASE WRAP-UP (P. 349) CONTAINS DISCUSSION QUESTIONS AND A SKILLS EXERCISE TO FURTHER ILLUSTRATE THE APPLICATION OF CHAPTER CONCEPTS TO THIS VIGNETTE.

Heinz Company manufactures and markets an extensive line of processed food products throughout the world, including ketchup and sauces, condiments, pet food, baby food, frozen potato products and low calorie products. The following is a recent letter sent to Heinz stockholders by its president.

Dear Fellow Shareholders:

I feel deeply privileged to have been selected as the new chief executive officer of H.J. Heinz Company and to lead one of the world's enduring corporations into a new century of growth.

Your management team has rededicated itself to the future through a formula we have dubbed "V5V" or "V × 5 = Victory." Through Vision, Voracity, Value, Volume and Velocity, we can achieve Victory.

Victory. Victory for Heinz means delivering superior shareholder value. It means realizing ambitious, but realistic, performance goals that we have set for the coming years, including consistent 10 to 12 percent annual earnings growth; 4 to 5 percent real unit growth; gross profit margins of more than 40 percent; a return on invested capital of more than 30 percent; and world-class "value chain" status from procurement to manufacturing to distribution.

Vision. To accomplish this requires *Vision*—the vision of a truly global Heinz, turning from reliance on affiliate strategies and manufacturing to global leverage of our eight core categories of food service: infant feeding; ketchup, sauces and condiments; pet food; tuna; weight control; frozen food; and convenience meals.

Voracity. We will propel our global vision with a new culture of *Voracity*. We are stimulating our management team's voracious appetite to succeed through "centralized decentralization." By this we mean our strategy will be global, directed by ambitious centralized goals. There will be decentralized local accountability, motivated by a creative, entrepreneurial zeal.

Value. Our global team is intently focused on delivering sustainable growth in shareholder *Value*. We anticipate continued progress in such key investment concerns as: increased sales and market shares, higher margins and greater capital efficiency.

This is a selection of Heinz Company's extensive product offerings around the world. Raw ingredients are gathered worldwide as well, including cereals from Russia and infant formula from the Czech Republic.

Volume. A primary factor in our company's valuation is top-line performance, fueled by greater *Volume* around the world. A mix of global expansion, improved marketing and new products will achieve this—all supported by increased margins and continued cost reduction. Opportunities abound in trends, such as meal solutions, nutraceuticals, the growing global popularity of pets, and the increasing world appetite for eating out.

Velocity. We are particularly impatient about pursuing change. Hence, the stress on *Velocity*. The transformation of Heinz will not be glacial; it will be lightning quick. We begin Fiscal 1999 with new senior management appointments to help drive our new philosophy forward immediately.

To summarize the "V5V" equation: Heinz will achieve victory through a vision based on global category management and growth; a voracious appetite for success; an unyielding focus on enhancing shareholder value; a dedication to volume growth fueled by cost containment; and a high-velocity commitment to change. This formula is the key to greater shareholder return and a dynamic future for Heinz as the most dependable growth and performance company in the global food industry.

William R. Johnson
President and Chief Executive Officer

What's Ahead

William R. Johnson is the new president and CEO of Heinz Company. With this new job, Johnson is facing a whole set of new professional challenges in leading Heinz into a new century of growth. The case, Johnson's letter, ends by noting that Heinz will achieve victory through the 5 Vs. The information in this chapter would be helpful to an individual such as Johnson as the basis for developing a useful leadership strategy to achieve such success. This chapter discusses the following:

1. How to define leadership
2. The difference between a leader and a manager
3. The trait approach to leadership
4. The situational approach to leadership
5. Leadership today
6. Current topics in leadership

DEFINING LEADERSHIP

Leadership is the process of directing the behavior of others toward the accomplishment of objectives.

Leadership is the process of directing the behavior of others toward the accomplishment of some objective. Directing, in this sense, means causing individuals to act in a certain way or to follow a particular course. Ideally, this course is perfectly consistent with such factors as established organizational policies, procedures, and job descriptions. The central theme of leadership is getting things accomplished through people.[1]

As indicated in chapter 14, leadership is one of the four main interdependent activities of the influencing subsystem and is accomplished, at least to some extent, by communicating with others. It is extremely important that managers have a thorough understanding of what leadership entails. Leadership has always been considered a prerequisite for organizational success. Today, given the increased capability afforded by enhanced communication technology and the rise of international business, leadership is more important than ever before.[2]

LEADER VERSUS MANAGER

Leading is not the same as managing. Many executives fail to grasp the difference between the two and therefore labor under a misapprehension about how to carry out their organizational duties. Although some managers are leaders and some leaders are managers, leading and managing are not identical activities.[3] According to Theodore Levitt, management consists of[4]

> the rational assessment of a situation and the systematic selection of goals and purposes (what is to be done); the systematic development of strategies to achieve these goals; the marshalling of the required resources; the rational design, organization, direction, and control of the activities required to attain the selected purposes; and, finally, the motivating and rewarding of people to do the work.

Leadership, as one of the four primary activities of the influencing function, is a subset of management. Managing is much broader in scope than leading and focuses on nonbehavioral as well as behavioral issues. Leading emphasizes mainly behavioral issues. Figure 15.1 makes

FIGURE 15.1	The most effective managers over the long term are also leaders

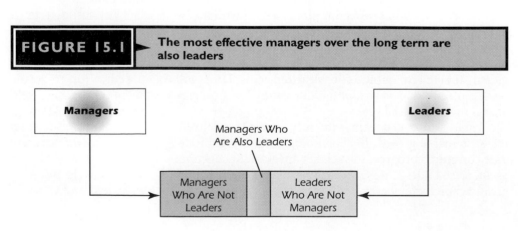

the point that although not all managers are leaders, the most effective managers over the long term are leaders.

Merely possessing management skills is no longer sufficient for success as an executive in the business world. Modern executives need to understand the difference between managing and leading and know how to combine the two roles to achieve organizational success. A manager makes sure that a job gets done, and a leader cares about and focuses on the people who do the job. To combine management and leadership, therefore, requires demonstrating a calculated and logical focus on organizational processes (management) along with a genuine concern for workers as people (leadership).[5]

THE TRAIT APPROACH TO LEADERSHIP

The **trait approach to leadership** is based on early leadership research that seemed to assume that a good leader is born, not made. The mainstream of this research attempted to describe successful leaders as precisely as possible. The reasoning was that, if a complete profile of the traits of a successful leader could be drawn, it would be fairly easy to identify the individuals who should and should not be placed in leadership positions.

Many of the early studies that attempted to summarize the traits of successful leaders were documented. One of these summaries concludes that successful leaders tend to possess the following characteristics:[6]

1. Intelligence, including judgment and verbal ability
2. Past achievement in scholarship and athletics
3. Emotional maturity and stability
4. Dependability, persistence, and a drive for continuing achievement
5. The skill to participate socially and adapt to various groups
6. A desire for status and socioeconomic position

Evaluations of these trait studies, however, have concluded that their findings are inconsistent. One researcher says that 50 years of study have failed to produce one personality trait or set of qualities that can be used consistently to discriminate leaders from nonleaders.[7] It follows, then, that no trait or combination of traits guarantees that someone will be a successful leader. Leadership is apparently a much more complex issue.

Contemporary management writers and practitioners generally agree that leadership ability cannot be explained by an individual's traits or inherited characteristics. They believe, rather, that individuals can be trained to be good leaders. In other words, leaders are made, not born. That is why thousands of employees each year are sent through leadership training programs.[8]

> The **trait approach to leadership** is an outdated view of leadership that sees the personal characteristics of an individual as the main determinants of how successful that individual could be as a leader.

BACK TO THE CASE

From the preceding material, a manager like William Johnson, the president of H.J. Heinz Company, should understand that his leadership activities relating to achieving "victory" are those activities that involve directing the behavior of organization members so that the company will achieve its success. A manager like Johnson also should understand that leading and managing are not the same thing. When managing, Johnson is involved with planning, organizing, influencing, and controlling. When leading, he is performing an activity that is part of the influencing function of management. To maximize his long-term success, Johnson should strive to be both a manager and a leader.

In assessing his leadership at Heinz, Johnson should not fall into the trap of trying to increase his leadership success by changing his personal traits or attitudes to mirror those of successful leaders that he might know. Studies based on the trait approach to leadership should indicate to Johnson that merely changing his characteristics will not guarantee his success as a leader.

The **situational approach to leadership** is a relatively modern view of leadership that suggests that successful leadership requires a unique combination of leaders, followers, and leadership situations.

Leadership studies have shifted emphasis from the trait approach to the situational approach, which suggests that leadership style must be appropriately matched to the situation the leader faces. The more modern **situational approach to leadership** is based on the assumption that each instance of leadership is different and therefore requires a unique combination of leaders, followers, and leadership situations.

This interaction is commonly expressed in formula form: $SL = f(L,F,S)$, where SL is *successful leadership*, *f* stands for *function of*, and *L*, *F*, and *S* are, respectively, the *leader*, the *follower*, and the *situation*.[9] Translated, this formula says that successful leadership is a function of a leader, follower, and situation that are appropriate for one another.

► LEADERSHIP SITUATIONS AND DECISIONS

THE TANNENBAUM AND SCHMIDT LEADERSHIP CONTINUUM Since one of the most important tasks of a leader is making sound decisions, all practical and legitimate leadership thinking emphasizes decision making. Tannenbaum and Schmidt, who wrote one of the first and perhaps most often quoted articles on the situational approach to leadership, stress situations in which a leader makes decisions.[10] Figure 15.2 presents their model of leadership behavior.

This model is actually a continuum, or range, of leadership behavior available to managers when they are making decisions. Note that each type of decision-making behavior depicted in the figure has both a corresponding degree of authority used by the manager and a related amount of freedom available to subordinates. Management behavior at the extreme left of the model characterizes the leader who makes decisions by maintaining high control and allowing subordinates little freedom. Behavior at the extreme right characterizes the leader who makes decisions by exercising little control and allowing subordinates much freedom and self-direction. Behavior in between the extremes reflects graduations in leadership from autocratic to democratic.

Managers displaying leadership behavior toward the right of the model are more democratic, and are called *subordinate-centered* leaders. Those displaying leadership behavior toward the left of the model are more autocratic, and are called *boss-centered* leaders.

Each type of leadership behavior in this model is explained in more detail in the following list:

1. *The manager makes the decision and announces it*—This behavior is characterized by the manager (a) identifying a problem, (b) analyzing various alternatives available to solve it, (c) choosing the alternative that will be used to solve it, and (d) requiring followers to implement the chosen alternative. The manager may or may not use coercion, but the followers have no opportunity to participate directly in the decision-making process.

FIGURE 15.2 ► Continuum of leadership behavior that emphasizes decision making

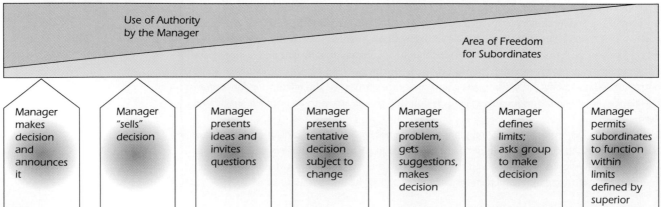

BOSS-CENTERED LEADERSHIP   SUBORDINATE-CENTERED LEADERSHIP

Use of Authority by the Manager

Area of Freedom for Subordinates

| Manager makes decision and announces it | Manager "sells" decision | Manager presents ideas and invites questions | Manager presents tentative decision subject to change | Manager presents problem, gets suggestions, makes decision | Manager defines limits; asks group to make decision | Manager permits subordinates to function within limits defined by superior |

2. *The manager "sells" the decision*—As above, the manager identifies the problem and independently arrives at a decision. Rather than announce the decision to subordinates for implementation, however, the manager tries to persuade subordinates to accept the decision.

3. *The manager presents ideas and invites questions*—Here, the manager makes the decision and attempts to gain acceptance through persuasion. One additional step is taken, however: Subordinates are invited to ask questions about the decision.

4. *The manager presents a tentative decision that is subject to change*—The manager allows subordinates to have some part in the decision-making process but retains the responsibility for identifying and diagnosing the problem. The manager then arrives at a tentative decision that is subject to change on the basis of subordinate input. The final decision is made by the manager.

5. *The manager presents the problem, gets suggestions, and then makes the decision*—This is the first leadership activity described thus far that allows subordinates the opportunity to offer problem solutions before the manager does. The manager, however, is still the one who identifies the problem.

6. *The manager defines the limits and asks the group to make a decision*—In this type of leadership behavior, the manager first defines the problem and sets the boundaries within which a decision must be made. The manager then enters into partnership with subordinates to arrive at an appropriate decision. The danger here is that if the group of subordinates does not perceive that the manager genuinely desires a serious group decision-making effort, it will tend to arrive at conclusions that reflect what it thinks the manager wants rather than what the group actually wants and believes is feasible.

7. *The manager permits the group to make decisions within prescribed limits*—Here the manager becomes an equal member of a problem-solving group. The entire group identifies and assesses the problem, develops possible solutions, and chooses an alternative to be implemented. Everyone within the group understands that the group's decision will be implemented.

MANAGEMENT AND THE INTERNET

K•B Uses Internet to Provide Information for Making Decisions

The Tannenbaum and Schmidt Leadership Continuum emphasizes involving subordinates in various levels of decision making. The successful application of this continuum is contingent upon an organization's providing to both managers and subordinates the information necessary to make sound decisions. As an organization, K•B Toy Stores, a toy retailer based in Pittsfield, Massachusetts, has devised a system to provide such information to decision makers.

K•B Toy Stores recently launched a wide-ranging corporate intranet that is already credited with bolstering the potential of employees to make more informed business decisions. The intranet was conceptualized about two years ago when the toy retailer planned to implement an information delivery system based on Lotus Notes and Lotus Domino. As planned, the primary strengths of the intranet were its ability to convert information into databases and its accessibility. Per this plan, K•B's intranet now can be accessed and used by employees via the Internet using any browser anywhere in the world.

An example of decisions being made at K•B involves temporary stores. Although K•B Toys operates 975 permanent stores nationwide, the company commonly experiments, as do other retailers, with opening temporary locations. Theoretically, selling merchandise beyond the existing store's four walls and in vacant mall space or free-standing units is a natural way to boost revenue during key shopping seasons like Christmas.

This temporary store concept, called K•B Express, entered the market in 1996 with an ambitious 200 sites in upscale malls, strip centers, and street sides. One year later, K•B Toys stuck with the best and dropped the rest, opening half as many stores during a recent holiday season, proving that less may be more. Undoubtedly, many people throughout the company are involved in deciding what stores to open and close. The company's new Internet-based information system enables people throughout the country to be viable and valuable participants in making such decisions.

K•B recently had record-breaking company sales. Chairman and CEO Michael Glazer attributed the company's record performance to delivering a blended merchandise program of popular name toys, value-oriented closeout goods, and a selection of margin-enhancing exclusives. Establishing and using the new Internet-based information system that enabled employees to make or participate in making more informed decisions undoubtedly also contributed to this success.

DETERMINING HOW TO MAKE DECISIONS AS A LEADER The true value of the model developed by Tannenbaum and Schmidt lies in its use in making practical and desirable decisions. According to these authors, the three primary factors, or forces, that influence a manager's determination of which leadership behavior to use in making decisions are as follows:

1. *Forces in the Manager*—Managers should be aware of four forces within themselves that influence their determination of how to make decisions as a leader. The first force is the manager's values, such as the relative importance to the manager of organizational efficiency, personal growth, the growth of subordinates, and company profits. For example, a manager who values subordinate growth highly will probably want to give group members the valuable experience of making a decision, even though he or she could make the decision much more quickly and efficiently alone.

   The second influencing force is level of confidence in subordinates. In general, the more confidence a manager has in his or her subordinates, the more likely it is that the manager's decision-making style will be democratic, or subordinate-centered. The reverse is also true: The less confidence a manager has in subordinates, the more likely it is that the manager's decision-making style will be autocratic, or boss-centered.

   The third influencing force within the manager is personal leadership strengths. Some managers are more effective in issuing orders than in leading group discussions, and vice versa. Managers must be able to recognize their own leadership strengths and capitalize on them.

   The fourth influencing force within the manager is tolerance for ambiguity. The move from a boss-centered style to a subordinate-centered style means some loss of certainty about how problems should be solved. A manager who is disturbed by this loss of certainty will find it extremely difficult to be successful as a subordinate-centered leader.

BACK TO THE CASE

The situational approach to leadership affords more insights on how William Johnson can help Heinz achieve success than does the trait approach. The situational approach would suggest that successful leadership for Johnson is determined by the appropriateness of a combination of three factors: (1) William Johnson as a leader, (2) Heinz's employees as followers, and (3) the situation(s) within the company that Johnson faces. Each of these factors plays a significant role in determining whether or not Johnson is successful as a leader.

One of the most important activities that a manager like Johnson performs as a leader is making decisions. He can make decisions in any number of ways, ranging from authoritarian to democratic. For example, Johnson could make the decision to sell Weight Watchers, an extensive line of low-fat, weight-control products owned by Heinz. The Weight Watchers line includes products like frozen chicken dinners and low-fat ice cream. On the other hand, Johnson could generally define the type of food lines he sees in the future of Heinz, discuss the situation with appropriate Heinz personnel, and allow personnel to come up with and implement its own conclusions about which food lines to keep and which to sell. Of course, Johnson could also be less extreme in his decision making, in that his leadership behavior could fall in the middle of the continuum. For example, he could suggest to appropriate Heinz personnel the type of company Heinz is to be, ask them to develop ideas for the type of food lines needed, and then make the decision on the basis of his own ideas and those of the staff.

2. *Forces in Subordinates.* A manager also should be aware of forces within subordinates that influence the manager's determination of how to make decisions as a leader.[11] To lead successfully, the manager needs to keep in mind that subordinates are both somewhat different and somewhat alike and that any cookbook approach to leading all subordinates is therefore impossible. Generally speaking, however, managers can increase their leadership success by allowing subordinates more freedom in making decisions when:

- ► The subordinates have a relatively high need for independence (People differ greatly in the amount of direction they desire)
- ► They have a readiness to assume responsibility for decision making (Some see additional responsibility as a tribute to their ability; others see it as someone above them "passing the buck")
- ► They have a relatively high tolerance for ambiguity (Some employees prefer to be given clear-cut directives; others crave a greater degree of freedom)
- ► They are interested in the problem and believe it is important to solve it
- ► They understand and identify with the organization's goals
- ► They have the necessary knowledge and experience to deal with the problem
- ► They have learned to expect to share in decision making (People who have come to expect strong leadership and then are suddenly told to participate more fully in decision making are often upset by this new experience. Conversely, people who have enjoyed a considerable amount of freedom usually resent the boss who assumes full decision-making powers)

If subordinates do not have these characteristics, the manager should probably assume a more autocratic, or boss-centered, approach to making decisions.

3. *Forces in the Situation*—The last group of forces that influence a manager's determination of how to make decisions as a leader are forces in the leadership situation. The first such situational force is the type of organization in which the leader works. Organizational factors like the size of working groups and their geographical distribution are especially important influences on leadership style. Extremely large work groups or wide geographic separations of work groups, for example, could make a subordinate-centered leadership style impractical.

The second situational force is the effectiveness of a group. To gauge this force, managers should evaluate such issues as the experience of group members in working together and the degree of confidence they have in their ability to solve problems as a group. As a general rule, managers should assign decision-making responsibilities only to effective work groups.

The third situational force is the problem to be solved. Before deciding to act as a subordinate-centered leader, a manager should be sure that the group has the expertise necessary to make a decision about the problem in question. If it does not, the manager should move toward more boss-centered leadership.

Joyce Roberts and Vic Williams operate Architectural Support Services Inc., an Atlanta-based firm that offers computer-aided design services to architects and engineers. Their decision-making style is based on the realization that employee contributions can have greater impact at smaller companies than at larger ones. Thus they have continued to delegate real authority to their young employees— mostly recent graduates who train each other and form their own work teams.

The fourth situational force is the time available to make a decision. As a general guideline, the less time available, the more impractical it is to assign decision making to a group because a group typically takes more time than an individual to reach a decision.

As the situational approach to leadership implies, managers will be successful decision makers only if the method they use to make decisions appropriately reflects the leader, the followers, and the situation.

DETERMINING HOW TO MAKE DECISIONS AS A LEADER: AN UPDATE

Tannenbaum and Schmidt's 1957 article on leadership decision making was so widely accepted that the two authors were invited by the *Harvard Business Review* to update their original work in the 1970s.[12] In this update, they warned that in modern organizations the relationship among forces within the manager, subordinates, and situation had become more complex and more interrelated since the 1950s and that this obviously made it harder for managers to determine how to lead.

The update also pointed out that new organizational environments had to be considered in determining how to lead. For example, such factors as affirmative action and pollution control—which hardly figured in the decision making of managers in the 1950s—have become significant influences on the decision making of leaders since the 1970s.

THE VROOM-YETTON-JAGO MODEL Another major decision-focused theory of leadership that has gained widespread attention was first developed in 1973 and refined and expanded in 1988.[13] This theory, which we will call the **Vroom-Yetton-Jago (VYJ) Model of leadership** after its three major contributors, focuses on how much participation to allow subordinates in the decision-making process. The VYJ Model is built on two important premises:

1. Organizational decisions should be of high quality (should have a beneficial impact on performance)
2. Subordinates should accept and be committed to organizational decisions that are made

Decision Styles   The VYJ Model suggests that there are five different decision styles or ways that leaders can make decisions. These styles range from autocratic (the leader makes the decision) to consultative (the leader makes the decision after interacting with the followers) to group-focused (the manager meets with the group, and the group makes the decision). All five decision styles within the VYJ Model are described in Figure 15.3.

The **Vroom-Yetton-Jago (VYJ) Model of leadership** is a modern view of leadership that suggests that successful leadership requires determining through a decision tree what style of leadership will produce decisions that are beneficial to the organization and accepted and committed to by subordinates.

FIGURE 15.3   The five decision styles available to a leader according to the Vroom-Yetton-Jago Model

DECISION STYLE	DEFINITION
AI	Manager makes the decision alone.
AII	Manager asks for information from subordinates but makes the decision alone. Subordinates may or may not be informed about what the situation is.
CI	Manager shares the situation with individual subordinates and asks for information and evaluation. Subordinates do not meet as a group, and the manager alone makes the decision.
CII	Manager and subordinates meet as a group to discuss the situation, but the manager makes the decision.
GII	Manager and subordinates meet as a group to discuss the situation, and the group makes the decision.

A = autocratic; C = consultative; G = group

Using the Model The VYJ Model, presented in Figure 15.4, is a method for determining when a leader should use which decision style. As you can see, the model is a type of decision tree. To determine which decision style to use in a particular situation, the leader starts at the left of the decision tree by stating the organizational problem being addressed. Then the leader asks a series of questions about the problem as determined by the structure of the decision tree until he or she arrives at a decision style appropriate for the situation at the far right side of the model.

Consider, for example, the very bottom path of the decision tree. After stating an organizational problem, the leader determines that a decision related to that problem has a low quality requirement, that it is important that subordinates be committed to the decision, and it is very uncertain whether a decision made solely by the leader will be committed to by subordinates. In this situation, the model suggests that the leader use the GII decision—that is, the leader should meet with the group to discuss the situation, and then allow the group to make the decision.

FIGURE 15.4 ► **The Vroom-Yetton-Jago Model**

QR	Quality Requirement:	*How important is the technical quality of this decision?*
CR	Commitment Requirement:	*How important is subordinate commitment to the decision?*
LI	Leader's Information:	*Do you have sufficient information to make a high-quality decision?*
ST	Problem Structure:	*Is the problem well-structured?*
CP	Commitment Probability:	*If you were to make the decision by yourself, is it reasonably certain that your subordinate(s) would be committed to the decision?*
GC	Goal Congruence:	*Do subordinates share the organizational goals to be attained in solving this problem?*
CO	Subordinate Conflict:	*Is conflict among subordinates over preferred solution likely?*
SI	Subordinate Information:	*Do subordinates have sufficient information to make a high-quality decision?*

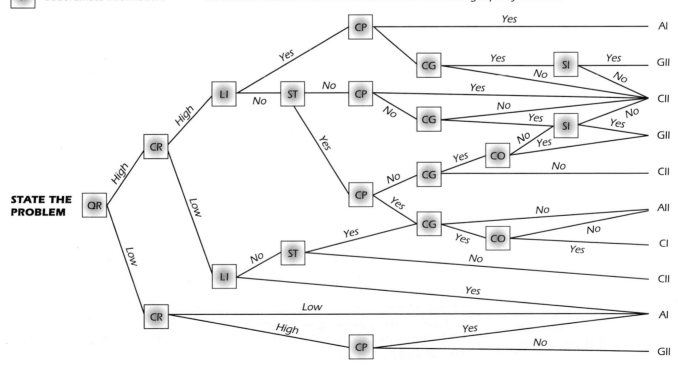

The VYJ Model seems promising. Research on an earlier version of this model has yielded some evidence that managerial decisions consistent with the model are more successful than are managerial decisions inconsistent with the model.[14] The model is rather complex, however, and therefore difficult for practicing managers to apply.

BACK TO THE CASE

Based on the previous information, in trying to decide exactly how to make his Heinz decisions as a leader, William Johnson should consider forces in himself as manager, forces in his Heinz subordinates, and forces in the specific organizational situation he faces. Forces within William Johnson include his own ideas about how to lead and his level of confidence in the Heinz employees that he is leading. If Johnson believes he is more knowledgeable about achieving *victory*, for example, than his staff is, he will be likely to make boss-centered decisions about what steps to take to create *victory* at Heinz. Forces within his subordinates such as the need for independence, the readiness to assume responsibility, and the knowledge of and interest in the issues to be decided, also affect Johnson's decisions as a leader. If his staff is relatively independent and responsible and its members feel strongly about what *victory* means and how it should be achieved, then Johnson should be inclined to allow his employees more freedom in deciding how to achieve that *victory*.

Forces within the company include the number of people making decisions and the problem to be solved. For example, if Johnson's staff is small, he will be more likely to use a democratic decision-making style, allowing his employees to become involved in such decisions as how to best achieve *victory*. He will also be likely to use a subordinate-centered leadership style if his staff is knowledgeable about what makes a company like Heinz victorious. The VYJ Model suggests that William Johnson should try to make decisions in such a fashion that the quality of decisions is enhanced and followers are committed to the decisions. Johnson can try to ensure that such decisions are made by matching his decision style (autocratic, consultative, or group) to the particular situation he faces.

►LEADERSHIP BEHAVIORS

The failure to identify predictive leadership traits led researchers in this area to turn to other variables to explain leadership success. Rather than looking at traits leaders should possess, the behavioral approach looked at what good leaders do. Are they concerned with getting a task done, for instance, or do they concentrate on keeping their followers happy and maintaining high morale?

Two major studies series were conducted to identify leadership behavior, one by the Bureau of Business Research at Ohio State University (referred to as the OSU studies), and another by the University of Michigan (referred to as the Michigan studies).

THE OSU STUDIES The OSU studies concluded that leaders exhibit two main types of behavior:

Structure behavior is leadership activity that (1) delineates the relationship between the leader and the leader's followers or (2) establishes well-defined procedures that the followers should adhere to in performing their jobs.

Consideration behavior is leadership behavior that reflects friendship, mutual trust, respect, and warmth in the relationship between leader and followers.

► **Structure behavior** is any leadership activity that delineates the relationship between the leader and the leader's followers or establishes well-defined procedures that followers should adhere to in performing their jobs. Overall, structure behavior limits the self-guidance of followers in the performance of their tasks, but while it can be relatively firm, it is never rude or malicious.

Structure behavior can be useful to leaders as a means of minimizing follower activity that does not significantly contribute to organizational goal attainment. Leaders must be careful, however, not to go overboard and discourage follower activity that *will* contribute to organizational goal attainment.

► **Consideration behavior** is leadership behavior that reflects friendship, mutual trust, respect, and warmth in the relationship between leader and followers. This type of behavior generally aims to develop and maintain a good human relationship between the leader and the followers.

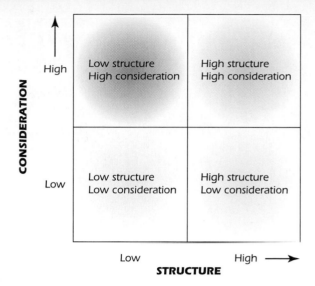

Leadership Style The OSU studies resulted in a model that depicts four fundamental leadership styles. A **leadership style** is the behavior a leader exhibits while guiding organizational members in appropriate directions. Each of the four leadership styles depicted in Figure 15.5 is a different combination of structure behavior and consideration behavior. For example, the high structure/low consideration leadership style emphasizes structure behavior and de-emphasizes consideration behavior.

The OSU studies made a significant contribution to our understanding of leadership, and the central ideas generated by these studies still serve as the basis for modern leadership thought and research.[15]

THE MICHIGAN STUDIES Around the same time the OSU leadership studies were being carried out, researchers at the University of Michigan, led by Rensis Likert, were also conducting a series of historically significant leadership studies.[16] After analyzing information based on interviews with both leaders and followers (managers and subordinates), the Michigan studies pinpointed two basic types of leader behavior: job-centered behavior and employee-centered behavior.

Job-Centered Behavior **Job-centered behavior** is leader behavior that focuses primarily on the work a subordinate is doing. The job-centered leader is very interested in the job the subordinate is doing and in how well the subordinate is performing at that job.

Employee-Centered Behavior **Employee-centered behavior** is leader behavior that focuses primarily on subordinates as people. The employee-centered leader is very attentive to the personal needs of subordinates and is interested in building cooperative work teams that are satisfying to subordinates and advantageous for the organization.

The results of the OSU studies and the Michigan studies are very similar. Both research efforts indicated two primary dimensions of leader behavior: a work dimension (structure behavior/job-centered behavior) and a people dimension (consideration behavior/employee-centered behavior). The following section focuses on determining which of these two primary dimensions of leader behavior is more advisable for a manager to adopt.

EFFECTIVENESS OF VARIOUS LEADERSHIP STYLES An early investigation of high school superintendents concluded that desirable leadership behavior is associated with high leader emphasis on both structure and consideration and that undesirable leadership

Leadership style is the behavioral pattern a leader establishes while guiding organization members in appropriate directions.

Job-centered behavior is leader behavior that focuses primarily on the work a subordinate is doing.

Employee-centered behavior is leader behavior that focuses primarily on subordinates as people.

Can a leader survive in high-risk circumstances when the environment is totally unfamiliar? Shelby Coffey, a former newspaper editor who has never worked in television, but was recently hired by ABC, home of such hits as the Rosie O'Donnell show, is about to find out. (Rosie's guest is Madonna.)

behavior is associated with low leader emphasis on both dimensions. Similarly, the managerial grid described in chapter 13 implies that the most effective leadership style is characterized by high consideration and high structure. Results of a more recent study indicate that high consideration is always preferred by subordinates.[17]

Comparing Styles   One should be cautious, however, about concluding that any single leadership style is more effective than any other. Leadership situations are so varied that pronouncing one leadership style as the most effective is an oversimplification. In fact, a successful leadership style for managers in one situation may prove ineffective in another situation. Recognizing the need to link leadership styles to appropriate situations, A. K. Korman notes in a classic article that a worthwhile contribution to leadership literature would be a rationale for systematically linking appropriate styles with various situations so as to ensure effective leadership.[18] The life cycle theory of leadership, which is covered in the next section, provides such a rationale.

The life cycle theory of leadership is a leadership concept that hypothesizes that leadership styles should reflect primarily the maturity level of the followers.

THE HERSEY-BLANCHARD LIFE CYCLE THEORY OF LEADERSHIP   The **life cycle theory of leadership** is a rationale for linking leadership styles with various situations so as to ensure effective leadership. This theory posits essentially the same two types of leadership behavior as the OSU leadership studies, but it calls them "task" and "relationships" rather than "structure" and "consideration."

Maturity   The life cycle theory is based on the relationship among follower maturity, leader task behavior, and leader relationship behavior. In general terms, according to this theory, leadership style should reflect the maturity level of the followers. Maturity is defined as the ability of followers to perform their job independently, to assume additional responsibility, and to desire to achieve success. The more of each of these characteristics that followers possess, the more mature they are said to be. (Maturity here is not necessarily linked to chronological age.)

The Life Cycle Model   Figure 15.6 illustrates the life cycle theory of leadership model. The curved line indicates the maturity level of the followers: Maturity level increases as the maturity curve runs from right to left. In more specific terms, the theory indicates that effective leadership behavior should shift as follows:[19] (1) high-task/low-relationships behavior to (2) high-task/high-relationships behavior to (3) high-relationships/low-task behavior to (4) low-task/low-relationships behavior, as one's followers progress from immaturity to maturity. In sum, a manager's leadership style will be effective only if it is appropriate for the maturity level of the followers.

FIGURE 15.6 ▶ The life cycle theory of leadership model

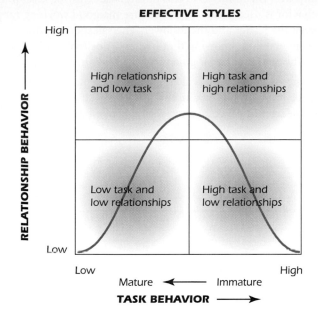

EFFECTIVE STYLES

Exceptions to the Model   There are some exceptions to the general philosophy of the life cycle theory. For example, if there is a short-term deadline to meet, a leader may find it necessary to accelerate production through a high-task/low-relationships style rather than use a low-task/low-relationships style, even if the followers are mature. A high-task/low-relationships leadership style carried out over the long term with such followers, though, would typically result in a poor working relationship between leader and subordinates.

Applying Life Cycle Theory   Following is an example of how the life cycle theory applies to a leadership situation:

▶ A man has just been hired as a salesperson in a men's clothing store. At first, this individual is extremely immature—that is, unable to solve task-related problems independently. According to the life cycle theory, the appropriate style for leading this salesperson at his level of maturity is high-task/low-relationships—that is, the leader should tell the salesperson exactly what should be done and how to do it. The salesperson should be shown how to make cash and charge sales and how to handle merchandise returns. The leader should also begin laying the groundwork for developing a personal relationship with the salesperson. Too much relationship behavior at this point, however, should be avoided, since it can easily be misinterpreted as permissiveness.

▶ As time passes and the salesperson gains somewhat in job-related maturity, the appropriate style for leading him would be high task/high relationships. Although the salesperson's maturity has increased somewhat, the leader still needs to watch him closely because he requires guidance and direction at times. The main difference between this leadership style and the first one is the amount of relationship behavior displayed by the leader. Building on the groundwork laid during the period of the first leadership style, the leader can now start to encourage an atmosphere of mutual trust, respect, and friendliness between herself and the salesperson.

▶ As more time passes and the salesperson's maturity level increases still further, the appropriate style for leading this individual will become high relationships/low task. The leader can now de-emphasize task behavior because the salesperson is of above-average maturity in his job and is capable of solving most job-related problems independently. The leader would continue to develop a human relationship with her follower.

▶ Once the salesperson's maturity level reaches its maximum, the appropriate style for leading him is low task/low relationships. Again, the leader deemphasizes task behavior because the follower is thoroughly familiar with the job. Now, however, the leader can also deemphasize relationship behavior because she has fully established a good working relationship with the follower. At this point, task behavior is seldom needed, and relationship behavior is used primarily to nurture the good working rapport that has developed between the leader and the follower. The salesperson, then, is left to do his job without close supervision, knowing that he has a positive working relationship with a leader who can be approached for guidance whenever necessary.

The life cycle approach more than likely owes its acceptance to its intuitive appeal. Although at first glance it appears to be a useful leadership concept, managers should bear in mind that there is little scientific investigation verifying its worth and therefore it should be applied very carefully.[20]

DAN CAULFIELD CHANGES HIS "HIGH TASK" LEADERSHIP STYLE

Modern leadership theory suggests that for leaders to be successful, their styles must suit particular situations. Supporting this theory, Dan Caulfield, a successful entrepreneur, recently discovered that he needed to change his leadership style to suit a situation that he faced.

Before starting Hire Quality, a $1.5 million recruitment firm for honorably discharged military personnel, Dan Caulfield was a supervisor of total quality control for a $1 billion Department of Defense test of the Javelin missile, a handheld antitank weapon. He led a staff of 24 controllers. Their job was to monitor military units that were testing the proposed new weapon in a war game. Before each war game exercise, he would carefully explain to the controllers what information to track. Caulfield actually told everyone what information to get and how to get it, and even told the data entry people how to key it in. This leadership style worked very well.

As most people would, Caulfield began leading at Hire Quality by using his previously successful high task style. He ran the company exactly as he had run the weapons test. He spent weeks training new staffers, telling them exactly what to do and how to do it. He drew up detailed instructions on everything from the steps to take to enlist job banks to the questions to ask job candidates. He held full staff meetings everyday at 8 AM and then again at 5 PM to find out exactly what was happening. He was making all the decisions. Overall, Caulfield's leadership style at Hire Quality was a disaster. Company performance plummeted and trusted employees resigned.

Fortunately, Caulfield quickly deduced that his leadership style was a detriment to the company. He decided to impose less structure on employees. He decided to give his talented and capable employees more independence to solve company problems. He began describing company objectives and allowing employees to decide how to proceed. As a result, employees began reacting more positively and company performance began to improve.

In essence, Caulfield's new leadership style turned his company toward success. Continuing to be a flexible leader should ensure that his success will continue.

BACK TO THE CASE

The OSU leadership studies should furnish a manager like William Johnson with insights on leadership behavior in general situations. According to these studies, Johnson can exhibit two general types of leadership behavior: structure and consideration. He will be using structure behavior if he tells Heinz's personnel what to do—for example, exactly how to design new, plastic containers for 9-Lives Cat Food. He will be using consideration behavior if he attempts to develop a more human rapport with his employees by discussing their concerns and developing friendships with them.

Of course, depending on how Johnson emphasizes these two behaviors, his leadership style can reflect a combination of structure and consideration ranging from high structure/low consideration to low structure/high consideration. For example, if Johnson stresses giving orders to employees and de-emphasizes developing relationships, he will be exhibiting high structure/low consideration. If he emphasizes a good rapport with his staff and allows its members to function mostly independently of him, his leadership style will be termed low structure/high consideration.

Although no single leadership style is more effective than any other in all situations, the life cycle theory of leadership furnishes William Johnson with a strategy for using various styles in various situations. According to this theory, Johnson should make his style consistent primarily with the maturity level of the Heinz organization members that he is leading. As Johnson's followers progress from immaturity to maturity, his leadership style should shift systematically from (1) high task/low relationships behavior to (2) high task/high relationships behavior to (3) high relationships/low task behavior to (4) low task/low relationships behavior.

FIEDLER'S CONTINGENCY THEORY Situational theories of leadership like the life cycle theory are based on the concept of **leader flexibility**—the idea that successful leaders must change their leadership styles as they encounter different situations. Can any leader be so flexible as to span all major leadership styles? The answer to this question is that some leaders can be that flexible, and some cannot. Unfortunately, there are numerous obstacles to leader flexibility. One is that a leadership style is sometimes so ingrained in a leader that it takes years to even approach flexibility. Another is that some leaders have experienced such success in a basically static situation that they believe developing a flexible style is unnecessary.

Leader flexibility is the ability to change leadership style.

Changing the Organization to Fit the Leader One strategy, proposed by Fred Fiedler, for overcoming these obstacles is changing the organizational situation to fit the leader's style, rather than changing the leader's style to fit the organizational situation.[21] Applying this idea to the life cycle theory of leadership, an organization may find it easier to shift leaders to situations appropriate for their leadership styles than to expect those leaders to change styles as situations change. After all, it would probably take three to five years to train a manager to use a concept like life cycle theory effectively, while changing the situation that leader faces can be done very quickly simply by exercising organizational authority.

According to Fiedler's **contingency theory of leadership**, leader-member relations, task structure, and the position power of the leader are the three primary factors that should be considered when moving leaders into situations appropriate for their leadership styles:

The **contingency theory of leadership** is a leadership concept that hypothesizes that, in any given leadership situation, success is determined primarily by (1) the degree to which the task being performed by the followers is structured, (2) the degree of position power possessed by the leader, and (3) the type of relationship that exists between the leader and the followers.

- ► *Leader-member relations* is the degree to which the leader feels accepted by the followers
- ► *Task structure* is the degree to which the goals—the work to be done—and other situational factors are outlined clearly
- ► *Position power* is determined by the extent to which the leader has control over the rewards and punishments followers receive

How these three factors can be arranged in eight different combinations, called *octants*, is presented in Table 15.1.

Figure 15.7 shows how effective leadership varies among the eight octants. From an organizational viewpoint, this figure implies that management should attempt to match permissive, passive, and considerate leaders with situations reflecting the middle of the continuum containing the octants. It also implies that management should try to match controlling, active, and structuring leaders with the extremes of this continuum.

Fiedler suggests some actions that can be taken to modify the leadership situation. They are as follows:[22]

1. In some organizations, we can change the individual's task assignment. We may assign to one leader very structured tasks which have implicit or explicit instructions telling him what to do and how to do it, and we may assign to another the tasks that are nebulous and vague. The former are the typical production tasks; the latter are exemplified by committee work, by the development of policy, and by tasks which require creativity.
2. We can change the leader's position power. We not only can give him a higher rank and corresponding recognition, we also can modify his position power by giving him subordinates

	Eight Combinations, or Octants, of Three Factors:
TABLE 15.1	**Leader-Member Relations, Task Structure, and Leader Position Power**

Octant	Leader-Member Relations	Task Structure	Leader Position Power
I	Good	High	Strong
II	Good	High	Weak
III	Good	Weak	Strong
IV	Good	Weak	Weak
V	Moderately poor	High	Strong
VI	Moderately poor	High	Weak
VII	Moderately poor	Weak	Strong
VIII	Moderately poor	Weak	Weak

who are equal to him in rank and prestige or subordinates who are two or three below him. We can give him subordinates who are experts in their specialties or subordinates who depend upon the leader for guidance and instruction. We can give the leader the final say in all decisions affecting his group, or we can require that he make decisions in consultation with his subordinates, or even that he obtain their concurrence. We can channel all directives, communications, and information about organizational plans through the leader alone, giving him expert power, or we can provide these communications concurrently to all his subordinates.

3. We can change the leader-member relations in this group. We can have the leader work with groups whose members are very similar to him in attitude, opinion, technical background, race, and cultural background. Or we can assign him subordinates with whom he differs in any one or several of these important aspects. Finally, we can assign the leader to a group in which the members have a tradition of getting along well with their supervisors or to a group that has a history and tradition of conflict.

FIGURE 15.7	**How effective leadership style varies with Fiedler's eight octants**

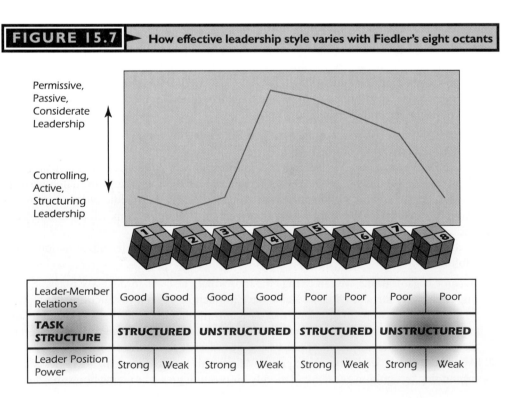

Fiedler's work certainly helps destroy the myths that there is one best leadership style and that leaders are born, not made. Further, his work supports the theory that almost every manager in an organization can be a successful leader if placed in a situation appropriate to that person's leadership style. This, of course, assumes that someone in the organization has the ability to assess the characteristics of the organization's leaders and of other important organizational variables and then to match the two accordingly.

Fiedler's model, like all theoretical models, has its limitations. But although it may not provide concrete answers, it does emphasize the importance of situational variables in determining leadership effectiveness. As said earlier, it may actually be easier to change the leadership situation or move the leader to a more favorable situation than to try to change a leader's style.[23]

THE PATH-GOAL THEORY OF LEADERSHIP The **path-goal theory of leadership** suggests that the primary activities of a leader are to make desirable and achievable rewards available to organization members who attain organizational goals and to clarify the kinds of behavior that must be performed to earn those rewards.[24] In essence, the leader outlines the goals that followers should aim for and clarifies the path that followers should take to achieve those goals and earn the rewards contingent on doing so. Overall, the path-goal theory maintains that managers can facilitate job performance by showing employees how their performance directly affects their reception of desired rewards.

Path-goal theory of leadership is a theory of leadership that suggests that the primary activities of a leader are to make desirable and achievable rewards available to organization members who attain organizational goals and to clarify the kinds of behavior that must be performed to earn those rewards.

Leadership Behavior According to the path-goal theory of leadership, leaders exhibit four primary types of behavior:

1. *Directive behavior*—Directive behavior is aimed at telling followers what to do and how to do it. The leader indicates what performance goals exist and precisely what must be done to achieve them.
2. *Supportive behavior*—Supportive behavior is aimed at being friendly with followers and showing interest in them as human beings. Through supportive behavior, the leader demonstrates sensitivity to the personal needs of followers.
3. *Participative behavior*—Participative behavior is aimed at seeking suggestions from followers regarding business operations to the extent that followers are involved in making important organizational decisions. Followers often help to determine the rewards that will be available to them in organizations and what they must do to earn those rewards.
4. *Achievement behavior*—Achievement behavior is aimed at setting challenging goals for followers to reach and expressing and demonstrating confidence that they will measure up to the challenge. This leader behavior focuses on making goals difficult enough that employees will find achieving them challenging, but not so difficult that they will view them as impossible and give up trying to achieve them.

Adapting Behavior to Situations As with other situational theories of leadership, the path-goal theory proposes that leaders will be successful if they appropriately match these four types of behavior to situations that they face. For example, if inexperienced followers do not have a thorough understanding of a job, a manager may appropriately use more directive behavior to develop this understanding and to ensure that serious job-related problems are avoided. For more experienced followers, who have a more complete understanding of a job, directive behavior would probably be inappropriate and might create interpersonal problems between leader and followers.

If jobs are very structured, with little room for employee interpretation of how the work should be done, directive behavior is less appropriate than if there is much room for employees to determine how the work gets done. When followers are deriving much personal satisfaction and encouragement from work and enjoy the support of other members of their work group, supportive behavior by the leader is not as important as when followers are gaining little or no satisfaction from their work or from personal relationships in the work group.

The primary focus of the path-goal theory of leadership is on how leaders can increase employee effort and productivity by clarifying performance goals and the path to be taken to achieve those goals. This theory of leadership has gained increasing acceptance in recent years.

In fact, research suggests that the path-goal theory is highly promising for enhancing employee commitment to achieving organizational goals and thereby increasing the probability that organizations will be successful. It should be pointed out, however, that the research done on this model has been conducted mostly on its parts rather than on the complete model.[25]

Back to the Case

The life cycle theory suggests that William Johnson should be flexible enough to behave as required by situations at Heinz. If Johnson finds it extremely difficult to be flexible, however, he should attempt to structure his situation so as to make it appropriate for his style. As suggested by Fiedler, if Johnson's leadership style is high task in nature, he generally will be a more successful leader in situations best described by octants 1, 2, 3, and 8 in Table 15.1 and Figure 15.7. If, however, Johnson's leadership style is more relationship oriented, he will probably be a more successful leader in situations representative of octants 4, 5, 6, and 7. Over all, Fiedler's work provides Johnson with insights on how to engineer situations at Heinz so they will be appropriate for his leadership style.

The path-goal theory of leadership suggests that in leading Heinz, Johnson should emphasize clarifying what rewards are available to followers in the organization, how those rewards can be earned, and eliminating barriers that could prohibit followers from earning the rewards. Johnson can use directive behavior, supportive behavior, participative behavior, and achievement behavior in implementing the path-goal theory.

LEADERSHIP TODAY

Leaders in modern organizations have been confronting many situations rarely encountered by organizational leaders of the past.[26] Today's leaders are often called upon to make massive personnel cuts in order to eliminate unnecessary levels of organizations and thereby lower labor expenses, to introduce work teams in order to enhance organizational decision making and work flow, to reengineer work so that organization members will be more efficient and effective, and to initiate programs designed to improve the overall quality of organizational functioning.

In reaction to these new situations, organizations are emphasizing leadership styles that concentrate on getting employees involved in the organization and giving them the freedom to use their abilities as they think best. This is a dramatically different type of leadership from that known in organizations of the past, which largely concentrated on controlling people and work processes. Figure 15.8 contrasts the "soul" of the new leader with the "mind" of the manager.

FIGURE 15.8 Characteristics of the emerging leader versus characteristics of the manager

LEADER	MANAGER
SOUL	**MIND**
Visionary	Rational
Passionate	Consulting
Creative	Persistent
Flexible	Problem-solving
Inspiring	Tough-minded
Innovative	Analytical
Courageous	Structured
Imaginative	Deliberate
Experimental	Authoritative
Independent	Stabilizing

The information in this section of the text points up the trend among today's leaders to get employees involved in their organizations and to give them the freedom to make and carry out decisions. The following People Spotlight feature describes how the CEO of Chrysler Corporation involves employees in the organization.

► PEOPLE SPOTLIGHT ◄ Robert Eaton Gets People Involved at DaimlerChrysler

The Chrysler division of DaimlerChrysler, a worldwide manufacturer of automobiles, trucks, and sport vehicles, experienced earnings of $3.7 billion—up 246 percent—and sales of $52.2 billion—up 20 percent. Both of these figures far surpassed the company's previous records. On the strength of this extraordinary performance, Chrysler paid 91,550 of its 125,825 employees a profit-sharing bonus averaging $8,000, also an all-time high.

DaimlerChrysler's chairman Robert Eaton attributes the company's recent success to its program of getting employees more seriously involved in company operations. For example, when Chrysler begins to create a new vehicle model or to revamp an old one, a team of about 700 people, comprising employees from engineering, design, manufacturing, marketing, and finance, is formed. A company vice president acts as "godfather" to the group, but all of the actual work is directed by team leaders below that rank, and the team organizes itself as it sees fit.

One of the most significant advantages of this method of operation is that it has greatly reduced the time it takes for Chrysler to get a new product to the marketplace. Once it took the company five years to develop a vehicle concept and to actually begin producing the vehicle. Now, using this new work process that focuses on people involvement, it takes Chrysler only two and a half to three years to begin producing a new vehicle. Moreover, the division projects that its concept-to-market time will shrink further in the future.

Four leadership styles have emerged in recent years to suit these new situations: transformational leadership, coaching, "superleadership," and entrepreneurial leadership.[27] Each of these new styles is discussed in the following sections.

► TRANSFORMATIONAL LEADERSHIP

Transformational leadership is leadership that inspires organizational success by profoundly affecting followers' beliefs in what an organization should be, as well as their values, such as justice and integrity.[28] This style of leadership creates a sense of duty within an organization, encourages new ways of handling problems, and promotes learning for all organization members. Transformational leadership is closely related to concepts like charismatic leadership and inspirational leadership.

Perhaps transformational leadership is receiving more attention nowadays because of the dramatic changes that many organizations are going through and the critical importance of transformational leadership in "transforming" or changing organizations successfully. Lee Iacocca is often cited as an exemplar of transformational leadership because of his success in transforming Chrysler Corporation from a company on the verge of going under into a successful company.[29]

THE TASKS OF TRANSFORMATIONAL LEADERS Transformational leaders perform several important tasks. First, they raise followers' awareness of organizational issues and their consequences. Organization members must understand an organization's high-priority issues and what will happen if these issues are not successfully resolved. Second, transformational leaders create a vision of what the organization should be, build commitment to that vision throughout the organization, and facilitate organizational changes that support the vision. In sum, transformational leadership is consistent with strategy developed through an organization's strategic management process.[30]

Managers of the future will continue to face the challenge of significantly changing their organizations, primarily because of the accelerating trend to position organizations to be more

> **Transformational leadership** is leadership that inspires organizational success by profoundly affecting followers' beliefs in what an organization should be, as well as their values, such as justice and integrity.

competitive in a global business environment. Therefore, transformational leadership will probably get increasing attention in the leadership literature. Although there is much practical appeal and interest in this style of leadership, more research is needed to develop insights about how managers can become successful transformational leaders.

►COACHING

Coaching is leadership that instructs followers on how to meet the special organizational challenges they face.

Coaching is leadership that instructs followers on how to meet the special organizational challenges they face. Operating like an athletic coach, the coaching leader identifies inappropriate behavior in followers and suggests how they might correct that behavior. The increasing use of teams has elevated the importance of coaching in today's organizations. Characteristics of an effective coach are presented in Table 15.2.

COACHING BEHAVIOR A successful coaching leader is characterized by many different kinds of behavior. Among these behaviors are the following:

► *Listens closely*—The coaching leader tries to gather both the facts in what is said and the feelings and emotions behind what is said. Such a leader is careful to really listen and not fall into the trap of immediately rebutting statements made by followers.

► *Gives emotional support*—The coaching leader gives followers personal encouragement.[31] Such encouragement should constantly be aimed at motivating them to do their best to meet the high demands of successful organizations.

TABLE 15.2 ► **Characteristics of an Effective Coach**	
Trait, Attitude, or Behavior	**Action Plan for Improvement**
1. Empathy (putting self in other person's shoes	*Sample:* Will listen and understand person's point of view. *Your own:*
2. Listening skill	*Sample:* Will concentrate extra-hard on listening. *Your own:*
3. Insight into people (ability to size them up)	*Sample:* Will jot down observations about people upon first meeting, then verify in the future. *Your own:*
4. Diplomacy and tact	*Sample:* Will study book of etiquette. *Your own:*
5. Patience toward people	*Sample:* Will practice staying calm when someone makes a mistake. *Your own:*
6. Concern for welfare of people	*Sample:* When interacting with another person, will ask myself, "How can this person's interests best be served?" *Your own:*
7. Minimum hostility toward people	*Sample:* Will often ask myself, "Why am I angry at this person?" *Your own:*
8. Self-confidence and emotional stability	*Sample:* Will attempt to have at least one personal success each week. *Your own:*
9. Noncompetitiveness with team members	*Sample:* Will keep reminding myself that all boats rise with the same tide. *Your own:*
10. Enthusiasm for people	*Sample:* Will search for the good in each person. *Your own:*

> *Shows by example what constitutes appropriate behavior*—The coaching leader shows followers, for instance, how to handle an employee problem or a production glitch. By demonstrating expertise, the coaching leader builds the trust and respect of followers.

►SUPERLEADERSHIP

Superleadership is leading by showing others how to lead themselves. If superleaders are successful, they develop followers who are productive, work independently, and need only minimal attention from the superleader.

In essence, superleaders teach followers how to think on their own and act constructively and independently.[32] They encourage people to eliminate negative thoughts and beliefs about the company and co-workers and to replace them with more positive and constructive beliefs. An important aspect of superleadership is building the self-confidence of followers by convincing them that they are competent, have a significant reservoir of potential, and are capable of meeting the difficult challenges of the work situation.

The objective of superleaders is to develop followers who require very little leadership. This is an important objective in the typical organization of today, whose structure is flatter than that of organizations of the past and which therefore has fewer leader-managers. Organizations cannot be successful in such a situation unless their members become proficient at leading themselves.

Superleadership is leadership that inspires organizational success by showing followers how to lead themselves.

►ENTREPRENEURIAL LEADERSHIP

Entrepreneurial leadership is leadership that is based on the attitude that the leader is self-employed. Leaders of this type act as if they are playing a critical role in the organization rather than a mostly unimportant one. In addition, they behave as if they are taking the risk of losing money, but will receive the profit if one is made. They approach each mistake as if it were a significant error rather than a smaller error that will be neutralized by the normal functioning of the organization.[33]

Each of these four contemporary leadership styles has received notable attention in recent management literature. Managers should realize that these four styles are not mutually exclusive; they can be combined in various ways to generate a unique style. For example, a leader can assume both a coaching and an entrepreneurial role. Figure 15.9 shows the various

Entrepreneurial leadership is leadership that is based on the attitude that the leader is self-employed.

| FIGURE 15.9 | Various combinations of transformational, coaching, superleader, and entrepreneurial leadership styles |

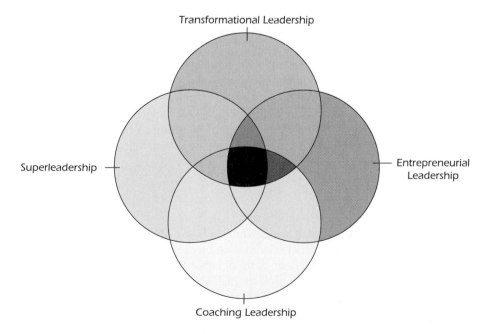

combinations of these four leadership styles that a leader can adopt. The shaded portion of the figure represents a leader whose style comprises all four.

Two currently popular leadership topics are leadership substitutes and women leaders. Both are discussed in the following sections under the heads "Substitutes for Leadership," "Women as Leaders," and "Ways Women Lead."

▶ SUBSTITUTES FOR LEADERSHIP

There are times when leaders do not have to lead or, for one reason or another, cannot lead. In these circumstances, situational substitutes can have as much influence on employees as any leader.

You have probably heard of or observed situations in which the nominal leader—for a number of reasons, including factors beyond the leader's control—had little or no impact on the outcome of a situation. Because so many factors can affect a situation, some people argue that leadership is really irrelevant to many organization outcomes. Under various conditions— for instance, strong subordinates, knowledge of the task, organizational constraints—subordinates may not need or even want leadership.

Substitute leadership theory attempts to identify those situations in which the input of leader behavior is partly or wholly canceled out by characteristics of the subordinate or the organization. Examples: A subordinate may have such high levels of ability, experience, education, and internal motivation that little or no leadership is required or desired; task characteristics may be so routine that the subordinate does not require much, if any, leadership; organizational characteristics such as group cohesion and a high degree of formalization may reduce the need for leadership. Recall, also, from our earlier discussion of life cycle theory the situation in which the leader delegates tasks to highly mature followers in a low-task/ low-relationship situation.[34]

Throughout this chapter, we have concentrated on a number of factors affecting leadership effectiveness. Much of this attention has centered on leadership characteristics, situations, and leader behavior. Substitute theory tends to downplay the importance of these dimensions. Why? Meindl and Ehrlich suggest one possible answer: Throughout history, human beings have had a tendency to romanticize leadership, treating it as more important than it actually is.[35] Substitute theory reminds us that—at least in some situations with some people in some organizations—things just seem to get done regardless of the quality of leadership.

▶ WOMEN AS LEADERS

One can read Stogdill's *Handbook of Leadership* (1974) and find barely any reference to women leaders, except as a subject deserving further research. This is probably because in 1970 only 15 percent of all managers were women. By 1989, this figure had risen to more than 40 percent. By 1995, women made up about 63 percent of the total workforce. Just how many women will become leaders in their companies or industries remains to be seen. Currently, only 3 of every 100 top jobs in the largest U.S. companies are held by women—about the same number as a decade ago. A Labor Department study of the early 1990s concluded that the so-called glass ceiling was keeping women from moving into leadership positions. The glass ceiling is the subtle barrier of negative attitudes and prejudices that prevents women from reaching seemingly attainable top-management positions.[36]

▶ WAYS WOMEN LEAD

Women who have broken through the glass ceiling have found that there is no one mold for effective leadership. In the past, women leaders modeled their leadership styles after successful male managers. Today's women managers, however, often describe their leadership styles as transformational—getting workers to transform or subordinate their individual self-interests into group consensus directed toward a broader goal. This leadership style attributes power to such personal characteristics as charisma, personal contacts, and interpersonal skills rather than to the organizational structure.

As CEO of clothing manufacturer Warnaco, Linda F. Wachner is the only woman currently heading a Fortune 500 industrial company. She practices a direct approach to both leadership and communication, often gathering marketing data by talking directly with salespeople in retail stores. "When people have a good leader who instills team spirit," she says, "... they live in an environment that demands excellence, energy, and keeping up of momentum...."

Men, on the other hand, are more likely to characterize their leadership as transactional. They see their jobs as involving a series of transactions between themselves and their subordinates. This leadership style involves exchanging rewards for services or dispensing punishment for inadequate performance.[37]

DIVERSITY SPOTLIGHT   For James G. Kaiser of Corning, Being Employee-Centered Includes a Focus on Diversity

James G. Kaiser is a senior vice president at Corning, Inc. Kaiser is responsible for keeping the Technical Products Division competitive in the global marketplace and for masterminding the strategic planning for his division's operations. In addition, he oversees research and development for new products and is responsible for seeking business partners with whom the company can pursue joint ventures. Lastly, Kaiser is in charge of a series of export and sales offices in several locations.

Kaiser considers himself to be a people-oriented leader. He is an African American manager who sees his race as an asset in managing people from different cultures because it gives him a broader perspective on the differences among various types of employees. He focuses formally on cultural diversity at Corning largely through the Executive Leadership Council, a group whose mission is to offer guidance and leadership to other up-and-coming African American executives. As president of Corning's Executive Leadership Council, Kaiser provides minority executives with a network and a discussion forum that help them to understand what the achievement of excellence means within and for the African American community and how they can personally excel.

Because Kaiser is an African American leader, it could be argued that he has special insights for advising and helping minority employees to be successful leaders. For their own long-run success, however, leaders like Kaiser must be careful not to become "specialists" who deal with only one culture, but rather "generalists" who develop the skills to successfully manage people from many different cultures.

BACK TO THE CASE

Based on the preceding information, during his tenure at Heinz, William Johnson could focus on being a transformational leader, a leader who inspires followers to seriously focus on achieving organizational objectives. As a transformational leader, he would strive to encourage new ideas, create a sense of duty, and encourage employees to learn and grow. As Heinz experiences more and more significant change, the importance of Johnson being a transformational leader increases.

Three other popular leadership styles also offer a manager like Johnson insights about how to lead at Heinz. As a coaching leader, Johnson can focus on instructing Heinz's followers to meet special challenges they face, such as expansion through global acquisition. In the role of a coaching leader, he would listen closely, give emotional support, and show by example what should be done. As a Superleader, Johnson would teach followers how to think on their own and act constructively and independently. As an entrepreneurial leader Johnson would act much like a self-employed owner of Heinz. He would act, for example, like an individual personally incurring the risk of developing a new "hot" ketchup sauce, but also benefiting from the profit if it is made.

Overall, a manager like Johnson must keep in mind that these leadership styles are aimed at getting people involved in an organization and giving them the freedom to use their abilities as they think best. Such leaders must always keep in mind that regardless of the type of leader they may be, they must earn and maintain the trust of their followers if they are to be successful in the long run.

ACTION SUMMARY

Reread the learning objectives below. Each objective is followed by questions. Answering these questions accurately will help you retain the most important concepts discussed in this chapter. After answering each question, check your answer against the answer key at the end of this chapter. (*Hint:* If you have any doubts regarding the correct response, consult the page number that follows the answer.)

Circle: From studying this chapter, I will attempt to acquire

1. A working definition of leadership.

a b c d e   **a.** The process of directing others toward the accomplishment of some objective is: (a) communication (b) controlling (c) leadership (d) managing (e) none of the above.

a b c d e   **b.** Directing must be consistent with: (a) organizational policies (b) procedures (c) job descriptions (d) none of the above (e) all of the above.

2. An understanding of the relationship between leading and managing.

T F   **a.** Leading and managing are the same process.

a b c d e   **b.** In the relationship between managers and leaders, one could say that: (a) all managers are leaders (b) all leaders are managers (c) some leaders are not managers (d) managers cannot be leaders (e) management is a subset of leadership.

3. An appreciation for the trait and situational approaches to leadership.

a b c d e   **a.** The following is true about the conclusions drawn from the trait approach to leadership: (a) the trait approach identifies traits that consistently separate leaders from nonleaders (b) there are certain traits that guarantee that a leader will be successful (c) the trait approach is based on early research that assumes that a good leader is born, not made (d) leadership is a simple issue of describing the traits of successful leaders (e) none of the above.

a b c d e   **b.** The situational approach to leadership takes into account: (a) the leader (b) the follower (c) the situation (d) a and b (e) a, b, and c.

4. Insights about using leadership theories that emphasize decision-making situations.

a b c d e   **a.** Forces in the manager that determine leadership behavior include: (a) the manager's values (b) the manager's confidence in subordinates (c) the manager's strengths (d) the manager's tolerance for ambiguity (e) all of the above.

a b c d e   **b.** Limiting the self-guidance of the follower and specifically defining procedures for the follower's task performance are called: (a) initiating behavior (b) structure behavior (c) maturity behavior (d) consideration behavior (e) relationship behavior.

T F   **c.** The VYJ Model suggests that a leader should match one of five decision-making styles to the particular situation the leader faces.

5. Insights about using leadership theories that emphasize more general organizational situations.

a b c d e   **a.** The ability of followers to perform their jobs independently and to assume additional responsibilities in their desire to achieve success is called: (a) maturity (b) authority (c) aggressiveness (d) assertiveness (e) consideration.

a b c d e   **b.** Usually upon entrance into an organization, an individual is unable to solve task-related problems independently. According to the life cycle theory, the appropriate style of leadership for this person is: (a) high task/low relationships (b) high task/high relationships (c) high relationships/low task (d) low task/low relationships (e) none of the above.

T F   **c.** According to the path-goal theory of leadership, a leader should carefully inform followers of the rewards that are available to them in the organization and then allow them to pick their own methods of earning the rewards.

6. An understanding of alternatives to leader flexibility.

a b c d e   a. According to Fiedler, the three primary factors that should be used as a basis for moving leaders into more appropriate situations are: (a) task behavior, consideration behavior, maturity (b) maturity, job knowledge, responsibility (c) the worker, the leader, the situation (d) leader-member relations, task structure, position power (e) task structure, leadership style, maturity.

T F   b. Fiedler's studies have proven true the myths that leaders are born, not made, and that there is one best leadership style.

7. An appreciation of emerging leader styles and leadership issues of today.

T F   a. Transformational leaders modify organizations by precisely carrying out strategic plans and emphasizing only slightly the values that followers may have.

a b c d e   b. The coaching leader: (a) listens closely (b) gives emotional support (c) shows by example (d) a and c (e) all of the above.

T F   c. The superleader and entrepreneurial leadership styles are basically the same.

T F   d. Even though there are situations in which a leader has little or no impact on the outcome, the leader is nevertheless an important part of management.

► INTRODUCTORY CASE WRAP-UP ◄

CASE DISCUSSSION QUESTIONS

"The President of H.J. Heinz Company Sends a Letter" (p. 325) and its related Back-to-the-Case sections were written to help you better understand the management concepts contained in this chapter. Answer the following discussion questions about this Introductory Case to further enrich your understanding of chapter content:

1. List and define five activities that William Johnson might perform as a manager moving his company toward *victory* as defined in the Introductory Case.

2. Do you feel that Johnson should use more of a boss-centered or subordinate-centered leader style in making decisions about achieving this *victory?* Why?

3. If you were Johnson, would understanding the transformational and the entrepreneurial leadership styles be valuable to you in leading Heinz employees to this *victory?* Explain fully.

SKILLS EXERCISE: APPLYING THE VYJ LEADERSHIP MODEL

The Introductory Case discussed some of William R. Johnson's plans as the new president of H.J. Heinz Company. Assume that you are Mr. Johnson and you want to decide whether or not to create a new line of instant fruit juices for infants. Use Figure 15.4 to help you decide which style you would use to make this decision. Be sure to explain the rationale you use to choose each branch of the VYJ decision tree.

► ISSUES FOR REVIEW AND DISCUSSION ◄

1. What is leadership?
2. How does leadership differ from management?
3. Explain the trait approach to leadership.
4. What relationship exists between successful leadership and leadership traits?
5. Explain the situational approach to leadership.
6. Draw and explain Tannenbaum and Schmidt's leadership model.
7. List the forces in the manager, the subordinates, and the situation that ultimately determine how a manager should make decisions as a leader.
8. How is the VYJ Model similar to Tannenbaum and Schmidt's model? How is it different?
9. What contribution did the OSU studies make to leadership theory?
10. Can any one of the major leadership styles resulting from the OSU studies be called more effective than the others? Explain.
11. Compare the results of the OSU studies with the results of the Michigan studies.
12. What is meant by *maturity* as it is used in the life cycle theory of leadership?
13. Draw and explain the life cycle theory of leadership model.
14. What is meant by *leader flexibility?*
15. Describe some obstacles to leader flexibility.
16. In general, how might obstacles to leader flexibility be overcome?
17. In specific terms, how does Fiedler suggest that obstacles to leader flexibility be overcome?
18. Based upon the path-goal theory of leadership, how would you advise a friend to lead?
19. Describe three challenges that a transformational leader must face.
20. Compare and contrast the coaching leader and the entrepreneurial leader.
21. Describe the leadership style indicated by the shaded portion of Figure 15.9.

1. **a.** c, p. 326
   b. e, p. 326
2. **a.** F, p. 326
   b. c, pp. 326–327

3. **a.** c, p. 327
   b. e, p. 328
4. **a.** e, p. 330
   b. b, p. 334
   c. T, p. 332

5. **a.** e, p. 334
   b. a, p. 335
   c. F, p. 341
6. **a.** d, p. 339
   b. F, p. 341

7. **a.** F, p. 343
   b. e, pp. 344–345
   c. F, p. 345
   d. F, p. 346

CASE STUDY: Come Fly the Turbulent Skies

In the highly competitive airline industry, airline company after airline company has crashed owing to lack of controls on costs or has been swallowed up by competitors. Delta Airlines, based in Atlanta, Georgia, is certainly not immune to all the ill winds blowing through the industry, but, so far, CEO Ron Allen seems to have kept the company on course.

Traditionally, Delta has promoted from within the company, and Allen is no exception. He entered Delta through the human resources department, became its president in 1982, and took on the mantle of CEO in 1987. As an insider, Allen personally knows the value of making plans and sticking to them, no matter how it might hurt employees in the short run. His loyalty, in short, is to the company shareholder and to the customer. At the same time, however, although Delta is ranked at the head of all domestic airlines, complaints about its customer service have risen sharply. Why? In part, because of cutbacks in frequent-flier benefits, use of fewer flight attendants, and the elimination of meals on the shortest flights.

Originally, Allen depended on such tried measures to ease Delta's financial problems. In 1993, however, he and his management team met daily for a period of six months to develop a long-range plan for the company. Throughout this period, they sought the opinions of middle management and front-line employees on Delta's status. By the end of the half-year planning session, it was obvious that layoffs would have to be instituted to get the company back on a balanced footing. For example, Delta acquired Western Airlines in 1987, and its employee ranks rose to 73,533 in 1993. Allen's most difficult leadership decision was to lay off 3,000 employees in a company that had once boasted that it did not know the meaning of the word "layoff." Thousands of other employees left after being offered early-retirement and other company-proposed plans. Since April 1994, Delta has cut its workforce by more than 10,000. As of January 1996, the number of employees was down to 59,000.

At the admitted expense of employee morale and goodwill, Allen pledged to continue cutting operating costs—eliminating the purchase of new aircraft, laying off pilots, and instituting a 5 percent pay reduction across the board. Such cuts led to outsourcing some jobs and reducing some employees to part-time status. Beset by financial woes and boasting the fewest unionized employees in the airline industry, Delta then became a prime target for union organizers. Even though full-time employees at Delta ranked among the highest paid in the industry, their wages and benefits had not risen since 1989. In effect, employees had taken a 20 percent cut in pay to hold their jobs and keep the company flying.

Meanwhile, Allen's cost cuts worked. In early 1996, he restored the 5 percent pay cut, gave nonunion employees a bonus amounting to 5 percent of their base pay, and brought back 665 customer-service employees who had been laid off. Allen is also reaching out to disaffected employees in other ways. To give them a voice in management, for example, he has created a flight attendants' group. To provide a sense of stability, he has announced that no full-time nonpilot employees will be subject to further layoffs. Many employees welcome Allen's changes and appreciate being given more responsibility—a natural result of running the company with fewer employees.

Of course, some changes are easier to make than others. If Delta is to experience less turbulent flying in the future, it must reach Allen's goal of improving employee morale and customer service. By the end of 1995, Delta had achieved annual cost savings of $1.6 billion. It has reevaluated some of its plans and is working to improve its poor on-time record. To upgrade customer service, Delta has built a new $30 million operations center.

Allen continues to have his critics, both in the ranks and outside the firm. He has been taken to task, for instance, for paying large bonuses (totaling $1.3 million) to his executives while Delta is still going through tough times. He counters that the management team he has put together is crucial to the company's long-term success and could easily make more money at another airline.

The competitive atmosphere of the airline industry demands strong leadership. Of the more than 100 airlines that were started after the industry was deregulated in 1978, very few remain flying today. ValuJet, a powerful Delta competitor in the Southeast, is an exception. At first, Allen tried to match ValuJet's discount prices and services, but these moves resulted in a loss of Delta's business customers. So Delta stopped trying to play ValuJet's game—and actually increased sales on ValuJet routes. Allen has learned a valuable lesson in leadership: When you're out in front, lead.

QUESTIONS

1. What situation led to the hard choices that Ron Allen had to make at Delta Airlines? Do these decisions highlight his leadership abilities? Explain.

2. Cite specific points to illustrate Allen's position on the boss-centered and subordinate-centered leadership scale. Is this balance effective in all decision-making situations? Explain.

3. Does Allen fall into one or more of the new categories of leadership: transformational, substitute, superleadership, and/or entrepreneurial? Explain.

SMALL BUSINESS 2000

Albert Black may not have been born a leader, but he certainly started early in life developing his interest in running a business. Albert Black started mowing lawns at the age of eight and founded his current company not long after finishing college. On Target Supply and Logistics today employs about 30 people and has sales in excess of $10 million annually.

This all sounds quite impressive, but things were not always so successful at On Target. In fact, Mr. Black worked a night job in addition to his role at On Target to provide the necessary cash to get the venture up and running and to gain the knowledge he believed was necessary to run a company. To better understand the strength and success of On Target, we need to understand the leadership philosophy that has guided this company from its beginning.

At least three things are important at On Target Supply and Logistics: personal responsibility for one's success, honesty and integrity, and focus on understanding and helping customers meet their needs. On the surface this may seem like pretty standard fare, but Albert Black has a strong opinion about this mission and a clear idea of how the company can meet it.

First, values Mr. Black learned as a child and knowledge he gained about business from his father's observations as a doorman are the foundation for his work philosophy and business ethics. Secondly, Mr. Black comes across as a man who believes that the job is probably never quite done. This comes across in the way he talks about what can be ac-

complished next. Thirdly, Mr. Black believes in himself and believes others should have similar high self-esteem.

On Target provides some great opportunities for its employees. Mr. Black provides some pretty strong encouragement to his employees to take advantage of the savings and education programs available from the company, to the point that those who do not might feel a bit uncomfortable. Mr. Black's approach has worked so far; will it work as On Target faces marketplace changes and other issues as it attempts to break the $10 million mark?

QUESTIONS

1. Do you think that Albert Black is a leader? Why or why not?
2. How did Albert Black go about preparing himself for the role he has today at On Target Supply and Logistics? What else do you think he might do now to maintain or improve his ability to lead the company?
3. What do you think of Albert's philosophy that employees at On Target realize three forms of income: Educational Income, Psychological Income, and Financial Income? Do you think that these are equally important to all employees?
4. In his comments about employees, we get the impression that Albert thinks everyone is, or should be, as excited about personal growth and development as he is. What is Albert's attitude toward the energy his employees commit to their own improvement? What do you think of this: Is it good or bad?

16

Motivation

STUDENT LEARNING OBJECTIVES

From studying this chapter, I will attempt to acquire

1. A basic understanding of human motivation

2. Insights about various human needs

3. An appreciation for the importance of motivating organization members

4. An understanding of various motivation strategies

CHAPTER OUTLINE

Introductory Case: *American Greetings Motivates through Lateral Moves*

THE MOTIVATION PROCESS
Defining Motivation
Process Theories of Motivation
Content Theories of Motivation: Human Needs

MOTIVATING ORGANIZATION MEMBERS
The Importance of Motivating Organization Members
Strategies for Motivating Organization Members

Across Industries: *Pharmaceuticals—Eli Lilly and Company Benefits from Job Rotation*

Quality Spotlight: *Apple Computer's Job Enrichment Excels*

Management and the Internet: *Managers Punish Pornographic-Related Behavior*

People Spotlight: *Job Satisfaction Is a More Powerful Motivator Than Money at Microsoft*

AMERICAN GREETINGS MOTIVATES THROUGH LATERAL MOVES

REMINDER: THE INTRODUCTORY CASE WRAP-UP (P. 372) CONTAINS DISCUSSION QUESTIONS AND A SKILLS EXERCISE TO FURTHER ILLUSTRATE THE APPLICATION OF CHAPTER CONCEPTS TO THIS VIGNETTE.

With few promotions to give out, companies are trying to motivate employees by shifting them sideways instead of up.

Consider American Greetings Corporation, the Cleveland greeting card and licensing concern. The company recently redesigned about 400 jobs in its creative division and asked workers and managers to reapply. Everyone was guaranteed a position, and no one took a pay cut.

Since the restructuring was completed, employees develop products in teams instead of assembly-line fashion. And they are free to transfer back and forth among teams that make different products, instead of working on just one product line, as they did in the past.

As a result, people who have spent careers specializing in Christmas and Easter cards can now sign up to work on birthday ribbons, humorous mugs, and Valentine's Day gift bags all in the same year. And artists whose only job was choosing dyes now try their hands at illustration and lettering.

"It unleashes a lot of their creative potential," says Dennis Chupa, a division vice president who engineered the shakeup. Added an employee: "A lot of people think it's a good time to make a change or work for someone different."

The main purpose of the restructuring was to cut production time by as much as half for some products, especially greeting cards that play on fleeting fads. But at the same time, American Greetings addressed an increasingly common problem: how to light fires under workers at a time when few promotions or pay raises are on the horizon.

Unless companies act now, workers whose eyes have glazed over during the recession will leave "so damn fast when the economy turns up that they're going to leave burn marks on the carpet," says Marilyn Moats Kennedy, editor of the newsletter *Kennedy's Career Strategist*. Lateral moves that require new skills may be companies' "only hope" for retaining talent.

Traditionally, lateral moves have smacked of demotion because they derailed what seemed like inevitable

The greeting card industry utilizes the diverse talents of many creative individuals. In order to cut production time and to keep employees motivated and creative, American Greetings Corporation recently restructured its operation to allow employees to work in teams and to transfer back and forth between different kinds of products.

promotions. The moves make more sense now that more hands are grabbing for fewer rungs on the corporate ladder. "If the channel above you is clogged, moving sideways can get you out of the traffic jam," says Robert Kelley, a business professor at Carnegie-Mellon University who has written about nontraditional career paths.

What's Ahead

> Dennis Chupa, the division vice president at American Greetings who was quoted in the Introductory Case, has engineered a reorganization of company workers. This reorganization is partially aimed at motivating employees at a time when few company promotions or pay raises are on the horizon. This chapter discusses why managers such as Chupa should focus on motivating workers and how this might be accomplished. It addresses two major topics:
>
> 1. The motivation process
> 2. Motivating organization members

THE MOTIVATION PROCESS

To be successful in working with subordinates, managers need to acquire a thorough understanding of the motivation process. To this end, the definition of motivation, various motivation models, and theories of people's needs are the main topics of discussion in this section of the chapter.

DEFINING MOTIVATION

Motivation is the inner state that causes an individual to behave in a way that ensures the accomplishment of some goal.[1] In other words, motivation explains why people act as they do. The better a manager understands organization members' behavior, the more able that manager will be to influence subordinates' behavior to make it more consistent with the accomplishment of organizational objectives. In essence, since productivity is a result of the behavior of organization members, motivating organization members is the key to reaching organizational goals.[2]

Several different theories about motivation have been proposed over the years. Most of these theories can be categorized into two basic types: process theories and content theories. **Process theories of motivation** are explanations of motivation that emphasize how individuals are motivated. They focus, essentially, on the steps that occur when an individual is motivated. **Content theories of motivation** are explanations of motivation that emphasize people's internal characteristics. They focus on the need to understand what needs people have and how these needs can be satisfied. The following sections discuss important process and content theories of motivation and establish a relationship between them that should prove useful to managers in motivating organization members.

PROCESS THEORIES OF MOTIVATION

There are four important theories that describe how motivation occurs:

1. Needs-Goal theory
2. Vroom expectancy theory
3. Equity theory
4. Porter-Lawler theory

These theories build on one another to furnish a description of the motivation process that begins at a relatively simple and easily understood level and culminates at a somewhat more intricate and realistic level.

THE NEEDS-GOAL THEORY OF MOTIVATION The **needs-goal theory** of motivation, diagrammed in Figure 16.1, is the most fundamental of the motivation theories discussed in this chapter. As the figure indicates, motivation begins with an individual feeling a need. This need is then transformed into behavior directed at supporting, or allowing, the performance of goal behavior to reduce the felt need. Theoretically, goal-supportive behavior and goal behavior itself continue until the felt need has been significantly reduced.

Motivation is the inner state that causes an individual to behave in a way that ensures the accomplishment of some goal.

Process theories of motivation are explanations of motivation that emphasize how individuals are motivated.

Content theories of motivation are explanations of motivation that emphasize people's internal characteristics.

The **needs-goal theory** is a motivation model that hypothesizes that felt needs cause human behavior.

FIGURE 16.1 ▶ The needs-goal theory of motivation

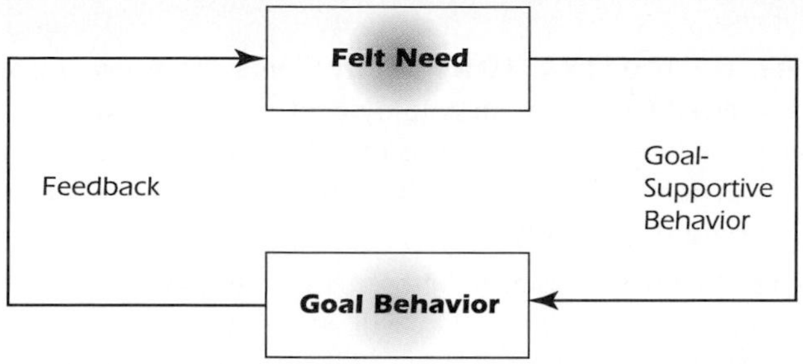

When an individual feels hunger, for example, this need is typically transformed first into behavior directed at supporting the performance of the goal behavior of eating. This supportive behavior could include such activities as buying, cooking, and serving the food to be eaten. The goal-supportive behaviors and the goal behavior itself—eating—generally continue until the individual's hunger substantially subsides. When the individual experiences hunger again, however, the entire cycle is repeated.

The Role of Individual Needs If managers are to have any success in motivating employees, they must understand the personal needs of those employees. When managers offer rewards that are not relevant to employees' personal needs, the employees will not be motivated. For example, if a top executive is already extremely well paid, more money is not likely to be an effective motivator. What is required is a more meaningful incentive—perhaps a higher-level title or an offer of partnership in the firm. Managers must be familiar with needs their employees have and offer them rewards that can satisfy these needs.[3]

THE VROOM EXPECTANCY THEORY OF MOTIVATION In reality, the motivation process is more complex than supposed by the needs-goal theory. The **Vroom expectancy theory** of motivation encompasses some of these complexities.[4] Like the needs-goal theory, the Vroom expectancy theory is based on the premise that felt needs cause human behavior. However, the Vroom theory also addresses the issue of **motivation strength**—an individual's degree of desire to perform a behavior. As this desire increases or decreases, motivation strength fluctuates correspondingly.

> The **Vroom expectancy theory** is a motivation theory that hypothesizes that felt needs cause human behavior and that motivation strength depends on an individual's degree of desire to perform a behavior.

Motivation and Perceptions Vroom's expectancy theory is shown in equation form in Figure 16.2. According to this theory, **motivation strength** is determined by the perceived value of the result of performing a behavior and the perceived probability that the behavior performed will cause the result to materialize. As both of these factors increase, so does motivation strength, or the desire to perform the behavior. In general, people tend to perform the behaviors that maximize their personal rewards over the long term.

> **Motivation strength** is an individual's degree of desire to perform a behavior.

To see how Vroom's theory applies to human behavior, suppose that a college student has been offered a summer job painting three houses at the rate of $200 a house. Assuming that the student needs money, her motivation strength, or desire, to paint the houses will be determined by two major factors: her perception of the value of $600 and her perception of the probability

FIGURE 16.2 ▶ Vroom's expectancy theory of motivation in equation form

$$\text{Motivation strength} = \begin{array}{c}\text{Perceived value of result}\\\text{of performing behavior}\end{array} \times \begin{array}{c}\text{Perceived probability that}\\\text{result will materialize}\end{array}$$

that she can actually paint the houses satisfactorily and thus receive the $600. As the student's perceived value of the $600 reward and perceived probability that she can paint the houses increase, the student's motivation strength to paint the houses will also increase.

EQUITY THEORY OF MOTIVATION **Equity theory,** the work of J. Stacy Adams, looks at an individual's perceived fairness of an employment situation and finds that perceived inequities can lead to changes in behavior. Adams found that when individuals believe they have been treated unfairly in comparison with their co-workers, they will react in one of the following ways to try to right the inequity:[5]

1. Some will change their work inputs to better match the rewards they are receiving. If they believe they are being paid too little, they will work less hard; if they believe they are being paid more than their co-workers, they will increase their work outputs to match their rewards.

2. Some will try to change the compensation they receive for their work by asking for a raise or by taking legal action.

3. If attempts to change the actual inequality are unsuccessful, some will try to change their own perception of the inequality. They may do this by distorting the status of their jobs or by rationalizing away the inequity.

4. Some will leave the situation rather than try to change it. People who feel they are being treated unfairly on the job may decide to quit that job rather than endure the inequity.

Perceptions of inequities can arise in any number of management situations—among them, work assignments, promotions, ratings reports, and office assignments—but they occur most often in the area of pay. All of these issues are emotionally charged, however, because they have to do with people's feelings of self-worth. What is a minor inequity in the mind of a manager can loom as extremely important in the mind of an employee. Effective managers strive to deal with equity issues because the steps that workers are prone to take to balance the scales are often far from good for the organization.

THE PORTER-LAWLER THEORY OF MOTIVATION Porter and Lawler developed a motivation theory that provides a more complete description of the motivation process than either the needs-goal theory or the Vroom expectancy theory.[6] Still, the **Porter-Lawler theory** of motivation (see Figure 16.3) is consistent with those two theories in that it accepts the premises that felt needs cause human behavior and that effort expended to accomplish a task is determined by the perceived value of rewards that will result from finishing the task and the probability that those rewards will materialize.

Equity theory of motivation is an explanation of motivation that emphasizes the individual's perceived fairness of an employment situation and how perceived inequities can cause certain behaviors.

The **Porter-Lawler theory** is a motivation theory that hypothesizes that felt needs cause human behavior and that motivation strength is determined primarily by the perceived value of the result of performing the behavior and the perceived probability that the behavior performed will cause the result to materialize.

FIGURE 16.3 ▶ **The Porter-Lawler theory of motivation**

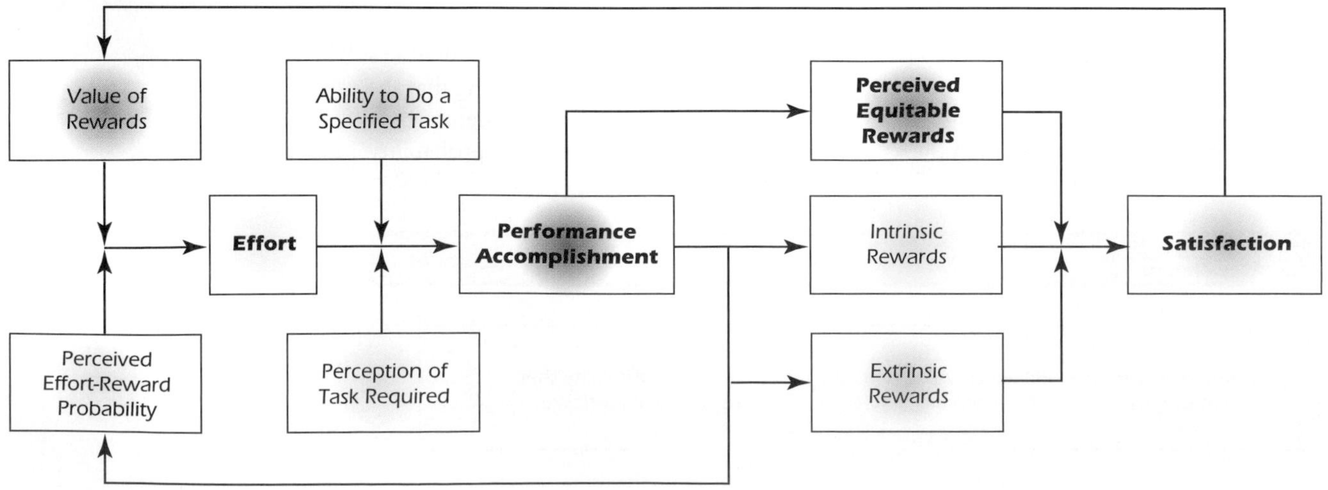

The Motivation Process In addition, the Porter-Lawler motivation theory stresses three other characteristics of the motivation process:

1. The perceived value of a reward is determined by both intrinsic and extrinsic rewards that result in need satisfaction when a task is accomplished. **Intrinsic rewards** come directly from performing the task, while **extrinsic rewards** are extraneous to the task. For example, when a manager counsels a subordinate about a personal problem, the manager may get some intrinsic reward in the form of personal satisfaction at helping another individual. In addition to this intrinsic reward, however, the manager also receives an extrinsic reward in the form of the overall salary the manager is paid.

2. The extent to which an individual effectively accomplishes a task is determined primarily by two variables: the individual's perception of what is required to perform the task and the individual's ability to perform the task. Naturally, effectiveness at accomplishing a task increases as the perception of what is required to perform the task becomes more accurate and ability to perform the task increases.

3. The perceived fairness of rewards influences the amount of satisfaction produced by those rewards. In general, the more equitable an individual perceives the rewards to be, the greater the satisfaction that individual will experience as a result of receiving them.

> **Intrinsic rewards** are rewards that come directly from performing a task.
>
> **Extrinsic rewards** are rewards that are extraneous to the task accomplished.

BACK TO THE CASE

Motivation is an inner state that causes individuals to act in certain ways that ensure the accomplishment of some goal. As division vice president at American Greetings, Dennis Chupa seems to understand the motivation process because he is focusing on influencing the behavior of his employees to make it consistent with his organization's objectives. That is, he is encouraging employees to be creative and efficient performers. The reorganization emphasizing lateral job moves that Chupa designed should be a valuable tool in making this encouragement effective.

To motivate employees, Chupa must keep five specific principles of human motivation clearly in mind:

1. Felt needs cause behavior aimed at reducing those needs
2. The degree of desire to perform a particular behavior is determined by an individual's perceived value of the result of performing the behavior and the perceived probability that the behavior will cause the result to materialize
3. The perceived value of a reward for a particular behavior is determined by both intrinsic and extrinsic rewards that result in need satisfaction when the behavior is accomplished
4. Individuals can effectively accomplish a task only if they understand what the task requires and have the ability to perform it
5. The perceived fairness of a reward influences the degree of satisfaction generated when the reward is received

►CONTENT THEORIES OF MOTIVATION: HUMAN NEEDS

The motivation theories discussed thus far imply that an understanding of motivation is based on an understanding of human needs. There is some evidence that most people have strong needs for self-respect, respect from others, promotion, and psychological growth.[7] Although identifying all human needs is impossible, several theories have been developed to help managers better understand these needs:

1. Maslow's hierarchy of needs
2. Alderfer's ERG theory
3. Argyris' maturity-immaturity continuum
4. McClelland's acquired needs theory

When General Motors workers struck at the Flint, Michigan plant in the summer of 1998, their concerns focused on subcontracting and other competitive issues. They were responding, in other words, to what they perceived as a security need, in this case, a buffer against a serious economic challenge to the operation.

MASLOW'S HIERARCHY OF NEEDS Perhaps the most widely accepted description of human needs is the hierarchy of needs concept developed by Abraham Maslow.[8] Maslow states that human beings possess the five basic needs described below, and theorizes that these five basic needs can be arranged in a hierarchy of importance—the order in which individuals generally strive to satisfy them. The needs and their relative positions in the hierarchy of importance are shown in Figure 16.4.

Physiological needs are Maslow's first set of human needs—for the normal functioning of the body, including the desires for water, food, rest, sex, and air.

Security, or safety, needs are Maslow's second set of human needs—reflecting the human desire to keep free from physical harm.

Social needs are Maslow's third set of human needs—reflecting the human desire to belong, including longings for friendship, companionship, and love.

► **Physiological needs** relate to the normal functioning of the body. They include the needs for water, food, rest, sex, and air. Until these needs are met, a significant portion of an individual's behavior will be aimed at satisfying them. Once the needs are satisfied, however, behavior is aimed at satisfying the needs on the next level of Maslow's hierarchy.

► **Security, or safety, needs** relate to the individual's desire to be free from harm, including both bodily and economic disaster.

Traditionally, management has best helped employees satisfy their physiological and security needs through adequate wages or salaries, which employees use to purchase such things as food and housing.

► **Social needs** include the desire for love, companionship, and friendship. These needs reflect a person's desire to be accepted by others. As they are satisfied, behavior shifts to satisfying esteem needs.

FIGURE 16.4 ► Maslow's hierarchy of needs

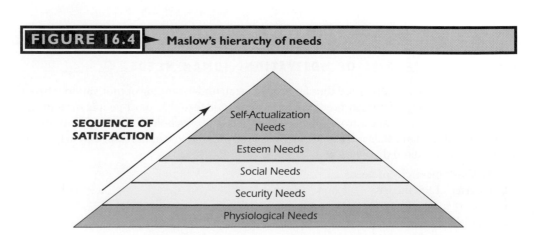

SEQUENCE OF SATISFACTION

Self-Actualization Needs

Esteem Needs

Social Needs

Security Needs

Physiological Needs

- **Esteem needs** are concerned with the desire for respect. They are generally divided into two categories: self-respect and respect from others. Once esteem needs are satisfied, the individual moves to the pinnacle of the hierarchy and emphasizes satisfying self-actualization needs.
- **Self-actualization needs** refer to the desire to maximize whatever potential an individual possesses. For example, in the nonprofit public setting of a high school, a principal who seeks to satisfy self-actualization needs would strive to become the best principal possible. Self-actualization needs occupy the highest level of Maslow's hierarchy.[9]

The traditional concerns about Maslow's hierarchy are that it has no research base, that it may not accurately pinpoint basic human needs, and that it is questionable whether human needs can be neatly arranged in such a hierarchy. Nevertheless, Maslow's hierarchy is probably the most popular conceptualization of human needs to date, and it continues to be positively discussed in management literature.[10] Still, the concerns expressed about it should remind managers to look upon Maslow's hierarchy more as a subjective statement than an objective description of human needs.

ALDERFER'S ERG THEORY Clayton Alderfer responded to some of the criticisms of Maslow's work by conducting his own study of human needs.[11] He identified three basic categories of needs:

1. Existence needs—the need for physical well-being
2. Relatedness needs—the need for satisfying interpersonal relationships
3. Growth needs—the need for continuing personal growth and development

The first letters of these needs form the acronym ERG, by which the theory is now known.

Alderfer's ERG theory is similar to Maslow's theory except in three major respects. First, Alderfer identified only three orders of human needs, compared to Maslow's five orders. Second, in contrast to Maslow, Alderfer found that people sometimes activate their higher-level needs before they have completely satisfied all of their lower-level needs. Third, Alderfer concluded that movement in his hierarchy of human needs is not always upward. For instance—and this is reflected in his frustration-regression principle—he found that a worker frustrated by his failure to satisfy an upper-level need might regress by trying to fulfill an already satisfied lower-level need.

Alderfer's work, in conjunction with Maslow's, has implications for management. Employees frustrated by work that fails to provide opportunities for growth or development on the job might concentrate their energy on trying to make more money, thus regressing to a lower level of needs. To counteract such regression, management might use job enrichment strategies designed to help people meet their higher-order needs.

ARGYRIS' MATURITY-IMMATURITY CONTINUUM Argyris' maturity-immaturity continuum also furnishes insights into human needs.[12] This continuum concept focuses on the personal and natural development of people to explain human needs. According to Argyris, as people naturally progress from immaturity to maturity, they move:

1. From a state of passivity as an infant to a state of increasing activity as an adult
2. From a state of dependence on others as an infant to a state of relative independence as an adult
3. From being capable of behaving only in a few ways as an infant to being capable of behaving in many different ways as an adult
4. From having erratic, casual, shallow, and quickly dropped interests as an infant to having deeper, more lasting interests as an adult
5. From having a short time perspective as an infant to having a much longer time perspective as an adult
6. From being in a subordinate position as an infant to aspiring to occupy an equal or superordinate position as an adult
7. From a lack of self-awareness as an infant to awareness and control over self as an adult

According to Argyris' continuum, then, as individuals mature, they have increasing needs for more activity, enjoy a state of relative independence, behave in many different ways, have deeper and more lasting interests, are capable of considering a relatively long time perspective,

Esteem needs are Maslow's fourth set of human needs—including the desires for self-respect and respect from others.

Self-actualization needs are Maslow's fifth, and final, set of human needs—reflecting the human desire to maximize personal potential.

Alderfer's ERG theory is an explanation of human needs that divides them into three basic types: existence needs, relatedness needs, and growth needs.

Argyris' maturity-immaturity continuum is a concept that furnishes insights into human needs by focusing on an individual's natural progress from immaturity to maturity.

occupy an equal position vis-à-vis other mature individuals, and have more awareness of themselves and control over their own destiny. Note that, unlike Maslow's needs, Argyris' needs are not arranged in a hierarchy. Like Maslow's hierarchy, however, Argyris' continuum is a primarily subjective explanation of human needs.

MCCLELLAND'S ACQUIRED NEEDS THEORY Another theory about human needs, called **McClelland's acquired needs theory,** focuses on the needs that people acquire through their life experiences. This theory, formulated by David C. McClelland in the 1960s, emphasizes three of the many needs human beings develop in their lifetimes:

1. *Need for achievement (nAch)*—the desire to do something better or more efficiently than it has ever been done before
2. *Need for power (nPower)*—the desire to control, influence, or be responsible for others
3. *Need for affiliation (nAff)*—the desire to maintain close, friendly personal relationships

The individual's early life experiences determine which of these needs will be highly developed and therefore dominate the personality.

McClelland's studies of these three acquired human needs have significant implications for management.

Need to Achieve McClelland claims that in some businesspeople the need to achieve is so strong that it is more motivating than the quest for profits. To maximize their satisfaction, individuals with high achievement needs set goals for themselves that are challenging, yet achievable. Although such people are willing to assume risk, they assess it very carefully because they do not want to fail. Therefore, they will avoid tasks that involve too much risk. People with a low need for achievement, on the other hand, generally avoid challenges, responsibilities, and risk.

Need for Power People with a high need for power are greatly motivated to influence others and to assume responsibility for subordinates' behavior. They are likely to seek advancement and to take on increasingly responsible work activities to earn that advancement. Power-oriented managers are comfortable in competitive situations and enjoy their decision-making role.

Need for Affiliation Managers with a high need for affiliation have a cooperative, team-centered managerial style. They prefer to influence subordinates to complete tasks through team efforts. The danger is that managers with a high need for affiliation can lose their effectiveness if their need for social approval and friendship interferes with their willingness to make managerial decisions.[13]

> ### BACK TO THE CASE
>
> Chupa undoubtedly understands the basic motivation concept that felt needs cause behavior. Before he can have a maximum effect on motivating organization members, however, he must also meet the more complex challenge of thoroughly acquainting himself with the various individual human needs of his employees.
>
> According to Maslow, people generally possess physiological, security, social, esteem, and self-actualization needs arranged in a hierarchy of importance. Argyris suggests that as people mature, they have increasing needs for activity, independence, flexibility, deeper interests, analyses of longer time perspectives, a position of equality with other mature individuals, and control over personal destiny. McClelland believes that the need for achievement—the desire to do something better or more efficiently than it has ever been done before—is a strong human need.
>
> As part of his reorganization efforts, Chupa guaranteed every worker a position with no pay cut. In so doing, he sought to satisfy employees' physiological and safety needs. Other features of Chupa's reorganization, like management development programs and a "best card verse of the month" program, could further motivate his employees by satisfying other needs they might have.

McClelland's acquired needs theory is an explanation of human needs that focuses on the desires for achievement, power, and affiliation that people develop as a result of their life experiences.

People are motivated to perform behavior to satisfy their personal needs. Therefore, from a managerial viewpoint, motivation is the process of furnishing organization members with the opportunity to satisfy their needs by performing productive behavior within the organization. In reality, managers do not motivate people. Rather, they create environments in which organization members motivate themselves.[14]

As discussed in chapter 14, motivation is one of the four primary interrelated activities of the influencing function performed by managers to guide the behavior of organization members toward the attainment of organizational objectives. The following sections discuss the importance of motivating organization members and present some strategies for doing so.

►THE IMPORTANCE OF MOTIVATING ORGANIZATION MEMBERS

Figure 16.5 makes the point that unsatisfied needs can lead organization members to perform either appropriate or inappropriate behavior. Successful managers minimize inappropriate behavior and maximize appropriate behavior among subordinates, thus raising the probability that productivity will increase and lowering the probability that it will decrease.

►STRATEGIES FOR MOTIVATING ORGANIZATION MEMBERS

Managers have various strategies at their disposal for motivating organization members. Each strategy is aimed at satisfying subordinates' needs (consistent with the descriptions of human needs in Maslow's hierarchy, Alderfer's ERG theory, Argyris' maturity-immaturity continuum, and McClelland's acquired needs theory) through appropriate organizational behavior. These managerial motivation strategies are as follows:

1. Managerial communication
2. Theory X–Theory Y
3. Job design
4. Behavior modification
5. Likert's management systems
6. Monetary incentives
7. Nonmonetary incentives

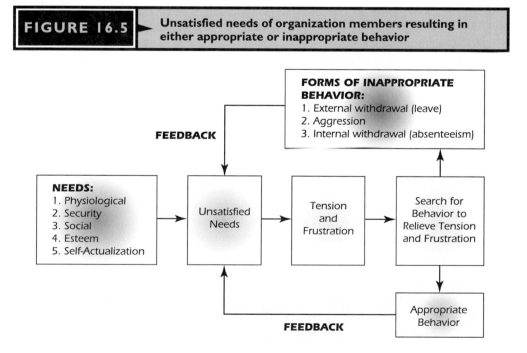

FIGURE 16.5 ► Unsatisfied needs of organization members resulting in either appropriate or inappropriate behavior

For Horst Stormer, director of physical research at AT&T Bell Laboratories, lunch is important to the communication process: He feels that the informal atmosphere, in which managers and employees can bounce ideas off one another without the usual pressure, contributes to teamwork and creativity. Although he does not claim to know precisely what "creativity" is, he is sure that it emerges when people communicate: "Nobody," he admits, "manages creativity. People are what gets managed."

The strategies are discussed in the sections that follow.

Throughout the discussion, it is important to remember that no single strategy will always be more effective for a manager than any other. In fact, most managers find that some combination of these strategies is most effective in the organization setting.

MANAGERIAL COMMUNICATION Perhaps the most basic motivation strategy for managers is simply to communicate well with organization members. Effective manager-subordinate communication can satisfy such basic human needs as recognition, a sense of belonging, and security. For example, such a simple managerial action as attempting to become better acquainted with subordinates can contribute substantially to the satisfaction of each of these three needs. To take another example, a message praising a subordinate for a job well done can help satisfy the subordinate's recognition and security needs.

As a general rule, managers should strive to communicate often with other organization members, not only because communication is the primary means of conducting organizational activities, but also because it is a basic tool for satisfying the human needs of organization members.

THEORY X–THEORY Y Another motivation strategy involves managers' assumptions about human nature. Douglas McGregor identified two sets of assumptions: **Theory X** involves negative assumptions about people that McGregor believes managers often use as the basis for dealing with their subordinates (for example, the average person has an inherent dislike of work and will avoid it whenever he or she can). **Theory Y** represents positive assumptions about people that McGregor believes managers should strive to use (for example, people will exercise self-direction and self-control in meeting their objectives.)[15]

McGregor implies that managers who use Theory X assumptions are "bad" and that those who use Theory Y assumptions are "good." Reddin, however, argues that production might be increased by using *either* Theory X or Theory Y assumptions, depending on the situation the manager faces: "Is there not a strong argument for the position that any theory may have desirable outcomes if appropriately used?" The difficulty is that McGregor had considered only the ineffective application of Theory X and the effective application of Theory Y. Reddin proposes a **Theory Z**—an effectiveness dimension that implies that managers who use either Theory X or Theory Y assumptions when dealing with people can be successful, depending on their situation.

The basic rationale for using Theory Y rather than Theory X in most situations is that managerial activities that reflect Theory Y assumptions generally are more successful in satisfying the human needs of most organization members than are managerial activities that reflect Theory X assumptions. Therefore, activities based on Theory Y assumptions are more apt to motivate organization members than are activities based on Theory X assumptions.

Theory X is a set of essentially negative assumptions about human nature.

Theory Y is a set of essentially positive assumptions about human nature.

Theory Z is the effectiveness dimension that implies that managers who use either Theory X or Theory Y assumptions when dealing with people can be successful, depending on their situation.

Once a manager such as Chupa understands that felt needs cause behavior and is aware of people's different types of needs, he is ready to apply this information to motivating his workforce. From Chupa's viewpoint, motivating employees means furnishing them with the opportunity to satisfy their human needs by performing their jobs. This is a very important notion because successful motivation tends to increase employee productivity. If Chupa does not give his employees the opportunity to satisfy their human needs on the job, they will probably develop low morale. Common signs of low morale in a company are workers who seldom initiate new ideas, go out of their way to avoid tough situations, and strongly resist innovation.

One strategy that the text recommends Chupa follow to further motivate American Greetings' workers is to take the time to communicate with his employees. Effective manager-employee communication satisfies employee needs for recognition, belonging, and security. Another strategy he could adopt is based on McGregor's Theory X–Theory Y concept. In following this strategy, Chupa would assume that work is as natural as play; that employees can direct themselves to accomplish organizational goals; that granting rewards encourages the achievement of American Greetings' objectives; that employees seek and accept responsibility; and that most employees are creative, ingenious, and imaginative. If Chupa manages by such assumptions, it should lead to the satisfaction of many of his employees' needs as defined by Maslow, Argyris, and McClelland.

JOB DESIGN A third strategy managers can use to motivate organization members involves designing jobs that organization members perform. The following two sections discuss earlier and more recent job design strategies.

Earlier Job Design Strategies A movement has long existed in American business to make jobs simpler and more specialized in order to increase worker productivity. The idea behind this movement is to make workers more productive by enabling them to be more efficient. Perhaps the best example of a job design inspired by this movement is the automobile assembly line. The negative result of work simplification and specialization, however, is job boredom. As jobs become simpler and more specialized, they typically become more boring and less satisfying to workers, and, consequently, productivity suffers.

Job Rotation. The first major attempt to overcome job boredom was **job rotation**—moving workers from job to job rather than requiring them to perform only one simple and specialized job over the long term. For example, a gardener would do more than just mow lawns; he might also trim bushes, rake grass, and sweep sidewalks.

> **Job rotation** is the process of moving workers from one job to another rather than requiring them to perform only one simple and specialized job over the long term.

Although job rotation programs have been known to increase organizational profitability, most of them are ineffective as motivation strategies because, over time, people become bored with all the jobs they are rotated into.[16] Job rotation programs, however, are often effective for achieving other organizational objectives, such as training, because they give individuals an overview of how the various units of the organization function.

ACROSS INDUSTRIES — Pharmaceuticals

ELI LILLY AND COMPANY BENEFITS FROM JOB ROTATION

Management research suggests that job rotation programs can provide organizations with many different types of significant benefits.

A recent study of a job rotation program at Eli Lilly and Company, a major pharmaceutical manufacturer, found support for the validity of this suggestion.

(continued)

Lilly has used job rotation longer and more often than most other large organizations. Although job rotation is not a formal program at Lilly, rotating employees from job to job has been viewed for many years as an integral part of the company's plan for professional development. In fact, one of Lilly's strongest recruiting tools in recent years has been its reputation for successfully implementing its job rotation program. Although management sees job rotation as an important training and development tool, moving around the organization isn't required of every employee. In general, providing employees with different, attractive job options has tended to increase overall employee job satisfaction as well as satisfaction with Lilly as a company.

At Lilly, job rotation has definitely proven to be a valuable training and development tool. History shows that job rotation at Lilly enhances employees' technical skills like accounting, finance, and operating procedures. In addition, Lilly's job rotation also enhances employees' fi-nancial, planning, communication, interpersonal, leadership, and computer skills. Naturally, although much valuable training is accomplished through job rotation at Lilly, the program does not focus on the development of *all* employee skills. For example, employees generally do not use job rotation at Lilly to improve their knowledge of the external business environment and how to develop other people.

The advantages of Lilly's job rotation program must be compared to its disadvantages. First, job rotation at Lilly sometimes results in increased workload and decreased productivity for the rotating employee as well as for the new work group to whom the employee is being rotated. This decreased productivity is normally due to the learning curve that can occur on new jobs, like time spent learning the new job, training costs related to the newly rotated employee, costly errors that employees often make while learning a new job, and integration of a new member into an established work group.

Job enlargement is the process of increasing the number of operations an individual performs in a job.

Job Enlargement. Another strategy developed to overcome the boredom of doing very simple and specialized jobs is **job enlargement,** or increasing the number of operations an individual performs in order to enhance the individual's satisfaction in work. According to the job enlargement concept, the gardener's job would become more satisfying as such activities as trimming bushes, raking grass, and sweeping sidewalks were added to his initial activity of mowing grass. Some research supports the contention that job enlargement does make jobs more satisfying, and some does not.[17] Still, job enlargement programs have generally proved more successful at increasing job satisfaction than have job rotation programs.

A number of other job design strategies have evolved since the development of job rotation and job enlargement programs. Two of these more recent strategies are job enrichment and flextime.

Hygiene, or **maintenance, factors** are items that influence the degree of job dissatisfaction.

Motivating factors, or **motivators,** are items that influence the degree of job satisfaction.

Job Enrichment Frederick Herzberg has concluded from his research that the degrees of satisfaction and dissatisfaction organization members feel as a result of performing a job are two different variables determined by two different sets of items.[18] The items that influence the degree of job dissatisfaction are called **hygiene,** or **maintenance, factors,** while those that influence the degree of job satisfaction are called **motivating factors,** or **motivators.** Hygiene factors relate to the work environment, and motivating factors to the work itself. The items that make up Herzberg's hygiene and motivating factors are presented in Table 16.1.

Herzberg believes that when the hygiene factors of a particular job situation are undesirable, organization members will become dissatisfied. Making these factors more desirable—for

TABLE 16.1 ▶ Herzberg's Hygiene Factors and Motivators	
Dissatisfaction: Hygiene or Maintenance Factors	**Satisfaction: Motivating Factors**
1. Company policy and administration	1. Opportunity for achievement
2. Supervision	2. Opportunity for recognition
3. Relationship with supervisor	3. Work itself
4. Relationship with peers	4. Responsibility
5. Working conditions	5. Advancement
6. Salary	6. Personal growth
7. Relationship with subordinates	

FIGURE 16.6 ▶ **Needs in Maslow's hierarchy of needs that desirable hygiene and motivating factors generally satisfy**

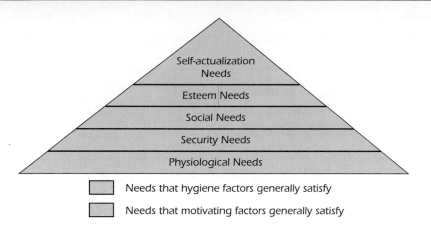

Self-actualization Needs

Esteem Needs

Social Needs

Security Needs

Physiological Needs

☐ Needs that hygiene factors generally satisfy

☐ Needs that motivating factors generally satisfy

example, by increasing salary—will rarely motivate people to do a better job, but it will keep them from becoming dissatisfied. In contrast, when the motivating factors of a particular job situation are high, employees usually are motivated to do a better job. In general, people tend to be more motivated and productive as more motivators are built into their job situation.

The process of incorporating motivators into a job situation is called **job enrichment.** Early reports indicated that companies such as Texas Instruments and Volvo had notable success in motivating organization members through job enrichment programs. More recent reports, though they continue to support the value of job enrichment, indicate that for a job enrichment program to be successful, it must be carefully designed and administered.[19]

Job Enrichment and Productivity. Herzberg's overall conclusions are that the most productive organization members are those involved in work situations that have both desirable hygiene and motivating factors. The needs in Maslow's hierarchy that desirable hygiene factors and motivating factors generally satisfy are shown in Figure 16.6. Esteem needs can be satisfied by both types of factors. An example of esteem needs satisfied by a hygiene factor is a private parking space—a status symbol and a working condition evidencing the employee's importance to the organization. An example of esteem needs satisfied by a motivating factor is an award given for outstanding performance—a public recognition of a job well done that displays the employee's value to the organization.

Job enrichment is the process of incorporating motivators into a job situation.

▶ **QUALITY SPOTLIGHT** ◀ Apple Computer's Job Enrichment Excels

Apple Computer has attempted to provide both hygiene factors and motivating factors for its employees because company executives firmly believe that highly motivated, satisfied employees produce high-quality products. Apple's job enrichment program serves as a good example of how management can take steps to enrich a work environment.

Creating the right work environment—pleasant but challenging—is the key to encouraging people to be productive at Apple. For example, management has established award systems for employees that incorporate both recognition for jobs well done and opportunities for growth and advancement. In addition, Apple management

has made hygiene factors acceptable to employees and takes pride in providing sufficiently generous salaries to its valued workers.

To take one example of the recognition programs at Apple, the company announces new products and projects through the employees who developed them instead of through a public relations office. This announcement process recognizes hardworking employees and makes them feel that they are making valuable contributions to the company. At Apple, rewards and recognition are an ongoing part of company life that helps management ensure the quality of its products, such as the Macintosh and Apple computers.

TABLE 16.2	Advantages and Disadvantages of Using Flextime Programs

Advantages	Disadvantages
Improved employee attitude and morale	Lack of supervision during some hours of work
Accommodation of working parents	Key people unavailable at certain times
Decreased tardiness	Understaffing at times
Fewer commuting problems—workers can avoid congested streets and highways	Problem of accommodating employees whose output is the input for other employees
Accommodation of those who wish to arrive at work before normal workday interruptions begin	Employee abuse of flextime program
Increased production	Difficulty in planning work schedules
Facilitation of employees scheduling of medical, dental, and other types of appointments	Problem of keeping track of hours worked or accumulated
Accommodation of leisure-time activities of employees	Inability to schedule meetings at convenient times
Decreased absenteeism	Inability to coordinate projects
Decreased turnover	

Flextime is a program that allows workers to complete their jobs within a workweek of a normal number of hours that they schedule themselves.

Flextime Another more recent job design strategy for motivating organization members is based on a concept called *flextime*. Perhaps the most common traditional characteristic of work in the United States is that jobs are performed within a fixed eight-hour workday. Recently, however, this tradition has been challenged. Faced with motivation problems and excessive absenteeism, many managers have turned to scheduling innovations as a possible solution.[20]

The main purpose of these scheduling innovations is not to reduce the total number of work hours, but rather to give workers greater flexibility in scheduling their work hours. The main thrust of **flextime,** or flexible working hours programs, is that it allows workers to complete their jobs within a workweek of a normal number of hours that they arrange themselves.[21] The choices of starting and finishing times can be as flexible as the organizational situation allows. To ensure that flexibility does not become counterproductive within the organization, however, many flextime programs stipulate a core period during which all employees must be on the job.

Advantages of Flextime. Various kinds of organizational studies have indicated that flextime programs have some positive organizational effects. Douglas Fleuter, for example, has reported that flextime contributes to greater job satisfaction, which typically results in greater productivity. Other researchers have concluded that flextime programs can result in higher motivation levels of workers. Because organization members generally consider flextime programs desirable, organizations that have such programs can usually better compete with other organizations in recruiting qualified new employees. (A listing of the advantages and disadvantages of flextime programs appears in Table 16.2.) Although many well-known companies, such as Scott Paper, Sun Oil, and Samsonite, have adopted flextime programs,[22] more research is needed before flextime's true worth can be conclusively assessed.

BACK TO THE CASE

Chupa can use two major job design strategies to motivate his employees at American Greetings. Through job enrichment, he can incorporate such motivating factors as opportunities for achievement, recognition, and personal growth into jobs. Chupa's program of allowing workers to transfer back and forth among work teams and to work on more than one product is a type of job enrichment because it gives employees opportunities for personal growth. However, for maximum success, hygiene factors at American Greetings—company policy and administration, supervision, salary, and working conditions, for example—must also be perceived as desirable by employees.

Another major job design strategy that Chupa can use to motivate his employees is flextime. With flextime, workers would have some freedom to schedule the beginning and ending of their workdays. Of course, this freedom would have to be limited by such organizational factors as seasonal demand and peak selling seasons.

BEHAVIOR MODIFICATION   A fourth strategy that managers can use to motivate organization members is based on a concept known as behavior modification. As stated by B. F. Skinner, the Harvard psychologist considered by many to be the "father of behavioral psychology," **behavior modification** focuses on encouraging appropriate behavior by controlling the consequences of that behavior.[23] According to the law of effect, behavior that is rewarded tends to be repeated, while that which is punished tends to be eliminated.

Although behavior modification programs typically involve the administration of both rewards and punishments, it is rewards that are generally emphasized because they are more effective than punishments in influencing behavior. Obviously, the main theme of behavior modification is not new.

> **Behavior modification** is a program that focuses on managing human activity by controlling the consequences of performing that activity.

Reinforcement   Behavior modification theory asserts that if managers want to modify subordinates' behavior, they must ensure that appropriate consequences occur as a result of that behavior. **Positive reinforcement** is a reward that consists of a desirable consequence of behavior, and **negative reinforcement** is a reward that consists of the elimination of an undesirable consequence of behavior.[24]

If arriving at work on time is positively reinforced, or rewarded, the probability increases that a worker will arrive on time more often. If arriving late for work causes a worker to experience some undesirable outcome, such as a verbal reprimand, that worker will be negatively reinforced when this outcome is eliminated by on-time arrival. According to behavior modification theory, positive reinforcement and negative reinforcement are both rewards that increase the likelihood that a behavior will continue.

> **Positive reinforcement** is a reward that consists of a desirable consequence of behavior.
>
> **Negative reinforcement** is a reward that consists of the elimination of an undesirable consequence of behavior.

Punishment   **Punishment** is the presentation of an undesirable behavioral consequence or the removal of a desirable behavioral consequence that decreases the likelihood that the behavior will continue. To use our earlier example, a manager could punish employees for arriving late for work by exposing them to some undesirable consequence, such as verbal reprimand, or by removing a desirable consequence, such as their wages for the amount of time they are late.[25] Although punishment would probably quickly convince most workers to come to work on time, it might have undesirable side effects, such as high absenteeism and turnover, if it is emphasized over the long term.

> **Punishment** is the presentation of an undesirable behavior consequence or the removal of a desirable one that decreases the likelihood that the behavior will continue.

MANAGEMENT AND THE INTERNET   Managers Punish Pornographic-Related Behavior

From a management viewpoint, punishing an employee is exposing that employee to some undesirable consequence because the employee has performed inappropriately. One inappropriate behavior that some modern managers are currently facing is that certain employees are accessing pornography on the Internet on company computers.

Elron Software, a company in Cambridge, Massachusetts, sells a program to help managers monitor the types of sites that employees are using. According to Elron, the number of sexually explicit sites on the Internet is estimated to be in the hundreds of thousands, and perhaps even millions, with more continually being created. Given the

(continued)

massive and growing number of pornographic sites, the task of listing them is impossible. Elron's software works by looking for suspicious words in the addresses of Web sites being accessed by a company's employees and alerting a manager when they are used. The obvious terms include sex, nude, porn, adult, XXX, play, and drugs. Managers can then access the sites to determine if they are indeed inappropriate and, if so, confront employees regarding the unwanted behavior.

Overall, managers are severely punishing employees who are accessing pornography on the Internet via company equipment. Faced with international controversies over pornography on the Internet, managers are sending strong messages to employees *not* to access pornographic sites. They are telling employees that such behavior can severely endanger company image and performance. Managers are within their rights to send such messages since freedom of speech under the First Amendment does not apply to the workplace. Essentially, employees have no right of privacy and no right of free speech using company resources.

Examples of employees reprimanded for accessing pornography on the Internet are commonplace. Pacific Northwest National Laboratory recently disciplined close to 100 employees for using lab computers on their own time to access pornographic sites on the Web. Kmart fired a Webmaster for spoofing the controversy over Internet pornography. At Sandia National Labs, 64 employees were disciplined for reading pornography on company time and their own time.

Applying Behavior Modification   Behavior modification programs have been applied both successfully and unsuccessfully in a number of organizations. Management at Emery Air Freight Company (now called Emery Worldwide), for example, found that an effective feedback system is crucial to making a behavior modification program successful.[26] This feedback system should be aimed at keeping employees informed of the relationship between various behaviors and their consequences.

Other ingredients of successful behavior modification programs are the following:[27]

1. Giving different levels of rewards to different workers according to the quality of their performances
2. Telling workers what they are doing wrong
3. Punishing workers privately in order not to embarrass them in front of others
4. Always giving out rewards and punishments that are earned to emphasize that management is serious about its behavior modification efforts

The behavior modification concept is also being applied to cost control in organizations, with the objective of encouraging employees to be more cost conscious. Under this type of behavior modification program, employees are compensated in a manner that rewards cost control and cost reduction and penalizes cost acceleration.[28]

LIKERT'S MANAGEMENT SYSTEMS   Another strategy that managers can use to motivate organization members is based on the work of Rensis Likert, a noted management scholar.[29] After studying several types and sizes of organizations, Likert concluded that management styles in organizations can be categorized into the following systems:

▶ *System 1*—This style of management is characterized by a lack of confidence or trust in subordinates. Subordinates do not feel free to discuss their jobs with superiors, and are motivated by fear, threats, punishments, and occasional rewards. Information flow in the organization is directed primarily downward; upward communication is viewed with great suspicion. The bulk of all decision making is done at the top of the organization.

▶ *System 2*—This style of management is characterized by a condescending master-to-servant–style confidence and trust in subordinates. Subordinates do not feel very free to discuss their jobs with superiors, and are motivated by rewards and actual or potential punishments. Information flows mostly downward; upward communication may or may not be viewed with suspicion. Although policies are made primarily at the top of the organization, decisions within a prescribed framework are made at lower levels.

▶ *System 3*—This style of management is characterized by substantial, though not complete, confidence in subordinates. Subordinates feel fairly free to discuss their jobs with superiors, and are motivated by rewards, occasional punishments, and some involvement. Information flows both upward and downward in the organization. Upward communication is often accepted, though at times it may be viewed with suspicion. Although broad policies and general decisions are made at the top of the organization, more specific decisions are made at lower levels.

▶ *System 4*—This style of management is characterized by complete trust and confidence in subordinates. Subordinates feel completely free to discuss their jobs with superiors, and are motivated by such factors as economic rewards based on a compensation system developed through employee participation and involvement in goal setting. Information flows upward, downward, and horizontally. Upward communication is generally accepted—but even where it is not, employees' questions are answered candidly. Decision making is spread widely throughout the organization and is well coordinated.

Styles, Systems, and Productivity   Likert has suggested that as management style moves from system 1 to system 4, the human needs of individuals within the organization tend to be more effectively satisfied over the long term. Thus, an organization that moves toward system 4 tends to become more productive over the long term.

Figure 16.7 illustrates the comparative long- and short-term effects of both system 1 and system 4 on organizational production. Managers may increase production in the short term by using a system 1 management style, because motivation by fear, threat, and punishment is generally effective in the short run. Over the long run, however, this style usually causes production to decrease, primarily because of the long-term nonsatisfaction of organization members' needs and the poor working relationships between managers and subordinates.

Conversely, managers who initiate a system 4 management style will probably face some decline in production initially, but will see an increase in production over the long term. The short-term decline occurs because organization members must adapt to the new system management is implementing. The production increase over the long term materializes as a result of organization members' adjustment to the new system, greater satisfaction of their needs, and good working relationships that develop between managers and subordinates.

This long-term production increase under system 4 can also be related to decision-making differences in the two management systems. Because decisions reached in system 4 are more likely to be thoroughly understood by organization members than decisions reached in system 1, decision implementation is more likely to be efficient and effective in system 4 than in system 1.

NBA Players Union President Patrick Ewing addresses the media during the player lockout of the fall 1998 season. Owners and players made several compromises late in the negotiations. Were monetary incentives the only issue for the players and the owners here?

FIGURE 16.7 ▶ **Comparative long-term and short-term effects of system 1 and system 4 on organizational production**

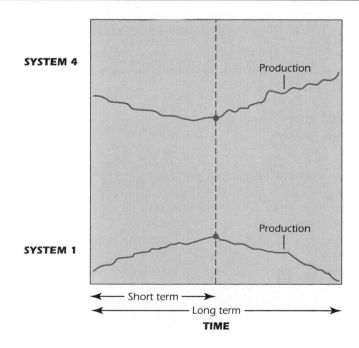

MONETARY INCENTIVES A number of firms make a wide range of money-based compensation programs available to their employees as a form of motivation. For instance, employee stock ownership plans (ESOPs) motivate employees to boost production by offering them shares of company stock as a benefit. Managers are commonly given stock bonuses as an incentive to think more like an owner and ultimately do a better job of building a successful organization. Other incentive plans include lump-sum bonuses—one-time cash payments—and gain-sharing, a plan under which members of a team receive a bonus when their team exceeds a goal. All of these plans link pay closely to performance. Many organizations have found that by putting more of their employees' pay at risk, they can peg more of their total wage costs to sales, which makes expenses more controllable in a downturn.[30]

NONMONETARY INCENTIVES A firm can also keep its employees committed and motivated by nonmonetary means. For instance, some companies have a policy of promoting from within. They go through an elaborate process of advertising jobs internally before going outside to fill vacancies. Another nonmonetary incentive emphasizes quality, on the theory that most workers are unhappy when they know their work goes to producing a shoddy product.[31]

This section of the text has presented information about providing both monetary and nonmonetary incentives to motivate employees. The following People Spotlight feature implies that nonmonetary incentives can be the more powerful motivator.

PEOPLE SPOTLIGHT | Job Satisfaction Is a More Powerful Motivator Than Money at Microsoft

Microsoft Corporation is a world-renowned developer of computer software. This is the company that has developed such popular software packages as Microsoft Windows, a computer operating system; Microsoft Word, a word-processing package; and Microsoft Excel, an electronic spreadsheet.

Microsoft has paid its employees exceedingly well over the years. For example, those with more than six years' seniority stand a very good chance of becoming independently wealthy. The typical salaried employee received a grant of 1,500 shares of Microsoft stock in 1982, which, with regular company stock additions, compounded and untouched, was valued at over $5 million in 1995. There are at present at least 10,000 rank-and-file employees in the company who

stand to gain over $3 billion altogether simply by exercising their options to buy almost 50 million shares of Microsoft stock.

Despite their incredibly high compensation, which makes many Microsoft employees financially independent, these employees have remained startlingly creative and productive over the years. Just what motivates them to continue to do a superb job when they don't need any more money? According to Mike Murray, the vice president for human resources and administration at Microsoft, the fact that these millionaire employees have remained highly productive proves that providing personally satisfying and interesting jobs is a far more effective motivator over the long run than simply handing out more and more money.

BACK TO THE CASE

Chupa can apply behavior modification at American Greetings by rewarding appropriate employee behavior and punishing inappropriate behavior. He would have to use punishment very carefully, however, for if he overuses it, he may destroy his good working relationship with his employees. If a behavior modification program is to be successful, Chupa will have to furnish employees with feedback concerning which behaviors are appropriate and which are inappropriate, reward them differently according to the quality of their performance, tell them what they are doing wrong, punish them privately, and consistently give rewards and punishments when earned.

To use Likert's system 4 management style to motivate employees over the long term, Chupa would have to demonstrate complete confidence in his workers and encourage them to feel completely free to discuss work problems with him. In addition, communication at American Greetings would have to flow freely in all directions within the organization structure, with upward communication generally discussed candidly. Chupa's decision-making process under system 4 would have to involve many employees. He could use the principle of supportive relationships as the basis for his system 4 management style.

No single strategy mentioned in this chapter for motivating organization members would necessarily be more valuable to managers like Chupa than any other of the strategies. In reality, Chupa would probably find that some combination of all of these strategies is most useful in motivating the workforce at American Greetings.

For updated information on the topics in this chapter, Internet exercises, links to related Internet sites, an interactive study guide, and more, visit our companion Web site at

http://www.prenhall.com/certo

Additional information can be found on the inside front and back covers of this text.

ACTION SUMMARY

Reread the learning objectives below. Each objective is followed by questions. Answering these questions accurately will help you retain the most important concepts discussed in this chapter. After answering each question, check your answer against the answer key at the end of this chapter. (*Hint:* If you have any doubts regarding the correct response, consult the page number that follows the answer.)

Circle:

From studying this chapter, I will attempt to acquire

1. A basic understanding of human motivation.

a b c d e   **a.** An individual's inner state that causes him or her to behave in such a way as to ensure accomplishment of a goal is: (a) ambition (b) drive (c) motivation (d) need (e) leadership.

T F   **b.** According to the needs-goal theory of motivation, a fulfilled need is a motivator.

a b c d e   **c.** The following most comprehensively describes how motivation takes place: (a) the Vroom expectancy theory (b) the needs-goal theory (c) the Porter-Lawler theory (d) all of the above (e) none of the above.

2. Insights about various human needs.

a b c d e   **a.** The following is a rank-ordered listing of Maslow's hierarchy of needs from lowest to highest: (a) self-actualization, social, security, physiological, esteem (b) social, security, physiological, self-actualization (c) esteem, self-actualization, security, social, physiological (d) physiological, security, social, esteem, self-actualization (e) physiological, social, esteem, security, self-actualization.

a b c d e   **b.** According to Argyris, as individuals mature, they have an increasing need for: (a) greater dependence (b) a shorter-term perspective (c) more inactivity (d) deeper interests (e) youth.

a b c d e   **c.** The desire to do something better or more efficiently than it has ever been done before is known as the need for: (a) acceleration (b) achievement (c) acclamation (d) actualization (e) none of the above.

3. An appreciation for the importance of motivating organization members.

T F   **a.** From a managerial viewpoint, motivation is the process of furnishing organization members with the opportunity to satisfy their needs by performing productive behaviors within the organization.

T F   **b.** The concepts of motivation and appropriate behavior are closely related.

4. An understanding of various motivation strategies.

a b c d e   **a.** The following is a Theory Y assumption: (a) the average person prefers to be directed (b) most people must be threatened and coerced before they will put forth adequate effort (c) commitment to objectives is a function of the rewards associated with achievement (d) the average person seeks no responsibility (e) all of the above.

b. The process of incorporating motivators into the job situation is called: (a) job enlargement (b) flextime (c) satisfying (d) job enrichment (e) Theory X.

c. Successful behavior modification programs can include: (a) giving rewards and punishments when earned (b) giving rewards according to performance quality (c) telling workers what they are doing wrong (d) punishing workers privately (e) all of the above.

INTRODUCTORY CASE WRAP-UP

CASE DISCUSSSION QUESTIONS

"American Greetings Motivates Through Lateral Moves" (p. 353) and its related Back-to-the-Case sections were written to help you better understand the management concepts contained in this chapter. Answer the following discussion questions about this Introductory Case to enrich your understanding of the chapter content:

1. Do you think it unusual for a manager like Chupa to spend a significant portion of his time motivating his workforce? Explain.

2. Which of the needs in Maslow's hierarchy of needs would the restructuring at American Greetings probably help satisfy? Why? If you have omitted one or more of the needs, explain why the reorganization probably would not satisfy those needs.

3. Can Chupa's restructuring succeed in both cutting production time and motivating workers? Explain fully.

SKILLS EXERCISE: ANALYZING WORKER NEEDS

The Introductory Case discussed how jobs were changed at American Greetings. Old jobs required people to work mainly by themselves and specialize in specific areas like Easter and Christmas cards. New jobs require people to work sometimes in groups in several different areas like Easter and Christmas cards, birthday ribbons, humorous mugs, and Valentine's Day gift bags. Between the new and old jobs, is there a difference in the human needs that workers have the opportunity to satisfy? If yes, explain the differences in detail. Use Maslow's hierarchy of needs to guide your analysis and related discussion.

ISSUES FOR REVIEW AND DISCUSSION

1. Define *motivation* and explain why managers must understand it.
2. Describe the difference between process and content theories of motivation.
3. Draw and explain a model that illustrates the needs-goal theory of motivation.
4. Explain Vroom's expectancy theory of motivation.
5. List and explain three characteristics of the motivation process described in the Porter-Lawler motivation theory that are not contained in either the needs-goal theory of motivation or Vroom's expectancy theories.
6. What is the main theme of the equity theory of motivation?
7. What does Maslow's hierarchy of needs tell us about the relationship between personal needs and workplace needs?
8. What concerns have been expressed about Maslow's hierarchy of needs?
9. What are the similarities and differences between Maslow's hierarchy of needs and Alderfer's ERG theory?
10. Explain Argyris' maturity-immaturity continuum.
11. What is the need for achievement?
12. Summarize the characteristics of individuals who have a high need for achievement.
13. Explain "motivating organization members."
14. Is the process of motivating organization members important to managers? Explain.
15. How can managerial communication be used to motivate organization members?
16. Describe Theory X, Theory Y, and Theory Z. What does each of these theories tell us about motivating organization members?
17. What is the difference between job enlargement and job rotation?
18. Describe the relationship of hygiene factors, motivating factors, and job enrichment.
19. Define *flextime* and *behavior modification*.
20. What basic ingredients are necessary to make a behavior modification program successful?
21. In your own words, summarize Likert's four management systems.
22. What effect do Likert's systems 1 and 4 generally have on organizational production in both the short and the long term? Why do these effects occur?
23. List three nonmonetary incentives that you personally would find desirable as an employee. Why would these incentives be desirable to you?

CASE STUDY: Why Bart Simpson Flies Western Pacific Airlines

Motivation is the inner state that causes an individual to behave in a way that ensures the accomplishment of some goal. Management policies at Ed Beauvais' new airline, Western Pacific, reflect his belief in the importance of a motivated workforce to a company's bottom line.

Convinced that low-cost, low-fare flights should make for a sound and profitable business, Beauvais spent a year reflecting on what had gone wrong with his previous venture, America West Airlines. He then looked to Oklahoma billionaire Edward Gaylord and oil heiress Margaret Hunt Hill for backing to try again. Beauvais' personal motivation was so convincing that they gave him $5.5 million each. Other investors kicked in an additional $17 million, and $48 million was raised from a public offering. Beauvais was back in business with Western Pacific Airlines.

Western Pacific is a low-cost airline similar in some ways to America West. Beauvais hopes both to borrow successful strategies from his experience with America West and to create new strategies for overcoming the difficulties that brought down his former airline. For one thing, Beauvais has been able to offer an unembellished travel option to potential customers by flying only Boeing 737-300s, thereby simplifying maintenance, training, and inventory control.

One of the mistakes that Beauvais will not repeat with Western Pacific is going head-to-head with Southwest Airlines, the inventors of low-cost airline travel. One of the strategies he hopes will bring success is maintaining routes out of Colorado Springs and only offering routes accessible to the 737s. This strategy gives Beauvais a chance to take advantage of the $5 billion Denver International Airport boondoggle. "Beauvais is right on top of a gold mine," says Michael Boyd, president of Aviation Systems Research Corporation.

Beauvais is counting on such customer- and equipment-based strategies to keep his new airline successful (eight months after Western Pacific began operations, Beauvais' initial $100,000 investment in stock was worth several million dollars). However, he is repeating one important and previously successful strategy—ensuring that his workforce is highly motivated. He strives, for instance, to create an atmosphere of respect and employee involvement. Employees are encouraged to become stockholders and are offered opportunities to buy stock at discounted rates. An owner-employee is more motivated to save the company money and to look for ways to improve service and cut costs, Beauvais figures. Owner-pilots take greater responsibility for their aircraft.

Employees are treated as individuals and encouraged to develop ideas in their own ways. Similarly, managers are instructed to coach, cheer on, and help employees shape their ideas. Employees are encouraged to communicate to all levels of the hierarchy with no fear of reprisals; thus there is a free flow of communication and a near-level playing field at Western Pacific. This open-door policy contributes to a highly motivated staff that is unafraid to speak up and eager to work together for the benefit of the company.

By offering a friendly and creative workplace where employees are allowed to manage themselves, Western Pacific is able to maintain a highly motivated, energetic workforce. Beauvais' flight attendants run contests and crack jokes aboard aircraft bearing pictures of the TV cartoon Simpsons, a 38-foot showgirl, and other images that advertisers pay $800,000 to display. Such goings-on bear out Ed Beauvais' philosophy: "We think folks should have a lot of fun when they fly with us." This approach holds for his employees as well as his customers.

Western Pacific employee benefit programs are designed to encourage employee input; they are people-oriented and employee-friendly. For example, the company offers maternity leave and counseling programs. Job-share and work-at-home programs are under consideration, as are programs to reward attendance with discounted tickets to special events. Another program being considered is a prepayment plan whereby employees may borrow against future salary to purchase big-ticket items, take vacations, or invest.

Such programs existed at American West Airlines, and Beauvais still believes that they are key to a motivated staff and a successful business. "If people enjoy working here, then the bottom line is they will provide the best customer service," says Director of Human Relations Glenn Goldberg.

QUESTIONS

1. How are the process theories of motivation implemented in the Western Pacific model?
2. Use Maslow's hierarchy to identify the needs addressed in Beauvais' approach to employee relations.
3. Would Beauvais be considered a Theory X, Theory Y, or Theory Z manager? Why?
4. Why do you think Beauvais considers his style of management to be critical to the success of the company?

Groups, Teams, and Corporate Culture

STUDENT LEARNING OBJECTIVES

From studying this chapter, I will attempt to acquire

1. A definition of the term *group* as used in the context of management

2. A thorough understanding of the difference between formal and informal groups

3. Knowledge of the types of formal groups that exist in organizations

4. An understanding of how managers can determine which groups exist in an organization

5. An appreciation for what teams are and how to manage them

6. Insights about managing corporate culture to enhance organizational success

CHAPTER OUTLINE

Introductory Case: *Work Groups Are Important to Progress at Rolls-Royce*

GROUPS

KINDS OF GROUPS IN ORGANIZATIONS
Formal Groups

Diversity Spotlight: *Managing a Diverse Salesforce Takes Special Insight at Equitable*

Ethics Spotlight: *Calvary Hospital Forms Ethics Committees*
Informal Groups

MANAGING WORK GROUPS
Determining Group Existence
Understanding the Evolution of Informal Groups

TEAMS
Groups versus Teams

Management and the Internet: *The Virtual Team*
Types of Teams in Organizations

Across Industries: *Motorcycle Manufacturing—Cross-Functional Teams Design New Products at Harley-Davidson*
Stages of Team Development
Team Effectiveness
Trust and Effective Teams

CORPORATE CULTURE
The Significance of Corporate Culture

WORK GROUPS ARE IMPORTANT TO PROGRESS AT ROLLS-ROYCE

REMINDER: THE INTRODUCTORY CASE WRAP-UP (P. 397) CONTAINS DISCUSSION QUESTIONS AND A SKILLS EXERCISE TO FURTHER ILLUSTRATE THE APPLICATION OF CHAPTER CONCEPTS TO THIS VIGNETTE.

In Crewe, England, Dennis Jones lifts a long slice of stainless steel and peers down the edge, squinting one eye as if aiming a rifle. He likes what he sees.

The piece is slightly bowed, he explains, to create the illusion from a distance of a straight line, "like a column on the Parthenon." "It's perfect for a Rolls Royce radiator grill," says Jones, who has built the units for 22 years in a shop at the company's factory here. "We can't afford to make many mistakes," he concedes.

In the early 1990s, however, Rolls-Royce did make some mistakes. Combined with a worldwide recession, a shift in tastes, even among customers for one of the world's ultimate status symbols, caused sales to slip; Rolls lost $54.5 million in 1991.

But by 1995, Rolls-Royce was at least on the threshold of a turnaround. An overall increase in retail sales of 10 percent was above the industry average and included an increase of 25 percent in North and South America. Chief executive Chris Woodwark attributes the improved performance to more focused marketing strategies, the introduction of competitive leasing programs, and greater responsiveness to customer needs. For instance, at the Mulliner Park Ward division, which operates under its own management, engineers work directly with customers to implement special and often unique requirements.

Streamlined operations have made it possible for engineers to respond more quickly to customer requests, and chairman Peter Ward readily admits that Rolls-Royce's improved performance has resulted in part from the adaptation of so-called "lean manufacturing" techniques pioneered by high-volume Japanese automakers.

Over the past several years, Ward has installed a computer-controlled production system, slashed 1,300 jobs, and reorganized workers into Japanese-style teams. Rolls-Royce now has its own version of such Japanese innovations as just-in-time parts delivery and continuous quality improvement.

Rolls-Royce officials attribute the company's recent turnaround to such factors as more focused marketing strategies, greater responsiveness to customer needs, and more efficient production techniques.

"We've really gone further than the Japanese," he asserts, adding that some of the moves are only bringing Rolls-Royce closer to its original structure. Before World War II, the car maker used a much more open system, with workers learning a variety of skills and having closer contact with management and engineers. This faded during the 1960s and 1970s, as unions sharply defined workers' tasks and the shop floor became more insulated from the management suite.

Not that any change is easy in a company as tradition-bound as Rolls-Royce, where workers are often second- or third-generation employees. The changes also are grating against Britain's class structure. Workers now routinely get pulled off the floor for "brown-paper sessions," in which engineers and workers sit together, dissecting and critiquing production processes on long sheets of brown paper taped to the wall. Company officials say some of the best worker input still comes, however, from yellow notes stuck on by workers when no one else is around.

What's Ahead

The Introductory Case highlights the important role that new work groups or teams are playing in solving problems at Rolls-Royce. The material in this chapter should give a manager like Peter Ward, Rolls-Royce's chairman, some insight into the broad area of work group management. This chapter proceeds as follows:

1. It defines groups
2. Next it discusses the kinds of groups that exist in organizations
3. Finally, it explains what steps managers should take to manage groups appropriately

The previous chapters in this section dealt with three primary activities of the influencing function: communication, leadership, and motivation. This chapter focuses on managing groups, the last major influencing activity to be discussed in this text. As with the other three activities, managing work groups requires guiding the behavior of organization members in ways that increase the probability of reaching organizational objectives.

GROUPS

A **group** is any number of people who (1) interact with one another, (2) are psychologically aware of one another, and (3) perceive themselves to be a group.

To deal with groups appropriately, managers must have a thorough understanding of the nature of groups in organizations.[1] As used in management-related discussions, a **group** is not simply a gathering of people. Rather it is "any number of people who (1) interact with one another, (2) are psychologically aware of one another, and (3) perceive themselves to be a group."[2] Groups are characterized by frequent communication among members over time and a size small enough to permit each member to communicate with all other members on a face-to-face basis. As a result of this communication, each group member influences and is influenced by all other group members.

The study of groups is important to managers because the most common ingredient of all organizations is people and the most common technique for accomplishing work through these people is dividing them into work groups. In a classic article, Cartwright and Lippitt list four additional reasons managers should study groups:[3]

1. Groups exist in all kinds of organizations
2. Groups inevitably form in all facets of organizational existence
3. Groups can cause either desirable or undesirable consequences within the organization
4. An understanding of groups can help managers raise the probability that the groups with which they work will cause desirable consequences within the organization[4]

KINDS OF GROUPS IN ORGANIZATIONS

Organizational groups are typically divided into two basic types: formal and informal.

FIGURE 17.1 ► A formal group

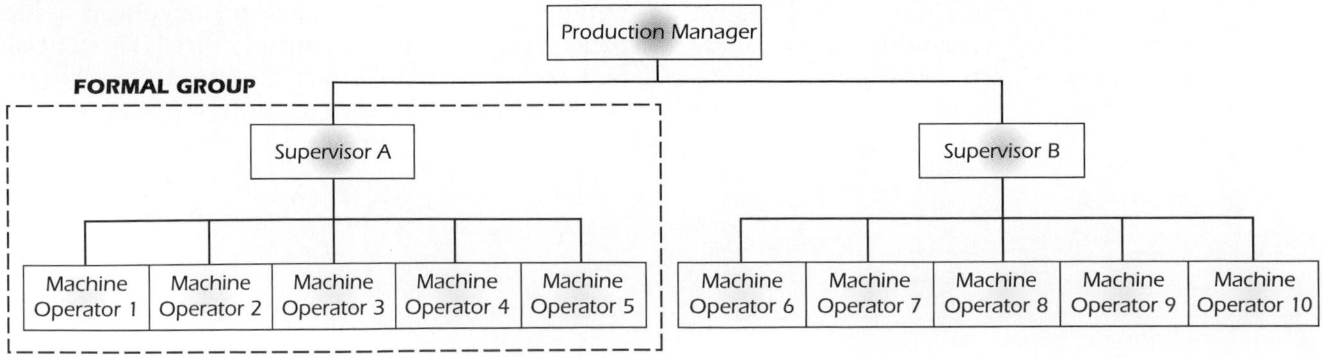

A **formal group** is a group that exists within an organization by virtue of management decree to perform tasks that enhance the attainment of organizational objectives.[5] Figure 17.1 is an organization chart showing a formal group. The placement of organization members in such areas as marketing departments, personnel departments, and production departments are examples of establishing formal groups.

Actually, organizations are made up of a number of formal groups that exist at various organizational levels. The coordination of and communication among these groups is the responsibility of managers, or supervisors, commonly called "linking pins."

A **formal group** is a group that exists in an organization by virtue of management decree to perform tasks that enhance the attainment of organizational objectives.

DIVERSITY SPOTLIGHT | Managing a Diverse Salesforce Takes Special Insight at Equitable

An example of a formal group that must be managed in many organizations is a salesforce. According to José S. Suquet, manager of Equitable Life Assurance Company's South Florida agency, managing a salesforce in a multicultural, multiethnic environment requires special insight and understanding. Suquet says that the key to management success is not to overcompensate for cultural diversity, but to be consistent across the board. His experience suggests that regardless of culture, employees need to feel that they are being treated fairly and that managers do not mark "favorites" for special treatment.

Experience also indicates that the first critical step in successfully managing a diverse salesforce is recruiting. Managers should not try to clone themselves, but rather should attempt to recruit people who reflect the market—that is, they should struggle to build a salesforce that represents the diverse ethnic market segments the company wishes to penetrate. Building such a salesforce should help to ensure that the organization's salespeople are able to communicate well with customers. To this end, managers should determine the language or languages that salespeople need to speak and be sensitive to customs, jargon, and individual needs that are relevant to a particular organizational situation. When leading a diverse salesforce, managers should also keep in mind that simply because employees have the same ethnic and cultural backgrounds does not automatically mean they will have the same opinions about organizational issues, approach problems in the same way, or be motivated by the same organizational incentives.

Formal groups are clearly defined and structured. The next sections discuss the following topics:

1. The basic kinds of formal groups
2. Examples of formal groups as they exist in organizations
3. The four stages of formal group development

KINDS OF FORMAL GROUPS Formal groups are commonly divided into command groups and task groups. **Command groups** are formal groups that are outlined in the chain of command on an organization chart. They typically handle routine organizational activities.

Task groups are formal groups of organization members who interact with one another to accomplish most of the organization's nonroutine tasks. Although task groups are usually made up of members on the same organizational level, they can consist of people from different levels in the organizational hierarchy. For example, a manager might establish a task group to consider the feasibility of manufacturing some new product and include representatives from various levels of such organizational areas as production, market research, and sales.[6]

A **command group** is a formal group that is outlined in the chain of command on an organization chart. Command groups handle routine activities.

A **task group** is a formal group of organization members who interact with one another to accomplish nonroutine organizational tasks. Members of any one task group can and often do come from various levels and segments of an organization.

BACK TO THE CASE

In order for a manager like Peter Ward to be able to lead work groups, he must understand the definition of the term *group* and grasp the idea that there are several types of groups that exist

(continued)

EXAMPLES OF FORMAL GROUPS Two formal groups that are often established in organizations are committees and work teams. Committees are the more traditional formal group; work teams have only recently gained acceptance and support in U.S. organizations. The part of this text dealing with the managerial function of organizing emphasized command groups; however, the examples here emphasize task groups.

Committees A **committee** is a group of individuals charged with performing some type of specific activity and is usually classified as a task group. From a managerial viewpoint, there are four major reasons for establishing committees:[7]

1. To allow organization members to exchange ideas
2. To generate suggestions and recommendations that can be offered to other organizational units
3. To develop new ideas for solving existing organizational problems
4. To assist in the development of organizational policies

Committees exist in virtually all organizations and at all organizational levels. As Figure 17.2 suggests, however, the larger the organization, the greater the probability that it will use committees on a regular basis. The following two sections discuss why managers should use committees and what makes a committee successful.

A **committee** is a task group that is charged with performing some type of specific activity.

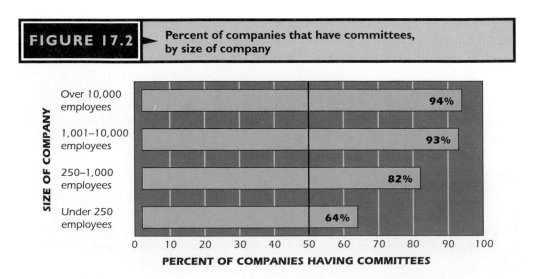

FIGURE 17.2 ▶ **Percent of companies that have committees, by size of company**

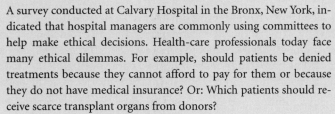

ETHICS SPOTLIGHT | Calvary Hospital Forms Ethics Committees

A survey conducted at Calvary Hospital in the Bronx, New York, indicated that hospital managers are commonly using committees to help make ethical decisions. Health-care professionals today face many ethical dilemmas. For example, should patients be denied treatments because they cannot afford to pay for them or because they do not have medical insurance? Or: Which patients should receive scarce transplant organs from donors?

To better handle such ethical dilemmas, hospital administrators are establishing ethics committees, and to get practical and worthwhile input from these committees, they are asking representatives from many different areas of health care to serve on them—nurses as well as physicians. Nurses are heavily involved in patient care, so their views on ethical questions can be extremely valuable.

The primary purpose of these committees is to help hospital administrators and other health-care professionals ensure that appropriate decisions are made in response to ethical dilemmas. Organization members seem willing to sit on ethics committees because participation allows them to express to management various ethical concerns they have about their work situation.

Why Managers Should Use Committees. Managers generally agree that committees have several uses in organizations.

► Committees can improve the quality of decision making. As more people become involved in making a decision, the strengths and weaknesses of various alternatives tend to be discussed in greater detail and the chances of reaching a higher-quality decision increase.

► Committees encourage the expression of honest opinions. Committee members feel protected enough to say what they really think because the group output of a committee cannot be associated with any one member of that group.

► Committees also tend to increase organization members' participation in decision making and thereby enhance the chances of widespread support of decisions. Another result of this increased participation is that committee members satisfy their social or esteem needs through committee work.

► Finally, committees ensure the representation of important groups in the decision-making process. Managers must choose committee members wisely, however, to achieve appropriate representation, for if a committee does not adequately represent various interest groups, any decision it comes to may well be counter to the interests of some important organizational group.

Although executives vary somewhat in their enthusiasm about using committees in organizations, a study reported by McLeod and Jones concludes that most executives favor using committees. The executives who took part in this study said they got significantly more information from organizational sources other than committees, but found the information from committees more valuable than the information from any other source. Nevertheless, some top executives express only qualified support for using committees as work groups, and others had negative feelings toward committees. Still, the executives who feel positive about committees or who display qualified acceptance of them in general outnumber those who look upon committees negatively.

What Makes Committees Successful. Although committees have become an accepted management tool, managerial action taken to establish and run them is a major variable in determining their degree of success.

Procedural Steps. Several procedural steps can be taken to increase the probability that a committee will be successful:[8]

► The committee's goals should be clearly defined, preferably in writing. This will focus the committee's activities and reduce the time members devote to discussing just what it is the committee is supposed to be doing.

► The committee's authority should be specified. Is it merely to investigate, advise, and recommend, or is it authorized to implement decisions?

- The optimum size of the committee should be determined. With fewer than 5 members, the advantages of group work may be diminished. With more than 10 or 15 members, the committee may become unwieldy. Although optimal size varies with the circumstances, the ideal number of committee members for most tasks seems to be from 5 to 10.
- A chairperson should be selected on the basis of ability to run an efficient meeting—that is, the ability to keep committee members from getting bogged down in irrelevancies and to see to it that the necessary paperwork gets done.
- Appointing a permanent secretary to handle communications is often useful.
- The agenda and all supporting material for the meeting should be distributed before the meeting takes place. When members have a chance to study each item beforehand, they are likely to stick to the point and be prepared to make informed contributions.
- Meetings should start on time, and their ending time should be announced at the outset.

People-Oriented Guidelines. In addition to these procedural steps, managers can follow a number of more people-oriented guidelines to increase the probability that a committee will succeed. In particular, a manager can raise the quality of committee discussions by doing the following:[9]

- *Rephrasing ideas already expressed*—This rephrasing ensures that the manager as well as other people on the committee clearly understand what has been said.
- *Bringing all members into active participation*—Every committee member is a potential source of useful information, so the manager should serve as a catalyst to spark individual participation whenever appropriate.
- *Stimulating further thought by members*—The manager should encourage committee members to think ideas through carefully and thoroughly, for only this type of analysis will generate high-quality committee output.

Groupthink. Managers should also help the committee avoid a phenomenon called "groupthink." **Groupthink** is the mode of thinking that group members engage in when the desire for agreement so dominates the group that it overrides the need to realistically appraise alternative problem solutions. Groups tend to slip into groupthink when their members become overly concerned about being too harsh in judging one another's ideas and lose their objectivity. Such groups tend to seek complete support on every issue to avoid conflicts that might endanger the "we-feeling" atmosphere.[10]

Groupthink is the mode of thinking that group members engage in when the desire for agreement so dominates the group that it overrides the need to realistically appraise alternate problem solutions.

A **work team** is a task group used in organizations to achieve greater organizational flexibility or to cope with rapid growth.

Work Teams   **Work teams** are another example of task groups used in organizations. Contemporary work teams in the United States evolved out of the problem-solving teams—based on Japanese-style quality circles—that were widely adopted in the 1970s. Problem-solving teams consist of 5 to 12 volunteer members from different areas of the department who meet weekly to discuss ways to improve quality and efficiency.

Special-Purpose and Self-Managed Teams. Special-purpose teams evolved in the early to middle 1980s out of problem-solving teams. The typical special-purpose team consists of workers and union representatives meeting together to collaborate on operational decisions at all levels. The aim is to create an atmosphere conducive to quality and productivity improvements.

Special-purpose teams laid the foundation for the self-managed work teams that arose in the 1990s, and it is these teams that appear to be the wave of the future. Self-managed teams consist of 5 to 15 employees who work together to produce an entire product. Members learn all the tasks required to produce the product and rotate from job to job. Self-managed teams even take over such managerial duties as scheduling work and vacations and ordering materials. Because these work teams give employees so much control over their jobs, they represent a fundamental change in how work is organized. (Self-managed teams will be discussed in some detail later in this chapter.)

Employing work teams allows a firm to draw on the talent and creativity of all its employees, not just a few maverick inventors or top executives, to make important decisions. As product quality becomes more and more important in the business world, companies will need to rely more and more on the team approach in order to stay competitive. Consider a recent situation at Yellow Freight Systems, a shipping company, whose management was intent on giving

Wal-Mart is building its first full-fledged supermarket. Will organizing work teams in this environment present any new challenges for management? What are some of the advantages the team structure might bring to the new venture, and to the members of the teams?

its customers excellent service. To address this concern, management established a work team made up of employees from many different parts of the company, including marketing, sales, operations, and human resources. The overall task of the work team was to run an excellence-in-service campaign that management had initiated.[11]

BACK TO THE CASE

Rolls-Royce's management could decide to form a committee to achieve some specific goal. A committee might be formed, for example, to offer recommendations on how to enhance the quality of the company's automobiles. This quality committee could encourage various Rolls-Royce departments to exchange quality improvement ideas and generate related suggestions to management. It could also improve Rolls-Royce's decision making in general by encouraging honest feedback from employees about quality issues in the organization. Such a committee could be used as well to urge Rolls-Royce's employees to participate more seriously in improving the quality of the automobiles made by the company. Finally, the committee could help Rolls-Royce's management ensure that all appropriate departments are represented in important quality decisions so that whenever Rolls-Royce takes an action to improve the quality of its automobiles, every important angle will be considered, including design, production, marketing, and sales.

Although committees *can* be useful, a poorly run committee wastes a lot of time. Therefore, when setting up a quality committee at Rolls-Royce, management should encourage committee members to take certain steps to enhance the committee's success. For example, the committee should clearly define its goals and the limits of its authority: Is the committee supposed to merely come up with quality improvement ideas, or is it also supposed to initiate a program for implementing those ideas?

The quality committee should not have too few or too many members. Issues such as the need to appoint an administrator to handle communications and a chairperson who works well with people must be addressed. The committee needs a chairperson who can rephrase ideas clearly so that everyone understands them and who can get members to participate in discussions and think about the issues without slipping into groupthink. A company like Rolls-Royce wants its committees to generate original ideas, not a unanimous opinion where the major virtue is that it enabled the committee to avoid conflict.

STAGES OF FORMAL GROUP DEVELOPMENT Another requirement for successfully managing formal groups is understanding the stages of formal group development. In a classic book, Bernard Bass suggested that group development is a four-stage process that unfolds as the group learns how to use its resources.[12] Although these stages may not occur sequentially, for the purpose of clarity, the discussion that follows will assume that they do.

The Acceptance Stage It is common for members of a new group to mistrust one another somewhat initially. The acceptance stage occurs only after this initial mistrust melts and the group has been transformed into one characterized by mutual trust and acceptance.

The Communication and Decision-Making Stage Once they have passed through the acceptance stage, group members are better able to communicate frankly with one another. This frank communication provides the basis for establishing and using an effective group decision-making mechanism.

The Group Solidarity Stage Group solidarity comes naturally as the mutual acceptance of group members increases and communication and decision making continue within the group. At this stage, members become more involved in group activities and cooperate, rather than compete, with one another. Members find belonging to the group extremely satisfying and are committed to enhancing the group's overall success.

The Group Control Stage A natural result of group solidarity is group control. In this stage, group members attempt to maximize the group's success by matching individual abilities with group activities and by assisting one another. Flexibility and informality usually characterize this stage.

As a group passes through each of these four stages, it generally becomes more mature and effective—and therefore more productive. The group that reaches maximum maturity and effectiveness is characterized by the following traits in its members:

- ► *Members function as a unit*—The group works as a team. Members do not disturb one another to the point of interfering with their collaboration.
- ► *Members participate effectively in group effort*—Members work hard when there is something to do. They seldom loaf, even if they have the opportunity to do so.
- ► *Members are oriented toward a single goal*—Group members work for the common purpose; they do not waste group resources by moving in different directions.
- ► *Members have the equipment, tools, and skills necessary to attain the group's goals*—Members are taught the various parts of their jobs by experts and strive to acquire whatever resources they need to attain group objectives.
- ► *Members ask and receive suggestions, opinions, and information from one another*—A member who is uncertain about something stops working and asks another member for information. Group members generally talk to one another openly and frequently.

BACK TO THE CASE

Managers in companies like Rolls-Royce must be patient and understand that it will take some time for a newly formed group to develop into a productive work unit. Like the members of any new group, the work teams at Rolls-Royce must learn to trust and accept one another, and then to freely communicate and exchange ideas within the group. Once acceptance and easy communication are established, group solidarity and control will naturally follow. In other words, the group members first get involved, then cooperate, and finally work to maximize the group's success.

All this is true as well of the quality committee we used as an example in the previous Back-to-the-Case section. Rolls-Royce's management must be patient and let the quality committee ma-

---

► INFORMAL GROUPS

Informal groups, the second major kind of group that can exist within an organization, are groups that develop naturally as people interact. An **informal group** is defined as a collection of individuals whose common work experiences result in the development of a system of interpersonal relations that extend beyond those established by management.[13]

As Figure 17.3 shows, informal group structures can deviate significantly from formal group structures. As is true of Supervisor A in the figure, an organization member can belong to more than one informal group at the same time. In contrast to formal groups, informal groups are not highly structured in procedure and are not formally recognized by management.

The next sections discuss the following subjects:

1. Various kinds of informal groups that exist in organizations
2. The benefits people usually reap from belonging to informal groups

An **informal group** is a collection of individuals whose common work experiences result in the development of a system of interpersonal relations that extend beyond those established by management.

KINDS OF INFORMAL GROUPS
Informal groups are divided into two general types: interest groups and friendship groups. **Interest groups** are informal groups that gain and maintain membership primarily because of a common concern members have about a specific issue. An example is a group of workers pressing management for better pay or working conditions. Once the interest or concern that instigated the formation of the informal group has been eliminated, the group will probably disband.

As its name implies, **friendship groups** are informal groups that form in organizations because of the personal affiliation members have with one another. Such personal factors as recreational interests, race, gender, and religion serve as foundations for friendship groups. As with interest groups, the membership of friendship groups tends to change over time. Here, however, membership changes as friendships dissolve or new friendships are made.

An **interest group** is an informal group that gains and maintains membership primarily because of a common concern members have about a specific issue.

A **friendship group** is an informal group that forms in organizations because of the personal affiliation members have with one another.

BENEFITS OF INFORMAL GROUP MEMBERSHIP
Informal groups tend to develop in organizations because of various benefits that group members obtain:[14]

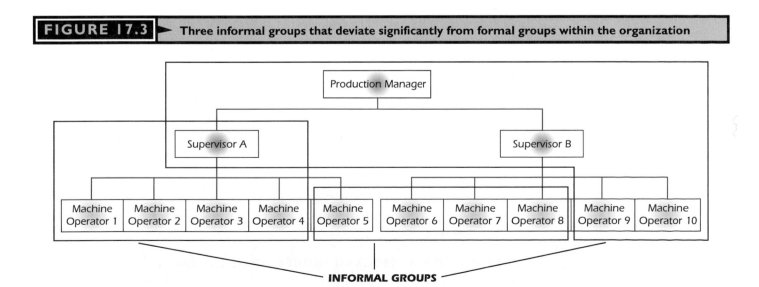

FIGURE 17.3 ► **Three informal groups that deviate significantly from formal groups within the organization**

1. Perpetuation of social and cultural values that group members consider important
2. Status and social satisfaction that people might not enjoy without group membership
3. Increased ease of communication among group members
4. Increased desirability of the overall work environment

These benefits may be one reason that employees who are on fixed shifts or who continually work with the same groups tend to be more satisfied with their work than employees whose shifts are continually changing.

BACK TO THE CASE

Issues pertaining to informal groups could affect the success of formal work groups at Rolls-Royce. Employees sometimes form interest groups because they are concerned about a certain issue. For example, certain minority employees might form a group to enhance their opportunities for professional growth at Rolls-Royce. In addition, employees form friendship groups, which ease communication and increase members' satisfaction in working for a company. Because such informal groups can improve the work environment for everyone involved, managers' encouragement of their development can be very advantageous for the company.

Perhaps Rolls-Royce's management can accelerate the maturing of its quality committee by drawing into it people who already know and trust one another through membership in one or more informal groups at Rolls-Royce—for example, members of a company bowling or softball team. The trust already developed among employees through past informal group affiliations could help the formal quality committee develop into a productive group more quickly.

MANAGING WORK GROUPS

To manage work groups effectively, managers must simultaneously consider the effects of both formal and informal group factors on organizational productivity. This consideration requires two steps:

1. Determining group existence
2. Understanding the evolution of informal groups

DETERMINING GROUP EXISTENCE

Sociometry is an analytical tool that can be used to determine what informal groups exist in an organization and who the members of those groups are.

The most important step that managers need to take in managing work groups is to determine what informal groups exist within the organization and who their members are. **Sociometry** is an analytical tool managers can use to do this. They can also use sociometry to get information on the internal workings of an informal group, including the identity of the group leader, the relative status of group members, and the group's communication networks.[15] This information on informal groups, combined with an understanding of the established formal groups shown on the organization chart, will give managers a complete picture of the organization's group structure.

SOCIOMETRIC ANALYSIS The procedure for performing a sociometric analysis in an organization is quite basic. Various organization members simply are asked, through either an interview or a questionnaire, to name several other organization members with whom they would like to spend free time. A sociogram is then constructed to summarize the informal relationships among group members. **Sociograms** are diagrams that visually link individuals within the population queried according to the number of times they were chosen and whether the choice was reciprocated.

A **sociogram** is a sociometric diagram that summarizes the personal feelings of organization members about the people in the organization with whom they would like to spend free time.

APPLYING THE SOCIOGRAM MODEL Figure 17.4 shows two sample sociograms based on a classic study of two groups of boys in a summer camp—the Bulldogs and the Red

FIGURE 17.4 → Sample sociograms

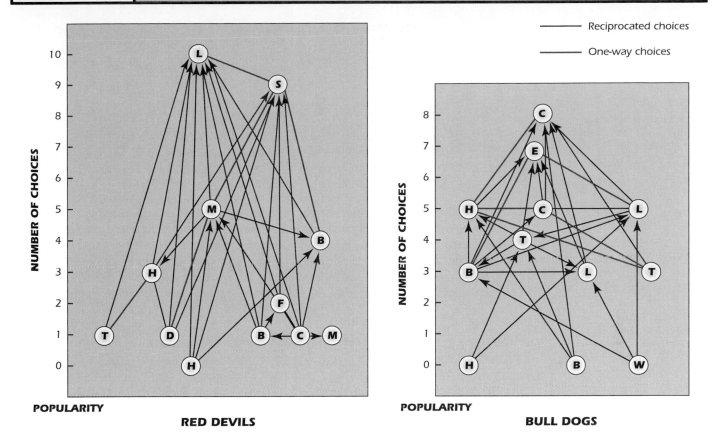

RED DEVILS

BULL DOGS

Devils. An analysis of these sociograms leads to several interesting conclusions. First, more boys within the Bulldogs than within the Red Devils were chosen as being desirable to spend time with. This probably implies that the Bulldogs are a closer-knit informal group than the Red Devils. Second, the greater the number of times an individual was chosen, the more likely it was that the individual would be the group leader. Thus individuals C and E in Figure 17.4 are probably Bulldog leaders, while L and S are probably Red Devil leaders. Third, communication between L and most other Red Devils members is likely to occur directly, whereas communication between C and other bulldogs is likely to pass through other group members.

Sociometric analysis can give managers many useful insights concerning the informal groups within their organization. Managers who do not want to perform a formal sociometric analysis can at least casually gather information on what form a sociogram might take in a particular situation. They can pick up this information through normal conversations with other organization members as well as through observations of how various organization members relate to one another.

►UNDERSTANDING THE EVOLUTION OF INFORMAL GROUPS

As we have seen, the first prerequisite for managing groups effectively is knowing what groups exist within an organization and what characterizes the membership of those groups. The second prerequisite is understanding how informal groups evolve. This understanding will give managers some insights on how to encourage the development of appropriate informal groups, that is, groups that support the attainment of organizational objectives and whose members maintain good relationships with formal work groups.

HOMANS' MODEL Perhaps the most widely accepted framework for explaining the evolution of informal groups was developed by George Homans.[16] Figure 17.5 broadly summarizes his theory. According to Homans, the informal group is established to provide satisfac-

FIGURE 17.5 ▶ Homans' ideas on how informal groups develop

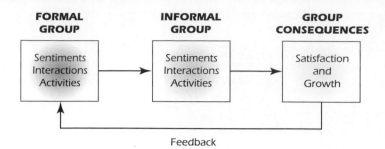

tion and growth for its members. At the same time, the sentiments, interactions, and activities that emerge within an informal group result from the sentiments, interactions, and activities that already exist within a formal group. Given these two premises, it follows that feedback on the functioning of the informal group can give managers ideas about how to modify the formal group so as to increase the probability that informal group members will achieve the satisfaction and growth they desire. The ultimate consequence will be to reinforce the solidarity and productiveness of the formal group—to the advantage of the organization.

Applying the Homans' Model　To see what Homans' concept involves, suppose that 12 factory workers are members of a formal work group that manufactures toasters. According to Homans, as these workers interact to assemble toasters, they might discover common personal interests that encourage the evolution of one or more informal groups that would maximize the satisfaction and growth of their members. Once established, these informal groups will probably resist changes in the formal work group that threaten the satisfaction and growth of the informal group's members. On the other hand, modifications in the formal work group that enhance the satisfaction and growth of the informal group's members will tend to be welcomed.

BACK TO THE CASE

For a company such as Rolls-Royce to be successful, managers must know how both formal and informal groups affect organizational productivity. Thus they need to determine what informal groups exist and who the group members are, as well as understand how these groups form. Armed with this information, managers can strive to make their work groups more effective.

One analytical tool Rolls-Royce's management can use to get information about informal groups within the company is sociometry. That is, managers can design a questionnaire asking their employees whom they spend time with and then construct a sociogram to summarize this information. Of course, managers might choose to do a more casual analysis by simply talking to their employees and observing how they interact with one another.

Rolls-Royce's managers should also realize that an organization's formal structure influences how informal groups develop within it. Assume, for example, that in one department at Rolls-Royce there are 30 people working on automobile design. Many of them are interested in sports, have become friends because of this common interest, and work well together as a result. When the department manager needs to make some changes in this design department, he or she should try to accommodate these informal friendship groups to keep their members satisfied. Actions that interfere with this productive friendship group—such as transferring one or more of its members out of the design department—should be taken only for very good reason.

The preceding sections of this chapter discussed groups—what they are, what kinds exist in organizations, and how such groups should be managed. This section focuses on a special type of group: teams. It covers the following topics:

1. Difference between groups and teams
2. Types of teams that exist in organizations
3. Stages of development that teams go through
4. What constitutes an effective team
5. Relationship between trust and team effectiveness

▶ GROUPS VERSUS TEAMS

The terms *group* and *team* are not synonymous. As we have seen, a group consists of any number of people who interact with one another, are psychologically aware of one another, and think of themselves as a group. A **team** is a group whose members influence one another toward the accomplishment of an organizational objective(s).

Not all groups in organizations are teams, but all teams are groups. A group qualifies as a team only if its members focus on helping one another to accomplish organizational objectives. In today's quickly changing business environment, teams have emerged as a requirement for success.[17] Therefore, good managers constantly try to help groups become teams. This part of the chapter provides insights on how managers can facilitate the evolution of groups into teams.

The text has defined "team" and emphasized the difference between a group and a team. The following Management and the Internet feature discusses a new type of organizational team—the virtual team—made possible mainly by the acquisition of advanced Internet technology by organizations.

> A **team** is a group whose members influence one another toward the accomplishment of (an) organizational objective(s).

MANAGEMENT AND THE INTERNET — The Virtual Team

Virtual teams are organizational teams whose members, though separated by several miles or even continents, are able to work together because they can communicate through modern Internet technology. The technological advancements that have made virtual teams possible include the Internet, fax machines, e-mail, videoconferencing, and computer software called groupware. The last electronically links team members via computer, allowing them to instantly trade and manipulate information.

Virtual teams are bound to become more prevalent in organizations into the next century because of the growing globalization and complication of business. Globalization requires organization members to work together across vast distances, and today's complex business problems demand the attention of the best minds in the organization, regardless of their physical location. The management challenge presented by virtual teams is how to get people to work together as a team even though they cannot meet face-to-face.

▶ TYPES OF TEAMS IN ORGANIZATIONS

Organizational teams take many different forms. The following sections discuss three types of teams commonly found in today's organizations: problem-solving teams, self-managed teams, and cross-functional teams.

PROBLEM-SOLVING TEAMS Management confronts many different organizational problems daily. Examples are production systems that are not manufacturing products at the desired levels of quality; workers who appear to be listless and uninvolved; and managers who are basing their decisions on inaccurate information.

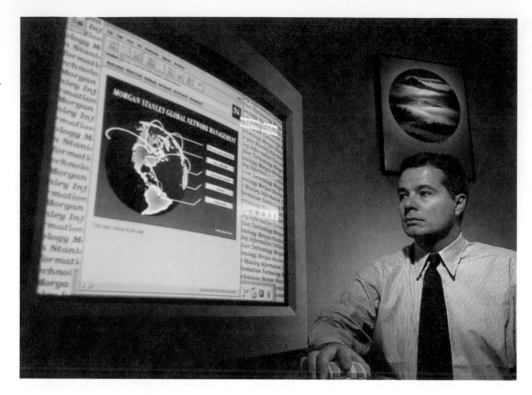

A **problem-solving team** is an organizational team set up to help eliminate a specified problem within the organization.

A **self-managed team** is an organizational team established to plan, organize, influence, and control its own work situation with only minimal direction from management.

For assistance in solving such formidable problems, management commonly establishes special teams. A team set up to help eliminate a specified problem within the organization is called a **problem-solving team.** The typical problem-solving team has 5 to 12 members and is formed to discuss ways to improve quality in all phases of the organization, to make organizational processes more efficient, or to improve the overall work environment.[18]

After the problem-solving team reaches a consensus, it makes recommendations to management about how to deal with the specified problem. Management may respond to the team's recommendations by implementing them in their entirety, by modifying and then implementing them, or by requesting further information to assess them. Once the problem that management asked the problem-solving team to address has been solved, the team is generally disbanded.

SELF-MANAGED TEAMS The **self-managed team,** sometimes called a *self-managed work group* or *self-directed team,* is a team that plans, organizes, influences, and controls its own work situation with only minimal intervention and direction from management. This creative team design involves a highly integrated group of several skilled individuals who are cross-trained and have the responsibility and authority to perform some specified activity.

Activities typically carried out by management in a traditional work setting—creating work schedules, establishing work pace and breaks, developing vacation schedules, evaluating performance, determining the level of salary increases and rewards received by individual workers, and ordering materials to be used in the production process—are instead carried out by members of the self-managed team. Generally responsible for whole tasks as opposed to "parts" of a job,[19] the self-managed team is an important new way of structuring, managing, and rewarding work. Since these teams require only minimum management attention, they free managers to pursue other management activities like strategic planning.

Reports of successful self-managed work teams are plentiful.[20] These teams are growing in popularity because today's business environment seems to require such work teams to solve complex problems independently, because American workers have come to expect more freedom in the workplace, and because the speed of technological change demands that employees be able to adapt quickly. Not all self-managed teams are successful of course. To ensure the success of a self-managed team, the manager should carefully select and properly train its members.[21]

Cross-functional teams operate in all kinds of situations. The members of this pit crew team must depend on one another to get the job done, with each one contributing his or her expertise in a particular task.

CROSS-FUNCTIONAL TEAMS A **cross-functional team** is a work team composed of people from different functional areas of the organization—marketing, finance, human resources, and operations, for example—who are all focused on a specified objective. Cross-functional teams may or may not be self-managed, though self-managed teams are generally cross-functional. Because cross-functional team members are from different departments within the organization, the team possesses the expertise to coordinate all the department activities within the organization that impact its own work.

A **cross-functional team** is an organizational team composed of people from different functional areas of the organization who are all focused on a specified objective.

ACROSS INDUSTRIES   Motorcycle Manufacturing

CROSS-FUNCTIONAL TEAMS DESIGN NEW PRODUCTS AT HARLEY-DAVIDSON

Harley-Davidson, Inc. designs, manufactures, and markets heavyweight motorcycles, motorcycle parts and accessories, and motorcycle collectibles and riding apparel. The company offers four popular motorcycle platforms: Sportster, Dyna, Softail, and Touring. In recent years, Harley-Davidson's products have gained much popularity, notoriety, and applause.

In addition, management at Harley-Davidson has been recognized worldwide for its successful use of progressive, cutting-edge management techniques. One specific area in which Harley-Davidson's management has received acclaim is its use of cross-functional teams to design new products. To some extent, cross-functional advice has always been considered within the new product design process at Harley-Davidson. Representatives from engineering, purchasing, manufacturing, and marketing have always had some influence on the future direction of new products.

More recently, management has underscored its commitment to cross-functional teams for designing new products by opening a new Product Development Center (PDC) near its plant in Wauwatosa, Wisconsin. For years the motorcycle maker has been consistently moving toward more emphasis on using cross-functional teams for new product development. The PDC accelerated this move by locating design engineers, purchasers, manufacturing personnel, and other crucial players in a single building. These team members work together daily and are totally dedicated to the new product development process on a full-time basis.

At Harley-Davidson, management's commitment to new product design via cross-functional teams is clear. Management uses the teams not only to generate the best possible product designs, but also to develop a sense of loyalty and commitment to the new designs that are developed.

FIGURE 17.6

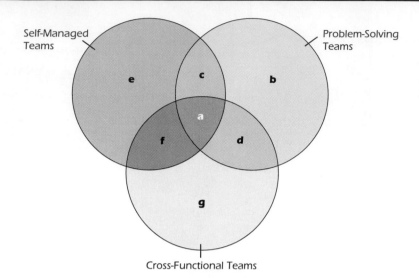

Self-Managed Teams

Problem-Solving Teams

e   c   b

a

f   d

g

Cross-Functional Teams

Some examples of cross-functional teams are teams established to choose and implement new technologies throughout the organization; teams formed to improve marketing effectiveness within the organization; and teams established to control product costs.[22]

This section discussed three types of teams that exist in organizations: problem-solving, self-directed, and cross-functional. It should be noted here that managers can establish various combinations of these three types of teams. Figure 17.6 illustrates some possible combinations that managers could create. For example, *a* in the figure represents a team that is problem-solving, self-directed, and cross-functional, while *b* represents one that is problem-solving, but neither cross-functional nor self-directed. Before establishing a team, managers should carefully study their own unique organizational situation and set up the type of team that best suits that situation.

STAGES OF TEAM DEVELOPMENT

More and more modern managers are using work teams to accomplish organizational tasks. Simply establishing such a team, however, does not guarantee it will be productive. In fact, managers should be patient when an established work team is not initially productive, for teams generally need to pass through several developmental stages before they become productive. Managers must understand this developmental process so they can facilitate it. The following sections discuss the various stages a team usually must pass through before it becomes fully productive.[23]

Forming is the first stage of the team development process, during which members of the newly formed team become oriented to the team and acquainted with one another as they explore issues related to their new job situation.

FORMING **Forming** is the first stage of the team development process. During this stage, members of the newly formed team become oriented to the team and acquainted with one another. This period is characterized by exploring issues related to the members' new job situation, such as what is expected of them, who has what kind of authority within the team, what kind of people are team members, and what skills team members possess.

The forming stage of team development is usually characterized by uncertainty and stress. Recognizing that team members are struggling to adjust to their new work situation and to one another, managers should be tolerant of lengthy informal discussions exploring team specifics and not regard them as time wasters. The newly formed team must be allowed an exploratory period if it is to become truly productive.

Storming, the second stage of the team development process, is characterized by conflict and disagreement as team members try to clarify their individual roles and challenge the way the team functions.

STORMING After a team has formed, it begins to storm. **Storming,** the second stage of the team development process, is characterized by conflict and disagreement as team members become more assertive in clarifying their individual roles. During this stage, the team seems to lack unity because members are continually challenging the way the team functions.

To help the team progress beyond storming, managers should encourage team members to feel free to disagree with any team issues and to discuss their own views fully and honestly. Most of all, managers should urge team members to arrive at agreements that will help the team reach its objective(s).

NORMING When the storming stage ends, norming begins. **Norming,** the third stage of the team development process, is characterized by agreement among team members on roles, rules, and acceptable behavior while working on the team. Conflicts generated during the storming stage are resolved in this stage.

Managers should encourage teams that have entered the norming stage to progress toward developing team norms and values that will be instrumental in building a successful organization. The process of determining what behavior is and is not acceptable within the team is critical to the work team's future productivity.

PERFORMING The fourth stage of the team development process is **performing.** At this stage, the team fully focuses on solving organizational problems and on meeting assigned challenges. The team is now productive: after successfully passing through the earlier stages of team development, it knows itself and has settled on team roles, expectations, and norms.

During this stage, managers should recognize the team's accomplishments regularly, for productive team behavior must be reinforced to enhance the probability that it will continue in the future.

ADJOURNING The fifth, and last, stage of the team development process is known as **adjourning.** Now the team is finishing its job and preparing to disband. This stage normally occurs only in teams established for some special purpose to be accomplished in a limited time period. Special committees and task groups are examples of such teams. During the adjourning stage, team members generally feel disappointment that their team is being broken up because disbandment means the loss of personally satisfying relationships and/or an enjoyable work situation.

During this phase of team development, managers should recognize team members' disappointment and sense of loss as normal and assure them that other challenging and exciting organizational opportunities await them. It is important that management then do everything necessary to integrate these people into new teams or other areas of the organization.

Although some work teams do not pass through every one of the development stages just described, understanding the stages of forming, storming, norming, performing, and adjourning will give managers many useful insights on how to build productive work teams. Above all, managers must realize that new teams are different from mature teams and that their challenge is to build whatever team they are in charge of into a mature, productive work team.

►TEAM EFFECTIVENESS

Earlier in this chapter, teams were defined as groups of people who influence one another to reach organizational targets. It is easy to see why effective teams are critical to organizational success. Effective teams are those that come up with innovative ideas, accomplish their goals, and adapt to change when necessary. Their individual members are highly committed to both the team and organizational goals. Such teams are highly valued by upper management and recognized and rewarded for their accomplishments.[24]

Figure 17.7 sketches the characteristics of an effective team. Note the figure's implications for the steps managers need to take to build effective work teams in organizations. *People-related steps* include the following:[25]

1. Trying to make the team's work satisfying
2. Developing mutual trust among team members and between the team and management
3. Building good communication—from management to the team as well as within the team
4. Minimizing unresolved conflicts and power struggles within the team
5. Dealing effectively with threats toward and within the team
6. Building the perception that the jobs of team members are secure

Norming, the third stage of the team development process, is characterized by agreement among team members on roles, rules, and acceptable behavior while working on the team.

Performing, the fourth stage of the team development process, is characterized by a focus on solving organizational problems and meeting assigned challenges.

Adjourning, the fifth and last stage of the team development process, is the stage in which the team finishes its job and prepares to disband.

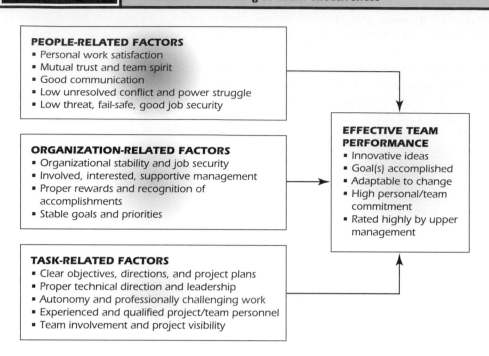

FIGURE 17.7 ▶ **Factors contributing to team effectiveness**

PEOPLE-RELATED FACTORS
- Personal work satisfaction
- Mutual trust and team spirit
- Good communication
- Low unresolved conflict and power struggle
- Low threat, fail-safe, good job security

ORGANIZATION-RELATED FACTORS
- Organizational stability and job security
- Involved, interested, supportive management
- Proper rewards and recognition of accomplishments
- Stable goals and priorities

TASK-RELATED FACTORS
- Clear objectives, directions, and project plans
- Proper technical direction and leadership
- Autonomy and professionally challenging work
- Experienced and qualified project/team personnel
- Team involvement and project visibility

EFFECTIVE TEAM PERFORMANCE
- Innovative ideas
- Goal(s) accomplished
- Adaptable to change
- High personal/team commitment
- Rated highly by upper management

Organization-related steps managers can take to build effective work teams include:

1. Building a stable overall organization or company structure that team members view as secure
2. Becoming involved in team events and demonstrating interest in team progress and functioning
3. Properly rewarding and recognizing teams for their accomplishments
4. Setting stable goals and priorities for the team

Finally, Figure 17.7 implies that managers can build effective work teams by taking six *task-related steps:*

1. Developing clear objectives, directions, and project plans for the team
2. Providing proper technical direction and leadership for the team
3. Establishing autonomy for the team and challenging work within the team
4. Appointing experienced and qualified team personnel
5. Encouraging team involvement
6. Building visibility within the organization for the team's work

▶ TRUST AND EFFECTIVE TEAMS

Probably the most fundamental ingredient of effective teams is trust. Trust is belief in the reliance, ability, and integrity of another. Unless team members trust one another, the team leader, and management, managers may well find that building an effective work team is impossible.[26]

Today there is significant concern that management is not inspiring the kind of trust that is essential to team effectiveness. In fact, subordinates' trust in their managers is critically low, and employee opinion polls indicate that it may well decline even further in the future.

Management urgently needs to focus on reversing this trend. There are many strategies managers can use to build trust within groups:[27]

▶ *Communicate often to team members*—This is a fundamental strategy. Keeping team members informed of organizational news, explaining why certain decisions have been made, and sharing information about organizational operations are examples of how managers should communicate to team members.

▶ *Show respect for team members*—Managers need to show team members that they are highly valued. They can demonstrate their respect for team members by delegating tasks to them, listening intently to feedback from the group, and acting on it appropriately.

▶ *Be fair to team members*—Team members must receive the rewards they have earned. Managers must therefore conduct fair performance appraisals and objectively allocate and distribute rewards. It should go without saying that showing favoritism in this area sows mistrust and resentment.

▶ *Be predictable*—Managers must be consistent in their actions. Team members should usually be able to forecast what decisions management will make before those decisions are made. Moreover, managers must live up to commitments made to team members. Managers who make inconsistent decisions and fail to live up to commitments will not be trusted by teams.

▶ *Demonstrate competence*—To build team trust, managers must show team members that they are able to diagnose organizational problems and have the skill to implement solutions to those problems. Team members tend to trust managers they perceive as competent and distrust those they perceive as incompetent.

◤ CORPORATE CULTURE

So far, this chapter has focused on managing smaller work groups. This section, in contrast, discusses corporate culture as an important ingredient for managing organization members as a total group.

Corporate culture is a set of shared values and beliefs that organization members have regarding the functioning and existence of their organization. What type of corporate culture is present in any organization can be discovered by studying that organization's special combination of status symbols, traditions, history, and physical environment. A management that understands the significance of all these factors can use them to develop a corporate culture that is beneficial to the firm.

> **Corporate culture** is a set of shared values and beliefs that organization members have regarding the functioning and existence of their organization.

STATUS SYMBOLS Looking at the status symbols of an organization—the visible, external signs of social position that are associated with the various positions in the firm—gives an observer a feeling for the organization's social hierarchy. The size and location of an organization member's office, as well as the member's access to executive clubs and reserved parking, indicates the status level of that member's job.

TRADITIONS AND HISTORY A firm's history and traditions can determine how workers in that particular firm act on a daily basis. Typically, traditions developed over time let workers know exactly what is expected of them. By developing traditions, therefore, managers can steer the everyday behaviors that go on in an organization.

PHYSICAL ENVIRONMENT The firm's physical environment makes a statement about its corporate culture. For instance, closed offices and few common areas where organization members can meet indicate a closed form of culture. On the other hand, a building with open offices and extensive common areas where employees can interact indicates a more open culture. Management that wants an open culture, then, will see to it that office doors are usually open; management that wants a more formal type of corporate culture will encourage closed office doors.

▶ THE SIGNIFICANCE OF CORPORATE CULTURE

The significance of corporate culture for management is that it influences the behavior of everyone within an organization and, if carefully crafted, can have a significant positive effect

The corporate culture at Interval Research in Palo Alto, California, is less a reflection of what the company does (conducting "pure research" on consumer goods and services for the information highway) than of how it goes about it. To build this futuristic kitchen, for example, researchers "collected" samples of people's everyday behavior in the real world. Then they brought it back to the office, where the workday consisted of freewheeling "informances"—informative performances in which staffers "play act" the imagined lives of imaginary consumers.

on organizational success.[28] If not properly managed, however, corporate culture can help doom an organization. Typically, top management and other present or past organizational leaders are the key agents influencing corporate culture.

The current management literature is full of advice about the way managers should handle corporate culture issues. One especially practical and helpful book suggests that there are five primary mechanisms for developing and reinforcing the desired corporate culture:[29]

▶ *What leaders pay attention to, measure, and control*—Leaders can communicate very effectively what their vision of the organization is and what they want done by consistently emphasizing the same issues in meetings, in casual remarks and questions, and in strategy discussions. For example, if product quality is the dominant value to be inculcated in employees, leaders may consistently inquire about the effect of any proposed changes on product quality.

▶ *Leaders' reactions to critical incidents and organizational crises*—The manner in which leaders deal with crises can create new beliefs and values and reveal underlying organizational assumptions. For example, when a firm faces a financial crisis but does not lay off any employees, the message is that the organization sees itself as a "family" that looks out for its members.

▶ *Deliberate role modeling, teaching, and coaching*—The behaviors of leaders in both formal and informal settings have an important effect on employee beliefs, values, and behaviors. For example, if the CEO regularly works very long hours and on weekends, other managers will probably respond by spending more time at work also.

▶ *Criteria for allocation of rewards and status*—Leaders can firmly communicate their priorities and values by consistently linking rewards and punishments to the behaviors that concern them. For example, if a weekly bonus is given for exceeding production or sales quotas, employees will recognize the value placed on these activities and focus their efforts on them.

▶ *Criteria for recruitment, selection, promotion, and retirement of employees*—The kinds of people who are hired and who succeed in an organization are those who accept the organization's values and behave accordingly. For example, if managers who are action oriented and who implement strategies effectively consistently move up the organizational ladder, the organization's priorities will come through loud and clear to other managers.

To influence the type of culture that exists within an organization, a manager must first determine what culture would be appropriate for the organization, and then take calculated and overt steps to encourage the establishment, growth, and maintenance of that culture. Merely allowing a corporate culture to develop without planned management influence can result in an inappropriate culture that limits the organization's success.

BACK TO THE CASE

In managing groups, Rolls-Royce's managers must understand that there is a crucial difference between a group and a team. While a group consists of people who interact with one another, are psychologically aware of one another, and think of themselves as a group, a team is a group whose members influence one another toward the accomplishment of organizational goals. Obviously, teams are more desirable from management's point of view, and an important managerial challenge is to turn work groups into teams.

Rolls-Royce's management can use problem-solving, self-managed, and cross-functional teams to solve specific organizational problems and to approach organizational issues from a variety of functional perspectives. The choice of teams—or combination of teams—would depend on the specific organizational circumstances.

Once a team is established, Rolls-Royce's management must be patient and recognize that teams usually need some time to develop into productive work units. The team development process generally proceeds from an initial forming stage to a fully effective performing stage. Management must understand each stage of the process, help teams progress through the stages, and empower them to do their jobs.

Rolls-Royce's managers should strive to develop *effective* teams—teams that generate innovative ideas, accomplish their goals, adapt to change, and are characterized by members who are dedicated both to the team and to the organization. It is essential also that Rolls-Royce's managers develop trust within their work teams by keeping team members informed about company events, showing respect for team members, being fair to them, being predictable in their own decision making, and demonstrating to team members that management is capable of solving organizational problems.

If Rolls-Royce wants to capitalize fully on the talents of its employees, management must work not only at turning work groups into effective work teams but also at making such teams a part of the corporate culture. That is, Rolls-Royce's organization members must come to share management's belief that effective teams are an important means to the company's success.

For updated information on the topics in this chapter, Internet exercises, links to related Internet sites, an interactive study guide, and more, visit our companion Web site at

http://www.prenhall.com/certo

Additional information can be found on the inside front and back covers of this text.

Reread the learning objectives below. Each objective is followed by questions. Answering these questions accurately will help you retain the most important concepts discussed in this chapter. After answering each question, check your answer against the answer key at the end of this chapter. (*Hint:* If you have any doubts regarding the correct response, consult the page number that follows the answer.)

Circle:

From studying this chapter, I will attempt to acquire

1. A definition of the term *group* as used in the context of management.

T F   **a.** A group is made up of people who interact with one another, perceive themselves to be a group, and are primarily physically aware of one another.

a b c d e   **b.** According to Cartwright and Lippitt, it is *not* true to say that: (a) groups exist in all kinds of organizations (b) groups inevitably form in all facets of organizational existence (c) groups cause undesirable consequences within the organization, so their continued existence should be discouraged (d) understanding groups can assist managers in increasing the probability that the groups with which they work will cause desirable consequences within the organization (e) all of the above are true.

2. A thorough understanding of the difference between formal and informal groups.

T F   **a.** An informal group is one that exists within an organization by virtue of management decree.

T F   **b.** A formal group is one that exists within an organization by virtue of interaction among organization members who work in proximity to one another.

3. Knowledge of the types of formal groups that exist in organizations.

a b c d e   **a.** The type of group that generally handles more routine organizational activities is the: (a) informal task group (b) informal command group (c) formal task group (d) formal command group (e) none of the above.

a b c d e   **b.** Managers should be encouraged to take the following steps to increase the success of a committee: (a) clearly define the goals of the committee (b) rephrase ideas that have already been expressed (c) select a chairperson on the basis of ability to run an efficient meeting (d) a and b (e) a, b, and c.

4. An understanding of how managers can determine which groups exist in an organization.

T F   **a.** The technique of sociometry involves asking people whom they would like to manage.

a b c d e   **b.** A sociogram is defined in the text as: (a) a letter encouraging group participation (b) a diagram that visually illustrates the number of times that the individuals were chosen within the group and whether the choice was reciprocal (c) a composite of demographic data useful in determining informal group choices (d) a computer printout designed to profile psychological and sociological characteristics of the informal group (e) none of the above.

5. An appreciation for what teams are and how to manage them.

T F   **a.** A cross-functional team can also be a problem-solving team, but it cannot be a self-managed team.

a b c d e   **b.** Which of the following is *not* a stage of team development: (a) storming (b) alarming (c) forming (d) performing (e) norming.

T F   **c.** Trust is probably the most fundamental ingredient of effective teams.

6. Insights about managing corporate culture to enhance organizational success.

T F   **a.** The concept of corporate culture usually does not include the set of beliefs that organization members have about their organization and its functioning.

a b c d e   **b.** Mechanisms that managers can use to influence corporate culture include: (a) what leaders pay attention to (b) criteria that leaders use to make organizational awards (c) criteria leaders use to select new employees (d) all of the above (e) none of the above.

CASE DISCUSSSION QUESTIONS

"**G**roups Are Important to Progress at Rolls-Royce" (p. 375) and its related Back-to-the-Case sections were written to help you better understand the management concepts contained in this chapter. Answer the following discussion questions about this Introductory Case to enrich your understanding of the chapter content:

1. What kinds of groups would the Japanese-style work teams at Rolls-Royce be classified as? Explain.
2. What advice would you give to a Rolls-Royce manager who is managing such a work team?

SKILLS EXERCISE: DESIGNING A WORK TEAM

In this chapter you studied the different kinds of teams that managers use in organizations. The Introductory Case explains how Rolls-Royce increased its good fortune by focusing its efforts on meeting customer needs. Assume that you are responsible for putting a team together at Rolls-Royce to ensure that this customer focus endures and is reflected in virtually all functions in the company. Use Figure 17.6 to help you determine the type of team you will establish. Which team do you choose? Why did you choose this team? In your discussion, be sure to include why you did not choose the other teams.

1. How is the term *group* defined in this chapter?
2. Why is the study of groups important to managers?
3. What is a formal group?
4. Explain the significance of linking pins to formal groups in organizations.
5. List and define two types of formal groups that can exist in organizations.
6. Why should managers use committees in organizations?
7. What steps can managers take to ensure that a committee will be successful?
8. Explain how work teams can be valuable to an organization.
9. Describe the stages a group typically goes through as it matures.
10. What is an informal group?
11. List and define two types of informal groups in organizations.
12. What benefits generally accrue to members of informal groups?
13. What is the relationship between work teams and informal groups?
14. Are formal groups more important to managers than informal groups? Explain.
15. Describe the sociometric procedure used to study informal group membership. What can the results of a sociometric analysis tell managers about members of an informal group?
16. Explain Homans' concept of how informal groups develop.
17. What is the difference between a group and a team? Is this an important difference for a manager to understand? Why?
18. Discuss how managers can develop effective teams in organizations.
19. What steps can managers take to develop trust in work teams? Is developing this trust important? Why?
20. Define corporate culture. Can managers actually build corporate culture? Explain.

1. **a.** F, p. 376
   b. c, p. 376
2. **a.** F, p. 377
   b. F, p. 377
3. **a.** d, p. 377
   b. e, pp. 379–380
4. **a.** F, p. 384
   b. b, p. 384
5. **a.** F, p. 389
   b. b, pp. 390–391
   c. T, p. 392
6. **a.** F, p. 393
   b. d, p. 394

On February 2, 1996, Apple Computer installed its fourth new chief—Gilbert Amelio, the CEO credited with turning around failing National Semiconductor Corporation. Amelio describes his turn-around magic in his book *Profit from Experience:* In essence, he creates a simple vision and pulls people together to back it, no matter what it takes. His plan has become known as the "chartreuse strategy" because, in the midst of turning around a division at Rockwell International, Amelio declared that he'd even paint the buildings chartreuse if that would draw people's attention to his insistence on cultural change.

At the time of the case, the board, shareholders, employees, and customers of Apple looked to Amelio to transform a floundering operation and rekindle a once-vital organization's hopes and commitments. Amelio certainly had his work cut out for him: Apple's share of the personal-computer market was down to 7.8 percent when he took office. If market share went any lower, the once brash technological innovator would be merely a niche player.

Amelio makes quick changes, but he is not a slash-and-burn artist. A physicist by training, he has a professorial bent and considerable personal charm. Although Amelio writes in his book that "layoffs are a sign of management failure," some observers believe that he has no choice but to make deep, fast cuts at what many critics consider a "flabby" company. His plans will also end Apple's waffling over broadly licensing Mac technology, reinventing Apple's Internet strategy, and terminating efforts that Amelio believes to be beyond the company's core business.

"The fact is," according to a *Business Week* magazine article, "despite its glowing reputation, Apple has rarely run smoothly—at least not for more than a few years at a time. The pattern of mismanagement that has characterized the company since its inception has caused Apple to bungle critical decisions and waver back and forth between strategies."

This disastrous pattern began with Apple's founders, Steven P. Jobs and Stephen Wozniak. While virtually inventing the PC industry with the Apple II, Jobs and Wozniak also created the renegade Apple corporate culture. Their guiding principles: Do your own thing, defy the pessimists, and ignore the Establishment. The crowning achievement of this attitude was a groundbreaking machine—the "insanely great" Mac—with which users fell in love.

According to a former Apple executive, however, this celebrated corporate culture had a dark side: It was "unharnessed and uncontrolled." Inevitably, this "dark side" led to clashes between Apple's free-wheeling creators and the experienced managers who had been hired to run the company's marketing and finance activities. First, disagreements between the two founders led to Wozniak's withdrawal from Apple. Then the clashes converged in an all-out battle between remaining founder Jobs and former PepsiCo executive John Sculley over the Mac's ultimate design.

Sculley came out on top. He immediately acted to protect the company with sweeping layoffs. Unfortunately, the rank and file resented the big-company systems that Sculley put in place. The new CEO also had to find a way to retain the dynamic engineers and programmers whose genius had kept Apple generally ahead of the technology curve. The solution: Don't tinker with the culture set in place by Jobs and Wozniak. By and large, that approach worked, but it had certain costs. The glorification of the so-called technical wizards made them difficult to supervise and fostered an atmosphere of arrogance that kept employees at all levels from responding seriously to competition.

Additionally, at least one grapevine joke had it that at Apple, protecting Apple's culture meant allowing an endless search for consensus. No decision was final; "even a vote of 15,000 to 1 can still be a tie." But the joke, it seemed, was ultimately on Apple. Year after year, key decisions were postponed, reversed, or avoided. Asks one former Apple executive, "Why can't somebody just say: 'I'm the leader. This is the way it's going to be. Thanks for the discussion, but if you don't want to do it, leave.' "

Still, Apple's fortunes took a turn for the good, and Sculley turned his attention to R&D. In fact, he took on the role of "techno-visionary," awarding himself the title of Chief Technology Officer in 1990. This was a major mistake. His pet project, the Newton, which was aimed at the needs of a converging computer/communications/media market, was released to widespread ridicule in 1993.

Apple's board did not laugh. They moved to fire Sculley and replaced him with Michael Spindler, whose no-nonsense attitude toward business seemed like the long-awaited voice of reason in Apple's chaotic culture. Like Sculley, Spindler began with massive layoffs. He also moved the firm toward a new, low-margin business model. The company responded to his strategy with four quarters of strong growth and a rebound in stock price. But Apple's cult of consensus and the new CEO's inconsistency quickly proved a deadly combination. Within a year, Spindler was caught in a cycle of delay, reversal, and missed opportunities.

At the time of the case, loyal Mac users, shareholders, employees, and the board all looked to Gilbert Amelio to "polish the Apple." He would have to solve the problem of Apple's culture if he was to be successful.

QUESTIONS

1. Describe the corporate culture created at Apple by Jobs and Wozniak. What were the pros and cons of that culture? What could have been done differently to maximize the pros and minimize the cons? Explain.

2. How did the Mac reflect the culture of the company? Discuss "decisions by indecision" made by Apple leadership that caused the Mac to lose its preeminence. Did these decisions reflect problems within Apple's corporate culture? Explain.

3. Examine the five suggestions for leaders who hope to manage corporate culture successfully. Evaluate Apple's management decisions in light of each. What mistakes were made and how could they have been corrected? What advice would you give Amelio?

SMALL BUSINESS 2000

Companies generally evolve and grow over time. Patterns for organizations sometimes are similar to those for individuals. Organizations begin with questions and uncertainty and learn and grow over time. Organizations develop relationships with other organizations outside of the company, such as vendors and customers. They also develop a set of characteristics which we might refer to as the firm's "personality." Much like when we hear a person's name and draw a mental picture of that person, we can often do the same thing when we hear reference to a particular company.

For companies, the puzzle is even more complicated by relationships, both formal and informal, which exist among the individuals and groups which make up a particular firm. Cactus and Tropicals is a business which serves as a good example of a firm with a personality and an attitude. Fortunately for Cactus and Tropicals' customers and employees, the company has a warm personality and a good attitude. If you asked Lorraine Miller, the founder and president of Cactus and Tropicals, about the firm's personality and attitude, she would probably tell you that the personality is one which allows for a pleasant and fun work environment and its attitude is that employees should have freedom to use their interests and talents.

Lorraine acknowledges that an owner, unless it is a very small venture, cannot run a business by herself. Cactus and Tropicals has over 45 part-time and full-time employees working in three basic organizations: the original business, retail plants; a gift shop; and a corporate plant care group. Although there is some similarity, the skills and talents needed to successfully run these three groups are not the same. Cactus and Tropicals is made up of a variety of people with an array of skills, yet it functions as a cohesive and profitable company. In this case you will have a chance to explore the individuals and groups that make up this company and give some thought to the culture that Lorraine and others have created at Cactus and Tropicals.

QUESTIONS

1. Identify at least three groups or teams which exist at Cactus and Tropicals. Discuss how/why you think they were formed and discuss the characteristics of the group or team.
2. You saw a brief segment with Lorraine talking to three group managers about the bonus program and the company's goals. For a long time Lorraine ran the company by herself. Discuss some things that you think Lorraine and these three employees might have dealt with as they became the company's "management team."
3. Describe the culture at Cactus and Tropicals. Think about and discuss why you think people would want to work there. Is this the kind of place where you might like to work? Why or why not?
4. Lorraine Miller seems to be the one who sets the tone for this company. She has now surrounded herself by a staff, many of whom seem to appreciate and share her vision of what the company should be and how it should run. Suppose Lorraine decided to still own the company but back away from day-to-day management to pursue another interest. What issues do you think the company would face going forward?

Understanding People: Attitudes, Perception, and Learning

STUDENT LEARNING OBJECTIVES

From studying this chapter, I will attempt to acquire

1. An understanding of employee workplace attitudes

2. Insights into how to change employee attitudes

3. An appreciation of the impact of employee perceptions on employee behaviors

4. Knowledge of employee perceptions of procedural justice

5. An understanding that adult learners are different from younger students

CHAPTER OUTLINE

Introductory Case: *Reviving Workplace Attitudes*

WHAT ARE ATTITUDES?
How Beliefs and Values Create Attitude
Attitude Surveys

Management and the Internet: *H.T.E. Uses the Internet to Study Employee Attitudes*

Quality Spotlight: *Nucor Steel*

PERCEPTION
Perception and the Perceptual Process
Attribution Theory: Interpreting the Behavior of Others
Perceptual Distortions

Across Industries: *Banking—National Westminster Bank Focuses on Erasing Traditional Bank Manager Stereotype*

Global Spotlight: *The Wide, Wide World of Cultural Perceptions*
Perceptions of Procedural Justice

LEARNING
Learning Strategies

INTRODUCTORY CASE

REVIVING WORKPLACE ATTITUDES

REMINDER: THE INTRODUCTORY CASE WRAP-UP (P. 417) CONTAINS DISCUSSION QUESTIONS AND A SKILLS EXERCISE TO FURTHER ILLUSTRATE THE APPLICATION OF CHAPTER CONCEPTS TO THIS VIGNETTE.

Claudia Younce, a 43-year-old nurse, considers herself gregarious and positive. She loves mending broken bodies and is passionate about nursing. But off and on between 1991 and 1993, Younce hit an impasse in her career: After the alarm buzzed in the mornings, she'd lie in bed daydreaming about what she'd rather do than go to work. Other symptoms surfaced. She noticed that she didn't chat as often with co-workers. She began to question whether nursing was truly her calling.

"I felt I wasn't getting much from my job," recalls Younce, who works at St. Elizabeth Medical Center, one of the five hospitals in Dayton, Ohio. "I liked my job, but there was something more I needed to be doing." Her experience was hardly unusual. Countless Americans experience times of frustration and dissatisfaction with their jobs and declining work attitudes. During these periods, their productivity usually falls and they perceive no meaning or purpose to their jobs. In fact, many people believe that quitting is the only way to relieve the stress. However, experts warn frustrated employees not to make a major move too quickly.

Experiencing workplace blues—a career low point—is common. The Bureau of Labor Statistics reports that more than 50 percent of workers are unhappy on the job. According to Priscilla Mutter, a career counselor in Dayton, people need to discover the cause of their frustrations in order to make the most of their job.

Employees often believe that managers and co-workers cause their frustrations at work. Yet it's usually their own response to others that creates problems, Mutter says. Once people discover the true source of their concerns, they should look around the company for other opportunities and consider going back to school to gain new skills or a new life interest. Every effort people make to better a work situation usually helps. "Even though work may not have changed, they're proactive and their work seems better," says Mutter. "They're taking charge of their lives and things look a lot brighter."

Claudia Younce, for example, wanted more from her career as a nursing supervisor. She visited two career

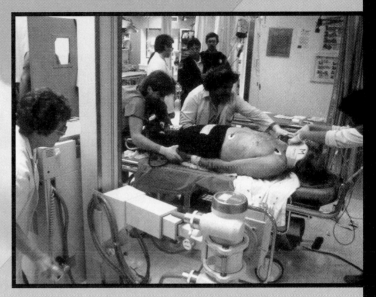

When nurses encounter stress in the workplace, they should be proactive in seeing their problems as something they can address.

counselors for advice. After some testing, the first counselor recommended that she consider another career—an idea that didn't sit well with Younce. She then went to Priscilla Mutter, who reinforced her career choice, but suggested that Younce pursue nonwork activities to create a balance in her life. More balance, Mutter suggested, would make her job more meaningful.

Younce thus began working with Starfish, a local organization that does volunteer work in developing countries. This summer, she will spend a month teaching nursing in South Africa. "I love to travel and I like helping people," says Younce. "Volunteering gives me something more to look forward to, and it broadens my outlook on life."

Younce also entered graduate school at the University of Cincinnati. Education not only fuels the part of her that loves to learn but also provides a chance to boost her career at the hospital. Now Younce gets out of bed every morning looking forward to work. Although her job responsibilities haven't changed at St. Elizabeth, she has largely healed herself by doing what made her happy. Although most people will never discover that "perfect" job, it's their *attitude* and view of work that *make the difference* in the world.

What's Ahead

In the Introductory Case, Claudia Younce, an employee who had skills and experience to be successful on the job, developed attitudes that negatively impacted her work. The information in this chapter provides insights for managers regarding how to enhance the productivity of organization members like Claudia through an understanding of people. More precisely, this chapter studies people by discussing the following topics:

1. Attitudes
2. Perception
3. Learning

The previous chapters in this section discussed people issues important to managing like influencing and communication, leadership, motivation, and groups and teamwork. This chapter continues the study of people issues important to managing by elaborating upon characteristics of individuals in organizations. Characteristics discussed in the following sections are attitudes, perception, and learning.

WHAT ARE ATTITUDES?

An **attitude** is a predisposition to react to a situation, person, or concept with a particular response.

An **attitude** is a predisposition to react to a situation, person, or concept with a particular response. This response can be either positive or negative. It is a learned reaction—one that results from an individual's past observations, direct experiences, or exposure to others' attitudes. For example, someone may say, "I love baseball," thus communicating to others a general attitude about the sport. Some baseball fans developed their love for the sport while playing it in childhood; direct experience shaped their attitude. Others never played the game but developed a love for the sport by watching games at the ballpark or on television. Still others had friends or family members who influenced their attitudes by communicating their love for the game.

Attitudes are internal and may be largely kept to oneself, or they may be made known to others through overt behaviors. Generally, attitudes have three primary components:[1]

1. *Cognitive*—information and beliefs about a particular person or object.
2. *Affective*—a positive or negative feeling about a particular person or object.
3. *Behavioral*—an intent or desire to behave in a certain way toward a particular person or object.

Again, a conversation among co-workers may help illustrate these differences:

Maria: Did you hear about the training program that starts next week?

Lex: Yes, I've read several reviews on that software. It may make my job much easier and help me to produce better newsletters and reports.

David: I hate going to training programs and having to learn new software. Just when you really get comfortable with one, they change to a new one.

Maria: Well, I intend to pick it up as quickly as possible so I can expand my skills and possibly bid for a higher-grade job.

In this brief exchange, Lex communicates one attitude about the specific training program. The information that he has learned about it has given him an attitude of awareness (a cognitive component), but no positive or negative feelings toward the program. David, however, expresses both awareness and a negative attitude (an affective component) toward the training program, probably based on his own past experiences or those of others. Maria not only has knowledge of the program (cognitive) and a positive feeling toward it (affective) but also has decided how she will approach it (a behavioral component).

HOW BELIEFS AND VALUES CREATE ATTITUDES

Beliefs are accepted facts or truths about an object or person that have been gained from either direct experience or a secondary source.

Overall, an individual's attitudes are a result of the beliefs and values held by the individual. **Beliefs** are accepted facts or truths about an object or person that have been gained from either direct experience or a secondary source. For example, what people believe about McDonald's restaurants or the Publisher's Clearinghouse Sweepstakes tends to form their attitudes about each and influences the way they react to each.

Values are levels of worth placed by an individual on various factors in the environment. Values tend to be broad views of life and are influenced by parents, peer groups, and associates. Values tend to guide one's actions and judgments across a variety of situations. Thus a person's workplace values may be defined as those concepts, principles, people, objects, or activities that he or she considers important. Values are those things for which a person may make sacrifices and work hard. In the workplace, such factors as compensation, recognition, and status are often regarded as common values.[2]

Values are the global beliefs that guide one's actions and judgments across a variety of situations.

One way in which the relationship among attitudes, values, and beliefs can affect people's behavior in the workplace is illustrated in Figure 18.1.[3] For example, direct past experiences or observations of others may have led our hypothetical manager to believe that software vendors usually exaggerate the virtues of their products. In fact, this person has developed a rule of thumb: New office software programs cost twice as much as their initial price (because of add-on charges, upgrades, training expenses, and so forth) and deliver only half the level of promised service. This general belief has led the manager to develop an attitude of distrust toward any new software. When the manager's skepticism is applied to a specific new product, this attitude influences his behavior—he denies the request for the software. We can see that the manager's decision-making process was not objective. Instead, the process was negatively biased because of an attitude—an attitude resulting from general beliefs and values formed by past experiences and observations.

► ATTITUDE SURVEYS

In election years, political candidates spend millions of dollars on public opinion surveys. In addition, the media publishes their own polls on candidates and issues. Why are such surveys done? In the case of the candidate, survey information can be used to plan future campaign strategy. The most important reason for such surveys, however, is that a professionally conducted poll will almost invariably predict the outcome of an election. Polls tend to be accurate because the people surveyed express *attitudes* on which they are likely to base *behavior*.

Managers also use attitude surveys. Faced with such employee problems as excessive turnover and absenteeism, low productivity, and poor-quality work, they may use surveys to predict employee behavior or determine the sources of existing problems. In the workplace, surveys are sometimes called "polling-attitude surveys" or simply "job-satisfaction surveys." In recent years, attitude surveys have gained in popularity because they often determine the sources of employee dissatisfaction. If an employer addresses problem areas identified in attitude surveys, organizational problems like low productivity and poor-quality products can often be reduced, employee morale improved, and productivity increased.

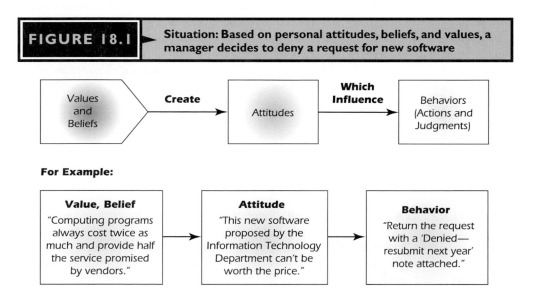

FIGURE 18.1 **Situation: Based on personal attitudes, beliefs, and values, a manager decides to deny a request for new software**

Values and Beliefs → **Create** → Attitudes → **Which Influence** → Behaviors (Actions and Judgments)

For Example:

Value, Belief	**Attitude**	**Behavior**
"Computing programs always cost twice as much and provide half the service promised by vendors."	"This new software proposed by the Information Technology Department can't be worth the price."	"Return the request with a 'Denied—resubmit next year' note attached."

Its "Intel Inside" campaign made Intel Corporation's Pentium chip a household name among computer-savvy consumers. In November 1994, however, when Intel learned of a minor flaw in its best-selling microprocessor, certain corporate values came up short. In particular, Intel failed to offer no-questions-asked replacements because its corporate culture valued growth and profitability and largely ignored the difficulties involved in marketing high-tech products directly to consumers.

MANAGEMENT AND THE INTERNET   H.T.E. Uses the Internet to Study Employee Attitudes

Attitude surveys can be extremely useful in helping managers pinpoint existing organizational problems. Dennis Harward, founder and president of H.T.E. Enterprises, recently used an attitude survey to gauge employee attitudes toward organizational communication. H.T.E. develops, markets, implements, and supports software applications designed for public sector organizations, like police and fire departments. Harward has had outstanding success recently. For the six months ended June 98, revenues rose 45 percent to $43.8 million. Net income during the same period rose 43 percent to $2.5 million.

Faced with the challenge of assessing and improving organizational communication within his company, Harward assembled an employee group along with an outside consultant to plan and implement a communication survey. The employee group represented major segments within the company and included representatives from areas like accounting, human resources, sales and marketing, operations, and strategic planning. Representing various organizational levels, employees within the group possessed titles like president, vice president, director, salesperson, and project manager. The consultant was a professor of management at a local graduate school of business.

As group meetings passed, the group made excellent progress. The group eventually settled on a survey that asked H.T.E. employ-

ees to rate several different organizational communication factors. These factors included receiving information from others, sending information to others, following-up on information sent, sources of information, and channels of communication. Although survey responses were completely anonymous, employees were also asked to identify themselves as a manager or nonmanager. Through this partial identity, the committee planned to see if managers saw communication at H.T.E. differently than nonmanagers.

The group decided to use the Internet to actually administer the survey. A Web services company, Websolvers Incorporated, was hired to design a Web site that would house or host the survey. According to plan, employees would access the survey on the Internet, answer it on-line, and then e-mail answers to Websolvers. Part of Websolvers' job was to e-mail all employee answers to the survey analyst. Basically, Websolvers was hired to eliminate any possibility that employees would think someone could identify their answers within H.T.E.

The implementation of the survey plan was virtually flawless. Naturally, the real value of the survey rests on its role in helping Harward to improve organizational communication at H.T.E. This survey experience, however, does support the notion that the Internet can play a useful and major role in conducting attitude surveys in organizations.

THEORY OF REASONED ACTION Research indicates that the attitudes employees hold toward their jobs and employers are quite stable over time: People with both generally positive and generally negative attitudes tend to retain them over time.[4] This finding is important to managers because it means they can feel reasonably confident that measuring attitudes is likely to produce useful information.

FIGURE 18.2 ▶ Theory of reasoned action

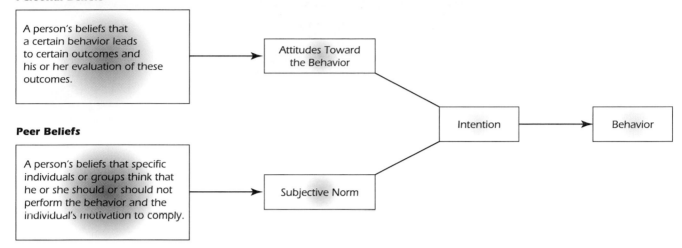

The Workplace Relationship Among Beliefs, Attitudes, Norms, Intentions, and Behaviors

At the same time, however, changing employees' attitudes toward specific aspects of their jobs is usually a challenging task for management. Researchers generally agree that while attitudes "influence" employee behaviors in the workplace, they are not perfect predictors of behaviors. Thus behavioralists Martin Fishbein and others have developed a model designed to provide a more complete examination of the attitude-behavior relationship. This model, called the **theory of reasoned action,** is summarized in Figure 18.2. According to the model, when a behavior is a matter of *choice,* the best predictor of the behavior is the person's *intention* to perform it. Intention is best predicted from two factors:

1. Person's attitude toward performing the behavior
2. Person's subjective norm—the perception that he or she is expected by peers or others to perform a certain behavior

According to this view, then, attitude is a person's positive or negative feeling toward performing a behavior.

The *reasoned action* model further suggests that a person's attitude can be predicted by his or her belief that a certain behavior will lead to certain outcomes. Also important is the value that the person places on those outcomes. Similarly, a person's subjective norm can sometimes be predicted from his or her belief that other individuals (supervisors, co-workers, friends) think that the person should (or should not) perform a behavior. Not surprisingly, when people have strong beliefs and attitudes about a certain behavior and perceive that it is expected of them, they are more likely to perform it. The reverse, of course, is also true.[5]

EMPLOYEE ATTITUDES   Many managers find employee attitudes complex and difficult to understand—and even more difficult to change. What job factors are important determinants of employee attitudes? Academic research and the hands-on experience of managers have produced at least three theories concerning the primary determinants of employee attitudes (see Figure 18.3).

The first approach focuses on the *design of the job* and stresses such factors as task design, work autonomy, and level of challenge. The second approach stresses *social influence,* assuming that employees' attitudes toward their jobs are affected by the attitudes or beliefs of their peers.

The third theory, called the *dispositional approach,* stresses personal characteristics that are fairly stable over time. This theory holds that people are *generally predisposed* to like or dislike both the overall quality of their jobs and such specific job characteristics as the work itself, supervision, compensation, and work rules. The dispositional approach does not deny potentially positive or negative situational influences—say, changes in supervision, work assignment, job design—but it holds that individuals enter the workplace with predisposed job attitudes

The **theory of reasoned action** states that when a behavior is a matter of *choice,* the best predictor of the behavior is the person's *intention* to perform it.

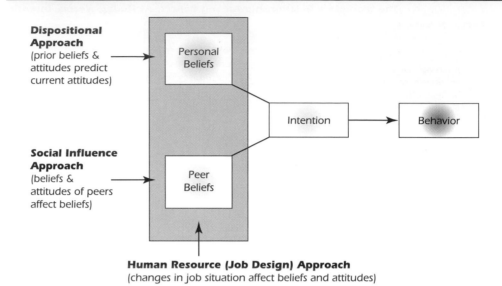

Dispositional Approach (prior beliefs & attitudes predict current attitudes) → Personal Beliefs

Social Influence Approach (beliefs & attitudes of peers affect beliefs) → Peer Beliefs

Intention → Behavior

Human Resource (Job Design) Approach (changes in job situation affect beliefs and attitudes)

formed from past experiences and personal beliefs. Changes such as pay increases, job redesign, and flexible hours can improve job attitudes, at least temporarily, but in the long run, the best predictor of employees' current job attitudes is their prior work attitudes.[6]

Attitude Theory and Reasoned Action   All three of these attitude theories can be adapted to the theory of reasoned action. Thus a change in job design may alter the general workplace situation to the extent that a worker's beliefs are changed. Social influence theory would say that the beliefs that predict a person's subjective norm will change when the beliefs and attitudes of the person's peers are changed. Finally, the dispositional approach would argue that a person's own prior beliefs and attitudes are the strongest predictor of job attitudes—and thus of intentions and behaviors while performing a newly designed job.

CHANGING ATTITUDES   Behaviors and attitudes can best be predicted by knowing two factors:

Among the changes that Motorola wants to see in the workplace attitudes of its employees are greater degrees of independent-mindedness, of equality in proposing creative ideas, and of teamwork in decision making. From its headquarters in Schaumberg, Illinois, to its offices in Honolulu and Tokyo, the company is thus pushing employee training as the key to both greater knowledge and upward mobility.

TABLE 18.1	► Basic Principles of the Human Resource Approach

Providing employee training

Communicating about human resource programs and policies

Helping new employees learn about their job and the company

Providing advancement opportunities within the company

Providing job security

Hiring qualified employees

Having enough people to get the job done

Asking my opinions about how one can improve one's own job

Asking my opinions about making the company successful

Asking for employee suggestions

Asking on employee suggestions

1. A person's beliefs
2. The social norms that influence a person's intentions

Managers may strive to change attitudes, intentions, and behaviors by changing workplace situations—that is, by changing such work factors as compensation, job design, and work hours. However, they must realize that employee attitudes are both fairly stable over time and slow to change. Thus, selecting employees who come to their positions with positive job attitudes might be the most effective way to build a workforce with a positive attitude.

Human Resource Approach   Research has also supported a related managerial philosophy often called the *human resource approach* to job satisfaction. Consistently providing personnel activities that are highly valued by employees will in the long run improve attitudes, intentions, and behaviors. This approach typically works because employees' attitudes are favorably affected by their belief that the organization is committed to providing a positive work environment. Studies have shown that employees who believe that their employer cares about them will reciprocate with more positive attitudes, reduced absenteeism, increased quality and productivity, and greater creative input.[7] Thus the basic principles of the human resource approach, which are listed in Table 18.1, can favorably influence employee attitudes when consistently applied by managers.

► QUALITY SPOTLIGHT ◄   Nucor Steel

F. Kenneth Iverson is the chief executive officer of Nucor Corporation. Nucor is America's seventh-largest steel company and the only one to consistently make a profit over the past 20 years. Nucor has increased its dividend annually and operated profitably in each quarter since 1968—this is quite an accomplishment in an industry that has lost money overall in more than half of those years. In addition, while the U.S. steel industry has laid off over 300,000 workers and shut down numerous plants in the past two decades, Nucor has not laid off a single worker. According to former U.S. Secretary of Labor Ann McLaughlin, "Every manager who wonders what it will take to compete in the twenty-first century needs to know the Nucor story."

Why has Nucor succeeded while the other U.S. steel firms have struggled? Ken Iverson proudly but without hesitation cites four practices that are directly related to the company's human resources policies:

1. *Employee Teams*—All tasks in Nucor's mills are performed by employee teams. Each team is in charge of complete tasks and receives a production bonus every week in which work standards are exceeded. This program is an excellent example of applied behavior modification with continuous reinforcement.

2. *Levels of Management*—Iverson believes that those closest to the work should make the decisions concerning that work whenever possible. Thus, the greater the autonomy given to teams, the fewer levels of management that are necessary.

(continued)

3. *Limited Staff*—Iverson also believes that staff tend to obstruct effective work teams. Nucor, therefore, operates 6 steel mills, 6 joist plants, and 2 products divisions with only 22 staff members. All staff are located at the corporate headquarters in Charlotte, North Carolina.

4. *No-Layoffs Policy*—For well over 20 years, Nucor has maintained a no-layoffs policy in an industry that has laid off over 350,000 U.S. workers. During lean times, Nucor prefers a "share the pain" policy. This plan reduces the number of days per week that a team works. In addition, management, including Iverson, also takes a pay reduction.

These principles have helped Nucor build an environment in which autonomous teams of employees strive for maximum productivity—a goal that, if achieved, maximizes bonuses and minimizes interference from management or staff. In addition, the teams have a great deal of job security because of the no-layoffs policy. As a result, Nucor employees have consistently maintained higher levels of productivity and far more positive work attitudes than their counterparts elsewhere in the steel industry.

As a practical matter, what does the manager do with the employee who has a "bad attitude"? Unfortunately, managerial experience and research both indicate that changing attitudes is very difficult. Fortunately, a "bad attitude" is often not the problem. Rather, the problem is usually unacceptable *behavior*. Attitude, of course, influences behaviors, as we have seen, but there are two good reasons why managers should not focus too sharply on attitudes:

1. Attitudes are *internal* and therefore cannot be accurately measured or observed
2. The beliefs, values, and norms that affect attitudes are complex and have been constructed over a lifetime

Behaviors, on the other hand, are not only observable but can also be documented and measured. Most importantly, managers can deal successfully with unacceptable performance.

Not surprisingly, then, the correct identification, analysis, and resolution of behavioral problems are an important task for managers. Of course, poor attitude or motivation is only one potential cause of unsatisfactory behavior or performance. Determining exactly *why* an employee is performing at an unsatisfactory level is critical because problems cannot be corrected unless their causes are known. Effective managers not only look for performance problems but also recognize that they stem from a variety of causes. Human resource specialists have identified at least four major causes of behavior problems:[8]

1. *Lack of Skills*—Organizations often place employees in jobs without giving them sufficient training. Once identified, the skills-deficiency problem can be remedied in one of three ways: (a) train the employee to remove the skill deficiency, (b) transfer the employee to a job that better uses his or her current skills, (c) terminate the employee.

2. *Lack of Positive Attitude*—Although there are numerous approaches to attitude and motivation problems, most strategies rest on one seemingly simple axiom: *Determine what the employee needs and offer it as a reward for good performance.* (Yet as most managers know, determining the needs of an employee and providing a corresponding change in job design or work environment is a challenging task.)

3. *Rule Breaking*—Rule breakers are employees who are occasionally absent or late to work without good reason, who violate dress codes, or who refuse to follow safety procedures. They have the necessary skills and normally do good work, but they disregard the organization's policies and regulations. The most effective approach to this form of behavior is to apply positive discipline. This means providing a written policy of expected behaviors and a written program detailing progressive disciplinary steps (for example, first offense—oral warning; second offense—written warning; third offense—suspension; fourth offense—termination).

4. *Personal Problems*—A final type of unsatisfactory behavior is associated with the *troubled employee*—one whose personal problems are so significant that they prevent the employee from performing satisfactorily at work. The troubled employee may suffer from a variety of problems, including emotional illness, financial crisis, alcohol or drug dependency, chronic physical problems, and family unrest.

PERCEPTION

The above material focused on individuals by discussing attitudes. This major chapter section continues the discussion of individuals by emphasizing perception. Topics discussed below are as follows:

1. Defining perception and the perceptual process
2. Attribution theory
3. Perceptual distortions

PERCEPTION AND THE PERCEPTUAL PROCESS

Perception is the psychological process of selecting stimuli, organizing the data into recognizable patterns, and interpreting the resulting information. The **perceptual process** is the series of actions that individuals follow in order to select, organize, and interpret stimuli from the environment. Every second of every day individuals are bombarded by countless stimuli through the human senses of sight, hearing, touch, smell, and taste. We attend to only a small portion of these stimuli.

Thus, as you can see in Figure 18.4, the perceptual process links the individual with his or her environment. Since we can only select and process a limited number of the stimuli, we are never aware of everything that occurs around us. Moreover, the limited stimuli that we do perceive are subjected to perceptual filters that are largely determined by our past experiences, attitudes, and beliefs. Just as importantly, stimuli that are inconsistent with our predispositions are often ignored or distorted. Thus we can become "close-minded" without realizing it.

> **Perception** is the psychological process of selecting stimuli, organizing the data into recognizable patterns, and interpreting the resulting information.
>
> The **perceptual process** is the series of actions that individuals follow in order to select, organize, and interpret stimuli from the environment.

ATTRIBUTION THEORY: INTERPRETING THE BEHAVIOR OF OTHERS

Attribution is the process by which people *interpret* the behavior of others by assigning to it motives or causes. For example, if an employee is routinely late to work, a manager might try to determine the cause of the behavior. Is it lack of motivation or lack of ability? Is it some personal factor or a situational factor such as the way the job is structured or scheduled? The

> **Attribution** is the process by which people *interpret* the behavior of others by assigning to it motives or causes.

FIGURE 18.4	► Process of perception

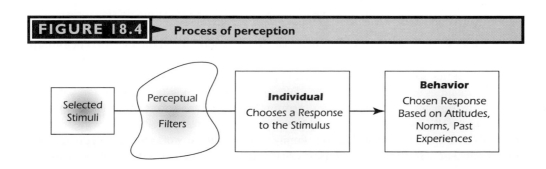

manager may believe that poor attitude is the cause of the behavior and try to motivate the employee to arrive on time. As a rule, managers do *not* consider situational factors. Why? Much of the conflict that occurs between managers and subordinates stems from the tendency of managers to act on their own perception and interpretation of a given situation, which may be quite different from those of subordinates; they may not even coincide with the facts of the situation. Managers can avoid inappropriate attributions in three ways:[9]

1. By making a greater effort to see situations as they are perceived by others
2. By guarding against perceptual distortions
3. By paying more attention to individual differences among subordinates

The underlying assumption of attribution theory is that managers are typically motivated to understand the *causes* of employee behavior. Naturally, they tend to question whether the behavior is the result of internal or external causes. *Internal* causes include attitude or motivation, ability, and lack of knowledge of the desired (correct) behavior. *External* causes include the difficulty of tasks and the actions of others, both of which may exert influence beyond the control of the individual. Research indicates that people generally focus on three factors when making attributions:[10]

1. *Consensus*—The extent to which they believe that the person being observed is behaving in a manner consistent with the behavior of his or her peers. High consensus exists when the person's actions reflect, or are similar to, the actions of the group; low consensus exists when the person's actions do not.
2. *Consistency*—The extent to which they believe that the person being observed behaves consistently—in a similar fashion—when confronted on other occasions with the same or similar situations. High consistency exists when the person repeatedly acts in the same way when faced with similar stimuli.
3. *Distinctiveness*—The extent to which they believe that the person being observed would behave consistently when faced with different situations. Low distinctiveness exists when the person acts in a similar manner in response to different stimuli. High distinctiveness exists when the person varies his or her response in different situations.

Thus a manager would be more likely to attribute an employee's behavior to external causes under at least three circumstances:

1. If other employees behave the same way
2. If the employee has behaved the same way in similar situations in the past
3. If this behavior is highly unusual or distinctive

Internal causes might be attributed if other employees do not behave in the same manner or if the employee usually behaves in the same manner under most circumstances.

► PERCEPTUAL DISTORTIONS

Managers, like everyone else, make judgments and decisions based on their perceptions. To help ensure that these judgments and decisions are worthwhile, managers must strive to avoid common perceptual distortions, including stereotypes, halo effects, projection, self-serving bias, attribution error, selective perception, and recency. Each of these distortions is discussed below.

A **stereotype** is a fixed, distorted generalization about members of a group.

STEREOTYPES A **stereotype** is a fixed, distorted generalization about members of a group. Stereotyping—which often stems from such aspects of diversity as race, gender, age, physical abilities/qualities, social background, and occupation— attributes incomplete, exaggerated, or distorted qualities to individual members of groups. Stereotyping results from the nature of our information-processing tendencies. As human beings, we process information through learned knowledge gained by means of past experience, observation, or contact with other individuals who influence us, such as our family, friends, and co-workers. Stereotyping, therefore, is not generalization. A stereotype is usually *learned* through outside sources rather than through direct individual experiences.

NATWEST BANK FOCUSES ON ERASING TRADITIONAL BANK MANAGER STEREOTYPE

Stereotypes are fixed, distorted generalizations about members of a group. Managers at NatWest Bank are attempting to dispel the traditional bank manager stereotype that they are cold, calculating, self-centered, and that they care very little about personal needs of employees. NatWest's management understands that it is impossible to gain maximum success if employees do not see bank managers as progressive, contemporary, and caring for employees as people.

NatWest is progressing so well that it is fast becoming an industry model for how to break the bank manager stereotype. Managers at Westminster are working toward developing a new image by focusing on developing their own abilities to inspire, listen to, and communicate with employees. Managers are also concentrating on having employees work in teams and are more focused on developing employee personal beliefs in and commitment to NatWest. In essence, managers are continually discussing employees and enlisting them in accomplishing company vision.

As a company, NatWest has made a significant resource commitment to breaking the traditional bank manager stereotype. For instance, the company has designed and implemented a two-year program of study to help its managers meet the stereotype-breaking challenge. The program covers topics like motivating employees and leadership. Also, the program includes managers from all bank levels and both on-the-job and off-the-job training. Overall, NatWest seems to have invested adequately to dispel the traditional bank manager stereotype. In reality, however, to ultimately eliminate the stereotype, individual managers must continually manage in a way that contradicts the stereotype.

HALO EFFECT   When a manager allows one particular aspect of an employee's behavior to influence his or her evaluation of all other aspects of that employee's behavior, the so-called **halo effect** has occurred. For example, the manager who knows that a particular employee always arrives at work early and helps to open the business may let the "halo" of the employee's dependability influence his or her perceptions of the employee in other areas—say, customer relations or products knowledge. Thus even if the employee is only mediocre in these areas, the manager perceives overall strength.

> The **halo effect** results from allowing one particular aspect of someone's behavior to influence one's evaluation of all other aspects of that person's behavior.

Of course, a negative halo—"devil's horns"—may also affect perceptions. If an accountant performs poorly only when working directly with plant managers on annual budget projects, a supervisor may allow this one negative behavior to cloud his or her judgment of the employee's other behaviors.

The halo problem can be minimized by supervisory training that focuses on the fact that it is not unusual for employees to perform well in some areas and less effectively in others.

PROJECTION   The unconscious tendency to assign (project) our own traits, motives, beliefs, and attitudes to others is called **projection.** Consider, for example, a manager who enjoys working as part of a quality-improvement team. This manager may strongly encourage subordinates to join similar teams, and then be disappointed in those who refuse to do so. This classic form of perceptual distortion assumes that others have the same needs and desires as oneself. Not surprisingly, this assumption is rarely accurate.

> **Projection** is the unconscious tendency to assign one's own traits, motives, beliefs, and attitudes to others.

SELF-SERVING BIAS AND ATTRIBUTION ERROR   In practice, when asked to identify the causes of an employee's poor performance, managers will usually choose internal causes, such as motivation, ability, or effort, rather than external causes, such as lack of support from others or circumstances beyond the employee's control. This tendency to overestimate internal causes of behavior and underestimate external ones is called **attribution error.** Interestingly, many of the same managers, when asked to identify the causes of their own performance, refer to external causes. This form of perceptual distortion is called **self-serving bias:** the tendency to attribute personal success to internal causes and personal failures to external causes.

> **Attribution error** is the tendency to overestimate internal causes of behavior and underestimate external ones when judging other people's behavior.

> The **self-serving bias** is the tendency to overestimate external causes of behavior and underestimate internal ones when judging one's own behavior.

SELECTIVE PERCEPTION   When bombarded with too many external stimuli, people may resort to perceptual filters in order to reduce their awareness of the stimuli. In particular, we tend to attend to stimuli that are consistent with our own motives, beliefs, and attitudes. Thus we are prone to collect information that not only supports our perceptions but also minimizes the emotional distress caused by unfamiliar or troublesome stimuli. This form of perceptual distortion is called **selective perception.**

Selective perception is the tendency to collect information that not only supports one's own motives, beliefs, and attitudes but also minimizes the emotional distress caused by unfamiliar or troublesome stimuli.

RECENCY For example, let's say that a manager notices a few unusually negative comments in the weekly stack of customer comment cards. However, because the majority of the cards contain positive comments about the service that the manager believes accurately reflect the work of her staff, she ignores the negative messages. A few weeks later, she notices a substantial number of negative comments. An investigation reveals that one newly hired employee is the cause of the negative comments—but this discovery comes too late to prevent negative impressions of the service among a good many customers. What went wrong here? The manager allowed her own perceptions to filter out early information that did not conform to her beliefs. Only later did she seek reliable data to check the accuracy of her perceptions.

> **GLOBAL SPOTLIGHT**   The Wide, Wide World of Cultural Perceptions

On a sea voyage, you are traveling with your spouse, your child, and your mother. The ship develops problems and starts to sink. Of your family, you are the only one who can swim, and you can save only one other individual. Whom will you save?

This question was posed to a group of men in Asia and the United States. In the United States, more than 60 percent of respondents said they would save the child, 40 percent the spouse, and none the mother. In the Asian countries, 100 percent of respondents said they would save the mother. Their rationale? You can always remarry and have more children, but you can never have another mother.

When doing business overseas, Americans cannot rely only on uniquely American perceptions and behavior patterns. What seems good in one place ("Father is getting to the age where he would probably be happier in the senior citizen home in Arizona") is scandalous in another ("Look at how Americans treat older people—it's awful").

Cross-cultural mistakes can be expensive. For example, many companies spend a minimum of $125,000 per year to employ one U.S. manager in an overseas position. Another less obvious factor is the human cost accrued when someone does poorly or returns early from an overseas assignment. Premature return of an employee and family may cost the company between $50,000 and $200,000 when replacement expenses are included. Mistakes of corporate representatives because of language or intercultural incompetence can jeopardize millions of dollars in negotiations and purchases, sales, and contracts, as well as undermine customer relations. No doubt, managers' cultural ineptitude damages organizational productivity and profitability.

The price of providing employees with education and training for intercultural effectiveness is miniscule compared to the financial losses that can occur because of personnel "faux pas" in cross-cultural business relations. The benefits from developing human resources can be enormous.

▶ PERCEPTIONS OF PROCEDURAL JUSTICE

Procedural justice is the perceived fairness of the process used for deciding workplace outcomes such as merit increases and promotions.

Perhaps the most important workplace perception formed by employees, however, is of **procedural justice:** the perceived fairness of the process used for deciding outcomes such as merit increases and promotions. The most important of these processes are performance appraisals, job applicant interviewing systems, pay systems, grievance or dispute-resolution systems, and participative decision making. Most employees continually evaluate for themselves not only the fairness of these systems but also their consequences.

PROCEDURES AND OUTCOMES Employees actually form separate perceptions about the organization's process for deciding outcomes on the one hand and the consequences on the other hand. *Procedural justice* examines the fairness of the process itself: Are decisions made according to clear standards? Is the process used consistently for everyone? Can I appeal the decision? Will I be able to have input? *Distributive justice,* on the other hand, examines only the outcome of a decision or policy: Did I receive the promotion? Did I get the raise? Research indicates that employees often view these two types of workplace justice quite differently.[11]

Obviously, then, employees expect managers to be fair in making selection and promotion decisions, in assigning tasks and scheduling work, in choosing people for training and promotion opportunities, in conducting performance appraisals, and in making pay decisions. Of all these processes the one most likely to affect attitudes and morale is performance appraisal. Probably because of the highly personal nature of the process, employees are especially sensitive to perceived unfairness in this area. Consequently, they base a large portion of their overall perceptions about procedural justice on their perceptions of performance appraisals.

A history of perceived fairness, therefore, can be a major asset to a manager in shaping employee perceptions of fairness, positive job attitudes, and productive behaviors. The manager with such a history is also often seen as honest, ethical, and trustworthy. Such a manager may, moreover, be judged less harshly when he or she is perceived as having made an unfavorable decision.[12]

DISPUTE RESOLUTION Another critical factor in employees' evaluations of fairness is how managers resolve disputes. Experienced managers are likely to use *mediation* techniques—they listen to the points of view of the parties involved, offer resources to help resolve the dispute, and encourage the parties to seek inventive solutions. Managers who resort to formal authority and simply impose their own settlements are less likely to be perceived as fair, regardless of the quality of their decisions.[13]

EMPLOYEE RESPONSES How do employees respond to perceptions of unfairness? Those with seniority usually decide that they have invested too many years in the organization either to leave or to cause a disturbance. Instead, they may respond by performing marginally until retirement. Newer employees are more likely to leave for (perceived) better opportunities elsewhere. The costs of unfair employee treatment are difficult to compute. Research has determined that employees' perceptions of unfair treatment are very strong predictors of job absence and turnover—two costly employee behaviors. Other consequences of unfair treatment include lower production quantity and quality, less initiative, diminished morale, lack of cooperation, spread of dissatisfaction to co-workers, fewer suggestions, and less self-confidence. Each result has a substantial organizational cost, whether direct or indirect.[14]

MEASURING EMPLOYEE ATTITUDES Considering the effects on the organization of employee responses to perceived unfairness, it is not surprising that managers often try to measure employees' perceptions of their treatment. However, measuring employee feelings is a complex and difficult process. Getting honest answers in interviews and group discussions is hardly assured; the most practical alternative is to use anonymous survey techniques. One advantage of using written questionnaires is that they make it easier to identify the dimensions of perceived unfairness. For example, results of a written survey can be compared across departments, jobs, and supervisors. A survey taken for Lens Lab, Inc., a national chain of eyeglass stores, found, overall, a high level of perceived fairness. However, in two of eight stores, the levels reported were significantly lower on two dimensions—work pace and pay administration. An investigation led to changes in policy and supervision at those stores, which resulted in higher levels of perceived fairness, and higher store profitability, the following year.

BACK TO THE CASE

In the Introductory Case, we saw that employees often perceive both managers and peers to be sources of their low morale and low productivity, though, many times, these perceptions are not entirely accurate. Rather, employees' perceptions of the workplace change as they gain more direct experiences and become acquainted with the attitudes of other employees. The response of employees to their own changing perceptions largely determines how happy and productive they will be on the job. Those who seek to control their lives and work situations as their perceptions change—like the nurse in the Introductory Case—will usually be happier and more productive on and off the job.

Learning is a more or less permanent change in behavior resulting from practice, experience, education, or training.

Learning can be defined as a relatively permanent change in behavior resulting from practice, experience, education, or training. Behavioral change includes the acquisition of skills, knowledge, and ability. In organizations, people learn specific job-related skills, knowledge, and abilities. They also learn about organizational norms—what is expected from them and how things are accomplished. Both of these learning situations affect employee beliefs, attitudes, intentions, and behaviors. This section will focus on two of the traditional approaches to learning that are of particular value in the workplace: operant and cognitive learning.

Operant learning is an approach that holds the behavior leading to positive consequences is more likely to be repeated.

OPERANT LEARNING **Operant learning,** also called operant conditioning, is based on the belief that behavior is a function of its consequences. If a person perceives that a behavior will lead to a positive consequence, that person will be more likely to repeat the behavior. For example, a salesperson who has taken a client to lunch at a favorite restaurant and has always subsequently received a large order from that client is likely to arrange a similar lunch meeting on the client's next visit. Conversely, if a person perceives that a behavior will likely lead to a negative consequence, that person will be more likely to avoid the behavior. An employee who receives a written disciplinary warning after submitting a report 24 hours late is more likely to submit the report on time next month.

Cognitive learning is an approach theory that focuses on thought processes and assumes that human beings have a high capacity to act in a purposeful manner, and so to choose behaviors that will enable them to achieve long-run goals.

COGNITIVE LEARNING The approach theory that focuses on thought processes is known as **cognitive learning.** This theory assumes that human beings have a high capacity to act in a purposeful manner, and so to choose behaviors that will enable them to achieve long-run goals. Thus employees will evaluate the work environment and choose behaviors that will enable them to achieve such goals as pay bonuses, promotions, and recognition.

Goal-Setting Strategies Cognitive learning theory is the basis for "goal-setting" strategies and has therefore become the most widely applied learning theory in the business world. Goal setting is the basis for individual incentive plans like commissions or piecework, group-incentive plans, and organizationwide incentive plans like profit sharing and gainsharing. The widespread use of goal setting in organizations is attributed to several advantages these strategies offer:[15]

1. *Directed Behavior*—Goals help people focus their daily decisions and behaviors in specific ways.
2. *Challenges*—Individuals are more motivated, and thus achieve higher levels of performance, when given specific objectives instead of such nondirective responses as "keep up the good work."
3. *Resource Allocation*—Critical decisions involving resources (people, time, equipment, money) are more consistent with organizational goals when goal-setting strategies are used.
4. *Structure*—The formal and informal organizational structure can be shaped to set communication patterns and provide each position with a degree of authority and responsibility that supports employee and organizational goals.

Basically, goal-setting strategies involve a systematic process wherein managers and subordinates discuss and agree upon a set of specific, jointly determined goals. If the process is functioning effectively, the final result will be a set of goals in keeping with the overall goals of the organization. Moreover, managers will have exact, measurable objectives by which to gauge each subordinate's performance. In this process, feedback on progress is periodically supplied, enabling workers to recognize and make necessary corrections in their work performance. Above all, the link among performance and evaluation and organizational rewards (goals) is made explicitly clear to the subordinate, with emphasis on *what* was achieved and *how*.

Goal Setting and Problem Solving Managers use goal setting to correct problems as well as achieve new objectives. For example, if the manager of a video store is told in her annual review that she should "cut down on the total number of employee hours," how will she react?

This vague reference to a perceived problem may cause the manager to do any one of a number of things, ranging from laying off several employees (and negatively affecting service) to simply worrying about the suggestion for a few days until it's forgotten. The problem: Her supervisor did not give her a specific measurable goal, require a plan of action, and provide a framework for feedback to see if the plan is working.

Moreover, the manager cannot be sure how achieving the goal (or failure to do so) will directly affect *her*—a necessary link in cognitive learning. Management by objectives (MBO), as discussed in detail in chapter 6, is perhaps the most common application of goal setting. In an MBO process, the supervisor and store manager would jointly discuss and agree upon a goal such as: "20 percent reduction of total employee hours per month to be achieved by reducing the number of 10:00 A.M.–5:00 P.M. personnel by 33 percent under a flextime program. The program is to be developed by the store manager, approved before implementation, and reported on monthly. This goal is one of three that will determine midyear bonuses."

Working with different types of people presents new challenges in goal setting, as women who break through to nontraditional occupations often discover. What kinds of goals might women in the construction industries have?

▶ LEARNING STRATEGIES

Many strategies have evolved that managers can use to enhance the learning of organization members. These strategies are positive strategy, avoidance strategy, escape strategy, and punishment and are discussed further in the following sections.

REINFORCEMENT STRATEGY Managers often use the principle of *reinforcement* when attempting to shape employee behavior. Reinforcement is based on operant conditioning theory: It is assumed that employees will repeat behavior that is reinforced or rewarded. Forms of reinforcement may include positive recognition by a supervisor, a "pass" on a checklist training item, or even simple praise ("You've mastered that, so let's move on to something new"). Of course, formal awards and monetary compensation also work. To shape or strengthen employee behavior, the manager can select from any combination of the following four reinforcement strategies:[16]

1. *Positive Reinforcement*—Any stimulus that causes a behavior to be repeated is a positive reinforcer. Common examples of positive reinforcement are praise, recognition, pay, and support. It is essential that the reinforcer directly follow the desired behavior. For example, if a manager witnesses an employee superbly handling an irate customer, immediate praise (or praise offered no later than the end of the day) is much more effective than a comment three months later during a performance appraisal.

2. *Avoidance Strategy*—Behavior that can prevent the onset of an undesired consequence often results from *avoidance learning*. In recent years, for example, many employers have adopted strict policies regarding the use of illegal drugs by employees. Research indicates that such strict "avoidance" policies have contributed to the overall decline in casual drug use, both in organizations and within the larger society. Indeed, one major pharmaceutical firm reported a drop in the number of job applicants testing positive for drug use from 7 percent in 1985 to less than 1 percent ten years later.[17]

3. *Escape Strategy*—When a manager provides an arrangement in which a desired response will terminate an undesired consequence, that manager is using the *escape strategy*. For example, a manager may first set employees the least desired task, such as cleaning and setting up equipment, and inform them that once the equipment has passed inspection, they can move on to a more desirable task.

4. *Punishment Strategy*—When an *undesired* behavior by an employee is followed by an undesired response by management, a punishment strategy is being used. Organizations commonly select such punishment strategies—usually they are called "disciplinary actions"—as oral and written warnings, demotion, suspension, and termination. The primary objective of a disciplinary program is to warn employees that certain undesired behaviors are considered serious enough to invoke discipline. The purpose, of course, is to motivate employees to comply with work rules and performance standards. A second objective is to establish and maintain a climate of respect and mutual trust between employees and managers.

For updated information on the topics in this chapter, Internet exercises, links to related Internet sites, an interactive study guide, and more, visit our companion Web site at

http://www.prenhall.com/certo

Additional information can be found on the inside front and back covers of this text.

ACTION SUMMARY

Read the learning objectives below. Each objective is followed by questions. Answering these questions accurately will help you retain the most important concepts discussed in this chapter. After answering each question, check your answer against the answer key at the end of this chapter. (*Hint:* If you have any doubts regarding the correct response, consult the page number that follows the answer.)

Circle:

From studying this chapter, I will attempt to acquire

1. An understanding of employee workplace attitudes.

   T F
   a. Attitudes are largely shaped by personal beliefs and values and the norms communicated by others.

   a b c d e
   b. People commonly communicate their attitudes through all the following methods *except:* (a) eyes (b) body language (c) thoughts (d) voice (e) behavior.

2. Insights into how to change employee attitudes.

   T F
   a. Employee workplace attitudes are fairly stable over time and slow to change.

   a b c d e
   b. Managers should keep in mind that of the following employee characteristics, only one is *external* and thus should be subject to potential disciplinary action: (a) bad attitude (b) negative intention (c) poor behavior (d) inappropriate values (e) false beliefs.

3. An appreciation of the impact of employee perceptions on employee behaviors.

   T F
   a. Managers can usually correctly attribute poor employee behavior to a lack of motivation.

   a b c d e
   b. When a manager evaluates an employee highly on all aspects of his or her job performance even though, in reality, the employee excels at only one aspect, the manager is guilty of (a) the halo effect (b) stereotyping (c) attribution error (d) selective perception (e) recency.

4. Knowledge of employee perceptions of procedural justice.

   T F
   a. Employee perceptions of the fairness of the processes used in reaching organizational decisions are often as important as the fairness of the decisions themselves.

   a b c d e
   b. Managers are most likely to be perceived as fair in their dispute-resolution strategy if they: (a) impose their own ideas for a settlement (b) stay out of all disputes (c) use mediation techniques (d) side with one party quickly (e) refer disputes to the human resource department.

5. An understanding that adult learners are different from younger students.

   T F
   a. Adult learners seek skills and knowledge that they can apply to their work or use to further their careers.

   a b c d e
   b. At Nucor Steel, employees have very positive work attitudes and production records owing to: (a) the use of employee teams (b) a "no-layoffs" policy (c) weekly production bonuses (d) limited levels of staff (e) all of the above.

CASE DISCUSSSION QUESTIONS

"Reviving Workplace Attitudes" (p. 401) and its related Back-to-the-Case sections discuss one of management's greatest challenges—poor job attitudes and burnout on the part of employees. Answer the following discussion questions about this Introductory Case to enrich your understanding of the chapter content:

1. Do you agree that most employees with "poor attitudes" blame managers and co-workers for their work problems?

2. What are some potentially effective methods, other than those presented in the case, that employees might use to take responsibility for improving their workplace attitude?

3. What services might an employer offer to employees to encourage them to improve their job attitudes?

SKILLS EXERCISE: USING REINFORCEMENT STRATEGIES

In this chapter you studied reinforcement strategies. The Introductory Case focuses on St. Elizabeth Medical Center, a hospital in Dayton, Ohio. Assume that as a head nurse in this hospital, you manage a nurse who never shows up for work on time. The nurse is always 15 to 20 minutes late. How would you use the four reinforcement strategies discussed in this chapter to encourage the nurse to arrive at work on time?

1. Define *attitude*.
2. Explain how people's own values and beliefs affect their job behaviors.
3. How do employees communicate their job attitudes to their co-workers?
4. In your own words, explain the theory of reasoned action.
5. Why are people with positive job attitudes often the best-liked employees?
6. How would you rate your current ability to maintain a positive attitude when you have a task to perform? Are you satisfied with your ability? How could you improve it?
7. What strategies should managers use in striving to improve employee attitudes?
8. What are the most common sources of unsatisfactory employee performance?
9. Do you really believe that hiring employees who have a positive attitude can be critical to the success of a company? Explain.
10. Do employees form mental sets about their managers that are at odds with reality?
11. Why do people "filter out" stimuli that do not match their perceptions?
12. Describe the differences between perceptions of objects and perceptions of people.
13. To provide for more effective communication, what seating arrangement should a manager utilize (around a desk or table) when discussing a behavioral problem with an employee?
14. How common is "attribution error" among managers when they are evaluating employees' behavioral problems?
15. List several employee stereotypes you have heard from co-workers.
16. How can a manager guard against selective perception?
17. Why do employees often form more negative perceptions of the organizations they work for after their first year on the job?
18. Which of the two traditional approaches to learning is more often used in organizations?
19. Describe several effective forms of managerial positive reinforcement.

1. **a.** T, p. 402
   b. c, p. 402
2. **a.** T, p. 405
   b. c, p. 405
3. **a.** F, p. 405
   b. a, pp. 410–411
4. **a.** T, pp. 411–412
   b. c, pp. 412–413
5. **a.** T, p. 414
   b. e, p. 407

There is no more disheartening experience for a corporate manager than to see his or her company exposed for wrongdoing by a national publication. Former chairman and CEO Daniel Gill of Bausch & Lomb had such an experience when *Business Week* published an article in October 1995 that accused the company of faked sales invoices, loose accounting practices, and ethics violations.

Rochester, New York–based Bausch & Lomb develops, manufactures, and markets products for the personal health, medical, and optical-care fields. It is widely known for its contact lenses and related products. The company's stock has long been a darling of Wall Street, but after ten years of increasing sales and income, earnings per share plunged in 1995.

Bausch & Lomb's problems did not begin with the *Business Week* article; they began in the field, where Gill's managers got the wrong perception of the company's expectations for them. A very demanding, numbers-oriented manager, Gill expected double-digit annual growth. He focused on the bottom line and quarterly results. Once target goals had been set, he and other top executives at Bausch & Lomb would not accept excuses for shortfalls.

In fact, Gill was known to say, "Make the numbers, but don't do anything stupid." Not surprisingly, since managers generally take their cues from the top, numbers became the key to success. Moreover, management incentives were based on sales targets rather than profitability. As a result, decisions were made to maximize short-term sales figures at the expense of long-run profitability. Ultimately, then, the attitude conveyed to field managers was that cutting corners was an acceptable tactic. Those who were just 10 percent shy of their targets were awarded much smaller bonuses than those who topped their targets. Finally, as field managers abandoned sound business practices and made decisions designed to maximize their personal bonuses, the results became costly to the company.

For example, both to perpetuate reported increases and to enhance personal bonuses, managers at B & L's Hong Kong unit inflated sales by faking invoices to real customers for Ray-Ban sunglasses; some of the same glasses were later sold at cut-rate prices to gray-market dealers. Because top management demanded increased sales figures, the attitude of the field managers was to continue the deceit in order to win top management's favor—and, of course, earn higher bonuses. Nor did Bausch & Lomb's problems end with inflated sales figures. The contact lens division shipped products never ordered, forcing distributors to take unnecessary inventory and violating accepted accounting practices. The Miami warehouse operation may have even laundered drug money.

Eventually, further *Business Week* reports alerted the Securities and Exchange Commission, which launched an investigation into the company's accounting procedures. After the investigation, the company instituted the most conservative practices possible. Quarter-end wheeling and dealing stopped, and a new bonus system was instituted to reflect long-term shareholder and corporate goals.

In addition, the board of directors began to take a more active interest in management. By naming William Balderston III, a former executive vice president of Chase Manhattan Bank and a board member since 1989, as chairman of the audit committee, the board hoped to send a strong message to management and control operating practices. According to Balderston, "We have carefully reviewed the company's recent audits and investigations into assertions regarding sales and accounting practices. While we have no reason to believe there is a systemic problem, we do take any questions about the company's operating methods extremely seriously." Nevertheless, the board made it clear to management that financial controls must be strengthened.

In keeping with these changes, Gill himself had announced that as part of its three-year strategic planning process, Bausch & Lomb would centralize management to gain greater global coordination in core businesses. On December 13, 1995, however, as a result of both shareholder complaints and the board's loss of confidence, Gill announced his retirement. On December 31, outside director William H. Waltrip took over as interim chairman and CEO.

Although the board claims that Gill's retirement was not forced, some analysts believe that he wanted to stay at Bausch & Lomb to clear his name. He still faces scrutiny by the SEC, and Waltrip has vowed to continue the board's probe. Gill claims to have only a general understanding of what happened, and continues to assert that no Bausch & Lomb executive would have placed numbers ahead of ethical practices. Meanwhile, however, there seems to be a disparity between what senior executives now believe happened and what managers down the line recollect. According to the latter, the signals they perceived gave them a license to commit unethical practices. According to one executive, "Gill blamed the problems on poor decisions by individual division presidents and said the divisions needed closer monitoring. It was like slapping the hands of children when they were really acting on Daddy's orders."

QUESTIONS

1. Did the behavior of Bausch & Lomb's field managers accurately reflect Gill's attitude and company policy? Explain.

2. Did Bausch & Lomb set the correct goals for its field managers? Was there a difference between the goals and managers' perception of them? In your opinion, how could Bausch & Lomb have prevented its field managers from getting the "wrong" perception of what was expected of them?

3. Gill disavowed knowledge of what was happening in the field. Should he have known? Should he have taken responsibility for the events? Might a change in his position have changed the actions of shareholders and the board? Explain.

4. Will changes in Bausch & Lomb's management solve the misperception problem? Explain. In what other ways is the board heading off possible problems?

This segment consists of a pretty serious discussion between Susan and Hal. We get the idea that Susan and John have not sorted out their differences. Actually, it is not clear whether John sees that there is really anything to worry about. Perhaps, as far as he is concerned, he is doing the job he was hired to do and over time things will smooth out between him and Susan.

Susan, on the other hand, sees "nothing but trouble" with John in the production manager slot. As she talks with Hal, we see at least two issues that Susan has: one directly related to John and his style of management; and the other related to the fact that Hal is less involved in the day-to-day operations at Quicktakes. Maybe Susan would be unhappy with anybody who was in the job—it just happens to be John. It would be helpful for us to know if these are Susan's feelings alone or if others in the company feel the same way. It's important for managers to understand when issues are individual in nature and when they affect a group of employees.

This segment shifts gears somewhat when Hal asks Susan to be part of a group he is assembling to identify issues in the company and provide suggestions to him for improvement. There are at least two lessons we get from Hal's attempt to change the direction of the discussion. First, we get an idea of how he decided to handle Susan's concerns. Second, we are introduced to a plan he has for getting feedback about the operations at Quicktakes. We do not know much, but it looks like he wants this advisory group to be made up of people who are not in his top management team. Think about how the group will interact. Also, consider whether it would be different if higher managers in the organization participated.

QUESTIONS

1. Susan came to Hal with what she believed is a problem at Quicktakes. By the end of the conversation, do you think Susan saw things the same way or differently from when she began talking with Hal?

2. After his discussion with Susan about John, Hal asks her to be part of a team he is establishing to identify issues and provide recommendations to him about the operations at Quicktakes? Why do you think Hal asked Susan to be on the team? Do you think asking her to be on the team was a good idea?

3. It seems like Hal dealt with Susan in a professional manner. He reacted to and expressed his interest in her concern. There are other ways Hal might have handled Susan's concerns. How else might he have dealt with this situation? What do you think are the strengths and weaknesses of your ideas?

4. Hal is setting up a team to identify issues and provide some possible solutions for problems that they identify at Quicktakes. This is basically a good idea but not one that is without risk. If you were advising Hal, what advice might you give him about setting up the team and in presenting them with his expectations of their work?

19

Principles of Controlling

STUDENT LEARNING OBJECTIVES

From studying this chapter, I will attempt to acquire

1. A definition of *control*

2. A thorough understanding of the controlling subsystem

3. An appreciation for various kinds of control and for how each kind can be used advantageously by managers

4. Insights into the relationship between power and control

5. Knowledge of the various potential barriers that must be overcome to implement successful control

6. An understanding of steps that can be taken to increase the quality of a controlling subsystem

CHAPTER OUTLINE

Introductory Case: *Controlling at Polaroid*

THE FUNDAMENTALS OF CONTROLLING
Defining Control
Defining Controlling

Across Industries: *Hotels—Marriott Hotels Set Performance Standards through the First Ten Program*

Management and the Internet: *NBC Focused on Reaching Future Profitability Standards by Adding Internet Focus*

People Spotlight: *Toyota Takes Corrective Action by Changing Its President*
Types of Control

Diversity Spotlight: *Feedback Control Induces Cosmetics Industry to Develop New Products for Diverse Population Segments*

THE CONTROLLER AND CONTROL
The Job of the Controller
How Much Control Is Needed?

POWER AND CONTROL
A Definition of Power
Total Power of a Manager
Steps for Increasing Total Power

PERFORMING THE CONTROL FUNCTION
Potential Barriers to Successful Controlling
Making Controlling Successful

CONTROLLING AT POLAROID

REMINDER: THE INTRODUCTORY CASE WRAP-UP (P. 438) CONTAINS DISCUSSION QUESTIONS AND A SKILLS EXERCISE TO FURTHER ILLUSTRATE THE APPLICATION OF CHAPTER CONCEPTS TO THIS VIGNETTE.

The Polaroid Corporation, maker of instant cameras and electronic imaging products, struggled with anemic sales and high production and labor costs. A company financial projection reflected that the company had operating losses of over $20 million for the year 1995. (For comparison purposes, the company made $1.4 million on sales of $462.6 million in 1994.)

In response to this negative situation, Polaroid's management announced that it was cutting the workforce by up to 5 percent, or 600 people. This action intended to lower production costs, thereby allowing the company to charge lower prices for its products on the theory that lower prices would boost company sales.

Management also announced that several other steps would be taken. First, Polaroid would consolidate several of its manufacturing facilities. The end result of this action would reduce the number of company plants. Second, the company sped up its entry into such emerging markets as China, India, and Southeast Asia in order to aggressively pursue new customers and higher sales. Third, Polaroid added emphasis on product development. Management especially stressed getting the most profitable new products to market.

Polaroid's management also announced that it would establish a new inventory control program to clamp down on the discounts the company gave to wholesale distributors and emphasized higher spending on advertising and marketing. The initial reaction to this move was expected to be negative, as wholesalers depleted their existing inventories rather than order new product without the discounts to which they have become accustomed. This would undoubtedly lower Polaroid's sales in the near term, but management anticipated that the long-run im-

Polaroid is hoping to hang on to its market in the face of increasing competition, not just from competing film manufacturers but also from digital cameras and one-hour photo developing shops. One possibility is to broaden the base of uses for its product, such as in documenting insurance claims.

pact of the new inventory control program on the company's profitability would be positive.

I. MacAllister Booth, Polaroid's president, believed that all these steps would boost profitability as the company pursued a more focused, aggressive approach to the market. He indicated that streamlining operations would make Polaroid more efficient and, ultimately, more profitable. Some industry analysts agree that the actions planned by Polaroid management would be necessary and would eventually lower costs and raise profits. Others, however, were more skeptical about the outcome of the announced actions. They thought that Polaroid had many other weaknesses that these steps do not address.

What's Ahead

The Introductory Case reports on how management is attempting to deal with high costs, low sales, and low profitability at Polaroid. The management function called *control* can help managers like those at Polaroid eliminate such problems. The material in this chapter explains why eliminating these problems at Polaroid would be controlling at that company and elaborates on the control function in general. The major topics in this chapter are as follows:

1. The fundamentals of controlling
2. The controller and control
3. Power and control
4. Performing the control function

THE FUNDAMENTALS OF CONTROLLING

As the scale and complexity of modern organizations grow, so does the problem of control in organizations. Prospective managers, therefore, need a working knowledge of the essentials of the controlling function.[1] To this end, the following sections provide a definition of control, a definition of the process of controlling, and a discussion of the various types of control that can be used in organizations.

►DEFINING CONTROL

Control is making something happen the way it was planned to happen.

Stated simply, **control** is making something happen the way it was planned to happen. As implied by this definition, planning and control are virtually inseparable functions.[2] In fact, these two functions have been called the Siamese twins of management. According to Robert L. Dewelt:[3]

> The importance of the planning process is quite obvious. Unless we have a soundly charted course of action, we will never quite know what actions are necessary to meet our objectives. We need a map to identify the timing and scope of all intended actions. This map is provided through the planning process.
>
> But simply making a map is not enough. If we don't follow it or if we make a wrong turn along the way, chances are we will never achieve the desired results. A plan is only as good as our ability to make it happen. We must develop methods of measurement and control to signal when deviations from the plan are occurring so that corrective action can be taken.

Murphy's Law is a lighthearted adage making the serious point that managers should continually control—that is, check to see that organizational activities and processes are going as planned. According to Murphy's Law, anything that can go wrong will go wrong.[4] This law reminds managers to remain alert for possible problems, because even if a management system appears to be operating well, it might be eroding under the surface. Managers must always seek feedback on how the system is performing and make corrective changes whenever warranted.

►DEFINING CONTROLLING

Controlling is the process managers go through to control. It is a systematic effort to compare performance to predetermined standards, plans, or objectives to determine whether performance is in line with those standards or needs to be corrected.

Controlling is the process managers go through to control. According to Robert Mockler, controlling is[5]

> a systematic effort by business management to compare performance to predetermined standards, plans, or objectives to determine whether performance is in line with these standards and presumably to take any remedial action required to see that human and other corporate resources are being used in the most effective and efficient way possible in achieving corporate objectives.

For example, production workers generally have daily production goals. At the end of each working day, the number of units produced by each worker is recorded so weekly production levels can be determined. If these weekly totals are significantly below weekly goals, the supervisor must take corrective action to ensure that actual production levels equal planned ones. If, on the other hand, production goals are being met, the supervisor should allow work to continue as it has in the past.[6]

The following sections discuss the controlling subsystem and provide more details about the control process itself.

THE CONTROLLING SUBSYSTEM As with the planning, organizing, and influencing functions described in earlier chapters, controlling can be viewed as a subsystem of the overall management system. The purpose of this subsystem is to help managers enhance the success of the overall management system through effective controlling. Figure 19.1 shows the specific components of the controlling subsystem.

THE CONTROLLING PROCESS As Figure 19.2 illustrates, there are three main steps in the controlling process:

1. Measuring performance
2. Comparing measured performance to standards
3. Taking corrective action

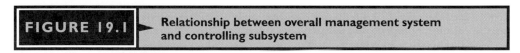

FIGURE 19.1 ▶ Relationship between overall management system and controlling subsystem

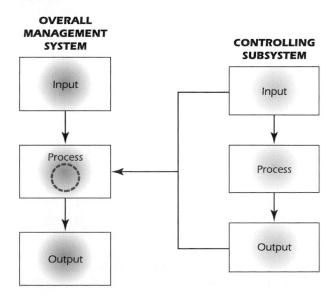

FIGURE 19.2 ▶ The controlling subsystem

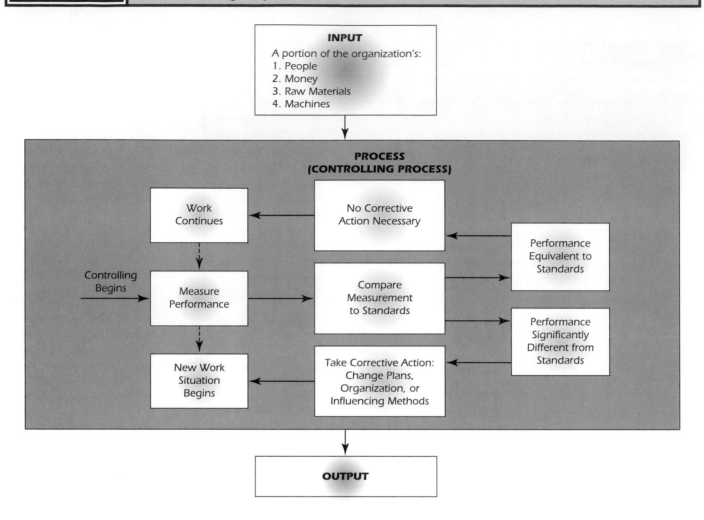

Measuring Performance Before managers can determine what must be done to make an organization more effective and efficient, they must measure current organizational performance.[7] But before they can take such a measurement, they must establish some unit of measure that gauges performance and observe the quantity of this unit as generated by the item whose performance is being measured.

How to Measure. A manager who wants to measure the performance of five janitors, for example, first must establish units of measure that represent janitorial performance—such as the number of floors swept, the number of windows washed, or the number of light bulbs changed. After designating these units of measure, the manager has to determine the number of each of these units accomplished by each janitor. This process of determining both the units of measure and the number of units associated with each janitor furnishes the manager with a measure of janitorial performance.

What to Measure. Managers must always keep in mind that there is a wide range of organizational activities that can be measured as part of the control process. For example, the amounts and types of inventory on hand are commonly measured to control inventory, while the quality of goods and services being produced is commonly measured to control product quality. Performance measurements can relate as well to various effects of production, such as the degree to which a particular manufacturing process pollutes the atmosphere.

The degree of difficulty in measuring various types of organizational performance, of course, is determined primarily by the activity being measured. For example, it is far more dif-

At retail outlets like this Best Buy store in Evanston, Illinois, inventory control often consists of addressing three related issues: (1) the information system gathers data needed to make merchandise decisions, (2) the valuation system determines the worth of merchandise in stock, and (3) the analysis system is designed to measure past performance and plan for future activities.

ficult to measure the performance of a highway maintenance worker than to measure the performance of a student enrolled in a college-level management course.

Comparing Measured Performance to Standards   Once managers have taken a measure of organizational performance, their next step in controlling is to compare this measure against some standard. A **standard** is the level of activity established to serve as a model for evaluating organizational performance. The performance evaluated can be for the organization as a whole or for some individuals working within the organization.[8] In essence, standards are the yardsticks that determine whether organizational performance is adequate or inadequate.[9]

A **standard** is the level of activity established to serve as a model for evaluating organizational performance.

| ► **ACROSS INDUSTRIES** ◄ | Hotels |

MARRIOTT HOTELS SET PERFORMANCE STANDARDS THROUGH THE FIRST TEN PROGRAM

This section emphasizes that in order to control, managers must compare measured performance to standards. Based on this comparison, managers take corrective action, if necessary, to make what is taking place in organizations more consistent with achieving organizational goals. This chapter feature discusses action taken by Marriott Hotels to set and enforce customer service standards.

Marriott International owns Marriott Hotels and is the world's leading hospitality company. Marriott Hotels has more than 4,700 units and serves more than four million customers a day. Marriott International operates the broadest portfolio of brands of any lodging company in the world through its company-owned chains. In addition to Marriott Hotels, these chains include The Ritz Carlton, Marriott Executive Residences, Courtyard by Marriott, Ramada In-

ternational, and Fairfield Suites by Marriott. Through all of its chains, Marriott International offers more than 229,000 rooms worldwide.

Recent financial results at Marriott International indicate that its focus on high-quality customer service is paying off. For the first half of 1998, total revenues rose 15 percent to $4.73 billion. For this same period, net income rose 24 percent to $190 million. Increased revenues reflect higher room revenues due to higher average room rates and the addition of properties. Overall, Marriott International's reputation is very positive among its customers.

One example of customer service focus at Marriott Hotels is the newly implemented First Ten program. Essentially, the First Ten program set a standard within the company for hassle-free check-in. The concept behind the program's name is simple: guests ideally should be in their hotel rooms within the first 10 minutes of their arrival. In

(continued)

Studying operations at General Electric will give us some insights into the different kinds of standards managers can establish. GE has established the following standards:

1. *Profitability standards*—In general, these standards indicate how much money General Electric would like to make as profit over a given time period—that is, its return on investment. More and more, General Electric is using computerized preventive maintenance on its equipment to help maintain profitability standards. Such maintenance programs have reduced labor costs and equipment downtime and thereby have helped raise company profits.

2. *Market position standards*—These standards indicate the share of total sales in a particular market that General Electric would like to have relative to its competitors. General Electric's market position standards were set by company chairman John F. Welch, Jr., in 1988, when he announced that henceforth any product his company offers must achieve the highest or second-highest market share compared to similar products offered by competitors or it would be eliminated or sold to another firm.

3. *Productivity standards*—How much that various segments of the organization should produce is the focus of these standards. Management at General Electric has found that one of the best ways of convincing organization members to commit themselves to increasing company productivity is simply to treat them with dignity and make them feel they are part of the General Electric team.

4. *Product leadership standards*—General Electric intends to assume a leading position in product innovation in its field. Product leadership standards indicate what must be done to attain such a position. Reflecting this interest in innovation, General Electric has pioneered the development of synthetic diamonds for industrial use. In fact, GE is considered the leader in this area, having recently discovered a method for making synthetic diamonds at a purity of 99.9 percent. In all probability, such diamonds will eventually be used as a component of super-high-speed computers.

5. *Personnel development standards*—Standards in this area indicate the type of training programs General Electric personnel should undergo to develop properly. General Electric's commitment to sophisticated training technology is an indication of the seriousness with which the company takes personnel development standards. Company training sessions are commonly supported by sophisticated technology like large-screen projection systems, computer-generated visual aids, combined video and computer presentations, and laser videos.

6. *Employee attitudes standards*—These standards indicate what types of attitudes General Electric managers should strive to inculcate in GE employees. Like many other companies today, General Electric is striving to build positive attitudes toward product quality in its employees.

7. *Social responsibility standards*—General Electric recognizes its responsibility to make a contribution to society. Standards in this area outline the level and types of contributions management believes GE should make. One recent activity that reflects social responsibility standards at General Electric is the renovation of San Diego's Vincent de Paul Joan Kroc center for the homeless, accomplished by work teams made up of General Electric employees. These teams painted, cleaned, and remodeled a building to create a better facility for a number of San Diego's disadvantaged citizens.

8. *Standards reflecting the relative balance between short- and long-range goals*—These standards express the relative emphasis that should be placed on attaining various short- and long-range goals. General Electric recognizes that short-range goals exist to enhance the probability that long-range goals will be attained.

NBC Focused on Reaching Future Profitability Standards by Adding Internet Focus

Profitability standards are defined in this section as the amount of profit that an organization would like to make over a given time period. The following discussion describes how National Broadcasting Company's (NBC) management had to focus on developing Internet-related revenue to help ensure reaching future profitability standards.

In a good week, NBC was selling $100 million of television advertising. That was more than the Internet search engine Yahoo! had in almost a year and about four times what MSNBC.com sold in two years. Although NBC's management recognized that the Internet as a media was still in its infancy, management also recognized that the future of selling advertising on the Internet could be a major source of future revenue growth and, as a result, future profit.

NBC's management was in a difficult situation. The company was gaining no Internet advertising revenue yet Internet advertising held the potential of being the "wave of the future" for advertising. As a result, management decided to change its strategy to include business ventures in the Internet arena.

NBC managed to craft an Internet strategy that was very aggressive without spending much cash. NBC made two well-publicized deals: the 1996 launch of MSNBC, the cable and online joint venture with Microsoft, and the more recent purchase of a controlling interest in Snap, a fledgling search engine site built by Internet startup CNET. NBC also created its own on-line programming, extending such television shows as *Saturday Night Live* onto the Net. NBC also acquired stakes in a host of Internet businesses, ranging from a popular music site to a new-media production company to a technology firm that delivers Internet video.

NBC's management has modified its organizational strategy to include a number of somewhat diverse Internet activities. The challenge now facing management is to generate ongoing profit from diverse online ventures. Look for NBC's Internet-related strategy to be changed again if management cannot meet this challenge.

Successful managers pinpoint all important areas of organizational performance and establish corresponding standards in each area.[10] For instance, American Airlines has set two very specific standards for appropriate performance of its airport ticket offices: (1) at least 95 percent of the flight arrival times posted should be accurate, meaning that actual arrival times do not deviate more than 15 minutes from posted times and (2) at least 85 percent of customers coming to the airport ticket counter should not have to wait more than 5 minutes to be serviced.

BACK TO THE CASE

Polaroid's management should view controlling activities within the company as a subsystem of the organization's overall management system. For management to achieve organizational control, Polaroid's controlling subsystem must receive an adequate portion of the people, money, raw materials, and machines available within the company.

The process portion of the controlling subsystem at Polaroid requires management to take the following three steps:

1. Measure the performance levels of various productive units
2. Compare these performance levels to predetermined performance standards for these units
3. Take any corrective action necessary to ensure that planned performance levels are consistent with actual performance levels

The Introductory Case indicates that one area in which Polaroid's management needs to develop standards is desired profitability. According to the case, there are two major reasons why Polaroid has been struggling with profitability in recent years: high production costs and low product sales. Because the company is not achieving a desirable level of profits, the control actions that management should take in this area would be aimed at lowering production costs and increasing sales competitiveness.

Servicing is an important element of the control process. Northwest Airlines recently experienced flight delays due to plane malfunctions that were traced to poor servicing procedures. What kinds of control processes might be in place here?

Corrective action is managerial activity aimed at bringing organizational performance up to the level of performance standards.

Problems are factors within an organization that are barriers to organizational goal attainment.

A **symptom** is a sign that a problem exists.

Taking Corrective Action   After actual performance has been measured and compared with established performance standards, the next step in the controlling process is to take corrective action if necessary.   **Corrective action** is managerial activity aimed at bringing organizational performance up to the level of performance standards. In other words, corrective action focuses on correcting organizational mistakes that are hindering organizational performance. Before taking any corrective action, however, managers should make sure that the standards they are using were properly established and that their measurements of organizational performance are valid and reliable.

Recognizing Problems. At first glance, it seems a fairly simple proposition that managers should take corrective action to eliminate **problems**—factors within an organization that are barriers to organizational goal attainment. In practice, however, it often proves difficult to pinpoint the problem causing some undesirable organizational effect. Let us suppose that a performance measurement indicates a certain worker is not adequately passing on critical information to fellow workers. If the manager is satisfied that the communication standards are appropriate and that the performance measurement information is both valid and reliable, the manager should take corrective action to eliminate the problem causing this substandard performance.

Recognizing Symptoms. But what exactly is the problem causing substandard communication in this situation? Is it that the worker is not communicating adequately simply because he or she doesn't want to communicate? Or is it that the job makes communication difficult? Or is it that the worker does not have the necessary training to communicate in an appropriate manner? Before attempting to take corrective action, the manager must determine whether the worker's failure to communicate is a problem in itself or a **symptom**—a sign that a problem exists.[11] For example, the worker's failure to communicate adequately could be a symptom of inappropriate job design or a cumbersome organizational structure.

Once the problem has been properly identified, corrective action can focus on one or more of the three primary management functions of planning, organizing, and influencing. That is, corrective action can include such activities as modifying past plans to make them more suitable for future organizational endeavors, making an existing organizational structure more suitable for existing plans and objectives, or restructuring an incentive program to ensure that high producers are rewarded more than low producers. Note that because planning, organizing, and influencing are closely related, there is a good chance that corrective action taken in one area will necessitate some corresponding action in one or both of the other two areas.

This section has discussed corrective action and described its role in the controlling process. The following People Spotlight feature on Toyota Motor Corporation illustrates that corrective action can involve changing organization members so that organizational standards can be more effectively maintained.

A stroke that forced the resignation of Tatsuro Toyoda, president of Toyota Motor Corporation, sent shock waves throughout the company. Toyota is Japan's largest automaker and the third largest automaker in the world. Toyota management was highly dissatisfied with the company's share of international automobile sales. In choosing a new president, therefore, management had to decide whether to go with someone who was likely to continue Toyoda's conservative, moderately successful posture or someone who promised to implement a bold new approach to international sales that might achieve the standards management desired.

The company appointed Hiroshi Okuda as president and thereby signaled that it would be "taking off the gloves" in the increasingly vicious arena of international car sales. The 62-year-old Okuda is a gregarious man who loves gambling and late night movies and holds a black belt in judo. In contrast to past Toyota presidents, he openly boasts that he is willing to use any and all company resources to beat competitors. Okuda sees himself as a warrior and, consistent with this image, recently announced that he will speed up new-product development, do whatever it takes to recover lost market share, and hasten Toyota's shift of product manufacturing to overseas locations.

Clearly, upper management at Toyota was convinced that the key to improving international sales was a new and very different type of president. It remains to be seen whether this corrective action was appropriate given Toyota's situation.

BACK TO THE CASE

In taking any corrective action at Polaroid, management must be certain that the action is aimed at organizational problems rather than at the symptoms of those problems. For example, if production costs are too high because workers are not trained well enough to operate their equipment properly, the symptom of high production costs will disappear when action is taken to improve training of production workers—which is the real problem.

Any corrective action taken at Polaroid must focus on further planning, organizing, or influencing efforts. For example, if production workers are being more carefully trained, how must Polaroid's scheduling of workers change? Will the company still need the same number of production supervisors when workers become more competent as a result of their improved training?

▶ TYPES OF CONTROL

Three types of management control are possible:

1. Precontrol
2. Concurrent control
3. Feedback control

What type is used is determined primarily by the work phase in which the control is needed.

PRECONTROL Control that takes place before work is performed is called **precontrol,** or *feed-forward control.*[12] Managers using this type of control create policies, procedures, and rules aimed at eliminating behavior that will cause undesirable work results. For example, the manager of a small record shop may find that a major factor in attracting return customers is having salespeople discuss records with customers. This manager might use precontrol by establishing a rule that salespeople cannot talk to one another while a customer is in the store. This rule is a precontrol because it is aimed at eliminating an anticipated problem: salespeople who are so engrossed in conversations with one another that they neglect to chat with customers about records. In sum, precontrol focuses on eliminating predicted problems.

Precontrol is control that takes place before some unit of work is actually performed.

Concurrent control is control that takes place as some unit of work is being performed.

CONCURRENT CONTROL Control that takes place as work is being performed is called **concurrent control.** It relates not only to employee performance but also to such nonhuman areas as equipment performance and department appearance. For example, most supermarkets have rigid rules about the amount of stock that should be placed on the selling floor. The general idea is to display generous amounts of all products on the shelves, with no empty spaces. A concurrent control aimed at ensuring that shelves are stocked as planned could consist of a stock manager's making periodic visual checks throughout a work period to evaluate the status of the sales shelves and, correspondingly, the performance of the stock crew.[13]

Feedback control is control that takes place after some unit of work has been performed.

FEEDBACK CONTROL Control that concentrates on past organizational performance is called **feedback control.**[14] Managers exercising this type of control are attempting to take corrective action by looking at organizational history over a specified time period. This history may involve only one factor, such as inventory levels, or it may involve the relationships among many factors, such as net income before taxes, sales volume, and marketing costs.

BACK TO THE CASE

In controlling at Polaroid, management should use an appropriate combination of precontrol, concurrent control, and feedback control. Precontrol would emphasize the elimination of factors that could cause low annual profitability at Polaroid before the year actually begins. Through concurrent control, management would be able to assess the company's profitability during a particular operating period. Finally, feedback control would enable Polaroid's management to control at the end of some operating period. By analyzing a segment of Polaroid's history, management could use feedback control to improve future performance.

An optimal mix of these types of control would certainly help to eliminate profitability problems at Polaroid before they became overwhelming. Polaroid's management must be careful, however, not to make the common mistake of emphasizing feedback control to the detriment of concurrent control and precontrol.

DIVERSITY SPOTLIGHT · Feedback Control Induces Cosmetics Industry to Develop New Products for Diverse Population Segments

For years, the cosmetics industry operated on the assumption that cosmetics sales are not influenced by recessions. As a result, firms like Maybelline Company and Fashion Fair historically developed their company plans with little regard for the U.S. economy.

Through feedback control, however, cosmetics companies recently came to the conclusion that economic downturns indeed influence cosmetics sales. An analysis of operating periods in the early 1990s indicated that the $4-billion-a-year cosmetics market had gone soft and that the main reason was the recession of that time.

Cosmetic firms swung into action to try to reignite cosmetics sales. Feedback control finally made the industry recognize the needs of a previously underserved diverse population—African American, Asian, Hispanic, and Native American women, who cannot wear mainstream makeup lines because the colors and formulations were developed for white skin. New products developed specifically for such ethnic customers are expected to give this previously "recession-proof" business a boost. Many cosmetics companies are either introducing separate brand lines aimed at ethnic customers or expanding present mainstream product lines to include a greater range of shades to accommodate those customers' coloring. Cosmetics industry consultant Allan Mottus estimates that makeup for women of color accounts for approximately 10 percent of the total market.

Organization charts developed for medium- and large-sized companies typically contain a position called *controller*. The sections that follow explain the job of the controller and discuss its relationship to the control function and how much control is needed within an organization.

►THE JOB OF THE CONTROLLER

The **controller** (also sometimes called the *comptroller*) is the staff person who gathers information that helps managers control. From the preceding discussion, it is clear that managers are responsible for comparing planned and actual performance and for taking corrective action when necessary. In smaller organizations, managers may also be completely responsible for gathering information about various aspects of the organization and developing necessary reports based on this information. In medium- or large-sized companies, however, the controller handles much of this work. The controller's basic responsibility is to assist line managers with the controlling function by gathering appropriate information and generating reports that reflect this information.[15] The controller usually works with information about the following financial dimensions of the organization:[16]

1. Profits
2. Revenues
3. Costs

> The **controller** is the staff person whose basic responsibility is to assist line managers with the controlling function by gathering appropriate information and generating necessary reports that reflect this information.

TABLE 19.1	Sample Job Description for a Controller in a Large Company

Objectives

The controller (or comptroller) is responsible for all accounting activities within the organization.

Functions

1. *General accounting*—Maintain the company's accounting books, accounting records, and forms. This includes:
   a. Preparing balance sheets, income statements, and other statements and reports
   b. Giving the president interim reports on operations for the recent quarter and fiscal year to date
   c. Supervising the preparation and filing of reports to the SEC

2. *Budgeting*—Prepare a budget outlining the company's future operations and cash requirements.

3. *Cost accounting*—Determine the cost to manufacture a product and prepare internal reports for management of the processing divisions. This includes:
   a. Developing standard costs
   b. Accumulating actual cost data
   c. Preparing reports that compare standard costs to actual costs and highlight unfavorable differences

4. *Performance reporting*—Identify individuals in the organization who control activities and prepare reports to show how well or how poorly they perform.

5. *Data processing*—Assist in the analysis and design of a computer-based information system. Frequently, the data-processing department is under the controller, and the controller is involved in management of that department as well as other communications equipment.

6. *Other duties*—Other duties may be assigned to the controller by the president or by corporate bylaws. Some of these include:
   a. Tax planning and reporting
   b. Service departments such as mailing, telephone, janitors, and filing
   c. Forecasting
   d. Corporate social relations and obligations

Relationship

The controller reports to the vice president for finance.

4. Investments

5. Discretionary expenses

The sample job description of a controller in Table 19.1 shows that the controller is responsible for generating information managers rely on when exercising the control function. Because the controller is seldom directly responsible for taking corrective action within the organization but instead advises managers on what sort of action to take, the controller position is considered a staff position.

►HOW MUCH CONTROL IS NEEDED?

Cost-benefit analysis is the process of comparing the cost of some activity with the benefit or revenue that results from the activity to determine the activity's total worth to the organization.

As with all organizational endeavors, control activities should be pursued if the expected benefits of performing such activities are greater than the costs of performing them.[17] The process of comparing the cost of any organizational activity with the expected benefit of performing the activity is called **cost-benefit analysis.** In general, managers and controllers should collaborate to determine exactly how much controlling is justified in a given situation.

Figure 19.3 graphs controlling activity at a certain company over an extended period of time. Note how controlling costs increase steadily as more and more controlling activities are performed. Also note that because the controlling function requires start-up costs, controlling costs are usually greater than the income generated from increased controlling at first. As controlling starts to correct major organizational errors, however, the income from increased controlling eventually equals controlling costs (point X_1 on Figure 19.3) and ultimately surpasses them by a large margin.

As more and more controlling activity is added beyond X_1, however, controlling costs and the income from increased controlling eventually become equal again (point X_2 on Figure 19.3). As more controlling activity is added beyond X_2, controlling costs again surpass the income from increased controlling. The main reason for this last development is that major organizational problems probably were detected much earlier, so most corrective measures at this point are aimed at smaller and less costly problems.

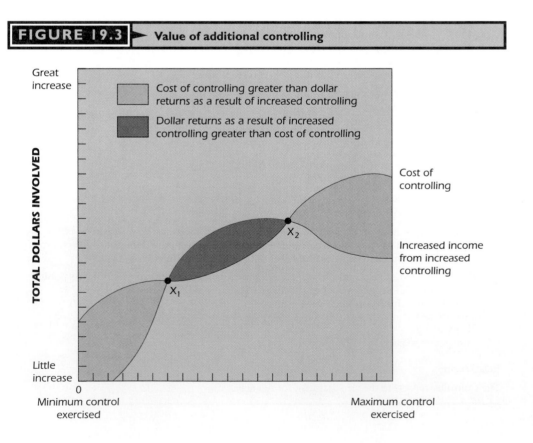

FIGURE 19.3 ► **Value of additional controlling**

The job of the controller at Polaroid is to gather information for reports that management can use to take corrective action. The controller does not take any corrective action, but simply advises management as to what actions should be taken.

Polaroid's management should determine, with the advice of the controller, exactly how much control is necessary throughout the company—that is, which production costs are most detrimental and how these expenses can be reduced. Management will probably find that controlling costs exceed savings from corrective actions in the beginning because of start-up expenses. But as major production and labor savings are achieved, the benefits from the control activities (enhanced profitability) will exceed their cost. Management should bear in mind throughout the control process that too much control results in a superabundance of paperwork throughout the company and often slows decision making to an undesirable level. In addition, controlling reaches a point of diminishing returns when the major organizational problems have all been successfully tackled and controlling is concentrating on even less significant problems. Beyond a certain point, controlling costs will again exceed savings achieved through corrective actions.

POWER AND CONTROL

To control successfully, managers must understand not only the control process but also how organization members relate to it. Up to this point, the chapter has emphasized the nonhuman variables of controlling. This section focuses on power, perhaps the most important human-related variable in the control process. The following sections discuss power by:

1. Presenting its definition
2. Elaborating on the total power of managers
3. Listing the steps managers can take to increase their power over other organization members

A DEFINITION OF POWER

Perhaps the two most often confused terms in management are *power* and *authority*. Authority was defined in chapter 11 as the right to command or give orders. The extent to which an individual is able to influence others so that they respond to orders is called **power.**[18] The greater this ability, the more power an individual is said to have.

Obviously, power and control are closely related. To illustrate, after comparing actual performance with planned performance and determining that corrective action is necessary, a manager usually gives orders to implement this action. Although the orders are issued by virtue of the manager's organizational authority, they may or may not be followed precisely, depending on how much power the manager has over the individuals to whom the orders are addressed.

TOTAL POWER OF A MANAGER

The **total power** a manager possesses is made up of two different kinds of power: position power and personal power. **Position power** is power derived from the organizational position a manager holds. In general, a manager moving from lower-level management to upper-level management accrues more position power. **Personal power** is power derived from a manager's relationships with others.[19]

Power is the extent to which an individual is able to influence others so that they respond to orders.

Total power is the entire amount of power an individual in an organization possesses. It is made up of position power and personal power.

Position power is power derived from the organizational position a manager holds.

Personal power is the power derived from a manager's relationships with others.

Managers can increase their total power by enhancing either their position power or their personal power or both. Position power is generally enhanced by a move to a higher organizational position, but most managers have little personal control over when they will move up in an organization. Managers do, however, have substantial control over the amount of personal power they hold over other organization members. John P. Kotter stresses the importance of developing personal power:[20]

> To be able to plan, organize, budget, staff, control, and evaluate, managers need some control over the many people on whom they are dependent. Trying to control others solely by directing them and on the basis of the power associated with one's position simply will not work—first, because managers are always dependent on some people over whom they have no formal authority, and second, because virtually no one in modern organizations will passively accept and completely obey a constant stream of orders from someone just because he or she is the "boss."

To increase personal power, a manager should attempt to develop the following attitudes and beliefs in other organization members:[21]

1. *A sense of obligation toward the manager*—If a manager succeeds in developing this sense of obligation, other organization members will allow the manager to influence them within certain limits. The basic strategy suggested for creating this sense of obligation is to do personal favors for people.

2. *A belief that the manager possesses a high level of expertise within the organization*—In general, a manager's personal power increases as organization members perceive that the manager's level of expertise is increasing. To raise perceptions of their expertise, managers must quietly make their significant achievements visible to others and build up a successful track record and a solid professional reputation.

3. *A sense of identification with the manager*—The manager can strive to develop this identification by behaving in ways that other organization members respect and by espousing goals, values, and ideals commonly held by them. The following description illustrates how a certain sales manager took steps to increase the degree to which his subordinates identified with him:[22]

> One vice-president of sales in a moderate-sized manufacturing company was reputed to be so much in control of his sales force that he could get them to respond to new and different marketing programs in a third of the time taken by the company's best competitors. His power over his employees was based primarily on their strong identification with him and what he stood for. Emigrating to the United States at age seventeen, this person worked his way up "from nothing." When made a sales manager in 1965, he began recruiting other young immigrants and sons of immigrants from his former country. When made vice-president of sales in 1970, he continued to do so. In 1975, 85 percent of his sales force was made up of people whom he hired directly or who were hired by others he brought.

4. *The perception that they are dependent on the manager*—The main strategy here is to clearly convey the amount of authority the manager has over organizational resources—not only those necessary for organization members to do their jobs but also those organization members personally receive in such forms as salaries and bonuses. This strategy is aptly reflected in the managerial version of the Golden Rule: "He who has the gold makes the rules."

BACK TO THE CASE

If Polaroid's managers are to be successful in controlling, they must be aware not only of the intricacies of the control process but also of how to deal with employees as they relate to that process. Polaroid's managers have to consider the amount of power they hold over organization members—that is, their ability to get workers to follow orders. Judging from the Introductory

Case, many of the orders managers at Polaroid are likely to issue would relate to implementing better production methods and improved selling techniques.

The total amount of power that Polaroid managers possess comes from both the positions they hold and their personal relationships with other organization members. Polaroid's top managers already have more position power than any other managers in the organization. Therefore, to increase their total power, they would have to enhance their personal power. Top management might attempt to do this by developing the following attitudes in other organization members:

1. A sense of obligation toward top managers
2. The belief that top management has a high level of task-related expertise
3. A sense of identification with top management
4. The perception that they are dependent on top management

PERFORMING THE CONTROL FUNCTION

Controlling can be a detailed and intricate function, especially as the size of an organization increases. The following two sections furnish valuable guidelines for successfully executing this complicated function. They discuss potential barriers to successful controlling and how to make controlling successful.

POTENTIAL BARRIERS TO SUCCESSFUL CONTROLLING

To avoid potential barriers to successful controlling, managers should take action in the following areas.[23]

Long-Term versus Short-Term Production A manager, in striving to meet planned weekly production quotas, might be tempted to "push" machines in a particular area so hard they cannot be serviced properly. This kind of management behavior would ensure that planned performance and actual performance are equivalent in the short term, but it might well cause the machines to deteriorate to the point where it is impossible to meet long-term production quotas.

Employee Frustration and Morale Worker morale tends to be low when management exerts too much control. Employees become frustrated when they perceive management is too rigid in its thinking and will not allow them the freedom they need in order to do a good job. Overcontrol may also make employees suspect that control activities are merely a tactic to pressure them to work harder and harder to increase production.

Filing of Reports Employees may perceive that management is basing corrective action solely on department records with no regard for extenuating circumstances. If this is the case, they may feel pressured to falsify reports so that corrective action pertaining to their organizational unit will not be too drastic. For example, employees may overstate actual production figures to make their unit look good to management; or they may understate the numbers to create the impression that planned production is too high, thereby tricking management into thinking that a lighter workload is justified.

A well-publicized instance of falsifying control reports involved the Federal Aviation Administration (FAA) and Eastern Airlines.[24] The FAA is a government organization charged with controlling airlines' safety. As part of the FAA's controlling process, airline companies must fill out service reports and return them to the FAA for monitoring and evaluation. Before Eastern went out of business, the company and its senior maintenance executives were charged by a federal grand jury with conspiring to falsify aircraft maintenance records and returning improperly maintained aircraft to passenger service. The indictment charged that on 52 different occasions company managers signed off on, or coerced aircraft mechanics and mechanics supervisors to sign off on maintenance that had not been completed. Management seems to have regarded the falsification of maintenance reports as a way of reducing maintenance costs and thereby boosting Eastern's poor profit performance. In essence, the pressure of poor profits at Eastern Airlines caused certain company managers to falsify service reports, making it impossible for the FAA to properly control the airline company.

Perspective of Organization Members Although controls can be designed to focus on relatively narrow aspects of an organization, managers must remember to consider any prospective corrective action not only in relation to the specific activity being controlled but also in relation to all other organizational units.

For example, a manager may determine that actual and planned production are not equivalent in a specific organizational unit because during various periods a low inventory of needed parts causes some production workers to pursue other work activities instead of producing a product. The appropriate corrective action in this situation would seem to be simply raising the level of inventory, but this would be taking a narrow perspective of the problem. The manager should take a broader perspective by asking the following questions before initiating any corrective action: Is there enough money on hand to raise current inventory levels? Are there sufficient personnel presently in the purchasing department to effect the necessary increase? Who will do the work the production workers are now doing when they run out of parts?

Means Versus Ends Control activities are not the goals of the control process; they are merely the means to eliminating problems. Managers must keep in mind throughout the control process that the information gathering and report generating done to facilitate taking corrective action are activities that can be justified only if they yield some organizational benefit that exceeds the cost of performing them.

►MAKING CONTROLLING SUCCESSFUL

In addition to avoiding the potential barriers to successful controlling mentioned in the previous section, managers can perform certain activities to make the control process more effective. To increase the quality of the controlling subsystem, managers should make sure that controlling activities take all of the following factors into account.

Specific Organizational Activities Being Focused On Managers should make sure the various facets of the control process are appropriate to the control activity under consideration. For example, standards and measurements concerning a line worker's productivity are much different from standards and measurements concerning a vice president's productivity. Controlling ingredients related to the productivity of these individuals, therefore, must be different if the control process is to be applied successfully.

Different Kinds of Organizational Goals According to Jerome, control can be used for such different purposes as standardizing performance, protecting organizational assets from theft and waste, and standardizing product quality.[25] Managers should remember that the control process can be applied to many different facets of organizational life and that, if the organization is to receive maximum benefit from controlling, each of these facets must be emphasized.

Timely Corrective Action Some time will necessarily elapse as managers gather control-related information, develop necessary reports based on this information, and decide what corrective action should be taken to eliminate a problem. However, managers should take the corrective action as promptly as possible to ensure that the situation depicted by the information gathered has not changed. Unless corrective actions are timely, the organizational advantage of taking them may not materialize.

Communication of the Mechanics of the Control Process Managers should take steps to ensure that people know exactly what information is required for a particular control process, how that information is to be gathered and used to compile various reports, what the purposes of the various reports actually are, and what corrective actions are appropriate given those reports. The lesson here is simple: For control to be successful, all individuals involved in controlling must have a working knowledge of how the control process operates.[26]

Polaroid's managers must be aware of the potential barriers to successful controlling and know what actions to take to increase the probability that controlling activities will be successful. They must, for instance, do all that they can to raise the probability that any new production techniques introduced will be performed efficiently, effectively, and without resistance.

To overcome potential control-related barriers at Polaroid, management must maintain a proper balance between short-term and long-term objectives, minimize any negative effects controlling may have on the morale of Polaroid's employees, eliminate all forces leading to the falsification of control-related reports, adopt a control perspective that appropriately combines narrow and broad organizational focuses, and stress that controlling is a means rather than an end.

To increase the probability that its controlling activities will be effective, Polaroid's management must ensure that the various facets of its controlling subsystem are appropriate for company activities, that components of the controlling subsystem are flexible enough to accommodate many purposes, that corrective action is based on timely information, and that the controlling subsystem is understood by all organization members taking part in its operation.

For updated information on the topics in this chapter, Internet exercises, links to related Internet sites, an interactive study guide, and more, visit our companion Web site at

http://www.prenhall.com/certo

Additional information can be found on the inside front and back covers of this text.

ACTION SUMMARY

Reread the learning objectives below. Each objective is followed by questions. Answering these questions accurately will help you retain the most important concepts discussed in this chapter. After answering each question, check your answer against the answer key at the end of this chapter. (*Hint:* If you have any doubts regarding the correct response, consult the page number that follows the answer.)

Circle:

From studying this chapter, I will attempt to acquire

1. A definition of *control*.

   a b c d e   **a.** Managers must develop methods of measurement to signal when deviations from standards are occurring so that: (a) the plan can be abandoned (b) quality control personnel can be notified (c) the measurement standards can be checked (d) corrective action can be taken (e) none of the above.

   T F   **b.** Control is making something happen the way it was planned to happen.

2. A thorough understanding of the controlling subsystem.

   a b c d e   **a.** The main steps of the controlling process include all of the following *except:* (a) taking corrective action (b) establishing planned activities (c) comparing performance to standards (d) measuring performance (e) all of the above are steps in controlling.

   T F   **b.** Standards should be established in all important areas of organizational performance.

3. An appreciation for various kinds of control and for how each kind can be used advantageously by managers.

   a b c d e   **a.** The following is *not* one of the basic types of management control: (a) feedback control (b) precontrol (c) concurrent control (d) exception control (e) all are basic types.

   a b c d e   **b.** An example of precontrol established by management would be: (a) rules (b) procedures (c) policies (d) budgets (e) all of the above are examples.

4. Insights into the relationship between power and control.

T F   **a.** According to Kotter, controlling others solely on the basis of position power will not work.

a b c d e   **b.** The extent to which an individual is able to influence others to respond to orders is: (a) power (b) sensitivity (c) authority (d) communication skills (e) experience.

5. Knowledge of the various potential barriers that must be overcome to implement successful control.

a b c d e   **a.** A control-related potential barrier to successful controlling is: (a) overemphasizing short-term production as opposed to long-term production (b) creative employee frustration leading to reduced workplace morale (c) the falsification of reports (d) narrowing the perception of organization members to the detriment of the organization (e) all of the above are potential barriers.

T F   **b.** Control activities should be seen as the means by which corrective action is taken.

6. An understanding of steps that can be taken to increase the quality of a controlling subsystem.

a b c d e   **a.** All of the following are suggestions for making controlling successful *except:* (a) managers should make sure the mechanics of the control process are understood by organization members involved with controlling (b) managers should use control activities to achieve many different kinds of goals (c) managers should ensure that control activities are supported by most organization members (d) managers should make sure that the information on which corrective action is based is timely (e) all of the above are suggestions.

T F   **b.** The standards and measurements pertaining to a line worker's productivity are much the same as the standards and measurements pertaining to a vice president's productivity.

◄ INTRODUCTORY CASE WRAP-UP ►

CASE DISCUSSSION QUESTIONS

" Controlling at Polaroid" (p. 421) and its related Back-to-the-Case sections were written to help you better understand the management concepts contained in this chapter. Answer the following discussion questions about this Introductory Case to enrich your understanding of the chapter content:

1. List four areas in which standards should be developed at Polaroid. Why would standards in these areas be important to company success?

2. Assume that Polaroid has a controller. From what the case tells about this company, describe five important duties of this controller. Be as specific as you can about how the controller's activities relate to this particular company.

3. What kind of power does Polaroid's management need to ensure that the new programs aimed at reducing production costs and improving sales will be implemented successfully? Explain.

SKILLS EXERCISE: DETERMINING SYMPTOMS AND PROBLEMS

The Introductory Case discusses several actions taken by Polaroid Corporation in response to anemic sales and high production and labor costs. List three of these activities and discuss whether each action is aimed at an organizational "symptom" or "problem," as discussed in this chapter. Explain your answer fully.

1. What is control?
2. Explain the relationship between planning and control.
3. What is controlling?
4. What is the relationship between the controlling subsystem and the overall management system?
5. Diagram and explain the controlling subsystem.
6. List and discuss the three main steps of the controlling process.
7. Define the term *standards*.
8. What is the difference between a symptom and a problem? Why is it important to differentiate between the two before taking any controlling action?
9. What types of corrective action can managers take?

10. List and define the three basic types of control that can be used in organizations.
11. What is the relationship between controlling and the controller?
12. What basis do managers use to determine how much control is needed in an organization?
13. What is the difference between power and authority? Describe the role of power in the control process.
14. What determines how much power a manager possesses?
15. How can a manager's personal power be increased?
16. Describe several potential barriers to successful controlling.
17. What steps can managers take to ensure that control activities are successful?

ACTION SUMMARY ANSWER KEY

1. **a.** d, p. 422
   b. T, p. 422
2. **a.** b, p. 423
   b. T pp. 425–427
3. **a.** d, p. 429
   b. e., p. 429
4. **a.** T, p. 434
   b. a, p. 433
5. **a.** e, pp. 435–436
   b. T, p. 436
6. **a.** c, p. 436
   b. F, p. 436

In February 1995, London-based Barings, an international investment bank with a 200-year tradition of providing financial services throughout the world, died an untimely death following the discovery of a $1.4 billion loss at one of its subsidiaries, Baring Futures Singapore (BFS). Most of that loss was attributed to the questionable dealings of a Singapore-based derivatives trader named Nick Leeson. A month earlier, it had been revealed that Leeson had imperiled Barings by taking large trading positions in Japan's Nikkei Index futures. Examiners also uncovered fictitious accounts Leeson had set up to cover his huge trading losses. But Nick Leeson was not the only cause of the demise of prestigious Barings Bank. Barings' death is an excellent example of the ultimate cost of a lack of management controls.

In Singapore, government-hired auditors "found the fall of Baring Futures Singapore was caused by 'institutional incompetence,' lack of understanding of futures business among senior executives, and a 'total failure of internal controls.'" The report also claimed that Barings CEO Peter Norris and other top officers not only tried to conceal Leeson's unauthorized dealings but also played down their significance.

In early 1993, Leeson had become BFS's general manager. Sometime later, he opened a special account, to conceal unauthorized trading. Leeson is said to have hidden the activity of his special account from his London superiors by creating fictitious accounts to cover huge losses until the market improved. Then, panicked by a continuing plunge in the Tokyo futures market, Leeson according to one source, began "doubling his bets in desperation."

In July and August 1994, an internal audit by Barings officials identified possible control problems at BFS. This report noted that Leeson supervised both the front and back offices at BFS, which allowed him both to make trades and to settle them. At first, Barings management in London did little, if anything, to rectify the situation. It seems that London feared that attempting to control BFS's operations might slow Barings' aggressive global expansion. Moreover, some London executives were too involved with a planned restructuring of BFS and/or intoxicated by their own prospective handsome annual bonuses to question Leeson's methods. Much of the money for those bonuses was generated by the Singapore subsidiary, which had provided almost two-thirds of Barings' total profit for the year. Indeed, Leeson could claim to have made nearly $30 million of the subsidiary's $157 million profit.

Because BFS was expected by London to produce disproportionately large profits from a relatively small capital base, Leeson strove not only to please his bosses but also to boost his own economic and social standing. A report issued later by the Bank of England's Board of Banking Supervisions speculated that had Leeson been successful, "he and his team would have received $24 million in bonuses."

Officials in Singapore claimed that Leeson "dominated the staff at BFS, who did his bidding, sometimes falsifying reports and transferring trades between Barings accounts." Barings management, however, consistently contended that they had no knowledge of false accounts. This discrepancy, continues the Singapore report, raises the question of how Mr. Leeson had obtained over $1.2 billion from the Barings Group without accounting for it."

It was not until someone noticed BFS's large exposure in future trading positions on the Nikkei Index that alarms began to go off. Fearing that one of BFS's customers might not be able to meet a margin call, London officials in January 1995 instructed BFS to reduce its exposure. Apparently that order was never carried out. The Singapore report later claimed that the large-exposures report submitted by Barings to the Bank of England (BOE), although inaccurate because of Leeson's false reporting, showed that the bank's maximum exposure had already exceeded the BOE's 25 percent large-exposure limit.

In late January 1995, Barings' auditors informed London of an apparent outstanding debt of $86 million due from a New York securities trader. In early February, two London Barings officials were sent to Singapore to look at the purported account receivable. They were unable to meet with Leeson until some 16 days later. After about a half-hour talk on February 23, Leeson left the BFS office and never returned. From his hotel in Kuala Lumpur, Malaysia, the next day, Leeson faxed his resignation to Singapore. Later that day, officials in Singapore discovered information that the $86 million account receivable was a fake.

Two days later, after the discovery of additional losses totaling an estimated $1.4 billion, the London High Court named a panel to manage Barings. Leeson and his wife, on their way to London, were arrested in Frankfurt on March 1. Three days later, a Dutch banking and insurance company, ING, bought Barings, thus ending the bank's 200-year-old tradition as a leading British international investment bank.

Leeson's rogue trading practices precipitated the bank's fall. Lack of control at all levels—by Barings top executives, the Bank of England, and the Singapore government—laid the groundwork for its demise.

QUESTIONS

1. List actions that Nick Leeson took that led to the demise of Barings. When should alarms have triggered control activity at Barings' London headquarters? What may have interfered with the process?

2. How were symptoms of problems at BFS hidden? Were some symptoms readily apparent? Explain. How might Barings' organizational goals have conflicted with control activities and corrective action at BFS?

3. In which areas of control—precontrol, concurrent control, and/or feedback control—was Barings remiss? Explain.

4. Describe Leeson's power at BFS. How did the power he accumulated play a role in circumventing control?

Making things happen is an accomplishment, but making things happen the way they are supposed to is an even greater accomplishment. The Medallion Funding Corporation has been making things happen for over 60 years. Now, under the direction of a third-generation manager, this family-operated venture has annual revenues in excess of $100 million. How does a cab company with one cab become one of New York City's largest lenders to women and minority-owned businesses?

The founder of Medallion Funding was an immigrant who bought a cab and went into business. At the time, a medallion to operate a cab in New York sold for $10; today, medallions trade in excess of $200,000. The founder, Leon Merstein, grew the business by adding cabs and drivers. His son took over the business and added more cabs. Alvin, the second generation Merstein in the business, also began lending funds to cab operators, allowing them an opportunity to own their own cabs. Andy, the third generation in the venture, has extended the lending operation to include loans of all types to businesses run by minority and women owners.

A driving theme in this venture is a quote by its founder who said, "In niches there's riches." The lesson in this seemingly casual quote is important. It suggests that businesses stay close to the business that they know. The Medallion Funding Corporation is a different company than the one founded by Leon Merstein, but its transition did not happen overnight. The company expanded and changed in incremental steps, always making marginal changes, not huge leaps, from its past.

Another valuable trait of the Medallion Funding Corporation is the order and care with which it seems to operate. The company invests in the staff, systems, and relationship building with the outside community that is critical for its survival. It is obvious that this venture plans for growth, commits the necessary resources, and launches the operation with clear and observable measures and systems. The company pays attention to what it wants and makes sure that it is achieving it.

QUESTIONS

1. How do you think the management and control of the Medallion Corporation has differed among the three generations of family members who have run it?

2. The founder of the company was quoted as giving two interesting anecdotal bits of advice to his successors, "In niches there's riches" and, "Stay in your own backyard." What do you think he meant in saying these things to his successors?

3. You observed the finance and collections department of this company. What types of controls did you observe? What else do you think might be done to improve the operation?

Production Management and Control

STUDENT LEARNING OBJECTIVES

From studying this chapter, I will attempt to acquire

1. Definitions of production, productivity, and quality

2. An understanding of the importance of operations and production strategies, systems, and processes

3. Insights into the role of operations management concepts in the workplace

4. An understanding of how operations control procedures can be used to control production

5. Insights concerning operations control tools and how they evolve into a continual improvement approach to production management and control

CHAPTER OUTLINE

Introductory Case: *The Quick Turn at USAir*

PRODUCTION
Defining Production
Productivity

Management and the Internet: *Sallie Mae Uses the Internet to Improve Productivity*
Quality and Productivity

Quality Spotlight: *Focusing on Quality at Adidas USA*
Automation

Across Industries: *Tools and Appliance Manufacturing—Black and Decker Uses Robot to Move Materials*
Strategies, Systems, and Processes

OPERATIONS MANAGEMENT
Defining Operations Management
Operations Management Considerations

Ethics Spotlight: *Firestone Exits LaVergne*

OPERATIONS CONTROL
Just-in-Time Inventory Control
Maintenance Control
Cost Control
Budgetary Control
Ratio Analysis
Materials Control

SELECTED OPERATIONS CONTROL TOOLS
Using Control Tools to Control Organizations
Inspection
Management by Exception
Management by Objectives
Breakeven Analysis
Other Broad Operations Control Tools

REMINDER: THE INTRODUCTORY CASE WRAP-UP (P. 468) CONTAINS DISCUSSION QUESTIONS AND A SKILLS EXERCISE TO FURTHER ILLUSTRATE THE APPLICATION OF CHAPTER CONCEPTS TO THIS VIGNETTE.

Ed Vilchis is in a hurry. So is his employer, USAir Group, Inc.

A ramp-agent supervisor at the company's Baltimore-Washington airport terminal, Vilchis used to have 45 minutes to see that bags moved off and on planes between flights. These days he and his crews have about half that (see below). "Once that plane rolls in, you basically attack it," says Vilchis, a 17-year USAir veteran. "You load it, fuel it, cater it, push it back, and it's gone."

What's the rush? It's all part of the "quick-turn" strategy being implemented by some U.S. airlines. To improve productivity and lower operating costs, these carriers are trying to cut the time that planes on nonconnecting flights stay on the ground. After all, planes earn money flying passengers, not sitting on the tarmac.

The strategy offers flyers one big advantage. Because of delays in boarding, "people were telling us they weren't getting their business done in one day," says a USAir spokeswoman. Stripping away amenities such as meals, pillows, and blankets means caterers and cleaners can turn around the flights more quickly and passengers can get where they're going faster, she maintains.

But flyers do lose some amenities, and there are other pitfalls. Some customers don't like the stricter boarding procedures. USAir, for example, has a "10-minute rule," which requires boarding 10 minutes or more before departure time. It also insists that all carry-on luggage fit into a "sizer box" at the gate, which is roughly the size of an overhead compartment. The box is intended to keep passengers from bringing on huge bags and holding up seating.

Some workers grumble about having to move faster. "They're not used to working this hard," says Tim Goodrich, a USAir ground-crew worker in Baltimore. "In the old days, you'd come to work and have 30 or 40 minutes before you did anything. Now, they've got to pick up the pace or get out."

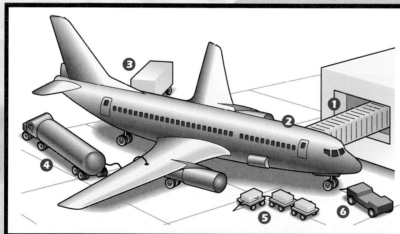

The quick turn at USAir.
Source: USAir Group, Inc., Boeing Co.

What's Ahead

The Introductory Case describes one airline company's attempt to raise productivity. It explains how USAir is shortening the amount of time that its planes stay on the ground between flights by speeding up procedures for preparing a plane for takeoff. This chapter is designed to help managers in a company like USAir increase employee productivity.

This chapter emphasizes the fundamentals of **production control**—ensuring that an organization produces goods and services as planned. The primary discussion topics in the chapter are as follows:

1. Production
2. Operations management
3. Operations control
4. Selected operations control tools

Production control ensures that an organization produces goods and services as planned.

PRODUCTION

To reach organizational goals, all managers must plan, organize, influence, and control to produce some type of goods or services. Naturally, these goods and services vary significantly from organization to organization. This section of the chapter defines production and productivity, and discusses the relationship between quality and productivity and automation.

DEFINING PRODUCTION

Production is the transformation of organizational resources into products.

Production is the transformation of organizational resources into products.[1] In this definition, *organizational resources* are all assets available to a manager to generate products, *transformation* is the set of steps necessary to change these resources into products, and *products* are various goods or services aimed at meeting human needs. Inputs at a manufacturing firm, for example, would include raw materials, purchased parts, production workers, and even schedules. The transformation process would encompass the preparation of customer orders, the design of various products, the procurement of raw materials, and the production, assembly, and (perhaps) warehousing of products. Outputs, of course, would consist of products fit for customer use.

"Production" occurs at service organizations as well. Inputs at a hospital, for instance, would include ambulances, rooms, employees (doctors, nurses, administrators, receptionists), supplies (medicines, bandages, food), and (as at a manufacturer) funds, schedules, and records. The transformation process might begin with transporting patients to the facility and end with discharging them. In between, the hospital would attend to patients' needs (nursing and feeding them, administering their medication, recording their progress). Naturally, the output here is health care.

PRODUCTIVITY

Productivity is the relationship between the total amount of goods or services being produced (output) and the organizational resources needed to produce them (input).

Productivity is an important consideration in designing, evaluating, and improving modern production systems. We can define **productivity** as the relationship between the total amount of goods or services being produced (output) and the organizational resources needed to produce them (input). This relationship is usually expressed by the following equation:[2]

$$\text{productivity} = \frac{\text{outputs}}{\text{inputs}}$$

The higher the value of the ratio of outputs to inputs, the higher the productivity of the operation.

Managers should continually strive to make their production processes as productive as possible. It is no secret that over the last 20 years the rate of productivity growth related to production management and innovation in U.S. manufacturing has lagged significantly behind that of countries such as Japan, West Germany, and France.[3] Some of the more traditional strategies for increasing productivity are as follows:[4]

1. Improving the effectiveness of the organizational workforce through training
2. Improving the production process through automation

3. Improving product design to make products easier to assemble
4. Improving the production facility by purchasing more modern equipment
5. Improving the quality of workers hired to fill open positions

► QUALITY AND PRODUCTIVITY

Quality can be defined as how well a product does what it is intended to do—how closely it satisfies the specifications to which it was built. In a broad sense, quality is the degree of excellence on which products or services can be ranked on the basis of selected features or characteristics. It is customers who determine this ranking, and customers define quality in terms of appearance, performance, availability, flexibility, and reliability. Product quality determines an organization's reputation.

During the last decade or so, managerial thinking about the relationship between quality and productivity has changed drastically. Many earlier managers chose to achieve higher levels of productivity simply by producing a greater number of products given some fixed level of available resources. They saw no relationship between improving quality and increasing productivity. Quite the contrary. They viewed quality improvement as a controlling activity that took place toward the end of the production process and largely consisted of rejecting a number of finished products that were too obviously flawed to be offered to customers. Under this approach, quality improvement efforts were generally believed to *lower* productivity.

Focus on Continual Improvement Management theorists have more recently discovered that concentrating on improving product quality throughout all phases of a production process actually improves the productivity of the manufacturing system.[5] U.S. companies were far behind the Japanese in making this discovery. As early as 1948, Japanese companies observed that continual improvements in product quality throughout the production process normally resulted in improved productivity. How does this happen? According to Dr. W. Edwards Deming, a world-renowned quality expert, a serious and consistent quality focus normally reduces nonproductive variables such as the reworking of products, production mistakes, delays and production snags, and inefficient use of time and materials.

Quality is the extent to which a product reliably does what it is intended to do.

Deming believed that for continual improvement to become a way of life in an organization, managers need to understand their company and its operations. Most managers feel they do know their company and its operations, but when they begin drawing flowcharts, they discover that their understanding of strategy, systems, and processes is far from complete. Deming recommended that managers question every aspect of an operation and involve workers in discussion before they take action to improve operations. He maintained that a manager who seriously focuses on improving product quality throughout all phases of a production process will initiate a set of chain reactions that benefits not only the organization but also the society in which the organization exists.

Focus on Quality and Integrated Operations Deming's flow diagram for improving product quality (Figure 20.1) contains a complete set of organizational variables. It introduces the customer into the operations process, and introduces the idea of continually refining knowledge, design, and inputs into the process in order to constantly increase customer satisfaction. The diagram shows the operations process as an integrated whole, from the first input to actual use of the finished product; a problem at the beginning of the process will impact the whole process and the end product. In Deming's scheme, there are no barriers between the company and the customer, between the customer and suppliers, between the company and its employees. Since the process is unified, the greater the harmony among all its components, the better the results will be.

An organization's interpretation of quality is expressed in its strategies. The following sections elaborate on the relationship between quality and production by discussing quality assurance and quality circles as part of organizational strategy.

Quality assurance is an operations process involving a broad group of activities that are aimed at achieving the organization's quality objectives.

QUALITY ASSURANCE **Quality assurance** is an operations process involving a broad group of activities aimed at achieving the organization's quality objectives.[6] Quality assurance is a continuum of activities that starts when quality standards are set and ends when quality goods and services are delivered to the customer. Although the precise activities involved in quality assurance vary from organization to organization, activities like determining the safest

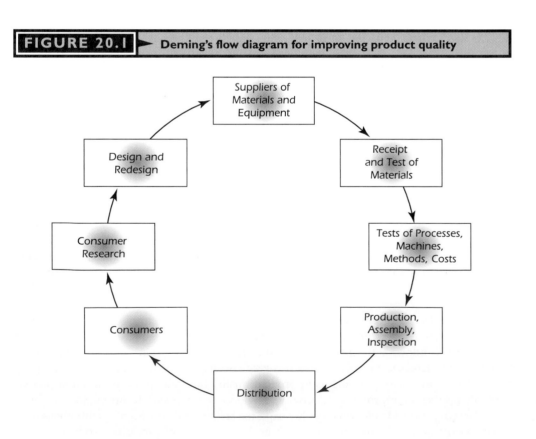

| **FIGURE 20.1** | Deming's flow diagram for improving product quality |

system for delivering goods to customers and maintaining the quality of parts or materials purchased from suppliers are part of most quality assurance efforts.

Statistical Quality Control   Statistical quality control is a much narrower concept than quality assurance. **Statistical quality control** is the process used to determine how many should be inspected to calculate a probability that the total number of products will meet organizational quality standards. An effective quality assurance strategy reduces the need for quality control and subsequent corrective actions.

"No Rejects" Philosophy   Quality assurance works best when management adopts a "no rejects" philosophy. Unfortunately, such a philosophy is not economically feasible for most mass-produced products. What is possible is training employees to approach production with a "do not make the same mistake once" mind set. Mistakes are costly. Detecting defective products in the final quality control inspection is very expensive. Emphasizing quality in the early stages—during product and process design—will reduce rejects and production costs.

QUALITY CIRCLES   The recent trend in U.S. organizations is to involve all company employees in quality control by soliciting their ideas for judging and maintaining product quality. This trend developed out of a successful Japanese control system known as *quality circles*. Although many U.S. corporations are now moving beyond the concept of the quality circle to that of the work team, as discussed in chapter 17, many ideas generated from quality circles continue to be valid.[7]

Quality circles are small groups of workers that meet to discuss quality assurance of a particular project and to communicate their solutions to these problems to management directly at a formal presentation session. Figure 20.2 shows the quality circle problem-solving process.

Most quality circles operate in a similar manner. The circle usually has fewer than eight members, and the circle leader is not necessarily the members' supervisor. Members may be workers on the project and/or outsiders. The focus is on operational problems rather than interpersonal ones. The problems discussed in the quality circle may be ones assigned by management or ones uncovered by the group itself.

Statistical quality control is the process used to determine how many products should be inspected to calculate a probability that the total number of products will meet organizational quality standards.

Quality circles are small groups of workers that meet to discuss quality-related problems on a particular project and communicate their solutions to these problems to management at a formal presentation session.

The bad news is that productivity is a little sluggish: General Electric cannot make quite enough Maxus washing machines to keep up with demand. The good news: With 40-percent fewer parts, a larger tub, and a new suspension that reduces both noise and vibration, the Maxus is a high-quality product. GE collected data from both market-research studies and service technicians in order to design its first really new washing machine in over 40 years, and managers attribute productivity snags to predictable but temporary start-up problems.

FIGURE 20.2 ▷ The quality circle problem-solving process

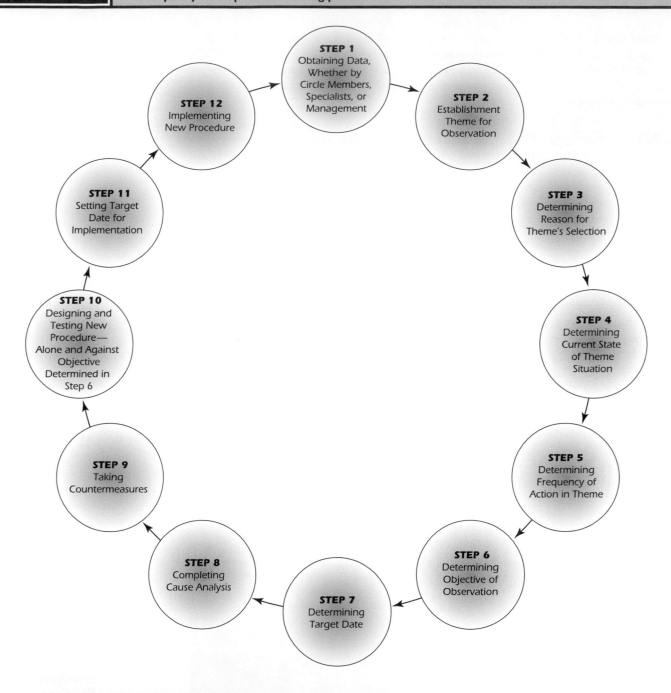

STEP 1
Obtaining Data,
Whether by
Circle Members,
Specialists, or
Management

STEP 2
Establishment
Theme for
Observation

STEP 3
Determining
Reason for
Theme's Selection

STEP 4
Determining
Current State
of Theme
Situation

STEP 5
Determining
Frequency of
Action in Theme

STEP 6
Determining
Objective of
Observation

STEP 7
Determining
Target Date

STEP 8
Completing
Cause Analysis

STEP 9
Taking
Countermeasures

STEP 10
Designing and
Testing New
Procedure—
Alone and Against
Objective
Determined in
Step 6

STEP 11
Setting Target
Date for
Implementation

STEP 12
Implementing
New Procedure

QUALITY SPOTLIGHT ◁ Focusing on Quality at Adidas USA

Adidas USA, Inc., an athletic apparel company, is best known for its athletic footwear. Events at Adidas illustrate that, without proper control aimed at enhancing profit, an organization may not last long enough to have the opportunity to focus on enhancing product quality.

Although Adidas USA lost significant amounts of money in the late 1980s, the company seemed to turn the corner in the early 1990s. It went from a $63 million loss in 1989 to a $2 million profit in 1990. This profit, although small, was highly significant because it was achieved despite an 11 percent drop in revenues, to $249 million. Staff reductions and an emphasis on collecting overdue receivables were important control measures that helped to produce the turnaround in earnings. The company also exercised control by analyzing product lines weekly to assess and increase the contributions to profit that each line was making.

Adidas' chief financial officer, Andrew P. Hines, conceded that these and other cost controls instituted by the company were primarily one-time measures. According to Hines, after the company was once again profitable, its challenge was to build lasting quality in both its staff and its products. Adidas USA dominated the U.S. market for athletic footwear in the 1970s, but strong competition and internal problems in the 1980s caused its market share to dwindle from more than 60 percent to 4 percent. Hines believed that such measures as creating a pay-for-performance plan, clarifying and documenting job responsibilities, and instituting critical training programs allowed Adidas to build more quality into its staff and its products.

In 1992, Adidas was acquired by Britain's Pentland Group, which plans to invigorate the Adidas brand name by upgrading products, improving distribution, and signing up more big-name endorsers.

► AUTOMATION

The preceding section discussed the relationship between quality and productivity organizations. This section introduces the topic of automation, which shows signs of increasing organizational productivity in a revolutionary way.[8]

Automation is defined as the replacement of human effort by electromechanical devices in such operations as welding, materials handling, design, drafting, and decision making. It includes robots—mechanical devices built to perform repetitive tasks efficiently—and **robotics**—the study of the development and use of robots.

Robotics is the study of the development and use of robots.

Over the past 20 years, a host of advanced manufacturing systems have been developed and implemented to support operations. Most of these are automated systems that combine hardware-industrial robots and computers—and software. The goals of new automation include reduced inventories, higher productivity, and faster billing and product distribution cycles. So far, the industrialized Asian countries appear to be doing the best job of making optimal use of company resources through automation.

ACROSS INDUSTRIES — Tools and Appliance Manufacturing

BLACK & DECKER USES ROBOT TO MOVE MATERIALS

This chapter emphasizes automation as the replacement of human effort through electromechanical devices in order to perform operations like materials handling both efficiently and effectively. In this section, events that have occurred at Black & Decker are used to illustrate how automation can be applied in manufacturing tools and appliances.

Black & Decker is a global marketer and manufacturer of quality power tools, hardware, and building products. These products are used in and around homes and for commercial applications and are marketed in more than 100 countries. The company has manufacturing operations in 14 countries. Black & Decker is the world's largest producer of electric power tools, including electric lawn and garden tools and residential security hardware.

Black & Decker recently faced a significant challenge at the end of its production line. In the shipping department at the company's power tool division in Brockville, Ontario, over 1,400 units of cased product, weighing as much as 70 pounds each, rolled off the production line in a typical day. The challenge was to find the best way to move these products out the door.

After considerable thought, management decided that an automated system should be developed to handle the finished goods—lawn mowers and work bench products. A Canadian robot manufacturer was chosen to help Black and Decker develop its new automation system. In its final form, the new system consists of a robot with a special tool at the end of its arm to grasp and move finished goods. The system also includes bar code scanning so that the robot knows how to adjust to the product being moved, conveyors on which the robot places finished goods, and appropriate safety barriers to prevent workers from being injured.

After several months of operation, the new automation system is a proven success. Productivity in the materials handling area improved dramatically, and operating costs decreased. In essence, the robot moves products tirelessly and is virtually maintenance-free.

► STRATEGIES, SYSTEMS, AND PROCESSES

According to Kemper and Yehudai, an effective and efficient operations manager is skilled not only in management, production, and productivity but also in strategies, systems, and processes. A *strategy* is a plan of action. A *system* is a particular linking of organizational components that facilitates carrying out a process. A *process* is a flow of interrelated events toward a goal, purpose, or end. Strategies create interlocking systems and processes when they are comprehensive, functional, and dynamic—when they designate responsibility and provide criteria for measuring output.[9]

Creating Web sites is a brand new and highly competitive industry in which systems for managing the flow of information and maintaining quality are continually being created to serve the needs of individual firms.

BACK TO THE CASE

Increasing productivity at USAir, as described in the Introductory Case, is mainly a matter of integrating resources such as people, equipment, and materials to provide better customer service.

Although productivity at USAir was far from disastrous, management seems to have decided that it was necessary to lower operating costs through improved productivity in order to stay competitive in the increasingly combative airline carrier business. USAir's first move to increase productivity has been the "quick-turn" strategy described in the Introductory Case—taking less time to ready a plane for takeoff after it has landed so customers will have shorter waits for flights. To improve productivity even further, USAir might consider implementing more effective training programs for employees and instituting more selective hiring procedures. In addition, company managers could evaluate the possibility of using robots to further shorten airport turnaround time. This strategy has the added advantage that robots would make fewer errors than humans.

To maintain and improve the quality of customer services like shorter turnaround time, USAir management could establish a quality assurance program that continually monitors services to ensure that they are at acceptable levels. Quality circles could be established to involve employees in the effort to improve customer service in both the specific area of turnaround time and in more general terms.

■ OPERATIONS MANAGEMENT

Operations management deals with managing the production of goods and services in organizations. The sections that follow define *operations management* and discuss various strategies that managers can use to make production activities more effective and efficient.

► DEFINING OPERATIONS MANAGEMENT

According to Chase and Aquilano, **operations management** is performance of managerial activities entailed in selecting, designing, operating, controlling, and updating production systems.[10] Figure 20.3 describes these activities and categorizes them as either periodic or continual. The distinction between periodic and continual activities is one of relative frequency of performance: Periodic activities are performed from time to time, while continual activities are performed essentially without interruption.

Operations management is the systematic direction (strategy) and control of operations processes that transform resources into finished goods and services; it is getting things done by working with or through other people.

► OPERATIONS MANAGEMENT CONSIDERATIONS

Overall, *operations management* is the systematic direction and control of operations processes that transform resources into finished goods and services.[11] The concept conveys three key notions:

► Operations management involves managers—people who get things done by working with or through other people

► Operations management takes place within the context of objectives and policies that drive the organization's strategic plans

► The criteria for judging the actions taken as a result of operations management are standards for effectiveness and efficiency

FIGURE 20.3 ► Major activities performed to manage production

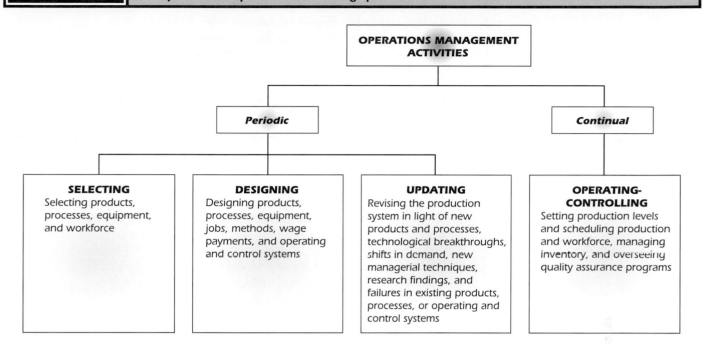

Effectiveness is the degree to which managers attain organizational objectives: "doing the right things." **Efficiency** is the degree to which organizational resources contribute to productivity: "doing things right." A review of organizational performance based on these standards is essential to enhancing the success of any organization.

Operations strategies—capacity, location, product, process, layout, and human resources—are specific plans of action designed to ensure that resources are obtained and used effectively and efficiently. An operational strategy is implemented by people who get things done with and through people. It is achieved in the context of objectives and policies derived from the organization's strategic plan.

CAPACITY STRATEGY **Capacity strategy** is a plan of action aimed at providing the organization with the right facilities to produce the needed output at the right time. The output capacity of the organization determines its ability to meet future demands for goods and services. *Insufficient capacity* results in loss of sales that, in turn, affects profits. *Excess capacity* results in higher production costs. A strategy that aims for *optimal capacity,* where quantity and timing are in balance, provides an excellent basis for minimizing operating costs and maximizing profits.

Capacity flexibility enables the company to deliver its goods and services to its customers in a shorter time than its competitors. This component of capacity strategy involves having flexible plants and processes, broadly trained employees, and easy and economical access to external capacity, such as suppliers.

Managers use capacity strategy to balance the costs of overcapacity and undercapacity. The difficulty of accurately forecasting long-term demand makes this balancing task risky. Modifying long-range capacity decisions while in production is both hard and costly. In a highly competitive environment, construction of a new high-tech facility might take longer than the life cycle of the product. Correcting overcapacity by closing a plant saddles management with high economic costs and even higher social costs—such as lost jobs that devastate both employees and the community in which the plant operates—that will have a long-term adverse effect on the firm.

The traditional concept of economies of scale led management to construct large plants that tried to do everything. The more modern concept of the focused facility has led management to conclude that better performance can be achieved in more specialized plants that concentrate on fewer tasks and are therefore smaller.

Effectiveness is the degree to which managers attain organizational objectives; it is doing the right things.

Efficiency is the degree to which organizational resources contribute to production; it is doing things right.

Capacity strategy is an operational plan of action aimed at providing the organization with the right facilities to produce the needed output at the right time.

Five Steps in Capacity Decisions Managers are more likely to make sound strategic capacity decisions if they adhere to the following five-step process:

1. Measure the capacity of currently available facilities
2. Estimate future capacity needs on the basis of demand forecasts
3. Compare future capacity needs and available capacity to determine whether capacity must be increased or decreased
4. Identify ways to accommodate long-range capacity changes (expansion or reduction)
5. Select the best alternative based on a quantitative and qualitative evaluation

Location strategy is an operational plan of action that provides the organization with a competitive location for its headquarters, manufacturing, services, and distribution activities.

LOCATION STRATEGY Location strategy is a plan of action that provides the organization with a competitive location for its headquarters, manufacturing, services, and distribution activities. A competitive location results in lower transportation and communication costs among the various facilities. These costs—which run as high as 20 to 30 percent of a product's selling price—greatly affect the volume of sales and amount of profit generated by a particular product. Many other quantitative and qualitative factors are important when formulating location strategy.

Factors in a Good Location A successful location strategy requires a company to consider the following major factors in its location study:

- Nearness to market and distribution centers
- Nearness to vendors and resources
- Requirements of federal, state, and local governments
- The character of direct competition
- The degree of interaction with the rest of the corporation
- The quality and quantity of labor pools
- The environmental attractiveness of the area
- Taxes and financing requirements
- Existing and potential transportation
- The quality of utilities and services

The dynamic nature of these factors could make what is a competitive location today an undesirable location in five years.

ETHICS SPOTLIGHT   Firestone Exits LaVergne

Firestone built a radial truck tire plant in LaVergne, Tennessee, in 1972. After a decade in LaVergne, faced with lower than anticipated demand, a hostile local union, and quality problems, Firestone announced that it was planning to sell the plant or to close it down if a buyer could not be found. The company had already shut down 7 of its 17 plants, so it was clear that management meant what it said and workers at the LaVergne plant would lose their jobs. In many observers' eyes, Firestone was reneging on its obligations to the community and to its own employees.

Bridgestone, a Japanese tire maker, was looking to locate in Tennessee. The state had been openly wooing Japanese companies for some time—Nissan was in Smyrna, Komatsu in Chattanooga, Sharp in Memphis, and Toshiba in the tiny town of Lebanon—so Bridgestone had ample reason to believe it would be welcome in Tennessee. Bridgestone sent negotiators to LaVergne to arrange to buy the plant from Firestone, provided they could come to rea-

sonable terms with the union. The union's leadership seemed to view the negotiations as an opportunity to win concessions, not make them. Both sides dug in their heels. Then, in a moment of ill-advised bravado, the local union president told the Japanese that they should go back to Japan. In many observers' eyes, the union was failing to take seriously its obligation to its members and to the community.

Bridgestone's negotiators did go home. Soon the local union's officers were summoned to Akron to meet with Firestone's top management and officers of the International Rubber Workers Union. This meeting between the union and management resulted in an invitation to Bridgestone negotiators to return to the bargaining table. This time both sides made commitments: Bridgestone pledged to recall laid-off workers, and the union agreed to a contract that eased work rules and promised to lobby members for its ratification. The $52 million sale went through.

PRODUCT STRATEGY **Product strategy** is an operational plan of action outlining which goods and services an organization will produce and market. Product strategy is a main component of an organization's operations strategy—in fact, it is the link between the operations strategy and the other functional strategies, especially marketing and research and development. In essence, product, marketing, and research and development strategies must fit together if management is to be able to build an effective overall operations strategy. A business' product and operations strategies should take into account the strengths and weaknesses of operations, which are primarily internal, as well as those of other functional areas concerned more with external opportunities and threats.

> **Product strategy** is an operational plan of action outlining which goods and services an organization will produce and market.

Cooperation and coordination among its marketing, operations, and research and development departments from the inception of a new product are strongly beneficial to a company. At the very least, it ensures a smooth transition from research and development to production, since operations people will be able to contribute to the quality of the total product, rather than merely attempt to improve the quality of the components. Even the most sophisticated product can be designed so that it is relatively simple to produce, thus reducing the number of units that must be scrapped or reworked during production, as well as the need for highly trained and highly paid employees. All of these strategies lower production costs and hence increase the product's price competitiveness or profits or both.

PROCESS STRATEGY **Process strategy** is a plan of action outlining the means and methods the organization will use to transform resources into goods and services. Materials, labor, information, equipment, and managerial skills are resources that must be transformed. A competitive process strategy will ensure the most efficient and effective use of these organizational resources.

> **Process strategy** is an operational plan of action outlining the means and methods the organization will use to transform resources into goods and services.

Types of Processes All manufacturing processes may be grouped into three different types. The first is the *continuous process,* a product-oriented, high-volume, low-variety process used, for example, in producing chemicals, beer, and petroleum products. The second is the *repetitive process,* a product-oriented production process that uses modules to produce items in large lots. This mass-production or assembly-line process is characteristic of the auto and appliance industries.

The third type of manufacturing process is used to produce small lots of custom-designed products such as furniture. This high-variety, low-volume system, commonly known as the *job-shop process,* includes the production of one-of-a-kind items as well as unit production. Spaceship and weapons systems production are considered job-shop activities.

Organizations commonly employ more than one type of manufacturing process at the same time and in the same facility.

Process strategy is directly linked to product strategy. The decision to select a particular process strategy is often the result of external market opportunities or threats. When this is true, the corporation decides what it wants to produce, then selects a process strategy to produce it. The product takes center stage and the process becomes a function of the product.

The function of process strategy is to determine what equipment will be used, what maintenance will be necessary, and what level of automation will be most effective and efficient. The type of employees and the level of employee skills needed are dependent on the process strategy chosen.

LAYOUT STRATEGY **Layout strategy** is a plan of action that outlines the location and flow of all organizational resources around, into, and within production and service facilities. A cost-effective and cost-efficient layout strategy is one that minimizes the expenses of processing, transporting, and storing materials throughout the production and service cycle.

> **Layout strategy** is an operational plan that determines the location and flow of organizational resources around, into, and within production and service facilities.

Layout strategy—which is usually the last part of operations strategy to be formulated—is closely linked, either directly or indirectly, with all other components of operations strategy: capacity, location, product, process, and human resources. It must target capacity and process requirements. It must satisfy the organization's product design, quality, and quantity requirements. It must target facility and location requirements. Finally, to be effective, the layout strategy must be compatible with the organization's established quality of work life.

A **layout** is the overall arrangement of equipment, work areas, service areas, and storage areas within a facility that produces goods or provides services.[12] There are three basic types of layouts for manufacturing facilities:

1. A **product layout** is designed to accommodate high production volumes, highly specialized equipment, and narrow employee skills. It is appropriate for organizations that produce and service a limited number of different products. It is not appropriate for an organization that experiences constant or frequent changes of products.

2. A **process (functional) layout** is a layout pattern that groups together similar types of equipment. It is appropriate for organizations involved in a large number of different tasks. It best serves companies whose production volumes are low, whose equipment is multipurpose, and whose employees' skills are broad.

3. The **fixed-position layout** is one in which the product is stationary while resources flow. It is appropriate for organizations involved in a large number of different tasks that require low volumes, multipurpose equipment, and broad employee skills. A *group technology layout* is a product layout cell within a larger process layout. It benefits organizations that require both types of layout.

Figure 20.4 illustrates the three basic layout patterns. Actually, most manufacturing facilities are a combination of two or more different types of layouts. Various techniques are available to assist management in designing an efficient and effective layout that meets the required specifications.

A **layout** is the overall arrangement of equipment, work areas, service areas, and storage areas within a facility that produces goods or provides services.

A **product layout** is a layout designed to accommodate a limited number of different products that require high volumes, highly specialized equipment, and narrow employee skills.

A **process (functional) layout** is a layout pattern based primarily on grouping together similar types of equipment.

A **fixed-position layout** is a layout plan appropriate for organizations involved in a large number of different tasks that require low volumes, multipurpose equipment, and broad employee skills.

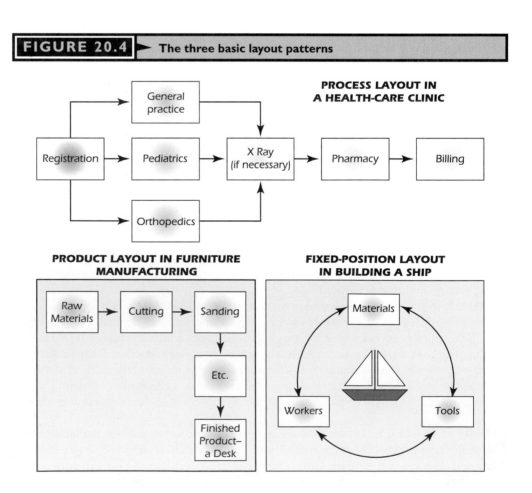

FIGURE 20.4 ▶ The three basic layout patterns

HUMAN RESOURCES STRATEGY *Human resources* is the term used for individuals engaged in any of the organization's activities. There are two human resource imperatives:

1. It is essential to optimize individual, group, and organizational effectiveness
2. It is essential to enhance the quality of organizational life

A **human resources strategy** is an operational plan to use the organization's human resources effectively and efficiently while maintaining or improving the quality of work life.[13]

As discussed in chapter 12, human resource management is about employees—who are the best means of enhancing organizational effectiveness. Whereas financial management attempts to increase organizational effectiveness through the allocation and conservation of financial resources, human resource management (personnel management) attempts to increase organizational effectiveness through such factors as the establishment of personnel policies, education and training, and procedures.

Operational Tools in Human Resources Strategy

Operations management attempts to increase organizational effectiveness by employing the methods used in the manufacturing and service processes. Human resources, one very important factor of operations, must be compatible with operations tasks.

Manpower planning is the primary focus of the operations human resources strategy. It is an operational plan for hiring the right employees for a job and training them to be productive. This is a lengthy and costly process. A human resources strategy must be founded on fair treatment and trust. The employee, not operations, must take center stage.

Job design is an operational plan that determines who will do a specific job and how and where the job will be done. The goal of job design is to facilitate productivity. Successful job design takes efficiency and behavior into account. It also guarantees that working conditions are safe and that the health of employees will not be jeopardized in the short or the long run.

Work methods analysis is an operational tool used to improve productivity and ensure the safety of workers. It can be performed for new or existing jobs. **Motion-study techniques** are another set of operational tools used to improve productivity.

Work measurement methods are operational tools used to establish labor standards. These standards are useful for planning, control, productivity improvements, costing and pricing, bidding, compensation, motivation, and financial incentives.

A **human resources strategy** is an operational plan to use the organization's human resources effectively and efficiently while maintaining or improving the quality of work life.

Manpower planning is an operational plan that focuses on hiring the right employees for a job and training them to be productive.

Job design is an operational plan that determines who will do a specific job and how and where the job will be done.

Work methods analysis is an operational tool used to improve productivity and ensure the safety of workers.

Motion-study techniques are operational tools that are used to improve productivity.

Work measurement methods are operational tools that are used to establish labor standards.

BACK TO THE CASE

In attempting to speed up plane turnaround, USAir's management is involved in operations management. Most of the issues mentioned in the Introductory Case pertain to the "periodic updating" segment of operations management activities—revising systems to provide better customer service. USAir's periodic updating should focus on the appropriate use of company resources like ticket agents, caterers, fuel trucks, and ramp agents. Once established, the new operations procedure must be continually monitored by USAir's management for both effectiveness—"doing the right things"—and efficiency—"doing things right."

Factors USAir's management must consider in making operations decisions are: *capacity strategy*, making sure that the airline has appropriate resources to perform needed functions at appropriate times; *location strategy*, making sure that airline resources are appropriately postured for work when the work must be performed; *product strategy*, making sure that appropriate customer services are targeted and provided; *process strategy*, making sure that USAir is employing appropriate steps in providing various customer services; *layout strategy*, making sure that the flow of USAir's resources in the process of providing customer services is desirable; and *human resources strategy*, making sure that USAir has appropriate people providing services to customers.

Once a decision has been taken to design an operational plan of action, resource allocations are considered. After management has decided on a functional operations strategy, using marketing and financial plans of action, it determines what specific tasks are necessary to accomplish functional objectives. This is known as *operations control*.

Operations control is an operational plan that specifies the operational activities of an organization.

Operations control is defined as making sure that operations activities are carried out as planned. The major components of operations control are *just-in-time inventory control, maintenance control, cost control, budgetary control, ratio analysis,* and *materials control.* Each of these components is discussed in detail in the following sections.

▶ JUST-IN-TIME INVENTORY CONTROL

Just-in-time (JIT) inventory control is a technique for reducing inventories to a minimum by arranging for production components to be delivered to the production facility "just in time" to be used.

Just-in-time (JIT) inventory control is a technique for reducing inventories to a minimum by arranging for production components to be delivered to the production facility "just in time" to be used. The concept, developed primarily by the Toyota Motor Company of Japan, is also called "zero inventory" or *kanban*—the latter a Japanese term referring to purchasing raw materials by using a special ordering form.[14]

JIT is based on the management philosophy that products should be manufactured only when customers need them and only in the quantities customers require in order to minimize the amounts of raw materials and finished goods inventories manufacturers keep on hand. It emphasizes maintaining organizational operations by using only the resources that are absolutely necessary to meet customer demand.

Best Conditions for JIT JIT works best in companies that manufacture relatively standardized products for which there is consistent demand. Such companies can comfortably order materials from suppliers and assemble products in small, continuous batches. The result is a smooth, consistent flow of purchased materials and assembled products, with little inventory buildup. Companies that manufacture nonstandardized products for which there is sporadic or seasonal demand, however, generally face more irregular purchases of raw materials from suppliers, more uneven production cycles, and greater accumulations of inventory.

Advantages of JIT When successfully implemented, JIT enhances organizational performance in several important ways. First, it reduces the unnecessary labor expenses generated by manufacturing products that are not sold. Second, it minimizes the tying up of monetary resources in purchases of production-related materials that do not result in timely sales. Third, it helps management hold down inventory expenses—particularly storage and handling costs. Better inventory management and control of labor costs, in fact, are the two most commonly cited benefits of JIT.

Characteristics of JIT Experience indicates that successful JIT programs have certain common characteristics:[15]

1. *Closeness of suppliers*—Manufacturers using JIT find it beneficial to use raw materials suppliers who are based only a short distance from them. When a company is ordering smaller quantities of raw materials at a time, suppliers must sometimes be asked to make one or more deliveries per day. Short distances make multiple deliveries per day feasible.

2. *High quality of materials purchased from suppliers*—Manufacturers using JIT find it especially difficult to overcome problems caused by defective materials. Since they keep their materials inventory small, defective materials purchased from a supplier may force them to discontinue the production process until another delivery from the supplier can be arranged. Such production slowdowns can be disadvantageous, causing late delivery to customers or lost sales.

3. *Well-organized receiving and handling of materials purchased from suppliers*—Companies using JIT must be able to receive and handle raw materials effectively and efficiently. Ma-

terials must be available for the production process where and when they are needed, because if they are not, extra costs will be built into the production process.

4. *Strong management commitment*—Management must be strongly committed to the concept of JIT. The system takes time and effort to plan, install, and improve—and is therefore expensive to implement. Management must be willing to commit funds to initiate the JIT system and to support it once it is functioning.

►MAINTENANCE CONTROL

Maintenance control is aimed at keeping the organization's facility and equipment functioning at predetermined work levels. In the planning stage, managers must select a strategy that will direct personnel to fix equipment either before it malfunctions or after it malfunctions. The first strategy is referred to as a **pure-preventive maintenance policy**—machine adjustments, lubrication, cleaning, parts replacement, painting, and needed repairs and overhauls are done regularly, before facilities or machines malfunction. At the other end of the maintenance control continuum is the **pure-breakdown policy,** which decrees that facilities and equipment be fixed only after they malfunction.

Most organizations implement a maintenance strategy somewhere in the middle of the maintenance continuum. Management usually tries to select a level and a frequency of maintenance that minimize the cost of both preventive maintenance and breakdowns (repair). Since no level of preventive maintenance can eliminate breakdowns altogether, repair will always be an important activity.

Whether management decides on a pure-preventive or pure-breakdown policy, or on something in between, the prerequisite for a successful maintenance program is the availability of maintenance parts and supplies or replacement (standby) equipment. Some organizations choose to keep standby machines to protect themselves against the consequences of breakdowns. Plants that use special-purpose equipment are more likely to invest in standby equipment than those that use general-purpose equipment.

Pure-preventive maintenance policy is a maintenance control policy that tries to ensure that machine adjustments, lubrication, cleaning, parts replacement, painting, and needed repairs and overhauls will be performed before facilities or machines malfunction.

Pure-breakdown (repair) policy is a maintenance control policy that decrees that machine adjustments, lubrication, cleaning, parts replacement, painting, and needed repairs and overhaul will be performed only after facilities or machines malfunction.

►COST CONTROL

Cost control is broad control aimed at keeping organizational costs at planned levels.[16] Since cost control relates to all organizational costs, it emphasizes activities in all organizational areas, such as research and development, operations, marketing, and finance. If an organization is to be successful, costs in all organizational areas must be controlled. Cost control is therefore an important responsibility of all managers in an organization.

Operations activities are very cost-intensive—perhaps the most cost-intensive of all organizational activities—so when significant cost savings are realized in organizations, they are generally realized at the operations level.

Operations managers are responsible for the overall control of the cost of goods or services sold. Since producing goods and services at or below planned cost levels is their principal objective, operations managers are commonly evaluated primarily on their cost control activities. When operations costs are consistently above planned levels, the organization may need to change its operations management.

Stages in Cost Control   The general cost control process has four stages:

1. Establishing standard or planned cost amounts
2. Measuring actual costs incurred
3. Comparing planned costs to incurred costs
4. Making changes to reduce actual costs to planned costs when necessary

Following these stages for specific operations cost control, the operations manager must first establish planned costs or cost standards for operations activities like labor, materials, and overhead. Next, the operations manager must actually measure or calculate the costs incurred for these activities. Third, the operations manager must compare actual operations costs to planned operations costs, and fourth, take steps to reduce actual operations costs to planned levels if necessary.

Introducing a new product for children entails facing many marketing and safety issues. Thus, in addition to the usual control processes for scheduling, budgeting, and quality, K'nex product designers must also factor in controls like product trials and safety checks.

A **budget** is a control tool that outlines how funds will be obtained and spent in a given period.

As described in chapter 9, a budget is a single-use financial plan that covers a specified length of time. An organization's **budget** is its financial plan outlining how funds in a given period will be obtained and spent.

In addition to being a financial plan, however, a budget can be the basis for *budgetary control*—that is, for ensuring that income and expenses occur as planned. As managers gather information on actual receipts and expenditures within an operating period, they may uncover significant deviations from budgeted amounts. If that be the case, they should develop and implement a control strategy aimed at bringing actual performance into line with planned performance. This, of course, assumes that the plan contained in the budget is appropriate for the organization. The following sections discuss some potential pitfalls of budgets and human relations considerations that may make a budget inappropriate.

POTENTIAL PITFALLS OF BUDGETS   To maximize the benefits of using budgets, managers must avoid several potential pitfalls. Among these pitfalls are the following:

1. *Placing too much emphasis on relatively insignificant organizational expenses*—In preparing and implementing a budget, managers should allocate more time for dealing with significant organizational expenses and less time for relatively insignificant organizational expenses. For example, the amount of time managers spend on developing and implementing a budget for labor costs typically should be much more than the amount of time they spend on developing and implementing a budget for office supplies.

2. *Increasing budgeted expenses year after year without adequate information*—It does not necessarily follow that items contained in last year's budget should be increased this year. Perhaps the best-known method for overcoming this potential pitfall is zero-base budgeting.[17] **Zero-base budgeting** is a planning and budgeting process that requires managers to justify their entire budget request in detail rather than simply refer to budget amounts established in previous years.

   Some management theorists believe that zero-base budgeting is a better management tool than traditional budgeting—which simply starts with the budget amount established in the prior year—because it emphasizes focused identification and control of each budget item. It is unlikely, however, that this tool will be implemented successfully unless management adequately explains what zero-base budgeting is and how it is to be used in the organization. One of the earliest and most commonly cited successes in implementing a zero-base budgeting program took place in the Department of Agriculture's Office of Budget and Finance.

3. *Ignoring the fact that budgets must be changed periodically*—Managers should recognize that such factors as costs of materials, newly developed technology, and product demand change constantly and that budgets must be reviewed and modified periodically in response to these changes.

   A special type of budget called a *variable budget* is sometimes used to determine automatically when such changes in budgets are needed. A **variable budget,** also known as a *flexible budget,* outlines the levels of resources to be allocated for each organizational activity according to the level of production within the organization. It follows, then, that a variable budget automatically indicates an increase in the amount of resources allocated for various organizational activities when production levels go up and a decrease when production goes down.

Zero-base budgeting requires managers to justify their entire budget request in detail rather than simply referring to budget amounts established in previous years.

A **variable budget** (also known as a *flexible budget*) is one that outlines the levels of resources to be allocated for each organizational activity according to the level of production within the organization.

HUMAN RELATIONS CONSIDERATIONS IN USING BUDGETS   Many managers believe that although budgets are valuable planning and control tools, they can result in major human relations problems in an organization. A classic article by Chris Argyris, for example, shows how budgets can build pressures that unite workers against management, cause harmful conflict between management and factory workers, and create tensions that result in worker inefficiency and worker aggression against management.[18] If such problems are severe enough, a budget may result in more harm to the organization than good.

Reducing Human Relations Problems   Several strategies have been suggested to minimize the human relations problems caused by budgets. The most often recommended strategy is to

TABLE 20.1	▶ Four Categories of Ratios		
Type	**Example**	**Calculation**	**Interpretation**
Profitability	Return on investment (ROI)	$\dfrac{\text{Profit after taxes}}{\text{Total assets}}$	Productivity of assets
Liquidity	Current ratio	$\dfrac{\text{Current assets}}{\text{Current liabilities}}$	Short-term solvency
Activity	Inventory turnover	$\dfrac{\text{Sales}}{\text{Inventory}}$	Efficiency of inventory management
Leverage	Debt ratio	$\dfrac{\text{Total debt}}{\text{Total assets}}$	How a company finances itself

design and implement appropriate human relations training programs for finance personnel, accounting personnel, production supervisors, and all other key people involved in the formulation and use of budgets. These training programs should emphasize both the advantages and disadvantages of applying pressure on people through budgets and the possible results of using budgets to imply that an organization member is a success or a failure at his or her job.

▶ RATIO ANALYSIS

Another type of control uses ratio analysis.[19] A *ratio* is a relationship between two numbers that is calculated by dividing one number into the other. **Ratio analysis** is the process of generating information that summarizes the financial position of an organization through the calculation of ratios based on various financial measures that appear on the organization's balance sheet and income statements.

Ratio analysis is a control tool that summarizes the financial position of an organization by calculating ratios based on various financial measures.

The ratios available to managers for controlling organizations, shown in Table 20.1, can be divided into four categories:

1. Liquidity ratios
2. Leverage ratios
3. Activity ratios
4. Profitability ratios

USING RATIOS TO CONTROL ORGANIZATIONS Managers should use ratio analysis in three ways to control an organization:[20]

▶ Managers should evaluate all ratios simultaneously. This strategy ensures that they will develop and implement a control strategy appropriate for the organization as a whole rather than one that suits only one phase or segment of the organization.

▶ Managers should compare computed values for ratios in a specific organization with the values of industry averages for those ratios. (The values of industry averages for the ratios can be obtained from Dun & Bradstreet; Robert Morris Associates, a national association of bank loan officers; the Federal Trade Commission; and the Securities and Exchange Commission.) Managers increase the probability of formulating and implementing appropriate control strategies when they compare their financial situation to that of competitors in this way.

▶ Managers' use of ratios should incorporate trend analysis. Managers must remember that any set of ratio values is actually only a determination of relationships that existed in a specified time period (often a year). To employ ratio analysis to maximum advantage, they need to accumulate ratio values for several successive time periods to uncover specific organizational trends. Once these trends are revealed, managers can formulate and implement appropriate strategies for dealing with them.

▶ MATERIALS CONTROL

Materials control is an operations control activity that determines the flow of materials from vendors through an operations system to customers. The achievement of desired levels of product cost, quality, availability, dependability, and flexibility heavily depends on the effective

Materials control is an operational activity that determines the flow of materials from vendors through an operations system to customers.

and efficient flow of materials. Materials management activities can be broadly organized into six groups or functions: purchasing, receiving, inventorying, floor controlling, trafficking, and shipping and distributing.

Procurement of Materials Over 50 percent of the expenditures of a typical manufacturing company are for the procurement of materials, including raw materials, parts, subassemblies, and supplies. This procurement is the responsibility of the purchasing department. Actually, purchases of production materials are largely automated and linked to a resources requirement planning system. Purchases of all other materials, however, are based on requisitions from users. The purchasing department's job does not end with the placement of an order; order follow-up is just as crucial.

Receiving, Shipping, and Trafficking Receiving activities include unloading, identifying, inspecting, reporting, and storing inbound shipments. Shipping and distribution activities are similar. These may include preparing documents, packaging, labeling, loading, and directing outbound shipments to customers and to distribution centers. Shipping and receiving are sometimes organized as one unit.

A traffic manager's main responsibilities are selection of the transportation mode, coordination of the arrival and departure of shipments, and auditing freight bills.

Inventory and Shop-Floor Control Inventory control activities ensure the continuous availability of purchased materials. Work-in-process and finished-goods inventory are inventory control subsystems. Inventory control specifies what, when, and how much to buy. Held inventories buffer the organization against a variety of uncertainties that can disrupt supply, but since holding inventory is costly, an optimal inventory control policy provides a predetermined level of certainty of supply at the lowest possible cost.

Shop-floor control activities include input/output control, scheduling, sequencing, routing, dispatching, and expediting.

While many materials management activities can be programmed, the human factor is the key to a competitive performance. Skilled and motivated employees are therefore crucial to successful materials control.

BACK TO THE CASE

Operations control activities help USAir's management make certain that customer services are carried out as planned. *Just-in-time inventory control,* for example, would ensure that pillows, blankets, ticketing materials, and packing materials are available just when customers need them. Putting money into large surpluses of these items would needlessly tie up company resources and reduce company profitability. *Maintenance control* would ensure that equipment (e.g., baggage conveyors) needed to provide customer services is operating at a desirable level. *Cost control* would ensure that USAir is not providing services to customers too expensively. *Budgetary control* would focus on acquiring company resources and using them to provide customer services as stipulated by USAir's financial plan.

Operations control at USAir can also include ratio analysis, or determining relationships between various factors on USAir's income statement and balance sheet to arrive at a good indication of the company's financial position. Through ratio analysis, USAir's management could monitor issues like customer services to determine their overall impact on company profitability, liquidity, and leverage. To assess the impact of providing various customer services on the financial condition of USAir, management would track ratios over time to discern trends.

Finally, operations control at USAir would need to include materials control to ensure that materials purchased from suppliers are flowing appropriately from vendors to customers in the form of customer services. For example, the goal of monitoring the drinks, snacks, and meals that caterers are providing to USAir's passengers would be to improve the quality of such items in terms of temperature, freshness, and nutritional value.

In addition to understanding production, operations management, and operations control, managers also need to be aware of various operations control tools that are useful in an operations facility. A **control tool** is a specific procedure or technique that presents pertinent organizational information in a way that helps managers and workers develop and implement an appropriate control strategy. That is, a control tool aids managers and workers in pinpointing the organizational strengths and weaknesses on which a useful control strategy must focus. This section discusses specific control tools for day-to-day operations as well as for longer-run operations.

A **control tool** is a specific procedure or technique that presents pertinent organizational information in a way that helps managers to develop and implement an appropriate control strategy.

► USING CONTROL TOOLS TO CONTROL ORGANIZATIONS

Continual improvement of operations is a practical, not a theoretical, managerial concern. It is, essentially, the development and use of better methods. Different types of organizations have different goals and strategies, but all organizations struggle daily to find better ways of doing things. This goal of continual improvement applies not just to money-making enterprises, but to those with other missions as well. Since organizational leaders are continually changing systems and personal styles of management, everyone within the organization is continually learning to live with change.

► INSPECTION

Traditionally, managers believed that if you wanted good quality, you hired many inspectors to make sure an operation was producing at the desired quality level. These inspectors examined and graded finished products or components, parts, or services at any stage of operation by measuring, tasting, touching, weighing, disassembling, destroying, and testing. The goal of inspection was to detect unacceptable quality levels before a bad product or service reached a customer. Whenever a lot of defects were found, management blamed the workers and hired more inspectors.

To Inspect or Not to Inspect   Today managers know that inspection cannot catch problems built into the system. The traditional inspection process does not result in improvement and does not guarantee quality. In fact, according to Deming, inspection is a limited, grossly overused, and often misused tool. He recommended that management stop relying on mass inspection to achieve quality, and advocated instead either 100 percent inspection in those cases where defect-free work is impossible or no inspection at all where the level of defects is acceptably small.

► MANAGEMENT BY EXCEPTION

Management by exception is a control technique that allows only significant deviations between planned and actual performance to be brought to a manager's attention. Management by exception is based on the *exception principle,* a management principle that appears in early management literature.[21] This principle recommends that subordinates handle all routine organizational matters, leaving managers free to deal with nonroutine, or exceptional, organizational issues.

Management by exception is a control tool that allows only significant deviations between planned and actual performance to be brought to a manager's attention.

Establishing Rules   Some organizations rely on subordinates or managers themselves to detect the significant deviations between standards and performance that signal exceptional issues. Other organizations establish rules to ensure that exceptional issues surface as a matter of normal operating procedure. Setting rules must be done very carefully to ensure that all true deviations are brought to the manager's attention.

Two examples of rules based on the exception principle are the following:[22]

1. A department manager must immediately inform the plant manager if actual weekly labor costs exceed estimated weekly labor costs by more than 15 percent
2. A department manager must immediately inform the plant manager if actual dollars spent plus estimated dollars to be spent on a special project exceed the funds approved for the project by more than 10 percent

Although these two rules happen to focus on production-related expenditures, detecting and reporting significant rules deviations can be established in virtually any organizational area.

If appropriately administered, the management-by-exception control technique ensures the best use of managers' time. Because only significant issues are brought to managers' attention, the possibility that managers will spend their valuable time working on relatively insignificant issues is automatically eliminated.

Of course, the significant issues brought to managers' attention could be organizational strengths as well as organizational weaknesses. Obviously, managers should try to reinforce the first and eliminate the second.

►MANAGEMENT BY OBJECTIVES

In management by objectives, which was discussed in chapter 5, the manager assigns a specialized set of objectives and action plans to workers and then rewards those workers on the basis of how close they come to reaching their goals. This control technique has been implemented in corporations intent on using an employee-participative means to improve productivity.

►BREAKEVEN ANALYSIS

Another production-related control tool commonly used by managers is breakeven analysis. **Breakeven analysis** is the process of generating information that summarizes various levels of profit or loss associated with various levels of production. The next sections discuss three facets of this control tool:

1. Basic ingredients of breakeven analysis
2. Types of breakeven analysis available to managers
3. Relationship between breakeven analysis and controlling

BASIC INGREDIENTS OF BREAKEVEN ANALYSIS Breakeven analysis typically involves reflection, discussion, reasoning, and decision making relative to the following seven major aspects of production:

1. *Fixed costs*—**Fixed costs** are expenses incurred by the organization regardless of the number of products produced. Some examples are real estate taxes, upkeep to the exterior of a business building, and interest expenses on money borrowed to finance the purchase of equipment.
2. *Variable costs*—Expenses that fluctuate with the number of products produced are called **variable costs.** Examples are costs of packaging a product, costs of materials needed to make the product, and costs associated with packing products to prepare them for shipping.
3. *Total costs*—**Total costs** are simply the sum of the fixed and variable costs associated with production.
4. *Total revenue*—**Total revenue** is all sales dollars accumulated from selling manufactured products or services. Naturally, total revenue increases as more products are sold.
5. *Profits*—**Profits** are defined as the amount of total revenue that exceeds the total costs of producing the products sold.
6. *Loss*—**Loss** is the amount of the total costs of producing a product that exceeds the total revenue gained from selling the product.
7. *Breakeven point*—The **breakeven point** is that level of production where the total revenue of an organization equals its total costs—that is, the point at which the organization is generating only enough revenue to cover its costs. The company is neither gaining a profit nor incurring a loss.

TYPES OF BREAKEVEN ANALYSIS There are two somewhat different procedures for determining the same breakeven point for an organization: algebraic breakeven analysis and graphic breakeven analysis.

Algebraic Breakeven Analysis The following simple formula is commonly used to determine the level of production at which an organization breaks even:

Breakeven analysis is a control tool that summarizes the various levels of profit or loss associated with various levels of production.

Fixed costs are expenses incurred by the organization regardless of the number of products produced.

Variable costs are expenses that fluctuate with the number of products produced.

Total costs are the sum of fixed costs and variable costs.

Total revenue is all sales dollars accumulated from selling the goods or services produced by the organization.

Profits are the amount of total revenue that exceeds total costs.

Loss is the amount of the total costs of producing a product that exceeds the total revenue gained from selling the product.

The **breakeven point** is that level of production where the total revenue of an organization equals its total costs.

$$BE = \frac{FC}{P - VC}$$

where

BE = the level of production at which the firm breaks even

FC = total fixed costs of production

P = price at which each individual unit is sold to customers

VC = variable costs associated with each product manufactured and sold

In using this formula to calculate a breakeven point, two sequential steps must be followed. First, the variable costs associated with producing each unit must be subtracted from the price at which each unit will sell. The purpose of this calculation is to determine how much of the selling price of each unit sold can go toward covering total fixed costs incurred from producing all products. Second, the remainder calculated in the first step must be divided into total fixed costs. The purpose of this calculation is to determine how many units must be produced and sold to cover fixed costs. This number of units is the breakeven point for the organization.

Say a book publisher faces the fixed and variable costs per paperback book presented in Table 20.2. If the publisher wants to sell each book for $12, the breakeven point could be calculated as follows:

$$BE = \frac{\$88,800}{\$12 - \$6}$$

$$BE = \frac{\$88,800}{\$6}$$

$$BE = 14,800 \text{ copies}$$

This calculation indicates that if expenses and selling price remain stable, the book publisher will incur a loss if book sales are fewer than 14,800 copies, will break even if book sales equal 14,800 copies, and will make a profit if book sales exceed 14,800 copies.

Graphic Breakeven Analysis Graphic breakeven analysis entails the construction of a graph showing all the critical elements in a breakeven analysis. Figure 20.5 is such a graph for the book publisher. Note that in a breakeven graph, the total revenue line starts at zero.

Advantages of Using the Algebraic and Graphic Breakeven Methods Both the algebraic and the graphic methods of breakeven analysis for the book publisher result in the same breakeven point—14,800 books produced and sold—but the processes used to arrive at this point are quite different.

Which breakeven method managers should use is usually determined by the situation they face. For a manager who desires a quick yet accurate determination of a breakeven point, the algebraic method generally suffices. For a manager who wants a more complete picture of the cumulative relationships between the breakeven point, fixed costs, and escalating variable

TABLE 20.2	Fixed Costs and Variable Costs for a Book Publisher		
Fixed Costs (Yearly Basis)		**Variable Costs per Book Sold**	
1. Real estate taxes on property	$1,000	1. Printing	$2.00
2. Interest on loan to purchase equipment	5,000	2. Artwork	1.00
		3. Sales commission	.50
3. Building maintenance	2,000	4. Author royalties	1.50
4. Insurance	800	5. Binding	1.00
5. Salaried labor	80,000		
Total fixed costs	$88,800	Total variable costs per book	$6.00

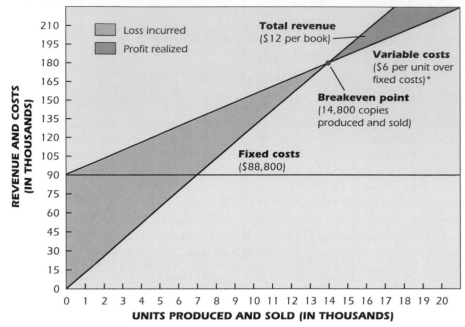

FIGURE 20.5 ▶ Breakeven analysis for a book publisher

* Note that drawing the variable costs line on top of the fixed costs line means that variable costs have been added to fixed costs. Therefore, the variable costs line also represents total costs.

costs, the graphic breakeven method is more useful. For example, the book publisher could quickly and easily see from Figure 20.5 the cumulative relationships of fixed costs, escalating variable costs, and potential profit and loss associated with various levels of production.

CONTROL AND BREAKEVEN ANALYSIS Breakeven analysis is a useful control tool because it helps managers understand the relationships between fixed costs, variable costs, total costs, and profit and loss within an organization. Once these relationships are understood, managers can take steps to modify one or more of the variables to reduce deviation between planned and actual profit levels.[23]

Increasing costs or decreasing selling prices has the overall effect of increasing the number of units an organization must produce and sell to break even. Conversely, the managerial strategy for decreasing the number of products an organization must produce and sell to break even entails lowering or stabilizing fixed and variable costs or increasing the selling price of each unit. The exact breakeven control strategy a particular manager should develop and implement is dictated primarily by that manager's unique organizational situation.

BACK TO THE CASE

There are several useful production control tools that USAir's management can use to ensure that various services are provided to customers as planned. First, management can have customer services inspected to determine which, if any, services should be improved and how to improve them. Second, USAir can use management by exception to control customer services. In this case, USAir's workers would handle all routine customer service issues and bring only exceptional matters to management's attention. To successfully use management by exception at USAir, it would be necessary to implement a number of carefully designed rules. One such rule might be that when five percent or more of luggage bags handled on a flight are damaged, a baggage handler must report this fact to a supervisor. The supervisor would then carefully inspect the baggage-handling process to see why this is happening—perhaps because of improper procedures or malfunctioning equipment—and management would take steps to correct the situation.

USAir might prefer to use management by objectives to control customer service issues. For example, management could set such customer service objectives as answering a ticket counter phone within five rings, ticketing a passenger within 5 minutes, and making sure that passengers do not wait longer than 30 minutes to buy a ticket at the airport. If such objectives are deemed both worthwhile and realistic, yet USAir's employees are not reaching them consistently, management would take steps to ensure that they are met.

Another control tool USAir's management might find highly useful is breakeven analysis. Breakeven analysis would furnish management with information about the various levels of profit or loss associated with various levels of revenue. To use this tool, USAir would have to determine the total fixed costs necessary to operate the airline, the price at which flights are sold, and the variable costs associated with various flights.

For example, if management wanted to determine how many tickets had to be sold before the company would break even on a particular flight, it could arrive at this breakeven point algebraically by following three steps. First, all fixed costs attributable to operating the flight—for example, airport facility rent—would be totaled. Second, all the variable costs of furnishing a flight to a passenger would be totaled, and from this total management would subtract the revenue that a ticket will generate. Variable costs include such expenses as meal costs, fuel costs, and labor needed to furnish the flight. Finally, the answer calculated in step 2 would be divided into the answer derived in step 1, and this figure would tell management how many tickets must be sold at the projected revenue level to break even.

USAir's management also could choose to determine the breakeven point by constructing a graph showing fixed costs, variable costs, and revenue per flight. Such a graph would probably give managers a more useful picture for formulating profit-oriented flight plans.

▶ OTHER BROAD OPERATIONS CONTROL TOOLS

Some of the best-known and most commonly used operations control tools are discussed in the following sections. The primary purpose of these tools is to control the production of organizational goods and services.[24]

DECISION TREE ANALYSIS **Decision tree analysis,** as you recall from chapter 7, is a statistical and graphical multiphase decision-making technique containing a series of steps showing the sequence and interdependence of decisions. Decision trees allow a decision maker to deal with uncertain events by determining the relative expected value of each alternative course of action. The probabilities of different possible events are known, as are the monetary payoffs that result from a particular alternative and a particular event. Decision trees are best suited to situations in which capacity decisions involve several capacity expansion alternatives and the selection of the alternative with the highest expected profit or the lowest expected cost is necessary.

> **Decision tree analysis** is a statistical and graphical multiphased decision-making technique that shows the sequence and interdependence of decisions.

PROCESS CONTROL Statistical process control, known as **process control,** is a technique that assists in monitoring production processes. Production processes must be monitored continually to ensure that the quality of their output is acceptable. The earlier the detection of a faulty production process, the better. If detection occurs late in the production process, the company may find parts that do not meet quality standards, and scrapping or reworking these is a costly proposition. If a production process results in unstable performance or is downright out of control, corrective action must be taken. Process control can be implemented with the aid of graphical charts known as control charts.

> **Process control** is a technique that assists in monitoring production processes.

VALUE ANALYSIS **Value analysis** is a cost control and cost reduction technique that aids managers controlling operations by focusing primarily on material costs. The goal of this analysis, which is performed by examining all the parts and materials and their functions, is to

> **Value analysis** is a cost control and cost reduction technique that examines all the parts, materials, and functions of an operation.

reduce costs by using cheaper components and materials in such a way that product quality or appeal is not affected. Simplification of parts—which lowers production costs—is also a goal of value analysis. Value analysis can result not only in cost savings but also in an improved product.

Value analysis requires a team effort. The team, if not companywide, should at least include personnel from operations, purchasing, engineering, and marketing.

Computer-aided design (CAD) is a computerized technique for designing new products or modifying existing ones.

COMPUTER-AIDED DESIGN Computer-aided design (CAD) systems include several automated design technologies. *Computer graphics* is used to design geometric specifications for parts, while *computer-aided engineering (CAE)* is employed to evaluate and perform engineering analyses on a part. CAD also includes technologies used in process design. CAD functions to ensure the quality of a product by guaranteeing not only the quality of parts in the product but also the appropriateness of the product's design.

Computer-aided manufacturing (CAM) is a technique that employs computers to plan and program equipment used in the production and inspection of manufactured items.

COMPUTER-AIDED MANUFACTURING Computer-aided manufacturing (CAM) employs computers to plan and program equipment used in the production and inspection of manufactured items. Linking CAM and CAD processes through a computer is very beneficial when production processes must be altered, because when CAD and CAM systems can share information easily, design changes can be implemented in a very short period of time.

In the machine-tool industry, which supplies equipment for manufacturing lines, computer-aided manufacturing now includes rapid-prototyping machines like this ultraviolet laser developed by 3D Systems of Valencia, California. These machines can fabricate parts directly from design data, in much the same way as a laser printer puts out data on a spreadsheet. This machine is building an oil pump by depositing one layer of powdered metal upon another.

BACK TO THE CASE

Decision tree analysis, process control, value analysis, computer-aided design, and computer-aided manufacturing were presented in the text as broader operations tools that are highly useful to managers exercising the control function. Of all these tools, value analysis would have the most application to USAir's service-oriented operation. USAir's management could use this cost control and cost reduction technique to examine the cost and worth of every component of customer service. To gain a complete picture of customer service components and their usefulness, USAir might establish a team comprising members from different customer service areas.

For instance, a team composed of a ticket agent, a flight attendant, a maintenance supervisor, and a baggage handler might explore different options for establishing comfortable cabin temperature while a plane is being loaded but before it taxis to the runway to await takeoff. If this team concludes, for example, that expediting the baggage-handling process would expose passengers to uncomfortable temperatures for shorter periods of time, management could take steps to speed up the process. Implementation of more efficient ways of handling baggage would result not only in better customer service but also in lower airline operating costs.

For updated information on the topics in this chapter, Internet exercises, links to related Internet sites, an interactive study guide, and more, visit our companion Web site at

http://www.prenhall.com/certo

Additional information can be found on the inside front and back covers of this text.

ACTION SUMMARY

Reread the learning objectives below. Each objective is followed by questions. Answering these questions accurately will help you retain the most important concepts discussed in this chapter. After answering each question, check your answer against the answer key at the end of this chapter. (*Hint:* If you have any doubts regarding the correct response, consult the page number that follows the answer.)

Circle:

From studying this chapter, I will attempt to acquire

1. Definitions of production, productivity, and quality.

a b c d e   **a.** Production is the transformation of organizational resources into: (a) profits (b) plans (c) forecasts (d) processes (e) products.

a b c d e   **b.** *Productivity* is the relationship between the amount of goods or services produced and: (a) profits (b) the organizational resources needed to produce them (c) quality (d) operations management activities (e) advanced manufacturing support.

T F   **c.** Quality is the extent to which a product reliably does what it is intended to do.

2. An understanding of the importance of operations and production strategies, systems, and processes.

a b c d   **a.** The flow of interrelated events moving toward a goal, purpose, or end is known as a: (a) system (b) process (c) strategy (d) plan.

a b c d   **b.** A particular linkage of mission, goals, strategies, policies, rules, human resources, and raw materials that facilitates carrying out a process is a: (a) system (b) process (c) strategy (d) plan.

3. Insights into the role of operations management concepts in the workplace.

T F   **a.** The criteria relevant for judging the actions taken as a result of operations management are effectiveness and efficiency.

a b c d   **b.** An operations strategy is achieved in a context of objectives and policies derived from the organization's: (a) capacity strategy (b) product strategy (c) strategic plan (d) human resources strategy.

a b c d   **c.** The reputation of an organization is determined by: (a) its size (b) its style of management (c) its profits (d) its product quality.

4. An understanding of how operations control procedures can be used to control production.

T F   **a.** Just-in-time inventory control is an inventory control technique based on the management philosophy that products should be manufactured when customers need them.

a b c d e   **b.** Potential pitfalls of using budgets as control tools include: (a) placing too much emphasis on relatively insignificant organizational expenses (b) changing budgets periodically (c) increasing budgeted expenses year after year without adequate information (d) a and c (e) a and b.

a b c d   **c.** Managers can use ratio analysis in the following way to control an organization:
a. Evaluate all ratios simultaneously to get a picture of the organization as a whole.

b. Compare computed values for ratios with values of industry averages.

c. Accumulate values for ratios for successive time periods to uncover specific organizational trends.

d. a, b, and c.

5. Insights concerning operations control tools and how they evolve into a continual improvement approach to production management and control.

T F **a.** By using inspection, managers can expect to catch any problems that are built into the system.

T F **b.** Management by exception is a control technique that allows only significant deviations between planned and actual performance to be brought to the manager's attention.

a b c d e **c.** The overall effect on the breakeven point of increasing costs or decreasing selling prices is that: (a) the number of products an organization must sell to break even increases (b) the amount of profit a firm will receive at a fixed number of units sold increases (c) the number of products an organization must sell to break even decreases (d) a and b (e) there is no effect on the breakeven point.

► INTRODUCTORY CASE WRAP-UP ◄

CASE DISCUSSSION QUESTIONS

"The QuickTurn at USAir" (p. 443) and its related Back-to-the-Case sections were written to help you better understand the management concepts contained in this chapter. Answer the following discussion questions about this Introductory Case to enrich your understanding of the chapter content:

1. Why is USAir attempting to raise productivity through shorter turnaround times? From your personal experience with airlines,

in what other ways do you think the company could increase productivity?

2. List three concepts discussed in this chapter that could help USAir's management increase productivity. Be sure to explain how each concept could help.

3. Which concept listed in question 2 do you think would have the most positive impact on increasing productivity? Explain fully.

SKILLS EXERCISE: APPLYING "NO REJECTS" IN A SERVICE INDUSTRY

The Introductory Case contains a diagram that outlines several steps to USAir's quick turn. Define what a "No Rejects" philosophy would mean for each of these processes. Be as detailed as you can.

► ISSUES FOR REVIEW AND DISCUSSION ◄

1. Define both *production* and *production control*.
2. Thoroughly explain the equation used to define productivity.
3. Discuss the relationship between quality and productivity.
4. What questions come to mind when you look at Deming's flow diagram for improving product quality?
5. What is quality assurance, and how is it related to statistical quality control?
6. Discuss how quality circles normally operate. What purpose do they serve?
7. Discuss the importance of automation in building productive organizations in the future.
8. Explain the term *operations management* as well as the major managerial activities involved in it.
9. List the three key concepts conveyed in the text discussion of operations management.
10. List the six operations strategies and explain how each contributes to continual increases in productivity.
11. What steps should management take to make sound strategic capacity decisions?

12. Discuss the three types of manufacturing processes.
13. Name the three basic types of layout patterns and give an example of each.
14. Discuss the two human resources strategy imperatives and the definition of a human resources strategy.
15. Discuss the management philosophy behind just-in-time inventory control.
16. Explain the difference between a pure-preventive maintenance policy and a pure-breakdown (repair) policy.
17. Explain why cost control is an important responsibility of every manager.
18. Define *budget*. How can managers use a budget to control an organization?
19. List three potential pitfalls of budgets.
20. What is ratio analysis?
21. What guidelines would you recommend to managers using ratio analysis to control an organization?
22. What is materials control, and how can it aid in production control?
23. What is a control tool?

24. Define *management by exception* and describe how it can help managers control production.

25. List and define seven major components of breakeven analysis.

26. How can managers use breakeven analysis to aid in controlling production?

27. List and define five other control tools.

CASE STUDY: Sun Also Rises

The key to success is having a good idea and the faith to pursue it. At least that's the bedrock of Sun Microsystems' corporate beliefs. For more than a decade, Scott McNealy, CEO of Sun, has maintained that the value of computing will be based upon computers networked together, and he has put his company's resources to work in pursuit of his vision.

Although the phenomenally successful Windows interface from Microsoft Corporation has often eclipsed the bright hopes of many technology companies, including PC pioneer Apple Computer, it has failed to deter Sun Microsystems from its network goals. In the 1980s, Sun workstations were easily accepted by engineers who needed the power of the network to do their work. In the early 1990s, Sun's sales faltered, but the Internet explosion refueled Sun's market. Company earnings jumped to $356 million in 1995, and revenues grew to $6 billion. Sun Microsystems now has a 35-percent market share of all computers used on the Internet. In the search for Internet standards, most large companies rely on Sun to provide them.

McNealy did not follow the usual path of engineer, or "techie," to the chief executive's suite at Sun. Instead, he came up through the ranks of manufacturing, and originally said he would have been content to own a machine shop and leave it as a legacy to his children. But in 1982, he was tapped by the president of Sun to come in and turn the manufacturing system around. The company was trying to deal with the enviable challenge of increasing production to keep up with exploding sales. (In 1984, sales jumped to $39 million, up from $9 million the year before.) McNealy did such a good job that, suddenly, production was moving ahead of sales. At this point, he moved over to marketing.

But then McNealy encountered a classical paradox: Success in sales led to a shortage of the cash needed to increase the level of production to meet the new level of sales. To raise the necessary money to expand the business, McNealy contacted a Sun Microsystems' customer, Eastman Kodak, to explore the possibility of a cash investment. Kodak executive vice president J. Philip Samper was so taken with McNealy's boldness and vision that he agreed. An unexpected condition of the agreement, however, was that McNealy be appointed president of Sun. The company's board of directors agreed to a temporary appointment, but as soon as sales took off, McNealy was formally installed as CEO. He was only 30 years old at the time.

Not surprisingly, Sun's success has made the company the target of other technology firms looking for a piece of the Internet pie. McNealy, however, is undeterred by attacks from competitors. Besides the success of Sun workstations as Web servers, he is counting on a new product called Java to loosen the viselike grip Microsoft and Intel Corporation have on the industry. The so-called Wintel standard seems to be unshakable for standalone computers, but Java allows a computer to reach across the expanse of the Internet and mimic the computer at the other end. Thus, instead of creating software to run in the dominant Windows environment, a company would be free to develop software in its own way and see it used in the freedom of the Internet.

Besides waging war with other technology companies over the Internet, McNealy must protect his home turf—the workstation. Corporations like Hewlett Packard, IBM, and DEC are encroaching on that part of Sun's business. Although Sun has lost some sales to Hewlett Packard, a redoubled commitment to support the customer seems to be paying off. In order to maintain a highly visible level of support, McNealy makes it a point to regularly call on the company's customers himself. He has also increased Sun's employee base by 50 percent in little more than a year's time. The emphasis on servers instead of workstations has helped the company increase revenues.

Finally, McNealy has always tried to instill an element of fun and camaraderie into Sun's corporate culture. Each April Fool's Day, for instance, reporters descend on corporate headquarters in Mountain View, California, to record the big event. The high point one year was the construction of a golf green inside the CEO's office. McNealy believes that fun is an essential part of the Sun equation. His hard-working employees need some amusing diversions to relieve their stress as they push to meet their CEO's ultimate goals.

QUESTIONS

1. What parts usually make up a successful corporate equation? Using information from this case study, create the specific formula for success at Sun Microsystems.

2. What are the benefits and liabilities of being first with a new product or technology?

3. Why is "vision" crucial in creating a successful technology company? Illustrate how Sun, Apple, IBM, Microsoft, and others are examples of vision—good or bad.

4. Chart McNealy's rise in the company and describe how this experience has helped make him a successful leader of a technology company.

Information Technology and the Internet

STUDENT LEARNING OBJECTIVES

From studying this chapter, I will attempt to acquire

1. An understanding of the relationship between data and information

2. Insights about the main factors that influence the value of information

3. Knowledge of some potential steps for evaluating information

4. An understanding of the importance of a management information system (MIS) to an organization

5. A feasible strategy for establishing an MIS

6. Information about what a management decision support system is and how it operates

7. An appreciation for the roles of computers and networks like the Internet in handling information

CHAPTER OUTLINE

Introductory Case: *Making Changes without the Right Information at Sunbeam?*

ESSENTIALS OF INFORMATION
Factors Influencing the Value of Information
Information Appropriateness
Information Quality
Information Timeliness
Information Quantity
Evaluating Information

THE MANAGEMENT INFORMATION SYSTEM (MIS)

Global Spotlight: *Pohang Iron & Steel Company Needs a Complex MIS*
Describing the MIS

Diversity Spotlight: *Target's MIS Focuses on Hispanic Workers*
Establishing an MIS

INFORMATION TECHNOLOGY
Computer Assistance in Using Information

THE MANAGEMENT DECISION SUPPORT SYSTEM (MDSS)

COMPUTER NETWORKS
The Local Area Network
The Internet

Management and the Internet: *Dell Computer Company Surfs the Internet to Service Customers and Build Its Image*

Across Industries: *Accounting—Technical Glitch at Arthur Andersen Renders E-Mail Useless*

MAKING CHANGES WITHOUT THE RIGHT INFORMATION AT SUNBEAM?

REMINDER: THE INTRODUCTORY CASE WRAP-UP (P. 497) CONTAINS DISCUSSION QUESTIONS AND A SKILLS EXERCISE TO FURTHER ILLUSTRATE THE APPLICATION OF CHAPTER CONCEPTS TO THIS VIGNETTE.

Sunbeam Corporation develops, manufactures, and markets consumer products in the areas of home appliances, home health care, and outdoor cooking. The company offers a very diverse product line ranging from electric blankets to gas grills.

Sunbeam Corp. recently announced the firing of Albert J. Dunlap as chairman and chief executive officer. Contrary to earlier projections, the company appeared headed for an operating loss. The ouster of Mr. Dunlap, whose aggressive layoffs and other cost-cutting tactics have made him one of corporate America's premier downsizers, was decided in an emergency meeting of Sunbeam's independent directors in New York. It marked the culmination of a week during which the board's support for him collapsed as its worries about his leadership and the company's deteriorating performance increased.

Mr. Dunlap, 60 years old, earned the nickname "Chain Saw Al" by obliterating thousands of jobs and firing managers who failed to deliver at several companies he ran over the past 15 years. Now Sunbeam's board decided that Mr. Dunlap was failing to turn around the Delray Beach, Fla., company.

Mr. Dunlap succeeded in slashing costs at Sunbeam, eliminating about half the company's 12,000 jobs. But he wasn't able to deliver on his promise to transform the company into a high-growth profit machine.

A series of disclosures about Sunbeam's worsening financial performance sapped investors' confidence. Despite

Sunbeam Corporation has long maintained its profile as a progressive firm driven by new-product evolution.

thumping assurances from Mr. Dunlap that his turnaround plan was working, the stock price sank steadily.

Given Mr. Dunlap's outstanding record of success in turning around other organizations, one can only wonder why he was unsuccessful at Sunbeam. Perhaps the information upon which he was basing his decisions was of low quality.

What's Ahead

The Introductory Case discusses how Albert J. Dunlap had a successful career as one of America's premier downsizers until he failed at Sunbeam. The case ends with the possibility that Dunlap failed because he based downsizing decisions on faulty information. This chapter presents material that should be useful to a manager like Dunlap who should scrutinize the overall worth of information before making important decisions based upon it. Major topics in this chapter are the following:

1. Essentials of information
2. The management information systems (MIS)
3. The management decision support system (MDSS)
4. Computer networks including both local area networks and the Internet.

Controlling is the process of making things happen as planned. Of course, managers cannot make things happen as planned if they lack information on the manner in which various events in the organization occur. This chapter discusses the fundamental principles of handling information in an organization by first presenting the essentials of information and then examining both the management information system (MIS) and information technology.

ESSENTIALS OF INFORMATION

Data are facts or statistics.

Information is the set of conclusions derived from data analysis.

The process of developing information begins with gathering some type of facts or statistics, called **data.** Once gathered, data typically are analyzed in some manner. In general terms, **information** is the set of conclusions derived from data analysis. In management terms, information is the set of conclusions derived from the analysis of data that relate to the operation of an organization. As examples to illustrate the relationship between data and information, managers gather data regarding pay rates that individuals are receiving within industries in order to collect information about how to develop competitive pay rates, data regarding hazardous-materials accidents in order to gain information about how to improve worker safety, and data regarding customer demographics in order to gain information about product demand in the future.[1]

The information that managers receive heavily influences managerial decision making, which, in turn, determines the activities that will be performed within the organization, which, in turn, dictate the eventual success or failure of the organization. Some management writers consider information to be of such fundamental importance to the management process that they define *management* as the process of converting information into action through decision making.[2] The next sections discuss the following aspects of information and decision making:

1. Factors that influence the value of information
2. How to evaluate information
3. Computer assistance in using information

►FACTORS INFLUENCING THE VALUE OF INFORMATION

Some information is more valuable than other information.[3] The value of information is defined in terms of the benefit that can accrue to the organization through its use. The greater this benefit, the more valuable the information.

Four primary factors determine the value of information:

1. Information appropriateness
2. Information quality
3. Information timeliness
4. Information quantity

In general, management should encourage generation, distribution, and use of organizational information that is appropriate, of high quality, timely, and of sufficient quantity. Following this guideline will not necessarily guarantee sound decisions, but it will ensure that important resources necessary to make such decisions are available.[4] Each of the factors that determines information value is discussed in more detail in the paragraphs that follow.

In 1993, Caterpillar, a maker of earthmoving vehicles based in Aurora, Illinois, returned to profitability after seven straight quarters of losses. One key was the use of computers to cut inventories by as much as 40 percent. Computers, for instance, monitor parts usage and transmit orders to suppliers on a strict as-needed basis.

►INFORMATION APPROPRIATENESS

Information appropriateness is defined in terms of how relevant the information is to the decision-making situation the manager faces. If the information is quite relevant, then it is said to be appropriate. Generally, as the appropriateness of information increases, so does the value of that information.

Figure 21.1 shows the characteristics of information appropriate for the following common decision-making situations:[5]

1. Operational control
2. Management control
3. Strategic planning

Information appropriateness is the degree to which information is relevant to the decision-making situation the manager faces.

FIGURE 21.1 ► Characteristics of information appropriate for decisions related to operational control, management control, and strategic planning

CHARACTERISTICS OF INFORMATION	OPERATIONAL CONTROL	MANAGEMENT CONTROL	STRATEGIC PLANNING
Source	Largely internal	⟶	External
Scope	Well defined, narrow	⟶	Very wide
Level of aggregation	Detailed	⟶	Aggregate
Time horizon	Historical	⟶	Future
Currency	Highly current	⟶	Quite old/historical
Required accuracy	High	⟶	Low
Frequency of use	Very frequent	⟶	Infrequent

OPERATIONAL CONTROL, MANAGEMENT CONTROL, AND STRATEGIC PLANNING DECISIONS *Operational control decisions* relate to ensuring that specific organizational tasks are carried out effectively and efficiently. *Management control decisions* relate to obtaining and effectively and efficiently using the organizational resources necessary to reach organizational objectives. *Strategic planning decisions* relate to determining organizational objectives and designating the corresponding action necessary to reach them.

As Figure 21.1 shows, characteristics of appropriate information change as managers shift from making operational control decisions to making management control decisions to making strategic planning decisions. Strategic planning decision makers need information that focuses on the relationship of the organization to its external environment, emphasizes the future, is wide in scope, and presents a broad view. Appropriate information for this type of decision is generally not completely current, but more historical in nature. In addition, this information does not need to be completely accurate because strategic decisions tend to be characterized by some subjectivity and focus on areas, like customer satisfaction, that are difficult to measure.

Information appropriate for making operational control decisions has dramatically different characteristics from information appropriate for making strategic planning decisions. Operational control decision makers need information that focuses for the most part on the internal organizational environment, emphasizes the performance history of the organization, and is well defined, narrow in scope, and detailed. In addition, appropriate information for this type of decision is both highly current and highly accurate.

Information appropriate for making management control decisions generally has characteristics that fall somewhere between the extreme of appropriate operational control information and appropriate strategic planning information.

UPS driver Kevin Smith can use a so-called electronic clipboard developed by McCaw Cellular Communications to track packages over a cellular network. The messages that he sends are converted into "packet-switched data" that improve upon both information timeliness and quantity.

►INFORMATION QUALITY

Information quality is the degree to which information represents reality.

The second primary factor that determines the value of information is **information quality**—the degree to which information represents reality. The more closely information represents reality, the higher the quality and the greater the value of that information. In general, the higher the quality of information available to managers, the better equipped managers are to make appropriate decisions and the greater the probability that the organization will be successful over the long term.

Perhaps the most significant factor in producing poor-quality information is *data contamination*. Inaccurate data gathering can result in information that is of very low quality—a poor representation of reality.[6]

►INFORMATION TIMELINESS

Information timeliness is the extent to which the receipt of information allows decisions to be made and action to be taken so the organization can gain some benefit from possessing the information.

Information timeliness, the third primary factor that determines the value of information, is the extent to which the receipt of information allows decisions to be made and action to be taken so the organization can gain some benefit from possessing the information. Information received by managers at a point when it can be used to the organization's advantage is said to be timely.

For example, a product may be selling poorly because its established market price is significantly higher than the price of competitive products. If this information is received by management after the product has been discontinued, the information will be untimely. If, however, it is received soon enough to adjust the selling price of the product and thereby significantly increase sales, it will be timely.

►INFORMATION QUANTITY

Information quantity is the amount of decision-related information a manager possesses.

The fourth and final determinant of the value of information is **information quantity**—the amount of decision-related information managers possess. Before making a decision, managers should assess the quantity of information they possess that relates to the decision being made. If this quantity is judged to be insufficient, more information should be gathered before the decision is made. If the amount of information is judged to be as complete as necessary, managers can feel justified in making the decision.

There is such a thing as *too* much information. According to Rick Feldcamp of Century Life of America, information overload—too much information to consider properly—can make managers afraid to make decisions and result in important decisions going unmade. Information overload is generally considered to be the major cause of indecision in organizations—commonly referred to as "paralysis by analysis."[7]

►EVALUATING INFORMATION

Evaluating information is the process of determining whether the acquisition of specified information is justified. As with all evaluations of this kind, the primary concern of management is to weigh the dollar value of benefit gained from using some quantity of information against the cost of generating that information.

IDENTIFYING AND EVALUATING DATA According to the flowchart in Figure 21.2, the first major step in evaluating organizational information is to ascertain the value of that information by pinpointing the data to be analyzed, and then determine the expected value or

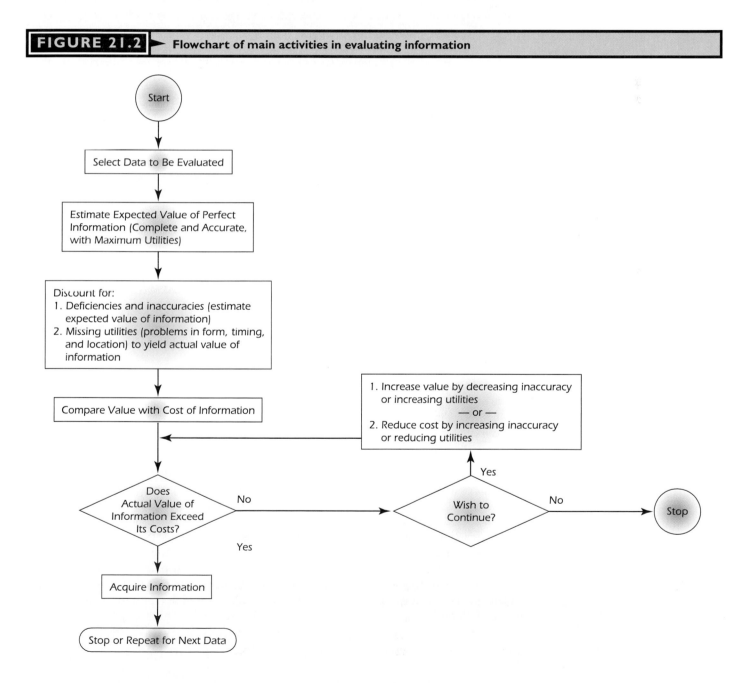

FIGURE 21.2 ► **Flowchart of main activities in evaluating information**

return to be received from obtaining perfect information based on these data. Then this expected value is reduced by the amount of benefit that will not be realized because of deficiencies and inaccuracies expected to appear in the information.

EVALUATING THE COST OF DATA Next, the expected value of organizational information is compared with the expected cost of obtaining that information. If the expected cost does not exceed the expected value, the information should be gathered. If it does exceed the expected value, managers either must increase the information's expected value or decrease its expected cost before the information gathering can be justified. If neither of these objectives is possible, management cannot justify gathering the information.

BACK TO THE CASE

According to the preceding material, information at Sunbeam Corporation can be defined as conclusions derived from the analysis of data relating to the way in which the company operates. The case implies that managers at Sunbeam Corporation will be better able to make sound decisions, including better control decisions, because of the successful data handling achieved by its information system. One important factor in evaluating the overall worth of Sunbeam Corporation's information handling system would be the overall impact of the system on the value of information that company managers would receive. A manager like Dunlap must see that investing in computers, satellites, and other data-handling devices at a reasonable cost can enhance the value of information that he receives and improve the appropriateness of downsizing decisions. That is, investments in improving information system components can enhance the appropriateness, quality, timeliness, and quantity of information that Dunlap can use to make downsizing decisions. In essence, Dunlap must believe and act on the notion that the benefits of making investments in computers and information systems will outweigh the costs of the equipment by significantly improving his downsizing decisions.

THE MANAGEMENT INFORMATION SYSTEM (MIS)

A **management information system (MIS)** is a network established within an organization to provide managers with information that will assist them in decision making. An MIS gets information to where it is needed.

In simple terms, a **management information system (MIS)** is a network established within an organization to provide managers with information that will assist them in decision making.[8] The following, more complete definition of an MIS was developed by the Management Information System Committee of the Financial Executives Institute:[9]

> An MIS is a system designed to provide selected decision-oriented information needed by management to plan, control, and evaluate the activities of the corporation. It is designed within a framework that emphasizes profit planning, performance planning, and control at all levels. It contemplates the ultimate integration of required business information subsystems, both financial and nonfinancial, within the company.

The typical MIS is a formally established organizational network that gives managers continual access to vital information. For example, the MIS normally provides managers with ongoing reports relevant to significant organizational activities like sales, worker productivity, and labor turnover. As this example implies, the purview of an MIS is usually limited to internal organizational events. Based upon information they gain via an MIS, managers make decisions that are aimed at improving organizational performance. Because the typical MIS is characterized by computer usage, managers can use an MIS to gain online access to company records and condensed information in the form of summaries and reports. Overall, the MIS is a planned, systematic mechanism for providing managers with relevant information in a systematic fashion.[10]

The title of the specific organization member responsible for developing and maintaining an MIS varies from organization to organization. In smaller organizations, a president or vice president may have this responsibility. In larger organizations, an individual with a title such as "director of information systems" may be solely responsible for appropriately managing an entire MIS department. The term *MIS manager* is used in the sections that follow to indicate the person within the organization who has the primary responsibility for managing the MIS. The term *MIS personnel* is used to designate the nonmanagement individuals within the organization who possess the primary responsibility for actually operating the MIS. Examples of nonmanagement individuals are computer operators and computer programmers. The sections that follow describe an MIS more fully and outline the steps managers take to establish an MIS.

GLOBAL SPOTLIGHT Pohang Iron & Steel Company Needs a Complex MIS

A management information system is used in managing activities at virtually all levels of an organization. Thus, although a given MIS may be relatively simple, managers at some organizations have to develop and use a very complex MIS, especially if their organizations are of significant size.

Management at the Pohang Iron & Steel Company in Korea faced the challenge of developing a complex MIS to manage Pohang's organizational activities efficiently and effectively. A complex MIS was needed primarily because of the large size of the company and the complexity of the activities involved in manufacturing steel. Pohang established an MIS that permits managers to monitor any phase of the steel production process. In addition, the system continually monitors about 60,000 items that are critical in controlling production costs and, at specified intervals, automatically updates the status of these items. To best interpret and react to information that flows on its MIS, management uses regularly scheduled video conferences with organization members in different locations. Pohang is the only Korean company to use regularly scheduled video conferences in this fashion. Pohang was founded in 1973 by the government of the Republic of Korea and is now the second largest and most competitive steel maker in the world. The company's success is largely credited to its development and use of its sophisticated MIS.

►DESCRIBING THE MIS

The MIS is perhaps best described by a summary of the steps necessary to properly operate it,[11] and by a discussion of the different kinds of information various managers need to make job-related decisions.

OPERATING THE MIS MIS personnel generally need to perform six sequential steps to properly operate an MIS.[12] (Figure 21.3 summarizes the steps and indicates the order in which they are performed.) The first step is to determine what information is needed within the organization, when it will be needed, and in what form it will be needed. Because the basic purpose of the MIS is to assist management in making decisions, one way to begin determining management information needs is to analyze the following:

1. Decision areas in which management makes decisions
2. Specific decisions within these decision areas that management must actually make
3. Alternatives that must be evaluated to make these specific decisions

For example, insights regarding what information management needs in a particular organization can be gleaned by understanding that management makes decisions in the area of plant and equipment, that a specific decision related to this area involves acquiring new equipment, and that two alternatives that must be evaluated relating to this decision are buying newly developed, high-technology equipment versus buying more standard equipment that has been around for some time in the industry.

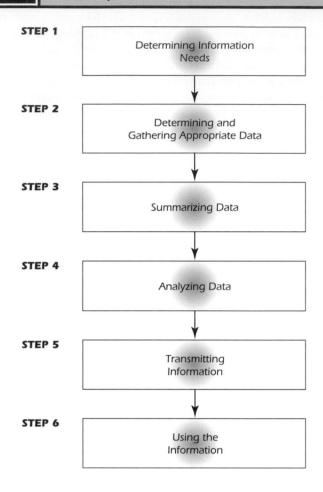

| FIGURE 21.3 | The six steps necessary to operate an MIS properly in order of their performance |

STEP 1 — Determining Information Needs

STEP 2 — Determining and Gathering Appropriate Data

STEP 3 — Summarizing Data

STEP 4 — Analyzing Data

STEP 5 — Transmitting Information

STEP 6 — Using the Information

DIVERSITY SPOTLIGHT   Target's MIS Focuses on Hispanic Workers

According to Target's vice president of public and consumer affairs, George Hite, and its president, Warren Feldberg, Target Stores is implementing aggressive expansion plans. Target, a consumer products retailer, has gained its success primarily by designing merchandise programs that reflect lifestyle trends. Company success has been significant enough to yield plans to add about 300 new stores over the next three years. Target managers are being prepared for expansion through comprehensive planning and a strong emphasis on management development.

Several MIS challenges face a company as substantial as Target. For example, management must have certain information: how competitive the company must be in order to hire an adequate number of workers; current trends in technology that might help Target become more efficient; financial results that the company is generating; the kind of continuing education necessary to build a productive workforce; international factors, such as the desirability of purchasing cheaper products abroad; and the level of workforce diversity that the company possesses and should aspire to.

The MIS at Target has provided management with a foundation of information upon which to make diversity-related decisions. For example, in southern California, the company is monitoring changing demographics of the population surrounding Target stores and attempting to build a workforce that reflects the diversity of that population. As a result, in southern California, Target is hiring a greater proportion of Hispanic workers. In order to help these workers become more productive, Target is offering them free English classes.

The second major step in operating the MIS is pinpointing and collecting data that will yield needed organizational information. This step is just as important as determining information needs of the organization. If collected data do not relate properly to information needs, it will be impossible to generate needed information.

After information needs of the organization have been determined and appropriate data have been pinpointed and gathered, summarizing the data and analyzing the data are, respectively, the third and fourth steps MIS personnel generally should take to properly operate an MIS. It is in the performance of these steps that MIS personnel find computer assistance of great benefit.

The fifth and sixth steps are transmitting the information generated by data analysis to appropriate managers and getting the managers to actually use the information. The performance of these last two steps results in managerial decision making. Although each of the six steps is necessary if an MIS is to run properly, the time spent on performing each step will naturally vary from organization to organization.

DIFFERENT MANAGERS NEED DIFFERENT KINDS OF INFORMATION For maximum benefit, an MIS must collect relevant data, transform that data into appropriate information, and transmit that information to the appropriate managers. Appropriate information for one manager within an organization, however, may not be appropriate information for another. Robert G. Murdick suggests that the degree of appropriateness of MIS information for a manager depends on the activities for which the manager will use the information, the organizational objectives assigned to the manager, and the level of management at which the manager functions.[13] All of these factors, of course, are closely related.

Murdick's thoughts on this matter are best summarized in Figure 21.4. As you can see from this figure, because the overall job situations of top managers, middle managers, and first-line managers are significantly different, the kinds of information these managers need to satisfactorily perform their jobs are also significantly different.

BACK TO THE CASE

In order for a company like Sunbeam Corporation to get maximum benefit from its computer assistance, management must appropriately build each main ingredient of its MIS. The MIS at a company like Sunbeam Corporation is the organizational network established to provide managers with information that helps them make job-related decisions. Such a system at a major company like Sunbeam Corporation would normally necessitate the use of several MIS personnel who would help determine information needs at the company, help determine and collect appropriate Sunbeam Corporation data, summarize and analyze these data, transmit analyzed data to appropriate Sunbeam Corporation managers, and generally help managers in interpreting received MIS information.

To make sure that managers get appropriate information, Sunbeam's MIS personnel must appreciate how different managers need different kinds of information. As an example, a top manager like Albert Dunlap would normally need information that summarizes trends like consumer tastes, competitor moves, and perhaps most importantly for a downsizer, summary reports for productivity and costs related to various organizational units. Middle managers would need information that focuses more on specific operating divisions or units within the company, such as all specifics regarding home appliance production. More lower-level managers, perhaps production supervisors, would normally need information about daily production rates, regular versus overtime labor costs, and the status of meeting production goals.

FIGURE 21.4 **Appropriate MIS information under various sets of organizational circumstances**

Organizational Level	Type of Management	Manager's Organizational Objectives	Appropriate Information from MIS	How MIS Information Is Used
1. Top management	CEO, president, vice president	Survival of the firm, profit growth, accumulation and efficient use of resources	Environmental data and trends, summary reports of operations, exception reports of problems, forecasts	Corporate objectives, policies, constraints, decisions on strategic plans, decisions on control of the total company
2. Middle management	Middle managers in such areas as marketing, production, and finance	Allocation of resources to assigned tasks, establishment of plans to meet operating objectives, control of operations	Summaries and exception reports of operating results, corporate objectives, policies, constraints, decisions on strategic plans, relevant actions and decisions of other middle managers	Operating plans and policies, exception reports, operating summaries, control procedures, decisions on resource allocations, actions and decisions related to other middle managers
3. First-line management	First-line managers whose work is closely related	Production of goods to meet marketing needs, supplying budgets, estimates of resource requirements, movement and storage of materials	Summary reports of transactions, detailed reports of problems, operating plans and policies, control procedures, actions and decisions of related first-line managers	Exception reports, progress reports, resource requests, dispatch orders, cross-functional reports

►ESTABLISHING AN MIS

The process of establishing an MIS involves four stages:

1. Planning for the MIS
2. Designing the MIS
3. Implementing the MIS
4. Improving the MIS

PLANNING FOR THE MIS The planning stage is perhaps the most important stage of the process. Commonly cited factors that make planning for the establishment of an MIS an absolute necessity are the typically long periods of time needed to acquire MIS-related data-processing equipment and to integrate it into the operations of the organization, the difficulty of hiring competent equipment operators, and the major amounts of financial and managerial resources typically needed to operate an MIS.[14]

The specific types of plans for an MIS vary from organization to organization. However, a sample plan for the establishment of an MIS at a large consumer-products company is shown in Figure 21.5. This hypothetical plan, of course, is abbreviated; much more detailed outlines of each of the areas in this plan would be needed before it could be implemented. Notice that

FIGURE 21.5 ▶ Plan for establishing a hypothetical MIS

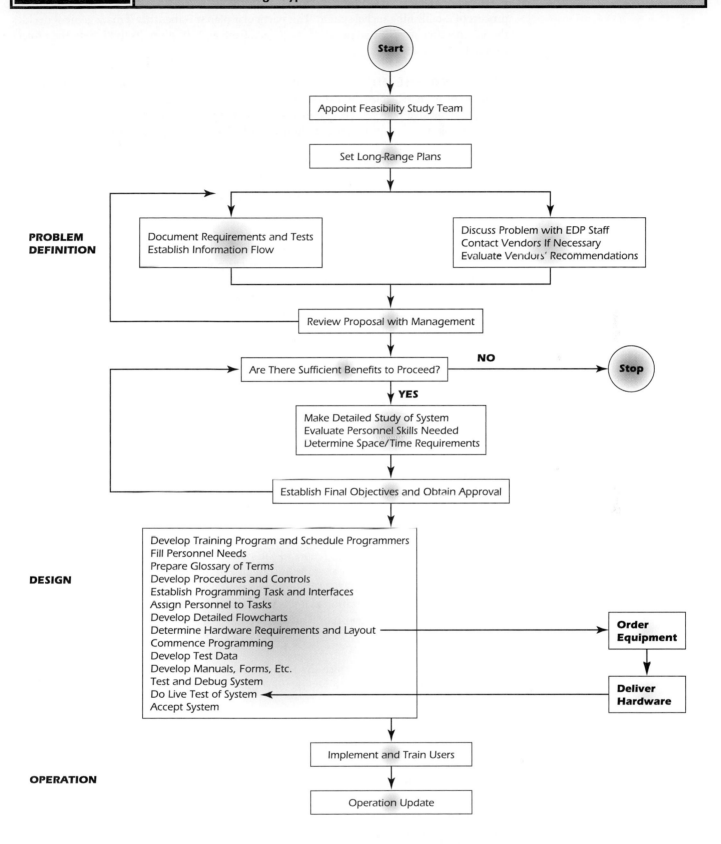

this plan includes a point (about a third of the way down the figure) at which management must decide if there is enough potential benefit to be gained from an MIS to continue the process of establishing such a system. This particular plan specifies that if management decides there is insufficient potential benefit to be gained from an MIS, given its total costs, the project should be terminated.

DESIGNING THE MIS Although data-processing equipment is normally an important component of management information systems, the designing of an MIS should not begin with a comparative analysis of the types of such equipment available. Many MIS managers mistakenly think that data-processing equipment and an MIS are synonymous.

Analyzing Managers' Decisions Stoller and Van Horn indicate that because the purpose of an MIS is to provide information that will assist managers in making better decisions, the designing of an MIS should begin with an analysis of the kinds of decisions the managers actually make in a particular organization.[15] These authors suggest that designing an MIS should consist of the following four steps:

1. Defining various decisions that must be made to run an organization
2. Determining the types of existing management policies that may influence the ways in which these decisions should be made
3. Pinpointing the types of data needed to make these decisions
4. Establishing a mechanism for gathering and appropriately processing the data to obtain needed information

IMPLEMENTING THE MIS The third stage in the process of establishing an MIS within an organization is implementation—that is, putting the planned-for and designed MIS into operation. In this stage, the equipment is acquired and integrated into the organization. Designated data are gathered, analyzed as planned, and distributed to appropriate managers within the organization. Line managers make decisions based on the information they receive from the MIS.

Making sure that the MIS is as simple as possible and serves the information needs of management is critical to a successful implementation of an MIS. If the MIS is overly complicated or does not meet management's information needs, the implementation of the system will encounter much resistance and will probably have only limited success.

Enlisting Management Support Management of the implementation process of the MIS can determine the ultimate success or failure of the system.[16] To help ensure that this process will be successful, management can attempt to find an executive sponsor—a high-level manager who understands and supports the MIS implementation process. The support of such a sponsor will be a sign to all organization members that the MIS implementation is important to the organization and that all organization members should cooperate in making the implementation process successful.

IMPROVING THE MIS Once the MIS is operating, MIS managers should continually strive to maximize its value. The two sections that follow provide insights on how MIS improvements might be made.

Symptoms of an Inadequate MIS To improve an MIS, MIS managers must first find symptoms or signs that the existing MIS is inadequate. A list of such symptoms, developed by Bertram A. Colbert, a principal of Price Waterhouse & Company, is presented in Table 21.1.[17]

Colbert divides the symptoms into three types:

1. Operational
2. Psychological
3. Report content

Operational symptoms and psychological symptoms relate, respectively, to the operation of the organization and the functioning of organization members. Report content symptoms relate to the actual makeup of the information generated by the MIS.

TABLE 21.1 ► **Symptoms of an Inadequate MIS**

Operational	Psychological	Report Content
Large physical inventory adjustments	Surprise at financial results	Excessive use of tabulations of figures
Capital expenditure overruns	Poor attitude of executives about usefulness of information	Multiple preparation and distribution of identical data
Inability of executives to explain changes from year to year in operating results	Lack of understanding of financial information on part of nonfinancial executives	Disagreeing information from different sources
Uncertain direction of company growth		Lack of periodic comparative information and trends
Cost variances unexplainable	Lack of concern for environmental changes	Lateness of information
No order backlog awareness	Executive homework reviewing reports considered excessive	Too little or excess detail
No internal discussion of reported data		Inaccurate information
Insufficient knowledge about competition		Lack of standards for comparison
Purchasing parts from outside vendors when internal capability and capacity to make are available		Failure to identify variances by cause and responsibility
Record of some "sour" investments in facilities, or in programs such as R&D and advertising		Inadequate externally generated information

Although the symptoms listed in the table are clues that an MIS is inadequate, the symptoms, by themselves, may not actually pinpoint MIS weaknesses. Therefore, after such symptoms are detected, MIS managers usually must gather additional information to determine what MIS weaknesses exist. Answering questions such as the following helps MIS managers to determine these weaknesses:[18]

1. Where and how do managers get information?
2. Can managers make better use of their contacts to get information?
3. In what areas is managers' knowledge weakest, and how can managers be given information to minimize these weaknesses?
4. Do managers tend to act before receiving information?
5. Do managers wait so long for information that opportunities pass them by and the organization becomes bottlenecked?

Typical Improvements to an MIS MIS inadequacies vary from situation to situation, depending on such factors as the quality of an MIS plan, the appropriateness of an MIS design, and the kinds of individuals operating an MIS. However, several activities have the potential of improving the MIS of most organizations:[19]

1. *Building cooperation among MIS personnel and line managers*—Cooperation of this sort encourages line managers to give MIS personnel honest opinions of the quality of information being received. Through this type of interaction, MIS designers and operators should be able to improve the effectiveness of an MIS.
2. *Constantly stressing that MIS personnel should strive to accomplish the purpose of the MIS— providing managers with decision-related information*—In this regard, it probably would be of great benefit to hold line managers responsible for continually educating MIS personnel on the types of decisions organization members make and the corresponding steps taken to make these decisions. The better MIS personnel understand the decision situations that face operating managers, the higher the probability that MIS information will be appropriate for decisions these managers must make.
3. *Holding, wherever possible, both line managers and MIS personnel accountable for MIS activities on a cost-benefit basis*—This accountability reminds line managers and MIS personnel that the benefits the organization receives from MIS functions must exceed the costs. In effect, this accountability emphasis helps increase the cost consciousness of both line managers and MIS personnel.

4. *Operating an MIS in a "people-conscious" manner*—An MIS, like the formal pyramidal organization, is based on the assumption that organizational affairs can and should be handled in a completely logical manner. Logic, of course, is important to the design and implementation of an MIS. However, MIS activities should also take human considerations into account. After all, even when MIS activities are well-thought-out and completely logical, an MIS can be ineffective simply because people do not use it as intended.

BACK TO THE CASE

Assume that Dunlap has just decided to establish an MIS within his company. Sunbeam Corporation, like any other company, would probably gain significantly by carefully planning the way in which its MIS would be established. For example, perhaps the answers to the following questions during the planning stage of Sunbeam Corporation's MIS would be useful. Is an appropriate computer-based system being acquired and integrated? Does the company need new MIS personnel or will present personnel require further training in order to operate the new MIS? Will managers need additional training in order to operate the new MIS?

About the design and implementation stages of Sunbeam's new MIS, Dunlap should seek answers to such questions as How do we design the new MIS based upon managerial decision making? How can we ensure that the new MIS as designed and implemented will actually exist and be functional?

Dunlap as well as MIS personnel should continually try to improve the new MIS. All users of the new MIS should be aware of the symptoms of an inadequate MIS and should be constantly attempting to pinpoint and eliminate corresponding MIS weaknesses. Suggestions for improving the new MIS could include (1) building additional cooperation between MIS managers, MIS personnel, and line managers; (2) stressing that the purpose of the MIS is to provide managers with decision-related information; (3) using cost-benefit analysis to evaluate MIS activities; and (4) ensuring that the MIS operates in a people-conscious manner.

■ INFORMATION TECHNOLOGY

Technology consists of any type of equipment or process that organization members use in the performance of their work.

Information technology is technology that focuses on the use of information in the performance of work.

Technology consists of any type of equipment or process that organization members use in the performance of their work. This definition includes tools as old as a blacksmith's anvil and tools as new and innovative as virtual reality. This section discusses one segment of technology, **information technology,** or technology that focuses on the use of information in the performance of work. Some recent information technology introductions are covered in more detail through the following topics: computer assistance in using information, the management decision support system (MDSS), and computer networks.

► COMPUTER ASSISTANCE IN USING INFORMATION

Managers have an overwhelming amount of data to gather, analyze, and transform into information before making numerous decisions. In fact, many managers in the United States as well as in the United Kingdom and other foreign countries are currently complaining that they are overloaded with information.[20] A computer is a tool managers can use to assist in the complicated and time-consuming task of generating this information.

A **computer** is an electronic tool capable of accepting data, interpreting data, performing ordered operations on data, and reporting on the outcome of these operations.

A **computer** is an electronic tool capable of accepting data, interpreting data, performing ordered operations on data, and reporting on the outcome of these operations. Computers give managers the ability to store vast amounts of financial, inventory, and other data so that the data will be readily accessible for making day-to-day decisions. These decisions can be quite diverse and focus on issues like billing customers more efficiently, keeping track of receivables that are past due, ordering materials in appropriate quantities, paying vendors on a timely basis, and making sure that planned projects are on schedule.

Computers are extremely helpful in generating information from raw data.

The sections that follow discuss the main functions of computers and possible pitfalls in using computers.

MAIN FUNCTIONS OF COMPUTERS A computer function is a computer activity that must be performed to generate organizational information. Computers perform five main functions:

1. Input
2. Storage
3. Control
4. Processing
5. Output

The relationships among these functions are shown in Figure 21.6.

Input The **input function** consists of computer activities through which the computer enters the data to be analyzed and the instructions to be followed to analyze the data appropriately. As Figure 21.6 shows, the purpose of the input function is to provide data and instructions to be used in the performance of the storage, processing, control, and output functions.

Storage The **storage function** consists of computer activities involved with retaining the material entered into the computer during the performance of the input function. The storage unit, or memory, of a computer is similar to the human memory in that various facts can be stored until they are needed for processing. In addition, facts can be stored, used in processing, and then restored as many times as necessary. As Figure 21.6 demonstrates, the storage, processing, and control activities are dependent on one another and ultimately yield computer output.

Processing The **processing function** consists of the computer activities involved with performing both logic and calculation steps necessary to analyze data appropriately. Calculation activities include virtually any numeric analysis. Logic activities include such analysis as comparing one number to another to determine which is larger. Data, as well as directions for processing the data, are furnished by input and storage activities.

The five main functions of computers are:

1. The **input function**—computer activities through which the computer enters the data to be analyzed and the instructions to be followed to analyze the data appropriately.

2. The **storage function**—computer activities involved with retaining the material entered into the computer during the performance of the input function.

3. The **processing function**—computer activities involved with performing the logic and calculation steps necessary to analyze data appropriately.

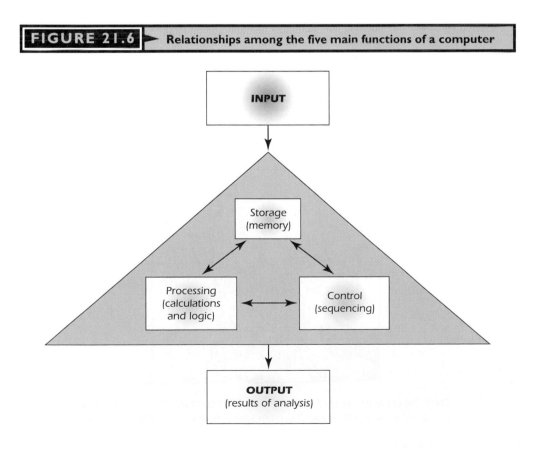

FIGURE 21.6 ▶ **Relationships among the five main functions of a computer**

INPUT

Storage
(memory)

Processing
(calculations
and logic)

Control
(sequencing)

OUTPUT
(results of analysis)

4. The **control function**—computer activities that dictate the order in which other computer functions are performed.

Control   Computer activities that dictate the order in which other computer functions are performed compose the **control function.** Control activities indicate the following:

1. When data should be retrieved after storage
2. When and how the data should be analyzed
3. If and when the data should be restored after analysis
4. If and when additional data should be retrieved
5. When output activities (described in the next paragraph) should begin and end

5. The **output function**—computer activities that take the results of input, storage, processing, and control functions and transmit them outside the computer.

Output   The **output function** comprises the activities that take the results of the input, storage, processing, and control functions and transmit them outside the computer. These results can appear in such diverse forms as data on magnetic tape or characters typed on paper. Obviously, the form in which output appears is determined primarily by how the output is to be used. Output that appears on magnetic tape, for example, can be used as input for another computer analysis but is of little value for analysis by human beings.

POSSIBLE PITFALLS IN USING COMPUTERS   The computer is a sophisticated management tool with the potential to make a significant contribution to organizational success. For this potential to materialize, however, the following possible pitfalls should be avoided:[21]

1. *Thinking that a computer is capable of independently performing creative activities*—A computer does not lessen the organization's need for a manager's personal creative ability and professional judgment. A computer is capable only of following precise and detailed instructions provided by the computer user. The individual using the computer must tell the computer exactly what to do, how to do it, and when to do it. Computers are simply pieces of equipment that must be directed very precisely by computer users to perform some function.

2. *Spending too much money on computer assistance*—In general, computers can be of great assistance to managers. The initial cost of purchasing a computer and the costs of updating it when necessary, however, can be high. Managers need to keep comparing the benefits obtained from computer assistance with the costs of obtaining it. In essence, an investment in a computer should be expected to help the organization generate enough added revenue not only to finance the computer but also to contribute an acceptable level of net profit.

Orlando Sentinel (May 1, 1989).

Sorry, but according to our brand-new $40,000 computer, we don't have any paintbrushes — and if we did, it wouldn't know how much to charge for one.

3. *Overestimating the value of computer output*—Some managers fall into the trap of assuming that they have "the answer" once they have received information generated by computer analysis. The preceding cartoon illustrates the kind of problems that can arise when organization members think that computers generate "the answer." Managers must recognize that computer output is only as good as the quality of data and directions for analyzing the data that human beings have put into the computer. Inaccurate data or inappropriate computer instructions yield useless computer output. A commonly used phrase to describe such an occurrence is "garbage in, garbage out."

BACK TO THE CASE

The computer would certainly be a valuable tool for Dunlap in making downsizing decisions as well as other decisions at Sunbeam. The computer can accept data within the company such as daily production levels of various products, perform operations on the data like percentage increases of various products shipped to customers daily or weekly, and quickly distribute the results of this analysis to managers. To be able to distribute such results to management, data must be put into Sunbeam's computers, and it must be stored as well as appropriately controlled and processed.

In addition to providing such valuable decision-related information as the production and shipping reports, computers at a company like Sunbeam can perform many other functions. As examples, computers can generate and track bills to Sunbeam's customers, generate payroll checks to employees, and write orders for materials as they are needed from suppliers. Despite the great worth of computers, Dunlap must keep in mind that computers, like any other management tool, have limitations. As an example, Dunlap must keep in mind that computer assistance at Sunbeam Corporation, as within any company, is only as good as the people running the computers, and that managers should not expect computers to independently perform creative activities.

THE MANAGEMENT DECISION SUPPORT SYSTEM (MDSS)

Traditionally, the MIS that uses electronic assistance in gathering data and providing related information to managers has been invaluable. This MIS assistance has been especially useful in areas where programmed decisions (see chapter 7) are necessary, because the computer continually generates the information that helps managers make these decisions. An example is using the computer to track cumulative labor costs by department. The computer can automatically gather and update the cumulative labor costs per department, compare these costs to corresponding annual budgets, and calculate the percentage of the budget that each department has reached to date. Such information is normally very useful in controlling department labor costs.

Closely related to the MIS is the **management decision support system (MDSS)**—an interdependent set of decision aids that help managers make nonprogrammed decisions (see chapter 7).[22] Figure 21.7 illustrates possible components of the MDSS and describes what they do. The MDSS is typically characterized by the following:[23]

1. *One or more corporate databases*—A **database** is a reservoir of corporate facts consistently organized to fit the information needs of a variety of organization members. These databases (also termed *corporate databases*) tend to contain facts about all of the important facets of company operations, including both financial and nonfinancial information. These facts are used to explore issues important to the corporation. For example, a manager might find facts from the corporate databases useful for forecasting profits for each of the next three years.

2. *One or more user databases*—In addition to the corporate database, an MDSS usually contains several user databases. A **user database** is a database developed by an individual manager or other user. Such databases may be derived from, but are not necessarily

A **management decision support system (MDSS)** is an interdependent set of computer-oriented decision aids that help managers make nonprogrammed decisions. The following characteristics are typical of an MDSS.

A **database** is a reservoir of corporate facts consistently organized to fit the information needs of a variety of organization members.

A **user database** is a database developed by an individual manager or other user.

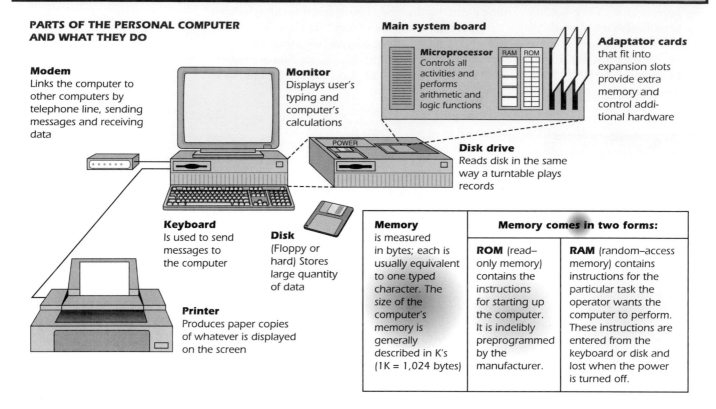

PARTS OF THE PERSONAL COMPUTER AND WHAT THEY DO

Modem
Links the computer to other computers by telephone line, sending messages and receiving data

Monitor
Displays user's typing and computer's calculations

Main system board

Microprocessor
Controls all activities and performs arithmetic and logic functions

RAM ROM

Adaptator cards
that fit into expansion slots provide extra memory and control additional hardware

POWER

Disk drive
Reads disk in the same way a turntable plays records

Keyboard
Is used to send messages to the computer

Disk
(Floppy or hard) Stores large quantity of data

Printer
Produces paper copies of whatever is displayed on the screen

Memory
is measured in bytes; each is usually equivalent to one typed character. The size of the computer's memory is generally described in K's (1K = 1,024 bytes)

Memory comes in two forms:	
ROM (read–only memory) contains the instructions for starting up the computer. It is indelibly preprogrammed by the manufacturer.	**RAM** (random–access memory) contains instructions for the particular task the operator wants the computer to perform. These instructions are entered from the keyboard or disk and lost when the power is turned off.

limited to, the corporate database. They tend to address specific issues peculiar to the individual user. For example, a production manager might be interested in exploring the specific issue of lowering production costs. To do so, the manager might build a simple user database that includes departmental facts about reject rates of materials purchased from various suppliers. The manager might be able to lower production costs by eliminating the purchase of materials from suppliers with the highest reject rates.

> A **model base** is a collection of quantitative computer programs that can assist MDSS users in analyzing data within databases.

3. *A set of quantitative tools stored in a model base.*—A **model base** is a collection of quantitative computer programs that can assist MDSS users in analyzing data within databases. For example, the production manager discussed in item 2 might use a correlation analysis program stored in a model base to accurately determine if there is any relationship between reject rates and the materials from various suppliers.

One desirable feature of a model base is its ability to allow the user to perform **"what if" analysis**—the simulation of a business situation over and over again, using somewhat different data for selected decision areas. For example, a manager might first determine the profitability of a company under present conditions. The manager might then ask *what* would happen *if* materials costs increased by 5 percent. Or *if* products were sold at a different price. Popular programs such as Lotus 1-2-3 and the Interactive Financial Planning System (IFPS)[24] allow managers to ask as many "what if" questions as they want to and save their answers without changing their original data.

> **"What if" analysis** is the simulation of a business situation over and over again, using somewhat different data for selected decision areas.

4. *A dialogue capability*—The ability of an MDSS user to interact with an MDSS is called **dialogue capability.** Such interaction typically involves extracting data from a database, calling up various models stored in the model base, and storing analysis results in a file.

> A **dialogue capability** is the ability of an MDSS user to interact with an MDSS.

Technological developments related to microcomputers have made the use of the MDSS concept feasible and its application available to virtually all managers today. In addition, the continual development of extensive software to support information analysis related to more subjective decision making is contributing to the popularity of these systems.

The preceding information about MDSS implies that Dunlap and other managers could use their own software to tap into corporate databases relevant to making decisions like downsizing. In order for Sunbeam to gain maximum advantage from an MIS, its managers should be able to use an MDSS efficiently and effectively. If Sunbeam's managers are not familiar with the MDSS concept, they can undergo training and could thus use the MDSS to help them make both programmed and nonprogrammed decisions.

In building and using the most advantageous MIS possible, management at a company like Sunbeam should ensure that MIS users within the company have adequate equipment to operate an MDSS, have adequate access to a corporate database, are properly employing user databases, have appropriate model bases available, and have adequate dialogue capability within the company's MDSS. If management is successful in ensuring that these issues reflect MDSS use within the company, then the probability is high that the company MDSS is being properly used. If, on the other hand, management is not successful in ensuring these issues reflect MDSS use within the company, management would probably be able to improve operations by encouraging organization members to appropriately use an MDSS.

COMPUTER NETWORKS

A **computer network** is a system of two or more connected computers that allows computer users to communicate, cooperate, and share resources. When working properly, a computer network is an information technology tool that encourages employees to maximize their potential and their productivity. The next sections discuss the two computer networks that have received the most attention recently from modern managers: local area networks and the Internet.

A **computer network** is a system of two or more connected computers that allows computer users to communicate, cooperate, and share resources.

► THE LOCAL AREA NETWORK

One type of computer network commonly used in modern organizations is called a **local area network (LAN)**. A LAN is a computer network characterized by software that manages how information travels through cables to arrive at a number of connected single-user computer workstations. One rule of thumb recommends that when an organization reaches the use of five independent computer workstations, the computers should probably be connected as a LAN.[25] At this number of computers, the cost of networking should be outweighed by the gain of important organizational advantages—for example, allowing computer users to communicate more efficiently and effectively with one another and enabling workers to share the use of expensive software.

Figure 21.8 indicates the growth of management interest in usage of LANs by illustrating the continuing upward trend of sales of equipment used to build LANs. Although this

A **local area network (LAN)** is a computer network characterized by software that manages how information travels through cables to arrive at a number of connected single-user computer workstations.

A LAN, or local area network, is a network for managing the flow of information to individual but connected workstations. Here a Microsoft employee monitors Microsoft's LAN.

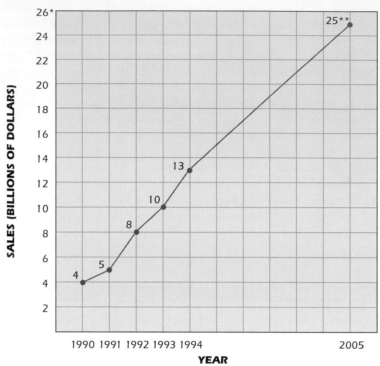

FIGURE 21.8 ▶ **Total dollar sales of equipment used to build LANs in organizations**

*Sales stated in billions of dollars
**Author estimate based on historical trends

growing enthusiasm for LANs has prompted many computer support companies to expand the array of LAN products they offer to organizations, managers should be cautious and refrain from investing in LAN products that do not satisfy a rigorous cost-benefit analysis.[26]

▶ THE INTERNET

The **Internet** is a large interconnected network of computer networks linking people and computers all over the world via phone lines, satellites, and other telecommunications systems.

The **Internet,** an information technology tool, is a large interconnected network of computer networks linking people and computers all over the world via phone lines, satellites, and other telecommunications systems. Simply stated, the Internet is an expansive computer network linking about 1 million smaller networks worldwide.[27] The following quote contains a worthwhile description of the Internet:[28]

> Probably the best model or analogy is that of a giant highway system that connects computers. The Internet connects all kinds of computers, no matter who made them, what programs run on them, or who they belong to—computers as large as the biggest supercomputers in the world or as small as a laptop PC. By connecting these computers, the Internet connects the people who use the computers. It's called the Internet because it connects not only the computers, but all the different kinds of regional and local networks that hook up these computers as well. Like the highway system, the Internet consists of interstates and state highways, and little roads. The number of computers and people linked by the Internet is now in the tens of millions and growing at an ever-faster rate.

Evolving out of a project conceived and initiated by the U.S. Department of Defense in the early 1970s to allow scientists and researchers to better communicate and exchange data, today the Internet provides over 30 million users with information and the ability to communicate worldwide. Forecasts indicate that by the year 2000, more than 100 million people will be using the Internet. In addition, as Table 21.2 shows, the number of managers registering their businesses on the Internet is growing very rapidly, with no signs of slowing.

TABLE 21.2	The Growing Number of Businesses Registering for Use of the Internet					
Types of Business	1990	1991	1992	1993	1994[1]	2000[3]
Financial services	3	17	46	125	281	18,000
Law	0	4	10	38	114	7,300
Advertising	0	1	1	7	21	1,300
Publishing	1	8	27	96	212	13,500
Entertainment	0	1	2	4	16	1,024
Venture capital	0	0	1	11	23	1,600
Total[2]	93	1,044	3,054	8,412	18,245	1,180,000

Source: Internet Info
[1]Through Aug 15.
[2]Includes other categories.
[3]Author projection based on historical trend.

Managers are using the Internet in many different ways. Some use it to continually monitor and gather late-breaking news that can impact their organization in the short run. For example, news regarding fluctuations in interest rates and the latest moves of competitors is readily available on the Internet. Other managers use the Internet to monitor and track government trends that can impact an organization's long-run viability. For example, issues like the evolving trade relationship between the United States and China or the latest turn in affirmative action legislation are easily monitored on the Internet. The following Management and the Internet feature describes how Dell Computer Corporation uses the Internet to reach customer service as well as company image objectives.

The following sections elaborate on the Internet by discussing the World Wide Web, e-mail, and intranets, illustrating how these factors help managers achieve organizational goals. Some managers even use the Internet to find new employees (see Figure 21.9).

MANAGEMENT AND THE INTERNET

Dell Computer Company Surfs the Internet to Service Customers and Build Its Image

Avowed computer nut Jay Snyder sits all day doing what he loves to do: surf the Internet. And he gets paid for it.

Mr. Snyder and six others make up Dell Computer Corporations' Internet SWAT team. They peruse traffic for any mention of Dell products, ready to swoop into "threads" of conversations to help solve customer problems, change negative perceptions, and protect the company's reputation.

"I am having way too much fun," Mr. Snyder says.

To Dell and other computer companies, though, the Internet is more than just sport. Every day, computer users post queries about what products others recommend. Every hour, the cyberspace chatter includes complaints that can damage a company's reputation.

"People aren't shy about their opinions on that thing," says Steve Smith, Dell's director of technical support.

The Internet is not the only place that computer-company employees are trolling and scrolling these days. Networks like CompuServe, America Online, and Prodigy have become increasingly important customer-service venues. Most major computer makers now have "forums" for questions and product information. Technical advisors offer answers and forward concerns to executives.

The electronic outlets are cheaper than phone banks, and company officials say they sometimes learn more from customers electronically than through telephone-service calls and traditional marketing surveys. "People can be pretty direct. You can be pretty cocky when you don't have to look someone in the eye," says Mal Ransom, Packard Bell Electronics Inc.'s marketing vice president, who sometimes takes to Prodigy and CompuServe himself to answer customers.

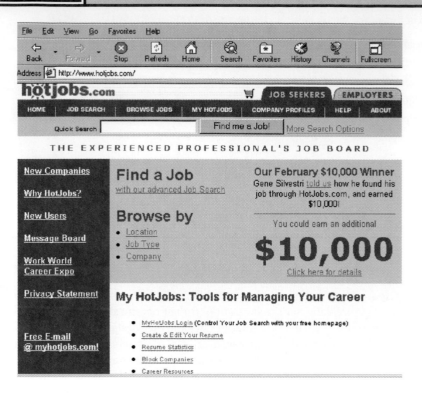

FIGURE 21.9 ► HotJobs is an Internet site where managers can list open positions and prospective applicants can review them

The **World Wide Web** is a segment of the Internet that allows managers to have an information location called a **Web site** available continually to Internet users. Each Web site has a beginning page called a **home page,** and each home page generally has several supporting pages called **branch pages** that expand on the thoughts and ideas contained in the home page.

THE WORLD WIDE WEB Perhaps the fastest-growing segment of the Internet is the World Wide Web.[29] The **World Wide Web** is a system that allows managers to have an information location called a **Web site** that is available 24 hours a day, 7 days a week, to anyone who is using the Internet. Each Web site has a beginning page called a **home page,** and each home page generally has several supporting pages called **branch pages** that expand on the thoughts and ideas contained in the home page. Special programming features allow Web site visitors to quickly visit branch pages and quickly return to a home page.

For example, Figure 21.10 is the actual home page of WebSolvers, a company that provides professional Web site services to managers across the world. With the click of a computer mouse on any words at the bottom of the home page, the site visitor quickly shifts to a branch page that provides more information regarding the highlighted topic. A similar click on the branch page quickly returns the visitor to the home page. For example, clicking on "Portfolio" on the WebSolvers home page will give the site visitor more information on a branch page about the company's customers and accomplishments. Another click on the branch page will quickly return the visitor to the WebSolvers home page.

The number of managers establishing Web sites has been growing exponentially, and it is predicted that the number will continue to increase rapidly in the foreseeable future. Managers are using Web sites to perform a wide array of activities ranging from soliciting venture capital to making business travel arrangements.[30]

Managers should not rush into establishing Web sites, but rather should take great care to design and implement a Web site that is consistent with organizational goals. Recall that the fundamental job of the manager is to reach organizational goals through the use of organizational resources. A properly designed and used Web site is an organizational resource that can help managers reach organizational goals like the following:

► *Marketing products more effectively*—Marketing is a very popular use of a Web site. Organizations already offer thousands of diverse products, including T-shirts, computers, books, financial services, travel advice and arrangements, and candy, on Web sites. An appropriately organized Web site can help managers promote products through an elec-

FIGURE 21.10 ▶ **The World Wide Web home page of WebSolvers**

tronic brochure that is cost-efficient, easily updated, and instantaneously distributed across the world.

▶ *Enhancing the quality of recruits to the organization*—A properly designed Web site enables management to recruit highly qualified people to the organization. Managers using Web sites appropriately can project the image of a progressive organization that keeps abreast of meaningful business trends and that uses any and all innovative tools available to ensure its success. This image should be useful in attracting the finest human resources.

▶ *Enhancing product quality*—An important part of establishing a high-quality product is the ability to offer high-quality service and to maintain communication with customers after the product is purchased. A Web site gives managers an effective and efficient vehicle for communicating with customers *after* an organization's product is purchased.

▶ *Communicating globally*—Many modern managers need to communicate across the globe. A Web site enables them to reach out quickly and easily to almost anywhere in the world—and communicating globally via a Web site is generally less costly than using the more traditional global communication vehicles. In addition, a Web site can bring international communities closer together.

▶ *Encouraging creativity in organization members*—Every successful organization maintains its success by devising creative solutions to problems. If appropriately designed and administered, a Web site can be a creative solution to myriad organizational problems. Perhaps more importantly, by establishing a Web site, management is sending a clear signal to all organization members that it is willing to provide technological tools for creatively solving problems, and also that it expects members to strive to develop their own creative solutions to their job problems.

E-MAIL E-mail[31] or **electronic mail** is a computerized information system that allows individuals the electronic capability to create, edit, and send messages to one another. Messages are sent to a recipient's "mailbox" where they can be read, saved, answered, forwarded, downloaded, or discarded. This section focuses on e-mail via the Internet, the fastest growing area of such messaging.

Evidence of the growing use of Internet e-mail abounds. For example, a recent report indicated that the U.S. Postal Service delivers 330 million first-class letters a day to the 270 million people living in the United States. On the other hand, America Online, a world-renowned Internet service provider, delivers 225 million "instant" e-mail messages daily to its 12.5 million subscribers.[32] The country's largest Internet provider appears to be rapidly catching up to

E-mail a computerized information system that allows individuals the electronic capability to create, edit, and send messages to one another.

the volume of daily mail sent via the traditional U.S. mail system. E-mail enthusiasts commonly refer to mail sent via the traditional system as "snail mail."

Using e-mail in organizations provides a means of communicating with unprecedented speed and convenience. Messages can literally be sent and received across the world within seconds from almost any location as long as a connection to the Internet can be procured. Overall, most agree that e-mail significantly enhances the efficiency and effectiveness of communication in organizations. As the following Across Industries feature illustrates, however, technical glitches can render e-mail and its accompanying advantages worthless.

Using e-mail in organizations can be very challenging. Because e-mail lacks the context of the body language, facial expression, and tone and pitch of voice that face-to-face or even telephone communication provides, electronic messages can be misread or misinterpreted if the words in messages aren't well chosen and to the point. Although some e-mail programs offer a kind of voice mail, they still are not perfect replications of the speaker's natural intonations. Keystroke versions of "happy faces" abound, for instance, **:**) for happy, and **:(** for sad, and so on, but they have little application in business writing. Also, because sending a message is as easy as clicking a button, the temptation is to fire off a message without stopping to give it a second reading, either for proofreading or for reconsidering your choice of words. Finally, because messages are so easy to send, the e-mail system in an organization, by its very nature, can increase the number of messages sent resulting in information overload. Table 21.3 contains a number of suggestions for how to e-mail appropriately.

Intranet is an internal corporate communication network that uses the structure and standards of the Internet to allow employees of a single firm to communicate and share information with each other electronically.

INTRANETS Intranets are internal corporate communications networks that use the structure and standards of the Internet to allow employees of a single firm to communicate and share information with each other electronically. Figure 21.11 is the home page for an actual intranet at HTE, Inc., a software company in Lake Mary, Florida. Although software to enable firms to set up their own intranets with relative ease is becoming more affordable, the high value of involving professional consultants in designing and building intranets is undeniable. Some of these new programs are Intranetics 97, Involv Intranet, e:Folders, and HotOffice. However, the task is not cheap. The primary costs are training employees how to use the intranet and identifying someone to manage it.[33]

Extranet is a program that expands an Intranet to allow organizational outsiders to perform such activities such as placing orders and checking on the status of their orders.

To give access to selected business partners, vendors, or clients, firms can expand their intranets with an **extranet** program that allows outsiders to place orders and check the status of their orders.[34] FedEx, for example, is expected to attempt a major business shift in the near future, to focus on its information systems that track and coordinate the delivery of packages, which is done through a type of extranet.[35]

TABLE 21.3	► Hints on How to E-Mail

1. Consider e-mail as you would a hard-copy letter. Proofread all your messages carefully before sending. If your program includes a spell-checker, learn how to use it.

2. Research and follow your company's policies about sending copies to the appropriate colleagues.

3. Remember that e-mail can be monitored in some firms, and that it has been retrieved from hard drives and used as evidence in court cases. Do not use e-mail to start or circulate rumors, repeat damaging information, or spread misinformation.

4. Be sure your message is clear and unambiguous. It should indicate whether or not you require a reply.

5. Do not reply to e-mails that are just confirmations or acknowledgments. Your e-mail will multiply unnecessarily if you do.

6. Write a letter when angry if you must, but do not send or save it.

7. Use a simple filing system for e-mails you need to save.

8. Do not send or reply to chain letters. They clog the system and have been known to shut down entire networks.

9. Be conservative about adding your name to mailing lists and newsletters.

10. Do your personal correspondence from your home computer.

FIGURE 21.11	► Intranet home page for HTE

One of the biggest concerns for intranet users is keeping the network secure, that is, preventing outsiders (or unauthorized insiders) from breaking into the system and accessing sensitive information. One way of doing this is to install a security system known as a *firewall*, which usually includes both hardware and software to block unauthorized users.

BACK TO THE CASE

The above material implies that Dunlap as well as other managers at Sunbeam can use computer networking to enhance the success of downsizing and other management decisions. A local area network could be designed to quickly report production data, for example, from various

(continued)

plant locations to a central computer where it would be combined, summarized, and analyzed. Such networking would allow Dunlap to quickly translate information into action focused not only on downsizing to eliminate unproductive company areas and related costs, but to enhance profitability by investing more in productive company areas.

Internet tools like the World Wide Web, e-mail, and an intranet could also be useful to Dunlap in downsizing as well as improving company profitability. The company Web site and its linked pages could be designed to accomplish purposes like promoting Sunbeam's products and helping customers locate retail outlets where the products are available. E-mail could be used to allow speedy communications among Sunbeam stakeholders like Dunlap and the Sunbeam management team, investors, customers, and nonmanagement employees. And finally, an intranet could be designed to allow employees abilities like speedy communication with one another and quick access to company databases to learn more about issues such as jobs available within the company, customer profiles, or manufacturing specifications.

For updated information on the topics in this chapter, Internet exercises, links to related Internet sites, an interactive study guide, and more, visit our companion Web site at

http://www.prenhall.com/certo

Additional information can be found on the inside front and back covers of this text.

ACTION SUMMARY

Reread the learning objectives below. Each objective is followed by questions. Answering these questions accurately will help you retain the most important concepts discussed in this chapter. After answering each question, check your answer against the answer key at the end of the chapter. (*Hint:* If you have any doubts regarding the correct response, consult the page number that follows the answer.)

Circle:

From studying this chapter, I will attempt to acquire

1. An understanding of the relationship between data and information.

a b c d e   **a.** Data can be: (a) information (b) opinion (c) premises (d) facts (e) gossip.

a b c d e   **b.** Information can be defined as conclusions derived from: (a) data analysis (b) opinion (c) premises (d) gossip (e) none of the above.

2. Insights about the main factors that influence the value of information.

a b c d e   **a.** All of the following are primary factors determining the value of information except: (a) appropriateness (b) expense (c) quality (d) timeliness (e) quantity.

T F   **b.** The appropriateness of the information increases as the volume of the information increases.

3. Knowledge of some potential steps for evaluating information.

a b c d e   **a.** All of the following are main activities in evaluating information except: (a) acquiring information (b) comparing value with cost of information (c) selecting data to be evaluated (d) using information in decision making (e) discounting expected value for deficiencies and inaccuracies.

T F   **b.** The primary concern of management in evaluating information is the dollar value of the benefits gained compared to the cost of generating the information.

4. An understanding of the importance of a management information system (MIS) to an organization.

T F   **a.** A management information system is a network established within an organization to provide managers with information that will assist them in decision making.

a b c d e   **b.** "Determining information needs" is which of the steps necessary to operate an MIS: (a) first (b) second (c) third (d) fourth (e) none of the above.

5. A feasible strategy for establishing an MIS.

a b c d e   **a.** All of the following are stages in the process of establishing an MIS except: (a) planning (b) designing (c) improving (d) implementing (e) all of the above are stages.

a b c d e   **b.** Which of the following activities has the potential of improving an MIS: (a) stressing that MIS personnel should strive to accomplish the purpose of an MIS (b) operating an MIS in a "people-conscious" manner (c) encouraging line managers to continually request additional information through the MIS (d) a and b (e) all of the above.

6. Information about what a management decision support system is and how it operates.

T F   **a.** A management decision support system is a set of decision aids aimed at helping managers make nonprogrammed decisions.

T F   **b.** There is basically no difference between a corporate database and a user database.

T F   **c.** Dialogue capability allows the MDSS user to interact with an MIS.

7. An appreciation for the roles of computers and networks like the Internet in handling information.

a b c d e   **a.** All of the following are main computer functions except: (a) input (b) storage (c) control (d) heuristic (e) output.

a b c d e   **b.** All of the following are possible pitfalls in using the computer except: (a) thinking that a computer is independently capable of creative activities (b) failing to realize that a computer is capable only of following precise and detailed instructions (c) training and retraining all computer operating personnel (d) spending too much money on computer assistance (e) overestimating the value of computer output.

T F   **c.** A LAN and the Internet are basically identical.

T F   **d.** A Web site can help managers achieve many different organizational goals.

INTRODUCTORY CASE WRAP-UP

CASE DISCUSSSION QUESTIONS

"**M**aking Changes Without the Right Information at Sunbeam?" (p. 471) and its related Back-to-the-Case sections were written to help you better understand the management concepts contained in this chapter. Answer the following discussion questions about this Introductory Case to further enrich your understanding of chapter content:

1. If you were Albert J Dunlap, what three functions would you use a computer to perform? Be as specific as possible.

2. List three decisions that an MDSS could help Dunlap to make. For each decision, describe the data that must be in the database in order to provide such help.

3. The main steps of the controlling process are measuring performance, comparing performance to standards, and taking corrective action. Discuss a possible role of an MIS at Sunbeam in each of these steps

---

SKILLS EXERCISE: APPLYING THE VYJ LEADERSHIP MODEL

The Introductory Case emphasized that Albert J. Dunlap, the top manager at Sunbeam Corporation, was fired because he could not achieve an acceptable profit level. Locate the company's Web site on the Internet. What features of the site could help the company be more profitable? Be sure to explain how each feature could help achieve the added profit. What features would you add to the present site to help achieve even greater profitability? Explain why you would add each feature. (*Note:* If you cannot locate the Sunbeam site, answer the same questions for a site of your choice.)

1. What is the difference between data and information?
2. List and define four major factors that influence the value of information.
3. What are operational control decisions and strategic planning decisions? What characterizes information appropriate for making each of these decisions?
4. Discuss the major activities involved in evaluating information.
5. What factors tend to limit the usefulness of information, and how can these factors be overcome?
6. Define *MIS* and discuss its importance to management.
7. What steps must be performed to operate an MIS properly?
8. What major steps are involved in establishing an MIS?
9. Why is planning for an MIS such an important part of establishing an MIS?
10. Why does the designing of an MIS begin with analyzing managerial decision making?
11. How should managers use the symptoms of an inadequate MIS as listed in Table 21.1?
12. How could building cooperation between MIS personnel and line managers improve an MIS?
13. How can management use cost-benefit analysis to improve an MIS?
14. Describe five possible causes of resistance to using an MIS. What can managers do to ensure that these causes do not affect their organization's MIS?
15. Is a computer a flexible management tool? Explain.
16. How do the main functions of a computer relate to one another?
17. Summarize the major pitfalls managers must avoid when using a computer.
18. How does an MDSS differ from an MIS? Define *"what if" analysis* and give an illustration of how a manager might use it.
19. How are local area networks and the Internet different? How are they similar? Explain fully.
20. Define a Web site and explain the relationship between a home page and branch pages.
21. Discuss three different organizational goals that a Web site might help a manager achieve. Be sure to clearly show how a Web site would help.
22. List three challenges to using e-mail and how to meet them.
23. Discuss the value of a firewall to an intranet.

1. **a.** d, p. 472
   b. a, p. 472
2. **a.** b, p. 472
   b. F, p. 473
3. **a.** d, p. 475
   b. T, p. 475

4. **a.** T, p. 476
   b. a, pp. 477–478
5. **a.** e, p. 480
   b. d, pp. 482–483

6. **a.** T, p. 485
   b. F, pp. 486–487
   c. F, p. 489

7. **a.** d, p. 487
   b. c, pp. 487–488
   c. F, p. 488
   d. T, pp. 492–493

CASE STUDY: The Internet Becomes a Technological Battlefield

The appearance of the Internet about 20 years ago as a U.S. Defense Department network did not foreshadow its boom as a commercial highway. Throughout the 1980s, the Internet continued to develop, connecting universities around the world—a "network of networks." Still, there was no strong commercial interest in this fast and powerful higher-ed linkup until Mosaic introduced color and graphics and point-and-click commands. Then the Internet stepped down from the towers of academia and into homes and offices all around the world. Powerful interests like Microsoft, Intel, and IBM, plus an array of start-up challengers like Netscape, Sun Microsystems, and Spyglass, got into the fray.

No wonder the stakes are high. Analysts estimate, for example, that the Internet industry will generate $13 billion in revenue by the year 2000, as companies sell the tools to make the "Net" a sound business medium. These tools will help companies and consumers buy and sell goods and services worth almost $20 billion. Meanwhile, managing the companies that guide businesses through the Internet of the future offers a challenge to both established high-tech firms and newcomers.

Netscape and Sun Microsystems have taken the lead in exploring the future, and thus have set the Internet standard. Older technology leaders—IBM, Oracle, Apple Computer, Silicon Graphics—have been forced to build Internet software compatible with Sun and Netscape platforms. Thus the industry has converged around Java, the Sun programming system that makes it possible to pull in little programs. Sun calls these programs "applets" or small applications. Why are they so valuable? They make it possible to create "active content" on a Web site—for instance, real-time weather radar maps or credit applications with built-in calculators. Dozens of companies are licensing JavaScript, Netscape's World Wide Web programming language that makes creating Java applets easier.

Netscape Communications founders are Jim Clark, once head of Silicon Graphics, and Marc Andreesen, creator of the pioneering Mosaic Web browser. Clark and Andreesen have followed a radical plan for the nascent Internet industry: They give away Netscape's powerful browser and make money selling software that supports companies using the Internet. Their goal is to become the "de facto standard" software for on-line commerce. Netscape's products guide the search for information across the Internet, provide companies with more viable means of building and maintaining their own World Wide Web Sites, and set up and improve security for growing on-line commercial enterprises. Netscape shipped its first product in December 1994, and by December 1995 was claiming that over 8,500 companies were using its technology to develop Web sites and software programs and services.

Moreover, the Netscape platform is not tied to the Microsoft operating systems that are standard in most PCs. Clark believes, therefore, that "the Internet basically blew apart [Microsoft's] whole strategy" for the 1990s. Sun CEO Scott McNealy doesn't believe Microsoft can get into the fray quickly enough to dominate the Internet. Microsoft's Bill Gates admits that his company has had to play "catch-up," but insists that Microsoft stands ready to lead the newest technological advances. Right now, for example, research and development dollars are pouring into the following Microsoft Internet projects:

1. Visual Basic or VB Script, which helps companies write applications that work across the Web
2. Internet Studio, a Web authoring language
3. Microsoft Network, a consumer Internet service
4. The Internet Information Server, which is included in Windows NT and manages Web information
5. Object Linking and Embedding (OLE) technology, which allows software "objects" to communicate across the Web, much like Java's applets

Unlike Java, OLE controls are ready-made. Thus using them does not require skilled programmers. Gates believes that ordinary businesses are more likely to want these ready-made components.

In addition, Gates does not worry that entering the Internet fray later than newcomers like Netscape and Sun did will matter in the end. For one thing, most new products are giveaways intended to build the market. According to Gates, the real money will come in the future, when managers reorganize their business operations around the Internet and consumers embrace on-line commerce. And in fact, commercial on-line services have begun to see the importance of Internet access to businesses and consumers. America Online, CompuServe, and Prodigy all offer gateways to the Internet in addition to their regular services. Some observers, however, believe that newer Internet service providers (ISP), such as Pipeline USA and Netcom On-Line Communication Services, offer more specialized and less expensive access.

The Internet may prove to be the computing shift of the 1990s. In the 1960s and 1970s, mainframe providers were the leaders. Ultimately, however, companies like IBM, Univac, Burroughs, and Control Data lost their momentum when the focus shifted to minicomputers. Names like Digital Computers and Data General rose to the top. In the 1980s, Microsoft and Intel led the movement to PCs. What's in store for managers in the 1990s? Will the PC go the way of its predecessors? Will the industry shift to the Internet and new names in technology? Will government regulation affect commerce on the Internet?

QUESTIONS

1. In the information age, how is managing a technology company different from managing other businesses? How is it similar?
2. What does all the excitement surrounding new Internet tools mean to the ordinary manager? What must a manager understand about these new products? Explain.
3. Scott McNealy (Sun Microsystems), Jim Clark (Netscape Communications), Bill Gates (Microsoft)—what do these managers have in common? How are they different? Based on the continuing commercial path of the Internet, who do you believe is the best manager? Why?
4. Dial into these home pages to keep track of the Internet competition and to find the newest information for making management decisions:
   www.microsoft.com
   www.netscape.com
   www.sun.com

SMALL BUSINESS 2000

Companies today must deal with many issues when it comes to information and information management. You might think that a simple solution is to collect everything you can and save it. On the surface this may make sense, but think about this for a minute. How useful is having something if you do not know where it is? How useful is information if it is not organized, if it is not stored in an easy-to-retrieve manner, if it cannot be accessed in a timely manner, or if no one has a real use for it?

The point is that information alone is of very little use. On the other hand, a well-designed and well-managed information system can be a key part of an organization's success. The King Company has found this to be true. The King Company is the U.S. distributor for the Lorus line of Seiko watches. Not only does the company use its information system to improve its own business performance, the information system helps its sole supplier, Seiko, and its major customers. King Company's customers include retailers as large as Wal-mart and as small as your corner drug store. Not bad for a company that started out of the trunk of the founder's car.

How does information management fit into King Company's operation? First, it allows for a sophisticated inventory management and order-filling operation that requires very little human intervention. With the assistance of its information capabilities, the company can enter and fill an order almost entirely through an automated system. Second, the company has a direct electronic interface with its customers. Orders, inquiries, billing, and even payment can be done without the generation of a single piece of paper. In fact some of its major customers require this capability before they will even consider using a vendor. The King Company also uses its information as a marketing tool. The company not only tracks what it has sold to its customers, but it also, in some cases, monitors its customers' sales on a daily basis. The knowledge from this activity supports short-term needs such as ordering and production planning but also has longer range value. Over time, the company can track product trends and make product line development decisions based on real market input.

In this video segment you will learn how one company designed a system to support its growth and one that would grow with it. The company controls its information management process to prevent the system from overloading with data that are not useful for the operation of the company. Remember, having volumes of useless information is not nearly as valuable as having a small pile that means something.

QUESTIONS

1. David Arnold added staff to manage information and technology in the early stages of the King Company's relationship with Seiko. What are some of the advantages and disadvantages of adding computer and information management processes early on in a company's development?

2. The King Company outsources part of its information system support (hardware and telecommunications) to a third-party vendor. Why do you think they do that?

3. The King Company collects a lot of information about its customers and the final purchasers of its products. Do you think there are any ethical issues in establishing such information transfers between vendors and customers? Why or why not?

This scene finds us in a meeting with Hal and several members of the production and post-production group. The focus of the meeting is a review of project status. As often happens at Quicktakes, this meeting starts with a diversion to matters not on the agenda. In this case, Hal sidetracks into a discussion of the company's information management system. Alex, in explaining why she is late to the meeting, tells us that the system is not performing as it needs to. From the discussion that follows, we get the idea that Quicktakes' information system was set up a few years ago, when options were limited. Back then, Quicktakes' staff was also smaller. Its information-management needs were probably different than they are today.

When we get back to the main agenda of the meeting, we find Hal going through a list of projects. The projects that Hal asks about are not as far along as he would like and are not necessarily on budget. Hal is asking for a lot of information that we might expect him to be able to pull out of a program set up to track project status. What is wrong with Hal collecting this information in a meeting? For one thing, meetings are expensive. Each person in the room has other responsibilities in the company. If the information were collected from the company's tracking systems, the meeting could be shortened and simply cover exceptions and issues. Information collection could be accomplished without using up valuable staff time. Think about the cost of this meeting by simply adding up what you think each of these people earn in an hour.

You might also think about what is being discussed in this meeting. Some of the issues of control may be more easily managed if the staff had individual project plans or budgets to follow. If three hours of editing is all that is usually built into a project schedule for a news release, the editor should know that he or she has to make quick work of it. Standardizing some of the more routine tasks that happen within projects might help improve efficiency at Quicktakes. Special cases could be planned for, but in creating the plan, exceptions would be considered, in both time and cost, before resources were used, not after the fact.

QUESTIONS

1. Quicktakes has some sort of automated information management system. We do not know a lot about it, but we know that it may not be working so well. From the video, we get an idea that they are using the system to support certain parts of their business and not others. Why do you think this is? What do you think Hal's priorities are regarding the information management system? Do you think he is right? What else might you advise him to think about?

2. Alexandra talks about outsourcing the maintenance of the information management system. We have seen in previous segments that Quicktakes does contract third parties to provide some services, so this is not an unusual idea. What issues would you consider in deciding to bring an outside vendor in to deal with information management? Do you think Hal will go for this? Why or why not?

3. You will hear about some problems Mary is having with a project. From what you have just learned about production management and control, consider the impact of how Mary has handled this project. What do you think Mary's approach means for others in the company? Do you think there is something that can be done to make things work better on other projects? Who's responsibility do you think it is to work with Mary and what do you think should be done?

Competitiveness: Quality and Innovation

STUDENT LEARNING OBJECTIVES

From studying this chapter, I will attempt to acquire

1. An understanding of the relationship between quality and total quality management

2. An appreciation for the importance of quality

3. Insights about how to achieve quality

4. An understanding of how strategic planning can be used to promote quality

5. Knowledge about the quality improvement process

CHAPTER OUTLINE

Introductory Case: *LEGO's MindStorms Market Research Causes Problem*

FUNDAMENTALS OF QUALITY
Defining Total Quality Management

Quality Spotlight: *"Quality Is Job 1" at Ford*
The Importance of Quality
Established Quality Awards
Achieving Quality

QUALITY THROUGH STRATEGIC PLANNING
Environmental Analysis and Quality
Establishing Organizational Direction and Quality
Strategy Formulation and Quality
Strategy Implementation and Quality
Strategic Control and Quality

THE QUALITY IMPROVEMENT PROCESS
The Incremental Improvement Process

People Spotlight: *Keeping People Involved in Incremental Improvement: Bearings, Inc.*
Reengineering Improvements

INNOVATION AND CREATIVITY

Management and the Internet: *Bill Gross Uses Creativity to Launch Idealab*
Creativity in Individuals
Encouraging Creativity in Organization Members

Across Industries: Candy Manufacturing—CEO at Guittard Chocolate Company Is Role Model for Creativity

LEGO's MindStorms Market Research Causes Problem

REMINDER: THE INTRODUCTORY CASE WRAP-UP (P. 523) CONTAINS DISCUSSION QUESTIONS AND A SKILLS EXERCISE TO FURTHER ILLUSTRATE THE APPLICATION OF CHAPTER CONCEPTS TO THIS VIGNETTE.

More than anything on his Christmas list, David Griffin wanted MindStorms, a $200 LEGO robot-construction set designed for kids age 11 and up. So, unable to wait for Christmas Day, he bought a set at a Toys "R" Us in Leominster, Mass.

In the 11-and-up demographic group, David Griffin is pretty far up: He is a 41-year-old computer engineer, and he is part of a large group of adult MindStorms buyers that *LEGO Group* AG did not anticipate when it put the set on the market. Surveys that LEGO collects with warranty-card returns show that nearly half of the people playing with the set are 25 to 45 years old.

"I really could have gone wild buying add-ons and accessories," Mr. Griffin confesses. "But I was making the purchase under the stern eye of my wife."

Before MindStorms came on the market in mid-September, LEGO expected to sell about 12,000 sets in the United States this year. But since it hit the shelves, demand has been so brisk that the Danish toy giant now expects sales of about 80,000, says John Dion, a LEGO spokesman. Even with ramped-up production, a number of retailers may not get MindStorms in time for Christmas.

"We're still waiting for product," says John Reilly, a spokesman for Consolidated Corporation's K•B toy chain. "I get about a dozen kids coming in every day asking for the new LEGO system," says David Hesel, owner of the Toy Shop in Concord, Mass., who has been told along with other small operators that he won't be getting any MindStorms until next year.

The toy is taking on an unusual life of its own among adult fans. On the Internet, they trade advice about how to break down the system and rebuild it better. Many older users are also swapping handmade programs that supersede the kit's basic software.

Well before it reached its target market, MindStorms, the new LEGO toy, benefited from infusions of creative effort and quality control. Courtesy of the LEGO Group

The 750-piece MindStorms set includes a palm-size microcomputer called the RCX, light and touch sensors, a bunch of Lego's trademark interlocking blocks and an infrared, wireless communications system that lets the RCX receive programming from a personal computer. Owners can build robots that walk, fight with other robots, pick up objects, and sound alarms when doors open.

Hobby programmers are trying to teach their MindStorms to do things LEGO never thought of. Mr. Griffin, who works for Compaq Computer Corp., says he wants to program his to run the vacuum cleaner. MindStorms hackers who exchange tips on the World Wide Web say they are trying to use the system to answer the phone and hang up on unwanted callers, or to help them operate hidden cameras.

What's Ahead

The Introductory Case focuses on how LEGO has offered the marketplace a new, revolutionary, highly desirable toy called MindStorms, but will not achieve high sales of the toy because company market research didn't accurately predict consumer interest in the product. The remainder of this chapter presents useful information for managers like those at LEGO who are interested in maintaining not only the quality of products, but also the quality of important internal company operations like market research. This chapter discusses

1. Fundamentals of quality
2. Quality through strategic planning
3. The quality improvement process

◤ FUNDAMENTALS OF QUALITY

Quality is the extent to which a product does what it is supposed to do—how closely and reliably it satisfies the specifications to which it is built.

Quality was defined in chapter 20 as how well a product does what it is supposed to do—how closely and reliably it satisfies the specifications to which it is built. In that chapter, quality was presented as the degree of excellence on which products or services can be ranked on the basis of selected features. This chapter expands on the topic of product quality.

▶ DEFINING TOTAL QUALITY MANAGEMENT

Total quality management (TQM) is the continuous process of involving all organization members in ensuring that every activity related to the production of goods or services has an appropriate role in establishing product quality.

Total quality management (TQM) is the continuous process of involving all organization members in ensuring that every activity related to the production of goods or services has an appropriate role in establishing product quality.[1] In other words, all organization members emphasize the appropriate performance of activities throughout the company in order to maintain the quality of products offered by the company. Under the TQM concept, organization members work both individually and collectively to maintain the quality of products offered to the marketplace.

Although the TQM movement actually began in the United States, its establishment, development, and growth throughout the world are largely credited to the Japanese. The Japanese believe that a TQM program should be companywide and must include the cooperation of all people within a company. Top managers, middle managers, supervisors, and workers throughout the company must strive together to ensure that all phases of company operations appropriately affect product quality. The company operations referred to include areas like market research, research and development, product planning, design, production, purchasing, vendor management, manufacturing, inspection, sales, after-sales customer care, financial control, personnel administration, and company training and education.

◤ QUALITY SPOTLIGHT ◢   "Quality Is Job 1" at Ford

Ford Motor Company has advertised for a number of years that "Quality Is Job 1" at Ford. Symbolic of that commitment is the company's refusal, a few years ago, to release its new Thunderbird model in time for *Motor Trend*'s Car of the Year competition; Ford chose to delay the Thunderbird's release because it had not yet solved certain quality problems. This decision is especially striking because the Thunderbird was the leading contender for the award that year, which would have meant millions of dollars in additional sales and some highly visible publicity for Ford.

Its commitment to quality has made Ford the leader among American automobile manufacturers in meeting the Japanese quality challenge. American automakers have been regaining market share in recent years largely because of the improved quality of their products.

The TQM concept has been adopted by a majority of Japanese firms. In fact, TQM is generally credited with being a major factor in establishing Japan as a major competitor in the world marketplace. Although U.S. firms have been moving toward accepting and implementing the TQM concept, there are still some basic differences between the traditional (U.S.) and Japanese positions on establishing and maintaining total quality.

TQM is a means to the end of product quality. The excellence or quality of all management activities (planning, organizing, in-

fluencing, and controlling) in an organization inevitably influences the quality of final goods or services offered by that organization to the marketplace. In general, the more effective its TQM
program, the higher the quality of goods and services the organization can offer to the marketplace. The Quality Spotlight feature
has been used throughout this text to illustrate how quality is related to planning, organizing, influencing, and controlling issues.

► THE IMPORTANCE OF QUALITY

Many managers and management theorists warn that U.S. organizations without high-quality
products will very soon be unable to compete in the world marketplace. A 1990 book by Armand V. Feigenbaum put the problem succinctly:[2]

> Quality. Remember it? American manufacturing has slumped a long way from the glory days
> of the 1950s and '60s when "Made in the U.S.A." proudly stood for the best that industry could
> turn out .... While the Japanese were developing remarkably higher standards for a whole host
> of products, from consumer electronics to cars and machine tools, many U.S. managers were
> smugly dozing at the switch. Now, aside from aerospace and agriculture, there are few markets
> left where the U.S. carries its own weight in international trade. For American industry, the
> message is simple: Get Better or Get Beat.

Producing high-quality products is not an end in itself. Rather, successfully offering high-
quality goods and services to the marketplace typically results in three important ends for the
organization:

1. A positive company image
2. Lower costs and higher market share
3. Decreased product liability costs

POSITIVE COMPANY IMAGE A reputation for high-quality products creates a positive image for an organization, and organizations gain many advantages from having such
an image. A positive image helps a firm recruit valuable new employees, accelerate sales of its
new products, and obtain needed loans from financial institutions. To summarize, high-
quality products generally result in a positive company image, which leads to numerous organizational benefits.

LOWER COSTS AND HIGHER MARKET SHARE Activities that support product
quality benefit the organization by yielding lower costs and greater market share. Figure 22.1
illustrates this point. As shown in the top half of this figure, greater market share or gain in
product sales is a direct result of customer perception of improved product quality. As shown
in the bottom half of the figure, organizational activities that contribute to product quality
result in such benefits as increased productivity, lower rework and scrap costs, and lower
warranty costs, which, in turn, result in lower manufacturing costs and lower costs of servicing products after they are sold. Figure 22.1 also makes the important point that both
greater market share and lower costs attributed to high quality normally result in greater organizational profits.

DECREASED PRODUCT LIABILITY COSTS Product manufacturers are increasingly facing costly legal suits over damages caused by faulty products. More and more frequently, organizations that design and produce faulty products are being held liable in the
courts for damages resulting from the use of such products. To take one dramatic example,
Pfizer, a company that develops mechanical heart valves, recently settled an estimated 180
lawsuits by heart-implant patients claiming that the valves used in their implants were
faulty.[3] Successful TQM efforts typically result in improved products and product performance, and the normal result of improved products and product performance is lower
product liability costs.

I. MARKET GAINS

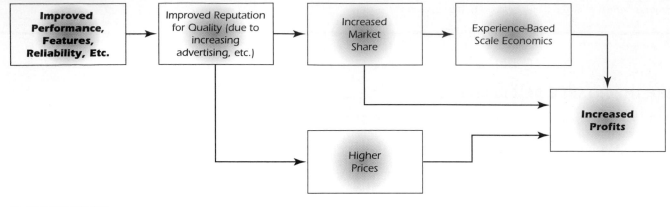

II. COST SAVINGS

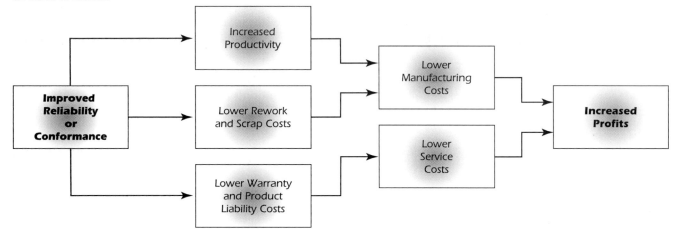

▶ **ESTABLISHED QUALITY AWARDS**

Recognizing all these benefits of quality, U.S. companies have been placing greater emphasis on manufacturing high-quality products in recent years. Several major awards have been established in the United States and abroad to recognize those organizations that produce exceptionally high-quality products and services.

The most prestigious international award is the Deming Award, established in Japan in honor of W. Edwards Deming, who introduced Japanese firms to statistical quality control and quality improvement techniques after World War II.

The most widely known award in the United States is the Malcolm Baldrige National Quality Award, awarded by the American Society of Quality and Control. This award was established in 1988.[4]

A few major awards recognize outstanding quality in particular industries. One example is the Shingo Prize for Excellence in American Manufacturing, sponsored by several industry groups, including the Association for Manufacturing Excellence and the National Association of Manufacturers, and administered by Utah State University. Another example, this one from the health-care industry, is the Healthcare Forum/Witt Award: Commitment to Quality.

The president of the United States and several states have established a variety of quality awards. NASA, for example, gives awards for outstanding quality to its exceptional subcontractors.

As these examples suggest, quality is an increasingly important element in an organization's ability to compete in today's global marketplace.

Based on the above information, product quality at LEGO can be defined as the extent to which customer needs are satisfied through the purchased toys. Total quality management, (TQM) would be the process of involving all workers from all organizational levels in providing a high-quality experience to customers.

Clearly, many different organization members at LEGO have significant roles in determining the quality of the entertainment that customers receive through purchased toys. Although the technological marvel of a toy like MindStorms is an obvious dimension of the quality of the experience that is provided customers, issues like customer support and friendliness to customers after the toy is purchased probably help build the perception of product quality in the customers' minds.

In essence, all individuals at LEGO, product designers who design toys, market researchers who study customer needs, and line workers who actually manufacture the toys, play a critical role in establishing the level of product quality that LEGO offers its customers.

In today's international marketplace, it is extremely important even for a company like LEGO to maintain a reputation of high product quality. Such a reputation typically results in a positive image for the company as a whole and can make it easier for management to recruit competent employees, reduce operating costs, and increase market share that can enhance company profits and decrease product liability costs.

►ACHIEVING QUALITY

Ensuring that all company operations play a productive role in maintaining product quality may seem like an overwhelming task. The task is indeed formidable, but several sets of valuable guidelines have been formulated to make it more achievable. Guidelines from five internationally acclaimed experts—Philip B. Crosby, W. Edwards Deming, Joseph M. Juran, Shigeo Shingo, and Armand V. Feigenbaum—on how to achieve product quality are summarized in the sections that follow.[5]

CROSBY'S GUIDELINES FOR ACHIEVING QUALITY

Philip B. Crosby is known throughout the world as an expert in the area of quality and is considered a pioneer of the quality movement in the United States.[6] His work provides managers with valuable insights on how to achieve product quality. According to Crosby, an organization must be "injected" with certain ingredients relating to integrity, systems, communications, operations, and policies before it will be able to achieve significant progress in product quality.

Crosby calls these ingredients the "vaccination serum" that prevents the disease of low companywide quality. The ingredients of Crosby's vaccination serum are presented in Table 22.1.

DEMING'S GUIDELINES FOR ACHIEVING QUALITY

W. Edwards Deming, who was originally trained as a statistician and began teaching statistical quality control in Japan shortly after World War II, is recognized internationally as a primary contributor to Japanese quality improvement programs. Deming advocated that the way to achieve product quality is to continuously improve the design of a product and the process used to manufacture it.[7] According to Deming, top management has the primary responsibility for achieving product quality.

Deming advised management to follow 14 points to achieve a high level of success in improving and maintaining product quality.[8]

Deming's 14 Points

1. Create and publish to all employees a statement of the aims and purposes of the organization. Management must continually demonstrate its commitment to this statement
2. Learn the new philosophy—this means top management and everybody else in the organization
3. Understand the purpose of inspection—for improvement of processes and reduction of cost
4. End the practice of awarding business on the basis of price tag alone

Integrity

A. The chief executive officer is dedicated to having the customer receive what was promised, believes that the company will prosper only when all employees feel the same way, and is determined that neither customers nor employees will be hassled

B. The chief operating officer believes that management performance is a complete function requiring that quality be "first among equals"—schedule and cost

C. The senior executives, who report to those in A and B, take requirements so seriously that they cannot stand deviations

D. The managers, who work for the senior executives, know that the future rests with their abilities to get things done through people—right the first time

E. The professional employees know that the accuracy and completeness of their work determine the effectiveness of the entire workforce

F. The employees as a whole recognize that their individual commitments to the integrity of requirements are what make the company sound

Systems

A. The quality management function is dedicated to measuring conformance to requirements and reporting any differences accurately

B. The quality education system (QES) ensures that all employees of the company have a common language of quality and understand their personal roles in causing quality to be routine

C. The financial method of measuring nonconformance and conformance costs is used to evaluate processes

D. The use of the company's services or products by customers is measured and reported in a manner that causes corrective action to occur

E. The companywide emphasis on defect prevention serves as a base for continual review and planning using current and past experience to keep the past from repeating itself

Communications

A. Information about the progress of quality improvement and achievement actions is continually supplied to all employees

B. Recognition programs applicable to all levels of responsibility are a part of normal operations

C. Each person in the company can, with very little effort, identify error, waste, opportunity, or any concern to top management quickly—and receive an immediate answer

D. Each management status meeting begins with a factual and financial review of quality

Operations

A. Suppliers are educated and supported in order to ensure that they will deliver services and products that are dependable and on time

B. Procedures, products, and systems are qualified and proven prior to implementation and then continually examined and officially modified when the opportunity for improvement is seen

C. Training is a routine activity for all tasks and is particularly integrated into new processes and procedures

Policies

A. The policies on quality are clear and unambiguous

B. The quality function reports on the same level as those functions that are being measured and has complete freedom of activity

C. Advertising and all external communications must be completely in compliance with the requirements that the products and services must meet

5. Improve constantly and forever the system of production and service
6. Institute training
7. Teach and institute leadership
8. Drive out fear. Create trust. Create a climate for innovation
9. Optimize the efforts of teams, groups, staff areas toward the aims and purposes of the company

10. Eliminate exhortations to the workforce
11. (a) Eliminate numerical quotas for production. Instead, learn and institute methods for improvement

    (b) Eliminate management by objectives. Instead, learn the capabilities of processes and how to improve them
12. Remove barriers that rob people of pride of workmanship
13. Encourage education and self-improvement for everyone
14. Take action to accomplish the transformation

JURAN'S GUIDELINES FOR ACHIEVING QUALITY Like Deming, Joseph M. Juran taught quality concepts to the Japanese and became a significant leader in the quality movement throughout the world. Juran's philosophy emphasizes that management should pursue the mission of quality improvement and maintenance on two levels:

1. The mission of the firm as a whole to achieve and maintain high quality
2. The mission of individual departments within the firm to achieve and maintain high quality

Juran insists that quality improvement and maintenance are a clear process requiring managers to become involved in the study of symptoms of quality problems, the identification of quality problems implied by the symptoms, and the application of solutions to these problems. For maximum effect of a quality effort, strategic planning for quality should be similar to the organization's strategic planning for any other organizational issue, such as finance, marketing, and human resources. That is, strategic planning for quality should include setting short- and long-term quality goals, comparing quality results with quality plans, and integrating quality plans with other corporate strategic areas.[9] More discussion on the relationship between quality and strategic planning follows.

SHINGO'S GUIDELINES FOR ACHIEVING QUALITY The late Shigeo Shingo served as president of Japan's Institute of Management Improvement and there distinguished himself as one of the world's leading experts on improving the manufacturing process. He and Taiichi Ohno are credited with creating the revolutionary Toyota Production Systems.

Shingo first learned quality production techniques from Americans, who advocated statistical techniques. He later broke with this approach, however, in favor of what he called "mistake-proofing," or in Japanese, *poka yoke.*

The essence of *poka yoke* is that a production system should be made so mistake-proof that it is impossible for it to produce anything except good products. Traditionally, quality efforts were largely confined to inspecting work after it was done—to catch and then fix defects, if possible. Even statistical quality control is dependent upon product inspection to diagnose problems with production systems. Recognizing the waste and cost of such inspections, Shingo developed methods to ensure that products are produced correctly the first time, every time.

Figure 22.2 shows an example of a *poka yoke* device designed to prevent errors in a brake wire clamp mounting.[10] Before the improvement, the mounting bridge would accommodate either left or right parts, regardless of which one was needed. This often caused confusion, leading to the installation of the wrong part. A *poka yoke* bridge was devised to set on mounts to ensure that only the correct part could be inserted.

FEIGENBAUM'S GUIDELINES FOR ACHIEVING QUALITY Armand V. Feigenbaum is credited with originating the term *total quality control,* today more often referred to as *total quality management,* or *TQM.* The basic idea of TQM is that every operation in an organization can benefit from the application of quality improvement principles. Defects are costly and unacceptable throughout the organization, not just on the manufacturing floor.[11]

FIGURE 22.2 ▶ *Poka yoke device*

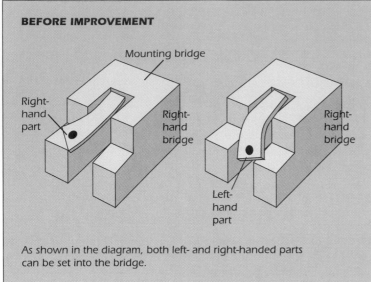

BEFORE IMPROVEMENT

As shown in the diagram, both left- and right-handed parts can be set into the bridge.

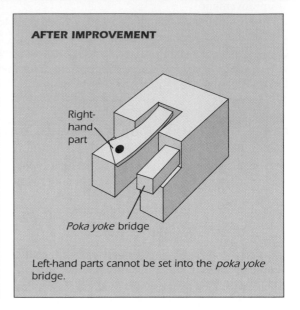

AFTER IMPROVEMENT

Left-hand parts cannot be set into the *poka yoke* bridge.

EFFECTS: Confusion of left and right parts was reduced to zero.

BACK TO THE CASE

The above information gives us insights about how an organization like LEGO can achieve high product quality. Based upon the ideas of Philip Crosby, LEGO's management can achieve its high product quality through focusing on complete dedication to quality, its quality-oriented systems, its communications—constantly discussing and monitoring quality, its sound quality-oriented operations decisions regarding issues like which suppliers to use, and its clear policies emphasizing guidelines for achieving a high-quality product.

Based on the ideas of Deming, LEGO can achieve its quality product by continually improving the design of its products and the process used, like market research, to actually provide the experience to its customers. Taking action like focusing on the purpose of improving product quality, promoting cooperation to facilitate the development of product quality, and emphasizing teamwork as a means to product quality are probably all management activities that are instrumental in achieving high product quality in the theme park.

Based upon the ideas of Juran, LEGO can achieve high-quality product by emphasizing that maintaining product quality is the challenge of the entire organization as well as of individual departments. In addition, LEGO can maintain product quality because all organization members constantly search for symptoms of quality problems and then take action to solve those quality problems.

It would be difficult to conclude that the thoughts of any one of these three theorists completely outline how an organization like LEGO can achieve product quality. Instead, managers should collectively use all of their ideas in formulating a best way to establish product quality within a particular organization.

QUALITY THROUGH STRATEGIC PLANNING

Managers in most organizations spend significant time and effort on strategic planning. Properly designed strategic planning can play an important role in establishing and maintaining product quality.[12] As you recall, strategic planning was defined earlier in this text as long-range planning that focuses on the organization as a whole. The following sections discuss the steps of the strategic management process and suggest how each step can be used to encourage product quality.

Part of the strategic planning process for dry cleaning entrepreneurs in general is assessing and limiting the environmental damage caused by the dumping of dry cleaning chemicals.

► ENVIRONMENTAL ANALYSIS AND QUALITY

The initial step in the strategic management process is environmental analysis. *Environmental analysis* was defined in chapter 8 as the study of the organizational environment to pinpoint factors that significantly influence organizational operations. In establishing the role of environmental analysis to enhance product quality, managers should pay special attention to quality-related environmental factors. Consumer expectations about product quality, the quality of products offered by competitors, and special technology under development that will enhance the quality of organizational activities are examples of such factors.

Suppliers are often emphasized during environmental analysis by managers who stress quality. Suppliers are those companies that sell materials used in the final assembly of a product by another company. For example, General Motors has many suppliers who furnish the company with parts that are used in the final assembly of GM automobiles. Managers need to keep in mind that the satisfactory performance of a final product will be only as good as the quality of parts obtained from company suppliers. Defective parts from suppliers can result in delayed delivery schedules, reduced sales, and lower productivity. Making a special study of suppliers during the environmental analysis allows managers to identify those suppliers who will help improve product quality by furnishing high-quality parts.

► ESTABLISHING ORGANIZATIONAL DIRECTION AND QUALITY

In this step of the strategic management process, the results of the environmental analysis are used to determine the path that the organization will take in the future. This path is then documented and distributed throughout the organization in the form of a mission statement and related objectives. Assuming that environmental analysis results indicate that product quality is important to the organization, a manager can use the organizational mission statement and its related objectives to give general direction to organization members regarding the focus on product quality.

The following is an example of a mission statement used to encourage total quality by Charles Steinmetz, president of All America, Inc., the largest privately owned pest control company in the United States:[13]

> All America Termite & Pest Control, Inc., operating as Sears Authorized Termite & Pest Control, was founded to provide the residential market a once-a-year pest control service as well as premium termite protection.
>
> The purpose of our company is to provide our customers the highest quality of customer service available in our industry while providing unlimited personal and financial potential to our employees.
>
> We will commit the time, energy, expertise, and resources needed to provide premier customer service. Furthermore, we realize there are no other choices, options, or alternatives in our pursuit of quality.

This requires us to give each customer full value for his or her money and to provide that value the first time and every time we have an opportunity to be of service.

We will resolve any customer problems quickly, whether real and apparent or hidden or imaginary. If for any reason we cannot satisfy any customer, we will stand behind our satisfaction or money-back guarantee.

Our commitment to our employees is no less important. We will provide all employees with the training necessary for them to become proficient at their job as well as proper equipment, safe materials, and a safe working environment.

We will provide ample personal and family benefits to provide reasonable security and offer unlimited compensation, significant opportunity for advancement, and an environment that limits success only by the limits of each employee's hard work, dedication, and capabilities.

A look at how different companies set the direction of their product quality effort reveals that different companies define product quality in very different ways. For example, some companies define it as a stronger product that will last longer, or as a heavier, more durable product. Other companies define product quality as the degree to which a product conforms to design specifications, or as product excellence at an acceptable cost to the company and an acceptable price to the consumer. In still other companies, quality is defined as the degree to which a product meets consumer requirements.

Whatever definition of product quality management decides on, this definition must be communicated to all organization members so they will work together in a focused and efficient way to achieve predetermined product quality.

▶ STRATEGY FORMULATION AND QUALITY

After determining organizational direction, the next step in the strategic management process is strategy formulation—deciding what actions should be taken to best deal with competitors. Incorporating product quality into the SWOT (Strengths, Weaknesses, Opportunities, Threats) analysis will help managers develop quality-based strategies. It may, for example, become apparent as a result of a SWOT analysis that organization members are not adequately trained to deal with certain product quality issues. Obviously, a strategy based on this organizational weakness would be to improve quality-oriented training.[14]

Several management strategies have proved especially successful in improving and maintaining high-quality operations and products. Among them are the following:

- ▶ *Value adding*—All assets and effort should, as far as possible, directly add value to the product or service. All activities, processes, and costs that do not directly add value to the product should, as far as possible, be eliminated because non–value-adding costs can be very wasteful. This particular strategy is largely responsible for the drastic reductions in staff positions in most large organizations in recent years. For instance, investment analysis does not add value to the product coming off the production line. Therefore, many companies are simplifying their investment strategies and placing greater emphasis on production processes.
- ▶ *Leadership*—The traditional vision of "The Boss," whip in hand, *driving* lazy, reluctant workers to ever-higher production goals set from on high by management, is disappearing. In quality-focused organizations, "associates" (no longer called "workers" in many quality-focused organizations) are *led*. Management sets the organizational vision and values, and then works with the associates to perfect the production process.
- ▶ *Empowerment*—Associates are organized into self-directed teams and empowered to do their jobs and even to change work processes if that will improve product quality. They are trained, retrained, and cross-trained in a variety of jobs. "Facilitators" (formerly called "supervisors") work with the associates to provide the resources necessary to meet customer needs.
- ▶ *Partnering*—The organization establishes "partnerships" with its suppliers and customers—that is, it actively works with them to find ways to improve the quality of its products and services. Management strives to reduce the number of suppliers to only those that can meet two requirements:

Scott Rohleder is vice president of CRC Products, Inc., a food-service equipment and supply distributor. Beginning in 1992, CRC initiated an electric partnering relationship with its biggest customer—the U.S. government. CRC has filed (electronically) a registration form with the government; in turn, CRC has access to government "electronic bid boards" and downloads orders from a private mailbox. CRC saves costs by filling orders earlier, combining orders, and buying inventory at lower prices.

1. Suppliers must prove themselves reliable and cost-effective
2. Suppliers must prove the sustained quality of their products

Many quality-focused companies formally certify their suppliers.

▶ *Gathering correct and timely information*—The new global marketplace is exacting and unsympathetic. Managers no longer have time to wait for indirect traditional financial reports of performance to make the decisions required to compete successfully.

Managers no longer have time to wade through mountains of tables, reports, and other documents to find the right information. Consequently, in a quality management environment, information systems provide managers with immediate access to critical nonfinancial and financial information, specifically tailored to the needs of the individual manager.

Computerized information systems are especially useful here. Everyone is trained in computers, from executive management through production staff.

Computer terminals are now as commonplace on factory floors as they are in offices.

▶ *Continuous improvement and innovation*—The clarion themes of the quality movement are continuous improvement and constant innovation. Last year's best performance is not good enough today, and today's best practices will not be good enough perhaps even a month from now.

Tom Peters reported in *Thriving on Chaos: Handbook for a Management Revolution* that in 1982, Toyota, the company that established the model for quality in automobile manufacturing, was implementing an average of *5,000* employee suggestions (i.e., improvements) every day. Note that this number does not include improvements initiated by management. Peters advocated, "as a starting point," that U.S. companies target the percentage of revenues stemming from new products and services introduced in the previous 24 months at 50 percent.[15] While these numbers might seem extreme—and they almost certainly are for some companies—they suggest the urgent need to tailor strategic planning to today's rapidly changing and ruthlessly competitive marketplace.

▶ STRATEGY IMPLEMENTATION AND QUALITY

When the results of environmental analysis indicate that product quality is important to an organization, product quality direction has been established through the organization's mission statement and its related objectives, and a strategy has been developed for achieving or maintaining product quality, management is ready to implement its product quality strategy. Implementation, of course, is putting product quality strategy into action.

This might seem like a straightforward step, but in reality it is quite complex. To succeed at implementing product quality strategy, managers must rise to some serious challenges. First of all, they must be sensitive to the fears and frustrations of employees who have to implement the new strategy. They must then provide the organizational resources necessary to implement the strategy, monitor implementation progress, and create and effectively use a network of individuals throughout the organization who can help overcome implementation barriers.

Two tools managers commonly employ to implement product quality strategy are policies and organization structure. Each of these tools is discussed in the following sections.

POLICIES FOR QUALITY A policy was defined in chapter 9 as a standing plan that furnishes broad, general guidelines for channeling management thinking toward taking action consistent with reaching *organizational* objectives. A quality-oriented policy is a special type of policy. A **quality-oriented policy** is a standing plan that furnishes broad, general guidelines for channeling management thinking toward taking action consistent with reaching *quality* objectives.

Quality-oriented policies can be made in virtually any organizational area. They can focus on such issues as the quality of new employees recruited, the quality of plans developed within the organization, the quality of decision-related information gathered and distributed within the organization, the quality of parts purchased from suppliers to be used in the final assembly of products, and the quality of the training used to prepare employees to work in foreign subsidiaries.

ORGANIZING FOR QUALITY IMPROVEMENT Juran says that "to create a revolutionary rate of quality improvement requires . . . a special organization structure." He suggests organizing a "quality council," consisting largely of upper managers, to direct and coordinate the company's quality improvement efforts.

A **quality-oriented policy** is a standing plan that furnishes broad, general guidelines for channeling management thinking toward taking action consistent with reaching quality objectives.

The quality council's main job is to establish an appropriate infrastructure, which would include:[16]

1. A process for nominating and selecting improvement projects
2. A process for assigning project improvement teams
3. A process for making improvements
4. A variety of resources, such as time for diagnosis and remedy of problems, facilitators to assist in the improvement process, diagnostic support, and training
5. A process for review of progress
6. A process for dissemination of results and for recognition
7. An appropriate employee merit rating system to reward quality improvement
8. Extension of business planning to include goals for quality improvement

Juran points out that upper management's role in quality improvement is to get actively involved in every element of the infrastructure—even to the point of serving on some improvement project teams.

Notice also that Juran's structure involves employees at all levels. All employees, including managers, serve on quality improvement teams. True, the quality council itself comprises mostly upper management, but it, too, may include other employees.

► STRATEGIC CONTROL AND QUALITY

Strategic control emphasizes monitoring the strategic management process to make sure that it is operating properly. In terms of product quality, strategic control focuses on monitoring company activities to ensure that product quality strategies are operating as planned. In achieving strategic control of product quality, management must measure how successful the organization has become in achieving product quality.

Philip Crosby states that in order to control product quality efforts, management needs to monitor several organizational areas. These areas include management's own understanding of and attitude toward quality, how quality efforts appear to others within the organization, how organizational problems are handled, the cost of quality as a percentage of sales, quality improvement actions taken by management, and how management summarizes the organization's quality position.

According to Crosby, organizations go through five successive stages of quality maturity as they approach the maximum level of quality in all phases of organizational activity:

1. *Uncertainty*—There is no comprehension of quality as a management tool. Problems are fought as they occur, with ad hoc methods.
2. *Awakening*—Quality management is recognized as a valuable tool, but the organization is still unwilling to provide adequate resources to attack quality problems.
3. *Enlightenment*—A quality improvement program is established. Top management becomes committed to the concept and implements all the steps necessary for the organization to face problems openly and resolve them in an orderly manner.

BACK TO THE CASE

According to the preceding information, strategic planning is a tool that managers in an organization like LEGO can use to achieve product quality. Strategic planning employs strategies and tactics to help management focus on what must be done to maintain product quality in both the long and the short run.

Management can use strategic planning to further product quality by emphasizing quality throughout the strategic management process. During environmental analysis, for example, management can strive to discover information, such as the level of quality that customers expect and technological improvements that might be employed to make the quality of products even greater. MindStorms is an example of such technological improvement to enhance product quality. Given such information, management can decide the direction that product quality should pursue and then use a mission statement and related goals to communicate this direction to all other organization members. Normally, related product quality strategy should then be developed, implemented, and controlled to make sure that it is working.

4. *Wisdom*—Management now thoroughly understands quality management. Quality problems are identified early, and employees are encouraged to suggest improvements to prevent defects from occurring.
5. *Certainty*—Quality management has become an essential part of the organization's system. Problems are almost always prevented, and quality improvement is a continuous activity.

THE QUALITY IMPROVEMENT PROCESS

Two approaches may be taken to improve quality. The first is the one advocated by most of the quality experts, including Deming, Juran, Crosby, and Feigenbaum. This process can be described as "incremental improvement"—or improve one thing at a time. Actually, many incremental improvements may be undertaken simultaneously throughout an organization; recall Toyota's average of instituting 5,000 improvements per day in 1982.

The second approach, advocated by Michael Hammer, consists of completely reengineering a process.[17] This approach requires starting with a clean slate. Management looks at operations and asks, "If we were to start over today, how would we do this?"

Each approach is discussed in detail in the following sections.

THE INCREMENTAL IMPROVEMENT PROCESS

Researchers and consultants have advocated a variety of incremental approaches to achieving excellent quality in products and processes. Despite their differences, almost all of these plans bear some remarkable similarities. Although a specific improvement process may not precisely follow the outline in Figure 22.3, most such processes at least approximate it.

► *Step 1: An area of improvement is chosen, which often is called the improvement "theme"*—
Either management or an improvement team may choose the theme. Examples are:
   ► Reduction in production cycle time
   ► Increase in the percentage of nondefective units produced
   ► Reduction in the variability of raw material going into production
   ► Increase in on-time deliveries
   ► Reduction in machine downtime
   ► Reduction in employee absenteeism

   Many other examples are possible, of course, but these suffice to make the point that an improvement objective must be chosen.

   Consider a pizza company whose delivery business is lagging behind that of its competitors, chiefly because of slow deliveries. The improvement theme in this case may be a reduction in delivery time (i.e., cycle time).
► *Step 2: If a quality improvement team has not already been organized, one is organized*—
Members of this team might include:
   ► One or more associates directly responsible for the work being done
   ► One or more customers receiving the benefits of the work
   ► One or more suppliers providing input into the work
   ► A member of management
   ► Perhaps one or more experts in areas particularly relevant to solving the problem and making the improvement

   For the pizza delivery company, the team might include two pizza builders, a driver, a university student customer, a local resident customer, and a store manager.

FIGURE 22.3 ▶ **The incremental approach to improving quality**

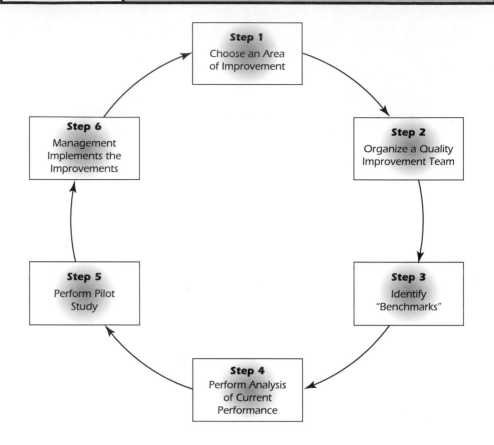

Step 3: The team "benchmarks" the best performers—that is, identifies how much improvement is required in order to match the very best performance—For example, the pizza company may discover in this step that the benchmark (i.e., the fastest average time between the moment an order is taken until the moment of front-door delivery) established by a competitor is 20 minutes.

Suppose the company's current average delivery performance is 35 minutes. That leaves a minimum possible improvement of 15 minutes on the average.

▶ Step 4: The team performs an analysis to find out how current performance can be improved to meet, or beat, the benchmark—Factors to be analyzed here include potential problems related to equipment, materials, work methods, people, and the environment, such as legal constraints, physical conditions, and weather. To return to the pizza delivery company, suppose the team discovered that the pizza-building process could be shortened by 4 minutes. Also suppose they found an average lag of 5 minutes between the time the pizza is ready and the time the delivery van picks it up. Finally, suppose the team discovered that a different oven could shorten cooking time by 7 minutes. Total potential savings in delivery time, then, would be 16 minutes—which would beat the benchmark by 1 minute.

▶ Step 5: The team performs a pilot study to test the selected remedies to the problem—In the pizza case, suppose the team conducted a pilot program for a month, during which the new pizza-building process was implemented, a new driver and van were added, and a new oven was rented. At the end of the month, suppose actual improvement was 17 minutes on average.

The question then becomes, Is the improvement worth the cost? In this case, the improved pizza-building process is improving other customer service as well, thereby increasing the company's overall sales capacity. By beating the benchmark, the company can establish a new delivery system standard—a significant marketing advantage. Suppose, then, that a cost/benefit study favors the changes.

▶ Step 6: Management implements the improvements—Making many such incremental improvements can greatly enhance a company's competitiveness. Of course, as more and more companies achieve better and better quality, the market will become more and more demanding. The key, therefore, is to continually improve both product and process.

This section discussed the incremental improvement process in organizations in general terms. The following People Spotlight feature provides insights about how to keep organization members involved in incremental improvement by discussing a very successful incremental improvement process at Bearings, Inc.

PEOPLE SPOTLIGHT | Keeping People Involved in Incremental Improvement: Bearings, Inc.

For over three years, operations at Bearings, Inc., have steadily improved as a result of a specially designed incremental improvement program. The program is both simple and effective. Bearings employees are asked to submit ideas for improving company operations, and ideas found to be worthwhile by management are implemented. What began as management's desire to informally solicit unedited ideas from the people who actually do the work has evolved into a program that steadily produces a swell of suggestions—one of which has trimmed $900,000 from the cost of running the program itself.

During the initial phase of the program, employees were simply invited to write down their ideas for improving company operations and to submit them to management. As the program became more formal, ideas were collected and printed in a quarterly report called *Quality Idea Briefs* and sent for review to over 4,000 organization members. Ideas presented in this report have focused on issues ranging from increasing customer satisfaction and sales to decreasing the cost of operations and the time it takes to manufacture bearings.

Submissions to *Quality Idea Briefs* have nearly tripled since the program began—in one recent year, over 8,000 ideas were submitted by workers. Bearings' success in getting workers to participate in the improvement program can probably be credited to the care management takes to inform workers of the exact status of their submitted ideas. Nearly 35 percent of all the ideas that made it into *Quality Idea Briefs* have been transformed into operating policy, and the workers who submitted the other 65 percent have been apprised of the reasons their ideas could not be implemented. Bearings workers feel proud when their ideas are accepted for implementation, and respected when management takes the time to explain to them why their ideas are inappropriate.

►REENGINEERING IMPROVEMENTS

Hammer argues that significant improvement requires "breaking away from . . . outdated rules and . . . assumptions . . . ." It demands a complete rethinking of operations. He, too, recommends that management organize a team representing the functional units involved in the process to be reengineered, as well as other units that depend upon the process.

One important reason for reengineering instead of attempting incremental improvements is the need to integrate computerized production and information systems. This is an expensive change, and one that is very difficult to accomplish piecemeal through an incremental approach.

Hammer outlines seven principles of reengineering:

► *Principle 1: Organize around outcomes, not tasks*—Traditionally, work has been organized around different tasks, such as sawing, typing, assembling, and supervising. This first principle of reengineering would, instead, have one person or team performing all the steps in an identified process. The person or team would be responsible for the outcome of the total process.

► *Principle 2: Have those who use the output of the process perform the process*—For example, a production department may do its own purchasing, and even its own cost accounting. This principle would require a broader range of expertise from individuals and teams, and a greater integration of activities.

► *Principle 3: Subsume information-processing work into the real work that produces the information*—Modern computer technology now makes it possible for a work process to process information simultaneously. For example, scanners at checkout counters in

Technicians slip the main span of a Centurion wing section into another during "fit check" operations that ensure quality for the innovative aircraft. The assembly of major framework sections was a milestone in the development of the lightweight remote control aircraft and a creative idea brought to fruition. The project was sponsored by a division of NASA's Dryden Flight Research Center.

grocery stores both process customer purchases and update accounting and inventory records at the same time.

▶ *Principle 4: Treat geographically dispersed resources as though they were centralized*—Hammer uses Hewlett-Packard as an example of how this principle works. Each of the company's 50 manufacturing units had its own purchasing department, which prevented the company from achieving the benefits of scale discounts. Rather than centralize purchasing, which would have reduced responsiveness to local manufacturing needs, Hewlett-Packard introduced a corporate unit to coordinate local purchases, so that scale discounts could be achieved. That way, local purchasing units retained their decentralized authority and preserved their local responsiveness.

▶ *Principle 5: Link parallel activities instead of integrating their results*—Several processes are often required to produce products and services. Too often, though, companies segregate these processes so that the product comes together only at the final stage. Meanwhile, problems may occur in one or more processes, and those problems may not become apparent until too late, at the final step. It is better, Hammer says, to coordinate the various processes so that such problems are avoided.

▶ *Principle 6: Put the decision point where the work is performed and build control into the process*—Traditional bureaucracies separate decision authority from the work. This principle suggests that the people doing the work are the ones who should make the decisions about that work. The salesperson should have the authority and responsibility to approve credit, for example. This principle saves time and allows the organization to respond more effectively and efficiently to customer needs.

Some managers worry that this principle will reduce control over the process. However, control can be built into the process. In the example cited, criteria for credit approval can be built into a computer program, so the salesperson has guidance for every credit decision.

▶ *Principle 7: Capture information once and at the source*—Computerized on-line databases help make this principle achievable. It is now easy to collect information when it originates, store it, and send it to those who need it.

Reengineering allows major improvements to be made all at once. While reengineering can be an expensive way to improve quality, today's rapidly changing markets sometimes demand such a drastic response.[18]

The preceding information gives insights regarding the quality improvement process that LEGO's management can follow within the company. For example, LEGO's management can emphasize the incremental improvement process. This process emphasizes choosing an area of improvement like market research, organizing a quality team to assess the market research area, having the team establish benchmarks indicating standards that market research activities should reach in the future, having the team study market research operations to see how current performance can reach or surpass benchmarks, having the team run a pilot study to see how proposed remedies to market research problems would actually work, and having the team implement remedies that are perceived to have value based on the results of the pilot study.

LEGO's management could also use reengineering to improve quality. Using this philosophy, management would not be searching for incremental improvements such as improving market research, but more revolutionary improvements—for instance, totally rethinking and redesigning LEGO's production process. Based on information in the case, incremental improvement would probably be a more appropriate philosophy for LEGO's management to follow than reengineering.

INNOVATION AND CREATIVITY

This chapter has discussed improving quality in organizations by explaining the incremental improvement process and reengineering. The last part of this chapter discusses innovation and creativity, two important keys to quality improvement in organizations. **Innovation** is defined as the process of taking useful ideas and turning them into useful products, services, or methods of operation. These useful ideas are the result of creativity, the prerequisite for innovation. **Creativity** is the ability to combine ideas in a unique way or to make useful associations among ideas.[19] In essence, creativity provides new ideas for quality improvement in organizations and innovation puts the ideas into action. This section focuses primarily on creativity in organizations, making sure that ideas necessary to fuel innovation are plentiful. Discussion focuses on creativity in individuals and encouraging creativity in organization members.

> **Innovation** is the process of taking useful ideas and turning them into useful products, services, or methods of operation.
>
> **Creativity** is the ability to combine ideas in a unique way or to make useful associations among ideas.

MANAGEMENT AND THE INTERNET — Bill Gross Uses Creativity to Launch Idealab

Creativity was the driving force behind Bill Gross' efforts to establish Idealab. Bill knew of the Internet and knew how to start companies. He simply put these two concepts together to form Idealab, a company that establishes start-up Internet companies.

Bill Gross established Idealabs as a novel base of operations. Since its inception, Idealab has been spinning Gross's raw ideas into independent companies. All are Internet-related start-ups, most of them based around Pasadena. There are 19 of them so far. At last count they employed about 400 people. Here's a partial list of the companies established by Idealab and the type of business performed by each company:

Answers.com—This Web site will answer any question in 24 hours.
CitySearch—This site provides Internet guides to local communities.
EntertainNet—A site that delivers news and other information about the entertainment industry within an organic screensaver.

Intranetics—Intranet systems for easy installation for small to medium companies.
PeopleLinks—A site loaded with communication tools. One tool allows chatters to switch to an anonymous telephone conversation.
SmartGames—A site that is actually a library of nonviolent, intellectually challenging games for brainy applications.

In posturing his companies for success, Gross is constantly contemplating competitive advantage in the new Internet world. Gross sees the key competitive weapons in this new world as intelligence and speed—not money. By intelligence, Gross means the ability to assemble the right group of creative talents. Speed is the ability to execute without making mistakes.

Within each individual, creativity is a function of three components.[20] These components are expertise, creative-thinking skills, and motivation. Figure 22.4 illustrates these three components and depicts how, when overlapping, they result in creativity.

Expertise, as depicted in Figure 22.4, is everything an individual knows and can do in the broad domain of his or her work. This knowledge pertains to work-related techniques and procedures as well as a thorough understanding of overall work circumstances. Take, for example, a produce worker in a supermarket. Her expertise includes basic abilities in trimming and cleaning fresh fruits and vegetables, building appealing product displays that encourage customers to buy products, and building customer relations. As with all organization members, the abilities of this produce worker can be acquired through formal education, experience, and interaction with peers and other professionals.

Creative thinking is the capacity to put existing ideas together in new combinations. Overall, creative thinking determines how flexibly and imaginatively individuals approach problems. This capacity depends mainly on an individual's personality and work habits. Continuing with the above example, the produce worker will tend to be more creative if she feels comfortable disagreeing with people about how the produce department presently functions. Such disagreement will often result in new thoughts about how to improve the department, such as keeping produce fresher for longer periods. In addition, she will tend to have more creative success if she keeps plodding along to face and solve department problems, such as buying new technology to keep product cool and not necessarily always looking for quick problem solutions. This enduring attention to problems will afford the produce worker the attention necessary to generate creative solutions to complex organizational problems.

Motivation, as depicted in Figure 22.4, refers to an individual's need or passion to be creative. If an individual feels a need to be creative, that individual is more likely to do so. Expertise and creative thinking are the individual's raw materials for being creative, but motivation determines whether or not an individual will actually be creative. An individual can be driven to be creative either extrinsically through organizational rewards and punishments, or intrinsically through personal interest and passion related to a situation. Normally, people will be most creative when motivated by personal interest, satisfaction, and the challenge of the work. Continuing with our supermarket example, the produce worker could have the expertise and critical thinking necessary to be creative, but unless she is motivated, she probably will not be creative. Generally the produce worker will be more motivated to be creative if she is personally interested in supermarket problems, tends to be personally satisfied by solving these problems, and sees solving the problems as challenging.

FIGURE 22.4 ▶ **The three components of creativity**

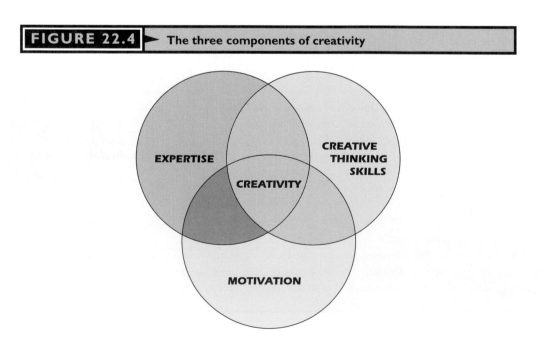

The above section discusses components of creativity: expertise, creative thinking skills, and motivation. This next section is based on the premise that managers can influence the existence of these components in individuals and provides sound advice that managers can use to encourage organization members to be creative.[21] To encourage individual creativity in organizations, managers should:

1. *Match individual expertise with work assignments*—Because expertise is an important component of creativity, managers should ensure that organization members are in work areas matched to their levels of expertise. Needless to say, if individuals do not have knowledge of how to adequately function in a job situation, being creative in that job will be virtually impossible. To promote productivity, work situations should be challenging and should require effort and focus. However, work situations significantly beyond an individual's level of expertise will result in frustration and confusion and will eliminate any creative potential that an individual might possess. If an individual's expertise is significantly below the requirements of a particular work situation, management might provide the individual with training necessary to raise the level of expertise, or transfer the individual to a more suitable work situation. Once the individual's expertise and the requirements of the work situation are made more equivalent, potential for individual creativity will be restored.

2. *Provide resources necessary for creativity*—In order for organization members to be creative, they need time and money—time in which to be creative and money to invest in assets such as help from consultants. Managers must allocate these resources carefully, knowing what creative challenges organization members face and how much time and money will be needed to meet the challenges. Unfortunately, many managers unknowingly discourage creativity in organizations by creating unrealistic work deadlines. Such deadlines not only discourage creativity, but tend to generate mistrust between managers and organization members and cause worker burnout.

3. *Reward creativity*—Managers can encourage creativity through organizational rewards. In essence, managers should reward workers when they are creative. Rewards should be given extrinsically, such as through annual performance appraisals or by assigning bonuses to be paid over time based on a percentage of the benefit that an individual's idea yields the organization. Managers can also assign rewards that focus on intrinsic motivation by recognizing the high value of creative efforts as well as the skill and perseverance necessary to generate creative solutions to problems. To magnify the impact of such rewards in encouraging personal creativity, managers should be creativity role models. As role models, managers should consistently focus attention on generating creative solutions to complex organizational problems.

► **ACROSS INDUSTRIES** ◄ | Candy Manufacturing

CEO AT GUITTARD CHOCOLATE COMPANY IS ROLE MODEL FOR CREATIVITY

As discussed in this section, managers should be role models for creativity in order to magnify the impact of rewards given to employees for creative ideas. Gary Guittard, CEO at Guittard's Chocolate Company, is an example of such a role model.

The Guittard Chocolate Company has been in operation for 130 years. The company has been owned and operated by four generations of Guittards at four different factory locations. Present operations are in Burlingame, California. Guittard produces 10-pound solid blocks of milk, dark, white, and other blends of chocolates to be used by others in producing smaller chocolate products.

Although the company is presently still doing well, a worrisome trend is observable. Throughout the industry, mergers and consolidation of chocolate suppliers are occurring at a steady and significant pace. At this time, Guittard is only one of two independent industrial chocolate suppliers nationwide. Major competitors are chocolate supply megacompanies.

Although President Gary Guittard admits that this consolidation scares him, he's confident that the company will survive. According to Guittard, the company will survive in the future by doing just what it's done in the past—having fun, being creative, and taking care of customers.

(continued)

Throughout his company, Gary Guittard is a role model for being creative. He is always looking for new ideas and encouraging his people to do the same. In fact, creativity at the top of this organization is often cited as a primary reason for the company's lasting success. Gerry Allen, vice president of operations, reflects this creative thrust by saying that creativity is a major reason that the company is able to respond to the quickly changing needs of customers. Ed Seguine, research and development director, echoes the importance of creativity at Guittard by saying that creativity applies to about every area of business operations and keeps the company in business.

BACK TO THE CASE

The above information implies that LEGO's management should use creativity and innovation to enhance organizational quality. New thoughts and ideas would come through creativity and putting the ideas into action would come through innovation. To encourage creativity at LEGO, management must help organization members to develop expertise in their work area, develop critical thinking skills, and be motivated to be creative.

MindStorms, as a product, is an example of how LEGO's management innovated based upon a creative idea to improve the quality of product offerings. Based on the case, LEGO's management obviously afforded appropriately skilled people the time and money necessary to generate the creative idea that spawned MindStorms. Now, management must reward those that spawned the idea and emphasize this new product as a model for how, in the future, creative ideas must grow and flourish at LEGO.

For updated information on the topics in this chapter, Internet exercises, links to related Internet sites, an interactive study guide, and more, visit our companion Web site at

http://www.prenhall.com/certo

Additional information can be found on the inside front and back covers of this text.

ACTION SUMMARY

Reread the learning objectives below. Each objective is followed by questions. Answering these questions accurately will help you to retain most important concepts discussed in this chapter. After answering each question, check your answer against the answer key at the end of the chapter. (*Hint:* If you have any doubts regarding the correct response, consult the page number that follows the answer.)

Circle: From studying this chapter, I will attempt to acquire

1. An understanding of the relationship between quality and total quality management.

    T F   **a.** Overall, product quality and total quality management are the same.

a b c d e   **b.** A TQM program is *not* characterized by: (a) a continual process (b) efforts by all organization members (c) a focus on only a few critical work activities (d) a focus on the production process (e) efforts to involve organization members.

2. An appreciation for the importance of quality.

    T F   **a.** High product quality can result in reduced costs but generally not increased market share.

    T F   **b.** Increasing product quality can reduce product liability costs for an organization.

3. Insights about how to achieve quality.

a b c d e   **a.** According to Crosby, in order to achieve quality, an organization must implement critical ingredients relating to: (a) integrity (b) systems (c) communications (d) operations (e) all of the above.

    T F   **b.** According to Deming, a company can improve its product quality by choosing suppliers based on quality rather than on price alone.

T F	**c.** According to Juran, a company can improve its product quality by focusing on the quality of the organization as a whole as well as the quality of individual departments.
a b c d e	**d.** According to Shingo, *poka yoke* means: (a) production (b) mistake-proofing (c) worker commitment (d) quality (e) diversity.
T F	**e.** According to Feigenbaum, defects are unacceptable only on the manufacturing floor.

4. An understanding of how strategic planning can be used to promote quality.

T F	**a.** Establishing an appropriate mission statement is important for achieving quality.
T F	**b.** Establishing and using appropriate policies and organization structure are important steps in quality-oriented strategy formulation.

5. Knowledge about the quality improvement process.

T F	**a.** The incremental improvement approach involves improving one thing at a time.
a b c d e	**b.** The following is a principle of the reengineering approach to improving quality: (a) organize around outcomes (b) link parallel activities (c) put decision points where the work is performed (d) capture information at the source (e) all are principles of reengineering for quality.
T F	**c.** In management, innovation usually precedes creativity.
a b c d e	**d.** To encourage creativity in organizations, managers can: (a) reward creativity (b) provide resources necessary for creativity (c) match individual expertise with work assignments (d) a and b (e) a, b, and c.

INTRODUCTORY CASE WRAP-UP

CASE DISCUSSSION QUESTIONS

"LEGO's MindStorms Market Research Causes Problem" (p. 503) and its related Back-to-the-Case sections were written to help you better understand the management concepts contained in this chapter. Answer the following discussion questions about the Introductory Case to further enrich your understanding of chapter content:

1. Can a successful TQM program at LEGO decrease the company's product liability costs? If not, why? If so, how?
2. Explain how Crosby's advice relates to ensuring high-quality company activities at LEGO in the future.
3. What steps can LEGO management take to ensure that creative ideas will continue to enhance the quality of company operations?

SKILLS EXERCISE: APPLYING TOTAL QUALITY MANAGEMENT (TQM)

TQM is a management philosophy that indicates that every operation in an organization can benefit from the application of quality improvement principles. The Introductory Case describes a situation wherein LEGO has missed and will miss sales of its new MindStorms robot construction set because the company did not anticipate significant purchases of the toy by adults. Assume that LEGO's market research department should be improved in order to prevent missed sales of any new toy in the future. Design a plan to improve the quality of LEGO's market research efforts. Be as specific as possible in stipulating and explaining the steps of your plan.

ISSUES FOR REVIEW AND DISCUSSION

1. What is the difference between product quality and total quality management (TQM)?
2. Is a successful TQM program important to an organization? Explain.
3. Discuss three benefits resulting from the achievement of high product quality.
4. What guidelines does Crosby offer organizations that want to achieve quality?
5. What guidelines does Deming offer on achieving quality?
6. What guidelines does Juran offer on achieving quality?
7. What guidelines does Shingo offer on achieving quality?
8. Discuss how establishing organizational direction as part of the strategic management process can be used to raise the chances of success of a product quality effort.
9. Can quality be a significant component of a company's strategy? Explain.
10. Discuss the significance of policies and organization structure as components of an effort to maintain product quality.
11. Using Crosby's "five successive stages of quality maturity" as a basis, how would you control TQM efforts in an organization?

12. Discuss how the strategies of partnering and empowerment can improve quality within an organization.

13. When organizing for quality, which structural changes would you anticipate would make the greatest contributions to achieving total quality?

14. Under which circumstances would you use the incremental improvement process to improve quality?

15. Under which circumstances would you use the reengineering approach to improve quality?

16. Discuss Hammer's principles of reengineering for improvement.

17. Would you be concerned with workforce diversity in a program aimed at enhancing product quality? Why or why not? If you would be concerned, what actions would you take?

18. Discuss the relationships among TQM, innovation, and creativity.

ACTION SUMMARY ANSWER KEY

1. **a.** F, p. 504
   b. c, pp. 504–505
2. **a.** F, p. 505
   b. T, p. 505

3. **a.** e, p. 507
   b. T, pp. 507–509
   c. T, p. 509
   d. b, p. 509
   e. F, p. 509

4. **a.** T, p. 511
   b. F, pp. 511–512

5. **a.** T, pp. 515–517
   b. e, pp. 517–518
   c. F, p. 519
   d. e, p. 521

CASE STUDY: Total Quality Management: Learning to Make It Work

Many U.S. companies, mostly manufacturers, adopted the total quality management (TQM) concept in the 1980s in order to compete with Japanese manufacturers. Now, however, more and more of them have begun to reassess their approach. This apparent change of heart does not mean that TQM programs have failed to show dramatic improvements in the overall quality of U.S. products and services. Rather, it means that some firms have simply reconsidered full commitment to what is often a lengthy ongoing process.

Things have changed since W. Edwards Deming and Joseph Juran first proposed their classic quality models in the 1950s. For example, although improved financial performance was not necessarily TQM's original goal, it certainly was a desirable side effect. Today's shareholders not only demand short-term results in company profitability, but also ask for a return on the firm's quality investment. "Quality management is hard to do," says Fred Smith, CEO of Fedex, a Baldrige Quality Award winner. "It takes a long time and constant reiteration, and every kind of management effort to keep it on track."

Contemporary quality management proponents argue that company operations can and should be improved continuously and that "quality" is, by definition, a long-term, never-ending commitment. In addition, the spectrum of managerial response to TQM varies widely. While there have been hundreds of successful cases in support of TQM, there are also many documented stories in which upper management simply misunderstood the commitment needed to implement a successful program. Other managers were too engrossed in implementing TQM policies and procedures to consider either the firm's overall profitability or the real meaning of "quality management." For example, according to *Business Week* magazine, managers at Varian Associates Inc., a Silicon Valley-based scientific-equipment manufacturer, "went about virtually reinventing the way it did business. But while Varian thought it was playing quality by the book, the final chapter did not feature the happy ending the company expected." Obsessed with meeting production schedules, for instance, the staff in the vacuum equipment department did not bother to return customers' phone calls.

TQM advocates contend that Varian managers failed to commit themselves to learning how to focus on quality. Phil Scanlan, vice president for corporate quality at AT&T, agrees. He compares learning quality management with learning how to use a personal computer: "I felt like learning was a problem that takes [time] away from doing the work," he recalls. "After I learned it, I used the PC to do the work. If you see [quality] as something you have to do instead of real work, then you don't get it."

Although less well-known than Deming and Juran, brothers Val and Don Feigenbaum focus on the nitty-gritty details of making quality work. Engineers by profession, the Feigenbaums are considered TQM's hands-on implementers. Their goal, they say, is to drive "failure costs" out of operations. *Failure costs* are the aggregate costs of failing to do things right. "Eliminating one inefficiency, a defect or an excessively complex process, reduces total product costs," notes Val. "Less money is spent on inspection, complaints, and product service, for instance." Moreover, observes Feigenbaum, as you reduce failure costs, "by definition you improve customer satisfaction." The Feigenbaums estimate that failure costs average 25 percent of gross sales in most major American companies. (At world-class companies, they are no more than 10 percent.)

For example, failure costs at Tenneco Inc. were running at 22 percent or about $2.9 billion, during the 1980s. In one decision, the Feigenbaums actually found that the company wasted 20 percent to 40 percent of the material used in manufacturing auto parts. Merely changing the way raw goods were fed into the machines eliminated the waste. Since 1991, Tenneco has cut a total of $1.8 billion in failure costs, resulting in an extra $900 million in operating income.

Depending on the level of management commitment, TQM may or may not satisfy upper-management and stockholder expectations of increased market share, sales, and profits. According to at least one analyst, "It is difficult to correlate TQM with those benefits. While the notion of increasing sales by offering high-quality products and services seemed reasonable, no models were developed within TQM to determine what effect, if any, improved product quality had on sales." In other areas, too, TQM was plagued by problems with management focus, and many TQM problems were simply not implemented in areas that would yield meaningful results. Invalid conclusions were often made because improvement priorities were driven by personal assumptions rather than by outside feedback.

Because many companies neglected to integrate effective customer-satisfaction research into the TQM process, managers could not identify effective customer expectations or weigh their priorities in responding to customer demands. In other words, because quality improvement was largely focused on the *product,* the intangible factors that influenced a purchase decision often went unnoticed.

The lesson, say TQM advocates, is sometimes learned the hard way, but it is worth learning: In order for companies to become successful in implementing TQM programs, managers must not only appraise operations systems but also figure out ways to meet the high expectations from two very demanding key constituencies—company shareholders and customers.

QUESTIONS

1. Based on the information in this case study, would you argue that the failure of TQM programs is in some way inherent in the process itself? Why or why not? Is there any way to ensure successful implementation? Explain.
2. Apply Crosby's vaccination serum for preventing poor total quality management to "cure" one of the companies described. In which area(s) do you believe the company might need the greatest help? Why?

VIDEO CASE STUDY: Quality: Building Competitive Organizations

Quality is no longer just "a good idea" for companies hoping to survive and grow. It is not that quality was ignored in the past, but it generally consisted of a "quality control" step in the manufacturing process. The quality check basically examined output to ensure that it met a predetermined standard. The approach was generally to check products and reject those that did not meet the standard. Although such an approach might be thought of as better than nothing, it allowed defective products to slip through and it was costly. As Dale Crownover of Texas Name Plate puts it, "Somebody pays for what you throw away."

The importance of quality and the ways in which firms manage their quality programs have become important topics for researchers, students, and managers of companies. A driving force behind an increased attention to quality comes from all of us, the users of company products and services. Customers often have more options today, and quality has been positioned as a source of competitive advantage.

Texas Name Plate has discovered and taken advantage of the value of quality throughout its operation. Dale Crownover initially believed that he was doing what was needed in the quality area until one day when a major customer helped him see the light. General Dynamics (a large military and aerospace manufacturer now a part of Lockheed) gave Texas Name Plate an ultimatum: either adopt certain quality processes and improve product defect rates or lose a customer. This wake-up call put Texas Name Plate on a companywide quality campaign that continues to run strong. Texas Name Plate is the smallest venture in Texas to win its states annual quality award, and it is competing for national recognition by applying for the Malcom Baldrige National Quality Award.

QUESTIONS

1. How do you think Dale Crownover would answer the following question: Who is responsible for quality at Texas Name Plate? Use examples from the video to support your answer.
2. Describe the difference between how quality was viewed and treated before and after the request for improvement from General Dynamics. Do you think a customer is entitled to make such a request?
3. Dale Crownover got very involved in the quality improvement program at Texas Name Plate. Do you think this is a good use of a company president's time? What do you think would have happened if he had not gotten so involved?

Management and Diversity

STUDENT LEARNING OBJECTIVES

From studying this chapter, I will attempt to acquire

1. A definition of diversity and an understanding of its importance in the corporate structure

2. An understanding of the advantages of having a diverse workforce

3. An awareness of the challenges facing managers within a diverse workforce

4. An understanding of the strategies for promoting diversity in organizations

5. Insights into the role of the manager in promoting diversity in the organization

CHAPTER OUTLINE

Introductory Case: *Ortho Pharmaceutical: "Showcase" for Cultural Diversity*

DEFINING DIVERSITY
The Social Implications of Diversity

ADVANTAGES OF DIVERSITY IN ORGANIZATIONS
Gaining and Keeping Market Share
Cost Savings
Increased Productivity and Innovation
Better-Quality Management

Diversity Spotlight: *General Electric Values Global Sensitivity*

CHALLENGES THAT MANAGERS FACE IN WORKING WITH DIVERSE POPULATIONS
Changing Demographics

Global Spotlight: *AT&T Connects the World*
Ethnocentrism and Other Negative Dynamics

Across Industries: *Family Dining—Shoney's Successfully Fights Racial Discrimination*
Negative Dynamics and Specific Groups

STRATEGIES FOR PROMOTING DIVERSITY IN ORGANIZATIONS
Workforce 2000
Equal Employment and Affirmative Action

Management and the Internet: *EEOC Uses Web Site to Inform Managers about Sexual Harassment*
Organizational Commitment to Diversity
Pluralism

THE ROLE OF THE MANAGER
Management Development and Diversity Training

ORTHO PHARMACEUTICAL: "SHOWCASE" FOR CULTURAL DIVERSITY

REMINDER: THE INTRODUCTORY CASE WRAP-UP (P. 547) CONTAINS DISCUSSION QUESTIONS AND A SKILLS EXERCISE TO FURTHER ILLUSTRATE THE APPLICATION OF CHAPTER CONCEPTS TO THIS VIGNETTE.

Few companies can match the cultural diversity record of Ortho Pharmaceutical. This company, part of Johnson & Johnson's $4 billion pharmaceutical manufacturing sector, produces, distributes, and markets women's health-care products, such as Ortho-Novum™ contraceptives and Retin-A™ skin ointment. Ortho is also "the most progressive client" of Elsie Cross, of Elsie Y. Cross Associates, a well-known diversity consultant. In fact, Ortho has become her diversity "showcase for the how and why of corporate culture change."

Currently, women and minorities at Ortho Pharmaceutical are being promoted in numbers representative of their numbers within the general workforce. According to a 1992 article in the *Los Angeles Times Magazine*, women hold 25 percent of management positions at Ortho, up from 22 percent in the year prior to the start of the corporate diversity program. Similarly, African Americans in managerial positions have increased from 6 percent to 13 percent, while all minorities jumped from 10 percent representation within managerial ranks to 18 percent. Although white males still hold a significant 63 percent of top positions at the company, Ortho's record of upward mobility for women and minorities is impressive.

Ortho Pharmaceutical's move toward diversity began when the company contacted the consulting firm of Elsie Y. Cross Associates in 1986. At that time, Gary Parlin, a white male, was Ortho's president. In spite of the affirmative action policies that were in place, Ortho had difficulty retaining women and minority employees. Moreover, the financial costs of such high turnover were extensive. Parlin worked with Cross and her staff to implement an organizational development assessment of the company's systems. Their assessment revealed that white males felt comfortable about their futures in the company, while women and minorities felt stifled and ignored and saw little opportunity for advancement.

The assessment also showed that company recruiters were not seeking a diverse pool of candidates. Once hired, women and minorities received little of the feedback, mentoring, or promotions made available to their white male counterparts. After collaborating with the Cross firm and implementing an extensive planned-change effort,

Diversity is valuable to an organization because it enables the organization to draw on all the rich contributions that a multicultural workforce has to offer and enlarges the pool of information available for making decisions.

management has found that employees now speak very differently of their experiences in the company. After six years, a black marketing research manager at Ortho was able to say, "This is a safe harbor. . . . Here I can be myself. I can say what I like, do what I like. I can disagree with people. At other companies, just to disagree meant political suicide." The kind of qualitative cultural changes referred to by this manager would be a plus for any corporation.

Although progress has been made, only one woman and one person of color currently sit on the board of directors, the company's top policymaking body. Responding to these concerns, an Ortho spokesperson said, "What we do here isn't easy. But if you value differences among people, incorporate those differences into the team, and then reward the team, change happens. Never fast enough, but it happens nonetheless."

What's Ahead

How will the increasing diversity of the U.S. workforce affect the responsibilities of managers? Is the importance of diversity exaggerated in contemporary management writing? Or can managers expect to play an ever-increasing role in the kinds of activities already occurring at Ortho Pharmaceutical? This chapter will help managers understand the challenges that a diverse workforce poses for American businesses. It examines the following topics:

1. The definition and social implications of diversity
2. Advantages of diversity in organizations
3. Challenges confronting managers who work with diverse populations
4. Managerial strategies for promoting diversity in organizations
5. The role of the manager in promoting effective workforce diversity

---

◼ DEFINING DIVERSITY

Diversity is the degree of basic human differences among a given population. Major areas of diversity are gender, race, ethnicity, religion, social class, physical ability, sexual orientation, and age.

Diversity refers to characteristics of individuals that shape their identities and the experiences they have in society. This chapter provides information about workforce diversity and discusses the strengths and problems of a diverse workforce. Understanding diversity is essential for managers today because managing diversity will undoubtedly constitute a large portion of the management agenda throughout the 1990s and well into the next century.[1]

This chapter describes some strategies for promoting social diversity in organizations. It also explains how diversity is related to the four management functions. Given the nature of this topic, you will find it necessary to integrate information you learned from other chapters into what is presented here. For example, you will need to consider the legal foundation for developing an inclusive workforce—affirmative action and Equal Employment Opportunity (EEO), discussed in chapter 12, and ideas about organizational change, discussed in chapter 17—as you study this chapter material.

▶ THE SOCIAL IMPLICATIONS OF DIVERSITY

Workforce diversity is not a new issue in the United States. People from various other regions and cultures have been immigrating to these shores since colonial times, so the American population has always been a heterogeneous mix of races, ethnicities, religions, social classes, physical abilities, and sexual orientations.[2] These differences—along with the basic human differences of age and gender—comprise diversity. The purpose of exploring diversity issues in a management textbook is to suggest how managers might include diverse employees equally, accepting their differences and utilizing their talents.

MAJORITY AND MINORITY GROUPS Managers must understand the relationship between two groups in organizations: majority groups and minority groups. The term **majority group** refers to that group of people in the organization who hold most of the positions that command decision-making power, control of resources and information, and access to system rewards. Note that the majority is not *always* the group with a numerical majority. The term **minority group** refers to that group of people in the organization who are smaller in number or who lack critical power, resources, acceptance, and social status. Together, the minority and majority group members form the entire social system of the organization.

Note that the minority group is not *always* lesser in number than the majority group. For example, women are seen as a minority group in most organizations because they do not have the critical power to shape organizational decisions and to control resources. Moreover, they have yet to achieve full acceptance and social status in most workplaces. In most health-care organizations, for instance, women outnumber men. Although men are numerical minorities, however, they are seldom denied social status because white males hold most positions of power in the health-care system hierarchy, such as physician and health-care administrator.

Majority group refers to that group of people in the organization who hold most of the positions that command decision-making power, control of resources and information, and access to system rewards.

Minority group refers to that group of people in the organization who are smaller in number or who possess fewer granted rights and lower status than the majority groups.

Managers are becoming more dedicated to seeking a wide range of talents from every group in American culture because they now realize that there are distinct advantages to doing so.[3] For one thing, as you learned in chapter 17, group decisions often improve the quality of decision making. For another, work groups or teams that can draw on the contributions of a multicultural membership gain the advantage of a larger pool of information and a richer array of approaches to work problems.

Ann Morrison carried out a comprehensive study of 16 private and public organizations in the United States. In the resulting book, *The New Leaders: Guidelines on Leadership Diversity in America,* she outlines the several other advantages of diversity, each of which is discussed here.[4]

►GAINING AND KEEPING MARKET SHARE

Managers today must understand increasingly diverse markets. Failure to discern customers' preferences can cost a company business in the United States and abroad. Some people argue that one of the best ways to ensure that the organization is able to penetrate diverse markets is to include diverse managers among the organization's decision makers.[5]

Diversity in the managerial ranks has the further advantage of enhancing company credibility with customers. A manager who is of the same gender or ethnic background as customers may imply to those customers that their day-to-day experiences will be understood. One African American female manager found that her knowledge of customers paid off when she convinced her company to change the name of a product it intended to sell at Wal-Mart. "I knew that I had shopped for household goods at Wal-Mart, whereas the CEO of this company, a white, upper-middle-class male, had not. He listened to me and we changed the name of the product."

Morrison cites a case in which one company lost an important opportunity for new business in a southwestern city's predominantly Hispanic community. The lucrative business ultimately went to a competitor that had put a Hispanic manager in charge of the project, who solicited input from the Hispanic community.

►COST SAVINGS

Companies incur high costs in recruiting, training, relocating, and replacing employees and in providing competitive compensation packages. According to Morrison, Corning Corporation's high turnover among women and people of color was costing the company an estimated $2 million to $4 million a year. Many managers that were questioned for her study felt that the personnel expenses associated with turnover—often totaling as much as two-thirds of an organization's budget—could be cut by instituting diversity practices that would give nontraditional managers more incentive to stay. When nontraditional managers remain with the organization, nontraditional employees at lower levels feel more committed to the company.

In addition to the personnel costs, executives are distressed by the high legal fees and staggering settlements resulting from lawsuits brought by employees who felt they had been discriminated against. For example, $17.65 million in damages was awarded to a woman employed by Texaco who claimed she had been passed over for a management promotion because of her gender. Executives are learning that such sums would be better spent on promoting diversity.

►INCREASED PRODUCTIVITY AND INNOVATION

Many executives quoted in Morrison's study believe productivity is higher in organizations that focus on diversity. These managers have found that employees who feel valued, competent, and at ease in their work setting enjoy coming to work and perform at a high level.

Morrison also cites a study by Donna Thompson and Nancy DiTomaso that concluded that a multicultural approach has a positive effect on employees' perception of equity. This, in turn, positively affects employees' morale, goal setting, effort, and performance. The managers in Morrison's study also saw innovation as a strength of a diverse workforce.

TABLE 23.1	▶ Advantages of a Diverse Workforce

- ▶ Improved ability to gain and keep market share
- ▶ Cost savings
- ▶ Increased productivity
- ▶ A more innovative workforce
- ▶ Minority and women employees who are more motivated
- ▶ Better quality of managers
- ▶ Employees who have internalized the message that "different" does not mean "less than"
- ▶ Employees who are accustomed to making use of differing worldviews, learning styles, and approaches in the decision-making process and in the cultivation of new ideas
- ▶ Employees who have developed multicultural competencies, such as learning to recognize, surface, discuss, and work through work-related issues pertaining to global, cultural, or intergroup differences
- ▶ A workforce that is more resilient when faced with change

Firms that take diversity seriously find they must sometimes adapt to employees' individual circumstances. The reward is often high employee loyalty and superior performance. Kelly Ramsey-Dolson, an accountant for Ernst & Young, maintains a full-time schedule with the flexibility to spend time with her son Jeffrey.

▶BETTER-QUALITY MANAGEMENT

Morrison also found that including nontraditional employees in fair competition for advancement usually improves the quality of management by providing a wider pool of talent. According to the research she cites, exposure to diverse colleagues helps managers develop breadth and openness.

The quality of management can also be improved by building more effective personnel policies and practices that, once developed, will benefit all employees in the organization, not just minorities. According to Morrison's study, many of the programs initially developed for nontraditional managers resulted in improvements that were later successfully applied throughout the organization. Ideas such as adding training for mentors, upgrading techniques for developing managers, and improving processes for evaluating employees for promotion—all concepts originally intended to help nontraditional managers—were later adopted for wider use. (See Table 23.1 for more information on the advantages of a diverse workforce.)

BACK TO THE CASE

A company that uses the diverse talents of a multicultural workforce to its advantage benefits along with the workers. Some experts believe that one of the best ways for a company to capture diverse markets is to make sure its decision makers are a diverse group. For example, health-care products such as Ortho Pharmaceutical's contraceptives may require varied marketing strategies to sell successfully in different cultures. By promoting decision makers who are sensitive to different cultural attitudes about contraceptives, Ortho stands a better chance of establishing product and marketing strategies attractive to various groups.

As it makes progress in its diversity program, Ortho Pharmaceutical can expect its productivity to increase, because workers who feel valued, competent, and at ease in their work setting will perform better than workers who feel the organization has little respect for their efforts. Moreover, by providing training that encourages nontraditional managers to remain with the organization, Ortho Pharmaceutical can expect to lower its personnel costs for recruiting, training, and replacing nontraditional employees.

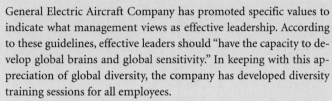

DIVERSITY SPOTLIGHT   General Electric Values Global Sensitivity

General Electric Aircraft Company has promoted specific values to indicate what management views as effective leadership. According to these guidelines, effective leaders should "have the capacity to develop global brains and global sensitivity." In keeping with this appreciation of global diversity, the company has developed diversity training sessions for all employees.

One especially innovative approach developed by General Electric Aircraft is a program titled "Leveraging Differences (Cultural Diversity)." This program, which uses an Interactive Video Disk (IVD), consists of the following five components:

1. An introduction explains how a company evolves from "homogeneous, to assimilative, to heterogeneous, and finally to multicultural"
2. "Walk a Mile in My Shoes" focuses on problems women face in the workplace
3. "Something I've Always Wanted to Ask You People" gives trainees a chance to express their curiosity about members of

other groups, specifically Asians, African Americans, Hispanics, and women
4. "You Decide" presents the trainee with a variety of problem-solving situations that have implications for diversity
5. A summary concludes the video with closing remarks by John Rittenhouse, General Electric's senior vice president

The strengths of this program on IVD are that the components are easily understandable by a wide range of employees, available for use on company time, and require responses from employees. "Leveraging Differences (Cultural Diversity)" reflects management's leadership values statement, which includes the following goals: selecting "the most talented team members available"; fully utilizing people "regardless of race, gender, ethnic origin, culture, or age"; and learning to see "the priority of all aspects of diversity to business success."

CHALLENGES THAT MANAGERS FACE IN WORKING WITH DIVERSE POPULATIONS

As you have seen, there are compelling reasons for an organization to encourage diversity in its workforce. For managers to fully appreciate the implications of promoting diversity, however, they must understand some of the challenges they face in managing a diverse workforce. Changing demographics and several issues arising out of these changes are discussed in the following sections.

CHANGING DEMOGRAPHICS

Demographics, defined in chapter 8 as the statistical characteristics of a population, are an important tool managers use to study workforce diversity. According to *Workforce 2000: Work and Workers for the Twenty-First Century,* a report done for the United States Department of Labor by the Hudson Institute, the workforce and jobs of the future will parallel changes in society and in the economy.

This report, published in 1987, projects that the following five demographic facts will be "most important" by the year 2000:[6]

1. The population and the workforce will grow more slowly than at any time since the 1930s
2. The average age of the population and the workforce will rise, and the pool of young workers entering the labor market will shrink
3. More women will enter the workforce
4. Minorities will make up a larger share of new entrants into the labor force
5. Immigrants will represent the largest share of the increase in both the general population and the workforce

Note how this study emphasizes the growth of nonwhites, women, immigrants, and older workers within the U.S. workforce. Figure 23.1 shows the distribution of new entrants in the labor force based on these demographic patterns.

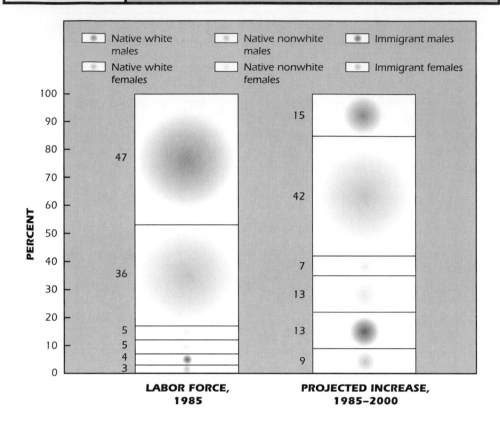

FIGURE 23.1 ▶ **Growth of nonwhites entering the U.S. labor force**

Legend:
- Native white males
- Native white females
- Native nonwhite males
- Native nonwhite females
- Immigrant males
- Immigrant females

LABOR FORCE, 1985
- 47
- 36
- 5
- 5
- 4
- 3

PROJECTED INCREASE, 1985–2000
- 15
- 42
- 7
- 13
- 13
- 9

PERCENT axis: 0, 10, 20, 30, 40, 50, 60, 70, 80, 90, 100

AT&T Connects the World

AT&T offers five consumer services to travelers and consumers living outside the United States: AT&T USADirect, AT&T World Connect, AT&T USADirect Service In-Language, AT&T Calling Card, and AT&T TeleTicket Service. The oldest service, USADirect, introduced in 1985, allows users to save on cost when calling the United States from 113 different countries. The newest service, USADirect Service In-Language, is offered to residents in 16 countries. Consumers using this service can make calls to the United States through operators who speak their languages. Both services are drawing more customers—and, consequently, increasing AT&T's need to hire diverse employees. Only 15 months after instituting USADirect Service In-Language, the company had to add 250 Spanish-speaking operators. Similar hiring increases occurred when the service was expanded to appeal to Polish and Hungarian speakers.

African consumers are a large market for the more established USADirect Service. According to Yaw Osei-Amoako, market devel-

opment manager for Africa in Morristown, New Jersey, more than 50,000 USADirect calls are made per week from Ghana—mostly by Ghanaians calling their U.S. relatives.

With respect to global diversity, Osei-Amoako, himself a Ghanaian, says, "Patience is the key virtue here. The Europeans understand this better than the Americans because of their colonial experience. Americans want to come in, make a deal, go home. The Africans want to get to know you personally, know all about your family, what you like, what you don't like, where you come from."

In Africa, USADirect Service In-Language was initially offered only in Liberia. Now it is available in 10 African countries. Africa is an emerging market that is also being pursued by Sprint and MCI. Its skills in global diversity may give AT&T a competitive edge in this market.

The changing demographics described in *Workforce 2000* set in motion certain social dynamics that can interfere with workforce productivity. If an organization is to be successful in diversifying, it must neutralize these dynamics.

ETHNOCENTRISM AND STEREOTYPING Our natural tendency is to judge other groups less favorably than our own. This tendency is the source of **ethnocentrism,** the belief that one's own group, culture, country, or customs are superior to others'. Two related dynamics are prejudices and stereotypes. A **prejudice** is a preconceived judgment, opinion, or assumption about an issue, behavior, or group of people.[7] **Stereotype** is a positive or negative assessment of members of a group or their perceived attributes. It is important for managers to know about these negative dynamics so they can monitor their own perceptions and help their employees view diverse co-workers more accurately.

DISCRIMINATION When verbalized or acted upon, these negative dynamics can cause discomfort and stress for the judged individual. In some cases, there is outright discrimination. **Discrimination** is the act of treating an issue, person, or behavior unjustly or inequitably on the basis of stereotypes and prejudices. Consider the disabled person who is turned down for promotion because the boss feels this employee is incapable of handling the regular travel required for this particular job. The boss' prejudgment of this employee's capabilities on the basis of "difference," and implementation of the prejudgment through differential treatment, constitutes discrimination.

Ethnocentrism is the belief that one's own group, culture, country, or customs are superior to others'.

A **prejudice** is a preconceived judgment, opinion, or assumption about an issue, behavior, individual, or group of people.

A **stereotype** is a positive or negative assessment of members of a group or their perceived attributes.

Discrimination is the act of treating an issue, person, or behavior unjustly or inequitably on the basis of stereotypes or prejudices.

ACROSS INDUSTRIES | Family Dining

SHONEY'S SUCCESSFULLY FIGHTS RACIAL DISCRIMINATION

This section discussed discrimination as treating an issue, person, or behavior unjustly or unfairly on the basis of stereotypes or prejudices. Management's recent struggle at Shoney's is evidence that management can successfully eliminate racial discrimination from an organization.

For more than 50 years, Shoney's Restaurants have been feeding America's families. Since starting back in 1947, the company has expanded to include over 750 locations in 33 states. In fact, Shoney's is the second largest family dining chain in the nation, and served 170 million guests in the last year alone. Shoney's may have grown, but the company is proud that a Shoney's Restaurant is still a place where folks gather to enjoy great food, great service, and great company. Shoney's Restaurants offer full table service and are open daily for breakfast, lunch, and dinner. It is famous for its breakfast bar, which includes more than 54 choices including bacon, eggs, and pancakes.

Not so long ago, Shoney's was synonymous with racial discrimination. To employees, the company stood for systematic denial of ca-

reer opportunities. To consumers, Shoney's meant mistreatment of minority customers—reminiscent of the days when America's lunch counters were ground zero in the nation's civil rights movement. In 1992, Shoney's paid $132.8 million to settle a class-action discrimination suit brought by 20,000 employees and rejected job applicants.

Recently, Shoney's appeared on *Fortune's* list of the best 50 companies for Asians, blacks, and Hispanics. With $1.2 billion in revenues last year, the company ranks 13th. How did this company go from a reputation of racial discrimination to being a role model for diversity? Company management acted quickly, decisively, and sincerely. Shoney's now operates under the premise that all employees should have an opportunity to move up if they are qualified and work hard. Now all openings are posted, which means more minority employees are seeking out, and getting, top jobs. Consider Julius Brinkley, a former cook at a Nashville Shoney's. For years he tried to enroll in training sessions that would qualify him for a better job. He is now an assistant dining room manager and believes that Shoney's really has "had a change of heart."

TOKENISM AND OTHER CHALLENGES Discrimination occurs when stereotypes are acted upon in ways that affect hiring, pay, or promotion practices—for example, where older employees are steered into less visible job assignments that are unlikely to provide opportunities for advancement. Other challenges facing minorities and women include the pressure to

Tokenism refers to being one of very few members of a group in an organization.

conform to the organization's culture, high penalties for mistakes, and tokenism. **Tokenism** refers to being one of very few members of your group in the organization.[8] "Token" employees are given either very high or very low visibility in the organization. One African American male indicated that he was "discouraged" by his white female manager from joining voluntary committees and task forces within the company—but at the same time criticized in his performance appraisal by her for being "aloof" and taking a "low-profile approach."

In other cases, minorities are seen as representatives or "spokespeople" for all members of their group. As such, they are subject to high expectations and scrutiny from members of their own group. One Latino male employee described how other Latinos in the company "looked up to him" for his achievements in the organization. In general, ethnocentrism, prejudices, and stereotypes inhibit our ability to accurately process information.

▶ NEGATIVE DYNAMICS AND SPECIFIC GROUPS

The following sections more fully discuss these negative dynamics as they pertain to women, minorities, older workers, and workers with disabilities.

WOMEN Rosabeth Kanter has researched the pressures women managers face. In her classic study of gender dynamics in organizations, she emphasized the high expectations women have of other women as one of those pressures.[9]

Gender-role stereotypes are perceptions about the sexes based on what society believes are appropriate behaviors for men and women.

Gender Roles Women in organizations confront **gender-role stereotypes,** or perceptions about people based on what our society believes are appropriate behaviors for men and women. Both sexes find their self-expression constrained by gender-role stereotyping. For example, women in organizations are often assumed to be good listeners. This attribution is based on our societal view that women are nurturing. Although this is a positive assessment, it is not true of all women or of any woman all the time—hence the negative side of this stereotypical expectation for women in the workplace.

Women professionals, for instance, often remark that they are frequently sought out by colleagues who want to discuss non–work-related problems. Women managers also describe the subtle sanctions they experience from both men and women when they do not fulfill expectations that they will be nurturing managers.

The "Glass Ceiling" and Sexual Harassment A serious form of discrimination affecting women in organizations has been dubbed the "glass ceiling."[10] The glass ceiling refers to an invisible "ceiling," or barrier to advancement. This term, originally coined to describe the limits confronting women, is also used to describe the experiences of other minorities in organizations. Although both women and men struggle to balance work and family concerns, it is still more common for women to assume primary responsibility for household management as well as their careers, and sometimes they are denied opportunities for advancement because of this stereotype.

Sexual harassment is another form of discrimination that disproportionately affects female employees. *Sexual harassment* is defined as any unwanted sexual language, behavior, or imagery negatively affecting an employee.[11]

Bicultural stress is stress resulting from having to cope with membership in two cultures simultaneously.

Role conflict is the conflict that results when a person has to fill competing roles because of membership in two cultures.

Role overload refers to having too many expectations to comfortably fulfill.

MINORITIES Racial, ethnic, and cultural minorities also confront inhibiting stereotypes about their group. Like women, they must deal with misunderstandings and expectations based on their ethnic or cultural origins.

Many members of ethnic or racial minority groups have been socialized to be members of two cultural groups—the dominant culture and their particular racial or ethnic culture. Ella Bell, professor of organizational behavior at MIT, refers to this dual membership as *biculturalism.* In her study of African American women, she identifies the stress of coping with membership in two cultures simultaneously as **bicultural stress.**[12] She also indicates that **role conflict**—having to fill competing roles because of membership in two cultures—and **role overload**—having too many expectations to comfortably fulfill—are common characteristics of bicultural stress. Although these are problems for many minority groups, they are particularly intense for women of color. This is because this group experiences negative dynamics affecting *both* minorities and women.

Socialization in one's culture of origin can lead to misunderstandings in the workplace. This is particularly true when a manager relies solely on the cultural norms of the majority group. According to the norms of American culture, for example, it is acceptable—even positive—to publicly praise an individual for a job well done. However, in cultures that place primary value on group harmony and collective achievement, this way of rewarding an employee causes emotional discomfort because employees fear that, if praised publicly, they will "lose face" in their group.

OLDER WORKERS   Older workers are a significant and valuable component of today's labor force.[13] The "baby boomers" born in the late 1940s and 1950s are now middle aged, while the previous generation of workers is approaching retirement. Organizations need to learn how to tap the rich knowledge and experience of these workers and how to help older workers avoid the occupational stagnation of later careers. These are especially important concerns given the *Workforce 2000* predictions that the supply of younger workers is dwindling and that huge numbers of baby boomers will reach the preretirement phase of their careers simultaneously, creating fierce competition for scarce jobs.

Stereotypes and Prejudices   Older workers present some specific challenges for managers. Stereotypes and prejudices link age with senility, incompetence, and lack of worth in the labor market.[14] Jeffrey Sonnenfeld, an expert on senior executives and older workers, compiled research findings from several studies of older employees. He found that managers view older workers as "deadwood," and seek to "weed them out" through pension incentives, biased performance appraisals, and other methods.

Actually, Sonnenfeld's compilation of research indicates that while older managers are more cautious, less likely to take risks, and less open to change than younger managers, many are high performers. Studies that tracked individuals' careers over the long term conclude that there is a peak in performance around age 45 to 50, and a second peak around 55 to 60. Performance in some fields (e.g., sales) either improves with age or does not significantly decline.

It is the manager's responsibility to value older workers for their contributions to the organization and to see to it that they are treated fairly. This requires an understanding of and sensitivity to the physiological and psychological changes that older workers are adjusting to. Supporting older workers also requires paying attention to how performance appraisal processes, retirement incentives, training programs, blocked career paths, union insurance pensions, and affirmative action goals affect this segment of the workforce.

WORKERS WITH DISABILITIES   People with disabilities are subject to the same negative dynamics that plague women, minorities, and older workers. For example, one manager confessed that before he attended diversity training sessions offered through a nearby university, he felt "uncomfortable" around disabled people. One disabled professional reported that she was always received warmly by phone and told that her background was exactly what companies were looking for, but when she showed up for job interviews, she was often rebuffed and informed that her credentials were insufficient.

The stereotyping, prejudice, and discrimination women and minorities often suffer in organizations are summarized in Figure 23.2. Managers who learn to recognize and deal with these negative dynamics will be better prepared to manage a diverse workforce.

STRATEGIES FOR PROMOTING DIVERSITY IN ORGANIZATIONS

This section looks at several approaches to diversity and strategies that managers can consider as they plan for promoting cultural diversity in their organizations. First, the six strategies for modern management offered by the Hudson Institute's *Workforce 2000* report are explored. Then the requirements of the Equal Employment Opportunity Commission, which is legally empowered to regulate organizations to ensure that management practices enhance diversity, are discussed, along with affirmative action. Finally, the wisdom of moving beyond these legal requirements and striving for pluralism is considered, and five approaches to pluralism are described.

WOMEN

• Gender-role stereotypes
  — expectations and prejudices

• Limits to organizational
  advancement (i.e., "glass
  ceiling")

• High expectations from and
  scrutiny by other women

CHALLENGES IN COMMON

• Discrimination in hiring, pay,
  and promotions

• Pressure to conform to the
  majority culture at the expense
  of one's own culture

• Hostile or stressful work
  environment:
  — too high visibility
  — too low visibility (e.g., tracked
    into jobs with low responsibility,
    status, or opportunity for advancement)

• Dynamics of tokenism

• Seen as representative spokesperson
  for all members of one's group

• Isolation or lower degree of social
  acceptance

• Lack of opportunities for mentoring
  and sponsorship

MINORITIES

• Racial stereotypes, ethnocentrism,
  and prejudices

• Bicultural stress

• High expectations from and
  scrutiny by other members
  of one's group

▶ WORKFORCE 2000

According to the authors of this Hudson Institute report, six major issues demand the full attention of U.S. business leaders and require them to take the following actions:[15]

1. *Stimulate balanced world growth*—The United States must pay less attention to its share of world trade and more to the growth of the economies of other nations of the world, including those nations in Europe, Latin America, and Asia with which the United States competes.

2. *Accelerate productivity increases in service industries*—Prosperity will depend much more upon how fast output per worker increases in health care, education, retailing, government, and other services than on gains in manufacturing.

Differently abled workers are being helped both by new laws and new technologies. For example, both the Rehabilitation Act of 1973 (which covers jobs connected with the federal government) and the Americans with Disabilities Act (which covers private-sector jobs) guarantee the right of access to training and job-performance equipment. Such laws require employers to make the reasonable accommodations that would permit the handicapped worker to perform at the minimum level of productivity expected of a nonhandicapped worker.

3. *Maintain the dynamism of an aging workforce*—As the age of the average American worker climbs toward 40, the nation must make sure that its workforce does not lose its adaptability and willingness to learn.

4. *Reconcile the conflicting needs of women, work, and families*—There has been a huge influx of women into the workforce in the last two decades, but organizational policies covering pay, fringe benefits, time away from work, pensions, welfare, and many other issues do not yet reflect this new reality.

5. *Fully integrate African American and Hispanic workers into the economy*—The decline in the number of "traditional" white male workers among the young, the rapid pace of industrial change, and the rising skill requirements of the emerging economy make the full utilization of minority workers a particularly urgent challenge between now and 2000.

6. *Improve the education and skills of all workers*—Human capital (knowledge, skills, organization, and leadership) is the key to economic growth and competitiveness.

As this *Workforce 2000* summary of the key strategies for modern management suggests, many of the most significant managerial challenges that lie ahead derive from dramatic demographic shifts and other complex societal issues. Organizations—and, ultimately, their leaders and managers—will need to clarify their own social values as they confront these dynamics. As you recall from chapter 8, *social values* refer to the relative worth society places on different ways of existence and functions.

The six strategies outlined in the report strongly imply that organizations need to become more inclusive—that is, to welcome a broader mix of employees and to develop an organizational culture that maximizes the value and potential of each worker. As with any major initiative, commitment to developing an inclusive organization begins at the top of the organizational hierarchy. However, on a day-to-day operational basis, each manager's level of commitment is a critical determinant of how well or how poorly the organization's strategies and approaches will be implemented.

►EQUAL EMPLOYMENT AND AFFIRMATIVE ACTION

As you recall from chapter 12, the Equal Employment Opportunity Commission (EEOC) is the federal agency that enforces the laws regulating recruiting and other management practices. That chapter discussed affirmative action programs designed to eliminate barriers against and increase opportunities for underutilized or disadvantaged individuals. These programs are positive steps toward promoting diversity and have created career opportunities for both women and minority groups.

Still, organizations can do much more. For example, some employees are hostile toward affirmative action programs because they feel these programs have been misused to create **reverse discrimination**—that is, they discriminate against members of the majority group in order to help groups that are underrepresented in the organization. When management implements appropriate legal approaches but stops short of developing a truly multicultural organization, intergroup conflicts are highly likely.

Reverse discrimination is the term used to describe inequities affecting members of the majority group as an outcome of programs designed to help underrepresented groups.

►MANAGEMENT AND THE INTERNET► | EEOC Uses Web Site to Inform Managers about Sexual Harassment

As you have learned in this chapter, the Equal Employment Opportunity Commission (EEOC) is a federal agency that enforces laws regarding fairness in recruiting and other management practices. The following information about sexual harassment is from the EEOC Web site and appears as an example of how managers can stay informed about EEOC issues by reviewing the EEOC's Web site.

Facts About Sexual Harassment

Sexual harassment is a form of sex discrimination that violates Title VII of the Civil Rights Act of 1964.

Unwelcome sexual advances, requests for sexual favors, and other verbal or physical conduct of a sexual nature constitutes sexual harassment when submission to or rejection of this conduct explicitly or implicitly affects an individual's employment, unreasonably interferes with an individual's work performance or creates an intimidating, hostile or offensive work environment.

Sexual harassment can occur in a variety of circumstances, including but not limited to the following:

The victim as well as the harasser may be a woman or a man. The victim does not have to be of the opposite sex.

The harasser can be the victim's supervisor, an agent of the employer, a supervisor in another area, a co-worker, or a non-employee.

The victim does not have to be the person harassed but could be anyone affected by the offensive conduct.

Unlawful sexual harassment may occur without economic injury to or discharge of the victim.

The harasser's conduct must be unwelcome.

It is helpful for the victim to directly inform the harasser that the conduct is unwelcome and must stop. The victim should use any employer complaint mechanism or grievance system available.

When investigating allegations of sexual harassment, EEOC looks at the whole record: the circumstances, such as the nature of the sexual advances, and the context in which the alleged incidents occurred. A determination on the allegations is made from the facts on a case-by-case basis.

Prevention is the best tool to eliminate sexual harassment in the workplace. Employers are encouraged to take steps necessary to prevent sexual harassment from occurring. They should clearly communicate to employees that sexual harassment will not be tolerated. They can do so by establishing an effective complaint or grievance process and taking immediate and appropriate action when an employee complains.

BACK TO THE CASE

Legal approaches alone cannot resolve all issues related to diversity. When Gary Parlin, the president of Ortho Pharmaceutical, consulted with Elsie Cross, his questions were aimed at discovering why his affirmative action policies were failing to retain minority employees. His company was investing time, energy, and money in recruiting, hiring, and training women and members of underrepresented groups only to lose them within a relatively short time. This is a common problem, and one that often goes unquestioned in organizations. Managerial monitoring of goal achievement and assessment of the effectiveness of present diversity policies are necessary to ensure that affirmative action is used to select and hire the best employees, rather than becoming simply a "paper tool" that does not lead to more effective business practices.

If a company's affirmative action policies are to be effective, managers must be held accountable for their implementation. As with any other organizational policy, these standards can be ignored, misused, or treated as a low priority. Sloppy recruitment and hiring practices are common misuses of affirmative action. Hiring women and minorities whose background, training, and personal goals are poorly matched to company needs and goals is sure to result in costly turnover. Inappropriate recruitment that emphasizes quotas rather than commitment to fair management practices damages both the company and minority employees.

►ORGANIZATIONAL COMMITMENT TO DIVERSITY

Figure 23.3 shows the range of organizational commitment to multiculturalism. At the bottom of the continuum are organizations that have committed resources, planning, and time to the ongoing shaping and sustaining of a multicultural organization. At the top of the continuum are organizations that make no efforts whatever to achieve diversity in their workforces. Most organizations fall somewhere between the extremes depicted in the figure.

Ignoring Differences   Some organizations make no effort to promote diversity and do not even bother to comply with affirmative action and EEOC standards. They are sending a strong message to their employees that the dynamics of difference are unimportant. By ignoring EEOC policies, they are sending an even more detrimental message to their managers: that it is permissible to maintain exclusionary practices.

FIGURE 23.3 ▶ Organizational diversity continuum

No diversity efforts:
- Noncompliance with affirmative action and EEOC

Diversity efforts based on:
- Compliance with affirmative action and EEOC policies
- Inconsistent enforcement and implementation (those who breach policies may not be sanctioned unless noncompliance results in legal action)
- Support of policies is not rewarded; organization relies on individual managers' interest or commitment

Diversity efforts based on:
- Compliance with and enforcement of affirmative action and EEOC policies
- No organizational supports with respect to education, training
- Inconsistent or poor managerial commitment

Diversity efforts based on:
- Narrowly defined affirmative action and EEOC policies combined with one-shot education and/or training programs
- Inconsistent managerial commitment; rewards not tied to effective implementation of diversity programs and goal achievement
- No attention directed toward organizational climate

Diversity efforts based on:
- Effective implementation of affirmative action and EEOC policies
- Ongoing education and training programs
- Managerial commitment tied to organizational rewards
- Minimal attention directed toward cultivating an inclusive and supportive organizational climate

Broad-based diversity efforts based on:
- Effective implementation of affirmative action and EEOC policies
- Organization-wide assessment and management's top-down commitment to diversity
- Managerial commitment tied to organizational rewards
- Ongoing processes of organization assessment and programs for the purpose of creating an organizational climate that is inclusive and supportive of diverse groups

Complying with External Policies   Some organizations base their diversity strategy solely on compliance with affirmative action and EEOC policies. They make no attempt to provide education and training for employees, nor do they use the organization's reward system to reinforce managerial commitment to diversity. Managers in some companies in this category breach company affirmative action and EEOC policies with impunity. When top management does not punish them, the likelihood of costly legal action against the organization rises.

Enforcing External Policies   Some organizations go so far as to enforce affirmative action and EEOC policies, but provide no organizational supports for education or training for diversity. Managerial commitment to a diverse workforce is either weak or inconsistent.

Responding Inadequately   Other organizations fully comply with affirmative action and EEOC policies, but define these policies quite narrowly. Organizational systems and structures are inadequate to support real organizational change. Education and training in diversity are sporadic, and managerial rewards for implementing diversity programs are inconsistent or nonexistent. Although these organizations may design some useful programs, they are unlikely to result in any long-term organizational change, so the organizational climate never becomes truly receptive to diverse groups.

Implementing Adequate Programs Some organizations effectively implement affirmative action and EEOC policies, provide ongoing education and training programs pertaining to diversity, and tie managerial rewards to success in meeting diversity goals and addressing diversity issues. However, such companies make only a minimal attempt to cultivate the kind of inclusive and supportive organizational climate diverse populations of employees will feel comfortable in.

Taking Effective Action The most effective diversity efforts are based on managerial implementation of affirmative action and EEOC policies that are developed in conjunction with an organization-wide assessment of the company's systems and structures. Such an assessment is necessary to determine how these systems and structures support or hinder diversity goals.

Generally, for such a comprehensive assessment to take place, top management must "buy" the idea that diversity is important to the company. Actually, support from the top is critical to all successful diversity efforts and underlies tying organizational rewards to managers' commitment to diversity. Ongoing assessment and continuing programs are also necessary to create an organizational climate that is inclusive and supportive of diverse groups.

BACK TO THE CASE

Managerial commitment is one of the most significant predictors of the success of company diversity initiatives. In the case of Ortho Pharmaceutical, it was Gary Parlin's interest in achieving excellence in all areas that prompted him to seek answers to a very costly company problem—high turnover among women and minority employees. Once an organizational assessment and diagnosis were made, Parlin discovered that there were serious performance breakdowns at the operational level.

He was quick to respond to the finding that recruiting problems were hindering the hiring of a diverse workforce. Having an overview and diagnosis of company strengths and weaknesses relating to diversity allowed Parlin and his staff of top managers to put in place an effective long-term plan for the company. Managerial commitment to this organizational plan resulted in a dramatic increase in upward mobility for women and minority workers at Ortho.

►PLURALISM

Pluralism is an environment in which cultural, group, and individual differences are acknowledged, accepted, and viewed as significant contributors to the entirety.

Pluralism refers to an environment in which differences are acknowledged, accepted, and seen as significant contributors to the entirety. A diverse workforce is most effective when managers are capable of guiding the organization toward achieving pluralism. Approaches, or strategies, to achieve effective workforce diversity have been classified into five major categories by Jean Kim of Stanford University:[16]

1. "Golden Rule" approach
2. Assimilation approach
3. "Righting-the-wrongs" approach
4. Culture-specific approach
5. Multicultural approach

Each approach is described briefly in the following sections.

"GOLDEN RULE" APPROACH The "Golden Rule" approach to diversity relies on the biblical dictate, "Do unto others as you would have them do unto you."[17] The major strength of this approach is that it emphasizes individual morality. Its major flaw is that individuals apply the Golden Rule from their own particular frame of reference without knowing the cultural expectations, traditions, and preferences of the other person.

One African American male manager recalled a situation in which he was having difficulty scheduling a work-related event. In exasperation, he volunteered to schedule the event on Saturday. He was reminded by another employee that many of the company's Jewish employees went to religious services on Saturday. He was initially surprised—then somewhat embarrassed—that he had simply assumed that "all people" attended "church" on Sunday.

ASSIMILATION APPROACH The assimilation approach advocates shaping organization members to fit the existing culture of the organization. This approach pressures employees who do not belong to the dominant culture to conform—at the expense of renouncing their own cultures and worldviews. The end result is the creation of a homogeneous culture that suppresses the creativity and diversity of views that could benefit the organization.

One African American woman in middle management said, "I always felt uncomfortable in very formal meetings. I tend to be very animated when I talk, and this is not the norm for the company. Until I became more comfortable with myself and my style, I felt inhibited. I was tempted to try to change my style to fit in."

"RIGHTING-THE-WRONGS" APPROACH "Righting-the wrongs" is an approach that addresses past injustices experienced by a particular group. When a group's history places its members at a disadvantage for achieving career success and mobility, policies are developed to create a more equitable set of conditions. For example, the original migration of African Americans to the United States was forced upon them as slaves. Righting-the-wrongs approaches are designed to compensate for the damages African Americans have suffered because of historical inequalities.

This approach most closely parallels the affirmative action policies discussed in chapter 12. It goes beyond affirmative action, however, in that it emphasizes tapping the unique talents of each group in the service of organizational productivity.

CULTURE-SPECIFIC APPROACH The culture-specific approach teaches employees the norms and practices of another culture to prepare them to interact with people from that culture effectively. This approach is often used to help employees prepare for international assignments. The problem with it is that it usually fails to give employees a genuine appreciation for the culture they are about to encounter.

Stewart Black and Hal Gergerson, in their study of managers on assignment in foreign countries, found that some identify much more with their parent firm than with the local operation.[18] One male manager, for instance, after spending two years opening retail outlets

The multicultural approach at Pitney-Bowes, the world's largest maker of postal equipment, is evident in its training programs. Nearly 20 languages are spoken at the company's Stamford, Connecticut, manufacturing plant; human resources managers also discovered that 40 percent of the plant's workers could read only at the fourth-grade level and that 65 percent needed basic-math training. Pitney-Bowes thus collaborated with a local community college to set up a seven-stage training program. Today, many employees now work on teams with engineers, order materials, and monitor product quality.

throughout Europe, viewed Europeans as "lazy and slow to respond to directives." Obviously, his training and preparation had failed to help him adjust to European host countries or to appreciate their peoples and cultures.

MULTICULTURAL APPROACH   The multicultural approach gives employees the opportunity to develop an appreciation for both differences of culture and variations in personal characteristics. This approach focuses on how interpersonal skills and attitudinal changes relate to organizational performance. One of its strengths is that it assumes the organization itself—as well as individuals working within it—will be required to change in order to accommodate the diversity of the organization's workforce.

The multicultural approach is probably the most effective approach to pluralism because it advocates change on the part of management, employees, and organization systems and structures. It has the added advantage of stressing the idea that equity demands making some efforts to "right the wrongs" so that underrepresented groups will be fairly included throughout the organization.

THE ROLE OF THE MANAGER

Managers play an essential role in tapping the potential capacities of each person within their departments. To do this requires competencies that are anchored in the four basic management functions of planning, organizing, influencing, and controlling. In this context, planning refers to the manager's role in developing programs to promote diversity, while organizing, influencing, and controlling, of course, take place in the implementation phases of those programs.

PLANNING   Recall from chapter 9 that planning is a specific action proposed to help the organization achieve its objectives. It is an ongoing process that includes troubleshooting and continually defining areas where improvements can be made. Planning for diversity may involve selecting diversity training programs for the organization or setting diversity goals for employees within the department.

Setting recruitment goals for members of underrepresented groups is a key component of diversity planning. If top management has identified Hispanics as an underrepresented group within the company, every manager throughout the company will need to collaborate with the human resources department to achieve the organizational goal of higher Hispanic representation. For example, a manager might establish goals and objectives for the increased representation of this group within five years. To achieve this five-year vision, the manager will need to set benchmark goals for each year.

ORGANIZING   Chapter 10 defined organizing as the process of establishing orderly uses for all resources within the management system. To achieve a diverse workplace, managers have to work with human resource professionals in the areas of recruitment, hiring, and retention so that the best match is made between the company and the employees it hires. Managerial responsibilities in this area may include establishing task forces or committees to explore issues and provide ideas, carefully choosing work assignments to support the career development of all employees, and evaluating the extent to which diversity goals are being achieved.

After managers have begun hiring from a diverse pool of employees, they will need to focus on retaining them. This means paying attention to the many concerns of a diverse workforce. In the case of working women and men with families, skillfully using the organization's resources to support their need for day care for dependents, allowing flexible work arrangements in keeping with company policy, and assigning and reassigning work responsibilities equitably to accommodate family leave usage are all examples of managers applying the organizing function.

INFLUENCING   Chapter 20 defined influencing as the process of guiding the activities of organization members in appropriate directions. Integral to this management function are an effective leadership style, good communication skills, knowledge about how to motivate others, and an understanding of the organization's culture and group dynamics. In the area of diversity, influencing organization members means that managers must not only encourage and support employees to participate constructively in a diverse work environment, but must themselves engage in the career development and training processes that will give them the skills to facilitate the smooth operation of a diverse work community.

Managers are accountable as well for informing their employees of breaches of organizational policy and etiquette. Let us assume that the diversity strategy selected by top management includes educating employees about organizational policies concerning diversity (e.g., making sure that employees understand what constitutes sexual harassment) as well as providing workshops for employees on specific cultural diversity issues. The manager's role in this case would be to hold employees accountable for learning about company diversity policies and complying with them. This could be accomplished by consulting with staff and holding regular group meetings and one-on-one meetings when necessary. To encourage participation in diversity workshops, the manager may need to communicate to employees the importance the organization places on this knowledge base. Alternatively, the manager might choose to tie organizational rewards to the development of diversity competencies. Examples of such rewards are giving employees public praise or recognition and providing workers with opportunities to use their diversity skills on desirable work assignments.

CONTROLLING Overseeing compliance with the legal stipulations of EEOC and affirmative action is one aspect of the controlling function in the area of diversity. Chapter 19 defines controlling as the set of activities that make something happen as planned. Hence the evaluation activities necessary to assess diversity efforts are part of the controlling role that managers play in shaping a multicultural workforce.

Managers may find this function the most difficult one of the four to execute. It is hard to evaluate planned-change approaches in general, and it is particularly hard to do so in the area of diversity. Many times the most successful diversity approaches reveal more problems as employees begin to speak openly about their concerns. Moreover, subtle attitudinal changes in one group's perception of another group are very difficult to measure. What *can* be accurately measured are the outcome variables of turnover, representation of women, minorities, and other underrepresented groups at all levels of the company, and legal problems stemming from inappropriate or illegal behaviors (e.g., discrimination and sexual harassment).

Managers engaged in the controlling function in the area of diversity need to continually monitor their units' progress with respect to diversity goals and standards. They must decide what control measures to use (e.g., indicators of productivity, turnover, absenteeism, or promotion) and how to interpret the information these measures yield in light of diversity goals and standards.

For example, a manager may need to assess whether the low rate of promotions for African American men in her department is due to subtle biases toward this group or group members' poor performance compared to others in the department. She may find she needs to explore current organizational dynamics, as well as create effective supports for this group. Such supports might include fostering greater social acceptance of African American men among other employees, learning more about the African American male's bicultural experience in the company, making mentoring or other opportunities available to members of this group, and providing them with some specific job-related training.

► MANAGEMENT DEVELOPMENT AND DIVERSITY TRAINING

Given the complex set of managerial skills needed to promote diversity, it is obvious that managers themselves will need organizational support if the company is to achieve its diversity goals. One important component of the diversity strategy of a large number of companies is diversity training. **Diversity training** is a learning process designed to raise managers' awareness and develop their competencies to deal with the issues endemic to managing a diverse workforce.

Diversity training is a learning process designed to raise managers' awareness and develop their competencies to deal with the issues endemic to managing a diverse workforce.

BASIC THEMES OF DIVERSITY TRAINING Chapter 12 refers to training as the process of developing qualities in human resources that will make them more productive and better able to contribute to organizational goal attainment. Some companies develop intensive programs for management and less intensive, more generalized programs for other employees. As stated in chapter 12, such programs generally focus on the following five components or themes:

1. Behavioral awareness
2. Acknowledgment of biases and stereotypes
3. Focus on job performance
4. Avoidance of assumptions
5. Modification of policy and procedure manuals

STAGES IN MANAGING A DIVERSE WORKFORCE Donaldson and Scannell, authors of *Human Resource Development: The New Trainer's Guide,* have developed a four-stage model to describe how managers progress in managing a diverse workforce.[19] In the first stage, known as "unconscious incompetence," managers are unaware of behaviors they engage in that are problematic for members of other groups. In the second stage, "conscious incompetence," managers go through a learning process in which they become conscious of behaviors that make them incompetent in their interactions with members of diverse groups.

The third stage is one of becoming "consciously competent": Managers learn how to interact with diverse groups and cultures by deliberately thinking about how to behave. In the last stage, "unconscious competence," managers have internalized these new behaviors and feel so comfortable relating to others different from themselves that they need to devote little conscious effort to doing so:

> Managers who have progressed to the "unconscious competence" stage will be the most effective with respect to interacting in a diverse workforce. Effective interaction is key to carrying out the four management functions previously discussed.

Table 23.2 summarizes our discussion of the challenges facing those who manage a diverse workforce. Managers, who are generally responsible for controlling organizational goals and outcomes, are accountable for understanding these diversity challenges and recognizing the dynamics described here. In addition to treating employees fairly, they must influence other employees to cooperate with the company's diversity goals.

Understanding and Influencing Employee Responses Managers cannot rise to the challenge of managing a diverse workforce unless they recognize that many employees have difficulties in coping with diversity. Among these difficulties are natural resistance to change, ethnocentrism, and lack of information and outright misinformation about other groups, as well as prejudices, biases, and stereotypes. Some employees lack the motivation to understand and cope with cultural differences—which, after all, requires time, energy, and a willingness to take some emotional risks.

Another problem is that employees often receive no social rewards (e.g., peer support and approval) or concrete rewards (e.g., financial compensation or career opportunities) for cooperating with the organization's diversity policies.

For all these difficulties, managers cannot afford to ignore or mismanage diversity issues because the cost of doing so is interpersonal and intergroup conflicts. These conflicts very often affect the functioning of the work group by destroying cohesiveness and causing communications problems and employee stress.

Managers who are determined to deal effectively with their diverse workforce can usually obtain organizational support. One primary support is education and training programs designed to help employees work through their difficulties in coping with diversity. Besides recommending such programs to their employees, managers may find it helpful to enroll in available programs themselves.

Getting Top-Down Support Another very important source of support for managers dealing with diversity issues is top management. Organizations that provide top-down support are more likely to boast the following features:

1. Managers skilled at working with a diverse workforce
2. Effective education and diversity training programs

TABLE 23.2	Organizational Challenges and Supports Related to Managing a Diverse Workforce

Organizational Challenges	Organizational Supports
Employees Difficulties in Coping with Cultural Diversity ▶ Resistance to change ▶ Enthnocentrism ▶ Lack of information and misinformation ▶ Prejudices, biases, and stereotypes **Reasons Employees Are Unmotivated to Understand Cultural Differences** ▶ Lack of time and energy and unwillingness to assume the emotional risk necessary to explore issues of diversity ▶ Absence of social or concrete rewards for investing in diversity work (e.g., lack of peer support and monetary rewards, unclear linkage between multicultural competence and career mobility) ▶ Interpersonal and intergroup conflicts arising when diversity issues are either ignored or mismanaged **Work Group Problems** ▶ Lack of cohesiveness ▶ Communication problems ▶ Employee stress	**Educational Programs and Training to Assist Employees in Working Through Difficulties** **Top-Down Management Support for Diversity** ▶ Managers who have diversity skills and competence ▶ Education and training ▶ Awareness raising ▶ Peer support ▶ Organizational climate that support diversity ▶ Open communication with manager about diversity issues ▶ Recognition for employee development of diversity skills and competencies ▶ Recognition for employee contributions to diversity goals ▶ Organizational rewards for managers' implementation of organizational diversity goals and objectives

3. An organizational climate that promotes diversity and fosters peer support for exploring diversity issues
4. Open communication between employees and managers about diversity issues
5. Recognition for employees' development of diversity skills and competencies
6. Recognition for employee contributions to diversity goals
7. Organizational rewards for managers' implementation of organizational diversity goals and objectives

BACK TO THE CASE

In most organizations, managers are given more extensive diversity training than other employees because they are the key to implementing diversity initiatives. They not only need to effectively apply the four management functions to diversity-related tasks; they also have to recognize their own levels of competency in this area.

Managers who know how to interact with people of other cultures and identify groups are more effective members of the management team than those who do not have this multicultural competence. They are better able to foster the kind of culture change that organizations like Ortho Pharmaceutical are determined to implement.

One of the major benefits of cultivating diversity is that the organization becomes safer for the expression of differences and more open to the kinds of new ideas that surface through disagreement and open communication. One African American market research manager at Ortho, for example, described the company as a place where he can disagree with others without being penalized. It is a place where he feels he can be himself—*and* be effective.

Today the distribution of women and minorities throughout Ortho Pharmaceutical is more equitable, but such improvements have not changed the company's culture very much, for this kind of subtle change takes time. To Ortho's credit, its top managers' promotion of diversity has extended beyond increasing the numerical presence of women and minorities at all organizational levels. Management seems to genuinely value difference, is willing to incorporate diverse employees into the management team, and has tied organizational rewards to diversity efforts. This complex long-term strategy is having positive results at Ortho.

For updated information on the topics in this chapter, Internet exercises, links to related Internet sites, an interactive study guide, and more, visit our companion Web site at

http://www.prenhall.com/certo

Additional information can be found on the inside front and back covers of this text.

ACTION SUMMARY

Reread the learning objectives below. Each objective is followed by questions. Answering these questions accurately will help you retain the most important concepts discussed in this chapter. After answering each question, check your answer against the answer key at the end of this chapter. (*Hint:* If you have any doubts regarding the correct response, consult the page number that follows the answer.)

Circle:

From studying this chapter, I will attempt to acquire

1. A definition of diversity and an understanding of its importance in the corporate structure.

   T F   **a.** Diversity refers to characteristics that shape people's identifies and the experiences they have in society.

   a b c d e   **b.** The following is *not* true of workforce diversity: (a) it is a new issue (b) it stems from workforce demographics (c) it involves developing an inclusive organization (d) it includes age and physical ability (e) it is a strength that can be built on.

2. An understanding of the advantages of having a diverse workforce.

   a b c d e   **a.** All of the following are advantages of a diverse workforce *except:* (a) employees who develop multicultural competencies (b) cost savings (c) similarity in thinking and approaches (d) increased productivity (e) improved ability to gain and keep market share.

   T F   **b.** A diverse workforce results in a "better quality of management" because managers are recruited from a wider pool of talent.

3. An awareness of the challenges facing managers within a diverse workforce.

   a b c d e   **a.** Challenges facing American corporations include all of the following *except:* (a) the need to look beyond traditional sources of personnel (b) the need to assess the opportunities suggested by demographic projections (c) the need to adapt to changes in the structure of the workforce (d) the need to prepare for a huge influx of younger workers by the year 2000 (e) the need to improve the educational preparation of all workers.

   a b c d e   **b.** The following is a potential challenge facing American business leaders: (a) reconciling the conflicting needs of women, work, and families (b) fully assimilating into the economy African American and Hispanic workers (c) maintaining the dynamism of an aging workforce (d) accelerating productivity increases in service industries (e) all of the above.

   a b c d e   **c.** The dynamics of coping with diverse populations include: (a) "the glass ceiling" (b) tokenism (c) bicultural stress (d) ethnocentrism (e) all of the above.

4. An understanding of the strategies for promoting diversity in organizations.

T F **a.** Following the appropriate affirmative action and EEOC guidelines will resolve intergroup conflicts and result in an effectively diverse organization.

a b c d e **b.** The following is true regarding strategies for promoting diversity in organizations: (a) organizations vary widely with respect to the strategies they employ (b) all organizations comply with affirmative action and EEOC guidelines (c) exclusionary practices have no effect on an organization (d) diversity programs always result in comprehensive culture change (e) all of the above.

5. Insights into the role of the manager in promoting diversity in the organization.

a b c d e **a.** A manager engaged in the four functions of management with respect to diversity might take all of the following actions *except:* (a) establishing hiring goals for specific underrepresented groups (b) granting family leave time (c) communicating the importance of diversity training (d) letting employees know they are not accountable for knowing diversity-related policies (e) assessing progress toward diversity goals.

T F **b.** In a diverse organization, the highest level of diversity competence is described as "conscious competence."

INTRODUCTORY CASE WRAP-UP

CASE DISCUSSSION QUESTIONS

"Ortho Pharmaceutical: 'Showcase' for Cultural Diversity" (p. 527) and its related Back-to-the Case sections were written to help you better understand the management concepts contained in this chapter. Answer the following discussion questions about this Introductory Case to enrich your understanding of the chapter content:

1. How important to an organization such as Ortho Pharmaceutical is the implementation of workforce diversity goals? Explain.

2. On the basis of the facts discussed in the Introductory Case, what strengths has Ortho Pharmaceutical gained from cultivating diversity within the company?

3. On the basis of the facts discussed in the Introductory Case, what organizational challenges does Ortho Pharmaceutical face? Discuss the organizational supports available to managers addressing these challenges.

SKILLS EXERCISE: DEFENDING ADVANTAGES OF A DIVERSE WORKFORCE

The Introductory Case outlines several workforce diversity issues at Ortho Pharmaceutical. As a manager at this company, use Table 23.1 as a guide for defending why its diverse workforce will contribute to its success. In your explanation, be sure to list the items in this table with which you agree and tell why. Also, list the items in this table with which you disagree and tell why.

ISSUES FOR REVIEW AND DISCUSSION

1. What is diversity?
2. Why is diversity an important contemporary management issue?
3. List the six challenges facing American businesses according to *Workforce 2000.*
4. Define *pluralism.*
5. Describe the five major approaches organizations can employ in responding to diversity.
6. List the advantages of a diverse workforce.
7. List the managerial challenges presented by a diverse workforce.
8. Give a detailed description of the dynamics encountered by diverse populations in the workplace.

9. Outline the organizational supports available to help managers address the challenges of a diverse workforce.
10. Describe the range of strategies organizations employ to implement workforce diversity.
11. Explain the concept of reverse discrimination.
12. What is the relationship between the four management functions and the implementation of diversity goals?
13. Why should managers undergo diversity training?
14. What is the meaning of "unconscious competence" and why is it desirable for managers?

1. **a.** T, p. 528
   b. a, p. 528
2. **a.** c, pp. 529–530
   b. T, p. 530

3. **a.** d, p. 531
   b. e, p. 531
   c. e, pp. 533–535

4. **a.** F, p. 537
   b. a, pp. 535–540

5. **a.** d, pp. 542–543
   b. F, p. 544

CASE STUDY: Levi Strauss: Valuing Diversity

In the 1987 study *Workforce 2000: Work and Workers for the Twenty-First Century,* an executive-shaking statistic was projected: By the year 2000, only 15 percent of the people entering the workforce will be American-born white males. Companies rushed to respond, hiring consultants and trainees to sensitize employees to racial and gender differences. Unfortunately, many of these efforts misfired—group stereotypes were rigidified, racial and gender groups were pitted against one another, or white males became workplace scapegoats for any and all inequalities.

Some companies have begun to change their approaches to the increasing diversity of the U.S. workplace. In fact, many have begun to make *diversity* the watchword for broader efforts to change corporate culture. Consider the case of Levi Strauss & Company. In 1994, instead of focusing simply on race or gender, Levi Strauss adopted a new management policy called by CEO Robert D. Haas "responsible commercial success." Under Haas' direction, a set of written corporate "aspirations" was created by top management to guide all major company decisions. According to a report in *Business Week* magazine, these guidelines describe a policy that not only "aspires" to create tangible opportunities for minority employees at Levi Strauss, but also sets out to "make each of [Strauss'] workers, from the factory floor on up, feel as if they are an integral part of the making and selling of blue jeans. [Management hoped] to ensure that all views on all issues are heard and respected."

In support of his "aspirations," Haas cited a study issued by Gordon Group, Inc., for the California Public Employees' Retirement System. According to this report, "Companies that involve employees more often in decision-making boast stronger market valuations than those that don't." However, Levi Strauss soon found that putting this idea into practice proved quite expensive. In 1985, Haas, who had become chairman and CEO the year before, decided to avert any possible takeover bids by taking Levi Strauss private in a leveraged buyout. His action saddled the company with $1.6 billion in debt, cost 6,000 jobs, and forced the closing of 26 plants. In the ensuing decade, however, Haas' action paid off. Since the buyout, profits have shaved corporate debt considerably. Record sales and earnings for the years between 1988 and 1993 culminated in a 36 percent rise in profits in 1993, and the estimated appreciation in stock values since 1985 is 1300 percent.

Implementing Haas' vision has not been easy, however. Perhaps distracted by an array of new managing techniques, Levi's has allowed its product development and customer service in the United States to slip since setting records in 1993. However, Haas believes the problem would be even worse were it not for the company's encouragement of the free exchange of ideas among its many employees. As Daniel M. Chew, Levi's director of corporate marketing, points out, "A diverse workforce, unafraid to volunteer idiosyncratic ideas and opinions, leads to better marketing decisions."

Consider Levi's "501 Blues" TV ads. They worked well with Levi's many hip, young customers. However, Levi's Hispanic employees were put off by them. They advised the company to pitch an image of family and friends—camaraderie rather than rugged individualism—to their community. These changes in the ads paid off: Sales in the Hispanic community boomed.

Many of Levi's employees view the company's new management policy changes with mixed feelings. Louis Kirtman, an African American who has worked as an executive at Levi's since the early 1980s, sees Haas' "aspirations" as positive. Before the change, Kirtman had seen African American executives whom he thought were highly qualified passed over for plum jobs at Levi's. In fact, his own career seemed stalled on a midlevel management plateau until 1994, when he became president of Levi's Britannia Sportswear division and stood only a step away from the company's senior management ranks.

Managing according to the new values is seen by many as a tough task, producing often contradictory results. The loss of old-boy networks, the pressure to assume new responsibilities and new ways of thinking, and the problems that result when values seem to interfere with bottom-line figures—all such changes can impose negative pressure. Empowerment and teamwork can be alien, uncomfortable concepts for those who have spent their working lives taking and giving orders.

Haas' controversial "aspirations" cannot yet be finally evaluated. Since 1984, the company has doubled the percentage of minority managers to 36 percent and has boosted the ranks of women in management from 32 to 54 percent. Recent marketing successes appear to support the belief that the cultivation of a workplace culture devoted to diversity and empowerment is making Levi's more responsive in the marketplace. Bankers are happy with the company's feat of shaving its debt to 4.6 percent of total capital. Haas admits that his company is "far from perfect. But," he insists, "the goal is out there, and it's worth striving for."

QUESTIONS

1. According to the text, diversity is the best way for a company to gain and keep market share. How does the experience of Levi Strauss bear this out? What kind of changes in minority management has Levi's seen in recent years? What corresponding changes in the company's marketing programs would you expect to see?

2. Levi's diverse workforce ethic could also pay off in international markets. Use information from the text to give reasons to support or refute this speculation.

3. Has Bob Haas' influence on his company's corporate community improved the company's bottom line? Explain.

In this segment we find Hal, Karen, and John discussing John's feelings about how his first three months on the job have gone. Do you remember the questions John had in his interview with Hal and Karen (part I) about planning and efficiency issues at Quicktakes? In this discussion we see John expressing concern about these issues again, as well as concerns related to issues of effectiveness.

An interesting aspect of John's comments is the perspective in which he formulates his ideas. John has identified some very specific concerns about how particular jobs or tasks are completed, but he also seems to be interested in a bigger picture. He seems to be interested in something more than how specific employees do their job. The discussion about effectiveness and efficiency quickly turns to a broader discussion of how the company's management looks at the importance of and relationship among certain jobs, and also at issues of motivation.

The meeting takes a turn in a different direction when John brings up an opportunity he sees in going after some markets where Quicktakes does not do much. It is interesting to find out that Quicktakes has previously tried to address this segment, culturally targeted video, with little success. The real interesting thing in this discussion is the subtle change in the way the talk goes. In previous discussions we saw the management team at Quicktakes just talking about planning issues, with little discussion of solutions. In this segment, we see Hal, Karen, and John talking about what might have limited success in the past and ways that they can try to make a second attempt in this market. The managers at Quicktakes seem to be getting interested in increasing the productivity, efficiency, and quality of what they are doing. Maybe you are not the only one using this textbook—sounds like Quicktakes is using it too!

QUESTIONS

1. John points out some concerns with certain parts of the business and how well certain jobs get done. Hal's reaction is to get the specific people responsible into the meeting. John discourages this and suggests that the problems might not really be related to the individuals involved. What do you think John is really saying? Do you think he is right? If you were hired by Quicktakes as a consultant to help with some of these issues, what might you recommend?

2. John identifies some issues in motivating people in the company to be more concerned about how efficiently things get done and the quality of what goes out the door. What types of policies or processes do you think are in place at Quicktakes to deal with these types of concerns? Do you think they are adequate? Why or why not?

3. You heard a discussion about issues Quicktakes has had in targeting culturally specific markets. Why do you think things might not have worked so well for them in these markets? What do you think about the ideas they are considering now? What else would you tell them to do?

GLOSSARY

Accountability refers to the management philosophy whereby individuals are held liable, or accountable, for how well they use their authority or live up to their responsibility of performing predetermined activities. *p. 243*

Activities are specified sets of behavior within a project. *p. 203*

Adjourning the fifth and last stage of the team development process, is the stage in which the team finishes its job and prepares to disband. *p. 391*

Affirmative action programs are organizational programs whose basic purpose is to eliminate barriers against and increase employment opportunities for underutilized or disadvantaged individuals. *p. 262*

Alderfer's ERG theory is an explanation of human needs that divides them into three basic types: existence needs, relatedness needs, and growth needs. *p. 359*

Appropriate human resources are the individuals in the organization who make a valuable contribution to management system goal attainment. *p. 256*

Argyris' maturity-immaturity continuum is a concept that furnishes insights into human needs by focusing on an individual's natural progress from immaturity to maturity. *p. 359*

Assessment center is a program in which participants engage in, and are evaluated on, a number of individual and group exercises constructed to simulate important activities at the organizational levels to which they aspire. *p. 265*

Attitude is a predisposition to react to a situation, person, or concept with a particular response. *p. 402*

Attribution is the process by which people *interpret* the behavior of others by assigning to it motives or causes. *p. 409*

Attribution error is the tendency to overestimate internal causes of behavior and underestimate external ones when judging other people's behavior. *p. 411*

Authority is the right to perform or command. *p. 239*

Behavior modification is a program that focuses on managing human activity by controlling the consequences of performing that activity. *p. 367*

Behavioral approach to management is a management approach that emphasizes increasing organizational success by focusing on human variables within the organization. *p. 32*

Beliefs are accepted facts or truths about an object or person that have been gained from either direct experience or a secondary source. *p. 402*

Bicultural stress is stress resulting from having to cope with membership in two cultures simultaneously. *p. 534*

Brainstorming is a group decision-making process in which negative feedback on any suggested alternative to any group member is forbidden until all group members have presented alternatives that they perceive as valuable. *p. 158*

Breakeven analysis is a control tool that summarizes the various levels of profit or loss associated with various levels of production. *p. 462*

Breakeven point is that level of production where the total revenue of an organization equals its total costs. *p. 462*

Budget is a control tool that outlines how funds will be obtained and spent in a given period. *p. 194, 458*

Bureaucracy is the term Max Weber used to describe a management system characterized by detailed procedures and rules, a clearly outlined organizational hierarchy, and impersonal relationships among organization members. *p. 216*

Business portfolio analysis is the development of business-related strategy based primarily on the market share of businesses and the growth of markets in which businesses exist. *p. 176*

Capacity strategy is an operational plan of action aimed at providing the organization with the right facilities to produce the needed output at the right time. *p. 451*

Career is a sequence of work-related positions occupied by a person over the course of a lifetime. *p. 12*

Career plateauing is a period of little or no apparent progress in the growth of a career. *p. 13*

Centralization refers to the situation in which a minimal number of job activities and a minimal amount of authority are delegated to subordinates. *p. 247*

Change agent is an individual inside or outside the organization who tries to modify an existing organizational situation. *p. 280*

Changing an organization is the process of modifying an existing organization to increase organizational effectiveness. *p. 278*

Classical approach to management is a management approach that emphasizes organizational efficiency to increase organizational success. *p. 26*

Classical organizing theory comprises the cumulative insights of early management writers on how organizational resources can best be used to enhance goal attainment. *p. 216*

Closed system is one that is not influenced by, and does not interact with, its environment. *p. 37*

Coaching is leadership that instructs followers on how to meet the special organizational challenges they face. *p. 344*

Code of ethics is a formal statement that acts as a guide for making decisions and acting within an organization. *p. 66*

Cognitive learning an approach theory that focuses on thought processes, assumes that human beings have a high capacity to act in a purposeful manner, and so to choose behaviors that will enable them to achieve long-run goals. *p. 414*

Command group is a formal group that is outlined in the chain of command on an organization chart. Command groups handle routine activities. *p. 377*

Commitment principle is a management guideline that advises managers to commit funds for planning only if they can anticipate, in the foreseeable future, a return on planning expenses as a result of the long-range planning analysis. *p. 166*

Committee is a task group that is charged with performing some type of specific activity. *p. 378*

Communication is the process of sharing information with other individuals. *p. 307*

Communication macrobarriers are factors hindering successful communication that relate primarily to the communication environment and the larger world in which communication takes place. *p. 309*

Communication microbarriers are factors hindering successful communication that relate primarily to such variables as the communication message, the source, and the destination. *p. 310*

Complete certainty condition is the decision-making situation in which the decision maker knows exactly what the results of an implemented alternative will be. *p. 154*

Complete uncertainty condition is the decision-making situation in which the decision maker has absolutely no idea what the results of an implemented alternative will be. *p. 154*

Comprehensive analysis of management involves studying the management function as a whole. *p. 30*

Computer is an electronic tool capable of accepting data, interpreting data, performing ordered operations on data, and reporting on the outcome of these operations. Computers are extremely helpful in generating information from raw data. *p. 484*

Computer-aided design (CAD) is a computerized technique for designing new products or modifying existing ones. *p. 466*

Computer-aided manufacturing (CAM) is a technique that employs computers to plan and program equipment used in the production and inspection of manufactured items. *p. 466*

Computer network is a system of two or more connected computers that allows computer users to communicate, cooperate, and share resources. *p. 489*

Conceptual skills are skills involving the ability to see the organization as a whole. *p. 11*

Concurrent control is control that takes place as some unit of work is being performed. *p. 430*

Consensus is agreement on a decision by all individuals involved in making that decision. *p. 147*

Consideration behavior is leadership behavior that reflects friendship, mutual trust, respect, and warmth in the relationship between leader and followers. *p. 334*

Content theories of motivation are explanations of motivation that emphasize people's internal characteristics. *p. 354*

Contingency approach to management is a management approach emphasizing that what managers do in practice depends on a given set of circumstances—a situation. *p. 36*

Contingency theory of leadership is a leadership concept that hypothesizes that, in any given leadership situation, success is determined primarily by (1) the degree to which the task being performed by the followers is structured, (2) the degree of position power possessed by the leader, and (3) the type of relationship that exists between the leader and the followers. *p. 339*

Control is making something happen the way it was planned to happen. *p. 422*

Control function is computer activities that dictate the order in which other computer functions are performed. *p. 486*

Controller is the staff person whose basic responsibility is to assist line managers with the controlling function by gathering appropriate information and generating necessary reports that reflect this information. *p. 431*

Controlling is the process managers go through to control. It is a systematic effort to compare performance to predetermined standards, plans, or objectives to determine whether performance is in line with those standards or needs to be corrected. *p. 422*

Control tool is a specific procedure or technique that presents pertinent organizational information in a way that helps managers to develop and implement an appropriate control strategy. *p. 461*

Coordination is the orderly arrangement of group effort to provide unity of action in the pursuit of a common purpose. It involves encouraging the completion of individual portions of a task in an appropriate, synchronized order. *p. 222*

Corporate culture is a set of shared values and beliefs that organization members have regarding the functioning and existence of their organization. *p. 393*

Corporate social responsibility is the managerial obligation to take action that protects and improves both the welfare of society as a whole and the interests of the organization. *p. 48*

Corrective action is managerial activity aimed at bringing organizational performance up to the level of performance standards. *p. 428*

Cost-benefit analysis is the process of comparing the cost of some activity with the benefit or revenue that results from the activity to determine the activity's total worth to the organization. *p. 432*

Cost leadership is a strategy that focuses on making an organization more competitive by producing products more cheaply than competitors can. *p. 178*

Creativity is the ability to combine ideas in a unique way or to make useful associations among ideas. *p. 519*

Critical path is the sequence of events and activities within a program evaluation and review technique (PERT) network that requires the longest period of time to complete. *p. 203*

Critical question analysis is a strategy development tool that consists of answering basic questions about the present purposes and objectives of the organization, its present direction and environment, and actions that can be taken to achieve organizational objectives in the future. *p. 175*

Cross-functional team is an organizational team composed of people from different functional areas of the organization who are all focused on a specified objective. *p. 389*

Data are facts or statistics. *p. 472*

Database is a reservoir of corporate facts consistently organized to fit the information needs of a variety of organization members. *p. 487*

Decentralization refers to the situation in which a significant number of job activities and a maximum amount of authority are delegated to subordinates. *p. 247*

Decision is a choice made between two or more available alternatives. *p. 144*

Decision-making process comprises the steps the decision maker takes to make a decision. *p. 150*

Decision tree is a graphic decision-making tool typically used to evaluate decisions involving a series of steps. *p. 156*

Decision tree analysis is a statistical and graphical multiphased decision-making technique that shows the sequence and interdependence of decisions. *p. 465*

Decline stage is the fourth and last stage in career evolution; it occurs near retirement age, when individuals of about 65 years of age show declining productivity. *p. 13*

Decoder/destination is the person or persons in the interpersonal communication situation with whom the source is attempting to share information. *p. 308*

Delegation is the process of assigning job activities and related authority to specific individuals in the organization. *p. 244*

Delphi technique is a group decision-making process that involves circulating questionnaires on a specific problem among group members, sharing the questionnaire results with them, and then continuing to recirculate and refine individual responses until a consensus regarding the problem is reached. *p. 159*

Demographics are the statistical characteristics of a population. Organizational strategy should reflect demographics. *p. 170*

Department is a unique group of resources established by management to perform some organizational task. *p. 217*

Departmentalization is the process of establishing departments within the management system. *p. 217*

Dialogue capability is the ability of an MDSS user to interact with an MDSS. *p. 488*

Differentiation is a strategy that focuses on making an organization more competitive by developing a product or products that customers perceive as being different from products offered by competitors. *p. 178*

Direct investing is using the assets of one company to purchase the operating assets of another company. *p. 87*

Discrimination is the act of treating an issue, person, or behavior unjustly or inequitably on the basis of stereotypes or prejudices. *p. 533*

Diversity is the degree of basic human differences among a given population. Major areas of diversity are gender, race, ethnicity, religion, social class, physical ability, sexual orientation, and age. *p. 528*

Diversity training is a learning process designed to raise managers' awareness and develop their competencies to deal with the issues endemic to managing a diverse workforce. *p. 543*

Divestiture is a strategy adopted to eliminate a strategic business unit that is not generating a satisfactory amount of business and has little hope of doing so in the future. *p. 180*

Division of labor is the assignment of various portions of a particular task among a number of organization members. Division of labor calls for specialization. *p. 222*

Domestic organization is a company that essentially operates within a single country. *p. 78*

Downward organizational communication is communication that flows from any point on an organization chart downward to another point on the organization chart. *p. 315*

Economics is the science that focuses on understanding how people of a particular community or nation produce, distribute, and use various goods and services. *p. 168*

Effectiveness is the degree to which managers attain organizational objectives; it is doing the right things. *p. 451*

Efficiency is the degree to which organizational resources contribute to production; it is doing things right. *p. 451*

E-mail is a computerized information system that allows individuals the electronic capacity to create, edit, and send messages to one another. *p. 493*

Employee-centered behavior is leader behavior that focuses primarily on subordinates as people. *p. 335*

Entrepreneurial leadership is leadership that is based on the attitude that the leader is self-employed. *p. 345*

Environmental analysis is the study of the organizational environment to pinpoint environmental factors that can significantly influence organizational operations. *p. 168*

Equal Employment Opportunity Commission (EEOC) is an agency established to enforce federal laws regulating recruiting and other employment practices. *p. 261*

Equity theory of motivation is an explanation of motivation that emphasizes the individual's perceived fairness of an employment situation and how perceived inequities can cause certain behaviors. *p. 356*

Establishment stage is the second stage in career evolution; individuals of about 25 to 45 years of age typically start to become more productive, or higher performers. *p. 12*

Esteem needs are Maslow's fourth set of human needs—including the desires for self-respect and respect from others. *p. 359*

Ethics is our concern for good behavior; our obligation to consider not only our own personal well-being but also that of other human beings. *p. 65*

Ethnocentric attitude reflects the belief that multinational corporations should regard home-country management practices as superior to foreign-country management practices. *p. 91*

Ethnocentrism is the belief that one's own group, culture, country, or customs are superior to others'. *p. 533*

Events are the completions of major project tasks. *p. 203*

Expected value (EV) is the measurement of the anticipated value of some event, determined by multiplying the income an event would produce by its probability of producing that income ($EV \times I = P$). *p. 155*

Exploration stage is the first stage in career evolution; it occurs at the beginning of a career, when the individual is typically 15–25 years of age, and it is characterized by self-analysis and the exploration of different types of available jobs. *p. 12*

Exporting is selling goods or services to another country. *p. 86*

Extranet is a program that expands an Intranet to allow organizational outsiders to perform such activities as placing orders and checking on the status of their orders. *p. 494*

Extrinsic rewards are rewards that are extraneous to the task accomplished. *p. 357*

Feedback is, in the interpersonal communication situation, the destination's reaction to a message. *p. 311*

Feedback control is control that takes place after some unit of work has been performed. *p. 430*

Financial objectives are organizational targets relating to monetary issues. They are influenced by return on investment and financial comparisons with competitors. *p. 111*

Fixed costs are expenses incurred by the organization regardless of the number of products produced. *p. 462*

Fixed-position layout is a layout plan appropriate for organizations involved in a large number of different tasks that require low volumes, multipurpose equipment, and broad employee skills. *p. 454*

Flat organization chart is an organization chart characterized by few levels and a relatively broad span of management. *p. 225*

Flextime is a program that allows workers to complete their jobs within a workweek of a normal number of hours that they schedule themselves. *p. 366*

Focus is a strategy that emphasizes making an organization more competitive by targeting a particular customer. *p. 179*

Forecasting is a planning tool used to predict future environmental happenings that will influence the operation of the organization. *p. 198*

Formal group is a group that exists in an organization by virtue of management decree to perform tasks that enhance the attainment of organizational objectives. *p. 377*

Formal organizational communication is organizational communication that follows the lines of the organization chart. *p. 315*

Formal structure is defined as the relationships among organizational resources as outlined by management. *p. 217*

Forming is the first stage of the team development process, during which members of the newly formed team become oriented to the team and acquainted with one another as they explore issues related to their new job situation. *p. 390*

Friendship group is an informal group that forms in organizations because of the personal affiliation members have with one another. *p. 383*

Functional authority consists of the right to give orders within a segment of the management system in which the right is normally nonexistent. *p. 242*

Functional objectives are targets relating to key organizational functions. They should be consistent with financial and product-market mix objectives. *p. 113*

Functional similarity method is a method for dividing job activities in the organization. *p. 235*

Gangplank is a communication channel extending from one organizational division to another but not shown in the lines of communication outlined on an organization chart. Use of Fayol's gangplank may be quicker, but could prove costly in the long run. *p. 226*

Gantt chart is a scheduling tool composed of a bar chart with time on the horizontal axis and the resource to be scheduled on the vertical axis. It is used for scheduling resources. *p. 202*

Gender-role stereotypes are perceptions about the sexes based on what society believes are appropriate behaviors for men and women. *p. 534*

General environment is the level of an organization's external environment that contains components normally having broad long-term implications for managing the organization; its components are economic, social, political, legal, and technological. *p. 168*

Geocentric attitude reflects the belief that the overall quality of management recommendations, rather than the location of managers, should determine the acceptability of management practices used to guide multinational corporations. The geocentric attitude is considered most appropriate for long-term organizational success. *p. 91*

Goal integration is compatibility between individual and organizational objectives. It occurs when organizational and individual objectives are the same. *p. 108*

Graicunas' formula is a formula that makes the span-of-management point that as the number of a manager's subordinates increases arithmetically, the number of possible relationships between the manager and the subordinates increases geometrically. *p. 224*

Grapevine is the network of informal organizational communication. *p. 318*

Grid organization development (grid OD) is a commonly used organization development technique based on a theoretical model called the *managerial grid*. *p. 286*

Group is any number of people who (1) interact with one another, (2) are psychologically aware of one another, and (3) perceive themselves to be a group. *p. 376*

Groupthink is the mode of thinking that group members engage in when the desire for agreement so dominates the group that it overrides the need to realistically appraise alternative problem solutions. *p. 380*

Growth is a strategy adopted by management to increase the amount of business that a strategic business unit is currently generating. *p. 179*

Halo effect results from allowing one particular aspect of someone's behavior to influence one's evaluation of all other aspects of that person's behavior. *p. 411*

Hierarchy of objectives is the overall organizational objectives and the subobjectives assigned to the various people or units of the organization. *p. 114*

Host country is the country in which an investment is made by a foreign company. *p. 84*

Human relations movement is a people-oriented approach to management in which the interaction of people in organizations is studied to judge its impact on organizational success. *p. 33*

Human relations skill is the ability to work with people in a way that enhances organizational success. *p. 33*

Human resource inventory is an accumulation of information about the characteristics of organization members; this information focuses on members' past performance as well as on how they might be trained and best used in the future. *p. 258*

Human resource planning is input planning that involves obtaining the human resources necessary for the organization to achieve its objectives. *p. 197*

Human resources strategy is an operational plan to use the organization's human resources effectively and efficiently while maintaining or improving the quality of work life. *p. 155*

Human skills are skills involving the ability to build cooperation within the team being led. *p. 10*

Hygiene, or maintenance, factors are items that influence the degree of job dissatisfaction. *p. 364*

Importing is buying goods or services from another country. *p. 86*

Individual objectives are personal goals that each organization member would like to reach as a result of personal activity in the organization. *p. 107*

Influencing is the process of guiding the activities of organization members in appropriate directions. It involves the performance of four management activities: (1) leading, (2) motivating, (3) considering groups, and (4) communicating. *p. 304*

Informal group is a collection of individuals whose common work experiences result in the development of a system of interpersonal relations that extend beyond those established by management. *p. 383*

Informal organizational communication is organizational communication that does not follow the lines of the organization chart. *p. 318*

Informal structure is defined as the patterns of relationships that develop because of the informal activities of organization members. *p. 217*

Information is the set of conclusions derived from data analysis. *p. 472*

Information appropriateness is the degree to which information is relevant to the decision-making situation the manager faces. *p. 473*

Information quality is the degree to which information represents reality. *p. 474*

Information quantity is the amount of decision-related information a manager possesses. *p. 474*

Information technology is technology that focuses on the use of information in the performance of work. *p. 484*

Information timeliness is the extent to which the receipt of information allows decisions to be made and action to be taken so the organization can gain some benefit from possessing the information. *p. 474*

Innovation is the process of taking useful ideas and turning them into useful products, services, or methods of operation. *p. 519*

Input function is computer activities through which the computer enters the data to be analyzed and the instructions to be followed to analyze the data appropriately. *p. 485*

Input planning is the development of proposed action that will furnish sufficient and appropriate organizational resources for reaching established organizational objectives. *p. 194*

Interest group is an informal group that gains and maintains membership primarily because of a common concern members have about a specific issue. *p. 383*

Intermediate-term objectives are targets to be achieved within one to five years. *p. 110*

Internal environment is the level of an organization's environment that exists inside the organization and normally has immediate and specific implications for managing the organization. *p. 173*

International joint venture is a partnership formed by a company in one country with a company in another country for the purpose of pursuing some mutually desirable business undertaking. *p. 87*

International management is the performance of management activities across national borders. *p. 76*

International market agreement is an arrangement among a cluster of countries that facilitates a high level of trade among these countries. *p. 88*

International organization is a company primarily based within a single country but having continuing, meaningful transactions in other countries. *p. 78*

Internet is a large interconnected network of computer networks linking people and computers all over the world via phone lines, satellites, and other telecommunications systems. *p. 490*

Intranet is an internal corporation communication network that uses the structure and standards of the Internet to allow employees of a single firm to communicate and share information with each other electronically. *p. 494*

Intrinsic rewards are rewards that come directly from performing a task. *p. 357*

Job analysis is a technique commonly used to gain an understanding of what a task entails and the type of individual who should be hired to perform that task. *p. 257*

Job-centered behavior is leader behavior that focuses primarily on the work a subordinate is doing. *p. 335*

Job description is a list of specific activities that must be performed to accomplish some task or job. *p. 234, 257*

Job design is an operational plan that determines who will do a specific job and how and where the job will be done. *p. 455*

Job enlargement is the process of increasing the number of operations an individual performs in a job. *p. 364*

Job enrichment is the process of incorporating motivators into a job situation. *p. 365*

Job rotation is the process of moving workers from one job to another rather than requiring them to perform only one simple and specialized job over the long term. *p. 363*

Job specification is a list of the characteristics of the individual who should be hired to perform a specific task or job. *p. 257*

Jury of executive opinion method is a method of predicting future sales levels primarily by asking appropriate managers to give their opinions on what will happen to sales in the future. *p. 199*

Just-in-time (JIT) inventory control is a technique for reducing inventories to a minimum by arranging for production components to be delivered to the production facility "just in time" to be used. *p. 456*

Lateral organizational communication is communication that flows from any point on an organization chart horizontally to another point on the organization chart. *p. 316*

Law of the situation indicates that managers must continually analyze the unique circumstances within their organizations and apply management concepts to fit those circumstances. *p. 17*

Layout is the overall arrangement of equipment, work areas, service areas, and storage areas within a facility that produces goods or provides services. *p. 454*

Layout strategy is an operational plan that determines the location and flow of organizational resources around, into, and within production and service facilities. *p. 453*

Leader flexibility is the ability to change leadership style. *p. 339*

Leadership is the process of directing the behavior of others toward the accomplishment of objectives. *p. 326*

Leadership style is the behavioral pattern a leader establishes while guiding organization members in appropriate directions. *p. 335*

Learning is a more or less permanent change in behavior resulting from practice, experience, education, or training. *p. 414*

Learning organization is an organization that does well in creating, acquiring, and transferring knowledge, and in modifying behavior to reflect new knowledge. *p. 40*

Lecture is primarily a one-way communication situation in which an instructor trains an individual or group by orally presenting information. *p. 268*

Level dimension of a plan is the level of the organization at which the plan is aimed. *p. 191*

License agreement is a right granted by one company to another to use its brand name, technology, product specifications, and so on in the manufacture or sale of goods and services. *p. 87*

Life cycle theory of leadership is a leadership concept that hypothesizes that leadership styles should reflect primarily the maturity level of the followers. *p. 336*

Line authority consists of the right to make decisions and to give orders concerning the production-, sales-, or finance-related behavior of subordinates. *p. 240*

Local area network (LAN) is a computer network characterized by software that manages how information travels through cables to arrive at a number of connected single-user computer workstations. *p. 489*

Location strategy is an operational plan of action that provides the organization with a competitive location for its headquarters, manufacturing, services, and distribution activities. *p. 452*

Long-term objectives are targets to be achieved within five to seven years. *p. 110*

Loss is the amount of the total costs of producing a product that exceeds the total revenue gained from selling the product. *p. 462*

Maintenance stage is the third stage in career evolution; individuals of about 45 to 65 years of age either become more productive, stabilize, or become less productive. *p. 13*

Majority group refers to that group of people in the organization who hold most of the positions that command decision-making power, control of resources and information, and access to system rewards. *p. 528*

Management is the process of reaching organizational goals by working with and through people and other organizational resources. *p. 6*

Management by exception is a control tool that allows only significant deviations between planned and actual performance to be brought to a manager's attention. *p. 461*

Management by objectives (MBO) is a management approach that uses organizational objectives as the primary means of managing organizations. *p. 117*

Management decision support system (MDSS) is an interdependent set of computer-oriented decision aids that help managers make nonprogrammed decisions. *p. 487*

Management functions are activities that make up the management process. The four basic management activities are planning, organizing, influencing, and controlling. *p. 7*

Management information system (MIS) is a network established within an organization to provide managers with information that will assist them in decision making. An MIS gets information to where it is needed. *p. 476*

Management inventory card is a form used in compiling a human resource inventory. It contains the organizational history of an individual and indicates how that individual might be used in the organization in the future. *p. 258*

Management manpower replacement chart is a form used in compiling a human resource inventory. It is people-oriented and presents a composite view of individuals management considers significant to human resource planning. *p. 259*

Management responsibility guide is a tool that is used to clarify the responsibilities of various managers in the organization. *p. 237*

Management science approach is a management approach that emphasizes the use of the scientific method and quantitative techniques to increase organizational success. *p. 34*

Management system is an open system whose major parts are organizational input, organizational process, and organizational output. *p. 38*

Managerial effectiveness refers to management's use of organizational resources in meeting organizational goals. *p. 9*

Managerial efficiency is the degree to which organizational resources contribute to productivity. It is measured by the proportion of total organizational resources used during the production process. *p. 9*

Managerial grid is a theoretical model based on the premise that concern for people and concern for production are the two primary attitudes that influence management style. *p. 286*

Manpower planning is an operational plan that focuses on hiring the right employees for a job and training them to be productive. *p. 455*

Materials control is an operational activity that determines the flow of materials from vendors through an operations system to customers. *p. 459*

Matrix organization is a traditional organizational structure that is modified primarily for the purpose of completing some kind of special project. *p. 283*

McClelland's acquired needs theory is an explanation of human needs that focuses on the desires for achievement, power, and affiliation that people develop as a result of their life experiences. *p. 360*

Means-ends analysis is the process of outlining the means by which various organizational objectives, or ends, can be achieved. *p. 116*

Message is encoded information that the source intends to share with others. *p. 308*

Message interference refers to stimuli that compete with the communication

message for the attention of the destination. *p. 310*

Minority group refers to that group of people in the organization who are smaller in number or who possess fewer granted rights and lower status than the majority groups. *p. 528*

Mission statement is a written document developed by management, normally based on input by managers as well as nonmanagers, that describes and explains the organization's mission. *p. 174*

Model base is a collection of quantitative computer programs that can assist MDSS users in analyzing data within databases. *p. 488*

Motion study finds the best way to accomplish a task by analyzing the movements necessary to perform that task. *p. 28*

Motion-study techniques are operational tools that are used to improve productivity. *p. 455*

Motivating factors, or motivators are items that influence the degree of job satisfaction. *p. 364*

Motivation is the inner state that causes an individual to behave in a way that ensures the accomplishment of some goal. *p. 354*

Motivation strength is an individual's degree of desire to perform a behavior. *p. 355*

Multinational corporation (MNC) is a company that has significant operations in more than one country. *p. 79*

Needs-goal theory is a motivation model that hypothesizes that felt needs cause human behavior. *p. 354*

Negative reinforcement is a reward that consists of the elimination of an undesirable consequence of behavior. *p. 367*

Nominal group technique is a group decision-making process in which every group member is assured of equal participation in making the group decision. After each member writes down individual ideas and presents them orally to the group, the entire group discusses all the ideas and then votes for the best idea in a secret ballot. *p. 159*

Nonprogrammed decisions are typically one-shot decisions that are usually less structured than programmed decisions. *p. 144*

Nonverbal communication is the sharing of information without using words. *p. 313*

Norming the third stage of the team development process, is characterized by agreement among team members on roles, rules, and acceptable behavior while working on the team. *p. 391*

On-the-job training is a training technique that blends job-related knowledge with experience in using that knowledge on the job. *p. 269*

Open system is one that is influenced by, and is continually interacting with, its environment. *p. 37*

Operant learning is an approach that holds that the behavior leading to positive consequences is more likely to be repeated. *p. 414*

Operating environment is the level of the organization's external environment that contains components normally having relatively specific and immediate implications for managing the organization. *p. 172*

Operational objectives are objectives that are stated in observable or measurable terms. They specify the activities or operations needed to attain them. *p. 115*

Operations control is an operational plan that specifies the operational activities of an organization. *p. 456*

Operations management is the systematic direction (strategy) and control of operations processes that transform resources into finished goods and services. *p. 450*

Organization chart is a graphic representation of organizational structure. *p. 216*

Organization development (OD) is the process that emphasizes changing an organization by changing organization members and bases these changes on an overview of structure, technology, and all other organizational ingredients. *p. 286*

Organizational communication is interpersonal communication within organizations. *p. 314*

Organizational mission is the purpose for which, or the reason why, an organization exists. *p. 174*

Organizational objectives are the targets toward which the open management system is directed. They flow from the organization's purpose or mission. *p. 104*

Organizational purpose is what the organization exists to do, given a particular group of customers and customer needs. *p. 104*

Organizational resources are all assets available for activation during normal operations; they include human resources, monetary resources, raw materials resources, and capital resources. *p. 8*

Organizing is the process of establishing orderly uses for all the organization's resources. *p. 212*

Output function is computer activities that take the results of input, storage, processing, and control functions and transmit them outside the computer. *p. 486*

Overlapping responsibility refers to a situation in which more than one individual is responsible for the same activity. *p. 236*

Parent company is the company investing in international operations. *p. 84*

Path-goal theory of leadership is a theory of leadership that suggests that the primary activities of a leader are to make desirable and achievable rewards available to organization members who attain organizational goals and to clarify the kinds of behavior that must be performed to earn those rewards. *p. 341*

People change is a type of organizational change that emphasizes modifying certain aspects of organization members to increase organizational effectiveness. *p. 286*

People factors are attitudes, leadership skills, communication skills, and all other characteristics of the organization's employees. *p. 282*

Perception is the psychological process of selecting stimuli, organizing the data into recognizable patterns, and interpreting the resulting information. *p. 310; is the interpretation of a message by an individual. *p. 409*

Perceptual process is the series of actions that individuals follow in order to select, organize, and interpret stimuli from the environment. *p. 409*

Performance appraisal is the process of reviewing past productive activity to evaluate the contribution individuals have made toward attaining management system objectives. *p. 271*

Performing the fourth stage of the team development process, is characterized by a focus on solving organizational problems and meeting assigned challenges. *p. 391*

Personal power is the power derived from a manager's relationships with others. *p. 433*

Physiological needs are Maslow's first set of human needs—for the normal functioning of the body, including the desires for water, food, rest, sex, and air. *p. 358*

Plan is a specific action proposed to help the organization achieve its objectives. *p. 190*

Plan for planning is a listing of all the steps that must be taken to plan for an organization. It ensures that planning gets done. *p. 134*

Planning is the process of determining how the management system will achieve its objectives. In other words, it determines how the organization can get where it wants to go. *p. 126*

Planning tools are techniques managers can use to help develop plans. *p. 198*

Plant facilities planning is input planning that involves developing the type of work facility an organization will need to reach its objectives. *p. 195*

Pluralism is an environment in which cultural, group, and individual differences are acknowledged, accepted, and viewed as significant contributors to the entirety. *p. 540*

Policy is a standing plan that furnishes broad guidelines for channeling management toward taking action consistent with reaching organizational objectives. *p. 192*

Polycentric attitude reflects the belief that because foreign managers are closer to foreign organizational units, they probably understand them better, and therefore foreign management practices should generally be viewed as more insightful than home-country management practices. *p. 91*

Porter-Lawler theory is a motivation theory that hypothesizes that felt needs cause human behavior and that motivation strength is determined primarily by the perceived value of the result of performing the behavior and the perceived probability that the behavior performed will cause the result to materialize. *p. 356*

Position power is power derived from the organizational position a manager holds. *p. 433*

Position replacement form is used in compiling a human resource inventory. It summarizes information about organization members who could fill a position should it open up. *p. 259*

Positive reinforcement is a reward that consists of a desirable consequence of behavior. *p. 367*

Power is the extent to which an individual is able to influence others so that they respond to orders. *p. 433*

Precontrol is control that takes place before some unit of work is actually performed. *p. 429*

Prejudice is a preconceived judgment, opinion, or assumption about an issue, behavior, individual, or group of people. *p. 533*

Premises are the assumptions on which an alternative to reaching an organizational objective is based. *p. 128*

Principle of the objective is a management guideline that recommends that before managers initiate any action, they should clearly determine, understand, and state organizational objectives. *p. 110*

Probability theory is a decision-making tool used in risk situations—situations in which the decision maker is not completely sure of the outcome of an implemented alternative. *p. 155*

Problems are factors within an organization that are barriers to organizational goal attainment. *p. 428*

Problem-solving team is an organizational team set up to help eliminate a specified problem within the organization. *p. 388*

Procedural justice is the perceived fairness of the process used for deciding workplace outcomes such as merit increases and promotions. *p. 412*

Procedure is a standing plan that outlines a series of related actions that must be taken to accomplish a particular task. *p. 193*

Process control is a technique that assists in monitoring production processes. *p. 465*

Process (functional) layout is a layout pattern based primarily on grouping together similar types of equipment. *p. 454*

Processing function is computer activities involved with performing the logic and calculation steps necessary to analyze data appropriately. *p. 485*

Process strategy is an operational plan of action outlining the means and methods the organization will use to transform resources into goods and services. *p. 453*

Process theories of motivation are explanations of motivation that emphasize how individuals are motivated. *p. 354*

Production is the transformation of organizational resources into products. *p. 444*

Production control ensures that an organization produces goods and services as planned. *p. 444*

Productivity is the relationship between the total amount of goods or services being produced (output) and the organizational resources needed to produce them (input). *p. 444*

Product layout is a layout designed to accommodate a limited number of different products that require high volumes, highly specialized equipment, and narrow employee skills. *p. 454*

Product life cycle is the five stages through which most products and services pass: introduction, growth, maturity, saturation, and decline. *p. 201*

Product-market mix objectives are objectives that outline which products—and the relative number or mix of these products—the organization will attempt to sell. *p. 112*

Product strategy is an operational plan of action outlining which goods and services an organization will produce and market. *p. 453*

Profits are the amount of total revenue that exceeds total costs. *p. 462*

Program is a single-use plan designed to carry out a special project in an organization that, if accomplished, will contribute to the organization's long-term success. *p. 194*

Program evaluation and review technique (PERT) is a scheduling tool that is essentially a network of project activities showing estimates of time necessary to complete each activity and the sequence of activities that must be followed to complete the project. *p. 203*

Programmed decisions are decisions that are routine and repetitive and that typically require specific handling methods. *p. 144*

Programmed learning is a technique for instructing without the presence or intervention of a human instructor. Small pieces of information requiring responses are presented to individual trainees, and the trainees determine from checking their responses against provided answers whether their understanding of the information is accurate. *p. 269*

Projection is the unconscious tendency to assign one's own traits, motives, beliefs, and attitudes to others. *p. 411*

Punishment is the presentation of an undesirable behavior consequence or the removal of a desirable one that decreases the likelihood that the behavior will continue. *p. 367*

Pure-breakdown (repair) policy is a maintenance control policy that decrees that machine adjustments, lubrication, cleaning, parts replacement, painting, and needed repairs and overhaul will be performed only after facilities or machines malfunction. *p. 457*

Pure-preventive maintenance policy is a maintenance control policy that tries to ensure that machine adjustments, lubrication, cleaning, parts replacement, painting, and needed repairs and overhauls will be performed before facilities or machines malfunction. *p. 457*

Quality is the extent to which a product does what it is supposed to do—how closely and reliably it satisfies the specifications to which it is built. *pp. 445, 504*

Quality assurance is an operations process involving a broad group of activities that are aimed at achieving the organization's quality objectives. *p. 446*

Quality circles are small groups of workers that meet to discuss quality-related problems on a particular project and communicate their solutions to these problems to management at a formal presentation session. *p. 447*

Quality-oriented policy is a standing plan that furnishes broad, general guidelines for channeling management thinking toward taking action consistent with reaching quality objectives. *p. 513*

Ratio analysis is a control tool that summarizes the financial position of an organization by calculating ratios based on various financial measures. *p. 459*

Recruitment is the initial attraction and screening of the supply of prospective human resources available to fill a position. *p. 256*

Relevant alternatives are alternatives that are considered feasible for solving an existing problem and for implementation. *p. 149*

Repatriation is the process of bringing individuals who have been working abroad back to their home country and reintegrating them into the organization's home-country operations. *p. 85*

Repetitiveness dimension of a plan is the extent to which the plan is to be used over and over again. *p. 190*

Responsibility is the obligation to perform assigned activities. *p. 234*

Responsibility gap exists when certain organizational tasks are not included in the responsibility area of any individual organization member. *p. 236*

Retrenchment is a strategy adopted by management to strengthen or protect the amount of business a strategic business unit is currently generating. *p. 180*

Reverse discrimination is the term used to describe inequities affecting members of the majority group as an outcome of

programs designed to help underrepresented groups. *p. 537*

Risk condition   is the decision-making situation in which the decision maker has only enough information to estimate how probable the outcome of implemented alternatives will be. *p. 154*

Robotics   is the study of the development and use of robots. *p. 449*

Role conflict   is the conflict that results when a person has to fill competing roles because of membership in two cultures. *p. 534*

Role overload   refers to having too many expectations to comfortably fulfill. *p. 534*

Rule   is a standing plan that designates specific required action. *p. 193*

Salesforce estimation method   predicts future sales levels primarily by asking appropriate salespeople for their opinions of what will happen to sales in the future. *p. 200*

Scalar relationships   refer to the chain-of-command positioning of individuals on an organization chart. *p. 226*

Scheduling   is the process of formulating a detailed listing of activities that must be accomplished to attain an objective, allocating the resources necessary to attain the objective, and setting up and following timetables for completing the objective. *p. 202*

Scientific management   emphasizes the "one best way" to perform a task. *p. 000*

Scope dimension   of a plan is the portion of the total management system at which the plan is aimed. *p. 191*

Scope of the decision   is the proportion of the total management system that a particular decision will affect. The broader the scope of a decision, the higher the level of the manager responsible for making that decision. *p. 146*

Security, or safety, needs   are Maslow's second set of human needs—reflecting the human desire to keep free from physical harm. *p. 358*

Selection   is choosing an individual to hire from all those who have been recruited. *p. 263*

Selective perception   is the tendency to collect information that not only supports one's own motives, beliefs, and attitudes but also minimizes the emotional distress caused by unfamiliar or troublesome stimuli. *p. 412*

Self-actualization needs   are Maslow's fifth, and final, set of human needs—reflecting

the human desire to maximize personal potential. *p. 359*

Self-managed team   is an organizational team established to plan, organize, influence, and control its own work situation with only minimal direction from management. *p. 388*

Self-serving bias   is the tendency to overestimate external causes of behavior and underestimate internal ones when judging one's own behavior. *p. 411*

Serial transmission   involves the passing of information from one individual to another in a series. *p. 316*

Short-term objectives   are targets to be achieved in one year or less. *p. 110*

Signal   is a message that has been transmitted from one person to another. *p. 308*

Single-use plans   are plans that are used only once—or, at most, several times—because they focus on unique or rare situations within the organization. *p. 192*

Site selection   involves determining where a plant facility should be located. It may use a weighting process to compare site differences. *p. 195*

Situational approach to leadership   is a relatively modern view of leadership that suggests that successful leadership requires a unique combination of leaders, followers, and leadership situations. *p. 328*

Social audit   is the process of measuring the present social responsibility activities of an organization. It monitors, measures, and appraises all aspects of an organization's social responsibility performance. *p. 62*

Social needs   are Maslow's third set of human needs—reflecting the human desire to belong, including longings for friendship, companionship, and love. *p. 358*

Social obligation approach   is an approach to meeting social obligations that considers business to have primarily economic purposes and confines social responsibility activity largely to conformance to existing legislation. *p. 57*

Social responsibility approach   is an approach to meeting social obligations that considers business as having both societal and economic goals. *p. 57*

Social responsiveness   is the degree of effectiveness and efficiency an organization displays in pursuing its social responsibilities. *p. 55*

Social responsiveness approach   is an approach to meeting social obligations that considers business to have societal and

economic goals as well as the obligation to anticipate potential social problems and to work actively toward preventing them from occurring. *p. 57*

Social values   are the relative degrees of worth society places on the manner in which it exists and functions. *p. 170*

Sociogram   is a sociometric diagram that summarizes the personal feelings of organization members about the people in the organization with whom they would like to spend free time. *p. 384*

Sociometry   is an analytical tool that can be used to determine what informal groups exist in an organization and who the members of those groups are. *p. 384*

Source/encoder   is the person in the interpersonal communication situation who originates and encodes information to be shared with another person or persons. *p. 307*

Span of management   is the number of individuals a manager supervises. *p. 224*

Stability   is a strategy adopted by management to maintain or slightly improve the amount of business a strategic business unit is generating. *p. 180*

Staff authority   consists of the right to advise or assist those who possess line authority. *p. 240*

Stakeholders   are all individuals and groups that are directly or indirectly affected by an organization's decisions. *p. 55*

Standard   is the level of activity established to serve as a model for evaluating organizational performance. *p. 425*

Standing plans   are plans that are used over and over because they focus on organizational situations that occur repeatedly. *p. 192*

Statistical quality control   is the process used to determine how many products should be inspected to calculate a probability that the total number of products will meet organizational quality standards. *p. 447*

Stereotype   is a fixed, distorted generalization about members of a group. *p. 410;* a positive or negative assessment of members of a group or their perceived attributes. *p. 533*

Storage function   is computer activities involved with retaining the material entered into the computer during the performance of the input function. *p. 485*

Storming   the second stage of the team development process, is characterized by conflict and disagreement as team members try to clarify their individual roles and challenge the way the team functions. *p. 390*

Strategic business unit (SBU) is, in business portfolio analysis, a significant organizational segment that is analyzed to develop organizational strategy aimed at generating future business or revenue. SBUs vary in form, but all are a single business (or collection of businesses), have their own competitors and a manager accountable for operations, and can be independently planned for. *p. 176*

Strategic control the last step of the strategy management process, consists of monitoring and evaluating the strategy management process as a whole to ensure that it is operating properly. *p. 180*

Strategic planning is long-range planning that focuses on the organization as a whole. *p. 166*

Strategy is a broad and general plan developed to reach long-term organizational objectives; it is the end result of strategic planning. *p. 167*

Strategy formulation is the process of determining appropriate courses of action for achieving organizational objectives and thereby accomplishing organizational purpose. Strategy development tools include critical question analysis, SWOT analysis, business portfolio analysis, and Porter's Model for Industry Analysis. *p. 175*

Strategy implementation the fourth step of the strategy management process, is putting formulated strategy into action. *p. 180*

Strategy management is the process of ensuring that an organization possesses and benefits from the use of an appropriate organizational strategy. *p. 167*

Stress is the bodily strain that an individual experiences as a result of coping with some environmental factor. *p. 290*

Stressor is an environmental demand that causes people to feel stress. *p. 292*

Structural change is a type of organizational change that emphasizes modifying an existing organizational structure. *p. 283*

Structural factors are organizational controls, such as policies and procedures. *p. 282*

Structure refers to the designated relationships among resources of the management system. *p. 216*

Structure behavior is leadership activity that (1) delineates the relationship between the leader and the leader's followers or

(2) establishes well-defined procedures that the followers should adhere to in performing their jobs. *p. 234*

Suboptimization is a condition wherein organizational subobjectives are conflicting or not directly aimed at accomplishing the overall organizational objectives. *p. 114*

Subsystem is a system created as part of the process of the overall management system. A planning subsystem increases the effectiveness of the overall management system. *p. 130*

Successful communication refers to an interpersonal communication situation in which the information the source intends to share with the destination and the meaning the destination derives from the transmitted message are the same. *p. 308*

Superleadership is leadership that inspires organizational success by showing followers how to lead themselves. *p. 345*

Suppliers are individuals or agencies that provide organizations with the resources they need to produce goods and services. *p. 172*

SWOT analysis is a strategy development tool that matches internal organizational strengths and weaknesses with external opportunities and threats. *p. 176*

Symptom is a sign that a problem exists. *p. 428*

System is a number of interdependent parts functioning as a whole for some purpose. *p. 37*

System approach to management is a management approach based on general system theory—the theory that to understand fully the operation of an entity, the entity must be viewed as a system. This requires understanding the interdependence of its parts. *p. 37*

Tactical planning is short-range planning that emphasizes the current operations of various parts of the organization. *p. 181*

Tall organization chart is an organization chart characterized by many levels and a relatively broad span of management. *p. 225*

Task group is a formal group of organization members who interact with one another to accomplish nonroutine organizational tasks. Members of any one task group can and often do come from various levels and segments of an organization. *p. 377*

Team is a group whose members influence one another toward the accomplishment of (an) organizational objective(s). *p. 387*

Technical skills are skills involving the ability to apply specialized knowledge and expertise to work-related techniques and procedures. *p. 10*

Technological change is a type of organizational change that emphasizes modifying the level of technology in the management system. *p. 283*

Technological factors are any types of equipment or processes that assist organization members in the performance of their jobs. *p. 282*

Technology consists of any type of equipment or process that organization members use in the performance of their work. *p. 484*

Testing is examining human resources for qualities relevant to performing available jobs. *p. 264*

Theory of reasoned action states that when a behavior is a matter of *choice* the best predictor of the behavior is the person's *intention* to perform it. *p. 405*

Theory X is a set of essentially negative assumptions about human nature. *p. 362*

Theory Y is a set of essentially positive assumptions about human nature. *p. 362*

Theory Z is the effectiveness dimension that implies that managers who use either Theory X or Theory Y assumptions when dealing with people can be successful, depending on their situation. *p. 362*

Time dimension of a plan is the length of time the plan covers. *p. 191*

Time series analysis method is a method of predicting future sales levels by analyzing the historical relationship in an organization between sales and time. *p. 200*

Tokenism refers to being one of very few members of a group in an organization. *p. 534*

Total costs are the sum of fixed costs and variable costs. *p. 462*

Total power is the entire amount of power an individual in an organization possesses. It is made up of position power and personal power. *p. 433*

Total quality management (TQM) is the continuous process of involving all organization members in ensuring that every activity related to the production of goods or services has an appropriate role in establishing product quality. *p. 504*

Total revenue is all sales dollars accumulated from selling the goods or services produced by the organization. *p. 462*

Training is the process of developing qualities in human resources that will enable them to be more productive. *p. 266*

Training needs are the information or skill areas of an individual or group that require further development to increase the productivity of that individual or group. *p. 267*

Trait approach to leadership is an outdated view of leadership that sees the personal characteristics of an individual as the main determinants of how successful that individual could be as a leader. *p. 327*

Transformational leadership is leadership that inspires organizational success by profoundly affecting followers' beliefs in what an organization should be, as well as their values, such as justice and integrity. *p. 343*

Transnational organizations also called *global organizations* take the entire world as their business arena. *p. 93*

Triangular management is a management approach that emphasizes using information from the classical, behavioral, and management science schools of thought to manage the open management system. *p. 39*

Unity of command is the management principle that recommends that an individual have only one boss. *p. 226*

Universality of management means that the principles of management are applicable to all types of organizations and organizational levels. *p. 11*

Unsuccessful communication refers to an interpersonal communication situation in which the information the source intends to share with the destination and the meaning the destination derives from the transmitted message are different. *p. 309*

Upward organizational communication is communication that flows from any point on an organization chart upward to another point on the organization chart. *p. 316*

User database is a database developed by an individual manager or other user. *p. 487*

Value analysis is a cost control and cost reduction technique that examines all the parts, materials, and functions of an operation. *p. 465*

Values are the global beliefs that guide one's actions and judgments across a variety of situations. *p. 403*

Variable budget (also known as a *flexible budget*) is one that outlines the levels of resources to be allocated for each organizational activity according to the level of production within the organization. *p. 458*

Variable costs are expenses that fluctuate with the number of products produced. *p. 462*

Verbal communication is the sharing of information through words, either written or spoken. *p. 313*

Virtual corporation is an organization that goes significantly beyond the boundaries and structure of a traditional organization. *p. 294*

Virtual office is a work arrangement that extends beyond the structure and boundaries of the traditional office arrangement. *p. 295*

Virtual organization is an organization having the essence of a traditional organization, but without some aspect(s) of traditional boundaries and structure. *p. 294*

Virtual teams are groups of employees formed by managers that go beyond the boundaries and structure of traditional teams. *p. 294*

Virtual training is a training process that goes beyond the boundaries and structure of traditional training. *p. 294*

Vroom expectancy theory is a motivation theory that hypothesizes that felt needs cause human behavior and that motivation strength depends on an individual's degree of desire to perform a behavior. *p. 355*

Vroom-Yetton-Jago (VYJ) Model of Leadership is a modern view of leadership that suggests that successful leadership requires determining through a decision tree what style of leadership will produce decisions that are beneficial to the organization and accepted and committed to by subordinates. *p. 332*

"What if" analysis is the simulation of a business situation over and over again, using somewhat different data for selected decision areas. *p. 488*

Work measurement methods are operational tools that are used to establish labor standards. *p. 455*

Work methods analysis is an operational tool used to improve productivity and ensure the safety of workers. *p. 455*

Work team is a task group used in organizations to achieve greater organizational flexibility or to cope with rapid growth. *p. 380*

World Wide Web is a segment of the Internet that allows managers to have an information location called a *Web site* available continually to Internet users. Each Web site has a beginning page called a *home page* and each home page generally has several supporting pages called *branch pages* that expand on the thoughts and ideas contained in the home page. *p. 492*

Zero-base budgeting requires managers to justify their entire budget request in detail rather than simply referring to budget amounts established in previous years. *p. 458*

ENDNOTES

CHAPTER 1

1. For an interesting discussion of how much return a company should be getting on its management resources see Robert Simons and Antonio Davila, "How High Is Your Return on Management?" *Harvard Business Review* (January/February 1998): 70–80; Peter F. Drucker, "Management's New Role," *Harvard Business Review* (November/December 1969): 54.
2. Eric S. Hardy, "The Prize," *Forbes*, May 19, 1997, 166–169.
3. Harris Collingwood, "The 10 Highest-Paid Female Executives," *Across the Board*, January 1998, 10.
4. Robert Albanese, *Management* (Cincinnati Southwestern, 1988), 8.
5. Gary Hamel and C.K. Prahalad, "Seeing the Future First," *Fortune*, September 5, 1994, 64–70.
6. For a recent example of tactics taken by Chase Manhattan Corporation to enhance its efficiency see Matt Murray, "Chase Combines International Units In Efficiency Move," *Wall Street Journal*, February, 19, 1998, C17.
7. William Wiggenhorn, "Motorola U: When Training Becomes an Education," *Harvard Business Review* (July/August 1990): 71–83.
8. Robert L. Katz, "Skills of an Effective Administrator," *Harvard Business Review* (January/February 1955): 33–41.
9. Ruth Davidhizar, "The Two-Minute Manager," *Health Supervisor 7* (April 1989): 25–29; for an article that demonstrates how important human skills are for middle managers, see also Philip A. Rudolph and Brian H. Kleiner, "The Art of Motivating Employees," *Journal of Managerial Psychology 4* (1989): i–iv.
10. Henri Fayol, *General and Industrial Management* (London: Sir Isaac Pitman & Sons, 1949).
11. B.C. Forbes, *Forbes*, March 15, 1976, 128.
12. Don Hellriegel, John W. Slocum, Jr., and Richard W. Woodman, *Organizational Behavior*, 6th ed. (St. Paul: West Publishing Company, 1992), 681.
13. John Ivancevich and Michael T. Matteson, *Organizational Behavior and Management* (Homewood, Ill.: BPI/Irwin, 1990), 593–95.
14. John W. Slocum, Jr., William L. Cron, and Linda C. Yows, "Whose Career Is Likely to Plateau?" *Business Horizons* (March/April 1987): 31–38.
15. Joseph E. McKendrick, Jr., "What Are You Doing the Rest of Your Life?" *Management World*, September/October 1987, 2; Carl Anderson, *Management: Skills, Functions, and Organizational Performance*, 2d ed. (Boston: Allyn and Bacon, 1988).
16. Paul H. Thompson, Robin Zenger Baker, and Norman Smallwood, "Improving Personal Development by Applying the Four-Stage Career Model," *Organizational Dynamics* (Autumn 1986): 49–62.
17. Kenneth Labich, "Take Control of Your Career," *Fortune*. November 18, 1991, 87–90; Buck Blessing, "Career Planning: Five Fatal Assumptions," *Training and Development Journal* (September 1986): 49–51.
18. Thomas J. Peters, Jr., "The Best New Managers Will Listen, Motivate, Support," *Working Woman*, September 1990, 142–43, 216–17.
19. For an interesting discussion of conflict of interest and dual-career couples, see Owen Ullmann and Mike McNamee, "Couples, Careers, and Conflicts," *Business Week* (February 21, 1994): 32–34.
20. For additional information see Sue Shellenbarger, "For the Burseks, Best Parent Regimen Is Back-to-Back Shifts," *Wall Street Journal*, February 25, 1998, B1; Jacqueline B. Stanfield, "Couples Coping with Dual Careers: A De-

scription of Flexible and Rigid Coping Styles," *Social Science Journal 35*, no. 1 (1998): 53–64; F.S. Hall and T.D. Hall, "Dual Careers—How Do Couples and Companies Cope with the Problems?" *Organizational Dynamics 6* (1978): 57–77.
21. For insights on how managers should deal with a multicultural workforce see "Ten Strategies for Managers in a Multicultural Workforce," *HR Focus 69*, no. 8 (August 1992): 6.
22. James F. Wolf, "The Legacy of Mary Parker Follett," *Bureaucrat 17* (Winter 1988–89): 53–57.
23. "Hazardous Materials Disaster Management," *Environmental Manager*, October 1994, pp. 7–9.
24. Philip M. Burgess, "Making It in America's New Economy," *Vital Speeches of the Day 60* (September 15, 1994): 716–19. For a useful discussion of special training issues related to such employees, see Adrienne S. Harris, "And the Prepared Will Inherit the Future," *Black Enterprise*, February 1990, 121–28.
25. Stephen J. Harrison and Ronald Stupak, "Total Quality Management: The Organizational Equivalent of Truth in Public Administration Theory and Practice," *Public Administration Quarterly 16* (Winter 1993): 416–29.

CHAPTER 2

1. James H. Donnelly, Jr., James L. Gibson, and John M. Ivancevich, *Fundamentals of Management* (Plano, TX: Business Publications, 1987), 6–8; Harold Koontz, Cyril O'Donnell, and Heinz Weihrich, *Management*, 8th ed. (New York: McGraw-Hill, 1984), 52–69; W. Warren Haynes and Joseph L. Massie, *Management*, 2d ed. (Upper Saddle River, NJ: Prentice Hall, 1969), 4–13.
2. David W. Hays, "Quality Improvement and Its Origin in Scientific Management," *Quality Progress*, May 5, 1994, 89–90.
3. Frederick W. Taylor, *The Principles of Scientific Management* (New York: Harper & Bros., 1947), 66–71.
4. For more information on the work of Frederick Taylor, see Edward Rimer, "Organization Theory and Frederick Taylor," *Public Administration Review 53* (May/June 1993): 270–72; Alan Farnham, "The Man Who Changed Work Forever," *Fortune*, July 21, 1997, 114.
5. Franz T. Lohrke, "Motion Study for the Blinded: A Review of the Gilbreths' Work with the Visually Handicapped," *International Journal of Public Administration 16* (1993): 667–68; For information illustrating how the career of Lillian Gilbreth is an inspiration for modern women managers see Thomas R. Miller and Mary A. Lemons, "Breaking the Glass Ceiling: Lessons from a Management Pioneer," *S.A.M. Advanced Management Journal 63*, no. 1 (Winter 1998): 4–9.
6. Edward A. Michaels, "Work Measurement," *Small Business Reports 14* (March 1989): 55–63.
7. Henry L. Gantt, *Industrial Leadership* (New Haven, CT: Yale University Press, 1916), 57.
8. For more information on the Gantt chart, see G. William Page, "Using Project Management Software in Planning," *Journal of the American Planning Association 55* (Autumn 1989): 494–99; Jeff Angus, "Software Speeds Up Project Management," *Informationweek*, September 8, 1997, 85–88.
9. Doug Green and Denise Green, "MacSchedule Has Rich Features at Low Price," *InfoWorld*, July 12, 1993, 88.

10. Gantt, *Industrial Leadership*, 85.

11. Chester I. Barnard, *Organization and Management* (Cambridge, MA: Harvard University Press, 1952). For more current discussion of Barnard's work, see Christopher Vasillopulos, "Heroism, Self-Abnegation and the Liberal Organization," *Journal of Business Ethics 7* (August 1988): 585–91.

12. Alvin Brown, *Organization of Industry* (Upper Saddle River, N.J.: Prentice Hall, 1947); Henry S. Dennison, *Organization Engineering* (New York: McGraw-Hill, 1931); Luther Gulick and Lyndall Urwick, eds., *Papers on the Science of Administration* (New York: Institute of Public Administration, 1937); J.D. Mooney and A.C. Reiley. *Onward Industry!* (New York: Harper & Bros., 1931); Oliver Sheldon, *The Philosophy of Management* (London: Sir Isaac Pitman and Sons, 1923).

13. Henri Fayol, *General and Industrial Management* (London: Sir Isaac Pitman and Sons, 1949).

14. Charles A. Mowll, "Successful Management Based on Key Principles," *Healthcare Financial Management 43* (June 1989): 122, 124.

15. Fayol, *General and Industrial Management*, 19–42. For an excellent discussion of the role of accountability and organization structure, see Elliott Jaques, "In Praise of Hierarchy," *Harvard Business Review 68* (January/February 1990): 127–133.

16. For an interesting discussion on how modern training programs are teaching managers to establish productive authority relationships in organizations, see A. Glenn Kiser, Terry Humphries, and Chip Bell, "Breaking Through Rational Leadership," *Training and Development Journal 44* (January 1990): 42–45. For an interesting discussion on how "chain of command" helps to minimize the negative impact of oil spills, see James Hunt, Bruce Carter, and Frank Kelly, "Clearly Defined Chain-of-Command Helps Mobilize Oil Spill," *Occupational Health & Safety,* June 1993, 40–45. For a discussion of the impact of remuneration on an organization, see Jeffrey Bradt, "Pay for Impact," *Personnel Journal,* January 1992, 76–79. For a discussion of centralization, see Paul T. Mill and Josephine Bonan, "Site-Based Management: Decentralization and Accountability," *Education Digest,* September 1991, 23–25.

17. For detailed summaries of these studies, see *Industrial Worker,* 2 vols. (Cambridge, MA: Harvard University Press, 1938); and F.J. Roethlisberger and W.J. Dickson, *Management and the Worker* (Cambridge, MA: Harvard University Press, 1939). For a more recent discussion of the Hawthorne Studies, see Bev Geber, "The Hawthorne Effect: Orwell or Buscaglia? *Training 23* (November 1986): 113–114.

18. Stephen Jones, "Worker Interdependence and Output: The Hawthorne Studies Reevaluated," *American Sociological Review,* (April 1990): 176–90.

19. Jennifer Laabs, "Corporate Anthropologists," *Personnel Journal* (January 1992): 81–91; Samuel C. Certo, *Human Relations Today: Concepts and Skills* (Burr Ridge, IL: Irwin, 1995), 4.

20. C. West Churchman, Russell L. Ackoff, and E. Leonard Arnoff, *Introduction to Operations Research* (New York: Wiley, 1957), 18.

21. Hamdy A. Taha, *Operations Research: An Introduction* (New York: Macmillan, 1988), 1–2.

22. James R. Emshoff, *Analysis of Behavioral Systems* (New York: Macmillan, 1971), 10. For an interesting account of how the scientific method can be applied to studying management problems like information system problems, see Allen S. Lee, "A Scientific Methodology for the MIS Case Studies," *MIS Quarterly 13* (March 1989): 33–50.

23. Catherine L. Morgan, "A Survey of MS/OR Surveys," *Interfaces 19* (November/December 1989): 95–103; H-J. Zimmermann, "Some Observations on Practicing Successful Operational Research," *The Journal of the Operational Research Society 49,* no. 4 (April 1998): 413–19.

24. The discussion concerning these factors is adapted from Donnelly, Gibson, and Ivancevich, *Fundamentals of Management*, 302–03; Efraim Turban and Jack R. Meredith, *Fundamentals of Management Science* (Plano, TX: Business Publications, 1981), 15–23.

25. Harold Koontz, "The Management Theory Jungle Revisited," *Academy of Management Review 5* (1980): 175–87. For an excellent illustration of how the contingency approach might apply to developing strategies for firms, see David J. Lemak and Wiboon Arunthanes, "Global Business Strategy: A Contingency Approach," *Multinational Business Review 5,* no. 1 (Spring 1997): 26–37.

26. Don Hellriegel, John W. Slocum, and Richard W. Woodman, *Organizational Behavior* (St. Paul, MN: West Publishing, 1986), 22.

27. J.W. Lorsch, "Organization Design: A Situational Perspective," *Organizational Dynamics 6* (1977): 2–4; Louis W. Fry and Deborah A. Smith, "Congruence, Contingency, and Theory Building," *Academy of Management Review* (January 1987): 117–32.

28. For a more detailed development of von Bertalanffy's ideas, see "General System Theory: A New Approach to Unity of Science," *Human Biology* (December 1951): 302–61.

29. L. Thomas Hopkins, *Integration: Its Meaning and Application* (New York: Appleton-Century-Crofts, 1937), 36–49; For an interesting illustration of how wholeness applies to managed care see Jill Wechsler, "Managed Care Firms Are Kicking Butts!" *Managed Healthcare 8,* no. 4 (April 1998): 32–36.

30. Joe Schwartz, "Why They Buy," *American Demographics 11* (March 1989): 40–41.

31. Ken Starkey, "What Can We Learn from the Learning Organization?" *Human Relations 51,* no. 4. (April 1998): 531–546.

32. David A. Garvin, "Building a Learning Organization," *Harvard Business Review 74,* no. 4. (July 1993): 78.

33. Peter Senge, *The Fifth Discipline. The Art & Practice of the Learning Organization* (New York: Doubleday/Currency, 1990). Used by permission of Doubleday, a division of Random House, Inc.

CHAPTER 3

1. For a good discussion of many factors involved in the modern meanings of social responsibility, see Frederick D. Sturdivant and Heidi Vernon-Wortzel, *Business and Society: A Managerial Approach,* 4th ed. (Homewood, Ill: Irwin, 1990), 3–24. The definition of corporate social responsibility is adapted from Keith Davis and Robert L. Blomstrom, *Business and Society: Environment and Responsibility,* 3d. ed. (New York: McGraw-Hill, 1975), 6. For illustrations of how social responsibility makes good economic sense, see David Woodruff, "Herman Miller; How Green Is My Factory," *Business Week* (September 16, 1992): 54–56; Ernest Beck, "Body Shop Founder Roddick Steps Aside as CEO," *Wall Street Journal,* May 13, 1998, B14.

2. Peter L. Berger, "New Attack on the Legitimacy of Business," *Harvard Business Review* (September/October 1981): 82–89.

3. Keith Davis, "Five Propositions for Social Responsibility," *Business Horizons* (June 1975): 9–24.

4. For extended discussion of arguments for and against social responsibility, see William C. Frederick, Keith Davis, and James E. Post, *Business and Society: Corporate Strategy, Public Policy, Ethics,* 6th ed. (New York: McGraw-Hill, 1988), 36–43.

5. For comments on a new way of exploring the relationship between the financial performance of an organization and its social responsibility activities see Sandra A. Waddock and Samuel B. Graves, "Finding the Link Between Stakeholder Relations and Quality of Management," *Journal of Investing 6,* no. 4 (Winter 1997): 20–24.

6. K.E. Apperle, A.B. Carroll, and J.D. Hatfield, "An Empirical Examination of the Relationship Between Corporate Social Responsibility and Profitability," *Academy of Management Journal* (June 1985): 446–63: J.B. McGuire, A. Sundgren, and T. Schneeweis, "Corporate Social Responsibility and Firm Financial Performance," *Academy of Management Journal,* (December 1988): 854–72; Vogel, "Ethics and Profits Don't Always Go Hand in Hand," *Los Angeles Times,* December 28, 1988, 7.

7. For Friedman's view, see "Freedom and Philanthropy: An Interview with Milton Friedman," *Business and Society Review* (Fall 1989): 11–18.

8. Milton Friedman, "Does Business Have Social Responsibility?" *Bank Administration,* April 1971, 13–14.

9. Eric J. Savitz, "The Vision Thing: Control Data Abandons It for the Bottom Line," *Barron's,* May 7, 1990, 10–11, 22.

10. For a discussion of radical environmentalism see Jeffrey Salmon, "We're All 'Corporate Polluters' Now," *Wall Street Journal,* July 2, 1997, A–14.

11. Joan E. Rigdon, "The Wrist Watch: How a Plant Handles Occupational Hazard with Common Sense," *Wall Street Journal,* September 28, 1992, 1.

12. Sandra L. Holmes, "Executive Perceptions of Corporate Social Responsibility," *Business Horizons* (June 1976): 34–40.

13. For insights regarding SC Johnson Wax's position on social responsibility involvement, see Reva A. Holmes, "At SC Johnson Wax Philanthropy Is an Investment," *Management Accounting,* August 1994, 42–45.

14. Bill Richards, "Nike Hires an Executive from Microsoft for New Post Focusing on Labor Policies," *Wall Street Journal,* January 15, 1998, B14.

15. Sturdivant and Vernon-Wortzel, *Business and Society,* 9–11.

16. Samuel C. Certo and J. Paul Peter, *The Strategic Management Process,* 3rd ed. (Chicago: Irwin, 1995), 219; Marianne M. Jennings, "Manager's Journal: Trendy Causes Are No Substitute for Ethics," *Wall Street Journal,* December 1, 1997, A22.

17. Carlo Wolff, "Living with the New Amenity," *Lodging Hospitality,* December 1994, 66–68.

18. Harry A. Lipson, "Do Corporate Executives Plan for Social Responsibility?" *Business and Society Review,* Winter 1974–75, 80–81.

19. S. Prakash Sethi, "Dimensions of Corporate Social Performance: An Analytical Framework," *California Management Review* (Spring 1975): 58–64.

20. For information on the growing trend for business to make contributions to support education, see Joel Keehn, "How Business Helps the Schools," *Fortune,* October 21, 1991, 161–71.

21. Frank H. Cassell, "The Social Cost of Doing Business," *MSU Business Topics,* Autumn 1974, 19–26.

22. Donald W. Garner, "The Cigarette Industry's Escape from Liability," *Business and Society Review 33* (Spring 1980): 22.

23. Meinolf Dierkes and Ariane Berthoin Antal, "Whither Corporate Social Reporting: Is It Time to Legislate?" *California Management Review* (Spring 1986): 106–21.

24. Condensed from Jerry McAfee, "How Society Can Help Business," *Newsweek,* July 3, 1978, 15. Copyright 1978 by Newsweek, Inc. All rights reserved. Reprinted by permission.

25. "Borden Chemicals Lashes Back at EPA," *Chemical Marketing Reporter,* November 7, 1994, 5, 19.

26. Leonard J. Brooks, Jr., "Corporate Codes of Ethics," *Journal of Business Ethics* (February/March 1989): 117–29.

27. For an interesting discussion of the ethical dilemma of fairly allocating an individual's time between work and personal life, see Paul B. Hoffmann, "Balancing Professional and Personal Priorities," *Healthcare Executive* (May/June 1994): 42.

28. Archie B. Carroll, "In Search of the Moral Manager," *Business Horizons* (March/April 1987): 7–15.

29. Sundeep Waslekar, "Good Citizens and Reap Rewards," *Asian Business,* January 1994, 52; see also Genine Babakian, "Who Will Control Russian Advertising?" *Adweek* [Eastern Edit.] August 1, 1994, 16.

30. John F. Akers, "Ethics and Competitiveness—Putting First Things First," *Sloan Management Review* (Winter 1989): 69–71; Natalie M. Green, "Creating an Ethical Workplace," *Employment Relations Today 24,* no. 2 (Summer 1997): 33–44.

31. "Helping Workers Helps Bottom Line," *Employee Benefit Plan Review,* July 1990.

32. Sandy Lutz, "Psych Hospitals Fight for Survival," *Modern Healthcare,* May 8, 1995, 62–65.

33. Patrick E. Murphy, " "Creating Ethical Corporate Structures," *Sloan Management Review* (Winter 1989): 81–87; Louis J. D'Amore, "A Code of Ethics and Guidelines for Socially and Environmentally Responsible Tourism," *Journal of Travel Research* (Winter 1993): 64–66.

34. James B. Treece, "Nissan Rattles Japan with Tough Ethics Code," *Automotive News,* May 4, 1998, 1, 49.

35. Richard A. Spinell, "Lessons from the Salomon Scandal," *America,* December 28, 1991, 476–77; Touche Ross, *Ethics in American Business* (New York: Touche Ross & Co., January 1988).

36. For additional insights on how to create an ethical workplace, see Larry L. Axline, "The Bottom Line on Ethics," *Journal of Accountancy* (December 1990): 87–91.

37. Alan L. Otten, "Ethics on the Job: Companies Alert Employees to Potential Dilemmas," *Wall Street Journal,* July 14, 1986, 25.

38. Gene R. Laczniak, "Framework for Analyzing Marketing Ethics," *Journal of Macromarketing* (Spring 1983): 7–18. See also Patricia Haddock and Marilyn Manning, "Ethically Speaking," *Sky,* March 1990, 128–31.

39. Saul W. Gellerman, "Managing Ethics from the Top Down," *Sloan Management Review* (Winter 1989): 73–79. For an interesting discussion of what management should do when charged with unethical actions, see John A. Byrne, "Here's What to Do Next, Dow Corning," *Business Week* (February 24, 1992): 33.

CHAPTER 4

1. For additional information on this topic, see Samuel C. Certo, *Human Relations Today: Concepts and Skills* (Chicago: Austen Press/Irwin, 1995), 352–75.

2. "Dossier: Telecommunications in Asia, Malaysia, Thailand," *International Business Newsletter,* June 1993, 12.

3. Robert N. Lussier, Robert W. Baeder, and Joel Corman, "Measuring Global Practices: Global Strategic Planning Through Company Situational Analysis," *Business Horizons 37* (September/October 1994): 56–63.

4. Alyssa A. Lappen, "Worldwide Connections," *Forbes,* June 27, 1988, 78–82.

5. Gale Eisenstodt, " 'We Are Happy,' " *Forbes,* May 8, 1995, 44–45.

6. "Global Investment: The Smart Money Is Flowing South," *Harvard Business Review 71* (September/October 1993): 13–14.

7. Ben J. Wattenberg, "Their Deepest Concerns," *Business Month* (January 1988): 27–33; American Assembly of Collegiate Schools of Business, *Accreditation Council Policies, Procedures, and Standards,* 1990–92, St. Louis, Mo.; Sylvia Nasar, "America's Competitive Revival," *Fortune,* January 4, 1988, 44–52.

8. For additional information regarding various forms of organization based on international involvement, see Arvind Phatak, *International Dimensions of Management* (Boston: Kent, 1993).

9. "Nu Horizons Electronics," *Fortune,* June 13, 1994, 121.

10. U.S. Department of Commerce, *The Multinational Corporation: Studies on U.S. Foreign Investment* 1 (Washington, D.C.: Government Printing Office).

11. Benjamin Gomes-Casseres, "Group versus Group: How Alliance Networks Compete," *Harvard Business Review 72* (July/August 1994), 62–74.

12. Grover Starling, *The Changing Environment of Business* (Boston: Kent, 1980), 140.

13. This section is based primarily on Richard D. Robinson, *International Management* (New York: Holt, Rinehart & Winston, 1967), 3–5.

14. 1971 Survey of National Foreign Trade Council, cited in Frederick D. Sturdivant, *Business and Society: A Managerial Approach* (Homewood, IL: Richard D. Irwin, 1977), 425. For an interesting discussion of diversification as an advantage to internationalizing, see Jeff Madura and Ann Marie Whyte, "Diversification Benefits of Direct Foreign Investment," *Management International Review 30* (First Quarter 1990): 73–85.

15. Barrie James, "Reducing the Risks of Globalization," *Long Range Planning 23* (February 1990): 80–88.

16. "NCR's Standard Contract Clause," *Harvard Business Review 72* (May/June 1994): 125.

17. Brenda Paik Sunoo, "Loosening up in Brazil," *Workforce 3* (May 1998): 8–9.

18. Roberta Maynard, "Importing Can Help a Firm Expand and Diversify," *Nation's Business* (January 1995) 11.

19. Karen Paul, "Fading Images at Eastman Kodak," *Business and Society Review 48* (Winter 1984): 56. For a discussion of how Eastman Kodak is attempting to reduce costs associated with its exporting, see Robert J. Bowman, "Cheaper by Air?" *World Trade 7* (October 1994): 88–91.

20. G. Sam Samdani, "Mobil Develops a Way to Extract Hg from Gas Streams," *Chemical Engineering 102* (April 1995): 17.

21. Robert Neff, "The Japanese Are Back—But There's a Difference," *Business Week,* Industrial/Technology Edition, October 31, 1994, 58–59.

22. Ken Korane, "Geo Metro: Economy Is Key" *Machine Design 67* (April 6, 1995): 146–48.

23. Francisco Granell, "The European Union's Enlargement Negotiations with Austria, Finland, Norway, and Sweden," *Journal of Common Market Studies 33* (March 1995): 117–41; Gwenan Roberts, "Swedish Lawyers Look South," *International Financial Law Review 14* (May 1995): 12–14; Jim Rollo, "EC Enlargement and the World Trade System," *European Economic Review 39* (April 1995): 467–73.

24. Jim Mele, "Mexico in '95: From Good to Better," *Fleet Owner,* January 1995, 56–60; William C. Symonds, "Meanwhile, to the North, NAFTA Is a Smash," *Business Week* (February 27, 1995): 66; Robert Selwitz, "NAFTA Expansion Possibilities," *Global Trade & Transportation,* October 1994, 17.

25. N. Carroll Mohn, "Pacific Rim Prices," *Marketing Research: A Magazine of Management & Applications,* Winter 1994, 22–27; Louis Kraar, "The Growing Power of Asia," *Fortune,* October 7, 1991, 118–31.

26. For an interesting account of organizing to go global, see Regina Fazio Maruca, "The Right Way to Go Global: An Interview with Whirlpool CEO David Whitwam," *Harvard Business Review 72* (March/April 1994): 134–45.

27. Howard V. Perlmutter, "The Tortuous Evolution of the Multinational Corporation," *Columbia Journal of World Business* (January/February 1969): 9–18; Rose Knotts, "Cross-Cultural Management: Transformations and Adaptations," *Business Horizons* (January/February 1989): 29–33.

28. Geert Hotstede, "Motivation, Leadership, and Organization: Do American Theories Apply Abroad?" *Organizational Dynamics 9* (Summer 1980): 42–63.

29. Walter Sweet, "International Firms Strive for Uniform Nets Abroad," *Network World,* May 28, 1990, 35–36.

30. To gain a feel for the broad range of activities occurring at a transnational company like Nestlé, see Joel Chernoff, "Advancing Corporate Governance in Europe," *Pensions & Investments,* June 12, 1995, 3, 37; E. Guthrie McTigue and Andy Sears, "The Safety 80," *Global Finance,* May 1995, 62–65; Robert W. Lear, "Whatever Happened to the Old-Fashioned Boss?" *Chief Executive,* April 1995, 71; Claudio Loderer and Andreas Jacobs, "The Nestlé Crash," *Journal of Financia! Economics 37* (March 1995): 315–39; Roberto Ceniceros, "Companies Aiding Workers, Starting to Assess Damage," *Business Insurance,* January 30, 1995, 22–23.

31. This section is mainly based on Thomas Donaldson, "Values in Tension: Ethics Away from Home," *Harvard Business Review 74,* no. 5 (September/October 1996): 48–62.

32. Anabelle Perez, "Sports Apparel Goes to Washington: New Sweatshop," *Sporting Goods Business 30,* no. 7 (May 12, 1997): 24.

33. Edward M. Mervosh and John S. McClenahen, "The Care and Feeding of Expats," *Industry Week 246,* no. 22 (December 1, 1977): 68–72.

34. Valerie Frazee, "Research Points to Weaknesses in Expat Policy," *Workforce 3,* no. 1 (January 1998): 9.

CHAPTER 5

1. James F. Lincoln, "Intelligent Selfishness and Manufacturing," Bulletin 434 (New York: Lincoln Electric Company).

2. John F. Mee, "Management Philosophy for Professional Executives," *Business Horizons,* (December 1956): 7.

3. Paul Psarouthakis, "Getting There by Goal Setting," *Supervisory Management* (June 1989): 14–15; David J. Campbell and David M. Furrer, "Goal Setting and Competition as Determinants of Task Performance," *Journal of Organizational Behavior 16,* no. 4 (July 1995): 377–90.

4. Hans Hinterhuber and Wolfgang Popp, "Are You a Strategist or Just a Manager?" *Harvard Business Review* (January/February 1992): 105–13.

5. For insights on how the Compaq Computer Corporation uses objectives to evaluate performance, see Alan M. Webber, "Consensus, Continuity, and Common Sense," *Harvard Business Review* (July/August 1990): 120.

6. Y.K. Shetty, "New Look at Corporate Goals," *California Management Review 22* (Winter 1979): 71–79. For more recent evidence that profitability, growth, and market share continue to be the most commonly set organizational objectives, see Luiz Moutinho, "Goal Setting Process and Typologies: The Case of Professional Services," *Journal of Professional Services Marketing,* 83–100.

7. For a description of how Levi Strauss attempts to keep individual objectives consistent with organizational objectives, see "Levi Strauss & Company Implements New Pay and Performance System," *Employee Benefit Plan Review,* January 1994, 46–48; Also see Mary Dee Hicks and David B. Peterson, "Steer Your People Straight," *Financial Executive 13,* no. 3 (May/June 1997): 44–45.

8. Peter F. Drucker, *The Practice of Management* (New York: Harper & Bros., 1954), 62–65, 126–29. For an interesting discussion of objectives set in the customer service area, see John Marshall, "Northwest Chain Store Enhances Customer Service and Lowers Operational Costs by Replacing Outdated POS Terminals," *Chain Store Age Executive,* June 1994, 92; For an interesting discussion on objectives and innovation, see Barton G. Tretheway, "Everything New Is Old Again," *Marketing Management 7,* no. 1 (Spring 1998): 4–13.

9. Theodore Levitt, "Marketing Myopia," *Harvard Business Review* (July/August 1960): 45.

10. Jay T. Knippen and Thad B. Green, "Directing Employee Efforts Through Goal-Setting," *Supervisory Management* (April 1989): 32–36.

11. Tom Brown, "What You 'Know' Could Be What Hurts You in Business," *Industry Week,* February 3, 1992, 13–19.

12. For a successful history of a company setting and meeting financial objectives over the long run, see Charles F. Knight, "Emerson Electric: Consistent Profits, Consistently," *Harvard Business Review* (January/February 1992): 57–70.

13. Joseph G. Louderback and George E. Manners, Jr., "Integrating ROI and CVP," *Management Accounting* (April 1981): 33–39. For a related discussion of financial objectives, see Gordon Donaldson, "Financial Goals and Strategic Consequences," *Harvard Business Review* (May/June 1985): 56–66.

14. Adapted, by permission of the publisher, from "How to Set Company Objectives," by Charles H. Granger, *Management Review* (July 1970). © 1970 by American Management Association, Inc. All rights reserved. See also Max D. Richards, *Setting Goals and Objectives* (St. Paul, MN: West Publishing, 1986).

15. Charles H. Granger, "The Hierarchy of Objectives," *Harvard Business Review* (May/June 1964): 64–74; Richard E. Kopelman, "Managing for Productivity: One-Third of the Job," *National Productivity Review 17,* no. 3 (Summer 1998): 1–2. Reprinted with the permission of American Management Association International. New York, N.Y. All rights reserved. http://www.amanet.org

16. See also Edwin A. Locke, Dong-Ok Chah, Scott Harrison, and Nancy Lustgarten, "Separating the Effects of Goal Specificity from Goal Level," *Organizational Behavior and Human Decision Processes* (April 1989): 270–87; Mike Deblieux, "The Challenge and Value of Documenting Performance," *HR Focus* (March 1994): 3; To better understand the role of setting objectives in compensation plans, see William J. Liccione, "Effective Goal Setting: A Prerequisite for Compensation Plans with Incentive Value," *Compensation & Benefits Management 13,* no. 1 (Winter 1997): 19–25.

17. For a discussion supporting the importance of making objectives operational or measurable, see Dan Logan, "Integrated Communication Offers Competitive Edge," *Bank Marketing* (May 1994): 63–67; Also see Nora Wood, "So You Say You Want a Revolution," *Incentive 172,* no. 6 (June 1998): 41–47.

18. James G. March and Herbert A. Simon, *Organization* (New York: Wiley, 1958), 191.

19. Drucker, *The Practice of Management;* see also Peter Drucker, Harold Smiddy, and Ronald G. Greenwood, "Management by Objectives," *Academy of Management Review 6* (April 1981): 225; Also see Paul N. Romani, "MBO by Any Other Name Is Still MBO," *Supervision 58,* no. 12 (December 1997): 6–8.

20. Robert L. Mathis and John H. Jackson, *Personnel: Human Resource Management* (St. Paul, MN: West Publishing, 1985), 353–55.

21. Robert Rodgers and John E. Hunter, "Impact of Management by Objectives on Organizational Productivity," *Journal of Applied Psychology* (1991): 322–35; Jerry L. Rostund, "Evaluating Management Objectives with the Quality Loss Function," *Quality Progress* (August 1989): 45–49; William H. Franklin, Jr., "Create an Atmosphere of Positive Expectations," *Administrative Management* (April 1980): 32–34; Peter Crutchley, "Management by Objectives," *Credit Management* (May 1994): 36–38; William J. Kretlow and Winford E. Holland, "Implementing Management by Objectives in Research Administration," *Journal of the Society of Research Administrators* (Summer 1988): 135–41.

22. Charles H. Ford, "Manage by Decisions, Not by Objectives," *Business Horizons* (February 1980): 17–18; Kretlow and Holland, "Implementing Management by Objectives in Research Administration," 135–41; For an interesting description of how firms in Sweden employ MBO, see Terry Ingham, "Management by Objectives—A Lesson in Commitment and Cooperation," *Managing Service Quality 5,* no. 6 (1995): 35–38.

CHAPTER 6

1. Harry Jones, *Preparing Company Plans: A Workbook for Effective Corporate Planning* (New York: Wiley, 1974), 3; Richard G. Meloy, "Business Planning," *The CPA Journal 63,* no. 8 (March 1998): 74–75.

2. Robert G. Reed, "Five Challenges Multiple-Line Companies Face," *Market Facts* (January/February 1990): 5–6; Brian Burrows and Ken G.B. Blakewell, "Management Functions and Librarians," *Library Management,* (1989): 2–61.

3. C.W. Roney, "The Two Purposes of Business Planning," *Managerial Planning* (November/December 1976): 1–6; Linda C. Simmons, "Plan. Ready. Aim," *Mortgage Banking 56,* no. 5 (February 1996): 95–96. For an interesting account of the planning function in an international setting, see Gabriel Ogunmokun, "Planning: An Exploratory Investigation of Small Business Organizations in Australia," *International Journal of Management 15,* no. 1 (March 1998): 60–71.

4. Wendy Zellner, "Moving Tofu into the Mainstream," *Business Week* (May 25, 1992): 94.

5. Harold Koontz and Cyril O'Donnell, *Management: A Systems and Contingency Analysis of Management Functions* (New York: McGraw-Hill, 1976), 130.

6. For an interesting discussion on how the importance of planning relates to even day-to-day operations, see Teri Lammers, "The Custom-Made Day Planner," *Inc.,* February 1992, 61–62.

7. Kenneth R. Allen, "Creating and Executing a Business Plan," *American Agent & Broker* (July 1994) 20–21.

8. For a discussion of U.S. shortsightedness in planning, see Michael T. Jacobs, "A Cure for America's Corporate Short-termism," *Planning Review* (January/February 1992): 4–9. For a discussion of the close relationship between objectives and planning, see "Mistakes to Avoid: From a Business Owner," *Business Owner* (September/October 1994): 11.

9. For an overview of strategic planning, see Bryan W. Barry, "A Beginner's Guide to Strategic Planning," *The Futurist 32*, no. 3 (April 1998): 33–36.

10. Excerpted, by permission of the publisher, from *1974–75 Exploratory Planning Briefs: Planning for the Future by Corporations and Agencies, Domestic and International,* by William A. Simmons, © 1975 by AMA-COM, a division of American Management Associations, 10–11. All rights reserved; For an illustration of technology's effect on planning, see Miriam Leuchter, "Sun Turns Up the Heat," *The Journal of Business Strategy 18,* no. 5 (September/October 1997): 44–46.

11. Henry Mintzberg, "A New Look at the Chief Executive's Job," *Organizational Dynamics* (Winter 1973): 20–40.

12. For similar questions focusing on strategic planning, see Hans Hinterhuber and Wolfgang Popp, "Are You a Strategist or Just a Manager?" *Harvard Business Review* (January/February 1992): 105–13; For an example of how a CEO plans organizational change, see Peter Spiegel, "Old Dog, New Tricks?" *Forbes,* June 1, 1998, 47.

13. James M. Hardy, *Corporate Planning for Nonprofit Organizations* (New York: Association Press, 1972), 37; For an interesting article that describes how CEOs gain assistance from their boards of directors, see Ben L. Lytle, "Putting Directors to Work Adding Value," *Directors and Boards 20,* no. 3 (Spring 1996): 10–12.

14. Milton Leontiades, "The Dimensions of Planning in Large Industrialized Organizations," *California Management Review 22* (Summer 1980): 82–86.

15. For a discussion of outside consultants who develop plans for business clients, see Donald F. Kuratko and Arnold Cirtin, "Developing a Business Plan for Your Clients," *National Public Accountant* (January 1990): 24–27.

16. The section "Qualifications of Planners" is adapted from John Argenti, *Systematic Corporate Planning* (New York: Wiley, 1974), 126; For an interesting look at the role of power and politics in the planning process, see Renee Berger, "People, Power, Politics," *Planning 63,* no. 2 (February 1997): 4–9.

17. These three duties are adapted from Walter B. Schaffir, "What Have We Learned about Corporate Planning?" *Management Review* (August 1973): 19–26.

18. For a discussion of how modern planners must focus more on gathering information related to the international environment, see William H. Davidson, "The Rule of Global Scanning in Business Planning," *Organizational Dynamics* (Winter 1991): 4–16. For insights on how a planner can use groups to solve problems, see Andrew E. Schwartz, "Group Decision-Making," *CPA Journal* (August 1994): 60–63. See also Thomas P. Houck, "Improving Efficiency in Your Audit Department," *Internal Auditing* (Winter 1994): 32–37.

19. Frank Corcell, "How to Identify a Sick Company in Time to Help It," *Practical Accountant* (October 1989): 90–99.

20. Michael Muckian and Mary Auestad Arnold, "Manager, Appraise Thyself," *Credit Union Management* (December 1989): 26–28.

21. Edward J. Green, *Workbook for Corporate Planning* (New York: American Management Association, 1970).

22. Z.A. Malik, "Formal Long-Range Planning and Organizational Performance," Ph.D. diss. (Rensselaer Polytechnic Institute, 1974).

23. James Brian Quinn, "Managing Strategic Changes," *Sloan Management Review 21* (Summer 1980): 3–20.

24. Kamal E. Said and Robert F. Sciler, "An Empirical Study of Long-Range Planning Systems: Strengths—Weaknesses—Outlook," *Managerial Planning 28* (July/August 1979): 24–28. See also John T. Sakai, "Japan as an Attractive Alliance Partner," *Directors & Boards* (Winter 1994): 42–44.

25. Paul J. Stonich, "Formal Planning Pitfalls and How to Avoid Them," *Management Review* (June 1975): 5–6.

26. Nigel Piercy, "Diagnosing and Solving Implementation Problems in Strategic Planning," *Journal of General Management* (Autumn 1989): 19–38. Concerning the emerging role of middle management in implementing customer satisfaction and profitability plans, see David Jackson and John Humble, "Middle Managers: New Purpose, New Directions," *Journal of Management Development 13* (1994): 15–21.

27. Peter F. Drucker, *Management: Tasks, Responsibilities, Practices* (New York: Harper & Row, 1973). See also Bernard W. Taylor III and K. Roscoe David, "Implementing an Action Program via Organizational Change," *Journal of Economics and Business* (Spring/Summer 1976): 203–08.

28. William H. Reynolds, "The Edsel: Faulty Execution of a Sound Marketing Plan," *Business Horizons* (Fall 1967): 39–46; Tony Grundy, "Strategy Implementation and Project Management," *International Journal of Project Management 16,* no. 1 (February 1998): 43–50.

29. Luis MaR. Calingo, "Achieving Excellence in Strategic Planning Systems," *Advanced Management Journal* (Spring 1989): 21–23. For more discussion on including the right people in the planning process, see Gary Hines, "Strategic Planning Made Easy, " *Training & Development Journal* (April 1991): 39–43.

CHAPTER 7

1. For an excellent discussion of various decisions that managers make, see Michael Verespej, "Gutsy Decisions of 1991," *Industry Week* (February 17, 1992): 21–31; For an interesting discussion of decision making in government agencies, see Burton Gummer, "Decision Making Under Conditions of Risk, Ambiguity, and Uncertainty: Recent Perspectives," *Administration in Social Work 2* (1998): 75–93.

2. Abraham Zaleznik, "What Makes a Leader?" *Success,* June 1989, 42–45; Daphne Main and Joyce C. Lambert, "Improving Your Decision Making," *Business and Economic Review 44,* no. 3 (April/June 1998): 9–12.

3. Mervin Kohn, *Dynamic Managing: Principles, Process, Practice* (Menlo Park, Ca.: Cummings, 1977), 38–62. For an interesting discussion of how to train managers to become better decision makers by slowing down the decision-making process, see Jack Falvey, "Making Great Managers," *Small Business Reports* (February 1990): 15–18. See also Herbert A. Simon, *The New Science of Management Decision* (New York: Harper & Bros., 1960): 5–8.

4. William H. Miller, "Tough Decisions on the Forgotten Continent," *Industry Week* (June 6, 1994): 40–44.

5. *The D of Research and Development* (Wilmington, DE: DuPont, 1966), 28–29; apparently, DuPont's basic tenets regarding how the scope of decisions influences how decisions should be made have evolved over many years; see, for example, George J. Titus, "Forty-Year Evolution of Engineering Research: A Case Study of DuPont's Engineering Research and Development," *IEEE Transactions on Engineering Management 41* (November 1994): 350–54.

6. Marcia V. Wilkof, "Organizational Culture and Decision Making: A Case of Consensus Management," *R&D Management* (April 1989): 185–99; For an interesting discussion of various tools used to build consensus, see Richard L. Luebbe and B. Kay Snavely, "Making Effective Team Decisions with Consensus Building Tools," *Industrial Management 39,* no. 5 (September/October 1997): 1–7.

7. Charles Wilson and Marcus Alexis, "Basic Frameworks for Decision," *Academy of Management Journal 5* (August 1962): 151–64.

8. For a discussion of the importance of understanding decision makers in organizations, see Walter D. Barndt, Jr., "Profiling Rival Decision Makers," *Journal of Business Strategy* (January/February 1991): 8–11. See also Ernest Dale, *Management: Theory and Practice* (New York: McGraw-Hill, 1973): 548–49.

9. "New OCC Guidelines for Appraising Management," *Issues in Bank Regulation* (Fall 1989): 20–22; For an interesting discussion of decision-making processes used in the United States versus those used in the United Kingdom, see Mark Andrew Mitchell, Ronald D. Taylor, and Faruk Tanyel, "Product Elimination Decisions: A Comparison of American and British Manufacturing Firms," *International Journal of Commerce & Management 8,* no. 1 (1998): 8–27.

10. For an extended discussion of this model, see William B. Werther, Jr., "Productivity Through People: The Decision-Making Process," *Management Decisions* (1988): 37–41.

11. These assumptions are adapted from James G. March and Herbert A. Simon, *Organizations* (New York: Wiley, 1958), 137–38.

12. William C. Symonds, "There's More than Beer in Molson's Mug," *Business Week* (February 10, 1992): 108.

13. Chester I. Barnard, *The Function of the Executive* (Cambridge, MA.: Harvard University Press, 1938).

14. For further elaboration on these factors, see Robert Tannenbaum, Irving R. Weschle, and Fred Massarik, *Leadership and Organization: A Behavioral Science Approach* (New York: McGraw-Hill, 1961), 277–78.

15. For more discussion of these factors, see F.A. Shull, Jr., A.I. Delbecq, and L.L. Cummings, *Organizational Decision Making* (New York: McGraw-Hill, 1970).

16. For a worthwhile discussion of forecasting and evaluating the outcomes of alternatives, see J.R.C. Wensley, "Effective Decision Aids in Marketing," *European Journal of Marketing* (1989): 70–79.

17. Timothy A. Park and Frances Antonovitz, "Econometric Tests of Firm Decision Making under Uncertainty: Optimal Output and Hedging Decisions," *Southern Economic Journal* (January 1992): 593–609; Mats Danielson, "A Framework for Analyzing Decisions Under Risk," *European Journal of Operational Research 104*, no. 3 (February 1, 1998): 474–84.

18. For a discussion of risk and decisions, see Sim B. Sitkin and Amy L. Pablo, "Reconceptualizing the determinants of Risk Behavior," *Academy of Management Review* (January 1992): 11. See also Michael J. Ryan, "Constrained Gaming Approaches to Decision Making under Uncertainty," *European Journal of Operational Research* (August 25, 1994): 70–81; To see how information can help reduce the risk in decision making, see Helga Drummond, " 'It Looked Marvelous In the Prospectus': TAURUS, Information and Decision Making," *Journal of General Management 23*, no. 3 (Spring 1998): 73–87.

19. Steven C. Harper, "What Separates Executives from Managers," *Business Horizons* (September/October 1988): 13–19; Russ Holloman, "The Light and Dark Sides of Decision Making," *Supervisory Management* (December 1989): 33–34.

20. The scope of this text does not permit elaboration on these three decision-making tools. However, for an excellent discussion on how they are used in decision making, see Richard M. Hodgetts, *Management: Theory, Process and Practice* (Philadelphia: Saunders, 1975), 234–66. For a discussion of the computer as a decision-making tool, see Robert Addleman, "Scientific Decision-Making," *Healthcare Forum* (March/April 1994): 47–50.

21. Richard C. Mosier, "Expected Value: Applying Research to Uncertainty," *Appraisal Journal* (July 1989): 293–96. See also Amartya Sen, "The Formulation of Rational Choice," *American Economic Review 84* (May 1994): 385–90; For an example of how companies use expected values when considering whether or not to drill oil wells, see James A. MacKay and Ian Lerche, "What an Option Is Worth for an Exploration Opportunity," *Oil & Gas Journal 93* no. 52 (December 25, 1995): 95–98.

22. Peter Boys, "Answers Grow on Decision Trees," *Accountancy* (January 1990): 86–89; For an example of how financial analysts use decision trees to reduce risk, see Joseph J. Mezrich, "When Is a Tree a Hedge?" *Financial Analysts Journal 50*, no. 6 (November/December 1994): 75–81.

23. John F. Magee, "Decision Trees for Decision Making," *Harvard Business Review* (July/August 1964). To see how decision trees can be applied to the problem of stress management, refer to Lin Grensing-Pophal, "If the Answer Is 'No,' Then 'Let It Go': Using the 'Stress Relief Decision Tree,' " *Manage* (July 1994): 18–20.

24. Rakesh Sarin and Peter Wakker, "Folding Back in Decision Tree Analysis," *Management Science 40* (May 1994): 625–28.

25. This section is based on Samuel C. Certo, *Supervision: Quality and Diversity Through Leadership* (Homewood, IL: Austen Press/Irwin, 1994), 198–202.

26. Clark Wigley, "Working Smart on Tough Business Problems," *Supervisory Management* (February 1992): 1.

27. Joseph Alan Redman, "Nine Creative Brainstorming Techniques, " *Quality Digest* (August 1992): 50–51; In K. Chung and Carl R. Adams, "A Study on the Characteristics of Group Decision Making Behavior: Cultural Difference Perspective of Korea vs. U.S.," *Journal of Global Information Management 5*, no. 3 (Summer 1997): 18–29.

28. David M. Armstrong, "Management by Storytelling," *Executive Female* (May/June 1992): 38–41.

29. André, Delbecq, Andrew Van de Ven, and D. Gustafson, *Group Techniques for Program Planning* (Glenview, IL: Scott, Foresman, 1975); Philip L. Roth, L.F. Lydia, and Fred S. Switzer, "Nominal Group Technique—An Aid for Implementing TQM," *CPA Journal* (May 1995): 68–69.

30. N. Delkey, *The Delphi Method: An Experimental Study of Group Opinion* (Santa Monica, CA: Rand Corporation, 1969); Delia Neuman, "High School Students' Use of Databases: Results of a National Delphi Study," *Journal of the American Society for Information Science 46* (1995): 284–98; Sibylle Breiner, Kerstin Cuhls, and Hariolf Grupp, "Technology Foresight Using a Delphi Approach: A Japanese-German Cooperation," *R&D Management* (April 1994): 141–53.

CHAPTER 8

1. Tony Grundy and Dave King, "Using Strategic Planning to Drive Strategic Change," *Long-Range Planning* (February 1992): 100–108; Andrall E. Pearson, "Six Basics for General Managers," *Harvard Business Review* (July/August 1989): 94–101.

2. Charles R. Greer, "Counter-Cyclical Hiring as a Staffing Strategy for Managerial and Professional Personnel: Some Considerations and Issues," *Academy of Management Review 9* (April 1984): 324–30; Dyan Machan, "The Strategy Thing," *Forbes*, May 23, 1994, 113–14.

3. Richard B. Robinson, Jr., and John A. Pearce II, "Research Thrusts in Small Firm Strategic Planning," *Academy of Management Review 9* (January 1984): 128–37; For a detailed discussion of strategy formulation in small family-owned businesses, see Nancy Drozdow and Vincent P. Carroll, "Tools for Strategy Development in Family Firms," *Sloan Management Review 39*, no. 1 (Fall 1997): 75–88.

4. This section is based on Samuel C. Certo and J. Paul Peter, *Strategic Management: Concepts and Applications* (Chicago: Austin Press/Irwin, 1995), 3–27.

5. Samuel C. Certo and J. Paul Peter, *The Strategic Management Process*, 4th ed. (Chicago: Austen Press/Irwin, 1995), 32; William Drohan, "Principles of Strategic Planning," *Association Management, 49*, no. 1 (January 1997): 85–87.

6. This section is based on William F. Glueck and Lawrence R. Jauch, *Business Policy and Strategic Management* (New York: McGraw-Hill, 1984), 99–110.

7. John F. Watkins, "Retirees as a New Growth Industry? Assessing the Demographic and Social Impact," *Review of Business* (Spring 1994): 9–14.

8. Bruce Henderson, "The Origin of Strategy," *Harvard Business Review* (November/December 1989): 139–43; For tips used to analyze competitors more effectively, see Dan Simpson, "Competitive Intelligence Can Be a Bad Investment," *Journal of Business Strategy 18*, no. 6 (November/December 1997): 8–9.

9. Peter Wright, "MNC—Third World Business Unit Performance: Application of Strategic Elements," *Strategic Management Journal 5* (1984): 231–40; Inga S. Baird, Marjorie A. Lyles, and J.B. Orris, "The Choice of International Strategies by Small Businesses," *Journal of Small Business Management 32*, no. 1 (January 1994): 48–60.

10. M. Klemm, S. Sanderson, and G. Luffman, "Mission Statements: Selling Corporate Values to Employees," *Long-Range Planning* (June 1991): 73–78.

11. Colin Coulson-Thomas, "Strategic Vision or Strategic Cons: Rhetoric or Reality," *Long-Range Planning* (February 1992): 81–89; Rhymer Rigby, "Mission Statements," *Management Today* (March 1998): 56–58.

12. This section is based primarily on Thomas H. Naylor and Kristin Neva, "Design of a Strategic Planning Process," *Managerial Planning* (January/February 1980): 2–7; Donald W. Mitchell, "Pursuing Strategic Potential," *Managerial Planning* (May/June 1980): 6–10; Benton E. Gup, "Begin Strategic Planning by Asking Three Questions," *Managerial Planning* (November/December 1979): 28–31, 35; Rainer Feurer and Kazem Chaharbaghi, "Dynamic Strategy Formulation and Alignment," *Journal of General Management 20*, no. 3 (Spring 1995): 76–91.

13. For a practical example of SWOT applied in the business world, see Robert H. Woods, "Strategic Planning: A Look at Ruby Tuesday," *Cornell Hotel & Restaurant Administration Quarterly* (June 1994): 41–49.

14. Philip Kotler, *Marketing Management Analysis, Planning and Control*, 7th ed. (Upper Saddle River, N.J.: Prentice Hall, 1991), 39–41.

15. Harold W. Fox, "The Frontiers of Strategic Planning: Intuition or Formal Models?" *Management Review* (April 1981): 8–14. See also J. Scott Armstrong and Roderick J. Brodie, "Effects of Portfolio Planning Methods on Decision Making: Experimental Results," *International Journal of Research in Marketing* (January 1994): 73–84; Robin Wensley, "Making Better Decisions: The Challenge of Marketing Strategy Techniques—A Comment on 'Effects of Portfolio Planning Methods on Decision Making: Experimental Results' by Armstrong and Brodie," *International Journal of Research in Marketing* (January 1994): 85–90.

16. This discussion of Porter's model is based on chapters 1 and 2 of Porter's *Competitive Strategy* (New York: The Free Press, 1980), and chapter 1 of

Porter's *Competitive Advantage: Creating and Sustaining Superior Performance* (New York: The Free Press, 1985); for an application of Porter's concepts, see William P. Munk and Barry Shane, "Using Competitive Analysis Models to Set Strategy in the Northwest Hardboard Industry," *Forest Products Journal* (July/August 1994): 11–18.

17. Ian C. MacMillan, Donald C. Hambrick, and Diana L. Day, "The Product Portfolio and Profitability—A PIMS-Based Analysis of Industrial-Product Businesses," *Academy of Management Journal* (December 1982): 733–55.

18. Bill Saporito, "Black & Decker's Gamble on Globalization," *Fortune,* May 14, 1984, 40–48; Walecia Konrad and Bruce Einhorn, "Famous Amos Gets a Chinese Accent," *Business Week* (September 28, 1992): 76.

19. Doron P. Levin, "Westinghouse's New Chief Aims to Push New Lines, Revitalize Traditional Ones," *Wall Street Journal,* November 28, 1983, 10.

20. William Sandy, "Avoid the Breakdowns Between Planning and Implementation," *Journal of Business Strategy* (September/October 1991): 30–33.

21. Thomas V. Bonoma, "Making Your Marketing Strategy Work," *Harvard Business Review* (March/April 1984): 69–76; For an interesting discussion that applies a contingency approach to strategy implementation, see Robert Waldersee and Simon Sheather, "The Effects of Strategy Type on Strategy Implementation Actions," *Human Relations 49*, no. 1 (January 1996): 105–23.

22. For a good discussion of the importance of monitoring the progress of the strategic planning process, see William B. Carper and Terry A. Bresnick, "Strategic Planning Conferences," *Business Horizons* (September/October 1989): 34–40; see also Stephen Bungay and Michael Goold, "Creating a Strategic Control System," *Long-Range Planning* (June 1991): 32–39.

23. For a detailed discussion of the characteristics of strategic and tactical planning, see George A. Steiner, *Top Management Planning* (Toronto, Canada: Collier-Macmillan, 1969), 37–39.

24. Russell L. Ackoff, *A Concept of Corporate Planning* (New York: Wiley, 1970), 4.

25. "The New Breed of Strategic Planner," *Business Week* (September 17, 1984): 62–67.

CHAPTER 9

1. Charles B. Ames, "Straight Talk from the New CEO," *Harvard Business Review* (November/December 1989):132–38.

2. Fremont E. Kast and James E. Rosenzweig, *Organization and Management: A Systems Approach* (New York: McGraw-Hill, 1970), 443–49. For a classic discussion on expanding this list of characteristics to 13, see P. LeBreton and D.A. Henning, *Planning Theory* (Upper Saddle River, NJ: Prentice Hall, 1961), 320–44. These authors list the dimensions of a plan as (1) complexity, (2) significance, (3) comprehensiveness, (4) time, (5) specificity, (6) completeness, (7) flexibility, (8) frequency, (9) formality, (10) confidential nature, (11) authorization, (12) ease of implementation, and (13) ease of control.

3. Jennifer A. Knight, "Loss Control Solution to Limiting Costs of Workplace Violence," *Corporate Cashflow* (July 1994): 16–17.

4. Kirkland Wilcox and Richard Discenza, "The TQM Advantage," *CA Magazine,* May 1994, 37–41.

5. From "Seize the Future—Make Top Trends Pay Off Now," *Success* (March 1990): 39–45.

6. For an interesting article outlining how currency exchange rates complicate budgets that relate to operations in more than one country, see Paul V. Mannino and Ken Milani, "Budgeting for an International Business," *Management Accounting* (February 1992): 36–41; see also J. Fred Weston and Eugene F. Brigham, *Essentials of Managerial Finance* (New York: Holt, Rinehart & Winston, 1971), 107; Mark M. Klein, "Questions to Ask Before You Sharpen Your Budget Knife," *Bottomline* (March 1990): 32–37; Pierre Filiatrault and Jean-Charles Chebat, "How Service Firms Set Their Marketing Budgets," *Industrial Marketing Management* (February 1990): 63–67.

7. Kjell A. Ringbakk, "Why Planning Fails," *European Business* (July 1970). See also William G. Gang, "Strategic Planning and Competition: A Survival Guide for Electric Utilities," *Fortnightly,* February 1, 1994, 20–23. For a good discussion on involving people in the planning process, see Margaret M. Lucas, "Business Plan Is the Key to Agency Success," *National Underwriter 94* (March 5, 1990): 15, 17.

8. For information that ranks U.S. cities on the possible site selection criterion of growth, see John Case, "Where the Growth Is," *Inc.,* June 1991, 66–79. See

also Walt Yesberg, "Get a Grip on Building Costs," *ABA Banking Journal 82* (March 1990): 90, 92; Robert Bowman, "Key Logistics Issues in Site Selection," *Distribution 88* (December 1989): 56–57.

9. Douglas P. Woodward, "Locational Determinants of Japanese Manufacturing Start-Ups in the United States," *Southern Economic Journal* (January 1992): 690–708.

10. Greg Nakanishi, "Building Business Through Partnerships," *HR Magazine* June 1991, 108–12; For an interesting description of a company that performs human resource planning for other companies, see Eryn Brown, "PeopleSoft: Tech's Latest Publicly Traded Cult," *Fortune,* May 25, 1998, 155–156.

11. Charles F. Kettering, "A Glimpse at the Future," *Industry Week* (July 1, 1991): 34.

12. William C. House, "Environmental Analysis: Key to More Effective Dynamic Planning," *Managerial Planning* (January/February 1977): 25–29. The basic components of this forecasting method, as well as of other methods, are discussed in Chaman L. Jain, "How to Determine the Approach to Forecasting," *Journal of Business Forecasting Methods & Systems* (Summer 1995): 2, 28.

13. Marshall L. Fisher et al., "Making Supply Meet Demand in an Uncertain World," *Harvard Business Review* (May/June 1994): 83–89; Tony Dear, "Fast and Slow Approaches to Sales Forecasting," *Logistics Focus 6* no. 4 (May 1998): 24–25.

14. Olfa Hemler, "The Uses of Delphi Techniques in Problems of Educational Innovations," no. 8499, RAND Corporation, December 1966; For an interesting article employing the Delphi method to analyze international trends, see Michael R. Czinkota and Ilkka A. Ronkainen, "International Business and Trade in the Next Decade: Report from a Delphi Study," *Journal of International Business Studies 28*, no. 4 (Fourth Quarter 1997): 827–44.

15. James E. Cox, Jr., "Approaches for Improving Salespersons' Forecasts," *Industrial Marketing Management 18* (November 1989): 307–11; Jack Stack, "A Passion for Forecasting," *Inc.,* November 1997, 37–38.

16. N. Carroll Mohn, "Forecasting Sales with Trend Models—Coca-Cola's Experience," *Journal of Business Forecasting 8* (Fall 1989): 6–8; For an interesting article that describes the use of time series analysis in predicting the alcohol consumption of Europeans, see David E. Smith and Hans S. Solgaard, "Global Trends in European Alcoholic Drinks Consumption," *Marketing and Research Today 26*, no. 2 (May 1998): 80–85.

17. For elaboration on these methods, see George A. Steiner, *Top Management Planning* (London: Collier-Macmillan, 1969), 223–27.

18. Willard Fazar, "The Origin of PERT," *The Controller* (December 1962). See also Harold L. Wattel, *Network Scheduling and Control Systems CAP/PERT* (Hempstead, N.Y.: Hostra University, 1964). For a discussion of software packages that draw preliminary PERT and Gantt charts, see Pat Sweet, "A Planner's Best Friend?" *Accountancy* (February 1994): 56, 58; Also see Curtis F. Franklin, Jr., "Project Managers Toolbox," *CIO 11*, no. 2 (October 15, 1997): 64–70.

19. R.J. Schonberger, "Custom-Tailored PERT/CPM Systems," *Business Horizons 15* (1972): 64–66. See also H.M. Soroush, "The Most Critical Path in a PERT Network," *Journal of the Operational Research Society 45* (March 1994): 287–300.

20. Avraham Shrub, "The Integration of CPM and Material Management in Project Management," *Construction Management and Economics 6* (Winter 1988): 261–72; Michael A. Hatfield and James Noel, "The Case for Critical Path," *Cost Engineering 40*, no. 3 (March 1998): 17–18.

21. For extended discussion of these steps, see Edward K. Shelmerdine, "Planning for Project Management," *Journal of Systems Management 40* (January 1989): 16–20.

CHAPTER 10

1. Douglas S. Sherwin, "Management of Objectives," *Harvard Business Review* (May/June 1976): 149–60. See also Lloyd Sandelands and Robert Drazin, "On the Language of Organization Theory," *Organizational Studies 10* (1989): 457–77.

2. Henri Fayol, *General and Industrial Management* (London: Sir Isaac Pitman and Sons, 1949), 53–54.

3. For a discussion emphasizing the importance of continually adapting organization structure, see Michael A. Vercspej, "When Change Becomes the Norm," *Industry Week* (March 16, 1992): 35–36.

4. Saul W. Gellerman, "In Organizations, as in Architecture, Form Follows Function," *Organizational Dynamics 18* (Winter 1990): 57–68; for a discussion of how evaluation can contribute to increased worker productivity, see Eugene F. Finklin, "Techniques for Making People More Productive," *Journal of Business Strategy* (March/April 1991): 53–56.

5. Max Weber, *Theory of Social and Economic Organization,* trans. and ed. A.M. Henderson and Talcott Parsons (London: Oxford University Press, 1947); Stanley Vanagunas, "Max Weber's Authority Models and the Theory of X-Inefficiency: The Economic Sociologist's Analysis Adds More Structure to Leibenstein's Critique of Rationality," *American Journal of Economics and Sociology 48* (October 1989): 393–400; Thomas A. Stewart, "Get with the New Power Game," *Fortune,* January 13, 1997, 58–62.

6. Sandra T. Gray, "Fostering Leadership for the New Millennium," *Association Management* (January 1995): L-78–L-82.

7. Lyndall Urwich, *Notes on the Theory of Organization* (New York: American Management Association, 1952).

8. For an interesting discussion of a nontraditional organization structure, see David M. Lehmann, "Integrated Enterprise Management: A Look at the Functions, the Enterprise, and the Environment—Can You See the Difference?" *Hospital Material Management Quarterly 19,* no. 4 (May 1998): 22–26.

9. Sally Helgesen, *The Female Advantage: Women's Ways of Leadership* (New York: Doubleday/Currency, 1990); Tom Peters, "The Best New Managers Will Listen, Motivate, Support," *Working Woman,* September 1990, 142–43, 216–17.

10. David Stamps, "Off the Charts," *Training 34,* no. 10 (October 1997): 77–83.

11. Geary A. Rummler and Alan P. Brache, "Managing the White Space on the Organization Chart," *Supervision* (May 1991): 6–12. For an article arguing in favor of having organizations designed by function, see Jack Cohen, "Managing the Managers," *Supermarket Business 44* (September 1989): 16, 244.

12. Roderick E. White and Thomas A. Poynter, "Organizing for Worldwide Advantage," *Business Quarterly 54* (Summer 1989): 84–89.

13. Y.K. Sherry and Howard M. Carlisle, "A Contingency Model of Organization Design," *California Management Review 15* (1972): 38–45. For additional discussion of factors influencing formal structure, see Paul Dwyer, "Tearing Up Today's Organization Chart," *Business Week* (November 18, 1994): 80–90.

14. For insights on how Ralph Larsen, CEO of Johnson & Johnson, views problems and how his view might influence the formal structure of his organization see Brian Dumaine, "Is Big Still Good?" *Fortune,* April 30, 1992, 50–60.

15. Carol Ann Dorn, "Einstein: Still No Equal," *Journal of Business Strategy* (November/December 1994): 20–23.

16. C.R. Walker and R.H. Guest, *The Man on the Assembly Line* (Cambridge, Mass.: Harvard University Press, 1952). For an excellent example of how technology can affect division of labor, see John P. Walsh, "Technological Change and the Division of Labor: The Case of Retail Meatcutters," *Work and Occupations 16* (May 1989): 165–83.

17. J. Mooney, "The Principles of Organization," in *Ideas and Issues in Public Administration,* ed. D. Waldo (New York: McGraw-Hill, 1953), 86. For a discussion of the importance of cooperation and coordination in division of labor, see Jason Magidson and Andrew E. Polcha, "Creating Market Economies Within Organizations," *The Planning Forum* (January/February 1992): 37–40. See also Peter Jackson, "Speed versus Heed," *CA Magazine,* November 1994, 56–57.

18. Bruce D. Sanders, "Making Work Groups Work," *Computerworld 24* (March 5, 1990): 85–89.

19. George D. Greenberg, "The Coordinating Roles of Management," *Midwest Review of Public Administration 10* (1976): 66–76; Stephen Ackroyd, "How Organizations Act Together: Interorganizational Coordination in Theory and Practice," *Administrative Science Quarterly 43,* no. 1 (March 1998): 217–21.

20. Henry C. Metcalf and Lyndall F. Urwich, eds., *Dynamic Administration: The Collected Papers of Mary Parker Follett* (New York: Harper & Bros., 1942), 297–99; James F. Wolf, "The Legacy of Mary Parker Follett," *Bureaucrat Winter* (1988–89): 53–57.

21. Leon McKenzie, "Supervision: Learning from Experience," *Health Care Supervisor 8* (January 1990): 1–11. For an interesting discussion of how span of management impacts a manager's perceived need for additional training, see James P. Guthrie and Catherine E. Schwoerer, "Individual and Contextual Influences on Self-Assessed Training Needs," *Journal of Organizational Behavior 15* (1994): 405–22.

22. Harold Koontz, "Making Theory Operational: The Span of Management," *Journal of Management Studies* (October 1966): 229–43; see also John S. Mc-Clenahen, "Managing More People in the '90s," *Industry Week 238* (March 1989): 30–38.

23. V.A. Graicunas, "Relationships in Organization," *Bulletin of International Management Institute* (March 1933): 183–87. L.F. Urwick, "V.A. Graicunas and the Span of Control," *Academy of Management Journal 17* (June 1974): 349–54; Luther Gulick, Lyndall Urwick, James D. Mooney, Henri Fayol, et al. "Papers on the Science of Administration," *International Journal of Public Administration 21,* no. 2–4 (1998): 441–641.

24. For discussion about why managers should increase spans of management see Stephen R. Covey, "The Marketing Revolution," *Executive Excellence 14,* no. 3 (March 1997): 3–4.

25. John R. Brandt, "Middle Management: 'Where the Action Will Be,'" *Industry Week* (May 2, 1994): 30–36.

26. Philip R. Nienstedt, "Effectively Downsizing Management Structures," *Human Resources Planning 12* (1989): 155–65; Robin Bellis-Jones and Max Hand, "Improving Managerial Spans of Control," *Management Accounting 67* (October 1989): 20–21.

27. S.R. Maheshwari, "Hierarchy: Key Principle of Organization," *Employment News, 21,* no. 49 (March 8–March 14): 1–2.

28. Cass Bettinger, "The Nine Principles of War," *Bank Marketing 21* (December 1989): 32–34; Donald C. Hambrick, "Corporate Coherence and the Top Management Team," *Strategy & Leadership 25,* no. 5 (September/October 1997): 24–29.

29. Henri Fayol, *General and Industrial Administration* (Belmont, Cal.: Pitman, 1949).

CHAPTER II

1. Andre Nelson, "Have I the Right Stuff to Be a Supervisor?" *Supervision 51* (January 1990): 10–12.

2. J.E. Osborne, "Job Descriptions Do More Than Describe Duties," *Supervisory Management* (February 1992): 8; see also G.F. Scollard, "Dynamic Descriptions: Job Descriptions Should Work for You," *Management World* (May 1985): 34–35; Charlene Marmer Solomon, "Repatriation Planning Checklist," *Personnel Journal* (January 1995): 32; Peggy Anderson and Marcia Pulich, "Making Performance Appraisals Work More Effectively," *The Health Care Supervisor 16,* no. 4 (June 1998): 20–27.

3. Robert J. Theirauf, Robert C. Klekamp, and Daniel W. Geeding, *Management Principles and Practices: A Contingency and Questionnaire Approach* (New York: Wiley, 1977), 334.

4. Deborah S. Kezsbom, "Managing the Chaos: Conflict Among Project Teams," *AACE Transactions* (1989): A.4.1–A.4.8; For an example of how overlapping responsibilities can impact a political organization see Carolyn Ban and Norma Riccucci, "New York State Civil Service Reform in a Complex Political Environment," *Review of Public Personnel Administration 14,* no. 2 (Spring 1994): 28–40.

5. Chuck Douros, "Clear Division of Responsibility Defeats Inefficiency," *Nation's Restaurant News* (February 21, 1994): 20.

6. Robert D. Melcher, "Roles and Relationships: Clarifying the Manager's Job," *Personnel 44* (May/June 1967): 34–41.

7. This section is based primarily on John H. Zenger, "Responsible Behavior: Stamp of the Effective Manager," *Supervisory Management* (July 1976): 18–24.

8. Stephen Bushardt, David Duhon, and Aubrey Fowler, "Management Delegation Myths and the Paradox of Task Assignment," *Business Horizons* (March/April 1991): 37–43; Jack J. Phillips, "Authority: It Just Doesn't Come with Your Job," *Management Solutions 31* (August 1986): 35–37.

9. Max Weber, "The Three Types of Legitimate Rule," trans. Hans Gerth, *Berkeley Journal of Sociology 4* (1953): 1–11; for a current illustration of this concept, see Gail DeGeorge, "Yo, Ho, Ho, and a Battle for Bacardi," *Business Week* (April 16, 1990): 47–48.

10. John Gardner, "The Anti-Leadership Vaccine," *Carnegie Foundation Annual Report,* 1965.

11. Chester I. Barnard, *The Functions of the Executive* (Cambridge, MA: Harvard University Press, 1938).

12. For an illustration of how line authority issues can impact the operation of the IRS, see Anonymous, "TEI Recommends Changes in IRS Appeals Large Case Program," *Tax Executive 48*, no. 4 (July/August 1996): 265.

13. Patti Wolf, Gerald Grimes, and John Dayani, "Getting the Most out of Staff Functions," *Small Business Reports 14* (October 1989): 68–70.

14. Harold Stieglitz, "On Concepts of Corporate Structure," *Conference Board Record 11* (February 1974): 7–13.

15. Wendell L. French, *The Personnel Management Process: Human Resource Administration and Development* (Boston: Houghton Mifflin, 1987), 66–68.

16. Derek Sheane, "When and How to Intervene in Conflict," *Personnel Management* (November 1979): 32–36; John M. Ivancevich and Michael T. Matteson, "Intergroup Behavior and Conflict," in their *Organizational Behavior and Management* (Plano, TX: Business Publications, 1987), 305–45.

17. Robert Albanese, *Management* (Cincinnati: South-Western Publishing, 1988), 313. For an excellent discussion of the role of accountability and organization structure, see Elliott Jacques, "In Praise of Hierarchy," *Harvard Business Review 68* (January/February 1990): 127–33.

18. "How Ylvisaker Makes 'Produce or Else' Work," *Business Week* (October 27, 1973): 112. For an interesting discussion of the importance of establishing an environment of accountability in a small women's specialty retail store, see Nan Napier, "Change Is Big Even for a Little Guy," *Business Quarterly* (Winter 1994): 21–27.

19. William H. Newman and E. Kirby Warren, *The Process of Management: Concepts, Behavior, and Practice,* 4th ed. (Upper Saddle River, N.J.: Prentice Hall, 1977), 39–40; These steps are also discussed in Jay T. Knippen and Thad B. Green, "Delegation," *Supervision 51* (March 1990): 7–9, 17. See also Robert Rohrer, "Does the Buck Ever Really Stop?" *Supervision* (July 1991): 7–8; Dave Wiggins, "Stop Doing It All Yourself! Some Keys to Effective Delegation," *Journal of Environmental Health 60*, no. 9 (May 1998): 29–30.

20. R.S. Drever, "The Ultimate Frustration," *Supervision* (May 1991): 22–23.

21. Ted Pollock, "Secrets of Successful Delegation," *Production* (December 1994): 10–11; Robert B. Nelson, "Mastering Delegation," *Executive Excellence 7* (January 1990): 13–14; Jimmy Calano and Jeff Salzman, "How Delegation Can Lead Your Team to Victory," *Working Woman,* August 1989, 86–87, 95.

22. Roz Ayres-Williams, "Mastering the Fine Art of Delegation," *Black Enterprise* (April 1992): 91–93.

23. Harold Koontz, Cyril O'Donnell, and Heinz Weihrich, *Essentials of Management,* 8th ed. (New York: McGraw-Hill, 1986), 231–33.

24. For an interesting discussion of whether or not to centralize the marketing function, see Richard Kitaeff, "The Great Debate: Centralized vs. Decentralized Marketing Research Function," *Marketing Research: A Magazine of Management & Applications,* Winter 1994, 59; Charlotte Sibley, "The Pros and Cons of Centralization and Decentralization," *Medical Marketing and Media 32*, no. 5 (May 1997): 72–76.

25. Steve Weinstein, "A Look at Fleming's New Look," *Progressive Grocer 74* (1995): 47–49.

26. H. Gilman, "J.C. Penney Decentralizes Its Purchasing," *Wall Street Journal,* May 8, 1986, 6.

27. Donald O. Harper, "Project Management as a Control and Planning Tool in the Decentralized Company," *Management Accounting* (November 1968): 29–33.

28. Information for this section is mainly from John G. Staiger, "What Cannot Be Decentralized," *Management Record 25* (January 1963): 19–21. At the time the article was written, Staiger was vice president of administration, North American Operations, Massey-Ferguson, Limited.

CHAPTER 12

1. For an interesting discussion of human resource department challenges see Robert Galford, Laurie Broedling, Edward E. Lawler III, Tim Riley, et al., "Why Doesn't This HR Department Get Any Respect?" *Harvard Business Review 76*, no. 2 (March/April 1998): 24–40.

2. To see how the performance of these steps can be shared in an organization see Brenda Paik Sunoo, "Growing Without an HR Department" *Workforce 77*, no. 1 (January 1998): 16–17.

3. Bruce Shawkey, "Job Descriptions," *Credit Union Executive 29* (Winter 1989/1990): 20–23; Howard D. Feldman, "Why Are Similar Managerial Jobs So Different?" *Review of Business 11* (Winter 1989): 15–22. For a discussion of the legal importance of job analysis, see James P. Clifford, "Job Analysis: Why Do It, and How Should It Be Done?" *Public Personnel Management 23* (1994): 321–40.

4. "Job Analysis," *Bureau of Intergovernmental Personnel Programs,* December 1973, 135–52; Gundars E. Kaupins, "Lies, Damn Lies, and Job Evaluations," *Personnel 66* (November 1989): 62–65; Jim Meade, "Identifying Criteria for Success Helps in Making Effective Hiring Decisions," *HR Magazine 43*, no. 5 (April 1998): 49–50.

5. James H. Martin and Elizabeth B. Franz, "Attracting Applicants from a Changing Labor Market: A Strategic Marketing Framework," *Journal of Managerial Issues* (Spring 1994): 33–53.

6. Fred K. Foulkes, "How Top Nonunion Companies Manage Employees," *Harvard Business Review* (September/October 1981): 90; John Perham, "Management Succession: A Hard Game to Play," *Dun's Review* (April 1981): 54–55, 58.

7. Walter S. Wikstrom, "Developing Managerial Competence: Concepts, Emerging Practices," *Studies in Personnel Policy,* no. 189, National Industrial Conference Board (1964): 95–105.

8. Patricia Panchak, "Resourceful Software Boosts HR Efficiency," *Modern Office Technology 35* (April 1990): 76–80.

9. Ray H. Hodges, "Developing an Effective Affirmative Action Program," *Journal of Intergroup Relations 5* (November 1976): 13. For a more philosophical argument supporting affirmative action, see Leo Goarke, "Affirmative Action as a Form of Restitution," *Journal of Business Ethics 9* (March 1990): 207–13.

10. R. Roosevelt Thomas, Jr., "From Affirmative Action to Affirming Diversity," *Harvard Business Review 68* (March/April, 1990): 107–17. For an argument on how using quotas to achieve affirmative action may harm business, see George Weimer, "Quotas and Other Dumb Ideas," *Industry Week* (April 6, 1992): 86; Dorothy J. Gaiter, "Blacks Mobilize to Defeat Foes of Affirmative Action," *Wall Street Journal,* June 8, 1998, A24.

11. For insights on how to select high performers, see Michael Rozek, "Can You Spot A Peak Performer?" *Personnel Journal* (June 1991): 77–78.

12. For more discussion of the stages of the selection process, see David J. Cherrington, *Personnel Management: The Management of Human Resources* (Dubuque, IA: Wm. C. Brown, 1987), 186–231.

13. This section is based on Andrew F. Sikula, *Personnel Administration and Human Resource Management* (New York: Wiley, 1976), 188–90. For information on various tests available, see O.K. Buros, ed., *The 8th Mental Measurements Yearbook* (Highland Park, N.J.: Gryphon Press, 1978).

14. For an example of an aptitude test for accident proneness see Hiroshi Matsuoka, "Development of a Short Test for Accident Proneness," *Perceptual and Motor Skills 85*, no. 3 (December 1997): 903–06.

15. Daniel P. O'Meara, "Personality Tests Raise Questions of Legality and Effectiveness," *HR Magazine,* January 1994, 97–100.

16. Clive Fletcher, "Testing the Accuracy of Psychometric Measures," *People Management 3*, no. 21 (October 23, 1997): 64–66. For a discussion of EEOC guidelines concerning appropriate pre-employment testing for Americans with disabilities, see Melanie K. St. Clair and David W. Arnold, "Preemployment Screening: No More Test Stress," *Security Management* (February 1995): 73.

17. David Littlefield, "Menu for Change at Novotel," *People Management* (January 26, 1995): 34–36; D.W. Bray and D.L. Grant, "The Assessment Center in the Measurement of Potential for Business Management," *Psychological Monographs 80* (1966): 1–27; Susan O. Hendricks and Susan E. Ogborn, "Supervisory and Managerial Assessment Centers in Health Care," *Health Care Supervisor 8* (April 1990): 65–75.

18. Barry M. Cohen, "Assessment Centers," *Supervisory Management* (June 1975): 30. See also Paul Taylor, "Seven Staff Selection Myths," *Management 45*, no. 4 (May 1998): 61–65.

19. Ann Howard, "An Assessment of Assessment Centers," *Academy of Management Journal 17* (March 1974): 117.

20. William Umiker and Thomas Conlin, "Assessing the Need for Supervisory Training: Use of Performance Appraisals," *Health Care Supervisor 8* (January 1990): 40–45.

21. Bass and Vaughn, *Training in Industry;* For discussion on using technology to improve lecture effectiveness see Anonymous, "Switches Offer Classroom Control," *Computer Dealer News 14*, no. 17 (May 4, 1998): 58.

22. David Sutton, "Further Thoughts on Action Learning," *Journal of European Industrial Training 13* (1989): 32–35.

23. Anne Fisher, "Don't Blow Your New Job," *Fortune* June 22, 1998: 159–62.

24. For more information on training techniques, see Cherrington, *Personnel Management,* 304–36.

25. Samuel C. Certo, "The Experiential Exercise Situation: A Comment on Instructional Role and Pedagogy Evaluation," *Academy of Management Review* (July 1976): 113–16. For a worthwhile discussion of the advantages of facilitation over lecturing for overcoming trainee resistance to learning, see Margaret Kaeter, "Coping with Resistant Trainees," *Training 31* (1994): 110–14. For more information on instructional roles in various situations, see Bernard Keys, "The Management of Learning Grid for Management Development," *Academy of Management Review* (April 1977): 289–97.

26. "Training Program's Results Measured in Unique Way," *Supervision* Editors-Supervision (February 1992): 18–19.

27. William Keenan, Jr., "Are You Overspending on Training?" *Sales and Marketing Management 142* (January 1990): 56–60.

28. For a review of the literature linking performance appraisal and training needs, see Glenn Herbert and Dennis Doverspike, "Performance Appraisal in the Training Needs Analysis Process: A Review and Critique," *Public Personnel Management* (Fall, 1990): 253–70. See also Mike Deblieux, "Performance Reviews Support the Quest for Quality," *HR Focus* (November 1991): 3–4.

29. Douglas McGregor, "An Uneasy Look at Performance Appraisal," *Harvard Business Review* (September/October 1972): 133–34; David A. Waldman and David E. Bowen, "The Acceptability of 360 Degree Appraisals: A Customer-Supplier Relationship Perspective," *Human Resource Management 37,* no. 2 (Summer 1998): 117–29.

30. Linda J. Segall, "KISS Appraisal Woes Goodbye," *Supervisory Management 34* (December 1989): 23–28.

31. Robert M. Gerst, "Assessing Organizational Performance," *Quality Progress* (February 1995): 85–88. See also George A. Rider, "Performance Review: A Mixed Bag," *Harvard Business Review* (July/August 1973): 61–67; Robert Loo, "Quality Performance Appraisals," *Canadian Manager 14* (December 1989): 24–26.

CHAPTER 13

1. John H. Zimmerman, "The Principles of Managing Change," *HR Focus* (February 1995): 15–16.

2. Rosabeth Moss Kanter, "The New Managerial Work," *Harvard Business Review* (November/December 1989): 85–92. For a review of planned change models as related to a nursing environment, see Constance Rimmer Tiffany, et al., "Planned Change Theory: Survey of Nursing Periodical Literature," *Nursing Management* (July 1994): 54–59.

3. John S. Morgan, *Managing Change: The Strategies of Making Change Work for You* (New York: McGraw-Hill, 1972), 99.

4. Bart Nooteboom, "Paradox, Identity, and Change in Management," *Human Systems Management 8* (1989): 291–300. For an interesting discussion of how to handle employee stress, see Alan Farnham, "Who Beats Stress Best—And How," *Fortune,* October 7, 1991, 71–86.

5. For a discussion of the value of outside change agents, see John H. Sheridan, "Careers on the Line," *Fortune,* September 16, 1991, 29–30. See also John H. Zimmerman, "The Deming Approach to Construction Safety Management," *Professional Safety* (December 1994): 35–37.

6. Myron Tribus, "Changing the Corporate Culture—A Roadmap for the Change Agent," *Human Systems Management 8* (1989): 11–22.

7. For an interesting case illustrating the changing nature of organization structure at Procter & Gamble, see Aelita G.B. Martinsons and Maris G. Martinsons, "In Search of Structural Excellence," *Leadership & Organization Development Journal 15* (1994): 24–28. See also Saul W. Gellerman, "In Organizations, as in Architecture, Form Follows Function," *Organizational Dynamics 18* (Winter 1990): 57–68.

8. C.J. Middleton, "How to Set Up a Project Organization," *Harvard Business Review* (March/April 1967): 73. See also George J. Chambers, "The Individual in a Matrix Organization," *Project Management Journal 20* (December 1989): 37–42, 50.

9. John F. Mee, "Matrix Organization," *Business Horizons* (Summer 1964).

10. Robert E. Jones, K. Michelle Jones, and Richard F. Deckro, "Strategic Decision Processes in Matrix Organizations," *European Journal of Operational Research 78* (1994): 192–203. See also Middleton, "How to Set Up a Project Organization," 74; Deborah S. Kezsbom, "Managing the Chaos: Conflict Among Project Teams," *AACE Transactions,* 1989, A.4.1–A.4.8; Harvey F. Kolodny, "Managing in a Matrix," *Business Horizons* (March/April 1981): 17–24.

11. This section is based primarily on R. Blake, J. Mouton, and L. Greiner, "Breakthrough in Organization Development," *Harvard Business Review* (November/December 1964): 133–55. For a discussion of other methods for implementing OD change, see William F. Glueck, *Organization Planning and Development* (New York: American Management Association, 1971).

12. Blake, Mouton, and Greiner, "Breakthrough in Organization Development."

13. W.J. Heisler, "Patterns of OD in Practice," *Business Horizons* (February 1975): 77–84.

14. Martin G. Evans, "Failures in OD Programs—What Went Wrong," *Business Horizons* (April 1974): 18–22.

15. David Coghlan, "OD Interventions in Catholic Religious Orders," *Journal of Managerial Psychology 4* (1989): 4–6. See also Paul A. Iles and Thomas Johnston, "Searching for Excellence in Second-Hand Clothes?: A Note," *Personnel Review 18* (1989): 32–35; Ewa Maslyk-Musial, "Organization Development in Poland: Stages of Growth," *Public Administration Quarterly 13* (Summer 1989): 196–214.

16. For an interesting discussion of resistance to change from inherited staff, see Margaret Russell, "Records Management Program-Directing: Inherited Staff," *ARMA Records Management Quarterly 24* (January 1990): 18–22.

17. This strategy for minimizing resistance to change is based on "How Companies Overcome Resistance to Change," *Management Review* (November 1972): 17–25. See also Hank Williams, "Learning to Manage Change," *Industrial and Commercial Training 21* (May/June 1989): 17–20; John P. Kotter and Leonard A. Schlesinger, "Choosing Strategies for Change," *Harvard Business Review* (March/April 1979): 106–13; Arnold S. Judson, *A Manager's Guide to Making Changes* (New York: Wiley, 1966), 118.

18. Newton Margulies and John Wallace, *Organizational Change: Techniques and Applications* (Chicago: Scott, Foresman, 1973), 14.

19. Edgar C. Williams, "Changing Systems and Behavior: People's Perspectives on Prospective Changes," *Business Horizons* (August 1969): 53.

20. Hans Selve, *The Stress of Life* (New York: McGraw-Hill, 1956). See also James C. Quick and Jonathan D. Quick, *Organizational Stress and Preventive Management* (New York: McGraw-Hill, 1984).

21. James D. Bodzinski, Robert F. Scherer, and Karen A. Gover, "Workplace Stress," *Personnel Administrator 34* (July 1989): 76–80; Richard M. Steers, *Introduction to Organizational Behavior* (Glenview, IL: Scott, Foresman, 1981), 340–41.

22. Corinne M. Smereka, "Outwitting, Controlling Stress for a Healthier Lifestyle," *Healthcare Financial Management 44* (March 1990): 70–75.

23. J. Clifton Williams, *Human Behavior in Organizations* (Cincinnati: South-Western, 1982), 212–13; Thomas L. Brown, "Are You Living in 'Quiet Desperation'?" *Industry Week* (March 16, 1992): 17.

24. Stewart L. Stokes, Jr., "Life after Rightsizing," *Information Systems Management* (Fall 1994): 69–71. For a discussion of other stressors, see "Workplace Stress," *HR Magazine,* Society of Human Resource Management, August 1991, 75–76.

25. For an interesting article addressing how managers can handle their own stress, see Thomas Brown, "Are You Stressed Out?" *Industry Week* (September 16, 1991): 21.

26. Fred Luthans, *Organizational Behavior* (New York: McGraw-Hill, 1985), 146–48.

27. Donald B. Miller, "Career Planning and Management in Organizations," *S.A.M. Advanced Management Journal 43* (Spring 1978): 33–43.

28. William H. Davidow and Michael S. Malone, *The Virtual Corporation* (New York: Harper Collier, 1992).

29. P. Maria Joseph Christie and Reuven R. Levary, "Virtual Corporations: Recipe for Success," *Industrial Management* (July/August 1998): 7–11.

30. Charles C. Snow, Raymond E. Miles, and Henry J. Coleman, Jr., "Managing 21st Century Network Organizations," *Organizational Dynamics* (Winter, 1992): 5–20; Shawn Tully, "The Modular Corporation," *Fortune,* February 8, 1993, 22–26.

31. Judith R. Gordon, *Organizational Behavior: A Diagnostic Approach* (Upper Saddle River, NJ: Prentice Hall, 1999), 385.

32. Christopher Barnatt, "Virtual Organizations in the Small Business Sector: The Case of Cavendish Management Resources," *International Small Business Journal, 15,* no. 4 (July/September 1997): 36–47.

33. Anthony M. Townsend, Samuel M. DeMarie, and Anthony R. Hendrickson, "Virtual Teams: Technology and the Workplace of the Future," *Academy of Management Executive 12,* no. 3 (August 1998): 17–29; M. Hammer and J. Champy, *Reengineering the Corporation* (New York: HarperCollins, 1993).

34. For other examples of types of virtuality in organizations see Daniel E. O'Leary, Daniel Kuokka, and Robert Plant, "Artificial Intelligence and Virtual Organizations, *Communication of the Ach 40* no. 1 (January 1997): 52–59.

35. This section draws heavily from Thomas H. Davenport and Keri Pearlson, "Two Cheers for the Virtual Office," *Sloan Management Review* (Summer 1998): 51–65.

CHAPTER 14

1. Derek Torrington and Jane Weightman, "Middle Management Work," *Journal of General Management 13* (Winter 1987): 74–89. For a useful discussion of how to influence people, see Martin Wilding, "Win Friends and Influence People by Being Sincere," *Marketing,* February 23, 1995, 16; Esther Bogin, "From Staff to Dream Team," *Financial Executive,* January/February 1995, 54–56.

2. Bernard Reilly and Joseph DiAngelo, Jr., "Communication: A Cultural System of Meaning and Value," *Human Relations 43* (February 1990): 29–40. See also Paul Sandwith, "Effective Communication," *Training and Development* (January 1992): 29–32; Christine Clements, Richard J. Wagner, and Christopher Roland, "The Ins and Outs of Experimental Training," *Training & Development* (February 1995): 52–56.

3. This section is based on the following classic article on interpersonal communication: Wilbur Schramm, "How Communication Works," *The Process and Effects of Mass Communication,* ed. Wilbur Schramm (Urbana, IL: University of Illinois Press, 1954), 3–10; For tips on how to increase communication skills, see T.J. Saftner, "Talk the Talk: How Well Do You Communicate?" *Career World 26,* no. 4 (January 1998): 24–27.

4. David S. Brown, "Barriers to Successful Communication: Part I, Macrobarriers," *Management Review* (December 1975): 24–29.

5. James K. Weekly and Raj Aggarwal, *International Business: Operating in the Global Economy* (New York: Dryden Press, 1987).

6. Davis S. Brown, "Barriers to Successful Communication: Part II, Microbarriers," *Management Review* (January 1976): 15–21; For study results having implications for e-mail as a communication microbarrier, see Norman Frohlich and Joe Oppenheimer, "Some Consequences of E-mail vs. Face-to-Face Communication in Experiment," *Journal of Economic Behavior & Organization 35,* no. 3 (April 15, 1998): 389–403.

7. Sally Bulkley Pancrazio and James J. Pancrazio, "Better Communication for Managers," *Supervisory Management* (June 1981): 31–37. See also Gene E. Burton, "Barriers to Effective Communication," *Management World* (March 1977): 4–8; John S. Fielden, "Why Can't Managers Communicate?" *Business 39* (January/February/March 1989): 41–44.

8. Lydia Strong, "Do You Know How to Listen?" *Effective Communications on the Job,* ed. M. Joseph Dooher and Vivienne Marquis (New York: American Management Association, 1956), 28. See also John R. White, "Some Thoughts on Lexicon and Syntax," *Appraisal Journal 57* (July 1989): 417–21.

9. Robert E. Callahan, C. Patrick Fleenor, and Harry R. Knudson, *Understanding Organizational Behavior: A Managerial Viewpoint* (Columbus, OH: Charles E. Merrill, 1986). For a discussion of the process of generating feedback, see Elizabeth Wolfe Morrison and Robert J. Bies, "Impression Management in the Feedback-Seeking Process: Literature Review and Research Agenda," *Academy of Management Review* (July 1991): 522–41.

10. For more on nonverbal issues, see I.T. Sheppard, "Silent Signals," *Supervisory Management* (March 1986): 31–33.

11. Verne Burnett, "Management's Tower of Babel," *Management Review* (June 1961): 4–11.

12. Reprinted, by permission of the publisher, from "Ten Commandments of Good Communication," by American Management Association AMA-COM. et al. from *Management Review* (October 1955). © 1955 American Management Association, Inc. All rights reserved. See also Robb Ware, "Communica-

tion Problems," *Journal of Systems Management* (September 1991): 20; "Communicating: Face-to-Face," *Agency Sales Magazine,* January 1994, 22–23.

13. Ted Pollock, "Mind Your Own Business," *Supervision,* May 1994, 24–26; Joseph R. Bainbridge, "Joint Communication: Verbal and Nonverbal," *Army Logistician 30,* no. 4: (July/August) 40–42.

14. Albert Mehrabian, "Communication Without Words," *Psychology Today,* September 1968, 53–55. For a practical article emphasizing the role of gestures in communication, see S.D. Gladis, "Notes Are Not Enough," *Training and Development Journal* (August 1985): 35–38. See also Nicole Steckler and Robert Rosenthal, "Sex Differences in Nonverbal and Verbal Communication with Bosses, Peers, and Subordinates," *Journal of Applied Psychology* (February 1985): 157–63; Andrew J. DuBrin, *Contemporary Applied Management* (Plano, TX: Business Publications, 1982): 127–34; W. Alan Randolph, *Understanding and Managing Organizational Behavior* (Homewood, IL: Richard D. Irwin, 1985), 349–50; Karen O. Down and Jeanne Liedtka, "What Corporations Seek in MBA Hires: A Survey," *Selections,* Winter 1994, 34–39.

15. Gerald M. Goldhaber, *Organizational Communication* (Dubuque, Iowa: Wm. C. Brown, 1983).

16. Kenneth R. Van Voorhis, "Organizational Communication: Advances Made during the Period from World War II Through the 1950s," *Journal of Business Communication 11* (1974): 11–18. See also Phillip J. Lewis, "The Status of 'Organizational Communication,' in Colleges of Business," *Journal of Business Communication 12* (1975): 25–28.

17. Paul Preston, "The Critical 'Mix' in Managerial Communications," *Industrial Management* (March/April 1976): 5–9; For discussion of implementing organizational communication reflecting a worldwide structure, see "Iridium Delays Full Start of Global System," *New York Times,* September 10, 1998, C6.

18. For a discussion of how to communicate failures upward in an organization, see Jay T. Knippen, Thad B. Green, and Kurt Sutton, "How to Communicate Failures to Your Boss," *Supervisory Management* (September 1991): 10.

19. "Upward/Downward Communication—Critical Information Channels," *Small Business Report 10* (October 1985): 85–88; Anne B. Fisher, "CEOs Think That Morale Is Dandy," *Fortune,* November 18, 1991, 70–71; For an article stressing the importance of upward and downward communication for managers, see W.H. Weiss, "Communications: Key to Successful Supervision," *Supervision 59,* no. 9 (September 1998): 12–14.

20. William V. Haney, "Serial Communication of Information in Organizations," in *Concepts and Issues in Administrative Behavior,* ed. Sidney Mailick and Edward H. Van Ness (Englewood Cliffs, N.J.: Prentice Hall, 1962), 150; For discussion involving implications of offsite patterns of communication, see Robert M. Egan, Wendy Miles, John R. Birstler, and Margaret Klayton-Mi, "Can the Rift between Allison and Penny Be Mended?" *Harvard Business Review 76,* no. 4 (July/August 1998): 28–35.

21. Alex Bavelas and Ermot Barrett, "An Experimental Approach to Organizational Communication," *Personnel 27* (1951): 366–71.

22. Polly LaBarre, "The Other Network," *Industry Week* (September 19, 1994): 33–36.

23. George de Mare, "Communicating: The Key to Establishing Good Working Relationships, " *Price Waterhouse Review 33* (1989): 30–37; Alan Zaremba, "Working with the Organizational Grapevine," *Personnel Journal 67* (July 1988): 38–42; Stanley J. Modic, "Grapevine Rated Most Believable," *Industry Week* (May 15, 1989): 11, 14.

24. Keith Davis, "Management Communication and the Grapevine," *Harvard Business Review* (January/February 1953): 43–49.

25. Linda McCallister, "The Interpersonal Side of Internal Communications," *Public Relations Journal* (February 1981): 20–23. See also Joseph M. Putti, Samuel Aryee, and Joseph Phua, "Communication Relationship Satisfaction and Organizational Commitment," *Group and Organizational Studies 15* (March 1990): 44–52. For an article defending the value of grapevines, see W. Kiechel, "In Praise of Office Gossip," *Fortune,* August 19, 1985, 253–54.

CHAPTER 15

1. Elise Goldman, "The Significance of Leadership Style," *Educational Leadership 55,* no. 7 (April 1998): 20–22.

2. David Nadler and Michael L. Tushman, "Beyond the Charismatic Leader: Leadership and Organizational Change," *California Management Review 32* (Winter

1990): 77–97; Peter R. Scholtes, *The Leader's Handbook: A Guide to Inspiring Your People and Managing the Daily Workflow* (New York: McGraw-Hill, 1998).

3. Abraham Zaleznik, "Executives and Organizations: Real Work," *Harvard Business Review* (January/February 1989): 57–64; Abraham Zaleznik, "Managers and Leaders: Are They Different?" *Harvard Business Review* (May/June 1977): 67–78.

4. Theodore Levitt, "Management and the Post-Industrial Society," *Public Interest* (Summer 1976): 73.

5. Patrick L. Townsend and Joan E. Gebhardt, "We Have Lots of Managers . . . We Need Leaders," *Journal for Quality and Participation* (September 1989): 18–20; Craig Hickman, "The Winning Mix: Mind of a Manager, Soul of a Leader," *Canadian Business* 63 (February 1990): 69–72; For discussion of how successful executives place more importance and emphasis on leadership than management, see Michael E. McGrath, "The Eight Qualities of Success," *Electronic Business* 24, no. 4 (April 1998): 9–10.

6. Ralph M. Stogdill, "Personal Factors Associated with Leadership: A Survey of the Literature," *Journal of Psychology* 25 (January 1948): 35–64.

7. Cecil A. Gibb, "Leadership," in *Handbook of Social Psychology*, ed. Gardner Lindzey (Reading, MA: Addison-Wesley, 1954); Eugene E. Jennings, "The Anatomy of Leadership," *Management of Personnel Quarterly 1* (Autumn 1961).

8. J. Oliver Crom, "What's New in Leadership?" *Executive Excellence* 7 (January 1990): 15–16.

9. For an interesting discussion of followers in a leadership situation, see Robert E. Kelly, "In Praise of Followers," *Harvard Business Review* (November/December 1988): 142–48; For discussion of a leader in a military situation, see Sherrill Tapsell, "Managing for Peace," *Management* 45, no. 5 (June 1998): 32–37.

10. Robert Tannenbaum and Warren H. Schmidt, "How to Choose a Leadership Pattern," *Harvard Business Review* (March/April 1957): 95–101.

11. William E. Zierden, "Leading Through the Follower's Point of View," *Organizational Dynamics* (Spring 1980): 27–46. See also Tannenbaum and Schmidt, "How to Choose a Leadership Pattern."

12. Robert Tannenbaum and Warren H. Schmidt, "How to Choose a Leadership Pattern," *Harvard Business Review* (May/June 1973): 162–80.

13. Victor H. Vroom and Philip H. Yetton, *Leadership and Decision-Making* (Pittsburgh: University of Pittsburgh Press, 1973); Victor H. Vroom and Arthur G. Jago, *The New Leadership* (Upper Saddle River, NJ: Prentice Hall, 1988).

14. Gary A. Yukl, *Leadership in Organizations,* 2d ed. (Upper Saddle River, NJ: Prentice Hall, 1989).

15. Vishwanath V. Baba and Merle E. Ace, "Serendipity in Leadership: Initiating Structure and Consideration in the Classroom," *Human Relations* 42 (June 1989): 509–25; Desmond Nolan, "Leadership Appraisals: Your Management Style Can Affect Productivity," *Credit Union Executive* 28 (Winter 1988): 36–37.

16. Rensis Likert, *New Patterns of Management* (New York: McGraw-Hill, 1961).

17. Andrew W. Halpin, *The Leadership Behavior of School Superintendents* (Chicago: University of Chicago Midwest Administration Center, 1959); Harvey A. Hornstein, Madeline E. Heilman, Edward Mone, and Ross Tartell, "Responding to Contingent Leadership Behavior," *Organizational Dynamics* 15 (Spring 1987): 56–65.

18. A.K. Korman, " 'Consideration,' 'Initiating Structure,' and Organizational Criteria—A Review," *Personnel Psychology* 19 (Winter 1966): 349–61. See also Rick Roskin, "Management Style and Achievement: A Model Synthesis," *Management Decision* 27 (1989): 17–22.

19. P. Hersey and K.H. Blanchard, "Life Cycle Theory of Leadership," *Training and Development Journal* (May 1969): 26–34.

20. Mary J. Keenan, Joseph B. Hurst, Robert S. Dennis, and Glenna Frey, "Situational Leadership for Collaboration in Health Care Settings," *Health Care Supervisor 8* (April 1990): 19–25. See also Claude L. Graeff, "The Situational Leadership Theory: A Critical View," *Academy of Management Review 8* (1983): 285–91; Robert P. Vecchio, "Situational Leadership Theory: An Examination of a Prescriptive Theory," *Journal of Applied Psychology* 72 (August 1987): 444–51; Jane R. Goodson, Gail W. McGee, and James F. Cashman, "Situational Leadership Theory: A Test of Leadership Prescriptions," *Group and Organizational Studies* 14 (December 1989): 446–61.

21. Fred E. Fiedler, "Engineer the Job to Fit the Manager," *Harvard Business Review* (September/October 1965): 115–22. See also Fred E. Fiedler, *A Theory of Leadership Effectiveness* (New York: McGraw-Hill, 1967).

22. From *A Theory of Leadership Effectiveness*, pp. 255–56 by F.E. Fiedler. Copyright © 1967 by McGraw-Hill, Inc. Used with permission of McGraw-Hill Company.

23. L.H. Peters, D.D. Harike, and J.T. Pohlmann, "Fiedler's Contingency Theory of Leadership: An Application of the Meta-analysis Procedures of Schmidt and Hunter," *Psychological Bulletin* 97 (1985): 224–85.

24. Robert J. House and Terence R. Mitchell, "Path-Goal Theory of Leadership," *Journal of Contemporary Business* (Autumn 1974): 81–98; Gary A. Yukl, *Leadership in Organizations.*

25. Alan C. Filley, Robert House, and Steven Kerr, *Managerial Process and Organizational Behavior* (Glenview, IL: Scott, Foresman, 1976), 256–60. For a worthwhile review of the path-goal theory of leadership, see Gary A. Yukl, *Leadership in Organizations.*

26. To learn how some managers are reacting to modern challenges, see Jaclyn Fierman, "Winning Ideas from Maverick Managers," *Fortune,* February 6, 1995, 66–80; For a fresh approach to leadership that modern managers are taking, see George Fraser, "The Slight Edge: Valuing and Managing Diversity," *Vital Speeches of the Day 64*, no. 8 (February 1, 1998): 235–40.

27. Andrew J. DuBrin, *Reengineering Survival Guide* (Cincinnati, Ohio, Thomson Executive Press, 1996), 115–29.

28. Karl W. Kuhnert and Philip Lewis, "Transactional and Transformational Leadership: A Constructive/Developmental Analysis," *Academy of Management Review* (October 1987): 648–57; Shirley M. Ross and Lynn R. Offermann, "Transformational Leaders: Measurement of Personality Attributes," *Personality and Social Psychology Bulletin,* October 1997, 1078–86.

29. For more discussion on specific steps that transformational leaders take, see Robert Miles, "Transformation Challenge," *Executive Excellence* 15, no. 2 (February 1998): 15.

30. Bernard M. Bass, *Leadership and Performance beyond Expectations* (New York: Free Press, 1985); Noel M. Tichy and David M. Ulrich, "The Leadership Challenge: A Call for Transformational Leadership," *Sloan Management Review* (Fall 1984): 59–68.

31. For more information on empathy and leadership, see William G. Pagonis, "The Work of the Leader," *Harvard Business Review* (November/December 1992): 118–26.

32. Charles C. Manz, "Helping Yourself and Others to Master Self-Leadership," *Supervisory Management* (November 1991): 19–38; Manz and Henry P. Sims, Jr., "SuperLeadership: Beyond the Myth of Heroic Leadership," *Organizational Dynamics* (Spring 1991): 28–40.

33. A profile of a successful female entrepreneurial leader in a multicultural situation is contained in Daniel J. McCarthy, Sheila M. Puffer, and Alexander I. Naumov, "Case study—Olga Kirova: A Russian Entrepreneur's Quality Leadership," *International Journal of Organizational Analysis 5,* no. 3 (July 1997): 267–90.

34. S. Kerr and J.M. Jermier, "Substitutes for Leadership: Their Meaning and Measurement," *Organizational Behavior and Human Performance 22* (1978): 375–403; C.C. Manz and H.P. Sims, Jr., "Leading Workers to Lead Themselves: The External Leadership on Self-Managing Work Teams," *Administrative Science Quarterly* (March 1987): 106–29.

35. J.R. Meindl and S.B. Ehrlich, "The Romance of Leadership and the Evaluation of Organizational Performance," *Academy of Management Journal 30 (1987):* 91–109.

36. Data in this section come from the following sources: Ralph M. Stogdill, *Handbook of Leadership* (New York: Free Press, 1974); U.S. Department of Labor, Bureau of Labor Statistics, 1989. *Employment and Earnings* (Washington, DC: Government Printing Office), 29; "Workforce 2000 Is Welcome Today at Digital," *Business Ethics* (July/August 1990): 5–16; Amy Salzman, "Trouble at the Top," *U.S. News and World Report,* June 17, 1991; Susan B. Garland, "Throwing Stones at the Glass Ceiling," *Business Week,* August 19, 1991, 29.

37. See the following articles: J.B. Rosener, "Ways Women Lead," *Harvard Business Review* (May/June 1990): 103–11; B.M. Bass Leadership. "Good, Better, Best," *Organizational Dynamics* (Winter 1985): 26–40.

CHAPTER 16

1. Philip A. Rudolph and Brian H. Kleiner, "The Art of Motivating Employees," *Journal of Managerial Psychology* 4 (1989): i–iv; Carole L. Jurkiewicz, Tom K. Massey Jr., and Roger G. Brown, "Motivation in Public and Private Organi-

zations: A Comparative Study," *Public Productivity & Management Review* 21, no. 3 (March 1998): 230–50.

2. Mike DeLuca, "Motivating Your Staff Is Key to Your Success," *Restaurant Hospitality* (February 1995): 20.

3. Craig Miller, "How to Construct Programs for Teams," *Reward & Recognition* (August/September 1991): 4–6; Walter F. Charsley, "Management, Morale, and Motivation," *Management World 17* (July/August 1988): 27–28.

4. Victor H. Vroom, *Work and Motivation* (New York: Wiley, 1964); Thomas L. Quick, "How to Motivate People," *Working Women 12* (September 1987): 15, 17.

5. J. Stacy Adams, "Towards an Understanding of Inequity," *Journal of Abnormal and Social Psychology 67* (1963): 422–36. For a rationale linking expectancy and equity theories, see Joseph W. Harder, "Equity Theory versus Expectancy Theory: The Case of Major League Baseball Free Agents," *Journal of Applied Psychology* (June 1991): 458–64; For group rewards as an alternative to individual rewards in human motivation, see Donald J. Campbell, Kathleen M. Campbell, and Ho-Beng Chia, "Merit Pay, Performance Appraisal, and Individual Motivation: An Analysis and Alternative," *Human Resource Management 37*, no. 2 (Summer 1998): 131–46.

6. L.W. Porter and E.E. Lawler, *Managerial Attitudes and Performance* (Homewood, Ill.: Richard D. Irwin, 1968). For more information on intrinsic and extrinsic rewards, see Pat Buhler, "Rewards in the Organization," *Supervision 50* (January 1989): 5–7.

7. Eric G. Flamholtz and Yvonne Randle, "The Inner Game of Management," *Management Review 77* (April 1988): 24–30.

8. Abraham Maslow, *Motivation and Personality*, 2d ed. (New York: Harper & Row, 1970). For an up-to-date discussion of the value of Maslow's ideas, see Edward Hoffman, "Abraham Maslow: Father of Enlightened Management," *Training 25* (September 1988): 79–82. See also Abraham Maslow, *Eupsychian Management* (Homewood, IL: Richard D. Irwin, 1965).

9. For a discussion of an empowerment tool managers can use to help employees satisfy esteem and self-actualization needs, see Chris Argyris, "Empowerment: The Emperor's New Clothes," *Harvard Business Review 76*, no. 3 (May/June 1998): 98–105.

10. For critiques of Maslow, see Jack W. Duncan, *Essentials of Management* (Hinsdale, Ill.: Dryden Press, 1975), 105; C.P. Alderfer, "An Empirical Test of a New Theory of Human Needs," *Organizational Behavior and Human Performance 4* (1969): 142–75; D.T. Hall and K. Nougaim, "An Examination of Maslow's Need Hierarchy in an Organizational Setting," *Organizational Behavior and Human Performance 3* (1968): 12–35; Hoffman, "Abraham Maslow: Father of Enlightened Management;" Dale L. Mort, "Lead Your Team to the Top," *Security Management 32* (January 1988): 43–45.

11. Clayton Alderfer, *Existence, Relatedness, and Growth* (New York: Free Press, 1972). For a reconstruction of Maslow's hierarchy, see Francis Heylighen, "A Cognitive-Systemic Reconstruction of Maslow's Theory of Self-Actualization," *Behavioral Science* (January 1992): 39–58.

12. Chris Argyris, *Personality and Organization* (New York: Harper & Bros., 1957). See also Charles R. Davis, "The Primacy of Self-Development in Chris Argyris's Writings," *International Journal of Public Administration 10* (September 1987): 177–207.

13. David C. McClelland and David G. Winter, *Motivating Economic Achievement* (New York: Free Press, 1969); David C. McClelland, "Power Is the Great Motivator," *Harvard Business Review* (March/April 1976): 100–10. See also Burt K. Scanlan, "Creating a Climate for Achievement," *Business Horizons 24* (March/April 1981): 5–9; Lawrence Holp, "Achievement Motivation and Kaizen," *Training and Development Journal 43* (October 1989): 53–63; McClelland, *The Achieving Society* (New York: Van Nostrand, 1961); McClelland and David H. Burnham, "Power Is the Great Motivator," *Harvard Business Review* (January/February 1995): 126–39.

14. Michael Sanson, "Fired Up!" *Restaurant Hospitality* (February 1995): 53–64.

15. Douglas McGregor, *The Human Side of Enterprise* (New York: McGraw-Hill, 1960). For a current illustration of how Theory X-Theory Y relates to modern business, see Kenneth B. Slutsky, "Viewpoint: Why Not Theory Z?" *Security Management 33* (April 1989): 110, 112. See also W.J. Reddin, "The Tri-Dimensional Grid," *Training and Development Journal* (July 1964). For a discussion of Theories X, Y, and Z as they relate to the adoption of new technology in organizations, see Richard T. Due, "Client/Server Feasibility," *Information Systems Management* (Summer 1994): 79–82.

16. For more discussion on the implications of job rotation in organizations, see Alan W. Farrant, "Job Rotation Is Important," *Supervision* (August 1987): 14–16.

17. L.E. Davis and E.S. Valfer, "Intervening Responses to Changes in Supervisor Job Designs," *Occupational Psychology* (July 1965): 171–90; M.D. Kilbridge, "Do Workers Prefer Larger Jobs?" *Personnel* (September/October 1960): 45–48.

18. This section is based on Frederick Herzberg, "One More Time: How Do You Motivate Employees?" *Harvard Business Review* (January/February 1968): 53–62.

19. Scott M. Meyers, "Who Are Your Motivated Workers?" *Harvard Business Review* (January/February 1964): 73–88; John M. Roach, "Why Volvo Abolished the Assembly Line," *Management Review* (September 1977): 50; Matt Oechsli, "Million Dollar Success Habits," *Managers Magazine 65* (February 1990): 6–14; J. Barton Cunningham and Ted Eberle, "A Guide to Job Enrichment and Redesign," *Personnel 67* (February 1990): 56–61; Richard J. Hackman, "Is Job Enrichment Just a Fad?" *Harvard Business Review* (September/October 1975): 129–38.

20. Bob Smith and Karen Matthes, "Flexibility Now for the Future," *HR Focus* (January 1992): 5.

21. D.A. Bratton, "Moving Away from Nine to Five," *Canadian Business Review 13* (Spring 1986): 15–17.

22. Douglas L. Fleuter, "Flextime—A Social Phenomenon," *Personnel Journal* (June 1975): 318–19; Lee A. Graf, "An Analysis of the Effect of Flexible Working Hours on the Management Functions of the First-Line Supervisor," Ph.D. diss. (Mississippi State University, 1976); Jill Kanin-Lovers, "Meeting the Challenge of Workforce, 2000," *Journal of Compensation and Benefits 5* (January/February 1990): 233–36; William Wong, "Rather Come in Late or Go Home Earlier? More Bosses Say OK," *Wall Street Journal*, July 12, 1973, 1.

23. B.F. Skinner, *Contingencies of Reinforcement* (New York: Appleton-Century-Crofts, 1969). See also E.L. Thorndike, "The Original Nature of Man," *Educational Psychology 1*, 1903; Fred Luthans and Robert Kreitner, *Organizational Behavior Modification and Beyond* (Glenview, IL: Scott, Foresman, 1985).

24. For an interesting discussion of accounting as a means of rewarding employees, see Mahmoud Ezzamel and Hugh Willmott, "Accounting, Remuneration, and Employee Motivation in the New Organization," *Accounting and Business Research 28*, no. 2 (Spring 1998): 97–110.

25. P.M. Padokaff, "Relationships between Leader Reward and Punishment Behavior and Group Process and Productivity," *Journal of Management 11* (Spring 1985): 55–73. For a practical discussion of punishment, see Bruce R. McAfee and William Pottenberger, *Productivity Strategies: Enhancing Employee Job Performance* (Upper Saddle River, NJ: Prentice Hall, 1982).

26. "New Tool: Reinforcement for Good Work," *Psychology Today* (April 1972): 68–69.

27. W. Clay Hamner and Ellen P. Hamner, "Behavior Modification on the Bottom Line," *Organizational Dynamics 4* (Spring 1976): 6–8.

28. James K. Hickel, "Paying Employees to Control Costs," *Human Resources Professional* (January/February 1995): 21–24.

29. Rensis Likert, *New Patterns of Management* (New York: McGraw-Hill, 1961). For an interesting discussion of the worth of Likert's ideas, see Marvin R. Weisbord, "For More Productive Workplaces," *Journal of Management Consulting 4* (1988): 7–14. The following descriptions are based on the table of organizational and performance characteristics of different management systems in Rensis Likert, *The Human Organization* (New York: McGraw-Hill, 1967), 4–10.

30. For a discussion of a novel monetary incentive program, see Charles A. Cerami, "Special Incentives May Appeal to Valued Employees," *HR Focus* (November 1991): 17; See also Reginald Shareef, "A Midterm Case Study Assessment of Skill-Based Pay in the Virginia Department of Transportation," *Review of Public Personnel Administration 18*, no. 1 (Winter 1998): 5–22.

31. Marilyn Moats Kennedy, "What Makes People Work Hard?" *Across the Board 35*, no. 5 (May 1998): 51–52.

CHAPTER 17

1. For an article illustrating the importance of managing groups in organizations, see Gregory E. Kaebnick, "Notes from Underground: Walter Corbitt Talks about Monitoring Paperwork for 35,000 Underground Storage Tanks," *Inform 3* (July/August 1989): 21–22, 48.

2. Edgar H. Schein, *Organizational Psychology* (Upper Saddle River, NJ: Prentice Hall, 1965), 67.

3. Dorwin Cartwright and Ronald Lippitt, "Group Dynamics and the Individual," *International Journal of Group Psychotherapy 7* (January 1957): 86–102.

4. For insights on how to be more successful in dealing with people in groups, see Anonymous, "Becoming More Persuasive," *Association Management 50*, no. 7 (July 1998): 24–25.

5. Edgar H. Schein, *Organizational Psychology*, 2d ed. (Upper Saddle River, NJ: Prentice Hall, 1970), 182.

6. For a recent study exploring diversity and task group processes, see Warren E. Watson, Lynn Johnson, and Deanna Merritt, "Team Orientation, Self-Orientation, and Diversity in Task Groups," *Group & Organization Management 23*, no. 2 (June 1998): 161–88.

7. For useful guidelines on how to make committees work, see Arthur R. Pell, "Making Committees Work," *Managers Magazine 64* (September 1989): 28.

8. Cyril O'Donnell, "Group Rules for Using Committees," *Management Review 50* (October 1961): 63–67. See also "Making Committees Work." *Infosystems,* October 1985, 38–39; For an example of problems created by committees not doing their jobs, see Joann S. Lublin and Elizabeth MacDonald, "Management: Scandals Signal Laxity of Audit Panels," *Wall Street Journal,* July 17, 1998, B1.

9. These and other guidelines are discussed in "Applying Small-Group Behavior Dynamics to Improve Action-Team Performance," *Employment Relations Today* (Autumn 1991): 343–53. For additional guidelines, see Peggy S. Williams, "Physical Fitness for Committees: Getting on Track," *Association Management 4* (June 1989): 104–11.

10. See Irving L. Janis, *Groupthink* (Boston: Houghton Mifflin, 1982). For insights on how to avoid groupthink, see Michael J. Woodruff, "Understanding—and Combatting—Groupthink," *Supervisory Management* (October 1991): 8.

11. For suggestions on how to build a team, see Edward Glassman, "Silence Is Not Consent," *Supervisory Management* (March 1992): 6–7; Robert B. Reich, "Entrepreneurship Reconsidered: The Team as a Hero," *Harvard Business Review* (May/June 1987): 77–83; Anonymous, "Teamwork Translates into High Performance," *HR Focus 75*, no. 7 (July 1998): 7.

12. Bernard Bass, *Organizational Psychology* (Boston: Allyn and Bacon, 1965), 197–98. For more insights on characteristics of productive groups, see Edward Glassman, "Self-Directed Team Building without a Consultant," *Supervisory Management* (March 1992): 6.

13. Raef T. Hussein, "Informal Groups, Leadership, and Productivity," *Leadership and Organization Development Journal 10* (1989): 9–16.

14. Keith Davis and John W. Newstrom, *Human Behavior at Work: Organizational Behavior* (New York: McGraw-Hill, 1985), 310–12. See also Muhammad Jamal, "Shift Work Related to Job Attitudes, Social Participation, and Withdrawal Behavior: A Study of Nurses and Industrial Workers," *Personnel Psychology 34* (Autumn 1981): 535–47.

15. For the importance of determining such information, see Dave Day, "New Supervisors and the Informal Group," *Supervisory Management 34* (May 1989): 31–33. For a classic study illustrating sociometry and sociometric procedures, see Muzafer Sherif, "A Preliminary Experimental Study of Intergroup Relations, in *Social Psychology at the Crossroads,* ed. John H. Rohrer and Muzafer Sherif (New York: Harper & Bros., 1951).

16. Homans, *The Human Group.*

17. William G. Dyer, *Teambuilding: Issues and Alternatives* (Reading, Mass.: Addison-Wesley, 1987), 4. See also Dawn R. Deeter-Schmelz and Rosemary Ramsey, "A Conceptualization of the Functions and Roles of Formalized Selling and Buying Teams," *Journal of Personal Selling & Sales Management* (Spring 1995): 47–60.

18. J.H. Shonk, *Team-Based Organizations* (Homewood, IL: Irwin, 1992).

19. Jack L. Lederer and Carl R. Weinberg, "Equity-Based Pay: The Compensation Paradigm for the Re-Engineered Corporation," *Chief Executive* (April 1995): 36–39.

20. Kevin R. Zuidema and Brian H. Kleiner, "Self-Directed Work Groups Gain Popularity," *Business Credit* (October 1994): 21–26.

21. Sami M. Abbasi and Kenneth W. Hollman, "Self-Managed Teams: The Productivity Breakthrough of the 1990s," *Journal of Managerial Psychology 9* (1994): 25–30.

22. For more information on cross-functional teams, see D. Keith Denton, "Multi-Skilled Teams Replace Old Work Systems," *HR Magazine,* September 1992, 48–56; Michael D. Hutt, Beth A. Walker, and Gary L. Frankwick, "Hurdle the Cross-Functional Barriers to Strategic Change," *Sloan Management Review* (Spring 1995): 22–30; John Teresko, "Reinventing the Future," *Industry Week* (April 17, 1995): 32–38; Margaret L. Gagne and Richard Discenza, "Target Costing," *Journal of Business & Industrial Marketing 10* (1995): 16–22.

23. Bruce W. Tuckman and Mary Ann C. Jensen, "Stages of Small Group Development Revisited," *Group and Organizational Studies 2* (1977): 419–27; Melissas Masikiewicz, "Are You a Team Player?" *Career World 26*, no. 6 (March 1998): 19–21.

24. Hans J. Thamhain, "Managing Technologically Innovative Team Efforts toward New Product Success," *Journal of Product Innovation Management* (March 1990): 5–18.

25. For insights about motivation and teams, see Gerben van der Vegt, Ben Emans, and Evert van de Vliert, "Motivating Effects of Task and Outcome Independence in Work," *Group & Organization Management 23*, no. 2 (June 1998): 124–43.

26. Jerre L. Stead, "People Power: The Engine in Reengineering," *Executive Speeches* (April/May 1995): 28–32.

27. Fernando Bartolome, "Nobody Trusts the Boss Completely—Now What?" *Harvard Business Review* (March/April 1989): 114–31.

28. Cass Bettinger, "Use Corporate Culture to Trigger High Performance," *Journal of Business Strategies,* (March/April 1989): 38–42.

29. The text discussion of these mechanisms is based on Edgar H. Schein, *Organizational Culture and Leadership* (San Francisco: Jossey-Bass, 1985), 223–43. For an example of using a new building to change corporate culture, see Anonymous, "Business: Places to Linger," *The Economist 348*, no. 8079 (August 1, 1998): 55–56.

CHAPTER 18

1. Martin Fishbein and Isek Ajyen, *Belief, Attitude, Intention and Behavior: An Introduction to Theory and Research* (Reading, Mass.: Addison-Wesley, 1975); For an example of a possible employee attitude toward jobs, see Brenda Paik Sunoo, "Optimists Love Their Jobs," *Workforce 77*, no. 5 (May 1998): 17.

2. Milton Kokeach, *The Nature of Human Values* (New York: Free Press, 1973); William K. Tracey, *The Human Resources Glossary* (New York: AMACOM, 1991), 366; For the generation X's value of intrinsic and extrinsic rewards, see John W. Andrews, "Membership Service—Part II: Retaining the Generation X," *Credit Union Executive, 38*, no. 4 (July/August 1998): 40–42.

3. John K. Schermerhorn, James G. Hunt, and Richard N. Osborn, *Managing Organizational Behavior,* 4th ed. (New York: Wiley, 1991), 115–17; Kevin Barksdale, "Why We Should Update HR," *Journal of Management 22*, no. 4 (August 1998): 526–30.

4. Barry M. Staw and Jerry Ross, "Stability in the Midst of Change: A Dispositional Approach to Job Attitudes," *Journal of Applied Psychology* (August 1985): 469–80.

5. Martin Fishbein and Mark Stasson, "The Role of Desires, Self-Predictions, and Perceived Control in the Prediction of Training Session Attendance," *Journal of Applied Social Psychology 20* (1990): 173–98; Robert P. Steel and Nestor K. Ovalle II, "A Review and Meta-Analysis of Research on the Relationship between Behavioral Intentions and Employee Turnover," *Journal of Applied Psychology* (November 1984): 873–86.

6. Staw and Ross, 469–80; For an example of how attitudes about race can influence behavior, see Bill Dedman, "For Some Reason, the Race Does Matter," *The Orlando Sentinel,* September 20, 1998, C3.

7. Angelo J. Kinicki, Kenneth P. Carson, and George W. Bohlander, "Relationships between an Organization's Actual Human Resource Efforts and Employee Attitudes," *Group & Organization Management 17* (June 1992): 135–52.

8. Michael R. Carrell, Norbert Elbert, and Robert Hatfield, *Human Resource Management,* 5th ed. (Upper Saddle River, NJ: Prentice Hall, 1995), 699–702.

9. M.J. Martinko and W.L. Gardner, "The Leader-Member Attribution Process," *Academy of Management Review 12* (1987): 235–49.

10. Richard M. Steers and J. Stewart Black, *Organizational Behavior* (New York: Harper Collins, 1994), 80–83.

11. Jerald Greenberg, "Looking Fair vs. Being Fair: Managing Impressions of Organizational Justice," *Research in Organizational Behavior,* ed. B.M. Staw and L.L. Cummings (Greenwich, CT: JAI Press, 1990).

12. L. Alan Witt and Jennifer G. Myers, "Perceived Environmental Uncertainty and Participation in Decision Making in the Prediction of Perceptions of the Fairness of Personnel Decisions," *Review of Public Personnel Administration* (May/August 1993): 48–55.

13. R. Karambayya, J. Brett, and A. Lytle, "Effects of Formal Authority and Experience on Third-Party Roles, Outcomes, and Perceptions of Fairness," *Academy of Management Journal 35* (1992): 426–38.

14. Carrell, Elbert, and Hatfield, 780–84.

15. Edwin A. Locke and G.P. Latham, *A Theory of Goal Setting and Task Performance* (Upper Saddle River, NJ: Prentice Hall), 1990.

16. Kenneth N. Wexley and Gary P. Latham, *Developing and Training Human Resources in Organizations* (New York: HarperCollins, 1991); For an interesting article discussing reinforcement of groups rather than individuals, see Donald J. Campbell, Kathleen M. Campbell, and Ho-Beng Chia, "Merit Pay, Performance Appraisal, and Individual Motivation: An Analysis and Alternative," *Human Resource Management 37*, no. 2 (Summer 1998): 131–46.

17. Joseph B. Treasfer, "Employer Drug Testing Driving Down Use in Society," *New York Times*, 1993, 21.

CHAPTER 19

1. For an illustration of the complexity of control in an international context, see Jean-Francois Hennart, "Control in Multinational Firms: The Role of Price and Hierarchy," *Management International Review*, Special Issue 1991, 71–96. See also Anonymous, "Defining Controls," *The Internal Auditor 55*, no. 3 (June 1998): 47.

2. K.A. Merchant, "The Control Function of Management," *Sloan Management Review 23* (Summer 1982): 43–55. For an example of how a control system can be used with a formal planning model, see A.M. Jaeger and B.R. Baliga, "Control Systems and Strategic Adaptations: Lessons from the Japanese Experience," *Strategic Management Journal 6* (April/June 1985): 115–34.

3. Robert L. Dewelt, "Control: Key to Making Financial Strategy Work," *Management Review* (March 1977): 18; For discussion relating planning and controlling to leadership, see Sushil K. Sharma and Savita Dakhane, "Effective Leadership: The Key to Success," *Employment News 23*, no. 10 (June 6–June 12, 1998): 1, 15.

4. For more discussion on Murphy's Law, see Grady W. Harris, "Living with Murphy's Law," *Research-Technology Management* (January/February 1994): 10–13.

5. Robert J. Mockler, ed., *Readings in Management Control* (New York: Appleton-Century-Crofts, 1970), 14.

6. For insights about the process that Delta Air Lines uses to control distribution costs, see Perry Flint, "Delta's 'Shot Heard 'Round the World,' " *Air Transport World* (April 1995): 61–62.

7. Francis V. McCrory and Peter Gerstberger, "The New Math of Performance Measurement," *Journal of Business Strategy* (March/April 1991): 33–38; Anonymous, "Measuring Performance Can Prevent Failure," *Metal Center News 38*, no. 7 (June 1998): 80–82.

8. James M. Bright, "A Clear Picture," *Credit Union Management* (February 1995): 28–29.

9. For a discussion of how standards are set, see James B. Dilworth, *Production and Operations Management: Manufacturing and Nonmanufacturing* (New York: Random House, 1986), 637–50. For more information on various facets of standards and standard setting, see the following: Len Eglo, "Save Dollars on Maintenance Management," *Chemical Engineering 97* (June 1990): 157–62; Alden M. Hayashi, "GE Says Solid State Is Here to Stay," *Electronic Business 14* (April 1, 1988): 52–56; Frank Rose, "A New Age for Business?" *Fortune*, October 8, 1990, 156–64; Edward Basset, "Diamond Is Forever," *New England Business 12* (October 1990): 40–44; David Sheridan, "Getting the Big Picture," *Training* (September 1990): 12–15; Thomas A. Foster and Joseph V. Barks, "The Right Chemistry for Single Sourcing," *Distribution 89* (September 1990): 44–52; Joseph Conlin, "The House That G.E. Built," *Successful Meetings 38* (August 1989): 50–58; Robert W. Mann, "A Building-Blocks Approach to Strategic Change," *Training and Development Journal 44* (August 1990): 23–25; Joel Chernoff, "Global Standards Due Soon," *Pensions & Investments 26*, no. 1 (January 12, 1998): 1, 29.

10. For an example of a company surpassing performance standards, see Peter Nulty, "How to Live by Your Wits," *Fortune*, April 20, 1992, 119–20.

11. For an illustration of the problem/symptom relationship, see Elizabeth Dougherty, "Waste Minimization: Reduce Wastes and Reap the Benefits," *R & D 32* (April 1990): 62–68.

12. Harold Koontz, Cyril O'Donnell, and Heinz Weihrich, *Essentials of Management* (New York: McGraw-Hill, 1986), 454–59.

13. For an example of concurrent control in the health-care industry, see Teri Lammers, "The Troubleshooter's Guide," *Inc.* (January 1992): 65–67.

14. For a discussion of the basic concepts of feedback control, see J. Greg Ziegler and J. Robert Connell, "For Optimum Control: Modify the Process, Not the Controls (Part 1)," *Chemical Engineering* (May 1994): 132–40.

15. Vijay Sathe, *Controller Involvement in Management* (Upper Saddle River, NJ: Prentice Hall, 1982).

16. James D. Wilson, *Controllership: The Work of the Managerial Accountant* (New York: Wiley, 1981). For an example of individuals in organizations with more specific and limited controlling responsibilities, see the discussion by the director of production control at Nissan in John Williams, "Total Logistics—The Profit Driver," *Logistics Focus* (August 1994): 20–24; For a discussion of cost control for stadium owners, see Lee Ann Gjertsen, "Stadiums Spawn Risk Management Challenges," *National Underwriter 102*, no. 32 (August 10, 1998): 7, 16.

17. For other ways in which cost-benefit analysis can be used by managers, see G.S. Smith and M.S. Tseng, "Benefit-Cost-Analysis as a Performance Indicator," *Management Accounting* (June 1986): 44–49; "The IS (Information System) Payoff," *Infosystems* (April 1987): 18–20.

18. To explore the relationship between nonverbal behavior and power, see Herman Aguinis, Melissa M. Simonsen, and Charles A. Pierce, "Effects of Nonverbal Behavior on Perceptions of Power Bases," *The Journal of Social Psychology 138*, no. 4 (August 1998): 455–69.

19. See Amitai Etzioni, *A Comparative Analysis of Complex Organizations* (New York: Free Press, 1961), 4–6. For a study discussing the utility of various types of power to managers, see Gary Yukl and Cecilia Falbe, "Importance of Different Power Sources in Downward and Lateral Relations," *Journal of Applied Psychology* (June 1991): 416–23.

20. John P. Kotter, "Power, Dependence, and Effective Management," *Harvard Business Review* (July/August 1977): 128.

21. Kotter, "Power, Dependence, and Effective Management," 135–36. For a discussion on how empowering subordinates can increase the power of a manager, see Linda A. Hill, "Maximizing Your Influence," *Working Woman* (April 1995): 21–22+.

22. Kotter, "Power, Dependence, and Effective Management," 131.

23. For further discussion of how to overcome the potential negative effects of control, see Ramon J. Aldag and Timothy M. Stearns, *Management* (Cincinnati, OH: South-Western Publishing, 1987), 653–54. See also Arnold F. Emch, "Control Means Action," *Harvard Business Review* (July/August 1954): 92–98; K. Hall and L.K. Savery, "Tight Rein, More Stress," *Harvard Business Review* (January/February 1986): 160–64.

24. James T. McKenna, "Eastern, Maintenance Heads Indicted by U.S. Grand Jury," *Aviation Week & Space Technology 133* (July 1990): 84–86.

25. W. Jerome III, *Executive Control: The Catalyst* (New York: Wiley, 1961), 31–34. See also William Bruns, Jr. and E. Warren McFarlan, "Information Technology Puts Power in Control Systems," *Harvard Business Review* (September/October 1987): 89–94; C. Jackson Grayson, Jr., "Management Science and Business Practice," *Harvard Business Review* (July/August 1973): 41–48.

26. For an article emphasizing the importance of management understanding and being supportive of organizational control efforts, see Richard M. Morris III, "Management Support: An Underlying Premise," *Industrial Management 31* (March/April 1989): 2–3.

CHAPTER 20

1. James B. Dilworth, *Production and Operations Management: Manufacturing and Non-Manufacturing* (New York: Random House, 1986), 3.

2. John W. Kendrick, *Understanding Productivity: An Introduction to the Dynamics of Productivity Change* (Baltimore: Johns Hopkins University Press, 1977), 114; For insights about what role productivity can play in a strike, see "What Price Peace?: GM Lost a Lot to the UAW, and Labor Relations Are Still Bad," *Business Week* (August 10, 1998): 24; For useful discussion on how to

motivate people to do more to enhance productivity, see Geoffrey Colvin, "What Money Makes You Do," *Fortune,* August 17, 1998 213–14.

3. Lester C. Thurow, "Other Countries Are as Smart as We Are," *New York Times,* April 5, 1981.

4. For an example of virtual offices created to increase worker productivity, see Michael K. Takagawa, "Turn Traditional Work Spaces into Virtual Offices," *Human Resources Professional* (March/April 1995): 11–14.

5. W. Edwards Deming, *Out of the Crisis* (Boston: MIT Center for Advanced Engineering Study, 1986); see also Rafael Aguayo, *Dr. Deming: The American Who Taught the Japanese about Quality* (New York: Carol Publishing Group, 1990), 160–64.

6. John J. Dwyer, Jr., "Quality: Can You Prove It?" *Fleet Owner* (April 1995): 36.

7. Gerry Davidson, "Quality Circles Didn't Die—They Just Keep Improving," *CMA Magazine,* February 1995, 6; see also John B. Miner, *Organizational Behavior: Performance and Productivity* (New York: Random House, 1988), 308–16.

8. John Peter Koss, "Plant Robotics and Automation," *Beverage World* (April 1995): 108.

9. Robert E. Kemper and Joseph Yehudai, *Experiencing Operations Management: A Walk-Through* (Boston: PWS-Kent Publishing Company, 1991), 48.

10. Richard B. Chase and Nicholas J. Aquilano, *Production and Operations Management: A Life Cycle Approach* (Homewood, IL: Richard D. Irwin, 1981), 4. For a worthwhile discussion of forecasting product demand as a continual operations management activity, see Jim Browne, "Forecasting Demand for Services," *Industrial Engineering* (February 1995): 16–17.

11. Roger W. Schmenner, "Operations Management," *Business Horizons 41,* no. 3 (May/June, 1998): 3–4.

12. For an example of the kinds of layout issues that concern printers in Europe, see Jill Roth, "Molto Bene," *American Printer* (March 1994): 54–58.

13. For ways to ensure that human resource strategy is progressive, see Kevin Barksdale, "Why We Should Update HR Education," *Journal of Management Education 22,* no. 4 (August 1998): 526–30.

14. Lee J. Krajewski and Larry P. Ritzman, *Operations Management: Strategy and Analysis* (Reading, MA: Addison-Wesley, 1987), 573. See also A. Ansari and Modarress Batoul, "Just-in-Time Purchasing: Problems and Solutions," *Journal of Purchasing and Materials Management* (August 1986): 11–15; Albert F. Celley, William H. Clegg, Arthur W. Smith, and Mark A. Vonderembse, "Implementation of JIT in the United States," *Journal of Purchasing and Materials Management* (Winter 1987): 9–15; For issues to consider when contemplating the use of just-in-time in marketing, see S. Altan Erdem and Cathy Owens Swift, "Items to Consider for Just-In-Time Use in Marketing Channels: Toward Development of a Decision Tool," *Industrial Marketing Management 27,* no. 1 (January 1998): 21–29.

15. John D. Baxter, "Kanban Works Wonders, but Will It Work in U.S. Industry?" *Iron Age* (June 7, 1982): 44–48.

16. For discussion of cost control focusing on corporate jets, see Mel Mandell, "Why Sharing Jets Is Cost Effective," *World Trade 11,* no. 7 (July 1998): 85.

17. George S. Minmier, "Zero-Base Budgeting: A New Budgeting Technique for Discretionary Costs," *Mid-South Quarterly Business Review 14* (October 1976): 2–8; see also Peter A. Phyrr, "Zero-Base Budgeting," *Harvard Business Review* (November/December 1970): 111–21; E.A. Kurbis, "The Case for Zero-Base Budgeting," *CA Magazine,* April 1986, 104–05; Linda J. Shinn and M. Sue Sturgeon, "Budgeting from Ground Zero," *Association Management 42* (September 1990): 45–48; Gregory E. Becwar and Jack L. Armitage, "Zero-Base Budgeting: Is It Really Dead?" *Ohio CPA Journal 48* (Winter 1989): 52–54; Aaron Wildausky and Arthur Hammann, "Comprehensive versus Incremental Budgeting in the Department of Agriculture," in *Planning Programming Budgeting: A Systems Approach to Management,* ed. Fremont J. Lyden and Ernest G. Miller (Chicago: Markham, 1968), 143–44.

18. Chris Argyris, "Human Problems with Budgets," *Harvard Business Review* (January/February 1953): 108.

19. This section is based primarily on J. Fred Weston and Eugene F. Brigham, *Essentials of Managerial Finance,* 7th ed. (Hinsdale, IL: Dryden Press, 1985). See also F.L. Patrone and Donald duBois, "Financial Ratio Analysis for the Small Business," *Journal of Small Business Management* (January 1981): 35.

20. For an excellent discussion of ratio analysis in a small business, see Patrone and duBois, "Financial Ratio Analysis," 35–40.

21. Lester R. Bittle, *Management by Exception* (New York: McGraw-Hill, 1964); Frederick W. Taylor, *Shop Management* (New York: Harper & Bros., 1911), 126–27.

22. These two rules are adapted from *Boardroom Reports 5* (May 1976): 4.

23. Robert J. Lambrix and Surenda S. Singhvi, "How to Set Volume-Sensitive ROI Targets," *Harvard Business Review* (March/April 1981): 174.

24. For a listing and discussion of quantitative tools and their appropriate uses, see Kemper and Yehudai, *Experiencing Operations Management,* 341–55. For a clear discussion, illustrations, and examples of linear programming, breakeven analysis, work measurement, acceptance sampling, payoff tables, value analysis, computer-aided design (CAD), computer-aided engineering (CAE), computer-aided manufacturing (CAM), manufacturing resource planning, program evaluation and review technique (PERT), capacity requirements planning (CRP), and input/output control, see Jay Heizer and Barry Render, *Production and Operations Management: Strategies and Tactics* (Needham Heights: MA: Allyn and Bacon, 1993).

CHAPTER 21

1. Garland R. Hadley and Mike C. Patterson, "Are Middle-Paying Jobs Really Declining?" *Oklahoma Business Bulletin 56* (June 1988): 12–14; A. Essam Radwan and Jerome Fields, "Keeping Tabs on Toxic Spills," *Civil Engineering 60* (April 1990): 70–72; Dean C. Minderman, "Marketing: Desktop Demographics," *Credit Union Management 13* (February 1990): 26.

2. Henry Mintzberg, "The Myths of MIS," *California Management Review* (Fall 1972): 92–97; Jay W. Forrester, "Managerial Decision Making," in *Management and the Computer of the Future,* ed. Martin Greenberger (Cambridge, MA and New York: MIT Press and Wiley, 1962), 37.

3. The following discussion is based largely on Robert H. Gregory and Richard L. VanHorn, "Value and Cost of Information." in *Systems Analysis Techniques,* ed. J. Daniel Conger and Robert W. Knapp (New York: Wiley, 1974), 473–89.

4. John T. Small and William B. Lee, "In Search of MIS," *MSU Business Topics* (Autumn 1975): 47–55.

5. G. Anthony Gorry and Michael S. Scott Morton, "A Framework for Management Information Systems," *Sloan Management Review 13* (Fall 1971): 55–70.

6. Stephen L. Cohen, "Managing Human-Resource Data Keeping Your Data Clean," *Training & Development Journal 43* (August 1989): 50–54.

7. Michael A. Verespej, "Communications Technology: Slave or Master?" *Industry Week* (June 19, 1995): 48–55; John C. Scully, "Information Overload?" *Managers Magazine,* May 1995, 2.

8. T. Mukhapadhyay and R.B. Cooper, "Impact of Management Information Systems on Decisions," *Omega 20* (1992): 37–49.

9. Robert W. Holmes, "Twelve Areas to Investigate for Better MIS," *Financial Executive* (July 1970): 24. A similar definition is presented and illustrated in Jeffrey A. Coopersmith, "Modern Times: Computerized Systems Are Changing the Way Today's Modern Catalog Company Is Structured," *Catalog Age 7* (June 1990): 77–78. For an interesting example of how a company can decentralize an MIS, see John E. Framel and Leo F. Haas III, "Managing the Dispersed Computing Environment at Mapco, Inc.," *Journal of Systems Management 43:* 6–12.

10. Kenneth C. Laudon and Jane Price Laudon, *Management Information Systems: Organization and Technology* (New York: Macmillan, 1993), 38.

11. For an article discussing how a well-managed MIS promotes the usefulness of information, see Albert Lederer and Veronica Gardner, "Meeting Tomorrow's Business Demands through Strategic Information Systems Planning," *Information Strategy: The Executive's Journal* (Summer 1992): 20–27.

12. This section is based on Richard A. Johnson, R. Joseph Monsen, Henry P. Knowles, and Borge O. Saxberg, *Management Systems and Society: An Introduction* (Santa Monica, CA: Goodyear, 1976), 113–20; James Emery, "Information Technology in the 21st Century Enterprise" *MIS Quarterly* (December 1991): xxi–xxiii.

13. Robert G. Murdick, "MIS for MBO," *Journal of Systems Management* (March 1977): 34–40.

14. F. Warren McFarlan, "Problems in Planning the Information System," *Harvard Business Review* (March/April 1971): 75.

15. David S. Stoller and Richard L. Van Horn, *Design of a Management Information System* (Santa Monica, CA: RAND Corporation, 1958).

16. Craig Barrow, "Implementing an Executive Information System: Seven Steps for Success," *Journal of Information Systems Management 7* (Spring 1990): 41–46.

17. Bertram A. Colbert, "The Management Information System," *Management Services 4* (September/October 1967): 15–24.

18. Adapted from Henry Mintzberg, "The Manager's Job: Folklore and Fact," *Harvard Business Review* (July/August 1975): 58.

19. William R. King and David I. Cleland, "Manager Analysis Teamwork in MIS," *Business Horizons 14* (April 1971): 59–68; Regina Herzlinger, "Why Data Systems in Nonprofit Organizations Fail," *Harvard Business Review* (January/February 1977): 81–86; John Sculley, "The Human Use of Information," *Journal for Quality and Participation* (January/February 1990): 10–13; Richard Discenza and Donald G. Gardner, "Improving Production by Managing for Retention," *Information Strategy: The Executive's Journal* (Spring 1992): 34–38.

20. David Harvey, "Making Sense of the Data Deluge," *Director 42* (April 1989): 139–40.

21. Robert Chaiken, "Pitfalls of Computers in a CPA's Office," *Ohio CPA Journal 46* (Spring 1987): 45–46; John E. Framel, "Managing Information Costs and Technologies as Assets," *Journal of Systems Management 41* (February 1990): 12–18; Martin D.J. Buss, "Penny-Wise Approach to Data Processing," *Harvard Business Review* (July/August 1981): 111; James A. Yardley and Parez R. Sopanwala, "Break-Even Utilization Analysis," *Journal of Commercial Bank Lending 72* (March 1990): 49–56.

22. Steven L. Mandell, *Computers and Data Processing: Concepts and Applications with BASIC* (St. Paul, MN: West Publishing, 1982), 370–91.

23. Mark G. Simkin, *Computer Information Systems for Business* (Dubuque, IA: William C. Brown, 1987), 299–301.

24. For additional information on these software packages, see *Lotus 1-2-3 Reference Manual* (Cambridge, MA: Lotus Development Corporation, 1985); Timothy J. O'Leary, *The Student Edition of Lotus 1-2-3* (Reading, MA: Addison-Wesley, 1989); *IFPS User's Manual* (Austin, TX: Execucom Systems Corporation, 1984).

25. Ron Evans, "Systems for Growing Firms," *Black Enterprise* (April 1995): 44–45.

26. Kathleen Kiley, "Spin-Offs Stake Claim in LAN Rush," *Catalog Age* (May 1995): 24; David Reeve, "How Much Is Too Much?" *Computing Canada* (May 11, 1994): 47.

27. Jill Ellsworth and Matthew V. Ellsworth, *Marketing on the Internet: Multimedia Strategies for the World Wide Web* (New York: Wiley, 1995), 3; James Coates, "A Mailbox in Cyberspace Brings the World to Your PC," *Chicago Tribune*, March 26, 1995, sec. 19, 1.

28. David Sachs and Henry Stair, *Hands-on Internet: A Beginning Guide for PC Users* (Upper Saddle River, NJ: Prentice Hall, 1994), 3.

29. Ellsworth and Ellsworth, *Marketing and the Internet*, xv.

30. Steve Williams, "The Internet—Exploring Its Uses for Economic Development," *Economic Development Review* (Winter 1995): 64–69; Gerry Khermouch, "Holiday Inn Books in the Net; Apollo 13 Launches in Cyberspace," *Brandweek*, June 19, 1995, 16.

31. The following two sections are based upon Samuel C. Certo, *Supervision* (New York: Irwin/McGraw-Hill, 2000).

32. Anonymous, "Fast Fact," *Fast Company*, October 1998, 84.

33. Emily Esterson, "Inner Beauties," *Inc. Technology* No. 4 (1998): 79–109.

34. Wayne Kawamoto, "Click Here for Efficiency," *Business Week Enterprise*, December 7, 1998, 12, 14.

35. Douglas A. Blackmon, "Will FedEx Shift from Moving Boxes to Bytes?" *Wall Street Journal*, November 20, 1998, B1, B8.

CHAPTER 22

1. "The Push for Quality," *Business Week* (June 8, 1987): 131.

2. A.V. Feigenbaum, *Total Quality Control* (New York: McGraw-Hill, 1983).

3. From Michael Schroeder, "Heart Trouble at Pfizer," *Business Week* (February 26, 1990): 47–48.

4. For a discussion of companies that have recently won the Malcolm Baldrige National Award, see Karen Bemowski, "1994 Baldrige Award Recipients Share Their Expertise," *Quality Progress* (February 1995): 35–40.

5. For more information on these three contributors, see Charles H. Fine and David H. Bridge, "Managing Quality Improvement," *Quest for Quality: Man-*

aging the Total System, ed. by M. Sepheri (Norcross, GA: Institute of Industrial Engineers, 1987), 66–74.

6. For some of Crosby's more notable books in this area, see Philip B. Crosby, *Quality Is Free* (New York: McGraw-Hill, 1979); *Quality Without Tears* (New York: McGraw-Hill, 1984); *Let's Talk Quality: 96 Questions You Always Wanted to Ask Phil Crosby* (New York: McGraw-Hill, 1989); and *Leading* (New York: McGraw-Hill, 1990).

7. Michael J. O'Connor, "A Way of Corporate Life," *Supermarket Business* (May 1995): 69–75.

8. Deming's 14 Points (January 1990 revision) reprinted by permission from *Out of Crisis* by W. Edwards Deming by permission of MIT and W. Edwards Deming. Published by MIT, Center for Advanced Engineering Study, Cambridge, MA 02139. Copyright 1986 by W. Edwards Deming.

9. Tracy Benson Kirker, "The Teacher's Still a Student," *Industry Week* (May 2, 1994): 37–38.

10. Alan Robinson, *Modern Approaches to Manufacturing Improvement: The Shingo System* (Productivity Press, 1990), 267–68. See also Gary S. Vasilash, "On Training for Mistake-Proofing," *Production* (March 1995): 42–44.

11. Tim Stevens, "Dr. Feigenbaum," *Industry Week* (July 4, 1994): 12–16.

12. Ross Johnson and William O. Winchell, *Strategy and Quality* (Milwaukee, WI: American Society for Quality Control, 1989), 1–2.

13. Company Mission Statement, All America Inc., 1991, used by permission.

14. For a discussion supporting the importance of training to a companywide quality effort, see "Dr. W. Edwards Deming," *EBS Journal* (Spring 1989): 3.

15. Tom Peters, *Thriving on Chaos: Handbook for a Management Revolution* (New York: Harper & Row, 1987), 88, 98, 326.

16. Joseph Juran, *Juran on Quality Leadership: How to Go from Here to There* (Juran Institute, Inc., 1987), 6.

17. Michael Hammer, "Reengineering Work: Don't Automate, Obliterate," *Harvard Business Review* (July/August 1990): 104–12.

18. For a discussion of why some reengineering attempts fail, see Michael Hammer, "Beating the Risks of Reengineering," *Fortune* (May 15, 1995): 105–14.

CHAPTER 23

1. For a discussion of diversity issues in the United Kingdom, see Ian Dodds, "Differences Can Be Strengths," *People Management* (April 20, 1995): 40–43. See also Raymond Pomerleau, "A Desideratum for Managing the Diverse Workplace," *Review of Public Personnel Administration 14* (Winter 1994): 85–100; For a list of companies well-known for their positive work in the area of diversity, see Roy S. Johnson, "The 50 Best Companies for Asians, Blacks and Hispanics," *Fortune 138*, no. 3 (August 3, 1998): 94–96.

2. Liz Winfeld and Susan Spielman, "Making Sexual Orientation Part of Diversity," *Training & Development* (April 1995): 50–51.

3. Judith C. Giordan, "Valuing Diversity," *Chemical & Engineering News*, February 20, 1995, 40.

4. Ann M. Morrison, "Leadership Diversity as Strategy," *The New Leaders: Guidelines on Leadership Diversity in America* (San Francisco: Jossey-Bass, 1992), 11–28.

5. Prem Benimadh, "Adding Value through Diversity," *Canadian Business Review* (Spring 1995): 6–11; Tara Parker-Pope, "Inside P&G, a Pitch to Keep Women Employees," *Wall Street Journal*, September 9, 1998, B1.

6. William B. Johnston and Arnold E. Packer, "Executive Summary," *Workforce 2000: Work and Workers for the Twenty-First Century* (Indianapolis: Hudson Institute, June 1987), xiii–xiv; For discussion of organizational impact of changing demographics, see Constance L. Hays, "McCormick Faces Changing Demographics, Changing Tastes," *New York Times*, February 20, 1998, D1.

7. Roosevelt Thomas, "Affirmative Action or Affirming Diversity," *Harvard Business Review* (1990): 110.

8. Rosabeth Moss Kanter, *Men and Women of the Corporation* (New York: Basic Books, 1977).

9. Rosabeth Moss Kanter, "Numbers: Minorities and Majorities," *Men and Women of the Corporation* (New York: Basic Books, 1977), 206–44; For a discussion of successful steps Price Waterhouse takes to keep women on the payroll, see Anonymous, "Secrets of Success," *HR Focus 74*, no. 8 (August 1997): 10.

10. Ann M. Morrison, *Breaking the Glass Ceiling: Can Women Reach the Top of America's Largest Corporations?* (Reading, MA: Addison Wesley, 1992).

11. Susan Webb, *Step Forward: Sexual Harassment in the Workplace* (New York: MasterMedia, 1991); Susan B. Garland, "Finally, a Corporate Tip Sheet on Sexual Harassment," *Business Week* (July 13, 1998): 39.

12. Ella Bell, "The Bicultural Life Experience of Career Oriented Black Women," *Journal of Organizational Behavior 11* (November 1990): 459–78.

13. Catherine Dorton Fyock and Anne Marrs Dorton, "Welcome to the Unretirement Generation," *HR Focus* (February 1995): 22–23; For insights on how to manage older employees, see Carol Hymowitz, "Young Managers Learn How to Bridge the Gap with Older Employees," *Wall Street Journal,* July 21, 1998, B1.

14. Jeffrey Sonnenfeld, "Dealing with the Aging Workforce," *Harvard Business Review 56* (1978): 81–92.

15. William B. Johnston and Arnold E. Packer, "Executive Summary," *Workforce 2000: Work and Workers for the Twenty-First Century* (Indianapolis: Hudson Institute, June 1987): xii–xiv.

16. Jean Kim, "Issues in Workforce Diversity," Panel Presentation at the First Annual National Diversity Conference (San Francisco, May 1991).

17. *The Holy Bible,* Authorized King James Version (Nashville: Holman Bible Publishers, 1984).

18. J. Stewart Black and Hal B. Gregersen, "Serving Two Masters: Managing the Dual Allegiance of Expatriate Employees," *Sloan Management Review* (Summer 1992): 61–71.

19. Les Donaldson and Edward E. Scannell, *Human Resource Development: The New Trainer's Guide,* 2d ed. (Reading, MA: Addison-Wesley, 1986), 8–9.

CREDITS

CHAPTER 1

Introductory Case: Gene Sloan, "Disney Goes Wild," *USA Today,* April 17, 1998, 1D; Mar Genther, "Disney's Call of the Wild," *Fortune,* April 13, 1998, 120–124; T. Trent Gegax, Booming Amusement Parks: The Theme Is Extreme," *Newsweek,* March 30, 1998, 12. **Table 1.1:** Harris Collingwood, "The 10 Highest-Paid Female Executives," *Across the Board,* January 1998, 10. **Figure 1.5:** Paul Hersey and Kenneth Blanchard, *Management of Organizational Behavior: Utilizing Human Resources,* 5th ed. © 1988, p. 8. Reprinted by permission of Prentice-Hall, Inc., Upper Saddle River, NJ. **Figure 1.6:** Douglas T. Hall, *Careers in Organizations.* © 1976 Scott, Foresman and Company. Reprinted by permission. **Table 1.2:** Reprinted, by permission of the publisher, from "Improving Professional Development by Applying the Four-Stage Career Model," by Paul H. Thompson, Robin Zenger Baker, and Norman Smallwood, *Organizational Dynamics* (Autumn 1986): 59. © 1986. American Management Association, New York. All rights reserved.

CHAPTER 2

Introductory Case: David Leonhardt, "McDonald's: Can It Regain Its Golden Touch?" *Business Week,* March 9, 1998, 70; Shannon Stevens, "McDonald's Realigns Marketing Arm," *Brandweek 39,* no. 11 (March 16, 1998): 4; Ralph Raffio, "Did Somebody Say . . .," *Restaurant Business 97,* no. 4 (February 15, 1998): 28–46. **Across Industries:** Anonymous, "L. L. Bean Scores Efficiency Gains with Data Collection Upgrade," *Modern Materials Handling 52,* no. 14 (December 1997): S12–S14. **Quality Spotlight:** Jeremy Main, "How to Win the Baldrige Award," *Fortune Magazine,* April 23, 1990, 101–116; Christopher W. I. Hart, Christopher Bogan, and Dan O'Brien, "When Winning Isn't Everything," *Harvard Business Review* (January/February 1990): 209. **Management and the Internet:** Michel Marriott, "The Sad Ballad of the Cybercafe," *New York Times,* April 16, 1998, G1. **People Spotlight:** Ben Nagler, "Recasting Employees into Teams," *Workforce 77,* no. 1 (January 1998): 101–106. **Case Study:** John A. Byrne "The Shredder," *Business Week,* January 15, 1996; Mary Kane, "Downsizing: Profit vs. Pain," *The Atlanta Journal-Constitution,* January 14, 1996, p. C1–2; "Scott Paper Company," *Hoover's Company Profile Database* (Austin, TX: The Reference Press, 1995).

CHAPTER 3

Introductory Case: Joseph Pereira, "Toy Maker Faces Dilemmas As Water Gun Spurs Violence," *Wall Street Journal.* June 11, 1992, B1, B9. Reprinted by permission of *Wall Street Journal,* 1992 Dow Jones & Company, Inc. All Rights Reserved Worldwide. Karen Benezra, "Hardee's Hopes to Soak Mac, BK Summer Kid Promos," *Brandweek,* February 28, 1994, 12; Anne G. Pepper, "Deadly Toys Aren't Good Business," *Japan 21st,* December 1994, 15. **Table 3.2:** Sandra L. Holmes, "Executive Perceptions of Social Responsibility," *Business Horizons* (June 1976). Copyright, 1976, by the Foundation for the School of Business at Indiana University. Reprinted by permission. **Global Spotlight:** Edgar S. Wollard, Jr. "The 'Soul' Factor in Corporate Growth and Prosperity," *Directors and Boards* (Winter 1989): 4–8. **Figure 3.1:** The Eli Broad College of Business, Michigan State University. **Diversity Spotlight:** Glenn Hasek, "Breaking Barriers: Education Erases

False Perceptions of Minority Opportunities," *Hotel & Motel Management 207* (February 24, 1992): 21–22. **Figure 3.2:** Kenneth E. Newgren, "Social Forecasting: An Overview of Current Business Practices," in Archie B. Carroll, Ed., *Managing Corporate Social Responsibility.* Copyright © 1977 by Little, Brown and Company (Inc.). Reprinted by permission of the author. **Figure 3.3:** Reprinted by permission of the *Harvard Business Review,* from "How Companies Respond to Social Demands" by Robert W. Ackerman (July/August 1973): 96. Copyright © 1973 by the President and Fellows of Harvard College; all rights reserved. **Figure 3.4:** John L. Paulszek, "How Three Companies Organize for Social Responsibility." Reprinted by permission from *Business and Society Review* (Summer 1973): 18. Warren, Gorham and Lamont, Inc., 210 South St., Boston MA. All rights reserved. **Across Industries:** Rhymer Rigby, "Tutti-Frutti Capitalists," *Management Today,* February 1998, 54–56. **Management and the Internet:** Thomas E. Weber, "On-Line: Intel Proposal Is Angering Web Publishers," *Wall Street Journal,* January 16, 1998, B1; Gary H. Anthes, "Businesses May Vie for 'Net Seal of Ethics' " *Computerworld 30,* no. 34 (August 19, 1996): 65. **Figure 3.5:** Reprinted by permission of Johnson & Johnson. **Figure 3.6:** Reprinted by permission from "Code of Ethics and Standards of Conduct" (Orlando, FL: Martin Marietta, n.d.): 3. **Case Study:** "Informed Consent" *Business Week,* October 2, 1995, 104–16; "Fatal Litigation," *Fortune,* October 30, 1995, 137–58.

CHAPTER 4

Introductory Case: Karen Benezra, "Baskin in Sara Lee's Glory," *Brandweek 35* (September 12, 1994): 4; Beth Lorenzini, "Sweets Chains Bundle Up in Nontraditional Sites," *Restaurants & Institutions 104* (July 15, 1994): 98–100; Richard Martin, "Baskin-Robbins Brings U.S. Ice Cream Back to Embargo-Free Ho Chi Minh City," *The Orlando Sentinel,* December 28, 1994, B-5. **Figure 4.1:** *Survey of Current Business 77,* no. 7 (July 1997): 84. **Table 4.1:** Brian Zajac, "Free Trade Payback," *Forbes,* July 15, 1996, 288. Edited from an orginal article in the February 1998 issue of *Managment Today* with the permission of the copyright owner, Haymarket Business Publications Ltd. **Table 4.2:** Gustavo Lombo, "The Land of Opportunity," *Forbes,* July 15, 1996, 293. Reprinted by permission of *Forbes Magazine.* **Table 4.3:** Neil H. Jacoby, "The Multinational Corporation," *Center Magazine 3* (May 1970): 37–55. Reprinted by permission. **Ethics Spotlight:** "Japanese New Earth 21 Plan," Peter Jennings on World News Tonight, *ABC Network* (December 14, 1992). **Management and the Internet:** Lewis Rose and John Feldman, "How to Stay within International Law on the Internet," *The Magazine for Magazine Management,* 1998, 249–250; Chris Gosnell, "Jurisdiction on the Net: Defining Place in Cyberspace," *Canadian Business Law Journal 29,* no. 3 (February 1998): 344–363. **Across Industries:** Adapted from Steve Barth, "Wheel World Solutions," *World Trade 11,* no. 5 (May 1998): 42–45. **Figure 4.4:** Richard D. Robinson, *International Management* (Hinsdale, IL: Dryden Press, 1967). Reprinted by permission. **People Spotlight:** Valerie Frazee, "Send Your Expats Prepared for Success," *Workforce 3,* no. 3 (May 1998): 15–16. **Case Study:** "A Conversation with Roberto Goizueta and Jack Welch," *Fortune,* December 11, 1995, 96–102; Milton Moskowitz, Michael Katz, and Robert Levering, *Everybody's Business: An Almanac* (San Francisco: Harper & Row, 1980), 16–20; Chris Roush, "Coca-Cola's Global Growth Takes Hit," *The Atlanta Journal-Constitution,* December 22, 1995, 1G; Kenneth Shea, "Top Quality Buys," *The Outlook* (New York: Standard & Poor's, October 11, 1995) S3.

CHAPTER 5

Introductory Case: Robert Lenzner and Peter Newcomb, "The Vindication of Sumner," *Forbes*, June 15, 1998, 50; Eben Shapiro, "Blockbuster's Return is on Fast Forward, Says CEO with Big Plans for Rentals," *Wall Street Journal,* April 7, 1998, A3. **Global Spotlight:** Ted Agresa, "Asea Brown Boveri—A Model for Global Management," *R & D 33* (December 1991): 30–34; Paul R. Sullivan, "Executive Excellence," *R&D 33* (September 1991): 9–10. **Figure 5.2:** Jon H. Barrett, *Individual Goals and Organizational Objectives: A Study of Integration Mechanisms,* 5. Copyright © 1970 by the Institute for Social Research, The University of Michigan. Reprinted with permission. **Management and the Internet:** Dean Takahashi, "Game Plan: Video-Game Makers See Souring Sales Now—and Lots of Trouble Ahead," *Wall Street Journal,* June 15, 1998, R10. **Across Industries:** Robert L. Simison, "Goodyear Is Expected to Unveil Manufacturing Technology Gains," *Wall Street Journal,* February 9, 1998, B7C. **Diversity Spotlight:** Samuel K. Skinner, "Workforce Diversity," *Bureaucrat 20* (Summer 1991): 29–31. **Figure 5.4:** Joseph L. Massie and John Douglas, *Managing.* © 1985, p. 244. Reprinted by permission of Prentice-Hall, Inc., Upper Saddle River, NJ. **Table 5.2:** Howard M. Carlisle, *Management Concepts and Situations,* 598. © 1976. Published by Science Research Associates. Reprinted by permission of the author. **Table 5.3:** Reprinted by permission from A. N. Geller, *Executive Information Needs in Hotel Companies* (New York: Peat Marwick Main, 1984): 17. © Peat Marwick Main & Co., 1984. **Figure 5.5:** From Samuel C. Certo, Stewart T. Husted, and Max E. Douglas, *Business,* 3rd ed., 205. Copyright © 1990 by Allyn and Bacon. Reprinted by permission of Prentice Hall. **Case Study:** The Atlanta Olympic Committee On-line (http://www.atlanta.olympic.org); The International Olympic Committee On-line (http://www.olympic.org); *The Atlanta-Journal Constitution* Olympic Reports On-line (http://www.ajc.com); "The Disposable Games," *The Atlanta-Journal Constitution,* December 8, 1995, K1.

CHAPTER 6

Introductory Case: James P. Miller, "DuPont Adds Women's Clothes to Its Mix," *Wall Street Journal,* January 9, 1995, B1, B2. **Across Industries:** James Risen, "Getting Back to Basics, C.I.A. Is Hiring More Spies," *The New York Times,* June 27, 1998, 9. **Management and the Internet:** Stephen Lawton, "Betting It All on the Web," *LAN Times 14,* no. 26 (December 18, 1997): 14. **Figure 6.5:** William R. King and David I. Cleland, "A New Method for Strategic Systems Planning," *Business Horizons* (August 1975): 56. Copyright, 1975, by the Foundation for the School of Business Administration at Indiana University. Reprinted by permission. **Ethics Spotlight:** Jean Marie Hubert van Engelshoven, "Corporate Environmental Policy in Shell," *Long-Range Planning 24* (December 1991): 17–24. **Quality Spotlight:** Bryan Siegal, "Organizing for a Successful CE Process," *Industrial Engineering 23* (December 1991): 15–19. **Case Study:** The Quaker Oats Company, *Hoover's Company Profile Database* (Austin, TX: The Reference Press, 1996); "Business Brief—Quaker Oats Co.: Fiscal 2nd-Quarter Loss Is Reported by Company," *Wall Street Journal,* February 7, 1996, B6; "Will Quaker Get the Recipe Right?" *Business Week,* February 5, 1996, 140–45.

CHAPTER 7

Introductory Case: Melanie Warner, "Gateway to Wealth," *Fortune,* September 8, 1997, 80; Roger O. Crockett, "Gateway Loses the Folksy Shtick," *Businessweek,* July 6, 1998, 80–84. **Management and the Internet:** Kara Swisher, "Software: A Web Pioneer Does a Delicate Dance with Microsoft," *Wall Street Journal,* February 12, 1998, B1. **Table 7.1:** Herbert A. Simon, *The Shape of Automation* (New York: Harper & Row, 1965): 62. Used with permission of the author. **Figure 7.3:** Republished with permission of E. I. du Pont de Nemours & Company. **Global Spotlight:** "United Technologies: Like Japan, but Different," *Economist* (UK) *317* (November 3, 1990): 76–77. **People Spotlight:** Kevin Kelly, "The New Soul of John Deere," *Business Week,* January 31, 1994, 64–66. **Across Industries:** Nikhil Deogun, "Ivester Sees Rise in Sales, Opportunity for Coke in Turmoil," *Wall Street Journal,* December 22, 1997, A4; Frederick Kempe, "While Some Count Their Losses in Asia, Coca-Cola's Chairman Sees Opportunity," *Wall Street Journal,* February 6, 1998, B6. **Figure 7.7:** Copyright © 1964 by the President and Fellows of Harvard College; all rights reserved. **Figure 7.8:** Samuel C. Certo, Supervision: Quality and Diversity Through Leadership (Chicago: Austen Press/Irwin, 1995), 202.

CHAPTER 8

Introductory Case: Mark Maremont, "Gillette's New Strategy Is to Sharpen Pitch to Women," *Wall Street Journal,* May 11, 1998, B1; Mark Maremont, "A Cut Above? Gillette Finally Reveals Its Vision of the Future, and It Has 3 Blades—But Firm's Bet that Shavers Will Pay a 30% Premium Is a Double-Edged Sword—Secrecy at 'Plywood Ranch,'" *Wall Street Journal,* April 14, 1998, A1. **Across Industries:** Lisa Bannon, "Mattel Plans to Double Sales Abroad," *Wall Street Journal,* February 11, 1998, A3, and Lisa Bannon, "Mattel Earnings Soar 82%, Lifted by Core Toy Lines," *Wall Street Journal,* February 4, 1998, B13. **Table 8.1:** (a) and (b) based on E. Meadows, "How Three Companies Increased Their Productivity," *Fortune Magazine,* March 10, 1980, 92–101. (c) based on William B. Johnson, "The Transformation of a Railroad," *Long-Range Planning 9* (December 1976): 18–23. **Figure 8.1:** Samuel C. Certo and J. Paul Peter, *Strategic Management: Concepts and Applications* (New York: McGraw-Hill, Inc., 1991). Reprinted by permission of The McGraw-Hill Companies. **Ethics Spotlight:** Joshua Levine, "Locking Up the Weekend Warriors," *Forbes* (October 2, 1989), 234–235. **Management and the Internet:** Kate Berry, "Travel Stock Jumps on Sales, Internet News," *Wall Street Journal,* April 20, 1998, B11. **Table 8.2:** Arvind V. Phatak, *International Dimensions of Management,* 2nd ed., 1989, 6. Copyright © 1989 by Wadsworth, Inc. Reprinted by permission of the publisher. **Quality Spotlight:** Julie Johnson, "New Mission Statement Creates Unity for Health Care System," *Trustee 45* (February 1992): 10, 23. **Figure 8.3:** © 1970 The Boston Consulting Group, Inc. All rights reserved. Published by permission. **Figure 8.4:** Reprinted by permission from p. 32 of *Strategy Formulation: Analytical Concepts* by Charles W. Hofer and Dan Schendel. Copyright © 1978 by South-Western College Publishing Company, a division of International Thomson Publishing. All rights reserved. **Figure 8.5:** Reprinted from *Competitive Advantage: Creating and Sustaining Superior Performance* by Michael E. Porter. Copyright 1985 by Michael E. Porter. **Case Study:** "The View from IBM," *Business Week,* October 20, 1995, 142–52; "Information Week Industry Update."

CHAPTER 9

Introductory Case: Guy Collins. "Fiat Will Build, Expand in Italy's Depressed South," *Wall Street Journal,* November 29, 1990, A9. Reprinted by permission of *Wall Street Journal,* © 1990 Dow Jones & Company, Inc. All Rights Reserved Worldwide. See also John Rossant, "After Gianni, There Are Mostly Questions," *Business Week,* July 10, 1995: 55; Rob Cleveland, "European Suppliers on Fast Track," *Ward's Auto World,* July 1995, 35–37; and Rossant: "The Man Who's Driving Fiat like a Ferrari," *Business Week* (January 23, 1995): 82–83. **Ethics Spotlight:** Yoshihiko Shimizu, "Toyota Buckles Down to Overtake GM," *Tokyo Business Today* (Japan) *59* (February 1991): 32–34. **Management and the Internet:** Stephanie Armour, "Firings Flag Firms' Need for Net Policy," *USA Today,* April 1, 1998, 1B; Jake Lloyd-Smith, "Salomon Gets Tough Over E-Mail Abuse," *South China Morning Post,* April 27, 1998, 1. **Tables 9.1/9.2:** E. S. Groo, "Choosing Foreign Locations: One Company's Experience," *Columbia Journal of World Business* (September/October 1977): 77. Used with permission. **Global Spotlight:** Mary B. Teagarden, Mark C. Sutler, and Mary Ann Von Glinow, "Mexico's Maquiladora Industry: Where Strategic Resource Management Makes a Difference," *Organizational Dynamics 20* (Winter 1992): 34–47. **Figure 9.4:** Bruce Colman, "An Integrated System for Manpower Planning," *Business Horizons* (October 1970): 89–95. Copyright 1970, by the Foundation for the School of Business at Indiana University. Reprinted by permission. **Across Industries:** Frederic M. Biddle, "Boeing Is Placing Bets on Smaller, Cheaper Airliners," *Wall Street Journal,* July 6, 1998, A22; Michael Skapinker, "Dip in Asian Aircraft Predicted," *Financial Times,* June 19, 1998, 7. **Figure 9.6:** Philip Kotler, *Marketing Managing Analysis Planning and Control.* © 1967, p. 291. Adapted by permission of Prentice-Hall, Inc., Upper Saddle River, NJ.

CHAPTER 10

Introductory Case: Susan O'Keefe, "Lucent: The Next Master of the Universe?" *32,* no. 4 (April, 1998): 28–38; "2 Key Posts Filled and Reorganization Planned," *New York Times,* October 25, 1997, 3; Robert Ristelhueber, "Shaking Up the Old Order," *Electronic Business 24,* no. 1 (January 1998): 66–67+. **Management and the Internet:** Steve Ditlea, "Click Here if You Care," *Mediaweek 8,* no. 18 (May 4,

1998): 54–56. **Global Spotlight:** Tim Davis, "Crowning Achievement," *Beverage World 111* (February 1992): 66, 78. **Quality Spotlight:** Robert F. Huber, "Mercedes Manufacturing Strategy Is to Keep the Company's Market Niche Full," *Production 103* (October 1991): 60–63. **Across Industries:** Mary M. Fanning, "A Circular Organization Chart Promotes a Hospital-Wide Focus on Teams," *Hospital & Health Services Administration 42*, no. 2 (Summer 1997): 243–254. **Case Study:** "Divide and Conquer?" *Business Week*, October 2, 1995, 56–57; "Just Three Easy Pieces," *Time*, October 2, 1995, 47–48; "Strategic Restructuring for the 21st Century," remarks by Robert Allen, September 20, 1995.

CHAPTER 11

Introductory Case: CNN Cable News Network "Pinnacle" interview, September 24, 1988, and Dennis P. Kimbro, "Dreamers: Black Sales Heros and Their Secrets," *Success 37* (May 1990): 40–41; Fonda Marie Lloyd, "A Cookie by Any Other Name," *Black Enterprise* (January 1995): 22; Hank Kim, "DiMassimo Gets Famous Amos Founder's $5 Mil. Muffin Account," *Adweek 38*, no. 13 (March 31, 1997): 41. **Management and the Internet:** Frank Hayes, "Where Have All Coders Gone?" *Computerworld 32*, no. 21 (May 25, 1998): 12; Brian Reed, "IS Departments: Wake Up and Get Online," *Hotel and Motel Management 211*, no. 11 (June 17, 1996): 27. **Table 11.1:** Reprinted, by permission of the American Management Association, from "Roles and Relationships Clarifying the Manager's Job," by Robert D. Melcher, *Management Review* (May/June/1967): 35, 38–39. © 1967 American Management Association, New York. **Ethics Spotlight:** Joseph Conlin, "The House That GE Built," *Successful Meetings 38* (August 1989): 50–58. **Diversity Spotlight:** Zachary Schiller, "No More Mr. Nice Guy at P&G—Not by a Long Shot," *Business Week* (February 3, 1992): 54–56. **Figure 11.3:** David B. Starkweather, The Rationale for Decentralization in Large Hospitals," *Hospital Administration 15* (Spring 1970): 139. Courtesy of Dr. P. N. Ghei, Secretary General Indian Hospital Association, New Delhi, India. **Across Industries:** Kelvin Childs, "Publishing Centralization Efficiency Move," *130*, no. 30 (July 26, 1997): 6–7. **Case Study:** "Wanted: Company Change Agents," *Fortune*, February 5, 1996, 60–61.

CHAPTER 12

Introductory Case: Susana Schwartz, "NW Mutual Improves Agent Recruitment Process," *Insurance & Technology 22*, no. 7 (July 1997): 14–16; "America's Most Admired Life Insurance Companies," *Fortune*, March 2, 1998. **Management and the Internet:** Robert Bellinger, "Job Recruiting All the Rage on Web," *Electronic Engineering Times* no. 1011 (June 8, 1998): 151–154. **Figure 12.2:** Reprinted with the permission of Macmillan Publishing Company from *The Management of People at Work: Readings in Personnel*, 2nd ed. by Dale S. Beach. Copyright © 1985 Adapted by permission of Prentice Hall, Upper Saddle River, NJ. **Figures 12.3, 12.4, 12.5:** Walter S. Wikstrom, "Developing Managerial Competence: Concepts, Emerging Practices," *Studies in Personnel Policy* No. 189, 9, 14. Used with permission. **Figure 12.6:** Reprinted by permission from L. C. Megginson, *Providing Management Talent for Small Business* (Baton Rouge, LA, Division of Research, College of Business Administration, Louisiana State University, 1961): 108. **Global Spotlight:** Anne Ferguson, "Compaq's Personnel Solution," *Management Today* (May 1989): 127–128; Prabhu Guptara, "Searching the Organization for the Cross-Cultural Operators," *International Management 41* (August 1986): 40–42. **Table 12.1:** Dale Feuer, "Where the Dollars Go." Reprinted from the October 1985 issue of *Training*, The Magazine of Human Resources Development, 53. Copyright 1985, Lakewood Publications, Inc., Minneapolis, MN 612-333-0471. All rights reserved. **Across Industries:** Bernie Knill, "Furniture Making, MES Style," *Material Handling Engineering 53*, no. 5 (May 1998): 42–46. **Table 12.2:** Compiled from Andrew F. Sikula, *Personnel Administration and Human Resource Management* (New York: John Wiley & Sons, 1976): 208–211. **Case Study:** "Buy! Employee Solutions, Inc.," *The Volume Investor Special Update*, June 8, 1995; Blomberg Business Wire, February 5, 1996.

CHAPTER 13

Introductory Case: Mahlon Apgar, IV, "The Alternative Workplace: Changing Where and How People Work," *Harvard Business Review* (May–June, 1998):

121–136; Stephanie Armour, "Success of Telecommuting Dispels Myth," *USA Today*, April 17, 1998, 2B; Anonymous, "How AT&T Took Telecommuting On-line," *The Management Accounting Magazine*, December 1996/January 1997, 14. **Figure 13.1:** Don Hellriegel and John W. Slocum, Jr. "Integrating Systems Concepts and Organizational Strategy," *Business Horizons 15* (April 1972): 73. Copyright, 1972, by the Foundation for the School of Business at Indiana University. Reprinted by permission. **Across Industries:** Steven Johnson, "Manager's Journal: Apple Gains on Microsoft," *The Wall Street Journal*, November 16, 1998, A38; Apple Company home page; David Kirkpatrick, "The Second Coming of Apple," *Fortune 138*, no. 9 (November 9, 1998): 86–92. **Ethics Spotlight:** Jonathan Lee, *Pulp & Paper 66* (March 1992): 198–200. **Figures 13.4, 13.5:** John F. Mee, "Matrix Organization," *Business Horizons* (Summer 1964): 71. Copyright, 1964, by the Foundation for the School of Business at Indiana University. Reprinted by permission. **Diversity Spotlight:** Beverly Geber, "The Disabled: Ready, Willing and Able," *Training 27* (December 1990): 29–36. **Figure 13.7:** Reprinted by permission of *Harvard Business Review*. From "Breakthrough in Organization Development" by Robert R. Blake, Jane S. Mouton, Louis Barnes, and Larry Greiner (November/December 1964): 136. Copyright © 1964 by the President and Fellows of Harvard College; all rights reserved. **Management and the Internet:** David Ashton, "Geography Lessons," *People Management 4*, no. 6 (March 19, 1998): 46–49, company Web site, and 1998 Annual Report. **Figure 13.8:** Thomas H. Davenport and Keri Pearlson, "Two Cheers for the Virtual Office," *Sloan Management Review* (Summer, 1998): 53. Copyright 1998 by Sloan Management Review Association. All rights reserved. **Table 13.1:** Carolyn Corbin, "Tips to Ensure Good Communication in a Virtual Office," *Workforce* (November 1997; supplement). Used with the permission of ACC. **Case Study:** Robert E. Allen. "Strategic Restructuring for the 21st Century." speech, September 20, 1995. AT&T On-line <http://www.att.com/news/speeches/95/950920.raa.html>; John J. Keller, "AT&T Will Eliminate 40,000 Jobs and Take a Charge of $4 Billion," *Wall Street Journal*, January 3, 1996, A3, A6; Deborah Lohse, "New Jersey to Be Hit Hard by Cutback at Largest Private Employer in State," *Wall Street Journal*, January 3, 1996, A3, A4; "AT&T Managers Ponder Their Future for Last Day." CNNfn On-line. December 29, 1995; <http://www.cnnfn.com/news/9512/29/att.managers/index.html>; "Out One Door and in Another," *Business Week*, January 22, 1996, 41.

CHAPTER 14

Table 14.1: Reprinted by permission from Stephen C. Harper, "Business Education: A View from the Top," *Business Forum* (Summer 1987): 25. Reprinted with permission. **Figures 14.3, 14.4:** Wilber Schramm, *The Process and Effects of Mass Communication*, © 1954 University of Illinois Press, Champaign, IL. Reprinted by permission. **Management and the Internet:** Roberta Fusaro, "Wimbledon Taps Notes for Web Site," *Computerworld 32*, no. 27 (July 6, 1998): 37–38. Reprinted with permission. **Across Industries:** David Bell, "How Local Government Managers Should Communicate in Organizations," *Public Management 79*, no. 7 (July 1997): 24–25. Reprinted with permission from the July 1997 issue of *Public Management* published by the International City/County Management Association ICMA, Washington DC. **Figure 14.5:** Permission of the publisher, from Alex Bavelas and Dermont Barrett, "An Experimental Approach to Organizational Communication," *Personnel* (March 1951): 370, © 1951 American Management Association, New York. All rights reserved. **Quality Spotlight:** Alan Salomon, "Bass Gains Base of Confidence," *Hotel & Motel Management 206* (November 25, 1991): 2, 42. **Figure 14.6:** Reprinted by permission of *Harvard Business Review*. An exhibit from "Management Communication and the Grapevine" by Keith Davis (September/October 1953): 45. Copyright © 1953 by the President and Fellows of Harvard College; all rights reserved. **Table 14.2:** Keith Davis, *Human Behavior at Work*, 396. Copyright © 1972 by McGraw-Hill, Inc. Used with permission of McGraw-Hill Book Company.

CHAPTER 15

Introductory Case: *Making It Happen*, H. J. Heinz Company Annual Report 1998, 4–7. **Figure 15.2:** Reprinted by permission of *Harvard Business Review*. From "How to Choose a Leadership Pattern" by Robert Tannenbaum and Warren H. Schmidt (May/June 1973). Copyright © 1973 by the President and Fellows of Harvard College; all rights reserved. **Management and the Internet:** Julie Ritzer Ross, "K-B Toys Expands Information-Exchange System," *Stores 80*, no. 1 (January

1998): 56–58; "Kay-Bee Turns in Record '97 Performance," *Discount Store News 37,* no. 3 (February 9, 1998): 75; Anonymous, "Temporary Temptations: Retailers Flirt with Seasonal Tenancy," *Chain Store Age 74,* no. 3 (March 1998): 173–174. **Figure 15.4:** Reprinted from *Leadership and Decision-Making* by Victor H. Vroom and Philip W. Yetton (Table 2.1, p. 13), by permission of the University of Pittsburgh Press. © 1973 by University of Pittsburgh Press. **Figure 15.5:** Reprinted from *The New Leadership: Managing Participation in Organizations* by Victor H. Vroom and Arthur G. Jago, 1988, Upper Saddle River, NJ: Prentice-Hall. Copyright 1987 by V. H. Vroom and A. G. Jago. Used with permission of the authors. **Figure 15.6:** Paul Hersey and Kenneth H. Blanchard, *Management of Organizational Behavior: Utilizing Human Resources,* 3rd ed., 103, © 1977. Reprinted by permission of Prentice-Hall, Inc., Upper Saddle River, NJ. **Across Industries:** Dan Caulfield, "Data Duty," *Inc Magazine 19,* no. 17 (November 18, 1997): 33–34. **Table 15.1:** F. E. Fiedler, *A Theory of Leadership Effectiveness,* 34. Copyright © 1967 by McGraw-Hill, Inc. Used with permission of McGraw-Hill Book Company. **Figure 15.7:** Reprinted by permission of the *Harvard Business Review.* From "Engineer the Job to Fit the Manager" by Fred Fiedler (September/October 1965). Copyright © 1965 by the President and Fellows of Harvard College; all rights reserved. **Table 15.2:** Andrew J. DuBrin, Participant Guide to Module 10: Development of Subordinates (McGregor, TX: Leadership Systems Corporation, 1985), P11. **Diversity Spotlight:** Kevin D. Thompson, "Blazing New Trails," *Black Enterprise 21* (January 1991): 54–57. **Case Study:** Steering Through Turbulence, *Atlanta Journal and Constitution,* January 14, 1996, F1–F2; "Morale Falters as Change Rocks Delta's Family," *Atlanta Journal and Constitution,* January 14, 1996, F5; "Turns Out This Critter Can Fly," *Fortune,* November 27, 1995, 51.

CHAPTER 16

Figure 16.3: Lyman Porter and Edward Lawler III, *Managerial Attitudes and Performance,* 165. Copyright © 1968 Richard D. Irwin Inc. Reprinted by permission. **Across Industries:** Lisa Cheraskin and Michael A. Campion, "Study Clarifies Job-Rotation Benefits," *Personnel Journal 75,* no. 11 (November 1996): 31–38; Tom Russell, "Reinvent Rotation Rule," *Government Executive 30,* no. 7 (July 1998): 62. **Table 16.1:** Reprinted by permission of *Harvard Business Review.* From "One More Time: How Do You Motivate Employees?" by Frederick Herzberg (January/February 1968). Copyright © 1968 by the President and Fellows of Harvard College; all rights reserved. **Quality Spotlight:** Jim Brahan, "A Rewarding Place to Work," *Industry Week 238* (September 18, 1989): 15–19. **Table 16.2:** Edward G. Thomas, "Workers Who Set Their Own Time Clocks," (Spring 1987): 50. Reprinted by permission from *Business and Society Review.* **Management and the Internet:** Denise Grady, "Keeping Track of Employees' On-Line Voyeurism," *New York Times,* May 7, 1998, 3; Mitch Wagner, "Firms Spell Out Appropriate Use of Internet for Employees," *Computerworld 30,* no. 6 (February 5, 1996): 55. **Case Study:** Interview with Glenn Goldberg, Director of Human Resources, Western Pacific Airlines; "If at First You Don't Secceed . . .", *Forbes,* February 12, 1996, 54–58.

CHAPTER 17

Introductory Case: Timothy Aeppel, "Rolls-Royce Tries to Restore Luster as Car Sales Fade, *Wall Street Journal,* May 26, 1992, B3. Reprinted by permission of *Wall Street Journal,* © 1992 Dow Jones & Company, Inc. All Rights Reserved Worldwide. **Diversity Spotlight:** Sherri K. Lindenberg, "Managing a Multi-Ethnic Field Force," *National Underwriter 95* (January 7, 1991): 16–18, 24. **Figure 17.2:** Reprinted by permission of *Harvard Business Review.* From "Committees on Trial" (Problems in Review) by Rollie Tillman, Jr. (May/June 1960): 163. Copyright © 1960 by the President and Fellows of Harvard College; all rights reserved. **Ethics Spotlight:** Colleen Scanlon and Cornelia Fleming, "Confronting Ethical Issues: A Nursing Survey," *Nursing Management 21* (May 1990): 63–65. **Figure 17.4:** Figure 11.5 from *Social Psychology* by Muzafer Sherif and Carolyn W. Sherif. Copyright © 1969 by Muzafer Sherif and Carolyn W. Sherif. Reprinted by permission of Addison-Wesley Educational Publishers, Inc. **Management and the Internet:** Beverly Geber, "Virtual Teams," *Training,* April 1995, 36–40. **Across Industries:** Tim Minahan, "Harley-Davidson Revs Up Development Process Purchasing," *124,* no. 7 (May 7, 1998): 18–23; Jay Koblenz, "Revving Up to the Motorcycle Craze," *Black Enterprise 29,* no. 1 (August 1998): 120–121; Tom Weir, "Facing a Wealth of Decisions Spend a Little Time with Ryan Leaf's $11.25 Mil-

lion Bonus," *USA Today,* August 26, 1998, 3C. **Figure 17.7:** Hans J. Thamhain, "Managing Technologically Innovative Team Efforts Toward New Product Success," *Journal of Product Innovation Management,* March 1990, 5–18. **Case Study:** "The Fall of an American Icon," *Business Week,* February 5, 1996, 34–44; "New Task at Apple: First Order, Then Orders," *Wall Street Journal,* February 5, 1996, A3–A4; "Inside Apple's Boardroom Coup," *Business Week,* February 19, 1996, 28–30.

CHAPTER 18

Introductory Case: Adapted from Terrence L. Johnson, "Workplace Enthusiasm Revivable," *Wall Street Journal,* June 4, 1995, G1, 12. **Table 18.1:** Angelo J. Kinicki, Kenneth P. Carson, and George W. Bohlander, "Relationships between an Organization's Actual Human Resource Efforts and Employee Attitudes," *Group & Organization Management,* June 1992, 142. Reprinted by permission of Sage Publishers. **Across Industries:** Jane Pickard, "Talent-Spotting NatWest Tackles Inverted Ageism," *People Management, 3,* no. 21 (October 23, 1997): 31. **Global Highlight:** Adapted by Michael R. Carrell, Norbert Elbert, *Human Resource Management* (Upper Saddle River, NJ: Prentice Hall, 1995); adapted from James A. McCaffrey and Craig R. Hafner, "When Two Cultures Collide: Doing Business Overseas," *Training and Development Journal,* October 1985, p. 26. © 1985; *Training and Development Journal,* American Society for Training and Development. Reprinted with permission. All rights reserved.

CHAPTER 19

Introductory Case: Barbara Carton, "Polaroid to Cut Work Force By Up to 5%," *Wall Street Journal,* February 6, 1995, 7A. **Across Industries:** Emily Knight and Gordon M. Amsler, "Checking In Under Marriott's First Ten Program," *National Productivity Review 17,* no. 4 (Autumn 1998): 53–56. Reprinted by permission of John Wiley & Sons, Inc. **Management and the Internet:** Marc Gunther, "NBC Is Old Media, but Its Web Plans Are Real Smart," *Fortune,* August 17, 1998, 191–94. Reprinted by special permission, Time, Inc. **Diversity Spotlight:** Lisa Lebowitz, "A Rainbow Coalition," *Working Woman 16* (December 1991): 72–74.

CHAPTER 20

Introductory Case: Carl Quintanilla, "New Airline Fad: Faster Airport Turnarounds," *Wall Street Journal,* August 4, 1994, B1, B2. **Management and the Internet:** Jaikumar Vijayan, "Legacy Access Lets Sallie Mae Go on Web," *Computerworld,* July 27, 1998, 61–62. **Figure 20.1:** Reprinted from *Out of Crisis* by W. Edwards Deming by permission of MIT and W. Edwards Deming. Published by MIT, Center for Advanced Engineering, Cambridge, MA 02139. Copyright 1986 by W. Edwards Deming. **Quality Spotlight:** Stephen Barr, "Adidas on the Rebound," *CFO: The Magazine for Senior Financial Executives* (September 1991): 48–56; Richard A. Melcher, "Now This Should Get Adidas on Its Feet," *Business Week,* July 20, 1992, 42. **Across Industries:** Anonymous, "Robot Curbs Heavy Lifting at Black and Decker," *Modern Materials Handling 53,* no. 4 (April 1998): 55–56. **Figure 20.3:** Richard B. Chase and Nicholas J. Aquilano, *Production and Operations Management: A Life Cycle Approach,* 4th ed., 5. © 1985 Richard D. Irwin, Inc. Reprinted by permission. **Ethics Spotlight:** Mary Walton, *Deming Management at Work: Six Successful Companies that Use the Quality Principles of the World Famous W. Edwards Deming* (New York: G. P. Putnam's Sons, 1991): 185–205; Kathleen Morris, "A Bridge Far Enough: Four Years after Buying Firestone Bridgestone Finally Gets Tough," *Financial World* (June 9, 1992): 52–54. **Figure 20.4:** Richard B. Chase and Nicholas J. Aquilano, *Production and Operations Management: A Life Cycle Approach,* 4th ed., 5. © 1985 Richard D. Irwin, Inc. Reprinted by permission. **Case Study:** Scott McNealy's Rising Sun, *Business Week,* January 22, 1996, pp. 66–73.

CHAPTER 21

Introductory Case: Martha Brannigan and James R. Hagerty, "Sunbeam, Its Prospects Looking Worse, Fires CEO Dunlap," *Wall Street Journal,* June 15, 1998,

A1, A14. **Figure 21.1:** Reprinted by permission from G. Anthony Gorry and Michael S. Scott Morton, "A Framework for Management Information Systems," *Sloan Management Review 13* (Fall 1971): 59. Reprinted by permission of the publisher. **Figure 21.2:** The Eli Broad College of Business, Michigan State University. **Global Spotlight:** Oles Gadacz, "Steel Giant Pioneers Korean IS," *Datamation 35* (June 1, 1989): 64g–64h. **Figure 21.4:** Adapted from Robert G. Murdick, "MIS for MBO," *Journal of Systems Management* (March 1977): 34–40. Used with permission of *Journal of Systems Management*, 24587 Bagley Road, Cleveland, OH 44138. **Diversity Spotlight:** Jay L. Johnson, "Target's New Dynamics," *Discount Merchandiser 31* (August 1991): 30–46; Terry E. Hedrick, "New Challenges for Government Managers," *Bureaucrat 19* (Spring 1990): 17–20. **Figure 21.5:** Reprinted by permission from R. E. Breen et al., *Management Information Systems: A Subcommittee Report on Definitions* (Schenectady, NY: General Electric Co., 1969): 21. **Figure 21.7:** "Parts of the Personal Computer and What They Do," *Time* (January 3, 1983), 39. Copyright 1982 Time Inc. Magazine Company. Reprinted by permission. **Table 21.2:** Jared Sandberg, "Technology: The Business Plan," *Wall Street Journal*, November 14, 1994, R14. Reprinted from Internet Info. **Across Industries:** Stephen Kreider Yoder, "Technology: The Business Plan," *Wall Street Journal*, November 14, 1994, R16. **Case Study:** "Win '95, Lose '96," *Business Week*, December 18, 1995, 34–35; "Promises of the Internet," *USA Today*, November 13, 1995, Section E; Don Clark, "Microsoft to Unveil Internet Products," *Wall Street Journal*, December 7, 1995, B8.

CHAPTER 22

Introductory Case: Joseph Pereira, "LEGO's Robot Set for Kids Grabs Crowds of Grown-Ups," *Wall Street Journal*, December 10, 1998, B1. Reprinted by permission. **Quality Spotlight:** Tom Peters, *Thriving on Chaos: Handbook for a Management Revolution* (New York: Harper & Row, 1987) 87. **Table 22.1:** © Copyright 1979. Crosby: *Quality Without Tears*. Reprinted with permission from McGraw-Hill. **Figure 22.1:** David A. Gavin, "What Does Product Quality Really Mean? *Sloan Management Review 26* (Fall 1984): 37. Reprinted by permission of the publisher. Copyright 1984 by the Sloan Management Review Association. All rights reserved. **Table 22.1:** Philip B. Crosby, *Quality Without Tears* (New York: McGraw-Hill, 1979): 8–9. Copyright 1979. Reprinted with permission of McGraw-Hill, Inc. **Figure 22.2:** From *Zero Quality Control: Source Inspection and the Poka Yoke System* by Shigeo Shingo. English translation copyright © 1986 by *Productivity Press, Inc.*, P.O. Box 13390, Portland, OR, 97213-0390, (800) 394-6868. Reprinted by permission. **Management and the Internet:** Jerry Useem, "The Start-Up Factory," *Inc 19*, no. 2 (February 1997): 40–52. **Figure 22.4:** Teresa M. Amabile, "How to Kill Creativity," *Harvard Business Review* (September-October 1998): 78. **Across Industries:** Susan Tiffany, "A Pledge for Independence," *Candy Industry 163*, no. 9 (September 1998): 8; Susan Tiffany, "Making a Case for Mergers," *Candy Industry 163*, no. 8 (August 1998): 12. **Case Study:** Theresa Flanagan, "Taking the Next Step," *Marketing Tools Magazine*, September 1995; "Is TQM Dead?" *USA Today*, October 17, 1995, 1b, 2b; David Greising, "Quality—How to Make It Pay," *Business Week*, August 8, 1994; John Waldes, "The Missing Link," *Marketing Tools Magazine*, March/April 1995; "Consultants, Never Mind the Buzz words. Roll Up Your Sleeves," *Business Week*, January 22, 1996.

CHAPTER 23

Table 23.1: Ann M. Morrison, *The New Leaders: Leadership Diversity in America*, adapted from pp. 18–27. Copyright 1992 by Ann M. Morrison and Jossey-Bass, Inc., Publishers. Reprinted by permission of Jossey-Bass, Inc., Publishers. **Diversity Spotlight:** Parker R. Goodwin, *Laying the Groundwork for Diversity Training at CAE-LINK: Demographic and Process Issues* (Reprinted by permission) Binghamton University (1993): 31–33. **Figure 23.1:** William B. Johnston and Arnold E. Packer, "Executive Summary," *Workforce 2000: Work and Workers for the 21st Century* (Hudson Institute, June 1987): 95. Reprinted by permission. **Global Spotlight:** "Connecting the World," *Focus for and about the People of AT&T* (September 1992). **Across Industries:** Anne Faircloth, "Shoney's Fights Racism," *Fortune*, August 3, 1998, 108–10. Reprinted by special permission, Time

Inc. From the Equal Employment Opportunity Commission Web site <http://www.eeoc.gov>. **Case Study:** "Managing by Values: Is Levi Strauss Approach Visionary—or Flaky?" *Business Week*, August 1, 1994, 46–47; "Taking Adversity Out of Diversity," *Business Week*, January 31, 1994, 54–55; "Tearing Up Today's Organization Chart," *Business Week*, November 18, 1994, 80–87; "Levi's Is Leaving China," *Business Horizons*, March/April 1995, 35–40.

PHOTO CREDITS

Chapter 1: p. 3 Scott Audette/AP/Wide World Photos; p. 6, Jim Bourg/Liaison Agency, Inc.; p. 7, Michael Greenlar/Michael Greenlar, Photographer; p. 7, Edward Gajdel Photography; p. 15, Jonathan Saunders; p. 16, John Abbott Photography; **Chapter 2:** p. 25, Ed Carreon/SIPA Press; p. 28, Brown Brothers; p. 28, Douglas Levere/Douglas Levere Photography; p. 29, Jay Brousseau; p. 32, Glentzer Photography; p. 36, David Butow/SABA Press Photos, Inc.; **Chapter 3:** p. 47, Liaison Agency, Inc.; p. 49, Steven Rubin/JB Pictures Limited/The Image Works; p. 54, R. Crandall/The Image Works; p. 63, AP/Wide World Photos; p. 68, Mark Lennihan/AP/Wide World Photos; **Chapter 4:** p. 75, Lois Raimondo/AP/Wide World Photos; p. 79, BFW, Inc.; p. 82, Alan Levenson; p. 88, Pascal Plessis/AP/Wide World Photos; p. 91, B. Daemmrich/The Image Works; p. 92, Greg Girard/Contact Press Images, Inc.; **Chapter 5:** p. 103, Porter Gifford/Liaison Agency, Inc.; p. 105, Spencer Grant/PhotoEdit; p. 106, Jason Furnari/Sygma; p. 112, Eli Reichman; p. 113, Chris Crosmeier Photography; **Chapter 6:** p. 125, Nancy Kaszerman/Shooting Star International Photo Agency; p. 130, Reid Horn; p. 133, Action Press/SABA Press Photos, Inc.; p. 134, Churchill & Klehr Photography; **Chapter 7:** p. 143, Gateway 2000, Inc.; p. 148, Alan Levenson; p. 151, Donal Philby/Tom Carroll Photography; **Chapter 8:** p. 165, David Young-Wolff/PhotoEdit; p. 169, Kaku Kurita/Liaison Agency, Inc.; p. 170, Greg Baker/AP/Wide World Photos; p. 171, Greg Girard/Contact Press Images, Inc.; **Chapter 9:** p. 189, Eligioi Paoni/Contrasto/SABA Press Photos, Inc.; p. 191, Michael L. Abramson/Michael L. Abramson Photography; p. 196, Bob Riha/Liaison Agency, Inc.; **Chapter 10:** p. 211, Terry Wild Studio; p. 212, Jeremy Woodhouse/New England Stock Photo; p. 213, Chris Sorensen Photography; p. 218, Bob Hower/Quadrant Photography; **Chapter 11:** p. 233, Churchill & Klehr Photography; p. 236, P. Hirth/T. Hartrich Eisenach/Transit Leipzig; p. 242, Andy Freeberg Photography; p. 248, Christopher Morrow/Stock Boston; **Chapter 12:** p. 255, The Northwestern Mutual Life Insurance Company; p. 262, Steven Rubin/JB Pictures Ltd./The Image Works; p. 269, Jeff Christensen/AP/Wide World Photos; **Chapter 13:** p. 277, AT&T Archives; p. 280, Curtis Compton/VF Corporation; p. 284, Robert Holmgren/Robert Holmgren Photography; p. 287, Mark Richards/Contact Press Images, Inc.; p. 293, Spencer Grant/PhotoEdit; **Chapter 14:** p. 303, Eaton Corporation; p. 305, Rich Frishman Photography and Videograph, Inc.; p. 308, Intel Museum Archives & Collection; p. 315, Matrix International, Inc.; p. 319, AP/Wide World Photos; **Chapter 15:** p. 325, H. J. Heinz Company; p. 330, Adam Nadel/AP/Wide World Photos; p. 331, David Strick/Outline Press Syndicate, Inc.; p. 336, AP/Wide World Photos; p. 346, John Abbott Photography; **Chapter 16:** p. 353, American Greetings Corporation; p. 358, AP/Wide World Photos; p. 362, Wyatt McSpadden Photography; p. 369, David Karp/AP/Wide World Photos; **Chapter 17:** p. 375, Tom Stoddart/Matrix International, Inc.; p. 381, J. Koontz/Picture Cube, Inc./Index Stock Imagery; p. 388, Andrew Brusso; p. 389, Todd V. Phillips/Picture Cube, Inc./Index Stock Imagery; p. 394, Louis Psihoyos/Matrix International, Inc.; **Chapter 18:** p. 401, L. Kolvoord/The Image Works; p. 404, Sepp Seitz/Woodfin Camp & Associates; p. 406, Mitsutaka Kurashina; p. 415, Spencer Grant/ Monkmeyer Press; **Chapter 19:** p. 421, James Hazelwood/James Hazelwood Photography; p. 425, Falf-Finn Hestoft/SABA Press Photos, Inc.; p. 428, AP/Wide World Photos; **Chapter 20:** p. 447, Lara Jo Regan/SABA Press Photos, Inc.; p. 450, Gary A. Conner/PhotoEdit; p. 457, Adam Nadel/AP/Wide World Photos; p. 466, Bob Sacha/Bob Sacha Photography; **Chapter 21:** p. 471, Terry Wild Studio; p. 473, Louis Psihoyos/Matrix International, Inc.; p. 474, Rex Rystedt Photography; p. 489, Rich Frishman Photography and Videograph, Inc.; **Chapter 22:** p. 503, Switzer Communications, Inc.; p. 511, Robert Holmgren/ Robert Holmgren Photography; p. 512, John Starkey/Black Star; p. 518, Dryden Flight Research Center/NASA Headquarters; **Chapter 23:** p. 527, SuperStock, Inc.; p. 530, Peter Menzel/Stock Boston; p. 536, Larry Ford Foto.

INDEX

NAME AND COMPANY INDEX

Ackoff, Russell L., 34, 182
Adams, J. Stacy, 356
Adidas USA, 448–49
Advertising Council, 214
Aetna, 255, 263
Akers, John F., 65
Alderfer, Clayton, 359
All America, 511–12
Allen, Gerry, 522
Allen, Robert E., 230, 299
Allen, Ron, 350
All England Lawn, Tennis & Croquet Club, 314–15
AltaVista, 132
Amelio, Gilbert, 281, 398
American Airlines, 427
American Can Company, 67
American Cereal Company, 141
American Greetings Corporation, 353, 354, 357, 363, 366–67, 370–71
American Home Products Corporation, 330
American Racing, 87
American Telegraph and Telephone Company (AT&T). See AT&T
America Online, 491, 493–94, 499
Amos, Wally "Famous," 233, 251
AMP, 76
AMS Plastics, 151
Andersen Consulting, 494
Andreesen, Marc, 498
Animal Kingdom, 3–4, 19
Antioco, John, 103, 104, 107, 108, 113, 116, 119
Apple Computer, 281, 365, 398
Applied Signal, 211
Aquilano, Nicholas J., 450
Architectural Support Services, 331
Argyris, Chris, 359–60, 458
Armstrong, David, 158–59
Armstrong International, 158–59
Army, U.S., 306
Arnoff, E. Leonard, 34
Artzt, Edwin L., 244
ASEA Brown Boveri (ABB), 106
Ashworth, Mark, 323

AT&T, 17, 211, 230, 265, 277, 278, 279, 281, 285, 288, 290, 293, 297, 299–300, 524, 532
AT&T Bell Laboratories, 362
Atlanta Chamber of Commerce, 122
Atlanta Committee for the Olympic Games (ACOG), 121–22
Atlantic Richfield, 50
Auburn Farms, 86

B. J.'s Men's Clothing, 200, 201
Baer, Jeffrey, 233, 234, 237, 238, 240, 244, 246
Baer, Ronald, 233, 234, 237, 238, 240, 244, 246
Balderston, William, III, 418
Ballmer, Steve, 305
Bank of England (BOE), 440
Barabba, Vincent, 162
Baring Futures Singapore (BFS), 440
Barings Bank, 440
Barnard, Chester, 30, 151, 239
Barrett, Dermot, 317
Barrett, Jon, 108
Baskin-Robbins, 75, 76, 77, 85–86, 94, 96–97
Bass, Bernard, 382
Bausch & Lomb, 418
Bavelas, Alex, 317
Beacon Sweets & Chocolates, 86
Bearings, 517
Beaulier, Blaise, 255
Beauvais, Ed, 373
Becherer, Hans W., 153
Bell, David, 316
Bell, Ella, 534
Ben & Jerry's Homemade, 62, 106
Best Buy, 425
Bethlehem Steel Co., 27
Bethune, Gordon M., 130
Better Business Bureaus, 66
BFW, 79
Black, Albert, 351
Black, Stewart, 541
Black & Decker, 179, 449
Blanchard, K. H., 336
Blockbuster Entertainment, 103, 104, 107, 108, 113, 116, 119
Boeing Company, 199

Bonfield, Peter, 208
Booth, MacAllister, 421
Borden Chemicals & Plastics, 64
Boyd, Michael, 373
BP America, 79
Bradley, David, 163
Branson, Richard, 133
Bridgestone, 110, 452–53
British Petroleum, 79, 80
British Telecommunications, 79, 80, 208
BRK Electronics, 81
Burger King, 166
Bush, George, 286

Cable and Wireless College, 294
Cable and Wireless Communications, 294
Cabletron, 132
Cactus and Tropicals, 399
Cadillac, 162–63
Calvary Hospital, 379
CAMI Automotive, 88
Cappelli, Peter D., 44
Carlisle, Howard M., 220
Cartwright, Dorwin, 376
Catera, 162–63
Caterpillar, 473
Cathy, Truett, 323
Caulfield, Dan, 338
Central Soya, 105
Century Life of America, 475
Challenger, John, 300
Chase, Richard B., 450
Chemical Bank, 67
Chevron, 79
Chiat/Day, 315
Chick-fil-A Restaurants, 323
Chrysler, 87, 88, 343
Chupa, Dennis, 353, 354, 357, 360, 363, 366–67, 370–71
Churchman, C. West, 34
Circle K Corporation, 103
Citicorp, 79
Clark, Jim, 498, 499
Cleland, David I., 134
Cloud 9 Shuttle, 187
Coca-Cola Company, 99–100, 154–55, 200

Coffey, Shelby, 336
Cohen, Ben, 62
Colbert, Bertram A., 482, 483
Coleman, Bruce, 197
Compaq Computer Company, 186, 252, 264
CompuServe, 491, 499
ConAgra, 112
Connelly, John F., 219
Continental Airlines, 130
Control Data Corporation, 50, 51, 65
Cooper, Lynn, 79
Corning Corporation, 347, 529
Council of Better Business Bureaus, 66
CP Railroad, 166
CRC Products, 512
Crosby, Philip B., 507, 510, 514
Cross, Elsie, 527, 538
Crown Cork & Seal Company, 219
Crownover, Dale, 45, 525
Crownover, Roy, 45
Cultural Toys, 123

Daewoo, 196
Daimler-Benz, 88
DaimlerChrysler, 16, 88, 223, 343
Dale, Ernest, 148
Danforth, Douglas D., 180
Davis, Al, 47
Davis, Keith, 48, 49, 318–19
Dayton-Hudson, 50
Deere & Company, 152, 153
Dell, Michael, 143
Dell Computer Corporation, 155, 157, 186, 491
Delta Airlines, 350
Deming, W. Edwards, 445–46, 461, 506–10, 524
DeSimone, L. D., 113
Dettloff, George, 303, 318
Dewelt, Robert L., 422
Digital Equipment Corporation, 132
DiNello, Gilbert, 47
Dion, John, 503
Disneyland, 319
DiTomaso, Nancy, 529
Dow Corning, 72
Dreamcast, 109
Drucker, Peter F., 108–9, 117, 137
Dun & Bradstreet, 111–12
Dunlap, Albert J., 44, 471, 472, 476, 479, 484, 487, 489, 495–96
DuPont Company (E. I. DuPont de Nemours and Company), 52, 53, 82, 105, 125, 126, 128, 131, 135, 138, 146, 147, 286
Dyer, Robert, 303, 307, 311, 314, 318, 320

Eastern Airlines, 435–36
Eastman Kodak, 86, 469
Eaton, Robert, 88, 343
Eaton Corporation, 303, 304, 307, 311, 314, 318, 320

Edsel, 137
Ehrlich, S. B., 346
800 Travel Systems, 172
Einstein, Albert, 222
Eisenhower, Dwight D., 99–100
Eisner, Michael, 3, 4
Eitelto, Maria, 54
Eli Lilly and Company, 363–64
Elron Software, 367–68
Elsie Y. Cross Associates, 527
Emery Worldwide, 368
Equitable Life Assurance Company, 377
Ewing, Patrick, 369
Exxon, 79, 258

Famous Amos Chocolate Chip Cookie Company, 180, 233, 237, 238, 240, 242, 244, 246, 250
Fand, Jimmy, 101
Fashion Fair, 430
Fayol, Henri, 11, 30–31, 32, 43, 198, 212, 226
Federal Express, 174, 494, 524
Feigenbaum, Armand V., 505, 509
Feigenbaum, Don, 524
Feldberg, Warren, 478
Feldcamp, Rick, 475
Fiat, 189, 190, 192, 198, 202, 204–5
Fiedler, Fred, 339–41, 342
Firestone, 452–53
Fishbein, Martin, 405
Fletcher, Philip B., 112
Fleuter, Douglas, 366
Flynn, Raymond, 47
Follett, Mary Parker, 17, 222–23
Forbes, B. C., 11
Ford, Henry, 11
Ford Motor Company, 79, 137, 166, 504–5
Friedman, Milton, 50–51

Gantt, Henry L., 26, 27, 29–30, 202–3
Gates, Bill, 143, 145, 208, 305, 499
Gateway Computers, 143, 144, 148, 150, 153, 155, 157, 160, 186, 293
Gatorade, 171
Gaye, Marvin, 233
Gaylord, Edward, 373
GE Appliances, 218
General Dynamics, 67
General Electric Aircraft Company, 531
General Electric Company (GE), 63, 79, 81, 177–78, 179, 241, 258, 426, 447
General Motors Corporation, 79, 87, 88, 126, 162–63, 190, 236, 278, 358, 511
General Portland Cement, 105
Georgia Power, 122
Gergerson, Hal, 541
Gerstner, Lou, 186
Gibara, Samir, 110, 111
Gilbreth, Frank and Lillian, 28–29
Gill, Daniel, 418

Gillette Company, 81, 165, 166, 167–68, 173, 181, 183
Glaser, Ron, 145
Glazer, Michael, 329
Goggin, William C., 72
Goizueta, Robert, 99–100
Goldberg, Glenn, 373
Goodyear Tire and Rubber Company, 110–11
Gotay, Israel, 445
Graicunas, V. A., 224–25
Grand Metropolitan, 80
Granger, Charles H., 112–13
Greenfield, Jerry, 62
Griffin, David, 503
Gross, Bill, 519
Group Attitudes Corporation, 312
Guittard, Gary, 521
Guittard Chocolate Company, 521

H. J. Heinz Company, 141, 325, 326, 327, 330–31, 334, 338–39, 342, 347
H. T. E. Enterprises, 404
Haas, Robert D., 548
Habitat for Humanity, 54
Hammer, Michael, 515, 517
Hammond, Mike, 143
Hanawa, Yoshikazu, 66
Hancock, John, 122
Haney, William V., 316
Hardee's Food Systems, 47
Harley-Davidson, 389
Harris Corporation, 211
Harward, Dennis, 404
Hasbro, 47
Heinz Company, 141, 325, 326, 327, 330–31, 334, 338–39, 342, 347
Helgesen, Sally, 217
Hellriegel, Don, 278
Hersey, P., 336
Hertz Corporation, 66
Herzberg, Frederick, 364–65
Hesel, David, 503
Hess, Bob, 241
Hewlett Packard, 469
Hewlett-Packard, 518
Hilbert, Stephen, 4
Hill, Margaret Hunt, 373
Hines, Andrew P., 449
Hire Quality, 338
Hite, George, 478
Hoare Govett, 189
Holiday Inn, 317
Holmes, Sandra, 52
Homans, George, 385–86
Honda Motor Co., 178, 191
Hopkins, L. Thomas, 38
Houghton, James, 35
House, William C., 198
HTE, 494, 495
Hudson, William J., 76
Hudson Institute, 531, 536

Iacocca, Lee, 343
IBM Corporation, 35, 79, 132, 155, 157, 186, 265, 293, 299, 314–15, 469, 498
Idealab, 519
Image Communications, 300
Incompatel, 132
Initiatives, 125, 126
Insect Control Services Company, 198, 199
Intel Corporation, 284, 308, 404, 498
International Olympic Committee (IOC), 121
Interval Research, 394
Itoh, Hiroyuki, 191
Iverson, F. Kenneth, 407–8
Ivester, M. Douglas, 154–55

J. C. Penney, 248, 265
Jacobsen, Judy, 73
Jacoby, Neil H., 79, 81
Jago, Henry P., 332–34
Jerome, W., III, 436
Job Link, 262
Jobs, Steven P., 281, 398
John Deere and Company, 152, 153
John Hancock Mutual Life, 255, 263
Johnson, General Robert Wood, 66
Johnson, William R., 325, 326, 327, 330–31, 334, 338–39, 342, 347
Johnson & Johnson, 66, 527
Jones, Dennis, 379
Juran, Joseph M., 509, 510, 524

Kaiser, James G., 347
Kanter, Rosabeth, 534
Kast, Fremont E., 190
Katz, Robert L., 10
Katzenbach, Jon R., 252–53
K*B Toy Stores, 329, 503
Kearns, David, 35
Keller Manufacturing Company, 270
Kelley, Robert, 353
Kemper, Robert E., 450
Kennedy, Marilyn Moats, 353
Ketchum Worldwide, 162
Kim, Jean, 540
Kimberly-Clark Corporation, 44
King, William R., 134
King Company, 500
Kirtman, Louis, 548
Kmart, 368
Knight-Ridder, 247
Kohl, Willem, 163
Koontz, Harold, 26, 127, 224, 246
Korean Air Cargo, 213
Korman, A. K., 336
Kotter, John P., 434

L. L. Bean, 28
Landes, Faye, 125
Langton, Bryan, 317

Larami Corporation, 47–51, 54, 58, 59, 63, 69
Laube, Sheldon, 242
Lawler, E. E., 356–57
Leeson, Nick, 440
LEGO, 503, 504, 507, 510, 514, 519, 522
Lens Lab, 413
Leven, Mike, 317
Levi Medica, 79
Levi Strauss & Company, 50, 548
Levitt, Theodore, 110, 326
Likert, Rensis, 335, 368–69
Lincoln Electric Company, 104–5
Linsenmann, Donald, 125
Lippitt, Ronald, 376
Lipson, Harry A., 57
Lockheed, 81
LSG/Sky Chefs, 32
Lucent Technologies, 211, 212, 215–16, 221, 223, 227, 229
Luddington, Jack S., 72
Lutheran General Health System, 174–75

McAfee, Jerry, 64
McCaw Cellular Communications, 230, 474
McClelland, David C., 360
McDonald's Corporation, 25, 30, 34, 41, 286, 402–3
McDonnell Douglas, 67
McGinn, Richard A., 211, 212, 215–16, 221, 223, 227, 229
McGregor, Douglas, 34, 271, 362, 363
Mach3, 165, 181
Mackey, John, 127
McKinsey and Company, 177, 252
McLeod, 379
McNealy, Scott, 6, 469, 499
Macintosh, 281, 365
Madison Park Greeting Card Company, 73
Magee, John F., 156
Malik, Z. A., 135
Margulies, Newton, 289
Marriott Hotels, 425–26
Martin Marietta, 67
Mashima, Karyn, 211
Maslow, Abraham, 33–34, 34, 357–60, 365
Massey-Ferguson, 249–50
Matsushita Electrical Industrial Co., 80, 82
Mattel, 167
Maybelline Company, 430
MCI Communications, 79, 207–8
Medallion Funding Corporation, 441
Mee, John F., 105, 283
Mehrabian, Albert, 313
Meindl, J. R., 346
Meltzer, Linda B., 207
Merstein, Alvin, 441
Merstein, Leon, 441
Michelin, 110
Microsoft Corporation, 145, 208, 370, 469, 489, 498, 499
Middleton, C. J., 283

Miles, Jake, 123
Miller, Lorraine, 399
Miller, Marvin, 270
MindStorms, 503, 504, 507, 514–15, 522
Mintzberg, Henry, 131–32
Mitsubishi Motors Corporation, 92
Mobil, 79
Mobil Research and Development Corporation, 87
Mockler, Robert, 422
Molson, 151
Monsanto Company, 330
Mooney, J. D., 30, 222
Morgan Stanley, 388
Morrison, Ann, 529, 530
Motorola, 211, 406
Motorola University's Education Systems Alliance, 36
Mottus, Allan, 430
MSNBC. com, 427
MTV Networks, 103
Murdick, Robert G., 479, 480
Murray, Mike, 370

NASA, 506, 518
National Broadcasting Company (NBC), 427
National Semiconductor Corporation, 398
NationsBank Corporation, 122, 262, 263
NatWest Bank, 411
Nelson, John, 257
Nestlé SA, 80, 93
Netcom On-Line Communication Services, 499
Netscape, 498–99
Newman, William H., 244
News Corporation, 207–8
New York City Transit Authority, 252
NIC Components Corp., 78
Nike, 54, 95, 178
Nintendo, 109
Nissan, 66
Norris, William, 51
Northwest Airlines, 428
Northwestern Mutual Life, 255, 256, 258, 263, 266, 268, 271, 272
Nucor Corporation, 407–8
Nu Horizons, 78

O'Donnell, Cyril, 26, 127, 246
Ohno, Taiichi, 509
Okuda, Hiroshi, 429
Oliver, Susanne, 189
On Target Supply and Logistics, 351
Opryland Hotel, 57
Ortho Pharmaceutical, 527, 528, 530, 538, 540, 545–46
Osei-Amoako, Yaw, 532
Osterman, Paul, 300
Our Lady of the Way Hospital, 226
Outback Steakhouse, 105

Packard Bell Electronics, 491
Palmer, Robert, 132
Paramount Pictures, 103
Parker, Kevin, 388
Parlin, Gary, 527, 538, 540
Payne, Tom, 280
PeopleSoft, 287
Pepsi Cola, 100
Perez, William D., 63
Perrier, 93
Pesce, Mary Ann, 165
Peters, Thomas J., 8, 15, 217, 513
Petróleos de Venezuela, 80
Philip Morris Co., 49, 79
Phillips, Richard L., 174
Pipeline USA, 499
Pirko, Tom, 141
Pitney-Bowes, 541
Playstation, 109
Pohang Iron & Steel Company, 477
Polaris, 203
Polaroid Corporation, 50, 105, 421, 422, 423,
    427, 429, 430, 433, 434–35, 437
Porter, Michael E., 175, 178–79, 356–57
President Enterprises, 180
Price, Timothy F., 208
Price Waterhouse, 242
Price Waterhouse & Company, 482
Procter & Gamble (P&G), 244
Prodigy, 491, 499
ProShare, 308
Proton, 92
Prudential Insurance of America, 255, 263

Quaker Oats Company, 130–31, 141, 171
Quicktakes, 23, 209, 301, 419, 501
Quinlan, Michael, 25, 30, 34, 41

R. J. Reynolds Tobacco Co., 49
Radisson Hotels International, 56
Ransom, Mal, 491
RealNetworks, 145
Reddin, W. J., 362
Reddy, Helen, 233
Redstone, Sumner, 103
Reebok, 95
Reilly, John, 503
Ricoh Company, 87
Ringbakk, K. A., 194
Rittenhouse, John, 531
Roberts, Bert C., 207, 208
Roberts, Joyce, 331
Rohleder, Scott, 512
Rolls-Royce, 375, 376, 377–78, 381–84,
    386, 395
Roney, C. W., 127
Rosenzweig, James E., 190
Royal Ahold, 80
Royal Dutch/Shell Oil, 79, 80
Russo, Patricia F., 15

S. C. Johnson & Son, 63
St. Elizabeth Medical Center
    (Dayton, Ohio), 401
Sallie Mae (Student Loan Marketing
    Association), 445
Salomon Smith Barney, 193–94
Samper, J. Philip, 469
Samsonite, 366
Sandia National Labs, 368
Sara Lee Corporation, 52, 75
Saturn, 162
Scanlan, Phil, 524
Schmidt, Laura, 255
Schmidt, Warren H., 328–29, 330, 332
Schramm, Wilbur, 308
Schrempp, Juergen, 88
Scotch-Brite, 113
Scott Paper Company, 44, 366
Sculley, John, 398
Sears Roebuck, 299
Sega Enterprises, 109
Selye, Hans, 290
Senge, Peter, 40
Sethi, S. Prakash, 57
Shapiro, Robert, 330
Sheaffer, John, 255, 256, 263
Shell Oil Company, 79, 136
Shetty, Y. K., 107, 220
Shingo, Shigeo, 509
SHL Systemhouse, 207
Shoney's Restaurants, 533
Shriver, Ron, 191
Signicast Corporation, 40
Skinner, B. F., 367
Slocum, John W., Jr., 278
Smale, John G., 162
Smith, Fred, 524
Smith, John F., Jr., 162, 163
Smith, Steve, 491
Smithburg, William D., 141
Snapple, 134, 141
Snyder, Jay, 491
Sonnenfeld, Jeffrey, 535
Sonoco Products Company, 282–83
Sony, 80, 109
Spindler, Michael, 398
Spyglass, 498
Stafford, John, 330
Standard Oil Company of Indiana, 61
Standard Oil of Ohio, 265
Starbucks, 170
Steinmetz, Charles, 511–12
Stempel, Robert, 162
Stickney, Douglas, 7
Stieglitz, Harold, 241
Stogdill, Ralph M., 346
Stoller, David S., 482
Stonich, Paul J., 136–37
Stormer, Horst, 362
Strong, Lydia, 311
Student Loan Marketing Association
    (Sallie Mae), 445

Stygian Chemical Company, 156, 157
Sunbeam Corporation, 471, 472, 476, 479,
    484, 487, 489, 495–96
Sun Microsystems, 138, 469, 498, 499
Sun Oil Company, 130, 131, 366
Super Soaker, 47–51, 54, 58, 59, 69
Suquet, José S., 377
Sutherland Foods, 141
Suzuki Motor Company, 88
Swanson, Colleen, 72
Swanson, John, 72

Taco Bell, 103
Tannenbaum, Robert, 328–29, 330, 332
Target Stores, 286, 478
Taylor, Frederick W., 27
Tellabs, 211
Tengelmann, 80
Tenneco, 524
Teslik, Sarah, 44
Texaco, 79, 529
Texas Instruments, 257, 365
Texas Name Plate, 45, 525
Thoman, Richard, 186
Thompson, Donna, 529
3D Systems, 466
3M Corporation, 113
Tile Connection, 101
Time Warner, 76–77
Toshiba Corporation, 76–77
Tosoh Corporation, 87
Toyoda, Shoichiro, 190
Toyoda, Tatsuro, 429
Toyota Motor Company, 80, 87, 190, 428,
    429, 456
Toys "R" Us, 47
Tyco Toys, 47

Ummel, Stephen L., 174–75
Uncle Noname Cookie Company, 233, 251
Unilever NV, 80
United Technologies, 149
Upshaw, Lynn, 162
Urocor, 231
USADirect Service In-Language, 532
USAir Group, 443, 444, 450, 455, 460,
    464–65, 466–67

ValuJet, 350
Van Grinsven, Michael, 255
Van Horn, Richard L., 482
Varian Associates, 524
VF Services, 280
Viacom, 103
Vilchis, Ed, 443
Virgin Atlantic Airways, 82, 133
Vohringer, Dieter, 223
Volvo, 365
Von Bertalanffy, Ludwig, 37
Vroom, Victor H., 332–34, 355–56

Wachner, Linda F., 346
Waitt, Ted, 143, 148
Wald, Jeff, 233, 234
Wallace, John, 289
Wal-Mart, 29, 148, 381
Walt Disney Company, 3, 19
Waltrip, William H., 418
Ward, Peter, 375, 376, 377–78
Warnaco, 346
Warner Lambert, 165, 173, 181
Warren, E. Kirby, 244
Waterman, Robert H., Jr., 8
Weber, Max, 216
WebSolvers, 492, 493
Weihrich, Heinz, 26, 246
Western Pacific Airlines, 373
Westinghouse, 180
Whole Foods Market, 127
Wikstrom, Walter S., 258–59
Williams, Vic, 331
Wimbledon, 314–15
Woodruff, Robert, 99
Woodwark, Chris, 375
Wozniak, Stephen, 398

XS New York, 37

Yehudai, Joseph, 450
Yellow Freight Systems, 380–81
Yetton, 332–34
York, Jerry, 186
Younce, Claudia, 401, 402, 416

Zarrella, Ronald, 162
Zeien, Alfred M., 81

SUBJECT INDEX

Acceptance stage of formal groups, 382
Accountability, 243–44
    for advancement of, 244
    case study, 244
Achievement, need for, 360
Achievement behavior, 341
Achievement tests, 264
Across Industries features, 17, 18, 247
    airplane manufacturing, 199
    automobile tire manufacturing, 110–11
    banking, 411
    candy manufacturing, 521–22
    e-mail, 494
    food processing, 62
    furniture manufacturing, 270
    government, 126
    health care, 226
    hotels, 425–26
    local government, 316
    mail order retailing, 28
    microcomputer manufacturing, 281
    motorcycle manufacturing, 389
    pharmaceuticals, 363–64
    recruitment, 338
    soft drink industry, 154–55
    tools and appliance manufacturing, 449
    toy manufacturing, 167
    transportation equipment, 87
Activities, in PERT network, 203
Adaptation, 278–79. *See also*
    Organizational change
Adjourning stage of team development, 391
Advisory role of staff personnel, 241
Affiliation—need for, 360
Affirmative action programs, 262, 537–38
African Americans, 17, 527, 534, 537
Airplane manufacturing, 199
Alderfer's ERG theory, 359
Algebraic breakeven analysis, 462–63
Allocating skill, 180
Appliance manufacturing, 449
Appropriate human resources, 256
Aptitude tests, 264
Argyris' maturity-immaturity continuum,
    359–60
Assessment centers, 265–66
Assimilation approach to pluralism, 541
Attitudes
    case studies, 401–2, 409
    changing, 406–8
    components of, 402
    definition of, 402
    measuring, 413
    reasoned action theory of, 404–6
Attitude surveys, 403, 404
Attribution errors, 411
Authority, 31, 239–44, 433
    acceptance of, 239
    case studies, 240, 242, 244, 252–53
    functional, 242–43
    job activities and, 239
    line, 240
    line-staff relationships and, 240–42
    in organization chart, 216–17
    staff, 240
    types of, 240
Automation, 449
Automobile tire manufacturing, 110–11
Avoidance learning, 415
Avoidance strategy, 415

Baldrige Award, 35
Banking, 411
BBBOnLine seal, 66
BCG Growth-Share Matrix, 176
Behavioral approach to management, 32–34
Behavior modification, 367–68
Beliefs
    attitudes and, 402–3
    definition of, 402
Benchmarks, 516

Bias. *See also* Prejudices
    self-serving, 411
Biculturalism, 534–35
Bicultural stress, 534
Bonuses, 30
Boss-centered leaders, 328
Brainstorming, 158–59
Branch pages, 492
Breakeven analysis, 462–64
    case study, 464–65
Breakeven point, 462
Budgetary control, 458–59
Budgets (budgeting), 194
    definition of, 458
    human relations considerations in using,
        458–59
    variable budget (flexible budget), 458
    zero-base, 458
Bureaucracy, 216
Business ethics. *See* Ethics, business
Business portfolio analysis, 176–78

Candy manufacturing, 521–22
Capacity strategy, 451
Capital resources, 9
Career counseling programs, 292–93
Career plateauing, 13
Careers
    definition of, 12
    dual-career couples, 15
    management, 12–16
    stages of, 12–13
    of women managers, 15
Central Intelligence Agency (CIA),
    126–27
Centralization, 31, 247–50
    case study, 250
Chain of command, 226–27
    Fayol's guidelines on, 226
Change agent, 280–81
Changing an organization. *See*
    Organizational change
Chief executives. *See also* Top management
    highest-paid, 4, 6
    planning and, 131–32
Child care, 263
Classical approach to management, 26
Classical organizing theory, 216
Classroom techniques, 269–70
Clean Air Act Amendments (1990), 52
Closed system, 37
Coaching, 269, 344–45, 394
Code of ethics, 66–67
Cognitive learning, 414
Command groups, 377
Commitment principle, 166
Committees, 378–80
Communication, 307–20
    case studies, 311, 314, 318, 320, 323
    control process and, 436
    definition of, 307

Communication—(continued)
  interpersonal. See Interpersonal
    communication
  multinational corporations and, 93
  time available for, 309–10
  in virtual offices, 296
  Web sites and, 493
Communication barriers, 309
Communication macrobarriers, 309
Communication microbarriers, 310
Communication stage of formal
    groups, 382
Competition, as component of the operating
    environment, 172
Competitiveness, 502–22
Competitors, as sources of human
    resources, 260
Complete certainty condition—decision
    making and, 154
Complete uncertainty condition—decision
    making and, 154
Comprehensive analysis of management, 30
Computer-aided design (CAD), 466
Computer-aided engineering (CAE), 466
Computer-aided manufacturing, 466
Computer graphics, 466
Computer networks, 489–96
  case study, 495–96
  definition of, 489
Computers, 484
  case study, 487
  main functions of, 485
  possible pitfalls in using, 486–87
Conceptual skills, 11
Concurrent control, 430
Conflict—in line-staff relationships, 242
Consensus, 147
  attributions and, 410
Consideration behavior, 334
Consistency—attributions and, 410
Consumer Product Safety Commission, 52
Content theories of motivation, 354,
    357–60
Contingency approach to management,
    36–37
Contingency theory of leadership, 339–41
Continual improvement, 445–46, 461
  quality and, 513
Continuous process, 453
Control
  amount needed, 432
  breakeven analysis and, 464
  concurrent, 430
  the controller and, 431–32
  definition of, 422
  feedback, 430
  power and, 433–34
  precontrol (feed-forward), 429
  strategic, 180
  types of, 429
Control function of computers, 486
Controller (comptroller), 431–32

Controlling, 420–37, 472
  barriers to, 435
  case studies, 421–22, 423, 427, 429, 430,
    433, 434–35, 437, 440, 441
  definition of, 422
  diversity and, 543
  as management function, 7–8
  performing the function of, 435–37
  process of, 423–24
  social responsibility activities, 62
  as a subsystem, 423
  successful, 436
Control role of staff personnel, 241
Coordination
  division of labor and, 222
  Follett's guidelines on, 222–23
  span of management and, 224
Corporate culture, 393–95
  case study, 395, 398, 399
Corporate social responsibility. See Social
    responsibility
Corrective action, 428, 436
Cost-benefit analysis, 432
Cost control, 457
Cost leadership, 178
Costs, in breakeven analysis, 462
Cost savings—diversity and, 529
Counseling role of staff personnel, 241
Creative thinking, 520
Creativity, 519–22
  case studies, 522
  decentralization and, 249
  encouraging, in organization members, 521
  in individuals, 520
  Web sites and, 493
Critical path of a PERT network, 203
Critical question analysis, 175
Cross-functional teams, 389
Cultural diversity. See Diversity
Culture. See also Corporate culture
  adjustment to a new, expatriates and, 85
  multinational corporations and, 92–93
Culture-specific approach to pluralism,
    541–42
Customer departmentalization, 220
Customers—as component of the operating
    environment, 172
Cybercafes, 37

Data
  definition of, 472
  evaluating the cost of, 476
  identifying and evaluating, 475–76
Databases, 487–88
Data contamination, 474
Decentralization, 247–50
  case study, 250
  at Massey-Ferguson, 249–50
  questions to ask to determine the amount
    of, 247
Decision makers, 148–49

Decision making, 143–60
  alternative solutions and, 151–52
  case studies, 143, 144, 150, 160, 162–63
  committees and, 379
  conditions for, 153–54
  by consensus, 147
  decentralization and, 248–49
  elements of the decision situation, 148–49
  gathering problem-related feedback, 152
  group, 158–60
  leadership and, 330–32
  organizational objectives and, 106
  process of, 150–52
  responsibility for, 146–47
  social responsiveness and, 55
  tools for, 155–56
Decision-making stage of formal groups, 382
Decisions
  definition of, 144
  nonprogrammed, 144, 145
  programmed, 144, 145
  scope of, 146
  types of, 144–45
Decision tree analysis, 465
Decision trees, 156–57
Decline stage of careers, 13
Decoder/destination, 308, 310
Delegation, 244–50. See also Centralization;
    Decentralization
  case studies, 246, 252–53
  definition of, 244
  obstacles to, 245–46
  steps in, 244–45
Delphi technique, 159–60, 199–200
Demographics, 170
  diversity and, 531
Department, 217
Departmentalization, 217–20
Destination, 308
  source's view of, 310
  view of the source by, 310
Dialogue capability, 488
Differentiation, 178
Direct investing, 87
Directive behavior, 341
Disabilities, workers with, 535
Discipline, 31
Discrimination, 533
  reverse, 537
Dispute resolution, 413
Distinctiveness, attributions and, 410
Distortions, perceptual, 410–12
Distributive justice, 412
Diversity, 17
  advantages of, 529–30
  case studies, 527–28, 530, 538, 540, 548
  challenges faced by managers, 531–35
  definition of, 528
  demographics and, 531
  discrimination and, 533
  ethnocentrism and, 533
  managers' role in, 542–45

organizational commitment to, 538–40
quality of management and, 530
social implications of, 528
stages in managing a diverse workforce, 544, 545
stereotyping and, 533
strategies for promoting, 535–42
    equal employment and affirmative action, 537–38
    organizational commitment, 538–40
    pluralism, 540–42
    Workforce 2000, 535–37
    tokenism and, 533–34
Diversity Spotlight features, 18
    Corning's focus on diversity, 347
    Equitable's diverse salesforce, 377
    General Electric values global sensitivity, 531
    McDonald's Corporation and disabled workers, 286
    objective for the whole organization at the Department of Transportation, 111
    Procter & Gamble's managers held accountable for advancement of minorities, 244
    social responsiveness and the Equal Opportunity Act at Opryland, 57
    Target's MIS and Hispanic workers, 478
Diversity training, 543–44
Division of labor, 222–23
Division of work, 31
Domestic organizations, 78
Downward organizational communication, 315
Dual-career couples, 15–16
DVD (digital video disc), 77

Economic function area, social responsibility measurements in, 62
Economics (economic issues), 168, 170
EDB (fungicide), 95
Educational institutions—as sources of human resources, 261
Effectiveness, 451
    managerial, 9
Efficiency, 451
    managerial, 9
    organizational—organizational objectives and, 106
E-mail (electronic mail), 493–94, 495
Emotional support, from coaching leaders, 344
Employee Advisory Programs (EAPs), 65
Employee attitudes. *See* Attitudes
Employee attitudes standards, 426
Employee-centered behavior, 335
Employee leasing, 275
Employees. *See* Human resources
Employment agencies—as sources of human resources, 260
Empowerment, quality and, 512

Entrepreneurial leadership, 345–46
Environmental analysis, 168, 511
Environmental Protection Agency, 52
Environment (environmental factors), 38
    critical question analysis and, 175
    general, 168
    internal, strategy management and, 173
    operating, strategy management and, 172
Equal Employment Opportunity Act (1972), 52
Equal Employment Opportunity Commission (EEOC), 52, 261–62, 537, 540–42
Equal Opportunity Act (1972), 57
Equal Pay Act (1963), 52
Equity theory of motivation, 356
Escape strategy, 415
Esprit de corps, 31, 32
Establishment stage of careers, 12
Esteem needs, 359
Ethics, business, 65–69
    code of, 66
    creating an ethical workplace, 67–69
    definition of, 65
    export of hazardous wastes and, 81
    government regulation and, 66
    importance of, 65
    international management and, 94–96
    productivity and, 65
    stakeholders and, 66
Ethics committees, 379
Ethics Spotlight features, 17–18
    attitude change at Sonoco, 282–83
    Calvary Hospital's ethics committees, 379
    environmental protection planning at Shell Oil Company, 136
    Firestone exits LaVergne, 452–53
    General Electric staff organizes renovation, 241
    hazardous waste sent by U. S. companies to Mexico, 81
    Quaker Oats cashes in on fitness fad, 171
    Toyota's philanthropy plan, 190
Ethnocentric attitude, 91
Ethnocentrism, 533
European Community (EC), 88–89
Events, in PERT network, 203
Existence needs, 359
Expatriates
    in multinational corporations (MNCs), 84, 85
    preparing, for foreign assignments, 95–96
Expected value (EV), 155–56
Expertise, 520
Exploitative orientation, decision makers with a, 148
Exploration stage of careers, 12
Exporting, 86
Extranets, 494
Extrinsic rewards—Porter-Lawler motivation theory and, 357

Fayol's guidelines on chain of command, 226
Federal Aviation Administration (FAA), 435–36
Feedback, interpersonal communication and, 311–12
Feedback control, 430
Feed-forward control, 429
Fiedler's contingency theory of leadership, 339–41
Financial objectives, 111–12
Firewall, 495
Fixed costs, in breakeven analysis, 462
Fixed-position layout, 454
Flat organization charts, 225
Flexible budget (variable budget), 458
Flextime, 366
Focus strategy, 179
Food and Drug Administration (FDA)— silicone breast implants and, 72
Food processing, 62
Forecasting, 198–201
    definition of, 198
    how it works, 198
    sales, 199–200
    types of forecasts, 199
Formal groups, 376–82
    case studies, 377–78, 381, 382–83
    committees, 378–80
    definition of, 377
    examples of, 378–81
    kinds of, 377
    stages of development of, 382
Formal organizational communication, 315–18
    encouraging, 319–20
Formal structure, 217–21
Forming stage of team development, 390
Friendship groups, 383
Frustration, employee, 435
Fully mobile workers, 295
Functional authority, 242–43
    case study, 244
Functional departmentalization, 218
Functional objectives, 113
Functional similarity method for dividing job activities, 235
Furniture manufacturing, 270

Gangplank, 226
Gantt chart, 29, 202
GE Multifactor Portfolio Matrix, 177–78
Gender, organization structure and, 217
Gender-role stereotypes, 534
General environment, 168
Geocentric attitude, 91–92
Geographic continuity, span of management and, 224
Geographic departmentalization, 218–19
Germany, 85
"Glass ceiling," 534
Globalization, 76

Global organizations, 93
Global Spotlight features, 17
   Asea Brown Boveri decides on global objectives, 106
   AT&T connects the world, 532
   Compaq Computer Company's international selection slip-ups, 264
   Crown Cork & Seal Company organizes by territory, 219
   cultural perceptions, 412
   DuPont protects the environment, 53
   Mexico as an attractive manufacturing site, 195
   Pohang Iron & Steel Company's need for a complex MIS, 477
   United Technologies executives detect a weakness among Japanese decision makers, 149
Goal integration, 108
Goals, organizational. *See* Organizational objectives
Goal-setting strategies—cognitive learning and, 414–15
"Golden rule" approach to pluralism, 540–41
Graicunas' formula, 224–25
Grapevine, 318–19
  case study, 320
Graphic breakeven analysis, 463
Grid organization development (grid OD), 286
Group control stage of formal groups, 382
Group decision making, 158–60
Groups, 376–86
  case studies, 377–78, 381, 382–83, 399
  case study, 375–76
  definition of, 376
  difference between teams and, 387
  formal, 376–82
  importance of studying, 376
  informal, 383–84
  kinds of, 376
  managing, 384–86
Group solidarity stage of formal groups, 382
Group technology layout, 454
Groupthink, 158, 380
Growth needs, 359

Halo effect, 411
Hawthorne Studies, 32–33
Hazardous wastes, export of, 81
Health care industry, 226
Hersey-Blanchard life cycle theory of leadership, 336–38
Herzberg's hygiene factors and motivators, 364
Hierarchy of objectives, 113–14
Highway Safety Act (1978), 52
Hispanic workers, 478, 529, 537
History of organizations, corporate culture and, 393

Hoarding orientation, decision makers with a, 149
Ho Chi Minh City, 75, 77
Home-based workers, 295
Home pages, 492
Host country, 84
Hotels (hoteling), 295, 425–26
Human relations, budgets and, 458–59
Human relations movement, 33–34
Human relations skill, 33
Human resource approach to job satisfaction, 407–8
Human resource inventory, 258–60
Human resource planning, 196–97
Human resources, 9, 254–72
  appropriate, 256
  case studies, 255, 256, 263, 275
  performance appraisal and, 271–72
  recruitment of. *See* Recruitment
  selection of, 263–66
  sources of, 258–61
  steps in providing, 256
  training, 266–71
Human resources strategy, in operations management, 455
Human rights, 95
Human skills, 10
Hygiene factors, 364

Ideal managerial style, 286
Implementation—of strategies, 180
Importing, 86
Incentives
  monetary, 370
  nonmonetary, 370
Incremental improvement process, 515–17
Individual objectives, 107
Influencing, 303–21. *See also* Communication
  case studies, 303, 304, 307, 311, 318, 323, 419
  definition of, 304
  diversity and, 542–43, 544
  as management function, 7
  in multinational corporations, 92
  social responsibility and, 61
  as a subsystem, 304–7
Informal groups, 383–86
  case study, 384, 386
  determining existence of, 384
  evolution of, 385–86
  Homans' model for, 385–86
  managing, 384–86
Informal organizational communication, 318–20
Informal structure, 217
Information. *See also* Data; Management information system (MIS)
  appropriateness of, 473
  case studies, 471, 476, 479, 484, 487, 489, 500
  definition of, 472
  evaluating, 475

  increasing need for, 309
  for management system analysis, 39
  need for increasingly complex, 309
  for operational control, management control, and strategic planning decisions, 474
  quality and, 513
  quality of, 474
  quantity of, 474–75
  timeliness of, 474
  value of, 472
Information technology, 484–87
  definition of, 484
Innovation, 519. *See also* Creativity
  diversity and, 529
  organizational objectives and, 109, 110–11
  quality and, 513
Input function of computers, 485
Input planning, 194
INROADS program, 57
In Search of Excellence (Peters and Waterman), 8
Inspection, 461
Integrated operations—quality and, 446
Interacting skill, 180
Interest groups, 383
Interference, message (noise), 310
Intermediate-term objectives, 110
Internal environment—strategy management and, 173
International component of the operating environment, 173
International joint ventures, 87–88
International management, 76–98. *See also* Multinational corporations (MNCs)
  ethics in in, 94
  fundamentals of, 76–77
  transnational organizations and, 93
  types of organizations involved in, 78
International market agreements, 88
International organizations, 78
Internet, the, 490–93
  case study, 498–99
Interpersonal communication, 307–15
  achieving effectiveness in, 312–13
  barriers to successful, 309
  case studies, 311, 314
  feedback and, 311–12
  in organizations, 314
  successful and unsuccessful, 308–9
  verbal and nonverbal, 313–14
Intranets, 494–95
Intrinsic rewards, Porter-Lawler motivation theory and, 357
Inventory control, 460
Investing—direct, 87

Japan, 85, 95
Job activities
  authority and, 239
  clarifying managers', 235, 237

dividing, 235
in job description, 234–35
Job analysis, 257
Job-centered behavior, 335
Job descriptions, 234–35
   recruitment and, 257
Job design, 455
   motivation of organization members
      and, 363
Job enlargement, 364
Job enrichment, 364, 365
Job rotation, 363–64
Job satisfaction
   human resource approach to, 407–8
   at Microsoft, 370
Job-shop process, 453
Job specification, 257
Joint ventures, 87–88
Jury of executive opinion method of sales
   forecasting, 199–200
Justice
   distributive, 412
   procedural, 412–13
Just-in-time (JIT) inventory control,
   456–57

Kanban, 456
K*B Toy Stores, 329

Labor, as component of the operating
   environment, 172
Languages other than English, 309
LANs (local area networks), 489–90
Lateral organizational communication,
   316–17
Law of the situation, 17
Layoffs, 299–300
Layout, 454
Layout strategy, 453–54
Leadership, 324–47
   case studies, 325–26, 327, 330–31, 334,
      338–39, 342, 347, 350–51
   coaching, 344–45
   current topics in, 346–47
   decision making and, 330–32
   definition of, 326
   entrepreneurial, 345–46
   Fiedler's contingency theory of, 339–41
   Hersey-Blanchard life cycle theory of,
      336–38
   managing versus, 326–27
   Michigan studies of leadership, 335
   in modern organizations, 342–46
   Ohio State University (OSU) studies
      of, 334
   path-goal theory of, 341
   quality and, 512
   situational approach to, 328–42
   substitutes for, 346
   superleadership, 345

Tannenbaum and Schmidt model of,
   328–32
   trait approach to, 327
   transformational, 343–44
   Vroom-Yetton-Jago (VYJ) model of,
      332–34
   women as leaders, 346–47
Leadership behaviors, 334–35
Leadership styles, 335
   effectiveness of various, 335–36
Learning, 414–16
   case study, 416
   cognitive, 414
   operant, 414
   strategies for, 415
Learning organization approach, 40
Lectures, 268–69
Legal component of the general
   environment, 171–72
Legislation, recruitment and, 261–63
Level dimension of a plan, 191
Levels of management@in2:
   decision making responsibility and, 146
   planning and, 182–83
License agreements, 87
Life cycle theory of leadership, 336–38
Likert's management systems, 368–69
Line authority, 240
Line-staff relationships, 240–42
Listening, 313, 319
   by coaching leaders, 344
   Ten Commandments for, 320
Local area networks (LANs), 489–90
Local government, 316
Location strategy, 452
Long-term objectives, 110
Long-term versus short-term production, 435
Losses—in breakeven analysis, 462
Lower-level management analysis, 26–27
Lower-level managers—planning and,
   182–83

Macrobarriers, communication, 309
MacSchedule, 29
Mail order retailing—at L. L. Bean, 28
Maintenance control, 457
Maintenance factors, 364
Maintenance stage of careers, 13
Majority groups, 528
Malcolm Baldrige National Quality Award, 35
Management
   behavioral approach to, 32
   classical approach to, 26–31
   comprehensive analysis of, 30
   contingency approach to, 36–37
   decision making responsibility and, 146
   definition of, 6–7
   Fayol's principles of, 30–31
   functions of, 7
   importance of, 4
   leadership versus, 326–27

planning and, 182–83
role of, 6
triangular, 39
universality of, 11
Management and the Internet features, 17,
   18–19
   Ad Council organizes to put Smokey the
      Bear on the Internet, 214
   Bill Gross uses creativity to launch
      Idealab, 519
   cybercafes, 37
   Dell Computer, 491
   EEOC and sexual harassment, 537–38
   ethical issues, 66
   H. T. E. studies employee attitudes, 404
   K*B Toy Stores' use of the Internet to
      provide information for making
      decisions, 329
   multinational corporations
      (MNCs), 82
   NBC's profitability standards, 427
   organizational objectives, 109
   planning, 132
   punishment of pornographic-related
      behavior, 367–68
   Sallie Mae's use of the Internet to
      improve productivity, 445
   Salomon Smith Barney's rules to deal
      with Internet, 193–94
   Texas Instruments' use of the Web to
      recruit engineers, 257
   800 Travel Systems' Internet
      strategy, 172
   unprogrammed decisions, 145
   virtual teams, 387
   virtual training at Cable and Wireless
      Communications, 294
   Wimbledon's communication with
      stakeholders, 314–15
Management by exception, 461–62
Management by objectives (MBO),
   117–19, 462
Management careers, 12–16
   promoting your own, 13–14
Management control decisions—information
   appropriate for, 474
Management decision support system
   (MDSS), 487–89
Management development—diversity
   training and, 543–44
Management games, 270
Management information system (MIS),
   476–84
   case study, 479, 484
   definition of, 476
   designing an, 482
   establishing an, 480
   implementing an, 482
   improving an, 482–84
   operating a, 477, 479
   planning for an, 480, 482
Management inventory card, 258–59

Management manpower replacement chart, 259
Management responsibility guide, 237
Management science—characteristics of applications of, 35–36
Management science approach, 34–36
Management skills, 10–11
Management styles—Likert's management systems and, 368–69
Management system, 38
    information to analyze, 39
Management task, 5
Managerial effectiveness, 9
Managerial efficiency, 9
Managerial grid, 286, 287
Manpower planning, 455
Manufacturing process departmentalization, 220
Maquiladoras, 195
Marketing, Web sites and, 492–93
Marketing-oriented decision makers, 149
Market position standards, 426
Market share, diversity and, 529
Maslow's hierarchy of needs, 358–59, 365
Master plan, 191
Materials, procurement of, 460
Materials control, 459–60
Matrix organizations, 283–85
Maturity level of the followers, 336
McClelland's acquired needs theory, 360
MDSS (management decision support system), 487–89
Means-ends analysis, 116
Measurements—social responsibility, 62
Mediation, 413
Message interference (noise), 310
Messages, 308
Mexico, 195–96
Michigan studies of leadership, 335
Microbarriers, communication, 310
Microcomputer manufacturing, 281
Middle management—planning and, 182
Mining Enforcement and Safety Administration, 52
Minority groups, 528. *See also* Diversity
    affirmative action programs and, 262, 537–38
    managers who are members of, 16–17
    negative dynamics and, 534–35, 536
    recruiting workers from, 16–17
MIS. *See* Management information system
MIS manager, 477
MIS personnel, 477
Mission statement, 174
Model base, 488
Models, mathematical, 36
Modular corporations. *See* Virtuality
Monetary incentives, 370
Monetary resources, 9
Monitoring skill, 180
Morale, 435
Motion studies, 28–29

Motivating factors (motivators), 364
Motivation, 352–71
    behavior modification, 367–68
    case studies, 353–54, 357, 360, 363, 370–71, 373
    content theories of, 354, 357–60
    creativity and, 520
    definition of, 354
    equity theory of, 356
    flextime, 366
    importance of, 361
    job design, 363
    job enlargement, 364
    job enrichment, 364–65
    job rotation, 363
    Likert's management systems, 368–69
    managerial communication, 362
    monetary incentives, 370
    needs-goal theory of, 354–55
    nonmonetary incentives, 370
    of organization members, 361–71
    Porter-Lawler theory of, 356–57
    process of, 354–60
    process theories of, 354–57
    strategies for, 361–70
    Theory X-Theory Y, 362, 363
    Vroom expectancy theory of, 355–56
Motivation strength, 355
Motorcycle manufacturing, 389
Multicultural approach to pluralism, 542
Multicultural workforce, 16–17. *See also* Diversity
Multimeaning words, as communication microbarrier, 310–11
Multinational corporations (MNCs), 78–93
    attitudes of managers toward foreign operations, 91–92
    complexities of managing, 81–82
    controlling, 93
    culture and, 92–93
    definition of, 78–79
    influencing people in, 92
    management functions and, 86–93
    organizing in, 89–90
    planning in, 86–88
    risk and, 84
    selection of managers for, 91
    workforce of, 84–85
Murphy's Law, 422

NAFTA (North American Free Trade Agreement), 89
National Highway Traffic Safety Administration, 52
Needs
    Alderfer's ERG theory of, 359
    Argyris' maturity-immaturity continuum of, 359–60
    Maslow's hierarchy of, 358–59, 365
    McClelland's acquired needs theory, 360

Needs-goal theory of motivation, 354–55
Negative reinforcement, 367
Network organizations. *See* Virtuality
Networks, computer. *See* Computer networks
New Earth 21, 81
Noise (message interference), 310
Nominal group technique, 159
Nonmonetary incentives, 370
Nonoperational objectives, 115
Nonprogrammed decisions, 144, 145
Nonverbal communication, 313–14
"No rejects" philosophy, 447
Norming stage of team development, 391
North American Free Trade Agreement (NAFTA), 89

Objectives
    individual, 107
    organizational. *See* Organizational objectives
Occupational Safety and Health Act (OSHA), 38
Occupational Safety and Health Administration, 52
Office of Federal Contract Compliance Programs, 52
Ohio State University (OSU) studies of leadership, 334
Older workers, 535
On-the-job training, 269
Open system, 37
Operant learning, 414
Operating environment—strategy management and, 172
Operational control decisions—information appropriate for, 474
Operational objectives, 115
Operations control, 456–67. *See also* Operations control tools
    budgetary control, 458–59
    cost control, 457
    definition of, 456
    just-in-time (JIT) inventory control, 456–57
    maintenance control, 457
    materials control, 459–60
    ratio analysis, 459
Operations control tools, 461–66
    breakeven analysis, 462–64
    case studies, 464–65, 466–67
    computer-aided design (CAD), 466
    computer-aided manufacturing, 466
    decision tree analysis, 465
    inspection, 461
    management by exception, 461–62
    management by objectives (MBO), 462
    process control, 465
    value analysis, 465–66
Operations management, 450–55
    capacity strategy, 451–52
    case studies, 455

dcfinition of, 450
human resources strategy, 455
layout strategy, 453–54
location strategy, 452
process strategy, 453
product strategy, 453
strategies in, 451–53
Operations research (OR). *See* Management science approach
Organizational change, 277–97
case studies, 277, 278, 281, 285, 288, 290, 293, 297, 299–300
definition of, 278
factors to consider in, 279–90
change agent, 280–81
determining what should be changed, 281–82
evaluation of thc change, 289
individuals affected by the change, 288
kind of change, 283–88
importance of, 278
resistance to, 288–89
stability *versus,* 278–79
stress and, 290–93
virtuality, 293–97
Organizational communication, 314–20
case studies, 318
formal, 315–18, 319–20
informal, 318–20
Organizational direction
quality and, 511–12
strategy management and, 174–75
Organizational mission, 174–75
Organizational objectives, 103–19
areas for, 108–9
attainment of, 116
case studies, 103, 107, 108, 121–23
controlling and, 436
critical question analysis and, 175
decision making and, 149
definition of, 104
diversity, 111
establishing, 110–15
financial, 111–12
functional, 113
goal integration and, 108
hierarchy of, 113
how to use, 116–17
importance of, 106
intermediate-term, 110
long-term, 110
management by (MBO), 117–19
means-ends analysis and, 116
mission and, 175
nonoperational, 115
operational, 115
planning and, 128–29
principle of the objective and, 110
product-market mix, 112–13
quality of, 114–15
short-term, 110
strategic planning and, 166

suboptimization and, 114
types of, 107
Organizational performance—measuring, 424–25
Organizational purpose, 104
Organizational resources, 8–9
Organization charts, 216–17
height of, 225
of multinational corporations, 89–90
scalar relationships on, 226
Organization development (OD), 286–88
Organization structure, 216–17
formal and informal, 217–21
gender and, 217
of multinational corporations, 89–90
Organizing, 210–27. *See also* Authority; Delegation; Responsibility
case studies, 211, 212, 215, 221, 223, 227, 230–31, 233
classical theory of, 216–27
definition of, 212
diversity and, 542
Fayol's guidelines for, 212
importance of, 212
as management function, 7
in multinational corporations, 89–90
for quality improvement, 513–14
steps of, 213–14
as subsystem, 215
Organizing skill, 180
Output function of computers, 486
Overlapping responsibility, 236

Pacific Rim area, 89
Parent company, 84
Participative behavior, 341
Partnering—quality and, 512–13
Path-goal theory of leadership, 341–42
People change, 286–88
People factors. *See also* Human resources
organizational change and, 282
People Spotlight features, 18
employee involvement at Deere & Company, 153
expatriates helped to adjust, 96
job satisfaction at Microsoft, 370
keeping people involved in incremental improvement at Bearings, Inc., 517
NationsBank helps women employees with child care, 263
Robert Eaton gets people involved at DaimlerChrysler, 343
Toyota takes corrective action by changing its president, 429
Perception(s), 409–13
attribution theory and, 409–10
case studies, 413, 418
as communication microbarrier, 310
definition of, 409
motivation and, 355
of procedural justice, 412–13

selective, 411–12
of unfairness, 413
Perceptual distortions, 410–12
Perceptual process, 409
Performance, organizational, 424–26
Performance appraisals, 271–72
case study, 272
handling, 271–72
management by objectives (MBO) and, 117
organizational objectives and, 106
of planners, 135
potential weaknesses of, 272
reasons for using, 271
Performing stage of team development, 391
Personal attitudes and values—of responsible managers, 238
Personality tests, 265
Personal power, 433
Personal problems, 408
Personnel development standards, 426
Pharmaceuticals, 363–64
Philanthropy plan, Toyota's, 190
Physical environment—corporate culture and, 393
Physiological needs, 358
Piece-rate system, 30
Planners, 132–35
duties of, 134–35
evaluation of, 135
qualifications of, 133
Planning, 124–38. *See also* Planners; Plans
advantages and potential disadvantages of, 127
for an MIS, 480, 482
areas of, 194–95
assistance in, 132
case studies, 125, 128, 131, 141
chief executives and, 131–32
communications, 312
definition of, 126
diversity, 542
evaluating developed plans, 134
human resource, 196–97
implementation-focused, 137
inclusion of the right people in, 137
input, 194
international market agreements and, 88
levels of management and, 182–83
as management function, 7
maximizing the effectiveness of, 136–37
in multinational corporations, 86–88
plans for, 134
plant facilities, 195–96
primacy of, 127–28
purposes of, 127
social responsibility activities, 58–59
solving problems in, 134–35
span of management and, 224
steps in process of, 128–29
strategic. *See* Strategic planning
as subsystem, 129–31

Planning organization, effective and efficient, 136–37
Planning subsystem, 129–31
Planning tools, 198–204
    forecasting tools, 198–201
Plans. *See also* Planning
    case studies, 189, 190, 192, 198, 202, 204–5, 207, 209
    definition of, 190
    dimensions of, 190–91
    failure of, 194
    for planning, 134
    single-use, 192, 194
    standing, 192
    types of, 192
Plant facilities planning, 195–96
Pluralism, 540–42
Policies, 192–93
    quality-oriented, 513
Political component of the general environment, 171
Polycentric attitude, 91
Porter-Lawler theory of motivation, 356–57
Porter's model for industry analysis, 178
Position power, 433
Position replacement form, 259
Position rotation, 269
Positive reinforcement, 367, 415
Power
    control and, 433–34
    definition of, 433
    need for, 360
Precontrol, 429
Prejudices, 533
    against older workers, 535
Premises, organizational objectives and, 128
Principle of the objective, 110
Probability theory, 155–56
Problems—recognizing, 428
Problem solving
    goal setting and, 414–15
    identifying an existing problem, 151
Problem-solving area—social responsibility measurements in, 62
Problem-solving teams, 387–88
Procedural justice, 412–13
Procedures, 193
Process control, 465
Processes, 450
Process (functional) layout, 454
Processing function of computers, 485
Process strategy, 453
Process theories of motivation, 354–57
Procurement of materials, 460
Product departmentalization, 218
Production
    definition of, 444
    long-term *versus* short-term, 435
Production control, 444
    case study, 464–65
Productivity

case studies, 443–44, 450
definition of, 444
diversity and, 529
job enrichment and, 365
Likert's management systems and, 369
organizational objectives and, 109
strategies for increasing, 444–45
Productivity standards, 426
Product layout, 454
Product liability, quality and, 505
Product life cycle, 201
Product-market mix objectives, 112–13
Product quality. *See* Quality
Product strategy, 453
Professional employer organizations (PEOs), 275
Profitability, organizational objectives and, 109, 110–11
Profitability standards, 426
Profits, in breakeven analysis, 462
Program evaluation and review technique (PERT), 203–4
Programmed decisions, 144, 145
Programmed learning, 269
Programs, 194
Projection, 411
Project organizations (matrix organizations), 283–85
Promotion, 394
Publishing industry—publishing industry, 247
Punishment, 367–68
Punishment strategy, 415
Pure-breakdown policy, 457
Pure-preventive maintenance, 457

Quality, 445, 446
    achieving, 507
    awards for, 506
    case studies, 503–4, 507, 510, 514–15, 519, 525
    Crosby's guidelines for achieving, 507
    definition of, 504
    Deming's guidelines for achieving, 507–9
    environmental analysis and, 511
    Feigenbaum's guidelines for achieving, 509
    importance of, 505
    improvement process, 515–19
    Juran's guidelines for achieving, 509
    of objectives, 114–15
    organizational direction and, 511–12
    organizing for improvement of, 513
    policies for, 513
    Shingo's guidelines for achieving, 509
    strategic control and, 514–15
    strategy formulation and, 512–13
    strategy implementation and, 513
    through strategic planning, 510–15
    total quality management (TQM), 504–6, 508
    Web sites and, 493

Quality assurance, 446–47
    "no rejects" philosophy and, 447
Quality circles, 447–48
Quality control—statistical, 447
Quality-of-life area—social responsibility measurements in, 62
Quality Spotlight features, 18
    Adidas USA, 448–49
    Apple Computer's job enrichment, 365
    DaimlerChrysler improves coordination to improve product quality, 223
    formal communication at Holiday Inn, 317
    including the right people in planning at Sun Microsystems, 138
    Lutheran General Health System's mission emphasizes quality, 174
    Nucor Steel, 407–8
    "Quality Is Job 1" at Ford, 504–5

Ratio analysis, 459
Ratios for Selected Industries, 111–12
Raw materials, 9
Readership of certain publications—as sources of human resources, 260–61
Reasoned action, theory of, 404–6
Receiving activities, 460
Recency, 412
Receptive orientation, decision makers with a, 148
Recruitment, 256–63, 338, 394
    case study, 263
    knowing sources of human resources and, 258–61
    knowing the job and, 257
    legislation and, 261–63
    of minority workers, 16–17
    Web sites and, 493
Reengineering improvements, 517–19
Regulation, government, ethical management practices and, 66
Reinforcement, 367
Reinforcement strategy, 415
Relatedness needs, 359
Relevant alternatives, 149
Repatriation, 85
Repetitiveness dimension of a plan, 190
Repetitive process, 453
Reports, filing of, 435–36
Resistance to change, 288–89
Resources, organizational, 8–9
Responsibility, 234–38
    case studies, 233, 234, 237, 238, 252–53
    clarifying the job activities of managers and, 237
    functional similarity method and, 235–36
    job descriptions and, 234–35
    management responsibility guide, 237
    managers' degree of, 238
    in organization chart, 216–17
    overlapping, 236

Responsibility gap, 236
Retirement of employees, 394
Return on investment (ROI), 111
Revenue—total, in breakeven analysis, 462
Reverse discrimination, 537
Rewards
    for creativity, 521
    Porter-Lawler motivation theory and, 357
"Righting-the-wrongs" approach to
    pluralism, 541
Risk condition—decision making and, 154
Robotics, 449
Role conflict, 534
Role modeling, 394
Role overload, 534
Role-playing activities, 270
Rule breaking, 408
Rules, 193

Safety needs, 358
Salesforce estimation method, 200
Sales forecasting, 199–200
Scalar chain, 31
Scalar relationships, 226
Scheduling, 202
Scientific management, 26–28
Scope dimension of a plan, 191
Scope of a decision, 146
Security needs, 358
Selection of human resources, 263–66, 394
    assessment centers and, 265–66
    case study, 266
    testing and, 264
Selective perception, 411–12
Self-actualization needs, 359
Self-managed teams, 380–81, 388
Self-serving bias, 411
Serial transmission, 316–17
Service role of staff personnel, 241
Sexual harassment, 534, 537–38
Shipping, 460
Shop-floor control, 460
Short-term objectives, 110
Signal, 308
Single-use plans, 192, 194
Site selection, 195–96
Situational approach to leadership, 328–42
Skills
    conceptual, 11
    human, 10
    management, 10–11
    technical, 10
Social audits, 63
    at Ben & Jerry's, 62
Social component of the general
    environment, 170
Social investment area—social responsibility
    measurements in, 62
Social needs, 358
Social obligation approach to meeting social
    responsibilities, 57

Social responsibility, 48–64
    approaches to meeting, 57
    areas of, 50
    arguments against, 50–51
    arguments for, 50
    communicating the degree of
        involvement, 54
    controlling activities, 62
    converting policies into action, 59
    Davis model of, 48–49
    determining existence of, 55
    influencing individuals and, 61
    management functions and, 58–63
    organizational objectives and, 109
    organizing activities, 60–61
    planning activities, 58–59
    required activities, 51–52
    social responsiveness in pursuing, 55
    society's assistance to business, 64
    standards for, 426
    voluntarily performed activities, 52–53
Social responsiveness, 55, 57
    decision making and, 55–56
Social values, strategy management and,
    170–71
Sociograms, 384–85
Sociometric analysis, 384
Sociometry, 384
Source (source/encoder), 307
    view of the destination by, 310
Span of management, 224–25
    Graicunas' formula and, 224–25
Special project committees, 269
Special-purpose teams, 380–81
Stability, organizational change versus, 278
Staff—line-staff relationships, 240–42
Staff authority, 240
Stakeholders, 55
    ethical management practices and, 66
Standards—comparing measured
    performance to, 425–27
Standing plans, 192
Statistical process control, 465
Statistical quality control, 447
Stereotypes, 410, 533
    against older workers, 535
Storage function of computers, 485
Storming stage of team development, 390–91
Strategic business units (SBUs), 176
Strategic control, 180
    quality and, 514
Strategic planning, 164–83
    case studies, 165–66, 173, 181, 186, 187,
        514–15
    definition of, 166
    quality through, 510–15
    tactical planning compared to, 181–82
Strategic planning decisions—information
    appropriate for, 474
Strategy(-ies), 450
    business portfolio analysis, 176–78
    capacity strategy, 451–52

    critical question analysis, 175
    definition of, 167
    focus, 179
    formulating, 175–80
    human resources strategy, 455
    implementation of, 180
    in operations management, 451
    layout strategy, 453–54
    location strategy, 452
    Porter's model for industry analysis, 178
    process strategy, 453
    product strategy, 453
    quality and, 512–13
    sample strategies, 179–80
    SWOT analysis, 176
    types of strategies, 178–79
Strategy management, 167–80
    environmental analysis and, 168
    general environment and, 168
    internal environment and, 173
    operating environment and, 172–73
    organizational direction and, 174
Stress
    bicultural, 534
    case study, 293
    definition of, 290
    helping employees handle, 292
    importance of studying, 290
    managing, 290–91
    organizational change and, 290–93
    performance and, 291
    unhealthy, 291–92
Stressors, 292–93
Structural change, 283
Structural factors—organizational change
    and, 282
Structure. See also Organization structure
    in classical organizing theory, 216–21
Structure behavior, 334
Suboptimization, 114
Subordinate-centered leaders, 328
Subordinates—responsible managers'
    behavior with, 238
Subsystem—planning, 129–31
Successful communication, 308
Superleadership, 345
Suppliers
    as component of the operating
        environment, 172
    decentralization and, 248
    Just-in-time (JIT) inventory control and,
        456–57
Supportive behavior, 341
Surveys—attitude, 403, 404
SWOT analysis, 176
Symptoms—recognizing, 428
System approach to management, 37
System(s), 450
    definition of, 37
    types of, 37
    "wholeness" and, 37–38
System theory, 37

Tactical planning, 181–82
Tall organization charts, 225
Tannenbaum and Schmidt Leadership
 Continuum, 328–32
Task groups, 377
Teaching, 394
Teams, 387–93
 case studies, 395, 399
 cross-functional, 389
 definition of, 387
 difference between groups and, 387
 effectiveness of, 391–93
 problem-solving, 387–88
 self-managed, 388
 stages of development of, 390–91
 types of, 387
 virtual, 387
Technical skills, 10
Technological change, 283
Technology
 definition of, 484
 information, 484–87
Technology (technological factors)
 in general environment, 172
 organizational change and, 282
Telecommuting—occasional, 295
Testing, 264–65
"Tethered" workers, 295
Theory X-Theory Y, 362, 363
Theory Z, 362
Time dimension of a plan, 191
Time series analysis method of sales
 forecasting, 200
Tobacco industry, 49, 55
Tokenism, 533–34
Tools and appliance manufacturing, 449
Top management (upper management). *See
 also* Chief executives
 planning and, 182

responsible managers' behavior with, 238
 support for planning, 136
Total costs—in breakeven analysis, 462
Total power, 433–34
 steps for increasing, 434
Total quality management (TQM), 504–6, 508
 case study, 524–25
Total revenue—in breakeven analysis, 462
Traditions
 corporate culture and, 393
 of foreign countries, 95
Trafficking, 460
Training, 266
 administering the program for, 268–70
 case study, 271
 designing the program for, 268
 determining need for, 267
 diversity, 543–44
 evaluating the program for, 270
 virtual, 294
Trait approach to leadership, 327
Transformational leadership, 343–44
Transnational organizations, 93
Transportation, Department of (DOT), 111
Transportation equipment, 87
Triangular management, 39
Trust, effective teams and, 392–93

Unity of command, 31, 226
Unity of direction, 31
Universality of management, 11
Unsuccessful communication, 309
Upper management. *See* Top management
Upward organizational communication, 316

Value adding, 512
Value analysis, 465–66

Values—attitudes and, 403
Variable budget (flexible budget), 458
Variable costs—in breakeven analysis, 462
Verbal communication, 313
Vietnam, 75
Virtuality (virtual organizations), 293–97
 case study, 297
 degrees of, 294
 virtual offices, 295–96
Virtual teams, 294, 387
Virtual training, 294
Vocational interest tests, 264–65
Vroom expectancy theory of motivation,
 355–56
Vroom-Yetton-Jago (VYJ) model of
 leadership, 332–34

Weber's bureaucratic model, 216
Web sites, 492–93
"What if" analysis, 488
"Wholeness"—systems and, 37–38
Women—negative dynamics and, 534, 536
Women employees, 262, 263
Women leaders, 346–47
Women managers, 15
*Workforce 2000: Work and Workers for the
 Twenty-First Century,* 531, 533, 535,
 536, 537
Work groups. *See* Groups
Work measurement methods, 455
Work methods analysis, 455
Work teams, 380–81
World Wide Web, 492–93

Zero-base budgeting, 458

Certo • Modern Management, 8/E • CD-ROM

READ THIS LICENSE CAREFULLY BEFORE OPENING THIS PACKAGE. BY OPENING THIS PACKAGE, YOU ARE AGREEING TO THE TERMS AND CONDITIONS OF THIS LICENSE. IF YOU DO NOT AGREE, DO NOT OPEN THE PACKAGE. PROMPTLY RETURN THE UNOPENED PACKAGE AND ALL ACCOMPANYING ITEMS TO THE PLACE YOU OBTAINED THEM FOR A REPLACEMENT COPY OF THE SOFTWARE. THESE TERMS APPLY TO ALL LICENSED SOFTWARE ON THE DISK EXCEPT THAT THE TERMS FOR USE OF ANY SHAREWARE OR FREEWARE ON THE DISKETTES ARE AS SET FORTH IN THE ELECTRONIC LICENSE LOCATED ON THE DISK:

1. GRANT OF LICENSE and OWNERSHIP: The enclosed computer programs ("Software") are licensed, not sold, to you by Prentice-Hall, Inc. ("We" or the "Company") and in consideration of your purchase or adoption of the accompanying Company textbooks and/or other materials, and your agreement to these terms. We reserve any rights not granted to you. You own only the disk(s) but we and/or our licensors own the Software itself. This license allows you to use and display your copy of the Software on a single computer (i.e., with a single CPU) at a single location for academic use only, so long as you comply with the terms of this Agreement. You may make one copy for back up, or transfer your copy to another CPU, provided that the Software is usable on only one computer.

2. RESTRICTIONS: You may not transfer or distribute the Software or documentation to anyone else. Except for backup, you may not copy the documentation or the Software. You may not network the Software or other-wise use it on more than one computer or computer terminal at the same time. You may not reverse engineer, disassemble, decompile, modify, adapt, translate, or create derivative works based on the Software or the Documentation. You may be held legally responsible for any copying or copyright infringement which is caused by your failure to abide by the terms of these restrictions.

3. TERMINATION: This license is effective until terminated. This license will terminate automatically without notice from the Company if you fail to comply with any provisions or limitations of this license. Upon termination, you shall destroy the Documentation and all copies of the Software. All provisions of this Agreement as to limitation and disclaimer of warranties, limitation of liability, remedies or damages, and our ownership rights shall survive termination.

4. LIMITED WARRANTY AND DISCLAIMER OF WARRANTY: Company warrants that for a period of 60 days from the date you purchase this SOFT-WARE (or purchase or adopt the accompanying textbook), the Software, when properly installed and used in accordance with the Documentation, will operate in substantial conformity with the description of the Software set forth in the Documentation, and that for a period of 30 days the disk(s) on which the Software is delivered shall be free from defects in materials and workmanship under normal use. The Company does not warrant that the Software will meet your requirements or that the operation of the Software will be uninterrupted or error-free. Your only remedy and the Company's only obligation under these limited warranties is, at the Company's option, return of the disk for a refund of any amounts paid for it by you or replace-ment of the disk. THIS LIMITED WARRANTY IS THE ONLY WARRANTY PROVIDED BY THE COMPANY AND ITS LICENSORS, AND THE COMPANY AND ITS LICENSORS DISCLAIM ALL OTHER WARANTIES, EXPRESS OR IMPLIED, INCLUDING WITHOUT LIMITATION, THE IMPLIED WARRANTIES OF MERCHANTABILITY AND FITNESS FOR A PARTICULAR PURPOSE. THE COMPANY DOES NOT WARRANT, GUARANTEE OR MAKE ANY REPRESENTATION REGARDING THE ACCURACY, RELIABILITY, CURRENTNESS, USE, OR RESULTS OF USE, OF THE SOFTWARE.

5. LIMITATION OF REMEDIES AND DAMAGES: IN NO EVENT, SHALL THE COMPANY OR ITS EMPLOYEES, AGENTS, LICENSORS, OR CONTRACTORS BE LIABLE FOR ANY INCIDENTAL, INDIRECT, SPECIAL, OR CONSEQUENTIAL DAMAGES ARISING OUT OF OR IN CONNECTION WITH THIS LICENSE OR THE SOFTWARE, INCLUD

ING FOR LOSS OF USE, LOSS OF DATA, LOSS OF INCOME OR PROFIT, OR OTHER LOSSES, SUSTAINED AS A RESULT OF INJURY TO ANY PERSON, OR LOSS OF OR DAMAGE TO PROPERTY, OR CLAIMS OF THIRD PARTIES, EVEN IF THE COMPANY OR AN AUTHORIZED REPRESENTATIVE OF THE COMPANY HAS BEEN ADVISED OF THE POSSIBILITY OF SUCH DAMAGES. IN NO EVENT SHALL THE LIABILITY OF THE COMPANY FOR DAMAGES WITH RESPECT TO THE SOFTWARE EXCEED THE AMOUNTS ACTUALLY PAID BY YOU, IF ANY, FOR THE SOFTWARE OR THE ACCOMPANYING TEXTBOOK. BECAUSE SOME JURISDICTIONS DO NOT ALLOW THE LIMITATION OF LIABILITY IN CERTAIN CIRCUMSTANCES, THE ABOVE LIMITATIONS MAY NOT ALWAYS APPLY TO YOU.

6. GENERAL: THIS AGREEMENT SHALL BE CONSTRUED IN ACCORDANCE WITH THE LAWS OF THE UNITED STATES OF AMERICA AND THE STATE OF NEW YORK, APPLICABLE TO CONTRACTS MADE IN NEW YORK, AND SHALL BENEFIT THE COMPANY, ITS AFFILIATES AND ASSIGNEES. HIS AGREEMENT IS THE COMPLETE AND EXCLUSIVE STATEMENT OF THE AGREEMENT BETWEEN YOU AND THE COMPANY AND SUPERSEDES ALL PROPOSALS OR PRIOR AGREEMENTS, ORAL, OR WRITTEN, AND ANY OTHER COMMUNICATIONS BETWEEN YOU AND THE COMPANY OR ANY REPRESENTATIVE OF THE COMPANY RELATING TO THE SUBJECT MATTER OF THIS AGREEMENT. If you are a U.S. Government user, this Software is licensed with "restricted rights" as set forth in subparagraphs (a)-(d) of the Commercial Computer-Restricted Rights clause at FAR 52.227-19 or in subparagraphs (c)(1)(ii) of the Rights in Technical Data and Computer Software clause at DFARS 252.227-7013, and similar clauses, as applicable.

Should you have any questions concerning this agreement or if you wish to contact the Company for any reason, please contact in writing:

Director New Media
Higher Education Division
Business Publishing Group
Prentice Hall, Inc.
One Lake Street
Upper Saddle River, NJ 07458

Should you have any questions concerning technical support of this product, please contact our technical support staff in writing at:

New Media Production and Technical Support
Higher Education Division
Prentice Hall, Inc.
One Lake Street
Upper Saddle River, NJ 07458

or call:

201-236-3477

or e-mail:

tech_support@prenhall.com